Newsmakers®

ISSN 0899-0417

Newsmakers®

The People Behind Today's Headlines

Laura Avery

Project Editor

2008
Cumulation

Includes Indexes from
1985 through 2008

GALE
CENGAGE Learning™

Detroit • New York • San Francisco • New Haven, Conn • Waterville, Maine • London

Newsmakers 2008, Cumulation

Project Editor: Laura Avery

Image Research and Acquisitions: Robyn Young

Editorial Support Services: Emmanuel T. Barrido

Rights Acquisition and Management: Sara Teller

Imaging: Lezlie Light

Composition and Electronic Capture: Amy Darga

Manufacturing: Cynde Bishop

For product information and technology assistance, contact us at
Gale Customer Support, 1-800-877-4253.
For permission to use material from this text or product,
submit all requests online at **www.cengage.com/permissions.**
Further permissions questions can be emailed to
permissionrequest@cengage.com

While every effort has been made to ensure the reliability of the information presented in this publication, Gale, a part of Cengage Learning, does not guarantee the accuracy of the data contained herein. Gale accepts no payment for listing; and inclusion in the publication of any organization, agency, institution, publication, service, or individual does not imply endorsement of the editors or publisher. Errors brought to the attention of the publisher and verified to the satisfaction of the publisher will be corrected in future editions.

EDITORIAL DATA PRIVACY POLICY. Does this publication contain information about you as an individual? If so, for more information about our editorial data privacy policies, please see our Privacy Statement at www.gale.cengage.com.

Gale
27500 Drake Rd.
Farmington Hills, MI, 48331-3535

ISBN-13: 978-0-7876-9624-5
ISBN-10: 0-7876-9624-2

ISSN 0899-0417

Contents

Obituaries

Introduction

Newsmakers provides informative profiles of the world's most interesting people in a crisp, concise, contemporary format. Make *Newsmakers* the first place you look for biographical information on the people making today's headlines.

Important Features

- **Attractive, modern page design** pleases the eye while making it easy to locate the information you need.

- **Coverage of all the newsmakers** you want to know about: people in business, education, technology, law, politics, religion, entertainment, labor, sports, medicine, and other fields.

- **Clearly labeled data sections** allow quick access to vital personal statistics, career information, major awards, and mailing addresses.

- **Informative sidelights essays** include the kind of in-depth analysis you're looking for.

- **Sources for additional information** provide lists of books, magazines, newspapers, and internet sites where you can find out even more about *Newsmakers* listees.

- **Enlightening photographs** are specially selected to further enhance your knowledge of the subject.

- **Separate obituaries section** provides you with concise profiles of recently deceased newsmakers.

- **Publication schedule and price** fit your budget. *Newsmakers* is published in three paperback issues per year, each containing approximately 50 entries, and a hardcover cumulation, containing approximately 200 entries (those from the preceding three paperback issues plus an additional 50 entries), *all at a price you can afford!*

- And much, much more!

Indexes Provide Easy Access

Familiar and indispensable: The *Newsmakers* indexes! You can easily locate entries in a variety of ways through our four versatile, comprehensive indexes. The Nationality, Occupation, and Subject Indexes list names from the current year's *Newsmakers* issues. These are cumulated in the annual hardbound volume to include all names from the entire *Contemporary Newsmakers* and *Newsmakers* series. The Newsmakers Index is cumulated in all issues as well as the hardbound annuals to provide concise coverage of the entire series.

- **Nationality Index**—Names of newsmakers are arranged alphabetically under their respective nationalities.

- **Occupation Index**—Names are listed alphabetically under broad occupational categories.

- **Subject Index**—Includes key subjects, topical issues, company names, products, organizations, etc., that are discussed in *Newsmakers*. Under each subject heading are listed names of newsmakers associated with that topic. So the unique Subject Index provides access to the information in *Newsmakers* even when readers are unable to connect a name with a particular topic. This index also invites browsing, allowing *Newsmakers* users to discover topics they may wish to explore further.

- **Cumulative Newsmakers Index**—Listee names, along with birth and death dates, when available, are arranged alphabetically followed by the year and issue number in which their entries appear.

Available in Electronic Formats

Licensing. *Newsmakers* is available for licensing. The complete database is provided in a fielded format and is deliverable on such media as disk or CD-ROM. For more information, contact Gale's Business Development Group at 1-800-877-4253, or visit our website at http://www.gale.cengage.com/bizdev.

Online. *Newsmakers* is available online as part of the Gale Biographies (GALBIO) database accessible through LexisNexis, P.O. Box 933, Dayton, OH 45401-0933; phone: (937) 865-6800, toll-free: 800-227-4908.

Suggestions Are Appreciated

The editors welcome your comments and suggestions. In fact, many popular *Newsmakers* features were implemented as a result of readers' suggestions. We will continue to shape the series to best meet the needs of the greatest number of users. Send comments or suggestions to:

The Editor
Newsmakers
Gale
27500 Drake Rd.
Farmington Hills, MI 48331-3535

Or, call toll-free at 1-800-877-4253

Mahmoud Abbas

President of the Palestinian National Authority

Born March 26, 1935, in Safed, British Mandate Palestine (now part of northern Israel); married Amina; children: three sons. *Education:* University of Damascus, Syria, B. A., 1950s; Moscow State University, Ph.D., 1980s.

Addresses: *Office*—c/o Permanent Observer Mission of Palestine to the United Nations, 115 E. 65th St., New York, NY 10021.

Career

Co-founded Fatah, 1954; elected to Palestine Liberation Organization executive committee and named head of PLO national and international relations department, 1980; negotiated Oslo Accords, 1993; prime minister of Palestinian National Authority, April 2003 (resigned, September 2003); elected president of the Palestinian National Authority, 2005.

Sidelights

Mahmoud Abbas, president of the Palestinian National Authority, has worked for years to achieve an independent Palestinian Arab nation and a peace agreement with Israel. After rising through the ranks of the Palestine Liberation Organization (PLO), Abbas was the key Palestinian negotiator of the 1993 Oslo Accords, which brought eight years of peace with Israel as well as limited self-government for Palestinians. But quarrels with other Palestinian leaders have wounded Abbas' attempts

to negotiate a permanent treaty that satisfies his people's grievances and ends Israel's four-decade occupation of Palestinian lands. During a stormy few months as Palestinian prime minister in 2003, Abbas struggled over power with former ally Yasir Arafat. After Arafat's death in 2004, Abbas succeeded him as president of the Palestinian National Authority. But conflicts with the radical Palestinian group Hamas have sapped Abbas' power and greatly complicated his attempts to find common ground with Israel.

Abbas, also known as Abu Mazen, was born on March 26, 1935, in Safed, a town that is now part of Israel. At the time, it was part of British Mandate Palestine, the territory that comprised present-day Israel, the West Bank, and Gaza. He was 13 when Israel was founded and the Arab-Israeli war of 1948 broke out. He and his family fled to Syria. "I remember everything," he once told Stephen Erlanger of the *New York Times.* "It was 1948 when we [were] deported from Safed to the Golan Heights to Damascus, and I remember every specific point. There was a war. We had to leave the city. The Israelis invaded the city, the Haganah at the time. We left our country."

Abbas earned a bachelor's degree in law from the University of Damascus in Syria in the early 1950s.

In the late 1950s, while living in the Persian Gulf nation of Qatar, Abbas helped organize a group of Palestinian Arab leaders who eventually became key leaders in the PLO. He and Arafat co-founded Fatah in 1954, which became the most dominant political faction in the PLO, with the goal of creating an Arab nation in Palestine. After the 1967 Six-Day War, in which Israel occupied Palestinian Arab territories, the PLO became more prominent. It established itself as the main representative of Palestinian Arabs and advocated their desire for their own nation. The PLO carried out several guerrilla and terrorist attacks on Israel. During this time, Abbas, Arafat, and the PLO's other leaders lived in exile in other Arab nations, such as Jordan, Lebanon, and Tunisia.

As Abbas rose in the PLO leadership, he got to know many Arab leaders and the heads of their intelligence services. He became a successful fundraiser for the PLO and assumed a key security position with the group. Meanwhile, he began a dialogue in the 1970s with Jewish pacifist and left-wing movements. In 1980, he was elected to the PLO executive committee and named to lead the organization's national and international relations department.

During the early 1980s, Abbas earned a doctorate in history in the then-Soviet Union. His doctorate and the book he adapted it into, *The Other Side: The Secret Relationship Between Nazism and Zionism*, attracted controversy as he rose to power. His comparison of Zionism, the ideology of Israeli Jewish nationalism, with Nazism was highly provocative simply because Nazis exterminated six million Jews in the 1940s. Also, some Jewish groups have argued that the book was an example of Holocaust denial. They said Abbas accused Jews of working with the Nazis and also minimized the number of victims of Nazi murders. Abbas denied the charges in 2003. "The Holocaust was a terrible, unforgivable crime against the Jewish nation, a crime against humanity that cannot be accepted by humankind," he said, according to BBC News.

Abbas spent the 1980s as a close adviser to Arafat and became known as a moderate voice within the PLO. In 1993, Abbas negotiated secretly with Israeli foreign minister Shimon Peres in Norway to reach a peace agreement. Their work resulted in the Oslo Accords, the 1993 agreement between Israel and the Palestinians that led to eight years of peace. The PLO renounced violence against Israel as part of the accords. Israel allowed for the creation of the Palestinian National Authority, which provided limited self-rule in the West Bank and Gaza, two Palestinian Arab territories Israel had occupied since the 1967 war.

After the peace agreement, Abbas briefly visited his old hometown in Israel in 1995. "I did go back, but secretly," he told Erlanger of the *New York Times*. "The Israeli ministry of interior helped me to go discreetly there. I was there for five or ten minutes only," he said. "I was very, very sad. I was very sad.... Every place, every quarter, every building I remember. I saw my house. But I didn't go inside." A refugee himself, Abbas passionately advocates for the right of Palestinians who left Israel in 1948 to return there or to be compensated for the loss of their homes—a major issue in all peace negotiations between the two sides.

Peace between Israel and the Palestinians broke down in the early 2000s after the failed talks between Arafat, the Palestinian National Authority's president, and Israeli Prime Minister Ehud Barak at Camp David, Maryland, in 2000. A new Palestinian uprising broke out in 2001. Abbas was opposed to the uprising, viewing it as extremely damaging to attempts to establish an independent Palestinian country.

Expectations were high in April of 2003 when Abbas became prime minister of the Palestinian National Authority, making him the second most powerful official in the government, below Arafat. In a speech to the Palestinian parliament just before it elected him, Abbas declared he was in favor of a "lasting peace" with Israel and renounced terrorism "by any party and in all its shapes," according to James Bennet of the *New York Times*. He called on various Palestinian radical groups to join the political process and defer to the Palestinian National Authority's decisions. "On this land and for this people, there is only one authority, one law, and one democratic and national decision that applies to us all." In a conciliatory gesture to Israel, he said, "We do not ignore the sufferings of the Jews throughout history. And in exchange, we hope the Israelis will not turn their backs on the sufferings of the Palestinians." He called for Israel to end its occupation of Palestinian lands. "The root of our suffering and the source of our pain is the occupation and its detestable oppressive policies," he said.

Many observers hoped Abbas would move the Palestinians and Israelis closer to peace; however, Arafat refused to cede much power to Abbas. The two quarreled over who would control the Palestinian security forces. It was the first time that Arafat had let a prime minister form a cabinet instead of forming one himself, and he had done it only in response to international pressure. In September, after several stormy months of conflict with Arafat, Abbas resigned.

Arafat died in November of 2004, and the PLO named Abbas its chairman. That made him the leading candidate to succeed Arafat as Palestinian president. He ran for the post as the candidate of the Fatah faction. In January of 2005, Palestinians elected him to a five-year term as president by a wide margin.

A month later, Abbas met with Israeli Prime Minister Ariel Sharon in Sharm el Sheik, Egypt. There, the two leaders agreed on a truce. Abbas soon declared that the war between Israel and the Palestinians was effectively over. "I believe we will start a new era," he told Erlanger of the New York Times.

However, Abbas' optimism was short-lived. By the time he took over Fatah, it had been in power for eleven years, and many Palestinians felt it had become ineffective and corrupt. In January of 2006, Fatah lost Palestinian elections to the more radical group Hamas. The Hamas victory left Abbas with much less power: He was in charge of the Palestinian National Authority's security forces and foreign policy, but little else. Israel and Western nations considered Hamas a terrorist group, and Hamas would not renounce violence or recognize Israel's right to exist, therefore Israel cut off the tax revenues that paid many salaries for Palestinian National Authority officials, and the United States and European Union cut off most aid to the Palestinians.

In March of 2007, Abbas and Hamas agreed to form a unity government, with both Hamas and Fatah in the cabinet. But it did not last long. Street fighting between Fatah and Hamas loyalists broke out in Gaza in June 2007, and ended with Hamas taking over Gaza. Abbas responded by dismissing Prime Minister Ismail Haniyah of Hamas, forming a new cabinet without Hamas, and solidifying his government's control over the West Bank. In September, Abbas told Lally Weymouth of the Washington Post that he supported the United States' attempt to isolate Hamas. "In the beginning, I believed that they were mistaken, but now we are in the same position. I am against Hamas," he said. That November, after three Hamas policemen shot and killed seven civilians at a Fatah rally in Gaza, Abbas called for Hamas to be ousted from power there. "We must topple this gang that took control of the Gaza Strip by force and that is exploiting the suffering and tragedies of our people," he said in a televised speech, according to Taghreed El-Khodary and Isabel Kershner in the New York Times.

In November of 2007, Abbas met with Israeli Prime Minister Ehud Olmert in Annapolis, Maryland, for a peace conference sponsored by the United States.

There, Abbas and Olmert agreed to negotiate a peace treaty by the end of 2008 that would outline how Arab Palestine would become an independent country. At the summit, Abbas declared emotionally that it was time for the two sides to confront the toughest issues between them. "I am not making an overstatement, Mr. President, if I say that our region stands at a crossroad that separates two historical phases: pre-Annapolis phase and post-Annapolis phase," Abbas said to Bush, according to Steven Lee Myers and Helene Cooper of the New York Times. "I say that this opportunity might not be repeated. And if it were to be repeated, it might not enjoy the same unanimity and impetus."

However, the peace talks soon hit several snags. Abbas suspended them for two months in 2008 to protest Israel's attacks on Gaza (a response to Hamas attacks). Also, a political scandal that threatened Olmert's job escalated. "Nothing has been achieved in the negotiations with Israel yet," Abbas declared in late May at a meeting of the Fatah Revolutionary Council, according to Mark Lavie of the Washington Post. Abbas and Olmert continued to talk, with another meeting between the two leaders scheduled for early June of 2008.

Selected writings

Non-fiction

The Other Side: The Secret Relationship Between Nazism and Zionism, 1983.

Sources

Periodicals

Newsweek, December 6, 2004, p. 32.

New York Times, April 30, 2003; February 14, 2005; November 16, 2007; November 28, 2007; May 11, 2008; May 30, 2008.

Washington Post, September 30, 2007, p. B4; May 25, 2008.

Online

"Mahmoud Abbas" Microsoft Encarta Online Encyclopedia, http://encarta.msn.com/encyclopedia_70171215.tif2/abbas_mahmoud.html (May 11, 2008).

"Palestine Liberation Organization" Microsoft Encarta Online Encyclopedia, http://encarta.msn.com/encyclopedia_76156684.tif4/Palestine_Liberation_Organization.h tml (May 30, 2008).

"Profile: Mahmoud Abbas" BBC News, http://news.bbc.co.uk/2/hi/middle_east/1933453.stm (May 11, 2008).

"Times Topics: Mahmoud Abbas" NYTimes.com, http://topics.nytimes.com/top/reference/timestopics/people/a/mahmoud_abbas/index.html?scp=1-spot&sq=mahmoud20abbas&st=cse (May 11, 2008).

—*Erick Trickey*

Amy Adams

Actress

Born Amy Lou Adams, August 20, 1974, in Aviano, Italy; daughter of Richard and Kathryn Adams. *Education:* Studied acting privately in Los Angeles.

Addresses: *Office*—c/o Sloane, Offer, Weber, & Dern, 9601 Wilshire Blvd., Ste. 735, Beverly Hills, CA 90210.

Career

Performer and server, Dinner Theatre and Country Dinner Playhouse, Boulder, CO, mid-1990s; performer, Chanhassen Dinner Theater, Chanhassen, MN, c. 1996-99. Film appearances include: *Drop Dead Gorgeous,* 1999; *Psycho Beach Party,* 2000; *Pumpkin,* 2002; *The Slaughter Rule,* 2002; *Serving Sara,* 2002; *Catch Me If You Can,* 2002; *The Last Run,* 2004; *Standing Still,* 2004; *The Wedding Date,* 2005; *Junebug,* 2005; *Moonlight Serenade,* 2006; *Pennies,* 2006; *Talladega Nights: The Ballad of Ricky Bobby,* 2006; *Underdog,* 2007; *Enchanted,* 2007; *Charlie Wilson's War,* 2007; *Sunshine Cleaning,* 2008; *Miss Pettigrew Lives for a Day,* 2008. Television appearances include: *Manchester Prep,* 2000; *The Last Run,* 2004; *Dr. Vegas,* 2004; and in episodes of *That '70s Show, Charmed, Buffy the Vampire Slayer, Providence, Smallville, The West Wing, King of the Hill, The Office,* and *Saturday Night Live.*

Awards: Critics' Choice Award for best supporting actress, Broadcast Film Critics Association, for *Junebug,* 2005; Spirit Award for best supporting actress, Film Independent, for *Junebug,* 2005.

Fitzroy Barrett/Landov

Sidelights

Amy Adams teetered on the brink of stardom for several years before delighting audiences in the 2007 Disney fairy tale *Enchanted.* The Colorado native had spent the better part of the past decade in Hollywood, consistently winning highly coveted roles and earning good reviews for her performances, but never truly becoming a household name or a sought-after studio asset. That changed with *Enchanted,* one of the top-grossing films of 2007, and Adam's star-making turn as Giselle. "Adams doesn't just bring her cartoonish character to life: she fills Giselle's pale cheeks with blood and feeling," asserted *New York Times* film critic Manohla Dargis, "turning a hazardously cute gimmick into a recognizable, very appealing human confusion of emotion and crinoline."

Adams was born in Italy in 1974 while her father was serving in the U.S. Air Force (USAF). She was born at the Aviano Air Base, and lived at another USAF base near the northern Italian city of Vicenza. The family, which grew to include seven children, returned to the United States and settled in Castle Rock, Colorado. Adams was a middle child, with two sisters and four brothers, and developed a love of performing at an early age thanks to her father's talent for writing skits for his large brood to perform—but not in public. At Douglas County High School, she was a member of the choir but not the drama club, telling Brad Goldfarb in *Interview*, "I was terrified to open my mouth! I was always jealous of those kids in high school who were so cocky and acted like they were going to take the world by storm. I loved to perform, but I just couldn't make that declaration." Preferring ensemble efforts, Adams was devoted to ballet and dance. She dreamed of a stage career, but gave up ballet as she neared the end of high school. "I didn't have enough natural talent," she admitted to Goldfarb. "I probably could've danced with a company, but I would have always had to work really hard just to keep a position."

After graduating from high school, Adams worked as a greeter at the local Gap store and as a waitress at Hooters. She eventually landed a job at the Dinner Theatre and Country Dinner Playhouse in Boulder. "We waited tables and then we would get up and do *A Chorus Line*," Adams recalled in the interview with Goldfarb. "The problem was, of course, that the show is performed without intermission, so when are people going to get their dessert? This was always a big problem. I was a really bad waitress, but I had the time of my life there."

Adams' talents were noticed by the director of the Chanhassen Dinner Theater near Minneapolis, Minnesota, who offered her a position with his theater troupe. She moved and spent three years there, appearing in musicals like *State Fair* and *Brigadoon* before an injury hobbled her temporarily. When she learned that a faux-documentary film about a local Minnesota beauty pageant was auditioning potential "contestants," she tried out and was cast in what became the cult-favorite dark comedy *Drop Dead Gorgeous*. Adams appeared alongside a few well-known names, such as Kirstie Alley and Ellen Barkin, along with rising stars Kirsten Dunst, Brittany Murphy, and Denise Richards. It was Alley who urged Adams to try her luck in Hollywood.

Adams relocated to the Los Angeles area at age 24, and just a few weeks later landed a starring role in a planned Fox Network series based on the successful movie *Cruel Intentions*. Adams was cast as the vixenish Kathryn Merteuil, played in the film version by Sarah Michelle Gellar, but once Fox network executives viewed the rather risqué footage of *Manchester Prep,* as the series was to be called, they ordered it delayed for the fall 1999 lineup and then canceled it altogether. With some added new footage, the project was turned into a straight-to-video release titled *Cruel Intentions 2.*

Losing a starring role in what looked to be a hot new teen drama was one of several setbacks that Adams experienced during her first few years in Los Angeles. She took television-series guest roles whenever possible, appearing in episodes of *That '70s Show, Charmed, Providence, Smallville,* and *Buffy the Vampire Slayer,* among others, and some weeks she went on as many as a dozen auditions. Her first real career break came when director Steven Spielberg cast her in *Catch Me If You Can,* the 2002 thriller with Leonardo DiCaprio as real-life con artist Frank Abagnale and Tom Hanks as the federal agent who tails him for years. Adams was cast as Brenda, the sweet teenager who volunteers at the hospital where DiCaprio's character begins impersonating a physician, then takes him home to meet her New Orleans district attorney father (Martin Sheen). Adams later told a *New York Times* writer that she was plagued by grave self-doubts about her level of experience in working alongside DiCaprio, Hanks, and Sheen, and to get through it had to force all negative thoughts from her mind. "You could have driven a truck over me," she told the paper's Margy Rochlin, "and had it not killed me, I would have come up as Brenda."

Adams hoped that her role in a well-received Spielberg movie would bring more film offers, but she was dismayed to find otherwise. Between 2003 and 2004, she appeared in just a few projects, among them a forgotten sex comedy called *The Last Run* and a CBS series that starred Rob Lowe as *Dr. Vegas,* which was canceled after just one season. In early 2005, however, Adams won rave reviews and a special jury prize at the Sundance Film Festival for her role in a small independent project called *Junebug.* The quiet family drama starred Alessandro Nivola as George, a young man who brings his new wife back home to meet his North Carolina family. Adams plays his talkative, naïve sister-in-law, who is fascinated by newcomer Madeleine, an British art dealer played by Embeth Davidtz. "Adams' performance in a role that could have easily devolved into caricature is complex and nuanced," asserted *Los Angeles Times* film critic Carina Chocano. "Ashley's faith and roots provide her with a rudder that Madeleine, for all her worldliness, lacks, and you get the sense that for all of Madeleine's self-sufficiency and independence, she would drown in Ashley's place."

Junebug earned Adams an Academy Award nomination in the Best Supporting Actress category, a race won by Rachel Weisz for *The Constant Gardener.* For her next role, the Debra Messing romantic comedy *The Wedding Date,* Adams returned to playing a thoroughly unlikable character, which she had not done since *Manchester Prep.* "I play Debra's younger half sister," she told fellow actress Selma Blair in *Interview.* "And honestly, they told me that I was too mean. We had to go back in looping and make her nicer."

The Oscar nomination for *Junebug* failed to bring any real onslaught of solid leading roles for Adams. After *The Wedding Date*, she appeared on three episodes of the hit NBC sitcom *The Office* as Katy, the purse seller, and showed up in a trio of forgettable films in 2006 before taking on a supporting part in Will Ferrell's *Talladega Nights: The Ballad of Ricky Bobby*. She also signed on as the voice of Polly in the animated feature *Underdog*.

Adams' true breakout role came in the Disney blockbuster *Enchanted*, released in time for the 2007 holiday season. She beat out 300 other hopefuls for the role of Princess Giselle in the animated/live-action feature film, and it was also her first opportunity to utilize her dinner-theater background and sing and dance in a role. Kevin Lima, *Enchanted*'s director, told Rochlin in the *New York Times* that Adams was a natural for the job for several reasons, but "what I was struck by is that she looks like a Disney character." For Adams, it seemed like destiny, too: "I was the dork in high school who was singing *The Little Mermaid* down the hallways," she told *Entertainment Weekly*'s Tim Stack. "So I'm well studied."

Giselle's animated sequences take place in the mythical land of Andalasia, where her love for a prince is thwarted by his nasty mother, a powerful queen, who pushes Giselle into a hole that magically transports her to the middle of New York City—at which point *Enchanted* becomes a live-action film. The PG film's humor relies on the proverbial fish-out-of-water jokes, while romance comes in the form of a single dad (Patrick Dempsey of *Grey's Anatomy*) and his young daughter, who rescue Giselle. "Adams proves to be an irresistibly watchable screen presence and a felicitous physical comedian, with a gestural performance and an emotional register that alternately bring to mind the madcap genius of Carole Lombard and Lucille Ball," wrote Dargis, the *New York Times* film critic. *Rolling Stone*'s reviewer Peter Travers declared that "it's star-is-born time" for Adams, describing her as the ideal Disney heroine and "the wish your heart makes when you want a storybook princess for the ages. She's wicked good."

Enchanted earned $49 million its opening weekend and became one of the top-grossing U.S. domestic releases of the year. That same holiday season, Adams also appeared in *Charlie Wilson's War* alongside three Oscar-winners—Philip Seymour Hoffman, Julia Roberts, and Tom Hanks—and gave another well-reviewed performance in *Miss Pettigrew Lives for a Day*, released early in 2008. Set in late 1930s London, the period piece recounts a day in the life of a starchy, down-on-her-luck English governess, played by Frances McDormand, who finagles an unlikely assignment as social secretary to Adams' character, Delysia Lafosse, a vain, self-absorbed nightclub singer busy stringing several men along.

After *Enchanted*, Adams suddenly found herself very much in demand. She appeared in several starring roles in 2008 and 2009 projects, beginning with *Sunshine Cleaning* alongside Emily Blunt (Anne Hathaway's fierce *Devil Wears Prada* colleague). Adams and Blunt play two sisters who start a crime-scene cleanup business. Adams also appeared with screen legend Meryl Streep in two works: *Doubt*, based on the John Patrick Shanley (*Moonstruck*) stage play of the same name about a church abuse scandal in which both women play Roman Catholic nuns, and *Julie & Julia*, slated for a 2009 release, based on writer Julie Powell's 2005 memoir about cooking her way through one of food writer Julia Child's famous cookbooks.

One of Adams' four brothers, Eddie, followed her out to Los Angeles and had an acting career before taking a job with the TMZ tabloid empire. Her longtime boyfriend is another actor, Darren Le Gallo, whom she met in an acting class in 2001. She maintains, however, that the best training she ever received came from working on the dinner-theater circuit, which she asserted "was great preparation for Hollywood," she told Rochlin in the *New York Times*. "Sitting in audition rooms with those catty girls and their little psych-out games? I have worked with some of the meanest people in the world. You can't do *anything* to intimidate me."

Sources

Entertainment Weekly, December 7, 2007, p. 10.
Interview, April 2005, pp. 130-36; February 2008, pp. 100-09.
Los Angeles Times, August 3, 2005.
Newsweek, January 7, 2008, p. 96.
New York Times, November 4, 2007; November 21, 2007; March 7, 2008.
Rolling Stone, November 15, 2007.
Star Tribune (Minneapolis, MN), June 17, 1999, p. 4B.
Sunday Times (London, England), April 16, 2006, p. 15.
USA Today, March 5, 2008, p. 1D.
Vogue, August 2005, p. 160.

—*Carol Brennan*

Yolanda Adams

Singer

Born Yolanda Yvette Adams, August 27, 1961, in Houston, Texas; daughter of Major and Carolyn Adams (both teachers); married first husband, 1988 (divorced); married Timothy Crawford Jr. (financial adviser and former NFL football player), 1997 (divorced, 2005); children: Taylor (daughter). *Education:* Graduated from Texas Southern University with a degree in broadcasting, early 1980s; took graduate classes in theology at Howard University, 1996.

Addresses: *Record company*—Columbia Records, 550 Madison Ave., New York, NY 10022. *Web site*—http://www.yolandaadams.org.

Career

Member of Southeast Inspirational Choir, mid-1970s to mid-1980s; released first album *Just as I Am,* 1987; became a radio morning show host, 2007; announced plans for Yolanda's Clozet clothing line, 2007.

Awards: Dove Awards for traditional gospel album of the year and traditional gospel recorded song of the year, Gospel Music Association, for *Through the Storm* and "Through the Storm," 1992; Dove Award for traditional gospel recorded song of the year, Gospel Music Association, for "Is Your All on the Altar," 1999; Grammy Award for best contemporary soul gospel album, Recording Academy, for *Mountain High ... Valley Low,* 1999; Image Award for outstanding contemporary gospel artist, NAACP, 2000; Image Awards for outstanding female artist, out-

standing contemporary gospel artist, outstanding song (for "Open My Heart"), and outstanding performance in a variety series or special (for the Soul Train Awards), NAACP, 2001; Grammy Award for best contemporary soul gospel album, Recording Academy, for *The Experience,* 2001; American Music Award for contemporary/inspirational artist, Dick Clark Productions, 2001; Soul Train Music Award for Best R&B soul single, female, Don Cornelius Productions, for "Open My Heart," 2001; Image Award for outstanding contemporary gospel artist, NAACP, 2002; BET Award for best gospel artist, Black Entertainment Television, 2002; BET Award for best gospel artist, Black Entertainment Television, 2003; Grammy Award for best gospel song, Recording Academy, for "Be Blessed," 2005; Grammy Award for best gospel performance, Recording Academy, for "Victory," 2006; Image Award for outstanding gospel artist, NAACP, 2006.

Sidelights

A leader of an exciting new wave of contemporary gospel music, Yolanda Adams has bent and mixed musical genres to spread her message of hope and devotion to God to as many listeners as she can. Adams' fashionable dress challenges traditional notions of a gospel singer, while her music embraces jazz, R&B, and hip-hop, and her accounts of how her faith helped her cope with two divorces remind her fans that religious people are not expected to live perfect lives. Always reaching out to new audiences, Adams expanded her career after 20 years as a singer, introducing her own clothing line and becoming a radio host.

Born in Houston, Adams was singing in her church choir by age four. Her mother, Carolyn, who studied music, exposed her and her five younger brothers and sisters to classical music, R&B, and jazz. Her father, Major, died from injuries sustained in a car crash when she was 13. She helped her mother raise her younger siblings, attending Texas Southern University so she could live at home. After graduating with a degree in broadcasting, Adams spent seven years working as a second-grade and third-grade teacher, but she also sang gospel music, touring and performing on the weekends with the Southeast Inspirational Choir. Her influences included classic gospel acts such as the Edwin Hawkins Singers and James Cleveland, R&B star Stevie Wonder, and jazz singer Nancy Wilson.

In 1986, producer Thomas Whitfield saw Adams sing with the choir and signed her to his small Sound of Gospel label. He recorded her first album, *Just as I Am*, and released it in 1987. Its modest success led Adams to the gospel label Tribute Records. In 1991, Tribute released her second album, *Through the Storm*, which became a national success. It won two Dove Awards from the Gospel Music Association, and she performed on *The Tonight Show* and *Arsenio Hall* to promote it. With the album's success, Adams no longer had enough time for both her musical and teaching careers. "I was so busy that I had to resign from teaching and go into ministry full-time," she told Andree Farias for an article on ChristianityToday.com. "It was a hard decision. I love young kids."

Between the first two albums, in 1988, Adams got married, but she later described the marriage as horrible. She left the relationship after nine months. Eventually, she began dating financial adviser and former professional football player Timothy Crawford Jr., a longtime friend whom she had met at age 16 when they both sang in church choirs around Houston. They married in 1997 and had a daughter, Taylor, in 2001.

Starting early in her career, Adams took a lot of risks for a gospel singer. Her 1993 album, *Save the World*, showed many secular influences, from jazz to R&B to Latin music. Adams proudly pointed to the Caravans, the wildly popular gospel group of the 1950s and 1960s, as a model. "[They] were on the cutting edge when they started out," Adams told Lisa Collins of *Billboard*. "Now they're what we call traditional gospel. Before, there were the basic hymns of the church. Then they came along and changed gospel music altogether." *Save the World*'s chart success vindicated Adams' creative gamble.

In 1995, with the release of *More than a Melody*, Adams was being celebrated as a leader in "a new gospel movement that is infusing and energizing gospel to record sales levels," as Collins of *Billboard* put it. Adams declared that she felt called to stretch the limits of gospel music. "We want to take gospel a step further, so that it's greeted in the marketplace by everybody, so I am making a conscious effort to not fit the mold," she told Collins. Another *Billboard* writer, Paul Verna, declared she had succeeded. His review of *More than a Melody* called her "a major talent" and "one of gospel's leading lights."

One look at Adams' song titles—"The Battle Is the Lord's," "The Good Shepherd"—makes it clear she is very devout. Yet she has little use for certain traditional images and expectations of gospel singers. The six-foot-one Adams often dresses with a sense of high fashion—her favorite designers include Donna Karan and Pamela Dennis—which helps her appeal to younger audiences. In 1998, Adams made a very unusual move for a modern gospel artist: She signed with a major label, Elektra Records. That, combined with her musical influences, led some conservative gospel fans to fear her work would turn secular. Adams insisted that the move to Elektra did not compromise her message, just broadened her audience. "We had about eleven record companies chasing us, and this is the only secular label that told me I didn't have to change a thing," Adams told Collins of *Billboard*.

Before her Elektra debut, Adams released one more album with Verity, the former Tribute label: *Songs from the Heart*, a collection of ten classic church hymns rearranged as modern R&B, jazz, and hip-hop. Less than a year later, Elektra released *Mountain High ... Valley Low*, promoting it heavily to gospel, R&B, and adult contemporary radio stations. "She's one of those rare vocalists with a range that rivals the best," Sylvia Rhone, the chairperson of Elektra, raved to Collins of *Billboard*. "I believe I could put her toe to toe with whoever one considers their favorite singer, and she could blow them away."

In 2000, Adams won a Grammy Award for best contemporary soul gospel album for *Mountain High ... Valley Low*. She also scored a major R&B hit with

"Open My Heart," a single from the album, produced and co-written by Jimmy Jam and Terry Lewis, who had previously worked with Janet Jackson. Its lyrics were addressed to God: "I need to talk to you and ask you for your guidance," she sang (as quoted by *Jet* magazine). "Just one word could make a difference in what I do Lord."

To follow her breakthrough, Elektra released three albums in little more than a year. The holiday album *Christmas with Yolanda Adams* appeared at the end of 2000, followed quickly in March of 2001 by a live album, *The Experience*, recorded the previous November during the "Sisters in the Spirit Tour" with fellow gospel performers Angela Christie, Shirley Caesar, and Mary Mary. "Adams revels in her faith, praising her Lord with a clear-throated yet understated intensity," wrote an appreciative Amy Linden in *People*. The live album spawned a single, a cover of R. Kelly's "I Believe I Can Fly."

Late in 2001, Elektra released an album of original material, *Believe*. Its slick R&B sound struck critics as an even bolder attempt to meld a gospel message with mainstream appeal. The first single, the uplifting ballad "Never Give Up," was produced by Jam and Lewis. Chuck Arnold of *People* gave *Believe* a mixed review. Because Adams was aiming to please "both gospel purists and R&B fans," he argued, "she can't totally cut loose in either genre." Michael Paoletta of *Billboard*, however, praised the album as "a seamless mix of gospel, R&B, hip-hop, and pop."

After so much productivity, Adams went four difficult years without releasing an album. She returned to the studio in 2003, but her next album's release was held up while Elektra Records merged into Atlantic Records. Meanwhile, her marriage to Crawford ended in 2005. She talked about her personal struggles at an outdoor concert in New York City's Central Park that August. "The past few years have been kind of hard for me," she said onstage (as quoted by reviewer Jeannette Toomer of the *New York Amsterdam News*). "I'll tell you what it feels like to have a broken heart, because I had one." She told the crowd that her faith helped her through her pain and disappointment, and she encouraged the audience not to dwell on past hurt: "Don't let your tomorrow be your yesterday."

Atlantic Records finally released Adams' next album, *Day by Day*, in 2005. From her hurt, Adams produced songs that insisted on hope: Song titles included "Be Blessed," "Someone Watching Over You," and "This Too Shall Pass." "I feel like we don't address depression, grief, and loss in gospel music," she told Farias of ChristianityToday.com. "We should, because we have the answer to those questions. Whenever I'm directing a lyric to a person, it is to get them to overcome." "Be Blessed" and another song from the album, "Victory," won Grammy awards.

Adams has been involved with several charities and causes. In 2005, she set up the Voice of an Angel Foundation, which encourages middle-school and high-school students to pursue careers as teachers. She has also worked with the U.S. Department of Health and Human Services to promote childhood immunizations in poor communities and has supported the Children's Defense Fund and a charity fighting juvenile diabetes.

In 2007, Adams embarked on a major change in her career. She became a morning show host on a gospel radio station in Houston. The show was syndicated and broadcast in more than a dozen cities on the Radio One network. "It's not a gospel show or an inspirational show, but an overall morning show," she said in her Web site's biography. "I wanted to create a clean alternative morning show for people of faith. People love the way we break down current events and our mix of music." The show played songs by a diverse range of artists, from Mariah Carey to George Benson to John Mayer.

Adams left Atlantic Records, which released a greatest hits disc as her last album on the label, and signed with Columbia Records. "I needed to come to a place where singers are loved and adored," she said in her Web site biography. "With everybody from Beyonce to Celine Dion, Columbia is that place. They really know what to do for people with voices." Meanwhile, she prepared for the debut of her own clothing line, Yolanda's Clozet, for tall women. Its jeans, T-shirts, and other items were to be sold online and at department stores.

That September, Adams performed with several other gospel stars at Madison Square Garden in New York City. Her performance impressed *New York Times* reviewer Kelefa Sanneh, especially her version of "Someone Watching Over You." Her improvisations reminded Sanneh of a preacher's. "She took a familiar musical phrase and embellished it, making it bigger and more forceful, and then, just when she seemed to have forgotten where she was going, returned to the theme," he wrote.

As 2007 ended, Adams' new Christmas album, *What a Wonderful Time*, was released. The album, produced by Jam and Lewis, included her versions of five Christmas classics, including "Do You Hear What I Hear?" and "Little Drummer Boy," and five original songs reflecting the spirit of the holiday season. Adams also planned to release a regular studio album, again produced by Jam and Lewis, in the first half of 2008. Her Web site reported that it would be an album of duets with legendary female singers.

Selected discography

Just as I Am, Sound of Gospel, 1987.
Through the Storm, Tribute, 1991.
Save the World, Tribute, 1993.
More than a Melody, Tribute, 1995.
Yolanda Live in Washington, Verity, 1996.
Shakin' the House: Live in L.A., Verity, 1996.
Songs from the Heart, Verity, 1998.
Mountain High ... Valley Low, Elektra, 1999.
The Best of Yolanda Adams, Verity, 1999.
Christmas with Yolanda Adams, Elektra, 2000.
The Experience, Elektra, 2001.
Believe, Elektra, 2001.
The Praise and Worship Songs of Yolanda Adams, Verity, 2003.
Day by Day, Atlantic, 2005.
The Essential Yolanda Adams, Jive Legacy, 2006.
The Best of Me, Atlantic, 2007.
What a Wonderful Time, Columbia, 2007.

Sources

Periodicals

Billboard, February 5, 1994, p. 33; July 8, 1995, p. 32; August 12, 1995, p. 64; August 19, 1995, p. 34; September 12, 1998, p. 47; September 26, 1998, p. 22; September 18, 1999, p. 15; December 8, 2001, p. 53; May 19, 2007, p. 93; May 26, 2007, p. 38.
Essence, February 1996, p. 64; July 2001, p. 106.
Heart & Soul, May 2001, p. 60.
Jet, June 12, 2000, p. 55.
New York Amsterdam News, August 18, 2005, p. 22.
New York Times, September 24, 2007.
People, April 16, 2001, p. 41; January 14, 2002, p. 35.
Texas Monthly, August 2007, p. 28.

Online

"Atlantic Records: Yolanda Adams: Bio," Atlantic Records, http://www.atlanticrecords.com/yolandaadams (November 23, 2007).
"One Day at a Time," ChristianityToday.com, http://www.christianitytoday.com/music/interviews/2006/yolandaadams-0106.html (November 23, 2007).
"Yolanda Adams," YolandaAdams.org, http://www.yolandaadams.org (November 27, 2007).

—*Erick Trickey*

Cecelia Ahern

Fitzroy Barrett/Landov

Author

Born September 30, 1981, in Dublin, Ireland; daughter of Bertie (a politician) and Miriam (a bank employee; maiden name, Kelly) Ahern. *Education:* Graduated with a degree in journalism and media communications from Griffith College, Dublin, Ireland, c. 2003.

Addresses: *Home*—Dublin, Ireland. *Office*—Cecelia Ahern, c/o Hyperion Editorial Department, 77 W. 66th St., 11th Fl., New York, NY 10023.

Career

Dance teacher in Dublin, Ireland, after 1997; member of the pop group Shimma, c. 1999; published first novel, *PS, I Love You,* 2004; co-creator, with Don Todd, of the ABC television comedy *Samantha Who?,* 2007.

Sidelights

Cecelia Ahern's debut novel, *PS, I Love You,* gained her extraordinary literary fame in her native Ireland at the age of just 22. The uplifting tale of love and loss spent months at the top of the Irish best-seller lists in 2004, and was even made into a Hollywood film that starred Hilary Swank. Ahern went on to craft several more equally appealing stories which critics sometimes classify as "chick-lit"—a category she rejects, Ahern told Ginanne Brownell in *Newsweek International.* "Chick lit isn't a nice term. Just because something is heartwarming and appeals to women does not mean it lacks intelligence."

Ahern is the daughter of prominent politician Bertie Ahern, who was serving as Ireland's taoiseach, or prime minister, when her first novel was accepted for publication in 2003. Between Ahern's birth on September 30, 1981, and the publication of her first novel, Ireland underwent a swift and utterly unprecedented transformation. In the early 1980s, the predominantly Roman Catholic nation was one of the poorer corners of Europe, hamstrung by a cultural conservativeness that even extended into the political sphere in the form of a constitutional ban on divorce. Political troubles also dominated Irish life: Ireland had been a sovereign state since 1921 after winning its independence from the English crown, but several pro-British, Protestant counties in the north chose to remain part of Britain. Thus the island nation was partitioned in two—the Roman Catholic Republic of Ireland and Northern Ireland, a smaller section dominated by pro-British Protestants. Sectarian violence flared once again in the late 1960s and continued over the next two decades. An underground organization, the Irish Republic Army (IRA), waged a campaign of political assassinations and bombings with the goal of uniting both Irelands; British military units and Northern Ireland paramilitary groups fought back with equal vigor. When Ahern was born in 1981, the year's dominant news story was the ongoing hunger strikes by IRA prisoners in Northern Ireland jails in which ten men died in a four-month period.

Ahern's father had risen through the ranks of Fianna Fáil, the political party whose name is sometimes translated as "Soldiers of Destiny," and was serving in the Dáil Éireann, or lower house of parliament, the year his second daughter was born. He became party leader in 1994, and then the youngest taoiseach in Ireland's history in 1997. In that role, Ahern's father played a crucial role in negotiating a lasting peace agreement between the IRA and Northern Ireland.

Ahern and her older sister, Georgina, grew up in the public eye, and their family's troubles were intensely scrutinized by the media. Their parents legally separated in 1987—the constitutional ban on divorce would not be lifted for another decade—and Bertie became involved in a 15-year relationship with Celia Larkin, who often accompanied him at official functions. This was a rather unusual arrangement, given Ireland's religious and social conservatism, but others noted that the tacit public acceptance of the still-married politician's partner was a sign that Ireland was undergoing a major cultural shift. Ahern and her sister reportedly saw little of Larkin, though they remained close to their father and spent every Sunday with him. Sometimes they attended sporting events, but other activities reflected their father's rising political fortunes. There were frequent official events, Ahern recalled in an interview with Louette Harding in the *Mail on Sunday*, "where we had to behave ourselves and be very good."

Ahern was a performer at an early age. She began tap-dance lessons in her early teens, moving on to hip-hop and even winning a national dance competition in 1997. Both during and after her time at Bruce College—a combination high school/junior college in Dublin—she taught dance, appeared on television and in stage shows, and joined a short-lived pop group called Shimma. Ahern eventually decided to enroll at Griffith College in Dublin to study for a journalism and media communications degree. There were few reports on her for nearly three years, until January of 2003, when news that she had secured a book deal with the U.K. division of HarperCollins was announced.

Ahern had finished her degree but was having little luck finding work in her field, so she began writing a love story. She showed a few chapters to her mother, who urged her to write more and then asked a golf-course acquaintance who was a literary agent for some advice. Ahern signed with the agent, and the unfinished manuscript sold for a little more than $200,000. Just two days earlier, she had started classes for a graduate program in film production, and was forced to drop out in order to finish the manuscript. The completed story captured the attention of U.S. publisher Hyperion Books, a unit of the Walt Disney Corporation, which signed Ahern to a two-book deal for an astonishing seven-figure sum, or at least one million U.S. dollars. The film rights to her debut novel, *PS, I Love You*, netted Ahern another $80,000 and then a further payout of $400,000 on the day filming started.

Published in early 2004, *PS, I Love You* recounts the story of young widow Holly Kennedy, who is grief-stricken by the sudden loss of her beloved husband after a fatal illness. She has said that she would be bereft if she were ever to lose him, and with this in mind he wrote and arranged to send ten letters to her in the ten months following his death. Each one contains a surprise or gift for Holly as well as a message of support and guidance for her new solo life.

Ahern's debut spent nearly five months at No. 1 on the Irish best-seller list, but more than a few critics were unkind and sniped that her success was due only to her family name, not her literary talents. "I've met people who've said, 'I didn't want to buy your book because I thought you only got the deal because of your father,'" Ahern once told a writer for the *Independent on Sunday*, "and I've met people who've bought the book because they've said they are big fans of my father. I would be stupid to say it had not helped, particularly in Ireland."

Ahern had already finished her second novel by the time she was on the publicity blitz for her debut. *Where Rainbows End* earned equally scathing reviews for its tale of long-distance friendship-turned romance, but a critic for *Booklist*, Kristine Huntley, reviewed its U.S. edition—titled *Rosie Dunne*—and found it an "engaging follow-up" to her debut. Huntley asserted that "readers will enjoy the breezy epistolary style and likable characters." In Ginanne Brownell's *Newsweek International* article, the literary editor of the *Irish Times* reflected upon the larger significance of Ahern's success, noting that until Ahern arrived on the scene, Ireland's best-selling women novelists had usually made their mark writing about beleaguered heroines who suffered because of political, religious, and economic repression. "With its economic transformation, Ireland has fast progressed from a victim culture to latte culture," Caroline Walsh explained to Brownell.

"To some extent, the women popular fiction writers have best encapsulated this, with Cecelia serving as her generation's head of this school."

Ahern's third novel, *If You Could See Me Now,* followed the trials of Elizabeth, who comes from a dysfunctional family long plagued by acts of casual but devastating abandonment. Her own mother walked out when Elizabeth was still very young, and now the adult Elizabeth must take care of her young nephew left behind by her thoughtless sister. The boy's imaginary playmate serves as a catalyst to help the family begin to heal. In Ahern's next work, *A Place Called Here,* a former police investigator known for her tracking skills goes missing herself, and finds herself in the dimension where all lost things are temporarily housed. It was published in the United States as *There's No Place Like Here.*

In Ahern's fifth book she deals with yet another unexplained phenomenon: 2008's *Thanks for the Memories* explores the issue of molecular memory. This is when marked personality changes occur in a recipient of a donor organ. In Ahern's novel, a pregnant woman falls down a flight of stairs, loses her baby, and receives a sizeable blood transfusion. Once recovered, she leaves her husband and strikes out on her new life, but finds that she is plagued by odd thoughts and has a newfound expertise in art history, which leads to romance. Again, British book critics for the mainstream newspapers and literary supplements savaged it, but Ahern's work was a best-seller in both Ireland and England, and optioned for film, as were her previous three titles.

Thanks for the Memories appeared in April of 2008 just as the political career of Ahern's father was coming to a close. Bertie Ahern announced that same month his coming resignation as taoiseach in the midst of an official inquiry regarding financial improprieties. Ahern herself, meanwhile, had been deemed one of Ireland's wealthiest citizens under 30, according to the Irish edition of the *Sunday Times.* She was worth an estimated $10 million, with her fortune amassed through book sales, movie deals, and her involvement in an television series for the ABC network in the United States (part of the same Disney corporate empire as her U.S. publisher, Hyperion). The sitcom *Samantha Who?* debuted on the network as part of its fall 2007 line-up and pulled in terrific ratings before the season was truncated by the Hollywood writers' strike of 2007-08. It was renewed it, however, for the 2008-09 season.

Ahern described the process of working with other writers and development executives at ABC as a stressful process in an interview with *Bookseller's*

Benedicte Page. Recalling the "three days of pitching to studios, I was so scared I almost dropped dead," she said, and was also counseled not to have too many hopes for the project. "Then it was picked up as a pilot and they said: 'There's a very slim chance it'll actually go to air,' and then it was picked up. At every stage, I've been going: 'I don't know what's going on!'"

Samantha Who? was the brainchild of Ahern and series co-creator Donald Todd, a television writing veteran whose credits include *ALF* and *Ugly Betty.* Christina Applegate was cast as the title character, a Chicago real estate executive who suffers retrograde amnesia after an accident. This means that she cannot remember anything about herself, and is unsettled to discover she was not a very well-liked person. "In flashback, she lives out the high-flying moments that won her pre-accident self a reputation as a no-regrets party girl who could be counted on for little except stingingly thoughtless behavior," noted *New York Times* reviewer Margy Rochlin.

Ahern has been romantically involved with athlete-turned-actor David Keoghan for several years. Her sister, Georgina, married Nicky Byrne, a member of the hugely successful Irish pop group Westlife, in the summer of 2000. The daughters still spend Sundays with their father, who by all accounts has been intensely supportive of his author-daughter's career. Neither he nor any other family member appear as fictionalized persona in any of her works, she asserts, a habit that stretches all the way back to *PS, I Love You.* "When I wrote it first, it wasn't for anyone," she told *Sunday Times* journalist John Burns. "The only people reading it were my mom and sister, so that was even more of an incentive not to put them in. They would have said, 'What am I doing in your book, take me out.'" Her books are also noteworthy for a chasteness that seems almost old-fashioned, but Ahern said in the same interview that the omission was understandable. "If I really really really wanted to put it (sex) in there, I would, but there would be that extra 'oh my God, look what the taoiseach's daughter has done,' and that would be really embarrassing."

Selected writings

PS, I Love You, HarperCollins UK (London, England), and Hyperion Books (New York City), both 2004.

Where Rainbows End, HarperCollins UK, 2004; published in the United States as *Rosie Dunne,* Hyperion, 2005.

If You Could See Me Now, Hyperion, 2006.

A Place Called Here, HarperCollins UK, 2006; published in the United States as *There's No Place Like Here,* Hyperion, 2007.
Thanks for the Memories, HarperCollins UK, 2008.
The Gift, HarperCollins UK, 2008.

Sources

Booklist, January 1, 2005, p. 811.
Bookseller, December 7, 2007, pp. 20-21.
Daily Mail (London, England), November 4, 2006, p. 26.
Independent on Sunday (London, England), April 13, 2008, p. 36.
Mail on Sunday (London, England), January 25, 2004, p. 30.
Mirror (London, England), January 21, 2004, p. 12.
Newsweek International, March 3, 2008.
New York Times, December 16, 2007.
Sunday Times (London, England), January 25, 2004, p. 5.
W, February 2004, pp. 60-61.

—*Carol Brennan*

Jananne al-Ani

Artist and photographer

Born in 1966 in Kirkuk, Iraq. *Education:* Byam Shaw School of Art, London, fine art diploma, 1986; University of Westminster, London, B.A., 1991; Royal College of Art, London, M.A., 1997.

Addresses: *Gallery*—South London Gallery, 65 Peckham Rd., London SE5 8UH, England.

Career

Multimedia artist and filmmaker; works first showed in the group exhibition *Women in View*, Brixton Art Gallery, London, England, 1987.

Awards: John Kobel Portrait Award, 1996; Arts Council Award, 1998; Artsadmin Artist Bursary, 1999; East International Award, 2000; London Arts Board Award, 2000-01.

Sidelights

Jananne al-Ani is one of a few well-known artists from an Islamic background within the international contemporary art scene. A multimedia practitioner whose works combine photography, video, and spoken word, al-Ani has spent much of her life in Britain, but lived in Iraq until she was 13. Her works often examine the status of women in Muslim societies, but they also force the viewer to address prejudices against women and Muslims everywhere in the world. Writing about a 2006 group show at New York's Museum of Modern Art that included her work, *New York Times* art critic Hol-

land Cotter asserted that "most of these artists are tagged Islamic because of their backgrounds. Yet much of their work is far less about Islam itself, as a religion or culture, than about their relationship to Islam—in some cases it is close and positive; in other cases, distant and critical. But in most instances, it is ambivalent—the opposite of how Islam is treated these days in the larger world."

Born in Kirkuk, Iraq, in 1966, al-Ani is the third of of four daughters of an Irish mother and Iraqi father. The family lived in northern Iraq, which was the center of several successive Mesopotamian empires after 2500 *b.c.e.* Along with her mother and three sisters, al-Ani moved to England in 1980, a year after Saddam Hussein and his Ba'ath Party seized power in Iraq and the same year that the eight-year-long Iran-Iraq War began.

Al-Ani studied art and earned several degrees. Her first was from the Byam Shaw School of Art, now part of Central Saint Martins College of Art and Design in London, and was a fine art diploma bestowed in 1986. Five years later, she earned another undergraduate degree, this one in Arabic languages and literature, from the University of Westminster, and in 1997 she completed work for her master's degree in photography from the Royal College of Art.

In the world of contemporary art, visual artists from Islamic backgrounds are still a relative rarity, even in multicultural Britain. This is tied to the longstanding tradition in Islam that forbids graven imagery, or the representation of a person, place, or animal. As a result, over the centuries Islamic art has been confined to intricate patterns, with a marked absence of traditional religious art as most in the West perceive the category. Another tenet of Islam is its urging for both men and women to be modest: In many Muslim societies, existing religious laws interpret this to mean that women must cover their hair or veil their face when in public; in some extreme cases they must cover their entire bodies in a head-to-toe garment known as a *burqa*. Al-Ani is one of the leading artists to examine the issues of the public and private selves for Muslim women, though she often points out that in previous centuries, women from many different cultures wore veils, not just Muslim societies.

Al-Ani took part in several group shows while still at the Royal College of Art, and her first solo exhibition was at the Harriet Green Gallery in London in 1997. Since then she has participated in several art events on both sides of the Atlantic, including the Smithsonian Institution in Washington, D.C. and London's Imperial War Museum. The Smithsonian show was titled "Constructing Identities: Recent Work by Jananne al-Ani" and featured images and videos of al-Ani, her three sisters, and their mother. In one piece, titled *Veil*, they wear traditional Iraqi veils in what Joanna Shaw-Eagle in the *Washington Times* called "the most mysterious and provocative image" of the show. The 1997 work used a slide projector and a large screen onto which images of the five women "appear, dissolve and reappear in hypnotic sequences that move from light to dark and back to light again," noted Shaw-Eagle.

Al-Ani's 2003 book *Veil: Veiling, Representation and Contemporary Art* was published by MIT Press as a compendium of essays and images as well as a companion piece to the group exhibition of the same name at the Museum of Modern Art, Oxford, England. That same year, al-Ani participated in a group show held at Haus der Kulturen der Welt in Berlin, Germany, but the group show *DisORIENTation* opened on the same day the U.S.-Iraq War started. Al-Ani's piece was titled, somewhat presciently, "Sounds of War." Malu Halasa, writing in the London *Guardian* explained that al-Ani's installation "intercuts war noises—missiles, sirens, swooping planes—with BBC special-effects, from cheering and booing to football-crowd noises." In the same article, al-Ani told Halasa that, because she left Iraq in 1980 at the start of the Iran-Iraq War, that conflict was relatively untroubling. "That was somewhere else, someone else's problem. Then the Gulf war comes in 1991 and suddenly everyone's involved."

In London in 2005, the Tate Britain invited al-Ani to show in their "Art Now" series, and she submitted a two-part video piece titled *The Visit*. One screen features her sisters and mother recounting and repeating narrative fragments about an unnamed man, while the second screen shows footage of a man in a suit wandering in what appears to be a vast and arid desert. A year later, she participated in a group show at New York's Museum of Modern Art headlined "Without Boundary: Seventeen Ways of Looking." Cotter, the *New York Times* art critic, paid particular attention to *Veil*, which had been seen at the Smithsonian show seven years earlier. "The veiling decreases from full to none if you read the pictures in the left-to-right direction of written English, and increases from none to complete if you read in the right-to-left direction of written Arabic," wrote Cotter. "It is possible to read the work as critical of orthodox Islamic custom. But Ms. al-Ani's historical reference is to European colonial photographs of 'exotic' Muslim women, which she turns into a visual essay on the artificiality of Western and Islamic identities."

Selected exhibitions

Solo

Harriet Green Gallery (London), 1997.
Margaret Harvey Gallery (St. Albans, England), 1998.
Imperial War Museum (London), 1999.
Constructing Identities: Recent Work by Jananne al-Ani, Arthur M. Sackler Gallery, Smithsonian Institution (Washington, D. C.), 1999.
Islamische Welten: Love Affairs, ifa-Galerie Berlin, Institut für Auslandsbeziehungen (Berlin, Germany), 2004.
Jananne al-Ani, Norwich Gallery (Norwich, England), 2004.
The Visit, Tate Britain (London), 2005.
Casino Luxembourg/Forum d'art contemporain, (Luxembourg), 2007.

Group

Women in View, Brixton Art Gallery (London), 1987.
Contact South Bank Photo Show, Royal Festival Hall (London), 1991.
No More Heroes Anymore, The Royal Scottish Academy (Edinburgh, Scotland), 1993.
After Eden, Ikon Gallery (Yoxall, England), 1996.
Modern Narrative: The Domestic and the Social, Artsway (Sway, England), 1997.
On Site, Lauderdale House (London), 1998.
Attitude: A History of Posing, Victoria and Albert Museum (London), 2000-01.
(Co-curator with Frances Kearney) *Fair Play*, Angel Row Gallery (Nottingham, England), 2002.

DisORIENTation, Haus der Kulturen der Welt (Berlin, Germany), 2003.

(Co-curator with David A. Bailey, Zineb Sedira, and Gilane Tawadros) *Veil: Veiling, Representation and Contemporary Art*, Museum of Modern Art (Oxford, England), 2003-04.

Without Boundary: Seventeen Ways of Looking, Museum of Modern Art (New York), 2006.

Sources

Periodicals

Christian Century, October 4, 2003, p. 43.
Guardian (London, England), March 29, 2003, p. 17.
New York Times, February 26, 2006.
Washington Times, November 27, 1999, p. 3.

Online

"Jananne Al-Ani: Veiling and Unveiling," LuxOnline, http://www.luxonline.org.uk/artists/jananne_al-ani/essay(2).html (May 15, 2008).

"Jananne Al-Ani: The Visit," LuxOnline, http://www.luxonline.org.uk/articles/the_visit(1).html (May 15, 2008).

—*Carol Brennan*

Marin Alsop

Conductor and musician

Born October 16, 1956, in New York, NY; daughter of LaMar (a violinist) and Ruth (a cellist) Alsop; children: one son. *Education:* Attended Yale University, 1972-75; The Juilliard School, New York, NY, bachelor's degree in music, 1977, master's degree in music, 1978, both in violin performance.

Addresses: *Office*—Baltimore Symphony Orchestra, Joseph Meyerhoff Symphony Hall, 1212 Cathedral Street #1, Baltimore, MD 21201.

Career

Freelance violinist, 1976—; founder/member of String Fever, 1981; founder/conductor of the Concordia Orchestra, New York City, 1984; conducting fellowship, Tanglewood Music Center, Lenox, MA, 1988-89; associate conductor, Richmond Symphony, Richmond, VA, 1988; music director, Eugene Symphony Orchestra, Eugene, OR, 1989-95; music director, Long Island Philharmonic, Melville, NY, 1989-95; music director, Cabrillo Music Festival, Santa Cruz, CA, 1992; music director, Colorado Symphony Orchestra, Denver, CO, 1993-2003; principal guest conductor, City of London Sinfonia, 1999—; principal conductor, Bournemouth Symphony Orchestra, Poole, England, 2002-07; music director, Baltimore Symphony Orchestra, 2007—; guest conductor with the New York Philharmonic, Philadelphia Orchestra, Chicago Symphony, Los Angeles Philharmonic, San Francisco Symphony Orchestra, Boston Pops Orchestra, London Symphony Orchestra, London Philharmonic, The Netherlands' Royal Concertgebouw Orchestra, Switzerland's Zurich Tonhalle, Orchestre de Paris, Bavarian Radio Symphony, Boston Symphony, Pittsburgh Symphony, and Tokyo Philharmonic.

Awards: Leopold Stokowski International Conducting Competition, American Symphony Orchestra, 1988; Koussevitzky Conducting Prize, Tanglewood Music Center, 1989; Distinguished Service Award, University of Oregon, 1997; Governor's Award for Excellence in the Arts, State of Colorado, 1998; Artist of the Year, *Gramophone,* 2003; Conductor's Award, Royal Philharmonic Society, 2003; MacArthur Fellowship, John D. and Catherine T. MacArthur Foundation, 2005; Classical BRIT Female Artist of the Year, British Phonographic Industry, 2005; BBC Radio 3 Listeners Award, Royal Philharmonic Society, 2006; European Women of Achievement Award, 2007.

Sidelights

Marin Alsop made history in 2007 when she took over as music director of the Baltimore Symphony Orchestra. Alsop, a woman working in the male-dominated world of orchestral conducting, is the first woman to lead a major U.S. orchestra. Prior to the appointment, the charismatic "maestra" made guest appearances with some of the world's leading orchestras, including the New York Philharmonic, Philadelphia Orchestra, Chicago Symphony, Los Angeles Philharmonic, London Symphony, London Philharmonic, Tokyo Philharmonic, Orchestre de Paris and The Netherlands' Royal Concertgebouw Orchestra.

While Alsop is credited with shrinking the gender barrier at the podium, she has spent her career downplaying the issue. Alsop wishes to be known as a great conductor, not a female conductor. "My success is probably due to the fact that I've never interpreted any rejection as gender-based," she told the London *Daily Telegraph*'s Geoffrey Norris. "I've always felt that the reason I didn't get something was that I wasn't good enough, and so I would go back and try to reassess what I was doing and make more progress. Once you start to feel that you're not getting there because of something that's completely out of your control, that's the beginning of the end."

An only child, Alsop was born on October 16, 1956, in the borough of Manhattan in New York City to musicians LaMar and Ruth Alsop. She grew up in Dobbs Ferry, New York. Her father, a violinist, and her mother, a cellist, both played for the New York City Ballet Orchestra. Her father was the concertmaster (lead violin). LaMar Alsop also played the saxophone, flute, clarinet, and viola, and was a world-class whistler, performing back up for many recordings and commercials. Alsop's mother also played piano and was a potter and weaver.

For Alsop, music was part of everyday life. On the Frequently Asked Questions section of her Web site, Alsop discussed her entry into the music world. "Unlike many of my friends who fell in love with music through their schools where they were allowed to pick an instrument and play in the orchestra, I was born with a job! My parents are both classical musicians and they could never ever imagine a life for their child that was not filled with music!" Alsop took up piano as a toddler and picked up the violin at age five. By seven, she was studying at the highly competitive New York-based Juilliard School and later studied classical guitar.

Early on, Alsop knew she wanted to be a conductor. The idea was planted in her mind after her father took her to see the New York Philharmonic, where she watched the legendary Leonard Bernstein at the podium. Speaking to the *Birmingham Post*'s Terry Grimley, Alsop recalled that defining moment. "I was about nine or ten. My dad took me to a young persons' concert and it was almost like a religious calling. I knew it right away. I was very bossy. My parents are both string players, professional musicians, and I always had a passion for music but was always interested in doing something they didn't do."

From that moment on, Alsop's mind was set. At 12 or 13 years old, she told one of her Juilliard teachers that she intended to become a conductor. The teacher told her that girls could not conduct. Alsop went home and told her father, who in turn marched out and bought her a box of batons so she could practice.

At age 16, Alsop entered Yale University but, in 1975, transferred back to Juilliard, earning a bachelor's degree in 1977 and a master's degree in 1978, both in violin performance. In 1976, Alsop began working as a freelance violinist playing with the New York Philharmonic, the New York Chamber Symphony, and the American Composers Orchestra, among others. She played alongside her parents with the New York City Ballet Orchestra. Alsop also made the rounds on Broadway, playing in several shows, including *Sweeney Todd* and *Showboat*. She did studio work, contributing to film scores and television commercials. She played on albums as well, once working with Grammy winner Billy Joel.

In 1979, Alsop began conducting studies with Vienna native Carl Bamberger, conductor of the New York Philharmonic. When Alsop came over for instruction, Bamberger rearranged his living room furniture to resemble an orchestra pit. In 1981, she founded String Fever, a ten-piece chamber ensemble devoted to playing and promoting Big Band swing. The band had four violins, two violas, two cellos, a bass player, and a drummer.

Meanwhile, Alsop continued to pursue her dream of becoming a conductor. To get face time as a conductor, Alsop formed her own ensembles. Luckily, her freelancing career was lucrative. In 1984, Alsop used $10,000 of her savings to start a string orchestra called Concordia. She appointed herself conductor. The group played all types of music, but specifically explored jazz and music from the 1920s and '30s that blurred the lines between classical and pop. The group provided a consistent outlet for Alsop to hone her skills and establish her own conducting style that would set her apart from her male peers.

Speaking to Sarah Urwin Jones of the London *Times*, Alsop put it this way: "A woman has to really think about how she gets sound out of the orchestra on the podium. If you want a really big dynamic range, you have to make a different gesture from a man, because otherwise people think that you're trying to be this huge person and they get scared of that. You're a woman possessed. Or a bitch. Whereas in a man it's seen as strong."

After working with her Concordia Orchestra for four years, Alsop won a fellowship to study conducting at the Tanglewood Music Center in Lenox, Massachusetts. She applied to the program several times and was rejected prior to winning. At Tanglewood, the summer home of the Boston Symphony Orchestra, Alsop was able to study under her hero, Bernstein, as well as with acclaimed conductors Gustav Meier and Seiji Ozawa.

For Alsop, studying under Bernstein was a dream come true. "He was unbelievable—hard to describe, but such a generous human being," Alsop told the *Birmingham Post*. "We hit it off tremendously when I first started with him at Tanglewood.... He was hugely embracing of me, but he couldn't figure out a woman conducting. He was of that generation—he didn't get it. He would say, 'When I'm in the hall, I close my eyes and I can't tell you're a woman.' "

It was at Tanglewood that Alsop began breaking down gender barriers. During the summer fellowship, she lived on the men's floor at the dormitory, across the hall from the percussionists. The musicians embraced her style and she became the star conductor of the 1988 season. Writing in the *Boston Globe*, Richard Dyer noted the warmth and accord with which the orchestra members welcomed Alsop. "They greeted her approach to the podium by batting their bows on their music stands, and when she had finished they joined the cheering and clapping of the audience, swelling the noise by stomping their feet."

Alsop's success at Tanglewood led to several guest conducting jobs. In 1988, she served as associate conductor of Virginia's Richmond Symphony and in 1989 she became music director of Oregon's Eugene Symphony. In 1989, Alsop was invited back to Tanglewood. At the end of the season, she was awarded the Koussevitzky Conducting Prize, given to the outstanding student conductor. Alsop was the first woman to receive the honor.

An invitation to the Boston Pops Orchestra followed and, in 1990, Alsop became the first woman to conduct a program of the Boston Pops at Symphony Hall. During an interview with the *Boston Globe*'s Marian Christy a few days before the historic performance, Alsop attributed her conducting success to her empathetic style. "My approach to the musicians is that I'm one of them. I have an idea of what it's like when a conductor doesn't appreciate you. When it happened to me, I had the feeling that I was doing menial labor. It was as if I was the kitchen help and had to come through the back door." Alsop knows firsthand that if musicians harbor resentments toward the conductor, the music will not flourish. She also understands that musicians are human, and, like all humans, they have good days and bad days. She understands that musicians cannot be forced to perform—they must be inspired.

Alsop, herself, has played for conductors who swore at her. The experience was educational because Alsop realized that the angrier the conductor got, the worse the music got. "We, the violinists, were demoralized," she told Christy. "Now, if the musicians aren't performing well, I say: 'Don't worry! It's going to be all right!' They don't believe you, of course, but they feel better. And when they feel better, they play better." In an effort to get the musicians to understand her approach, Alsop begins rehearsals by telling the musicians the story behind the music or a story about the composer.

Throughout the 1990s and early 2000s, Alsop stayed busy hopping from orchestra to orchestra as a guest conductor. She also served as music director of the Long Island Philharmonic from 1989 to 1996 and as music director of the Colorado Symphony Orchestra from 1993 to 2003. In 2002, Alsop made history when she became principal conductor of the Bournemouth Symphony, thus becoming the first woman to lead a major British symphony.

In 2005, Alsop was appointed music director of the Baltimore Symphony Orchestra, scheduled to take over the reigns in 2007. The orchestra was suffering from debt and dwindling attendance. The announcement caused an uproar and many of the players told the symphony board to keep looking. Some publicly questioned Alsop's musical depth, fearing she might water down the programs. Alsop was known for performing some less serious orchestral works at various venues. The Baltimore musicians contacted her former colleagues and some musicians who had worked with Alsop said they did not enjoy the experience. Alsop acknowledged that she had made some mistakes early on in her career but had learned from them. During the ordeal, Alsop met with the musicians privately, in a candid meeting, to air all grievances. She also reminded them that they did not really know the real Alsop. Afterward, she signed the contract.

When the Baltimore Symphony gave its first performance under Alsop in September 2007, the Music Center at Strathmore was filled to capacity. She put the orchestra through the paces, opening with "Fearful Symmetries," a 25-minute-long piece by American composer John Adams, followed by Gustav Mahler's five-movement Symphony No. 5. *Washington Post* reviewer Tim Page liked the show. "Alsop is a lot of fun to watch," he wrote. "Like her great mentor, Leonard Bernstein, when she is conducting she seems a map of the score—vigorously alive, sensitive to every passing idea, riding the waves." He did note that the slow-tempo "Adagietto" of Mahler's piece failed to inspire. In the end, though, Page wrote that "the Baltimore Symphony sounded terrific, with its crooning saxes, loamy croaks from the lower brass, surging strings and taut percussion, and you don't get such eager and colorful playing without a guide." By the midway mark of the season, attendance was up.

For Alsop, music is life. She believes every child should study an instrument. On her Web site, she explained why: "Learning an instrument develops innumerable skills: physically it develops hand-eye coordination; it teaches children that nothing comes overnight and that practice is the key to success; it teaches them how to motivate themselves and budget their time and be responsible to themselves to practice! These are lessons that stayed with me for life and helped me become successful!"

Sources

Periodicals

Birmingham Post, March 22, 2001, p. 17.
Boston Globe, September 3, 1988, p. 9 (Living); May 26, 1990, p. 20 (Living); May 30, 1990, p. 39 (Living).
Daily Telegraph (London, England), March 22, 2001, p. 27.
New Yorker, January 7, 2008.
New York Times, October 9, 2005, p. 1 (Music).
Times (London, England), February 9, 2007, p. 16 (Features).
Washington Post, September 29, 2007, p. C1.

Online

"Biographical Timeline," Marin Alsop, http://www.marinalsop.com/timeline.php (January 27, 2008).
"Marin Alsop Biography," Marin Alsop, http://www.marinalsop.com/longbio.php (January 27, 2008).
"Media F.A.Q.," Marin Alsop, http://www.marinalsop.com/mediafaq.php (January 27, 2008).

—Lisa Frick

Martin Amis

Author

David Levenson/Getty Images

Born Martin Louis Amis, August 25, 1949, in Oxford, England; son of Kingsley William (an author) and Hilary Amis; married Antonia Phillips, 1984 (divorced, 1993); married Isabel Fonseca, 1996; children: Delilah Seale (with Lamorna Heath), Louis, Jacob (from first marriage), Fernanda, Clio (from second marriage). *Education:* Exeter College, Oxford, B.A. (with honors), 1971.

Addresses: *Agent*—The Wylie Agency, 250 W. 57th St., Ste. 2114, New York, NY 10107. *Home*—London, England, and Uruguay.

Career

Editorial assistant, *Times Literary Supplement*, 1972-75, fiction and poetry editor, 1974; *New Statesman*, assistant literary editor, 1975-77, literary editor, 1977-79; first novel, *The Rachel Papers*, published by J. Cape, 1973; Manchester Centre for New Writing, University of Manchester, professor of creative writing, 2007—. Contributor to anthologies and to numerous periodicals.

Awards: Somerset Maugham Award, Society of Authors, for *The Rachel Papers*, 1974; James Tait Black Memorial Prize for biography, University of Edinburgh Department of English Literature, for *Experience*, 2000; National Book Critics Circle Award for criticism, for *The War against Cliché: Essays and Reviews, 1971-2000*, 2001.

Sidelights

Martin Amis is one of Britain's most famous living literary figures, a writer as lauded for his books as he is reviled for the acclaim they have brought him. The son of novelist Kingsley Amis, he has produced a string of postmodern novels and strongly opinionated essays since his career began, which have earned him a reputation as the quintessential English malcontent. In 2006, his tenth novel, *House of Meetings*, was published to glowing reviews in the British press, which hailed it as a return to his earlier, more succinct prose and plotting style.

Amis was born on August 25, 1949, in Oxford, England, 12 months and ten days after the birth of his older brother, Philip. The Amis parents had met at Oxford when Kingsley was working on his degree and fell in love with art student Hilary Ann Bardwell; they married in 1948 when she became pregnant with Philip. A sister, Sally, was born in 1954. By then Kingsley was teaching at the University College of Swansea, Wales, and his fiction debut, *Lucky Jim*, appeared that same year. The novel made Amis' father famous overnight, and was hailed as a comic masterpiece of postwar British literature. Its plot centers on the dejected, disillusioned title character, a lecturer at a lesser university whose career prospects hinge upon his cultivating a good relationship with his mentor. The snobbish professor and his music-loving family were allegedly modeled after the Bardwell clan.

Amis's parents' marriage deteriorated over the next decade as Kingsley's literary fame grew and, with it, his penchant for alcohol and extramarital affairs. He was a disciplined writer, however, and his son recalled the household rules in an interview with Lewis Burke Frumkes of *Writer* magazine. "When I was growing up, it was only in the direst emergency that you knocked on the study door of my father, who'd whip around in his chair and say, 'What?'—although he was very soft and friendly when he wasn't in his study."

The family moved to New Jersey when Kingsley taught at Princeton University for a year, where the eight-year-old Amis was ridiculed when he wore shorts to school on the first day. Back in London, he attended a grammar school in South Kensington, then a boarding school, where he showed himself to be entirely uninterested in much beyond drugs and comic books. When Amis was 17 years old, his father's second wife—novelist Elizabeth Jane Howard—encouraged him to take up classic English writers. She also worked to get him into a "cram school" to help him prepare for university entrance exams, which he aced to the surprise of many.

Amis earned a bachelor's degree in English, with honors, from Exeter College of Oxford University in 1971, and went to work as an editorial assistant at the venerable *Times Literary Supplement,* the separate book-review section of the *Times* of London. His debut novel, *The Rachel Papers,* was published by his father's publisher, J. Cape, in 1973. The tale of a rakish young man hoping to enter Oxford on a scholarship but distracted by the two young women with whom he is romantically involved, *The Rachel Papers* earned an unfavorable comparison to J.D. Salinger's *Catcher in the Rye* from *Times* reviewer David Williams, who conceded that Amis "is very funny though, has a mensa mind beyond any doubt, and can make nice phrases by the score." The novel was adapted for the big screen years later, with the story updated for the 1980s and becoming one of the cult-classic teen romance films of the decade.

Amis' second novel, *Dead Babies,* was followed by *Success* in 1978, by which time he was working in his final year as literary editor of the *New Statesman.* His first work of nonfiction was *Invasion of the Space*

Invaders, a 1982 tome with an introduction by filmmaker Stephen Spielberg. Its essays discussed films, contemporary politics, and the current video-game craze. Sharp-tongued and famously opinionated, Amis also began to accrue a following on the other side of the Atlantic for his novels, which the *New York Times'* Michiko Kakutani commended as a distinctly "recognizable fictional world. It is a place defined by Swiftian excess and metropolitan satire, a place where variously shabby characters partake of lust and violence and guilt in hopes of being allowed a second chance."

Amis' next novel, the tale of a debauched would-be filmmaker, was set in both New York and London. *Money: A Suicide Note* was published by J. Cape in 1984, and cemented his reputation, at age 35, as one of Britain's leading literary talents of his generation; many were surprised when it failed to be nominated for that year's Booker Prize for Fiction, Britain's most prestigious literary honor. Eric Korn in the *Times Literary Supplement* lauded "the astonishing narrative voice he has devised, the jagged, spent, street-wise, gutter-wise, guttural mid-Atlantic twang, the buttonholing, earbending, lughole-jarring monologue" of its anti-hero, the slovenly, chain-smoking television commercial director John Self, who is struggling to bring his script to life. At one point, a writer named "Martin Amis" is brought in to fix it.

Amis' next novel, *London Fields,* appeared in 1989 and was set in a London ten years into the future. Its central character is an American writer, ill with cancer, who moves to London as the world teeters on the brink of both the millennium and impending nuclear disaster. Critics consider it to be one of Amis' finest works, with multiple plotlines that remain strong throughout, unlike some of his other novels. It was followed by *Time's Arrow, or The Nature of the Offense* in 1991, whose plot centered around the Holocaust. This was the first work of his to be nominated for the Booker Prize.

In the early 1990s, the British press seemed to turn on Amis. Part of the disenchantment came after stories surfaced that he left his wife of several years and their two young sons for another woman, and then famously ditched his British literary agent of 23 years, Pat Kavanagh, for the American agent Andrew Wylie. Adding another element to the drama was the fact that Kavanagh was married to one of Amis' closest friends, the novelist Julian Barnes. Wylie then negotiated an immense book deal for Amis' next work, just completed, that set a new record in publishing of half a million British pounds, or about $794,500. Sales of Amis' works had never been particularly strong, and publishing-industry insiders noted that his forthcoming novel would probably not earn back that amount in sales. The press derided Amis as ungentlemanly in the kinder reports, and un-English in the vitriolic screeds. Furthermore, much ink was given over to the fact that Amis had used some of the advance money to have major cosmetic dental work done, and had it done by an American dentist, too.

The novel in question, *The Information*, was published in 1995 and also prompted some sniping, for some thought it had been modeled after Amis' friendship with Barnes. Its tale centered around two longtime friends who are both novelists; the less successful one attempts to sabotage the other's career, which backfires and serves to bring even more acclaim onto his rival. Roz Kaveney, critiquing it for the *New Statesman & Society*, found some positive elements, noting that "the descriptions of Richard's and Gwyn's books make one amusedly glad to be reading any other novel—even this one," but asserted that much of its contrivances were recycled from Amis' previous works. Kaveney concluded by declaring that "no reviewer should blame Amis for making a lot of money. We are entitled to express concern that a brilliant career has come to this: the overpriced sale of second-hand shoddy."

Amis' father died later in 1995, after a career that had spanned 40 years, 20 novels, and several collections of essays and poetry. Later in life, reportedly guilt-stricken over the end of his marriage to Amis' mother, Kingsley's drinking intensified, and he often reached a point in the evening where he became unable to walk. Divorced from his second wife, he entered into an unusual arrangement with Bardwell, now married to a titled but impoverished member of the House of Lords, whereby she and Lord Kilmarnock lived in separate quarters in her ex-husband's London home and cared for him. Amis summed up his literary relationship with his father in an interview with Charles McGrath in the *New York Times* in 2007. "He was always saying, 'I think you need more sentences like "He put down his drink, got up and left the room,"' and I thought you needed rather fewer of them."

Over the next decade Amis continued to produce works of fiction like 1997's *Night Train*—a police procedural—and *Yellow Dog*, a 2003 novel about a pornography addict that was the target of so much critical scorn that it was said to have prompted Amis to move to Uruguay with his second wife, Isabel Fonseca, who had ties to the South American country. There were also several works of nonfiction published over the years, including 1993's *Visiting Mrs. Nabokov and Other Excursions* and a 2000 memoir, *Experience*. In the latter work, Amis wrote of meeting a daughter he had never known until the mid-1990s, when she was 19 years old.

Amis earned mixed reviews for his 2002 book, *Koba the Dread: Laughter and the Twenty Million*, an examination of Soviet leader Josef Stalin and the years of praise given to the leader of the world's only Communist state by leftists in the West. The revelations that came after Stalin's death in 1953 that he persecuted millions of his own citizens in a war of terror through sham trials, labor camps, and government-instigated famines was a blow to the left from which it has yet to recover, Amis argues in the book. The work also incited a minor literary feud with a friend of Amis', journalist Christopher Hitchens.

In April of 2006, the *New Yorker* published Amis' short story "The Last Days of Muhammad Atta," an imagined tale of the final days of the alleged ringleader of the 9/11 hijackers, which was an excerpt from a novel in progress. Asked why he made Atta a subject of fiction by *Newsweek International* writer Silvia Spring, Amis replied that it was Atta's "face, so rich and malevolent that it haunted me." Later that year Amis published an 11,000-word essay in the London *Observer* on the eve of the fifth anniversary of 9/11. He drew upon his as-yet-unfinished novel about radical Islamic operatives and discussed the war in Iraq, Palestinian suicide bombings, and the West's ineffectual responses to the threat of militant Islamicism. Several passages were inflammatory, but this one was often singled out: "I will never forget the look on the gatekeeper's face, at the Dome of the Rock in Jerusalem, when I suggested, perhaps rather airily, that he skip some calendric prohibition and let me in anyway," Amis writes in the essay. "His expression, previously cordial and cold, became a mask; and the mask was saying that killing me, my wife, and my children was something for which he now had warrant."

The essay, titled "The Age of Horrorism," ignited major debate and prompted strong rejoinders from scholars of Middle Eastern politics and Islam. The furor served to inadvertently publicize Amis's next work, the 2006 novel *House of Meetings*, which is set in a Soviet gulag camp and features a doomed romantic triangle. The *Economist* praised it as a comeback for the writer, declaring that "Amis has suddenly—and unexpectedly, even to his publishers—turned in a work of real worth, a novel that not so much makes the spine tingle as the heart race at its passion and richness."

For Amis' next novel, 2008's *The Pregnant Widow*, he described it in one interview as autobiographical and touching upon the themes of Islamicism and feminism. Having moved back to London with his family in 2006 after two and a half years in Uruguay, he was nearing the age of 60 and untroubled by the attacks he regularly received in the British press. "Nearly everyone I know likes me," he told the *Guardian*'s Sally Vincent, "and nearly everyone who doesn't know me hates my guts."

Selected writings

Fiction

The Rachel Papers, J. Cape (London, England), 1973; Knopf (New York, NY), 1974.

Dead Babies, J. Cape, 1975; reprinted as *Dark Secrets*, Panther (London, England), 1977.

Success, J. Cape, 1978.

Other People: A Mystery Story, J. Cape, 1981.

Money: A Suicide Note, J. Cape, 1984; Viking (New York, NY), 1985.

London Fields, J. Cape, 1989.

Time's Arrow, or The Nature of the Offense, J. Cape, 1991.

The Information, HarperCollins (London, England), 1995..

Night Train, J. Cape, 1997.

Heavy Water and Other Stories, J. Cape, 1998.

Yellow Dog, J. Cape, 2003.

Vintage Amis (selected works), Vintage (London, England), 2004.

House of Meetings, J. Cape, 2006; Alfred A. Knopf, 2007.

The Pregnant Widow, J. Cape, 2008.

Nonfiction

Invasion of the Space Invaders (introduction by Stephen Spielberg), Hutchinson (London, England), 1982.

The Moronic Inferno and Other Visits to America (articles, reviews and interviews), J. Cape, 1986.

Einstein's Monsters (essay and short stories), J. Cape, 1987.

Visiting Mrs. Nabokov and Other Excursions (essays), J. Cape, 1993; Harmony Books, 1994.

Experience: A Memoir, J. Cape, 2000.

The War against Cliché: Essays and Reviews, 1971-2000, J. Cape, 2001.

Koba the Dread: Laughter and the Twenty Million, J. Cape, 2002.

Sources

Economist, October 14, 2006, p. 88.

Guardian (London, England), March 18, 1995, p. 12.

New Statesman & Society, March 24, 1995, p. 24.

Newsweek International, November 6, 2006.

New York, January 22, 2007, pp. 88-89.

New York Times, August 20, 1981; February 4, 1990; April 22, 2007.

Observer (London, England), September 10, 2006; September 17, 2006, p. 10.

Times (London, England), November 22, 1973, p. 13.

Times Literary Supplement, November 26, 1982, p. 1290; October 5, 1984, p. 1119.

Writer, October 2000, p. 14.

—*Carol Brennan*

Javier Bardem

Actor

Born Javier Angel Encinas Bardem, March 1, 1969, in Las Palmas de Gran Canaria, Canary Islands, Spain; son of Carlos Encinas and Pilar Bardem (an actress). *Education:* Attended the School of Arts and Crafts, Madrid, Spain, 1988.

Addresses: *Agent*—Elyse Scherz, Endeavor, 9601 Wilshire Blvd., 3rd Fl., Beverly Hills, CA 90210; Jose Marzilli, Jose Marzilli Represente de Actors, Rafael Calvo 42, Ste. 5, 28010 Madrid, Spain.

Career

Actor in films, including: *El poderoso influjo de la luna* (uncredited), 1980; *Las edades de Lulú* ("The Ages of Lulu"), 1990; *Tacones lejanos* ("High Heels"), 1991; *Amo tu cama rica*, 1992; *Jamón, jamón* ("Ham, Ham"), 1992; *Huidos*, 1993; *El amante bilingüe* ("The Bilingual Lover"), 1993; *Huevos de oro* ("Golden Balls"), 1993; *La teta y la luna* ("The Tit and the Moon"), 1994; *Días contados* ("Numbered Days"), 1994; *El detective y la muerte* ("The Detective and Death"), 1994; *Pronòstic reservat*, 1994; *Boca a boca* ("Mouth to Mouth"), 1995; *La madre* ("The Mother"), 1995; *Éxtasis* ("Ecstasy"), 1996; *Más que amor, frenesí* ("Not Love, Just Frenzy"), 1996; *El amor perjudica seriamente la salud* ("Love Can Seriously Damage Your Health"), 1996; *Mambrú*, 1996; *Airbag*, 1997; *Carne trémula* ("Live Flesh"), 1997; *Perdita Durango* ("Dance with the Devil"), 1997; *Torrente, el brazo tonto de la ley* ("Torrente, the Dumb Arm of the Law"; uncredited), 1998; *Entre las piernas* ("Between Your Legs"), 1999; *Los lobos de Washington* ("Washington Wolves"), 1999; *Segunda piel* ("Second Skin"), 1999; *Before Night Falls*, 2000; *Sin noticias de Dios* ("Without

News of God"), 2001; *The Dancer Upstairs*, 2002; *Los lunes al sol* ("Mondays in the Sun"), 2002; *Collateral*, 2004; *Mar adentro* (released in the United States as *The Sea Inside*), 2004; *Goya's Ghosts*, 2006; *Hécuba, un sueño de pasión* (documentary), 2006; *No Country for Old Men*, 2007; *Love in the Time of Cholera*, 2007; *Vicky Cristina Barcelona*, 2008. Television appearances include: *Segunda ensenanza*, c. 1986 and *El dia por delante*, 1989, as well as several guest appearances on television programs. Executive producer, *Los lobos de Washington* ("Washington Wolves"), 1999.

Awards: Silver Lion, Venice Film Festival, for *Jamón, jamón*, 1992; Goya Award for best supporting actor, Spanish Film Academy, for *Dias contados*, 1995; Goya Award for best actor, Spanish Film Academy, for *Boca a boca*, 1996; People's Award for best European actor, European Film Academy, 1997; Coppa Volpi Award for best actor, Venice Film Festival, award for best actor, National Board of Review, award for best actor, National Society of Film Critics, award for best male lead, Southeastern Film Critic Association, 2000, and Spirit Award for best male lead, Film Independent, 2001, all for *Before Night Falls*; Goya Award for best actor, for *Los lunes al sol*, 2003; award for best actor, Venice Film Festival, for *Mar adentro*, 2004; Academy Award for best supporting actor, Golden Globe Award for best performance by an actor in a supporting role, and Screen Actors Guild Award for best supporting actor, all 2008, all for *No Country for Old Men.*

Sidelights

Though Javier Bardem spent his life being surrounded by actors, he initially had no interest in pursuing the profession. "I didn't even want to become an actor," the Oscar winner confessed to John Malkovich in *Interview.* "I wanted to be a painter, but I was lazy. I started working as an extra on movies just to make some money and keep on with my painting lessons, but one day I realized I'd make more money in movies than by painting in the street." Bardem followed the footsteps of his mother and grandfather and became a regular on the Spanish screen. In the early 2000s, Bardem began making English-language films, selecting such diverse roles as writers, lovers, and serial killers. He became a major film star in Spain during the 1990s, and in the early 2000s, rose to prominence in Hollywood. Bardem was the first Spaniard to be nominated for an Academy Award for best actor, and in 2008, he won the Oscar for best supporting actor.

Due to the variety of roles Bardem has played, he is often called "an actor's actor," "an artist's actor," and a chameleon. In a description of his role in *The Dancer Upstairs,* in which Bardem plays a police officer, Owen Gleiberman of *Entertainment Weekly* noted how different this performance was than his previous depiction of a persecuted writer: "Anyone who loved Bardem's performance in *Before Night Falls* will want to see what a true chameleon of the spirit he is," the critic wrote. Jesse Katz of *Los Angeles Magazine* commented on the same trend: "Detective and drug dealer, doctor and invalid, straight hunk and queer poet—Javier Bardem is the ultimate chameleon, an actor who more often than not makes himself unrecognizable." Though Bardem has been offered a host of formulaic roles, including a villain role in a James Bond film, the actor has chosen roles he feels have more depth, refusing to be typecast.

Born on March 1, 1969, in Las Palmas, the Canary Islands, Spain, Bardem was primarily raised by his mother. His father, who held a macho outlook on life, did not approve of acting as a profession. Bardem attended Madrid's School of Arts and Crafts, preparing to become a painter. He also played rugby, making Spain's national team. Opportunities to perform in movies, however, continued to come easily, and by the time he was 18, acting had become his primary profession. Many of his early roles

were given to him due to his good looks, and often, his roles, such as his appearance in *Huevos de oro,* which translates to "Golden Balls," were very sexual. He told Malkovich about his mother's response to the film. "I was naked and having sex—she was like, 'Okay, I like it. You have a career here, but maybe you should try to do another kind of role.'" He and his mother acted together in the film *Las edades de lulu.*

The opportunity for Bardem to do a more serious film came with *Jamón, jamón,* in which he plays a trucker who wants to become a bullfighter, but instead becomes an underwear model. The character was very macho—a character type that would become uncommon in Bardem's future work. Bardem received a Silver Lion award for the movie, and his acting career began in earnest. He performed in such roles as a paralyzed policeman in *Carne trémula* ("Live Flesh") and a drug addicted informant in *Días contados* ("Numbered Days").

Feeling that there was not enough work in the film industry in Spain, Bardem began seeking out English-speaking roles. He continued working in Spanish productions, including *Boca a boca,* a comedy that was later released in the United States. The film that landed him the most recognition in America, however, was *Before Night Falls,* in which he played a Cuban writer who flees to the United States. In playing the character of Reinaldo Arenas, who was persecuted in Cuba not only for his writing but also for being homosexual, Bardem left behind macho roles and portrayed Arenas through his ailing health and eventual death from AIDS. "Nobody who witnesses the scene is likely to forget Bardem's stunning believability in it," wrote Steve Daly in an *Entertainment Weekly* review of the movie.

In order to learn about Arenas' identity, Bardem spent two weeks in Cuba, interviewing people who had been friends of the poet. "Cubans were very open with me and not afraid to talk. I met people who had been transvestites at the Copacabana nightclub in the '60s, people who were in El Morro [prison], people from the writers' union. I was really shocked at what I learned," he told B. Ruby Rich of the *Advocate.* The experience in Cuba helped him not only understand the character, but also aided him in picking up the Cuban accent he would need for both his Spanish and English lines. The dialect was difficult to learn, and Bardem spent hours with a vocal coach and listened to recordings of Arenas reading his autobiography. The result was convincing, and Bardem received his first Oscar nomination for the performance.

Roles in American movies continued. He played the lead role in John Malkovich's *The Dancer Upstairs,* in which he portrayed a police officer fighting terrorism led by a cult leader. In order to keep his acting in English convincing, Bardem relied on his physical acting, not trusting solely in the language. "When I read in English, I need to see that there is a character to build," he explained to Malkovich in *Interview*. "I pay attention to the physicality of it, to the body language, to try to create some kind of behavior that's not close to my own, so I can be surrounded by elements besides the language."

Bardem balanced his growing American career with continued roles in Spain, including the part of an unemployed Santa in *Los lunes al sol* ("Mondays in the Sun"), for which he won Spain's Goya Award in 2002. Lisa Schwarzbaum said in a review of *Los lunes al sol* for *Entertainment Weekly* that the film "pulses with the star power of the extraordinary Javier Bardem." In *Mar adentro*, which was released in the United States as *The Sea Inside*, Bardem played the part of another writer, this one a paraplegic who pled with the Spanish government for the right to end his life. As a very physical actor, playing the role with very little body language was a challenge for Bardem, who gained weight, lost hair, and wore layers of make up to make him appear 55 years old. "Bardem, in an extraordinary performance, convinces us of the essence of Sampedro's character ... by almost entirely relying on his voice and facial expressions," wrote Philip Booth in the *Sarasota Herald Tribune*.

"I'm just very fortunate to have found these two different characters in two great movies," Bardem told Andrew Dansby in the *Houston Chronicle* about playing both Arenas and Sampedro. "I do think they're related somehow. They gave their own lives to raise questions that were up in the air." He also saw irony in playing two writers, and he shared his thoughts with Elvis Mitchell of *Interview*. "It's weird that both are writers because I consider myself very low intellectually. That's not modesty—it's the truth. When real-life characters like Reinaldo Arenas or Ramon Sampedro, who are so intellectually prepared and emotionally experienced, come my way, I get scared. In both cases I was much younger than the individuals I was portraying, so it was like, 'I don't have the experience to know what they do.'" Choosing the hard roles, particularly in *Mar adentro* contributed to Bardem's growing reputation as an actor's actor. "I do try to choose things I think are important, though—things that can teach us something about what it is to be human, which is why I like to make movies about real people," Bardem told Mitchell.

Given those preferences, Bardem had some concerns about accepting the role of Chigurh, a serial killer, in the Coen brothers' adaptation of Cormac McCarthy's novel, *No Country for Old Men*. When he received the script, he was delighted at the prospect of working with the Coen brothers, whose work he had long admired. "Then I saw the violence in it," he said to Mitchell in a later interview, noting the European distaste for violence in film. Bardem had always been comfortable with sex on the screen, but not violence—a preference he had discussed with critics after he filmed *Before Night Falls*. Coming around to the role was difficult. He told Mitchell, "I talked to the Coen brothers about my concerns, and they explained to me why it was important for the story to be told in exactly the terms I was trying to criticize.... The statement behind the movie is about that—the lack of meaning in violence." The role was another challenge for Bardem, who had little faith in his spoken English and didn't drive, because the role required him to do both. But the most difficult aspect was showing a character who is more force of nature than human. "I guess there was the challenge, which is to try to bring what he represents," he explained on *Day to Day*, "which is kind of an icon of a symbolic figure of what violence is and put that into a human behavior."

After the film's release, critics lauded Bardem's performance, and he received a Golden Globe and an Oscar for the role. Jenelle Riley of *Back Stage West* noted, "Tell Bardem it's impossible to imagine anyone else in the role and he laughs. 'That's funny, because before I played it, no one could imagine me doing it.'" But though the movie increased his fame, Bardem maintained his modesty, often crediting the Coens for his work in the role. He explained in *Hollywood Reporter* that he maintains a sense of detachment from response to his work. "At the end of the day, your job is going to be judged by a lot of people, so you have to really be strong in your personal view of things, otherwise you can be destroyed," he explained.

The year *No Country for Old Men* was released, Bardem appeared in a very different role in the movie adaptation of Gabriel García Márquez's *Love in the Time of Cholera*. He also worked on Woody Allen's film *Vicky Cristina Barcelona*, a comedy, providing a third drastically different role within two years of filming. He described the part to Mitchell in *Interview*: "I play a painter who lives in Spain. Two tourists come from the States, and there's a love relation between all of us—including my character's ex-wife, who is played by Penelope Cruz. The movie has a very pointed perspective about relationships. Making that movie was an intense experience, because, as everyone knows, with Woody Allen you do the whole scene in one sequence, and I had to improvise in a foreign language."

In addition to his acting, Bardem also produced the 1999 film *Los lobos de Washington* ("Washington Wolves"), in which he also starred. He served on the jury of the Cannes Film Festival in 2005. Bardem continues to work on American films, though Spain is his home. In 2008, he proposed to his *Vicky Cristina Barcelona* co-star Cruz, and the two planned a marriage for late that year.

Sources

Books

Almanac of Famous People, 9th ed., Gale (Detroit, MI), 2007.
Contemporary Theatre, Film, and Television, vol. 75, Gale (Detroit, MI), 2007.

Periodicals

Advocate, December 19, 2000, p. 55.
Back Stage West, December 6, 2007, p. 6A.
Entertainment Weekly, February 23, 2001, p. 30; May 9, 2003, p. 55; August 15, 2003, p. 54; February 1, 2008, p. 36.
Hollywood Reporter, November 27, 2007, p. S4.
Houston Chronicle (Houston, TX), January 30, 2005, p. 8.
Interview, January-April 2001, p. 61; May 2003, p. 100; March 2005, p. 152; November 2007, p. 92.
Los Angeles Magazine, February 2005, p. 51.
New York Times, December 11, 2007, p. E2.
Sacramento Bee (Sacramento, CA), November 17, 2007.
Sarasota Herald Tribune (Sarasota, FL), February 4, 2005, p. 22.

Online

"Day to Day: Bardem on Working with the Coen Brothers," National Public Radio, http://www.npr.org/templates/story/story.php?storyId=18184544.tif (April 15, 2008).
"Javier Bardem," Internet Movie Database, http://www.imdb.com/name/nm0000849/ (May 18, 2008).

—*Alana Joli Abbott*

Francine Benes

Courtesy of Dr. Francine Benes

Neuroscientist and psychiatrist

Born May 8, 1946, in New York City; daughter of Joseph William and Emma Mary Benes. *Education:* St. John's University, New York, B.A., 1967; Yale School of Medicine, Ph.D. in cellular biology, 1972; City of Hope National Medical Center, CA, postdoctoral training in single-cell neurochemistry, early 1970s; Yale Medical School, M.D., 1978.

Addresses: *Office*—McLean Hospital, 115 Mill St., Belmont, MA 02478.

Career

Founded the Laboratory for Structural Neuroscience at McLean Hospital, Belmont, MA, 1982; assistant professor of psychiatry, Harvard Medical School, Boston, MA, 1982-87; director, Program in Structural and Molecular Neuroscience, McLean Hospital, Belmont, MA, 1992—; director of the Harvard Brain Tissue Resource Center, 1996—; professor, Harvard Medical School, 1997—.

Member: National Wildlife Federation; Humane Society of the United States; editorial board of *Biotechniques,* 1990-96; chair, McLean Hospital Affirmative Action Committee, 1993-94; Board of Directors, Walden Pond Reservation Trust, Concord, MA, 2001—; National Institute of Medicine, 2004—.

Awards: Shervent S. Frazier Lifetime Achievement Award, 1999; National Institute of Mental Health Merit Award, 2000-02; Lieber Prize for Outstanding Achievement in Schizophrenia Research, National Association for Research in Schizophrenia and Depression, 2002; Institute of Medicine inductee, National Academies, 2004; Kempf Fund Award for Research Development in Psychobiological Psychiatry, American Psychiatric Association, 2006; William Silens Lifetime Achievement in Mentoring Award, Harvard Medical School, 2006.

Sidelights

As director of the Harvard Brain Tissue Resource Center, neuroscientist Francine Benes oversees a collection of nearly 6,000 brains. Her facility—commonly known as the Brain Bank—stockpiles human brains for medical researchers around the globe. The Brain Bank receives about one brain a day and is specifically interested in collecting three types of brains: "normal" brains from disease-free people; brains from people with neurodegenerative disorders such as Alzheimer's, Parkinson's, and Huntington's diseases; and brains from those diagnosed with mental illnesses—particularly schizophrenia and bipolar disorder.

As a scientific sleuth, Benes has dedicated her career to investigating the biology of mental illness. "The brain is biology's last, vast frontier," Benes told the *Boston Phoenix*'s Alicia Potter. "And within brain studies, those aspects of the brain that give rise to thinking and feeling, cognitive function, and our ability to reason really constitute the final mystery of biological science." Over the course of her career, Benes has completed groundbreaking research on schizophrenia. In 2004, Benes was recognized for her work by being elected to the prestigious Institute of Medicine, part of the National Academy of Sciences. In the field of medicine, this honor ranks among the highest.

Benes was born on May 8, 1946, in New York City to Joseph and Emma Benes. She was raised in the borough of Queens. As a child, Benes figured she would grow up and go into education or social work. That all changed in eighth grade when Benes had a teacher who created personal poems for each student. "The poem she wrote for me was about me becoming a scientist," Benes recalled in an article on CNN.com. "I had never thought about being a scientist, but from then on I realized it was something to strive for." Benes attended St. John's University in New York, graduating with her bachelor's degree in 1967. Five years later, Benes earned her Ph.D. in cellular biology from the Yale School of Medicine.

Benes became interested in mental illness after attending a neuroscience conference at a Colorado ski resort in 1973. While there, she heard a speech about schizophrenia. The presenter proposed that the mental illness might be caused by a dopamine disturbance. Dopamine is a neurotransmitter. In the 1970s, the idea that schizophrenia could be caused by bad circuitry was a radical notion. Psychiatrists at the time thought schizophrenia was more likely a character flaw brought on by poor parenting. Speaking to the *Boston Globe*'s Pagan Kennedy, Benes described her reaction to the talk. "I was standing in the back of the room, and it blew me away. Schizophrenia could now be visualized in terms of the circuitries of the brain."

The next morning, while riding the ski lift, Benes talked the matter over with a neuropathologist. The man disagreed with the presenter's views and told Benes that nothing abnormal had been detected in the brains of people with schizophrenia. He insisted the idea had been studied earlier in the century and that nothing unusual was found. Benes recalled her reaction in an article for CNN.com. "All I could think of was how could you find nothing? If you really seriously look, you've got to find something, so I just got intrigued with this, and I decided that I was going to devote my career to the study of schizophrenia."

At this point, having spent eight years studying cellular biology, Benes decided to become a psychiatrist so she could study schizophrenia. After earning her medical degree from Yale in 1978, Benes began a residency at McLean Hospital, one of the nation's top-rated psychiatric hospitals. McLean, located in Belmont, Massachusetts, is affiliated with Harvard Medical School. After her residency, Benes stayed at McLean and established the Laboratory for Structural Neuroscience in 1982. Accompanied by several other researchers, Benes began doing postmortem schizophrenia research.

Speaking to *Psychology Today*, Benes is quoted as ssaying she felt "pure awe" the first time she saw a brain. "I was a graduate student at Creedmore State Hospital when I saw a postmortem brain being carried down the hall. I asked if I could watch them prepare it. All I could think was that about 10 minutes before, the person might have been alive. And now we were holding the organ of the body that in essence made them who they were."

In 1996, Benes became director of the Brain Bank, succeeding its founder, Edward Bird, who had established it in 1978. The Brain Bank collects about 350 brains a year and annually distributes thousands of individual specimens to researchers around the world. When a brain arrives, one hemisphere is usually preserved in formaldehyde, while the other is dissected into slices and freeze-dried in liquid nitrogen. The specimens are stored in a place staffers have dubbed "the Tupperware room," where shelves hold plastic containers of brain slices.

Researchers have used brains from the bank to pinpoint the gene that causes the progressive neuromuscular disorder known as Huntington's disease. The brains have also been used in research that has led to treatments for Parkinson's. Aside from collecting brains, the laboratory oversees the National Brain Data Bank. This collection of data—available to the public—consists of thousands of genetic profiles on brains from people with psychiatric and neurological disorders. Scientists who receive tissue samples from the Brain Bank are asked to submit their findings to the data bank.

Besides directing the Brain Bank, Benes has continued her research on schizophrenia and has found evidence to support the idea that subtle wiring defects in the brain play a role in schizophrenia and bipolar disorder. Benes has also discovered that degenerative changes in the brain are not associated with schizophrenia and bipolar disorder, as with Alzheimer's disease. Her findings are being used by researchers to study new treatments and prevention strategies. In 1997, Benes traveled to Stockholm, Sweden, to present her research at a Nobel Symposium on Schizophrenia held at Karolinska University. Benes' work attracted so much attention that the National Institute of Mental Health awarded her $4 million over a ten-year period to carry on her research on schizophrenia and manic-depressive disorder. Benes believes breakthroughs are on the horizon—and so do her colleagues.

"With each important discovery, Benes continues to provide new hope to the countless individuals and their families whose lives have been robbed of the basic human qualities that most people take for granted," her colleague, Bruce Cohen, is quoted as saying in *Reintegration Today*. "The path to treatment is long and winding; however, with individuals like Francine Benes leading the way, that path is filled with promise."

Sources

Periodicals

Boston Globe, December 13, 1998, p. 1 (Northwest Weekly); June 13, 2004, p. 34.

Psychology Today, July-August 2004, p. 26.
Reintegration Today, Winter 2005, p. 5.

Online

"Doctor Controls Harvard's Brain Trust," CNN.com, http://www.cnn.com/2005/HEALTH/08/30/profile.brain/index.html (October 11, 2007).
"Francine Benes: Brain Collector," *Harvard University Gazette*, http://www.hno.harvard.edu/gazette/2002/10.03/05-bigpic.html (October 11, 2007).
"Francine Benes, MD, PHD," McLean Hospital, http://www.mclean.harvard.edu/about/bios/detail.php?username=fbenes (October 11, 2007).
"How to Get Ahead in Science: The Future of Neurology Lies in a Room Full of Tupperware in Belmont," *Boston Phoenix*, http://bostonphoenix.com/archive/features/99/04/08/BRAINS.html (October 11, 2007).

Other

Additional information was obtained from a press biography from Dr. Francine Benes.

—*Lisa Frick*

Andy and Rachel Berliner

Founders of Amy's Kitchen

Andy Berliner born c. 1947, in Chicago, IL; son of meat buyer and a legal secretary; first marriage ended in divorce; married Rachel Berliner, 1985; children: Amy. Rachel Berliner born c. 1954; daughter of a private investigator and a librarian; first marriage ended in divorce; married Andy Berliner, 1985; children: Amy. *Education:* Andy Berliner: Earned degrees in biology and psychology from Purdue University. Rachel Berliner: Studied art at Santa Monica City College.

Addresses: *Office*—Amy's Kitchen, Inc., P.O. Box 449, Petaluma CA 94953.

Career

Andy Berliner worked for Magic Mountain Tea Company, San Rafael, CA. Rachel Berliner worked as a physician's assistant. Together, founded Amy's Kitchen, c. 1987.

Sidelights

Andy and Rachel Berliner founded Amy's Kitchen, an organic foods company, in 1987 in the kitchen of their northern California home. Two decades later, the bustling organic foods enterprise is the No. 1 brand in the natural/organic category of the frozen foods industry and also makes a line of standard groceries that have proved equally profitable. "The consumer might not think so, but people in the food industry find it amazing to see that we make our products just like they would make it at home," Andy Berliner told Rex Daven-

port in a company profile that appeared in *Refrigerated & Frozen Foods*, an industry trade magazine. "As opposed to how food is manufactured in most plants. I have been in food plants and have seen food running through pipes, having modified food starch or flavors added and then being cooked and deposited in a tray. We don't do that."

Andy Berliner was a native of Chicago who had grown up in a staunch meat-eating household, with a father who worked as a meat buyer. After studying biology and psychology at Purdue University in Indiana, Andy Berliner moved to the Sonoma, California, area in the early 1970s, and was working as a manager at the Magic Mountain Tea Company in San Rafael, one of the first successful herbal-tea companies, when he met Rachel in 1979 on a meditation retreat in India while he was married to his first wife.

Rachel Berliner grew up in the Los Angeles area, the daughter of a private investigator father and a mother who was a librarian, and both parents encouraged healthy eating habits in their children. "My mother always said, 'If you can't pronounce an ingredient on a label, it's a good idea not to eat it,'" she told Julie K. L. Dam and Vicki Sheff-Cahan in *People.* Her brother and father were vegetarians, but Rachel Berliner did not become one until her teen years, when she met a champion of the cause who traveled around with a live lamb. "I was 16 years old, and I never really connected that what I was eating was once a live animal," she recalled in an interview with the *San Francisco Chronicle*'s Cynthia Wollman. "I just wasn't aware of that." After studying art at Santa Monica City College, Rachel

Berliner married and worked as a physician's assistant for a homeopathic doctor.

Both Andy's and Rachel's first marriages eventually ended, and the couple wed in 1985. Strict vegetarians, they even grew their own vegetables, but when they were awaiting the birth of their first child in 1987, they realized they might be forced to change their eating habits. "The more pregnant Rachel got, the less energy there was for gardening and cooking," Andy Berliner told Wollman in the *San Francisco Chronicle* interview, but he recalled that when they visited the convenience-food section of their local health-food store, they "were shocked at the poor quality of prepared meals that were natural and organic," he said. They decided that there must be other families like theirs who wanted healthy food but simply did not have the time to prepare such meals every day.

Amy's Kitchen, named after their newborn daughter, was launched in 1987 with their first product, a vegetarian pot pie made from organic vegetables. They started the company with a loan from Rachel's mother and cash from selling a watch, some gold coins, and even one of their cars; they also refinanced their house. Once the business was underway, they realized they needed to establish a line of credit line. "Every bank turned us down," Rachel Berliner remembered when she was interviewed by Susan McGinnis, a writer for the magazine *Kiwi*, but they finally convinced a loan officer at a small bank in their hometown to approve them. "We said we'd be their biggest customer someday," she remembered—a promise that they kept.

Amy's Kitchen grew slowly, with new frozen goods such as spinach pizza and vegetarian enchiladas added to their top-selling pot pies. The groceries were available in health food stores nationwide. In 1999 they introduced a line of non-frozen foods, such as canned soups and chili, pasta sauces, and salsa. In 2001 sales for the company passed the $100 million mark, and thanks to a surge in interest in organic, healthy foods among more mainstream consumers, that figure doubled just five years later. Twenty years after creating their first recipe, the Berliners adhered to all of the same guidelines on which they founded their company. The 100-plus

line of Amy's Kitchen groceries are made by hand and with the same principles—no additives or artificial ingredients, and with all-organic source materials. "We are deeply involved in the entire agricultural process," Andy Berliner said in the *Refrigerated & Frozen Foods* article by Davenport. "So, if we want to create a new product that wasn't planned, we have to see if we can find the ingredients or have it grown quickly enough. It helps that we are in California."

The Berliners still run a family business, albeit one with 1,600 employees and 2006 sales of $200 million. When they moved forward with plans to open a second manufacturing facility plant in Oregon, their decision prompted a phone call from California governor Arnold Schwarzenegger asking them to reconsider—but Oregon had cheaper utility rates and a lower cost of living than northern California. Amy's Kitchen is a progressive company that offers a profit-sharing plan for employees, as well as English-language and citizenship classes for foreign-born staffers; there is even a college scholarship program for the children of employees. The "Amy" in Amy's Kitchen grew up and entered Stanford University, but still worked in the food plant during her summer breaks. "My first memory of solid food," Amy Berliner once told Dam and Sheff-Cahan in the *People* interview, "was looking at Amy's Kitchen macaroni and cheese and thinking, 'Yummy!' I had no idea I was the Amy." Thirteen years old at the time of that article, she was proud of being her parents' inspiration. "It's nice for people to know that Amy's Kitchen is family owned," she said in the same interview. "I love reading the consumer letters. I write back. I want them to know that my family really cares about them."

Sources

Frozen Food Age, June 2007, p. S25.
Kiwi, July-August 2007, p. 45(3).
New York Times, November 8, 2000; February 23, 2002.
People, December 18, 2000, p. 151.
Refrigerated & Frozen Foods, January 2004, p. 28.
San Francisco Chronicle, January 25, 2002, p. 9.

—*Carol Brennan*

Ben Bernanke

Chairman of the Federal Reserve

Born Benjamin S. Bernanke, December 13, 1953, in Augusta, GA; son of Philip (a pharmacist and theater manager) and Edna (a teacher) Bernanke; married Anna Friedmann, May 29, 1978; children: Alyssa, Joel. *Education:* Harvard University, B.A., 1975; Massachusetts Institute of Technology, Ph.D., 1979.

Addresses: *Office*—c/o Federal Reserve Board, 20th St. and Constitution Ave., NW, Washington, D.C. 20551.

Career

Assistant professor of economics, Stanford University, 1979-83; associate professor of economics, Stanford University, 1983-85; professor of economics and public affairs, Princeton University, 1985-96; Howard Harrison and Gabrielle Snyder Beck professor of economics and public affairs and chair of the economics department, Princeton University, 1996-2002; served on the Federal Reserve System's Board of Governors, 2002-05; chairman of the President's Council of Economic Advisors, 2005-06; Chairman of the Federal Reserve, 2006—.

Awards: Allyn A. Young Prize for best undergraduate honors thesis in economics, Harvard University, 1975; John H. Williams Prize for outstanding Harvard senior majoring in economics, Harvard University, 1975; Graduate Fellow, National Science Foundation, 1975; Hoover Institution National Fellow, Hoover Institution of Stanford University, 1982-83; Research Fellow, Alfred P. Sloan Foundation, 1983-84; fellowship, John Simon Guggenheim Memorial Foundation, 1999.

Sidelights

Ben Bernanke was selected as the Chairman of the Board of Governors of the Federal Reserve in 2006, filling the shoes of former Chairman Alan Greenspan. His appointment was met with a market surge, reflecting the confidence many economists felt at his appointment to what is arguably one of the most powerful positions in the United States government. Given the 19-year legacy of Greenspan, Bernanke has often been compared to the former chairman, both positively and negatively, as his ideas about inflation targeting and his dedication to speaking plainly and making the Federal Reserve—also known as the Fed or the Federal Reserve System—less obscure run counter to the previous administration.

Bernanke was born on December 13, 1953, in Augusta, Georgia, and grew up in Dillion, South Carolina. His parents, a pharmacist and a teacher, encouraged Bernanke's education early on. By the age of three, he could add and subtract; he learned to read as a kindergartener and skipped the second grade. At the age of 12, he won the South Carolina spelling bee and went on to compete in the national competition. As a teen, Bernanke assisted rabbinical students in offering services for the small Jewish community in Dillon, South Carolina. In high school, he taught himself to speed read and learned calculus on his own, since it was not offered at his school; in 1971, he earned the highest scoring Scholastic Aptitude Test score of the year in South Carolina, earning 1,590 out of a possible 1,600 points. An avid fan of baseball, Bernanke became interested in statistics, and developed a dice-based baseball game. He was the valedictorian of his graduating class.

Bernanke attended Harvard University for his undergraduate degree in economics, which he earned summa cum laude in 1975. To help support himself through college, he worked at various jobs, including as a waiter at a South of the Border restaurant and as a construction worker. After graduating, he attended the Massachusetts Institute of Technology, where he earned his Ph.D. in economics in four years. His dissertation focused on the Great Depression, an era that particularly fascinated Bernanke. In the *Wall Street Journal*, Bernanke was quoted as having said, "If you want to understand geology, study earthquakes. If you want to understand economics, study the biggest calamity to hit the U.S. and world economies." *Newsweek* reporters Daniel McGinn and Richard Wolffe quoted another of Bernanke's comments about his interest in the era: "I guess I am a Great Depression buff, the way some people are Civil War buffs. To understand the Great Depression is the Holy Grail of macroeconomics." The paper criticized the Fed's failure to keep the banks steady after the stock market crashed in 1929, and earned Bernanke attention throughout academic circles.

As an academic, Bernanke taught at both Stanford and Princeton, where he became known for his spirit of teamwork inside his department. As the chair of the Department of Economics at Princeton, he was known for a sense of equality with his peers, engaging all members of the department as contributors to the team. In what is usually a competitive academic environment, Bernanke earned "almost universal admiration from colleagues, both for his intellectual prowess and for his personable manner," Tom Buerkle wrote in *Institutional Investor International Edition*.

"What sets Bernanke apart from many other academic economists is his ability to forge consensus," wrote Rich Miller and Richard S. Dunham in an article for *BusinessWeek*. Along with focusing on team dynamics in his department at Princeton, Bernanke also made efforts to build a sense of collaboration on the Montgomery Township school board, which

was his first public position. That position gave him experience in dealing with both angry parents and angry taxpayers. "I learned something, I think, about public service, about working with other people, and dealing with sometimes emotional or otherwise highly charged issues," he told *U.S. News and World Report*.

That his only public position had been as a school board member made him a surprising candidate for the Federal Reserve's Board of Governors. While serving as a governor, Bernanke became known for his outspoken concerns on deflation and his ideas on how the Fed should counter it. He was also noted for his congenial relationship with Fed staffers and aides, asking questions about data and their analyses. Chairman Alan Greenspan would often jump in with his own explanation and, while Bernanke would listen, he would tend to follow Greenspan's thoughts with, "Be that as it may ... I'd still like the staff to get back to me," according to Miller and Dunham in *BusinessWeek*. Bernanke did not challenge Greenspan, but continually requested additional information and sought differing views in order to develop a more complete understanding of economic situations.

In 2005, Bernanke left the Board of Governors to become Chairman of the President's Council of Economic Advisors. Within a year of being named to that position, President George W. Bush nominated Bernanke for the position of Chairman of the Board of Governors when Greenspan announced his retirement. Atypical of most nominations, both Democrats and Republicans were largely pleased, in part because Bernanke kept his own political opinions quiet. "I didn't know he was a Republican until he got appointed to the Fed," Cornell economist Robert Frank, who had written papers with Bernanke, told Buerkle in *Institutional Investor International Edition*. In the same article, Edward Gramlich, an economics professor at the University of Michigan and former Fed governor, called Bernanke "very nonpolitical."

Not only was Washington enthusiastic about Bernanke's appointment, but the market itself seemed to take a positive stance. As *Newsweek* contributors McGinn and Wolffe noted, "Economists applauded the choice, the stock market rose, and even in partisan Washington, it was hard to find anyone who disapproved." Bernanke announced in his acceptance of the nomination, as quoted by National Public Radio's *Morning Edition*, that he intended to maintain the "standard for excellence in economic policy-making" that Greenspan set while in office, but it was quickly obvious that Bernanke intended to make some changes in the way things were run. The first difference, and possibly the one that made Bernanke Bush's choice as Greenspan's replacement, was Bernanke's commitment to transparency. Bush was quoted on *Morning Edition* as saying of Bernanke, "His speeches were widely admired for their keen insight and clear, simple language." N. Gregory Mankiw, a Harvard professor who formerly held Bernanke's position on the President's Council of Economic Advisors, told *Newsweek,* "Some academics find it hard to leave academia and talk more broadly, but Ben is so tremendously articulate." This attitude went directly counter to the precedent set by Greenspan, who was known for his obscure comments. He once quipped, according to Daniel Kadlec in *Time,* "If I seem unduly clear to you, you must have misunderstood what I said."

Bernanke has also taken the stance that the best strategy for fighting inflation is a predictable approach. While a Fed governor, he proposed selecting a target rate for inflation, letting investors, media, and the market know that when inflation fell below three percent, for example, the Fed would raise it, and if it went above, they would lower it. Greenspan long rejected this strategy, feeling that it would not allow for the flexibility necessary to manage spikes in prices due to natural disasters or other short-term occurrences.

Despite these ideological differences, the president of the Federal Reserve Bank of New York, Tim Geithner, expressed to Maria Bartiromo of *BusinessWeek* that he anticipated most policies to carry through from Greenspan to Bernanke. "I suspect that even though the way the meetings are run will change, you will see continuity in policy," Geithner said. He continued, "Ben is a champion of transparency in monetary policy, but he also recognizes that there are limits to what we know about the economic forecast and what that means to monetary policy. And he understands that we can't give the markets more clarity about the forecast or about future policy than we have ourselves."

Supporters of Bernanke were quick to emphasize his expertise after he was selected as Greenspan's replacement. "He combines a deep understanding of monetary theory with broad policy experience," wrote *BusinessWeek* contributor Robert J. Barro. David Wyss, chief economist of Standard & Poor's, told an interviewer for *BusinessWeek Online,* "Bernanke has probably the best academic qualifications for chairman in Fed history," and called Bernanke "one of the leading experts in monetary theory." Wyss went on to say, "If Bernanke has a weakness,

it's his inexperience in practical finance, since he hasn't been in the private sector, and his tenure at the Fed board was relatively brief." But while Bernanke quickly gained praise, others noted that the bond market in the United States weakened upon the announcement of Bernanke's appointment. Representatives from Baring Asset Management felt "Bernanke's reign could bring further volatility to U.S. inflation," according to an article in *Money Marketing. U.S. News & World Report* contributor Paul J. Lim summed up the public doubts, writing, "There's a growing feeling among market mavens that Bernanke, despite widespread support evidenced by the market's strong rally the day of his appointment, still needs to build up immediate credibility in his first few months in office."

Upon reaching the six-month mark in office, it was obvious that the economy was in transition, something Bernanke told members of Congress. According to Barbara Kiaviat of *Time,* the economy was not the only thing changing: "The Fed itself is feeling the Bernanke effect," Kiaviat wrote. "Listening, mulling, debating, airing opinions of all stripes ... that style is spilling over into the way economists at the Fed communicate as they forge the nation's monetary policy." But while the clarity of communication made an impact and positive impression on most, Bernanke had to learn to manage his bluntness, watching one comment make the market soar, and then watching it fall again when he corrected the assumptions investors had made. Other transitions in the economy were not so easy to pinpoint, and Bernanke and the Fed have struggled to find out why the housing market is continuing to decrease when other consumer prices are increasing. In late 2007, the Fed dropped interest rates in an effort to stave off the recession that Bernanke felt to be threatening, and while some economists felt the gambit would work, others worry changing the focus from "fighting inflation to preventing panic," as Robert J. Samuelson described it in *Newsweek,* might not be the right decision.

Despite the seriousness of his position, Bernanke enjoys playing basketball or rooting for his favorite baseball team—the Boston Red Sox—in his spare time. He has also made an effort to change clothing trends. "My proposal that Fed governors should signal their commitment to public service by wearing Hawaiian shirts and Bermuda shorts has so far gone unheeded," Miller and Dunham quoted Bernanke as saying in *BusinessWeek.* When jokingly criticized by Bush for wearing tan socks with a dark suit, Bernanke responded by presenting Vice President Dick Cheney and others in the administration with tan socks of their own.

In a speech that Bernanke delivered to the National Economists Club, he described the difficulties of predicting economic trends. "If making monetary policy is like driving a car," he said, "then the car is one that has an unreliable speedometer, a foggy windshield, and a tendency to respond unpredictably and with a delay to the accelerator or the brake." Bernanke lives with his wife, Anna, and their children, Joel and Alyssa, in Washington, D.C.

Sources

Periodicals

BusinessWeek, November 7, 2005, p. 36; November 7, 2005, p. 146; May 15, 2006, p. 110.
Institutional Investor International Edition, November 2005, pp. 7-8.
Money, August 1, 2003, p. 55.
Money Marketing, November 3, 2005, p. 26.
Newsweek, November 7, 2005, p. 54; October 1, 2007, p. 39.
Time, November 7, 2005, p. 49; July 31, 2006, p. 54.
U.S. News & World Report, December 29, 2003; November 7, 2005, p. 59; November 7, 2005, p. 66.
Wall Street Journal, December 7, 2005.

Online

"Analysis: Bernanke Chosen to Succeed Fed's Greenspan," NPR's *Morning Edition,* http://www.npr.org/templates/story/story.php?storyId=4973231 (March 12, 2008).
"Answers About Bernanke," *BusinessWeek Online,* http://www.businessweek.com/investor/content/oct2005/pi20051024.tif_7872_pi015.htm (March 12, 2008).
"Biography of Dr. Ben S. Bernanke," White House, http://www.whitehouse.gov/cea/bbernankebio.html (March 12, 2008).

—Alana Joli Abbott

Anthony Bourdain

Chef, television personality, and author

Born June 25, 1956, in New York, NY; son of Pierre (a record-company executive) and Gladys (a copy editor) Bourdain; married Nancy Putkoski, c. 1985 (divorced, 2005); married Ottavia Busia, 2007; children: Ariane (from second marriage). *Education:* Attended Vassar College, c. 1973-75; graduated from the Culinary Institute of America, 1978.

Addresses: *Home*—New York, NY. *Office*—Brasserie Les Halles, 411 Park Avenue S., New York, NY 10016.

Career

Worked in the kitchen of The Dreadnought, Provincetown, MA, early 1970s, and in the following New York City restaurants: The Rainbow Room, c. 1978-80; Work Progress after 1981; Gianni's; The Supper Club, started as sous-chef, c. 1988, became chef; held executive chef positions at the following restaurants: Vince and Linda at One Fifth, after May 1995; Coco Pazzo Teatro, summer of 1996; Sullivan's, after October 1996; Brasserie Les Halles, c. 1997. First novel, *Bone in the Throat,* published by Villard Books, 1995. Host of the television series *Cook's Tour,* 2002, and *Anthony Bourdain: No Reservations,* 2005—, both for the Travel Channel.

Sidelights

Celebrity chef Anthony Bourdain has produced just one cookbook in his career, and vows he will never host his own television cooking show. Instead he travels around the world sampling the most exotic—and at times, stomach-turning—fare available for his popular Travel Channel show, *Anthony Bourdain: No Reservations.* He no longer supervises the nightly dinner rush at the popular Brasserie Les Halles in New York City, but admitted in an interview with the London *Observer*'s Euan Ferguson that he sometimes missed the camaraderie of the kitchen. "Cooking is such an intimate thing," he reflected about his longtime profession, which he detailed in a 2000 bestseller, *Kitchen Confidential: Adventures in the Culinary Underbelly.* "There's no lying in the kitchen. You can't massage or spin your ability; you can't even lie about your personal life, because problems come through."

Bourdain was born on June 25, 1956, in New York City, and grew up in Leonia, a town in New Jersey's Bergen County. His father was a record-label executive, and his mother was a copy editor with the *New York Times.* When Bourdain was a child, the family spent a summer in a fishing village in southwestern France where his father had grown up. One morning, they joined a local oyster fisherman on his daily trip, and it was aboard that boat that Bourdain sampled his first oyster. "It tasted of seawater ... of brine and flesh ... and, somehow ... of the future," he wrote in he wrote in *Kitchen Confidential.* "This, I knew, was the magic I had until now been only dimly and spitefully aware of."

In the early 1970s, Bourdain went on to Vassar College in Poughkeepsie, New York, though he later admitted he lacked the discipline necessary for academics, and dropped out after two years. He spent the summer of 1974 working at The Dreadnought, a seafood restaurant in Provincetown, Massachusetts. Here he found his future career, recalling in an interview with *Newsweek*'s Jerry Adler the awe with which he viewed the restaurant's cooks, who "carried these huge dangerous knives, they wore tattoos and headbands and they drank like madmen, stole everything they could get their hands on and slept with all the waitresses and half the customers…. That was the life I wanted."

In 1975, Bourdain enrolled at the Culinary Institute of America, a renowned training ground for chefs in Hyde Park, New York. He graduated in 1978, settled in New York City, and began the first of his many Manhattan restaurant jobs. In 1981, a friend of his became chef at a SoHo eatery called Work Progress, and hired Bourdain as well as a pal from their Provincetown restaurant days. "Hardly a decision was made without drugs," Bourdain wrote in *Kitchen Confidential.* "We worked long hours and took considerable pride in our efforts—the drugs, we thought, having little effect on the end-product."

Bourdain's substance abuse progressed through marijuana, cocaine, and then finally heroin, and he held a number of successively less prestigious chef's jobs after he left the failing Work Progress, including a new place on Bleecker Street whose ex-convict owner had been set up in the business by organized-crime figures whom he had refused to rat out to federal authorities; the restaurant was a gesture of gratitude from the mobsters. When the restaurant finally opened, they were packed, but short-staffed. "Guys I'd read about later in the papers as running construction in the outer boroughs, purported killers, made men, who lived in concrete piles on Staten Island and Long Beach and security-fenced estates in Jersey … slathered mayo and avocado slices on pita bread behind the counter, and bussed tables in the dining room," Bourdain recalled in *Kitchen Confidential.* "I have to say I liked them for that."

Bourdain's career prospects improved after he finally gave up the hard drugs. "I'd be the last person in the world to say don't take drugs for moral reasons," he reflected years later in an interview with Gaby Huddart for *Caterer & Hotelkeeper.* "But when cocaine is the main priority in your life, it's not conducive to making good food." His career trajectory took him from sous-chef at a place called The Supper Club in the late 1980s, to executive chef at a dining room called Vince and Linda at One

Fifth. In between jobs, he wrote two novels, both set in fictional restaurants with ties to the underworld. The first was *Bone in the Throat,* published in 1995, which Marilyn Stasio of the *New York Times* called a "satirical and prodigiously self-assured first novel." He followed it two years later with another tongue-in-cheek crime thriller, *Gone Bamboo.* By this point, Bourdain had changed jobs yet again, this time to a Manhattan landmark called Sullivan's located inside the Ed Sullivan Theater. Asked by Enid Nemy in the *New York Times* if his co-workers knew of his second career as an author, he said that "my cooks view my writing career with suspicion. It isn't tangible. There's something a little shady about it."

Bourdain eventually landed at Brasserie Les Halles on Park Avenue South, as executive chef of the French-bistro-fare provider. Back in 1997, he had told Nemy that he fantasized about writing his first work of nonfiction, a behind-the-scenes tell-all book. In April of 1999, the esteemed *New Yorker* published what would become one of the chapters of that book. Headlined "Don't Eat before Reading This (The Workings of a Professional Kitchen)," the article divulged several sneaky cost-cutting practices even the best New York City restaurants were known to employ. Bourdain advised against ordering fish on a Monday, for example, revealing that it had probably been delivered three days earlier by the seafood supplier. *Kitchen Confidential: Adventures in the Culinary Underbelly* was published in the spring of 2000 and spent 14 weeks on the *New York Times* best-seller list. Writing in the London *Observer,* Ferguson said it is a book "written with magnificent flair" as well as "the first real account of proper life in a restaurant kitchen, the cheating and the burns and the drugs and the short-cuts and the sex and the threats, and the tears, and the savage triumphs."

In *Kitchen Confidential,* Bourdain recounted his experiences as a dishwasher at The Dreadnought up through his success at Les Halles, detailing his period of drug abuse and the camaraderie and insults the line cooks, sous-chefs, and assorted other kitchen employees commonly hurl at one another in the chaotic atmosphere of a restaurant kitchen in full-swing dinner rush. Of the brutal bullying that new hires were usually subjected to, Bourdain explained to Huddart in *Caterer & Hotelkeeper* that it was simply a way of testing the person's mettle. "Better to find out early if someone can handle the pressure of the kitchen by yelling at them, than to discover they freak out on the first busy Saturday night a few weeks in."

Bourdain's tell-all caused such a stir that filmmaker David Fincher (*Fight Club*) optioned the movie rights, and there was talk about Brad Pitt starring.

Meanwhile, the chef returned to writing, crafting *Typhoid Mary: An Urban Historical* for the Bloomsbury publishing house in 2001. He retold the tale of a notorious public-health incident in New York City in the early 1900s, when an Irish immigrant cook named Mary Mallon infected some 33 victims with the deadly typhoid fever virus, three of whom died. He also wrote another nonfiction work published that same year, *A Cook's Tour: In Search of the Perfect Meal*. For this joint project between his publisher, Bloomsbury, and the Food Network, Bourdain spent several months traveling to exotic locales to sample the local fare. In Morocco, he ate sheep's testicles and, in Vietnam, he ate the still-beating heart of a cobra snake, as well as more standard fare such as the 20-course meal he enjoyed at the acclaimed French Laundry restaurant in California's Napa Valley. A camera crew traveled with him, and the 22 episodes of the first season began airing on the Food Network in January of 2002 as *Cook's Tour: Global Adventures in Extreme Cuisines*.

Bourdain was adamant that he would never host his own cooking show. Not long after *Kitchen Confidential* was published, he told *Entertainment Weekly* writer Karen Valby that "I really hate the concept of celebrity chefs. I know chefs who are getting voice coaches now! I have enough reasons to hate myself without looking at myself in the mirror and saying 'I employ a hairstylist.'" At times, he has publicly derided the most popular television chefs. In an *Esquire* interview, he told Manny Howard that one popular Cajun-cuisine Food Network star was "the Antichrist. I'm consumed with fantasies of causing him harm. His food is crap. His act is crap. He's an offense to everything I stand for." Mario Batali, however, "strikes me as a line cook," Bourdain said. "That's the highest compliment you could pay a chef."

Bourdain did produce one cookbook, *Anthony Bourdain's Les Halles Cookbook: Strategies, Recipes, and Techniques of Classic Bistro Cooking*, which appeared in 2004. A year later, in July of 2005, he debuted with a new television series on the Travel Channel with the title *Anthony Bourdain: No Reservations*. It repeated much of the premise of his earlier international tour, taking a camera crew along with him with the mission of eating as the locals do. "What I do is not complicated," he told David Carr in the *New York Times*. "Any stranger who shows an honest curiosity about what the locals think is the best food is going to be welcomed. When you eat their food and you seem happy, people sitting around a table open up and interesting things happen." Bourdain and his camera crew sometimes experienced less-than-idyllic conditions, however, such as the time in the summer of 2006 when they were filming in Beirut, Lebanon, and were stranded amidst a military conflagration between Lebanese and Israeli forces that went on for several days. They kept filming, however, showing the behind-the-scenes drama, and the episode was nominated for an Emmy Award.

Bourdain remains with Les Halles, but has delegated the daily operations to another chef. He continues to write for a variety of publications, including *Gourmet* and the *New York Times*, and several of his articles were collected in a 2006 volume, *The Nasty Bits: Collected Varietal Cuts, Usable Trim, Scraps, and Bones*. "Bourdain is a vivid and witty writer, but his greatest gift is his ability to convey his passion for professional cooking," asserted Bruce Handy in a *New York Times* review. "With one eye on the kitchen and the other on the dining room, he never loses sight of how the terrestrial inevitably informs the divine." In 2007, his memoir of the past three years of travels for *No Reservations* was published by Bloomsbury as *No Reservations: Around the World on an Empty Stomach*. He recounted stories that never made it to the air, accompanied by photographs of many of his most memorable journeys.

Bourdain married for the second time in 2007, just days after the birth of his first child. For Ariane, his new daughter, Bourdain finally gave up his long-time cigarette habit. Somewhat improbably, the man once dubbed the "bad boy chef" seemed to mellow a bit. "I regret saying a lot of those things now," he told *Fresno Bee* reporter Joan Obra about the barbs that made *Kitchen Confidential* so controversial. "First of all, a lot has changed. Since cooking became a glamour profession, there's a lot more hope and pride in kitchens.... A lot of that nonsense would be looked down on that used to be standard operating procedure."

Selected writings

Bone in the Throat, Villard Books (New York City), 1995.
Gone Bamboo, Villard Books, 1997.
Kitchen Confidential: Adventures in the Culinary Underbelly, Bloomsbury (New York City), 2000.
Typhoid Mary: An Urban Historical, Bloomsbury, 2001.
A Cook's Tour: In Search of the Perfect Meal, Bloomsbury, 2001; published in paperback as *Cook's Tour: Global Adventures in Extreme Cuisines*, Ecco/HarperCollins (New York City), 2002.
The Bobby Gold Stories, Bloomsbury, 2003.
(With José de Meirelles and Philippe Lajaunie) *Anthony Bourdain's Les Halles Cookbook: Strategies, Recipes, and Techniques of Classic Bistro Cooking*, Bloomsbury, 2004.

The Nasty Bits: Collected Varietal Cuts, Usable Trim, Scraps, and Bones, Bloomsbury, 2006.

No Reservations: Around the World on an Empty Stomach, Bloomsbury, 2007.

Sources

Caterer & Hotelkeeper, November 1, 2001, p. 44.
Entertainment Weekly, December 7, 2001, p. 29.

Esquire, June 2000, p. 38.
Fresno Bee, February 14, 2007, p. E1.
Guardian (London, England), August 12, 2000, p. 6.
Newsweek, May 15, 2000, p. 54.
New York Times, August 6, 1995; September 10, 1997; September 17, 2005; May 28, 2006.
Observer (London, England), April 30, 2006, p. 44.

—*Carol Brennan*

Wayne Brady

Actor and talk-show host

Born June 2, 1972, in Orlando, FL; married Mandie Taketa (an actress), April 3, 1999 (divorced, 2007); children: Maile Masako.

Addresses: *Office*—c/o Don't Forget the Lyrics, P.O. Box 900, Attn: FOX Broadcasting Publicity Dept., Beverly Hills, CA 90213-0900.

Career

Actor on television, including: *Superboy*, 1990; *I'll Fly Away*, 1993; *In the Heat of the Night*, 1993; *On Promised Land* (movie), 1994; *Kwik Witz*, 1996; *Vinyl Justice*, 1998; *Whose Line Is It Anyway*, ABC, 1998-2003; *Hollywood Squares*, 1999-2003; *Geppetto* (movie), 2000; (also producer and writer) *The Wayne Brady Show*, 2001, then syndicated, 2002-04; *Dick Clark's New Year's Rockin' Eve*, 2001, 2002; *American Dreams*, 2003; *The Electric Piper* (movie), 2003; *Going to the Mat* (movie), 2004; *Reno 911!*, Comedy Central, 2004; *I Do, They Don't* (movie), 2005; *Kevin Hill*, 2005; *Stargate SG-1*, 2005; *Girlfriends*, 2006; *Celebrity Duets*, 2006; *30 Rock*, 2007; (host) *Don't Forget the Lyrics*, 2007—. Stage appearances include: *Wayne Brady & Friends*, U.S. cities, 2000-04; *Chicago*, Broadway production, 2004; *Making **it Up*, Venetian, Las Vegas, NV, 2007—; *A Chorus Line*; *A Raisin in the Sun*; *Jesus Christ Superstar*; *I'm Not Rappaport*; *The Only Game in Town*; *Blade to the Heat*, Mark Taper Forum, Los Angeles, CA. Film appearances include: *Clifford's Really Big Movie* (voice), 2004; *Stuart Little 3: Call of the Wild* (voice), 2005; *Roll Bounce*, 2005; *The List*, 2006; *Crossover*, 2006; *The Adventures of Brer Rabbit* (voice), 2006. Served as host of Miss America Pageant, 2002; 30th Annual Daytime Emmy Awards, 2003; Broadway on Broadway, 2004; 8th Annual Soul Train Christmas Starfest, 2005; That's What I'm Talking About, VH1, 2006; Countdown to the American Music Awards. Also worked at Disney World as a character performer for Tigger and Goofy; performed in shows at Universal Studios Florida theme park, including *Beetlejuice*, *Ghostbusters*, and *Rock 'n' Roll Revue*; appeared with a comedy troupe in Orlando, FL, and with House Full of Honkies, Los Angeles, CA.

Awards: Rookie of the Year, Saks Theatre, 1992; Daytime Emmy Awards for outstanding talk show and outstanding talk show host, for *The Wayne Brady Show*, National Television Academy, 2003; Emmy Award for outstanding individual performance in a variety or music program for *Whose Line Is It Anyway?*, Academy of Television Arts & Sciences, 2003; Daytime Emmy Award for outstanding talk show host, for *The Wayne Brady Show*, National Television Academy, 2004.

Sidelights

An Emmy Award-winning television show host, Wayne Brady is also a popular actor with an upbeat point of view, strong singing voice, and dancing ability which allows him to work in a variety of genres. Gifted at the art of improv, he first came to international attention for his appearances on the Drew Carey-hosted *Whose Line Is It Anyway?* in the late 1990s and early 2000s. Brady's success on the show eventually led to his own short-lived talk show, *The Wayne Brady Show,* a stint on Broadway in *Chicago,* and small film roles beginning in 2004.

Born on June 2, 1972, in Orlando, Florida, Brady was raised by his grandmother, Valerie Petersen, and was a shy child with a stuttering problem. By the time he attended Dr. Phillips High School, he was a member of the ROTC and seemed destined to join the military. However, after appearing in a school play, Brady caught the acting bug and joined the drama club. Brady told Steve Hedgpeth of New Jersey's *Star-Ledger,* "When I was 16, I was in ROTC. I hadn't made up my mind about a career yet. But as soon as I found out that my calling was being an actor, there was never any doubt. I knew that I was leaving myself open to some extreme butt-kicking, but there was nothing else I could possibly do."

Brady put all his energy into his new career focus as he completed his high school education and moved into community theater. In addition to appearing with a comedy troupe in Orlando, he also worked at Disney World as a character performer and performed in shows at Universal Studios Florida theme park, including *Beetlejuice, Ghostbusters,* and *Rock 'n' Roll Revue.* Brady had roles in stage productions like *A Raisin in the Sun,* toured in musicals like *Jesus Christ Superstar,* and appeared in locally filmed television series like *Superboy,* as well.

To fully pursue his career goals, Brady moved to Las Vegas, then Los Angeles in the early 1990s. In California, he began appearing with an improv group called House Full of Honkies. Brady also landed guest spots in television series such as *I'll Fly Away* and *In the Heat of the Night,* as well as a 1994 television movie *On Promised Land.*

Brady's career really took off in 1998 when he began appearing in the American version of *Whose Line Is It Anyway?,* hosted by Carey. Carey had seen the long-running, popular British version of the show, and brought it to the United States to high ratings. Brady was a regular on *Whose Line* for several years, demonstrated both his quick wit and singing ability. His work on the show led to an Emmy Award nomination for him in 2000 and an Emmy Award in 2003, the same year it was canceled. Of the show's affect on his career, he told Scott D. Pierce of the *Deseret News* that *Whose Line* "pretty much changed my entire life. It changed everything about my life. Not one thing, past certain personal things, was the same."

Brady's work on *Whose Line* led to new career opportunities. In the early 2000s, he toured the United States in an improv show entitled *Wayne Brady & Friends* with four other improv actors and a keyboard player. It was first performed in comedy clubs in 2000, then made its way into bigger theaters and attracted audiences in the thousands in 2001. Brady continued to regularly tour with the show over the next several years.

Also in 2001, Brady launched his own television show, *The Wayne Brady Show.* This weekly prime-time program on ABC included elements of a variety show, such as a full band, dancers, improv and sketch comedy, a supporting cast, and special guests, and had a brief, seven-episode run. Admitting he owed a debt to variety series from the 1960s and 1970s, Brady told Robin Vaughan of the *Boston Herald,* "It really involves stuff I most enjoy doing, the blending of music and comedy. It's a melding of some classic comedy shows of the past. Having grown up on the Flip Wilson and Carol Burnett shows, I think we pay a little homage to them. But I think if anything what we'll try to do is have a classic feel with a very now energy."

While ABC declined to pick up *The Wayne Brady Show* for a longer run, the show was re-tooled by the network in 2002 to become more of a talk show with celebrity guests. Brady still included comedy and musical elements as well on the syndicated daily program. *The Wayne Brady Show* paid homage to classic television, with Mike Douglas and Merv Griffin inspiring Brady. When *The Wayne Brady Show* debuted in the fall of 2002, it received the best ratings of the five new talk shows on the air. Brady won an Emmy as best talk show host for his work on *The Wayne Brady Show* in 2003.

As Brady's television career was taking off, he was tapped to host a number of impressive gigs. In 2001 and 2002, he served as the host of the annual classic show *Dick Clark's New Year's Rockin' Eve* in 2001 and 2002. Also in 2002, Brady was selected to host the Miss America Pageant. He was the first African American to host the American institution. Before the pageant aired, he told Walt Belcher of the *Tampa Tribune* that though he hesitated to take the job, "I realized that I would be part of television history as the first African American to be the host, so I'm honored to be a small part of pop culture. And the format does allow me to entertain, and so I hope to bring some fun to the pageant."

Because of declining ratings, *The Wayne Brady Show* was canceled after its second season ended in 2004. By this time, Brady had expanded his acting repertoire by appearing television movies like *The Electric Piper,* doing guest spots on shows like *American Dreams* and *Reno 911!,* and providing a voice for his first film, *Clifford's Really Big Movie.* After *The Wayne Brady Show* ended, Brady made his Broadway debut by joining the cast of *Chicago* for a limited run as Billy Flynn in the fall of 2004.

In 2005, Brady temporarily shook off his good guy, daytime television-friendly persona with an appearance on the popular *Chappelle's Show* on Comedy Central. In addition to hosting a mock episode, Brady appeared in a sketch where he swore, used drugs, and played a pimp. Brady received much attention for his work in the sketch and his acting career continued to take off. Though he continued to work in television in guest spots and movies, Brady acted in a variety of films, including *Stuart Little 3: Call of the Wild, Roll Bounce,* and *The List.* In 2006's street basketball-focused *Crossover,* he played the seedy agent Vaughn.

Brady returned to series television in 2006 when he served as the host of the reality series *Celebrity Duets* on FOX. In 2007, after touring in his solo improv show and launching a regular show in Vegas, he began hosting a game show on FOX entitled *Don't Forget the Lyrics.* The show was a karaoke-type competition where competitors sing along with a band and a teleprompter for part of a song, but must complete it on their own when the music and lyrics are cut. Because of its popularity, *Don't Forget the Lyrics* was expected to run at least through early 2008.

No matter what happens in his career, Brady was grateful to keep working. He told the *Chicago Sun-Times'* Mike Thomas, "I really believe that as long as you're a nice person, you give due where it's due, and you keep your nose to the grindstone, that you can always work. Maybe someday it won't be on a big TV show, or it will just be doing theater, but as long as I'm working. I think a lot of people get sucked into the negative side of show business, and that's not me."

Sources

Books

Marquis Who's Who, Marquis Who's Who, 2008.
Who's Who Among African Americans, 21st ed., Gale, 2008.

Periodicals

Associated Press Online, September 19, 2002; May 10, 2004; July 4, 2007.
Boston Herald, March 21, 2001, p. O43.
Calgary Herald (Alberta, Canada), August 31, 2005, p. E1.
BPI Entertainment News Wire, January 9, 2004.
Business Wire, January 29, 2002.
Chicago Sun-Times, May 15, 2002, p. 49.
Columbus Dispatch (Columbus, OH), November 12, 2003, p. 8F.
Deseret News (Salt Lake City, UT), November 11, 2003, p. C8.
Globe and Mail (Canada), August 4, 2001, p. 9.
Hollywood Reporter, June 20, 2007.
Jet, February 10, 2003, p. 56; September 18, 2006, p. 60.
Orlando Sentinel (FL), August 29, 2006.
Star-Ledger (Newark, NJ), August 5, 2001, p. 11.
St. Louis Post-Dispatch (MO), August 7, 2001, p. F1.
Tampa Tribune (FL), September 20, 2002, p. 4.
Telegraph Herald (Dubuque, IA), October 15, 2004, p. C17.
Vancouver Province (British Columbia, Canada), February 23, 2007, p. B7.
Washington Post, July 14, 2007, p. C1.
zaptoit, December 6, 2007.

—*A. Petruso*

Jim Broadbent

Eddie Gallacher/Alpha/Landov

Actor

Born May 24, 1949, in Lincoln, Lincolnshire, England; son of Roy (an artist, furniture maker, and amateur actor) and Doreen (a sculptor and amateur actress; maiden name, Findlay) Broadbent; married Anastasia Lewis (an actress), 1987; children: Tom (stepson), Paul (stepson). *Education:* London Academy of Music and Dramatic Art, 1972.

Addresses: *Contact*—Broadbent Theatre, Snarford Road, Wickenby, Lincolnshire, England LN3 5AW. *Home*—Lincolnshire and London, England. *Management*—Ms. George Lee, International Creative Management Ltd., Oxford House, 76 Oxford St., London, England W1D 1BS. *Web site*—http://www.broadbent.org.

Career

Actor in films, including: *The Life Story of Baal*, 1978; *The Shout*, 1978; *Breaking Glass*, 1980; *Dead on Time*, 1983; *The Hit*, 1984; *Brazil*, 1985; *The Good Father*, 1985; *Running Out of Luck*, 1987; *Superman IV: Quest for Peace*, 1987; *Vroom*, 1988; *Life is Sweet*, 1991; *Enchanted April*, 1992; *The Crying Game*, 1992; *Widows' Peak*, 1994; *Princess Caraboo*, 1994; *Bullets Over Broadway*, 1994; *Richard III*, 1995; *The Secret Agent*, 1996; *The Borrowers*, 1997; *The Avengers*, 1998; *Little Voice*, 1998; *Topsy-Turvy*, 1999; *Big Day*, 1999; *Bridget Jones's Diary*, 2001; *Moulin Rouge!*, 2001; *Iris*, 2001; *Gangs of New York*, 2002; *Nicholas Nickleby*, 2002; *Bright Young Things*, 2003; *Around the World in 80 Days*, 2004; *Vanity Fair*, 2004; *Bridget Jones: The Edge of Reason*, 2004; *Chronicles of Narnia: The Lion, the Witch and the Wardrobe*, 2005; *Art School Confidential*, 2006; *And When Did You Last See Your Father?*,

2007; *Indiana Jones and the Kingdom of the Crystal Skull*, 2008; *Harry Potter and the Half-Blood Prince*, 2008. Television appearances include: *Black Adder*, 1983; *Only Fools and Horses*, 1983, 1985, 1991; *Gone to Seed*, 1992; *The Peter Principle*, 1997, 2000; *Longford*, 2006. Stage appearances include: *A Doll's House*, c. 1953; *Illuminatus*, 1976; *Ecstasy*, 1979; *Goose-Pimples*, 1981; *A Flea in Her Ear*, Old Vic, London, 1989; also appeared in productions with the Royal Shakespeare Company, Royal National Theatre, and the National Theatre of Brent.

Awards: Volpi Cup for best actor, Venice Film Festival, for *Topsy-Turvy*, 1999; British Film Award for best actor, Evening Standard, for *Topsy-Turvy*, 2001; award for best supporting actor, Los Angeles Film Critics Association, for *Moulin Rouge!*, 2001; film award for British actor of the year, London Critics Circle, for *Topsy-Turvy*, 2001; film award for best performance by an actor in a supporting role, British Academy of Film and Television Awards (BAFTA), for *Moulin Rouge!*, 2001; award for best supporting actor, National Board of Review, for *Iris*, 2001; Audience Award for best supporting actor, Chlotrudis Society for Independent Film, for *Moulin Rouge!*, 2002; Golden Satellite Award for best performance by an actor in a supporting role in a comedy or musical, International Press Academy, for *Moulin Rouge!*, 2002; award for best acting by an ensemble,

National Board of Review, for *Nicholas Nickleby*, 2002; Academy Award for best supporting actor, Academy of Motion Picture Arts and Sciences, for *Iris*, 2002; Golden Globe for best supporting actor in a motion picture, Hollywood Foreign Press Association, for *Iris*, 2002; television award for best actor, BAFTA, for *Longford*, 2007; award for best actor, Broadcasting Press Guild, for *Longford*, 2007; International Emmy Award for best performance by an actor (tie), International Academy of Television Arts and Sciences, for *The Street*, 2007; Golden Globe for best performance by an actor in a mini-series or made-for-TV motion picture, Hollywood Foreign Press Association, for *Longford*, 2008.

Sidelights

While the name Jim Broadbent may not sound familiar, his face surely is. A versatile character actor, Broadbent has spent more than 35 years playing a steady stream of characters on stage, television, and film. The British actor has appeared in more than 100 film and television productions, receiving acclaim on both sides of the Atlantic. Broadbent won an Academy Award in 2002 for his supporting role in the biographical drama *Iris*, a story about a married couple's bout with Alzheimer's. He has also won two British Academy of Film and Television Arts Awards. Known as a BAFTA, it is the British equivalent of an Academy Award.

Broadbent has transformed himself into countless characters over the years, but a few performances stand out. He is well-respected for his portrayal of the quirky, devilish, and flamboyant showman Harold Zidler in the 2001 theatrical romp *Moulin Rouge!* Zidler was the buffoonish, red-headed master of ceremonies at the famed Parisian Moulin Rouge theater, where most of the story took place. This standout performance, during which he danced to Madonna's "Like a Virgin," earned him a BAFTA. He is also memorable as the title character's silly and saccharine father in 2001's *Bridget Jones's Diary*, a role he reprised for the sequel, 2004's *Bridget Jones: The Edge of Reason*.

Fellow actor David Schneider says Broadbent has been successful in his career because he knows how to stay present. "Jim is instinctively in the moment," Schneider told James Rampton of the London *Independent*. "You don't feel he comes to rehearsals with a bag of ideas that he then hammers roughly onto the script. He tries things, and because his instinct is good, they normally work. He makes you laugh each time he does a line and that's rare. On one hand, you're impressed, on the other, you're jealous."

Broadbent was born on May 24, 1949, in Lincoln, Lincolnshire, England. A twin sister died at birth. He was raised alongside his older siblings Barney and Julie. His parents, Roy and Dee Findlay Broadbent, made their living as artists and amateur actors. His father made furniture and his mother created sculptures. Roy Broadbent moved to the Lincoln area after the start of World War II. A conscientious objector, he opposed Britain's involvement in the war and escaped to Lincolnshire, where he helped found a pacifist commune that attracted a number of bohemian artists and actors. In time, they formed an amateur theater company called the Lindsey Rural Players. The group converted an abandoned Royal Air Force Nissen hut into a theater and staged productions. A Nissen hut is similar to a Quonset hut. It is a semi-circular-shaped structure made of corrugated steel.

Roy helped run the amateur-dramatics society and cast four-year-old Jim in a production of *A Doll's House*, a thought-provoking drama by Norwegian playwright Henrik Ibsen. As a child, Broadbent spent a lot of time at the theater. He matured right along with the Lindsey Rural Players, who, by the late 1960s, had a new home in a renovated chapel in Wickenby. Today, their home theater is called the Broadbent Theatre, named in honor of Roy Broadbent.

Broadbent attended school at Leighton Park, a Quaker boarding school in Reading, England. He excelled at art and acting; however, a favorite pastime involved hanging out at the local pubs and he was eventually expelled from the school. "I was always clowning around at school because I didn't like the academic stuff," Broadbent told the *Mirror*'s Mel Hunter. The school allowed Broadbent to take his final exams early, then banned him from campus.

After leaving Leighton Park, Broadbent enrolled in art school but soon decided he lacked the skills necessary to make an impact in the art world. He decided to pursue acting and applied to the London Academy of Music and Dramatic Art. The independent drama school proved to be a good fit. "As soon as I got there I felt at home," Broadbent told the *Daily Mail*'s Sarah Chalmers.

After graduating in 1972, Broadbent worked as an assistant stage manager at London's Open Air Theatre in Regent's Park. He landed a few small roles at the outdoor theater, once playing a Sprite and Sailor in an adaptation of Shakespeare's *The Tempest*. There were times he lacked for money and supported himself washing dishes at the Bank of England cafeteria and working as a housecleaner. Over the next decade, Broadbent spent time on stage with the Royal Shakespeare Company and the National Theatre.

Broadbent first made waves in 1976 when Ken Campbell cast him in his epic fantasy *Illuminatus*, a production of the Science Fiction Theater of Liverpool. During the multi-hour production—*Illuminatus* ran 12 hours—Broadbent played 12 different characters that showcased his impeccable bent for comedy.

Afterward, Broadbent began creeping onto the big screen. In 1978, he played bit roles in the British films *The Life Story of Baal* and *The Shout*. Broadbent continued his stage work as well. He worked with British writer/director Mike Leigh, appearing in productions of *Ecstasy*, 1979, and *Goose-Pimples* in 1981.

In the 1980s, Broadbent co-founded the National Theatre of Brent with his friend, Patrick Barlow. Together, the actors staged two-man shows of comedic classics such as *The Greatest Story Ever Told, The Complete Guide to Sex, The Messiah,* and *Revolution*. These productions gave Broadbent the opportunity to play a wide host of characters, including God, Robespierre, John the Baptist, and Marie Antoinette.

Over the next few years, Broadbent scored numerous roles on British television programs. He appeared on the BBC's *Only Fools and Horses* as detective Roy Slater. This was a recurring role and he appeared sporadically on the show between 1983 and 1991. Around this same time, Broadbent made his leap across the Atlantic, making his first U.S. film debut in 1987's *Superman IV: The Quest for Peace* starring Christopher Reeve.

Broadbent garnered more recognition after being reunited with Leigh who cast Broadbent in the lead of his 1991 flick *Life is Sweet*. Leigh wrote and directed the film. In this film, Broadbent played a dorky father whose dream is to run a lunch wagon. Broadbent then switched gears, following with a role in 1992's enormously successful psychological thriller *The Crying Game*. Though Broadbent played only a subsidiary role—as a bartender—his performance stood out and he began to receive offers to appear in U.S. studio films. In 1994, Woody Allen cast Broadbent in his big-screen production of *Bullets Over Broadway*. Broadbent played a very memorable Warner Purcell, a theater star with a serious eating disorder.

Broadbent next earned his first lead in a sitcom, playing inept bank manager Peter Duffley in *The Peter Principle,* which aired on the BBC from 1995 to 2000. Broadbent's off-the-cuff performance and ability to create in the moment propelled the comedy to receive commendable ratings.

Again joining forces with writer/director Leigh, Broadbent appeared in 1999's *Topsy-Turvy*, where he gave a spectacular performance portraying real-life British lyricist W. S. Gilbert and his trials and tribulations working alongside the famed composer Sir Arthur. For this performance, Broadbent earned best actor accolades at the 1999 Venice Film Festival.

By the early 2000s, Broadbent had become well-known among U.S. filmmakers and he scored a number of supporting roles in films alongside big-name stars. In 2001, he appeared with Renee Zellweger, portraying her father in *Bridget Jones's Diary*. That same year, he created a buzz with his performance in *Moulin Rouge!*, starring alongside Nicole Kidman and Ewan McGregor.

Broadbent's breakout film success came with 2001's *Iris*. In this film, Broadbent played John Bayley, husband to ailing Alzheimer's patient Iris Murdoch, an English novelist and scholar. Judi Dench portrayed the failing Murdoch. The movie was based on a real-life story and adapted from two memoirs written by Bayley. To prepare for the role, Broadbent listened to a tape of Bayley being interviewed by a doctor for a British radio program called *In the Psychiatrist's Chair*. "That provided a huge insight," Broadbent told the *Independent*'s Richard Barber. "His character was revealed through his vocal mannerisms: the light voice, the slight stutter, the humour, the diffidence, the strength." Broadbent listened to the interview over and over in an effort to copy Bayley's distinct stammer. Bayley was startled by Broadbent's dead-on portrayal—the two never met before filming. Broadbent's own experience provided additional perspective for the role—his mother suffered from Alzheimer's and he was able to tap into that helpless heartache he felt during her decline. The performance earned Broadbent a number of awards. He won a Golden Globe for best supporting actor, besting nominees Ben Kingsley, Jude Law, and Steve Buscemi. In addition, he won an Academy Award for best actor in a supporting role.

In 2002, Broadbent worked alongside Martin Scorsese, appearing in the director's nineteenth-century gangster flick *Gangs of New York* as the corrupt U.S. politician William "Boss" Tweed. In this film, Broadbent got to work with Daniel Day Lewis, Leonardo

DiCaprio, and Cameron Diaz. In 2004, he appeared as Lord Kelvin in *Around the World in 80 Days*, based on the novel by Jules Verne.

In 2006, Broadbent returned to the small screen, snagging the title role in the made-for-TV biopic *Longford*. Broadbent played the long-suffering British politician Lord Longford. For this role, Broadbent was awarded a BAFTA TV Award for Best Actor.

By the mid- to late-2000s, Broadbent was in high demand in Hollywood. He grabbed a supporting role in 2008's highly anticipated Indiana Jones sequel, *Indiana Jones and the Kingdom of the Crystal Skull*, playing college dean Charles Stanforth. That same year, he appeared in *Harry Potter and the Half-Blood Prince* as retired magic teacher Horace Slughorn. For 2009, Broadbent was set to appear in *Inkheart*, a movie based on the "Inkworld" trilogy by novelist Cornelia Funke. He was to play Fenoglio.

Despite his success and extensive work obligations in the United States, Broadbent has no desire to move to Hollywood. He enjoys a slow-paced life in England. During his free time, he likes to play golf and do some woodworking. He also enjoys spending time with his artist-turned-actress wife, Anastasia Lewis. The couple met in 1983. After marrying in 1987, Broadbent became a stepfather to her two sons, Tom and Paul. Speaking to the *Birmingham Post*'s Noreen Barr, Broadbent said he enjoys being home so he can take part in helping run the house. "When I'm working I can't do anything domestic so when I'm not working I fill it with domesticity—cooking and doing my share of the shopping."

As for the future, Broadbent intends to keep plodding along with no set goals in mind. Speaking to the London *Independent*, Broadbent said he sees no sense in plotting out a lot of career goals because following a predirected course might mean missing opportunities. He has let his career unfold at will and has been happy with the outcome. "Well, I never had an ambition, for example, to play the man who ran the Moulin Rouge in a big-screen musical.... No, my only game plan is to keep the options open and seize the surprises when they present themselves."

Sources

Periodicals

Birmingham Post, February 9, 2002, p. 53; October 1, 2007, p. 13.
Daily Mail (London, England), March 26, 2002, pp. 10-11.
Daily Telegraph (London, England), January 12, 2008, p. 13.
Independent (London, England), May 24, 1997, p. 6; December 23, 2003, pp. 4-5.
Los Angeles Times, December 22, 2001, p. F1.
Mirror, January 22, 2002, p. 6.

Online

"Famous Yellowbelly—Jim Broadbent," BBC, http://www.bbc.co.uk/lincolnshire/content/articles/2005/08/24/famous_yellowbelly_jim_broadbent_feature.shtml (May 7, 2008).
"A Jim Broadbent Biography," Broadbent Theatre, http://www.jimbroadbent.org (May 7, 2008).
"Jim Broadbent: The Heartbreak Kid," *Daily Telegraph*'s *Seven* magazine, http://www.telegraph.co.uk/arts/main.jhtml?xml=/arts/2007/09/23/sv_jimbroadbent.xml&page=1 (May 7, 2008).

—*Lisa Frick*

Gordon Brown

Prime Minister of Britain

Born James Gordon Brown, February 20, 1951, in Glasgow, Scotland; son of John Ebenezer (a minister) and Elizabeth Brown; married Sarah Jane Macauley, August 3, 2000; children: Jennifer Jane, John, James Fraser. *Education:* Edinburgh University, M.A., 1972; Ph.D., 1982.

Addresses: *Office*—The Rt. Hon. Gordon Brown MP, 10 Downing St., London SW1A 2AA, England.

Career

Edinburgh University, rector, 1972-75, lecturer after 1976; lecturer, Glasgow College of Technology, 1976-80; current affairs editor, Scottish Television, 1980-83; first elected to the British House of Commons 1983; British Labour Party, chair of Scottish Council, 1983-84, opposition chief secretary at the Treasury, 1987-89, opposition trade and industry secretary, 1989-92, shadow Treasury chancellor, 1992-97, chancellor of the exchequer, 1997-2007, elected party chair, May 2007, became prime minister, June 2007.

Sidelights

In June of 2007, Gordon Brown became Britain's newest prime minister, or head of government, after winning the leadership post of his country's Labour Party. A Scot known for his keen intelligence and famously abrupt demeanor, he was dubbed the "Iron Chancellor" when he served in the cabinet, but as prime minister Brown has won high marks for his leadership style, which many political pun-

dits note is the antithesis of former Prime Minister Tony Blair's. "Those qualities once deemed weaknesses—his lack of glitz and sparkle—have come to seem like strengths," wrote Jonathan Freedland of Brown in the *New York Review of Books*.

Brown was born on February 20, 1951, in Glasgow, Scotland, and was the second of three sons of John Brown, a Church of Scotland minister. In 1954, Reverend Brown took a post at the St. Bryce parish in Kirkcaldy, a city in the Fife area that surrounds the Firth of Forth. During Brown's youth, Fife suffered a steep economic decline occasioned by the closing of several factories in the area. Parishioners regularly turned up at the "manse," as the rectory where the pastor and his family live is called in British parlance, to ask his father for help. A commitment to others was instilled in Brown and his brothers at a young age. On one occasion his parents left him home alone and a visitor turned up. "So as my parents taught me, I say, what do you want—help yourself! And when they come back, the town's most notorious burglar is sitting in the kitchen," he confessed in an interview with Bel Mooney for the *Times* of London.

A gifted student, Brown was put on a fast-track university-entrance program at Kirkcaldy High School when he was just ten years old, and was

ready to enter Edinburgh University at age 16. That same year, he penned an essay on the program in which he described himself as "a guinea-pig," according to a *Times* of London article by Ben Macintyre, and "the victim of a totally unsighted and ludicrous experiment in education, the result of which was to harm materially and mentally the guinea-pigs.... I was lucky and passed, but many of my friends met with dismal failure, despair and a sense of uselessness."

Despite the demands of the academic program, Brown still found time to excel in sports. He became a talented rugby player during his teen years, but his athletic career was cut short when he suffered a detached retina in his eye after a particularly brutal collision on the playing field. He underwent surgery three times, remaining in the hospital for up to a month each time in a dark room and keeping as still as possible. His vision in that eye could not be saved, however, and he was eventually fitted with an artificial eye. A few years later he noticed the same symptoms in his other eye; by this time the treatment options were more advanced, and the sight in his right eye was saved.

At Edinburgh University, Brown studied history and was active in student political organizations. Around campus he became known as "Red Gordon" for his leftist sympathies, and in 1972, the same year he earned his master's degree, he was elected rector of the school. In this capacity, he chaired the school's governing body, and famously challenged the University for not fully breaking ties with their academic peers in South Africa and Rhodesia, two nations that denied political rights to its black majority population. Brown's first mention in a national newspaper came in a *Times* of London article from 1973 headlined "University clash with student rector" over the inclusion of representatives from both nations at an upcoming Congress of Commonwealth Universities conference.

While working toward his doctorate degree, Brown taught at Edinburgh University and later at the Glasgow College of Technology. His doctoral dissertation examined the role of the Scottish Labour Party in British politics in the decade following World War I, and he was himself a member of this offshoot of the larger Labour Party of Britain. He first ran for a seat in parliament in May of 1979, but lost, as did scores of other Labour Party incumbents and challengers. The Conservative (Tory) Party, led by Margaret Thatcher, swept to victory that year and, with their win, Thatcher became Britain's first female prime minister.

In 1980, Brown switched careers and became a current affairs editor for Scottish Television. He also rose within the Scottish Labour Party, becoming its chair by 1983 and also winning a seat in the House of Commons in that year's general elections. Another young rising name in the party who had also won a seat was Tony Blair, an Oxford-trained lawyer and onetime rock musician. As junior members, they shared an office in Westminster, where the Houses of Parliament meet, and both would rise within the party ranks and shape its future. The two were close allies for the next 14 years as the Tories remained in power through general elections in 1987 and 1992. Brown became known as a finance specialist within the Labour Party, and challenged Tory policies as the shadow (or opposition counterpart) to the chancellor of the exchequer in Thatcher's government. The chancellor's office oversees all aspects of the British economy, including the treasury, taxes, and annual budget.

For some years, Brown's name had been discussed as a future Labour Party chief. In the British system, the party that wins the majority in the general election forms a government, with the party leader becoming prime minister. Brown's longtime mentor was a fellow Scot, John Smith, and in 1992, when the leadership post became vacant, Brown chose not to run against Smith, who was an older, more experienced politician with wide support among both English and Scottish Labour MPs. Smith won, but died two years later after suffering a fatal heart attack. At this juncture, Brown was expected to announce his candidacy for the Labour leadership, but he did not. Tony Blair did, and won the balloting at the 1994 party conference. Three years later, Blair and the Labour Party won the 1997 general election, marking the return of the party to power for the first time since 1979. Blair named Brown to become his cabinet's chancellor of the exchequer.

Later, rumors arose that Blair and Brown had struck a quiet, informal agreement shortly after Smith's death and a few weeks before the next party conference that would elect Blair as party chief. The terms of the arrangement varied: One thread asserted that should Blair lead Labour to victory and become prime minister, he would grant Brown an unprecedented degree of power as chancellor; another thread claimed that Blair would lead Labour to victory, and then serve just one term in office before stepping aside to let Brown advance to the party leadership and the prime minister's office. The pact was said to have been made over a meal at a North London restaurant called Granita in May of 1994, and was chronicled in a 2003 fictionalized film, *The Deal*. The symbiotic relationship between Blair and Brown was also discussed in a 2005 book, *Brown's Britain*, whose author, Robert Peston, was believed to have relied on sources close to Brown for the information. Peston's book also alleged that by that time, the two were no longer speaking to one another.

Blair did not step down, but he did come close to being forced out of office after giving his support to U.S. President George W. Bush in the American leader's bid to win European allies for the coming invasion of Iraq in March of 2003. Britain was the sole European power to condone the invasion and provide a significant number of troops, and Blair had made the decision against strong opposition, both from the public as well as warnings from within his own party that his leadership abilities were being questioned.

Brown, meanwhile, had earned mostly positive marks for his stewardship of Britain's economy. He reduced some taxes, enacted Bank of England reforms, and took a firm stand on the controversial matter of whether the country would adopt the European Union's single currency unit, the Euro. In June of 2004, he became the longest continuous serving chancellor since Nicholas Vansittart held the office from May of 1812 to December of 1822. Some sources note that Brown's tenure has witnessed the longest period of sustained economic growth in British history.

By the time of the next general elections in May of 2005, Blair had mended fences, and the Labour Party won again. In September of 2006, Blair announced he would leave office within a year, and the following May gave a firm date. That same month, the nomination process for the party leadership formally began, but there were no strong challengers to the 308 nominations that the Brown received. He took part in a series of hustings, or public debates, in which he outlined his vision for the future of Britain. On June 22, the ballot nominating process ended, and two days later Brown was declared the new leader of the Labour Party. On June 27, Blair stepped down as prime minister and Brown formally met with Queen Elizabeth II in private, as is the tradition in British politics. The monarch asks the new prime minister to form a government.

There were several challenges for Brown during his first year in office. These began when a major terrorist plot was foiled in London just two days after he took office, followed by a failed suicide-bomb attack at the Glasgow International Airport via a sport utility vehicle. Later came a mortgage scandal involving a major lender in England, Northern Rock, and revelations of misdeeds involving campaign donations to the Labour Party in exchange for peerage titles. In foreign policy, Brown adopted a distinctly different attitude toward the White House than his predecessor, which became apparent when Brown made his first formal visit to the United States as prime minister in late July of 2007 to meet Bush at the presidential retreat in Camp David, Maryland. "Gone were the chinos, first names, and chummy informality of the Bush-Blair summits," noted Freedland in the *New York Review of Books*. "At Brown's request, prime minister and president wore suits and addressed each other formally. Brown wanted to convey that the relationship from now on would be strictly business."

Brown married in 2000 at the age of 49. His wife, Sarah Macauley, had enjoyed a successful career as a partner in a London public relations firm prior to her marriage. Their first child, a daughter named Jennifer Jane, was born in December of 2001 two months prematurely; she died of a brain hemorrhage several days later. The tragedy prompted an outpouring of public support for the characteristically stoic chancellor, who did not return to his office at the Treasury for much of January. In 2003, Sarah Brown gave birth to a son they named John, followed in 2006 by a second child, James, who was diagnosed with cystic fibrosis at four months old. The Browns have established a foundation named after their daughter, the Jennifer Jane Brown Research Trust, for research into the prevention of neonatal deaths.

Brown may remain in office at least until 2010, when he is required to call a general election. When Blair was still in office in 2005, the Labour government surpassed any of its previous records for holding power, and Brown seems determined to continue that legacy. In interviews, he has voiced regret that his work in London kept him away from Kirkcaldy and his aging parents for so many years, both of whom died in their 80s. Of his father, who passed away in 1998, the prime minister has reiterated what a lasting influence his father's charitable actions had on him as a public servant. "He went through his life liked by everybody; I don't think he made one single enemy," Brown told Suzie Mackenzie in an interview that appeared in the *Guardian*. "That's a long way from politics, I can tell you."

Sources

Guardian (London, England), September 25, 2004, p. 14.
Independent (London, England), June 28, 2007.
New York Review of Books, October 25, 2007.
New York Times, May 10, 2007; December 5, 2007.
Time, May 21, 2007, p. 54.
Times (London, England), March 20, 1973, p. 4; November 8, 2006, p. 4; May 19, 2007.

—*Carol Brennan*

Rhonda Byrne

Television producer and writer

Born 1955, in Melbourne, Australia; daughter of Ronald; married (divorced); children: Hailey.

Addresses: *Contact*—c/o 1235-A North Clybourn Ave., Ste. 416, Chicago, IL 60610.

Career

Began career as a producer/writer for the Nine Network; co-founded own production company, Prime Time Productions, 1994; created *The Secret* documentary, 2005; published *The Secret* book, 2006.

Sidelights

While Rhonda Byrne began her career working in television in Australia, she came to international prominence for her DVD and book entitled *The Secret*. In these products, Byrne revealed her philosophy called the Law of Attraction to help people get what they want out of life. *The Secret* became a phenomenon, selling more than two million DVDs and four million books within the first year of release. Though Byrne rarely gave interviews, she believed her success showed that she practiced what she preached.

Born in 1955 in Melbourne, Australia, Byrne was a successful television producer and writer working in Australia, first with the Nine Network, where she worked on a version of *The Tonight Show* for many years. In 1994, she co-founded her own production company, Prime Time Productions. Byrne was then involved in the production of such reality programs for Australian television as *World's Greatest Commercials, Great Escapes, OZ Encounters—UFO's in Australia, Marry Me,* and the true crime series, *Sensing Murder.* It was around the time of filming *Sensing Murder* that Byrne dealt with turmoil that came to inspire her to create *The Secret.*

Her father died in 2004, and her mother became deeply despondent and shared her overwhelming feelings with her daughter. Then the production of *Sensing Murder* depressed Byrne herself, both because of the subject matter and numerous problems that cropped up during the production. Her relationship with her production team became problematic, then she learned that the financial status of her production company was such that she did not have enough money to finish two more films that had to be completed that year.

Byrne's daughter Hailey learned of her mother's problems and showed her a book by Wallace Wattles from 1910. In *The Science of Getting Rich,* the author argued that the thoughts people had could define their lives. Bad thoughts led to bad situations, while good thoughts led to positive results. Doing research on Wallace's law of attraction, Byrne discovered it lay in ancient philosophy and had been affecting people for centuries.

Byrne then decided to do a television show on her findings and the philosophy of the law of attraction. Originally created in conjunction with Australia's Channel 9, Byrne interviewed a number of teachers and philosophers who embraced the belief system espoused by Wallace. She conducted most of these interviews in the United States even as her funding became questionable. Her first television distribution deal fell through, and the funding for each step of the project was not in place from the beginning. Still, Byrne finished her documentary on a $3 million budget in 2005.

Though Channel 9 dropped out and did not air the documentary until after it became a success, Byrne found an audience first on video-streaming on the Internet. Interest spread by word of mouth. She later released a DVD version of what came to be known as *The Secret* DVD movie in 2006. Within a year of this DVD release, Byrne had sold more than two million copies. A book version, published about six months later, was similarly successful. Several million books were purchased within six months of publication.

Some, like Jack Canfield, the co-author of the *Chicken Soup for the Soul*, believed the success of *The Secret* lay with Byrne herself. Touching on the reason for the phenomenon, Canfield wrote in *Time*, "It is primarily because Byrne's love and joy permeate every frame and every page. Her intention was pure and simple—to uplift as much of humanity as she could reach, and so far she has reached millions."

Touting her philosophy, Byrne told Carol Memmott of *USA Today* that "Everyone has to have their own experience to believe. People should start with little things like deciding a cup of coffee will come to you or that you'll see a feather. There's no difference between attracting a feather and anything else you want. It's as easy to attract one dollar as it is $10,000."

Many found the ideas in *The Secret* to be encouraging and prudent. Byrne herself claimed that people wrote in with such success stories as getting rid of chronic pain, finding a longed-for mate, and diseases disappearing. Because of such stories and massive sales, Byrne appeared on a two-show *Oprah* special, as well as the talk shows of Larry King and Ellen DeGeneres, which only increased interest in *The Secret*. More books by other authors inspired by *The Secret* were also published.

But as Byrne became an internationally known figure, others began criticizing her and *The Secret*. American self-help gurus Jerry and Esther Hicks

had been promoting a similar philosophy for years and appeared on the first version of the DVD. They later claimed that they had a falling out with Byrne after a promised sales cut of ten percent on DVD never materialized. Esther Hicks was removed from the film, and the couple declined to sue for breach of contract citing their life philosophy.

Skeptics also derided *The Secret*'s emphasis on material wealth and possessions. Others believed the book and DVD were worthless. American psychologist John Norcross told Peter Sheridan of the *Express*, "It's pseudo-scientific psychobabble. About 10 per cent of self-help books are rated by mental health professionals as damaging. This is probably one."

Despite the many detractors, Byrne became a multi-millionaire and believed in what she revealed in *The Secret*. She told Colin Vickery of Australia's *Herald Sun*, "I was trying to change things on the outside and you can't. You've got to feel it on the inside and everything else will change."

Selected writings

The Secret, Atria Books, 2006.

Sources

Periodicals

Express (United Kingdom), March 2, 2007, p. 34.
Newsweek, March 5, 2007, p. 52.
Publishers Weekly, August 13, 2007, p. S4.

Online

"Company Biography," The Secret, http://www.thesecret.tv./behind-the-secret-company.html (November 11, 2007).

"Cosmic secret pays out earthly dollars for controversial guru," *Sydney Morning Herald*, http://www.smh.com.au/news/national/how-cosmic-secret-made-millions/2007/02/28/11723387.tif10029.html (November 11, 2007).

"Making *The Secret*—A Brief History," The Secret, http://www.thesecret.tv./behind-the-secret-making-of.html (November 11, 2007).

"Rhonda Byrne—The Time 100," *Time*, http://www.time.com/time/specials/2007/time100/article/0,28804,1595326_1615737_1615871,00.html (November 11, 2007).

"*Secret* attracts plenty of attraction," *USA Today,* http://www.usatoday.com/life/books/news/2007-02-14-the-secret_x.htm (November 11, 2007).

"The Secret Life of Rhonda," *Herald Sun,* http://www.news.com.au/heraldsun/story/0,21985,21062184.tif-5006022,00.html (November 11, 2007).

—*A. Petruso*

Meg Cabot

Author

Born Meggin Patricia Cabot, February 1, 1967, in Bloomington, IN; daughter of A. Victor (a college professor) and Barbara Cabot; married Benjamin D. Egnatz (a financial writer), April 1, 1993. *Education:* Indiana University, B.A., 1991.

Addresses: *Agent*—Laura Langlie, 275 President St., Ste. 3, Brooklyn, NY 11231. *Contact*—Meg Cabot, P.O. Box 4904, Key West, FL 33041-4904. *Home*—Key West, FL.

Career

Assistant dormitory manager, New York University, c. 1991-2000; published first novel, *Where Roses Grow Wild*, as Patricia Cabot, 1998; signed with HarperCollins to publish *The Princess Diaries*, 1999; *The Princess Diaries* adapted into a feature film by Walt Disney Pictures, 2001; signed with the Scholastic Corporation to publish books for children and young adults, 2007.

Sidelights

Meg Cabot writes the immensely successful *Princess Diaries* young-adult novels, about an ordinary teen who is stunned to learn she is heir to the throne of a small European kingdom. The first in the series appeared in 2000, went on to spend the better part of a year on the *New York Times* bestseller list, and was translated for the big screen into an equally profitable film franchise. Cabot is a prolific writer who produced at least one *Princess* sequel every year for the next decade, while also writing other teen-friendly tales that have earned her a devoted, ardent following. Her book's "heroines," noted *Sunday Times* journalist Amanda Craig, "are ordinary girls who discover they are a princess, or a psychic, or an all-American girl who happens to save the president's life, and who then have to deal with the commonplace problems of envy, ostracism, loneliness, and confusion."

Born in Bloomington, Indiana, in 1967, Cabot was a writer at an early age, faithfully keeping a diary and progressing on to writing short stories in her teens. Her mother worked as an illustrator and her father was a professor of business and computer science in their college town. In an article Cabot wrote for *CosmoGirl* in 2005, she confessed that her genial and well-liked father was actually an alcoholic who hid bottles of bourbon throughout the house—which Cabot and her brothers would then discard when they found them. "Dad insisted he didn't have a problem, and Mom, like so many spouses of alcoholics, didn't know what to do about it—so she did nothing," Cabot wrote. "We spent many Christmas Eves pushing the family car out of whatever ditch my dad had managed to drive it into after refusing to let Mom drive, insisting he was 'fine.'" Finally, her father agreed to enter a substance abuse treatment program, and the family all underwent counseling.

Cabot earned a fine-arts degree from her hometown's Indiana University and moved to New York City in late 1990. She intended to pursue a career as an illustrator, but had a difficult time finding work in the highly competitive job field. "It was really intimidating and awful," she told Kristin Kloberdanz in an interview that appeared in *Book*. Eventually she found a secure job—with the added perk of a free Manhattan apartment, too—at New York University as an assistant manager for one of its undergraduate dormitories. She also began writing short stories and found success in 1998 when St. Martin's Press published her first romance novel, *Where Roses Grow Wild*, under the pseudonym Patricia Cabot.

The kernel of a story that blossomed into the *The Princess Diaries* had its roots in the discomfort Cabot felt when her widowed mother began dating one of her former college professors. In original draft of the story, New York City teenager Mia Thermopolis is merely a tomboy unnerved by the fact that her mother is involved with Mia's math teacher at Albert Einstein High School. When Cabot's friend read it as a favor and confessed it was a little dull, Cabot decided to turn it into a lost-royalty fable—a staple of myths and fairy tales throughout the history of literature.

Cabot's manuscript was rejected by several U.S. publishers before HarperCollins finally agreed in 1999 to publish it; however, before it went to press, Disney acquired the film rights and the filming of the story was set to begin a month before *The Princess Diaries* appeared in print. After the novel was published in October of 2000, Cabot's book went on to spent 38 weeks on the *New York Times* best-seller list. In one of its first reviews, *Booklist*'s Chris Sherman asserted that, in her young-adult debut, Cabot demonstrated "a knack for creating fully realized teen and adult characters that readers will miss when the story ends." Thanks to the book's success, however, the saga of Mia Thermopolis and her unexpected destiny would not be coming to an end in the foreseeable future.

The Princess Diaries introduces readers to Mia, her best friend Lilly, and her cat Fat Louie through Mia's journal entries. A tomboy and a vegetarian who is deeply interested in environmental issues, Mia is also a typical 15-year-old with a crush on two boys, one of whom is Lilly's brother. Every summer, her mother ships her off to the palatial estate in France where her formidable "Grandmere" lives; this also gives Mia the chance to spend time with her father, whom she believes is a politician in Genovia, a small but wealthy European principality between France and Italy. Cabot's fictional kingdom shares several similarities with the actual principality of Monaco, also wedged between France and Italy. For more than a quarter-century it also had an American-born princess in the form of film star Grace Kelly, who married Monaco's reigning prince in 1956 in one of the most famous weddings of the twentieth century.

In the first *Princess Diaries* book, Mia learns she is heir to the throne when father reveals that, because of recent medical setbacks, he cannot produce any more children. He says that he is actually the Crown Prince of Genovia, and Grandmere is the current ruler. Mia, then, is next in the line of succession. The rest of the book chronicles her struggle to accept this news and maintain some semblance of a "normal" life back in the United States. "Wrapped up in the pink and glitter is a surprisingly tough, old-fashioned message to adolescent girls about keeping your sense of your own self-worth, being loyal to your friends and resolutely independent of the images of youth promulgated by pop stars," declared Craig in the *Sunday Times* article.

Cabot's debut young-adult novel became even more of a success when the movie version proved a box-office hit and launched the career of Anne Hathaway, who played Mia. Cabot was still working at New York University when the movie premiered, but left the job and, eventually, New York City thanks to the success of her teen novels. Mia's saga continued through ten books, including the fourth installment, *Princess in Waiting*, 2004's *Perfect Princess*, and the ninth and penultimate sequel, *Princess Mia*, published in 2007. This last-cited title finds Mia in her senior year of high school but troubled by relationship issues and a long-buried secret in Genovian political history.

Cabot has written several other books for young adults, including those in "The Mediator" series, under the pen name Jenny Carroll, and others aimed at a slightly older readership, such as *Queen of Babble*, a 2006 tale of a young woman looking for romance on a European sojourn. Cabot has fared less well in adapting her own work for the big screen. A short story that became the 2005 Michelle Trachtenberg movie *Ice Princess* is one example. She submitted several drafts before giving up, characterizing the process as "60 studio executives telling me what to do," in an interview with Sue Corbett for *Publishers Weekly*. "It was clear a death was going to occur if I ever did that again." Cabot noted in the same interview that "there are two types of writers: egg layers and egg polishers. I am such an egg layer. I turn in the first draft and I'm done. They come back to me with revisions, and I hate them. I know this sounds terrible, but the idea of working on a book for more than a month? That's torture."

Cabot writes from Key West, Florida, where she lives with her husband, Ben Egnatz. They left New York City after the traumatic events of September 11, 2001, and lucked into a unique, mural-filled home that dates back to 1860 and is one of the oldest buildings in Florida. The resort town of Key West, meanwhile, suits Cabot's requirements as an ideal place to live. One important factor is that the town—the southernmost zip code in the continental United States—is bike-friendly, because Cabot has never learned to drive.

Cabot and Egnatz eloped in 1993, telling their friends and families that they were vacationing in Europe. Instead they had made prior arrangements to wed in a small town in the Italian Riviera—the very same place that would fill in for Mia's Genovia a few years later. There was no bridal shower, department-store gift registry, nor bachelor and bachelorette parties, but in an article Cabot penned for *Marie Claire*, she asserted that "we were happy to trade all that for what we did get—a bridal wreath of garlic flowers made by the local children, which materialized outside our door on our wedding day ... and the moonlit serenade beneath our bedroom window that evening—courtesy of the soccer team" coached by the mayor who had married them earlier in the day.

Cabot's official Web site scores hundreds of individual hits every day, and her e-mail inbox tallies as many as 200 letters on some days. With her devoted readership and pitch-perfect ear for teen angst, Cabot is sometimes compared to Judy Blume, the popular young-adult novelist whose books were best sellers in the 1970s. Cabot even contributed a chapter to the anthology *Everything I Needed to Know About Being a Girl I Learned from Judy Blume,* a 2007 collection of essays by female writers chronicling their own teenage devotion to much-loved Blume titles like *Are You There, God? It's Me, Margaret?* and *Forever.* Cabot's essay "Cry, Linda, Cry: Judy Blume's *Blubber* and the Cruelest Thing in the World," recounted how Blume's 1974 novel about cliquish female bullying, *Blubber,* helped her come to terms with the mean classmate who bullied her when they were ten-year-olds. "I was willing to let others have their way in an effort to get them to like me," Cabot confessed, and said that reading Blume's book helped her become a bit more assertive. Her bully then backed off, and from then on Cabot made it a habit to defend classmates who were targeted by others.

Cabot easily recalls these vivid details from her life because of the diaries and journals she has kept so faithfully over the years. In an article she penned for *CosmoGirl,* she wrote how miraculous it was that she could flip back to a night in February of 1983 and revisit what was troubling her: eating too many Oreos while babysitting and fretting over a boy. She also said that she has carted the several milk crates that hold her diaries and notebooks from home to home across several states, and even paid for storage facilities at times. "While they're valuable to me now as a source of material for the books I write to make a living, they have always been even more valuable—priceless, actually—as the emotional connection between the girl I used to be," she notes, "to the woman I've become."

Selected writings

"The Princess Diaries" novels

The Princess Diaries, HarperTeen (New York City), 2000.

The Princess Diaries Volume II: Princess in the Spotlight, HarperTeen, 2001.

The Princess Diaries Volume III: Princess in Love, HarperTeen, 2002.

The Princess Diaries Volume IV: Princess in Waiting, HarperTeen, 2003.

The Princess Diaries Volume IV and a Half: Project Princess, HarperCollins, 2003.

Princess Lessons, HarperTeen, 2003.

Perfect Princess, HarperTeen, 2004.

The Princess Diaries Volume V: Princess in Pink, HarperTeen, 2004.

Mia Tells It like It Is (contains *The Princess Diaries* and *The Princess Diaries Volume II: Princess in the Spotlight*), HarperTeen, 2004.

The Highs and Lows of Being Mia (contains *The Princess Diaries Volume III: Princess in Love* and *The Princess Diaries Volume IV: Princess in Waiting*), HarperTeen, 2004.

The Princess Diaries Volume VI: Princess in Training, HarperTeen, 2005.

The Princess Diaries Volume VII and a Half: Sweet Sixteen Princess, HarperTeen, 2006.

The Princess Diaries Volume VII: Party Princess, HarperCollins, 2006.

Valentine Princess: A Princess Diaries Book, HarperTeen, 2007.

The Princess Diaries Volume VIII: Princess on the Brink, HarperTeen, 2007.

The Princess Diaries Volume IX: Princess Mia, HarperTeen, 2007.

"The Mediator" Series" under pseudonym Jenny Carroll

Shadowland, HarperTeen, 2000.
Ninth Key, HarperTeen, 2001.
Reunion, HarperTeen, 2001.

Darkest Hour, HarperTeen, 2001.
Haunted, HarperTeen, 2003.
Twilight, HarperTeen, 2005.

Other

All American Girl, HarperCollins (New York City), 2002.
(As Meggin Cabot) *The Boy Next Door* (first in the "Boy" series), HarperCollins, 2002.
Nicola and the Viscount, Avon (New York City), 2002.
(As Meggin Cabot) *She Went All the Way,* Avon, 2002.
Victoria and the Rogue, Avon, 2003.
(As Meggin Cabot) *Boy Meets Girl* (second in the "Boy" series), Avon, 2004.
Teen Idol, HarperCollins, 2004.
Holiday Princess (nonfiction), illustrated by Chesley McLaren, HarperTeen, 2005.
Every Boy's Got One (third in the "Boy" series), Avon, 2005.
Ready or Not: An All-American Girl Novel, Harper-Collins, 2005.
Avalon High, HarperCollins, 2006.
How to Be Popular, HarperTempest (New York City), 2006.
(As Jenny Carroll) *Missing You* (fifth in the 1-800-Where-R-You? series), HarperTeen, 2006.
Queen of Babble, William Morrow (New York City), 2006.
Size 12 Is Not Fat: A Heather Wells Mystery, Avon, 2006.
Size 14 Is Not Fat Either, Avon, 2006.

Pants on Fire, HarperTeen, 2007.
Also author of romance novels under pseudonym Patricia Cabot, beginning with *Where Roses Grow Wild,* published by St. Martin's Press, 1998; also author of "1-800-Where-R-You" series under pseudonym Jenny Carroll; contributor of "Cry, Linda, Cry: Judy Blume's *Blubber* and the Cruelest Thing in the World" to *Everything I Needed to Know About Being a Girl I Learned from Judy Blume,* edited by Jennifer O'Connell, Pocket Books, 2007.

Sources

Books

"Cry, Linda, Cry: Judy Blume's Blubber and the Cruelest Thing in the World," in *Everything I Needed to Know About Being a Girl I Learned from Judy Blume,* Pocket Books (New York City), 2007.

Periodicals

Book, March-April 2003, p. 34.
Booklist, September 15, 2000, p. 233.
CosmoGirl, December 2005, p. 152; February 2007, p. 114.
Marie Claire, June 2005, p. 240.
New York Times, August 3, 2001.
Publishers Weekly, July 17, 2006, p. 62.
Sunday Times (London, England), October 10, 2004, p. 9.

—*Carol Brennan*

Cristina Carlino

Founder of Biomedic Clinical Care/Philosophy cosmetics

Born c. 1961, in Phoenix, AZ; daughter of Mario (an optometrist) and Patricia (an artist) Carlino. *Education:* Completed cosmetology school, c. 1982.

Addresses: *Office*—Philosophy, Inc., 3809 E. Watkins St., Phoenix, AZ 85034.

Career

Facialist after 1982, and creator of a private makeup line; licensed skincare provider for a Los Angeles plastic surgeon after 1985; founded Biomedic Clinical Care, a skin-care line, 1990; founded Philosophy, Inc., a skin-care and cosmetics company, 1996; sold BioMedic to L'Oreal, 2001; sold stake in Philosophy, Inc. to The Carlyle Group, 2007.

Sidelights

Cristina Carlino founded the innovative company Philosophy, Inc. in 1996, and built it into one of the leading department store and home-shopping network brands before selling a stake in it to the private-equity investment firm The Carlyle Group in 2007. The Arizona native still holds a significant personal share of her business, and continues to sell Philosophy's all-natural, plant-based wares on QVC, the cable channel devoted to home shopping.

Born in the early 1960s, Carlino grew up in the Phoenix area as the daughter of an optometrist father and an artist mother. Sandwiched between an older sister and younger brother, Carlino suffered from severe acne and weight problems in her teens, and distress over her looks was compounded by her parents' divorce when she was 14. After that, she ballooned to 210 pounds, and recalled her final years of high school as "painful," she told *People* writers Julie K. L. Dam and Karen Brailsford. "I sank into a very deep and dark depression."

Carlino found the solution to her skin-care problems after finishing cosmetology school: In 1982, her mother and a friend loaned her $6,700 to start her own business as a facialist, and she also concocted her own line of makeup. In 1985, she moved to the Los Angeles area and took a job with a plastic surgeon as his office's licensed skin-care professional. In the late 1980s, she devised the "15-Minute MicroPeel," which repaired signs of premature aging and sun damage. Dubbed the lunch-hour peel by industry insiders, the procedure used a razor to take off the top layer of skin on the face, then dosed it with alpha hydroxy acids before finishing with an application of dry ice.

The MicroPeel resulted in noticeably improved skin texture, and caught on with appearance-conscious trendsetters. In 1990, Carlino founded BioMedic Clinical Care with a loan from her sister, and created a entire range of skin-care products in addition to the MicroPeel. Her business was thriving, and she was living back near her family in Arizona, but she was dejected during the Christmas holidays of 1994, especially when her boyfriend at the time had decided to spend the break elsewhere. On Christmas Day, she went for a hike up Piestewa Peak in the Phoenix Mountains. It was then she realized, she told Dam and Brailsford in the *People* interview, that "my problems had nothing to do with my looks. There didn't need to be one more diet, one more hairstyle. There needed to be a contribution from me."

Carlino teamed up with David J. Watson, her brother-in-law who had invested in BioMedic, to launch Philosophy in early 1996. Its skin-care line and makeup products had all-natural ingredients made from plant extracts, but what set Carlino's new venture apart from the competition was the modern look of its packaging and the clever names for its wares. A face cream was called "Hope in a Jar," a line once used derisively by the founder of the Revlon empire, while an undereye cream was named "Eye Believe." The slogans under each were also unique, and written by Carlino herself. Eye Believe, for example, urged users to "stop looking for lines and you won't see so many," while Hope in a Jar's tag line cautioned that while "science can give us better skin only humanity can give us better days." As Carlino explained in an interview with Mary Vandeveire for the Phoenix-area *Business Journal,* her goal in coming up with the puns and stand-out lower-faced black typeface for the packaging was twofold. "You're competing against people $1 billion bigger than you, but it's also an opportunity," she said. "When you don't have a huge marketing department, you have to dig deeper. An advertising company could not have come up with [Philosophy's packaging.] It was too corny."

Like BioMedic, Carlino's Philosophy products gained a cult following and the company grew quickly. After just a year in business, the 250-unit Philosophy range was being sold at Nordstrom, Barneys New York, and Saks Fifth Avenue. At one point, she and Watson decided to hire a real advertising agency instead of doing everything themselves—but changed their minds when vintage family photographs they had selected were replaced with images of models. "The best decision was the day the advertising came back in-house," Carlino confessed to the *Business Journal*'s Vandeveire, citing the dual lessons she learned as "don't second-guess yourself…. Never release some of the creative control."

The moment of insight that Carlino had experienced when hiking that day in the Phoenix Mountains took shape in another unique angle for Philosophy's

business plan: Carlino donated a percentage of profits to charitable organizations. Those numbers grew significantly in 1999 when she and Philosophy made their debut on QVC, the home-shopping channel. A year later, Philosophy opened its first freestanding store in Tempe, Arizona, supplementing scores of in-store boutiques in the cosmetic aisles of major department stores like Macy's and Nordstrom.

In May of 2001, Carlino sold BioMedic to cosmetic conglomerate L'Oreal, which sells it under the same name but within its La Roche-Posay family of products. Carlino also began to retool Philosophy, Inc. by ending some store contracts and shedding some of the underperforming items. "In the beginning, we had too much product and too many doors," she said in a 2002 interview with Julie Naughton for *WWD.* "My goal isn't to be the biggest, but to do what's right for us."

Over the next few years Philosophy, Inc. became a profitable presence on QVC and rose to be the sales leader among all the channel's beauty brands. In January of 2007, Carlino sold part of Philosophy, Inc. to The Carlyle Group, a private equity firm based in Washington, D.C., for a reported $450 million price tag. With the deal she exchanged her chief executive officer title for a new one, executive chair, but her new role allowed her to concentrate on product development, not financial operations. "I feel like I've been given a blank chalkboard and there's nothing I'm better with," she told Molly Prior, a journalist for *WWD.* Later that year she spent some of her windfall on a $12 million apartment in the 995 Fifth Avenue Building in Manhattan, the former Stanhope Hotel located across the street from the Metropolitan Museum of Art.

Sources

Allure, March 1, 2005, p. 112.
Business Journal (Phoenix, AZ), September 12, 1997, p. 45.
New York Times, January 18, 1998; April 20, 2008.
New York Times Magazine, December 19, 2004.
People, October 18, 1999, p. 155.
WWD, August 23, 2002, p. 7; January 31, 2007, p. 2.

—*Carol Brennan*

Stephen L. Carter

Law professor and author

Born Stephen Lisle Carter, October 26, 1954; son of Lisle (a law professor and college administrator) and Emily (an administrator) Carter; married Enola Aird (an organization director); children: Leah, Andrew. *Education:* Stanford University, B.A., 1976; Yale University, J.D., 1979.

Addresses: *Office*—Yale Law School, PO Box 208215, New Haven, CT 06520-8215.

Career

Law clerk to presiding justice, U.S. Court of Appeals (D.C. circuit), 1979-80; law clerk to Thurgood Marshall, U.S. Supreme Court, 1980-81; admitted to the Washington, D.C., Bar, 1981; associate, Shea & Gardner, Washington, D.C., 1981-82; Yale University, New Haven, CT, assistant professor, 1982-84, associate professor, 1984-86, professor, 1986-91, William Nelson Cromwell professor of law, 1991—; published first nonfiction work, *Reflections of an Affirmative Action Baby*, 1991; published first novel, *The Emperor of Ocean Park*, 2002.

Awards: Named one of the Ten Outstanding Young Americans, United States Jaycees, 1987; Anisfield-Wolf Book Award for fiction, for *The Emperor of Ocean Park*, 2003.

Sidelights

While Yale law professor Stephen L. Carter was respected for his nonfiction works on race and religion in American society, he came to wider prominence in 2002 when he published his first novel after receiving a multi-million dollar fiction deal. In *The Emperor of Ocean Park,* Carter explored the lives of academic African Americans in a New England university setting. Carter followed *The Emperor of Ocean Park* with another novel in 2007, the murder mystery *New England White,* which foregrounds two minor characters from his first novel and is similarly set in a New England university town. Despite his success as a novelist, however, Carter had no plans to leave Yale or discontinue his academic scholarship.

Born on October 26, 1954, Carter was the second of five children of Lisle and Emily Carter. Raised in Washington, D.C., and Ithaca, New York, Carter was the son of an academic: His father was a law professor who served as an administrator for Cornell and the University of the District of Columbia and worked in human services posts in the administrations of John F. Kennedy and Lyndon B. Johnson. His mother worked for a Georgia state senator and for the Urban Coalition. His paternal grandmother, Eunice, was a prominent lawyer.

The young Carter had fiction writing aspirations from an early age. He told Leonard Picker of *Publishers Weekly,* "When I was a little boy, I used to buy spiral notebooks at the corner store and write little novels in them. From that time, I always wanted to write fiction." Embracing the legacy of his family, Carter went to Stanford, where he earned his undergraduate degree and still thought about writing novels. He served as the managing editor of *The Stanford Daily* as well but decided on a law career.

After graduating from Stanford in 1976, Carter applied to law schools. Race played a factor in his admissions. He was initially rejected by Harvard Law School because admission officials assumed he was white. When they found out that Carter was African American, they offered him admission. Carter turned Harvard down to enter Yale University's law school, though he was probably admitted because of his race. He earned his J.D. in 1979.

With law degree in hand, Carter spent the next two years clerking for federal judges. First, he served for a year as a clerk for a judge on the U.S. Court of Appeals, Washington, D.C. circuit. Then Carter became a clerk for Supreme Court Justice Thurgood Marshall for another year. After spending a year as an associate with the D.C. law firm Shea & Gardner, Carter turned to academia.

Carter was hired at Yale as an assistant professor in 1982. He moved quickly through the tenure-track ranks, spending two years as an assistant professor then another two years as an associate professor. Carter became a full professor in 1986. At the time, he was one of the youngest tenured professors in the history of Yale and the first African-American tenured professor there. Carter received another honor in 1991, when he was given an endowed chair. At that time, he was named the William Nelson Cromwell Professor of Law.

Also in 1991 Carter published his first book, *Reflections of an Affirmative Action Baby*. Here Carter relates his own experiences as an educated African American who experienced racism in academic and professional settings. He had been both labeled and patronized because of his race, a type of unexpected, acceptable racism found among white intellectuals. Carter also believed that affirmative action encourages people to be regarded as members of a racial group instead of as individuals.

Reviewing the book for the *New York Times*, David J. Garrow explained Carter's goal: "*Reflections of an Affirmative Action Baby* is Mr. Carter's powerfully written and persuasive attempt to illuminate both the significant personal costs that accrue even to those like himself who are acknowledged beneficiaries of affirmative action programs ... as well as what he correctly terms 'the deepening divisions in the black community over the issue of affirmative action.'"

Two years later, Carter published a second book about another controversial subject: religion in the United States. In *The Culture of Disbelief: How American Law and Politics Trivialize Religious Devotion*, he looked at religion and politics through the filter of U.S. legal culture. Carter emphasized the hostility toward religion and believed that legal culture turned away from religion.

In a review in the *Washington Post*, Thomas Morawetz explained that Carter "protests that our law and politics trivialize religious belief, treating it as a hobby. He argues that the constitutional mandate of separation of church and state has been misconstrued to protect politics from religion, rather than to protect religion from politics." Picking up on this theme, Larry Witham of *Insight on the News* noted: "Carter advocates eloquently on behalf of ordinary people of religious faith who, with their children, confront a public sector that views their convictions as hobbies rather than as taproots of morality and salvation."

Continuing to criticize a certain kind of liberalism from a Christian, African-American perspective, Carter published two other titles on the subject in 1998: *The Dissent of the Governed: A Meditation on Law, Religion, and Loyalty* and *Civility: Manners, Morals, and the Etiquette of Democracy*. Reviewing both books for the *New York Times*, Michael Lind wrote: "Carter elaborates his critique of a liberalism that in his judgment all too often becomes illiberal in its attitude toward those who dissent from the secular worldview of the American elite."

Arguing that religious morality does have a place in U.S. public debate in *Dissent*, Carter also emphasized his belief that religious people can sometimes have good reason for committing acts of defiance. In *Civility*, Carter explored related territory by exploring the concepts of civility and incivility at different points in history. Again touching on religious themes in the book, he analyzed the concepts and their effect on American life.

Religion and politics again took center stage in Carter's next book, 2000's *God's Name in Vain: The Wrongs and Rights of Religion in Politics*. Going back to the ideas he explored in *The Culture of Disbelief*,

Carter developed his argument that religion and religious dialogue add much to public debate and have caused social and political change throughout U.S. history. Yet Carter also conceded that tying religion to politics has negatively affected personal religiosity. Furthermore, he used *God's Name in Vain* to explain fundamental links between politics and religion.

After *God's Name in Vain*, Carter went in an entirely different direction with his writing: fiction. On the basis of the first draft of a novel that he had been thinking about for 20 years and actively working on for several years, in 2001 he signed a two-book deal worth $4.2 million with Alfred A. Knopf. The film rights were sold for $1 million soon after as well as foreign rights for a number of countries. Carter then revised the manuscript for what became his first novel, the legal thriller *The Emperor of Ocean Park.*

The novel explored the often invisible lives of black professionals through the life of Talcott Garland, a narrator with a similar background to the author's though Carter denied any real link to the character. Garland is a law professor whose father, a conservative judge, was once denied a seat on the Supreme Court. After his father's death, Garland must deal with the fallout from secret deals his father made. Writing about *The Emperor of Ocean Park*, Dinitia Smith of the *New York Times*, stated that the novel "is populated by characters who embody all the contradictions of the new, integrated America. Affluence and education have propelled them into white society, but they are also profoundly African American, conscious of their history and culture."

The Emperor of Ocean Park was generally well received by critics and audiences. *Time*'s Lev Grossman wrote, "Talcott's clear-eyed observation of his peers, both white and black, give *Emperor* a serious social conscience most books of its ilk lack." While critics took issue with the superficial characterizations and the convoluted storyline, reviews like the one in *Economist* noted, "The novel's humor obliterates these faults. Much of the action takes place on campus, and Mr. Carter is as witty as David Lodge about academic vendettas, and more venomous. His scholars ooze goodwill as they scheme to ruin their colleagues' careers, reputations, and marriages."

Some detractors derided the book's length (654 pages) and the author's long-winded style. Reviewing the book in *Newsweek*, David Gates wrote, "*Ocean Park* has problems that no amount of cutting and editing could have cured. For one thing, not a lot actually happens besides conversations and cogitations in which clues are dropped, picked up and anatomized ... and the puzzle pieces do their clicking." Despite such sentiments, the novel had an initial run of 500,000 copies, many favorable reviews, and was a bestseller. Carter told Grossman of *Time*, "I never dreamed the reception would be anything like what happened. I assumed it would more or less drop without a ripple."

Five years after *The Emperor of Ocean Park* appeared, Carter published his second novel, *New England White*. Focusing on two minor characters from the first novel, Carter switched from a first-person to third-person narrative in a mystery thriller that again focused on upwardly mobile African Americans. At the center are Lemaster Carlyle, an immigrant from Barbados who has just become the first black president of a respected university, and his wife, Julia. Their lives are filled with social clubs and other activities until they are connected to the murder of Kellen Zant, a university colleague. Julia becomes drawn into investigating the death of Zant, a former lover.

New England White received mixed reviews as critics again commented on Carter's convoluted organization and wordiness. In the *Los Angeles Times*, Paula L. Woods wrote that the novel "fails to satisfy, not because of its length ... or the complex conspiracy at its heart, but because of the heavy-handed plotting and deductive leaps of faith the novel asks of readers that become hard to stomach. That said, one must acknowledge that Carter is a thoughtful writer." Some believed it suffered in comparison to the first, as fellow author Joyce Carol Oates noted in the *New Yorker*, "Though there is much to admire in *New England White*, especially in the interstices of the mystery plot, the novel seems to lack the vigor, intensity, and air of authenticity of its predecessor."

After publishing his second novel, Carter planned on returning to the genre he knew best. After *The Emperor of Ocean Park* came out in 2002, he told David Mehegan of the *Boston Globe*, "I don't know what the future holds. I'll write the second book, and then I plan to continue writing nonfiction. I don't want to stop being a law professor—I love teaching."

Selected writings

Nonfiction

Reflections of an Affirmative Action Baby, Basic Books, 1991.

The Culture of Disbelief: How American Law and Politics Trivialize Religious Devotion, Basic Books, 1993.
The Confirmation Mess, 1994.
Integrity, Basic Books, 1996.
The Dissent of the Governed: A Meditation on Law, Religion, and Loyalty, Harvard University Press, 1998.
Civility: Manners, Morals, and the Etiquette of Democracy, Basic Books, 1998.
God's Name in Vain: How Religion Should and Should Not Be Involved in Politics, Basic Books, 2000.

Novels

The Emperor of Ocean Park, Knopf, 2002.
New England White, Knopf, 2007.

Sources

Books

Complete Marquis Who's Who Biographies, Marquis Who's Who, 2007.

Periodicals

Boston Globe, June 12, 2002, p. C1.
Economist (US), June 15, 2002.
Historian, Spring-Summer 2002, p. 734.
Insight on the News, November 15, 1993, p. 35.
Los Angeles Times, June 27, 2007, p. E1.
Newsweek, June 10, 2002, p. 56.
New Yorker, July 2, 2007, p. 74.
New York Times, September 1, 1991, sec. 7, p. 1; May 10, 1998, sec. 7, p. 12; May 27, 2002, p. E1.
Press Enterprise (Riverside, CA), June 13, 2002, p. A20.
Publishers Weekly, October 16, 2000, p. 70; May 14, 2007, p. 29.
Time, June 10, 2002, p. 62.
Washington Post, October 3, 1993, p. X8.

Online

Contemporary Authors Online, Thomson Gale, 2007.

—A. Petruso

Cecil Castellucci

Photo by Craig Wadlin. Courtesy of Cecil Castellucci

Author, filmmaker, and musician

Born October 25, 1969, in New York, NY; daughter of scientists. *Education:* Concordia University, B.F.A., 1993; studied theater at École Florent (Paris, France), and with the Groundlings troupe of Los Angeles.

Addresses: *Home*—Los Angeles, CA. *Office*—P.O. Box 29095, Los Angeles, CA 90039.

Career

Member of the rock band Bite after 1990; cofounder of the band Nerdy Girl; has also recorded under the name Cecil Seaskull. Founding member of the Alpha 60 Film Club, 2001; appearance in *Starwoids* documentary, 2001; field producer, *Big Urban Myth Show,* MTV Networks, 2002; actor, screenwriter, and director of the film *Happy Is Not Hard to Be,* 2005. First young-adult novel, *Boy Proof,* published by Candlewick Press, 2005.

Sidelights

Cecil Castellucci moved from a career as an indie-rock musician and filmmaker to a successful young-adult novelist as the author of *Boy Proof* and *Queen of Cool.* In 2007, she wrote her first graphic novel, *The P.L.A.I.N. Janes,* with DC Comics illustrator Jim Rugg. Seemingly unafraid to tackle new creative challenges throughout her career, Castellucci admitted to being unnerved by having to stay mindful of how her text merged with images. "I had to learn how to write a story all over again," she confessed to George Gene Gustines in a *New York Times* interview. "I did have a week or two when I thought I don't know what I'm doing."

Castellucci was born in 1969 in New York City to scientist-parents who traveled widely. In 1979, when she was nine years old, the family was in Brussels, Belgium, and witnessed a bomb attack by operatives of the Irish Republican Army—an event she would later adapt for the plot of *The P.L.A.I.N. Janes.* A self-professed nerd, in middle school Castellucci inexplicably found herself part of the alpha-female clique at her school. Years later, she described the dual life she led for a time in an article she penned for *Horn Book* titled "My Brother's Bookshelf," noting that while she tried hard to fit in, she still remained somewhat of a rebel. "I wore a man's shirt and tie to school and talked to the boys who liked Star Wars and played Dungeons & Dragons. I realized that my bedroom, where my girlfriends came over and inspected my stuff, had to be just so or I would be turfed from the group. That meant a jewelry box, pretty hair things, girly dolls, and only the right kind of books," she wrote. "There were books I could never let my popular friends see," which were her favorite science-fiction and fantasy favorites, and so she kept them in her brother's room.

Castellucci attended New York City's LaGuardia High School of the Performing Arts, a specialized public high school near Lincoln Center for students hoping for a career in the performing arts. From there, she went on to Montreal's Concordia University, where she earned a fine-arts degree in film production and played in the rock band Bite in the early 1990s. For a time, they were the only all-female band on the Montreal indie-rock scene. "I didn't even really want to be in a band," she told Rupert Bottenberg in an interview for the *Montreal Mirror.* "Everyone was just afraid to sing, and I was like, 'I've got a big mouth, I'll sing!'"

After a falling-out with the band, Castellucci went on to found another act she called Nerdy Girl, which issued an eponymous 1994 EP and a 1997 full-length LP titled *Twist Her.* After the band went through several changes in its line-up, it disbanded and Castellucci moved to Los Angeles, where she took classes with the noted improvisational comedy troupe the Groundlings. She also recorded one more album, *Whoever,* under the name Cecil Seaskull, and appeared in the 2001 documentary film *Starwoids* as one of the scores of fans who camped out in front of Grauman's Chinese Theater for tickets to see *Star Wars Episode I: The Phantom Menace* before its 1999 premiere. "It was a ridiculous thing to do, but at the same time, it was Star Wars, and Star Wars was the reason that I even thought you could become a person who told stories when you grew up," she told Bottenberg in the *Montreal Mirror.*

Castellucci's career as a writer began with the performance-art pieces she wrote, "The Shirt and Other Awkward Stories," "The Ladies' Room," and "My Heart, the Whore." From there, she wrote a screenplay based on a questionnaire she had sent out to struggling actors, which she made into the feature film *Happy Is Not Hard to Be* with the help of the Alpha 60 Film Club she co-founded in 2001. As the film neared completion, she decided to use some of her songwriting royalties toward a workshop on writing for children in Banff, Alberta. She needed to submit 40 pages of fiction with the application to the workshop, and visited a friend who worked at a Los Angeles bookstore for advice. As she recalled in an interview with Jennifer M. Brown of *Publishers Weekly,* her friend Steve told her, "You should write a book called Boy Proof and have a guy in it named Max," she said. "Steve loves me as a person but he thinks of me as boy proof," and she admitted that once she heard the phrase "'boy proof,' it all came together."

Boy Proof was published by Candlewick Press in 2005 and marked Castellucci's debut as a young-adult novelist. The story centers on Victoria, who calls herself Egg, after the heroine of her favorite science-fiction movie *Terminal Earth.* Egg even sports a shaved head and a white cape like her on-screen role model, which makes her somewhat of a rebel at the Los Angeles private school she attends. Focused on earning top grades, a side career as a photographer for the school paper, and her science-fiction world, Egg is immune to the charms of the opposite sex, which in her mother's words is "boy proof." The plot hinges upon a cautious friendship she develops with a new student, Max Garter, who has a similarly iconoclastic streak. Other elements of the story include the disintegration of her parents' marriage; her mother is an actress whose career has languished since Egg was born, and her father is an award-winning special-effects artist.

Reviews for *Boy Proof* were largely positive. "As we follow Egg's adventures (and misadventures) in this honest, amusing novel," wrote the *Philadelphia Inquirer's* Katie Haegele, "we get to watch a hatchling emerge. She doesn't have to give up her heroines or their postapocalyptic worlds entirely, but she does learn that it's not the worst thing if your heroes turn out to be creeps." A contributor to *Publishers Weekly* commended Egg's narrative voice, which the writer asserted recounts an "inner struggle and prickly exterior.... Castellucci effortlessly paints a picture of Hollywood as a setting that shapes her characters as much as they shape it."

After *Boy Proof* was accepted by Candlewick but before it appeared in print, Castellucci attended a Los Angeles-area literary event where she met the novelist Aimee Bender. As Castellucci recalled in an interview with Cynthia Leitich Smith on Smith's blog, Cynsations, "when I told her that I had sold my first novel, she said 'Write your second one before your first one comes out.' I was like, 'Why?' and she was like, 'Because that way you won't freak out.'" Castellucci took the advice to heart, and began working on her next young-adult novel, *Queen of Cool,* which was published by Candlewick Press in 2006.

Queen of Cool is another coming-of-age tale, this one centering on 16-year-old Libby Brin, whose affluent lifestyle and jaded friends bring on a sense of ennui that culminates in odd behavior: At her private high school's formal dance, she strips out of her dress, "puts a paper bag over her head, and streaks (in her underwear) through the gym—then asks herself, 'What is wrong with me?'" noted a *Publishers Weekly* review. The ensuing ruckus prompts Libby to become a volunteer at the Los Angeles Zoo, where the new friends she meets causes her to re-evaluate her idea of who's cool and who's not.

Again, Castellucci's novel won kudos from critics. "Though there's nothing revolutionary about Libby's transformation," noted Christine M. Heppermann in *Horn Book,* "her observations are sharp and convincing." *Booklist's* Shelle Rosenfeld also weighed in with laudatory words. "Relayed in Libby's lively, intimate voice, this story is a quick, engaging read," she wrote. Asked by Leitich Smith why she had chosen to make the zoo a centerpiece of the story, Castellucci replied that for a period of time "I was just kind of obsessed with the L.A. Zoo. I had gone to visit one day when I was having an emotional freak out," she recalled, and came across the condor exhibit. None of the majestic birds were on public view, however, which "made me really sad. I got the idea for a scene, in a flash, about this girl who is totally cool who goes on a field trip to the zoo and sees a baby condor die while it's hatching and her life is changed."

Castellucci's next book was *Beige,* her third for young-adult readers. Here she drew upon part of her Montreal experiences in crafting a protagonist, Katy, who is a straight-arrow French-Canadian teen. Katy has been estranged from her father for much of her life, but her mother's work as an archaeologist forces her to spend the summer in Southern California with him. A member of notorious early-punk act called Suck that is now on the verge of a comeback, Katy's father tries to bond with her, but she tells him she is disinterested in music. A bandmate's daughter, Lake, is recruited to befriend her, but Lake—also a musician—dubs Katy "Beige" for being so boring. "Castellucci gives a fresh spin to the familiar exiled-teen plot," noted Cindy Dobrez in a *Booklist* review. A writer for *Publishers Weekly* noted that the coming-of-age tale rang true as Katy "slowly finds a place in their world, affecting them with her kindness and 'learning to be loud.'"

Castellucci revisited the terror she experienced as a child in Brussels in re-creating the event that launches her first graphic novel, *The P.L.A.I.N. Janes.* Illustrated by Jim Rugg, the title was published by DC Comics in 2007 as part of its new Minx imprint of graphic novels aimed at female readers. In the fictional "Metro City," teenaged Jane is injured by bomb that goes off outside of a café. She helps a young man to safety, but he winds up in a coma and lingers unidentified in the hospital. Jane has his sketchbook, however, and writes "John Doe" letters about her new suburban life, because her parents—unnerved by the attack—have chosen to move out of the city.

Jane's transition to suburban living is aided by her three new friends, also named Jane. There is Jayne, who is instantly dubbed "Brain Jane," drama-loving Theater Jane, and athletic Sporty Jane, whose real name is Polly Jane. The quartet call themselves P.L.A.I.N., or People Loving Art in Neighborhoods, and stage secret guerrilla art attacks in their neighborhood. "The core of this timely novel, though, is Jane's struggle to see the beauty of the world rather than its dangers," noted Claire E. Gross

in a *Horn Book* review. Castellucci's words and Rugg's illustrations, noted a contributor to *Publishers Weekly,* "nimbly make their larger point—that fear is an indulgence we must give ourselves permission to overcome—without ever preaching."

Castellucci admitted that writing *The P.L.A.I.N. Janes* was somewhat cathartic for her after her long-ago experience in Brussels. "It seemed like this was a good opportunity to explore those fearful feelings that I had growing up," she told Gustines in the *New York Times* interview. "They've always been a part of my makeup and fears." Like any creative type, she remains chained to her worst fear—that she will lose the gift of her imagination. "Sometimes I lay around staring at the ceiling," she told Smith on the Cynsations blog interview, "thinking, 'OK that's it. I've had my last idea. I'm done. It's over. I'm a big fat fraud.'"

Selected writings

Boy Proof, Candlewick Press (Cambridge, MA), 2005.
Queen of Cool, Candlewick Press, 2006.
Beige, Candlewick Press, 2007.
The P.L.A.I.N. Janes (graphic novel; illustrated by Jim Rugg), DC Comics (New York City), 2007.

Sources

Periodicals

Booklist, February 15, 2006, p. 90; September 1, 2007, p. 103.
Horn Book, March-April 2006, p. 182; July-August 2007, p. 390; September-October 2007, p. 528.
New York Times, November 25, 2006.
Philadelphia Inquirer, September 13, 2006.
Publishers Weekly, February 21, 2005, p. 176; June 27, 2005, p. 27; February 20, 2006, p. 158; April 9, 2007, p. 56; June 18, 2007, p. 56.
School Library Journal, April 2005, p. 129; August 2007, p. 112.

Online

"Author Interview: Cecil Castellucci on The Queen of Cool," Cynsations, http://cynthialeitichsmith. blogspot.com/2006/01/author-interview-cecil-castellucci-on.html (February 6, 2008).
"Wordy Girl," *Montreal Mirror,* http://www.montrealmirror.com/2005/102005/watn19.html (February 6, 2008).

—Carol Brennan

Gina Centrello

**Publisher of Random House
Ballantine Publishing Group**

Born c. 1959 in the United States; married; children: two.

Addresses: *Office*—Random House Publishing Group, 1745 Broadway, New York, NY 10019.

Career

Copy editor, Pocket Books, early 1980s; executive vice president and publisher, Pocket Books, 1993-94; president and publisher, Pocket Books, 1994-99; president and publisher, Ballantine Books, 1999-2003; president and publisher, Random House Ballantine Publishing Group, 2003—.

Awards: "Top 50 Women to Watch," *Wall Street Journal,* 2004.

Sidelights

During her 25-year book-publishing career, Gina Centrello made a name for herself as a marketing guru, able to create mainstream bestsellers and transform stagnant imprints into profitable units. In 2003, Centrello became president and publisher of Random House, the world's largest commercial publisher of English-language books. The appointment was prestigious given that Random House, home to such stalwart authors as William Faulkner, Truman Capote, and Maya Angelou, has rolled out more Pulitzer and Nobel Prize-winning tomes than any other publisher.

Centrello's rise to the top spot was not without controversy, particularly since her appointment came at the expense of Random House's highly respected publisher and editor-in-chief Ann Godoff; however, Centrello proved she had a loyal following of her own. "I find her one of these refreshing people in publishing who is not interested in being a publishing persona, but interested in being the best possible publisher, both for the sake of her company and her authors," author Richard North Patterson told John Schwartz of the *New York Times.* "It makes her an absolute dream to work with."

Centrello was born around 1959. She entered the publishing world in the early 1980s and rose rapidly through the ranks. Her first job was as a copy editor at Pocket Books, a division of Simon & Schuster known for its mass-market, rack-sized paperbacks. By 1994, Centrello, just 35, was running the company, having been promoted to president and publisher. At the time, Pocket Books made its money by reprinting literature, mysteries, and popular nonfiction works. Centrello helped the company diversify and become a noteworthy publisher of original works.

Under Centrello, Pocket rolled out a number of profitable bestsellers targeted at a wide range of readers, including books by conservative talk-show host Rush Limbaugh, who was popular in the early 1990s. Pocket also picked up publication rights for spinoffs based on MTV's Beavis and Butthead cartoon series. Centrello boosted profits by publishing reprints from popular novelists such as Larry Mc-Murtry, Mary Higgins Clark, Ann Rule, and Jackie Collins. As a publisher, Centrello had a knack for figuring out what the public would buy. A surprise hot-selling item released under Centrello included the 1998 printing of the report by independent counsel Kenneth Starr, which delved into the Clinton White House. All copies of the book's initial run were snatched up the first day it appeared in bookstores.

In 1993, Pocket Books scored a coup by obtaining rights to the Amy Fisher story. The teenage Fisher gained notoriety in 1992 when she shot her married lover's wife in the head. The book, *Amy Fisher: My Story*, was co-written by Fisher and Shella Winter. Centrello sped up production when rumors began to fly that Fisher's lover, Joey Buttafuoco, was going to be indicted on charges of statutory rape because of his affair with a minor. To beef up sales, Centrello wanted to roll out the book at the same time the indictment was handed down.

"So this place became Amy central," Centrello told the *New York Times*' Esther B. Fein. "Pocket has done a lot of crash books in paperback, so we have the experience, but it was mad. I wouldn't say it was a circus. It was more like controlled hysteria, but definitely hysteria." The work paid off when the book was published and instantly landed on the *New York Times*' non-fiction best-seller list.

After 17 years with Pocket Books, Centrello left in 1999, becoming president and publisher of Ballantine Books. At the time, Ballantine had been concentrating efforts on reprints and was losing about $7 million a year. Centrello encouraged Ballantine to focus on publishing original works and she helped sign several up-and-coming authors to the label. These included former trial lawyer Richard North Patterson, author of *To Protect and Defend*, and historical fiction writer Jeff Shaara, son of Pulitzer Prize-winner Michael Shaara and author of *Gods and Generals*. Under Centrello's direction, Ballantine snatched up rights to books by romance and historical fiction writer Julie Garwood and psychologist and writer Jonathan Kellerman. Buffered by the new work, Ballantine turned a profit of more than $20 million in 2002.

In 2003, Bertelsmann AG, which owned both Random House and Ballantine, decided to merge the two entities. Random House publisher Godoff was served walking papers and Centrello was promoted to president and publisher of the new Random House Ballantine Publishing Group. Random House had a reputation for publishing highbrow, literary works, while Ballantine was more into mass-market thrillers and romances. The appointment caused controversy among those loyal to Random House, particularly from those who viewed literature as an art and not a profit-making endeavor.

Many insiders feared Centrello would water down Random House's literary focus in pursuit of profits. One agent discussed reservations with the *New York Times*' Lynn Hirschberg. "Gina is a marketing person. She does not know writers. Random House is a literary imprint. In the past, and under Ann Godoff, that was the main priority. With Gina, financial success will be the main priority. That scares a lot of people." At the time, it was no secret that Godoff was forced out partly because her division consistently failed to make profit targets.

Those who had worked with Centrello thought she was a perfect fit for the job. Former boss and fellow publisher Irwyn Applebaum noted that Centrello was refreshing, down-to-earth and not given to the snobbery that pervades the publishing world. Centrello's actions speak for themselves. She is known as a hard worker. Instead of going out to schmooze agents and other industry insiders over long, expensive lunches, Centrello is more likely to order a pizza and spend her lunchtime at her desk, working through publishing schedules.

Like many women in the corporate world, Centrello has had to balance work and family life. She tries to get to the office before 8 a.m. so she can be home for dinner and read to her two children before bed. After they are tucked in, she works more, this time from the comforts of her home.

After taking over at Random House, Centrello knew she had a job to do—maintain the publisher's integrity and make money. "Publishing well and publishing profitably are not mutually exclusive," she told the *New York Times*' Schwartz. After three years on the job, Centrello appeared to be on track. According to Random House's fiscal report, sales grew 6.5 percent in 2006. That year, the North American division of Random House had 201 *New York Times* bestsellers, including 37 that topped the chart.

Sources

Periodicals

New York Post, January 17, 2003, p. B37.
New York Times, April 21, 1993, p. C15; January 17, 2003, p. C1; February 24, 2003; July 20, 2003, p. 28 (Section 6); June 11, 2007, p. C1.
Publishers Weekly, December 12, 1994, pp. 10-11; March 1, 1999, p. 11.
Wall Street Journal, November 8, 2004, p. R5; January 18, 2005, p. B1.

Online

"Random House Sales and Profits Up, According to 2006 Fiscal Report," *Book Business*, http://www.bookbusinessmag.com/story/story.bsp?sid=50017&var=story (February 20, 2008).

—Lisa Frick

Joba Chamberlain

Professional baseball player

Born Justin Chamberlain, September 23, 1985, in Lincoln, Nebraska; son of Harlan Chamberlain; children: Karter. *Education:* Attended University of Kansas—Kearney and University of Kansas—Lincoln.

Addresses: *Office*—c/o New York Yankees, Yankee Stadium, Bronx, NY 10451.

Career

Pitcher, West Oahu CaneFires, Hawaiian Winter League, 2006; drafted by New York Yankees, 2006; played for Single-A Tampa, Double A-Trenton, and Triple A-Scranton/Wilkes Barre, 2007; joined Yankees bullpen, 2007; relief pitcher for the Yankees, 2007—.

Awards: Third-Team All American, 2005; First-Team All Big 12, 2005; Big 12 newcomer pitcher of the year, 2005; Second-Team ABCA All-Midwest Region, 2005; Big 12 pitcher of the week, March 1, 2005; Collegiate Baseball national pitcher of the week, March 1, 2005; First-Team Preseason All-American, 2006; pitcher of the week, Florida State League, May 14, 2007 and May 28, 2007; fan choice for athlete with biggest future impact, *ESPN: The Magazine*, 2007.

Sidelights

Joba Chamberlain did not have the typical background of a star baseball player. He was not a varsity player in high school. He did not begin col-lege immediately with a full scholarship on a team. It took Chamberlain time to hit his stride as a player and as a pitcher, but once he did, he moved up from the minors to the majors with a speed that surprised even him. Chosen as the 41st draft pick by the Yankees in 2006, Chamberlain began his year on the winter league in Hawaii, then moved into the Florida State League, the Eastern League on the Single-A team the Atlanta Thrashers, the International League, and up into the Yankees bullpen, from where he began a pitching career that had him labeled by the press as a phenomenon poised for stardom.

Chamberlain was born in Lincoln, Nebraska, the son of Harlan Chamberlain, a security manager at a state penitentiary who had suffered from polio in his youth. When Chamberlain was just a boy, Harlan progressed to a secondary stage that many polio survivors suffer, and his left side was mostly paralyzed. Chamberlain learned early on the value of determination, watching his father live the lessons he strove to teach. Despite his weaknesses, Harlan worked with Chamberlain on baseball drills, using a box full of used equipment that they had found at a yard sale for three dollars. Harlan would position himself on the stoop of their small home and have Chamberlain throw him balls—any that were inaccurate enough for Harlan not to catch from his scooter, Chamberlain would have to run after and retrieve.

During high school, Chamberlain was not accepted on junior varsity as a sophomore, and instead was picked for the reserve team. He might have given up then, but Harlan encouraged him to serve as a role model for the younger players, as well as broaden his horizons. Chamberlain performed in high school musicals and learned to hoop dance. The hoop dance was not the only part of his Winnebago Indian heritage Harlan encouraged: Chamberlain attended powwows and spent time on the reservation with his extended family and his mother (his parents divorced when Chamberlain was only three). Harlan also encouraged Chamberlain to stay involved in the sport he loved by working as a ball boy, picking up after star players, and staying active in the team's environment.

From high school to college, Chamberlain shed his extra pounds and grew taller, learning how to better use his body in the sport. He started pitching his senior year of high school but was passed over by recruiters due to only average performance. Rather than going to college immediately, Chamberlain worked maintenance on ball fields, earning extra income and staying close to the sport. He was recruited from a baseball camp for Division II college University of Nebraska—Kearney and given a scholarship. By working out on his own as well as working out with the team, he dropped the extra weight that had plagued him, and the speed of his pitches increased enough that University of Nebraska—Lincoln recruited him as a transfer. His 2005 season had him poised for a top ten pick in the majors, but after the 2006 season, during which he underperformed due to a triceps injury, his status was less certain. He made the overall draft at 41, and was selected by the Yankees—a move that some thought was meant to sweeten potential trades for the team. But the Yankees held on, and Chamberlain leapt from the Class A league in Tampa all the way to the Yankees bullpen, moving in as a relief pitcher in the last two months of the Major League season.

Some questioned the quick move, but fans cried for Chamberlain to be moved up when Kyle Farnsworth, the pitcher who had been the Yankees' best bet for setting up their closer Mariano Rivera, surrendered two runs in one inning in a game against the Baltimore Orioles. Chamberlain had been trained as a starter in Nebraska, but soon after he moved into the bullpen, the move was considered a

success, albeit with rules. Because Chamberlain had not had as much experience in the league, he was not to pitch back-to-back days, and he would not pitch for two days any time he pitched two innings. Called the "Joba Rules," they were consistent through most of the season, holding until the final games of the playoffs.

Despite all of the media attention, Chamberlain remained humble about his position and the excitement he caused. "I don't get reminded of it until all of you [the media] tell me," he said to Kat O'Brien of Melville, New York, paper *Newsday*. But his fellow players noticed. Pedro Martinez said that Chamberlain reminded him a bit of himself, and said in the Bergen County *Record*, "I wouldn't doubt that that guy will be a dominant pitcher. Right now really from now on." Yankees pitching coach Ron Guirdy noted in the same article, "Anybody who drives so much from his legs, when you put that together with a great arm and solid mechanics, you've got something pretty special." Part of their response comes from Chamberlain's performance, but a writer for the *New York Post* noted that Chamberlain's attitude also contributes equal parts fun and work: "He can be loud and he can bust chops, but when it comes to learning his craft, Chamberlain is very serious," the reporter wrote. Doug Mientkiewicz, a Yankee baseman, commented on Chamberlain's attitude in the *New York Post*: "He gives us an attitude and an edge. He essentially says, 'Here's my best. What can you do with it?'"

Chamberlain's season was not without some controversy. During an August game against the Boston Red Sox, Chamberlain threw two wild pitches over the head of Red Sox player Kevin Youkilis, which earned him a suspension. Chamberlain and manager Joe Torre said that the bad pitches were unintentional, and Chamberlain paid the fine. "A couple balls slipped," Chamberlain told *UPI News Track*. "Youkilis plays the game hard, and it was nothing against him. There's no chance I'm trying to do that." Chamberlain's suspension was soon over, and Chamberlain continued to play as the Yankees made their way into the playoffs. But during one of their playoffs games against the Cleveland Indians, Chamberlain was swarmed with midges, and the tiny insects interfered with his performance, allowing the Indians to tie the game. "I'm never going to make an excuse but they were bad," Chamberlain told the *Buffalo News*. But not one to let himself out of responsibility, he continued, "I've got to do a better job executing my pitches."

After losing to the Indians in the playoffs, the Yankees turned their focus to the next season. The owner turned over the business to his two sons, and manager Joe Torre left the team for the Los Angeles Dodgers. Chamberlain's contract meant he would be staying, but there was no consensus on whether he would be a starter or whether he would continue to set up for closer Rivera. But while his position on the team for the 2008 season is still up in the air, Chamberlain is ready to go wherever he's asked. Back before his position on the Yankees was certain, Harlan Chamberlain told Mitch Sherman of the *Omaha World-Herlad*, "No matter where he plays, he's going to step up. That's the way it's been since he was four years old."

When asked about his job by Gary Smith of *Sports Illustrated,* Chamberlain gestured to the ball field where he was being interviewed. "This is what I do for a living. I get to come here on a weekend day and watch a major league game for free—and maybe even get to pitch in it. What could be better than that?" He expressed his other great hope to Pat Borzi of the *New York Times*: Chamberlain has a son of his own back home in Nebraska. Speaking of his father, Chamberlain said, "If I can be half the man and half the father he was, I'll be very, very happy and have a great life."

Sources

Periodicals

Buffalo News, October 6, 2007.
Business Wire, December 5, 2007.
Daily Oklahoman, May 25, 2006.
News Day (Melville, NY), August 14, 2007; August 30, 2007.
New York Observer, August 13, 2007.
New York Post, September 29, 2007, p. 58; October 4, 2007, p. 107; October 8, 2007, p. 87; October 9, 2007, p. 78, p. 81, p. 99; December 16, 2007, p. 90.
New York Times, September 8, 2007, p. D5.
Omaha World-Herald, August 22, 2006; September 6, 2006; July 8, 2007; July 31, 2007; September 22, 2007.
Record (Bergen County, NJ), September 14, 2007, p. S1; January 11, 2008, p. S10.
Sports Illustrated, October 8, 2007, p. 52.
UPI News Track, August 31, 2007.

Online

"Joba Chamberlain," Huskers.com, http://www. huskers.com/ (February 21, 2008).
"Player File: Joba Chamberlain," Official Site of the New York Yankees, http://mlb.mlb.com/team/player_career.jsp?player_id=501955 (February 21, 2008).

—*Alana Joli Abbott*

Dov Charney

Chief Executive Officer of American Apparel

Born January 31, 1969, in Montreal, Canada; son of Morris (an architect) and Sylvia (an artist) Charney. *Education:* Attended Tufts University, c. late 1980s.

Addresses: *Office*—American Apparel, Inc., 747 Warehouse St., Los Angeles, CA 90021.

Career

Founded T-shirt manufacturing company in Columbia, SC, 1989; moved business to Los Angeles, c. 1996 and renamed it American Apparel, Inc.; opened first American Apparel store in Los Angeles, 2003; company acquired by Endeavor Acquisition Corporation, 2006.

Sidelights

Dov Charney is the founder and chief executive officer of American Apparel, Inc., a rapidly growing company with more than 150 stores in North America and Europe, along with outposts as far away as Israel and South Korea. The company's brand identity is closely linked to Charney, who sometimes sports an extravagant handlebar mustache and is known for making provocative, sometimes sexually charged statements in the media. "A complicated, charismatic and occasionally controversial figure," wrote Jaime Wolf in a lengthy *New York Times Magazine* profile in 2006, "Charney is so acutely in tune with the cultural moment that he is

somehow able to use the plain blank T-shirts that he sells to convey potent messages concerning contemporary sex and politics."

Charney was born in Montreal, Canada, in 1969, into an accomplished Israeli-immigrant family. His uncle was renowned architect Moshe Safdie, who designed one of the city's architectural landmarks, the Habitat 67 housing complex. Safdie was the brother of Charney's mother, Sylvia, an artist, and Charney's father, Morris, was also an architect. During his high school years, Charney attended Choate Rosemary Hall, a private boarding school in Wallingford, Connecticut, and went on to enroll in Tufts University in the Boston area, but he left before earning his degree.

Charney was obsessed with T-shirts at an early age. When visiting relatives in Florida, he was astounded by the marked differences between those sold in the United States by companies such as Hanes and the ones available to Canadian shoppers, which he could tell were made from inferior cotton. He began buying the Hanes in bulk and reselling them to a friend who had a printed T-shirt business targeting concert-goers and hockey fans outside the Montreal Forum. In 1989, Charney moved to Columbia, South Carolina, where he set up a T-shirt-manufacturing company, but it failed and entered Chapter 11 bankruptcy status. A business associate who had his own apparel business, Rick Klotz of Fresh Jive, convinced Charney to move to Los Angeles and set up shop there.

The first American Apparel T-shirts came out of Charney's new factory located just off Interstate Highway 10, also known as the Santa Monica Freeway, in 1997. Charney was convinced that he could corner the market by producing a T-shirt from good-quality cotton, knit with a tighter weave that held its shape over time, and styled to have a slimmer fit and longer length. In a 2000 profile that appeared in the *New Yorker,* Charney explained to writer Malcolm Gladwell: "The finest T-shirts are six dollars a piece wholesale. The [worst] shirts are like two dollars. We're going to come in at three and have the right stuff. I'm making the perfect fit. I'm going to manufacture this like gasoline."

While American Apparel was originally a wholesaler of T-shirts, in the summer of 2003 Charney rented a storefront in order to stage a gallery exhibition for an artist friend and put out some of his company's T-shirts for sale, too. They sold quickly, and out of that gritty, hipster venue was born Charney's idea for a retail empire. He set up white-box, gallery-like spaces in arty neighborhoods such as Nolita in New York City and Chicago's Wicker Park and by mid-2007 had 145 American Apparel stores around the world. The stores sold the company's wares, which had expanded to include tank tops, leggings, shorts, and underwear, and were somewhat daring in their décor, which relied heavily on large color photographs—taken by Charney in many cases—of his employees or other young adults wearing American Apparel items along with risqué images from pornography magazines of the 1970s. The photographs became the basis for a national advertising campaign and had "a flashbulb-lighted, lo-fi sultriness to them," wrote Wolf in the *New York Times Magazine* article. "They look less like ads than photos you'd see posted on someone's Myspace page."

Business journalists writing about Charney liked to focus on that edgy, soft-core porn vibe that seemed emblematic of the brand identity, but some writers also noted that the CEO was a maverick in the U.S. apparel-manufacturing business, paying the 5,000 workers at his Los Angeles factory well above the average wage for the industry and offering a slew of generous benefits, including on-site meals and a masseuse along with free English lessons for immigrants. Sewers of American Apparel shirts and other items became the highest-paid mass-produced garment workers in the world, and as the company met the demand for more stores, the headquarters became the largest garment manufacturing establishment in the United States.

Most apparel companies use overseas manufacturers to make their wares, which keeps costs low, but Charney explained his philosophy to David Greenberg in an interview for the *Los Angeles Business Journal,* noting that banks that provide loans to start-up manufacturers like he once was would "rather you open a line of credit for a one-shot deal and pull the goods in from China than have you buy knitting and sewing machines and do it here." Despite the comparative high costs of Charney's business, his vision seemed to be working, and company sales were estimated at $275 million in 2006. American Apparel became a publicly traded company in December of that year. The structure of its initial public offering was somewhat unusual, with Charney's privately held company becoming part of a publicly traded one called Endeavor Acquisition Corporation, which was an investment group.

After the deal, rumored to be in the neighborhood of $380 million, Charney planned to open hundreds of new stores and said he hoped to make American Apparel as ubiquitous in malls and other retail spaces as Abercrombie & Fitch. He was also exploring the idea of a print magazine and a new kind of store for his target urban-hipster customer that would sell electronics and basic staples. "American Apparel is the new normal," he told Wolf in the *New York Times Magazine* interview. "It's fun to say, 'He's wild and crazy,' but I'm not wild and crazy. This is the way the adult generation is going to live. They're not preoccupied by monogamy. Exciting things can happen. They're mobile; they can travel; they're willing to take chances; they're open-minded and ready for change. That's what the boomers presented for America, and that's what this new generation presents for us. I want to be in business with them."

Sources

BusinessWeek, June 27, 2005, p. 88.
Los Angeles Business Journal, May 31, 2004, p. 18.
Newsweek International, August 21, 2006.
New Yorker, April 24, 2000.
New York Times, December 19, 2006.
New York Times Magazine, April 23, 2006.

—*Carol Brennan*

Kenny Chesney

Singer and songwriter

Born Kenneth Arnold Chesney, March 26, 1968, in Knoxville, TN; married Renee Zellweger (an actress), May 9, 2005 (annulled, December 20, 2005). *Education:* East Tennessee State University, undergraduate degree, 1991.

Addresses: *Contact*—Kenny Chesney Fan Club, PO Box 128529, Nashville, TN 37212-8529.

Career

Performer at Chuckie's Trading Post and Quarterback's Barbecue, Johnson City, TN; resident performer at The Turf, Nashville, TN; signed publishing deal with Acuff-Rose, 1992; signed recording contract with Capricorn, 1993; released first album, *In My Wildest Dreams*, 1993; signed recording contract with RCA subsidiary BNA, c. 1995.

Awards: Top New Vocalist Award, Academy of Country Music, 1997; Top Male Vocalist Award, Country Music Association, 2002; Single of the Year Award, Academy of Country Music, for "The Good Stuff," 2003; Album of the Year Award, Country Music Association, for *When the Sun Goes Down*, 2004; Male Video of the Year Award, Country Music TV, for "I Go Back," 2005; Entertainer of the Year Award, Country Music Association, 2005; Entertainer of the Year Award, Country Music Association, 2006; *Billboard* Music Award for country artist of the year, 2006; Entertainer of the Year Award, Country Music Association, 2007; People's Choice Award for favorite male singer, 2007; Male Video of the Year Award, Country Music TV, for "You Save Me," 2007.

Sidelights

Kenny Chesney became a country music superstar in the early 2000s, primarily on the basis of his extraordinarily energetic and popular live shows. The multiple award-winning artist also garnered attention for his many multi-platinum selling records and by reviving interest in the country genre. Known for having a rock edge to his sound, Chesney stated he was firmly a country artist. He told the *Florida Times-Union*'s Nick Marino: "I sing country music. But you listen to our records, a lot of them are pretty edgy.... But when I sing it, it's country. There's no doubt about it."

Born on March 26, 1968, in Knoxville, Tennessee, Chesney was raised in the small community of Luttrell, which was also the home of country legend Chet Akins. Chesney enjoyed music from an early age. While he was growing up he preferred rock music, but he was also a fan of certain country artists such as Conway Twitty. He told the *Virginian-Pilot*'s Frank Roberts: "The heart and soul—there was so much heart in everything he [Twitty] did. He was so unbelievable." Sports were also an important part of Chesney's life. He was a starting end in football while attending Gibbs High School in Luttrell.

Music did not appear as a career choice for Chesney until college. While studying advertising and marketing at East Tennessee State University, Chesney had a country-music epiphany. He told Tonya Parker Morrison of the *South Bend Tribune,* "I never really gave country music a passing thought. Then, one day, I was on my way to class at East Tennessee State and I heard Merle sing 'That's the Way Love Goes.' That was it, brother! Slowly but surely, I moved away from sports and business and into the music life."

While still in school, Chesney began appearing in clubs in Johnson City, where East Tennessee State is located. Though most of the clubs were blues-oriented, he stuck with his infatuation with country music and began attracting much attention from local fans beginning with his initial performances. Chesney found a regular audience for him at Chuckie's Trading Post and Quarterback's Barbecue in Johnson City.

After Chesney earned his degree in advertising from East Tennessee State University in 1991, he moved to Nashville to break into the country music scene there. He did not find an immediate audience for his music, but his strong songwriting abilities led to a songwriting contract. Thus, Chesney first broke into country music as a songwriter, not a singer, by signing a publishing deal with Acuff-Rose in 1992.

While Chesney had a developing songwriting career, he still loved to perform. Not in demand as a performer, he was forced to take the stage in seedy, low-end venues. Chesney remained determined to have a career as a singer; his persistence paid off when he became a resident performer at The Turf in Nashville. Capricorn Records started a new country music division and signed Chesney as a performer in 1993.

Chesney released his first album on Capricorn that year, *In My Wildest Dreams,* though it was not particularly popular. Chesney believed that the label did not promote him enough, but critics praised the album. It sold about 100,000 copies. The label then folded, and Chesney signed a contract with RCA's BNA subsidiary in the mid-1990s.

Chesney released his next albums on BNA. He followed *In My Wildest Dreams* with *All I Need to Know* and *Me & You.* As he changed labels, Chesney was still working on developing his sound, but he found more success. His second album, *All I Need to Know,* was a smash hit. Chesney's third album *Me & You* went gold and spawned a number-one single with "When I Close My Eyes."

In 1999, Chesney looked back on and reflected to Bill Blankenship of the *Topeka Capital-Journal* about these early releases. Chesney said, "The first three albums that I did, I really think I was just part of a bunch of guys out there making music. Don't get me wrong. I'm very proud of those records.... But with time and consistency, slowly but surely, I've been able to separate myself from that bunch and build a career as opposed to just having some songs out there that do well and that's it."

Chesney slowly built up his career in this manner through the 1990s. By the release of his fourth album, *I Will Stand,* Chesney had a solid reputation for putting on an energetic live show as well. He told Roberts of the *Virginian-Pilot,* "I like to have a good time when I get on stage. I stay cooped up on that bus, so when I get to do a show, I'm excited as anybody. It's a fast-paced show, even though I have ballads. I get the audience involved."

Chesney's next album, *Everywhere We Go,* was released in 1999 and went double platinum. Chesney also had at least two number-one singles off the album: "You Had Me From Hello" and "How Forever Feels." "You Had Me from Hello" was Chesney's fifth number-one record, but the first one he wrote himself, making it all the more special for the artist.

Chesney also opened for country legend George Strait in 1999 and 2000, increasing Chesney's already high profile. During the tour, Chesney had a run-in with the law on a stop in Buffalo, New York. Chesney was accused of stealing a horse belonging to the Erie County's sheriff's office. Chesney claimed he had permission to ride the animal, and the incident got out of hand. The officer asked for the horse back, and Chesney refused in jest. The misunderstanding blew up, involving Chesney, country music star Tim McGraw, and Mark Russo, an entourage member. All three were accused of various crimes, with Chesney being charged with disorderly conduct. He was later acquitted.

After meeting a career goal by releasing a greatest hits record in 2000, Chesney did not release an album for two years. Yet the country music singer was able to continue to build his career, primarily through his now-legendary live performances. Before *No Shoes, No Shirt, No Problems* was released in 2002, Chesney had a few hit singles from the album and was able to tour to promote it by headlining arena concerts. He continued to emulate rock artists in his live shows, telling Marino of the *Florida Times-Union,* "My goal is to be like Aerosmith and AC/DC. They still go out there and kick butt every night on stage."

When *No Shoes, No Shirt, No Problems* did come out, it was also a smash, not only among country music fans, but with music fans in general. Young, non-country music fans increasingly showed up at his concerts. The record debuted as number one on *Billboard*'s country album charts as well as the pop charts and eventually went triple platinum. Critics raved about Chesney's maturity as a songwriter and performer, with strong lyrics, clever stories, and more personal and emotional sincerity. A few tracks received particular attention, including "Big Star," which talks about women with problems they overcome. Such songs showed him to be a serious artist.

Chesney believed the success of *No Shoes, No Shirt, No Problems* was important not only for him since it reflected his growth as an artist, but for his genre as a whole. He told Robert Kreutzer of the *Press Enterprise*, "The fact that I debuted at No. 1 was a shot in the arm for country music. It raised the bar. For people to think country music is dead is wrong. And, for a short time, for me to outshow everybody that's out there, that's a big thrill."

As Chesney became not just a gigantic country artist but a mainstream music star, he had the highest-grossing country tour in the United States and one of the most popular tours of any genre in 2002. He sold more than 1.8 million tickets for $24 million in sales on his tour that year, and did similar business for his tour in 2003. With such high-profile exposure came more accolades, including being named the sexiest male country singer alive by *People* magazine.

Despite his continued achievements, Chesney remained humble and was aware his success could be gone just as quickly. He told the *Winston-Salem Journal*'s Ed Bumgardner, "I've worked hard to get here, and, to be honest, I still can't believe it all isn't going to disappear tomorrow—and it might. I looked at my band as we walked out on stage the other night ... and I told them, 'Guys, take a long look at this, enjoy it and remember it forever, because it isn't always going to be like this.'"

Chesney continued to push the envelope with his subsequent releases. After a 2003 Christmas album, *All I Want for Christmas Is a Real Good Tan*, Chesney's next major release *When the Sun Goes Down*, continued to expand the definition of country. While the album included the expected country ballads, it also featured Calypso rhythms, influenced by his love of the Caribbean, and a duet with Uncle Kracker, a rap-rocker. The more up-tempo album also featured more songs written by Chesney. *When the Sun Goes Down* also sold more than three million copies.

In 2005, Chesney went more introspective with his *Be As You Are*. Unlike previous records, Chesney wrote or co-wrote nearly all the tracks. More deeply reflecting the peace he felt at his second home in the British Virgin Islands, songs such as "Island Boy" and "Key Lime Pie" describe people and places in his life there. He told John Gerome of the Associated Press, "A lot of the people in those places have really touched me and showed me I don't have to push so hard all of the time." The music was also more simple and stripped down, unlike the heavy production of his previous efforts.

While Chesney's career remained red hot as he evolved, he became a media sensation for more personal reasons. After only knowing actress Renee Zellweger a few months, the couple married on a beach in the British Virgin Islands on May 9, 2005. The marriage was short-lived as Chesney admitted he was not ready for marriage. It was annulled on the grounds of fraud on December 20, 2005, setting off an even more dramatic tabloid frenzy.

Chesney retreated to his music, releasing a live album in 2006, *Live: Live Those Songs Again*, and a new studio release in 2007, *Just Who I Am: Poets & Pirates*. The new album did not feature any of his own songs but was the expected mix of ballads and up-tempo numbers, all reflecting his emotional state. Chesney also had another number-one single, "Never Wanted Nothing More." Yet the country music star admitted he was unsure he was ready to record again because of his personal problems, though the studio provided some solace in the storm.

Despite such setbacks, Chesney planned on having a long career, even if it is primarily as a performer. He told Bumgardner of the *Winston-Salem Journal*, "I'm not out to save the world, but I am out to entertain as much of it as I can. I want to still be doing this when I am 60, just like the Rolling Stones. I just hope to look a little better than Keith Richards. That's why I work out."

Selected discography

In My Wildest Dreams, Capricorn, 1993.
All I Need to Know, BNA, 1995.
Me & You, BNA, 1996.
I Will Stand, BNA, 1997.
Everywhere We Go, BNA, 1999.
Greatest Hits, BNA, 2000.
No Shirt, No Shoes, No Problems, BNA, 2002.
All I Want for Christmas Is A Real Good Tan, BNA, 2003.

When the Sun Goes Down, BNA, 2004.
Be As You Are (Songs from an Old Blue Chair), BNA, 2005.
The Road & the Radio, BNA, 2005.
Live: Live Those Songs Again, BNA, 2006.
Just Who I Am: Poets & Pirates, BNA, 2007.

Sources

Books

Complete Who's Who Biographies, Marquis's Who's Who, 2007.

Periodicals

Associated Press, February 18, 2004; January 25, 2005; September 10, 2007.

Florida Times-Union (Jacksonville, FL), April 5, 2002, p. WE-11.
Miami Herald (FL), September 7, 2007.
Milwaukee Journal Sentinel, July 1, 2003, p. 1E.
Omaha World Herald (NB), August 22, 2002, p. 5.
Plain Dealer (Cleveland, OH), August 5, 2005, p. 4.
Press Enterprise (Riverside, CA), May 24, 2002, p. AA13.
South Bend Tribune (IN), November 10, 2000, p. C1.
Topeka Capital-Journal (KS), October 15, 1999, p. C1.
Virginian-Pilot (Norfolk, VA), August 7, 1997, p. E3.
Winston-Salem Journal (Winston Salem, NC), February 14, 2003, p. E1.

—*A. Petrusso*

Julie Christie

Actress

Born Julie Frances Christie, April 14, 1941, in Chukua, Assam, India; daughter of Frank (a tea plantation foreman) and Rosemary (a painter, maiden name Ramsden) Christie; married Duncan Campbell (a journalist), November 2007. *Education:* Studied art in France; attended Brighton Technical College and Central School of Music and Drama, London, mid-1950s.

Addresses: *Agent*—Endeavor Agency, 9601 Wilshire Blvd., 10th Fl., Beverly Hills, CA 90212. *Home*—London, England, and Llandyssil, Montgomeryshire, Wales.

Career

Made stage debut with the Frinton Repertory Company, Essex, England, 1957; made television debut in the British series *A for Andromeda*, 1962. Film appearances include: *Crooks Anonymous*, 1962; *The Fast Lady*, 1962; *Billy Liar*, 1963; *Young Cassidy*, 1965; *Darling*, 1965; *Doctor Zhivago*, 1965; *Fahrenheit 451*, 1966; *Far from the Madding Crowd*, 1967; *Petulia*, 1968; *In Search of Gregory*, 1969; *The Go-Between*, 1970; *McCabe and Mrs. Miller*, 1971; *Don't Look Now*, 1973; *Shampoo*, 1975; *Nashville*, 1975; *The Demon Seed*, 1977; *Heaven Can Wait*, 1978; *Memoirs of a Survivor*, 1981; *The Return of the Soldier*, 1982; *Heat and Dust*, 1983; *Miss Mary*, 1986; *Power*, 1986; *Secret Obsession*, 1987; *Fools of Fortune*, 1990; *Dragonheart*, 1996; *Hamlet*, 1996; *Afterglow*, 1997; *No Such Thing*, 2001; *Snapshots*, 2002; *I'm with Lucy*, 2002; *Troy*, 2004; *Finding Neverland*, 2004; *Harry Potter and the Prisoner of Azkaban*, 2004; *The Secret Life of Words*, 2005; *Away from Her*, 2006; *New York, I Love You*, 2008.

Awards: Academy Award for best actress, Academy of Motion Picture Arts and Sciences, for *Darling*, 1966; award for best actress, New York Film Critics, for *Darling*, 1966; award for best actress, National Board of Review, for *Darling*, 1966; film award for best British actress, British Academy of Film and Television Arts Award, for *Darling*, 1966; Spirit Award for best female lead, Film Independent, for *Afterglow*, 1998; British film award for best actress, Evening Standard, for *Afterglow*, 1999; award for best actress, National Board of Review, for *Away from Her*, 2007; award for best actress in a motion picture, Screen Actors Guild, for *Away from Her*, 2008; Golden Globe Award for best performance by an actress in a motion picture drama, Hollywood Foreign Press Association, for *Away from Her*, 2008.

Sidelights

British screen siren Julie Christie was one of the top-earning female stars of the 1960s and '70s, commanding $400,000 per picture after causing a sensation in two major releases of 1965, *Darling* and *Doctor Zhivago*. In the first, Christie portrayed an amoral London beauty and earned an Academy Award for Best Actress in a Leading Role at the age of 24. The other film was a big-budget romance set during revolutionary-era Russia, and though it was panned by critics at the time it, too, became a cult classic over time. Christie appeared in a few major Hollywood films of the 1970s, but later went into semi-retirement, emerging from her sheep farm in Wales only occasionally. She earned her fourth Oscar nomination in 2008 for her role in *Away From Her*, the tale of a woman descending into the fog of Alzheimer's disease.

Christie was born in 1941—though some sources also claim 1940 as the year of her birth—in the Indian state of Assam, where her father worked as a foreman on a tea plantation. When she reached elementary-school age, she was sent off to school in England, a separation she recalled as quite difficult. Her parents' marriage eventually ended, and her mother settled in Wales, where Christie spent her time off from school. At the age of 16, she moved to Paris to study art, then returned to England for a course at the Central School of Music and Drama in London to train for the stage. She made her professional debut with the Frinton Repertory Company in Essex, England, and was hired for her first television role in the British science fiction series *A for Andromeda* in 1962.

After small roles in two British films, Christie was cast by an up-and-coming young English director, John Schlesinger, as the female lead in *Billy Liar*. The title character, played by Tom Courtenay, is a young man who endures a life so dreary that he imagines an entire fantasy world in his mind; Christie played Liz, the young woman who urges him to break free of his humdrum life. Her performance won rave reviews from critics, including a *Times* of London writer who asserted that, as Liz, Christie "has the rare quality of obliterating everything else from the screen whenever she walks across."

Schlesinger also cast Christie in his next film, *Darling*, which became one of the most talked-about films of 1965. Its plot tracked the rise of a young English model, Diana, who dates her way up through the middle classes to immense wealth. Her conquests include a married television journalist (played by Dirk Bogarde), a callous advertising executive (Laurence Harvey) and, finally, an Italian prince. Half-comedy, half-tragedy, and a fully realized portrayal of the jaded values of the jet-set European lifestyle, *Darling* attempted to show that, though morals had loosened considerably, the world into which Diana plunges is a shallow and soulless one.

Darling baffled some critics, and not all of them assessed it as an Oscar-worthy performance. "The heroine, as played by Julie Christie, is a vigorous, vivacious sort, full of feline impulses and occasional disarming charms, but uncommunicative of the urges that make her tick," declared *New York Times* critic Bosley Crowther. A reviewer for the *Times* of London, however, wrote that "Christie, with slender experience and tremendous potential, remains magnetically viewable throughout.... And she captures the heroine's qualities exactly: the emotional shallowness of the spoilt child and the effortless sensuality of the grown woman."

Christie became the "darling" of the celebrity-movie-media axis with that role, her status as a new screen icon cemented further with her appearance in another major movie of 1965, *Doctor Zhivago*, which was released just before Christmas. Clocking in at three hours and 17 minutes, the $11 million film from director David Lean was the highly anticipated adaptation of a Boris Pasternak novel about the Russian civil war. Its title character, played by Omar Sharif, is a physician and poet whose loyalties are tested by the upheavals of the era. Christie was cast as Lara, the woman he loves and chases across war zones during the violent struggles that followed the 1917 Bolshevik Revolution.

Directed by David Lean, *Doctor Zhivago* featured stunning cinematography in its massive crowd and battle scenes, and sweeping images of vast wintry landscapes. It won five Academy Awards and was nominated in five additional categories, but Christie won her first Oscar for *Darling*, and caused somewhat of a stir at the April of 1966 ceremony when she wore wide-legged palazzo pants to the event, allegedly making her the first woman to accept an Academy Award statuette wearing pants. Later that year, her next picture, the screen version of the Ray Bradbury's chilling science-fiction tale *Fahrenheit 451*, was released; this time, she worked with acclaimed French director François Truffaut, but the movie was a flop.

In 1967, Christie's third movie with Schlesinger, *Far from the Madding Crowd*, co-starred her with British actor Terence Stamp, with whom she would become romantically involved. Adapted from the classic Thomas Hardy novel, *Far from the Madding Crowd* earned some abysmal reviews, but Christie's portrayal of the willful nineteenth-century heroine Bathsheba Everdene would also later be judged in a more favorable light. Salon.com writer Stephanie Zacharek called it "a picture that captured the bleak beauty of Hardy perfectly.... Christie again balances that graciously composed façade with an innocence that's buried deep; she shows a kind of cautious openness to the world around her. What makes her Bathsheba so moving is that no matter how many trials she faces, she never seems to be on the verge of cracking."

During the making of *Petulia,* a bleak romance that paired her with George C. Scott as an adulterous California socialite, Christie became involved with Warren Beatty, one of Hollywood's most sought-after leading men known for his smoldering appeal both on-screen and off. For the next several years, the pair dated, shared a home in the pricey California beach enclave of Malibu, and made films together. They appeared in the 1971 Robert Altman western *McCabe and Mrs. Miller,* with Christie cast as the bordello owner who reluctantly falls for Beatty's naïve McCabe. This was the only joint work of theirs filmed when they were still a couple; however, she appeared as a cosseted Hollywood housewife in Beatty's 1975 debut as a screenwriter, *Shampoo,* in which he starred as a rakish hairdresser named George. Zacharek, the Salon.com writer, asserted that "Christie's performance in *Shampoo* is one of the most mournfully luminous things ever put on film. Her vulnerability courses through the movie like a barely audible heartbeat, even when, or especially when, she's trying to treat George indifferently."

Christie's last film with Beatty was *Heaven Can Wait,* a 1978 Oscar-winner about a man who dies before his time, but returns to earth in the body of someone else. By then she had worked with Altman again—in his 1975 classic *Nashville*—and made a movie with another acclaimed filmmaker, Nicolas Roeg, the cinematographer on four of her previous films. Known for his dark, somewhat disturbing films, Roeg cast Christie in *Don't Look Now,* his 1973 story about a couple who move to Venice—a city built on water—to escape their grief over the drowning death of their young daughter. Canadian actor Donald Sutherland played her husband, and one of his intimate scenes with Christie is cited in histories of the screen as one of the steamiest ever committed to film; rumors even swirled that their liaison was actually real, a piece of gossip that all principals involved later denied.

A few years later, as her sojourn in California was coming to an end, Christie was slated to appear in *American Gigolo,* another drama noted for its steamy love scenes; the 1980 film made Richard Gere a household name, but his on-screen paramour was played by former model Lauren Hutton. Christie had dropped out of the project when John Travolta appeared to want to oust Gere for the lead, but when the role went to Gere anyway Christie was already committed to other projects. This was also the point in her life where she removed herself from the Hollywood scene by buying a piece of property in Wales—which she noted had been the only true childhood home she remembered—on which she ran a sheep farm. She emerged once a year or so to make a movie, and became increasingly involved in various political causes, including animal rights and nuclear disarmament. She would later give Beatty partial credit for awakening her interest in social justice, and, although the two were no longer a couple, he had reportedly wanted her to co-star with him in *Reds,* the 1981 epic of a real-life couple, John Reed and Louise Bryant Reed, both American Communists who devoted themselves to the cause of the Russian Revolution in the years following World War I. Christie declined the role, believing an American actor should play Bryant, and the role went to Diane Keaton instead. Beatty nevertheless dedicated *Reds* "to Jules."

None of the movies that Christie appeared in after this period ever achieved the same social impact of her earlier works, and she usually steered clear of leading roles. Her credits during the 1980s and '90s include the British India-set *Heat and Dust* from 1983 and *Hamlet,* the Kenneth Branagh-directed Shakespeare adaptation. Director Alan Rudolph convinced her to take the starring role in his 1997 movie *Afterglow,* which earned her another Academy Award nomination. She had a brief part as the mother of Brad Pitt's Achilles in the 2004 epic *Troy,* and in a 2007 interview with the *New Yorker*'s Anthony Lane she described this particular job as "absolute heaven. I got to do one whole day in a Maltese bay, a blissful bay, sitting in one of those director's chairs with Brad Pitt, who is a charming and thoughtful young man. What could be nicer?"

Christie also appeared in *Harry Potter and the Prisoner of Azkaban* in 2004, and a year later in *The Secret Life of Words* with Sarah Polley. The younger star then persuaded Christie to take the lead role in what would be Polley's directorial debut, *Away from Her,* in 2006. Based on an Alice Munro story titled "The Bear Came Over the Mountain," *Away from Her* was the heartwrenching tale of a woman diagnosed with Alzheimer's disease who decides to release her husband from the obligation of caring for her at home by moving into a care facility. The flaws in their longtime marriage re-emerge as Fiona's memory falters and sometimes returns her to earlier, painful moments of her life. Christie was again nominated for an Oscar, and agreed to attend the event only reluctantly. As she told several journalists in the run-up the ceremony, she disliked the red-carpet chaos, especially the custom of wearing designer gowns and borrowed jewelry. "Models wear designer things, so you become like a salesperson," she told *Sunday Times* journalist Garth Pearce. "There are actual signs outside the ceremony that say, 'Turn around.' Why? Because they want you to advertise the dress."

A month before the Oscar ceremony, rumors arose that Christie had traveled to India with her long-time partner, *Guardian* columnist Duncan Campbell, where they were wed. In characteristic fashion, Christie refused to confirm the rumor. The couple live in Wales, but Christie also keeps a place in London—not in the posh part of the city, but in the gritty, artistic milieu of the East End. Later in 2008 she appeared in *New York, I Love You,* an anthology of New York City-set love stories featuring an immense cast of stars, from Blake Lively of *Gossip Girl-*fame to Kevin Bacon. In one interview, Christie conceded that she likes making films, just dislikes the attendant publicity that is also part of the contractual commitment to the project for the lead actors. "I think celebrity is the curse of modern life, or at least advertising, which it is a branch of," she told Tim Adams, a journalist with the London *Observer.* "And I don't like being part of something dirty. I know that sounds prissy. But I talk to some young stars and say: Why do you do all these publicity things? They say they have signed up to it. I suppose I have never wanted to sign up."

Sources

Periodicals

InStyle, April 1, 2003, p. 252.
Los Angeles Magazine, February 2008, p. 94.
New Yorker, May 7, 2007, p. 24.
New York Times, August 4, 1965; November 21, 1965; December 23, 1965, p. 21; April 18, 2007.
Observer (London, England), April 1, 2007, p. 4.
People, February 9, 1998, p. 119.
Sunday Times (London, England), February 3, 2008, p. 4.
Times (London, England), August 14, 1963, p. 11; September 16, 1965, p. 16.

Online

Biography Resource Center Online, Gale, 2008.
"Julie Christie," Salon.com, http://archive.salon.com/people/bc/2001/06/12/julie_christie/index.html (May 18, 2008).

—*Carol Brennan*

Rafael Correa

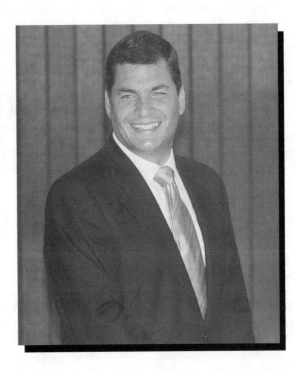

President of Ecuador

Born Rafael Correa Delgado, April 6, 1963, in Guayaquil, Ecuador; married Anne Malherbe. *Education:* Economics degree, Catholic University of Santiago de Guayaquil, 1987; master of arts in economics, Catholic University of Louvain (Belgium), 1991; master of science in economics, University of Illinois at Urbana-Champaign, 1999; doctorate in economics, University of Illinois at Urbana-Champaign, 2001.

Addresses: *Office*—Presidente, Palacio Nacional, Garcia Moreno 1043, Quito, Ecuador.

Career

Industrial specialist for the Center of Industrial Development of Ecuador, 1984-87; volunteer for a rural development mission in Sumbahua, Ecuador, 1987-88; financial director and associate professor of economics at the Catholic University of Santiago de Guayaquil, 1988-89; administrative director of finance for educational projects in Ecuador, Inter-American Development Bank, 1992-93; associate professor of economics at the Catholic University of Santiago de Guayaquil, 1992-93; economics professor, University of San Francisco in Quito, 1993-97, 2001-05; Ecuadorian finance minister, 2005; elected president of Ecuador, 2006; sworn in as president, 2007.

Sidelights

Rafael Correa, who was sworn in as president of Ecuador in January of 2007, is one of many South American leaders elected in the 2000s on a platform of left-wing, populist politics. Though he is an economist who earned his doctorate in the United States, he opposes the U.S.-led "Washington consensus," which advocates free markets, international free trade, and strict repayment schedules for developing countries' international debt. When Correa took office, Ecuador, a small, mountainous country of 13 million people, had gone ten years without a president serving a full term. Correa promised a change in the country's troubled politics, and 80 percent of the country voted in favor of his proposal to have the constitution rewritten. But the referendum sparked a power struggle between Correa, the National Congress, and two courts. As the country prepared to rewrite its constitution, observers were watching whether Correa would use the process to amass more power, as other populist South American leaders have.

Correa was born in Guayaquil, on the coast of Ecuador. He grew up in a modest home; his mother worked as a manager for a supermarket chain. His father spent three years in prison for smuggling drugs (a fact that was not publicly revealed until Correa was president). Correa attended Catholic schools, including the Catholic university in his hometown, which helped shape his sympathy for the poor. After college, he volunteered on a rural development mission. After a year working as a financial manager and instructor at his alma mater, he moved to Belgium to study economics at a Catholic university there. While in Belgium, he met his future wife, Anne Malherbe. After earning a master's degree, he returned to Ecuador, worked briefly for the Inter-American Development Bank, and taught economics at a university in the Ecuadorian capital of Quito. He spent four years in the United States, earning a doctorate at the University of Illinois at Urbana-Champaign, where he often challenged the economic doctrine of free trade and free markets. His thesis studied globalization's effects on development and poverty. He returned to Ecuador in 2001 and resumed teaching economics there.

In April of 2005, Correa was named Ecuador's finance minister. He declared that instead of using an oil fund to make payments on Ecuador's international debt, he would use it on an anti-poverty program. He also established ties with the radical Venezuelan government and denounced the World Bank. That put him in conflict with Ecuador's President, Alfredo Palacio. Less than four months after joining the government, Correa was forced to resign.

Correa ran for president of Ecuador in 2006, a bold decision, since the troubled, tumultuous country had gone through eight presidents in ten years, none of them remaining in office for a full term. Correa vowed to oppose multinational corporations that he said had left Ecuador in poverty. He also attacked Ecuador's ruling political class as corrupt, promising to convene a constituent assembly to rewrite the constitution and possibly dissolve the National Congress. At rallies, playing off the fact that "correa" means "belt" in Spanish, he would take a belt, beat it on a car, and say he would administer a beating to those companies and politicians. "The belt is coming for all those political classes," he declared, according to Juan Forero of the *Washington Post*.

Though Correa said he wanted good relations with the United States, he vowed to end stalled trade talks with that country, arguing that a free trade agreement would be bad for Ecuador. He also said he would not renew a lease on a U.S. military base in Ecuador when it expired in 2009. He promised to cut Ecuador's ties to international lending organizations such as the World Bank and International Monetary Fund, and he said that if international lenders did not cut the payments on Ecuador's $10 billion debt in half, he would stop paying.

Correa pledged to forge closer diplomatic ties with the radical president of Venezuela, Hugo Chavez, a dedicated foe of United States foreign policy. After Chavez gave a fiery speech at the United Nations, calling U.S. President George W. Bush the devil, Correa went further. Calling Bush the devil would offend the devil, Correa said, because Bush was dimwitted and had damaged his own country. "Hugo Chavez is a friend of mine," Correa told reporters, according the *Washington Post*'s Forero. "We are part of the trend that is cutting throughout Latin America," he added. "We are looking for a united Latin America that can confront a globalization that is inhumane and cruel."

Ecuadorians, disappointed that market reforms and conventional politicians had not cured their country's economic ills, rallied around Correa. In about a month in the fall of 2006, he rose from third place to first in the polls. Observers debated whether, if elected, he would follow a radical nationalist and socialist path similar to Chavez, or whether, despite his rhetoric, he would pursue a center-left mix of free-market economic strategies and government anti-poverty programs similar to those of Brazilian President Luiz Inacio Lula da Silva.

Correa took second place in the first round of voting in October of 2006, with 23 percent of the vote, behind banana company owner Alvaro Noboa, the richest man in Ecuador. On election night, Noboa argued that Correa wanted to turn Ecuador into another Cuba. "Rafael Correa's posture is communist, dictatorial," he charged, according to the *Washington Post*'s Forero. Perhaps to allay such fears, Correa toned down his rhetoric during the runoff campaign and focused more on promising housing programs and small grant programs for the poor. He won the November runoff easily.

At his inauguration in January of 2007, Correa held up a sword that Chavez gave him and promised to work for an "economic revolution," according to the *Chicago Tribune*. He said he would try to renegotiate Ecuador's international debt. Ecuador would put the needs of its poor first, he said, and only make whatever debt payments it could after that.

Immediately after taking office, Correa issued a declaration calling for a referendum to approve forming a constituent assembly to rewrite the constitution. Correa argued it was a way to fight corruption in the political system, but critics accused him of trying to bypass the National Congress and acquire more power. The Congress voted to approve the referendum, but Correa later rewrote the referendum language, triggering an intense political crisis. On one side were Correa and a majority of the judges on the Supreme Electoral Tribunal, which approved the referendum's new language. On the other side were a majority of the National Congress and the Supreme Court. Congress voted to impeach the tribunal judges, arguing that the rewrite of the referendum language was unconstitutional, and the tribunal responded by firing the 57 lawmakers that had voted for impeachment. Correa sided with the judges, police surrounded the National Congress to keep the opposition lawmakers out, and new lawmakers were appointed. The Supreme Court ordered the fired lawmakers reinstated, but the Congress, which included the fired congresspeople's replacements, fired the Supreme Court judges. In April, Ecuadorians approved the referendum by more than 80 percent of the vote.

Meanwhile, Correa quickly doubled cash payments to the poor to $30 a month, increased housing subsidies for the poor, and gave out $350 "microcredit" grants. He also increased education and health spending. Despite his ambivalence about paying Ecuador's debt, he issued a $135 million payment in February of 2007. But in April, he asked the local representative of the World Bank to leave Ecuador, as retaliation for the bank's denial of a $100 million loan to the country while Correa was finance minister. Correa also said that Ecuador had paid off its debt to the International Monetary Fund and would sever its ties to the fund.

In May, Correa announced he would form a truth commission to look into allegations that government forces had committed human rights abuses in the 1980s, 1990s, and 2000s, especially during the term of right-wing president Leon Febres Cordero in the 1980s. In July, Correa and the National Congress clashed again. The Congress voted down his bill that would have given the government more control over banks. Correa accused several lawmakers of corruption, saying that some had accepted bribes to oppose his bill and that others had asked members of his government for jobs in exchange for their votes.

In August, he reiterated that he would not renew the United States' lease on an air base in Ecuador when it expires in 2009. The United States uses the base for surveillance planes that search for drug smuggling activity across South America. Correa suggested that the surveillance planes should move to Colombia.

As fall 2007 arrived, Correa's conflicts with other political factions in Ecuador were headed toward a climax. Elections to choose the constituent assembly

were scheduled for September 30. "Ecuador needs a second independence," Correa said in August, according to the *Angus Reid Global Monitor*. "We need to separate ourselves from the corruption." Once elected, the assembly was to have until spring of 2008 to write a new constitution, which would have to be approved by the voters. Meanwhile, the truth commission report was also due in the first half of 2008.

Selected writings

Non-fiction

La Vulnerabilidad de la Economia Ecuatoriana (The Vulnerability of the Ecuadorian Economy), United Nations Development Program, 2004.

Sources

Periodicals

Chicago Tribune, September 28, 2006, sec. News, p. 16; October 13, 2006, sec. Business, p. 3; January 16, 2007, sec. News, p. 7; May 5, 2007, sec. News, p. 12; August 12, 2007, sec. News, p. 24.
Economist, April 19, 2007.
New York Times, November 28, 2006, p. A3; January 16, 2007, p. A4.
Washington Post, October 15, 2006, p. A15; October 16, 2006, p. A15; November 26, 2006, p. A15; March 9, 2007, p. A15; April 16, 2007, p. A14; April 24, 2007, p. A18; April 27, 2007, p. D5; July 8, 2007, p. A16.

Online

"Ecuador calls for honest constituent assembly," *Angus Reid Global Monitor.* http://www.angus-reid.com/polls/index.cfm/fuseaction/viewItem/itemID/16872 (August 18, 2007).
"Ecuador's Congress sacks judges," BBC News, http://news.bbc.co.uk/1/hi/world/americas/6590245.stm (August 18, 2007).
"Ecuador Referendum Row Escalates," BBC News, news.bbc.co.uk/2/hi/americas/6429191.stm (August 18, 2007).
"Presidencia de la Republica: Presidente," National Government of the Republic of Ecuador, http://www.presidencia.gov.ec/modulos.asp?id=192 (August 18, 2007).
"Profile: Ecuador's Rafael Correa," BBC News, news.bbc.co.uk/2/hi/americas/6187364.stm (August 18, 2007).

—*Erick Trickey*

Daniel Craig

Carl de Souza/AFP/Getty Images

Actor

Born March 2, 1968, in Chester, England; son of Tim (a bar manager) and Carol Olivia (a teacher) Craig; married Fiona Loudon (an actress; divorced); children: Ella (with Loudon). *Education:* With the National Youth Theater school, 1984-88; graduated from the Guildhall School of Music and Drama, 1991.

Addresses: *Agent*—ICM, Oxford House, 76 Oxford St., London W1N 0AX, England.

Career

Actor in films, including: *The Power of One*, 1992; *Obsession*, 1997; *Love is the Devil*, 1998; *Elizabeth*, 1998; *Love and Rage*, 1998; *The Trench*, 1999; *I Dreamed of Africa*, 2000; *Hotel Splendide*, 2000; *Some Voices*, 2000; *Lara Croft: Tomb Raider*, 2001; *The Road to Perdition*, 2002; *The Mother*, 2003; *Sylvia*, 2003; *Enduring Love*, 2004; *Layer Cake*, 2004; *The Jacket*, 2005; *Munich*, 2005; *Casino Royale*, 2006; *Infamous*, 2007; *The Invasion*, 2007; *The Golden Compass*, 2007. Television appearances include: *Sharpe's Eagle*, Central Television, 1993; *Our Friends in the North*, BBC, 1996; *Moll Flanders*, Granada Television, 1996; *Sword of Honour*, Channel 4, 2001; *Copenhagen*, BBC, 2002. Stage appearances include: *No Remission*, Lyric Studio Hammersmith, London, England, 1992; *Angels in America*, Royal National Theater, London, 1993; *The Rover*, Women's Playhouse Trust, London, 1996; *Hurly Burly*, Old Vic, London, 1997.

Awards: Best actor, Evening Standard British Film Awards, for *Casino Royale*, 2007.

Sidelights

Legions of devoted fans of the James Bond espionage-thriller movies were appalled when a relatively unknown British actor, Daniel Craig, was cast as the next action hero of the immensely successful, long-running film franchise. Craig's blond hair and blue eyes seemed to make him an unlikely choice to play Bond, the British intelligence operative known as Agent 007, and the actor found himself the target of some intense sniping during the making of *Casino Royale*, his 2006 debut as Bond. Upon its release, however, Craig's performance immediately put to rest any doubts over his suitability for the part, with a majority of critics hailing him as the best Bond since Sean Connery—the first actor to take the role—set a near-impossible benchmark of sophisticated, deadly on-screen cool for all subsequent Bonds to follow. Even the famously disdainful London media establishment had a hard time finding a flaw in Craig's performance; the *Guardian's* Peter Bradshaw ventured that the actor may have actually surpassed Connery, noting that "Craig brings off cinema's most preposterous role with insouciant grit."

Craig was born in 1968 in the walled English city of Chester, but grew up in Liverpool, a larger city to the north. His father ran a pub, and was later divorced from Craig's mother, an art teacher who was active in Liverpool's fringe-theater community. As a kid, Craig spent a great deal of time with his mother and her friends at the somewhat infamous Everyman Theatre, where the majority of the venue's productions "involved walking around in the nude," he told John-Paul Flintoff in a *Sunday Times* interview. His first stage experiences were in more standard works for the stage at school, like the musical *Oliver!*. He also loved the cinema, and the first James Bond movie he encountered on the big screen was 1973's *Live and Let Die*, which his father took him to see.

A stage talent and a fearless rugby player but an admittedly poor student, Craig left school for good at the age of 16 with the intent of winning a place at a drama school. All of the prominent British academies rejected him, however, including the Royal Academy of Dramatic Art, the Old Vic, and the Guildhall School of Music and Drama, all in London. In 1984 he managed to win a place at the National Youth Theatre, a performance company and actors' training ground whose alumni include Helen Mirren, Ben Kingsley, and Orlando Bloom. A few years later, Craig re-applied to the Guildhall School and was accepted; fellow students there included Ewan McGregor and Joseph Fiennes.

After graduating from Guildhall in 1991, Craig appeared in various London stage productions, and made his film debut the following year in *The Power of One*, a drama about apartheid-era South Africa. He also won parts in British television movies and series, with his breakout role coming in a highly acclaimed miniseries for the British Broadcasting Corporation (BBC) in 1996, *Our Friends in the North*. The story followed a quartet of friends across a 30-year span of their lives in Newcastle and London; Craig was cast as the dissolute Geordie Peacock. The role led to a solid part in a 1998 art-house drama, *Love Is the Devil*, in which he played Georgie Dyer, a real-life petty criminal who became romantically attached to the painter Francis Bacon in the 1960s before meeting a tragic end.

Craig also appeared in the 1998 period drama *Elizabeth* alongside Cate Blanchett as the sixteenth-century English monarch. It would be the last time he took on such a role, explaining a few years later to *Times* of London journalist Jasper Rees that he wished to avoid "dressing up in costumes and pansying around. It doesn't appeal to me. It never did. When I left drama school the only jobs were for boys in floppy fringes who went to Eton. I fitted in because I could do a slightly posh accent." Instead, Craig was making a name for himself in small, in-dependent, and often critically acclaimed films such as *The Trench* and *Hotel Splendide* while taking on the occasional, much more lucrative paycheck for roles like the archeologist Alex West in 2001's *Lara Croft: Tomb Raider*. He remained certain, however, of the ultimate direction of his career. "I have no hunger for Hollywood," he told Glasgow *Herald* journalist Gavin Docherty. "I have got no sights set there. I like European films. We don't make millions of [dollars]. Hollywood looks to Europe for clues. Because we make cheaper films with great actors who want to work with directors."

One of those directors was a veteran of the London stage, Sam Mendes, who won an Academy Award for directing the 1999 feature film *American Beauty*. Mendes' next Hollywood project was *The Road to Perdition* in 2002, and he cast Craig in a supporting role. Craig then won a coveted but controversial role as the British poet Ted Hughes in *Sylvia* in 2003, playing the husband of American poet Sylvia Plath with Gwyneth Paltrow in the title role. A year later, he starred in a little-seen but enthusiastically received drama called *Layer Cake*, as a London cocaine dealer who is midway up the sales chain and has managed to earn enough to retire. His more powerful bosses, however, pull him into a twisted mystery involving a missing debutante and a pilfered drug shipment. Reviewing it in the *Village Voice*, Michael Atkinson found *Layer Cake*'s storyline ridiculously improbable and asserted "there's little acting involved" among a cast that included Michael Gambon and Sienna Miller, "but Craig's vulnerable yet supercool demeanor carries the old-school fiction lightly along."

Layer Cake failed to make an impression at the box office, but it was seen by a few influential entertainment-industry figures. Among them was film producer Barbara Broccoli, who held the rights to the James Bond "Agent 007" character and stories, the second-most lucrative franchise in film history after *Star Wars*. Broccoli and her producing partner were searching for a new Bond, and were drawn to Craig after seeing his performance in *Layer Cake*. They offered him the lead in a highly anticipated new 007 story, *Casino Royale*, which would be the twenty-first in the series but was the debut tale from novelist Ian Fleming that introduced the intrepid British agent. The novel's film rights had been mired in a legal battle for years, and two screen adaptations for the story existed: one for television in 1954—a year after Fleming's novel was published—and then an odd 1967 film featuring David Niven and Woody Allen which actually spoofed the Bond genre, its over-the-top spy games, and its hero's debonair charm. The actual Bond films were by then runaway cinematic hits beginning with Connery's debut in *Dr. No* in 1962.

Accepting the Bond role has proved a double-edged sword for the actors who have taken it on, even Connery. The Scottish actor originated the role but was forever hampered by it over the course of his long career. After four more films, he bowed out and was replaced by Australian actor George Lazenby for *On Her Majesty's Secret Service*, but returned for a sixth movie before Roger Moore took over in 1973 in *Live and Let Die*. Lazenby's career stalled after producers dubbed his voice, and fans railed against Roger Moore's casting, but the latter's seven turns in the role would later be hailed as another quintessential Bond. Two other actors, Timothy Dalton and Pierce Brosnan, failed to achieve the cult-status aura of either Connery or Moore, though the franchise continued to reap rich rewards at the box office. The 1990s-era films with Brosnan descended into typically Hollywood explosive action films, relying more on expensive special effects than the character's clever one-upmanship. When Broccoli and her partner finally acquired *Casino Royale* in 1999—a deal that involved a trade-off between movie studios for the original Fleming rights in exchange for some revenues from a planned *Spider-Man* series—they announced their intentions to retool the series and bring a new actor into the role.

Craig's name was mentioned as a possible contender, as were those of his former Guildhall classmate McGregor, Clive Owen, Goran Visnjic, and Hugh Jackman. The lesser-known Craig bested the others, but with the October of 2005 announcement that filming was about to commence suddenly found himself in the midst of an enthusiastic and at times vicious debate over the role—especially in Britain, where Bond had achieved the status of a national icon. He faced intense criticism which even spilled over onto a Web site, craignotbond.com, for being too short for the part at five feet, eleven inches, as well as too blond and in the opinion of some, not nearly handsome enough. Internet rumors swirled around the *Casino Royale* shoot, including the claim that Craig did not know how to drive the manual-transmission Aston Martin racer that served as Bond's automotive accessory. The British tabloids picked up some of the gossip and began to join in, dubbing him "James Bland."

When *Casino Royale* premiered in November of 2006, however, Craig's critics were chastened, and film reviewers echoed the sentiment that the newest Bond had proved himself utterly captivating in the role. Shot on locations that included Venice, the Bahamas, and the Czech Republic, the film featured Craig earning his "007" designation and license to kill from his bosses at the British Secret Intelligence Service, then dallying at a posh Caribbean resort, locking horns with his superior M (Judi Dench),

and finally landing in a high-stakes poker game at a lavish Montenegran casino in which he must ensure that the villain Le Chiffre (Mads Mikkelsen) loses. In typical Bond fashion, he romances multiple women but his involvement with Vesper Lynd (Eva Green), a British treasury department official, almost proves a career-ending error in judgment.

More than one film reviewer claimed Craig's Bond marked a return to the famously excellent 007 films of the 1960s and '70s. "Bond became a jokey superhero in a dinner jacket" after Connery left, noted Owen Gleiberman in *Entertainment Weekly,* and asserted that this latest incarnation "relaunches the series by doing something I wouldn't have thought possible: It turns Bond into a human being again—a gruffly charming yet volatile chap who may be the swank king stud of the Western world, but who still has room for rage, fear, vulnerability, love." Writing in the *New York Times,* Manohla Dargis delivered similar plaudits for Craig's performance, noting that the newest Bond "fits Fleming's description of the character as appearing 'ironical, brutal and cold' better than any actor since Mr. Connery."

Casino Royale ended the year as the top-grossing British film of 2006, and even the Blu-ray high-definition DVD edition, released in March of 2007, set an industry record by passing the 100,000 sales mark in the new format just a few short weeks after its release. The movie itself was nominated for a slew of British Academy of Film and Television Arts (BAFTA) awards, including Best Actor, but Craig lost out to a heavily favored Forest Whitaker as Ugandan dictator Idi Amin in *The Last King of Scotland.*

Not surprisingly, Craig was signed to reprise his role in the next Bond project, murkily titled *Bond 22* and slated for a November of 2008 release; 007 aficionados in cyberspace now preoccupied themselves with determining which of the Fleming tales would turn out to be the real title. Craig, meanwhile, was tying up other commitments before heading to location. These included the first in Philip Pullman's "His Dark Materials" fantasy trilogy, *The Golden Compass,* in which the actor grew a long beard for the part of Lord Asriel. Divorced and the father of a daughter, Ella, born in the early 1990s, Craig is famously reticent about his personal life in interviews with the press. *Casino Royale* vaulted him onto an entirely different plane, he admitted in an interview with Liz Hoggard for the London *Observer.* "The truth is I can't really go out at the moment," the once hard-drinking actor said. "It's not anything bad, and it will die down eventually. And if it stops me walking into too many bars, that's no bad thing."

Sources

Entertainment Weekly, August 18, 2006, p. 44; November 24, 2006, p. 79.
Guardian (London, England), November 10, 2006.
Herald (Glasgow, Scotland), December 30, 2000, p. 6.
Independent (London, England), September 17, 1998, p. 13; October 15, 2005.
New York Times, November 17, 2006.

Observer (London, England), November 19, 2006, p. 14; December 31, 2006, p. 12.
Sunday Times (London, England), October 8, 2006, p. 30.
Times (London, England), January 17, 2004, p. 21; November 4, 2006, p. 8.
Village Voice, May 10, 2005.

—*Carol Brennan*

Scott Crump

Courtesy of Stratasys Inc.

Chief Executive Officer of Stratasys, Inc.

Born S. Scott Crump, c. 1954; son of Ralph E. Crump (a chemical engineer, businessman, and venture capitalist); married Lisa; children: one daughter. *Education:* Washington State University, B.S. (mechanical engineering), 1976; University of California at Los Angeles, business degree.

Addresses: *Office*—Stratasys, Inc., 14950 Martin Dr., Eden Prairie, MN 55344.

Career

IDEA, Inc., Seattle, WA, co-founder and vice president of sales, 1982-88, director and shareholder, 1982-2005; Stratasys, Inc., Eden Prairie, MN, co-founder, chief executive officer, president, treasurer, and director, 1988—, chief financial officer, 1990-97.

Awards: Entrepreneur of the Year Award (Manufacturing category in the Minnesota and Dakotas Division), Ernst & Young, 2005; named one of the best chief executive officers in the United States by DeMarche Associates, Inc., 2007.

Sidelights

The co-founder of Stratasys, Inc. and an engineer, Scott Crump developed his patented fused deposition modeling (FDM) process and sold small rapid prototyping machines widely used in industry by engineer and designers. The primary executive of his company, Stratasys eventually became the world-wide leader in the rapid prototype trade and a solid success story on Wall Street.

Born around 1954, Crump was the son of Ralph E. Crump, who had a career as a chemical engineer and in business. His father was later a venture capitalist who used his funds to help start a number of companies. As a child, Crump was a tinkerer who refurbished a car for his mother at the age of 14. Crump followed in his father's footsteps by studying engineering, though the mechanical variety, at Washington State University in the 1970s. To pay for college, he refurbished Volkswagens and sold them. He graduated in 1976, and later earned a business degree from the University of California at Los Angeles.

In 1982, Crump was the co-founder of IDEA, Inc. (later known as Structural Instrumentation Inc. and then SI Technologies, Inc.), a Seattle-based company which made force, load, and pressure transducers, automated packaging machinery, and electronic equipment for the transportation industry. He also served as the company's vice president of sales. Crump remained in the positions through 1988. In addition, Crump served as a director and held stock in the company through 2005, when it was sold to Vishay Intertechnologies.

In 1988, Crump and his wife, Lisa, moved to the Minneapolis-St. Paul area and founded Stratasys. Crump took on numerous leadership positions within the company, including chief executive officer, president, and treasurer. In 1990, Crump temporarily took on another position in Stratasys, serving as chief financial officer. Crump held the position through 1997. Crump founded the company to sell his patented rapid-prototyping method which he had devised in his garage workshop while trying to make a toy frog for his young daughter. His idea was to improve the mechanical design process, a feat he accomplished by inventing FDM and devising related machines.

Crump's rapid prototyping machines directly converted computer-aided designs into three-dimensional models made of proprietary thermoplastic or wax modeling material through the FDM process in only a few hours. Previously, the production of such models would take weeks or months. During the early years of Stratasys, it lost millions of dollars. In 1991, the first year the Crumps offered their rapid prototyping machines on the market, the company had $900,000 in sales.

Stratasys was one of only a few companies selling such technology at the time, though many competitors were entering what was becoming a major business. With rapid prototyping machines, companies could develop products which reached market faster and explore different options with prototypes because of the decreased costs and greater flexibility associated with rapid prototyping machines. Crump's machines had some advantages over his competitors. While others almost exclusively sold large machines meant for use in a laboratory or industrial shop, Stratasys sold smaller machines which used nontoxic materials safe for an office or school environment.

By 1994, sales had increased to $3.8 million, but Stratasys was still losing money selling the machines and modeling materials. Despite the losses, Stratasys went public in October of 1994. At that time, the stock was trading at five dollars per share, a figure which did not vastly increase until early in 1995. The stock price had nearly tripled a year after its initial public offering and the company had a market value of $60 million. The reason for Stratasys's turnaround was an ever-increasing demand for its machines by companies in the automotive, consumer products, and medical products industries. Even NASA (National Aeronautics and Space Administration) bought one to potentially use on the space shuttle.

Crump's company continued to thrive in 1996 when sales jumped to $26 million and a 34 percent share of the market. Though Stratasys' stock price rose through early 1997, a few missteps—a new product introduced by the company having technical problems and pricing difficulties in a European market, among others—led to a quarterly loss and a temporary decline in stock price by the spring. However, because the rapid prototyping business was expanding at a speedy rate and with the introduction of new products, Stratasys soon rebounded.

Under Crump's leadership, Stratasys continued to thrive over the next decade despite greater competition because of never-ending demand for its continually improved and refined line of machines. The 2002 introduction of the Dimension line, which sold for less than $30,000 and could produce prototypes in minutes, greatly enhanced sales. In 2004 alone, the company had $50 million in revenue.

By 2005, Stratasys was the recognized leader in the rapid prototype industry world-wide, selling twice as many machines as its nearest competitor, the Burlington, Massachusetts-based Z Corporation. However, Stratasys remained essentially a small business with only about 200 employees, but one which did business around the world and remained a staple of Wall Street trading. Stratasys retained their position as world leader for several years, with revenues, net income, profits, and stock prices continuing to rise in 2007.

Crump rode the wave of Stratasys' success with a relatively relaxed attitude. He told Neal St. Anthony of the Minneapolis *Star Tribune* in 2004, "The last 15 years have been challenging, a lot of fun, and because I like to work, it's been very interesting. Any success I've had I attribute to the excellent team and the passion the people have brought to Stratasys. That's been very gratifying."

Sources

Periodicals

Business Wire, June 16, 2005; June 7, 2007.
Forbes, September 20, 2004, p. 208.
FSB, October 1, 2005, p. 59.
New York Times, September 21, 2004, p. G2.
Star Tribune (Minneapolis, MN), October 16, 1995, p. 2D; September 22, 1997, p. 2D; November 2, 2004, p. 1D; August 2, 2007, p. 1D.

Online

"Scott Crump—Bio," http://www.rpjp.or.jp./Crump0io.htm (August 12, 2007).

—A. Petruso

Alfonso Cuarón

Film director, screenwriter, and film producer

Born Alfonso Cuarón Orozco, November 28, 1961, in Mexico City, Mexico; son of Alfredo Cuarón (a cardiologist); married Mariana Elizondo (an actress), 1980-93 (divorced); married Annalisa Bugliani, 2001; children: three. *Education:* Attended the Centro Universitario de Estudios Cinematograficos.

Addresses: *Contact*—Cha Cha Cha, c/o Universal Pictures, 100 Universal City Plaza, Universal Studios, CA 91608. *Home*—London and Italy.

Career

Director of films, including: *Cuarteto para el fin del tiempo* (also writer), 1983; *Sólo con tu pareja* (also writer and producer), 1991; *A Little Princess,* 1995; *Great Expectations,* 1998; *Y tu mamá también* (also writer and producer), 2001; *Harry Potter and the Prisoner of Azkaban,* 2004; *Children of Men* (also writer), 2006; *The Shock Doctrine* (also writer and producer), 2007; *The Possibility of Hope* (also producer), 2007. Producer of films, including *El Laberinto del fauno* (*Pan's Labyrinth*), 2006. Director of television series, including *Hora Marcada,* 1988-90; and *Fallen Angels,* 1993.

Awards: Silver Ariel Award for best original story, for *Sólo con tu pareja,* 1992; CableACE Award for best directing in a drama series, for the "Murder, Obliquely" episode of *Fallen Angels,* 1993; Los Angeles Film Critics Association's New Generation Award, for *A Little Princess,* 1995; Jury Award for best foreign language film, Ft. Lauderdale International Film Festival, for *Y tu mamá también,* 2001; FIPRESCI Prize, Havana Film Festival, for *Y tu mamá también,* 2001; Premios ACE Award for best director-cinema, for *Y tu mamá también,* 2001; best screenplay, Venice Film Festival, for *Y tu mamá también,* 2001; Luminaria Award for best Latino film, Santa Fe Film Festival, for *Y tu mamá también,* 2001; MTV north feed favorite film, MTV Movie Awards-Latin America, for *Y tu mamá también,* 2002; Golden Slipper Award for best youth feature film, Zlin International Film Festival for Children and Youth, for *Y tu mamá también,* 2002; Aurora Award, Tromso International Film Festival, for *Y tu mamá también,* 2002; Glitter Awards, Best Feature—International Gay Film Festivals and Best Feature U.S. Film Festivals, for *Y tu mamá también,* 2003; Independent Spirit Award for best foreign film, for *Y tu mamá también,* 2003; BAFTA (British Academy of Film and Television Arts Awards) Children's Award for best feature film, for *Harry Potter and the Prisoner of Azkaban,* 2004; Laterna Magica Prize, Venice Film Festival, for *Children of Men,* 2006; best adapted screenplay and best director, Austin Film Critics Association, for *Children of Men,* 2007; BAFTA Film Award for best film not in the English language, for *El Laberinto del fauno,* or *Pan's Labyrinth,* 2007; best adapted screenplay, Online Film Critics Society, for *Children of Men,* 2007; ShoWest Award for international achievement in filmmaking, 2007; USC Scripter Award, for *Chil-*

dren of Men, 2007; best director, Vancouver Film Critics Circle, for *Children of Men*, 2007.

Sidelights

Mexican-born filmmaker Alfonso Cuarón jumped into the spotlight in 2001 with a raunchy, teen road-trip comedy, *Y tu mamá también*, which translates as "And Your Mother, Too." The Spanish-language movie smashed box-office records in Mexico and racked up awards at film festivals around the globe. Cuarón received so much attention that Warner Bros. asked him to direct the third installment of the big-budget Harry Potter series—2004's *Harry Potter and the Prisoner of Azkaban*. In 2007, Cuarón received two Academy Award nominations for *Children of Men*, which he directed and co-wrote. Though Cuarón did not win, the nominations illustrate the magnitude of his influence.

"What I admire in Alfonso is that he doesn't play it safe, in anything," writer-director Guillermo del Toro told the *Sacramento Bee*'s Dixie Reid. "This guy has a sex-road movie (*Y tu mamá también*), a beautiful childhood movie (*A Little Princess*), a fantasy movie (*Harry Potter and the Prisoner of Azkaban*) and a bleak, dystopian film like *Children of Men*. He is reinventing himself with every movie."

Cuarón was born on November 28, 1961, in Mexico City, Mexico. His cardiologist father, Alfredo, was employed by the United Nations. Around the time Cuarón turned 12, he received a camera and began taking snapshots. In time, he traded the still-frames for video, creating his own home movies. Obsessed with films, Cuarón spent his high school years at the local movie houses studying the films of the day. He attended the Centro Universitario de Estudios Cinematograficos, where he studied philosophy and filmmaking.

Cuarón's first jobs involved Mexican television. From 1988 to 1990, he worked as a writer, cinematographer, and director for the Latin American soap opera *Hora Marcada*. He also began dabbling in the film industry, working on full-length English-language films that were being shot in Latin America. Cuarón was an assistant director for 1987's *Gaby—A Love Story* and 1989's *Romero*, the story of El Salvador's outspoken archbishop Oscar Romero, as portrayed by Raul Julia.

Cuarón gained attention in his homeland for the film *Sólo con tu pareja*, a romantic comedy that deals with AIDS. The title translates to "Only with Your Partner," a government safe-sex slogan. Cuarón co-wrote the screenplay with his younger brother, Carlos. The film follows the exploits of Tomas, a bed-hopping playboy, played by Daniel Gimenez Cacho, and the scorned lover who gets back at him by falsifying his medical report to make him think he has AIDS.

Sólo con tu pareja became Mexico's highest-grossing film of 1992. Writing in the *New York Times*, film critic A. O. Scott was mostly positive in his review, though he noted that Cuarón failed to adeptly mix the film's light humor with its darker underpinnings. Scott conceded, "Still it is hard not to admire the younger man's cheeky self-confidence, and hard not to enjoy the dexterity of his camera movements and the flair with which he attempts both low comedy and high melodrama." *Sólo con tu pareja* won a 1992 Ariel Award for Best Original Story; the Ariels are the most prestigious film awards given in Mexico.

After *Sólo con tu pareja*, Cuarón was invited to Hollywood to work on the Showtime series *Fallen Angels*. The series, mimicking the downbeat Hollywood crime dramas of the 1940s and '50s, was set in post-World War II Los Angeles. Cuarón directed one 1993 episode, for which he earned a CableACE Award for best direction.

Cuarón made his U.S. film-directing debut with 1995's *A Little Princess*, which won the L.A. Film Critics New Generation Award. *A Little Princess* tells the story of a privileged, precocious girl living in India at the turn of the 20th century. When her British army captain father goes off to fight in World War I, she is shipped off to a New York City boarding school. There, she captures the hearts of the other girls—much to the annoyance of the stern headmistress—by telling magical tales of life in India. The father ends up missing in action, leaving the girl stranded at the boarding school and forced into the role of servant to the headmistress who despises her.

Cuarón followed with 1998's *Great Expectations*. In this modern adaptation of the classic Dickens novel, the orphan Pip has been replaced by an orphan painter named Finn, played by Ethan Hawke. Finn is obsessed with Estella, played by Gwyneth Paltrow. While the story received a huge makeover from the original novel—it is set in Florida and New York instead of Victorian England—Cuarón remained true to the poor-boy-pursues-wealthier-girl storyline set out by Dickens. In the end, the movie did little to boost Cuarón's stature as an up-and-coming star, though it generated some positive words. Writing in *Newsweek,* David Ansen said the movie, "while not a total success, produces its own share of memorably enchanted moments."

After *Great Expectations,* Cuarón returned to Mexico to begin work on *Y tu mamá también,* which he co-wrote with his brother. This twisted, coming-of-age story features teen protagonists—Tenoch, the son of a corrupt politician, and his pal Julio, the son of a single, working-class mom. Diego Luna portrayed Tenoch and Gael Garcia Bernal played the part of Julio. With their girlfriends away on vacation, the boys set off for an elusive beach with an older woman, Luisa, played by Maribel Verdu. Luisa is married to Tenoch's cousin and is running away because he has cheated on her.

The threesome sets out in a borrowed station wagon across Mexico's back roads on an adventure that is ripe with heartbreaking confessions, lewd sex, drinking, and pot-smoking. While the trio's escapades often involve hilarity, it is clear there are darker elements behind the facade, driving the later sober revelations. One of the film's themes is the search for identity. Cuarón uses the characters' coming-of-age stories as a metaphor for Mexico, itself. Cuarón believes Mexico, as a country, is moving from adolescence to maturity. He used the film as a vehicle for commenting on that transformation.

Two-time Oscar nominee and camera master Emmanuel Lubezki shot the film, using long, unbroken takes. Lubezki has shot all of Cuarón's films. Before Lubezki got behind the camera, though, Cuarón brought in Bernal and Luna and had them run through a series of improvisations. Bernal and Luna met their film companion, Verdu, only once before the cameras rolled because Cuarón wanted the actors to develop their relationships on the road, just like their characters. Using the road-trip technique to tell the characters' stories allowed Cuarón to tell stories about Mexico as well. The station wagon drives past military checkpoints and shanty towns, quietly revealing the poor peasants the Mexican economy has left behind.

Cuarón had trouble getting *Y tu mamá también* released in Mexico. The government gave the film a rating that allowed only those over 18 to see it, though neighboring nations set lower age limits. When officials refused to give Cuarón a definition for the rating, he sued because he believed the rating had more to do with censorship than content. "They were shocked, because nobody has ever complained to them," Cuarón told *New York Times* writer Karen Durbin, noting that officials harassed moviegoers. "For the first time ever they sent inspectors to the theaters. It was amazing. They would demand ID's from everyone, even people in their 30's and 40's. And if you could not show proof of your age, you couldn't go in."

The government's attempt to limit moviegoers backfired as crowds gathered to watch the controversial film. Many sex educators and parent associations came out in favor of the movie, saying teens should be allowed to see it to facilitate a dialogue about sex and drugs. One group of high school students gained admittance by threatening to take off their clothes outside the movie theater if they were not allowed inside. *Y tu mamá también* was released in the United States without a rating and received countless awards, including a best screenplay award at the 2001 Venice Film Festival.

With the success of *Y tu mamá también,* Cuarón became a hot property. As a result, he was asked to direct 2004's *Harry Potter and the Prisoner of Azkaban.* Chris Columbus had directed the first two Potter films but declined the third. Cuarón was shocked by the invitation. "I was a little surprised at the beginning, a little suspicious about the whole thing," he told *Cinema Confidential.* "I knew that there was a movie and the huge success of Harry Potter but I never read the books and I hadn't seen the films. So when I read the script, immediately I wanted to read the book and when I read the book, I said I had to do this movie. It's just the material. The material is so great."

On first glance, Cuarón seemed an unlikely candidate to direct a Potter film, given the adult material he explored in his previous films. However, Warner Bros. was looking for someone to delve into the darker sides of Harry's journey into puberty. The third book, *Harry Potter and the Prisoner of Azkaban,* is much darker than its predecessors. The characters are older. Harry is 13, on the brink of adolescence and wrestling with inner turmoil and confusion. The book also introduces darker, spine-chilling characters—such as the evil Dementors who have the ability to suck people's souls from their bodies.

Like *Y tu mamá también,* Cuarón said *Harry Potter and the Prisoner of Azkaban* is a movie about identity. Speaking to the *New York Times'* Sarah Lyall, Cuarón described the film this way: "It's about a kid trying to come to terms with being a teenager, with being 13 and having an awareness of things. It's the moment when you realize that the monster is not under the bed or in the closet, but inside you—and the only weapon to fight that monster also resides inside you."

Cuarón shifted the focus of the movie from special effects to the characters. Before filming began, Cuarón required the main actors—Daniel Radcliffe, who plays Harry Potter, Emma Watson, who plays Hermione Granger, and Rupert Grint, who plays Ron Weasley—to write autobiographical essays from their character's point of view. In 2004, *Harry Potter and the Prisoner of Azkaban* grossed $795.5 million worldwide, placing second to *Shrek 2*.

Cuarón followed with 2006's *Children of Men*, a science-fiction flick based loosely on a novel by P. D. James. Cuarón co-wrote the screenplay and directed. Set in England in 2027, the film offers a bleak perspective of the future. Mass infertility has spread around the globe, leaving humanity on the brink of extinction. The world's youngest person, 18, is killed by a mob for refusing to sign an autograph and all hope seems lost. Terrorism runs rampant; many nations have collapsed. Immigrants seek refuge in England because the government is still functioning, but officials lock them up in cages alongside the streets. Amid the despair and warring factions, there is a glimmer of hope when a young African refugee turns up pregnant. A disillusioned bureaucrat, Theo Faron, played by Clive Owen, is given the task of finding a safe haven for the woman to ensure the baby is born.

The film is unique in that Cuarón used many lengthy, sustained shots with few close-ups. He wanted the dystopian environment to be one of the film's characters and felt that close-ups would favor the actors over the environment. In addition, Cuarón offers viewers minimal explanations for what is happening. As Cuarón told *Combustible Celluloid*'s Jeffrey M. Anderson: "I cannot stand explanation in movies. I cannot stand exposition. I prefer participation. You set up a situation and audiences have to make their own conclusions. I was not interested in explaining infertility, because if you start explaining, it becomes about that."

Cuarón went on to say that he believes too many directors are hand-feeding moviegoers. "Cinema has become a medium that you can watch with your eyes closed. You go to a movie theater, you close your eyes and you follow the whole thing. They tell you what they are doing, and you hear dialogue. It is losing its meaning as cinema, a cinema that has its own language." Cuarón hopes viewers do not understand everything in his films so they go home and think about them.

As for the future, it is safe to say Cuarón will be making pictures for years to come. In 2007, he joined forces with two other Mexican directors—del Toro and Alejandro Gonzalez Inarritu—to form a production label, Cha Cha Cha. The trio inked a five-picture package worth $100 million with Universal Pictures. Universal will fully finance the films and share ownership with the directors. Cuarón is slated to direct one of the five features.

Sources

Periodicals

Daily News of Los Angeles, March 14, 2002, p. U4.
Hollywood Reporter, March 12, 2007, p. 28.
Latino Leaders, September-October 2007, p. 24.
Newsweek, February 2, 1998, p. 61.
New York Times, March 17, 2002, p. AR17; May 9, 2004, p. 4 (Arts & Leisure); September 20, 2006, p. E5.
Orlando Sentinel (Orlando, FL), June 6, 2004.
Sacramento Bee, December 31, 2006, p. TK8.
San Francisco Chronicle, March 31, 2002, p. 27 (Sunday Datebook).

Online

"Interview: Children of Men Director Alfonso Cuarón," *Cinematical,* http://www.cinematical.com/2006/12/25/interview-children-ofmen-director-alfonso-cuaron/ (October 5, 2007).
"Interview: Director Alfonso Cuarón on *Harry Potter & The Prisoner of Azkaban,*" *Cinema Confidential,* http://www.cinecon.com/news.php?id=0406011 (October 5, 2007).
"Interview with Alfonso Cuarón," *Combustible Celluloid,* http://www.combustiblecelluloid.com/interviews/alfonsocuaron/shtml (October 5, 2007).
"Mexico's 3 Amigos do the Cha Cha Cha with Universal," Reuters, http://www.reuters.com/article/entertainmentNews/idUSN21274537.tif20070521.tif (November 11, 2007).

—Lisa Frick

Miley Cyrus

Actress and singer

Born Destiny Hope Cyrus, November 23, 1992, in Nashville, TN; daughter of Billy Ray (a country music singer and actor) and Leticia Cyrus.

Addresses: *Contact*—c/o The Disney Channel, 3800 W. Alameda Ave., Burbank, CA 91505.

Career

Actress on television, including: *Doc,* 2003; *Hannah Montana,* 2006—; *The Suite Life of Zack and Cody,* 2006; *The Emperor's New School,* 2007; *High School Musical 2* (movie), 2007; *The Replacements,* 2007. Film appearances include: *Big Fish,* 2003; *Hannah Montana: One in a Million,* 2008; *Hannah Montana/ Miley Cyrus: Best of Both Worlds Concert Tour,* 2008.

Sidelights

In 2006, Miley Cyrus became a tween and teen sensation when her television series *Hannah Montana* debuted on the Disney Channel and immediately became one of the most popular shows on the network. The young actress—the daughter of popular country singer Billy Ray Cyrus, who played her father on the show—also sang on *Hannah Montana* and released several popular albums under her character's name as well as her own. Cyrus' popularity as a singer and actress was confirmed by her sold-out concert tours in 2007 and 2008 which saw scalpers charging thousands of dollars for tickets.

Cyrus was born Destiny Hope Cyrus on November 23, 1992, in Nashville, Tennessee, the daughter of Billy Ray and his wife, Leticia, commonly known as

Tish. That year, the relatively unknown Billy Ray Cyrus had what was most likely the biggest hit of his career, "Achy Breaky Heart." While his career was taking off, his new daughter was displaying a sunny personality which earned her the nickname, "Smiley." Smiley was soon shortened to Miley, which became the name by which she was commonly known.

As a child, Cyrus was interested in music and acting. From an early age, Cyrus wrote songs and sang around the house as much as she could. She also took acting lessons on occasion, and appeared in school plays in Nashville. She made her professional debut on her father's PAX television series, *Doc,* in 2003. Later that year, she had also had a small role as Ruthie in the film *Big Fish,* directed by Tim Burton. While Cyrus did not act for a few years after these roles, she continued working on her music as she attended school and lived a relatively normal life.

In 2005, Cyrus was able to use both her acting and musical gifts in a new creative pursuit. That year, she and 1,000 others auditioned for a new show aimed at young viewers on the Disney Channel— what became *Hannah Montana.* Though Cyrus was going for the role of sidekick Lilly, she was cast as the titular character in *Hannah Montana* after a six-month audition process. Writing in the *New York Times*, Jacques Steinberg explained that "What ultimately won her the job, the producers and network executives say, was her cool confidence ..., her intuitive comic timing ... and a husky singing voice not unlike Mary Chapin Carpenter's." Cyrus was also tapped to sing the show's theme song.

In the show, Cyrus' character lived a double life. During the day, she was Miley Stewart, a normal teenager who dealt with typical middle school and family problems. At night, she was the blond wig-wearing Hannah Montana, a famous singing pop star. While her father Robby Stewart (played by her real-life father, who won the role after her daughter was cast) directed her career, only two of Miley Stewart's friends have any idea about her other identity. Much of the comedy of the show centered around keeping this secret.

Cyrus admitted playing both characters was a challenge. She told David Kronke of the *Daily News of Los Angeles*, "As an actor, it's really fun because you get to experience different things from different perspectives. As a person, it's a little harder. It's double the work—not only for me but for the wardrobe people, the hair and makeup people and everyone else. It's hard but really fun to be the character. The cool part is I've gotten to add my own take to it. I relate to both of them so easily."

Hannah Montana made its debut in March 2006 and was a hit from its first airings. The show made its debut after a repeat airing of the popular Disney movie *High School Musical* and attracted 5.4 million viewers. When *Hannah Montana* began appearing in its regular time slot, the show averaged 3.5 million viewers, but viewer numbers later increased as it gained popularity. It soon became the most watched show for six to 14 year olds on cable, and the most popular show on the Disney Channel.

By the time Cyrus began appearing on *Hannah Montana*, she had written about 100 songs, and a handful of them were used on the show. Singing as Hannah Montana, Cyrus released a soundtrack album for the series in October of 2006. The album featured eight songs from the show. The other five tracks were related to the show, and included "I Learned from You," a duet with her father. After it debuted at number one on the *Billboard* album charts, Cyrus toured in support of the record as the opening act for the Cheetah Girls, another popular act created by Disney. The soundtrack eventually went at least triple platinum.

In 2007, *Hannah Montana* continued to grow in popularity with television audiences. Cyrus had other acting roles in 2007, including guest spots on *The Replacements* and *The Emperor's New School*. Cyrus also had a cameo in the second installment of the Disney Channel's movie franchise, *High School Musical 2.*

Cyrus built on the show's popularity by designing some pieces of the *Hannah Montana* clothing line put out by Disney as well as releasing another album, the two-disc set *Hannah Montana, Vol. 2: Meet Miley Cyrus,* in June of 2007. This collection featured both songs Cyrus wrote and sung under her own name as well as more songs from the show she performed as Hannah Montana. Like *Hannah Montana, Hannah Montana, Vol. 2: Meet Miley Cyrus* debuted at number one on the *Billboard* album charts and sold more than a million copies in its first week of release, garnering platinum status. Cyrus thus became the youngest recording artist ever with two number-one albums released within a year. *Hannah Montana, Vol. 2: Meet Miley Cyrus* stayed in the top five on the charts for at least eleven consecutive weeks and eventually achieved double platinum status.

This time when Cyrus toured in support of *Hannah Montana, Vol. 2: Meet Miley Cyrus,* she was the headliner. In her fall and winter North American tour, Cyrus sang both as herself and Hannah Montana on the tour, dubbed "Hannah Montana and Miley Cyrus: The Best of Both Worlds," with the Jonas Brothers as her opening act. When the tour was announced in early fall, ticket demand far outstripped supply for all dates. Most stops sold out in minutes, and scalpers were able to sell tickets for five times the face value or more, with some tickets costing hundreds or even thousands of dollars.

Reviewing the tour's stop in the Bay Area in November of 2007, pop culture critic Peter Hartlaub of the *San Francisco Chronicle* noted: "Though parts of the stage show lacked polish, for the most part the concert delivered everything a parent could want for an impressionable child who judging from the piercing screams was probably experiencing the highlight of her young life. It was relatively wholesome, musically tolerable, and certainly had plenty of production value. Some of the adults may have walked away wondering what the big fuss was about, but none of the kids looked the least bit disappointed."

Cyrus' "Best of Both Worlds" tour extended into 2008 with a new opening act, Aly and AJ. It became one of the top-grossing North American concert tours. A controversy emerged in January of 2008 when a YouTube video showed that Cyrus briefly used a body double in the middle of her set to facilitate the changeover from Hannah Montana to Cyrus herself. Though Cyrus' publicist acknowledged the use of a body double and explained the situation fully, some fans were outraged by the deception.

Feeling no long-lasting ill effects from the hullabaloo, Cyrus put out two records in 2008, *The Best of Both Worlds,* a live disc from her tour, and a new disc based on the television show, *Hannah Montana 2: Non-Stop Dance Party.* She also released a concert movie available only on video, *Hannah Montana: One in a Million,* and a popular 3D concert film in movie theaters, *Hannah Montana/Miley Cyrus: Best of Both Worlds Concert Tour.* When the latter was released on Super Bowl weekend, it became the highest-grossing Super Bowl weekend movie ever; however, the film created another controversy because Cyrus and her father were depicted not wearing their seatbelts in one shot.

Amidst all her success, Cyrus decided to legally change her name from Destiny Hope Cyrus to Miley Ray Cyrus in early 2008. Her new middle name was a nod to her father's middle moniker and to his importance in her life. While Cyrus was ranked in *Forbes'* list of top 20 highest-paid celebrities under the age of 25, her family, especially her father, ensured that she would remain grounded amidst her success. Billy Ray Cyrus told Chuck Barney of the *Contra Costa Times,* "Our No. 1 rule is love what you do, be happy and be true to yourself and the music. I always say, 'If you're not having fun, it ain't working.'"

Selected discography

(As Hannah Montana) *Hannah Montana,* Walt Disney, 2006.

Hannah Montana, Vol. 2: Meet Miley Cyrus, Disney, 2007.

(Some tracks as Hannah Montana) *The Best of Both Worlds,* Disney, 2008.

(As Hannah Montana) *Hannah Montana 2: Non-Stop Dance Party,* Disney, 2008.

Sources

Periodicals

Associated Press, December 13, 2007.
Associated Press Worldstream, January 12, 2008.
Baltimore Sun, January 8, 2008.
Business Wire, July 3, 2007; September 12, 2007.
Columbus Dispatch (OH), September 18, 2007, p. 1A.
Contra Costa Times (CA), October 28, 2007.
Daily News of Los Angeles, June 27, 2007, p. U9.
New York Times, April 20, 2006, p. E3.
Pittsburgh Post-Gazette, January 3, 2008, p. W16.
San Francisco Chronicle, November 3, 2007, p. E1.
Seattle Times, October 28, 2007.

Online

"Miley Cyrus," Billboard.com, http://www.billboard.com/bbcom/bio/index.jsp?pid=772285 (February 23, 2008).

"Miley Cyrus," Internet Movie Database, http://www.imdb.com/name/nm1415323/ (February 23, 2008).

"Miley Cyrus Makes Name Change Official," *People,* http://www.people.com/people/article/0,,20174585.tif,00.html (February 21, 2008).

"Miley Cyrus Seat Belt Flap Debated," Associated Press, http://ap.google.com/article/ALeqM5gHVfWItglOzymvQ-e-gTRt7qQMugD8UV 0T981 (February 23, 2008).

—A. Petruso

Paula Deen

Television personality, chef, and author

Born Paula Ann Hiers, January 19, 1947, in Albany, GA; daughter of Earl (a gas station owner) and Corrie (a souvenir shop manager) Hiers; married Jimmy Deen (a car dealer), November 28, 1965 (divorced, 1992); married Michael Anthony Groover (a docking pilot), March 6, 2004; children: Bobby, Jamie (from first marriage), two stepchildren.

Addresses: *Office*—The Lady & Sons, 102 W. Congress St., Savannah, GA 31401.

Career

Worked as a bank teller and as a hospital biller, mid- to late-1980s; founded The Bag Lady (a lunchtime catering business), Savannah, GA, 1989; opened first restaurant, The Lady, in Savannah, GA, 1991; opened Lady & Sons restaurant in Savannah, 1996; published first cookbook, *The Lady & Sons Savannah Country Cookbook,* 1998; host of *Paula's Home Cooking* on the Food Network, 2002—; co-publisher with Hoffman Media of the magazine *Cooking with Paula Deen;* made film debut in *Elizabethtown,* 2005; published autobiography, *Paula Deen: It Ain't All about the Cookin',* 2007.

Sidelights

Paula Deen hosts of one of the Food Network's most popular cooking shows, *Paula's Home Cooking.* Deen has also authored several cookbooks that showcase the Southern cuisine that made her famous, but it was her 2007 autobiography that endeared her to audiences. In *Paula Deen: It Ain't All about the Cookin',* she discussed her unhappy first marriage, financial setbacks, and the panic attacks that kept her from leaving her house for years when her children were young. "Backed against the wall, I cooked everything my granny taught me and then some," she wrote in her autobiography. "Fried chicken, collard greens, country fried steak—my family ate *good.*"

Deen was born on January 19, 1947, in Albany, Georgia, and spent the first years of her life in the town's River Bend resort area, where her grandparents owned a motel and restaurant. When she was six, her parents bought a nearby gas station and souvenir shop, and the family moved into living quarters behind the store. "We had no bathroom; our toilet was a big old slop jar inside a pink wicker chair," she wrote in her autobiography. Sometimes, she took her two-year-old brother "Bubba" to school with her if the babysitter was unable to come and her mother needed to be at the store. She learned to cook from her grandmother, who was skilled in the Southern repertoire upon which Deen would build her career.

When Deen graduated from Albany High School, she asked her parents to allow her to move to Atlanta to enroll in modeling school. They were aghast at the idea, she recalled in an interview with Jim Auchmutey for the *Atlanta Journal-Constitution.* "'No daughter of mine is going to Atlanta and live by herself in that big city,'" Deen quoted her father as saying. "He wanted me to enroll in dental hygiene school. I didn't want to smell stinky breath, so I said I'm not doing that, I'll just get married."

Deen married her senior-year boyfriend, Jimmy Deen, who was a student at Auburn University but eventually dropped out to become a car salesperson. Not long after their wedding in November of 1965, Deen's father fell ill. He underwent heart surgery at the age of 40, suffered a stroke, then died from injuries sustained in a car accident brought on by another stroke in June of 1966. Four years later, Deen's 44-year-old mother died from cancer, and Bubba, now a teenager, came to live with her. She had two young boys of her own by then, and though she was just 23 years old, she became convinced that she would be the next to die. For years, she told *People*'s Mike Lipton, "I got up, got my children off to school and sat and waited to die."

Deen suffered from debilitating panic attacks whenever she left the house, and carried a brown paper bag in her purse to breathe into, to prevent hyperventilating. She recalled the worst years between 1977 and 1983, when she was barely able to leave the house at all. To pass the time, she cooked. "I could concentrate on what was in my pots and block out what was in my head," she told Julia Moskin in the *New York Times.* "Some days I could get to the supermarket, but I could never go too far inside. I learned to cook with the ingredients they kept close to the door." She also said these were times of severe financial hardship for her family. "My definition of success was, I would be successful if I could buy groceries for my family on Tuesday and my paycheck wasn't until Friday," she told Jennifer Sergent in the *Cincinnati Post.* "I thought people that didn't have to buy groceries on payday were rich."

Finally, Deen saw an episode of Phil Donahue's popular daytime television talk show that featured recovered agoraphobics. "I thought nobody else could be this crazy, and here was Phil Donahue devoting a whole program to it," she wrote in *It Ain't All about the Cookin'.* Financial worries also helped her move forward, because she needed to find a job after her husband's car dealership failed and they lost their home. She worked as a bank teller, but was robbed at gunpoint on one of her last days at work just as she was preparing to move to Savannah, Georgia. The 1986 robbery was so traumatic an experience that she stayed in bed for two months

once she relocated. Around the time she turned 40, with one son away at college and the other living with Bubba in Albany to finish his senior year of high school, Deen decided to make a change. "I looked in the mirror one day and said, 'You cannot live another day like this,'" she recalled in the *People* interview with Lipton. "It was like putting on a light switch."

Deen forced herself to drive around her block, going a little further each time, and found a job in a hospital, but her husband's income declined further, and she was forced to look for a new source of money in order to avoid foreclosure on their house yet again. A friend told her about a woman who came around to the hair salons and sold snacks to customers out of a basket, and Deen thought she could do better by making bag lunches and selling them to office workers. Even her grandmother tried to discourage her, reminding her how tough the food-service business could be, and her husband only reluctantly gave her the $200 she needed to start, which paid for groceries, a cooler, and the city license for her business, which she called The Bag Lady. Her friends at the hospital were some of her first customers, and her sons made the deliveries.

In 1991, Deen leased a kitchen and dining space inside a Savannah Best Western hotel, and opened her own restaurant, which she called The Lady. Her sons' girlfriends were the first waitresses, and she continued to run the sandwich business with her sons' help; however, her marriage finally ended. In 1996, she relocated her restaurant to a larger location in Savannah, and renamed it The Lady & Sons. Savannah had, by then, become a new tourist destination thanks to the success of a John Berendt's best-selling murder mystery, *Midnight in the Garden of Good and Evil*, which was set in the city and incited interest in its charming architecture and storied past. One of the visitors was an editor for Random House in New York City, who read Deen's self-published first cookbook and offered her a contract.

The Lady & Sons Savannah Country Cookbook was published by Random House in 1998, and Deen went on QVC, the home-shopping channel, and sold 70,000 copies of it in a single day. Her editors in New York arranged a visit by Food Network chef Gordon Elliott, who dined at The Lady & Sons and was impressed by Deen's personal warmth. That led to an appearance on his television show, *Doorknock Dinners*, and, in November of 2002, *Paula's Home Cooking* debuted on the Food Network and immediately began pulling in impressive ratings.

Deen became a major celebrity in Savannah, a tourist attraction in her own right with one company running a "Paula Deen Tour" for her fans. Around the same time, she began dating a neighbor on the piece of waterfront property she had bought, and her March of 2004 wedding to Michael Groover, a semi-retired docking pilot, was filmed for a Food Network special and became the highest-rated show on the network of the entire year. Her empire expanded later that year to include a second restaurant she opened with her brother called Uncle Bubba's Oyster House.

Deen's naturalness before the television cameras—she never uses a script—appealed to the casting director for a 2005 movie, *Elizabethtown*. Directed by Cameron Crowe, the film is the story of a young man, played by Orlando Bloom, who returns to his Kentucky roots for a funeral; Deen played his dynamic Aunt Dora, a renowned cook. She was initially wary about the idea of acting, fearing she might not pull it off, but as she recalled in an interview with Judith Evans in the *St. Louis Post-Dispatch*, once she and Crowe spoke by phone he reassured her. "He said, 'Paula, I just want you to be yourself,'" Deen told Evans. "I said, 'I can handle that.'"

On *Paula's Home Cooking*, Deen is known for liberally sampling her creations with obvious relish, and her Southern drawl and idioms have endeared her to viewers. But critics argue that Deen's typical Southern fare, with its reliance on animal fats and sugar, is unhealthy. "Our ancestors ate this way from the cradle," she replied when *Houston Chronicle* writer Diane Cowen asked her about it. "But the thing is those people worked. So I think we need to take care of it with exercise and moderation. If you want to eat a hoecake, eat a hoecake—just don't eat six hoecakes."

Deen provides a recipe for hoecakes—which are made with cornmeal and buttermilk and then deep-fried—in her 2005 cookbook, *Paula Deen & Friends: Living It Up, Southern Style*. In 2006, she inked a deal with Smithfield Foods for her own line of groceries, and that same year her two sons debuted in their own Food Network show, *Road Tasted*, which focuses on regional American cuisine. Deen thanked her sons for their loyalty and help in the early years of her business in her 2007 memoir, *Paula Deen: It Ain't All about the Cookin'*, written with Sherry Suib Cohen, which debuted in the No. 2 spot on the *New York Times* non-fiction best-seller list. In it, she candidly revealed her unhappy first marriage and years of agoraphobia, but also admitted her occasional bad judgment, such as the affair she carried on with a married man for several years when she was between marriages. "I'm very ashamed of that," she told Auchmutey in the *Atlanta Journal-Constitution*

interview. "I know I'm not the only woman it's happened to. We get so lonely and our self-esteem gets so low that we think we don't deserve anything better."

Deen is often cited as a successful example of someone who found their true career only later in life. "It's such a blessing," she told *Roanoke Times* journalist Lindsey Nair about starting her career after 40—"a time of life when you almost think you're not wanted or needed anymore.... I hope that I offer hope, because there is nothing worse than the feeling of hopelessness, and I had those feelings for so long. But we are not limited by our age." In her autobiography, she provided advice in the final chapters for readers thinking about starting their own venture, but also made sure to divulge that her two sons, her brother, and her Aunt Peggy, who often drove from Albany to help her make sandwiches, were crucial to the success of her empire. Deen quoted her son Bobby, who reflected, "The best thing about our business is being able to be with our family so much. The hardest thing about our business is having to be with family so much."

Selected writings

The Lady & Sons Savannah Country Cookbook, Random House (New York City), 1998.
The Lady & Sons, Too! A Whole New Batch of Recipes from Savannah, Random House, 2000.
The Lady & Sons Just Desserts: More Than 120 Sweet Temptations from Savannah's Favorite Restaurant, Simon & Schuster (New York City), 2002.
Paula Deen's Kitchen Classics: The Lady & Sons Savannah Country Cookbook and The Lady & and Sons, Too!, Random House, 2005.
(With Martha Nesbit) *Paula Deen & Friends: Living It Up, Southern Style*, Simon & Schuster, 2005.
(With Martha Nesbit) *Paula Deen Celebrates! Best Dishes and Best Wishes for the Best Times of Your Life*, Simon & Schuster, 2006.
(With Sherry Suib Cohen) *Paula Deen: It Ain't All about the Cookin'* (autobiography), Simon & Schuster, 2007.

Sources

Books

Deen, Paula, *It Ain't All about the Cookin'*, Simon & Schuster, 2007.

Periodicals

Atlanta Journal-Constitution, April 11, 2005, p. B1; April 22, 2007, p. M1.
Cincinnati Post, January 29, 2003, p. B1.

Daily News (Los Angeles, CA), May 11, 2005, p. U10.
Houston Chronicle, March 19, 2006, p. 3.
New York Times, February 28, 2007.
People, August 22, 2005, p. 113.
Roanoke Times, August 22, 2007, p. 1.

St. Louis Post-Dispatch, October 12, 2005, p. 1.
Virginian Pilot, June 6, 2007, p. F4.

—*Carol Brennan*

Dana Delany

Actress

Born Dana Welles Delany, March 13, 1956, in New York, NY; daughter of Jack and Mary Delany. *Education:* Wesleyan University, bachelor's degree, late 1970s.

Addresses: *Management*—Brillstein Entertainment Partners, 9150 Wilshire Blvd., Ste. 350, Beverly Hills, CA 90212.

Career

Actress in television, including: *Love of Life,* 1979-80; *As the World Turns,* 1981; *Threesome* (movie), 1984; *Liberty* (movie), 1986; *Magnum, P.I.,* 1986-87; *Sweet Surrender,* 1987; *China Beach,* 1988-91; *A Promise to Keep* (movie), 1990; *Wild Palms* (miniseries), 1993; *Donato & Daughter,* 1993; *The Enemy Within* (movie), 1994; *Choices of the Heart: The Margaret Sanger Story* (movie), 1995; *Fallen Angels,* 1995; *For Hope* (movie), 1996; *Wing Commander Academy,* 1996; *Superman* (voice), 1996-2000; *The Rescuers,* 1998; *The Patron Saint of Liars* (movie), 1998; *Sirens* (movie), 1999; *Resurrection* (movie), 1999; *Shake, Rattle and Roll* (miniseries), 1999; *Final Jeopardy* (movie), 2001; *Pasadena,* 2001-02; *Presidio Med,* 2002; *A Time to Remember,* 2003; *Baby for Sale* (movie), 2004; *Kidnapped,* 2006-07; *Desperate Housewives,* 2007—. Film appearances include: *The Fan,* 1981; *Almost You,* 1985; *Where the River Runs Black,* 1986; *Masquerade,* 1988; *Patty Hearst,* 1988; *Moon Over Parador,* 1988; *Housesitter,* 1992; *Light Sleeper,* 1992; *Tombstone,* 1993; *Exit to Eden,* 1994; *Live Nude Girls,* 1995; *Fly Away Home,* 1996; *Wide Awake,* 1998; *The Curve,* 1998; *The Outfitters,* 1999; *The Right Temptation,* 2000; *Mother Ghost,* 2002; *Getting to Know You,* 2005; *Drunkboat,* 2007. Stage

appearances include: *A Life,* Morosco Theatre, Broadway, 1980-81; *Blood Moon,* Production Company Theatre, New York City, then Los Angeles, CA, 1983-84; *Translations,* Plymouth Theatre, Broadway, 1995; *Dinner With Friends,* Variety Arts Theatre, New York City, Geffen Playhouse, Los Angeles, Wilbur Theatre, Boston, all 2000; *Much Ado About Nothing,* Old Globe Theatre, San Diego, CA, 2003. Also worked as a cocktail waitress, museum ticket seller, and antique shop assistant.

Awards: Emmy Award for best actress in a drama series, Academy of Television Arts and Sciences, for *China Beach,* 1989 and 1992.

Sidelights

Best known for her work on the television series *China Beach, Pasadena,* and *Desperate Housewives,* actress Dana Delany also has extensive film credits and a background in theater. Among her best known films are *Tombstone* and *Housesitter.* Delany began her career on soap operas and the New York stage.

Born on March 13, 1956, in New York City, Delany was raised in wealth and privilege with her brother and sister in Stamford, Connecticut. Her family gained its financial position because her grandfather invented a toilet flush valve, the Delany valve, in 1928. Delany received her education at the prep school Phillips Academy in Andover, Massachusetts, as part of the first class to admit girls. She became interested in theater there. Delany then attended Wesleyan University in Connecticut, where she earned her undergraduate degree in the late 1970s.

After leaving school, Delany moved to New York City to become an actress. She briefly worked as a cocktail waitress, then was employed at the Metropolitan Museum of Art as a ticket seller. Delany was also an assistant at an antiques shop before landing her first role. She began her career on a soap opera, *Love of Life,* playing Amy Russell from 1979-80. After *Love of Life* was cancelled, Delany moved to the stage. She spent 1980 to 1981 appearing in the Broadway production of *A Life,* then spent a year on another soap, *As the World Turns,* as Haley Wilson in 1981.

Many actors and actresses consider soaps a good training ground, but Delany was not as enamored by the experience. She told Karen Heller of the *Toronto Star,* "Well, I loved soaps in college, but when I was on them I found I was learning some bad habits that I thought were very detrimental to my career. You take shortcuts. You don't make the choices to try the interesting things—at least I didn't. You just try to see how little work you can get away with. It was very dangerous."

Because of her experiences, Delany decided to leave *As the World Turns* and attend an acting school in New York City to receive more training in her craft. Returning to acting in 1983, she appeared in the Production Company's *Blood Moon,* written by Nicholas Kazan. Delany played a naïve pre-med student who tries to gain life experience in the first act, but is raped and tries to take revenge on her attacker in the second. Reviewing the play, Mel Gussow of the *New York Times* commented, "she has two roles to play and she does them both with authority."

When *Blood Moon* moved to Los Angeles, Delany went with the production and stayed. She focused on television roles for much of the 1980s, including playing the titular character's girlfriend for two seasons on *Magnum, P.I.* In 1987, Delany had a central role on the short-lived situation comedy, *Sweet Surrender.* She also did the occasional film such as 1985's *Almost You* and 1986's *Where the River Runs Black.* By 1988, Delany had featured roles in three bigger films: *Masquerade, Patty Hearst,* and *Moon Over Parador.*

In 1988, Delany had the first break of her career when she began playing the main character and moral center of the acclaimed television program *China Beach.* The drama focused on the lives of women serving in the armed forces during the Vietnam War and stationed in a U.S. base near Da Nang. While the series had low ratings, critics roundly praised the show and it developed a cult following of enthusiastic fans who appreciated its sophistication, deft handling of war time relationships, and fresh perspective on the conflict.

Delany's portrayal of Colleen McMurphy, an unsentimental nurse, was highly regarded. The *Washington Post's* Tom Shales wrote of her performance, "As McMurphy, Dana Delany is fascinating—pure and simple. Or rather, pure and complex.... As McMurphy, she is full of provocative surprises, able to make swings from implacable to vulnerable with complete conviction. Some performers are just innately and inescapably watchable, and she's one of them."

Despite numerous awards, including two Emmy Awards for Delany, and a rabid fan and critical base of support, *China Beach* was cancelled by ABC in 1991, but proved popular in reruns which aired on Lifetime in the early 1990s. Delany's work in the role touched many viewers, including veterans, even as it neared the end of its run. A year after the show was cancelled, she told *Parade's* James Brady, "[In 1991], when I was up for an Emmy Award, a man wrote me to say that, after seeing the show, he stopped drinking and went into treatment—and he sent me his Purple Heart just in case I lost. And I did. So now I have his Purple Heart, which is a lot more important."

After the demise of *China Beach,* Delany appeared in a number of films in the early 1990s. In 1992, she appeared in two films: *Housesitter,* a comedy with Steve Martin and Goldie Hawn; and *Light Sleeper,* opposite Willem Dafoe and Susan Sarandon. Delany's roles were diverse: She appeared in the 1993 Wyatt Earp western *Tombstone* as traveling actress Josephine Marcus, then played an S&M dominatrix in the panned comedy *Exit to Eden* in 1994.

While having big-screen success in this time period, Delany also took on television roles, primarily in movies and miniseries. Of working in both film and television, she told Steve Bornfeld in the *Seattle Post-Intelligencer,* "As an actress, you really need to do both these days. Television has been very good to me and I'm not a snob. And the roles are better for women than they are in films."

In 1993, she was delighted to play Charles Bronson's daughter—and superior—in the violent cop movie *Donato & Daughter*. The pair have tension because of the death of her brother, a cop, but are forced to work together to catch a serial killer. That same year, Delany appeared in the miniseries *Wild Palms*, created by Oliver Stone. Though *Wild Palms* was dismissed by critics, she enjoyed her work on the stylized melodrama. In 1995, Delany played the founder of Planned Parenthood, Margaret Sanger, in the biographical television movie *Choices of the Heart: The Margaret Sanger Story*.

After a return to the stage in 1995 in the New York production of *Translations*, Delany continued to move between film and television in the mid to late 1990s. In the 1995 film *Live Nude Girls*, she played a smug married woman who reunites at a dinner with her female friends since childhood to talk about their lives. She also took on challenging television movie roles like 1998's *The Patron Saint of Liars* and the 1999 sci-fi remake of *Resurrection*. In the former, she played a married pregnant woman who leaves her husband to live at a home for unwed mothers, while in the latter she was the central character who gains healing powers after living through a car crash which killed her husband. In this time period, Delany also provided the voice of Lois Lane in the animated *Superman* series.

In the early 2000s, Delany appeared in a few smaller films, such as 2002's *Mother Ghost* and 2005's *Getting to Know You*, but primarily focused on television. In addition to roles in television movies such the 2001 thriller *Final Jeopardy*, she took starring roles in a number of television series. One high profile role came in 2001 with the prime-time soap opera *Pasadena*. Delany played Catherine Greeley McAllister, an uptight, high society woman who is part of an old money family with many dark secrets.

The actress drew on her own background growing up in Stamford, Connecticut for the role. She told Valerie Kuklenski of the *Daily News of Los Angeles*, "I just had to remember what it was like living in Connecticut and then I got it.... People hide everything in Connecticut. I grew up in that atmosphere of 'everything's fine; let's not talk about problems.'" Yet Delany enjoyed the role, telling Bart Mills of the *Boston Herald*, "I love the character because she's so far from what I am. I've always been aware of the need to give back, and here I am playing someone so unconcerned about others.... Americans sometimes like to pretend everyone here is equal, but we're not, not at all."

Though the dark soap received critical kudos, it failed to attract an audience and was cancelled after only a handful of episodes aired. Delany moved into another television show the following season, playing Dr. Rae Brennan in the short-lived medical drama, *Presidio Med*. Created by the team behind *China Beach*, Delany's oncologist character was envisioned as Colleen McMurphy ten years later. Despite the pedigree and impressive ensemble cast which included Blythe Danner, the edgy show was canceled during its first season as well.

After the demise of *Presido Med*, Delany did some stage work, including appearing in *Dinner with Friends* in three cities and as Beatrice in a San Diego production of *Much Ado About Nothing* in 2003. Playing Beatrice marked the first time she performed Shakespeare. She then took roles in television movies, like the family drama *A Time to Remember* and the adoption drama *Baby for Sale*.

In 2007, Delany returned to series television by taking a role in the established hit prime-time drama *Desperate Housewives*. The actress had auditioned for the series in 2004 and had been offered the role of Bree. Delany turned it down three times, and Marcia Cross became the perfect housewife. As *Desperate Housewives* was a hit, Delany regretted not taking the part, but she had misgivings after *Pasadena* and she had just finished a demanding project. Series co-creator Marc Cherry remembered Delany when he added a new character for the 2007-08 season, the complex Katherine Mayfair.

Delany's Mayfair lived on Wisteria Lane more than a decade ago, was friends with Susan Mayer, moved away under mysterious circumstances, and has moved back with her teenaged daughter and a younger husband. Her secrets were central to the show's plotline in the 2007-08 season, though Delany was expected to remain with the show for several more seasons. Praising her work in *Desperate Housewives*, John Caramanica of the *Los Angeles Times* wrote, "Delany is sharp, vibrant, and, most crucially, emotional, even if her character is meant to be essentially emotionless. Her hair, her eyes, her teeth—every part of her comes together to connote terror lurking just beneath the surface."

Delany appreciated the opportunity afforded to her by the show and television in general. She told Karen Tay of Auckland, New Zealand's *Sunday Star-Times*, "I have to say almost all my best work has been on television, just because the roles were more interesting. Television has always been a great medium for women and the fact that *Desperate Housewives* offers these great roles for women over 40 is such as dream, you know. Because it gets harder the older you get and luckily I haven't had to deal with that yet."

Sources

Books

Complete Marquis Who's Who Biographies, Marquis Who's Who, 2007.

Periodicals

Associated Press, March 7, 1995; July 2, 2004.

BPI Entertainment News Wire, December 30, 1993.

Boston Globe, February 9, 1996, p. 50.

Boston Herald, October 5, 2001, p. S36.

Buffalo News (Buffalo, NY), March 14, 1999, p. 14TV.

Chicago Sun-Times, October 14, 1994, p. 43.

Daily News (New York, NY), April 2, 1998.

Daily News of Los Angeles, September 27, 2001, p. L3.

Hamilton Spectator (Hamilton, Ontario, Canada), April 9, 2001, p. C10.

Los Angeles Times, April 13, 2008, p. E17.

New York Times, January 14, 1983, p. C6; November 23, 2003, sec. 13, p. 4.

Parade, May 10, 1992, p. 18.

Pittsburgh Post-Gazette (Pittsburgh, PA), August 17, 2007, p. D1.

Record (Bergen County, NJ), October 2, 2002, p. F8.

San Diego Union-Tribune, August 28, 2003, p. 4.

Seattle Post-Intelligencer, September 21, 1993, p. B5.

Sunday Star-Times (Auckland, New Zealand), February 17, 2008, p. 13.

Toronto Star, July 10, 1989, p. C4.

Toronto Sun, October 9, 1994, p. S3.

USA Today, April 16, 1990, p. 3D; November 2, 1990, p. 1D.

Washington Post, April 26, 1988, p. B1.

Windsor Star (Windsor, Ontario, Canada), January 15, 2003, p. B7.

—A. Petruso

Novak Djokovic

Stephen Dunn/Getty Images

Professional tennis player

Born May 22, 1987, in Belgrade, Serbia; son of Srdjan (a restaurant operator) and Dijana (a restaurant operator) Djokovic.

Addresses: *Contact*—201 ATP Tour Blvd., Ponte Vedra Beach, FL 32082. *Home*—Monte Carlo, Monaco.

Career

Began playing tennis, c. 1991; turned pro, 2003; won first Association of Tennis Professionals (ATP) title, Dutch Open, Amersfoort, Netherlands, 2006, and followed up with another win, the Moselle Open, Metz, France, 2006; won five ATP singles titles in 2007, including Australia's Next Generation Adelaide International, the Miami Masters, Portugal's Estoril Open, Canada Masters (Rogers Cup) and BA-CA Tennis Trophy, Vienna, Austria; won Australian Open, Melbourne, 2008; won Indian Wells Masters, Indian Wells, CA, 2008; won Rome Masters, Italy, 2008.

Awards: Most Improved Player, ATP Awards, 2006.

Sidelights

Serbian tennis standout Novak Djokovic hit the pro circuit in 2003 and enjoyed a rapid rise through the rankings despite being one of the youngest players on the tour. At the start of the 2007 season, the Association of Tennis Professionals ranked Djokovic 16th in the world. He ended the season at third after notching an amazing victory over Swiss master and world No. 1 Roger Federer in the Rogers Cup. The next year, Djokovic proved the triumph was no fluke. In 2008, Djokovic won the Australian Open after knocking out defending champion Federer in the semifinals and besting Frenchman Jo-Wilfried Tsonga in the finals. The victory ensured Djokovic's place in history as the first Serbian to win a Grand Slam singles title.

Tennis legend Martina Navratilova told the *Sydney Morning Herald*'s Linda Pearce that Djokovic has many admirable qualities that will keep him at the top of the game for years to come. "I love his head—he's such a smart guy out there," Navratilova said. "I like his attitude, on and off the court."

Djokovic was born on May 22, 1987, in Belgrade, Serbia, to Srdjan and Dijana Djokovic. Although Djokovic is the first member of his family to play tennis, sports run deep in his bloodline. Djokovic's father, Srdjan, skied competitively and taught lessons at a ski school in the Serbian resort town of Kopaonik. Kopaonik is one of the largest mountain ranges in Serbia. It was there that he met Djokovic's mother, who also taught skiing.

Following in his parents' footsteps, Djokovic took up skiing as a youngster. By this time, his parents were running a pancake and pizza restaurant in Kopaonik. When Djokovic was about four years old, a construction team built some tennis courts near the family restaurant. Jelena Gencic opened a tennis camp there and in no time, Djokovic was on the court. Speaking to Emma John of the *Observer*, Gencic described an early encounter with the aspiring youngster. "He arrived half an hour early with a big tennis bag. Inside his bag I saw a tennis racket, towel, bottle of water, banana, wrist-bands, everything you need for a game." Gencic asked Djokovic if his mother had packed his bag and he said that he had. When Gencic asked Djokovic how he knew what to pack, he replied, "I watch TV."

As an adolescent, Djokovic remained loyal to his workout routine, despite the crisis going on in his country. In 1999, NATO forces began bombing Serbia in an effort to persuade Serbian President Slobodan Milosevic to withdraw his troops, which were at war with the Albanians in Kosovo. NATO forces targeted Belgrade, the city where Djokovic lived. The air raids continued for more than two months but never scared Djokovic off the court. He honed his backhand and practiced his serves even as warning sirens pierced the air and bombs burst in the distance.

Djokovic's father believes the experience helped Djokovic develop the nerves of steel and exceptional concentration skills that help him win on the court today. "Novak was very scared then, but he never showed it," Srdjan Djokovic told the *New York Times'* Juliet Macur. "Now he is scared of nothing." Djokovic's mother told Macur that Djokovic's tennis gave the family focus, which helped them survive. "I think tennis saved us," she said. "If we didn't have tennis, we would have spent the days scared, always looking to the sky, wondering when the bombs would come."

At age 12, Djokovic left home to train with former Croatian standout Nikola Pilic at his tennis academy in Munich, Germany. Before long, he was competing across Europe. In 2002, Djokovic was one of the hottest 16-and-under players on the European Tennis Association circuit, winning the U-16 championship at La Baule, France.

In 2003, Djokovic turned pro and played mostly in the Futures and Challenger circuits, ending the year with an ATP ranking of 676. In 2006, he earned his first ATP tour victory at the Dutch Open, followed with a second victory at the Moselle Open in Metz, France. In 2007, Djokovic's career took off—he won his first Masters Series event with a victory at the Miami Masters and followed up with another Masters victory at the Rogers Cup with an upset over Federer, the world's No. 1 player. Djokovic had never beaten Federer before. Within a few weeks, Djokovic reached his first-ever Grand Slam final at the U.S. Open, where he faced Federer again. Shaky—and playing before a crowd 23,000-strong—a nervous Djokovic, just 20, lost the final. He did, however, win five titles that year and ended the season ranked third, making him the youngest player in the top 20.

The year 2008 proved to be a breakout year for Djokovic as he beat Federer in the Australian Open semifinals and went on to defeat Tsonga in the finals. This gave Djokovic his first Grand Slam title. Djokovic was the youngest player in 23 years to win the Australian Open, and the first Serbian. He went on to win two more Masters events—at Indian Wells and Rome.

On the court, Djokovic is flashy and fun—people like to watch him play. Skinny and known for bouncing the ball 10 to 15 times before a serve, the 6-foot-2-inch, 176-pound rightie has a smooth, two-fisted backhand he can shoot down the line. Djokovic's success has inspired a new generation of Serbian children to take up the sport—including his younger brothers, Marko and Djordje. The Djokovic boys are all about four years apart. Djordje Djokovic is said to be more talented than his brothers. Perhaps the two will face each other on the court someday.

In an interview before the Pacific Life Indian Wells tournament, posted on the event Web site, Djokovic said that winning the Australian Open was fantastic. "You get the feeling that everything you have done, you know, in your life, has paid off in one tournament. Everybody's dream is to win a Grand Slam, any Grand Slam, and I've done it. Still I'm only 20 years old and still have a long way to my lifetime goal, which is to be No. 1, and hopefully I can stay healthy and play professional tennis in another ten, 15 years."

Sources

Books

Complete Marquis Who's Who Biographies, Marquis Who's Who, 2008.

Periodicals

New York Times, June 3, 2007, p. 8 (sports).

Observer (London, England), January 6, 2008, p. 20 (sports).

Sun Herald (Sydney, Australia), September 30, 2007, p. 92 (sports).

Sydney Morning Herald (Sydney, Australia), January 12, 2008, p. S38; January 25, 2008, p. S32; January 29, 2008, p. S30.

Times (London, England), January 22, 2008, p. 70 (sports).

Online

"Biography," Novak Djokovic Web site, http://www.novak-djokovic.com/eng/about_nole/more.php (April 13, 2008).

"Djokovic Upsets Federer to Cap Rogers Cup Title Run," *SI.com,* http://sportsillustrated.cnn.com/ (August 13, 2007).

"Djokovic Wins Australian Open," *SI.com,* http://sportsillustrated.cnn.com/ (January 28, 2008).

"Novak Djokovic," Pacific Life Open, http://www.pacificlifeopen.com/4/players/interviews/2008/djokovic314.asp (April 13, 2008).

—Lisa Frick

Roddy Doyle

AP Images

Author

Born May 8, 1958, in Kilbarrack, Ireland; son of Rory (a printer and teacher) and Ita Bridget (Bulger) Doyle; married Belinda Moller (an arts publicist), c. 1989; children: Rory, Jack, one daughter. *Education:* Graduated from the University College, Dublin, c. 1980.

Addresses: *Office*—Penguin Group (USA), Inc., c/o Viking Press Publicity, 375 Hudson St., New York, NY 10014.

Career

Greendale Community School, Dublin, Ireland, English and geography teacher, 1980-93; formed King Farouk publishing company and published his first novel, *The Commitments,* 1987; full-time writer, 1993—; wrote first television play, *The Family,* BBC, 1994; co-produced film, *When Brendan Met Trudy,* 2000; also served on Irish Film Board.

Awards: Booker Prize for Fiction, for *Paddy Clarke Ha Ha Ha,* 1993; Kerry Group Irish Fiction Award, for *Paula Spencer,* 2007.

Sidelights

Best known for such novels as *The Commitments* and the Booker Prize-winning *Paddy Clarke Ha Ha Ha,* Irish author Roddy Doyle has built a solid career as a novelist writing with honesty about his native country, especially its working-class people. Doyle also turned several of his novels into screen-

plays and wrote several plays as well. Considered the most famous author living in Ireland and sometimes compared to James Joyce by American critics, Doyle worked as a school teacher in Dublin before becoming an author.

Doyle was born in 1958, in Kilbarrack, Ireland, a few miles outside of Dublin. He was one of four children of Rory and Ita Doyle, who raised their brood there as the town became engulfed by the growing city. His father worked as a printer for the *Irish Independent* and later as a teacher of printing at a trade college, Dublin's School of Printing. Doyle had a happy, middle-class childhood, but was often treated poorly at school by his teachers at nearby Sutton's St. Finton's Christian Brothers School. After graduating from University College in Dublin, Doyle began working as a teacher himself, at Greendale Community School in Kilbarrack in 1980. He taught English and geography at the grammar school for the next 13 years.

While working as a teacher, Doyle began his writing career. His first efforts were plays and an unpublished novel, *Your Granny's a Hunger Striker.* He produced his first novel to see print, *The Commitments,* in the late 1980s. He wrote it in six months while living in a one-room apartment. The novel was about a group of working-class teenagers in contemporary Dublin who form a soul band. It centered around the band's organizer and leader, Jimmy Rabbitte, and the other seven members of his family who played a significant role in the plot.

Because publishers were not initially not interested in the novel, Doyle borrowed £5000 (about $10,300) and with a friend created a company, King Farouk, to self-publish *The Commitments* in 1987. Doyle then sold the initial 1,000 copy run himself. Within two years, the company was dissolved as Doyle's book was picked up by British and American publishers. *The Commitments* received much critical praise and was translated into a number of languages, including Japanese and Czech.

Other members of the Rabbitte family took center stage in Doyle's two subsequent novels. *The Snapper* focuses on Jimmy's single sister, Sharon, as the 20-year-old deals with being impregnated by a married, middle-aged neighbor. It also explores the effect of the pregnancy on her father, Jimmy, Sr. Next, in 1991's *The Van*, Jimmy Sr. starts a mobile food business with a friend to supplement the family's income in the face of chronic unemployment. This novel made the short list for the Booker Prize.

The three novels formed the "Barrytown Trilogy," as each was set in this fictional working class area of Dublin. The books also consisted nearly entirely of dialogue, rich in local slang and cursing that some reviewers considered almost lyrical in its execution. While many in Ireland praised the book and Doyle's depiction of their country and its people, others were not as impressed. He told Diane Turbide of *Maclean's* "I've been criticized for the bad language in my books—that I've given a bad image, and it's always somebody else's definition of what is good."

While writing the trilogy, Doyle built on the success of the novels by moving into screenwriting. He co-wrote the script for the film version of *The Commitments,* which was directed by Alan Parker. It was released in the United States to much acclaim in 1991. Doyle also wrote the screenplay for the film based on *The Snapper,* which was directed by Stephen Frears and came out in 1993. Doyle wrote the script for the screen take on *The Van* as well.

As Doyle's secondary career took off, he resigned from teaching to focus on writing full time in 1993. That same year, he published his fourth novel, *Paddy Clarke Ha Ha Ha*. In this book, also set in Barrytown but in the 1960s, Doyle explores the life of the title

character, a ten-year-old boy, and the way he perceives the world. For example, one scene involves Paddy and his friends holding a funeral for a deceased rat, while others highlight his ideas for taunting his younger brother.

More complexly, *Paddy Clarke* explores his parents' tense marital problems as he sees their relationship fall apart. Though not explicitly about Doyle's own childhood, he drew on his own memories of what it was like to be a child in the time period. The depth and strength of Doyle's writing led to him winning the prestigious Booker Prize for the book in 1993.

While novels continued to be Doyle's main creative outlet, he also continued to work in other genres. In 1994, his four-part television play, *The Family,* was produced by the BBC and aired on the Irish network, RTE. In the short series, he explored alcoholism and domestic violence in working-class families in his native country. While a creative success, the television event proved important to Ireland and was said to help sway Irish voters to approve the legalization of divorce later that year.

Doyle followed *Paddy Clarke* with 1996's *The Woman Who Walked Into Doors.* In this novel, Doyle moved into even darker territory by describing the life of a housewife who is trapped in a physically and emotionally abusive marriage and is also an alcoholic. Paula Spencer, the primary character, pours out her sad life story aware of her own self-pity, through Doyle's usual acute ear for dialogue. Of the novel, Carmen Callil wrote in London's *Financial Times,* "*The Woman Who Walked into Doors* throbs with what it must really be like to love a man who beats you almost to death, and what it must be like to be a man who loves his wife but who, with the smallness of heart dictated by his circumstances, cannot stop his own violence."

Ignoring criticisms that he had grown dark and depressing in his works, Doyle's next novel, 1999's *A Star Called Henry,* continued to explore Ireland's darker side. A historically based book set in the early twentieth century, Doyle's central character is born in a Dublin slum to a brothel bouncer and alcoholic mother. A large child, Henry Smart becomes involved in the Irish Rising as a teenager and soon becomes a violent killer in the name of revolutionary Irish political action.

While many American critics praised the book, Irish and British critics were divided on his nearly mythological creation and many found the book offensive. One reviewer who found *A Star Called*

Henry evident of Doyle's evolution as a writer was the *Independent*'s John Walsh. He wrote, "*A Star Called Henry* is a quantum leap for this cautious and unpretentious storyteller. His earlier naturalism has been replaced by a kind of heartless exuberance, shot through with magic realism, in which the tones of Barrytown and Paddy Clarke are still just as discernible."

Doyle planned for *A Star Called Henry* to be the first novel of a trilogy about Henry and Irish history over the course of the twentieth century dubbed "The Last Roundup." Taking a break from novels after the first installment's publication, Doyle returned to visual media. He wrote several teleplays and screenplays in the late 1990s and early 2000s, including the light romantic comedy *When Brendan Met Trudy*, which was released in 2000. In addition to writing the script, Doyle also served as the film's co-producer.

Still putting his planned trilogy of novels on hold, Doyle focused on other written enterprises for a time as well. Inspired by his three children, he published two children's books in succession, 2000's *The Giggler Treatment* and 2001's *Rover Saves Christmas*. Doyle continued to work in the genre intermittently, adding a third title, *Meanwhile Adventures*, later in the decade.

Amidst the children's books, Doyle wrote a memoir, 2002's *Rory and Ita*, about his parents. In the intimate text, Doyle chronicles the stories of their lives, alternating chapters between the memories of his mother and his father. The chapters had a natural flow because they were based on taped discussions Doyle had with his parents. Of his process, Doyle told the *Irish Times*' Donald Clarke, "[I]t's wholly my book, in that from the beginning it was my idea. I decided on the structures. I decided what questions to ask my parents. I took all these tapes and fashioned a book out of it." While Doyle regarded the book as a labor of love which many critics found fascinating, others found the tome more of interest to family members or friends rather than the general public.

Finally returning to "The Last Roundup" trilogy, Doyle published the second novel in the series in 2004. Titled *Oh, Play That Thing*, it is set in the United States during the Jazz Age because Henry has been forced to live in exile in New York City and Chicago. Doyle listened incessantly to jazz while writing the novel, and even had his protagonist befriend a young Louis Armstrong. The myth of Doyle's braggart Henry grew larger in the novel, where he continues his wild ways working with gangsters and opening speakeasies.

Instead of immediately completing the trilogy, Doyle moved in a different direction for his next novel. He decided to write a sequel to *The Woman Who Walked Into Doors* a decade after it went into print. Published in 2007, *Paula Spencer: A Novel* also picks up the story ten years in the future. Paula's abusive husband, Charlo, has been killed and she is a widow who still supports herself by cleaning offices. Now sober, Paula fights to stay clean while dealing with the effects of her choices on her family.

The book received praise, with a number of critics commented especially on his still-strong dialogue. Writing in the *Financial Times*, Callil noted "Doyle's dialogue, both spoken and stream of consciousness, is the core of the genius of his writing and of the happily politically incorrect imagination he uses to choose each perfectly pitched word."

For all his success, Doyle worked to remain connected to the real world and ordinary people to retain his human touch as a writer. He understood that he was fortunate to be in the position he was in as an author and Irish celebrity. Doyle told Nicci Gerrard of the *Observer*, "I have worked very hard for it, but I'm very lucky, yes. It could not have happened. I don't work to any commissions. I do what I want to do. My novels come from within me; they are things I feel I want to do."

Selected writings

Novels

The Commitments, King Farouk (Dublin, Ireland), 1987; Heinemann (London, England), 1988; Random House (New York City), 1989.

The Snapper, Secker and Warburg (London, England), 1990; Penguin (New York City), 1992.

The Van, Secker and Warburg, 1991; Viking (New York City), 1992.

Paddy Clarke Ha Ha Ha, Secker and Warburg, 1993; Viking, 1993.

The Woman Who Walked Into Doors, Viking, 1996.

A Star Called Henry, Viking, 1999.

Oh, Play That Thing, Viking, 2004.

Paula Spencer: A Novel, Viking, 2007.

Screenplays

(With Dick Clement and Ian La Frenais) *The Commitments*, Twentieth Century-Fox, 1991.

The Snapper, 1993.

The Van, 1997.

Famine, Crom Films, 1998.
When Brendan Met Trudy (also co-producer), 2000.

Television plays

The Family, BBC, 1994.
Two Lives: Hell for Leather, 1999.

Plays

Brownbread, Secker & Warbug, 1987.
War, Passion Machine (Dublin, Ireland), 1989.
Brownbread and War, Penguin Books, 1994.

Children's books

The Giggler Treatment, Arthur A. Levine Books (New York City), 2000.
Rover Saves Christmas, Arthur A. Levine Books, 2001.
Meanwhile Adventures, Scholastic Paperbacks (New York City), 2006.

Memoir

Rory and Ita, Viking, 2002.

Sources

Books

Contemporary Authors, New Revision Series, vol. 128, Gale (Detroit, MI), 2004, pp. 112-18.

Periodicals

Financial Times (London, England), August 26, 2006, p. 32.
Gazette (Montreal, Quebec, Canada), December 28, 2002, p. H4.
Globe and Mail (Canada), September 11, 1999, p. C7.
Independent (London, England), September 4, 1999, p. 5; September 17, 2004, pp. 20-21.
Irish Independent, May 31, 2007.
Irish Times, December 24, 1999, p. 54; November 2, 2002, p. 73.
Maclean's, August 30, 1993, p. 50.
New York Times, September 22, 1999, p. E1.
Observer, April 15, 2001, p. 3.
Washington Post, February 4, 1994, p. C1.
Weekly Standard, July 8, 1996/July 15, 1996, p. 37.

Online

"Roddy Doyle," Internet Movie Database, http://www.imdb.com/name/nm0236486/ (August 11, 2007).

—A. Petruso

Zac Efron

Actor

Born Zachary David Alexander Efron, October 18, 1987, in San Luis Obispo, CA; son of David (an electrical engineer) and Starla (a power plant employee) Efron.

Addresses: *Office*— c/o The Disney Channel, 3800 W. Alameda Ave., Burbank, CA 91505. *Agent*—TalentWorks, 3500 West Olive Ave., Ste. 1400, Burbank, CA 91505. *Management*—Alchemy Entertainment, 9229 Sunset Blvd., Ste. 720, Los Angeles, CA 90069.

Career

Actor in television, including: *Firefly*, FOX, 2002; *The Big Wide World of Carl Laemke* (pilot), 2003; *ER*, NBC, 2003; *Triple Play* (pilot), 2004; *The Guardian*, CBS, 2004; *Miracle Run* (movie), Lifetime, 2004; *Summerland*, The WB, 2004-05; *CSI: Miami*, CBS, 2005; *If You Lived Here, You'd Be Home By Now* (movie), 2006; *NCIS*, CBS, 2006; *High School Musical*, The Disney Channel, 2006; *The Suite Life of Zack and Cody*, The Disney Channel, 2006; *Heist* (pilot), 2006; *The Replacements*, 2006; *High School Musical 2*, The Disney Channel, 2007. Film appearances include: *The Derby Stallion*, 2005; *Hairspray*, 2007. Stage appearances include: *Gypsy*, Pacific Conservatory of the Performing Arts, CA, c. 2000; *Peter Pan*; *Little Shop of Horrors*; *Auntie Mame*.

Awards: Teen Choice Award (with Vanessa Anne Hudgens) for TV-choice chemistry, for *High School Musical*, 2006; Teen Choice Award for TV-choice breakout star, for *High School Musical*, 2006; Hollywood Film Award (with others) for ensemble of the

AP Images

year, Hollywood Film Festival, for *Hairspray*, 2007; Young Hollywood Award for one to watch, Movieline, for *Hairspray*, 2007.

Sidelights

The star of the hit Disney Channel movies *High School Musical* and *High School Musical 2*, Zac Efron used the popularity of the movies to build his acting career. His appearances in the movies led to his being cast in a film musical, the 2007 remake of the hit indie comedy *Hairspray*. Praised for his abilities as a performer, he began acting as a young teenager, first appearing on stage and then primarily in roles on television. With fans around the world, Efron was regarded the ideal face for Disney. Helmi Yusof of Singapore's *Strait Times* wrote of Efron, "A model of decency, restraint and politeness, he was peachy-perfect (in terms of ratings) for tweens."

Efron was born on October 18, 1987, in San Luis Obispo, California. He was the son of David and Starla Efron. His father worked as an electrical engineer at a nuclear power plant, while his mother worked as a secretary at the same place. Efron was raised in Arroyo Grande, California, with his younger brother, Dylan. His family was firmly middle class, and he was not particularly interested in show business as a young child. Efron told Lesley O'Toole of London's *Daily Mail*, "I had a protected childhood. I was lucky."

Efron's acting career began when he was about eleven years old. He had already been displaying an unexpected singing ability, which impressed his parents. Young Efron could listen to any song on the radio and after memorizing the lyrics, sing it back with perfect pitch and tone. This skill compelled his parents to sign him up for singing lessons. A piano teacher also encouraged his abilities and helped him land theater roles.

Showing promise as an actor and singer, young Efron was cast in a theatrical production of *Gypsy* at the Pacific Academy of the Performing Arts. It ran for 90 performances, and Efron decided he wanted an acting career. He continued to appear on stage in roles in regional productions of *Peter Pan, Little Shop of Horrors,* and *Mame,* among others. He primarily regarded acting as something he did for fun.

Efron's work on the stage attracted the attention of professional talent agents. Signing with an agent, Efron began making the three-hour drive to Los Angeles with his mother to audition for roles. He made the leap to television in his early teens. Efron began with guest spots on shows such as *Firefly* in 2002 (his first television role), *ER* in 2003, and *The Guardian* in 2004. Efron also had parts in pilots such as *The Big Wide World of Carl Laemke* in 2003 and *Triple Play* in 2004, but neither show was picked up for full production.

In 2004, Efron landed his first regular role on a television show when he was cast as Cameron Bale on The WB series *Summerland*. Efron played his girl-crazy character for a season. While appearing on *Summerland*, Efron expanded his acting abilities by challenging himself in the roles he assumed. For example, in 2004, he played Steven Morgan, an autistic child in the Lifetime television movie *Miracle Run*.

Though Efron's acting career continued to grow, he did not take it particularly seriously until he reached the age of 18. About this time, he appeared in his first film, 2005's *The Derby Stallion*. Returning to television, he then appeared in the 2006 television movie *If You Lived Here, You'd Be Home By Now* and in guest spots on shows such as *NCIS* and *The Suite Life of Zack and Cody*. More importantly, Efron had the breakout role of his young career in the 2006 television movie, *High School Musical*.

Airing on the Disney Channel for the first time in January of 2006, the low-budget *High School Musical* became a massive ratings juggernaut. It drew ever-increasing audiences with repeated airings on the network and attracted passionate young viewers. Originally *High School Musical* was not expected to be much more than another movie on the Disney Channel. Efron told Richard Ouzounian of the *Toronto Star*, "We made the movie with low expectations. And, initially, there was no phenomenon. But after we signed the contracts for the second movie, suddenly, pandemonium broke loose and there we were on *Good Morning, America*."

High School Musical eventually became a worldwide hit, attracting at least 200 million viewers in more than 100 countries, and it was regarded as the most successful movie made for television ever. The compact disc of the movie's soundtrack was also the bestseller of the year. Efron was but one young performer who saw his star rise because of his work in the G-rated *High School Musical,* as his Troy Belton was the male lead. In the movie, he played the captain of the basketball team who is compelled to audition for the school's musical production, nabs the lead, and finds love with new student Gabriella (played by Vanessa Anne Hudgens). Critics often compared the plot to the popular film *Grease.*

There was a backlash with the success, however. Efron became a target because he was not actually singing in the movie. *High School Musical* featured another male voice mixed in with his own. Some sources claim his singing voice was totally dubbed with the voice of Drew Seeley because the singing parts were not really compatible with Efron's range. He also did not really appear on the soundtrack album. Because this information became public, Efron was sometimes put in an awkward situation in interviews and had to diverge from the message Disney wanted its young stars to promote. He told Ramin Setoodeh of *Newsweek:* "We were all given talking points. When *High School Musical* became successful, that's when we found ourselves having to backtrack."

While Efron's career was taking off through the *High School Musical* phenomenon, he continued his education. He was a good student and considered himself somewhat nerdy. Efron graduated from his local Arroyo Grande High School in 2006. Putting any ideas about college aside, Efron focused on his burgeoning career. As *High School Musical* continued to air on the Disney Channel, Efron looked to build on his success with his first major film role.

Efron landed a part in the remake of *Hairspray,* released in 2007. Originally a film directed by John Waters in 1988, *Hairspray* had been adapted as a hit

Broadway musical which ran for about five years. Efron appeared in the filmed remake based primarily on the musical. He played Link Larkin, a popular boy in school who dances on the local television program, *The Corny Collins Show*. Efron's Link falls in love with Tracy Turnblad, an overweight girl from the wrong side of the tracks who can dance and does not share racial prejudices held by many white people of the time. Playing Link allowed Efron to show off his dancing, acting, and singing ability.

Efron was cast in part because he would attract his fans from *High School Musical*. One of *Hairspray*'s producers, Neil Meron, told Ben Nuckols of the Associated Press that Efron was "not only right for the role, but God bless him, he brings with him all of teen idol-dom."

Later in 2007, Efron also garnered attention for his role in the follow-up *High School Musical 2*. Like its predecessor, this production was extremely popular among Disney Channel viewers, aired worldwide, and was merchandized in every possible way. In the movie, Efron's Troy and the other teen characters from *High School Musical* spend the summer vacation after their junior year at East High working at a country club in Albuquerque where school diva Sharpay is a member. Much romance ensues amid the singing and dancing as Sharpay tries to lure Troy from his girlfriend, Gabriella.

Efron compared the plot to the film *Dirty Dancing*, as it was a bit more mature in terms of plot and music than *High School Musical*. He was also allowed to sing without any vocal support in *High School Musical 2*, a negotiating point for his appearance in the sequel. He contributed his own vocals to this movie's soundtrack as well.

Critics praised Efron's work in the role and *High School Musical 2* as a whole. Mary McNamara wrote in the *Los Angeles Times*, "*High School Musical 2* is zippier, bouncier, prettier, more soulful, and even more musical than its predecessor, and that's saying something." Commenting specifically on Efron, she noted, "Efron brings more emotional heft to Troy than was evidence in *HSM*.... Efron has all the handsome enthusiasm and grace of an old-fashioned movie musical star."

Efron's acting career continued to develop after *High School Musical 2*. He was in discussion regarding starring in *High School Musical 3*, which would cover the East High students' senior year and might be produced for the big screen, as well as another film,

the comedy *Seventeen*. Efron was also being considered for a role in a remake of the 1984 film *Footloose*. He ultimately planned on moving away from musicals, telling O'Toole of London's *Daily Mail*, "I could act, sing, and fake my way through a dance. But singing and being in musicals wasn't what I set out to do. It happened along the way, but I don't want it to be a major part of my career." He definitely did not want to have a singing career.

Hollywood was divided on what path Efron should take in order to have a long-term, successful career as an actor, but insiders agreed it would not be easy. Casting director Joseph Middleton told Rachel Abramowitz of the *Los Angeles Times*: "Everything is pretty much open to him. There's no stigma attached yet. You're going to have those directors for whom he's going to have to prove himself. He may not be offered the part, but he will have the opportunity to read for the part, and he's a really good actor."

No matter where his career took him, Efron remained fundamentally humble. He told Ouzounian of the *Toronto Star*, "They tell kids that what's really important in life is following your dreams and truly being yourself. Hey, if it happened to me, then, man, it can happen to anybody." He also insisted success had not changed him. Efron told Yusof of Singapore's *Strait Times*, "I haven't changed much since my career took off in a big way. Sure, I get to travel more as an actor now. But I'll still go home after that and do the same things. I'm still a regular kid."

Selected discography

(Contributor) *High School Musical*, Disney, 2006.
(Contributor) *High School Musical 2*, Disney, 2007.
(Contributor) *Hairspray* (soundtrack), New Line Records, 2007.

Sources

Books

Contemporary Theatre, Film, and Television, vol. 74, Thomson Gale, 2007.

Periodicals

Associated Press, July 19, 2007.
Daily Mail (London, England), August 31, 2007, p. 48.

Los Angeles Times, August 16, 2007, p. C1; August 17, 2007, p. E1; August 27, 2007, p. E1.

Newsweek, August 6, 2007, p. 56.

Strait Times (Singapore), August 31, 2007.

Toronto Star, August 4, 2007, p. E3.

Toronto Sun, July 22, 2007, p. TV2.

Washington Post, August 12, 2007, p. N1.

Online

"Zac Efron," Internet Movie Database, http://www.imdb.com/name/nm1374980/ (November 6, 2007).

—*A. Petruso*

Alber Elbaz

Fashion designer

Born Albert Elbaz, in 1961, in Casablanca, Morocco; son of a hairdresser and Allegria Elbaz (a painter and waitress). *Education:* Earned degree from Shenkar College of Textile Technology and Fashion, c. 1986.

Addresses: *Home*—Paris, France. *Office*—Jeanne Lanvin S.A., 15, rue du Faubourg Saint-Honoré, 75008 Paris, France.

Career

Designer for an evening- and bridalwear company, George F, in New York City, c. 1986-89; assistant to designer Geoffrey Beene, c. 1989-96; creative director, Guy Laroche, Paris, 1996-99; designer for Rive Gauche ready-to-wear line, Yves Saint Laurent Couture, Paris, 1998-99; designer for Krizia Top, c. 2000; creative director for women's ready-to-wear and accessories, House of Lanvin, Paris, 2001—.

Awards: Best international designer, Council of Fashion Designers of America, 2005; Légion d'honneur, Republic of France, 2007.

Sidelights

In 2001, Moroccan-born designer Alber Elbaz took over as the design director of Lanvin, and began turning out women's collections that have given France's oldest house of couture a much-needed twenty-first century remake. Elbaz's newest seasonal offerings at Lanvin are almost always greeted effusively by the fashion press, and his dresses are a favorite of affluent, anonymous clients and red-carpet celebrities alike. However, the rotund, unassuming tastemaker remains a remarkably unpretentious figure in the cutthroat, ego-driven world of high-end fashion. "I compare my job to being the maitre d' at the Ritz," he told *Times* of London journalist Lisa Armstrong. "You try to direct everyone but the minute you feel you're one of the crowd and start acting snobby it's very dangerous." In 2007, he became one of the rare handful of foreign-born luminaries ever to be awarded France's prestigious Légion d'honneur medal.

Elbaz was named "Albert" by his parents when he was born in 1961, but later dropped the "t" to ensure its proper, French-language pronunciation. His early years were spent in the legendary Moroccan city of Casablanca, but his Jewish parents later resettled their four children in Tel Aviv, Israel. His father was a hairdresser, and died when Elbaz was 15, which forced his artist-mother to take a job as a waitress to support the family. Elbaz inherited his mother's creative talents, and was drawing by the time he reached school age. He was particularly fascinated by women's clothes, even at an early age. "When I was nine, I gave my teacher a notebook full of pictures of all the clothes she wore during that year," he recalled in an interview with the *Independent*'s Susannah Frankel. An asthma sufferer, he was also markedly uninterested in sports, telling Frankel that "when we were divided into teams for any kind of sport, nobody wanted me. I was always left till last and then it was like—you take Alber. My mother told me once that she asked them if it was normal for her son—her macho son—to be drawing all the time instead of playing football."

As a young man, Elbaz completed a mandatory stint in the Israeli Defense Forces, but his poor health resulted in an army job arranging cultural events for troops and at retirement homes for senior citizens. Following his discharge, he spent four years at the Shenkar College of Textile Technology and Fashion in Ramat Gan near Tel Aviv, and after graduating in the mid-1980s moved to New York City with $800 his mother had given him. He found work for a Garment District company that made eveningwear and bridal dresses, which he realized was a rather humble way to begin his career in fashion. "Coming from the country I came from, I had no choice," he told Frankel in the *Independent*. "There was no glamour, no wow; you just got there, did the patterns, checked the prices. It was more like doing a jigsaw puzzle than an act of creation. That taught me about fashion as a business."

After two years there, Elbaz came to the attention of Dawn Mello, who was at the time an executive vice president at Gucci, the luxury-goods label. Mello was searching for a new designer to help revamp Gucci's less-than-stylish image at the time, and though she felt the sketches Elbaz submitted were not in the right direction she wanted for Gucci, she recognized his budding talent and introduced him to American designer Geoffrey Beene, who hired him as a design assistant. Beene ran a highly successful atelier and was considered one of the leading American fashion visionaries, respected for his technical skills as well as a habit of turning out well-made collections that rejected prevailing trends in favor of a cool classicism. Elbaz would spend seven formative years at Beene, later telling *Sunday Times* journalist Colin McDowell, "I learnt everything from Mr. Beene."

In 1996, Elbaz moved to Paris to take a job as creative director for Guy Laroche, a French fashion house whose eponymous designer had died a few years earlier. Elbaz designed four collections for Laroche over the next two years which were deemed a hit at the biannual Paris Fashion Week previews, where designers present their newest wares for store buyers and journalists. Reviewing this debut in the *New York Times*, Constance C. R. White noted that

"Elbaz worked for Geoffrey Beene for seven years, so his [new] employers no doubt thought him up to the task of mastering the precise cut that is in part responsible for the definitive French look." Of his fall/winter 1997 line, White judged it a success, asserting that "Elbaz has a nice touch on the whole. He has brought a breath of fresh air to a house about to die of asphyxiation."

In June of 1998, Elbaz won one of the most coveted titles in French—and international—couture when designer Yves Saint Laurent hired him to revive the company's ready-to-wear line, sold under the Rive Gauche label. Both the reclusive Saint Laurent and his business partner Pierre Berge believed Elbaz to be gifted enough to take on the job at the company, which had been breaking new ground in women's fashions since the early 1960s, having popularized first the pant suit for women later that decade and then ethnic-inspired clothing in the 1970s. The new designer's highly anticipated collections presented on Paris runways throughout 1999 were met with mixed reviews. Living up to the standards of a living legend was impossible, Elbaz later reflected in an interview with Sally Singer for *Vogue*. "I felt like the son-in-law in that house. I got into a family, a royal family, and I had to perform. Everything I did I questioned myself: Is it too Saint Laurent or not enough Saint Laurent? That is wrong in design. It should be fluid."

Elbaz retreated from view for most of 2000, avoiding the gossipy hotbed of the fashion world by traveling across India and the Far East; he even contemplated a return to school to fulfill his parents' career dream for him—to become a doctor. He returned, however, when he was offered a post with the Italian sportswear and accessories-maker Krizia to create a new line for the label called Krizia Top, but he lasted just three months and left after creative disagreements with Mariuccia Mandelli, the label's founder. In the fall of 2001, he was hired as creative director for women's ready-to-wear and accessories at the House of Lanvin, an even more venerable French house whose 1889 origins made it the country's oldest house of couture still in operation.

Founded by dressmaker and milliner Jeanne Lanvin, the house was now owned by a Taiwanese publishing tycoon, Shaw-Lan Wang, who promised Elbaz full creative freedom. Elbaz's first Lanvin collection debuted in March of 2002 in Paris, and earned accolades from the fashion press, with Cathy Horyn of the *New York Times* assessing the clothes as "handsome, with distinctive details, like silver sequins scattered over a scissored chiffon evening dress. The day clothes had an uncomplicated chic missing from fashion.... Elbaz obviously did his homework. The clothes have enough identifying references to the style of Jeanne Lanvin, but he left room to add his own perspective. It was a great debut."

Elbaz's next effort, the spring ready-to-wear line shown later in 2002 in Paris, also earned rave reviews, especially the bejeweled or beribboned black dresses. "The fashion press quickly fell in love with this image of sweet gentility and Lanvin, a label that had been pretty much forgotten, has become one of the highlights of Paris fashion week," declared *Guardian* writer Hadley Freeman. Elbaz's collections that followed scored equally impressive plaudits for their originality and cohesive reinterpretation of Lanvin's long, illustrious legacy. *Vogue* lauded his spring/summer 2005 collection as the pace-setter for that season, singling out his belted trench coats and ballerina skirts as "classical, elegant, and modern.... These were alluring clothes with those special details that make a woman want to feast on their chic."

Two years after Elbaz took over at Lanvin, sales for its ready-to-wear collections had increased tenfold, and the company was on firm financial footing thanks to its cautionary spending on advertising dollars—unlike many top fashion houses, which have marketing budgets in the millions range. Instead, word of mouth and a well-heeled roster of fashionista clients had landed Elbaz's designs at Lanvin on the habitual must-have lists for scores of well-dressed trendsetters on both sides of the Atlantic. Noting his infamous ouster by the high-profile Tom Ford at Yves Saint Laurent, the *New York Times*'s fashion critic Horyn asserted that "Elbaz's success at Lanvin serves as a kind of vindication for talent over the cult of personality." In 2005, he was honored with the international designer of the year award from the Council of Fashion Designers of America, one of the industry's highest honors.

Elbaz's dresses have graced the red-carpet appearances of a long list of international stylesetters, from actresses Nicole Kidman and Gwyneth Paltrow to fashion icons like the model Kate Moss and film director Sofia Coppola. He has made pointed remarks in the press about the latter-day practice of licensing designer labels for mass-produced luxury goods, as many top design houses have done to increase brand visibility and boost profit. "When I work with my customers, I see the comfort, happiness, and

even safety that a woman gains from putting on a beautiful dress," he told the *Sunday Times'* McDowell. "You can't achieve that with the overproduction that comes from a commercial ambition to fill five floors of a designer tower with merchandise." His sole concession to commerce has been the development of a fragrance, Rumeur, launched in 2006.

Elbaz has also stated on several occasions that he has no higher ambitions than to stay on at Lanvin for a few more years then retire permanently, noting that his boss, Madame Wang, took a risk in hiring him after the Yves Saint Laurent debacle, and that he feels a strong sense of gratitude to her. Loyalty was a value he learned to prize from his stint in the Israeli Defense Forces, he told *New York Times* writer Elizabeth Hayt. "In the army, you know someone is behind you. You depend on him. Fashion is a business, but not a Swiss watch business. It's very personal. As a designer, sometimes they like you, and other times they throw you to the dogs. Loyalty impresses me."

Elbaz is an avowed workaholic who considers a vacation an unnecessary stress-inducing event. Instead he works 12-hour days, and then retires to his Paris home to read or watch television. Even his relatively long stint at Lanvin, and the resounding praise for his designs, has not inured him to the vagaries of the fickle fashion world. "The big difference between now and five years ago is that it's more neurotic," he told Lisa Armstrong in a *Harper's Bazaar* interview in 2005. "More scary, I'm just waiting for tragedy. You can't imagine the agony after each show."

Sources

Guardian (London, England), October 2, 2004, p. 58.
Harper's Bazaar, September 2005, p. 382.
Independent (London, England), September 16, 2006, p. 14.
New York Times, March 17, 1997; November 8, 1998; March 11, 2002; October 5, 2004.
New York Times Magazine, September 25, 2005, p. 32.
Sunday Times (London, England), January 14, 2007, p. 20.
Times (London, England), May 17, 2004, p. 11.
Vogue, December 2004, p. 88; March 2005, p. 512.
WWD, March 8, 1999, p. 12. .

—*Carol Brennan*

Lynda Fassa

Founder of Green Babies, Inc.

Born c. 1963; married Hossein Fassa (a company executive); children: Layla, Mina, Nadia.

Addresses: *Home*—Westchester, NY. *Office*—Green Babies, Inc., 28 Spring St., Tarrytown, NY 10591-5025.

Career

Worked as a model after the age of 16, and in advertising and marketing before founding Green Babies, Inc., 1994; first book, *Green Babies, Sage Moms: The Ultimate Guide to Raising Your Organic Baby*, published by New American Library, 2008.

Sidelights

Founded in 1994, Lynda Fassa's Green Babies, Inc. was one of the first makers of organic-cotton clothing for infants and children. Since then, Fassa and her business-partner husband have carefully grown their venture to meet increasing consumer demand for safer, less environmentally toxic products. In 2008, she wrote her first book, *Green Babies, Sage Moms: The Ultimate Guide to Raising Your Organic Baby*, a comprehensive how-to guide for embracing a greener lifestyle for mothers-to-be and new parents.

Fassa began modeling at age 16, and had a thriving career in Paris by the early 1980s with one of the top agencies, Ford Models. She later moved on to advertising and marketing, married Hossein Fassa, who was director of a well-known drama school, and settled in New York City. The first of their three daughters, Layla, was born in 1993, and Fassa soon realized how wrong her prenatal imagining of the blissful new life with a happy baby had been—Layla was a colicky newborn who cried often and for hours on end. Fassa finally figured out that her daughter was allergic to the cotton that was a part of nearly everything she wore. As Fassa wrote in *Green Babies, Sage Moms,* one day she came across a *New York Times* article "about Texas farmers reverting to organic cotton farming, working the land as past generations had. I learned about the perils of conventional cotton; how, unbeknownst to most folks, this great American crop was causing sickness in farm workers and devastating the agricultural landscape because of the amount of chemicals it guzzled."

Fassa tracked down some of that organic cotton in knitted, fabric-bolt form, and sewed her first all-organic baby clothes by hand. She also taught herself to how to screen-print with art-store supplies, and began making rompers with colorful, bold graphics and clever sayings. One of her first successful items was a romper that bore the slogan, "Give Peas a Chance." Initially, she made all the items by hand in the East Village apartment she shared with her husband and daughter, and sold them by visiting Manhattan baby-clothing boutiques. Eventually she found a family-owned sewing operation in one of the outer boroughs and began contracting out the work, which allowed her to design a full range of baby gear and children's wear.

A few years later, after the birth of a second daughter, Fassa and her husband moved out of the city and settled in Tarrytown, one of the quaint villages of the Hudson River Valley north of Manhattan. Their business continued to grow in the late 1990s as consumers became more aware of organic farming and its short- and long-term benefits, and Hossein Fassa left his job to help his wife run Green Babies full time. The business eventually grew too big for their home, and they set up an office in an old fire station in nearby Irvington, another Hudson Valley town.

The Fassas nearly went out of business, however, after the first dot-com boom of the late 1990s went bust, taking under a new online retailer that was one of their biggest accounts at the time. "I would definitely never ever do this again if I knew how difficult it was," Fassa told Barbara Whitaker in a *New York Times* interview in 2004. A year later, however, Green Babies won an important new client, and one with an enviable track record: The thriving health-food grocery chain Whole Foods began to introduce apparel in its stores, and Green Babies was one of the oldest all-organic clothing brands it carried. Whole Foods' expansion into apparel and accessories seemed to show just how much consumer tastes had changed since Fassa launched her business back a decade earlier, as Americans committed to eating organic began to embrace the idea of an all-organic lifestyle.

Sensing a hunger for even more information, Fassa wrote her first book, *Green Babies, Sage Moms: The Ultimate Guide to Raising Your Organic Baby*, as a bible for new parents. Published in 2008, her how-to guide featured a wealth of practical information specific to pregnancy and protecting one's child from environmental toxins, from the threats posed by prenatal hair-salon visits to where to find non-toxic crib bedding. She also included recipes for all-natural, pesticide-free baby food, and her advice was interspersed with contributions from other green experts.

According to Fassa, common household cleaning products pose just one of the dangers to everyone, not just pregnant women and newborns. In a situation similar to the baffling colic suffered by her first daughter, Fassa herself turned out to have a sensitivity to certain chemicals. She had long been conscious that she had an aversion to household chores, and even suffered headaches on heavy-duty cleaning days. "I know this sounds really dumb, but I did not associate it with what I was using," she told David Schepp, a reporter for the *Journal News* of White Plains. "I just associated it with the act of cleaning." In her book, she provides scores of recipes for safe, economical cleaning products made from vinegar, baking soda, and other common household staples.

Fassa is still committed to the same principles embodied by that first batch of organically grown Texas cotton she bought. She points out that organic farming may even bring a potential economic revolution in Africa, where a few progressive nations have returned to growing crops by centuries-old organic methods. Responsible, chemical-free farming is a rebuke to the large U.S. agribusiness giants, she notes, which peddle genetically modified seeds that require "synthetic pesticides and fertilizers; some were even genetically engineered to produce only sterile seeds," she writes in *Green Babies, Sage Moms.* "The natural cycle of 'grow, sell and save to replant' was broken and farmers were forced to use their profits to buy more seeds, pesticides, and fertilizers from the same food giants year after year. Like sharecroppers, the farmers remained impoverished as they grew crops that someone else would profit from."

Fassa and her husband have three daughters and are pleased that consumers are so much more knowledgeable about organic crops than back when they began Green Babies. The next step, she told Schepp, is to bring public policy in line with consumer awareness. "The green movement is the revolution," she said in the *Journal News* interview. "This is the new Renaissance, and we need to be leading it, not just staggering along behind."

Selected writings

Green Babies, Sage Moms: The Ultimate Guide to Raising Your Organic Baby, New American Library, 2008.

Sources

Periodicals

Booklist, January 1, 2008, p. 30.
Children's Business, August 2001, p. 22.
Fort Wayne News Sentinel (Fort Wayne, IN), June 22, 2005.
Journal News (White Plains, NY), December 25, 2007.
New York Times, February 15, 2004; March 5, 2006.
White Plains Times (White Plains, NY), August 10, 2007.

Online

"A Clean Sweep," Grist, http://www.grist.org/ feature/2007/09/21/cleaning/ (May 13, 2008).
"Who We Are," Green Babies, http://www.green babies.com/who_we_are.htm (May 13, 2008).

—*Carol Brennan*

Drew Gilpin Faust

AP Images

President of Harvard University

Born Catharine Drew Gilpin, September 18, 1947, in New York, N.Y.; daughter of McGhee Tyson Gilpin (a horse breeder) and Catharine Ginna (Mellick) Gilpin; married Stephen Faust (divorced, 1976); married Charles Ernest Rosenberg (a professor), June 7, 1980; children: Jessica Marion (from second marriage), Leah (stepdaughter). *Education:* Bryn Mawr College, B.A., 1968; University of Pennsylvania, M.A., 1971, Ph.D., 1975.

Addresses: *Office*—Office of the President, Harvard University, Massachusetts Hall, Cambridge, MA 02138.

Career

University of Pennsylvania, Philadelphia, senior fellow, 1975-76, assistant professor, 1976-80, associate professor of American civilization, 1980-84, chairman of department, 1980-83 and 1984-86, professor 1984-88, Stanley Sheerr Professor of History, 1988-89, director of women's studies, 1996-2000, Annenberg Professor of History, 1989-2000; Harvard University, Cambridge, MA, professor of history, beginning 2001, founding dean of the Radcliffe Institute for Advanced Study, beginning 2001, professor of Afro-American studies, beginning 2002, Lincoln Professor of History, beginning 2003, president, 2007—.

Sidelights

In February of 2007 Drew Gilpin Faust was chosen as the 28th president of Harvard University, the oldest institution of higher learning in the United States whose founding even pre-dates America's as a nation. Faust had been at the school just a few years, having spent much of her academic career at the University of Pennsylvania, where she was a professor of history and specialist in the U.S. Civil War period. She was 59 years old at the time of her new appointment, and had come of age in an era when women were not even allowed as full students at Harvard and the other schools of the Ivy League. "One of the things that I think characterizes my generation—that characterizes me, anyway, and others of my generation—is that I've always been surprised by how my life turned out," she told *New York Times* writer Sara Rimer. "I've always done more than I ever thought I would. Becoming a professor—I never would have imagined that."

Born in New York City in 1947, Faust was named after her mother, Catharine Mellick Gilpin, but her family called her by her middle name, Drew, from an early age. The Gilpins lived in Clarke County, Virginia, where her father, McGhee Gilpin, was a breeder of thoroughbred horses. It was an affluent county in the northern part of the state, known for its nineteenth-century architecture and picturesque estates. Faust grew up with three brothers, and had a difficult time adjusting to the different behavioral standards of the era that were demanded of Southern women, even young girls, who were expected to be quiet, demure, and remain close to home even as adults. She had memorable battles with her mother over these issues, and recalled that she was often told, "it's a man's world, sweetie, and the sooner you learn that the better off you'll be," she recalled in the *New York Times* interview with Rimer.

Faust also began questioning the segregated nature of her Southern world when she was still very young, and recalled hearing a news report one day over a statewide movement in Virginia to reject the landmark ruling of the U.S. Supreme Court in 1954 in the famous *Brown v. Board of Education* case, which outlawed segregated schools. Upon listening to the news report, she suddenly realized that she had no black classmates at her Millwood elementary school, and even asked one of her family's African-American household employees that if she painted her face black, would that mean she would not be allowed into her school? His evasive answer let her know this was a topic on par with religion or sex—that is, never discussed in polite society—and her interest in the civil rights movement began to grow. She even sent a letter to U.S. President Dwight D. Eisenhower as a fifth-grader in 1957 in which she voiced her support for integration. The letter wound up in the Eisenhower Presidential Library, and many years later Faust tracked it down. "Please Mr. Eisenhower please try and have schools and other things accept colored people," she had urged, according to a 2003 article she wrote for *Harvard Magazine*.

In her teens, Faust attended Concord Academy, a private boarding school in Concord, Massachusetts, that was an all-women institution at the time. In the early 1960s, many of the nation's elite schools remained closed to women, and she might have entered Princeton University as a "legacy," meaning she had family members who had graduated—in this case, her father and several others—and was to be granted preferred admissions status, but the New Jersey school did not admit its first women undergraduates until 1969. This was a year after Faust graduated with an undergraduate degree in history from Bryn Mawr College in Pennsylvania, considered one of the top women's schools of the era.

During her college years, Faust continued the social activism of her teen years, when she took part in civil-rights marches and anti-Vietnam War rallies. At Bryn Mawr, she and other students agitated to abolish what were known as "parietal rules" which, she explained in a commencement address she delivered at the school in 2001, "were the restrictions that required us to be back in the dorm by 2 a.m. and that did not permit men in the halls except dur-

ing certain very limited hours," she said in her speech, which appeared on the college's Web site. "I take some satisfaction in the fact that not only was women's freedom from these rules achieved but this is now so taken for granted no one even knows what parietals were."

Faust went on to earn two graduate degrees from the University of Pennsylvania, completing her doctorate in American civilization in 1975. Often referred to in its shortened form of Penn, this was also one of the eight "Ivy League" schools, along with Princeton, Harvard, and five other East Coast colleges, but had a longer record in admitting female students and hiring female faculty members. After earning her Ph.D, she remained at the school as a senior fellow, and was hired as an assistant professor in 1976. Four years later, she was promoted to associate professor of American civilization and the department chair, and her career began to flourish. She was active on several campus committees, made contacts off-campus in professional organizations, and began writing well-received books on life in the pre-Civil War South, such as 1982's *James Henry Hammond and the Old South: A Design for Mastery*, the biography of a slaveholder.

Faust became a full professor at Penn in 1984, and the Annenberg Professor of History five years later. She also served as director of the women's studies program for a time in the late 1990s. Another book, *Mothers of Invention: Women of the Slaveholding South in the American Civil War*, was published in 1996 to effusive reviews in the academic press, and then reissued in trade paperback form a year later. In it, Faust drew upon the correspondence and diaries of 500 Southern women whose lives were drastically uprooted by the war and the end of slavery. Reviewing it for the *Historian*, Wendy Hamand Venet noted that Faust "provides convincing evidence that Confederate women, far from supporting Southern independence uncritically, resented the changes that the war forced upon them. Slavery became a burden, as mistresses reluctantly attempted to manage an increasingly unruly slave labor force in the absence of their husbands. Many had to cope with household drudgery for the first time in their lives when African Americans fled to advancing Union armies."

Faust was recruited by Harvard University and joined its faculty in 2001 as a professor of history. She was also hired to serve as the founding dean of the Radcliffe Institute for Advanced Study. Radcliffe College was once the women's school of Harvard, and when she arrived to head it the Institute was just a small, flagging unit on a campus rich with esteemed academic organizations, such as its Center for European Studies. Over the next five years, Faust worked to turn it into a respected center of interdisciplinary scholarship for researchers on gender.

Faust became Harvard's Lincoln Professor of History in 2003, and was named to head two separate task-force committees created by Harvard's president, Lawrence H. Summers, in 2005 in the wake of his controversial remarks about women and their intellectual aptitude. Speaking at a conference of the National Bureau of Economics Research (NBER) in January of 2005 Summers's speech discussed several possible reasons in response to the question of why there were so few female chairs of departments in math, engineering, and science. The difficulty presented by working extremely long hours in the first two decades of their careers, when many women were also new parents, was one reason they lagged behind the professional paces of their male colleagues, but Summers also noted that there was still ongoing research about "intrinsic aptitude," meaning that women were simply not born with the same intellectual capabilities as men. Summers' remarks made national headlines and rocked the Harvard campus and many others, too, where women had struggled to achieve the pay, perks, and respect commensurate with their achievements since the 1970s. Furthermore, it was not the first controversy in Summers' tenure as Harvard's president, and he was disliked by many faculty members for his autocratic style. Despite the creation of the task-force committees, whose goals were to hire and promote more women in the sciences, Summers was forced to resign in early 2006, effective June 30 of that year.

Faust's name was one of several advanced as possible successors, including former U.S. Department of Health and Human Services Secretary Donna Shalala, and Shirley Ann Jackson, the first African-American woman to earn a doctorate from the prestigious Massachusetts Institute of Technology. A Nobel Prize-winning chemist, Thomas R. Cech, was also on the list of finalists, but when he announced he was removing himself from the final list of candidates, Faust suddenly emerged as the most likely choice of the Harvard Corporation board, a six-member panel that governs the school, and the announcement that she was to become Harvard's next president was made over the second weekend in February.

Faust became the first woman to lead the school, which was founded in 1636 and is the oldest institution of higher learning in the United States. Even the governing board, founded in 1650 and formally known as the "President and Fellows of Harvard College," used a charter of governance that made it the oldest corporation in all of the Americas. Faust, noted *Christian Science Monitor* journalist Ben Arnoldy, "will not only sit at the pinnacle of higher education, but will oversee a budget on a par with top corporations. Of the 20 female CEOs in the Fortune 1000, only one runs a firm with assets greater than Harvard's." Unusually, Faust was also the first Harvard president without a Harvard degree to hold the office since 1672.

Faust joined an illustrious list of women heading Ivy League schools: Of the eight colleges or universities, fully half now were led by female presidents. Her husband, Charles Ernest Rosenberg, is a specialist in the history of American medicine and teaches at Harvard, and their daughter, Jessica, is a Harvard graduate. As president, Faust had even more ambitious plans for the generation of students to come. "None of us imagined that, in our lifetimes, four out of eight Ivy League presidents would be women, let alone considered that those presidents would be us," she was quoted as saying in an article by David Pluviose for *Diverse Issues in Higher Education*. "Now it is all the more important that this expansion of opportunity be demonstrable for members of other groups who have been discriminated against throughout history."

Selected writings

Nonfiction

A Sacred Circle: The Dilemma of the Intellectual in the Old South, 1840-1860, Johns Hopkins University Press, 1977.

The Ideology of Slavery: The Proslavery Argument in the Antebellum South, Louisiana State University Press, 1981.

James Henry Hammond and the Old South: A Design for Mastery, Louisiana State University Press, 1982.

The Creation of Confederate Nationalism: Ideology and Identity in the Civil War South, Louisiana State University Press, 1988.

Southern Stories: Slaveholders in Peace and War, University of Missouri Press, 1992.

A Riddle of Death: Mortality and Meaning in the American Civil War, Gettysburg College, 1995.

Mothers of Invention: Women of the Slaveholding South in the American Civil War, University of North Carolina Press, 1996; Vintage Books, 1997.

Sources

Periodicals

Christian Science Monitor, February 12, 2007, p. 1.
Chronicle of Higher Education, February 23, 2007.
Diverse Issues in Higher Education, March 22, 2007, p. 19.
Financial Times, April 27, 2007, p. 6.
Harvard Magazine, May-June 2003.
Historian, Spring 1998, p. 624.
New York Times, February 10, 2007; February 12, 2007.

Online

"Bryn Mawr College Convocation Address by Drew Gilpin Faust, Saturday, May 19, 2001," Bryn Mawr College, http://www.brynmawr.edu/news/2007-02-11/faust_speech.shtml (August 1, 2007).

—*Carol Brennan*

Dario Franchitti

Professional race car driver

Born May 19, 1973, in Edinburgh, Scotland; son of George (an ice-cream company owner) and Marina Franchitti; married Ashley Judd (an actress), December 12, 2001.

Addresses: *Home*—Franklin, TN. *Office*—c/o Indy Racing League, 4565 W. 16th St., Indianapolis, IN 46222.

Career

Won Scottish Junior Karting Championship, 1984, and British Junior Karting Championship, 1985 and 1986; joined Formula Vauxhall Series, c. 1990, and Formula Vauxhall Lotus circuit, 1992; raced in the English Formula Three circuit, 1994; with AMG Racing as a driver for German Touring Car series, 1995-97; became Championship Auto Racing Team (CART) driver, 1997, with Hogan Racing team; joined Team KOOL Green Honda/Reynard (later known as Andretti Green Racing), 1998; won Indianapolis 500, 2007.

Sidelights

Scottish race-car driver Dario Franchitti won the Indianapolis 500 in May of 2007, one of the most lucrative prizes in motor sports. His victory came as a surprise in the rain-plagued race, but was nonetheless enthusiastically celebrated by Franchitti, who is married to Hollywood star Ashley Judd. "I've been waiting for this day, and today it's finally good to get noticed," he was quoted as saying by Lars Anderson in *Sports Illustrated*.

Franchitti was born in 1973 in Edinburgh, Scotland, to Italian-heritage parents who were second-generation immigrants to the British Isles, and grew up in the suburb of Whitburn. His father owned several ice-cream parlors in Edinburgh, and was an amateur race car driver, a passion that Franchitti inherited. His career began as a youngster in go-kart competitions, and in 1984 the eleven-year-old Franchitti won the Scottish Junior Karting Championship. He followed it with two wins in the British Junior Karting Championships in 1985 and 1986, and by 1989 had progressed to a second-place finish in the British Senior Karting Championship that year.

Racing in the Formula Vauxhall Series as a junior driver, Franchitti scored a few impressive wins and came to the attention of Scottish auto-racing legend Jackie Stewart, who became his informal coach. Before he became Stewart's protégé, "I just drove every lap as hard as I could," Franchitti said in an interview with Andrew Longmore for the *Independent on Sunday*. "Jackie taught me to be faster and more consistent over the whole of a race." In 1992, Franchitti joined the Formula Vauxhall Lotus circuit, and won his first championship cup a year later. After a stint with the English Formula Three circuit, Franchitti was recruited by a prestigious outfit, AMG Racing, which is the sportscar-competition division of German automaker Mercedes-Benz. He spent two years driving a Mercedes C-class in German Touring Car series events, but failed to win any major competitions.

In 1997 Franchitti signed with Hogan Racing, a major player on the United States-based Championship Auto Racing Team (CART) circuit, and moved to the United States. A year later, he began driving for Team KOOL Green Honda/Reynard, which would later morph into Andretti Green Racing after a change in sponsors. He and Juan Pablo Montoya were the top two drivers in the CART series in 1999, but a pre-season test outing at a racetrack in Miami early in 2000 resulted in a broken pelvic bone and concussion that kept him from competing for much of 2000. In 2001, he won just one race, the Marconi Grand Prix of Cleveland, Ohio.

In the United States, the Championship Auto Racing Teams (CART) feature the best-known drivers, who are nevertheless relatively unknown outside of motor-racing enthusiasts. In Europe, the equivalent upper-echelon racing teams are the Formula One stars, whose exploits are chronicled endlessly in the tabloid press and who enjoy name recognition on par with that of soccer players and pop singers. Franchitti's decision to decamp to the U.S. circuit meant that he remained a relative unknown back in Scotland, where CART events are neither held nor followed in the sports pages, but he did begin to gain some press when he began dating Hollywood film actress Ashley Judd, daughter of country-music legend Naomi Judd.

In the 2002 season, Franchitti finished in fourth place, and also made his Indy 500 debut. This annual Memorial Day weekend event is the biggest auto-racing championship in the United States, and its television viewers make it one of the largest single-day sporting events in the world. Named for the Indianapolis Motor Speedway, the 500-mile race is the premier event in the Indy Racing League (IRL). IRL teams drive "formula" or open-wheel vehicles—denoting cars with oversized wheels on the outside of the vehicle designed to enhance performance at speeds with reach 225 miles per hour—much like the Formula One cars of European motor sports.

Franchitti finished in 19th place in the 2002 Indy 500, and after recovering from a motorcycle accident in 2003, won two Indy Car events in Wisconsin and Colorado in 2004. The next two years featured solid, but not winning finishes for Team Andretti Green, owned by Michael Andretti, son of racing legend Mario Andretti. He and his teammates took their starting positions at the 91st Indy 500 on May 27, 2007, under the threat of rain, and did 113 laps before the downpour began and the race was halted for more than two hours. When it resumed it went to 166 laps before race officials halted it for good and declared Franchitti the winner. His teammate, Tony Kanaan, had actually been in the lead, but was penalized for one of his pit-stops when the crew changed all of his tires, instead of just the flat one. It was a surprise victory for Franchitti against a crowded field, including two-time winner Helio Castroneves; prior to this, Franchitti had never made it past a sixth-place finish in four previous Indy 500 races.

Franchitti's wife ran down to greet him in her bare feet when he was declared the 2007 Indy 500 winner. He and Judd wed at Skibo Castle in Scotland in December of 2001, and settled in Franklin, Tennessee, a Nashville suburb that is also home to a long roster of contemporary country-music stars. Later that season, Franchitti walked away from a spectacular crash at the Firestone Indy 400 event in Brooklyn, Michigan, that involved five other vehicles and sent his own airborne. "I was just hoping it wasn't going to hurt when it came down," he replied in a post-race press conference when asked what he was thinking at that moment, according to the *Detroit Free Press*.

Well aware of the dangers of his sport, Franchitti still mourns the loss of his closest friend, driver Greg Moore, who died in a 1999 crash at the last CART event of the season in California. "Greg was the guy I competed with the hardest on the track, and he was the guy I had the most fun with away from the track, " he told David Tremayne, a journalist for the London newspaper the *Independent* just after his 2007 Indy 500 win. "He was going to be a champion many times over."

Sources

Detroit Free Press, August 6, 2007.
Guardian (London, England), September 9, 2002, p. 20.
Independent (London, England), May 29, 2007.
Independent on Sunday (London, England), April 18, 1999, p. 14.
New York Times, May 28, 2007.
Sports Illustrated, June 4, 2007, p. 60.
Sunday Times (London, England), March 26, 2000, p. 5.

—*Carol Brennan*

Lew Frankfort

Chief Executive Officer of Coach

Yoshikazu Tsuno/AFP/Getty Images

Born March 19, 1946, in New York, NY; son of a police officer and a homemaker; married Bobbie, c. 1976; children: Tamara, Alana, Sam. *Education:* Hunter College, B.A., 1967; Columbia University, M.B.A., 1969.

Addresses: *Home*—New York, NY. *Office*—Coach Inc., 516 W. 34th St., New York, NY 10001-1394.

Career

Commissioner, New York City Agency for Child Development, 1973-79; Coach Leatherware, Inc., vice president for business development, 1979-85, president, 1985-93, chair and chief executive officer, 1995—; also held various positions with the Sara Lee Corporation, Coach's parent company, 1985-2000, including chief executive officer of Coach Leatherware and Champion Products, 1991, chief executive officer of Sara Lee Accessories, 1991-94, and Sara Lee Corporation senior vice president, 1994-2000.

Sidelights

Lew Frankfort has spent much of his career with Coach Leatherware, Inc., the premium accessories brand, and has turned the company into a dominant force in American fashion. Board chair and chief executive officer (CEO) since 1995, he was also one of the highest paid CEOs in the United States who did not run a Wall Street firm such as an investment bank. Few criticized his exorbitant salary, however, for Coach loyalists and investors alike

were thrilled with both the product and the company's performance. Frankfort, noted *New York Times* retail-sector writers Michael Barbaro and Eric Dash, "has transformed Coach, once a niche player, into an international megabrand peddling luxury leather purses, flip-flops, and backpacks. He also pioneered an entirely new retailing category, known as affordable luxury. It was Coach, after all, that made it permissible, if not compulsory, for women to own not just one $250 handbag but several."

Frankfort was born on March 19, 1946, and grew up in the New York City borough of the Bronx. His father was a New York City police officer, and his mother was a homemaker. In his earliest years, Frankfort suffered from a speech impediment that garbled his words, but it abated by the time he began kindergarten. He was a political science major at Hunter College and, after graduating in 1967, went on to a graduate business degree at Columbia University. For a time, he took the standard route for recent M.B.A.-holders, with a job at an investment bank, but he soon realized he wanted a career that offered more meaningful work. Turning to the public sector, he was hired by the administration of New York's mayor, John V. Lindsay, and in 1973 he rose to become commissioner of the city's Agency for Child Development. He stayed on through the next mayoral administration but began searching for a new job when he was passed over for a promotion when a new mayor was elected in 1977.

Frankfort's public-service experience impressed Miles Cahn, the longtime head of Coach Leatherware. The company was founded in New York City in 1941 as a small leather-goods manufacturer whose workers produced mainly wallets and billfolds by hand. Cahn began at the company a few years later and eventually took over; he also added a new line of distinctive women's handbags made from leather specially treated in the same way that baseball mitts are and which grow supple with age. Cahn hired Frankfort as vice president for business development at Coach. In this new role, Frankfort began a profitable mail-order business and opened the company's first freestanding retail stores.

Coach was sold to the Sara Lee Corporation in 1985, and Frankfort became president of the Coach division. He held various other titles over the next decade, including chief executive officer of Coach Leatherware and Champion Products, chief executive officer of Sara Lee Accessories, senior vice president with Sara Lee, and president and chief executive officer of the Sara Lee Champion, Intimates & Accessories group. Frankfort focused, however, primarily on Coach, and in the late 1980s, the brand began to enjoy stronger sales thanks to his efforts. Despite the fact that the handbags never went on sale, certain Coach styles reached near-ubiquitous status by the early 1990s and even enjoyed a cult cache in Japan.

Frankfort was made chair and chief executive officer of Coach Leatherware in 1995, taking on the task of revitalizing a brand that had become so popular that sales had peaked and then began to decline, as younger, fashion-conscious buyers began favoring handbags from new designers such as Kate Spade. In 1996, he hired Reed Krakoff as the new president and creative director for Coach, who had successfully retooled the apparel brand Tommy Hilfiger USA. Krakoff created new lines, some made from a combination of fabric and leather that were more affordable; came up with a "C" logo that gave the brand's image a fresh, updated look; and opened new stores with a sleek new design.

Sara Lee spun off Coach into a publicly traded company in 2000, traded under the ticker symbol COH. Under Frankfort, Coach had continued to post impressive sales despite the fluctuations in consumer tastes over the years. This transition and market strength occurred at the same time that expensive designer "It" bags began to emerge as the must-have accessory of the season, but Coach still held on to an impressive market share of the high-end leather-goods business. Furthermore, as an independent, publicly traded company, it posted terrific earnings, rising from $64 million to $494 million between 2001 and 2006. During that same period, the price of its stock soared from $6 to $51.

Frankfort is believed to be the highest-paid CEO outside of Wall Street's banking and investment-firm ranks. In 2006, he earned $44.4 million, which put him in the same salary range as the heads of Citigroup and Goldman Sachs; that figure was also double the amount earned by Ralph Lauren himself. But as Frankfort pointed out in press interviews, about 90 percent of his pay was tied to Coach's stock performance, and had it not performed well for its investors, he would have wound up in the lowest pay rankings for American CEOs.

Married and the father of three grown children, Frankfort has houses in New Jersey and the Long Island summer resort of the Hamptons, and in 2004 he bought a coveted corner apartment in the Beresford, a famous building on Central Park West. The four-story apartment is located in one of the Beresford's three distinctive towers. Recalling his humble origins as the son of a cop, he is candid in some interviews about a recurring nightmare that occasionally disrupts his sleep—that he lives on a hill overlooking the Bronx streets of his childhood, and "with one misstep," he told *Business Week*'s Robert Berner, "I would slide and my house would slide right back into the Bronx."

Sources

Periodicals

BusinessWeek, June 9, 2003, pp. 86-87; March 29, 2004, p. 98; January 24, 2007.
Forbes, September 3, 2001, p. 86.
Investor's Business Daily, January 26, 2004, p. A3.
New York Times, April 8, 2007.
WWD, November 18, 2002, p. 18.

Online

BusinessWeek Online, January 24, 2007.

—*Carol Brennan*

Simon Fuller

Entertainment entrepreneur and television producer

Born May 17, 1960, in Hastings, England; son of a teacher.

Addresses: *Contact*—19 Entertainment Ltd., 33 Ransomes Dock, 35-37 Parkgate Rd., London, SW11 4NP, England. *Home*—London, England; France; Beverly Hills, CA. *Web site*—http://www.19.co.uk/.

Career

Began career managing British bands and disco halls, c. 1970s; talent scout for Chrysalis Records, early 1980s; founded and ran own entertainment management group, 19 Entertainment, 1985—; created highly successful British reality television show *Pop Idol,* 2001, and *American Idol,* 2002; director at CKX Entertainment, 2005—.

Awards: Named to *Time* magazine's Top 100 list of the world's most influential people, 2007.

Sidelights

British entertainment mogul Simon Fuller is the mastermind behind the outrageously popular *Idol* franchise, the most successful television format in entertainment history. Fuller launched *Pop Idol* in Britain in 2001 and has since seen spin-offs reach into 30 countries. *American Idol,* as the series is called in the United States, draws more than 40 million viewers during its season finale each year. Fuller began his career more than 20 years ago as a record producer and manager and has overseen such acts as Annie Lennox, Carrie Underwood, and the Spice Girls. He has collected more No. 1 hits than any other manager in music history. In 2007, *Time* magazine named Fuller to its "Top 100" list of the most influential people in the world. According to the *Guardian,* in 2007, Fuller was worth an estimated 450 million British pounds—or about $900 million.

Fuller was born on May 17, 1960, in Hastings, England. His ties to the entertainment industry reach back to his grandfather, who worked as a stand-up comic and acrobat. For a time, Fuller's father was a member of the Royal Air Force. Later, he worked as an overseas schoolteacher, and the young Fuller spent a portion of his childhood living on the Mediterranean island of Cyprus and also in the West African country of Ghana. Speaking to the *Observer*'s Caspar Llewellyn Smith, Fuller acknowledged that living abroad in unfamiliar territories helped him develop an ease and grace with new people and new situations, which has helped in his people-oriented career. "It made me very open-minded and ready to accept new experiences."

Eventually, Fuller's family settled back in Hastings, England. During his teen years, Fuller ran his school's music club and managed a band for some classmates. Fuller's interest in music prompted him into an early career running local discos, a job he worked in lieu of attending college. This was during the highly popular punk-rock era, a movement that exploded in England during the late 1970s. Fuller found himself listening to bands such as the Clash, the Buzzcocks, and the Jam.

In time, Fuller landed a job as a talent scout for Chrysalis Records, the British label behind the Grammy Award-winning British rockers Jethro Tull. In 1985, Fuller quit Chrysalis Records and set out on his own as manager of synthesizer master Paul Hardcastle, a British musician who was launching a solo music career after playing keyboards for other bands. In 1985, Hardcastle released "19," an entrancing anti-Vietnam war anthem that hit No. 1 on the British charts. Energized by the success of his client, Fuller named his management company 19 Entertainment in honor of Hardcastle's hit single. The next big name Fuller signed was singer-songwriter Cathy Dennis, who composed several early 1990s pop hits. After the Eurythmics split in 1990, Fuller began managing Annie Lennox's highly successful solo career. With a handful of flourishing clients, Fuller was a millionaire by the age of 30.

In the mid-1990s, Fuller made a name for himself as manager of the British female pop group the Spice Girls. Fuller cannot claim credit for putting the group together; he simply took over the reins and embarked on a strategic marketing campaign that kept the Spice Girls in the media spotlight, which in turn made their albums sell. With the Spice Girls, Fuller ushered in a new management style. Rather than concentrate on their music, Fuller focused on their commercial possibilities, turning the band into a brand and landing the Spice Girls lucrative sponsorship deals with Pepsi, Polaroid, Sony, and Impulse deodorant. Under Fuller's guidance, the Spice Girls became an international brand with their "girl power" catchphrase. Each member of the quintet adopted a charming alias that matched her personality. These nicknames were used as a marketing ploy, played up in interviews, videos, and press releases. Geri Halliwell thus became "Ginger Spice," Melanie Brown was dubbed "Scary Spice," Victoria Adams was "Posh Spice," Melanie Chisholm became "Sporty Spice," and Emma Bunton was christened "Baby Spice." The nicknames helped boost the group's appeal by offering a range of personalities with which fans identified.

As per Fuller's suggestion, the Spice Girls made appearances at music industry events long before they released their first song. As a result, hype surrounding the Spice Girls was running high when they re-leased their 1996 debut single "Wannabe," which hit No. 1 in the United Kingdom and went on to top the charts in more than 30 countries. Under Fuller's watchful eye, the group sold about 40 million albums worldwide, though some critics derided their music as bubblegum pop. "Simon Fuller's great skill is to turn people into brands," one market analyst told the Observer's Oliver Marre. "And for that, it doesn't really matter who the people are, as long as they're willing and there's a platform around."

The Spice Girls were willing to do whatever Fuller said—for a while. In time, their careers took off, but their relationship with Fuller soured. There were rumors he kept tabs on them with private detectives and also allegedly harped on the women about their diets. There was also tension surrounding his relationship with Baby Spice. Some analysts say, however, that what really upset the Spice Girls was the fact that under Fuller's management deal, he was bringing in more money than any individual Spice Girl. As their manager, Fuller took a 20 percent cut on all Spice Girls merchandise. Despite their international success, the singers fired Fuller in 1997 then struggled to manage their own affairs. Less than two years later, the group had split.

Undaunted, Fuller moved on to his next project—the creation of S Club 7, also known as the S Club. Fuller launched the mixed-gender pop group after auditioning thousands of British twenty-something hopefuls and choosing seven finalists based on their talents, personalities, and potential public appeal. Fuller created S Club 7 with the intention of marketing it in various entertainment media. Fuller orchestrated the group's career so members would appear as television personalities before releasing any songs. In 1999, the S Club 7 series aired on British television. Working behind the scenes, Fuller sold the TV program to dozens of countries before the group released its first single. In time, the S Club notched four No. 1 singles in the United Kingdom. Fuller used the successful format for an offshoot called S Club Juniors, which released an album in 2002.

Not all of Fuller's plans have worked out as successfully. In 1999, he tried to launch a punk-girl group called 21st Century Girls, but it never made much impact on the music world. Some critics were happy. They say Fuller is spoiling the music industry with his manufactured stars. "He's not really in the music business at all," one insider told the Observer's Jamie Doward. "He's in the TV business. And the things he's involved with clog up the music industry's arteries. There are only so many spots on radio station play lists, there's only so much space in magazines. His TV-driven projects relegate music to be a spin-off, not a core product."

In the early 2000s, Fuller carved out a lucrative niche in reality-television programming when he created the *Idol* concept. *Pop Idol* hit the British airwaves in 2001. The show featured contestant auditions from across Britain, including talented performers as well as the poorest singers, giving the judges the opportunity to mock them. In the final stage, the singers performed on live television, allowing viewers to cast their votes. Fuller's company, 19 Entertainment, developed the show and sold versions of it to 30 countries, from Norway to China. *Australian Idol, Latin American Idol,* and *Vietnam Idol* have all hit the airwaves. Fuller's company takes a share of the profit from each offshoot.

In the United States, *American Idol* debuted in the summer of 2002 to instant success, becoming one of the most-watched shows on prime-time television. While viewers ultimately get to cast their votes for the best young idol, the show is overseen by a trio of judges who comment on each performer. These judges include former pop star Paula Abdul, music producer Randy Jackson, and music executive Simon Cowell, who has since become infamous for his rants. At the conclusion of the first season, Kelly Clarkson was named the winner. The former cocktail waitress from small-town Texas signed a record deal. Initially, she was managed by Fuller, as part of the deal. Fuller's management company gets first dibs at signing any winner, taking a 15 to 20 percent cut of the winner's income. In the years that followed her win, Clarkson recorded several hit singles and in 2006 won two Grammy Awards.

Besides earning money managing the winners from each *Idol* offshoot, Fuller's company also earns revenue from merchandise like T-shirts and the arena-filling *Idol* concert tours. In addition, Fuller also hires the songwriters whom he manages to write songs for the new talent. As such, Fuller perpetually creates more work—and more money—for himself. As a multimillionaire, Fuller owns several houses, including a five-bedroom, eight-bath beauty in Beverly Hills. He also has a hand-built Mercedes Maybach that cost upwards of $700,000 and a Dassault Falcon jet. Revenues from *American Idol* should continue to roll in for years to come. Fox-TV pays a seven-figure licensing fee for each episode. In addition, Sony BMG pays $5 million a season to 19 Entertainment, as well as a percentage of sales, just for the opportunity to record the winners. The show is set to stay on the airwaves through at least 2009. If the show hits pre-set ratings benchmarks, there is an automatic renewal option through 2011.

In 2003, Fuller bested Beatles manager Brian Epstein for the most top hits in circulation at once when his artists held the top three slots on the U.S. singles chart and the No. 1 position on the album chart. Over the course of his career, Fuller has been responsible for more than 100 No. 1 hits on charts around the globe. In 2005, Fuller sold 19 Entertainment for about $190 million to U.S. billionaire Robert Sillerman, who in turn named Fuller a director of his CKX entertainment empire. Fuller, however, still retained autonomy with 19, and CKX became its parent company.

In the early 2000s, Fuller became manager to British soccer star David Beckham and his wife, Victoria, who was formerly managed by Fuller as Posh Spice back when she was Victoria Adams. Fuller negotiated Beckham's 2007 move from England to play for the U.S.-based Los Angeles Galaxy. It was one of the biggest sports deals in history, worth an estimated $250 million. Besides an annual salary, the package included merchandise and endorsement contracts. Fuller created hype by getting Beckham on the cover of *Sports Illustrated* in conjunction with his American debut. In addition, Fuller orchestrated a reality television program following Beckham's career move to play soccer on U.S. soil. At the same time, Fuller was promoting Victoria Beckham, branding the Beckham name. She accepted a deal to appear in an episode of ABC TV's *Ugly Betty*. Insiders wonder if Fuller was trying to launch a movie career for her. In addition, Fuller also snagged a management contract in 2006 to oversee the interests of the players on England's national football team.

As for the future, Fuller would like to launch another reality show, possibly called *The Greatest Show on Earth*, which would take winners of the various *Idol* shows and pit them against each other in a contest to become the "world's pop idol." Fuller was also tinkering with the idea of launching a program called *Second Chance Idol*, which would feature past former stars competing to revive their careers.

While critics try to paint a picture of Fuller as a selfish and domineering manager, those who know him say he is polite—and even boring. Fuller regularly turns down interviews, preferring to stay quietly behind the scenes. This reclusiveness has turned him into somewhat of an enigma. One thing that is certain, however, is that Fuller knows he is good at what he does. "My business is creating fame and celebrity and I'm one of the best in the world," he told Peter Sheridan of the *Express*. "I reflect what's out there and if there's a demand for something I recognize it. I don't think I'm crass. I stand by everything I do."

Sources

Periodicals

BusinessWeek, May 30, 2005, p. 63.

Express (United Kingdom), August 2, 2007, p. 20.

Hollywood Reporter, November 30, 2005, p. 4.

Independent (London, England), November 2, 2003, p. 23.

Los Angeles Times, August 7, 2006, p. E1.

National Post (Toronto, Canada), October 7, 2002, p. AL5.

Observer (United Kingdom), July 27, 2003, p. 25; April 18, 2004, p. 5; January 14, 2007, p. 33.

Time, January 27, 2003, p. A14.

Online

"Simon Fuller," *Guardian,* http://www.guardian.co.uk/media/2007/jul/09/mediatop1002007.mondaymediasection36 (November 18, 2007).

"Simon Fuller: Guiding Pop Culture," BBC News, http://news.bbc.co.uk/1/hi/entertainment/music/2999872.stm (November 18, 2007).

—Lisa Frick

Clara Furse

Chief Executive Officer of London Stock Exchange

Born Clara Hedwig Frances Siemens, September 16, 1957, in Montreal, Quebec, Canada; daughter of Herman W. (an aluminum company executive) and Cornelie Siemens; married Richard Furse (a banker), 1981; children: two sons, one daughter. *Education:* London School of Economics, B.S., c. 1979.

Addresses: *Office*—London Stock Exchange plc, Paternoster Square, London EC4M 7LS, England.

Career

Agricultural commodities trader with Heinold Commodities Ltd. 1979-83; Phillips & Drew/UBS, began in 1983, became director, 1988, executive director, 1992-95, managing director, 1995-96, and global head of futures, 1996-98; deputy chair of London Financial Futures and Options Exchange (LIFFE), 1997-99; group chief executive, Credit Lyonnais Rouse, 1998-2000; chief executive officer, London Stock Exchange plc, 2001—.

Sidelights

In 2001, Clara Furse was hired to head the London Stock Exchange (LSE), one of the largest share-trading centers in the world. The first woman ever to serve as chief executive there, Furse, who is known for a sharp intellect combined with formidable management style, has beaten back a series of takeover bids from rivals in both Europe and the United States who covet the LSE's cache. "Many have taken to calling her Queen Boadicea, the name

of an ancient British monarch commemorated with a statue on Westminster Bridge for a revolt she led in 61 A.D. against Roman rule," wrote Suzanne Kapner in a *New York Times* of Furse. "Like Boadicea, whose name means 'victory' but has become synonymous with terror and savagery, Mrs. Furse has developed a reputation for toughness."

The daughter of an aluminum executive, Furse was born Clara Hedwig Frances Siemens in Montreal, Canada, in 1957. On her father's side were wealthy industrialists who had founded an electrical-goods empire in Germany in the nineteenth century, but their descendants were forced to flee Germany when the Nazi Party rose to power. Furse's grandfather and other relatives were then jailed when Nazi Germany invaded the Netherlands during World War II. Her father's job took them to Colombia and Denmark, but the family had settled in England by the time Furse reached her teens. After finishing at St. James's School in Malvern, she went on to earn a degree in economics from the prestigious London School of Economics.

Furse began her career in the financial markets in 1979 as an agricultural commodities trader. In 1983, she moved on to a branch of UBS, a financial services company whose name represents one of its founding companies, the Union Bank of Switzerland. Five years later, she was named a company director and became an executive director in 1992. Her career rise had come thanks to her prowess in overseeing the derivatives market for the bank, a specialized area of finance sometimes called the futures market. As Kirstie Hamilton explained in a London *Sunday Times* article, London's "futures traders are not pin-striped gentlemen—they are louts in brightly coloured jackets. While equity traders deal from behind banks of computer screens, until recently futures trading was conducted in rough-and-tumble fashion in pits on the floor of the exchange. A woman venturing on to the floor could expect cat calls and leers at the very least; whatever their sex, only the tough survived."

Furse was promoted to managing director at UBS in 1995 and global head of its futures division a year later. In 1997, she took a concurrent post as deputy chair of London Financial Futures and Options Exchange (LIFFE), the hub of the derivatives market in Britain. During her two-year stint at LIFFE, she pushed for the installation of an electronic tradition system, instead of the traditional verbal "open out-call" format used by floor traders. She held her ground over tremendous resistance to change, and LIFFE's chief executive, Daniel Hodson, actually resigned over the battle. Her mettle won the attention of the directors of a French bank, Credit Lyonnais Rouse, however, and she was tapped as the new group chief executive for the derivatives division in 1998. During her two years on the job, she enacted serious cost-cutting measures to help rescue the ailing Credit Lyonnais Rouse, including elimination of 60 percent of the workforce.

In a surprise announcement, Furse was named as the newest chief executive for the London Stock Exchange in January of 2001. The LSE is one of the oldest institutions in the City, as the central square mile of London is called which is home to its banking and financial services sector. Founded in 1760 as an informal club for share-traders at the nearby Jonathan's Coffee House, and the LSE became the London Stock Exchange in 1773. By the time Furse became its chief executive, the LSE was the busiest exchange in Europe in terms of volumes of shares traded daily. Its internal workings, however, were plagued by internecine squabbles and financial mismanagement. The three chief executives who held the job before Furse had not lasted very long, nor were they judged to have had much of success in overseeing the LSE.

For generations, the LSE was owned solely by the stockbrokers who had seats on the exchange, and it developed a reputation as a clubby, insular body that was wary of outsiders. When Furse came on board, a new, more transparent era began, and for the first time shares of the LSE were listed on the exchange itself. This meant that investors other than LSE stockbrokers could own a stake in it and, therefore, had more say in its management and future direction. During the next few years Furse oversaw a period of great financial growth at the LSE, with its share price and earnings performing well. It became an attractive property, and she fought off a series of takeover bids from Swedish, German, and Australian suitors; even the U.S. giant NASDAQ (National Association of Securities Dealers Automated Quotations) was tempted to make an offer, but Furse rejected the bids as not high enough for such a prestigious, venerable institution.

Furse's critics assert that she has not pursued mergers with or acquisitions of other exchanges aggressively enough, but the man who appointed her to the job, chairperson Don Cruikshank, backed her strategy, telling *Guardian* journalist Simon Bowers that "people don't realise how tough it is to be the aggressor when you're up against German, French, Spanish competitors—all of whom have enjoyed government protections. If Clara was to turn around and make a bid for Nasdaq it would need to be approved by the U.S. government." Finally, in 2007 LSE did make its first purchase, acquiring Milan's Borsa Italia for $2 billion.

Furse has been married since 1981 to a former Barings Bank executive and has three children. Occasionally the demands of her job force her to put in long hours, and as the Christmas holidays of 2006 approached, she was forced to cancel Caribbean vacation plans as the potential crisis regarding the NASDAQ offer loomed. She held a drawing at the office for the villa in St. Lucia she had already booked, and a LSE secretary won the prize. In a rare interview, Furse dismissed the idea that being a woman in the financial-services world was a challenge. "I've never found there to be an anti-female thing in the City," she told Julia Kollewe in the *Independent*. "Maybe I've been lucky but I don't think so."

Sources

Economist, January 27, 2001, p. 8.
Financial Times, January 27, 2001, p. 11.
Guardian (London, England), August 24, 2007, p. 23.
Independent (London, England), November 5, 2005, p. 50.
New York Times, June 3, 2001; January 28, 2005.
Sunday Times (London, England), January 28, 2001, p. 5.

—*Carol Brennan*

Helene Gayle

Dominic Bracco II/UPI/Landov

Epidemiologist and pediatrician

Born Helene Doris Gayle, August 16, 1955, in Lancaster, NY; daughter of Jacob (an entrepreneur) and Marietta (a psychiatric social worker) Gayle. *Education:* Barnard College, B.A., 1976; University of Pennsylvania, M.D., 1981; Johns Hopkins University, Baltimore, MD, M.P.H., 1981.

Addresses: *Home*—Atlanta, GA. *Office*—151 Ellis St. NE, Atlanta, GA 30303.

Career

Pediatric resident, Children's Hospital National Medical Center, Washington, DC, 1981-84; resident with Epidemic Intelligence Service, Centers for Disease Control and Prevention (CDC), Atlanta, GA, 1984-86; medical epidemiologist, CDC, Division of HIV/AIDS, 1984-92; medical researcher, U.S. Agency for International Development, AIDS Division, Washington, DC, 1992-95; director, CDC, National Center for HIV, STD, and TB Prevention, 1995-2001; director of the HIV, TB, and Reproductive Health Program, Bill and Melinda Gates Foundation, Seattle, WA, 2001-06; president, International AIDS Society, 2004-06; president and chief executive officer, Cooperative for Assistance and Relief Everywhere (CARE) USA, Atlanta, GA, 2006—.

Sidelights

Helene Gayle is a renowned epidemiologist and one of the world's foremost experts in Acquired Immune Deficiency Syndrome (AIDS). Her career has included executive posts with the Cen-

ters for Disease Control and Prevention (CDC) in Atlanta and the Gates Foundation, but in 2006 she became president and chief executive officer of CARE USA. The first woman and first African American to head the humanitarian organization, Gayle joined CARE at a time when it had recently revised its mission to one that focused on helping poor women around the world. "Women are more likely to sink additional income they have back into their families," Gayle explained to *New York Times* writer Stephanie Strom about why CARE was committing itself to a specific gender. When given a bit of financial help, she noted, even in the poorest corners of the world mothers will use it "to send their children to school, whereas men tend to spend such income more egocentrically."

Gayle was born in 1955, in Lancaster, New York, near Buffalo. She arrived midway through a close-knit family of five and into a household headed by a mother who was a social worker and a father who ran a barber and beauty-supply business. The Gayles actively encouraged their children to share their own interest in the larger world and also exposed them to the city's cultural treasures on a regular basis through museum visits and symphony performances. At the age of 12, Gayle was struck by a car and spent time in a full-body cast, but she recovered fully. During her high school years at Bennett High School, she served as head of the black student union group at the school.

After considering then rejecting a possible career in politics, Gayle entered New York City's Barnard College in 1972 as a psychology and pre-med major. She went on to earn two medical degrees from prestigious schools—the University of Pennsylvania and Johns Hopkins University. The latter institution, in Baltimore, also granted her a graduate degree in public health. Gayle's specialty in medicine was pediatrics, and she spent three years as a resident at the Children's Hospital National Medical Center in Washington, D.C. In 1984, she won a spot in the two-year residency program of the Epidemic Intelligence Service of the Centers for Disease Control and Prevention (CDC) in Atlanta.

At the time that Gayle began at the Epidemic Intelligence Service, there was tremendous fear that Acquired Immune Deficiency Syndrome (AIDS), caused by the human immunodeficiency virus (HIV), would decimate global population in just a few short decades. After completing her CDC residency in 1986, she spent the next six years as a medical epidemiologist at the CDC's Division of HIV/AIDS, emerging as an expert in pediatric AIDS. Thanks to education, prevention, and research efforts, AIDS failed to become the No. 1 killer in the developed world, as many had predicted, and Gayle was part of that first wave of researchers who conducted important studies and authored scientific papers that became part of the standard body of knowledge for those who treat or work to prevent the disease.

In 1992, Gayle took a post as a medical researcher with the AIDS Division of U.S. Agency for International Development, but she returned to the CDC in 1995 when she was hired to head its National Center for HIV, STD, and TB Prevention. This position called upon her scientific training as well as her public-relations skills; the high-profile post put her in a position to recommend policy and decide new initiatives in fighting AIDS as well as other sexually transmitted diseases and another highly communicable, potentially fatal sickness, tuberculosis.

In 2001, Gayle moved on to the Bill and Melinda Gates Foundation in Seattle, Washington, which had recently emerged as one of the world's most generous philanthropic organizations. Started by the founder of the Microsoft computer empire and his wife, the Gates Foundation had just committed $300 million for worldwide HIV and AIDS prevention.

Gayle was invited to head the Foundation's HIV, TB and Reproductive Health Program, which focused on education and prevention programs. She also served as president of the International AIDS Society for two years. In discussing the wide-ranging nature of her job, Gayle told Linda Villarosa in a New York Times interview: "Though cultures and societies are different, working with commercial sex workers in Thailand is not dissimilar to working with populations of gay men here. Around the world the epidemic affects people who are the most vulnerable because they have been stigmatized, isolated, and marginalized by their society. So many of the challenges are the same."

In April of 2006, Gayle took over as president and chief executive officer of CARE USA. The organization's name is an acronym for "Cooperative for Assistance and Relief Everywhere," and it dates back to the end of World War II and a desire by many Americans to help the war-ravaged population of Western Europe, many of whom faced starvation in the months immediately following the close of hostilities. Its boxes of food and medical supplies became known as "care packages," and the organization continued its outreach efforts in later decades, expanding to help any who had been displaced by war or were simply living in abject poverty. Based in Atlanta, CARE had 12,000 employees, many of whom worked out of its satellite aid offices around the world.

CARE's new "I Am Powerful" campaign was already in place when Gayle joined. Its print ads feature images of women and girls from around the world who have benefited from CARE initiatives; the program is aimed at showing women in the developed world how they can help reduce world poverty. Gayle oversaw a budget of nearly $600 million annually meted out to its various programs. "Our main focus is to bring people out of poverty," she told Ernie Suggs of the Atlanta Journal-Constitution. "We are talking about people with no access to clean water, electricity, or health facilities. They don't have schools. All of the things we as Americans take for granted, even if you are poor."

Sources

Atlanta Journal-Constitution, April 4, 2007, p. B1.
Buffalo News, December 12, 2005, p. B1.
Ebony, November 1991, p. 38; December 2006, p. 146.
New York Times, August 28, 2001; May 3, 2007.

—Carol Brennan

Lou Gentine

Sargento Foods, Inc.

Chairman and Chief Executive Officer of Sargento Foods

Born Louis Peter Gentine in 1947, in Plymouth, WI; son of Leonard A. (a business executive) and Dolores A. (Becker) Gentine; married Michele Ann Miller, December 27, 1969; children: Thomas Anthony, Louis Peter II, Kelly Marie. *Education:* University of Notre Dame, BBA, 1970.

Addresses: *Office*—Sargento Foods, Inc., 1 Persnickety Pl., Plymouth, WI 53073-3544.

Career

Price Waterhouse, Hartford, CT, staff accountant, 1970-73; Sargento Cheese (later known as Sargento, Inc., and Sargento Foods, Inc.), Plymouth, WI, controller, 1973-74, vice president of finance, 1974-77, executive vice president of administration, 1977-81, president, 1981—, chairman and chief executive officer, c. 1995—.

Member: Board, First Wisconsin National Bank of Sheboygan; board, National Cheese Institute; board, Boys and Girls Club of Milwaukee; board, Oldenburg Group; vice chairman of the International Dairy Foods Association, 2002; chairman, National Cheese Institute, 2002; chairman, International Dairy Foods Association, 2003; chairman, National Cheese Institute, 2003.

Sidelights

The chairman and chief executive officer of Sargento Foods, Inc., Lou Gentine is the second generation of his family to run the cheese and cheese-related products producer. Taking the helm of Sargento after his father, Gentine oversaw innovation and expansion of the company. It remained one of the foremost producers of retail cheese products in the United States for decades and also sold its wares worldwide.

Born on December 18, 1947, in Plymouth, Wisconsin, Gentine was the third son of Leonard and Dolores Gentine. His father initially worked in the funeral business, then ran a cheese shop and mail-order gift company, the Plymouth Cheese Counter, before co-founding Sargento Cheese Company in 1953 with cheese maker Joseph Sartori. The company initially focused on converting bulk natural cheeses, especially those not usually available in supermarkets, and selling them there. With innovative production and marketing—such as introducing packaged pre-shredded and sliced cheeses to consumers in 1958—Sargento became quite successful.

Gentine attended the University of Notre Dame, where he studied accounting. After earning his BBA in accounting in 1970, he moved east to work as a staff accountant at Price Waterhouse in Hartford, Connecticut. During his tenure at Price Waterhouse, Gentine also joined the United States Air Reserve. He continued his service to his country after leaving Price Waterhouse in 1973. (Gentine left the reserves as a first lieutenant in 1977.)

From the first, Gentine knew his time at Price Waterhouse was limited. He told Steve Prestegard of *Marketplace Magazine,* "I had all the intention of going back to [Sargento]. Each of my brothers and my sister were involved in the company in one job or another, and I think we were all interested in the growth of the company."

In 1973, Gentine returned to Plymouth and joined Sargento as a controller. Within a year, he was promoted to vice president of finance. After three years in this post, Gentine was named the executive vice president of administration. In 1981, Gentine took over as president of Sargento, the holding company for four divisions (Sargento Cheese, Sargento Food Service, Duralam, and Special Food Groups) of the company.

Like his father before him, Gentine emphasized innovation. In addition to introducing such products as a Fancy Shredded Cheese line in 1981, string cheese in 1983, and Nacho Shredded Cheese in 1984, Sargento was the first company to use zippered resealable packaging for its shredded and sliced cheese in 1986. Sargento was the only company to have zippered resealable packaging for several years, though other companies soon copied their idea.

Because of such innovations, Sargento was the number-two brand of natural cheese in the United States by 1991. Not content to rest on its laurels, the company continued to add new products, such as reduced fat cheeses in 1991. Sargento also underwent significant expansion, including building several new plants in the early 1990s. In addition, Gentine decided to expand its international market; in 1996 it created a division to focus on international sales.

With the success of such innovation and expansion, Gentine took on more executive responsibilities at Sargento. He became chief executive officer in the mid-1990s, and later added the title of chairman of the board in the years after his father's death in 1996. By 1999, Sargento Foods counted both retail and industrial consumers and annual sales of $375 million.

As the leader of Sargento, Gentine emphasized the importance of family. Sargento had been owned by members of the Gentine family and their stockholders since 1965 when Leonard Gentine had bought out his partner. Like his father, Gentine also looked on his nearly 1,000 employees as family. He supported worker-focused initiatives intended to benefit the local community. In addition, Gentine offered tuition reimbursement for all employees who decided to continue their formal education.

Gentine told *Dairy Foods'* Donna Berry: "My father always said that in order to be successful, you have to surround yourself with good people and treat them like family, and we've lived up to that philosophy. Our employees are an extension of our family and they share our passion for cheese and our love for succeeding as an industry leader. We consider our employees to be our greatest assets and offer them as many opportunities as possible to grow and prosper."

In addition to running Sargento, Gentine served on the board of directors of several companies, including the First Wisconsin National Bank of Sheboygan, the National Cheese Institute, Boys and Girls Club of Milwaukee, and the Oldenburg Group. Gentine also served on industry-related councils. In 2002, he was elected the vice chairman of the International Dairy Foods Association as well as the chairman of the National Cheese Institute. Gentine was elected chairman of both the International Dairy Foods Association and the National Cheese Institute in 2003.

Though Gentine participated in many such activities, his primary focus remained his company. In 2003, he began appearing in ads for Sargento. Gentine became Sargento's public face and voice in a series of television and radio commercials. He also began appearing on billboards and the back of Sargento cheese packages sold at the retail level. The move was made in part to increase the company's then flat sales. By 2006, sales had increased to $550 million annually.

Despite some ups and downs, Gentine believed Sargento had been influential in increasing the consumption of cheese products among Americans. He told Berry of *Dairy Foods,* "Since my father started the company, we've focused on giving consumers what they want—the best-tasting cheese for making meals and snacks their families will enjoy. Per capita cheese consumption has practically quadrupled in the past 50 years, and we believe the company has had a lot to do with that."

Sources

Books

Standard & Poor's Register of Directors and Executives, McGraw-Hill, 2007.

Who's Who in America, 46th ed., Marquis Who's Who, 2004.

Periodicals

Brandweek, September 29, 2003, p. 12.
Cheese Market News, February 14, 1992, p. 1.
Dairy Field, November 2002, p. 12; January 2004, p. 11.
Dairy Foods, August 1, 2003.
Dairy Today, January 2, 2006.
Marketplace Magazine, June 22, 1999, p. 12.

Wisconsin State Journal (Madison, WI), August 20, 1996, p. 4B.

Online

"Sargento's President and CEO, Lou Gentine, to Speak at Concordia's Business Leadership Series," Concordia University Wisconsin, http://www.cuw.edu/News_Events/media/business_leadership_fall2007.html (November 4, 2007).

—A. Petrusso

Carlos Ghosn

Francois Durand/Getty Images

Chief Executive Officer of Nissan and Renault

Born March 9, 1954, in Porto Velho, Brazil; married Rita; children: Caroline, Nadine, Maya, Anthony. *Education:* École Polytechnique, engineering degree, 1974; École des Mines de Paris, engineering degree, 1978.

Addresses: *Office*—Renault S.A., 13-15 quai Le Gallo, 92513 Boulogne-Billancourt Cédex, France.

Career

Plant manager, Michelin, Le Puy, France; head of research and development—industrial tires, Michelin, Ladoux, France; chief operating officer of South American Operations, Michelin, Rio de Janeiro, Brazil; president and chief operating officer, Michelin North America, 1989-96, chairman, 1990-96; executive vice president, Renault S.A., 1996-99; chief operating officer, Nissan Motor Company, Tokyo, Japan, 1999-2000, president, 2000, chief executive officer, 2001—, co-chairman, 2003—; president and chief executive officer in charge of Renault and Nissan, 2005—.

Awards: Industry leader of the year, *Automotive News,* 2000, 2001; man of the year, honorary doctorate, Cranfield University School of Management (U. K.), 2002; *Fortune Magazine* (Asia), 2003; honorary doctorate, American University of Beirut (Lebanon), 2003; honorary doctorate, Kyushu University (Japan), 2003; Golden Plate Award, Academy of Achievement, 2004; industry leader of the year, Automotive Hall of Fame, 2004; honorary doctorate,

Waseda University (Japan), 2005; Knight Commander of the British Empire (KBE), 2006; honorary doctorate, University of South Carolina.

Sidelights

The product of an international upbringing, automotive executive Carlos Ghosn heads both the Japan-based Nissan and its French alliance partner, Renault. In the early 2000s, he was lauded for the successful execution of his turnaround plan for Nissan. While the Japanese automaker had been struggling with falling sales and profits, Ghosn led the company back to both competitiveness and profitability. Because of his triumph with Nissan, Ghosn was asked to head Renault and was allowed to lead both companies beginning in 2005. Though Nissan soon struggled again, Ghosn was expected to right the ship.

Born on March 9, 1954, in Port Velho, Brazil, Ghosn was the son of a Lebanese father and French mother. Ghosn was raised in Brazil and Lebanon, attending high school in the latter country. Ghosn received his college education in France. He studied engineering at the École Polytechnique, earning a degree in 1974, and the École des Mines de Paris, earning a degree in 1978.

Ghosn began his career with Michelin, the French-based tire manufacturer. He first served as a plant manager in Le Puy, France, then became the head of research and development for industrial tires at Michelin's Ladoux, France, offices. He was transferred to Brazil where he became the chief operating officer of South American Operations. There, Ghosn began developing a reputation as a turnaround innovator, a reputation he took to his next career stop for Michelin.

In 1989, Ghosn moved to the United States where he became the president and chief operating officer of Michelin North America. In 1990, he added the title of chairman. During his time at Michelin, his company bought Uniroyal-Goodrich, and Ghosn played an active role in integrating the former competitors. Ghosn also developed a reputation as an effective cost cutter while working there.

Ghosn left Michelin in 1996 to return to France and join French automaker Renault S.A. as executive vice president. He continued to show his ability to cut costs while working at Renault, where he earned the nickname "Le Cost Killer." Ghosn's most significant cost-cutting measures came in 1997 when he instituted a company-wide program which led to the closing of the Belgian Vilvoorde plant as well as firing 3,500 redundant workers. There were riots in Belgium because of his actions, and many European politicians denounced him. Yet Renault became profitable again later that year.

Ghosn also played a role in Renault acquiring a significant stake in the nearly bankrupt Nissan Motor Company in 1999. He told Andrew English of London's *Daily Telegraph*, "From the beginning we saw this opportunity but through a real partnership. Also, when we analysed Nissan, we saw that even though the company had very mediocre performance, there were a lot of strengths: good engineering skills, good reliability of the products, very good manufacturing systems. These were all assets that, if appropriately managed, would turn in your favor."

In July of 1999, Ghosn was transferred from Renault to its new alliance partner, Nissan. As the company's new chief operating officer, he faced a daunting challenge as the automaker was troubled, deeply in debt, lacked profitability, and had a declining global market share. Within three months, Ghosn laid down the gauntlet and announced his Nissan Revival Plan to turn the company around and make it one of the best auto makers on Earth in three years. He also promised that he and his top managers would resign if the automaker was not profitable in 2001.

As his plan was being implemented, Ghosn was promoted. In 2000, he became president of the company, and in 2001, he was promoted again to chief executive officer (CEO). Ghosn was the first foreigner to become CEO of a major Japanese company. During his first few years at Nissan, Ghosn had to answer related questions about the integration of culture between the French and the Japanese. He believed that in his company's case, quick integration happened out of necessity.

Ghosn told Victoria Emerson of the *Journal of World Business*, "The Nissan Revival Plan came very fast and established strong objectives. It didn't leave any room for mediation on the differences about cultures. We were all mobilized and engaged in the revival of the company. What we see today is that differences in culture as being used more and more as ways of listening to what different people can bring to the table to achieve our objectives for the future."

When Nissan announced its numbers at the end of the business year in March of 2001, the company silenced any doubters about Ghosn's plan as it posted its best financial results ever. Operating profits tripled to the equivalent of $2.38 billion. Ghosn's company succeeded in part because it reduced purchasing costs, cut some 21,000 jobs, sold some of its assets, and boosted sales by four percent. While the Nissan Revival Plan was reaping immediate benefits, Ghosn still wanted to cut the company's debt to less than $5.8 billion and turn an operating profit equal to 4.5 percent of sales, both by March of 2003. Ghosn also was thinking beyond his three-year plan, and in his Plan 180 (also known as Nissan 180), hoped to sell one million more vehicles worldwide by introducing 28 new models as well as get the company completely out of debt in 2005.

As Ghosn continued to meet his goals with his Nissan Revival Plan in 2002 with record profits of $3 billion and a reduction in debt, he was lauded in Japan. In 2002, he was the subject of a manga (comic book) series produced in Japan entitled *The True Life of Carlos Ghosn*. In the comic, Ghosn was immortalized as a superhero who saved Nissan. The story integrated episodes of his life with Nissan's celebrated turnaround, and sold more than a half million copies per issue. Other automakers also noticed Ghosn's success, and there were constant rumors that he would leave Nissan and Renault for greener pastures. Renault worked to ensure that he would remain with the company.

In May of 2002, it was announced that Ghosn would become the CEO of Renault when the company's chief executive Louis Schweitzer stepped down from that post in 2005. Ghosn was also to remain in charge of Nissan as an overseer. Before this shift in power took place, Ghosn was promoted within Nissan to become the company's co-chairman in 2003. That year, Nissan again announced record profits and cut debts to zero. Ghosn's company also beat the targeted eight percent profit margin. In the first year of the 180 Plan, the only goal that remained was boosting sales by one million vehicles from levels at the start of the initiative.

As the Renault leadership changeover neared, Ghosn worked on appointing a successor, who would hold the COO position, to oversee day-to-day operations. In 2004, he began shuffling his duties by dropping a number of responsibilities in Tokyo while taking charge of North American operations. One reason for the change was a concern that Nissan sales goals were not being met in the United States, especially on SUVs and pickup trucks, as well as quality problems and the need to balance sales with incentives to ensure profit.

As scheduled, Ghosn returned to Renault to become the company's president and chief executive officer, while retaining his nonresident CEO position at Nissan, in the spring of 2005. By the end of September of 2005, Nissan had completed its Plan 180, reaching its last goal of increasing sales by one million cars. Yet the following month, sales suffered and there were concerns that Nissan might start flagging again.

Despite such problems, auto analysts believed that Ghosn would be the ideal candidate to turn around struggling American automaker General Motors. By 2006, both General Motors and Ford were considering pursuing Ghosn to ally with, if not jump ship for, their companies. Of the idea that he would leave for a new post, Ghosn told James Brooke of the *New York Times*, "It is very flattering, but at the same time you know that you are as good as your last quarter results or your last six-month results or your last year results. I know very well the rules. As long as you perform, you are good. Your management is as good as your performance."

In 2006, Ghosn hoped to continue the success he built at Nissan with a new three-year plan, Commitment 2009, for Renault. This turnaround plan set high sales targets, increased profit margins goals, and ensured the third generation Laguna was among the top three models in its class for product and service quality. By 2007, it was hoped that these targets would be helped by Renault's popular new entry sold in emerging markets worldwide, the

Logan. Yet Renault's sales suffered on the whole in the first half of the year, and the company was losing market share. Ghosn vowed sales would soon increase. More new products were slated to be introduced by Renault in 2009, further cementing Ghosn's belief that Renault would experience a significant surge by 2010.

Ghosn also faced challenges in 2007 when Nissan did not increase profits for the first time in six years. While the company was still profitable through 2006, sales slowed as few new products were introduced and the rising cost of commodities cut into profits. Ghosn believed Nissan would turn around in 2007 and 2008 as Nissan introduced new products like the crossover SUV Rogue. He also gave into consumer demand in the United States for more environmentally conscious cars by announcing the introduction of cleaner-burning diesel engines in 2010.

In addition, Ghosn faced criticisms from the changes he was making at Renault. Pressure he was putting on staff was linked to suicides at the company's technical center in Guyancourt, France. He also was blamed for the introduction of work from home and desk sharing policies, a radical change in the company's conservative corporate culture. There were also concerns that his holding two highly demanding positions on two continents was resulting in ineffective leadership in both companies and contributing to the problems they faced. Ghosn remained confident, telling James B. Treece of the *Automotive News*, "You learn from your failures. So from time to time, when you miss, I don't think it is a disaster. If you fail to learn, that's a disaster." To that end, Ghosn began staging a comeback for both companies at the end of 2007.

When Ghosn began devising his plans and other projects, he took an unusual approach: He started with a blank piece of paper. He told Kimimasa Mayama of the *Independent on Sunday*, "Believing by seeing is easy. Believing without seeing anything is much more difficult, even when you are the main dealer of the action. You have to move fast, but at the same time be very cautious. Any step can lead to disaster. The most difficult part is when you see something other people don't see and can't back it up by evidence. You question yourself. Am I doing the right thing? Am I going in the right direction?" With all his success, Ghosn has proven that he knows the answers to these questions.

Sources

Books

Marquis Who's Who, Marquis Who's Who, 2007.

Periodicals

Automotive News, July 9, 2001, p. 1; December 17, 2001, p. 23; May 5, 2003, p. 40; March 15, 2004, p. 3; July 9, 2007, p. 14.

Automotive News Europe, April 5, 2004, p. 24; February 7, 2005, p. 14; June 11, 2007, p. 2.

BusinessWeek, July 8, 2002, p. 53; July 22, 2002, pp. 46-49; March 17, 2003, pp. 52-53.

Daily Telegraph (London, England), February 1, 2003, p. 4.

Globe and Mail (Canada), February 8, 2007, p. G2.

Guardian Unlimited (London, England), October 24, 2006.

Independent on Sunday (London, England), May 18, 2003, p. 7.

Journal of World Business, Spring 2001.

National Post (Canada), January 15, 2002, p. FP10; May 10, 2002, p. FP12.

Newsweek (International ed.), December 17, 2007.

New York Post, August 24, 2006, p. 47.

New York Times, February 9, 2003, sec. 3, p. 6; November 19, 2005, p. C4; April 19, 2007, p. C3.

Toronto Star, June 22, 2001, p. D5.

Online

"Logan plays key role in Ghosn's Renault turnaround," just-auto.com, http://www.just-auto.com/articlerelated.aspx?id=90597&lk=nap (March 1, 2007).

—*A. Petruso*

Dana Gioia

AP Images

Chairman of the National Endowment for the Arts and poet

Born Michael Dana Gioia, December 24, 1950, in Hawthorne, CA; son of Michael (a cab driver and owner of a shoe store) and Dorothy (a telephone operator; maiden name, Ortiz) Gioia; married Mary Hiecke, February 23, 1980; children: Michael (deceased), Theodore, Michael Frederick. *Education:* Stanford University, B.A. (with high honors), 1973; Harvard University, M.A., 1975; Stanford University, M.B.A., 1977.

Addresses: *Office*—National Endowment for the Arts, 1100 Pennsylvania Ave. NW, Washington, DC 20506.

Career

Poet, essayist, editor, translator, and arts administrator. Began as assistant product manager for Country Time lemonade, General Foods, 1977; group product manager for Kool-Aid, General Foods, after 1983; Corporate Development group, General Foods, after 1985; published first book of poetry, *Daily Horoscope*, 1986; vice president, General Foods, 1990-92; appointed to chair the National Endowment for the Arts, 2003, reappointed, 2006. Contributor to periodicals, including the *New Yorker, Kenyon Review, Hudson Review, San Francisco Magazine* and *Poetry*.

Awards: Frederick Bock Award, *Poetry* magazine, 1985; American Book Award, Before Columbus Foundation, for *Interrogations at Noon*, 2002.

Sidelights

It seems improbable that the marketing executive who created Jell-O Jigglers would go on to head the federal agency that funds arts and cultural programs in the United States, but Dana Gioia's career has indeed included both of these roles. Before President George W. Bush appointed him to chair the National Endowment for the Arts (NEA) in 2002, the California native was also a published poet, critic, and essayist. Contrary to what some of the NEA's most vocal critics assert, its programs "are not elitist undertakings," Gioia told Peggy McGlone of the Newark *Star-Ledger*. "The arts are ways in which people develop and realize the fullness of their own humanity. If you take the arts away from an educational system, or a community, you have left that community impoverished."

Born on December 24, 1950, in Hawthorne, California, in southern Los Angeles county, Gioia is the son of a Sicilian Italian father who drove a taxicab and owned a shoe store, and a Mexican-American mother who worked for years as a telephone operator. Many members of Gioia's extended family lived in their neighborhood, and the first paid job that he held was as a helper for his uncles' construction business. Devoted to music, he considered a future career as a composer while a student at Serra High School in Gardena, but chose to major in English at Stanford University with a goal toward becoming a writer who taught at the college level.

Perhaps because of his multicultural heritage, Gioia seemed to pick up languages easily, and spent one of his college years in Vienna, Austria, where he became fluent in German. He graduated from Stanford in 1973—the first person in his family to earn a college degree—and went on to Harvard University, which granted him a master's degree in comparative literature in 1975. By this point he realized he would likely be unhappy in academia, especially as a poet, for nearly all of the college English departments favored a certain kind of non-rhyming verse, and the twinned worlds of teaching and publishing had become clubby, safe havens. "It's bad as a society if you have all your poets at a university," Gioia explained to *BusinessWeek* writer Nanette Byrnes. "There should be a broader life experience open to writers. I was being taught a professional language that was spoken by about 600, 700 people in the world."

Gioia considered another career path, this one modeled after the late American poet Wallace Stevens, who won the Pulitzer Prize for poetry in 1955 but had spent the previous decades as an insurance executive in Hartford, Connecticut. Returning to Stanford to earn a graduate business degree in 1977, Gioia then took a job with the General Foods Corporation in suburban New York City. He worked on the Country Time lemonade, Kool-Aid, and Jell-O teams, and often put in long hours. Despite the demands of his job, Gioia forced himself to spend at least three hours nightly either reading or writing. His first published work was a limited edition—about 70 copies were printed—fine press book titled *Two Poems*, which appeared in 1982 from the short-lived Bowery Press.

In 1990, Gioia was made a vice president at General Foods, but left the corporate world two years later. Some of his decision to leave was spurred by a family tragedy, when the four-month-old son he had with his wife Mary, a fellow Stanford business grad, died of sudden infant death syndrome (SIDS). He also found some unexpected success with a May 1991 essay in *Atlantic Monthly* magazine titled "Can Poetry Matter?" In it, Gioia criticized the insular world of professional poetry, and urged several remedies that could return poetry to a place of relevance for ordinary Americans, he argued. High-school and undergraduate-level students should emphasize recitation, not analysis, for one. "Poems should be memorized, recited, and performed," he wrote in the article. "The sheer joy of the art must be emphasized. The pleasure of performance is what first attracts children to poetry, the sensual excitement of speaking and hearing the words of the poem."

Gioia moved back to California with his family in 1996 and continued to write and publish. In 2002, President Bush named him to succeed the late Michael Hammond, who had died after just a week on the job as chairperson of the NEA. The federal arts-funding agency had a troubled legacy in the latter part of its four-decade history. Created in 1965 as part of Lyndon B. Johnson's Great Society program, the NEA was regularly targeted by some Republicans in Congress as a waste of taxpayer money. The lawmakers often used examples of NEA-funded art or cultural programs that might be likely to anger religious conservatives to drum up outrage. By the time Gioia took over, the NEA's annual budget had dropped from $176 million in 1992 to just $98 million.

Under Gioia's leadership, the NEA has implemented several new initiatives that seem to have escaped criticism. There was the 2003 "Shakespeare in America" tour in which four works by the playwright were staged in a pair of communities in each of the 50 states. A program that brought opera performances to U.S. military bases was another success, and Gioia scored somewhat of a personal triumph with Poetry Out Loud, a national poetry recitation competition. In 2006, President Bush reappointed him to another term as NEA, a decision confirmed by unanimous vote in the Senate.

By then Gioia had personally met with most of the Senate and the House. For meetings with the latter lawmakers, he brought with him a list of high schools in their district that used educational materials purchased with NEA grants in order to illustrate what kind of work his agency does. In a 2007 interview with *New York Times* journalist Patricia R. Olsen, he likened his NEA job to the period of his corporate career when he managed the Jello-O brand and came up with Jell-O Jigglers after months of trying out various recipes the company had collected over the years. "I had all the men on the team make them with me. We figured if we could make them, anyone could.... My job at the National Endowment for the Arts is oddly similar: to understand how to take all the agency's resources and, in addition to everything else we're doing, come up with a few ideas that are transformative."

Selected writings

Poetry

Two Poems, Bowery Press (New York City), 1982.
Summer, Aralia Press (West Chester, PA), 1983.
Daily Horoscope, Graywolf Press (St. Paul, MN), 1986.
The Gods of Winter, Graywolf Press, 1991.
Interrogations at Noon, Graywolf Press, 2001.

Other

(Editor) *The Ceremony and Other Stories,* by Weldon Kees, Graywolf Press, 1984.
Can Poetry Matter?: Essays on Poetry and American Culture, Graywolf Press, 1992.
(Editor with William Logan) *Certain Solitudes: Essays on the Poetry of Donald Justice,* University of Arkansas Press (Fayetteville), 1997.
(Librettist) *Nosferatu* (opera; music by Alva Henderson), 2001.
Disappearing Ink: Poetry at the End of Print Culture, Graywolf Press, 2004.

Sources

Atlantic Monthly, May 1991.
BusinessWeek, November 13, 2006.
Forbes, March 21, 1988, p. 170.
New York Times, October 28, 2007.
Star-Ledger (Newark, NJ), June 22, 2003, p. 1.

—Carol Brennan

Ira Glass

Radio host and author

Born March 3, 1959, in Baltimore, MD; son of Barry (an accountant) and Shirley (a psychologist) Glass; married Anaheed Alani (an editor), August, 2005. *Education:* Earned undergraduate degree from Brown University, 1982.

Addresses: *Home*—New York, NY. *Office*—c/o Showtime Networks, 10880 Wilshire Blvd., Ste. 1101, Los Angeles, CA 90024.

Career

National Public Radio, summer intern, c. 1978, and audiotape editor, newscast writer, and producer at its Washington, D.C. studios, 1982-89; reporter for WBEZ-FM, Chicago, 1989-95; co-host of *The Wild Room* on WBEZ, 1990-95; creator, producer, writer, and host of *This American Life*, 1995—; writer and television host of *This American Life*, Showtime, 2007—; editor of the essay anthology, *The New Kings of Non-Fiction*, published by Riverhead Books, 2007.

Sidelights

Ira Glass is the host of the long-running *This American Life* radio program that has aired on public radio stations across the United States since 1997. A decade later, the program made its television debut on the Showtime cable network but remained a staple of public radio and one of its highest-rated weekly broadcasts. "Glass' voice, a bit whiny-sounding, inflecting at times like a teen's, is terrifically idiosyncratic and chummy," asserted Florangela Davila in the *Seattle Times*, "and as a host he allows the stories to take hold of him. That, in turn, frosts the radio program with a kind of honesty and truthfulness, making the stories that much more embraceable."

Glass was born in 1959, sandwiched between a pair of sisters, and grew up in Baltimore, Maryland. His father Barry was an accountant, while Glass' mother, Shirley, worked as a psychologist. Glass entered Northwestern University in the Chicago area following his high school graduation then transferred to Brown University in Rhode Island. He also switched majors along the way, from pre-med to semiotics, which he described to Marshall Sella of the *New York Times Magazine* as "a sadly pretentious body of theory about language and narrative."

Glass' career took shape with an internship he landed at National Public Radio (NPR) headquarters in Washington, D.C., one summer during college. After earning his degree from Brown in 1982, he went back to NPR, working as an audiotape editor for the rest of the decade. "I cut tape for ten years before I went on the air myself," he confessed in an interview with Joel Reese of the *Daily Herald* of Arlington Heights, Illinois. "It took a long time for me to learn how to write competently for the radio. Like, sort of longer than anyone in the history of broadcasting, I believe.... I wasn't that good at being on the air, and I was really shy about hearing my voice on the air."

In 1989, Glass relocated to Chicago to be near his girlfriend at the time, cartoonist Lynda Barry (*Ernie Pook's Comeek*). Hired as a reporter for NPR's Chicago affiliate, WBEZ-FM, he went on to produce some notable radio programs for WBEZ in the early 1990s. The first was a pair of year-long reports that tracked reform efforts at two troubled public schools in the city. He also produced a holiday segment by a then-unknown writer, David Sedaris, that aired in December of 1992 on "Morning Edition." In it, Sedaris recounted his humiliating experiences working as a department store elf in New York City a year earlier. "The Santaland Diaries" quickly propelled Sedaris to a two-book contract with a major publisher.

From 1990 to 1995 Glass served as co-host of *The Wild Room,* a Friday-night, free-form documentary-style program on WBEZ that showcased Chicagoland writers and artists. That show was an early incarnation of *This American Life,* which came out of an idea that Glass took to the Corporation for Public Broadcasting, the entity that funds both NPR and another public radio network Public Radio International (PRI), which operates out of Minneapolis. The show began airing on WBEZ in November of 1995 as *Your Radio Playhouse,* but after a few months its name was changed to *This American Life.* Originally featuring local writers and radio-documentary storytellers, Glass' show took on a more national identity in 1997 when PRI agreed to offer it for distribution to public radio stations across the United States.

From its onset, *This American Life* attracted a devoted listening audience who tuned in to hear Glass' unusual, somewhat nasally voice introducing and prodding forward the quirky tales—some true, some fiction—recounted in separate segments. Each hour-long program was arranged around a theme, such as "Other People's Mail" or "Hoaxes," and the three or four stories were grouped into acts, much like a stage play. "We're documenting things with no particularly uplifting social mission," Glass told Deborah Solomon in the *New York Times* about the thrust of his show. "The mission is that of an ambitious novel or movie: to point out universal feelings and moments."

From the outset, *This American Life* was notable for bringing in new listeners to PRI and NPR affiliates, who called their local public radio stations during semi-annual fund-raising drives to pledge their support for it. Writing in the *Atlantic Monthly,* Michael Hirschorn called *This American Life* "the voice of a generation too young to buy into the broader public-radio mission ('This is the sound of Guatemalan basket weavers; their way of life is threatened....') and too smart or old for the braying of commercial radio." Glass believed the kernel of

This American Life's appeal was the old-fashioned nature of the format, exemplified by "the fact that there are so many things you can do on radio that are so much harder to do well in any other medium," he told Cara Jepsen in an interview that appeared in *Book.* "Certain things are just more powerful, when done as talking, without pictures."

Sedaris occasionally appeared on *This American Life,* and the show made some new stars as well, such as author and comedian Sarah Vowell and John Hodgman, who later personified the Personal Computer in a series of humorous television ads for Apple Computer and began appearing as a correspondent on *The Daily Show with Jon Stewart* on Comedy Central. Glass was also courted relentlessly by film and television producers, and once he even penned an article for the Web magazine *Slate.com* about a trip he made out to Hollywood to meet with television executives. He, along with a television producer and a filmmaker he knew, were taken around by an agent from William Morris, who told the trio that "some execs at these meetings will have actually prepared for the meetings," Glass recounted in the article. "They'll have listened to tapes she's sent of *This American Life* .... But many of them won't have prepared. It's our job, she says, to politely ignore it if they know nothing about our work." As Glass continued in the Slate diary, the agent then told them that "the way one handles this situation is to tell them everything you think they *need* to know about your work, prefaced with the phrase 'As you know already.'"

These early experiences with the corporate giants of the entertainment industry made Glass hesitate before committing to anything, and he has admitted in several interviews that for many years he did not even own a television set. But *This American Life* continued to attract avid listeners, some with impressive credentials. Pulitzer Prize-winning playwright David Mamet lauded its charms in a 2001 *Time* magazine article which called it the best program on American radio. Its executive producer and host, Mamet wrote, "seems to have reinvented radio"; he also noted that Glass "finds—uncovers—drama and humor in the most pedestrian of places."

Glass eventually inked a deal with Warner Bros. to develop stories that originally appeared on *This American Life* broadcasts. One of the first properties to move forward dated back to 2001 and a story called "Minors" from Susan Burton, a contributing editor on *This American Life.* It recounted her experiences one holiday season when she and her sister were stranded at an airport during a snowstorm. The result was the 2006 comedy, *Unaccompanied Minors,* for which Glass served as executive producer. By then he had finally agreed to do a television version of *This American Life,* which happened only when a network—in this case the Showtime cable channel—conceded to some stringent demands from Glass and his crew. "We insisted that they find us filmmakers to collaborate with," Glass told Mary Carole McCauley in his hometown newspaper, the *Baltimore Sun,* about the four years between Showtime's first approach and 2006, when the television deal was written. "We figured we'd never hear from them. And then they came back with all these great people. That posed a problem for us—suddenly, we had to take them seriously."

In another interview, Glass explained that he and his team of writers and segment producers were also worried that the quirkiness of their radio show would fail to translate onto the screen. "We asked for assurances from Showtime and got it in our contract with them that if we thought it didn't work, that at the end of the pilot, even though they would have spent hundreds of thousands of dollars, then we could ask them to kill it," he told *New York Times* writer David Carr. The final version seemed to click, however, and the television version of *This American Life* debuted on Showtime in March of 2007. It was a half-hour show, and Glass still fulfilled his role as host, introducing the stories and narrating segues—though in the screen version he did so from behind a desk which improbably turned up on location for each story.

Glass has often admitted in interviews that despite the fact that the audio broadcasts of *This American Life* seemed to flow almost effortlessly, they were in fact relentlessly edited. Moving over to a visual medium, he soon realized, meant the stories took even longer to complete. Yet he was also pleasantly surprised by one factor, as he told Gerri Miller in *American Jewish Life Magazine*. "The sheer power of seeing somebody's face as they tell a story and all the information you get, that was something I never expected," Glass said.

Glass' contract for six episodes for Showtime was extended for another six after *This American Life* earned some enthusiastic reviews. As Davila, the *Seattle Times* journalist noted, "The best radio stories are already chock-full of imagery, but the rewards here are also seeing a man's watery eyes, a teen's shiny forehead, a senior citizen's shaky hand. It all looks so easily crafted, and it's hard to imagine these stories told in any better way." Critiquing it for the *New York Times*, Carr asserted, "What connects the shows—both the television and radio versions—is an uncommon empathy for subject. Viewers often find themselves rooting for whoever is featured going through the traditional arc of setup, epiphany, and denouement."

This American Life was still heard on more than 500 public radio stations and by an audience estimated at 1.7 million listeners. Glass, who married in 2005, relocated with his wife, Anaheed Alani, to New York City in 2006. In Chicago, he was recognized by voice at least once a day, but "in New York, I'm never recognized ever," he told *Entertainment Weekly*'s Ari Karpel. "People here don't listen to radio in the same way because they're not in their cars." He did concede, however, that his new city has "better take-out food."

Both Glass and Alani are self-professed atheists, though she was raised in a Muslim family and he in a Jewish one; he even attended Hebrew *shul* as a youngster back in Baltimore. He noted that the rabbi at the temple his family attended on High Holidays made a strong impression on him—and perhaps even inspired *This American Life*. "Rabbi Seymour Esrog was really funny, a great storyteller," he recalled in the interview with Miller in *American Jewish Life Magazine*. "He was so good that even the kids would stay and watch him. He'd tell a funny anecdote, something really moving, and go for a big finish. That's what the show is."

Sources

Periodicals

American Jewish Life Magazine, March-April 2007.
Atlantic Monthly, September 2007, p. 142.
Baltimore Sun, March 22, 2007.
Book, March 2001, p. 48.
Chicago Tribune, November 15, 2005.
Daily Herald (Arlington Heights, IL), December 5, 2000, p. 1.
Entertainment Weekly, April 13, 2007, p. 27.
New Yorker, April 16, 2007, p. 164.
New York Times, March 4, 2007; March 21, 2007.
New York Times Magazine, April 11, 1999.
Seattle Times, March 18, 2007, p. K1.

Online

"Ira Glass," for "Diary: A Weeklong Electronic Journal," Slate.com, http://www.slate.com/id/29923/entry/29924/ (October 29, 2007).
"Radio Host: Ira Glass," Time.com, http://www.cnn.com/SPECIALS/2001/americasbest/pro.iglass.html (October 29, 2007).

—*Carol Brennan*

Christina Gold

Sebastian D'Souza/AFP/Getty Images

President and Chief Executive Officer of Western Union

Born Christina Engelsman, September 12, 1947, in Renkum, Netherlands; emigrated to Canada as a child; daughter of a military officer and a painter/nurse; married Peter Gold (an attorney). *Education:* Earned degree in geography from Carleton University, 1969.

Addresses: *Office*—First Data Corporation, 6200 S. Quebec St., Greenwood Village, CO 80111.

Career

Worked at a coupon-center clearinghouse, Ottawa, Ontario, Canada, after 1969; joined Avon Canada as an inventory control clerk, and moved on to a positions in marketing, sales, finance, and management between 1970 and 1989; became chief executive officer and president of Avon Canada, 1989, and president of Avon North America, 1993; board chair, chief executive officer, and president, Excel Communications, Inc., Dallas, TX, 1999-2002; senior executive vice president, First Data Corporation, Greenwood, CO, 2002; president and chief executive officer, Western Union, Greenwood, CO, 2006—.

Sidelights

Christina A. Gold spent nearly 30 years with Avon Products, Inc., the international direct-sales giant, rising from an inventory clerk in Canada to head of Avon's North American operations. Her skills in managing a far-flung empire eventually brought her to Western Union, where she advanced to the dual posts of president and chief executive officer in early 2006. At the Colorado-based Western Union, Gold oversees a company with $4 billion in revenues annually from its thriving money transfer, bill payment, and prepaid services offerings.

Gold was born on September 12, 1947, as the second of three children in her family when they were living in the Dutch town of Renkum. Her Dutch father was a military officer and former Olympic gymnast, and moved the family to his wife's native country, Canada, in the early 1950s. Gold's first years of elementary school were difficult, given her slim English-language skills, and once she mastered her second language the shyness remained. She attended Carleton University in Ottawa, and graduated in 1969 with a degree in geography.

Gold's first job was a clerical one at a coupon-center clearinghouse in the Canadian federal capital, but she quit when she was hired at Avon Canada as an inventory control clerk, which she took "because it paid $100 a week, $10 more than I was making," she told *New York Times* journalist Claudia H. Deutsch. She moved on to a better job with the company in marketing, but in 1972 Avon Canada was folded into Avon's U.S. operations. By this time

Gold was married to an attorney with a private practice in Montreal, which made relocating to Avon headquarters in New York City for any potential job transfer unfeasible, and so she stayed on at Avon's Montreal offices and accepted a job in sales promotions there.

A human resources executive named Mun Lavigne took notice of Gold's talent and work ethic, and became an influential mentor for her during this period of her career. Lavigne suggested that she take a lesser position as a supervisor, which would give her some crucial management experience. He even brought her along with him to meetings with Avon executives in New York City, and coached the still-shy Gold through her first presentation at headquarters. "I was afraid of the people who worked for me, so imagine how I felt about addressing management," she recalled in the *New York Times* interview with Deutsch. During the 1980s, she rose rapidly through management ranks, and was named chief executive officer and president of Avon Canada in 1989. Four years later, she was tapped to head Avon North America, the division that included the United States, Canada, and Puerto Rico, and this time she moved to New York City and commuted back and forth from Montreal, where her husband still lived.

Gold was the first woman to serve as president at Avon North America, but was part of a growing wave of female executives rising at the once male-dominated company. Yet Avon was struggling to adjust to a new era in other ways as well: For a generation Avon had dominated the direct-sales beauty industry with thousands of part-time representatives—once known as "Avon Ladies"—selling Avon's makeup, skin care, fragrances, and jewelry through an informal network of friends, families, and co-workers. As more women entered the full-time job market, Avon's sales dropped along with the numbers of active sales agents. When Gold arrived in New York City in late 1993, there were still 400,000 Avon Ladies in the United States, but droves had already quit because the sales incentives Avon offered to its top sellers had been replaced by a savings-bond program.

Gold reinstituted several perks for sellers, and oversaw the introduction of a new 1-800 telephone line, which allowed customers to bypass the Avon Lady entirely. Avon also added lingerie, vitamins, and an improved giftware line to its offerings, and within a year sales figures had improved significantly. Under Gold, noncosmetics sales reached $765 million in 1995, up from $140 million in 1993. She was considered one of the top three contenders to head Avon worldwide as its next board chair and chief executive officer, but was bypassed in favor of Andrea Jung, who headed Avon's global marketing division, in 1999. Gold moved on to a long-distance phone company in Dallas, Texas, as chief executive officer and president, but in the spring of 2002 was recruited by the First Data Corporation, the parent company of Western Union, to serve as senior executive vice president responsible for global operations, marketing, and sales.

First Data was a spinoff of American Express, operated as a payment-processing company for credit card issuers, and had bought Western Union in 1994. Western Union was founded in 1851 and dominated the communications sector for another 100 years as the main provider of telegraph services in the United States. These were messages sent electronically from one Western Union office to another, and then transcribed and hand-delivered to the designated recipient. By the 1980s, however, the company's fortunes were in serious decline, and it instead began to focus on its money-transfer business.

In early 2006, Western Union was spun off from First Data Corporation, and Gold was named president and chief executive officer (CEO) of the new stand-alone Western Union. She foresaw immense continued growth for the money-transfer business, which had reached 275 million transactions annually, especially with her company's recent acquisition of Vigo Remittance Corporation, an electronic money-transfer company that dominated the New York-New Jersey market. Millions of workers in the United States use such services to send money back to their families in Latin America and throughout the world.

Gold's new role as CEO included frequent travel to China to meet with government officials there in order to secure new business. She appears regularly on *Fortune* magazine's annual list of the "50 Most Powerful Women in Business," and remains close friends with Lavigne, now in his eighties, with whom she and her husband spend Christmas in Canada every year. She relaxes by playing video games, telling *New York Times* reporter Patricia R. Olsen that on one occasion her now-retired husband Peter "went to buy me the latest PlayStation game and the clerk asked how old his child was. He told the man: 'You don't want to know. It's my wife.'"

Sources

Brandweek, December 4, 1995, p. 26.
ColoradoBiz, November 2005, p. 58.
Crain's New York Business, June 2, 1997, p. 1.

Denver Post, October 5, 2003.
Forbes, December 2, 1996, p. 135.
New York Times, April 3, 1994; January 23, 2005; January 27, 2006.

—*Carol Brennan*

Philip Green

Retail executive

Born Philip Nigel Ross Green, March 15, 1952, in the South London borough of Croydon, England; son of Simon (a property developer and electrical retailer) and Alma (a laundry-business owner) Green; married Christina (Tina) Palos, August, 1990; children: Chloe, Brandon.

Addresses: *Home*—London, England. *Office*—Topshop, Colegrave House 70 Berners St., London, W1T 3NL, England.

Career

Wholesale footwear seller in London, late 1960s; worked for family's electrical retail business; opened two designer-discount stores, Bond Street Bandit and 41 Conduit Street, c. 1979-80; bought and sold a chain of London denim stores, Jean Jeanie, 1985-86; chair and chief executive officer, Amber Day, c. 1986-88; bought and sold several other retail properties during the 1990s, including Owen Owen, Olympus Sports, Shoe Express, Sears Group; bought British Home Stores, 2000; bought Arcadia Group (includes Topshop, Topman, Wallis, Miss Selfridge, Dorothy Perkins, and Outfit), 2002.

Sidelights

Knighted on June 17, 2006, Sir Philip Green serves as chief executive officer of Topshop, the British clothing retailer whose flagship outpost in the heart of London's retail district is one of the busiest stores in the world. Topshop's fashion-forward styles are affordably priced and have even become a favorite of celebrities, models, and fashion-industry elite, while Green has won kudos for rescuing the flagging clothier and turning it into a hip brand—a status exemplified by his joint venture with supermodel Kate Moss for her own clothing line at Topshop, which launched in 2007.

Despite his impressive financial acumen, Green is known as a maverick and has had a controversial relationship with the British press, which is fond of writing about his lavish lifestyle. In 2005, he made his first appearance on the *Forbes* "Rich List," and the U.S. magazine estimated the net worth of this retail executive, who left school at age 16, at $5 billion (by June of 2006, he was worth around $7 billion). He credits his success to a work ethic he learned at an early age, telling a reporter for London's *Sunday Times*, "I come from a very old school and have learnt most of the business myself. I've taught myself everything, from making garments to fitting out stores."

Green was born into a Jewish family in 1952 and grew up in Croydon and North London. His mother, Alma, ran a chain of laundromats but took over her husband's business when Simon Green—a property developer who became an electrical retailer—died unexpectedly of a heart attack in the early 1960s. By then Green was already installed at his boarding school for Jewish students in Oxfordshire, Carmel College, which he had entered at the age of eight. In his teens, he served as captain of Carmel's rugby and cricket teams, but he fared poorly in the classroom and left at the age of 16.

Green went to work for his family's business, but he also cut a deal with a friend of theirs who was a shoe importer, to purchase a wholesale lot of women's boots. He then made enough money selling them to stores to finance a long jaunt through the United States and Asia. Returning to London, he continued working in retail, and in the late 1970s he bought the contents of a clothing store that was going out of business and then opened his own space in the posh Mayfair district of London. He became known for selling top-of-the-line designer clothing at a discounted price at both his Bond Street Bandit store and the other, named for its address at 41 Conduit Street. In 1981, he entered into a partnership with British film star Joan Collins that attempted to capitalize on the designer-jean craze, but "Joan Collins Jeans" proved a year late to the game, and it folded with a spectacular loss a year later, as did another business venture of Green's called Cupcraft.

Green eventually sold 41 Conduit Street, netting $30,000 from the sale, and in 1985 bought a debt-ridden denim retailer, Jean Jeanie, with multiple locations in London, and fixed its financial situation enough that he sold it six months later for $3 million. His next post was as chair and chief executive officer of clothing chain Amber Day, but this was a publicly traded company, and when the board became unhappy with his performance they fired him. In the early 1990s, he acquired a department store chain called Owen Owen and sold off its dozen locations to larger department store companies such as Debenham's. In 1995, in another highly publicized deal, he led a buyout bid for Olympus Sports, which was at the time Britain's largest seller of athletic goods and apparel. The price tag was one British pound, but Green and his fellow investors had agreed to take on a debt load of several million dollars. Again, Green engineered an impressive turnaround, and in 1998, when the company was sold for $550 million to another sporting-goods firm, Green earned $73 million on the deal.

By this point Green was a well-known figure in the British business press, but the media attention and his hard-charging lifestyle began to catch up with him. In 1995, at the age of just 43, he came close to suffering a heart attack, and a year later he was attacked by three men on the street outside his home in the posh London area of Hampstead, one of whom held a sword to his throat. Married by then, with two small children, he and his wife relocated to Monaco, and Green began commuting to London for his workweek. He was sometimes criticized for being a "tax exile," that is, a wealthy citizen who registers a primary address in another country and lives there just enough days out of the year to avoid paying the onerous British personal income tax. These duties are especially high for incomes over six figures.

Green made a number of further acquisitions in the late 1990s, including Shoe Express and the Sears Group, which was not related to the U.S. department store chain of the same name but was a retail outfit that also had financial-services holdings. This particular acquisition was a hostile takeover bid for $1 billion, but in a few months Green and his group had sold off the various components and made $340 million for their trouble. He then made a well-publicized bid in 2000 for Marks & Spencer, Britain's number-one retailer, but the deal fell through at the last minute. He had better luck later that year with his purchase of British Home Stores, known as "BHS," for a purchase price of $380 million for its 156 stores. BHS was the number-five retailer in the country, but known as a somewhat staid provider of clothing and basic household necessities such as linens and dishes. He reverted it to a privately held company through a buyout of stock shares and began to implement immediate measures that revived its moribund sales.

In 2002 Green made his most spectacular acquisition when he bought the Arcadia Group, which owned a number of mass-market retail clothing store brands. Obtaining Bank of Scotland financing to the tune of $1.6 billion and investing $1.3 million of his own assets, he took control of Arcadia's nearly 2,500 stores, which include a well-known women's "cheap chic" powerhouse called Topshop. Founded at the onset of the Swinging London scene in 1964, Topshop had become a pariah in the fashion world by the 1980s, but it began to revive a bit with a new look for its stores and its own line of clothing. Within a short time, Green put his stamp on Topshop as well as the other clothing retailers in the Arcadia stable, such as Miss Selfridge and Wallis, and sales began to jump correspondingly. "Green astounded the City—London's financial district—with the speed at which he turned BHS and Arcadia around and paid back much of the $1.9 billion of debt he used to take them private," noted Kiri Blakeley, a writer for *Forbes Global*. "He did it so effortlessly that the cry went up that he'd 'stolen' the franchises for much less than their worth."

Green began selling off his other holdings in order to concentrate on Topshop and the rest of the Arcadia brands, and was known as an involved boss who paid regular visits to all the stores, sometimes at midnight to check out the clean-up efforts and displays readied for the next day. He also enjoyed a somewhat fearsome reputation as a famously efficient chief executive officer, with a loathing of lengthy presentations and an aversion to leaving the office for meals. "You'd be surprised what you can get done in an hour, if you've got a purpose," he told Samantha Conti in *WWD*. "I am 1,000 percent focused on what I do. I'm not into lunches and I'm not into meetings. I don't do any of that corporate stuff or waste my time with charts, meetings, or market research."

Topshop's lines were so fashion-forward—as well as affordable—that the chain soon began to gain a reputation among the fashion elite. Green was known for cultivating famous shoppers, such as film star Lindsay Lohan and R&B diva Beyonce, and taking them for a late-night visit to Topshop's flagship store on Oxford Circus. The 90,000-square-foot store has four stories, and its back door takes deliveries three times daily to keep the merchandise in stock; an astounding 28,000 shoppers a day visit it. By contrast, a New York City landmark such as Bloomingdale's, with a much larger footprint, hosts about 45,000 visitors daily. It is estimated that three out of every five British women shop regularly at Topshop or Arcadia's other stores, making Green perhaps the most influential trendsetter in the country. In 2007, shoppers lined up overnight to be the first in the door when model Kate Moss's exclusive Topshop line debuted, which quickly sold out.

Green has an opulent lifestyle that is somewhat of a rarity for British CEOs, who generally keep much lower, less flashy profiles. He owns a $20 million, Italian-made yacht called the *Lionheart* and uses his $45 million Gulfstream jet to fly back home to Monaco on Friday afternoons. The R&B group Destiny's Child performed at his son's 2005 bar mitzvah party in Monaco, and Green regularly hosts a birthday bacchanal every March for himself. In 2007, to celebrate turning 55, he flew two planeloads of guests to an exclusive resort in the Maldives. Later that year, however, the British press printed allegations that Topshop manages to keep its prices low because of contracts with manufacturers on another island in the Indian Ocean, Mauritius, where employment agents recruit foreign workers to toil in near-slavery conditions.

Even Green's wife did not like him when they first met in the mid-1980s in London, where Tina Palos had emigrated from South Africa to open a clothing boutique. "I thought he was dreadful," she told *Daily Mail* journalist Kathryn Knight in a rare interview. "I remember him asking me who I was. I said I ran a boutique called Harabels and he said, rather dismissively, 'Well I've never heard of it.' I thought: 'What an arrogant man.'" One legend about his acquisition of Arcadia holds that his daughter Chloe, just nine years old at the time, begged him to buy it.

Topshop's appeal, however, seems universal. Altogether, Green oversees 40,000 employees and a retail empire with more than 2,300 stores in the United Kingdom and an additional 360 foreign franchises. There were plans to extend those numbers with the opening of the first Topshop in New York City by 2008. "I think everybody, from every end of the market place, from young through to old, wants to be fashionable," he said in an interview with Polly Vernon for London's *Observer*. "Everybody. Women want to feel like they're wearing the right merchandise, regardless of age. They want to be trendy."

Sources

Daily Mail (London, England), June 3, 2005, p. 22.
Forbes Global, March 15, 2004, p. 58.
Guardian (London, England), March 12, 2007, p. 3.
New York Times, June 21, 2006.
Observer (London, England), February 11, 2007, p. 32.
Sunday Times (London, England), September 1, 2002, p. 13; August 12, 2007, p. 3.
Times (London, England), October 19, 1981, p. 10.
WWD, March 24, 2003, p. 16; May 3, 2006, p. 1.

—Carol Brennan

Julie Greenwald

President of Atlantic Records

Born in 1970; married Lewis Largent (a former MTV veejay); children: Tallulah Rose. *Education:* Tulane University, B.A.

Addresses: *Office*—Atlantic Records Group, 1290 Avenue of the Americas, New York, NY 10104.

Career

Teacher in New Orleans, LA, c. 1991-92; Def Jam Records, personal assistant to the president, 1992, later head of marketing; Island Def Jam Music Group, senior vice president of marketing, 1999-2002, then executive vice president, 2002-04; president, Island Records, 2002-04; president, Atlantic Records, New York, NY, 2004—.

Sidelights

Record company executive Julie Greenwald was one of the few women to run a music label in the United States and one of the youngest. Beginning her career at Def Jam as an assistant to its president, she eventually founded the label's effective marketing department. After a stint as the president of Island Records, Greenwald became the president of the Atlantic Records Group in 2004. In her time in the music industry, Greenwald was known for her toughness as well as her devotion to the artists with which she worked.

Born in 1970, Greenwald was the third of four daughters in her Jewish family. Raised in the Catskills, she later entered Tulane University. While a college student, Greenwald was already a music fan, favoring such bands as 10,000 Maniacs and The Smiths. After graduating with her B.A. from Tulane, she spent a year teaching as part of Teach for America in the Calliope projects of New Orleans.

Moving to New York City to be with her boyfriend after the year was up, Greenwald joined Def Jam Records as a personal assistant to the president of the label, Lyor Cohen, in 1992. Showing skill in her work for Cohen, Greenwald was given numerous promotions within Def Jam as well as a stake in the company. Greenwald eventually became the head of marketing and promotions at the hip-hop and rap-oriented label.

Greenwald's work in marketing was widely respected as she established and built up the marketing team there. She was credited for contributing to the development of the talent on the label as well as the success of such Def Jam artists as Public Enemy, LL Cool J, and DMX. Greenwald's efforts helped sell millions of records and earn the talent numerous gold and platinum records. One of her most successful marketing ideas for the label was Month of the Man, which promoted solo rappers Redman and Method Man. The promotion led to two albums and a franchise worth $20 million. Greenwald also put together the Survival of the Nest tour, featuring DMX, Onyx, and Ja Rule, in 1998.

In 1999, Greenwald was promoted to senior vice president of marketing for Def Jam's newly created parent, Island Def Jam Music Group. There, Greenwald continued to build a strong marketing department. She oversaw marketing campaigns for a number of leading Def Jam artists including Jay-Z as well as Island rock musicians such as Bon Jovi, Nickelback, Sum 41, and Ryan Adams.

Greenwald moved to two new positions within Island Def Jam in 2002. She was named the president of Island Records and executive vice president of the parent company, Island Def Jam Music Group. She also oversaw not only marketing for the whole group, but all aspects of the rock and pop-oriented Island's operation including A&R (artists and repertoire) and promotions. While Def Jam had had more success at the time than Island, one reason for moving Greenwald into the position was to build up Island and the rock side which had been lagging behind its rap/hip-hop counterpart. She spent two years working with Island artists with some success.

In 2004, Greenwald was on maternity leave when she decided to leave her positions at Island Def Jam for a job within Warner Music. Her mentor, Cohen, was now employed there as the head of U.S. operations, and Warner Music was undergoing a restructuring after a change in ownership. Greenwald was named the president of the Atlantic Records Group, a subsidiary of Warner Music, and continued to primarily focus on marketing and promotions.

Upon taking the position, Greenwald had to cut more than 20 percent of the staff as Warner was consolidating the Atlantic and Elektra labels as part of a larger cost-cutting effort. The number of artists and releases handled by Atlantic was also being reduced to better maximize effort and profits. Despite the cuts, Atlantic soon thrived under Greenwald's leadership and within two years had increased its market share by 14 percent. By 2006, Atlantic was the number-three label in the United States in terms of market share. In one week in March of 2006 alone, Atlantic artists Juvenile and James Blunt had the top two spots on the *Billboard* album chart.

Still focused on the artists at Atlantic, Greenwald played an integral role in launching the careers of the band the Killers and the solo career of Rob Tho-
mas, the frontman of Matchbox 20. Other success stories for Atlantic and Greenwald covered a variety of music genres and included Gnarls Barkley, Panic! at the Disco, Staind, and Death Cab for Cutie. Greenwald especially focused on building up the urban side of the label with gold records coming for Yung Joc, Cassie, and Young Dro in 2006. One reason for their success was Greenwald's forward-thinking broad marketing campaigns. For example, she arranged strategic brand alliances, such as ringtone deals, long before an album's launch.

No matter what, the talent remained the central focus of Greenwald's attention as label chief. Upon being hired at Atlantic, she told Catherine Hong of *W*, "I'm going to do everything I need to do for these artists. I will kill, maim, rape, and pillage for them."

Sources

Books

Marquis Who's Who, Marquis Who's Who, 2006.

Periodicals

Billboard, January 19, 2002, p. 88; June 11, 2005; September 2, 2006; December 9, 2006.

Business Wire, January 7, 2002.

Craig's New York Business, January 31, 2005, p. 21.

Daily Variety, January 4, 2002, p. 1; March 29, 2004, p. 10.

New York Post, March 23, 2004, p. 33; March 19, 2006, p. 31.

PR Newswire, March 31, 2004.

W, February 2005, p. 106.

Online

"Fast Talk: Brands on the Run," Fastcompany.com, http://www.fastcompany.com/magazine/112/fast-talk-greenwald.html (August 12, 2007).

—*A. Petruso*

Rogan Gregory

Fashion designer

Born September 17, 1972, in Boulder, CO; son of Stanford (an industrial artist) and Helen Gregory.

Addresses: *Office*—Rogan, 91 Franklin St., New York, NY 10013.

Career

Worked as a designer for Levi's, Daryl Kerrigan, and Calvin Klein; co-founder and owner of Rogan, 2001—, and Loomstate, 2004—, and designer for Litl Betr, 2005—; creative director for the clothing line Edun, 2004—; opened first store, Rogan, in New York City, 2006; founded home-furnishings line, Rogan Objects, 2006.

Sidelights

Rogan Gregory founded the denim line Rogan in 2001, along with two friends, and serves as the designer behind what *New York Times* journalist David Colman called "the in-crowd jeans label whose formula of realness, coolness and conscience has caused his company to grow faster than Mr. Gregory was ready for." Operating out of an office in New York City's Chinatown neighborhood, Gregory's company also has several other ventures, including a menswear line and a clothing partnership with Bono, singer for the Irish band U2, and Bono's wife Ali Hewson.

Born in Boulder, Colorado, in the early 1970s, Gregory is the son of Stanford Gregory, an industrial artist and sculptor, and his wife, Helen. Gregory be-

gan helping his father at an early age in making totem poles out of flag poles and car parts, among other projects, but "as I got to be 12 or 13, I became more of his art critic," he said in an interview with Eric Wilson for the *New York Times*. As a youngster, he lived with his family in places as diverse as the American Midwest and North Africa, and he moved to New York City in 1994. For the next few years, he worked for the denim giant Levi's as well as at Calvin Klein, and he also did a stint with Irish-born New York designer Daryl Kerrigan. He started his own company in 2001 with two founding partners, and launched a denim line that bore his first name. "Rogan" capitalized on the new craze for distressed denim, or jeans that were deliberately made to look vintage. "People spend too much time in sterile environments," Gregory explained about the appeal of such styles to Austin Bunn in the *New York Times* in 2002. "They get up, go to the gym and the office, and they move from one air-conditioned room to another. People are into the authenticity of vintage jeans because they don't want to look like they spend all day at a computer."

Gregory's premium jeans soon caught on with customers in Europe and Japan, and stateside became known for astronomical retail prices that inched toward $450. Even Gregory was astonished at what the market would bear. He told *New York* online magazine writer Adam Sternbergh that he once introduced a limited edition line: "I made them as perfectly as I could. Which for me means essentially destroying the fabric, to the point where if you wear them for a month, they'll disintegrate. And I literally sold them out in a week. And they'll completely disintegrate. You wear them for a couple of weeks and go out one night and there'll be a giant tear. I mean, it's embarrassing. I was surprised that people would pay that amount of money for something that literally falls apart."

Gregory began to think more about the cotton he used in his jeans from an environmental perspective, particularly how it was grown and dyed. In 2004, he launched a separate clothing line, called Loomstate, which offered T-shirts and other basic clothing staples made from organically grown cotton. "It just seemed like the logical thing to do," he explained to Marin Preske in a *Good* magazine article that appeared on the HuffingtonPost.com Web site. "We're concerned about the food we eat and where it comes from, and it should be the same with the clothes on our backs."

Gregory's progressive ideas soon brought him into contact with Bono, the frontman for the Irish rock band U2 who is known for his humanitarian activism. Bono and his wife, Ali Hewson, were interested in boosting the number of manufacturing jobs in some of the hardest-hit areas of the planet. Gregory told Preske that Bono and his wife "wanted to do production in Africa. So they approached us about helping them with design and a sustainable platform for the line." The new venture, for which Gregory served as creative designer, was called Edun ("nude" spelled backwards). Edun offered an affordable line of men's and women's clothing manufactured in Lesotho, Uganda, and other places in Africa, and made from organically grown cotton whenever possible. Its mission was to offer an alternative for consumers who were aware that most of the clothing the Western world wears is often made in sweatshop conditions and in some cases by child labor. The labels sewn into Edun's clothes sum up the company's motto: "We carry the stories of the people who make our clothes around with us." As Gregory explained to *WWD* writer Rosemary Feitelberg, "In the end, you have a lot of options with clothing and the choices you can make with your money."

Gregory signed on with Edun in 2004, and the first collection appeared in the spring of 2005. The clothes are sold in stores such as Saks Fifth Avenue in the United States and Harrods and Selfridges in Britain, and Gregory admitted that the first few years were difficult. Transportation issues in some parts of Africa were one obstacle, as was the fact that many of the factories with which Edun contracted had an unusually high number of workers who were HIV-positive, reflecting the deadly grip that HIV and AIDS have in parts of southern Africa. Finding enough organically grown cotton was yet another issue. "Three years later, we've got our heads above water," he told *Wall Street Journal*'s Christina Binkley in the fall of 2007. "It's hard enough to start a company, let alone to do it with organic fabric and make it in Africa."

Continuing to branch out, Gregory launched Litl Betr, a menswear line of suits, ties, and sweaters, in early 2005. In 2006, he opened his first freestanding retail store in New York City's Tribeca neighborhood, and he also introduced Rogan Objects, a home furnishings line made from salvaged wood and other recycled materials. But it was his premium denim, roughed up to look dirty and old, on which Gregory had built his mini-empire, which he found somewhat ironic. "I've been wearing the same thing my entire life," he told Sternbergh in the *New York* magazine article in 2006. "But ten years ago, people gave me a hard time. If I was checking into a hotel, they wouldn't believe that I was actually staying there. Now it's accepted that just because that dude doesn't look like some fancy-pants—well, you never know."

Sources

Periodicals

Daily News Record (Los Angeles, CA), February 14, 2005, p. 30.

New York Times, December 1, 2002; April 17, 2005; March 2, 2006.

Wall Street Journal, October 18, 2007, p. D8.

WWD, February 5, 2005, p. 14; October 24, 2005, p. 5.

Online

"Up with Grups," *New York Magazine*, http://www.nymag.com/news/features/16529 (October 29, 2007).

"Victimless Fashion," HuffingtonPost.com, http://www.huffingtonpost.com/good-magazine/victimless-fashion_b_65359.html (October 31, 2007).

—*Carol Brennan*

Armando Guebuza

President of Mozambique

Born Armando Emílio Guebuza, January 20, 1943, in Murrupula, Nampula province, northern Mozambique; married Maria da Luz Guebuza (maiden name, Dai); children: Mussumbuluko, Ndambi, Norah, Valentina.

Addresses: *Office*—Office of the President, Avenida Julius Nyerere 2000, Maputo CP 285, Mozambique.

Career

Joined the Front for the Liberation of Mozambique (Frelimo), c. 1963, and rose through its military forces to the rank of lieutenant general; served as Mozambique's Minister of the Interior, c. 1975-84, and Transport Minister, c. 1987; chief negotiator at the 1992 Rome General Peace Accords to resolve Mozambique's 17-year civil war; became secretary-general of Frelimo, 2002; became Frelimo's winning presidential candidate, December 2004.

Sidelights

When Armando Guebuza was elected president of the southern African nation of Mozambique in 2004, he became just the third person to serve as head of state in its history as an independent nation. Mozambique's long struggle for independence and the devastation of the civil war that followed have shaped Guebuza's life and that of the nation's, and the scars from those wars had not yet fully healed. "Only united we can overcome poverty and all the other difficulties our country is facing today," Guebuza said in his victory speech, according to Tom Nevin in a 2005 report that appeared in *African Business.*

Guebuza was born Armando Emílio Guebuza on January 20, 1943, in northern Mozambique. His given names reflect the country's long legacy as a colony of Portugal; traders from the European sea-faring power had been active along Mozambique's Indian Ocean coastline as far back as the early 1500s. Blacks in Mozambique, descended from aboriginal San and Bantu-speaking peoples, were exploited for centuries as a laboring class and had no political voice. This system continued even after World War II—while other European nations were granting independence to their overseas colonies, Portugal was by then a right-wing dictatorship, and Mozambique, along with other properties like Angola and Macau, was declared an overseas province, bringing a flood of immigrants hoping to escape the repressive atmosphere in Portugal itself. As other African nations were finally achieving black self-rule, Mozambique was becoming an increasingly white society, and there were fears that it would become like its neighbor, South Africa, which was under the harsh rule of a white separatist government that kept its widely reviled policy of apartheid in place only by force.

The situation in Mozambique gave rise to a guerrilla movement for independence that was based on Marxist theories. Calling itself the Front for the Liberation of Mozambique, but better known by its acronym "Frelimo," it began to win over villagers and enjoyed support from the Soviets and other Communist nations. Guebuza joined Frelimo at the age of 20 and rose to a prominent position in its leadership cadre during the war for Mozambique's independence that began on September 25, 1964. Only when the Portuguese regime in Lisbon fell did Frelimo succeed in taking control of Mozambique, and independence was declared on June 25, 1975. Mozambique's first president was Guebuza's Frelimo colleague Samora Machel, who immediately implemented several Marxist-style programs, such as nationalization of all industries and collectivization of agricultural production. These economic programs were poorly managed, often staffed by disinterested Russian specialists, and Mozambique's already devastated economy sunk into further decline as agricultural production plummeted and, with that, its vital export revenues.

Machel's government made up for lost exports by becoming dependent on economic ties to South Africa, including labor contracts that sent Mozambican men to toil in South Africa's hellish gold and diamond mines. Inside Frelimo—now a political party—there was a concerted opposition to such links to the apartheid regime, and Guebuza was apparently a key figure among these senior party officials. A July 1976 report in the *New York Times* from correspondent John F. Burns noted that since independence Mozambique was a place of still-roiling unrest, political repression, and widespread poverty. "Rumors of an impending coup, current for months, died down after reports that Armando Guebuza, the Interior Minister and acknowledged leader of the radical faction, had been stabbed by Mr. Machel's bodyguards after a disagreement in the presidential palace in May."

Despite that incident, Guebuza served as Interior Minister in Machel's cabinet, and earned the nickname *Vinte-quatro/Vinte* (Portuguese for "24-20") for the infamous policy enacted by his office: Any Portuguese person could be delivered a so-called "24-20" summons, which gave them just 24 hours to leave the country and permitted them to take just 20 kilograms of luggage out of Mozambique. Meanwhile, a divisive civil war with another guerrilla group called Renamo (the acronym for the Portuguese-language "Mozambican National Resistance") was continuing to make Mozambique one of the African continent's most violent and unstable places. The country descended into further chaos when Machel and several members of the government died in a mysterious 1986 plane crash in South Africa.

Following the death of Machel, Guebuza served on the ten-member presidential council that ran the country for the next few weeks, and then served as Mozambique's Transport Minister under the Frelimo veteran who succeeded Machel. Joaquim Chissano would lead the country for the next 18 years as president, guiding the country out of its long and disastrous civil war and ruinous Marxist policies. Regarding the conclusion of hostilities with Renamo, Chissano appointed Guebuza to serve as chief negotiator at the 1992 Rome peace accords that helped bring an end to the internal conflict in 1995.

Chissano declined to run for a third term as president in 2004 elections, and Guebuza became the Frelimo candidate. He won with 63 percent of the vote, beating the Renamo candidate Alfonso Dhlakama. Sworn in as president on February 2, 2005, Guebuza took over a nation of 20 million that is the sixth poorest in the world. Its potential for economic success is dependent on its relatively untapped mineral resources, and Guebuza has actively sought out foreign investment.

The remaining symbol of Portuguese rule in Mozambique was the Cahora-Bassa hydroelectric dam on the Zambezi River, the largest dam in sub-Saharan Africa. Finished in 1975, it was sabotaged by Renamo during the civil war and needed extensive repairs. Portugal remained a majority stakeholder, but after 20 years of negotiations, the government in Lisbon agreed to a complicated $950 million deal that finally gave Mozambique control of Cahora-Bassa. The handover ceremony in November of 2007 in the village of Songo was a momentous occasion attended by Portugal's minister for finance and thousands of Mozambicans. "This is our second independence," Guebuza told the crowd, according to another report by Nevin, the *African Business* journalist. The president noted that back in 1975 Frelimo had decided to declare independence even though Cahora-Bassa, a key part of the country's infrastructure, had not yet been secured by Frelimo forces. "However, like the struggle for our national liberation that took 12 years, we remained convinced that one day we would win because we knew we were right in our demands."

Sources

African Business, February 2005, p. 48; January 2008, p. 54.
Economist, December 1, 2007, p. 61.
New York Times, July 25, 1976; January 27, 1987; December 5, 2004.
Pretoria News (Pretoria, South Africa), September 27, 2006, p. 5.

—*Carol Brennan*

Amy Gutmann

President of the University of Pennsylvania

Born November 19, 1949, in Brooklyn, NY; daughter of Kurt and Beatrice Gutmann; married Michael W. Doyle (a professor of law and international affairs), 1976; children: Abigail. *Education:* Radcliffe College, B.A. (magna cum laude), 1971; London School of Economics, M.S., 1972; Harvard University, Ph.D., 1976.

Addresses: *Home*—Philadelphia, PA. *Office*—University of Pennsylvania, 100 College Hall, Philadelphia, PA 19104-6380.

Career

Assistant professor of politics, 1976-81, associate professor of politics, 1981-86, professor of politics, 1987-2004, director of political philosophy program, 1987-89, Andrew W. Mellon Professor, 1987-90, director of ethics and public affairs programs, 1990-95 and 1997-2000, dean of faculty, 1995-97, academic advisor to president, 1997-98, University Center for Human Values (founding director), 1990-2004, Laurance S. Rockefeller Professor of Politics, 1990-2004, provost, 2001-04, all at Princeton University; president and professor of political science, University of Pennsylvania, 2004—. Also author of several books and contributor to academic journals.

Member: Executive commitee, Association of Practical and Professional Ethics, 1990—; board and executive committee, Princeton University Press, 1996-2004; board of directors, Schuylkill River Development Corporation, 2004—; National Security Higher Education Advisory Board, 2005—; executive committee, Greater Philadelphia Chamber of Commerce, 2005—; board of directors, the Carnegie Corporation of New York, 2005—; board of directors, the Vanguard Group, 2006—; board of trustees, National Constitution Center, 2007—.

Awards: Ralph J. Bunche Award, American Political Science Association, for *Color Conscious: The Political Morality of Race,* 1997; Book Award, North American Society for Social Philosophy for *Color Conscious: The Political Morality of Race,* 1997; Gustavus Myers Center for the Study of Human Rights in North America Award, 1997; Bertram Mott Award, American Association of University Professors, 1998; President's Distinguished Teaching Award, Princeton University, 2000; Centennial Medal, Harvard University, 2003; Alumunae Recognition Award, Radcliffe Institute for Advance Study, Harvard University, 2006.

Sidelights

In 2004, Amy Gutmann became the second woman chosen to lead the University of Pennsylvania, a first in the Ivy League. A political science professor who rose to the number-two post at Princeton University, Gutmann was also a distinguished specialist in political philosophy and gained a reputation as a strong, consensus-building executive. "I feel as I've never been able to feel before in my life—that I'm putting years of research and knowledge into practice," she told *Philadelphia Inquirer* reporter Susan Snyder in 2007 after news that her contract had been extended until 2014. "I'm leading an enormous institution forward in ways that everybody can affirm makes a big difference to society."

Gutmann was born in 1949 to Jewish parents living in Brooklyn at the time. Her father fled Nazi Germany in 1934 and spent several years in Bombay, India, before coming to the United States. Gutmann's American-born mother had hoped to attend college, but her plans to become a teacher were thwarted by the Great Depression and the necessity of having to work to support her struggling family. Life for the Gutmanns was easier by the time their only child was born and, like her mother, she dreamt of becoming a teacher. "When I was in kindergarten, the only thing I remember is that I wanted to be a kindergarten teacher, and then I went to high school and wanted to be a high-school teacher," Gutmann told John Prendergast in the *Pennsylvania Gazette* about her earliest career ambitions. "In college, I wanted to be a college teacher."

Gutmann grew up in Monroe, New York, an hour's drive from New York City, in a rural working-class community where Jewish families were rare. When her father died of a heart attack before she started her senior year of high school, she and her mother worried about how to finance her college plans. "A college recruiter comes to my high school and, as I later discover, my principal tells him that I won't need any financial aid," Gutmann recalled in a 2003 speech on diversity in higher education that was reprinted in the *Princeton Alumni Weekly*. "He apparently assumed that since we're Jewish, we are rich. I was fortunate enough to receive a full scholarship to college, and my mother, ironically enough, was hired as secretary to my high school principal."

Gutmann was such a talented student that she scored first place in the New York State Regents' exam in math, and was valedictorian of her 1967 graduating class of Monroe-Woodbury High School. Her scholarship was to Harvard-Radcliffe College, and she had collected enough advance credits to enter as a sophomore. When she arrived at the Cambridge, Massachusetts, school, Radcliffe was shedding its long history as the women's college attached to Harvard, and the administrative, academic, and even residential-dormitory barriers

were being dismantled. All college campuses, even the elite Ivy League schools like Harvard, witnessed episodes of protest and unrest during this era as opposition to the war in Vietnam escalated along with support for civil rights and other social-justice issues, and the atmosphere prompted Gutmann to abandon her plans for a math degree. Instead she graduated magna cum laude in 1971 with a degree in political science, and went on to earn her master's degree from the prestigious London School of Economics a year later.

Returning to Cambridge, Gutmann entered the doctoral program in political science at Harvard, and, as she neared completion of her dissertation and planned to return to England as a Fulbright scholar, she heard of an opening at Princeton's department of politics, as its political science department is called. She applied for it at a time when U.S. colleges and universities were eager to bring more women into tenure-track positions, and "I got the offer before I finished my dissertation," Gutmann told *New York Times* journalist Anne Ruderman. "It was my first job interview ever."

Gutmann joined the faculty of Princeton as an assistant professor of politics in 1976, the same year she married Michael Doyle, a fellow graduate student whom she had met while at Harvard; he was also hired by Princeton. After five years, she advanced to associate professor status, and earned tenure in 1987, the same year she became director of Princeton's political philosophy program. She also headed its ethics and public affairs programs for most of the 1990s, and even briefly served as the school's dean of faculty, though she gave it up to return to teaching and research.

During this period of her career, Gutmann published several titles. She edited works that were collections of scholarly essays by others on democracy, multiculturalism, the U.S. courts, and welfare. Her first author credit came in 1980 for *Liberal Equality*, published by Cambridge University Press. Her 1987 work, *Democratic Education*, examined the role of educational instructions in a democratic society. For several books, she collaborated with a Harvard scholar, Dennis Thompson, with whom she had taught a course at Princeton. Their joint works include *Democracy and Disagreement*, *Identity in Democracy*, and *Why Deliberative Democracy?* The third title refers to a concept they formulated called deliberative democracy which, Gutmann explained to Prendergast in the *Pennsylvania Gazette*, is "a way of moving forward on hard issues" like crime, health care in America, and even education. Deliberative democracy ensures that "all voices are heard. If you engage the perspectives of all of the people whose lives are affected by these issues, it is possible to arrive at a consensus that is defensible. Not unanimous, but defensible."

Gutmann's achievements at Princeton include helping to found the University Center for Human Values in 1990 and serving as its director for the next 14 years. In 2001, her name was mentioned as a possible candidate to become the first female president of her alma mater, Harvard—a school whose first joint commencement exercises with its women's college, Radcliffe, had happened just a year before she earned her undergraduate degree. In 1994, Judith Rodin became the first female president of an Ivy League school (University of Pennsylvania); seven years later Ruth Simmons became president of Brown University, and Shirley Tilghman was appointed to lead Princeton. Tilghman named Gutmann to serve as provost, the number-two job at the school, but Gutmann's first month on the job was shaped by the tragedy of September 11, 2001, when the New York City's World Trade Center and the Pentagon in Washington, D.C. were attacked. "I had thought there was no time left in the day, but apparently I was wrong," Gutmann recalled about her busy first weeks as provost in the *New York Times* interview with Ruderman. "Needless to say, I could not have anticipated writing a memorial prayer."

Gutmann won high marks as Princeton provost, and emerged as a leading candidate for the University of Pennsylvania president's job, from which Rodin was retiring. Founded by Benjamin Franklin in 1740, the Philadelphia school is the fourth-oldest institution of higher learning in the United States. After a surprisingly brief search process, trustees of Penn—as the school is known informally—announced in January of 2004 that Gutmann would become the school's eighth leader. She also achieved a new Ivy League first as the first female president to succeed a female predecessor.

Gutmann's long and well-documented support for diversity issues was said to have been one of the key factors in Penn's decision. Much larger than most of its Ivy League counterparts in student body and the number of graduate schools, Penn is an urban campus with close links to the Philadelphia and southern New Jersey region. The school is also Philadelphia's largest private employer. During her first week on the job in July of 2004, Gutmann sent out an e-mail to the 93,000 living University of Pennsylvania degree-holders, asking for their suggestions. She received hundreds of responses, which served as an example of "deliberative democracy" at work. "The idea of Penn being an ex-

tended family is something that is very dear to my heart," she added in the interview with Prendergast for the *Pennsylvania Gazette*. "This will be my family, and I intend to interact a lot with it and do everything I can to cultivate the kind of loyalty that is necessary to make us an even greater institution."

In her inaugural address as president, Gutmann announced what she called the Penn Compact, whose trio of goals included increasing the diversity of the student body, bringing in top-caliber faculty, and expanding Penn's presence in the city, the nation, and even the world. One example of the Compact in action was Community Partnership Celebration days, where Penn students volunteered at Philadelphia public schools. During her first few years on the job, Gutmann also initiated a new campus development plan, called Penn Connects, to expand eastward to the Schuylkill River by revitalizing a former industrial zone. It was also designed to make the campus less of an inaccessible "ivory tower" facility for Philadelphia residents.

In the fall of 2007, Gutmann announced that Penn had overhauled its financial aid system. Students from households with incomes of $60,000 a year or less became eligible for full tuition grants to cover the cost of one year of college, which, with room and board, had reached $46,000. It marked a far cry from the tuition rate hike that brought fees to $2,000 at Harvard-Radcliffe in 1967, the year she began college, but, even adjusted for inflation, the high costs of attending such prestigious schools put them out of reach for many hard-working parents of bright students, as she had once been. With that in mind, Penn also announced that beginning with the academic year 2008-09, students from households with incomes below $100,000 would also be eligible for loan-free aid packages. "Even before we did the low-income initiative, we knew that middle-income families were facing a squeeze," a report by *Philadelphia Inquirer* writer Kathy Boccella quoted her as saying. "You begin with those with greatest need. But if you stop there, you're not doing everything you can do."

In 2007 Gutmann's contract as president was extended for another five years past its 2009 expiration date, giving her a full decade on the job. The announcement of the extension was viewed as a vote of confidence for both her leadership and the success of Penn's massive endowment-enhancement campaign already in progress. Titled "Making History," the fund-raising program had already given Penn's endowment a significant boost to $6.6 billion—though that paled in comparison to Harvard's endowment of nearly $35 billion—and was crucial to the success of the Penn Compact to help a more diverse section of students attend the school while also luring prominent scholars and researchers to its faculty.

Gutmann earns a salary of $675,000 annually as Penn's president, along with benefits and the use of an official residence called Eisenlohr on Walnut Street. Her husband is a Columbia University professor of law and international affairs, and their daughter, Abigail Gutmann Doyle, was following in both parents' footsteps by planning to enter academia after earning her doctorate in chemistry from Harvard. Gutmann is a popular and respected university president, winning high marks from students, faculty, and alumni. The sole negative criticism associated with her came after a Halloween party held at Eisenlohr in the fall of 2006, a long-standing Penn tradition. Some 700 costumed students attended that year, and having a photograph with the University president is also a time-honored tradition. Gutmann posed with an engineering student dressed as a suicide bomber who also toted a toy automatic gun. When the photograph circulated on the Internet, some questioned her judgment in seeming to condone terrorism. In response, her office released a statement that read, according to the *Weekly Standard*, that "the costume is clearly offensive and I was offended by it. As soon as I realized what his costume was, I refused to take any more pictures with him, as he requested. The student had the right to wear the costume just as I, and others, have a right to criticize his wearing of it."

Sources

Periodicals

Newsweek International, October 22, 2007.
New York Times, September 30, 2001.
Pennsylvania Gazette, September-October 2004.
Philadelphia Inquirer, January 22, 2004; October 23, 2007; December 18, 2007.
USA Today, June 5, 2006, p. 3B.
Weekly Standard, November 13, 2006.

Online

"Why Does Diversity Matter?," *Princeton Alumni Weekly*, http://www.princeton.edu/~paw/web_exclusives/bonus_stories/bonus_030403gutmann.html (May 14, 2008).

—*Carol Brennan*

Rafi Haladjian

Co-founder of Violet

Born c. 1962, in Beirut, Lebanon. *Education:* Studied linguistics.

Addresses: *Office*—Violet, 18 Rue du Faubourg du Temple, 75011 Paris, France.

Career

Began career with Minitel, the France Telecom proto-Internet service, 1983; co-founder, FranceNet/Fluxus (an Internet service provider),

1994; sold FranceNet/Fluxus to British Telecom, 2001; co-founder of Ozone and Violet, 2002.

Sidelights

Rafi Haladjian is one of the founders of Violet, the Paris-based company that makes the innovative Nabaztag "smart-home" device. The Nabaztag is an appealing white plastic rabbit that connects to the home's wireless system. It can receive text messages from outside the home or be programmed to announce commands, among its myriad of uses. "It's more like a living creature than an appliance," Haladjian told Thomas Jackson of *Forbes Life*. "People become emotionally attached to it."

The "Nabaztag" brand name is in homage to Haladjian's Armenian heritage as the Armenian word for "rabbit." He was born in Beirut, Lebanon, and his family moved to France when he was a teenager. For a time, he studied linguistics, and began his career in the telecommunications field in 1983 during the Minitel era. A joint venture of Britain and France's state-owned telephone monopolies, Minitel was a pre-Internet online service that became immensely successful in France thanks to the fact that France Telecom gave out its terminals—consisting of a monitor, keyboard, and telephone modem—for free. The Minitel revolution helped pave the way for future online service providers like Compuserve and America Online in the era before the World Wide Web.

Around 1994, Haladjian became involved in the start-up FranceNet, the Internet service provider (ISP) for the country. Its name was changed to Fluxus in 2000, and it was sold to British Telecom a year later. With the money from the deal, "I was wondering what to do next," Haladjian told Hrag Vartanian in an article for *AGBU* magazine—the organ of the Armenian General Benevolent Union—that appeared on the Armeniapedia.org Web site. "Then I found that the internet wasn't the last step in the evolution of the way we use things to access networks. In my opinion, pervasive networks and smart objects were the next step."

Haladjian began two ventures: one was Ozone, whose ultimate goal was to loop Paris into Europe's wireless internet (Wi-Fi) network. Ozone kept its infrastructure-building costs low by soliciting residents to let them allow rooftop access for the wireless towers in exchange for free wireless service. Violet was the second company that Haladjian cofounded, and its mission was to develop new ways

to capitalize on this Wi-Fi service. Its first product was the Dal, a computerized lamp launched in 2004 that would become the predecessor of the Nabaztag bunny. It connected to the home or office wireless network, and could be programmed to blink different colors related to various functions; for example, if stock market trading was tumbling that day, the Dal flashed a certain color. It sold for about $937, however, and failed to catch on with early-adapter consumers.

The idea for the Nabaztag "bunny" was entirely accidental. "I just happened to have a toy rabbit on my desk, and my cofounders and I thought, 'What if we stuffed it with Wi-Fi?'" Haladjian recounted about Violet's next product in an interview with *Fast Company* writer David Lidsky. Once Haladjian and his business partner, Olivier Mével, realized the genius of using a bunny as their flagship product, they went ahead with the prototype. A rabbit has multiple associations, Haladjian explained to Vartanian, such as "a smart rabbit like Bugs Bunny, a sexy rabbit like the Playboy bunny or the rabbit in Alice in Wonderland." They also decided to use the Armenian word for rabbit, rationalizing that many successful high-tech items bore foreign names, like the Tamagotchi virtual pet from Japan.

The Nabaztag bunny caught on quickly after its launch in June of 2005 in France, partly because of its much lower price than the Dal lamp. The initial shipment from the factory in Shenzhen, China, was 4,800 and it sold out in Paris stores less than two weeks later. Another shipment, double that amount, also sold out. The product was launched in Britain later that summer, and was tested by Charles Arthur, a journalist for the *Guardian*. Arthur found some fault with the device, including the fact that the cartoon-like, ten-inch bunny is irresistible to very small children. Arthur said that his one-year-old son pulled out the ears that serve as the Nabaztag wireless antenna, "an indignity it suffered in immobile silence, though once the ears were reattached it slowly whirled them back into place, guaranteeing the process would be repeated." Arthur also criticized what he found was "the impenetrability of its colour-coded blinking," asserting that the Nabaztag's "lack of text gave it the air of an object from the anti-literate world of *Fahrenheit 451*," referring the 1951 science-fiction novel in which all books were banned by a totalitarian state.

Haladjian saw the Nabaztag as the next stage in the long-awaited smart home, in which everyday tasks could be programmed automatically by a series of devices connected to a network. "Your alarm clock, coffee maker, and heater should all adjust in a synchronized manner to the time at which you want to get up," he explained to *International Herald Tribune* journalist Thomas Crampton. "The ultimate goal is to link all devices within a home and even a city for your convenience."

A second-generation version of the Nabaztag was launched in the United States in the fall of 2007 as the Nabaztag/tag. One of the new features was the inclusion of programmable ID tags—similar to the fuel-station keychain icons that automatically record one's purchase at the pump—which could be used by a child coming home from school; waving the tag would send a text message to a parent at work alerting them to the fact the youngster was safely at home. He and Mével also planned to make the Nabaztag code open-source, thus available to users who were also software programmers so that they could come up with their own features. As Haladjian told Crampton in the *International Herald Tribune* interview, "my customers will direct this journey."

Sources

Periodicals

Fast Company, December 19, 2007.
Forbes Life, December 11, 2006, p. 87.
Guardian (London, England), May 18, 2006, p. 4.
International Herald Tribune, July 18, 2005, p. 8.
New York Times, December 6, 2006.
Sydney Morning Herald (Sydney, Australia), August 14, 2006.

Online

"Rafi Haladjian," Armeniapedia.org, http://www.armeniapedia.org/index.php?title=Rafi_Haladjian (February 11, 2008).

—*Carol Brennan*

Victoria Hale

Robert Pitts/Landov

Chemist and pharmaceutical executive

Born c. 1961, in Maryland; daughter of government employees; married Ahvie Herskowitz (a cardiologist). *Education:* University of Maryland, B.S., 1983; University of California—San Francisco, Ph.D., 1990.

Addresses: *Office*—Institute for OneWorld Health, 50 California St., Ste. 500, San Francisco, CA 94111.

Career

Clinical trial research associate, Johns Hopkins Hospital oncology center, c. 1983-85; senior reviewer, U.S. Food and Drug Administration, 1990-94; research scientist, Genentech Inc., 1994-97; co-founder, Axiom Biomedical Inc., 1999; chief scientific officer, Axiom Biomedical Inc., 1999-2000; founder, Institute for OneWorld Health, 2000; chairperson and chief executive officer, Institute for OneWorld Health, 2000—; adjunct associate professor of biopharmaceutical sciences, University of California—San Francisco, 2002; advisor, World Health Organization (WHO); expert reviewer, National Institutes of Health (NIH).

Awards: Executive of the Year, *Esquire* magazine, 2005; award for social entrepreneurship, Skoll Foundation, 2005; fellow, Ashoka Innovators for the Public, 2006; MacArthur Fellow, John D. and Catherine T. MacArthur Foundation, 2006.

Sidelights

Victoria Hale is the founder of the Institute for OneWorld Health, an innovative new nonprofit pharmaceutical company that strives to bring life-saving drugs to the developing world. Based in San Francisco, OneWorld Health is the first such firm of its type in the United States, and has the potential to prevent millions of needless deaths. Hale was inspired to launch her visionary project in part from a joke a cab driver once made when she told him she was a pharmaceutical scientist. "You guys have all the money," she recalled him saying, and Hale realized he had a point, she told *Fast Company*'s Alison Overholt. "Our industry does have all the money. We decide which drugs to make—and it's always about the profit margin. I decided right there that it would have to be me that separated profit from the scientific process of deciding which drugs are to move forward."

Born in the early 1960s, Hale was the first of three daughters in her family, and grew up in suburban Washington, D.C. Both of her parents worked for the federal government, and she recalled that her interest in medicine was sparked at an early age from her own medical issues. "I had been a sickly child with a lot of ear and sinus infections," she told *New York Times* reporter Elizabeth Olson. "Relief came from the antibiotics I was given, and I wanted to do for other people what my pharmacist did for me."

Hale earned her undergraduate degree in pharmacy from the University of Maryland in 1983, then worked for two years at Johns Hopkins Hospital, one of the country's most prestigious medical centers for both teaching and treatment. In its oncology center she worked on clinical trials for new drugs, which spurred her to continue her education at the University of California's doctoral program in pharmaceutical chemistry in San Francisco. She earned her Ph.D. in 1990 and was hired by the U.S. Food and Drug Administration (FDA) as a senior reviewer for new drug applications.

The world's major drug companies spend millions of dollars every year searching for new or improved cures for diseases and chronic conditions, but firms like Pfizer, AstraZeneca, and Merck are for-profit enterprises. This means that their research and development spending is lavished on drugs with the highest profit potential, because conducting the large-scale clinical trials necessary to gain approval from the FDA and regulatory agencies in other parts of the world is a costly and lengthy process. As a result, many new innovative drug treatments that come onto the market are usually ones with millions of potential customers, such as medicines for heart disease and arthritis sufferers. Once a drug is approved, the company that introduced it is granted a patent for a specified period of time—usually ten years—to recoup their investment in research and development. Global giants like Pfizer and GlaxoSmithKline do have divisions that work on drugs for other kinds of diseases that affect people in the developing world, but generally less than ten percent of the company's entire research budget is spent on such endeavors.

From 1994 to 1997 Hale was a research scientist with Genentech Inc., a San Francisco Bay-area company that pioneered biotech drugs such as the first synthetically produced insulin for diabetes sufferers. She and her husband, a cardiologist, founded their own consulting firm in the late 1990s to support themselves as well as fund the future nonprofit firm that Hale was hoping to launch. They were inspired in part by friends of theirs who asked for help in researching possible drug remedies for their 13-year-old daughter who had been diagnosed with a rare form of cancer that affects just a few thousand Americans every year. Hale and her husband learned that there was a promising drug for it, but

it was still in the laboratory stage and had never moved on to the large-scale drug trial required for FDA approval. Hale knew from her own work experience that there were many other potential treatment breakthroughs for other diseases, but there were so few sufferers that companies did not consider it feasible to begin the patent-application and clinical-safety trial processes.

Hale founded the Institute for OneWorld Health in San Francisco in 2000, serving as its chairperson and chief executive officer. Its mission is to identify a disease, then ask companies that have already conducted research to donate those proprietary findings to OneWorld Health; because Hale's venture is a nonprofit, the companies then receive a tax write-off for their generosity. She then searches for grant money or outright donations to help bring the drug to the market. The Bill and Melinda Gates Foundation is one of the most generous supporters of OneWorld Health, and both the National Institutes of Health (NIH) and the World Health Organization (WHO) also help by running clinical trials.

The first drug that OneWorld Health developed was paromomycin, a treatment for visceral leishmaniasis, which affects 1.5 million sufferers around the world in places like India's impoverished Bihar state. In 2006, just after India's government approved paromomycin for use, Hale was given one of the genius grants from the John D. and Catherine T. MacArthur Foundation. More formally called the MacArthur Foundation fellowships, the annual awards bestow $500,000 on U.S. scientists, musicians, artists, or others who are deemed to have the potential to make a difference in the world. By then OneWorld Health was already working on its next projects: a treatment for Chagas disease, which kills 50,000 annually in Central and South America; an anti-diarrheal potion that could prove a lifesaver to millions of children in the developing world; and artemisinin, a miracle malaria cure from an herb known for centuries in China and made from the sweet wormwood plant, but too expensive to produce in large amounts. OneWorld Health was working with researchers to come up with a cost-effective way to genetically engineer artemisinin by tricking bacteria cells into producing it in the lab.

As Hale noted in an article she wrote for *Newsweek*, industry professionals have been generous and supportive of OneWorld Health and its goals. "That's been enormously gratifying, of course, but not surprising," she reflected. "Most pharmaceutical researchers got into the business because they wanted to ease suffering and save lives. Systems may be flawed, but most people want to do the right thing. All they need—all any of us need—is to create a path."

Sources

Esquire December 2005, p. 222.
Fast Company, February 2003, p. 38.
New Statesman, October 17, 2005, p. 18.

Newsweek, December 6, 2004, p. 80.
New York Times, December 31, 2006.

—*Carol Brennan*

Laurell K. Hamilton

Author

Born Laurell Kaye Klein, February 19, 1963, in Heber Springs, AR; daughter of Susie Klein; married Gary Hamilton (divorced); married Jonathon Green, 2001; children: Trinity (from first marriage). *Education:* Degrees in English and biology from Marion College.

Addresses: *Agent*—Merrilee Heifetz, c/o Writers House, 21 West 26th St., New York, NY 10010. *Home*—St. Louis County, Missouri. *Web site*—http://www.laurellkhamilton.org.

Career

Worked as editor for Xerox Corp., c. late 1980s to early 1990s; author of Anita Blake vampire hunter series, 1993—; author of Merry Gentry PI series, 2000—.

Awards: PEARL (Paranormal Excellence Award for Romantic Literature) for *A Kiss of Shadows*, 2000.

Sidelights

In 1993, Laurell Hamilton published *Guilty Pleasures*, which introduced readers to the supernatural world of Anita Blake—a smart and sassy vampire hunter who inhabits a modern-day world where vampires, zombies, werewolves, witches, and magic are commonplace. Fifteen years and 15 volumes later, the dark fantasy-horror-mystery-romance series was still selling strong, making bestseller lists with regularity and earning Hamilton a reputation as one of literature's first ladies of horror.

"Laurell Hamilton's Anita Blake: Vampire Hunter series has to rank as one of the most addictive substances on earth," science fiction and fantasy reviewer Kim Fawcett noted in an article posted on the SF Site. Fawcett went on to describe Blake as "one of the most entertaining characters to come around in a while." Though most authors would be content to create one hit character, Hamilton stretched herself and in 2000 launched the Merry Gentry series about a contemporary faerie princess-turned-detective. By 2007, she had published six books in that series.

Hamilton was born Laurell Kaye Klein on February 19, 1963, in Heber Springs, Arkansas. Her mother, Susie Klein, relocated to Sims, Indiana, shortly after giving birth to Hamilton and being abandoned by Hamilton's father. They moved in with Hamilton's grandmother, Laura Gentry. When Hamilton was six, her mother died in a car crash caused by another motorist running a stop sign. After the accident, Hamilton's uncle took her to see her mother's crunched-up car, and her fascination with the darker sides of life came shining through. Hamilton crawled inside and touched the bloodstains. "No one protected me from that," she told the *Chicago Tribune*'s Sharman Stein. "I did not flinch. I remember all the details."

This event marked a turning point in Hamilton's life—a time when childhood innocence was lost as she came to realize that the adults around her could not shield her from the real world. Speaking to the *St. Louis Post-Dispatch*'s Dave Dorr, Hamilton acknowledged that she would be a different person had her mother not died. With no parents, Hamilton felt like an anomaly. "By the time I was in first grade, my mother was dead and my father was gone. It was just my grandmother and me. I was the only one in first grade without a mom or dad and no brothers or sisters. There were mother-daughter picnics and father-daughter banquets I missed."

Hamilton's introduction to vampires came through her grandmother, who entertained Hamilton by recounting ghost stories that originated in the hills of Arkansas where she was raised. At 13, Hamilton's interest in creatures of the night was piqued after she stumbled upon *Pigeons from Hell*, a collection of horror stories by Robert E. Howard. "It was the first heroic fantasy I'd read," Hamilton told the *Post-Dispatch*'s Dorr. "It was fights, swords, monsters. I decided not only did I want to become a writer, it was this I wanted to write."

Obsessed with horror stories, Hamilton stayed up late on weekends to catch *Creature Feature*, a 1970s television program that presented clips from classic monster movies of the 1930s to 1950s. Later, Hamilton became fixated on *The Natural History of the Vampire*, a book she checked out from the high school library so many times she had parts memorized.

After high school, Hamilton attended Marion College—now Indiana Wesleyan University—and earned degrees in English and biology. The science studies gave Hamilton a good background in anatomy and blood, which later proved useful in her writing. She married her college sweetheart, computer scientist Gary Hamilton, and they eventually settled in St. Louis. For a time, Hamilton worked as an editor for the Xerox Corp., rising at 5 a.m. to write because she was too exhausted in the evenings to do so. She began publishing short stories. "When I first started writing, I did two pages a day, five or six days a week," Hamilton told *Science Fiction Weekly*'s Michael McCarty. "Why two pages? Because on my worst day I could do two pages before I had to get to work in corporate America. I was working a full-time job when I started my first book...."

Hamilton's first book, 1992's *Nightseer*, tells the tale of a sorcerer and prophet, Kereios, whose mother is slain by a nemesis when Kereios is a youngster. The story follows Kereios when she is older and is working to avenge her mother's death. The book did little to get Hamilton noticed. In a review on the SF Site, Steven H. Silver called the novel "a reminder of why many first novels disappear from the shelves, only to be found in used bookstores."

Unfazed by the lack of enthusiasm for her work, Hamilton continued writing and created the world of vampire hunter Anita Blake. The first book in the series, *Guilty Pleasures*, hit bookstores in 1993. The series is set in St. Louis, the same town where Hamilton lives, and features creatures of the night who frequent a vampire strip club known as Guilty Pleasures. The loner-type protagonist, Anita Blake, has a day job as a necromancer—someone who raises the dead. With the help of a blood sacrifice, Blake raises the dead so they can answer questions about disputed wills and estate conflicts. Sometimes, she is called to raise the dead so they can identify their murderers.

By night, Blake works as a licensed vampire executioner. In this world, vampires have civil rights, but if they kill someone an executioner like Blake is summoned to hunt them down. "Anita's world is based on ours," Hamilton told *Science Fiction Weekly*. "As if we went to bed tonight, and when we woke up tomorrow, vampires, zombies, ghouls, werewolves, everything that goes bump in the night, were real. And the modern world had to deal with them, bang. I wanted to play in modern America with the addition of monsters from folklore and mythology."

Hamilton published *Laughing Corpse*, a sequel, in 1994, and fans were clamoring for more. Through word-of-mouth, vampire cultists spread news about Hamilton's fantasy-horror world. Speaking to J. Stephen Bolhafner of the *St. Louis Post-Dispatch*, Hamilton credited her fans—and the Web—for her success. "I'm not sure where I'd be if there wasn't an Internet, actually. One of the first ways that people began to talk about me to each other was over the Internet."

During the next dozen years, Hamilton churned out volumes at a rate of about one per year. Over the course of the series, Blake has evolved. In the first books, Blake believes that monsters are tyrants, and she has no trouble despising and disposing of them. Over time, Blake begins to realize that some of the monsters she hunts are kinder than the humans. She also sees that some of the humans are more hideous than the monsters. Blake continues her work as an executioner, yet at the same time she develops a soft side for these creatures and ends up in romantic relationships with some of them. Along the way, a romantic triangle develops between Blake, a master vampire named Jean-Claude, and an alpha werewolf named Richard.

Hamilton introduced sex in the sixth book, 1997's *The Killing Dance*. Initially, Hamilton was reluctant to add an erotic element to her books and had to be talked into it by one of her editor's friends. Hamilton realized that as she explored Blake's growing attraction to and affection for the monsters of her world, romantic entanglements were inevitable. Nonetheless, Hamilton had a hard time writing about sex. "In the beginning, the scenes were difficult to write," Blake told the *Atlanta Journal-Constitution*'s Teresa K. Weaver. "I was uncomfortable and a little embarrassed. I'd written graphic violence for the five preceding books, but sex made me want to flinch."

As the sex scenes picked up, the books drew the attention of romance readers. Much of Hamilton's fan mail comments on the erotic scenes. Many are complimentary; however, Hamilton also receives criticism and threats from people who consider the scenes too graphic and too twisted. Sometimes, Hamilton uses a bodyguard on book tours. This was the case after the publication of 2001's *Narcissus in Chains*, which is filled with steamy sex and graphic violence. As Hamilton made appearances at book signings and readings, critics lined up to antagonize her and question her sexual desires. "It was vicious," Hamilton told *Publishers Weekly* writer Dorman T. Schindler. "Europeans, almost without exception, think the sex is fine but the violence is too great. And Americans are not bothered by the violence at all—they're bothered by the *sex*! It's okay [in America] to die on stage or in the movies, but God forbid you make love."

Hamilton's idea to explore both the good and evil sides of people and monsters came in part from her experiences. Growing up, she was close to her grandfather, Elbert Gentry, who showered her with love, yet he also spent 20 years beating her grandmother before they divorced. "It's why I do monsters," Hamilton told the *Chicago Tribune*. "The same person who helped me catch butterflies was beating the heck out of my grandmother.... But I loved him and he loved me. The juxtaposition of gentle and cruel: It's hard to wrap a kid's mind around it."

Several years into the Anita Blake series, Hamilton branched out and created another alternate universe, one where humans and magical faeries coexist. The first book in this series, *A Kiss of Shadows*, was published in 2000. The series—which is a mix of supernatural fantasy, detective adventure, and sex—follows the exploits of Merry Gentry, a faerie who is hiding out in Los Angeles, trying to pass as human because her aunt wants her dead. She finds work as a private investigator specializing in supernatural crime.

Along the way, Hamilton divorced her husband and in 2001 married Jonathon Green in a ceremony presided over by a Wiccan high priestess. Hamilton's husband is 12 years her junior. The two met in 1993 at a sci-fi fantasy convention. At the time, Hamilton was married and Green was still in high school. They saw each other occasionally at conventions, where they would hang out and talk about science fiction, religion, politics, and philosophy. They were friends for eight years before dating.

For Hamilton, creating novels has become a full-time, fulfilling occupation. "Writing is a job," she told the *Atlanta Journal-Constitution*. "I write every day from 9 a.m. to whenever I break for lunch. In the afternoon, I either work with my husband on a collaborative project or something else of my own, if the muse is insistent. We work until our daughter gets home from school." While Hamilton writes, she listens to music, including Depeche Mode, U2, Audioslave, Thornley and Nickelback. Sometimes she prefers musicals or Christmas music.

The Anita Blake series became so popular that Dabel Brothers Productions, in conjunction with Marvel Comics, adapted her first three books into a comic series, with Hamilton co-writing with Stacie Ritchie. The project started in 2006. At first, Hamilton was nervous about writing in a genre that relies on so few words. To help with the transition, Hamilton's husband bought her comics and movie scripts to study. As Hamilton read them, she came to realize that comic script revolves around dialogue. "Script is just dialogue," Hamilton told Laurel Maury of *Publishers Weekly*. "I do dialogue really well and really fast. Writing script was a much happier, much easier transition than I ever imagined." Hamilton even created a prequel to the Blake series, which will appear only in comic format. Hamilton enjoyed the artistic collaboration that went into creating the comics. "Working on the comic was invigorating," she told Maury. "Writing a book is a very solitary thing. For the most part, I'm alone in my office with my imaginary friends."

In 2007, Hamilton published *The Harlequin*, the fifteenth volume in her vampire hunter series. Another volume was set for publication in 2008. Though fans may worry, Hamilton has said that she does not see herself running out of ideas any time soon. By the time Hamilton finished the first installment, she had plot ideas for 15 to 17 more books. "I've still not gotten even halfway through the list, because the books I've written have birthed new ideas, new characters and taken the series in directions I never dreamt," Hamilton told *Science Fiction Weekly*. "New book ideas keep coming, because Anita's world is so fresh, alive, real, in the way that the best fictional worlds can be."

Selected writings

Nightseer, Ace Books, 1992.
Guilty Pleasures, Ace Books, 1993.
Laughing Corpse, Ace Books, 1994.
Circus of the Damned, Ace Books, 1995.
The Lunatic Cafe, Ace Books, 1996.
Bloody Bones, Ace Books, 1996.
The Killing Dance, Ace Books, 1997.
Burnt Offerings, Ace Books, 1998.
Blue Moon, Ace Books, 1998.
Obsidian Butterfly, Ace Books, 2000.
A Kiss of Shadows, Del Rey Books, 2000.
Narcissus in Chains, Berkley Books, 2001.
A Caress of Twilight, Ballantine, 2002.
Cerulean Sins, Berkley Books, 2003.
Incubus Dreams, Berkley Books, 2004.
Seduced by Moonlight, Ballantine, 2004.
A Stroke of Midnight, Ballantine, 2005.
Danse Macabre, Berkley Books, 2006.
Micah, Penguin, 2006.
Mistral's Kiss, Ballantine, 2006.
A Lick of Frost, Ballantine, 2007.
The Harlequin, Berkley Books, 2007.
Blood Noir, Orbit, 2008.

Sources

Periodicals

Atlanta Journal-Constitution (Atlanta, GA), June 5, 2007, p. E1.
Chicago Tribune, October 31, 1996, p. 1 (Tempo).
Publishers Weekly, September 20, 2004, p. 42.
St. Louis Post-Dispatch, February 22, 1996, p. 1F; October 10, 2001, p. E1; August 20, 2006, p. E1.

Online

"Anita Blake Stakes Out Comics," *Publishers Weekly,* http://www.publishersweekly.com/article/CA6458792.html (October 1, 2007).
"Blue Moon," SF Site, http://www.sfsite.com/12b/blu47.htm (October 29, 2007).
"Laurell K. Hamilton Biography," Laurell K. Hamilton Web site, http://www.laurellkhamilton.org/Laurell/LKHBiography.htm (October 1, 2007).
"Laurell K. Hamilton Steps into the Light for an Interview with a Vampire Writer," *Science Fiction Weekly,* http://www.scifi.com/sfw/issue313/interview.html (October 1, 2007).
"Nightseer," SF Site, http://www.sfsite.com/06b/nite35.htm (October 27, 2007).

—Lisa Frick

Lewis Hamilton

AP Images

Professional race car driver

Born January 7, 1985 in Stevenage, Hertfordshire, England; son of Anthony and Brenda Hamilton.

Addresses: *Home*—Switzerland. *Office*—McLaren Technology Centre, Chertsey Rd., Woking, Surrey, GU21 4YH England.

Career

Driver for Vodafone McLaren Mercedes, 2007—. Signed by McLaren and Mercedes-Benz to Young Driver Support Programme, 1998. Placed in various amateur races, including Cadet Class: Super One British Champion, 1995; Cadet Class: winner of McLaren Mercedes Champions of the Future Series, 1996 and 1997; Sky TV Kart Masters Champion, 1996; Five Nations Champion, 1996; Junior Yamaha: Super One British Champion, 1997; Junior Intercontinental A (JICA): second place in McLaren Mercedes Champions of the Future series, 1998; fourth place, Italian Open Championship, 1998; Intercontinental A (ICA): Italian "Industrials" Champion, 1999; JICA: Vice European Champion, 1999; winner, Trophy de Pomposa, 1999; fourth place, Italian Open Championship, 1999; Formula A: European Champion, winner of all four rounds, 2000; World Cup Champion, 2000; Karting World Number 1, 2000; winner, Masters at Bercy, 2000; British Formula Renault winter series, fifth overall, 2001, third, 2002, champion, 2003; fifth place, Formula Renault Euro-Cup Championship, 2002; F3 Euroseries, fifth place, 2004, champion, 2005; winner, Bahrain F3 Superprix, 2004; winner, F3 Masters at Zandvoort, 2005; winner, Pau F3 Grand Prix, France, 2005; winner, Monaco F3 Grand Prix, 2005; GP2 Series: Champion with ART Grand Prix, 2006; double win, Nürburgring, 2006; winner, Monaco GP2 race, 2006; double win, Silverstone, 2006; third place, Australian Grand Prix, 2007; second place, Bahrain Grand Prix, 2007; second place, Spanish Grand Prix, 2007; second place, Monaco Grad Prix, 2007; winner, Canadian Grand Prix, 2007; winner, U.S. Grand Prix, 2007; third place, French Grand Prix, 2007; winner, Hungarian Grand Prix, 2007; second place, Turkey Grand Prix, 2007; second place, Italian Grand Prix, 2007; fourth place, Belgian Grand Prix, 2007; winner, Japanese Grand Prix, 2007; winner, Australian Grad Prix, 2008; third place, Spanish Grand Prix, 2008; second place, Turkish Grand Prix, 2008; winner, Monaco Grand Prix, 2008.

Awards: Hawthorn Memorial Trophy, Motor Sports Association; Driver of the Year, Motorsport Aktuell; Sports Person of the Year, Squar Mil Sport Awards; Sportsman of the Year and Best International Newcomer Award, Sports Journalist Association; Racing Driver of the Year, Italian Confartigianato Motori; Most Inspiring Public Figure Award, Pride of Britain; Sportsman of the Year, *GQ UK*; Man of the Year, *GQ Germany*; Golden Steering Wheel Award for Outstanding Achievement, Bild Am Sonntag; Motorsport Award, Autocar Awards; British Sporting Excellence, Walpole Awards for British Excellence; Driver of the Year, Man of the Year, Rookie of the

Year, Qualifier of the Year, and Personality of the Year, all *F1 Racing* magazine; Best British Competition Driver, Best International Racing Driver, and Rookie of the Year, Autosport Awards; Gold Star Winner, BRDC Annual Awards; and Sports Personality of the Year, BBC East Sports Awards; all 2007; Sport Award, Britain's Best Awards, 2008.

Sidelights

In addition to being the first black driver in Formula One's 61-year history, Lewis Hamilton very nearly became the first rookie driver to win the Formula One World Championship, failing to meet the high score by a single point. Brought onto the McLaren team under champion and veteran Fernando Alonso, Hamilton was expected to have a good first season on the track. He surpassed everyone's expectations, having one of the best first seasons for a rookie in the history of Formula One.

Born on January 7, 1985, Hamilton did not have an easy early life. Named after U.S. sprinter and Olympian Carl Lewis, Hamilton was raised in the home of his mother following his parents' divorce two years after he was born. His father, Anthony Hamilton, whose family had immigrated to England from Grenada, remained active in Hamilton's life and was the first to notice Hamilton's potential as a driver. After giving Hamilton a remote-controlled car, the elder Hamilton was determined to encourage the young driver's developing skills. When Hamilton was nine, already a cart champion, he moved in with his father and stepmother.

Hamilton's father encouraged him to begin go-karting when he was only six years old. In order to support Hamilton's growing commitment to the hobby, the elder Hamilton worked three jobs, buying his son a go-kart and helping him to enter in races. "I've always believed in Lewis," the elder Hamilton was quoted as saying in *USA Today*. "I've always believed he was a great person and a great driver."

At the age of ten, Hamilton won the British Junior Kart Championship, and many other successes followed. It was while being presented with a trophy for one of his wins in 1994 that he met McLaren head Ron Dennis. "I want to drive for you one day," Hamilton informed the team leader, according to *AutoWeek*. That was enough to get Dennis' attention, and two years later, McLaren began sponsoring Hamilton's races, providing advice and training to the young driver. Hamilton has credited that meeting with giving him the opportunity to suc-

ceed as a Formula One driver. "Who knows if I hadn't bumped into Ron and made the impression that I did?" he mused in *USA Today*.

McLaren backed Hamilton through the European go-karting circuit while Hamilton finished high school. When he graduated from karting to single-seat cars, he finished third in the British Formula Renault series. The next year, he won the Formula Renault, capturing ten races. His first year in the Formula Three Euroseries, he finished fifth, winning one race; his second year in that series, he was the champion, the winner of 15 races.

But despite his successes, Hamilton was never in a hurry to jump start his career. "My ambition isn't to get to F1 early," he said at 15 years old to Tim Blair of *Time International*. "It's just to get there." But even as a child, he was noticed by the racing community. When he was only 13, he was featured on the cover of *AutoWeek*, a magazine that proclaimed Lewis as a future star. "Trust me, that kid is good!" said world-class driver Keke Rosberg in *AutoWeek* during Hamilton's early career.

After winning the GP2 title in 2006, Hamilton was offered a position as a McLaren driver for the 2007 racing season under teammate and champion Fernando Alonso. This was an ideal set up for Hamilton: it gave him the chance to test his skills without the pressure of having to win. "I hoped to do well," Hamilton reflected of his season start in the *Houston Chronicle*. "I hoped maybe I'd get a podium at some point." Those modest expectations were blown away when Hamilton qualified fourth in the first race of the season, then second in his second, behind teammate Alonso. "It's sort of hard to believe he's a rookie, isn't it?" Dennis commented in *AutoWeek* after the 1-2 McLaren win. Hamilton placed second in three more consecutive races before winning his first professional race at the Canadian Grand Prix. In only the sixth professional race of his career, Hamilton dominated the track.

The quick move up in the ranks attracted the attention of the media, who, because of his race and skill, began comparing Hamilton to golf's Tiger Woods. But Dennis told *AutoWeek* that race never entered into discussions with Hamilton. "Already, people are starting to speak in terms of an F1 Tiger Woods, and while that's obviously quite a compliment in itself, it's not relevant to our objective," Dennis explained. "Lewis is driving for McLaren because we considered him the best driver available to us as Fernando's teammate." Hamilton responded similarly. "It's obviously nice to be compared to someone like Tiger Woods," he said in an interview with *AutoWeek*, "but I just have to remember I'm not Tiger Woods, I'm Lewis Hamilton. And it's Formula One, not golf." The reaction was typical of Hamilton, who was noted for his modesty. Dennis commented of Hamilton in *AutoWeek*, "I had more arrogance at every step of my career than he has now. I don't know where he finds the ability to motivate himself and have self-belief without turning it into arrogance."

Hamilton's record would have been an easy thing to get arrogant about. But in typical modest fashion, after his first win, Hamilton told *USA Today*, "It still hasn't really sunk in that I have won my first race. It was an amazing weekend for me, and it's fantastic that we are racing again already." It was especially fantastic for Hamilton, who won the following race as well, dominating the U.S. Grand Prix and taking the lead in score for the Formula One standings. "What an amazing trip," he said in *USA Today*, "to come [to North America] for the first time and then have the two best races of my life." Downplaying his successes in *AutoWeek*, he explained that he didn't listen much to the media buzz. "At the end of the day, I'm still the same driver, the same person, and I'm here to do the same job," he said.

Hamilton's wins caused some tension with teammate Alonso, and McLaren may have encouraged Hamilton to fall back in some of his races. In the press, Hamilton spoke of their friendly competition, and Alonso, too, was quick to downplay their conflict. "Many things are said about our relationship which are not true," the senior driver said in *Financial Times*. "We are in competition—we love competition and we enjoy this battle when we are here. Sometimes we win and sometimes we lose, this is how real competition should be." But Alonso and team leader Dennis were reported exchanging hard words, and Hamilton, driven by their rivalry, used a maneuver in attempting to pass Alonso that caused him to skid off the track. Hamilton also had some difficulties in the European Grand Prix, in which he hit a wall, but was uninjured, and in Shanghai, driving during the rain, he stayed on his rain tires too long and skidded out. Those mistakes cost him his lead in the standings, and though he recovered well, he ended the season finishing second to Alonso in the Monaco Grand Prix. He was pulled over to refuel during the race, far earlier than he needed to, costing him the race. His comments to the press at his surprise in McLaren's pit tactics drove the wedge further between the two racers, and Alonso left McLaren after finishing the season and took a position on the Renault team.

Joining McLaren for the 2008 season was Heikki Kovalainen, who was once a karting rival of Hamilton's. The two drivers were immediately on good terms, and though McLaren's "equal treatment for drivers" policy was noted in *AutoWeek*, the contributor suspected that Hamilton, with his record from the previous year, would become the defacto leader. Some in the circuit worried that Hamilton might suffer from a sophomore slump, and that his rookie season might have been more of a fluke than a preview of things to come. But the first race of 2008 put their minds to rest: Hamilton took first place at the Australian Grand Prix. His teammate Kovalainen took fifth. In the second race, the Malaysian Grand Prix, Kovalainen finished ahead of Hamilton, taking third place while Hamilton took fifth.

Struggling to do well in the third race, Hamilton made a mistake that cost him his lead in points: he crashed into Alonso's Renault. The move cost both drivers time; Alonso finished 10th while Hamilton finished 13th, a full lap behind the winner. Neither driver earned points. Hamilton spoke with the *Times Online* about the difference in pressure between his first and second season. "I put a lot on myself in wanting to do well for the team," he said. But as for everyone else's expectations, Hamilton pays little attention. "I don't think it distracts me or makes it harder for me to do my job. I just want to win more than ever." The mistake in Bahrain only firmed his determination, and he recovered in Spain, where he placed third, coming in behind two Ferrari drivers.

In Turkey, Hamilton finished in second place, helping to close the gap on Ferrari's lead, and putting himself and the McLaren team back into third place in the standings. Hamilton was especially pleased with his performance, which was his best ever run on the Turkish track. "It's not about winning," he said of his performance, quoted on CNN.com, "it's about feeling you extract 100 percent from yourself and the car and I did that."

In addition to his success on the race track, Hamilton has also found success in the bookstores. "Not many people have been interested in Formula 1 recently, but Lewis Hamilton's success is going to change that," publisher Mark Booth said in the middle of the 2007 season when Hamilton's autobiography and photographic memoir came up for bid. When his book *My Story* was released in November of 2007, it sold nearly 15,000 copies in its first week on sale, making it number one in sports books in England that week.

Hamilton has also been sought out for sponsorship offers, and has been featured in a number of advertisements. "Hamilton combines looks, personality and charisma with the elusive quality of being a genuine winner," said Dominic Curran, director at Karen Earl Sponsorship, in *Marketing Week*. His popularity among brands was expected to rival that of tennis pro David Beckham, husband of former Spice Girl Victoria Beckham, and golf champion Tiger Woods, to whom Hamilton had been compared so often at the start of his career. "He's young, good looking, and unusually has the potential to appeal across both genders," said Havas Sports UK managing partner Keith Impey in *Marketing Week*. "The more wins, the more publicity, and the more brands across the genders he will appeal to."

During the off season of 2007, Hamilton moved from England to Switzerland, seeking greater privacy and tax shelter. Hamilton continues to race for the McLaren team.

Sources

Periodicals

Auto Week, December 4, 2006, p. 71; March 26, 2007, p. 4; March 26, 2007, p. 44; April 16, 2007, p. 46; June 25, 2007, pp. 60-61; March 3, 2008, p. 20; March 24, 2008, p. 40.
Bookseller, July 13, 2007, p. 13; November 16, 2007, p. 41.
Ebony, September 2007, p. 36.
Financial Times, October 20, 2007, p. 12.
Houston Chronicle (Houston, TX), June 18, 2007, p. 3.
Independent (London, England), May 18, 2008.
Marketing Week, October 25, 2007, p. 24.
New York Times, July 22, 2007, p. 6.
Observer (Manchester, England), May 18, 2008, p. 7.
Time International, March 5, 2001, p. 50.
USA Today, June 11, 2007, p. 1C; June 15, 2007, p. 11C; June 18, 2007, p. 10C.

Online

Biography Resource Center Online, Gale Group, 2007.
Formula One Online, http://www.formula1.com/ (May 19, 2008).
"Hamilton Determined to Put Bahrain Nightmare Behind Him," *Times*, http://www.timesonline.co.uk/tol/sport/formula_1/article3810500.ece (May 19, 2008).
"Hamilton Primed for Success in Monaco," CNN.com, http://www.cnn.com/2008/SPORT/05/13/Hamilton.monaco/ (May 13, 2008).
"Hamilton Wins 'Britain's Best' Award," *Home of Sport*, hptt://www.homeofsport.com/f1/news/item.aspx?id=22042 (May 19, 2008).
Lewis Hamilton Fan site, http://www.lewishamilton.com (May 18, 2008).
"Lewis Hamilton," *McLaren*, http://www.mclaren.com/theteam/lewis-hamilton.php (May 18, 2008).

—*Alana Joli Abbott*

Katharine Heigl

Actress

Born Katherine Marie Heigl, on November 24, 1978, in Washington, DC (some sources say New Canaan, CT); daughter of Paul (an accountant) and Nancy (a personal manager) Heigl; married Josh Kelley (a musician), December 23, 2007.

Addresses: *Agent*—William Morris Agency, One William Morris Place, Beverly Hills, CA 90212. *Home*—Los Angeles, CA.

Career

Actress on television, including: *Roswell,* The WB, 1999-2001, UPN, 2001-2002; *Wuthering Heights* (movie), 2003; *Critical Assembly* (movie), 2003; *Evil Never Dies* (movie), 2003; *Love Comes Softly* (movie), 2003; *Vegas Dick* (movie), 2003; *Love's Enduring Promise* (movie), 2004; *Romy and Michele: In the Beginning* (movie), 2005; *Grey's Anatomy,* 2005—. Film appearances include: *That Night,* 1992; *King of the Hill,* 1993; *My Father the Hero,* 1994; *Under Siege 2: Dark Territory,* 1995; *Prince Valiant,* 1997; *Stand-Ins,* 1997; *Bride of Chucky,* 1998; *100 Girls,* 2000; *Valentine,* 2001; *The Ringer,* 2005; *Side Effects,* 2005; *Zyzzyx Rd.,* 2006; *Caffeine,* 2006; *Knocked Up,* 2007; *27 Dresses,* 2008.

Awards: Emmy Award for outstanding supporting actress in a drama series, Academy of Television Arts and Sciences, for *Grey's Anatomy,* 2007.

Sidelights

Katharine Heigl first gained notice in ABC's top-rated medical drama, *Grey's Anatomy,* but within two years of that show's 2005 debut she was being hailed as the next Julia Roberts for her comedic film roles. She played the heroine in two romantic comedies—the surprise summer hit of 2007, *Knocked Up,* and *27 Dresses,* released the following January. She was anything but a newcomer, however, having appeared in a slew of television movies and little-seen horror flicks over the past decade. "I always imagined what it might be like to have this success," she told *Houston Chronicle* journalist Sandy Cohen, but admitted fame had its drawbacks. "You feel watched all the time, and it feels like you can't be yourself, like you can't go to the grocery store unless you're wearing a cute outfit and look perfect."

Heigl was born Katherine Marie Heigl on November 24, 1978, in Washington, D.C., but grew up in New Canaan, Connecticut, as the youngest of four. In September of 1986, when she was seven, her 15-year-old brother was thrown from the back of a pick-up truck and died seven days later from his injuries. "The worst part was watching the devastation of my family," she recalled in an interview with

Vanity Fair's Leslie Bennetts. "They weren't the same people anymore." Some family friends of her parents belonged to the Church of Jesus Christ of Latter-Day Saints—more commonly referred to as the Mormon church—and were especially empathetic during this difficult period, and this led to a decision by Heigl's parents, Paul and Nancy, to join the church. Heigl also converted, but gave up practicing the faith after she moved to California. "I give my parents unbelievable credit for pulling it together, and I give the Mormon church a lot of credit for helping them to do that," Heigl told Bennetts.

Heigl began modeling just as she was about to enter her teens, and appeared in television commercials for Cheerios and Sears. She made her film debut in *That Night*, a 1992 teen romance that starred Eliza Dushku and Juliette Lewis. A year later, she appeared in the little-seen 1993 Steven Soderbergh movie *King of the Hill*, set in a run-down hotel during the Great Depression. Her first starring role came in an ill-advised project that featured French film legend Gérard Depardieu as her on-screen father. Heigl played a spoiled American teenager who has not seen her French father in years. To make up for lost time, he takes her on a lavish trip to the Bahamas, where they are mistaken for a couple, and this plot device drives the remainder of *My Father the Hero*. Critics savaged it, with Lisa Schwarzbaum writing in *Entertainment Weekly* that "every ostensibly funny moment leaves an aftertaste of creepy discomfort."

Heigl's next role was opposite action-adventure star Steven Seagal in 1995's *Under Siege 2: Dark Territory*. She graduated from New Canaan High School in 1996, and moved to Los Angeles with her mother, who, by then, was divorced from Heigl's father. In 1997, she appeared in the comic-book adaptation *Prince Valiant* and also in *Stand-Ins*, a tale of four young women trying to break into Hollywood in the 1940s. She played Jade in *Bride of Chucky* in 1998 and won her first regular television role on the successful teen drama *Roswell*, which debuted on The WB network in 1999. Her character, Isabel Evans, was one of four aliens sent to live among humans in the New Mexico community of the series title.

Roswell lasted three seasons, and then Heigl's career seemed to stall in the television-movie genre. She was in an MTV adaptation of the Emily Brontë classic *Wuthering Heights* in 2003, as well as a four more small-screen movies—*Critical Assembly*, *Evil Never Dies*, *Love Comes Softly*, and *Vegas Dick*. Her career perked up in 2004 when she was offered one of the lead roles in a new ABC drama set in a Seattle hospital. *Grey's Anatomy* was named for its narrator,

Meredith Grey (Ellen Pompeo), who is one of several new interns at Grace Hospital. Heigl was cast as Isobel "Izzie" Stevens, a former lingerie model who struggles to be taken seriously by her peers and supervisors after racy photos of her previous career surface.

Grey's Anatomy debuted in late March of 2005 and was given a strong spot in the Sunday night line-up, right after *Desperate Housewives*. It was quickly dubbed "Sex and the City Hospital" for its focus on the doctors' personal lives, and inevitably compared to the most successful hospital drama in television history. "Nobody's apt to forget *ER* because of this," wrote *Variety*'s Brian Lowry in his review of the pilot, "but the mix of a youthful cast, crisp dialogue, romance, the Darwinian workplace struggle to survive, and life-or-death situations combine to make the show appealing and watchable in spite of its familiarity." After roles in so many horror films and little-seen comedies, Heigl was happy to have landed such a part. "I'm really grateful because the character I play is smart and ambitious," she told Cohen in the *Houston Chronicle* interview. "And not ambitious in a bad way, getting ahead at the expense of someone else. She's ambitious in her own self, pushing herself to be her best."

Grey's Anatomy quickly became one of the top-rated shows on network television, and finished its second season in May of 2006 in the No. 5 spot. In the fall of 2006, it moved to a Thursday-night slot, which did little to diminish its fan base. That same season, however, reports surfaced of squabbling on the set between Isaiah Washington, who played one of the older supervising doctors, and T. R. Knight, whose character, Dr. George O'Malley, harbored an unrequited crush on Heigl's Izzie during the first season. The tension led to an incident that involved Washington, Knight, and Patrick Dempsey, who was the show's heartthrob character, Dr. Derek Shepherd, but almost always referred to as "Dr. McDreamy." Once the media heard of the scuffle, Washington apologized for uttering a derogatory epithet at Knight, who a few days later stated publicly for the first time that he was gay.

The controversy appeared to have quieted down, but in January of 2007, Heigl and her *Grey's Anatomy* castmates appeared at a press conference immediately following the Golden Globes, the annual Hollywood Foreign Press Association awards show. They were visibly excited to have won for best dramatic television series, and the series' creator, Shonda Rhimes, answered questions about the female cast members' gowns and jewelry before being asked about the October incident. At that point, Washington stepped up to the microphone and "denied that he ever used the slur to describe Mr. Knight, at the same time repeating the word," reported *New York Times* writer Edward Wyatt. "Fellow cast members who were with Mr. Washington appeared shaken, quickly going from jubilant to solemn." Following the press conference, Heigl was interviewed by a television reporter and said that Washington "needs to just not speak in public," the *New York Post* quoted her as saying.

Behind the scenes, Heigl and Knight had developed a close friendship, and she later recalled that Washington's use of the slur and Knight's subsequent admission that he was gay was a stressful time for her. "I was terrified for him," she told John Griffiths in the *Advocate,* and cited a list of worries she had about his admission of his sexual orientation, including "that he would be ridiculed, that he would be picked on, that he would [be] ostracized—all the reasons why people don't come out. But I was so proud of his strength. It's such a cliché to say this, but he handled it courageously."

There were hints that same season that Heigl was involved in her own behind-the-scenes battle with network executives and *Grey's Anatomy* producers over the terms of her contract, which was up for renewal. The negotiations were stalled for several months, with Heigl reportedly unhappy that the proposed raise was not on par with what Pompeo and Dempsey were earning. She was still appearing in films when her schedule permitted, in 2006 taking roles in *Zyzzyx Rd.,* a Las Vegas-set thriller, and *Caffeine,* a little-seen ensemble piece set in a London coffee house.

In May of 2007, Heigl's film career was suddenly jolted forward thanks to her starring role in *Knocked Up,* the new comedy from writer-director Judd Apatow (*The 40-Year-Old Virgin*). She was cast as Alison Scott, whose job as a TV entertainment reporter is threatened when a drunken evening with a guy she meets at a bar results in an unexpected pregnancy. For the rest of the film, she guides Ben Stone, the immature slob/father-to-be played by Seth Rogen, to a more responsible lifestyle. Their woes are offset by the dysfunctional marriage of Debbie (Leslie Mann), who is Alison's older sister, and her hapless mate Pete (Paul Rudd). Heigl earned terrific reviews for her work, with *Rolling Stone*'s Peter Travers proclaiming her "an exciting new star with real acting chops and a no-bull quality that ups her potential." Writing for Salon.com, Stephanie Zacharek found *Knocked Up* to be "a romantic comedy that's unafraid to face human suffering dead on. And yet, in the end, it's all the more joyous for that." Zacharek noted that while "Rogen is an unlikely romantic-comedy lead.... Heigl is wonderful here: She gives Alison just the right mix of youthful vulnerability and fierce, mom-to-be determination."

The year 2007 proved to be a busy one for Heigl: In addition to filming episodes for the fourth season of *Grey's Anatomy,* she won her first Emmy Award for her role on the series, and completed work on her first genuine lead role in a romantic comedy, *27 Dresses.* She also married her fiancé, musician Josh Kelley, whom she had met in 2005 when she was cast in his video for his song "Only You." The wedding took place in Park City, Utah, just before Christmas and less than a month before the premiere date for *27 Dresses.*

In *27 Dresses,* Heigl plays Jane, a perennial bridesmaid and loser at love. She harbors a secret crush on her boss, played by Ed Burns, that goes unnoticed. Jane's sister meets him and the attraction is instant. Jane dreads her next bridesmaid's role at their impending nuptials, compounded by the unwanted attention a journalist (James Marsden) is giving her. Again, Heigl won praise for her comic timing, with the *New York Times* film critic A. O. Scott panning the film itself but noting that "Heigl certainly works hard to convince the audience of the existence of a universe in which she could be the dowdier, shyer member of a pair of sisters." It was a sentiment echoed by another reviewer, *Entertainment Weekly*'s Owen Gleiberman, who wrote that Heigl has "some of the nervous, high-strung sensuality of the young Kathleen Turner—and she makes Jane a live presence, even if it's a bit much to ask us to believe that a woman this attractive could be this nerdishly self-sacrificing a sop."

Heigl's snappish comment about her *Grey's Anatomy* castmate Washington—whose contract was not renewed for the fourth season—was not the last remark she would make that showcased her independent streak. In January of 2008, she appeared on that month's *Vanity Fair,* and in the interview she faulted the characterization as Alison in *Knocked Up.* Heigl considered it "a little sexist," she told Bennetts, the author of the cover story. "It paints the women as shrews, as humorless and uptight, and it paints the men as lovable, goofy, fun-loving guys."

Sources

Periodicals

Advocate, June 19, 2007, p. 38.
Cosmopolitan, December 2006, p. 36.
Entertainment Weekly, February 18, 1994, p. 95; January 18, 2008, p. 62.
Houston Chronicle, November 23, 2006, p. 6.
New York Post, January 18, 2007, p. 123.
New York Times, March 25, 2005; January 22, 2007; January 18, 2008.

Rolling Stone, May 30, 2007.
USA Today, May 21, 2007, p. 1D.
Variety, March 24, 2005, p. 6; January 7, 2008, p. 35.

Online

"Katherine Heigl talks about marriage, ratings ploys, and why she thinks *Knocked Up* is sexist,"

Vanity Fair, http://www.vanityfair.com/services/presscenter/pressrelease/katherine_heigl200801 (January 22, 2008).
"Knocked Up," Salon.com, http://www.salon.com/ent/movies/review/2007/06/01/knocked_up/index.html?CP=IMD&am p;DN=110 (January 22, 2008).

—*Carol Brennan*

Felix Hernandez

Jason Wise/MLB Photos via Getty Images

Professional baseball player

Born Felix Abraham Hernandez, April 8, 1986, in Valencia, Venezuela; son of Felix Sr. (a truck driver) and Mirian Hernandez; children: Mia (with his girlfriend, Mariella).

Addresses: *Office*—Seattle Mariners, Safeco Field, 1250 First Ave. South, Seattle, WA 98134.

Career

Signed with Seattle Mariners, 2002; pitcher for minor-league teams in the Seattle Mariners organization, 2003-04; pitcher for Mariners' Triple A team in Tacoma, 2005; pitcher for Seattle Mariners, 2005—.

Sidelights

When Felix Hernandez joined the Seattle Mariners' pitching rotation in August of 2005, he was only 19 years old, the youngest major-league pitcher since the 1970s. He was widely considered baseball's best pitching prospect, with a 97-mile-per-hour fastball, a strong curve ball, and a change-up that he used rarely but could aim very precisely. The six-foot-three pitcher's confidence impressed fans: He had the words "Felix el Cartelua," roughly translated as "Felix the Badass," stitched on his glove. The Venezuelan rookie, part of the huge wave of Latin American players that swept into the major leagues in the 2000s, showed flashes of brilliance in his 2005 starts and early in 2007, but injuries and youthful nervousness under pressure led him to a mediocre record in 2006. His pitching in 2007, impressive by most standards, helped the Mariners contend for the playoffs, but he and his coaches alike agreed that he had not yet reached his full potential.

Hernandez was born in 1986 in Valencia, Venezuela, the country's third largest city, 70 miles from the capital of Caracas. His early baseball hero was fellow Venezuelan Freddy Garcia, who pitched for the Mariners and the Chicago White Sox. In 2001, when Hernandez was 14, Mariners scouts saw him pitch and quickly pegged him as a hot prospect, impressed with his speedy fastball, sharp curveball, and mature confidence on the pitcher's mound. "Right away, we knew he would be a special player," Emilio Carrasquel told Dave Sheinin of the *Washington Post*. "He was so much better than anyone else. I called Bob Engle [the Mariners' director of international scouting] and said, 'Bob, you better come right away. We cannot miss this kid.'"

Other teams showed interest too, but Hernandez chose the Mariners. In July of 2002, he signed with Seattle for a bonus of $710,000. "I liked watching Seattle, and they tried the hardest to get me," Hernandez explained to Albert Chen of *Sports Illustrated*.

Even before Hernandez joined the major leagues, baseball insiders were buzzing about his talent. In

April of 2005, *Baseball America* put him on its cover and compared him to Dwight Gooden, the New York Mets pitching legend who also joined the majors as a teenager. Herndanez spent much of 2005 with Seattle's Triple A farm team in Tacoma, where he won nine games, lost four, struck out 100 in 88 innings, and compiled a league-leading 2.25 earned run average.

Hernandez debuted in the major leagues on August 4, 2005, at age 19, the youngest starting pitcher in the majors since 1978. Pitching five innings for the Mariners against the Detroit Tigers, he only gave up one run, and the Tigers only hit three balls out of the outfield against him. "What's most impressive is his poise," his veteran teammate Jamie Moyer told Chen of *Sports Illustrated*. "In Detroit he loaded the bases with no one out but pitched himself out of it, giving up just one run. He's got the self-assurance to match his stuff." In his second start, Hernandez shut out the Minnesota Twins for eight innings for a 1-0 win. After four starts, he had a 2-1 record with a very impressive 1.24 ERA and 30 strikeouts. He finished the season 4-4 with a 2.67 ERA. Hitters had only a .203 average against him.

As the 2006 season began, the Mariners worried about how to preserve Hernandez's health, even as they relied on him to try to reverse their team's fortunes after two losing seasons. By 2006, baseball managers knew that young pitchers who threw too many innings in a season often injured their arms, hampering the rest of their careers. Since Hernandez was even younger than most rookie pitchers, the team promised to carefully regulate how much he pitched. Shin splints that kept him from pitching for parts of March and April added to the concern.

Early in the season, Hernandez struggled. By mid-May he had lost four games and won only one, and his ERA was a disappointing 5.40. In five out of six straight starts, he was pulled out of the game before the sixth inning. Coaches said the early injury had set him back. "He got into some bad habits because of the injury," Mariners pitching coach Rafael Chaves told Chen of *Sports Illustrated*. "He was trying to generate all his power from his upper body, instead of his legs."

Hernandez, ever confident, insisted he was fine. He spoke to Chen of *Sports Illustrated* in English, which he was learning quickly. "I feel great," he said. "I feel more comfortable [than last year], knowing the hitters better. Right now I'm making bad pitches at the bad time. One or two pitches different, [and] it's a different game." His strikeout rate, almost ten per nine innings, was better than in 2005, and his top pitch speed, 97 miles per hour, was the same.

Yet Hernandez finished 2006 with a losing record, 12-14, and a mediocre 4.52 ERA. By early September, hitters had batted only .221 against him with the bases empty, but .329 with runners on base. That was a sign that Hernandez often grew nervous in clutch situations, overthrowing and losing command of his pitches.

During the off-season, at home in Venezuela, Hernandez underwent a workout regimen and lost 20 pounds. When the 2007 season began, he excited fans and the baseball press all over again. On Opening Day, he shut out the Oakland Athletics for eight innings, giving up three hits and striking out 12. In an internationally televised April 11 start in Boston, Hernandez was matched against Daisuke Matsuzaka, a star pitcher from Japan making his major-league debut. Hernandez stole the show, pitching seven no-hit innings before giving up a single in the eighth inning, beating the Red Sox 3-0 with a one-hit shutout. Hernandez's performance "announced his arrival as perhaps the most dominant young pitcher in the game," declared Dave Sheinin of the *Washington Post*. But on April 19, Hernandez left a game in Seattle in the first inning, complaining of tightness in his elbow. His injury, a strained forearm muscle, caused extreme worry among Mariners fans and the press, but he returned from the disabled list in mid-May. When he pitched 3 2/3 innings in Seattle on May 15, he gave up three earned runs and seven hits, yet relieved Mariners fans still gave him a standing ovation when he left the game.

It took Hernandez a while to recover from his time on the disabled list; he posted a 6.31 ERA in his first five starts after returning. But by July, he was back in top form, shutting out Oakland in eight innings two more times that month. The Mariners' pitching coach had helped improve his pitching strategy, warning him not to use his fastball too much in early innings. With Hernandez pitching well, the Mariners contended for a wild-card spot in the American League playoffs, but eventually fell short, with an 88-74 record.

Hernandez, who made $420,000 in 2007, pitched the last game of the season, going 8 2/3 innings as Seattle beat the Texas Rangers 4-2. He finished with a respectable 14-11 with a 3.92 ERA, but told Geoff Baker of the *Seattle Times* that the April injury had kept him from doing better. "It was bad for me," he said. "My first two games, I was feeling great. When I came off the [disabled list], for five or six games I was horrible. I couldn't throw strikes."

As the season ended, and Mariners coaches looked toward 2008, they said Hernandez would improve once he became a craftier pitcher and stopped giving up so many hits when ahead on 0-2 ball-strike counts. Meanwhile, Hernandez's top goal for 2008 was simpler: to avoid a serious injury. "First of all, I want to stay healthy all year," he told Baker.

Sources

Periodicals

Chicago Tribune, April 22, 2007, Sports section, p. 2; July 8, 2007, Sports section, p. 10.

Seattle Times, May 16, 2007; June 15, 2007; July 17, 2007; September 20, 2007; October 1, 2007.

Sports Illustrated, August 22, 2005, p. 74; August 29, 2005, p. 29; April 3, 2006, p. 54; May 15, 2006, p. 70; September 4, 2006, p. 55.

Washington Post, April 12, 2007, p. E7; April 18, 2007, p. E1; April 19, 2007, p. E6.

Online

"ESPN: Felix Hernandez Stats, News, Photos," ESPN.com; http://sports.espn.go.com/mlb/players/stats?playerId=6194 (November 23, 2007).

—Erick Trickey

Lazaro Hernandez and Jack McCollough

Donato Sardella/WireImage/Getty Images

Fashion designers for Proenza Schouler

Born Lazaro Hernandez, c. 1979, in Miami; son of Fulgencio (an oil company representative) and Estella (a beauty shop owner) Hernandez. Born Jack McCollough, c. 1979, in Montclair, N.J.; son of Huston (an investment banker) and Joan McCollough. *Education:* Hernandez: Attended University of Miami, c. 1998; Parsons The New School for Design, B.A., 2002. McCollough: Attended San Francisco Art Institute, c. 1998; Parsons The New School for Design, B.A., 2002.

Addresses: *Contact*—PR Consulting, 304 Hudson St., 6th Flr., New York, NY 10013. E-mail—mailproenzaschouler.com. *Office*—Proenza Schouler, 120 Walker St., 6th Flr., New York, NY 10013. *Web site*—http://www.proenzaschouler.com.

Career

Hernandez and McCollough met at Parsons The New School for Design, c. 1999; co-founded Proenza Schouler, 2002; served as co-designers for the company, 2002—.

Awards: Swarovski's Perry Ellis Award for Ready-to-Wear, CFDA (Council of Fashion Designers of America), 2003; contest winner, CFDA/Vogue Fashion Fund, 2004; Womenswear Designer of the Year (shared with Oscar de la Renta), CFDA, 2007.

Sidelights

Since founding the apparel company Proenza Schouler in 2002, fashion designers Lazaro Hernandez and Jack McCollough have quickly distinguished themselves as emerging leaders in the world of style. Their fashions—with lush yet mod embellishments—are youthful, showy, and finely tailored. When Proenza Schouler first hit the market, its clothes were available only at high-end luxury stores like Barneys New York and Bergdorf Goodman. In 2007, however, Proenza Schouler launched a more affordable limited-edition collection through Target.

The brand is a favorite among A-list celebrities, including Demi Moore, Kirsten Dunst, and Maggie Gyllenhaal, who each have walked down the red carpet at the Academy Awards sporting the Proenza Schouler label. A vote of market confidence came in 2007 when the Valentino Fashion Group put down $3.7 million to purchase a 45 percent stake in the company, helping solidify a bright future for the already successful duo.

Hernandez was born in Miami in the late 1970s to Cuban immigrants Fulgencio and Estella Hernandez. Fulgencio Hernandez worked as an oil company representative, while Estella Hernandez operated a beauty salon. As a child, Hernandez spent innumerable hours in his mother's shop, taking in the customers and noticing their various styles of dress. "All there was to do was to sit reading *Vogue, Elle,* and *Cosmo,*" Hernandez told *People* magazine. "That imagery got stuck in my head."

Initially, Hernandez wanted to become a doctor and enrolled as a pre-med student at the University of Miami. In 1998, he visited New York and caught the fashion bug after meeting some designers and realizing he could probably forge a satisfying career in the industry. He transferred to New York's famed Parsons The New School for Design where he met another young aspiring designer—Jack McCollough.

McCollough, the son of Huston and Joan McCollough, was born in the late 1970s and grew up in Montclair, New Jersey. His father worked as an international investment banker for Merrill Lynch. McCollough took an early interest in tailoring and received his first sewing machine at 14. As a youngster, he identified with the hippie movement and sported dreadlocks. McCollough attended Walnut Hill, an independent boarding school for the arts located near Boston. He studied visual arts, intending to become a glassblower. After graduating from Walnut Hill in 1997, McCollough briefly studied at the San Francisco Art Institute before enrolling at Parsons in 1998. Soon after, he met Hernandez and the two became fast friends.

Another serendipitous event that helped foster the designers' careers occurred in 2000 when Hernandez boarded a flight at Miami airport and eyed *Vogue* editor Anna Wintour stepping aboard the plane. Wintour was a leading inspiration in Hernandez's choice to pursue a career in fashion. Hernandez grabbed a napkin and scribbled a note to Wintour discussing his devotion to the industry and his respect for her work. Within weeks, Hernandez received a call from a Michael Kors representative offering him an internship at the prolific label. The representative said Wintour had recommended him for the job. McCollough honed his skills working an internship at Marc Jacobs.

Hernandez and McCollough persuaded their Parsons instructors to let them do a joint thesis project. "They had such incredible synergy," former Parsons fashion design chairman Tim Gunn told *New York* magazine's Amy Larocca. "During their junior year, it became really clear that they shared a vision and a philosophy." At Parsons, the dazzling duo honed their craft under the direction of Gunn, who went on to become the mentor for contestants on the Bravo show *Project Runway.*

As part of their final project, the pair created a collection of clothing and dubbed their label Proenza Schouler (pronounced Pro-EN-za SKOOL-er). The name is derived from their mothers' maiden names. Barneys fashion director Julie Gilhart was so impressed she bought the whole lot. Instantly, Proenza Schouler moved from a senior-year project to a full-fledged design firm. Gilhart liked how the clothes seemed effortlessly sophisticated. In order to produce a run of the collection for Barneys, Hernandez and McCollough borrowed money from their parents. Soon, other stores were inquiring about their designs.

Their collections are truly collaborations. Hernandez and McCollough spend time and effort melding their ideas. The designers have developed a process. After they roll out a new collection, they take a vacation. When they are ready to begin designs for the next season, they sit down and discuss their moods. Then, they go their separate ways, each doing research by poring over photographs and drawings and pulling together a collection of images that evoke positive emotions. When they really like something, they copy it and tuck it in an inspiration book, sharing copies with the other. Next, they begin sketching, working independently for several weeks before comparing designs. At this point, they say they find a lot of similarities to work with. But there is also compromise. As Hernandez told Larocca: "One of us might be feeling long when the other one is feeling short. So then we're just, like, 'Let's do both.' Like, miniskirts with long coats over it."

This unique process seems to work. Over the past few years, the label has expanded its territory and moved into international markets. Proenza Schouler rolled out a shoe collection with the Italian manufacturer Iris, developed a watch for Movado and a camera case for Hewlett-Packard. In 2007, the label expanded its accessibility with a limited-edition line at Target. That year, the Proenza Schouler runway collection included a $1,150 blazer, but at Target, fans could get a blazer for $39.99. When the Target selection sold out, the items showed up on eBay, often selling for several times the initial price.

In the early days, Hernandez and Lazaro lived and worked together in a New York City loft. They have since moved into separate apartments. At times, fashion-world rumblings have suggested the two are more than just business partners. Speaking to Phoebe Eaton of *Harper's Bazaar,* Lazaro classified their relationship as "undefined."

Vogue editor André Leon Talley is not surprised by the pair's meteoric success. "These are not just *stylists,*" he told *New York* magazine. "Their greatest strength is their appreciation of the construction of clothes: the tailoring, the linings, the seams—all are done perfectly, and that's what makes them great."

Sources

Periodicals

Flare, March 2008, pp. 56-58.
Harper's Bazaar, September 2007, pp. 550-53.
People, December 15, 2003, pp. 101-02.

Wall Street Journal, September 7, 2007, p. B1.
WWD, April 4, 2006, p. 11.

Online

"1+1=1: Deconstructing the Collaborative Process of the Proenza Schouler Boys," *New York* magazine, http://nymag.com/nymetro/shopping/fashion/spring05/11014/ (May 9, 2008).
"Two Stylish," *New York* magazine, http://nymag.com/nymetro/shopping/fashion/features/n_8809/ (May 9, 2008).

—*Lisa Frick*

Rachel Herz

Research psychologist

Born Rachel Sarah Herz, April 20, 1963, in Ithaca, NY; daughter of Carl Samuel (a mathematics professor) and Judith Emily Scherer (an English professor) Herz; married. *Education:* Queen's University, B.A., 1985; University of Toronto, M.A., 1987, Ph.D., 1992.

Addresses: *Office*—Brown University, Department of Psychiatry and Human Behavior, 89 Waterman St., Providence, RI 02912.

Career

Postdoctoral fellow in psychology, University of British Columbia, 1992-94; assistant member, Monell Chemical Senses Center, Philadelphia, 1994-2000; Brown University, visiting professor, department of psychology, 2000-05, and Brown University School of Medicine, visiting professor, 2005; published first book, *The Scent of Desire: Discovering Our Enigmatic Sense of Smell,* 2007.

Sidelights

Research psychologist Rachel Herz is a leading researcher in a relatively new field of olfactory research, which examines the biological and evolutionary aspects of how human beings perceive and process smell. Affiliated with Brown University in Providence, Rhode Island, since 2000, Herz has conducted dozens of experiments that attempt to gauge how and why human beings react so viscerally to certain scents. She discussed many of these trials in her first book for a general audience, *The Scent of*

Desire: Discovering Our Enigmatic Sense of Smell, published in 2007. "The way I like to think about it is that emotion and olfaction are essentially the same thing," she explained to Laura Spinney of London's *Independent* about why we perceive some odors as pleasant while others are repulsive. "The part of the brain that controls emotion literally grew out of the part of the brain that controls smell."

Herz was born in 1963 in Ithaca, New York, but she and her younger brother moved several times during their early childhood years, including two stints in Paris. She was seven when her parents—both academics—settled in Montreal, Canada, and took teaching positions there. Her own college years were spent first at Queen's University in Kingston, Ontario, where she earned her undergraduate degree in psychology in 1985, and then at the University of Toronto, where she earned two advanced degrees in her field. After receiving the doctorate in 1992, Herz won a Canadian government grant from the Natural Sciences and Engineering Research Council for postdoctoral work at the University of British Columbia. In 1994, she joined the faculty of the Monell Chemical Senses Center in Philadelphia, the first scientific institute for multidisciplinary research on taste, smell, and chemosensory irritation in the world when it was founded in 1968. She spent six years there before joining the faculty of Brown

University in 2000 where she first held a visiting professorship with the department of psychology, and then with the School of Medicine since 2005.

At Brown, Herz teaches a course called "Olfaction and Human Behavior," and conducts scientific studies whose findings have been published in an array of professional journals. As she explained in an article she wrote for the July 2000 issue of *The Sciences*, a professional journal, "olfactory information is ... the key form of communication for all the most critical aspects of behavior—recognizing kin, finding a reproductively available mate, locating food, and determining whether an animal or object is dangerous. Smell was the first sense to evolve," she asserted. Herz's experiments explore various aspects of this basic human function. One involved manipulating how scents were labeled, and observed how an unpleasant label can cause subjects to perceive an odor as foul, even when they had rated the exact same smell as very pleasant with another label. Another addressed the matter of whether humans can smell odors while sleeping, and the resulting negative findings reaffirmed a crucial public-safety need for auditory smoke alarms in homes, because the even the uniquely pungent, acrid odor of smoke would not be detected by deeply sleeping inhabitants.

Another one of Herz's research trials used functional Magnetic Resonance Imaging (fMRI) technology, a form of brain scan. In this case, she gave her subjects a scent, and then an image associated with the same scent. The fMRI could detect which of the two triggered the stronger responses in the amygdale, the area of the brain that processes emotion and emotional memory. The scent, rather than the image, provoked a more intense response in the brain, but Herz was intrigued by the responses that came when she asked the subjects of their recollections associated with the scent. "People don't remember any more detail or with any more clarity when the memory is recalled with an odor," she explained to Spinney in the *Independent* article. "However, with the odor, you have this intense emotional feeling that's really visceral."

Herz's work has also investigated the memory evocation known as the "Proust phenomenon," named after French writer Marcel Proust and his most famous work, the 1913 novel *Remembrance of Things Past*. A key element of the novel is the bite its narrator takes into a madeleine cookie he has dipped in linden-blossom tea; both the scent and the taste bring the memory of an event from his past flooding back to him in rich detail. In an article she wrote about this famous literary moment for *The Sciences*,

Herz asserted that "it is that connection to long-forgotten events that makes the Proust phenomenon so exhilarating. The rush of vivid, emotionally charged memory linked to a lost love or a childhood event can make the past appear more powerful than the present. That such vividness could be merely an illusion—a product of the intimate tangle of smell, memory, and emotion—seems no reason not to revel when coming across the right scent."

Herz's first book for a mainstream audience, *The Scent of Desire: Discovering Our Enigmatic Sense of Smell*, was published in 2007. In it, she recounts her scores of studies and the often-surprising findings they yield, and noted in an interview on her Web site that her next book would likely be an examination of the role that scent plays in sexual attraction. Her own personal experience in this realm dates back to the Nino Cerutti fragrance worn by her first boyfriend, she said. "Although the last time I smelled it on him was almost 25 [years] ago I use this scent now as a memory test and every few years I sniff the empty bottle that I've kept at my parents' house to see if I can conjure up the memory of those early days. It still works." She has also saved a since-discontinued perfume her mother wore when Herz was a child. "Whenever I go to these fragrance bottles and uncork the genie inside, I always feel infused with a wonderful, powerful happiness. My emotions are at least partly due to the fact that I am still amazed at how smell, like none of my other senses, can transport me to a different time and place."

Selected writings

The Scent of Desire: Discovering Our Enigmatic Sense of Smell, HarperCollins, 2007.

Sources

Periodicals

Dallas Morning News, April 8, 2002.
Houston Chronicle, January 3, 2007, p. 1.
Independent (London, England), March 24, 2004, p. 8.
The Sciences, July 2000, p. 34.

Online

"A Conversation with Rachel Herz," Rachel Herz's Official Site, http://www.rachelherz.com (August 3, 2007).

—*Carol Brennan*

India Hicks

Thos Robinson/Getty Images

Interior designer and author

Born India Amanda Caroline Hicks, September 5, 1967, in London, England; daughter of David Hicks (an interior designer) and Pamela Mountbatten; children: Felix, Amory, Conrad (with boyfriend, David Flint Wood [an artist and writer]). *Education:* Earned photography degree in Boston, MA.

Addresses: *Home*—Harbour Island, Bahamas. *Office*—c/o Crabtree & Evelyn, 102 Peake Brook Rd., P.O. Box 167, Woodstock, CT 06281-0167.

Career

Worked as a photographer's agent in Paris, and as a model in New York City, 1980s and '90s; co-owner of a boutique hotel in the Bahamas, and operator of two guest cottages on Harbour Island, Bahamas; also owns boutique, Sugar Mill; first book, *Island Life: Inspirational Interiors,* published by Stewart, Tabori & Chang, 2003; Crabtree & Evelyn, spokesperson, 2006—, and creator of exclusive fragrance line, India Hicks Island Living, 2007.

Sidelights

Iconic British stylesetter India Hicks is known as one of the rebel daughters of the English aristocracy. The onetime model and well-heeled itinerant finally settled down in the Bahamas in the mid-1990s and began a family as well as several business ventures there. The daughter of a celebrated English interior designer, Hicks avoids the title herself, partly because she is not formally trained, but her keen eye and aesthetic sensibility are on display in a pair of coffee-table books, *Island Life* and *Island Beauty.* In 2007, she launched her own fragrance line, India Hicks Island Living, in partnership with Crabtree & Evelyn. Though she is not technically a royal, Hicks is 475th in line to the throne of England—actually one place ahead of Prince Philip, husband of the reigning monarch Elizabeth II.

Born in 1967, Hicks was the third child and second daughter born to Lady Pamela Hicks and David Hicks, a successful interior designer whose groundbreaking use of color and pattern helped advance British home decor into the modern era. Hicks' father avoided chintz and other fussy relics of the Victorian age, instead using bold colors to play off natural light. During the 1960s and '70s, he was known as the England's top society interior designer, with commissions that included rooms in Buckingham Palace and Windsor Castle. On her mother's side, Hicks was a Mountbatten, once known as Battenberg. This was a long line of German princes, one of whom married a daughter of Queen Victoria back in the nineteenth century. Hicks' grandfather was the famous Louis, Lord Mountbatten, who served as the Viceroy of India and supervised the transition of that country from

British colonial possession to independence. Hicks, who followed sister Edwina and brother Ashley, was named in honor of India, the country.

Hicks' young life was blighted by the tragic death of Lord Mountbatten, to whom she was quite close, in August of 1979. She and other family members were visiting him at the Mountbatten property, Classiebawn Castle, in Northern Ireland, when a bomb exploded on his fishing boat as he was heading into Donegal Bay. He died, as did Hicks's 14-year-old cousin, Nicholas Knatchbull, along with a local youth serving as a crew member. An 83-year-old baroness, related by marriage to the Mountbattens, died the following day. The bomb had been planted by members of the Irish Republican Army (IRA), and the event was a turning point in its struggle to achieve independence. Mountbatten was a decorated war hero and beloved figure in contemporary Britain. Hicks actually heard the explosion and recalled years later that just before her grandfather had sailed away, he had told her, "Look after my dog," she said in a *Daily Mail* interview with Alice Fowler. She brought the black labrador retriever, Juno, aboard with her on the Royal Air Force helicopter that came to bring her and other family members back to London. "We were given headphones to protect our ears, and I was asking for a pair for Juno," she recalled. "I kept saying: 'He told me to look after his dog.'"

Two years later, a more celebratory event rocked the British monarch with the July 29 wedding of Prince Charles to Lady Diana Spencer at St. Paul's Cathedral, London. Because Hicks was the goddaughter of Prince Charles, she was chosen as one of Diana's five bridesmaids, and footage of her attending the bride was seen by an estimated one billion viewers around the world that day. "We helped her get dressed," Hicks recalled when asked about the momentous occasion by *Evening Standard* journalist Marianne MacDonald. "She was in jeans and tiara, the TV next to her, and she kept shooing everyone away so she could watch it." Hicks also noted that Diana, who was just a few years older than she at the time, "got to the bottom of the staircase at Clarence House in her wedding dress, and everything was on such a tight schedule, and said, 'I need a glass of water.' Twenty-three footmen ran to get her a glass of water." Years later, however, Hicks confessed to CNN's Larry King that she was "a tomboy" and that she "hated the whole thing." Her own bridesmaid's dress, she continued was "awful," but she conceded, "now, as an adult, I appreciate enormously that I was part of a bit of history like that."

Hicks and Princess Diana came from similar backgrounds, though the Spencer clan had roots far older in the English land-owning aristocracy than the Mountbattens. Young women from such backgrounds were typically raised by nannies and sent to boarding school at a young age. "I saw a lot of my mother on her own and not a great deal of my parents together," she told Fowler in the *Daily Mail* article. Hicks attended the all-girl North Foreland Lodge, now the Sherfield School, in Hampshire, where she did well in her studies. She went on to the co-educational Gordonstoun School in Scotland but ran into trouble and was briefly suspended when she was caught entertaining two boys in her room. While there, she began dating Aris Comninos, who was part-Greek and would later become a professional stuntperson for the Bond 007 film franchise. Their relationship would last nearly a decade.

After leaving Gordonstoun, Hicks traveled through India in 1983 and lived a nomadic life for the next decade. She earned a degree in photography in Boston, moved to Paris to work as a photographic agent, and wound up becoming a model herself. She was a favorite of American designer Ralph Lauren in the early 1990s but began to feel disenchanted with the beauty industry. She still spurned, however, the traditional path expected of her, which was to settle down in England by marrying a man off a list of eligible titled men her father had been compiling since she was a child.

In the mid-1990s, Hicks met a former London advertising executive, David Flint Wood, while on vacation in the Bahamas. Flint Wood had been a longtime friend of her sister Edwina's and had abandoned his high-profile lifestyle in London for a quieter one running the only hotel on Harbour Island, located off Eleuthera Island. Hicks' family had property on Windermere Island, which was adjacent to Eleuthera, and since her childhood she had loved visiting the tropical paradise. Once they met again, she and Flint Wood became romantically involved, and the announcement of her unexpected pregnancy set off shock waves in the British media, especially when she flippantly characterized herself as "just some girl up the duff," a British slang expression for being pregnant.

Whereas a woman near 30 who chose not to marry the father of her child was not unusual in the West, it was for someone so closely connected to the royal family and British establishment. Hicks granted several interview requests and explained her position on the matter. "Having a child with someone is the biggest commitment you can make," she told *Daily Mail* journalist Anne De Courcy. "It's hard to explain without sounding critical of what has worked so well for so many people I know. Nor would I like anyone to think I'm not marrying as a sort of rebel thing, or because I'm not fully committed to David.... I think it's just a very personal gut feeling that I'm probably better off without going through the marriage thing." She also added that "I find the idea of a big white wedding in England highly claustrophobic. It's wonderful for some people but just not something I'm suited to. Maybe if I was 22 I'd be thinking differently, but now I'm 30 I don't want it." Nearly all journalists asked her to divulge the reaction of her godfather, Prince Charles, and she characterized him to De Courcy as "very pleased and supportive and glad for me," though she added "my father did have difficulty in accepting it to begin with. Dad was quite an old-fashioned person and was worried by me not being married. But, much to his credit, he overcame that."

Hicks's father died in 1998, several months after the car crash that tragically killed the Princess of Wales. When CNN's King interviewed Hicks some years later and asked her where she was when learned of Diana's death, she replied that she and Flint Wood were in England, having traveled there for the church christening ceremony of their first son, and, she said, "we heard it on the radio. We were in the middle of the English countryside, on a very quiet morning," she recalled, noting that Flint Wood "said he thought he'd heard this, but he must have misunderstood what he'd heard. And then later, we realized that it was actually something that had happened."

Hicks and Flint Wood have three sons—Felix, Amory, and Conrad—and on the eve of her fortieth birthday in September of 2007 she announced they were expecting a fourth child. By then she had turned her free-spirited Bahamian lifestyle into a branded venture: She and Flint Wood renovated their Caribbean plantation-style house, called Hibiscus Hill, and it was regularly featured in U.S. and U.K. design magazines, and then they built two rental cottages on the property, which features Harbour Island's famous pink sand beaches. They are co-owners of a small boutique hotel called The Landing but are not involved in its day-to-day operations, and they have a boutique on the island, Sugar Mill. In 2003, Stewart, Tabori & Chang published her first book, *Island Life: Inspirational Interiors*, which was written with Flint Wood. *Island Beauty*, with photographs by David Loftus, was published in 2006 and features Hicks' prescriptions for a natural and healthier lifestyle, including traditional Bahamian folk remedies and her own recipes for all-natural cleansers and shampoos.

That same year, Hicks signed with retailer Crabtree & Evelyn, which makes personal-care products and scents from a range of botanical-based ingredients.

She became its spokesperson, and in 2007 she launched her own fragrance line with the company called India Hicks Island Living. The products, for both home and body, retail for $18 to $80 and are divided into two scent families: Spider Lily and Casuarina, named after two fragrant plants that are typical of the Bahamian landscape. "From the beginning, I wanted to capture the unique smells of living here," she told Catherine Piercy in *Vogue*. "And that has got everything to do with the freshness of the ocean air, the scent of the palm fronds, the lush tropical flowers."

Hicks maintains that ten years on, she still has no plans to marry Flint Wood or return to England permanently—especially now that her sons are so acclimatized to island life. "From the boys' point of view, it's paradise—they're very free and rather savage as a result," she said in an interview with London *Sunday Times* writer Amanda Craig. "There's no smog, no car seats. I come back to England and it's so pressurised about what schools your children go to and there's an enormous pressure on kids to perform."

Selected writings

(With David Flint Wood) *Island Life: Inspirational Interiors*, Stewart, Tabori & Chang (New York City), 2003.
Island Beauty, with photographs by David Loftus, Stewart, Tabori & Chang, 2006.

Sources

Periodicals

Daily Mail (London, England), June 27, 1998, p. 6; October 13, 2003, p. 11.
Evening Standard (London, England), March 26, 2004, p. 44.
Sunday Times (London, England), July 1, 2001, p. 8.
Vogue, February 2007, p. 175.
WWD, January 5, 2007, p. 8.

Online

"Interview with India Hicks, Prince Charles's Goddaughter," *Larry King Live*, CNN.com (transcript of March 25, 2004, broadcast), http://edition.cnn.com/TRANSCRIPTS/0403/25/lkl.00.html (September 20, 2007).

—*Carol Brennan*

Anya Hindmarch

Michael Crabtree/Bloomberg News/Landov

Accessories designer

Born May 7, 1969, in England; daughter of Michael (a plastics company owner) and Susan Hindmarch; married James Seymour (a retail executive), 1996; children: Hugo (stepson), Rupert (stepson), Octavia (stepdaughter), Felix, Otto.

Addresses: *Home*—London, England. *Office*—The Stable Block, Plough Brewery, 516 Wandsworth Rd., London SW8 3JX, England.

Career

Launched eponymous label, 1987; opened first store in London, 1993, followed by stores in New York City, Los Angeles, Tokyo, and Hong Kong; launched Blue Label line of purses, 1999; launched footwear line, 2002.

Awards: Best British Accessories Designer, British Fashion Council, 2001.

Sidelights

British accessories designer Anya Hindmarch inadvertently found herself in the midst of a media frenzy over the special-edition grocery-shopping tote she created in 2007, with its clever anti-logo that touted, "I'm Not A Plastic Bag." Though its success inspired a bit of backlash, with cynics pointing out it was made in China—where manufacturing costs are low—and from non-organic cotton, Hindmarch was hopeful that her $15 tote was a harbinger of change and the beginning of the end for the supermarket plastic bag, each of which takes 500 years to decompose. "When you throw something away, there is no away," she pointed out in an interview with *Times* of London journalist Lisa Armstrong. "Currently each of us in [Britain] uses 167 bags a year. If we've made people think about that, then job done."

Born in 1969, Hindmarch grew up in a family with a strong entrepreneurial streak. Her father, Michael, owned a plastics company, and both her brother and sister would go on to launch their own companies as young adults. She attended a convent school in Essex and hoped to have a career as an opera singer, though she knew she first had to conquer her fear of performing in public. At the age of 18, she traveled to Italy for what the British call the "gap year," some time off between secondary school, as high school is known there, and college. The craze in Italian cities that year was for a draw-string duffle bag, which trend-conscious young women were carrying in lieu of a purse; Hindmarch returned to England with one and then looked in the telephone book for a manufacturer who could copy it. She took her prototype to the offices of *Harpers & Queens*, a leading British fashion magazine, and convinced them to sell it through one of their promotional offers. Hindmarch wound up selling 500 of the duffel bags, and with that her company was born in 1987.

Hindmarch returned to Italy to look for more items to bring back to sell, but she failed to find anything she felt would be a similar hit. Despite her lack of design experience or artistic training, she began sketching out her first line of handbags and began to land accounts with women's boutiques and department stores. "There were times in the early days when I was sitting alone at my dining room table, packing boxes, fighting through invoices and trying to design the occasional bag in between when I wondered what I was doing," she told Lisa Armstrong in an earlier *Times* of London interview. "But I knew I never wanted to work for anyone else."

In the first few years of her business, Hindmarch designed quirky purses. One was shaped like a clock, for example, while another had bamboo handles shaped like dogs. By 1993, she had grown the company well enough to open her first free-standing store, located on Walton Street in the posh Sloane Square neighborhood of London. In 1999, her company launched a lower-priced range of bags, sold as Blue Label. Two years later in 2001 she entered into her first serious philanthropic venture with Be a Bag, which allowed customers to create their own unique Blue Label handbag via a screen-printed photograph of their choice. Proceeds were donated to the Lavender Trust, a British breast-cancer awareness charity.

Hindmarch launched a footwear line in 2002 in partnership with an Italian shoe manufacturer, and she continued to open more stores around the world. Though her wares were a favorite of fashion-conscious women and celebrities, Hindmarch did not become a genuine household name until 2007, when her special-edition canvas tote imprinted with the tongue-in-cheek logo, "I'm Not A Plastic Bag," began to gain a flood of media attention. The shopping tote had long been in use in Europe, where grocery stores regularly charged customers for plastic bags, and by a more environmentally aware segment of consumers in the United States and Canada, but such totes were distinctly utilitarian and rarely had any pretension to fashion. Hindmarch wanted to create an item that could be used for hauling groceries home but appealed to the style-conscious as well, and designed her blue-script-on-white bag in partnership with a British organization for social change called We Are What We Do, which publicizes ways citizens can make small changes in their daily routines that have a cumulatively beneficial effect on the environment, such as turning off the water while brushing one's teeth.

A limited run of 20,000 of Hindmarch's bags went on sale in April of 2007 at Sainsbury's, a major British supermarket chain, and advance press prompted a slew of interest; people began lining up seven hours before the sale began at 9 a.m. The bags sold for $15 each but proved such a hot item that some were soon fetching $400 on the online auction Web site eBay. Despite the private profit that came from such secondhand sales, Hindmarch was pleased that the bags had seemed to catch on so quickly. "It's all good because this whole project is about awareness," she told Jessica Iredale in an interview that appeared in *WWD.* "It actually ends up with the bag being much talked about and much worn, and subliminally, it's a billboard that brainwashes people into changing how they behave."

Hindmarch married James Seymour in 1996, a widower with three children, and her stepchildren eventually began campaigning for new siblings. Felix and Otto joined Hugo, Rupert, and Octavia at the home in Chelsea that is minutes away from Hindmarch's company offices. Seymour was once an executive with Jigsaw, a high-end British retail chain, but he left to work for Hindmarch's business. Hindmarch claims that she handles her dual role as a mother of five and full-time executive and designer by being compulsively organized. She confesses to being a fanatical listmaker. "I have a master list, it's written in pencil and has sections," she told *Sunday Times* writer Claudia Croft. "You have the Immediate list, then As Soon as Possible, then Long-term Projects. There's a section for blue-sky ideas on the left and I put some things in smaller writing. I understand it, but other people go nuts." She also added that this trait was intrinsically linked to her designs. "I'm a freak. I love to be given a messy cupboard and organize it into sections. Handbags are like that. They are mobile filing cabinets."

Sources

Evening Standard (London, England), November 15, 2002, p. 58; March 20, 2007, p. 3.
New York Times, July 18, 2007.
Sun (London, England), March 14, 2007, p. 8.
Sunday Times (London, England), April 16, 2006, p. 10.
Time, August 13, 2007, p. 49.
Times (London, England), April 3, 2000, p. 14; May 9, 2007, p. 9.
WWD, July 19, 2007, p. 3.

—*Carol Brennan*

Carl Hodges

Scientist and entrepreneur

Born in 1937; married Elizabeth Swilling; children: four. *Education:* Graduated from University of Arizona, 1959.

Addresses: *Office*—Seawater Foundation, 4500 N. 32nd Street, Ste. 203, Phoenix, AZ 85018; Seaphire International, Inc., 4455 E. Camelback Rd., Ste. B200, Phoenix, AZ 85018.

Career

Supervisor, Solar Energy Research Laboratory, University of Arizona, 1967-92; director, University of Arizona Environmental Research Laboratory; founded Seawater Foundation, 1977; president, Planetary Design Corporation (resigned, 1991); president and CEO of Seaphire International, 1985.

Sidelights

Carl Hodges has spent 40 years on the forefront of research and development focused on solving problems related to the environment. As one of the original founders of the Environmental Research Laboratory at the University of Arizona, Hodges has worked on pioneering projects for companies such as Coca-Cola, Union Carbide, and Mattel, for the governments of Abu Dhabi, Iran, and Morocco, as well as for the United States Department of Energy and National Aeronautics and Space Administration (NASA). His vision and entrepreneurship have launched programs that could stop environmental degradation while also generating much-needed income for areas of the world suffering from poverty.

Born in 1937, Hodges spent the majority of his career as the director of University of Arizona's Environmental Research Laboratory. His studies have focused on global warming and its effects on water, arable land, fisheries and biodiversity. He graduated from the school in 1959 with a degree in atmospheric physics and a determination to help solve the problems facing the world of the future. He is married to Elizabeth Swilling, with whom he has four children.

Concerned about global warming and interested in finding alternative ways to generate revenue for impoverished nations, through the auspices of the Environmental Research Laboratory, Hodges began studying ways to use sea water to generate crops. One of the first ventures was a joint project with the University of Sonora in Mexico. In 1965, the University of Arizona and the University of Sonora constructed a desalination plant in hopes of finding an economically feasible way to remove salt from seawater to make it useful for farming. The research facility discovered that the process was unattainable at a large scale so the desalination plant was reengineered as an area for cultivating shrimp. This process was found to be highly successful and was one of the first projects exported for use in other countries. In the 1980s, Hodges also helped create a teaching and research facility on the Sea of Cortez that focuses on collaboration between Mexico and the United States with regard to the natural and cultural resources of the area.

From his research, Hodges found that it was much more viable to try and find ways to use salt water rather than figuring out methods of removing the salt content from sea water. He spent many years researching and developing salt-tolerant crops. Eventually he found a combination of animals and plants that made for a viable farm operation. There are more than 20,000 miles of desert coast that could be used for Hodges' specific kind of farming. Hodges explained to Kurt Shillinger of the *Star Tribune* the important contribution his work could make to the world, "If we could develop the coasts we could feed billions."

A visionary researcher, Hodges is also a tireless entrepreneur. In 1992, Hodges retired from his work at the University of Arizona and began to focus on running his company. In 1998, his Seaphire International company signed a deal with the Eritrean government to build the first seawater farm. While the deal was easy, the initial start up was a bit rocky due to a border war between Eritrea and Ethiopia. Hodges showed up with the first shrimps and the seeds for the specialty crop called salicornia and immediately had to make a decision between his personal safety and following his vision. While colleagues left the country, Hodges stayed behind to take care of the baby shrimp.

The farm system built in Eritrea on the west coast of the Red Sea consists of pumps and ponds that draw seawater inland. The first pond houses shrimp; after the shrimp pond the water flows to one that grows a type of fish called tilapia. From the tilapia pond the water moves on to irrigate salicornia (also known as sea asparagus, it is a delicacy in Europe). The water then irrigates experimental groves of mangrove trees. The shrimp, tilapia, salicornia, and mangroves are all exportable and in-demand. Hodges hopes that in the long run, many of these farms all along the coasts will stem the rising seas while also solving the problem of providing food for growing populations. In 2002, Hodges reported on his company's venture at a conference in Germany. His results led conference organizer Birgit Wirsing to comment to *European Innovation*, "Many people have a vision but see no way to realize it. He told us that he had thought about his vision for more than 30 years, and finally he has made it come true."

According to the Seawater Foundation Web site, in 2003 Seawater Farms Eritrea employed more than 700 people. The farm grew enough shrimp to make large weekly shipments to Europe and the Middle East. The salicornia crops were also established and were being used to produce oils for cosmetics and cooking. A wetland that had been built to contain the farm water after it passed through all its uses had attracted more than 200 species of birds. Unfor-tunately, an unstable political climate led to the project being abandoned the same year that the report was issued.

Throughout his career Hodges has tirelessly innovated and his vision of the future has attracted the attention of other visionaries. In 1992, he served as a consultant for Biosphere 2. The project sought to create a livable, secure, and independent ecosystem for scientific study. A group of people was selected to live inside the specially created dome and attempt to survive only on what was available inside. Conflicts between those inside as well as problems with management outside led to the entire project being discredited. For the Epcot Center at Disney World's exhibit Millennium Village, Hodges served as the consultant for the interactive exhibits for Eritrea and Saudi Arabia. Built in 1999, the Millennium Village was a temporary exhibit built as part of Disney World's celebration of the new millennium.

In 2005, based on the success of his Seawater Farms Eritrea, Seawater Foundation was awarded a $5 million contract by the World Bank Group to establish a mangrove tree farm in Mexico. The joint project between the government of Mexico, the University of Sonora, and the Seawater Foundation would also explore the viability of building a farm similar to the one built in Eritrea. In 2007, the success of the project led to a profile of Hodges in the green issue of *Vanity Fair*, which concluded, "By injecting life into the earth's proliferating desert landscapes, projects like the seawater farms of Carl Hodges may turn out to be just the kind of magic act the world sorely needs."

Sources

Periodicals

African Business (London, England), October 2002, p. 54.
Star Tribune (Minneapolis, MN), March 18, 2001, p. 4A.

Online

"Academic entrepreneurship—what works," *European Innovation*, http://cordis.europa.eu/aoi/article.cfm?article=190&lang=EN (July 2, 2007).
"The Future's Farmer," *Vanity Fair*, http://www.vanityfair.com/politics/features/2007/04/hodges200704 (August 2, 2007).

—Eve Hermann

David Horvath and Sun-Min Kim

Founders of Pretty Ugly LLC

Born David Horvath, May 28, 1971, in Summit, NJ; married Sun-Mim Kim, November 2005; children: one. Born Sun-Min Kim, June 8, 1976, in South Korea; married David Horvath, November 2005; children: one. *Education:* Horvath and Kim: Each earned an illustration degree from Parsons The New School for Design, New York City, 2001.

Addresses: *Office*—Pretty Ugly LLC, 45 Fernwood Ave., Edison, NJ 08837. *Web site*—http://www. uglydolls.com.

Career

Horvath worked for Toys International, Los Angeles, c. 2001; freelance illustrator, early 2000s. Together, began making Uglydolls, c. 2002; formed Pretty Ugly LLC, c. 2002.

Awards: Together: Specialty Toy of the Year, Toy Industry Association, 2006; Seal of Approval Award, National Parenting Center, for the Uglydoll card game, 2006; Parents' Choice Award, Parents' Choice Foundation, 2007; Platinum Award, Oppenheim Toy Portfolio, for the Uglydoll card game, 2007.

Sidelights

In the early 2000s, David Horvath and Sun-Min Kim began peddling a line of weird stuffed creatures that were adorably homely, yet cute and vulnerable. Called Uglydolls, the snaggle-toothed plush monsters enjoyed a meteoric rise in popularity. By 2006, sales topped $2.5 million and, in 2008, the company sold its one-millionth doll. The strange characters come from a place Horvath and Kim dubbed "Uglyverse"—this is a universe where ugly means unique or special. Creatures include Wage, Jeero, Wedgehead, and Ice Bat, among others. Some have one eye, while others have three. Many have fangs. They all have distinctive personalities. Each Uglydoll comes with a mini-biography on its tag, describing its favorite foods, likes and dislikes, hobbies and so forth.

Eric Nakamura, owner of the L.A.-based Asian pop-culture store Giant Robot, was the first retailer to carry the dolls. "Uglydolls are a constant seller," he told *Time* magazine's Nadia Mustafa. "They hit an emotional chord in people." Nakamura believes they are popular in part because they force people to confront the eternal question of defining what ugly is and what it is not.

Horvath was born on May 28, 1971, in Summit, New Jersey, though he enjoyed a bi-coastal upbringing as the family moved frequently between New York City and Los Angeles. Horvath's mother worked as a designer for Mattel. As a child, Horvath was always interested in the unique prototypes his mother brought home, but upon seeing the toys on the store shelves, he lost interest. Horvath thought that somewhere along the way, the toys seemed to lose their magic. Early on, Horvath knew he wanted to make toys but did not want to work for a large corporation.

Horvath also liked to draw. He decided to study illustration and entered New York City's Parsons The New School for Design. In 1997, he met Kim, a fellow illustration student at Parsons. Horvath said he chased Kim around for a year before she would give him the time of day.

Kim was born on June 8, 1976, and grew up in Seoul, South Korea. She was always crafty and imaginative. As a child, she built dollhouses out of cardboard and clay. After graduating from Parsons in 2001, Horvath and Kim went their separate ways. In the aftermath of 9/11, Kim's parents urged her to return to Korea. Heartbroken, Horvath was left alone in the United States. He bounced around for a while, working in Los Angeles at Toys International. He also worked as an illustrator, opening a studio in New York City.

Horvath thought he might find fame as an illustrator. He was inspired by Rodney Greenblat, the American fine artist who drew the characters for the 1990s PlayStation game "Parappa the Rapper." Influenced by the game and its quirky characters—like the blue-skinned Katy Kat and Chop Chop, a martial arts master with a stinky green onion head—Horvath created his own cast of characters.

One of those characters was a blobbish creature with far-set eyes and triangular teeth extending from a somber, not-quite-grinning and not-quite-frowning mouth. Horvath inked the character, named Wage, onto the love letters he sent Kim. He took illustrations of the creature—and others like it—to toy companies and was told his characters had no viable market. Horvath felt devastated.

Kim used the illustrations on her love letters to create a foot-tall plush version of Horvath's character. "I knew it would make David happy to see his character alive in the real world," she told Time. "So for Christmas I sewed Wage into a doll." Horvath showed the stuffed creation to Nakamura, who immediately ordered a batch for his store. Speaking to Time, Nakamura recalled his intrigue. "The prototype had great energy and didn't ask too much in terms of analyzing it as a form or design concept. It was just easy to like."

Horvath and Kim delivered 20 of the dolls to Nakamura. The dolls sold out in two days so Kim made more. Soon, they added Babo, Wage's not-too-smart but incredibly loyal best friend. In Korean, babo means fool. Seeing a market for their creations, Horvath and Kim got down to business. At the time, Kim still lived in Korea. She did the sewing while Horvath created the tags and website and searched for boutiques to sell their quirky creatures. Over the course of 18 months, Kim sewed 1,500 dolls.

They also created new characters. Horvath made sketches, then sent them to Kim who brought them to life. In an interview with Jason Arber for the online magazine Pixelsurgeon, Horvath credited Kim for the dolls' success. "If someone else were to take my illustrations and turn them into plush dolls, it wouldn't come out the same way. Sun-Min took my drawings and turned them into the most amazing toys I have ever seen. In many cases Sun-Min would take bits from one drawing and pieces of another and put them all together to create an all new doll."

Horvath and Kim reunited in 2003 when they exhibited their dolls at the International Toy Fair held in New York. The Uglydolls were a hit and the couple was blown away by the number of retailers who expressed interest. As the operation grew, the couple opened a warehouse in New Jersey. The dolls, which sell for about $25, are hand-sewn in Korea and assembled in China. Over the next few years they launched companion products, including T-shirts, key chains, vinyl figures, stationary, and journals.

Each year, the company expands its territory into new stores. Uglydolls are sold globally in 2,500 retail stores, including FAO Schwarz and Barneys. They can also be found in gift shops at the New York City Museum of Modern Art and the Musée des Arts Decoratifs in Paris.

Major corporations have offered to buy the company, but Horvath and Kim are not selling. In fact, they refuse to place Uglydolls in chain stores because they want to preserve their history. Horvath does not want them turned into a mass-produced, mass-marketed cash machine. Speaking to the National Post's Neil Dunlop, Horvath put it this way: "They were not made on purpose so you would buy it, but as a genuine act of love that came without greed or wanting to get something from it."

Horvath believes that is part of the reason for their success. As for the future, he would love to see Uglydolls break into television. They have been featured in several books co-written and drawn by Horvath and Kim. Most are guides to the "Uglyverse."

Selected writings

How to Draw Uglydoll Kit: Ugly Drawings in a Few Easy Steps, Walter Foster (Laguna Hills, CA), 2006.

Ugly Guide to Things That Go and Things That Should Go But Don't, Random House Books for Young Readers (New York City), 2008.

The Ugly Guide to the Uglyverse, Random House Books for Young Readers, 2008.

Sources

Periodicals

Entrepreneur, June 2007, p. 38.
Houston Chronicle (Houston, TX), July 29, 2005, p. 1

National Post (Canada), December 13, 2004, p. FP9.
New York Times, March 23, 2008, p. ST10.
New York Times Magazine, February 15, 2004, p. 28.
Playthings, May 2005, p. 22.
Time, Winter 2006, p. 38.

Online

"About," Uglydolls.com, http://www.uglydolls.com (April 20, 2008).

"David Horvath," *Pixelsurgeon*, http://www.pixelsurgeon.com/interviews/interview.php?id=71 (May 22, 2008).

—Lisa Frick

Khaled Hosseini

Author and physician

Born March 4, 1965, in Kabul, Afghanistan; son of a diplomat and a high school teacher; immigrated to United States, 1980; married Roya; children: two. *Education:* Santa Clara University, B.A., 1988; University of California, San Diego, M.D., 1993.

Addresses: *Agent*—Elaine Koster Literary Agency, 55 Central Park W., Ste. 6, New York, NY 10023.

Career

Practicing physician specializing in internal medicine, 1996-99, with the Permanente Medical Group, 1999-2004; first novel, *The Kite Runner,* published by Riverhead Books, 2003, and adapted for film, 2007. Active in volunteer work for Paralyzed Veterans of America and Aid the Afghan Children; United Nations Refugee Agency, goodwill ambassador, 2006—.

Sidelights

Khaled Hosseini has been called the most famous Afghan in the world thanks to his 2003 novel *The Kite Runner.* A tale of boyhood friendship and betrayal set in Hosseini's native Afghanistan during its past three tumultuous decades, the book went on to become a runaway bestseller, with more than eight million copies sold—half of them in the United States, the author's adopted home. *The Kite Runner* was also made into a 2007 film, whose premiere in Afghanistan was delayed by threats of violence against its actors. "The controversy reflects that

things in Afghanistan have changed to some extent, certainly in the last year or two," Hosseini said in an interview with Erika Milvy for Salon.com. "Things have become more violent. It's a more dangerous place than it was. It has slid back and there's a new element of criminality and violence there."

The first of five children, Hosseini was born in 1965, in Kabul, Afghanistan's capital city. His father was a diplomat with the country's foreign ministry, and his mother taught at a high school for young women. In 1970, the family moved to Tehran, Iran, when his father was assigned to the Afghan embassy there. They returned to Kabul three years later, the same year that a coup ousted the longtime king of Afghanistan, Mohammed Zahir Shah. In 1976, Hosseini's father was posted to France, and they remained in Paris when a Communist takeover of Afghanistan's government occurred in 1978. The family applied for and received political asylum in the United States in 1980.

The Hosseinis brought few possessions or assets with them, and relied on government assistance for a time after their arrival in San Jose, California. Hosseini earned his undergraduate degree in biology from Santa Clara University in 1988, and then went on to the medical school of the University of

California at San Diego. After a residency in internal medicine at Cedars-Sinai Medical Center in Los Angeles, he became a practicing physician in 1999 with the Permanent Medical Group in Mountain View, California. He married and became a father, but found the time to write short stories in which he tried to recapture the fading memories of his childhood in Kabul. After the Communist takeover, Afghanistan had disintegrated into full-scale war that raged for much of the 1980s, with United States-backed anti-communist guerrilla fighters known as the mujahideen fighting the Soviet occupiers. A period of civil war ensued after Soviet troops pulled out in 1989.

A few of Hosseini's stories had been published in literary journals and one was even nominated for a Pushcart Prize, but it was his father-in-law's praise for a short story called "The Kite Runner"—accompanied by the wish that it had been a longer tale—that prompted Hosseini to try his hand at writing a novel. "If there is one thing we doctors have been trained for, it's getting by with less than ideal hours of sleep," he wrote in the British medical journal *Lancet*. "So for 15 months, I woke up at [5 a.m.], drank cupfuls of black coffee, and created the world of Amir and Hassan."

Those two names were the pair of boys whose stories dominate *The Kite Runner*, which was finished in June of 2002 and published by Riverhead Books exactly one year later. The novel begins in 1975 in the Kabul household of Baba, a wealthy merchant whose wife died in childbirth. Baba's son is Amir, who longs to be closer to his emotionally distant father, and fears his father blames him for his mother's death. Yet Baba dotes on Hassan, the little boy who lives in a mud shack on their property with his disabled father, Ali. Ali has been a longtime servant of the family, and is of a different ethnic group, the Hazara. Amir's family, by contrast, are Pashtun, who held most positions of power in the country during the era. The boys are close friends as youngsters, with Hassan worshipping his more privileged friend and often defending him from the neighborhood bullies, while Amir resents his father's affection for the servant boy.

The title of *The Kite Runner* refers to a popular pastime among Afghan children, kite fighting. Participants tie shards of glass and affix glue to their kite strings in an attempt to knock down the competitors' kites; the kite runner chases down the kites that have been cut down. Hassan is the most talented of the runners, and Amir sends him to retrieve his winning kite, which is the most coveted prize in the annual winter tournament. When Has-

san seems to be delayed, Amir goes to look for him, and spies him crouching in an alley as he is taunted by other boys. Amir hides from the group, but witnesses the ringleader—the half-German neighborhood bully who crows that the new, post-monarchy regime in Afghanistan will eliminate the Hazara ethnic minority as Nazi Germany attempted to do with Europe's Jews—sodomize Hassan.

Amir is traumatized by what he saw, and his silence only deepens the psychic wound. At home, he rebuffs Hassan and begins to resent him, and finally tells his father that Hassan stole his birthday money. It is a lie, but the loyal Hassan admits to the deed to protect his adored friend. Ali, however, is hurt by the accusation against his son, and the two leave Baba's household forever. Soon after this, Soviet troops invade Afghanistan, and Amir and Baba are forced to flee across the border. They resettle in America, where Amir becomes a successful writer but is still haunted by his act of betrayal against Hassan. To him, the secret is a heavy weight that he has never confessed to anyone, not even his Afghan-born wife. One day, after Baba has died, he receives a call from his father's old friend, Rahim, who urges him to come to visit him in Pakistan. There, Rahim reveals some long-buried secrets about Amir's family, and tells him that Hassan and his wife were killed by the harsh Islamic fundamentalist Taliban regime. Rahim asks Amir to go back to Kabul to find Hassan's son.

Hosseini's debut novel won effusive praise from critics. Writing in the London *Independent*, Aamer Hussein called it "a first novel of unusual generosity, honesty and compassion." The *Boston Herald*'s Judith Wynn asserted that Hosseini "neatly balances the novel's two themes of immigrant dislocation and personal redemption.... Well-paced suspense, engaging characters, riveting incidents and pungent dialogue make *The Kite Runner* soar." Edward Hower of the *New York Times Book Review* found it a "powerful first novel [that] tells a story of fierce cruelty and fierce yet redeeming love." Commenting on the third section of the novel in which Amir returns to Afghanistan and encounters the horrors of the Taliban, Hower noted that this part "is full of haunting images: a man, desperate to feed his children, trying to sell his artificial leg in the market; an adulterous couple stoned to death in a stadium during the halftime of a football match; a rouged young boy forced into prostitution, dancing the sort of steps once performed by an organ grinder's monkey."

The Kite Runner's paperback edition appeared in 2004, and propelled the title to the best-seller lists for nearly all of 2005, 2006, and even into 2007. In

2005, Hosseini's debut novel was the third best-selling book in the United States. It also proved a hit with readers worldwide, and was translated into more than three dozen languages; there was even a bootleg translation into Farsi, which made it an underground bestseller in Iran.

Hosseini's second novel, *A Thousand Splendid Suns*, was published in May of 2007. This time, he weaves a portrait of Afghan culture, politics, and society through the intertwined stories of two women, Mariam and Laila. Mariam comes from a poor family and is married off to a man in Kabul. Rasheed, her abusive husband, expects her to wear the head-to-toe-covering garment known as the burka when out in public. Mariam is unable to carry a pregnancy to term, which further enrages Rasheed. She watches, with interest, the life of her young neighbor, Laila, who comes from a progressive-minded family and even attends school. The story takes place as the Soviet occupation of Afghanistan is giving way to chaotic fighting by warlords, which is finally quelled by the totalitarian Taliban regime. Laila's family is one of the many casualties of the conflict and, having nowhere else to turn, she is adopted by Rasheed and then becomes his second wife.

Hosseini's novel again earned high marks from book reviewers. "Where Hosseini's novel begins to sing is in depicting the slowly growing friendship of the two wives in the face of the horrific abuse from their shared husband," wrote Natasha Walter in the *Guardian*. She also noted that "Hosseini does not challenge the usual western view of Afghanistan, but he does enrich it—he adds greater knowledge and understanding to it, and makes the Afghans come alive as loving, feeling individuals." Comparing it with its predecessor, a *Time* critic wrote that "*A Thousand Splendid Suns* probably won't be as commercially successful as Hosseini's first novel, but it is, to put it baldly, a better book," asserted Lev Grossman. "*The Kite Runner* ran heavily to unredeemable sinners and spotless saints, [while] in *Suns* the characters are more complex and paradoxical—more human."

The film version of *The Kite Runner* was released later in 2007. The story was adapted for the screen by David Benioff, and directed by Marc Forster of *Monster's Ball* and *Finding Neverland* fame. Because of Afghanistan's ongoing troubles, the film was shot in China, but Hosseini and Forster agreed that much of the dialogue would be in Dari, the main language of Afghanistan, with English subtitles added. The film's December premier in Afghanistan was delayed several weeks when conservative elements in the country learned of the 30-second sexual assault scene in the story. The parents of the child actor claimed that they had been unaware of this part of the story, and all three young actors involved in it became the targets of threats. Some demanded that the scene be excised from the movie, which Paramount refused to do.

The debacle did little to counter assertions that Hosseini's homeland was a repressive country deeply troubled by its own shameful past. Still, Hosseini hoped that its larger message would come through, he told Milvy in the Salon.com interview, referring to the scene in which "Amir, in a moment of distress and personal anguish, goes to a mosque and prays. How many times have we seen Muslim characters in a film pray—in that kind of very spiritual moment, piously? Usually when they do, in the next scene they're blowing something up."

The success of *The Kite Runner* enabled Hosseini to give up his career as a physician in 2004 in order to write full time. In 2006, he became a goodwill ambassador for the United Nations Refugee Agency, which works to repatriate the several million Afghans displaced since the 1979 Soviet invasion. Speaking about the success of *The Kite Runner*, he told Lorraine Ali in *Newsweek International* that "my story took place in Afghanistan, but this same story is being played out everywhere, all over the world. Iraq is a dramatic example, but I get letters from Africa, and I was just speaking to refugees in Chad. The nature of the conflict may be different, but the end result is so tragically similar. The people who have no control over what's happening ultimately end up paying the price."

Selected writings

The Kite Runner, Riverhead Books (New York, NY), 2003.
A Thousand Splendid Suns, Riverhead Books, 2007.

Sources

Periodicals

Boston Herald, June 15, 2003, p. A20.
Guardian (London, England), December 18, 2004, p. 31; May 19, 2007, p. 16.

Independent (London, England), September 20, 2003, p. 30.

Lancet, September 20, 2003, p. 1003.

Newsweek International, December 17, 2007.

New York Times Book Review, August 3, 2003, p. 4.

Publishers Weekly, March 19, 2007, p. 34.

Time, May 28, 2007, p. 68.

Online

"The 'Kite Runner' Controversy," Salon.com, http://www.salon.com/ent/movies/feature/2007/12/09/hosseini/ (February 1, 2008).

—*Carol Brennan*

Dawn Hudson

President and Chief Executive Officer of Pepsi-Cola North America

Born Dawn E. Hudson, November 27, 1957, in Worcester, MA; daughter of Kenneth Dunlap and Nancy (Selin) Hudson; married Bruce Beach (president of an executive search firm), August 31, 1980; children: Morgan (daughter), Kendall (daughter). *Education:* Graduated Dartmouth College, 1979.

Addresses: *Office*—700 Anderson Hill Rd., Purchase, NY 10577.

Career

Advertising account representative, Compton Advertising, 1979-82; product manager, Clairol, 1982-83; account supervisor, management supervisor partner, Tatham-Laird & Kudner, Chicago, 1983-86; advertising representative, DDB Needham, Chicago, 1986-94; executive vice-president and director of client services, DDB Needham Worldwide, New York, 1994-96; managing director, D'Arcy, Masius, Benton & Bowles, 1996; executive vice-president of sales and marketing, Frito-Lay, 1996-98; senior vice president strategy & marketing, Pepsi-Cola North America, 1998-2002; president, Pepsi-Cola North America, 2002-05; president and chief executive officer, Pepsi-Cola North America, 2005—.

Awards: B*East award, American Advertising Federation; twice awarded Top 50 Marketers, Advertising Age; Hall of Achievement, American Advertising Federation.

Sidelights

In 2005, Dawn Hudson was listed at number 41 on Fortune's list of America's 50 most powerful female chief executives. As chief executive officer and president of Pepsi-Cola North America, Hudson has focused her passion for advertising and her skillful ability to judge consumer demand into an amazing career. She rose through the ranks of some of the nation's top advertising agencies, working on challenging and high-profile accounts such as Clairol, Proctor and Gamble, and Maybelline. Keith Reinhard, chairman of DDB Worldwide, one of Hudson's previous employers, told Thom Forbes of *Advertising Age*, "Dawn gets it.... She was way ahead of the curve in terms of what everybody is now talking about—the need for thinking about a brand in its totality."

Born in 1957, Hudson is the oldest of three daughters who grew up in Massachusetts. Extremely competitive and driven, Hudson competed in tennis while growing up while also nurturing a desire to follow a different path from that of her parents. She explained to Constance L. Hays of the *New York Times*, "You want to chart your own course."

Hudson's course led her to attend Dartmouth College. The campus had recently been opened to women and at the time she was one of 100 women on a campus that was 95 percent male. Her experience at Dartmouth led to her believe in the power of networking and maintaining connections. She believes in using her network and encourages other women to assist each other by providing feedback and mentoring.

In 1979, as she was about to graduate from school and was trying to figure out what direction to take at that point, a friend encouraged her to apply for a job with Compton Advertising who was on campus that day. Hudson quickly put together her resume and ran over to interview. She was hired and began working at Compton doing commercials. She spent three years on the advertising end before she was promoted to brand manager for Clairol, a position she was given in part because she had taken French classes in college.

After several years with Compton, Hudson ended up moving to Chicago to work with Tatham-Laird & Kudner. Her primary account was working with Proctor and Gamble, a company she had also done work for at Compton. In 1986, she moved over to work with DDB Needham where eventually she rose to the position of managing partner. Her projects there included work for General Mills, Maybelline, and Ralston Purina. In 1994, a desire to be closer to family back East and a promotion brought Hudson to DDB Needham's New York office where she took the position of executive vice president and client services director.

In 1996, she was offered a position with the advertising agency D'Arcy, Masius, Benton, and Bowles where she was named managing director. By that time she had formed a relationship with Frito-Lay, having worked on a retooling of their advertising campaigns in the early 1990s. She was passionate then about the direction the campaign should go, which was counter to what most of the team was recommending. She felt so strongly that she ended up putting in an urgent call to the president of Frito-Lay at the time, Steve Reinemund. He listened and then directed the team to follow her suggestions which led to the successful campaign for Rold Gold starring Jason Alexander of the sitcom *Seinfeld.* Reinemund explained to *Advertising Age*'s Forbes, "She felt very passionate about what we needed to do and she was clearly right." The ad campaign was responsible for moving Frito-Lay's market share up from eleven percent to 30 percent.

Her work made an impression on Reinemund and in October of 1996 she was offered a position with Frito-Lay as head of sales and marketing. She jumped at the opportunity. Within two years she moved over to Pepsi-Cola North America, taking on the role of senior vice-president of marketing and strategy. Her work in that role included overseeing the "Joy of Cola" campaign which featured pop singer Britney Spears. She also had a hand in introducing two new drinks to the market: Mountain Dew Code Red and Pepsi Twist.

Hudson is always on the move. She finds time for leisure activities like reading, skiing, playing tennis, and going to the zoo with her two daughters, Morgan and Kendall. Her husband, Bruce Beach, who spent many years at home with their two daughters is also the president of an executive search firm. Hudson believes strongly that it is necessary to lead a well-rounded life. She explained to Hays in the *New York Times* interview, "Part of being a good marketer is just being a regular person." Two losses in her life may have brought home this idea of balance between work and home. When she was 23 her father died of a heart attack and five years later her younger sister died from congenital heart disease. She told Forbes in the *Advertising Age* interview, "To lose two people in your five-member family in a five-year time frame, you've got to look at the glass as half-full and keep pressing on."

In 2002, Hudson was named president of Pepsi-Cola North America. Her responsibilities included marketing, sales, and strategic direction as well as building and maintaining relationships with bottlers and the food-service industry. The new level of accountability was a welcome challenge to Hudson, who says she thrives on competition. In 2004, talking to Forbes in *Advertising Age*, she said she was most excited about finding a way to weave together Pepsi Cola's three branches—Pepsi's beverage operations, Frito-Lay, and Quaker food service—into a strong leader of the food and beverage industry.

In 2005, Hudson was awarded another promotion and took on the additional title of chief executive officer (CEO) for Pepsi-Cola North America. As CEO she was now responsible for all beverages under the Pepsi umbrella. The following year she played a part in Pepsi's acquisition of Izze Beverage, a small company based in Boulder, Colorado, whose fruit-juice-based carbonated beverages had become very popular.

By 2006, Hudson's rise in the industry had been acknowledged by her place on *Fortune* magazine's list of the 50 most powerful chief executive women in the United States. Two years in a row she was listed in *Forbes* magazine as one of the top 100 most powerful women. Her skill at understanding target audiences as well as the products has served her well throughout her career. In response to peers who think she somehow knows what's going on in the minds of her target audiences, Hudson replied to Kate MacArthur of *Advertising Age,* "You might find me on a snowboard, but I'll never say I know what a teenager is thinking."

Sources

Advertising Age, June 26, 2000, p. S18; November 8, 2004, pp. P5-P8.

New York Times, January 31, 1999, p. 2.

—*Eve Hermann*

Jennifer Hudson

Singer and actress

Born Jennifer Kate Hudson, September 12, 1981, in Chicago, IL; daughter of Samuel Samson (a bus driver) and Darnell Hudson. *Education:* Attended Langston University and Kennedy-King College.

Addresses: *Agent*—William Morris Agency, 151 El Camino Dr., Beverly Hills, CA 90212. *Home*—Chicago, IL.

Career

Worked at Burger King, and on a Disney cruise ship, 2003. Actress in films, including: *Dreamgirls,* 2006. Also appeared on the third season of *American Idol,* FOX, 2004.

Awards: Academy Award for best performance by an actress in a supporting role, Academy of Motion Picture Arts and Sciences, for *Dreamgirls,* 2007; Golden Globe for best performance by an actress in a supporting role in a motion picture, Hollywood Foreign Press Association, for *Dreamgirls,* 2007.

Sidelights

Toward the end of 2006, Chicago native Jennifer Hudson became one of the most talked-about new celebrities in the entertainment industry thanks to her starring role in the long-awaited film adaptation of *Dreamgirls,* the hit Broadway musical. Critics showered the *American Idol* reject—infamously ousted during the television talent-search contest's third season in 2004—as a winning combination of vocal talent and intensely photogenic looks that helped make *Dreamgirls* the must-see movie of the holiday season. In the story's opening moments, noted *Entertainment Weekly*'s Owen Gleiberman, Hudson's character leads her 1960s all-girl R&B trio act on stage, takes the mic, then "sings the way that a lion roars, blasting the roof off with her full-throated gospel vibrations." Writing in *Newsweek,* reviewer David Ansen commended the novice's big-screen debut, asserting "the movie belongs to Hudson as the proud, self-destructive Effie."

Born in Chicago in 1981, Hudson grew up in Englewood as the last of three children of her mother, Darnell Hudson, and a bus-driver father, Samuel Samson, who died when Hudson was still in her teens. Her maternal grandmother, Julia Kate Hudson, was a strong influence on Hudson when she was a child, and she followed her into the church choir. Hudson's solo debut was an inauspicious one, however, because she forgot the words to "Must Jesus Bear the Cross Alone?". Later, she managed her perpetual stage jitters in a novel way, explaining to *Los Angeles Magazine* writer Mary Melton that "until I was 19, I sang with my eyes closed."

Hudson spent time at Langston University, Oklahoma's only historically black college, but later returned to the Chicago area and took classes at Kennedy-King College. She worked at Burger King while appearing in community theater productions before auditioning for and winning a job on a Disney cruise ship in 2003, which marked her professional debut. Back home, her mother suggested she get in line for the next round of *American Idol* casting tryouts, and Hudson traveled to Atlanta and was surprised to make the cut for the hit show's third season. She was teamed with two other young African-American women, one of them Fantasia Barrino, as the weekly series progressed in early 2004, but was subject to harsh criticism from judge Simon Cowell. She was famously ousted by viewer voting results on April 21, 2004, and recalled that the entire experience was a brutal one. Cowell had said to her, "You get one shot … you ain't never gonna be seen again," according to Cori Murray in *Essence.* Hudson was even criticized for her choice of outfits. "He talked about me bad, but maybe I needed to be talked about," she admitted to *New York Times* writer Lola Ogunnaike. "At that time I didn't really understand the language of fashion."

Hudson spent some months appearing in concerts on an *American Idol* tour, and considered that singing cover tunes to preteen fans of the show might indeed be her last time in the public eye. "I'd say, 'Lord, if I don't get another chance, thank you for this—at least I got to taste it,'" she recalled in the *Essence* interview with Murray. She did relocate to the Los Angeles area for a few months in order to try out for some roles, and turned up alongside almost 800 other female hopefuls vying for a part in the planned film version of *Dreamgirls,* the hit Broadway musical from the 1980s. Its story was roughly based on that of the Supremes' rise to stardom on Detroit's Motown record label. The Supremes' solidly built and torchy lead vocalist was Florence Ballard, who was eventually pushed aside for the slimmer, lighter-skinned Diana Ross, and Ross went on to have a major career in Hollywood and as a solo recording artist.

Hudson was called back to audition several times for the part of Effie White, the Florence Ballard of the fictional Dreamettes, before finally winning the role. The film also starred Beyoncé Knowles as the Diana Ross-type character, along with Jamie Foxx and Eddie Murphy, and was directed by Bill Condon, who had previously adapted another storied Broadway musical, *Chicago,* for the big screen. Hudson's screen debut in *Dreamgirls* was greeted with effusive reviews for her performance even before the movie premiered in December of 2006, and its opening box-office weekend was boosted by the cast's appearance on Oprah Winfrey's daytime talk show. Winfrey had seen the movie in previews, and adored it, but Hudson recalled that when she was told she had a phone call and it was Oprah on the line, "I thought it was my manager playing around," she confessed in an interview with Sean Smith in *Newsweek.* "It took about 30 seconds before I realized, 'Oh, my God, this is Oprah for real!'"

Dreamgirls' tour-de-force moment comes midway through the story, when Effie learns that their manager—Foxx's character, who is also Effie's boyfriend—is moving Deena into the lead vocalist slot, and has been romancing her on the side as well. Effie's farewell number as a Dreamette, "And I'm Telling You (I'm Not Going)," won rave reviews from critics and cemented Hudson's future as an entertainment tour-de-force in her own right. Gleiberman, writing in *Entertainment Weekly,* called it a "grandly shattering … piece of musical acting," while *Newsweek'*s David Ansen noted that "with her powerhouse voice, Hudson turns [it] into a heartbreaking yelp of anguish so potent one preview audience gave it a standing ovation. That's not supposed to happen in movie theaters."

Hudson won both a Golden Globe and the Academy Award for Best Supporting Actress for her role in *Dreamgirls,* and the world's top fashion designers were eager to provide her with custom evening gowns. The 25-year-old newcomer, with her curvy figure, was suddenly hailed as America's newest style icon, and even appeared on the cover of *Vogue,* making her only the third African-American woman who was not a fashion model to grace the American edition. She continued to sign on to work on other films, including *Winged Creatures* and *Sex and the City: The Movie,* both scheduled for a 2008 release. She was rumored to be in talks for a planned biopic of soul legend Aretha Franklin, and confessed she still had not become fully adjusted to all the attention. "Sometimes they have to pull me off the red carpet, " she admitted to Ogunnaike in the *New York Times* interview. "The first thing I do when I get home from an event is get on the computer and look at my pictures."

Sources

Advocate, December 19, 2006, p. 36.
Entertainment Weekly, December 22, 2006, p. 54.
Essence, March 2007, p. 129.
Los Angeles Magazine, January 2007, p. 34.
Newsweek, December 11, 2006, p. 96, p. 98.
New Yorker, December 25, 2006, p. 150.
New York Times, February 25, 2007.
People, May 10, 2004, p. 22.
Vogue, March 2007, p. 542.

—*Carol Brennan*

Eddie Izzard

Actor and comedian

Born Edward John Izzard, February 7, 1962, in Aden, South Yemen, Africa; son of Harold John (a chief auditor for British Petroleum) and Dorothy Ella (a nurse) Izzard. *Education:* Attended University of Sheffield, Sheffield, United Kingdom.

Addresses: *Agent*—Karon Maskill, 33 Cranwich Road, London, N16 5HZ. *Web site*—http://www.eddieizzard.com.

Career

Stand-up comedy performances include: *Live at the Ambassadors*, 1993; *Unrepeatable*, 1994; *Definite Article*, 1996; *Glorious*, 1997; *Dress to Kill*, 1998; *Circle*, 2002; *Sexie*, 2003. Stage appearances include: *The Cryptogram*, 1994; *900 Oneonta*, 1994; *Edward II*, 1995; *Lenny*, 1999; *A Day in the Death of Joe Egg*, Comedy Theatre, England, 2001, Roundabout Theatre Company, New York, 2003; *Trumbo*, 2003. Television appearances include: *Aristophanes: The Gods are Laughing*, 1995; *Tales from the Crypt*, 1996; *Rex the Runt*, 1998; *Pythonland*, 1999; *40*, 2003; *The Riches*, 2007. Film appearances include: *The Secret Agent*, 1996; *Velvet Goldmine*, 1998; *The Avengers*, 1998; *Mystery Men*, 1999; *Circus*, 2000; *Shadow of the Vampire*, 2000; *The Cat's Meow*, 2001; *All the Queen's Men*, 2001; *Revenger's Tragedy*, 2002; *Blueberry*, 2004; *Five Children and It*, 2004; *Ocean's Twelve*, 2004; *Romance & Cigarettes*, 2005, *My Super Ex-Girlfriend*, 2006; *Ocean's Thirteen*, 2007; *Across the Universe*, 2007.

Awards: British Comedy Award for best stand-up comedian, 1993 and 1996; Emmy Award for outstanding individual performance in a variety or mu-sic program, Academy of Television Arts & Sciences, for *Dress to Kill*, 2000; Emmy Award for outstanding writing for a variety, music, or comedy program, Academy of Television Arts & Sciences, for *Dress to Kill*, 2000; Outer Critics Circle Award for outstanding actor in a play, for *A Day in the Death of Joe Egg*, 2003.

Sidelights

What does it take to be compared to the quirky comic geniuses in the troupe known as Monty Python? For stand-up comedian Eddie Izzard, wearing women's clothes and theorizing on the thought processes of squirrels has helped him garner an international reputation equal to the cross-dressing British comedians who were popular in the 1970s. Izzard's talents are not only apparent in his wide-ranging stand-up performances. He has also proven himself as an actor on stage, in film, and on television. He has been nominated for a Tony award and won Emmy awards. His prolific output belies the fact that many of his performances are extemporaneous ramblings based on a loose outline. Sheryl Garratt of the *Guardian* described Izzard's eccentric lure: "He's an action transvestite, an executive transvestite, a male tomboy.... Having established where he fits into the real world, he then proceeds to make it irrelevant by pulling the audience into a parallel universe of his own creating, taking an infectious, almost childlike joy in making strange leaps of logic and absurd connections."

Born Edward John Izzard on February 7, 1962, in Aden, South Yemen, Africa, Izzard is the younger of two sons of Harold and Dorothy Izzard. Izzard's father spent his life working for British Petroleum, beginning his career as a filing clerk and working his way up to become chief auditor for the international company. A transfer took Izzard's father to South Yemen, where he met Dorothy, a nurse, and the two were married. In 1963, the family moved to Bangor, Ireland, where they lived for four years until tensions in Northern Ireland led the family to move to Skewen, South Wales. Izzard remembers his early years in Ireland as happy ones. Unfortunately, soon after the family moved to South Wales, tragedy struck.

In 1967, the same year as their move, Izzard's mother was diagnosed with cancer and died soon afterward. At the age of six, Izzard lost his mother and was subsequently sent to boarding school. The loss of his mother was a devastating blow, one that he continues to mourn. He told the *Guardian*'s Garratt, "Hitler died at a later age than my mother. It proves that there is no God." Boarding school provided little comfort in the face of his loss. Izzard claims to have cried until he was eleven years old. The first school he attended was known for being tough and Izzard claims to have been physically disciplined most of his time there. When his father moved again, Izzard was placed in a more liberal school. While dealing with his pain, he managed to discover a love of acting. He was also an avid soccer player, a member of the Boy Scouts, and an army cadet.

At age seven, Izzard decided he wanted to become an actor. Not long after deciding this, he was exposed to the comedy of Peter Cook, Peter Sellers, and Monty Python, all of whom had shows on television. In high school he made valiant attempts to pursue his dream, but he was never chosen for starring roles. His passion drove him to audition for the National Youth Theatre, for which he was turned down. He even attempted to sneak onto the grounds of Elstree Studios, a prominent film studio, in the hopes of being discovered. He was discovered, but it was by security, and he was kicked off the lot.

Izzard ended up attending the boarding school Eastbourne College to finish out his pre-college years. It

was here that he began to come into his own as an actor. He began landing better roles, which included turns in plays such as *Comedy of Errors, Cabaret,* and *The Proposal.* Andrew Boxer, who produced most of the plays at Eastbourne, told Garratt in the *Guardian* article of Izzard's desire to be in *The Proposal,* "It really mattered to him to do that play. Kids at that age aren't usually that good at bringing their own ideas to it, they want to be told. Eddie was one of the few people who could. He was very determined."

When Izzard was 18, he attended Sheffield University. His studies were focused on accounting and math but he also continued to spend time acting. In 1981, his first show was staged in Edinburgh and was titled *Fringe Flung Lunch.* Four years later he formed a small theater company with his friend, Rob Ballard. As the company grew, Izzard and Ballard were drawn to expand their horizons and headed to London. There the two formed a comedy duo called the Official Touring Company of Alpha Centauri. They would call themselves the Officials for short and performed on the street. Izzard described the experience to Garratt of the *Guardian,* "It was awful, humiliating…. People treat you like beggars." He was discovered, but the offers were for spots on children's shows. Izzard was leery of getting typecast as a children's performer and turned down the offers.

In 1987, Ballard went on to do other work, so Izzard performed solo. The previous year he had also begun performing in clubs. For his street performances, Izzard learned to ride a unicycle. He would ride and just talk, telling stories until he ran out of breath or his voice gave out. He explained to Garratt of the *Guardian,* "I learned to go on and on without stopping … just to keep the energy high and stop them walking away. I'd point at people and impose scenarios on them." The combination of solo street performance and stand-up in the clubs gave Izzard the experience he needed to gain confidence and find his own rhythm and style, one that peers described as responsive and free.

Having honed his performance style, Izzard was ready to move on. In 1991, he was invited to perform live for the AIDS benefit titled *Hysteria 3.* The show was televised and eventually released on video. He gained recognition from the performance and found the confidence to move out of the club circuit. What he did was untested: He booked theaters for multi-night runs. In 1992, he performed a two-week run at the Shaw Theatre in London. A year later he performed a 13-week run of shows at the Ambassador Theater in New York City. The run ended up being a huge success with audiences. Previous hits had only been attained with the help of the comedian having a television show, so Izzard had beaten the odds.

Spurred on by his successful run at the Ambassador and another hit with *Definite Article* in 1996, Izzard decided to take his act across the pond again and see how American audiences responded. Despite positive reviews and reactions to his New York shows, Izzard found that he was not gaining footing in the United States. In fact, it took until 1999 when HBO began airing his *Dress to Kill* performances from the year before that he made his breakthrough. *Dress to Kill* earned him two Emmy Awards, one for best writing and one for best performance. The live performances brought him to the attention of comedian Robin Williams, who helped produce his shows on the West Coast. While not a fan of performing for television, Izzard has made a concerted effort to make all of his tours available on video. Other popular shows of his include 1997's *Glorious*, 2002's *Circle*, and 2003's *Sexie*.

Izzard claims that comedy is secondary to his desire to be a respected actor. With the recognition he had gained with his stand-up, he was able to garner stage roles. In 1994, he starred in the world premiere of playwright David Mamet's *The Cryptogram* as well as the black comedy *900 Oneonta*. Other stage roles included the lead role in 1995's *Edward II* and 2003's *Trumbo*. In 1999, he took on the role of the controversial 1960s-era comedian Lenny Bruce in the play about him titled *Lenny*. In 2001, he played the male lead in the revival of *A Day in the Death of Joe Egg* at the Comedy Theatre in London, England. Two years later the play opened with the same cast in New York at the Roundabout Theater Company. His performances in New York earned him a Tony nomination.

Not long after he began touring in the United States, he secured a film agent and began campaigning for roles. In 1996, he secured a small role in *The Secret Agent*, a film starring Bob Hoskins and Patricia Arquette. Two years later he appeared in both *Velvet Goldmine* and *The Avengers*. Throughout the 1990s, Izzard continued to make regular appearances in films, if only in small roles. In 2001, he took on the role of silent movie actor Charlie Chaplin in the film *The Cat's Meow*, which retells the true, though contested, story of a death on the yacht of William Randolph Hearst, a prominent publisher in

the early part of the 20th century. That was quickly followed by a lead role in the film *All the Queen's Men*, co-starring television star Matt LeBlanc.

In the spring of 2007, Izzard made his television debut in a new series for the FX channel. The show, titled *The Riches*, follows an itinerant family of con artists who take on the identity of a suburban family that they find dead in a car crash. Izzard stars as the father who fakes his way into a position at a law firm. Co-starring British actress Minnie Driver, the show was met with enthusiasm by audiences and critics.

Never one to rest on his laurels, Izzard has a grand desire to perform around the world in the native languages of the places he visits. In 1997, he achieved the first level of that goal by performing for six nights in Paris, France, speaking almost entirely in French. He also likes to interject Latin and German into his regular performances. Other languages he hopes to perform in are German, Russian, Arabic, and Spanish.

Izzard has continually tested his limits and exhibited a personal braveness that he is very proud of in himself. One of his most daring moves was coming out to the public that he is a transvestite, a man who likes to wear women's clothes. This revelation was closely followed by his first performance in a dress. Although it has been suggested that his cross-dressing is a gamble to gain attention, Izzard denies it thoroughly. In many statements he has made it clear that his desire to wear women's clothes is something that is innate. He claims that transvestitism is genetic, as much a part of his being as the color of his eyes. Izzard makes no apologies for who he is. He wears what he feels like wearing, when he feels like wearing it. Some days he is inspired to wear make-up and skirts. Other days he wears jeans, a T-shirt, and no make-up.

The hardest part of being transvestite was coming out to his father. The two men share a love for soccer and it was after having attended a game that Izzard told his father. Izzard was surprised to find that his father was so accepting. He explained to Garratt in the *Guardian* interview, "That was very hard. Worrying about it. I didn't want to give him a hard time. But he was very cool about it, which wasn't what I was expecting."

With a seemingly endless list of goals, Izzard works hard to check off one item after another on that list. His popularity as a stand-up comedian grows while he looks forward to even better roles in film and television. It seems clear that Izzard is ready, willing, and able to conquer the entertainment world.

Sources

Advocate, October 29, 2002, pp. 56-57.

Guardian (London, England), November 21, 1998, p. 6.

New York Times, October 8, 2003, p. E1.

—*Eve Hermann*

Bharrat Jagdeo

AP Images

President of Guyana

Born January 23, 1964, in Unity, Demerara, Guyana; married Varshni Singh, July 26, 1998. *Education:* Earned graduate degree in economics from Peoples' Friendship University of Russia, 1990.

Addresses: *Office*—Office of the President, New Garden St., Georgetown. Guyana.

Career

Republic of Guyana, Macroeconomic Planning Division, State Planning Secretariat, economist, 1990-92, special advisor to minister of finance, 1992-93, junior minister of finance, 1993-95, minister of finance, 1995-99; appointed president of the Republic of Guyana, 1999, elected president, 2001, reelected, 2006.

Sidelights

When 35-year-old Bharrat Jagdeo became president of Guyana in August of 1999, he became the youngest head of state in all of the Americas. A Soviet-educated economist who had most recently served as Guyana's finance minister, Jagdeo was committed to unifying the lingering racial tensions in this small, South American, Atlantic seaport nation, and improving its struggling economy. "I feel that Guyana's future lies to the south, as well as the north," he said in an interview with *Washington Times* writer Larry Luxner about some of his government's initiatives after three years on the job. "We have the unique opportunity of opening a door for the Caribbean into South America, and of being a gateway for Brazil's northern states to the Atlantic."

Jagdeo was born on January 23, 1964, in a village called Unity in the country's Demerara region. He is of East Asian descent, which makes him a member of the largest single ethnic group in Guyana at more than 40 percent of the population. Guyana, located at the northeastern tip of the South American continent, is a long way from the Indian subcontinent, but for many years both lands were under British rule, and Indians arrived in Guyana as indentured servants to work the sugar plantations after 1834, when slavery was outlawed and many Afro-Guyanese refused to toil in the fields any longer, even for wages. Guyana gained its independence from Britain in 1966, but remains the only English-speaking nation in South America. Sugar and rice exports still play a leading role in its economy, along with bauxite, an aluminum ore, and its population of 750,000 is one of the poorest in the Western Hemisphere.

Guyanese politics are dominated by two parties: the People's National Congress (PNC) and the People's Progressive Party (PPP). Jagdeo's party is the PPP, which is also the traditional party of the Indo-Guyanese. It was founded in 1950 by Cheddi Jagan as a left-wing group, but shifted in ideology over the years and came to support more moderate political goals, such as free-market reform and the privatization of formerly nationally run industries.

Jagdeo was interested in politics at an early age, joining a PPP youth group before receiving his party membership card at the age of 16. The PPP was still a Marxist-oriented party at the time, with ties to the Soviet Union, and Jagdeo traveled abroad for his college degree, spending several years in Moscow at the Peoples' Friendship University of Russia, which was established to train leaders of Third World nations.

After earning a graduate degree in economics in 1990, Jagdeo returned to Guyana and settled in the capital city, Georgetown. He found a government job with the Macroeconomic Planning Division as an economist, and in 1992 was made special advisor to the country's minister of finance. He was named junior minister of finance a year later, and then minister of finance in 1995 in the Jagan government. He remained a cabinet member after the late Jagan was succeeded by his U.S.-born wife, Janet Jagan, in the December of 1997 elections. The PNC—Guyana's other main party—claimed the balloting was fraudulent, however, and refused to recognize Janet Jagan as president. An independent audit declared the election to have been a valid one, however, but the continuing battle was one with strong racial overtones, for the PNC was the considered the voice of the Afro-Guyanese population, much in the same way that Jagdeo's PPP represented its East Asian-heritage citizens' political goals.

Janet Jagan's health declined, and in August of 1999 Jagdeo was named to succeed her by the Prime Minister, Sam Hinds, who was also serving as acting president after Jagan suffered a heart attack. The ongoing political strife over the 1997 elections results had not abated in the 20-month interim, and the PNC's leader, Desmond Hoyte, refused to recognize Jagdeo as president, too. "The opposition's attitude does bother me somewhat," Jagdeo admitted in an interview with Canute James of the *Financial Times*. "Guyana's leaders should not let petty issues divide them. I extended a hand of cooperation to the opposition, it was not accepted, but we have to move on. The invitation stands."

In March of 2001, Jagdeo was elected president for a five-year term by direct vote, and was reelected for another term in August of 2006. During these years, he has worked to improve Guyana's economic outlook by attracting foreign investment and strengthening ties with neighboring nations, including Brazil and Venezuela. His reelection in 2006 marked the first time in several decades that Guyanese voting had not been marked by violence and protests. He viewed his next five years as a continuance of his mission to help raise the standard of living for citizens of the tiny, embattled nation, and unify a long-divided populace. As he told Luxner in the *Washington Times* article, "we still have this colonial legacy of a divided people," and he cited as one of his two main challenges "forging the people together into a Guyanese identity."

Several months later, Guyana suddenly became the topic of international news headlines when agents of the U.S. Federal Bureau of Investigation uncovered a plot to plant explosives at Kennedy International Airport in New York City, and arrested four men—three Guyanese, and the fourth a Guyanese-born U.S. citizen, one of whom had worked as a cargo handler at the airport. Another of the quartet had served in Guyana's National Assembly, but Jagdeo moved quickly to assert that his country was far from a breeding ground for guerrilla movements run by radical Muslims. More than half of all Guyanese belong to various Christian denominations, with another 37 percent identifying themselves as Hindu; less than ten percent claim Islam as their faith. Jagdeo urged the West to consider his country "true partners in this fight against terrorism, because terrorism is alien to the Caribbean value," Jacqueline Charles of the *Miami Herald* quoted him as saying. "I don't know of this radicalism. It is alien to our people."

Sources

Financial Times, November 23, 1999, p. 7; March 16, 2001, p. 3.
Miami Herald, June 11, 2007.
New York Post, January 27, 2007, p. 3.
New York Times, June 3, 2007.
Washington Times, February 12, 2002, p. A10.

—Carol Brennan

Jonas Brothers

Pop group

Group formed in 2005 in Wyckoff, New Jersey; members include Kevin Jonas (born November 5, 1987), guitarist and vocalist; Joseph Jonas (born August 15, 1989), vocalist, guitarist, drummer, and piano player; and Nicholas Jonas (born September 16, 1992), vocalist and keyboardist; all sons of Kevin, Sr. (a Christian minister) and Denise Jonas.

Dave Hogan/Getty Images

Addresses: *Record company*—Hollywood Records, 500 S. Buena Vista St., Burbank, CA 91521. *Web site*—http://www.jonasbrothers.com.

Career

Nicholas Jonas was a Broadway performer in *Beauty and the Beast*, 2002, and *Les Misérables*, 2003; Kevin Jonas appeared in commercials as a child; Joseph Jonas appeared in *La Boheme*, 2002-03; brothers also performed together at Christian events and anti-drug rallies; Nicholas Jonas signed with Columbia Records as a solo artist, 2004, and released self-titled album, c. 2005. The Jonas Brothers band formed, 2005; signed with Columbia, 2005; released *It's About Time*, 2006; moved to Hollywood Records, 2007; released *Jonas Brothers*, 2007; toured with Miley Cyrus, 2007; toured as headliners in 2007 and 2008; signed Live Nation agreement, 2008; starred in several Disney Channel projects including *Camp Rock*, a television movie, 2008, *Jonas Brothers: Living the Dream*, a television series, 2008, and *J.O.N.A.S!*, a television series, 2008.

Sidelights

A teen pop sensation, the Jonas Brothers are often compared to Green Day, but considered a cleaner version of the band. After struggling with their first label, the brothers—Kevin, Joe, and Nick—signed with Hollywood Records, toured with Miley Cyrus, and became a music phenomenon in 2007. They eventually signed a deal with Live Nation, and had their own movie and television series on the Disney Channel. Writing in the Syracuse, New York *Post-Standard*, Carrie Stetler called their popular music "sunny power pop brimming with good attitude and sensitive yearning."

The brothers are the sons of Kevin Jonas, Sr., and his wife, Denise. They were raised in Wyckoff, New Jersey, where their father was a minister at a Christian church. The brothers—including the youngest brother Frankie (later dubbed "Bonus Jonas") who was not part of the band—originally attended East Christian School in North Haledon, New Jersey, but were later home schooled and sang at Christian events and anti-drug assemblies at schools for fun.

Nick was the first in the family to have a serious musical career. After being heard singing in a barbershop, he was signed by a manager as a young boy. Nick then appeared in several Broadway musicals as an elementary school student, including *Beauty and the Beast* and *Les Misérables*. Then, a holiday song co-written with his father, "Joy to the World (A Christmas Prayer)," was featured on a benefit album and played on Christian radio stations. His brothers also had some success as well, with Kevin appearing in television commercials and Joe appearing in a stage show, Baz Luhrmann's *La Boheme*.

On the strength of his singing, Nick signed a solo deal with Sony in 2004. His brothers, Kevin and Joe, decided to help write songs for his album. While incoming Columbia Records president Steve Greenberg was not impressed with Nick's album, he saw potential with the brothers, as he had when he discovered the pop sensation Hanson (also a trio of brothers) years ago. Greenberg told *Billboard*'s Mikael Wood, "I didn't like the record he'd made. But his voice struck out, so I met with him and found out he had two brothers."

Columbia signed the brothers together as an act in 2005. Greenberg explained to Wood of *Billboard*, "I liked the idea of putting together this little garage-rock band and making a record that nodded to the Ramones and '70s punk. So Michael Mangini and I went into the studio with the Jonas Brothers and did it." Kevin explained their sound was different than Nick's as a solo artist, telling the *Village Voice*, "Nick's sound was a little more adult contemporary, but our sound changed as a group. We're definitely a rock and roll band."

After being signed to Columbia, the Jonas Brothers spent the next two years working on their debut album. They wrote some 60 songs, and then rewrote them. They collaborated on their songs with leading songwriters like Desmond Child, Adam Schlesinger, and StarGate along the way. While the experience was frustrating and they feared the album would never be released, *It's About Time* finally came out in August of 2006 in limited release after being delayed several times.

By the time the album came out, the Jonas Brothers were already seen as part of the next wave of boy bands, albeit ones which played their instruments and contributed to their own material. While firmly in the rock category, the brothers sung in harmonies about teen topics like doing homework and going online. As committed Christians, the Jonas Brothers also sang about their faith.

The first single, "Mandy," was pushed on the Internet and MTV's *Total Request Live*, but attracted little attention. The Jonas Brothers tried to build their fan base by touring with hot young bands like the Veronicas, Backstreet Boys, and Jesse McCartney.

While the brothers attracted some female fans, the album did not do well in the first few months of release and was not available in many stores.

The brothers were frustrated by the lack of support from their label and had a meeting with Columbia executives. Greenberg had already left the label, and his ideas for grass-roots support went with him. Their manager, Phil McIntyre, told Wood of *Billboard*, "It was important to find out what their game plan was before we did anything. We had a very frank meeting with them in which they said they were not ready to go to the next level of setting up the project."

In early 2007, the Jonas Brothers decided Columbia was not working for them and looked for a new record deal. After being dropped by Columbia, they signed with Hollywood Records, a label associated with Disney, which was looking for a boy band to fill a teen-pop niche. Their debut album was re-released on Hollywood Records, and became the first boy rock band pushed by Disney.

Despite the problems with Columbia and the transition to a new label, the Jonas Brothers had their breakthrough hit in February of 2007 with "Year 3000," a song which was added to *It's About Time* at the behest of the record company, which thought the album needed a strong single. "Year 3000" had originally been a hit in the United Kingdom in 2002 for the band Busted. For the Jonas Brothers, "Year 3000," was a smash on Radio Disney and as a single download on iTunes. It also became a Top 40 hit on *Billboard* charts.

Soon after signing with Hollywood Records, the Jonas Brothers began working on their next album. They worked with producer John Fields (who had worked with Jimmy Eat World, Switchfoot, and the Backstreet Boys) on new songs, spent three weeks recording them in Seedy Underbelly studio in Los Angeles, and released their second album in September of 2007. Entitled *Jonas Brothers,* they had a hit with "S.O.S." The single was number one on iTunes. The album itself sold 360,000 copies between August and December of 2007, then more than a million by early 2008, and was certified platinum. By March of 2008, they sold 2.5 million digital tracks.

While the Jonas Brothers were attracting more attention for their music, a key to their success came when they served as the opening act for pop phenomenon Miley Cyrus in 2007. Cyrus had a popular television series on the Disney Channel, *Hannah*

Montana (on which the brothers made a guest appearance), and numerous sold-out tours. Opening for Cyrus brought the Jonas Brothers a whole new audience, which they built on with their own tour dates later in 2007.

Because of the constant touring in 2007, the brothers found it challenging to schedule studio time to record their next record. They cut a deal with Gibson Guitar, a company they already endorsed, to change their tour bus into a recording studio during a series of West Coast dates. Using the bus allowed them to record at least 15 new tracks in record time with Fields while continuing to tour. The songs featured new influences like Elvis Costello, the Beatles, the Animals, and the Rascals. The album—described by Kevin to Elysa Gardner of *USA Today* as "a hopeful, good-time kind of record"—was scheduled for release in August of 2008.

Although the Jonas Brothers were considered an emerging act, the depth of their success and potential for growth was confirmed when they signed a two-year, multimillion dollar worldwide touring deal with Live Nation. They immediately began touring in early 2008, and many dates were sold out in minutes. Explaining their appeal, Live Nation's Jason Garner told Jac Chebatoris of *Newsweek*, "They're good-looking guys, they write their own songs and it's music that you can't get of your head. This is a band who is doing everything right."

Reviewing a show in their adopted home of Los Angeles, Mikael Wood of the *Los Angeles Times* wrote, "the Jonases are tremendously more polished performers than predecessors such as New Kids on the Block; even if they relied on their four-piece backing band for most of the music's muscle, the brothers' singing and playing reflected the degree of sophistication their media-savvy fan base now expects."

The brothers also extended their deal with Disney to appear in Disney Channel projects. In the spring of 2008, a reality series based on their 2008 Look Me in the Eyes tour was scheduled to air on Disney. Entitled *Jonas Brothers: Living the Dream,* the short-form reality show depicted their lives both on stage and off. Other family members, including their parents and little brother, also made appearances.

In the summer of 2008, they appeared in the movie *Camp Rock,* which aired on the Disney Channel, ABC Family, and ABC. In the film, Joe plays a bad-boy rocker whose bandmates in the fictional Connect

Three, played by Kevin and Nick, send him to summer music camp. There, he meets a girl who is trying to find herself and falls in love. Of the film, Joe told Alan Scully of the *Patriot Ledger*, "The movie we filmed had a lot do to with music, so we were able to connect with our characters because we did play a band in the movie. And I did play a musician. It was definitely different for us, but we had a lot of fun."

The Jonas Brothers were also getting their own fictional television series, *Junior Operatives Networking As Spies* or *J.O.N.A.S.* on Disney. It was to be filmed beginning in September of 2008, and air at a later date. In the show, the three brothers play rock stars by day and secret government spies at night. In addition to their work on Disney, the brothers also appeared on a Baby Bottle Pops commercial and signed on as sponsors of Breakfast Breaks.

Though the Jonas Brothers were popular, they realized that being a teen sensation had its limitations and hoped to become mainstream successes. Joe told Moser of *Tulsa World*, "I think the thing that's really going to help us is the fact that we write our own songs and we're in the studio when they're produced, and we're writing songs for other artists right now. And I think that that's really a major part in everything we do in the future and right now. But we are brothers, so we can't really break up."

While the Jonas Brothers were hugely successful, they remained down to earth and grounded in their beliefs and family. *Seattle Times'* Marian Liu wrote "In person, the brothers are extremely polite, definitely more cordial than typical rock stars. They are gracious and say a lot of thank-yous. They seem genuinely enthusiastic about meeting fans, and hold up a squeaky clean image, perfect for their pint-size fans and their parents. The brothers attribute this to a strong family base and their faith." Kevin told Liu, "We try to be the people that our parents raised us to be."

Selected discography

It's About Time, Daylight/Columbia, 2006.
Jonas Brothers, Hollywood, 2007.

Sources

Periodicals

Advertising Age, March 3, 2008, p. 10.
Billboard, September 10, 2005; February 24 2007; December 1, 2007.
CosmoGIRL!, June 1, 2008, p. 77.
Los Angeles Times, February 4, 2008, p. E4; April 1, 2008, p. C1.
Newsday (New York, NY), December 27, 2007, p. B2.
Newsweek, February 4, 2008, p. 56.
Patriot Ledger (Quincy, MA), February 28, 2008, p. ONE19.
Post-Standard (Syracuse, NY), April 16, 2007, p. D3.
Record (Bergen County, NJ), September 3, 2007, p. F4.
Salt Lake Tribune, February 4, 2008.
Seattle Times (Seattle, WA), February 1, 2008.
Star Tribune (Minneapolis, MN), February 17, 2008, p. 1F.
Tulsa World (Tulsa, OK), March 14, 2008, p. D6.
USA Today, March 27, 2008, p. 1D, p. 8D.
Village Voice, May 3, 2006.

Online

"Jonas Brothers," VH1.com, http://www.vh1.com/artists/az/jonas_brothers/albums.jhtml (May 18, 2008).

—A. Petruso

Miranda July

Noel Hines/Landov

Filmmaker, artist, and author

Born Miranda Jennifer Grossinger, February 15, 1974, in Barre, VT; daughter of Richard Grossinger (a writer, publisher, and publishing company cofounder) and Lindy Hough (a writer, publisher, and publishing company cofounder). *Education:* Attended the University of California at Santa Cruz.

Addresses: *Contact*—PO Box 26596, Los Angeles, CA 90026.

Career

Co-created girlzine *Snarla* as a teen; put on play *The Lifer,* c. 1990; recorded album with The Need, *Margie Ruskie Stops Time,* 1996; created live-action performance pieces *Love Diamond,* 1998, and *Swan Tool,* 2000; published short story in the *Paris Review,* 2003; released first feature film as writer, director, and actress, *Me and You and Everyone We Know,* 2005; published first short-story collection, *No One Belongs Here More than You,* 2007.

Awards: Gecko Award—international competition, Cinematexas International Short Film Festival, for *Nest of Tens,* 2000; Best Debut Award—Experimental, New York Expo of Short Film, for *Nest of Tens,* 2000; Main Prize, Oberhausen International Short Film Festival, for *Nest of Tens,* 2001; Prize of the Ministry for Development, Culture, and Sports, Oberhausen International Short Film Festival, for *Nest of Tens,* 2001; Young Critics Award for best feature, Cannes Film Festival, for *Me and You and Ev-*eryone We Know,* 2005; Prix Regards Jeune for best feature film, Cannes Film Festival, for *Me and You and Everyone We Know,* 2005; Golden Camera, Cannes Film Festival, for *Me and You and Everyone We Know,* 2005; Critics Week Grand Prize, Cannes Film Festival, for *Me and You and Everyone We Know,* 2005; Russell Smith Award, Dallas-Fort Worth Film Critics Association, for *Me and You and Everyone We Know,* 2005; Audience Award for best feature, Newport International Film Festival, for *Me and You and Everyone We Know,* 2005; Jury Award for best director, Newport International Film Festival, for *Me and You and Everyone We Know,* 2005; Audience Award for best narrative feature, San Francisco International Film Festival, for *Me and You and Everyone We Know,* 2005; SKYY Prize, San Francisco International Film Festival, for *Me and You and Everyone We Know,* 2005; Special Jury Prize—dramatic, Sundance Film Festival, for *Me and You and Everyone We Know,* 2005; Best First Time Director Award, Philadelphia Film Festival, for *Me and You and Everyone We Know,* 2005; Chicago Film Critics Association Award for most promising performer, for *Me and You and Everyone You Know,* 2006; Frank O'Connor International Short Story Award, Frank O'Connor International Short Story Festival, for *No One Belongs Here More than You,* 2007.

Sidelights

As a respected performance artist, filmmaker, and short-story writer, Miranda July has created in various artistic mediums, but always with an emotionally charged, often quirky, usually sincere edge. While working primarily in video and audio performance art through the 1990s, she came to greater recognition in the early 2000s. July first got her short stories printed in journals such as the *Paris Review,* then in 2005 made a critically acclaimed, award-winning independent film, *You and Me and Everyone We Know.* In 2007, she published her first book, *No One Belongs Here More than You.* Of July's work, Karen Durbin wrote in the *New York Times,* "At her most unnerving, Ms. July upends the rocklike surface of social norms to show us the creepy, crawly bits we keep hidden underneath. But more than anything, her fearless, often playful output suggests the freewheeling creativity of a child—an enviable quality that seldom survives."

Born Miranda Jennifer Grossinger on February 15, 1974, in Barre, Vermont, July was the daughter of Richard Grossinger and Lindy Hough. Raised primarily in Berkeley, California, her parents were both authors and publishers who co-founded a small publishing company, North Atlantic Books. The press published self-help and out-there nonfiction throughout July's youth. July remembered her parents as creative but confessing too much personal information to her as a child. She told Kimberly Cutter of *New York Magazine,* "I wasn't neglected at all, but my parents didn't have the best boundaries in the world. I was privy to pretty much everything about their lives. I think that's definitely where my desire to be the one who understands comes from."

In this environment, July began her own creative endeavors as a young child. With a friend, the six-year-old July began recording herself talking about sexual matters. At the age of seven, she began recording her own voice and half of a conversation. Young July would play the tape back and have a conversation with herself. By the time July reached her teen years, her artistic endeavors moved to the written word. She created her own girlzine with a friend. Dubbed *Snarla,* July and her friend wrote creatively about their real-life experiences.

It was through the magazine that July came up with her monthly surname. A character used in the zine had the name, and July took it on as her pen name. It was first used when she was 16 years old, when her play *The Lifer* debuted at a punk club in Berkeley in a show for family and friends. July also took on her unusual teenage surname because she said the month best encourages her creative juices.

Completing high school, July entered the University of California at Santa Cruz, where she studied film for a year and a half. Unhappy with some of the classes she was taking, July dropped out and moved to Portland, Oregon, and began focusing exclusively on her creative endeavors in the artist-friendly city. July's need to create had become her mission. She told Nathan Ihara of the *LA Weekly:* "[M]y sense of self-worth is totally tied up in making things. It's definitely the hell of my life. It's the worse thing, that pressure, in a way. ... I had a period of like three months when I was 22 or so where I didn't make anything. At the end, I thought, 'Never again.'"

By the age of 23, July no longer needed to take a day job to support herself; she was creating both audio and video pieces. Some of her audio pieces found their way onto two CDs she recorded for the Kill Rock Stars label, *Ten Million Hours a Mile* and *The Binet-Simon Test.* July was also part of a more mainstream rock band called The Need, and a few of the tracks on *Margie Ruskie Stops Time* feature her work with the group.

July eventually became more involved as a performance and conceptual artist who primarily worked in video and similar media. Among her video-live action performance pieces are *Swan Tool* and *Love Diamond.* In the latter, a 90-minute production, she explores the concept of the seeming futility of life. While an actor plays a professor, the rest of the characters are performed by July, including its center, Tini Santini, a troubled girl, who is being interrogated in a pseudo-scientific manner.

Love Diamond led to more high-profile work for July. A curator at the Whitney Museum, Debra Singer, saw a presentation of the piece and asked July to create a new work for the museum's 2002 biennial. July came up with a live performance and, more importantly, sound installations which were aired in one of the Whitney's elevators. Entitled "The Drifters," it consisted of 16 brief audio narratives that were quite humorous.

Another influential person heard the elevator audio art, and July was asked to create more works for the next Whitney biennial. As July garnered a wider audience, National Public Radio also commissioned her audio works to air on its show *The Next Big Thing.* Next came two short stories, "Birthmark" and "Making Love in 2003," which were published in the *Paris Review,* though July had only begun writing short stories in 2001.

A few years later, July began working on a screenplay for what became her first feature film. Having been selected for a spot at the Sundance Institute's screenwriting lab, July began work on the script for what became *Me and You and Everyone We Know*. When she arrived at the institute, her script was in a primitive state. Writer/director Miguel Arteta worked with her to improve the script and turn it into a true feature film.

Of the writing process for *Me and You and Everyone We Know*, July told the *Times'* Wendy Idle, "I didn't sit down with a plot. I would just sit down each day with the feeling that I had. So if I was feeling hopeful I would reach for the feeling through these stories and try to articulate it through these characters. And then gradually it built up this web that became a structure. But I didn't worry myself with the structure until the heart of it was there."

In 2005, July's film *Me and You and Everyone We Know* was released. July wrote, directed, and had a co-starring role in the film, which won multiple awards at such prestigious film festivals as Cannes and Sundance. *Me and You and Everyone We Know* focuses on the burgeoning romantic relationship between a lonely conceptual artist Christine Jesperwon, played by July, and Richard, played by John Hawkes. Richard is a recently, reluctantly separated shoe salesman who sometimes has custody of his sons. Exploring the idea of community in modern urban life, the film also incorporates Christine's job as a escort driver who assists seniors. The film shows her developing relationship with a widower who has fallen in love with a terminally ill woman. A thus far unrecognized performance artist, Christine creates the woman's memorial service for her client. Through clever persistence she also persuades a gallery to show some of her video work.

Noting *Me and You and Everyone We Know*'s "wide-eyed, quizzical approach to the world" in its depiction of odd behaviors, A. O. Scott of the *New York Times* wrote of the film and its filmmaker: "Though her movie has a clear narrative line, and might even be classified as romantic comedy, it is also a meticulously constructed visual artifact, diffidently introducing the playful, rebus-like qualities of installation art to the conventions of narrative cinema." To July, the film was still very much her own. She told Liam Lacey of the *Globe and Mail:* "It's amazing how much it's still intimate. When I hear all this hype it feels peculiar, as if people were complimenting you for the way you smell."

While many filmmakers would take the exposure and positive press from their first feature to use as leverage for their second, July decided to focus on other projects in the short term. She still planned to

make a second feature, but not on anyone's time table but her own. Denying other people's expectations, including those of Hollywood, July returned to her own performances to emphasize her creative autonomy, though she did move from Portland to Los Angeles. She also focused on completing a collection of short stories, several of which appeared in *Zoetrope, Tin House,* and the *New Yorker.*

The 2007 short story collection, *No One Belongs Here More than You,* received as much acclaim as *Me and You and Everyone We Know.* As in the film, July explores in these stories the longing for connection and related emotional responses. For example, in one story, an older man working in a purse factory becomes obsessed with a teenage girl he has never met. In another, two young female lovers find their infatuated relationship falls apart and comes back together. In "Mon Plaisir," a married couple with problems find their love is gone while they work as extras on a movie set.

Reviewing *No One Belongs Here More than You,* in *Vogue,* Megan O'Grady wrote: "The result, laden with offbeat, emotionally isolated characters—a woman gives swimming lessons in her living room; another develops an obsession with Prince William—might initially invite comparison to [fiction writer] Lorrie Moore, but its mordantly funny commentary on modern-day relating is classic July."

Going deeper, Tiffany Lee-Youngren wrote in the *San Diego Union-Tribune:* "the vast majority of the characters in July's stories are social rejects, outcasts and lonelyhearts, people who form more inappropriate relationships, make inappropriate comments, and find themselves in inappropriate situations almost by force of habit. These are not people for whom divine insight comes easy." *No One Belongs Here More than You* also caught the attention of literati: It won the 2007 Frank O'Connor Award.

For July, there was synergy between her book and other art works. One short story in the collection "Important Things We Don't Understand and Definitely Are Not Going to Talk About" received particular praise. In this story, a woman whose boyfriend focuses on his own enlightenment to the detriment to their relationship comes up with the list referred to in the story's title. Around the same time that *No One Belongs Here More than You* was published, July created the performance-art piece also called *Important Things We Don't Understand and Definitely Are Not Going to Talk About,* which she began performing in 2006.

As she began writing her second screenplay and perhaps a novel, July remained creatively diverse. No matter what the medium, creativity was a key element to July's essence. She told Katherine Monk of the *Times Colonist*, "Art is now my main way of experiencing my life. It's the best way I know how to love and take care of myself. I'm hardworking, but you really have to take care of that part of yourself—the part that makes things—and you have to show it all kinds of love. Otherwise, you can't survive and do what you do."

Selected discography

(With The Need) *Margie Ruskie Stops Time*, Kill Rock Stars, 1996.
Ten Million Hours a Mile, Kill Rock Stars, 1997.
The Binet-Simon Test, Kill Rock Stars, 1998.

Selected works

Love Diamond, originally appeared at Portland Institute of Contemporary Art, 1998-2000.
The Swan Tool, originally appeared at Portland Institute of Contemporary Art, 2000-02.
"The Drifters," The Whitney Museum, New York City, 2002.
How I Learned to Draw, various sites, 2002-03.
Things We Don't Understand and Definitely Are Not Going to Talk About, various sites, 2006.

Selected writings

Short story collections

No one belongs here more than you. Scribner, 2007.

Sources

Periodicals

Globe and Mail (Canada), July 22, 2005, p. R6.
Guardian Unlimited, September 24, 2007.
Interview, July 1, 2005, p. 80.
LA Weekly, May 17, 2007.
Los Angeles Times, May 6, 2007, p. F13; May 27, 2007, p. R8.
New York Magazine, May 21, 2007.
New York Times, June 17, 2005, p. E13; June 19, 2005, sec. 2, p. 13.
Times (London, England), August 11, 2005, sec. 2, p. 20.
Times Colonist (Victoria, British Columbia), August 8, 2005, p. D3.
San Diego Union-Tribune, August 5, 2007, p. E5.
Vancouver Province (Canada), July 27, 2005, p. B4.
Vogue, May 2007, p. 179.

Online

"Miranda July," Internet Movie Database, http://www.imdb.com/name/nm0432380/ (November 7, 2007).

—A. Petruso

Cristie Kerr

Professional golfer

Robert Laberge/Getty Images

Born October 12, 1977, in Miami, FL; daughter of Michael (an elementary school teacher) and Linda (a legal secretary) Kerr; married Erik Stevens (a developer), December 9, 2006.

Addresses: *Contact*—LPGA, 100 International Golf Dr., Daytona Beach, FL 32124-1092. *Web site*—http://www.birdiesforbreastcancer.com/.

Career

Amateur career wins include: Florida State Junior Girls Championships, 1993, 1994, 1995; Dade County Youth Fair Tournament, 1994; Harder Hall Women's Championship, 1995; Women's Western Amateur Championship, 1995; Florida State Women's Championship, 1995; South Atlantic Women's Amateur title, 1996. LPGA wins include: Longs Drugs Challenge, 2002; Junior Orange Bowl Classic, 2004; Doral Publix Junior Classic, 2004; Women's Western Junior Championship, 2004; Takefuji Classic, 2004; ShopRite LPGA Classic, 2004; State Farm Classic, 2004; Michelob ULTRA Open, 2005; Wendy's Championship for Children, 2005; Franklin American Mortgage Championship, 2006; CN Canadian Women's Open, 2006; John Q. Hammons Hotel Classic, 2006; U.S. Open, 2007.

Awards: Named American Junior Golf Association Player of the Year, 1995; U.S. Curtis Cup Team, 1996; U.S. Solheim Cup Team, 2002, 2003, 2005; LPGA Komen Award for breast cancer charity work, 2006.

Sidelights

Once dubbed the Tiger Woods of women's golf, Cristie Kerr hit the Ladies Professional Golf Association (LPGA) tour as a 19-year-old rookie in 1997. After a meteoric rise through the junior and amateur ranks, Kerr was expected to take the tour by storm. Her initial performance, however, was underwhelming. Kerr teed off in more than 130 LPGA events before securing her first victory, which finally came in 2002. As Kerr grew older and her maturity level began to match her skill level, she transformed herself into a formidable force on the green and staged a comeback by winning the 2007 U.S. Women's Open and mounting a challenge to Annika Sorenstam's reign as the queen of the women's golf world.

Kerr was born on October 12, 1977, in Miami, Florida, to Michael and Linda Kerr. Her father was a teacher and her mother worked as a legal secretary. As a youngster, Kerr caddied for her father and took an interest in the sport. By age ten, she was playing. "I fell in love with golf the first time I had a club in my hand," Kerr told the *Miami Herald*'s Mike Phillips. At the time, Kerr was already involved in another sport—bowling—and was one of the top-ranked youth bowlers in the state. She begged her father for golf lessons and at the age of 12, Kerr became the youngest person to ever quality for the U.S. Golf Association Junior girls' championship. At 13, Kerr made her mark as the youngest qualifier for the Women's Amateur Public Links championship, even making the two-day cut to appear in the finals.

Kerr attended Miami Sunset High School, where she anchored the boys' golf team. As a girl competing with boys—some of whom did not want her to be a part of their team—Kerr had trouble fitting in. Because she was slightly chunky, classmates taunted her with jeers of "Fatso" and "four-eyes." To get through this rough patch of adolescence, Kerr concentrated on her game and found she could get even with the name-callers by beating them on the golf course. In 1994, Kerr became the first girl to win the boys' division of the well-respected Dade County Youth Fair Tournament. Kerr beat the nation's top-ranked junior boy by a total of four shots.

As a teenager, Kerr spent her summers on the road, golfing with her dad and competing in various matches around the country. Funding Kerr's junior golf career proved hard for her parents—they spent $50,000 on her golf in 1995. As the costs mounted, the Kerrs remained dedicated to financing their daughter's dream. "We did it with everything we earned, with loads of credit cards, and with help from other family members," Kerr's mom told the *Sun-Sentinel*'s Randall Mell. "Every extra dollar outside of the mortgage, the electric bill, and the telephone bill was going to Cristie's golf."

By the time Kerr graduated from high school, she had won 22 of her last 25 amateur events and decided to forgo college to turn pro. She entered the tour in 1997. That rookie season, she competed in 27 events and not once finished in the top 10. Kerr played so poorly she lost her tour card and had to go back to "qualifying school" before she could play the next year. In addition to struggling on the greens, Kerr had trouble connecting with fellow golfers who found her cocky and temperamental. Intensely blunt, Kerr put off other players. Speaking to *Golf World*'s Ron Sirak, Kerr acknowledged that her immaturity got in the way of her career. "From a growing-up standpoint it might have been good to go to college for a year or two," she said. "At the time when I came out here there weren't many people my own age, so it was hard to be accepted by some of the older players, especially getting a lot of press and stuff."

Tournament after tournament, Kerr failed to make her mark on the LPGA. In 1999, her parents divorced, and Kerr suffered through the season with back pain that forced her to withdraw from several events. Feeling down and out, Kerr decided to make a change. She hired a dietician and began working out, eventually shedding about 60 pounds from her nearly 5-foot-4-inch frame. "I just wanted to change my image, how I felt about myself," Kerr told the *Palm Beach Post*'s Craig Dolch. "I just got sick of being fat and not playing as well as I wanted to."

The transformation followed Kerr to the golf course. In 2000, Kerr notched eight top-10 finishes and placed second at the U.S. Women's Open. She finished the season ranked fifteenth on the money list with earnings of $530,751—this was nearly double her earnings for her first three years combined. In 2002, Kerr grabbed her first LPGA victory, at the Longs Drugs Challenge. As Kerr moved from tentative newcomer to confident veteran, more wins came her way. Buoyed by three wins in 2004, she finished fifth on the money list. In 2005, Kerr grabbed two LPGA wins, following with three in 2006.

The year 2006 also saw Kerr marry developer Erik Stevens and earn an LPGA Komen Award for her work raising money for her charity, Birdies for Breast Cancer, which she founded after her mother was diagnosed with the disease in 2003. Kerr also stayed busy off the course with endorsements. Since rising through the ranks and re-imaging herself, Kerr landed deals to represent Lacoste, Titleist/Foot Joy, and Mutual of Omaha.

In July of 2007, Kerr entered the 62nd U.S. Women's Open at the Pine Needles Lodge & Golf Club in North Carolina. She had not won all season. In the final round, Kerr faced tough competition from Mexico's Lorena Ochoa, at the time the No. 1-ranked player in the world. Kerr and Ochoa were tied with five holes remaining, but Kerr went on to secure the win, swinging her way to a two-shot victory. Kerr shot a 5-under-par 279 to Ochoa's 71-281. The win earned her $560,000. "This is a long time coming," fellow golfer Natalie Gulbis told the *Miami Herald*'s Jeff Shain shortly after Kerr's win. "She's been arguably the top American player for many years."

Sources

Periodicals

Golf World, May 20, 2005, pp. 36-37.
Houston Chronicle, July 2, 2007, p. 1.
Miami Herald, April 22, 1994, p. 1D; July 3, 2007.
New York Times, July 2, 2007, p. 1 (Sports).
Palm Beach Post, September 18, 2002, p. 1C.
Sports Illustrated, October 30, 2000, p. G15.
Sun-Sentinel, August 1, 1989, 1C.

Online

"Cristie Kerr," LPGA.com, http://www.lpga.com/content/2007PlayerBiosPDF/Kerr-07.pdf (October 2, 2007).

"Overlooked No More, Kerr Wins U.S. Open," Golf.com, http://www.golf.com/golf/tours_news/article/0,28136,1639178-0,00.html (July 2, 2007).

—*Lisa Frick*

Fred Krupp

AP Images

Executive Director of the Environmental Defense Fund

Born March 21, 1954, in Mineola, NY; son of Arthur L. (a businessman) and Rosalind (a high school teacher; maiden name, Mehr) Krupp; married Laurie Louise Devitt (a public health nutritionist), August 21, 1982; children: Alexander Mehr, Zachary Devitt, Jackson O'Connor. *Education:* Yale University, B.S., 1975; University of Michigan, J.D., 1978.

Addresses: *Home*—Connecticut. *Office*—Environmental Defense Fund, 257 Park Ave. S., New York, NY 10010-7304.

Career

General counsel, Connecticut Fund for the Environment, 1978-84; partner, Albis & Krupp (law firm), 1978-83; partner, Cooper, Whitney, Cochran & Krupp (law firm), 1984; executive director, Environmental Defense Fund, 1984—.

Member: President's Commission on Environmental Quality, 1991-92; President's Council on Sustainable Development, 1993-99; President's Advisory Committee on Trade Policy and Negotiations, 1994-2002; board, H. John Heinz III Center for Science, Economics, and Environment, 1999-2005; board, John F. Kennedy School of Government Environment Council; Leadership Council, Yale School of Forestry and Environmental Studies.

Sidelights

Fred Krupp serves as executive director of the Environmental Defense Fund (EFD), a nonprofit environmental advocacy group that is one of the largest and most influential organizations of its kind in the United States. During a tenure there that has stretched more than a quarter-century, Krupp has gained a reputation as a pioneer in what is sometimes called third wave environmentalism, or attacking the issue of environmental degradation from an economic standpoint. The most famous example of this tactic came in the early 1990s, when Krupp convinced executives at McDonald's that it would be more beneficial in the long term to phase out its foam containers, which were becoming a staple of landfills.

Krupp was born in 1954 in Mineola, New York, but grew up in Verona, New Jersey. His father, Arthur, ran a company that recycled waste rags into roofing materials, and his mother Rosalind was a history teacher at a local high school. Entering Yale University, Krupp was first mentioned in the media in November of 1972 on the day after the first federal election in which 18-year-olds were allowed to cast their ballot in a presidential election. In an article that discussed the reaction on college campuses about lowering the voting age from 21 to 18, Krupp told *New York Times* reporter Michael T. Kaufman, "There is no sense of this being a historical occasion. Everybody just takes it for granted."

The comment—used by Kaufman to begin the article's first paragraph—seemed to foreshadow a future career in providing terrific sound bytes to the media on current events. After graduating from Yale in 1975, Krupp went on to earn a law degree from the University of Michigan. Moving to Connecticut, he went into private practice but also founded the Connecticut Fund for the Environment (CFE). In the late 1970s, the CFE filed a lawsuit against the Upjohn Corporation, makers of fungicides, dyes, and other chemical products at its plant in North Haven, a suburb of New Haven. The lawsuit was aimed at halting the company's decades of dumping toxins into the heavily polluted Quinnipiac River, and it eventually succeeded.

As general counsel for the CFE, Krupp came to the attention to the Environmental Defense Fund, which was closely following the CFE's suit against Upjohn. The national nonprofit organization was founded in 1967 by several Long Island scientists who noticed that birds of prey, like eagles and raptors, were in sudden population decline. Investigating the matter, the quartet of researchers found that DDT, a highly toxic pesticide use to eliminate mosquito populations, was entering the food chain and causing the eggshells of the birds' young to weaken to the point of uselessness. The EFD pushed for a federal ban on DDT, which went into effect in 1972. By 1984, the organization was searching for a new leader, and Krupp was offered the job as executive director. He was just 30 years old at the time, and accepted immediately, as he told Susan Reed in *People* magazine. "I thought if I waited, they might come to their senses," he joked.

When Krupp took over at the Environmental Defense Fund, its informal motto was "Sue the Bastards," according to *Wall Street Journal* writer David Wessel. This eventually gave way to a less adversarial approach, the third wave environmentalism, which relied on economic justifications to convince companies to adopt more earth-friendly practices. One of Krupp's most notable successes came in 1990, when the McDonald's Corporation—the world's largest chain of fast-food restaurants—finally agreed to phase out its polystyrene clamshell, the plastic foam box that had been keeping Big Macs and other McDonald's grill items warm since the mid-1960s. Though the clamshell had long been the target of environmental activists, Krupp decided to investigate the matter one day when he was dining at a McDonald's with his two young sons. "Alex and Zach were eating their Happy Meals and I was looking at all this packaging—six little Chicken McNuggets come in a big foam clamshell," he told Connie Koenenn in an interview that appeared in the *Albany Times Union*. "My idea was that if McDonald's made major changes they could help set a new environmental ethic of what is acceptable and what isn't," he told Koenenn. "I decided I would write a letter to McDonald's, tell them they could solve these problems, and suggest that I talk to them about it."

Krupp went on to have several more important coups at the helm of Environmental Defense. He brought together officials at FedEx and alternative-energy researchers to launch the courier company's first fuel-efficient, low-emission delivery truck in its fleet. He has also served on presidential advisory commissions and councils under both Republican and Democratic administrations of the White House. Typical of his advocacy is a 2002 *New York Times* op-ed column on a significant new piece of California legislation to reduce greenhouse gas emissions from automobiles in the state. The measure was the target of a massive, automotive-maker-funded public-relations campaign to overturn the new fuel-standard requirements, claiming that the new laws were aimed at eventually outlawing sport-utility vehicles. "What if, instead, the auto industry were to take the resources it will devote to waging political warfare on the new legislation," Krupp wrote, "and use that money and the talents of its engineers to accelerate the development of technology to limit greenhouse gas emissions from cars and trucks?... As in the past, automotive engineers are likely to prove far more ingenious in producing new technological answers than their bosses give them credit for."

When Krupp began at the Environmental Defense Fund in 1984, its budget was $3 million, its New York City headquarters had 50 employees, and its membership rolls totaled 35,000. Twenty-three years later, Krupp oversaw a budget of $65 million, 300 employees, and a membership roster that was nearly ten times larger. He lives in Connecticut with his wife since 1982, Laurie Louise Devitt, and their three children. As Wessel wrote in the *Wall Street Journal* profile, "a 1991 *Rolling Stone* article described Mr. Krupp as 'slightly nerdy but persuasive.' His wife's response, as he recalls it today, wasn't exactly an ego booster: 'I didn't realize that [the reporter] actually met with you in person.'"

Sources

Albany Times Union, November 14, 1990, p. B12; May 22, 2005, p. B8.

New York Times, November 8, 1972, p. 98; July 20, 2002.

People, April 15, 1991, p. 61.

Time, April 3, 2006, p. 57.

Wall Street Journal, March 1, 2007.

—*Carol Brennan*

Shia LaBeouf

Actor

Born Shia Shaide LaBeouf, June 11, 1986, in Los Angeles, CA; son of Jeffrey (a performer and rodeo clown) and Shayna (a ballet dancer and visual artist) LaBeouf.

Addresses: *Agent*—Teresa Valente, c/o Beverly Hecht Agency, 12001 Ventura Place, Ste. 320, Studio City, CA 91604. *Contact*—Shia LaBeouf Fan Club, P.O. Box 450802, Kissimmee, FL 34745-0802. *Home*—Burbank, CA.

Career

Actor in films, including: *Charlie's Angels: Full Throttle,* 2003; *Dumb & Dumberer: When Harry Met Lloyd,* 2003; *Holes,* 2003; *I, Robot,* 2004; *Constantine,* 2005; *The Greatest Game Ever Played,* 2005; *A Guide to Recognizing Your Saints,* 2006; *Bobby,* 2006; *Disturbia,* 2007; *Surf's Up* (voice), 2007; *Transformers,* 2007. Television appearances include: *Caroline in the City,* 1998; *Suddenly Susan,* 1999; *Touched by an Angel,* 1999; *The X-Files,* 1999; *ER,* 2000; *Even Stevens,* 2000-03.

Awards: Daytime Emmy Award for outstanding performer in a children's series, for *Even Stevens,* 2003; best actor, Gijón International Film Festival, for *A Guide to Recognizing Your Saints,* 2006; Hollywood Film Award for ensemble of the year, Hollywood Film Festival, for *Bobby,* 2006; special jury prize (dramatic), Sundance Film Festival, for *A Guide to Recognizing Your Saints,* 2006; ShoWest award for male star of tomorrow, 2007.

Sidelights

Many child actors get their start with Disney only to disappear from the entertainment world once they become adults. Shia LaBeouf is an exception. In 2000, LaBeouf, just 14, became a favorite of the pre-teen set after landing on the Disney Channel's *Even Stevens,* which became a hit show. Over the next few years, as he crept into adulthood, LaBeouf took on heavier roles that showcased his great range, appearing in thrillers, biographical pictures, animations, and action flicks.

In 2007, LaBeouf proved he could anchor a film when his low-budget thriller *Disturbia* opened at No. 1 at the box office, drawing a larger audience than the Halle Berry/Bruce Willis suspense thriller *Perfect Strangers,* which opened the same weekend. "Shia's not your pretty-boy hunky guy [with] perfect hair. He has that young John Cusack thing— quirky and smart," *Disturbia* director D. J. Caruso told *Entertainment Weekly*'s Missy Schwartz.

LaBeouf was born on June 11, 1986, in Los Angeles, California, to Jeffrey and Shayna LaBeouf. His first name, pronounced SHY-ah, comes from his grandfather, a veteran of the Catskills comedy circuit. La-Beouf grew up poor in Echo Park, a Los Angeles neighborhood riddled with street crime and gang violence. He attended a school made up largely of Latinos and African Americans. The LaBeouf family never had much money—his parents worked sporadically. LaBeouf has often joked that he is from a long line of artists who never quite made it. His heroin-addicted Cajun father sometimes worked as a rodeo clown or a comedian. He also sold snow cones and toured with the Doobie Brothers, a popular rock group from the 1970s. LaBeouf's Jewish mother, Shayna, was a ballerina. Forced to give up dancing due to an injury, she became a visual artist and jewelry designer. Speaking to *Time*'s Rebecca Winters Keegan, LaBeouf described his parents as old hippies. "They're not really worker bees. They're artists who just didn't have enough bureaucrat in them to get it all wrapped up in a nice little package to be able to feed to the American public."

Early on, Jeffrey LaBeouf pushed his son into street performance, hoping to earn some quick cash from his small son's quips and tricks. Little Shia LaBeouf became the star of his family's traveling street act. The elder LaBeouf stole a maid's cart from a local hotel, spruced it up with paint and streamers, and filled it with hot dogs and shaved ice. He dressed his son up as a clown, then headed for the park. "I hated selling hot dogs," LaBeouf told *Time*'s Winters. "I hated dressing up in clown. But the minute somebody would buy into my thing and buy a hot dog from my family because of my shtick, my parents would look at me like, 'All right, man.' Besides performing, I've never had that validation from anything else I've ever done in my life."

Alongside his father, LaBeouf spent his childhood watching Steve McQueen movies and going to Rolling Stones concerts. He also attended AA meetings, where he began smoking and playing cards at ten. Eventually, LaBeouf's parents divorced and the family's money situation worsened. Fed up with being poor, LaBeouf wondered how he could earn some money. One day at the beach, he admired a friend's surf gear and found out the youth was an actor. "He always had the coolest stuff," LaBeouf told *Los Angeles Times* writer Susan King. "His mom drove a nice car. He had a nice watch and nice clothing. He always had a nice surfboard." After the friend told LaBeouf that he made his money appearing on *Dr. Quinn, Medicine Woman*, LaBeouf decided to become an actor.

LaBeouf makes it clear that he pursued acting only for the money. "It wasn't about art," he told *USA Today*'s Scott Bowles. "It was about making money

to get somewhere and be somebody." Taking matters into his own hands, LaBeouf flipped through the Yellow Pages looking for an agent. When he got Teresa Valente on the phone, LaBeouf pretended to be a middle-aged talent manager from Europe, representing England's best up-and-coming talent. Valente knew she was talking to a child but was nonetheless intrigued. She was used to parents calling, insisting their kids needed representation because they were the next big thing; she never had a child call before. So, Valente took a chance on LaBeouf. She paid for head shots and toted him to audition after audition. By this time, LaBeouf's father, a Vietnam vet, was stuck in a VA hospital, struggling through withdrawal.

LaBeouf joined an improv group and tried his hand at stand-up. He had already been doing a comedy routine at some local nightspots. LaBeouf's routine was always the same. He went onstage looking young and innocent, wearing overalls and a bowl haircut. But then he spoke, channeling an irritable, foul-mouthed 50-year-old through his childish body. LaBeouf's off-color humor shocked audiences. He continued to audition for bit parts and landed appearances on the situation comedy *Suddenly Susan*, the family drama *Touched by an Angel*, the FOX hit *The X-Files*, and the NBC drama *ER*.

At 13, LaBeouf secured a starring role on the Disney family comedy *Even Stevens*. The show, which first aired in 2000, followed the sibling rivalry between class clown Louis Stevens—played by LaBeouf—and his older, perfectionist sister, Ren, played by Christy Carlson Romano. LaBeouf's steady performance as Louis earned him a 2003 Daytime Emmy for Outstanding Performer in a Children's Series.

The show folded in 2003, but that year LaBeouf made a jump to the big screen, playing supporting roles alongside some of Hollywood's biggest stars. He appeared in *Dumb and Dumberer: When Harry Met Lloyd* and *Charlie's Angels: Full Throttle*. LaBeouf's breakout role for 2003, however, was the Disney feature *Holes*, based on the best-selling teen novel by Louis Sachar. In the film, LaBeouf played Stanley Yelnats. As a juvenile wrongly accused of a crime, Stanley is sent to a detention camp in Texas where kids are mysteriously forced to dig five-foot-deep holes all day, every day. On the set, LaBeouf befriended veteran actor Jon Voight—father of actress Angelina Jolie—who played one of the camp warden's assistants. Voight coached LaBeouf on his acting and got him to realize that he should look for fulfillment from the work, not just a paycheck. *Holes* made $67 million and director Andrew Davis credited LaBeouf with its success. "I need[ed] a cross between Dustin Hoffman, Tom Hanks, and Gene Wilder in a kid's body," Davis told *Entertainment Weekly*'s Nancy Miller. "We looked at Shia and knew he was the right kid."

As LaBeouf moved into the spotlight, he carefully guarded his image and told the *Orange County Register*'s Barry Koltnow that he planned to avoid the pitfalls many young actors fall into. "To not party is part of the plan. I have made a calculated effort to stay away from the party scene because that can have as much impact on your career as your performances. If the industry takes you lightly because you're always partying, then they will take your work lightly as well." To stay out of trouble, LaBeouf spends his free time attending Dodgers games and playing video games with friends. LaBeouf does admit to one bad habit, smoking, and reporters often note another, cussing.

The brown-eyed, lanky-framed LaBeouf appeared opposite Will Smith in 2004's *I, Robot* and with Keanu Reeves in 2005's *Constantine*. Disney, banking on LaBeouf's popularity, snapped him up for the lead role in another project, *The Greatest Game Ever Played*. The film, released in 2005, is a biographical picture that follows the real-life tale of underdog golfer Francis Ouimet as he competes in the 1913 U.S. Open. Playing Ouimet gave LaBeouf the opportunity to prove he could move beyond juvenile films.

In 2006, LaBeouf appeared in writer-director Dito Montiel's *A Guide to Recognizing Your Saints*, an indie film about how a would-be gangster escapes street life in Queens, New York. That year, LaBeouf also appeared alongside Anthony Hopkins in *Bobby*, a fictionalized account that revisits the 1968 assassination of Robert F. Kennedy.

For LaBeouf, 2007 proved to be a breakout year when he opened three major films in a four-month period. LaBeouf provided the voice behind the cocky surfing penguin Cody Maverick in the computer-animated flick *Surf's Up*. Unlike most animated films where actors get scripts, the producers wanted the film to have a documentary feel so the stars were forced to ad-lib their lines. Work on the film involved sitting in the studio several hours a day joking and improvising alongside co-star Jeff Bridges.

In a complete change of pace, LaBeouf also starred in the Michael Bay sci-fi thriller *Transformers*, based on the popular 1980s Hasbro action figures. LaBe-

ouf played Sam Witwicky, a teenager whose yellow Camaro transforms into an Autobot named Bumblebee from the planet Cybertron. Unwittingly, LaBeouf's character finds himself at the center of a feud between some warring alien robots. Steven Spielberg served as the executive producer for this $145 million action thriller, jam-packed full of special effects. During filming, the set often resembled a war zone. There were tanks on the ground, Black Hawk helicopters in the air, and Navy SEALS firing off bazookas.

For LaBeouf, the film was more physically than mentally challenging. "In a Michael Bay movie, you're blowing up a building, dropping a helicopter, lighting five guys on fire—all before lunch," LaBeouf told *Hollywood Reporter*'s Jacqueline Marmo. To prepare, LaBeouf ran several miles a day and did calisthenics to get in shape. During filming, LaBeouf ran from guard dogs, dodged bullets, scurried through flames, and was set on fire. The scariest action scene required LaBeouf to hang from the side of a building by a wire.

LaBeouf's biggest success that year, however, was the D.J. Caruso-directed film *Disturbia*. In this Hitchcockian-themed film, LaBeouf played a depressed, rough-around-the-edges teen named Kale who gets in a tussle with a teacher and ends up sentenced to house arrest. Kale—forced to live with a transmitter on his ankle that alerts police if he leaves his home—gets cabin fever and begins spying on his neighbors. He comes to believe one of them is a serial killer. The film surprised Hollywood its first weekend when it brought in $22 million in ticket sales to open at No. 1 at the box office.

The same weekend *Disturbia* opened, LaBeouf conquered another Hollywood milestone—he hosted *Saturday Night Live*. "I'm very fortunate," LaBeouf told Bob Strauss of the *Daily News of Los Angeles*. "When you start this business, the pinnacles are ... meeting Spielberg, working with Scorsese, winning an Oscar, doing *Saturday Night Live*, things like that. And, at 20, some of those things are off my list. It's jarring, it's very weird."

Soon after the release of his 2007 films, LaBeouf was back in front of the camera, this time working for Spielberg, who cast the young hotshot actor in the fourth Indiana Jones installment. It was rumored that LaBeouf would play Harrison Ford's son in the film. The much-anticipated sequel was scheduled for release in 2008.

As for the future of his career, LaBeouf told the *Hollywood Reporter*'s Marmo that he plans to continue choosing films in various genres so he does not get typecast. "I want to do drama and comedy. I want to do all of it because that's human. People are funny, and they're not funny, and they're dramatic and confused. If I was just to play one emotion my whole career, I wouldn't have a very long career. My whole goal is longevity—not necessarily fame and stardom. I want to be working until I'm 70. I want to be Michael Caine. And the only way I can be Michael Caine is to do everything and not do the same thing back-to-back."

Sources

Periodicals

Daily News of Los Angeles, April 8, 2007, p. U4.
Entertainment Weekly, August 15, 2003, pp. 28-30; April 27, 2007, p. 14.
Hollywood Reporter, March 15, 2007, p. S13.
Interview, October 2006, p. 128.
Los Angeles Times, April 12, 2007, p. E6; July 1, 2007, p. E5.
Orange County Register, April 13, 2007, p. 1M.
People, May 19, 2003, p. 128.
Time, July 16, 2007, p. 63.

Online

"Shia LaBeouf is riding a wave of success," MSNBC.com, http://www.msnbc.msn.com/id/19074228.tif (June 27, 2007).
"Shia LaBeouf makes waves in Hollywood," *USA Today,* http://www.usatoday.com/life/people/2007-06-05-shia-labeouf_N.htm (June 27, 2007).

—Lisa Frick

Frank Langella

Actor

Born January 1, 1940, in Bayonne, NJ; son of Frank Langella (a business owner); married Ruth Weil, June 14, 1977 (divorced, 1996); children: one son, one daughter. *Education:* Syracuse University, B.S., 1959; studied acting with Elia Kazan at the Lincoln Center Repertory Company.

Addresses: *Agent*—Special Artists Agency, 9465 Wilshire Blvd., Ste. 890, Beverly Hills, CA 90212-2607.

Career

Actor on stage, including appearances with Yale Repertory Theatre, 1971-72; McCarter Theatre, Princeton, NJ, 1972; Guthrie Theater Company, Minneapolis, MN, 1972-73. Stage appearances include: *The Immoralist,* New York City, 1963; *The Old Glory,* New York City, 1964-65; *Good Day,* New York City, 1965-66; *The White Devil,* New York City, 1965-66; *Yerma,* Broadway production, 1966-67; *The Devils,* Los Angeles, 1967; *A Cry of Players,* Broadway production, 1968-69; *Cyrano de Bergerac,* 1971; *Seascape,* Broadway production, 1974-75; *Dracula,* Broadway production, 1977-80; *Passion,* Broadway production, 1983; *Designing for Living,* Broadway production, 1984-85; *Hurlyburly,* Broadway production, 1985; *Sherlock's Last Case,* Washington, D.C. then Broadway production, 1987; *The Tempest,* New York City, 1989; *Scenes from an Execution,* Los Angeles, CA, 1993; *The Father,* Broadway production, 1996; *Present Laughter,* Broadway production, 1996-97; *Fortune's Fool,* Broadway production, 2002; *Match,* Broadway production, 2004; *Frost/Nixon,* Broadway production, 2006-07. Film appearances include: *Diary of a Mad Housewife,* 1970; *The Twelve Chairs,* 1970; *The Deadly Trap,* 1971; *The Wrath of God,* 1972; *Dracula,* 1979; *Those Lips Those Eyes,* 1980; *Sphinx,* 1981; *The Men's Club,* 1986; *Masters of the Universe,* 1987; *And God Created Women,* 1988; *True Identity,* 1991; *1492: Conquest of Paradise,* 1992; *Dave,* 1993; *Brainscan,* 1994; *Junior,* 1994; *Bad Company,* 1995; *Cutthroat Island,* 1995; *Eddie,* 1996; *Lolita,* 1997; *Small Soldiers,* 1998; *The Ninth Gate,* 1999; *Stardom,* 2000; *Sweet November,* 2001; *House of D,* 2004; *Breaking the Fifth,* 2005; *How You Look to Me,* 2005; *Return to Rajapur,* 2006; *Good Night and Good Luck,* 2005; *Superman Returns,* 2006; *Starting Out in the Evening,* 2007; *Frost/ Nixon,* 2008. Television movie appearances include: *Benito Cereno,* 1967; *The Mark of Zorro,* 1974; *The Seagull,* 1975; *The American Woman: Portraits of Courage,* 1976; *Eccentricities of a Nightingale,* 1976; *Sherlock Holmes,* 1981; *I, Leonardo: A Journey of the Mind,* 1983; *Liberty,* 1986; *The Doomsday Gun,* 1994; *Moses,* 1996; *Kilroy,* 1999; *Jason and the Argonauts,* 2000; *Cry Baby Lane,* 2000; *111 Gramercy Park,* 2003; *Now You See It ...,* 2005; *The Water Is Wide,* 2006; *10.5: Apocalypse,* 2006. Productions as stage director include: *John and Abigail,* Stockbridge, MA, 1969; *Passione,* Broadway production, 1980; *Cyrano de Bergerac,* New York City, 1997-98. Productions as a stage producer include: *After the Fall,* New York City, 1984; *Sherlock's Last Case,* Washington, D.C. then Broadway production, 1987.

Member: Actors' Equity Association; Screen Actors Guild.

Awards: OBIE Award for best performance, *Village Voice*, for *The Old Glory*, 1965; OBIE Award for distinguished performance, *Village Voice*, for *Good Day*, 1966; OBIE Award for distinguished performance, *Village Voice*, for *The White Devil*, 1966; Drama Desk Award for outstanding performance, for *A Cry of Players*, 1968; National Board of Review Award for best supporting actor, for *Diary of a Mad Housewife*, 1970; Tony Award for best featured actor in a play, American Theatre Wing, for *Seascape*, 1975; Drama Desk Award for outstanding featured actor in a play, for *Seascape*, 1975; Drama League Award for *Dracula*, 1978; Drama Desk Award for outstanding actor in a play, for *The Father*, 1996; Tony Award for best featured actor in a play, American Theatre Wing, for *Fortune's Fool*, 2002; Drama Desk Award for outstanding actor in a play, for *Frost/Nixon*, 2007; Outer Critics Circle Award for outstanding actor in a play, for *Frost/Nixon*, 2007; Tony Award for best actor in a play, American Theatre Wing, for *Frost/Nixon*, 2007.

Sidelights

After making a splash on the New York stage and silver screen in the 1960s and 1970s, actor Frank Langella experienced a career renaissance in 2006 and 2007 for his lauded performances in the stage production *Frost/Nixon* and the indie film *Starting Out in the Evening*. The actor won several awards for his work over the years, including three Tonys, and was often praised by critics for his ability to inhabit the characters he played. Langella recognized that his career had ups and downs, telling the *New York Times'* Michiko Kakutani, "I think I've always been a success. But some things get noticed and some things don't. My career has been a strangely unpredictable one: I keep being rediscovered and counted out, then rediscovered again. But I accept that."

Born on January 1, 1940, in Bayonne, New Jersey, Langella was named after his father. His father was the owner of a steel drum reconditioning business, and Langella and his two siblings were raised in an atmosphere of privilege. From an early age, Langella knew he wanted to be an actor, although, for a time in his youth, he hoped he could make a living horseback riding. Acting and the theater were attractive to the young Langella, who often felt overlooked in his family and among his peers. He told the *Washington Post*'s Dave Richards, "If you tend to be a loner, there is a place you can go and be tremendously involved, and that's in the bright lights of the theater. You feel very much loved and em-braced and part of the world.... I was the weakest link in an overpowering family. In the theater, I could be someone else. Or myself in disguise."

To pursue his acting goals, he attended Syracuse University. There, Langella studied drama with Sawyer Falk, but received his B.S. in speech pathology. Langella then moved to New York City to pursue an acting career, where he struggled for a time though his family financially supported him. He appeared in summer stock productions and toured Long Island-based 4-H Clubs. In 1963, he was a member of the first training program at the Lincoln Center Repertory Company.

That year, Langella made his New York debut in the Off-Broadway production of *The Immoralist* as Michel. Langella impressed audiences, and, in the mid-1960s, had three OBIE award-winning roles: in 1965's *The Old Glory*, 1966's *Good Day*, and 1966's *The White Devil*. He was on his way to being recognized as one of the best young stage actors in the United States.

After another award-winning turn as a young William Shakespeare in *A Cry of Players* in 1968, Langella was typecast for a time into young men on a search or quest in his life. This typecasting shifted in 1970 after his role in the film, *Diary of a Mad Housewife*. Langella was praised for his portrayal of George, the caddish lover with a cruel steak in the critically acclaimed film. When *Diary of a Mad Housewife* was released, the actor was regularly offered similarly mean-spirited roles. Langella was also lauded for his work in the Mel Brooks-directed film *The Twelve Chairs*, released in 1970.

Because of the success of these two films as well as his stage work, Langella was seen as a sex symbol, widely interviewed in magazines and regularly featured in gossip columns. He was expected to be a breakout film star, but his next few films were essentially failures. Langella came to be seen as a soon-to-be has-been. His stage work even took him away from New York for several years, as he appeared regionally in various productions with prestigious companies such as Yale Repertory, the McCarter Theatre, and the Guthrie Theater Company.

A more humbled Langella returned to New York City by the mid-1970s. He told *New York Times'* Kukutani, "I know it all rests with me. I've learned by making mistakes, just about every mistake you could make—the wrong choices, the wrong goals, going down the wrong road. I know it sounds like a cliché, but I don't regret any of them."

In 1975, Langella had his breakthrough role as a talking lizard named Leslie in his Broadway debut, the hit play *Seascape*. Winning both a Tony and a Drama Desk award for his performance, Langella was again a highly regarded actor. In the late 1970s, Langella also received critical kudos for his work in the title role in Edward Gorey's revisionist *Dracula* on Broadway. While he again became something of sex symbol, he also was typecast for a time for his work in the role. He also appeared in the title role of the 1979 film based on the Broadway play.

Langella's film career continued to be strong in the early 1980s by his taking on more challenging roles. For example, he starred as Harry Crystal in the film *Those Lips, Those Eyes* in 1980. Drawing on his own experiences as a stage actor who sometimes struggled to survive, Langella's Crystal is a mediocre song-and-dance actor who has had limited success in middling shows and summer stock productions. Critics appreciated Langella's work, noting, as Kakutani of the *New York Times* reported, "only a first-class actor could portray such a second-rate performer with such panache."

In 1980, Langella also directed his first play in New York City, the poorly reviewed *Passione*. Throughout the 1980s, Langella moved back and forth between stage and screen, while continuing to expand his horizons by directing and producing on occasion. In 1985, he optioned a script about the famous fictional sleuth Sherlock Holmes, which proved to be a major project for him. The following year, Langella was both the producer and star of a new version of Arthur Miller's *After the Fall*.

Langella was both the producer and star of *Sherlock's Last Case* when it was finally produced in the late 1980s. The play was a hit in runs in Washington, D.C., and on Broadway. While working out his characterization of Sherlock in rehearsals, Langella also had to manage the $1.2 million production. He was able to do so successfully because of his own maturity. As he put together the Washington production before its opening, Langella told Richards of the *Washington Post*, "I just think about the list of things that have to be done today and take it as it comes. Sometime in the last three or four years, I stopped needing to control everything. It was the beginning of liberation for me.... Lately, I've begun to realize the less you try to manipulate others, the more life comes to you. You're not squeezing it tight. You're letting it happen."

Sherlock's Last Case received generally positive reviews. Louise Sweeney in the *Christian Science Monitor* wrote of Langella's work in the Washington production, "Langella's Holmes is also silkily charming, elegantly tailored, and the first Sherlock to bring a subtle sexiness to the role." While the Associated Press' Michael Kuchwara was less impressed with the production overall, he raved about Langella's work. Kuchwara wrote, "Langella was born to wear that deerstalker, smoke that pipe and play that violin. He has a commanding stage presence and has got the correct Holmes attitude down just right. The actor, who has the best glare on Broadway, is egocentric without being alienating, a difficult trick to accomplish."

With the success of the play, Langella's film career again underwent a brief revival. He appeared as the villain Skeletor in 1987's *Masters of the Universe*, based on the popular Mattel toys, then appeared as a politician in a re-make of *And God Created Women* in 1988. Langella returned to the New York stage in 1989 to perform in an Off-Broadway production of William Shakespeare's *The Tempest*.

In the 1990s, Langella appeared in a number of films, primarily in small roles. His first film role of the decade came in 1991 with *True Identity*, based on a *Saturday Night Live* sketch. Langella's film career was really ignited for a time by his work as the malicious Chief of Staff Bob Alexander in the presidential comedy *Dave*, released in 1993. He went to appear in such comedies as 1994's *Junior* and 1996's *Eddie*. Langella also put in noteworthy performances in the pirate film *Cutthroat Island* and a new version of the controversial novel, *Lolita*. In 1999, he appeared in the failed supernatural thriller *The Ninth Gate*, directed by Roman Polanski. Langella took on television roles as well, including playing weapon-building Gerald Bull in the 1994 HBO original movie *Doomsday Gun*, based on real events in the 1980s.

In 1996 Langella starred in the Broadway revival of August Strindberg's *The Father*, a psychological drama about a paranoid father. Playing the title role, the actor received some of the best reviews of his career, though the production as a whole was not as well-received. Langella then moved into another hailed role on Broadway, playing the world-weary Garry Essendine in a revival of Noel Coward's *Present Laughter* in late 1996 and early 1997.

As Langella entered his sixties in 2000, his acting career continued to thrive. In 2002, he co-starred in a Broadway revival of the Ivan Turgenev play, *Fortune's Fool*. Langella played the charming, but snake-like fop, nobleman Tropatochov, opposite Alan Bates, who played the nicer Kuzovkin. Langella garnered a Tony Award for his performance. Two years later, Langella was similarly lauded for his work in the new comedy *Match*. Writing in the *New York Times*, Ben Brantley commented of his work: "A convincingly contradictory mix of small-town American folksiness and aesthetic worldliness, Mr. Langella makes you feel, as only a fine actor can, that his character is both deeply familiar and original. You're ready to follow this manic, hopeful, charming, and pathetic creature wherever he wants to take you."

Langella found even greater acclaim—and earned his third Tony Award—playing Richard Nixon in the stage play *Frost/Nixon*. It was based on a series of interviews the famous British journalist David Frost did with Nixon after he resigned from the presidency. Reviewing the production in *New York Magazine*, Jeremy Carter wrote "When Langella lopes onstage, he at first seems [a] broad a caricature.... But as the performance deepens, what really strikes you—especially coming from Langella, one of the world's greatest scenery-chewers—is his subtlety, his coiled restraint." Langella reprised Nixon in the film version of the play, released in 2008 and directed by Ron Howard.

Langella's work was well-received in the independent film *Starting Out in the Evening*. Filmed in less than three weeks and released in 2007, there was talk of an Academy Award nomination for his work as the once-famous novelist Leonard Schiller. Langella's Schiller is nearing the end of his life, trying to finish his last novel, and must deal with family drama and life change when a comely graduate student enters his life. Langella believed he understood why audiences embraced his performance as Schiller, telling Sam Allis of the *Boston Globe*, "The movie has for some reason touched people. It has something to do with the universality of trying in all of us. I find it beautiful that at 74 Leonard said, 'Oh, I've learned something. I think I'll put this book away and I'll start again.'"

As Langella lined up more film roles, including the *The Box*, he remained thoughtful about the cyclicism of his career. He told Michael Phillips of the *Chicago Tribune*, "You act to try to lessen the noise. And eventually you discover, if you're lucky, that acting is a skill and a craft, and not just a way of barfing up your neuroses. The demons that used to really taunt me and rule my life don't anymore. And new ones come along: mortality, death, the questions.... Looking back I'm proud I wasn't afraid of embracing change. I think my work is more complicated now than it's ever been. And maybe that's because I didn't ever decide: 'This is what people want to see me do.'"

Sources

Books

Contemporary Theatre, Film, and Television, vol. 60, Thomson Gale, 2005.
Marquis Who's Who, vol. 160, Marquis Who's Who, 2008.
Who's Who in the Theatre, 17th ed., Gale Research, 1981.

Periodicals

Associated Press, August 21, 1987; November 15, 1989.
Associated Press Worldstream, April 4, 2002.
Boston Globe, March 10, 2000, p. D5; December 9, 2007, p. N9.
Chicago Tribune, December 28, 2007.
Christian Science Monitor, October 6, 1980, p. 23; August 18, 1987, p. 20.
Daily News of Los Angeles, November 23, 2007, p. L9.
Houston Chronicle, May 25, 1993, p. 3.
Los Angeles Times, November 23, 2007, p. E2.
New York Magazine, May 7, 2007.
New York Post, November 16, 2007, p. 40.
New York Times, September 4, 1980, p. C15; February 11, 1996, sec. 2, p. 5; December 2, 1996, p. C11; March 31, 2002, sec. 2, p. 7; April 9, 2004, p. E1.
Post-Standard (Syracuse, NY), January 22, 1996, p. B3.
Toronto Star, December 22, 1995, p. D8.
USA Today, August 23, 1991, p. 4D.
Virginian-Pilot (Norfolk, VA), July 23, 1994, p. 1.
Washington Post, June 21, 1987, p. G1.

—A. Petruso

Justine Larbalestier

Author and editor

Born c. 1968 in Sydney, Australia; daughter of anthropologists; married Scott Westerfeld (an author), 2001. *Education:* University of Sydney, research fellow in English, early 1990s.

Addresses: *Agent*—Jill Grinberg Literary Management, 244 Fifth Ave., 11th Fl., New York, NY 10001. *Home*—Sydney, Australia, and New York, NY.

Career

First book, *The Battle of the Sexes in Science Fiction* published by Wesleyan University Press, 2002.

Sidelights

Justine Larbalestier is a writer of science-fiction and fantasy novels for young adults who divides her time between her native Australia and New York City. The title of a 2007 *Village Voice* article described Larbalestier and her husband, author Scott Westerfeld, as "the East Village 'It' Couple of Young-Adult Lit." Taken together, noted Carol Cooper, the *Village Voice* journalist, their books "send the same fundamental message—take time to find out who you are, because individuality is power. They suggest that human nature is inherently flawed, but that properly understood, even these flaws can be turned to your advantage."

Born in Sydney, Australia, to a pair of anthropologist parents, Larbalestier lived in several Australian locales during her formative years, including two Aboriginal settlements of the island nation's Northern Territory state. As a result of this transience during her earlier years, Larbalestier wrote on the biography that appears on her Web site, "the world has always seemed an odd and fascinating place to me." In the late 1990s, she moved to New York City, where she met Westerfeld at a science-fiction reading in a bar.

Larbalestier's first book was a work of nonfiction, *The Battle of the Sexes in Science Fiction* (2002), which was published when she was a research fellow with the Department of English at the University of Sydney. Its chapters discuss the role of women writing in the genre and how female characters are portrayed by male writers. Writing and researching it, she noted in her introduction, had taken up much of the past decade of her life, and took her to Toronto, San Francisco, and New York City in order to research historical collections of science fiction in each of the cities. "Larbalestier offers a fresh look, without bitterness, at science fiction's lengthy engagement with issues of sex, sex roles, and gender rivalry," asserted Cooper in another *Village Voice* issue, who summarized the work as "a solid compendium of rare facts and fannish artifacts." *The Battle of the Sexes* was nominated for a Hugo Award, the annual honors given out to the year's best science fiction writing.

Larbalestier moved on to young-adult fiction when she learned that Penguin Books was launching a new young-adult imprint called Razorbill. She submitted a proposal with three chapters of what became the first book in her "Magic or Madness" trilogy. The eponymous debut was named one of the top ten fantasy-science fiction reads of 2005 for young adults by *Booklist*. *Magic or Madness* is told in the first-person narrative voice by 15-year-old Reason Cansino, an Australian teen who comes from a long line of wizards, witches, and other practitioners of magic. Reason's given name, however, is a reflection of her mother's strong opposition to magic, a wariness with which Reason has been inculcated from an early age. When her mother suffers a mental breakdown, Reason is taken in by her witchy grandmother, Esmeralda. In Esmeralda's kitchen, Reason discovers a portal that suddenly teleports her from Sydney to New York City. "Readers looking for layered, understated fantasy will follow the looping paths of Larbalestier's fine writing ... with gratitude and awe," asserted *Booklist* critic Jennifer Mattson. Larbalestier's fiction debut also earned a glowing review from *School Library Journal's* Melissa Moore, who noted that "Larbalestier's sense of place and refreshing exploration of magic as a force for both good and evil make this novel unusual."

The second book in the "Magic or Madness" trilogy was 2006's *Magic Lessons*, which follows the further adventures of Reason and her friends Tom, who is Esmeralda's apprentice, and Jay-Tee, her New York City pal. A romance with Jay-Tee's brother Danny results in an unplanned pregnancy while Reason is still struggling to solve the conundrum presented by a sword given to her by a mysterious Cansino ancestor. "Larbalestier creates complex relationships among her characters," wrote Beth L. Meister in a *School Library Journal* review.

The title character in *Magic's Child*—the final book in the trilogy—is Reason's newborn, and in this third installment Reason struggles with the knowledge that if she chooses to use the sword that bestows her with magical powers, she will die before reaching her twentieth birthday. If she avoids using her inherited gifts, she will likely descend into madness, as her mother did. As Mattson noted in a *Booklist* review of this 2007 title, there were some flaws in the resolution of the trilogy's multiple plotlines, but other elements, such as the characterizations and dialogue, "give reason to hope for more from Larbalestier as her storytelling powers mature."

In an interview that appeared on the Web site Cynsations, Larbalestier admitted to writer Lawrence Schimel that writing a trilogy was tricky. "I asked several people to read *Magic Lessons* [book 2 of the trilogy] who hadn't read book 1 to see if they could follow the story," she recalled. "Arrogantly, I was expecting them to tell me it worked just fine on its own. Nope. I had to do several major rewrites after I got their comments." Schimel also echoed the sentiments of most reviewers in noting that the dialogue and narrative voices that Larbalestier crafts for her teen characters seem pitch-perfect, and asked how she achieved that feat. "Like many people, my teenage years weren't exactly fabulous," she replied. "They are etched deep in my memory, accessing them is dead easy. It's being an adult that's hard."

Larbalestier has also served as editor of *Daughters of Earth: Feminist Science Fiction in the Twentieth Century*, a 2006 anthology of science-fiction tales dating back to the 1920s, and another novel, titled *How to Ditch Your Fairy*, which was published by Bloomsbury in 2008. She and Westerfeld—author of the popular young-adult "Uglies" series about a world in which plastic surgery is compulsory—wed in 2001 and have homes in Sydney and New York City, but they also enjoy settling in at remote locales in Central or South America to write their books. In the Cynsations interview, Schimel asked Larbalestier about being married to a fellow writer, and she replied they were only "competitive about stupid things, like, who can spit the farthest, bounce the highest, predict cricket scores, stuff like that, but never about writing."

Selected writings

"Magic or Madness" trilogy

Magic or Madness, Penguin/Razorbill (New York City), 2005.
Magic Lessons, Penguin/Razorbill, 2006.
Magic's Child, Penguin/Razorbill, 2007.

Other

The Battle of the Sexes in Science Fiction (nonfiction), Wesleyan University Press (Middletown, CT), 2002.
(Editor) *Daughters of Earth: Feminist Science Fiction in the Twentieth Century*, Wesleyan University Press, 2006.
How to Ditch Your Fairy (novel), Bloomsbury (New York City), 2008.

Sources

Periodicals

Booklist, March 15, 2005, p. 1286; April 15, 2005, p. 1467; April 1, 2006, p. 33; April 15, 2007, p. 38.
Publishers Weekly, May 20, 2002, p. 52.
School Library Journal, March 2005, p. 213; October 2005, p. S82; June 2006, p. 161; July 2006, p. 36; May 2007, p. 136.
Village Voice, July 16, 2002; December 18, 2007.

Online

"Biography," Justine Larbalestier.com, http://www.justinelarbalestier.com/bio.htm (May 8, 2008).
"SCBWI Bologna 2006 Author Interview: Justine Larbalestier," Cynsations, http://cynthialeitichsmith.blogspot.com/2006/02/scbwi-bologna-2006-author-interview_17.html (May 15, 2008).

—Carol Brennan

Isaac Larian

Mike Segar/Reuters/Landov

Chief Executive Officer of MGA Entertainment

Born March 28, 1954, in Kashan, Iran; immigrated to the United States, 1971; married; children: Jasmine, Cameron, additional child. *Education:* California State University, Los Angeles, B.S., 1978.

Addresses: *Office*—MGA Entertainment, Inc., 16300 Roscoe Blvd., Ste. 200, Van Nuys, CA 91406.

Career

Co-founded ABC Electronics (later known as Micro Games America, then MGA Entertainment), 1979; launched Bratz dolls line, 2001.

Awards: Entrepreneur of the Year Award, Ernst & Young, 2004.

Sidelights

The creative force behind the Bratz dolls, Isaac Larian is the founder and chief executive officer of MGA Entertainment. Beginning his career by selling consumer electronics and hand-held electronic games, his company found its greatest success with the Bratz, which essentially overcame Barbie as the world's most popular toy. Of his success with the dolls, Larian told Denise Abbott of *Hollywood Reporter,* "As an entrepreneur, a lot of my decisions are based on instinct and gut feeling. They don't all pan out—but this one certainly did."

Larian was born in 1954 in Kashan, Iran, into a Jewish family, and was raised in the small Jewish community based in Tehran. In 1971, Larian left Iran for

California to study civil engineering at California State in Los Angeles. He worked as a dishwasher there to save money for his education. Because of the Iranian revolution in the late 1970s, returning home and working there as he originally planned became an impossibility. Larian remained in the United States and took a different direction in his life and career.

After completing his degree in 1978, Larian, his brother, Farhad, and a brother-in-law co-founded ABC Electronics in 1979. This mail-order company dealt primarily in consumer electronics. Larian's company really took off in 1987 when he gained the U.S. importing license for the Japanese company Nintendo. When ABC Electronics narrowed its focus to selling only Nintendo's hand-held electronic games, its name was changed to Micro Games America; it later became MGA Entertainment, Inc.

Over the years, Larian expanded MGA's product line to include radio-controlled toys and robotic plush animals. One of his company's first dolls was My Dream Baby, inspired by his own then nine-year-old daughter, Jasmine. The extremely realistic doll used special technology to grow from infant to toddler size and move from crawling to walking. Each doll also grew at its own rate and reacted to its owner. It was introduced in the fall of 2000.

The origins of what would be MGA's biggest-selling product came from a conversation with a buyer from Wal-Mart. The buyer challenged Larian to create a doll to beat Barbie and Wal-Mart would buy it. Though others dismissed his idea, Larian forged forth and created the Bratz. He was helped by his children and their cousins in his bi-weekly Kitchen Sink Focus Group. In this informal focus group, he showed them products in development at MGA and talked with them about what kind of toys they wanted.

The result of the challenge was the Bratz dolls. In June of 2001, MGA Entertainment introduced the Bratz, Barbie-like dolls with a more modern, street, hip, urban attitude. The nine-inch dolls had thigh-length hair, exaggerated lips and eyes with makeup as well as street-inspired clothing. Like My Dream Baby, Larian's daughter Jasmine was especially important to the doll's development. One of the original Bratz dolls, Yasmin, was also named for her.

From the first, the Bratz were a hit, high on the list of most-wanted toys at Christmas for many years after their introduction. Targeted at a slightly older demographic than Barbie—seven to eleven year olds as opposed to Barbie's four to six year old—Bratz also appealed to teens and young adults. Approximately 30 months after the Bratz were introduced, 150 million of Bratz and Bratz-related products had been sold worldwide. They soon outsold Barbies in many markets.

Despite their instant popularity, the Bratz dolls were criticized by some psychologists and parents for their effect on children, primarily because the dolls were perceived to be sexualized. Larian dismissed these concerns, believing they were popular because of generational changes that had made Barbies seem more old-fashioned. He also emphasized the racial and cultural diversity of the Bratz which included black, Hispanic, white, and Asian dolls. His research also showed that kids saw the Bratz as being their age while Barbies were perceived as adults. He told Charles Laurence of *Sunday Telegraph*, "It's a new generation. Kids are living in a different world. What puzzles me is why other people haven't worked it out for themselves. I know kids, and they love my toys."

Larian built on the popularity of Bratz by adding a line of male Bratz dolls, more Bratz girls, limited-edition Bratz in themed sets, and tons of accessories for the dolls. A significant source of income came from licensing the brand for posters, clothes, foot-wear, fashion accessories, and books, as well as other products. There were 200 licenses worldwide by 2003, with more coming in subsequent years. Larian was discerning in what products he would allow the Bratz to appear on since he emphasized responsibility and ethics in his toys. For example, he turned down a chance to put the Bratz on a cigarette lighter in Japan because he did not want the dolls associated with smoking.

The success of MGA Entertainment led to numerous accolades for the company, including being named the Supplier of the Year by Wal-Mart in 2003. That same year, it was given Vendor of the Year Awards from Toys R Us and Target. Larian himself was honored in 2004 as Entrepreneur of the Year by Ernst & Young. MGA Entertainment's exponential growth continued in 2004, as it remained the fastest growing consumer entertainment company in the world with $1 billion in retail sales alone that year. Still expanding the Bratz empire, Larian struck a deal with Twentieth Century-Fox for the distribution of Bratz movies. First to hit the market was direct-to-DVD animated *The Bratz Go Hollywood*, created by MGA Entertainment before the deal was made.

In addition to the Bratz, Larian ensured MGA was diversified. His company created many toys targeted at boys, including *Spider-Man 2: The Movie* products, R/C Vehicles, and Boys Action. Not content to rest on the success of the Bratz, Larian's company introduced another line of dolls that year, 4-Ever Best Friends, which were targeted at a younger audience than Bratz. Bratz and related accessories still formed the majority of MGA sales, and were in short supply as demand outstripped supply in Christmas 2004. By 2005, the Bratz had 350 licensees, and the company expanded Bratz items to include cosmetics, bedding, digital music players, and other electronic items to retain its core consumers. A television show and more films were in the works, and a related fashion magazine was introduced in the fall of 2005.

In 2005, as MGA Entertainment's growth slowed slightly, Larian took on Mattel, the company which created Barbie. He sued them on several fronts, including unfair competition and intellectual property infringement. Larian accused Mattel of creating a new line of dolls, called My Scene, which imitated looks, packaging, and themes of his Bratz dolls. Larian also claimed that Mattel intimidated retailers and licensees for doing business with his company and tried to control the doll hair supply. A year later, Mattel countersued, accusing MGA of stealing company secrets, including plans for what became the Bratz doll line as well as expansion-related information. Specifically, Mattel believed that former employees, including doll designer Carter Bryant, created the Bratz dolls while working for Mattel and hid the concept. Bryant and the others later took jobs with MGA.

While the suit was ongoing, Larian focused on expanding his company. To increase MGA Entertainment's sales and profits, Larian worked to expand his company's international sales. By 2006, MGA was opening direct sales offices in countries like Mexico and Canada, with more planned in certain European countries. Larian made the choice because he and his company felt their previous licensed distributors there were not maximizing the company's potential and they could do it better themselves despite the higher costs involved.

In 2006, Larian said believed that the Bratz's full potential would be reached in three or four years, though the dolls and related products were already pulling in $600 to $800 million annually for MGA. To ensure the long-term stability of the company, he continued to expand its product base to include more toy lines and by becoming the licensee for the *Shrek* movies and Marvel comic characters. MGA's future was also to include more product lines like sporting goods, bikes, and soft goods such as clothing and shoes.

Explaining Larian's success, Jim Gianopulos, the co-chairman of Fox Filmed Entertainment, told Christina MacDonald of the *Hollywood Reporter*, "Isaac Larian is a visionary entrepreneur. He understands consumer, the retail infrastructure, and creative properties, which is a great combination." Larian also believed in himself, telling Australia's *Sunday Herald Sun*, "I was always a big dreamer. The human mind and energy is so vast and powerful that I believe you can make everything possible if you truly believe in it.... If I can do it, everyone else can."

Sources

Advertising Age, November 17, 2003, p. S17.

BusinessWeek, May 2, 2005, p. 76; December 18, 2006, p. 13.

Business Wire, February 10, 2000; January 7, 2004; February 12, 2004; March 3, 2004; July 13, 2004.

Chicago Sun-Times, March 5, 2004, p. 55.

Daily Variety, June 20, 2006, p. A.

Hollywood Reporter, June 8, 2004; June 21, 2005.

Independent on Sunday (London, England), December 19, 2004, p. 2.

Los Angeles Times, November 21, 2006, p. C1.

New York Times, October 13, 2005, p. C1.

Playthings, June 1, 2006, p. 8.

Sunday Herald Sun (Australia), April 9, 2006, p. F3.

Sunday Telegraph (London, England), December 21, 2003, p. 1.

—*A. Petruso*

Sandra Lee

Television personality and author

Born Sandra Lee Waldroop, July 3, 1966, in Santa Monica, CA; daughter of Wayne and Vicky Waldroop; married Bruce Karatz (a real estate developer and corporate executive), 2001 (divorced, 2006). *Education:* Attended the University of Wisconsin, mid-1980s, and the Cordon Bleu Institute, Ottawa, Canada, c. 1998.

Addresses: *Home*—Los Angeles, CA, and New York, NY. *Office*—Food Network, 1180 Avenue of the Americas, 11th Fl., New York, NY 10036.

Career

Worked as a waitress and for an import-expert company in California, late 1980s; founded Kurtain Kraft, a homewares line, c. 1992; created line of homewares sold at Target and Wal-Mart; first cookbook, *Sandra Lee Semi-Homemade Cooking,* published by Miramax Books, 2002; television show *Semi-Homemade Cooking with Sandra Lee* debuted on the Food Network, October, 2003.

Sidelights

Television personality Sandra Lee is the host of the popular *Semi-Homemade Cooking* series on the Food Network, a spin-off of her bestselling *Semi-Homemade* cookbooks. Lee provides recipes that use store-bought packaged foods artfully doctored up with fresh ingredients, and her ingenuous quick-fix creations have given her cult-hero status among busy families. A lithe, blond Californian, she has sometimes been called "the next Martha Stewart,"

but Lee avoids such comparisons, instead describing herself as "the new-generation homemaker," she told *Parade* writer Iris Krasnow. "I'm the one who can show you how to get it all done, have a satisfying career and a satisfying home life and not feel overly stressed. I want women to be able to accomplish anything."

Lee was born in the mid-1960s, and grew up in Sumner, Washington, near Tacoma. She was the first of five children born to a mother barely out of her teens, who then left Lee and her second daughter with her mother-in-law in Santa Monica, California. This happened when Lee was still a toddler, and she grew up thinking that her grandmother, Lorraine Waldroop, was her mother. From her she learned some valuable skills that would provide the building blocks for her career. "My grandmother was perfect," Lee recalled in the interview with Krasnow in *Parade.* "I think of her decorating our birthday cakes. She built us a sandbox in her yard. We didn't have shovels, so she gave us serving spoons to use in the sand."

Lee's mother returned with a new husband around the time that Lee was about to begin first grade, and the family lived in Marina del Rey, a nearby Southern California community, for a time. Then her stepfather took a job in Washington State, and the family moved north. Her mother had three more children by then, but was often ill with migraine headaches; as the oldest child in the family, Lee became responsible for many of the household chores. Her mother, whom she refers to in her 2007 memoir as Vicky, "spent her days lying on the couch, taking pills and screaming at us," Lee wrote in for a book excerpt published by *Family Circle*. "When the welfare check arrived, I'd bike to the bank to deposit it. Then I paid our bills to ensure our gas and electricity weren't shut off." When Lee entered her teens, tensions between Vicky and her reached a crisis point, and she went to live with her biological father in Wisconsin.

After graduating from high school, Lee enrolled at the University of Wisconsin's LaCrosse campus with the goal of becoming a physical therapist, but found she was much more interested in the business courses she took. Working two jobs, she eventually dropped out of college and moved to Los Angeles, where her aunt and uncle lived; the couple had once tried to adopt Lee and her sister Cindy when Vicky abandoned them at Lorraine's, and she had remained close to them over the years. She found a job with an import-export company and began attending home-goods trade shows and county fairs as part of her work. Her living quarters were a single room in a house in the beachfront community of Malibu, and to decorate it she made some window treatments without a sewing machine by using wire coat hangers, which she bent into forms and then wrapped with swaths of fabric. When her aunt and uncle visited, they were so impressed with the result that her uncle suggested she talk to a welder friend of his, who might be able to replicate the wire forms.

The welder made the forms, and Lee took three weeks off from her jobs to sell her wares at the Los Angeles County Fair in Pomona. She won the blue ribbon in home decorations at the fair, and launched her Kurtain Kraft business with proceeds from her sales. With her sister Kimmy she traveled to other California county fairs in a van—for which she had traded her prized sports car—and gave demonstrations on how to use her Kurtain Kraft forms. The line sold so well on the fair circuit that Lee earned enough to make her own infomercial, and then launched her home-products line on the QVC home-shopping channel.

Lee's wares—which grew to include wall-stencil kits and garden pots already filled with seeds and fertilizer—expanded to mass retailers like Wal-Mart and Target, and she decided to branch out into cooking in the late 1990s. She enrolled at one of the famed Cordon Bleu cooking schools—in her case the Ottawa, Canada, outpost of the French culinary academy—but was dismayed by the complicated recipes. "They had us making bouillabaisse for three weeks," she explained to Mary Boone, a writer for the Tacoma *News Tribune*, "with the idea that we'd freeze it and have a year's worth of this wonderful homemade stew, and I started thinking that's good and fine, but what if you don't have three weeks to make soup? What if you have a job and kids and a husband and house?"

Lee began working on a cookbook that used convenience foods to create dishes that appeared to have been made from scratch. She called it the 70/30 strategy, laying out her philosophy to Colorado Springs *Gazette* writer Teresa J. Farney: "You purchase 70 percent of ready-made products, add 30 percent of your own ingenuity, personality and inspiration, and then take 100 percent of the credit!" Also known as convenience cuisine or speed-scratch cooking, this genre of cookbooks had been launched in early 1999 with Anne Bryn's immensely successful *Cake Mix Doctor*, which provided dessert recipes that relied on store-bought cake mixes.

By this point Lee had become the spokesperson for a home builder, KB Home, and then began dating its chief executive officer, Bruce Karatz. "Most women dream about a husband. "I never wanted to be married," she told Margot Dougherty in a *Los Angeles Magazine* interview, recalling that in previous relationships, "I kept thinking, 'Oh no, you are cramping my ... business!'" She and Karatz were wed in 2001 in a lavish wedding, but the always-frugal Lee spent her funds wisely. "I bought my own wedding dress off the rack for $800," she told Kimberly Cutter in *W*. "My husband was so appalled."

Through Karatz, Lee met art dealer Barbara Guggenheim, and showed her the first draft of her cookbook. Guggenheim was married to entertainment lawyer Bert Fields, who notified magazine editor Tina Brown about Lee's potential as the next Martha Stewart. At the time, Brown was editor of *Talk* magazine, which was part of the Miramax Studios empire founded by Harvey and Bob Weinstein. Brown arranged a meeting with Harvey Weinstein, who signed Lee immediately to a multimedia contract.

Lee's first book was *Sandra Lee Semi-Homemade Cooking*, and was published in the fall of 2002. It became a *New York Times* bestseller, and led to the debut of her own show on the Food Network, *Semi-Homemade Cooking with Sandra Lee,* in October of 2003. She was given a prime slot between two highly rated shows on the channel: Paula Deen's *Paula's Home Cooking* and *Rachael Ray's 30 Minute Meals.* "When I first started doing the show it took all day to get a single episode shot," Lee recalled in *Family Circle.* "I taught myself to talk to the camera as if I were speaking to Kimmy or my best friend Colleen."

Lee actually trademarked the term "semi-homemade," and went on to produce several more cookbooks, including 2003's *Sandra Lee Semi-Homemade Desserts* and *Semi-Homemade Grilling* in 2005, all of which boosted her popularity with busy working parents. "Her approach merely underlines a way of cooking that is rapidly growing in American culture," wrote Amanda Hesser in the *New York Times.* "While cake mixes and convenience foods have been around for decades, it is only recently that attitudes toward using them have shifted from embarrassment to allegiance."

Lee's Food Network show was a hit with viewers, and she became one of the channel's most popular personalities. She was often dubbed the next Martha Stewart, especially when Stewart's powerful multimedia empire seemed to be on the verge of collapsing when the original domestic diva was tarnished by an insider-trading scandal and was sentenced to prison for lying to federal investigators. There were several crucial differences, however, as Dougherty, the *Los Angeles Magazine* writer, pointed out. "Stewart addresses the tasteful sophisticate who's comfortable in the potting shed and at the stove, the woman with time on her hands. Lee gives hints to the young newlywed or the overextended mother who knows her way around Wal-Mart, harbors no ill will toward Velveeta, and wants to take the basics—soups, sandwiches, and apricot brandy—and make them her own."

Lee explained her reliance on brand names in her recipes as an aid to her readers and viewers, not a product endorsement. "If a recipe for potato salad doesn't turn out, maybe it's because you used sweet and sour mustard that was just too sugary," she explained to Boone in the Tacoma *News Tribune,* and asserted that by giving instructions to use specific brands, "I'm making cooking pretty much foolproof." Using convenience foods, she noted in another interview, was a way to spend less time in the kitchen. "The question isn't what's for dinner," she told Cutter in *W.* "The question is, 'What did you do today? Tell me about your day.' The point is to have more time to spend with your family, and what I offer is a way for people to do that without having to feed their kids McDonald's."

Lee's 70/30 philosophy has been disdained by some food writers, who criticize her recipes and reliance on brand-name items from supermarket shelves as a strategy that makes her recipes actually more expensive that making a comparable item from scratch. In Lee's cookbooks, noted Hesser in the *New York Times,* "she encourages a dislike for cooking, and gives people an excuse for feeding themselves and their families mediocre food filled with preservatives." But Lee's most outspoken critic was celebrity chef and television personality Anthony Bourdain, who served as a guest writer on food journalist Michael Ruhlman's blog, Ruhlman.com, in early 2007. Bourdain gave a rundown on the merits of various Food Network stars, praising some but excoriating Lee and Rachael Ray, another quick-meal advocate. Bourdain faulted Lee for relying on processed, preservative-laden foods high in fat, and termed her show "simply irresponsible programming."

In late 2007, Lee returned to the home-furnishings market after inking a deal with Waverly, the fabric and wallpaper manufacturer, and also published her memoir, *Sandra Lee: Made from Scratch.* She and Karatz divorced after five years of marriage, and she divides her time between Los Angeles and New York City, near to the Millbrook, New York, house—dubbed Sandyland by staffers—where her Food Network show is taped. She dedicated her first cookbook to her late grandmother, who had played such a formative role in life, and keeps a pair of Lorraine's shoes. "She said, 'Honey, until you walk in someone else's shoes, you don't know,'" Lee explained to Dougherty in the *Los Angeles Magazine* interview. "So I put them there to remind me."

Selected writings

Sandra Lee Semi-Homemade Cooking, Miramax Books (New York City), 2002.
Sandra Lee Semi-Homemade Desserts, Miramax, 2003.
Sandra Lee Semi-Homemade Grilling, Meredith Books (Des Moines, IA), 2006.
Sandra Lee Semi-Homemade Cooking Made Light, Meredith Books, 2006.
Sandra Lee Semi-Homemade Cool Kids Cooking, Meredith Books, 2006.
(With Laura Morton) *Sandra Lee: Made from Scratch* (memoir), Meredith Books, 2007.

Sources

Periodicals

Daily News (Los Angeles, CA), December 7, 2002, p. U14.
Family Circle, November 1, 2007.

Gazette (Colorado Springs, CO), March 5, 2003, p. FOOD1.

Los Angeles Business Journal, January 9, 2006, p. 3.

Los Angeles Magazine, December 2003, p. 121.

New York Times, October 1, 2003.

Parade, December 2, 2002.

Publishers Weekly, October 13, 2003, p. 73.

News Tribune (Tacoma, WA), October 23, 2002.

USA Today, May 5, 2006, p. 4D.

W, December 2002, p. 108.

Online

"Meet Sandra Lee," FoodNetwork.com, http://www.foodnetwork.com/food/sandra_lee/0,1974,FOOD_16936,00.html (January 19, 2008).

"Nobody Asked Me, But…," Ruhlman.com, http://blog.ruhlman.com/ruhlmancom/2007/02/guest_blogging_.html (January 19, 2008).

—Carol Brennan

Doris Lessing

Author

Born Doris May Tayler, October 22, 1919, in Kermansha, Persia; daughter of Alfred Cook (a farmer) and Emily Maude (a former nun and nurse; maiden name, McVeagh) Tayler; married Frank Charles Wisdom (a civil servant), 1939 (divorced, 1943); married Gottfried Anton Nicholas Lessing, 1945 (divorced, 1949); children: John (deceased), Jean (from first marriage); Peter (from second marriage).

Addresses: *Agent*—c/o Jonathan Clowes, Ltd., 10 Iron Bridge House, London NW1 8BD England.

Career

Worked as a nursemaid, a lawyer's secretary, a Hansard typist, switchboard operator, and a Parliamentary Commissioner's typist while living in Rhodesia, 1934-49; author, 1950—; published first book, *The Grass Is Singing*, 1950; published "Children of Violence" series, 1952-69; published "Canopus in Argos: Archives" series, 1979-83.

Member: Honorary fellow, National Institute of Arts and Letters, Modern Language Association, foreign honorary member, American Academy of Arts & Letters, 1974—; friend, Institute for Cultural Research.

Awards: Somerset Maugham Award, Society of Authors, for *Five: Short Novels*, 1954; Prix Médicis étranger Award, France, for *The Golden Notebook*, 1976; Austrian State Prize for European Literature, 1981; German Federal Republic Shakespeare Prize, 1982; W. H. Smith Literary Award, W. H. Smith retailer, for *The Good Terrorist*, 1986; Palermo Prize for *The Good Terrorist*, 1987; Premio Internazionale Mondello for *The Good Terrorist* 1987; Grinzane Cavour Award, Italian Cultural Institute, for *The Fifth Child*, 1989; honorary doctorate, Princeton University, 1989; honorary doctorate, Durham University, 1990; distinguished fellow, University of East Anglia, 1991; honorary doctorate, Warwick University, 1994; honorary doctorate, Bard College, 1994; James Tait Black Memorial Book Prize, University of Edinburgh, for *Under My Skin*, 1995; book prize, *Los Angeles Times*, for *Under My Skin*, 1995; honorary doctorate, Harvard University, 1995; named Woman of the Year, Norway, 1995; honorary doctorate, Open University, 1999; honorary doctorate, University of London, 1999; David Cohen British Literary Prize, 2001; Asturias Prize for Literature, Prince of Asturias Foundation, 2001; named Companion of Honour, British Royal Society of Literature, 2001; Golden PEN Award for Lifetime Distinguished Services, 2002; Nobel Prize for Literature, 2007.

Sidelights

The 2007 winner of the Nobel Prize for Literature, Doris Lessing has had a controversial career during which her fiction, nonfiction, plays, and poems touched on topics such as politics, interpersonal relationships, colonist Africa, the lives of women, mystical ideas, and mental breakdown. The author was hailed by Lesley Hazleton in the *New York Times* in 1982 as "widely considered one of the most honest, intelligent, and engaged writers of the day." Unafraid to take chances, Lessing counted intense realism, science fiction, and horror among the fictional genres she explored to greater or lesser success.

Lessing was born on October 22, 1919, in Kermansha, Persia. She is the daughter of British citizens Alfred Cook Tayler and his wife, Emily Maude McVeagh, a former nun. Her father was a World War I veteran who had reached the rank of captain and lost his leg in battle. At the time of her birth, he was working for the Imperial Bank of Persia, and had moved his family there after finding post-war Britain uninhabitable. On a whim, after attending an exposition in Britain, Tayler moved his family (including Lessing's younger brother, Harry) to the British colony of Southern Rhodesia in 1924, where he became a farmer despite a lack of experience in farming.

Lessing's childhood there was difficult and lonely, enveloped by the wide landscape and her poorly matched parents' unhappy marriage. The headstrong girl attended a Dominican convent school in Salisbury, Rhodesia, for four years until the age of 14, but was not impressed by the quality of teaching and returned home to pursue her education on her own. Lessing found what interested her, read everything she could on that topic, and then would move on to the next subject. While living in Rhodesia, she worked much of the time, and not only on the family farm. Throughout her childhood and early adulthood, Lessing was also employed as a nursemaid, a lawyer's secretary, a Hansard typist, and a Parliamentary Commissioner's typist.

Lessing worked in some of these positions in Salisbury, a city she returned to when she was 18 years old. While living a conventional life, she married her first husband, Frank Wisdom, in 1939 and had two children with him. Wisdom was a kind but uninteresting man, but Lessing felt smothered and realized over the course of her four-year marriage that she was not cut out for marriage and motherhood. The couple divorced in 1943, and she left her son and daughter with her husband. After the failure of her first marriage, Lessing became an active supporter of Communism and soon married again. In 1945, she impulsively wed Gottfried Lessing, a political refugee from Germany, and had another son, Peter. Again realizing she did not want to be married, Lessing divorced her husband in 1949 and left Africa.

Lessing then moved to London with her son, and already had her first novel in hand. She published her first book in 1950, *The Grass Is Singing*, and established herself as an important literary figure with the book's success. The novel reflected her awareness of race and color prejudice in Africa, something that contributed to the end of her first marriage.

In addition to putting out a collection of stories in 1952, *This Was the Old Chief's Country*, Lessing began her first series, "Children of Violence," that same year. The five novel series—which included *Martha Quest, A Proper Marriage, A Ripple from the Storm, Landlocked,* and *The Four-Gated City*—was also known as the "Martha Quest novels" and were published irregularly over the 1950s and 1960s. In the books, Lessing explored ideas of colonialism, racism, and psychology as Quest lives out her socialist beliefs and deals with color prejudice in Africa. Lessing also touched on autobiographical elements of her childhood in Rhodesia, including a depiction of her father and his striving to make his Rhodesian farm work through Quest's father.

As evidenced in the novels and the primary character, psychology and psychiatry became an interest of Lessing's in the mid-1950s. By 1956, Lessing abandoned her support of Communism after being disillusioned by the Soviet invasion of Hungary and Nikita Khrushchev's public denouncement of Stalinism. She soon was intensely interested in radical psychiatry, especially the ideas of R. D. Laing. She spent the next few years immersed in the topic and allowed it to greatly influence her thinking as a person and an author.

During this time period, Lessing also wrote what became her classic novel, *The Golden Notebook*. Published in 1962, the book depicts women of strength living independent lives and later became a celebrated feminist text, although Lessing later distanced herself from such a political idea. Despite Lessing's feelings, the novel had strong sales well into the 1990s and was translated into 18 languages.

By the mid-1960s, Lessing left radical psychiatry behind as she became disenchanted by Laing and his cohort, the American radical writer Clancy Sigal. She found a new primary intellectual force in Sufism, a mystical Middle Eastern spiritual philosophy she discovered by reading Idries Shah's 1964 book *The Sufis*. Sufis believe that one must be involved with the world to help reach universal harmony with the Absolute Being's spirit. In other words, Sufism takes the concept of cosmic evolution for mankind as an essential idea. Lessing did not consider herself a Sufi, per se, but a student of the philosophy. Sufism began seeping into her books of the late 1960s and early 1970s, reaching an apex in 1979.

In 1979, Lessing began publishing the second series of her career, in a genre thought to be the antithesis of her previous focus on intense realism: science fiction. Dubbed the "Canopus in Argos: Archives" series, she produced five books in four years: *Shikasta Re: Colonized Planet Five, The Marriage Between Zones Three, Four, and Five, The Sirian Experiments: The Report of Ambien II, of the Five, The Making of the Representative for Planet Eight,* and *Documents Relating to the Sentimental Agents in the Volyen Empire.* The series still touched on classic Lessing themes of social and sociological concerns as well as explored ideas which showed the distinct influence of Sufi philosophy on the author. Yet readers and critics alike were mystified by her desire to work in this genre and many found the books themselves difficult.

After completing "Canopus in Argos: Archives," Lessing continued to produce novels with regularity in the 1980s. While still doing some science fiction, she returned to her realistic roots as well. One novel of note was 1985's *The Good Terrorist,* which focused on a gullible woman, Alice Mellings, in post-World War II London. She belongs to a cluster of self-declared revolutionaries who want to join up with a larger group which will have them, preferably the Irish Republican Army or the Russians. Mellings is the mother figure of the group, providing them refuge in her home while dealing with her own sadness and desire for connection. Critics linked Mellings to Quest, with Anne Collins in *Maclean's* commenting, "the poignancy of the book and its compelling emotional power spring from the character of Alice."

Lessing continued to produce challenging works in the late 1980s and early 1990s, including the novel *The Fifth Child* and collection of sketches and short stories *The Real Thing.* The former is a horror story about a monster child born to a self-absorbed, nice, middle class family in London in the 1960s to 1980s. The birth and subsequent psychotic actions of Ben tears the family apart, creating a nightmare world, which can be interpreted as reflecting greater problems in society. When *The Fifth Child* was published in 1988, it was considered an instant classic and evoked strong reactions among readers and critics about its deeper meaning. In contrast, *The Real Thing* is more naturalistic, using her adopted home of London as the common bond between many of the

pieces as she shares observations about her life and typical Lessing stories about women and their relationships with men.

By the mid-1990s, Lessing became more personal in her writing. Leaving aside fiction for a time, she focused on nonfiction. In addition to a work on her visits back to Zimbabwe (as Southern Rhodesia was now known), she wrote her autobiography. Two well-received volumes came out in 1994 and 1997, *Under My Skin: Volume 1 of My Autobiography, to 1949* and *Walking in the Shade: Volume Two of My Autobiography, 1949—1962,* respectively. Lessing covered her childhood and young adulthood in Africa in *Under My Skin,* and focused primarily on her experiences in the male-dominated London literary scene and with Communism in the 1950s in the latter book.

While Lessing concentrated on touring and writing nonfiction for much of the 1990s, she produced at least one novel of significance. Her first novel since *The Fifth Child* was *Love, Again,* published in 1996. The novel centers on a 65-year-old woman, Sarah, who was widowed in young adulthood with two children to raise and falls in love with two men young enough to be her offspring. Sarah has worked at a fringe theatre for much of her life, and has feelings for a show's lead and director. While each has feelings for her, they will not sleep with her. Critics praised the book, believing it was somewhat autobiographical in nature.

Lessing continued to produce fiction at a steady rate in the late 1990s and early 2000s. The 2001 novel *The Sweetest Dream* (2002, U.S. edition) is a sweeping novel about the last five decades of Great Britain as experienced through three generations of women, their lives, and a common interest in the leftist movement. Reviewing the novel for London's *Sunday Telegraph,* Anne Chisholm found the book difficult to read, but noted the author's growth. Chisholm wrote, "Doris Lessing never lacked the moral courage or been afraid to change her mind. Here, she reconsiders and even rejects many of the ideas which have conditioned her life and writing."

Lessing explored the human condition in the four short novels which make up 2004's *The Grandmothers.* Three of them touch on love, while the fourth marks a return to science fiction. In 2006, her novel *The Story of General Dann and Mara's Daughter, Griot and the Snow Dog* went back to the characters she introduced in the 1999 novel *Mara and Dann: An Adventure.* Both were science fiction adventures set in the future during an ice age.

While Lessing continued to write as she neared 90 years of age, she was indifferent to learn that she had won the 2007 Nobel Prize in Literature for her impressive body of work. Linton Weeks of the *Washington Post* quoted her as saying "I can't say I'm overwhelmed with surprise.... I'm 88 years old and they can't give the Nobel to someone who's dead, so I think they were probably thinking they'd better give it to me now before I've popped off." Despite her cynicism, many critics believed she deserved the honor, which she accepted in a January of 2008 ceremony in London.

Lessing continued to write after receiving the award, including a 2008 novel that presents an alternate history about her parents, *Alfred and Emily*. When she was given the Nobel, Philip Hensher of the *Spectator* summed up her importance, stating "She is one of the greatest novelists in English."

Selected writings

Fiction

The Grass Is Singing, Crowell (New York City), 1950.
This Was the Old Chief's Country, M. Joseph (London), 1952.
Martha Quest (first in "Children of Violence" series), M. Joseph, 1952.
Five: Short Novels, M. Joseph, 1953.
A Proper Marriage (second in "Children of Violence" series), M. Joseph, 1954.
Retreat to Innocence, M. Joseph, 1956.
Habitat of Loving, Crowell, 1958.
A Ripple from the Storm (third in "Children of Violence" series), M. Joseph, 1958.
The Golden Notebook, Simon & Schuster (New York City), 1962.
A Man and Two Women, Simon & Schuster, 1963.
African Stories, Simon & Schuster, 1965.
Landlocked (fourth in "Children of Violence" series), MacGibbon & Kee (London), 1965.
The Four-Gated City (fifth in "Children of Violence" series), MacGibbon & Kee, 1969.
Briefing for a Descent into Hell, Knopf (New York City), 1971.
The Temptation of Jack Orkney and Other Stories, Knopf, 1972.
The Summer Before the Dark, Knopf, 1973.
The Memoirs of a Survivor, Knopf, 1975.
To Room Nineteen: Collected Stories, Vol. 1, Jonathan Cape (London), 1978.
The Temptation of Jack Orkney: Collected Stories, Vol. 2, Jonathan Cape, 1978.
Shikasta Re: Colonized Planet Five (first in the "Canopus in Argos: Archives" series), Knopf, 1979.

The Marriages between Zones Three, Four, and Five (second in the "Canopus in Argos: Archives" series), Knopf, 1980.
The Sirian Experiments: The Report of Ambien II, of the Five (third in the "Canopus in Argos: Archives" series), Knopf, 1981.
The Making of the Representative for Planet 8 (fourth in the "Canopus in Argos: Archives" series), Knopf, 1982.
Documents Relating to the Sentimental Agents in the Volyen Empire (fifth in the "Canopus in Argos: Archives" series), Knopf, 1983.
(As Jane Somers) *The Diary of a Good Neighbor*, Knopf, 1983.
(As Jane Somers) *If the Old Could ...*, Knopf, 1984.
The Good Terrorist, Knopf, 1985.
The Fifth Child, Knopf, 1988.
The Doris Lessing Reader, Knopf, 1989.
The Real Thing: Stories and Sketches, HarperCollins (New York City), 1992.
Love, Again HarperCollins, 1996.
Mara and Dann: An Adventure, HarperCollins, 1999.
The Old Age of El Magnificato, Flamingo (London), 2000.
Ben, in the World, HarperCollins, 2000.
The Sweetest Dream, HarperCollins, 2002.
The Grandmothers: Four Short Novels, HarperCollins, 2004.
The Story of General Dann and Mara's Daughter, Griot and the Snow Dog, HarperCollins, 2006.
The Cleft, HarperCollins (New York City), 2007.
Alfred and Emily, Fourth Estate (London), 2008.

Nonfiction

Going Home, M. Joseph, 1957.
In Pursuit of the English: A Documentary, Simon & Schuster, 1961.
Particularly Cats, Simon & Schuster, 1967.
(Edited by Paul Schlueter) *A Small Personal Voice: Essays, Reviews, Interviews*, Knopf, 1974.
Prisons We Choose to Live Inside, Harper & Row (New York City), 1987.
The Wind Blows Away Our Words, Vintage (New York City), 1987.
Particularly Cats ... And Rufus, Knopf, 1991.
African Laughter: Four Visits to Zimbabwe, HarperCollins, 1992.
Under My Skin: Volume 1 of My Autobiography, to 1949, HarperCollins, 1994.
Walking in the Shade: Volume Two of My Autobiography, 1949—1962, HarperCollins, 1997.
Time Bites, HarperCollins, 2004.

Plays

Mr. Dollinger, produced in Oxford, England, 1958.
Each In His Own Wilderness, produced in London, England, 1958.
The Truth About Billy Newton, produced in Salisbury, England, 1961.
Play with a Tiger, M. Joseph (London, England), 1962.

Poems

Fourteen Poems, Scorpion Press (London, England), 1959.

Sources

Books

Complete Marquis Who's Who Biographies, Marquis Who's Who, 2008.
Concise Major 21st Century Writers, vol. 3, Thomson Gale, 2006.

Periodicals

Boston Globe, October 26, 1997, p. N1.
Economist, October 22, 1994, p. 103.
Evening Standard (London, England), January 31, 2008, p. A21.
Herald (Glasgow, Scotland), May 3, 2008, p. 9.
Independent (London, England), April 13, 1996, p. 10.
Maclean's, September 23, 1985, p. 65; June 6, 1988, p. T4; August 24, 1992, p. 62; April 15, 1996, p. 64.
Newsweek, May 22, 1978, p. 75.
New York Times, July 25, 1982, sec. 6, p. 21; June 14, 1988, p. C21; November 2, 1994, p. C1; February 3, 2004, p. E3.
Ottawa Citizen, February 8, 1998, p. E6.
Spectator, November 15, 2003, pp. 51-52; October 20, 2007, p. 71.
Sunday Telegraph (London, England), September 16, 2001, p. 12.
USA Today, December 1, 1994, p. 9D.
Vancouver Sun (Vancouver, British Columbia, Canada), March 11, 2006, p. F16.
Washington Post, December 29, 1994, p. C1; October 12, 2007, p. C1.
Washington Post Book World, September 22, 1985, p. 4.

Online

Contemporary Authors Online, Thomson Gale, 2007.

—A. Petruso

Arthur D. Levinson

Chief Executive Officer of Genentech

Born Arthur David Levinson, March 31, 1950, in Seattle, WA; son of Sol and Malvina Levinson; married Rita May Liff, December 17, 1978; children: son Jesse, daughter Anya. *Education:* University of Washington, B.S., 1972; Princeton University, Ph.D., 1977.

Addresses: *Office*—Genentech, 1 DNA Way, South San Francisco, CA 94080-4990.

Career

Joined Genentech in 1980 as senior research scientist; director of Cell Genetics department, 1987-89; vice president of Research Technology, 1989-90; vice president of Research, 1990-93; senior vice president, 1993-95; president and chief executive officer, 1995—.

Awards: Corporate Leadership Award, National Breast Cancer Coalition, 1999; named one of the Best Managers of 2003 by *BusinessWeek*.

Sidelights

Arthur D. Levinson began his career with the northern California biotechnology company Genentech as a molecular biologist and rose to become its chief executive officer (CEO). Scientist-turned-CEOs are somewhat rare in the corporate world, but Levinson has won the trust of Wall Street analysts and investors alike for helping make Genentech a leader in its field. "I'd like to defy con-

ventional thinking," he told *Forbes* journalist Zina Moukheiber. "It's easier for a scientist to understand business concepts than it is for a businessperson to understand scientific concepts."

Levinson was born in 1950 in Seattle, Washington, and planned on a career as an astronomer or doctor. He attended the University of Washington, where in his junior year he took a course taught by a prominent genetic scientist, Lee Hartwell, who had done groundbreaking work into the origins of cancer from a cellular standpoint. Levinson became so intrigued by the course that he switched majors to molecular biology, which investigates the interactions between the various systems of a cell, such as DNA, RNA, and the production of proteins. After receiving his undergraduate degree in 1972 Levinson went on to Princeton University, where he earned his doctorate degree in 1977.

Prior to joining Genentech, Levinson did postdoctoral research at the University of California at San Francisco, and wrote a much-discussed scientific paper on the biochemistry of cancer. There he also gained a reputation as somewhat of a maverick, known for occasionally donning a pith helmet and carrying a toy rifle in presentations or for group photos to impart his belief that scientists needed to have keen hunting instincts in order to make progress in their work. In 1980, he surprised many of his academic colleagues by moving to the private sector as a senior research scientist at Genentech. The South San Francisco company was a relatively new firm, founded just four years earlier, and Levinson was one of the first researchers hired there. The company was established with the aim of devising new ways to replicate DNA proteins to create a new class of biologics, the drugs that mimic the body's own natural disease-fighting properties. Genentech's first success was the manufacture of synthetic human insulin, which went on the market in 1982. Previously, diabetics injected insulin made from the pancreatic glands of cows, pigs, horses, or fish.

During the 1980s, Levinson pioneered mammalian-cell manufacturing at Genentech, which was an experimental idea at the time and not considered cost-effective enough to pursue in earnest. Until then, biotech drugs were manufactured by growing the compounds inside bacteria cells. Levinson experimented with hamsters, and his and Genentech's breakthroughs helped make the use of rodent cells standard in the industry. In 1987, he became director of Cell Genetics at Genentech, where he was involved in cloning the HER2 gene, which is linked to an advanced form of breast cancer. That work led to Genentech's breakthrough drug, Herceptin, which targeted that HER2 gene. In 1989, Levinson was named vice president of Research Technology, and became a senior vice president in 1993.

Levinson advanced to the post of president and chief executive officer at Genentech in 1995 when its board ousted G. Kirk Raab after a number of issues had surfaced. Some years earlier, Genentech had struck a deal with Hoffmann-La Roche when it was in financial trouble; the Swiss pharmaceutical giant invested in Genentech, a publicly traded company, in exchange for a 60 percent stake. Raab resigned over negotiations with Hoffmann-La Roche that would give the Swiss company a greater stake in Genentech. There were also other problems at the company, including a pending lawsuit over kickbacks its sales representatives allegedly paid to physicians, and federal criminal charges about promotion of off-label uses to physicians for another Genentech success story, human growth hormone.

One of Levinson's first acts as CEO was to hold a mass meeting of its 3,000-plus employees in which he urged everybody to move forward and act responsibly. Over the next few years, he implemented several changes at Genentech to ensure that legal problems would no longer trouble the company. The pace of Genentech's scientific breakthroughs also accelerated rapidly under Levinson's guidance, and its immensely successful new biotech drugs include the aforementioned Herceptin, which came onto the market in 1998; Xolair, an asthma treatment, and Raptiva, a psoriasis drug, both in

2003; and Avastin, approved first for colon cancer patients in 2004 and later for sufferers of lung cancer. None are marketed directly to consumers in television commercials, with Genentech preferring to convince physicians and other medical professionals about the drugs' efficacy. "These ads with people running through flowers and dancing are distasteful," Levinson told *BusinessWeek*'s Arlene Weintraub.

Hoffmann-La Roche is still a majority shareholder of Genentech, but allows Levinson to run the company as he sees fit. That independence has helped Genentech post impressive numbers, including $2.4 billion in earnings in 2006. Now with a workforce of 11,000 employees, Genentech has a prestigious reputation among scientists and researchers, and receives around 15,000 resumes every month. Its employees are encouraged to spend 25 percent of their work hours on research projects of personal interest, and are free to use all of the top-of-the-line scientific technology at the company in doing so. "You don't get 40 motivated people by telling them to get behind someone else's idea," Levinson explained to *Financial Times* writer Victoria Griffith.

Levinson has a small office, measuring just 9 by 12 feet, and favors jeans, not suits. He sits on the Board of Apple Computer, and has a son and daughter with his wife Rita, a childhood playmate. At Genentech, the rather unusual corporate culture that was present when he began working there in the early 1980s remains in place under his watch: Employees are expected to work long hours, but are known to unwind at annual Friday-afternoon parties, and the company is known for its elaborate office pranks. When a joke cover for the 2005 annual corporate report was submitted as a mock-up during a meeting, Levinson liked the gallery of images from Genentech costume parties over the years so much that he had it set as the back cover for the actual shareholders' report. "You'd think with the kind of success we've had that more people would see us as a model," he told Griffith, "but I just don't see a lot of companies moving in our direction."

Sources

BusinessWeek, October 6, 2003, p. 72; May 17, 2005.
Financial Times, February 11, 2005, p. 12.
Forbes, July 26, 1999, p. 133.
U.S. News & World Report, February 19, 2007, pp. 46-50.

—*Carol Brennan*

Phillip Lim

Fashion designer

Born c. 1974, in Thailand; emigrated to the United States; son of a professional poker player and a seamstress. *Education:* Studied home economics at California State University, Long Beach, early 1990s.

Addresses: *Office*—3.1 Phillip Lim, 260 W. 39th St., 9th Fl., New York, NY 10018.

Career

Held retail jobs at Benetton and Barneys New York in Southern California, late 1980s-early 1990s; began as intern for designer Katayone Adeli, became design assistant; founding creative director, Development, 2000-04; launched 3.1 Phillip Lim, 2005.

Awards: Swarovski Award for Emerging Talent, Council of Fashion Designers of America, 2007.

Sidelights

New York-based fashion designer Phillip Lim has steadily gained a devoted clientele for his streamlined clothing, sold under the label 3.1 Phillip Lim, that steers clear of the latest trends. In June of 2007, his status as a newcomer to watch was confirmed by his win of the highly coveted Swarovski Award for Emerging Talent from the Council of Fashion Designers of America. Weeks later, Lim opened his first freestanding retail store in New York City's Soho district. His clothes have earned enthusiastic praise in the fashion press, and com-parisons to the equally cult-status favorite, Marc Jacobs. "The girls I design for are very modern, very feminine girls who are very strong-willed," he told Maureen Callahan of the *New York Post.*

Lim was born in the early 1970s to a Chinese couple who were living in Thailand at the time, which has a large ethnic-Chinese population. The family moved on to neighboring Cambodia, but was forced to flee when a devastating civil war erupted. Lim and his five brothers and sisters eventually settled in the Southern California seaside community of Huntington Beach in Orange County. His father earned a living as a professional poker player—Lim would later say he inherited some of his father's risk-taking personality—while his mother worked long hours as a seamstress. At home, she made her children's clothes, and Lim recalls that he insisted his be unfussy and made from a narrow range of fabric shades. "I would direct my mother when she made my clothes," he said in an interview with *New York* magazine writer Amy Larocca. "I look at pictures of myself when I was 5 years old and I think that, yes, that is exactly what I like."

Lim's nascent interest in fashion led to a job at Ben-etton during his high school years, and he enrolled at California State University's Long Beach campus as a finance major to appease his parents, who hoped for professional careers for all of their children. Eventually he balked one day, as he said in the *New York Post* interview with Callahan. "One day in accounting we were going through equations and graphs and I was just like, I can't do this. I can't do this! I was getting physically ill," he recalled, and immediately switched to home economics classes instead. His mother was predictably upset when he told her of his career plans, he said in another interview, this one with *Times* of London writer Lisa Armstrong. "All she foresaw was 18 hours a day of struggling for $3 a hour," Lim recalled. "I said, 'It's not gonna be like that, I'm not going to be a seamstress.'"

Lim moved on to a job at Barneys New York, the premium retailer, at its Costa Mesa, California, outpost in Orange County. Unpacking boxes one day in the storeroom, he came across a shipment of clothing from a young, Iranian-American designer, Katayone Adeli, who had also grown up in California. Adeli's designs had a minimalism that appealed to Lim, and so he called the telephone number on the box to inquire about a possible internship. Lim eventually became Adeli's design assistant, but lost the post when Adeli decided to move her business to New York City. Lim was committed to remaining in California, and found his next role when a friend with a surfwear business offered to back him in a new label. Launched in the fall of 2000, Lim's line was sold under the name "Development" and featured interesting, modern pieces for the women's contemporary market. He and his business partners parted ways a few years later over creative differences. "I wanted to make more intricate things, special things, because I saw that everyone else was throwing stones on T-shirts and calling them contemporary, and I just wanted to elevate the quality," he told Callahan in the *New York Post* interview. "And the company was growing healthy, but they wanted to grow faster, meaning a sacrifice, and I wasn't ready to do that."

Lim's experiences at Development had introduced him to a woman who became one of his closest friends, Wen Zhou. Of Chinese heritage, too, she was the daughter of a seamstress and displayed a canny knack for business even in her teens, and was the chief executive officer of her own fabric company by the age of 21. When Lim lost his job with Development in late 2004, Zhou bought him a plane ticket to visit her in her New York City. "By Friday she said, 'Okay. That's enough. I'm tired of you crying,'" Lim told *New York*'s Larocca. "'Let's start a company.'" Wen invested $750,000 of her own assets, gave Lim a room in her apartment and told him to come up with a collection in two months' time. They named their venture "3.1 Phillip Lim," because both were 31 years old at the time.

Lim's first 3.1 collection immediately interested buyers from two important stores, his onetime employer, Barneys New York, and Fred Segal, the Los Angeles-based retailer known for its cutting-edge fashion. Zhou's investment paid off, with 3.1 Phillip Lim selling $2.8 million in its first six months in business, and signing up 150 stores interested in carrying his line. The fashion press began writing enthusiastic paeans to Lim's cool, clean silhouettes and luxurious, but wearable and surprisingly affordable clothes. Lim added handbags, shoes, and other accessories in 2006, and a menswear line debuted in time for the spring 2007 season. For fall 2007, sales reached the $12 million mark for that season's line alone, and Lim's label was now in 300 stores.

In July of 2007, Lim opened his first freestanding retail store on Mercer Street in New York City's Soho neighborhood. The retail space was finished ahead of time and even came in slightly below cost—both rarities in fashion and retail that Lim attributes to his and Zhou's combined vigilance. "I'm a very balanced person. I understand what the bottom line is," he told Nandini D'Souza of *WWD*. "It's not like every day Wen is like, 'Phillip, you're over budget.' Actually, I'm always under budget and always ahead of time."

Sources

Daily News Record, April 23, 2007, p. 16.
New York, July 30, 2007.
New York Post, January 30, 2006, p. 36.
New York Times, June 7, 2007.
Times (London, England), May 2, 2007, p. 9.
WWD, January 3, 2006, p. 24S; July 12, 2007, p. 6.

—*Carol Brennan*

David Lindsay-Abaire

AP Images

Playwright and screenwriter

Born David Lindsay, c. 1970, in Boston, MA; married Christine Abaire (an actress); children: Nicholas. *Education:* Earned a degree in drama from Sarah Lawrence College, c. 1992; completed the Lila Acheson Wallace American Playwrights Program at the Juilliard School.

Addresses: *Home*—Brooklyn, NY.

Career

Worked summers in a circuit-board factory; first play, *Mario's House of Italian Cuisine,* staged at his high school, Milton Academy, c. 1984; *A Show of Hands* premiered at Sarah Lawrence College; *A Devil Inside* produced at the SoHo Repertory Theater, New York City, January, 1997; other plays include *Fuddy Meers,* 1999; *Kimberly Akimbo,* commissioned for the South Coast Repertory Theater, Costa Mesa, CA, 2001; *Wonder of the World,* 2001; *Rabbit Hole,* 2006; author of scripts for the Broadway stage-musical versions of *High Fidelity,* 2006, and *Shrek,* 2008; credited as a writer on two films, *Robots* (2006) and *Inkheart* (2007).

Awards: Pulitzer Prize for drama for *Rabbit Hole,* 2007.

Sidelights

Playwright David Lindsay-Abaire won the 2007 Pulitzer Prize for Drama for his acclaimed Broadway play, *Rabbit Hole.* The tale of a family grieving over the unexpected death of their only child, the drama was Lindsay-Abaire's first serious-minded work for the stage and earned strong praise from critics for its deft touch with such delicate subject matter. It starred *Sex and the City*'s Cynthia Nixon as the unraveling mother around whom the story revolves, a role was slated to be reprised by Nicole Kidman in film adaptation planned for 2009.

Born in the early 1970s, David Lindsay grew up in the predominantly working-class section of South Boston, Massachusetts, known as the longtime home to Irish-American families like his. He would add the "Abaire" to his surname after marrying Christine Abaire. His mother worked in a factory, and his father at the Boston-area fruit-delivery hub in nearby Chelsea. At the age of 12, Lindsay won a scholarship to Milton Academy in Milton, Massachusetts, a suburb of Boston. This prestigious private school dated back to 1798 and had an alumni roster that included members of the Kennedy political dynasty. As a day student at Milton, Lindsay was a standout wrestler but quit the team when he decided to try out for the school play in ninth grade. Not long afterward, he wrote his first play after a friend suggested they collaborate on a project, asserting "'you should write it because you're the funny one,'" Lindsay-Abaire recalled in an interview with Jenelle Riley for *Back Stage West.* "Having never written a play before, I said okay. Then I wrote an 11th-grade play and a 12th-grade play."

Lindsay-Abaire went on to Sarah Lawrence College in the New York City area, where he studied acting, but took some playwriting courses to fill in his schedule. After this initial training, his first effort was staged at the school, and the warm reception of this play, *A Show of Hands,* helped decide his career direction. "The audience really seemed to like it," he told another *Back Stage* interviewer, Raven Snook. "It dawned on me that playwriting seemed so much easier than acting."

After graduating from Sarah Lawrence, Lindsay-Abaire began entering playwriting contests that he found in the *Dramatists Sourcebook,* a compendium of theater companies, competitions, and literary agents. He won a contest sponsored by the Trustus Theatre in Columbia, South Carolina, and traveled there for the honor; while there, the second-place finisher suggested he apply to the Juilliard School, one of the most esteemed performing-arts training institutions in the United States. Its Lila Acheson Wallace American Playwrights Program was notoriously difficult to win admission to, but came with an enticing perk, no tuition fee. "I explained that I didn't have the money for graduate school and he told me that there was no tuition," Lindsay-Abaire recalled in the interview with Snook about this conversation with the other playwright. "I was like 'Wait, it's free? I applied right away.'"

Lindsay-Abaire was one of the handful—between three and five new students every year—of playwriting hopefuls who entered the Wallace program, where his teachers were two well-known figures, Marsha Norman—who won a Pulitzer Prize in 1983 for her drama *'night, Mother*—and Christopher Durang, author of the first play that Lindsay-Abaire ever appeared in back at Milton Academy in his ninth-grade year: *A History of the American Film.* The Wallace program does not grant a degree or grade its participants' work, but it does offer an invaluable chance for participants to hone their craft, especially with guidance from occasional visiting teachers such as Terrence McNally. As a program participant, Lindsay-Abaire was required to submit ten pages of a script each week to the program's master class. Two days later, Juilliard drama students would do a read-through of the pages in a workshop-style setting.

After finishing the two-year Wallace program, Lindsay-Abaire began in the late 1990s to make a name for himself with plays at the SoHo Repertory Theater. One of them was *A Devil Inside,* described by *New York Times* writer D. J. R. Bruckner as "a fair test of how convincingly lunatic every member of the cast can be," with dialogue "calculated to sound like improvisation by dazed people addicted to bad jokes." Other works of Lindsay-Abaire's from this period include *The L'il Plays* and *Snow Angel,* but it was the debut of his comedy *Fuddy Meers* at the Manhattan Theatre Club in the autumn of 1999 that gained the young playwright his first serious critical attention. Vincent Canby, the estimable *New York Times* reviewer, hailing him as "a smart new playwright to be watched," compared the lively, farcical tone of the play to some of Durang's works. Canby wrote: "Mr. Lindsay-Abaire is, possibly, an original. He also can write lines that haunt as they amuse."

The title of *Fuddy Meers* derives from the speech impediment of one of its characters, who has suffered a stroke. The lead figure is disabled by a different, most unusual affliction, however: this pleasant, polite homemaker named Claire awakens each morning with amnesia. She wanders off with a shady man who takes her to meet a woman who claims to be her mother. "*Fuddy Meers* is, on one level, the sort of abused-woman-at-the-crossroads tale that is a mildewed staple of television movies," noted Ben Brantley, another critic from the *New York Times.* "On another level, it's a wisecracking, self-conscious dysfunctional family comedy, which is about all comedies seem to be these days."

Around this same period, Lindsay-Abaire signed a deal with a major Hollywood studio, 20th Century-Fox, to write screenplays. Because he had never written for film, his contacts there suggested that he write one just for practice, but they were excited at the road-trip/comedy he turned in, and for a time the name of British actor Hugh Grant was discussed for the lead. An executive shuffle at the studio put the project on hold, and then Lindsay-Abaire was asked to make major revisions that would have considerably altered the story structure. He did wind up working on two other scripts that were produced several years later—*Robots* and *Inkheart*—though he claimed his actual contribution to each was negligible. "In Hollywood, you're just a guy for hire," he told Snook in the interview for *Back Stage.* "They pay you through the nose and in return you have no power. They do what they want with your script and they give you pages of notes and they contradict themselves 17 times over."

Lindsay-Abaire's next play was *Kimberly Akimbo,* which was commissioned for the South Coast Repertory Theater in Costa Mesa, California. It premiered there in April of 2001 and was staged at the

Manhattan Theatre Club a year later. Its story centers on a young woman afflicted with a rare genetic condition that causes her to age prematurely. The lead role was played by Marylouise Burke, who had appeared in most of Lindsay-Abaire's plays. Again, the *New York Times'* Brantley gave it a glowing review, terming it a play that manages to be several things: "a shrewd satire, a black comedy and a heartbreaking study of how time wounds everyone. And while its tone initially suggests a dysfunctional family sitcom … the production keeps confounding your expectations of how you're going to respond to a given scene."

Lindsay-Abaire's next work, which premiered at the Manhattan Theatre Club in late 2001, scored an impressive big-name star for its lead. *Wonder of the World* featured *Sex and the City* actor Sarah Jessica Parker—on break from the hit HBO series—as a mild-mannered schoolteacher who finds something odd in her husband's dresser drawer, which prompts her to suddenly walk out on the marriage. She boards a bus bound for Niagara Falls, determined to fulfill a long list of goals she carries with her that represent a life she once hoped to experience. Reviews of the play were mixed, however. "The deftly bizarre jokes, the outlandish symbols, the double-edged tone of voice are all in plain view," noted the *New York Times'* Brantley, comparing this work to *Fuddy Meers*. "But they only rarely cohere into a three-dimensional landscape."

In 2003, Lindsay-Abaire enrolled in a musical-theater workshop at the New Dramatists theater company in New York City. He explained why in an interview with the *New York Times'* John Hodgman. "Having never really collaborated with anyone, I thought I should learn how to sit in a room with people and work with them," he reflected, and went on to explain that the workshop "basically laid out the rules of how to work together, and I went by the rules, and I had a really good time." The learning experience led to new work, including the musical adaptation of *High Fidelity,* the novel by Nick Hornby that was turned into a 2000 film starring John Cusack. He also signed on to pen the script for a stage-musical version of the successful animated movie *Shrek*.

Lindsay-Abaire's Pulitzer Prize-winning drama *Rabbit Hole* showed touches of comedy, but as Brantley's *New York Times* review noted, the drama about the unexpected death of a small child "inspires such copious weeping among its audience that you wonder early on if you should have taken a life jacket." The play premiered at the Manhattan Theatre Club in February of 2006, this time with another *Sex and the*

City star, Cynthia Nixon, in the lead. Nixon played Becca, the woman whose son, Danny, died several months earlier when he was hit by a car and who is finding it exceedingly difficult to cope. Her husband, Howie, secretly watches old videotapes of Danny, while her mother—played by Tyne Daly—tries to commiserate with her over the fact that Becca's brother died of a drug overdose several years earlier. Further complicating Becca's grief is the fact that her irresponsible sister is now pregnant. When the high school student responsible for the accident appears on their doorstep with a science-fiction story he has written about an alternate, parallel universe—the "rabbit hole" of the title and a reference to Lewis Carroll's *Alice in Wonderland*—finally a semblance of closure seems to come for all.

Rabbit Hole earned Lindsay-Abaire accolades, with many critics noting that the absurdist humor of his previous plays had vanished. Instead, wrote David Rooney in *Variety*, "the playwright has crafted a drama that's not just a departure but a revelation—an intensely emotional examination of grief, laced with wit, insight, compassion and searing honesty." Brantley, writing in the *New York Times*, gave it a glowing review, finding it an impressive departure and a career turning point. "The sad, sweet release of *Rabbit Hole* lies precisely in the access it allows to the pain of others, in its meticulously mapped empathy," Brantley declared; he also praised the playwright, cast, and director Daniel Sullivan. "This anatomy of grief doesn't so much jerk tears as tap them, from a reservoir of feelings common to anyone who has experienced the landscape-shifting vacuum left by a death in the family."

Lindsay-Abaire explained the origins of *Rabbit Hole* in the interview with Riley for *Back Stage West*, recalling that when he was at Juilliard, Marsha Norman—whose Pulitzer Prize-winning drama *'night, Mother* centered on a final telephone conversation between a mother and her grown daughter who is determined to commit suicide that night—had once told her students "that if we wanted to write a good play, we should write about the thing that scares us most in the world," Lindsay-Abaire said, and he remembered thinking at the time that he felt unable to tap into that. "A few years later I had a son, and when he was three years old, I heard a couple stories about friends of friends who had children die very suddenly and unexpectedly." In contemplating such an event befalling his own household, Lindsay-Abaire recalled, he could barely grasp the depths of grief that a parent would suffer. "Then I thought, 'Oh, this is what Marsha was talking about.'"

Selected writings

Plays

A Devil Inside, produced at the SoHo Repertory Theater, New York City, January 1997.

Fuddy Meers, produced at the Manhattan Theatre Club, New York City, November 1999.

Wonder of the World, produced at the Manhattan Theatre Club, November 2001; published by Overlook/Tusk (New York City), 2005.

Kimberly Akimbo, commissioned for the South Coast Repertory Theater, Costa Mesa, CA, premiered April 2001, also produced at the Manhattan Theatre Club, November 2002.

Rabbit Hole, produced at the Manhattan Theatre Club, February 2006.

Sources

Back Stage, September 28, 2001, p. 7.

Back Stage West, October 5, 2006, p. 11.

New York Times, January 23, 1997; February 25, 1999; November 3, 1999; November 21, 1999; November 2, 2001; February 5, 2003; February 13, 2005; February 3, 2006.

Variety, November 5, 2001, p. 32; February 6, 2006, p. 85.

—Carol Brennan

Liesel Litzenburger

Author

Born c. 1967, in Petoskey, MI; married Hank. *Education:* Earned B.A. from the University of Michigan; Western Michigan University, M.F.A., 1993.

Addresses: *Home*—Grand Rapids, MI. *Office*—c/o Random House, 1745 Broadway, New York, NY 10019.

Career

Editor of trivia book series; creative-writing instructor at various colleges, including Saginaw Valley State University, University of Michigan, Interlochen Arts Academy, St. Mary's College, and New College (Sarasota, FL); assistant professor of creative writing, Central Michigan University, 2001—; published first novel, *Now You Love Me,* 2001; book reviewer for the *Chicago Tribune, Detroit Free Press,* and other publications.

Sidelights

Liesel Litzenburger's debut novel was barely noticed in the mainstream press, but *Now You Love Me* did manage to land her a deal with Random House. Her second book, *The Widower,* earned generally positive reviews upon its release in 2006 and even prompted a re-issue of her first title. "Everything that's happened has been a pleasant surprise," the college writing professor said in an interview with Marta Salij for the *Detroit Free Press.*

Born in Petoskey, Michigan, Litzenburger is a sixth-generation Michiganian and grew up in the nearby summer resort community of Harbor Springs—a town largely deserted in the winter months save for its old-timer families, hers among them. She was an avid reader as a child, and well aware of a famous literary connection in her family: Twentieth century American writer Ernest Hemingway spent childhood summers near Harbor Springs, and Litzenburger's grandmother was a close friend of Hemingway's sister, who still lived in the original Walloon Lake summer home belonging to the Hemingway family. Litzenburger's own family's legacy included an appreciation for a narrative thread, as she wrote in a biography that appeared on her official Web page: She noted that she hailed from "a long line of storytellers; I'm just the first one to get the sentences down on the page."

Litzenburger's family briefly decamped from northern Michigan to Fort Worth, Texas, but later returned to the Walloon Lake area. In the early 1980s, when she was in high school, she visited Brazil as an exchange student—an experience eerily foreshadowed in the first piece of fiction she ever wrote back when she was eight or nine years old. The story, as she recalled on her Web site, "involves a kidnapping and espionage plot in Brazil. Ironically, when I ended up in Brazil years later, I found myself living in a town that looked a lot like the one I had invented in that childhood novel. I think the line between writing and life can sometimes be pleasantly blurred."

At the University of Michigan, Litzenburger studied English, and after earning her undergraduate degree went to work as an editor for a trivia-book series. She returned to school for a graduate degree in writing at Western Michigan University, which she earned in 1993, and then held a variety of college teaching jobs while churning out short stories for literary journals and book reviews for the *Chicago Tribune* and *Detroit Free Press,* among other publications. By 2001 she had landed a job at Central Michigan University as an assistant professor of creative writing, and stints in writers' workshops at the MacDowell Colony and Yaddo helped her bring her first novel, *Now You Love Me,* to completion. The 2001 debut was published by Carnegie-Mellon University Press and sold a respectable number of copies, despite a lack of marketing budget common to such small academic publishing houses. The title was, however, discovered by a well-known editor at Random House named Shaye Areheart, who signed Litzenburger and helped bring her next work, *The Widower,* to fruition in 2006.

This time, Litzenburger's book benefited from a modest publicity campaign that resulted in good reviews from several sources, including the *New York Times.* Critics liked her tale of a lonely orchard owner in northern Michigan who is nursed back to health by his longtime employee after the death of his wife. The story takes place in a rural Upper Peninsula community where nearly everyone knows one another—and one another's family secrets—and centers on Swan Robey, age 37, despondent after an auto accident on an icy road has killed his wife and resulted in injuries that confine him to bed. His apple-harvesting associate is Grace Blackwater, who has been secretly in love with him for some time. The plot moves forward with the return of her uncle, Joseph Geewa, to town after two decades in prison for a crime in which the weapon remains undiscovered. That mystery, along with the discovery of an abandoned infant in Robey's orchard, propels the story toward its conclusion and unites this trio of lonely characters.

A few reviewers felt that Litzenburger had wrapped up *The Widower* a bit too tidily, such as *New York Times Book Review* critic Julia Scheeres, but commended her style. "Although Litzenburger's plot may be troublesome, her prose often soars," Scheeres asserted. "When a character steps into the frigid winter night, her lungs 'feel like they've been swabbed out with rubbing alcohol.' A woman met in a bar smells of 'dried pine needles and gasoline, like something about to catch fire.' A blackbird swoops past a window 'like a thrown shoe.'" It was a sentiment echoed, first in *Booklist* by Carol Haggas, who wrote that "despite a surfeit of too neat coincidences, Litzenburger's elegiac debut novel abounds with searching lyricism," and then in *Publishers Weekly,* whose reviewer granted that though the novel "leans heavily on implausible encounters, Litzenburger's prose lends luster and mystery to an otherwise conventional story." A writer for the newspaper of Litzenburger's new hometown, Mary Ann Sabo in the *Grand Rapids Press,* called the book "a beautiful meditation on fate and love." Sabo commended "one particularly lovely chapter" in which Litzenburger "shifts the narration duties from Swan to Grace to Ray and then back, as effortlessly as a relay team hands its baton from one runner to the next. She takes tremendous care with words and ideas, layering them effortlessly to create these beautiful, wounded souls."

Thanks to the success of *The Widower,* Litzenburger's first novel was reissued several months later. This time, *Now You Love Me* scored several prominent reviews, including a recommendation from *Entertainment Weekly.* The plot centered on nine-year-old Annie, who finds herself on an odd journey with her unbalanced mother and little brother in a car stolen out of their neighbor's driveway. Using a single narrative perspective—that of a preternaturally wise Annie—"lends both innocence and distance to the drama," declared *Entertainment Weekly* writer Jennifer Armstrong. It also allowed Litzenburger to present Paige, Annie's unconventional mother, in a more appealing way. "She's lovable," Litzenburger explained to Salij in the interview for the *Detroit Free Press* about the novel. "Sure, she's never going to win Mother of the Year, but she's a free spirit, and I think a lot of women want to be her."

Selected writings

Now You Love Me, Carnegie-Mellon University Press (Pittsburgh, PA), 2001; Crown Publishing/Three Rivers Press (New York City), 2007.
The Widower, Shaye Areheart Books/Crown Publishing (New York City), 2006.

Sources

Periodicals

Booklist, June 1, 2006, p. 37.
Detroit Free Press, October 15, 2006; May 8, 2007.
Entertainment Weekly, March 2, 2007, p. 72.
Grand Rapids Press, September 3, 2006, p. J5.
New York Times Book Review, September 10, 2006, p. 33.
Publishers Weekly, June 12, 2006, p. 31.

Online

"Biography," Liesel Litzenburger—The Official Site, http://www.lieselonline.com/bio.htm. (July 9, 2007).

—Carol Brennan

Adam Lowry and Eric Ryan

Founders of Method Home Care

Lowry: Born c. 1974. Ryan: Born c. 1972; married; children: one daughter. *Education:* Lowry: Graduated from Stanford University. Ryan: Graduated from the University of Rhode Island.

Addresses: *Office*—Method, 637 Commercial St., San Francisco, CA 94111.

Career

Lowry: Worked in product development for several companies; developed software, computer models, and interfaces for the Carnegie Institute of Washington. Ryan: Worked for such advertising agencies as Fallon, San Francisco; worked as marketing consultant for Saturn, the Gap, Old Navy, and Colgate. Together: Founded Method Home Care, 2000; sold first Method products, 2001; began selling Method at Target, 2002; Method reached 10,000 stores, 2003; Method named the seventh-fastest-growing private company in the United States by *Inc.,* 2006.

Sidelights

As the co-founders of Method Home Care, Adam Lowry and Eric Ryan successfully launched a new line of trendy cleaning products. Method products have gentle aromatherapy scents, fewer harsh chemicals than cleaners commonly found in supermarkets, and are both non-toxic and environmentally friendly. Having introduced the first Method products in 2001, the pair found success within two years and by 2006, were recognized as a dynamic force in what had been static industry. As *SF Weekly*'s Matt Palmquist explained, "Ryan and Lowry see Method as more than just a breath of fresh air. They view their company as a means to redefine the very essence of cleaning, transforming ugly objects that hide under the sink into chic, must-have countertop accessories."

Both Lowry and Ryan grew up in Grosse Pointe, Michigan, where they were friends in high school before going off to different colleges. Lowry moved to California to study chemistry at Stanford, while Ryan went to the University of Rhode Island. After graduating from college, they both moved to San Francisco without knowing the other lived there.

Lowry's work experience consisted of creating patented products for several companies as well as developing software, computer models, and interfaces for the Carnegie Institute of Washington. A business entrepreneur since middle school, Ryan had a career in advertising and marketing. He worked for ad agencies such as Fallon, and also used his well-honed marketing expertise, nose for consumer trends, and knowledge of corporate brand imaging as a marketing consultant. Among the firms he consulted for were Saturn, the Gap, and Old Navy. Ryan also helped launch a new toothpaste for Colgate.

Lowry and Ryan did not realize they were living in the same city until they returned to Michigan for Thanksgiving in 1997 and ran into each other on a plane. During that fateful meeting, they learned they lived only about a block apart. Shortly thereafter, a roommate of Lowry's moved out and Ryan accepted Lowry's invitation to move in. By this time, Lowry was unemployed and, like Ryan, longing to start his own business. After discussing their options in a 1999 ski trip in northern Michigan, they found themselves taking about cleaning products. Lowry and Ryan concluded that such products were more about killing germs and pests than caring for the home. They decided to create cleaning products that people who loved their home would want to buy.

Returning to San Francisco, Lowry and Ryan delved into research about the history of household cleaning products as well as the current marketplace. A few companies like Proctor & Gamble dominated the market, and there had been little innovation in the previous half century. Companies were afraid to change products which consumers had been buying for generations for fear of alienating their customer base.

After spending a year deciding if cleaning products were really what they wanted to do, Ryan quit his job and the pair rented an office. Using all their savings as well as investment funds from family and friends, the pair launched Method Home Care. Ryan focused on marketing and design, while Lowry did the product development and chemical processes.

Lowry developed Method's chemical formulations with an environmental conscience. Instead of using bleaches, antibacterial agents, and other oxidizing ingredients, he favored active ingredients which were absorptive and attached themselves only to dirt. Many of Method's active ingredients were derived from coconut and palm oils, making them safe to use around children and pets. They also worked well, a fact that initially surprised his partner, Ryan. For color, Lowry limited his choices to stable but environmentally friendly dyes. Method's line of cleaning products employed essential oils and plant extracts to make them smell better and more organic than most every-day cleaners, which have harsh, artificial smells.

In 2001, Lowry and Ryan made their first sale to a retail store in suburban San Francisco: Mollie Stone's Market. The store's manager agreed to give them two shelves of retail space for their interesting bottle and oddly hued all-purpose spray cleaner.

They returned a few days later to find that people had actually purchased their then-hand packaged product, a mind-blowing concept to the young entrepreneurs. Ryan told Palmquist in the *SF Weekly* interview, "It was surreal to think of people taking your product, putting it in a cart, and using it at home. Imagine that."

After this first sale, Lowry and Ryan began placing their product in other groceries, primarily gourmet stores, in San Francisco. As their sales grew, they hired Alastair Dorward to be the company's chief executive officer and guide Method into a well-managed national, if not international, company. Bigger grocery chains began noticing their success. Albertsons was the first national chain to stock Method in certain stores. Safeway followed soon after. One big breakthrough came in 2002 when giant retailer Target agreed to stock Method products.

Aiming at customers in their twenties and thirties, Lowry and Ryan did not just have a line of good-smelling, gentle-but-effective cleaners, but also packaged them in a hip, clean way similar to packaging found in personal care products. By the time Target became interested, the pair had approached well-known designer Karim Rashid to reinvent the packaging for their dish soap to make it look chic. Rashid came up with a curved bottle, shaped somewhat like a bowling pin, which dispensed product out of its base. Rashid became the company's chief creative officer, and after a very successful six-month test run, Target began stocking Method products in all its stores.

By 2003, the Method line was available in at least 10,000 stores in the United States and posted about $10 million in annual sales. That year, Lowry and Ryan also expanded to Europe, with consumers in London the first to be able to buy Method products. By adding Target as a retail outlet, Lowry and Ryan were able to gain more investors, including the Simon Property Group and the Sumitomo Corporation of America.

Over the years, Method's product line grew. One early product was Kitchen, an orange all-purpose kitchen cleaner which had an odor dubbed "bamboo" because of it smelled like the rain forest where bamboo was grown. Another product called Glass, the company's glass cleaner, was blue and smelled like coral. Lowry and Ryan's first dish soap was available in four scents: mandarin, cucumber, mint, and lavender. They later added other items to the Method family of products such as hand soap, shower spray, floor cleaner, room sprays, air fresheners, soy candles, a laundry line, and cleaning wipes, each with a signature pleasant smell. For Ryan, however, packaging was what helped sell the product in stores as they kept their advertising for Method to a minimum. He told Donna Howell of *Investor's Business Daily*, "We believe packaging is our biggest ad vehicle."

Despite continued growth, Lowry and Ryan realized that their overall market share was small relative to Procter & Gamble, which had about $43 billion in annual sales in 2002. While they feared that such companies might create knock-offs of Method's carefully crafted products, the cost of recreating and marketing such products would be a costly risk which might not pay off. Instead of worrying about what such large companies might do, Lowry and Ryan concentrated on growing their own niche in the industry and vowed to remain private. They continued to add more retailers, including nationwide chains Linens 'n Things and Wal-Mart, and their sales grew rapidly. By 2006, annual sales had grown to an estimated $44 million on 132 products. That year, it was named the seventh fastest growing private company in the United States by *Inc.*

Because of the elegant packaging and the quality of Method's product, Ryan believed that he and Lowry's company made people happy. Of the aesthetics of Method, Ryan told Rob Walker of the *New York Times*, "It just makes you get enjoyment out of an object that you never expected to get enjoyment from, because it makes you smile when you look at it, or it's fun to touch. So it's not that it looks beautiful, but when you actually interact with it, it makes a chore a little less of a chore. Who wouldn't want that?"

Sources

Periodicals

Brand Packaging, June 2003.
Inc., February 2006, p. 102.
Investor's Business Daily, January 5, 2004, p. A8.
National Post (Toronto, Ontario, Canada), March 8, 2002, p. B7.
New York Times, February 29, 2004, p. 42.
San Francisco Chronicle, October 8, 2006, p. C1.
SF Weekly, December 24, 2003.
Vanity Fair, May 2007, p. 254.

Online

"Selling cool in a bottle," CNNMoney.com, http://cnnmoney.com (August 3, 2007).

—A. Petruso

John Mackey

Chief Executive Officer of Whole Foods

Born in 1953 in Texas; son of William S. (an accounting professor and hospital-management company executive) Mackey; married Deborah Morin (a software consultant and yoga instructor). *Education:* Attended Trinity University, the University of Texas—Austin, and one other college, c. 1971-78.

Addresses: *Home*—Austin, TX. *Office*—Whole Foods Market, Inc., 550 Bowie St., Austin, TX 78703-4644.

Career

Opened health-food store and restaurant, Safer Way, in Austin, TX, 1978; opened Whole Foods Natural Market in Austin, 1980, and became chief executive officer of Whole Foods Markets, Inc., with a 1992 initial public offering of company stock.

Sidelights

John Mackey is the founder and chief executive officer of Whole Foods Markets, Inc., the largest organic- and natural-foods grocery store chain in the United States. Known for their immense size and commitment to educating consumers about the foods they eat, Mackey's stores have a devoted customer base, and his company enjoys some of the highest profit margins and growth figures in the entire grocery industry. A rather uncommon CEO, Mackey is unapologetic about his commitment to social justice and environmental causes, and he believes that companies like his can be leaders and ef-

fect positive societal change. "Business is always painted as the bad guys," he asserted in a *New York Times Magazine* profile by Jon Gertner. "They're the ones who are greedy, selfish, the ones who despoil the environment. They're never the heroes. Business ... never will be accepted by society as long as business says it has no responsibility except for maximizing profits."

Mackey was born in 1953 in Texas, and grew up in the Houston area. His father was an accounting professor but later became chief executive officer of a hospital-management company. Following his graduation from high school in 1971, Mackey attended three different schools, including the University of Texas at Austin, studying philosophy and religion because, he told Wendy Zellner in a *BusinessWeek* interview, "I was searching for the meaning of life." He eventually settled into an experimental living arrangement known as a commune, which were in fashion in the 1960s and '70s. At this Austin commune, called Prana, he was first introduced to vegetarianism and became a convert himself. "It was the first time I realized what you ate could affect how you felt," he told *Business Week*'s Zellner.

In 1978, with then-girlfriend Renee Lawson Hardy, Mackey opened his first health-food store. Their seed money came from a small inheritance of Hardy's, and another $20,000 borrowed from Mackey's father, and several more thousands of dollars invested by other family members and friends. Called Safer Way, the store was located in a three-story building in Austin; the couple opened a health-food restaurant on the second floor, while the third floor served as their living quarters. "We didn't even have a shower," he recalled in a *Fast Company* story by Charles Fishman. "Renee and I would take showers in the Hobart dishwasher in the restaurant, you know, using the spray hose."

Mackey eventually decided to scuttle the restaurant business and join forces with two other investors to open a much larger Austin store in 1980, called the Whole Foods Natural Market. It caught on quickly with local residents, partly because it offered convenient one-stop shopping—Whole Foods sold all the standard health-food store items that were free of preservatives, processed flour, refined sugars, and other additives, but the store also stocked some foods that were traditionally spurned by other health-food stores on principle, such as sugar, coffee, and even red meat. The enterprise was nearly ruined by severe flooding in Austin in the spring of 1981, which put the shelves under eight feet of water, but loyal customers stopped by to help clean up the mess, and Whole Foods reopened for business just a month later.

In the 1980s, Mackey and his partners expanded Whole Foods into other Texas cities, such as Houston and Dallas, and then moved into Louisiana, North Carolina, and northern California. The company became publicly traded in January of 1992 with an initial public offering of stock, traded on the NASDAQ under the ticker "WFMI." The infusion of cash allowed Mackey to expand the number of Whole Foods stores, either by building new ones or acquiring competitors. Several smaller chains around the country—including Fresh Fields on the East Coast and the California-based Mrs. Gooch's—were folded into the growing Whole Foods empire.

Rebellious and a maverick by nature, Mackey was determined to create a workplace based on the model of the commune, where all worked together, resources were shared equally, and a common goal served as an underlying principle. Intrigued by Japanese management styles, Mackey read scores of books on the subject during the 1980s and borrowed the team-based approach used by many major Japanese manufacturers for managing his workers. Each Whole Foods store had eight teams, and any new hire went through a month-long trial period before

their suitability for permanent employment was put to a vote by the other team members. Two-thirds approval was necessary, and team members often sought out the hardest workers to join, because regular wage increases and bonuses were linked to team performance.

Even Whole Foods' corporate board was called the National Leadership Team, and Mackey rarely overruled the decisions of its 24 members. He also proved surprisingly movable on certain issues: When a hardline animal-rights activist challenged him at one stockholders' meeting, he began investigating her assertions by reading all available literature on the issue, and he came to see her point of view when she claimed Whole Foods was not doing enough to avoid the horrors that plague many farms that raise animals for food. He was stunned, for example, to learn that the supplier of ducks to Whole Foods for the past decade housed the birds inside, and at his urging the farm began to construct ponds.

Mackey's company continued to grow, and in the first years of the new century consistently posted impressive sales numbers on a per-square-foot basis. Wall Street analysts also liked the fact that there was phenomenal sales growth from year to year even for existing Whole Foods stores. There have been a few missteps along the way, however, such as the 2006 revelation that for the past eight years Mackey had been posting messages in a Yahoo message board devoted to finance issues, consistently praising Whole Foods and deriding its competitors, such as the Colorado chain Wild Oats, which it later acquired.

Detractors and even some ardent Whole Foods loyalists complain about the chain's prices, and it even has an unofficial nickname, "Whole Paycheck." "Everyone thinks we cater to the rich, but it's really not true," Mackey told *Fortune* in 2007. "We cater to the well-educated. The reason is that for people to change their dietary habits requires that they be well informed."

Sources

BusinessWeek, December 7, 1998, p. 79.
Fast Company, July 2004, p. 70.
Fortune, July 23, 2007, p. 72.
New York Times, July 16, 2007.
New York Times Magazine, June 6, 2004.

—*Carol Brennan*

Eli Manning

Scott Wintrow/Getty Images

Professional football player

Born January 3, 1981, in New Orleans, LA; son of Archie (a professional football player) and Olivia Manning; married Abby McGrew, April 19, 2008. *Education:* University of Mississippi, B.A., 2004.

Addresses: *Office*—c/o New York Football Giants, Giants Stadium, East Rutherford, NJ 07073.

Career

Signed to play college football at the University of Mississippi, 1998; became starting quarterback at the University of Mississippi, 2001; drafted number one overall in the National Football League (NFL) draft, 2004; signed with the New York Giants and became starting quarterback, 2004; won Super Bowl XLII, 2008.

Awards: Johnny Unitas Golden Arm Award, Johnny Unitas Golden Arm Educational Foundation, 2003; Maxwell Award, Maxwell Football Club, 2003; Super Bowl Most Valuable Player Award, 2008.

Sidelights

The winner of the Most Valuable Player Award at the 2008 Super Bowl, Eli Manning is the All-Star quarterback for the New York Giants. Manning led his team to victory over the New England Patriots, who had not previously lost a game in the 2007-08 season and playoffs. The six-foot, four-inch tall, 205-pound Manning had played college foot-

ball at the University of Mississippi, also known as Ole Miss, was the son of former National Football League (NFL) quarterback Archie Manning, and the brother of Super Bowl-winning quarterback Peyton Manning.

Born on January 3, 1981, in New Orleans, Louisiana, Manning was the son of Archie and his wife, Olivia. The youngest of three brothers, he was obsessed with football from an early age. He practiced the quarterback's five-step drop from the age of five, and helped his elder brothers with their game. While football was his focus, Manning was also interested in other sports and played baseball as well as basketball by the time he reached high school.

Manning attended Isidore Newman High School in New Orleans, where he was a stand-out football player who started for three seasons and threw more than 7,000 yards more than the course of his high school career. As a senior, Manning led his team to an 11-1 record and the state quarterfinals. His personal statistics were also impressive, completing 134 of 229 passes for 2,336 yards and 29 touchdowns. He received more than 100 college football scholarship offers, but his choice was simple.

While his elder brother, Peyton, had declined to follow in his father's footsteps and played at the University of Tennessee, Manning verbally committed to play for his father and elder brother Cooper's alma mater, the University of Mississippi (known as Ole Miss), at the end of 1998. Manning began attending the school in the fall of 1999. During his redshirt freshman year, Manning faced some off-field challenges as he was arrested for public drunkness, failure to comply, and possession of alcohol by a minor in February of 2000.

After serving as a backup who saw little playing time his first eligible playing year, Manning was named the Rebels starting quarterback for the 2001 season after stepping in unexpectedly in the team's bowl game at the end of the previous season. His first significant playing time for Ole Miss came in the 2000 Music City Bowl when he was sent in at the beginning of the fourth quarter. At the time, Ole Miss trailed the University of West Virginia 49-16. Under Manning's guidance, the Rebels scored three times as he threw for 167 yards. While Ole Miss still lost, the final score was a more palatable 49-38.

When Manning took over as Ole Miss's quarterback, he was inevitably measured up against his father, considered the greatest quarterback ever to play at the school. Manning shook off comparisons, telling Doug Segrest of the Birmingham News "As long as I'm playing football, I'll hear the comparisons. It's not something I worry about. I try to be my own man. I can be a leader on this team. But if I'm a leader, it's because of what I've done here with my teammates. Not what anyone else has done before me."

Manning lived up to the hype in his first starting game against Murray State in September of 2001. He set several school records in the 49-14 victory with 18 completed passes and five touches in the game. Manning continued to have an impressive playing career over the next three seasons. In his senior season in 2003, he threw for 3,341 yards and 27 touchdowns, leading his team to a 9-3 record and a berth in the Cotton Bowl. He finished third for the Heisman Trophy for the 2003 season, and won several awards, including the Johnny Unitas Golden Arm Award and the Maxwell Award. By the time his career at Ole Miss ended, he held 54 team records.

Based on his pedigree and college career, Manning was a highly touted NFL prospect. He was expected to be selected number one overall, but that pick was held by the San Diego Chargers. Manning and his people made it clear that he would not sign with the Chargers and would sit out the whole season if

necessary, but the team selected him anyway. Less than an hour later, San Diego traded Manning to the New York Giants for another highly touted quarterback draftee, Philip Rivers, and three draft picks. Manning soon signed a six-year deal with New York worth $74 million, including incentives and a $20 million signing bonus.

Playing for the Giants presented new challenges for Manning, including the pressures of being part of one of the largest media markets in the world. His rookie year was difficult as he adjusted to the level of play in the NFL. After backing up Kurt Warner to start the season, Manning was named the team's starter for the last seven games of the 2004 season, winning only one of them, showing both moments of brilliance and making huge mistakes. By the end of this trying season, he completed only 95 of 197 passes for 1,043 yards.

Despite such setbacks, Manning remained even-keeled and sure of himself. He told Aaron Kurlioff of the New Orleans Times-Picayune, "This is something new for me, where I haven't played the way I've wanted to. But you know, it's just a part of learning. It's a part of getting a feel for this game, the NFL. It's not something that can be fixed overnight, where the next day you just understand everything. It's a process of getting better. And that's my concern right now."

Manning improved greatly in his second year, playing with more confidence and taking charge as the quarterback. He started all 16 games in 2005, seemingly progressing in each one of them. He ultimately completed 294 of 557 passes for 3,762 yards. While Manning managed only six touchdowns as a rookie, he had 24 touchdowns in 2005. He was still learning, however, as he also had 17 interceptions. Despite uneven numbers, Manning led the Giants to an 11-5 record, their division title, and an appearance in the post-season.

In 2006, Manning also started 16 games, completing 201 of 522 passes for 3,244 for 24 touchdowns and 18 interceptions. One standout from the season was a September game in which he faced his brother Peyton's team, the Indianapolis Colts, for the first time. Manning's Giants lost to his brother's Colts, 26-21. Despite this loss, Manning was emerging as a usually strong, sometimes erratic, quarterback who played smart, although his team often did not always reach his level of play. The Giants made the post-season as a wild card, but lost to the Philadelphia Eagles.

While the Giants had personnel uncertainties and were not a lock to make the playoffs coming into 2007, Manning continued to be a steady performer.

He started all 16 games, completing 297 of 529 passes for 3,336 yards. Yet Manning threw 23 touchdowns and 20 interceptions on the season. He played well in the last regular season game against the New England Patriots, but New York still lost 38-35. Despite an uneven ten win and six loss season, the Giants made the post-season again as the wild card.

In this post-season, Manning gained confidence as he led his team to repeated victories. First, the Giants defeated the Tampa Bay Buccaneers in the wild card game, 24-14, then bested the Dallas Cowboys 21-17. Manning shined in critical situations in the latter game, despite playing with a sore shoulder. Reaching Super Bowl XLII by defeating the Green Bay Packers in the NFC (National Football Conference) championship game, Manning and the Giants were the underdogs to the New England Patriots, who had not lost a game all season long. Despite the odds, Manning led New York to a 17-14 victory and was named the game's most valuable player.

The victory did not change Manning. He told Mark McGuire of the Albany *Times Union*, "I guess you're a Super Bowl champion. That's the difference. It doesn't change my attitude or my personality or my goals for next season." Manning's life did change in one way after the end of the season. He married his college girlfriend, Abby McGrew, in Mexico in April of 2008.

Manning was ready for the next season, and planned on taking the same approach to return to the Super Bowl. Arthur Staple of the *Calgary Herald* quoted him as saying "Just because you have success and you win a championship doesn't mean you stop for a year, or you become content with what you've done. If anything, I think it should make you strive even harder or more to try and get here again…. Last year is behind you, and we've celebrated for that month or two that you have off, and now it's back to work to see if you can do it again."

Sources

Periodicals

Associated Press, December 18, 1998; August 15, 2001; April 21, 2008.
Atlanta Journal-Constitution, December 13, 2003, p. 3C.
Birmingham News (Birmingham, AL), May 27, 2001; September 6, 2001.
Boston Herald, January 29, 2008, p. 70.
Business Wire, December 15, 2003.
Calgary Herald (Calgary, Alberta, Canada), February 5, 2008, p. E6.
Houston Chronicle, January 1, 2004, p. 4.
Kansas City Star (Kansas City, MO), January 18, 2008.
Los Angeles Times, January 6, 2008, p. D1; February 3, 2008, p. D13; February 4, 2008, p. D11.
New York Post, September 21, 2005, p. 74.
New York Times, January 6, 2006, p. D1; September 11, 2006, p. D1; September 19, 2006, p. D1; December 12, 2006, p. D1.
Times-Picayune (New Orleans, LA), April 25, 2004, sec. National, p. 1; December 18, 2004, sec. Sports, p. 1; July 9, 2005, sec. Sports, p. 1.
Times-Union (Albany, NY), February 5, 2008, p. B1.
University Wire, February 4, 2000.
USA Today, December 22, 2004, p. 6C.

Online

"Eli Manning," NFL.com, http://www.nfl.com/players/elimanning/profile?id=MAN473170 (May 19, 2008).

—*A. Petruso*

JoAnn E. Manson

AP Images

Physician and researcher

Born JoAnn Elisabeth Manson, April 14, 1953, in Cleveland, OH; daughter of S. Stanford (an engineer) and Therese Palay (a medical social worker) Manson; married Christopher N. Ames (an attorney), June 12, 1979; children: Jenn, Jeffrey, Joshua. *Education:* Harvard University, A.B., 1975; Case Western Reserve University School of Medicine, Cleveland, OH, M.D., 1979; Harvard University School of Public Health, M.P.H., 1984; Harvard University School of Public Health, Dr.P.H., 1987.

Addresses: *Contact*—Brigham and Women's Hospital, 900 Commonwealth Ave. E., 3rd Floor, Boston, MA 02215-1204. *Home*—Beverly, MA.

Career

Resident in internal medicine, Harvard Medical School, 1979-82; fellowship in endocrinology, University Hospital, Boston, 1982-84; research fellowship, Brigham and Women's Hospital, Boston, 1984-87; staff physician/consulting endocrinologist, Harvard Vanguard Medical Associates, 1986-2003; co-director of women's health in preventive medicine, Brigham and Women's Hospital, 1993—; chief of preventive medicine, Brigham and Women's Hospital, 1999—; professor of medicine, Harvard Medical School, 1999—; Elizabeth Brigham professor of women's health, Harvard Medical School, 2003—.

Member: Fellow, American College of Physicians; fellow, American College of Epidemiology; American Medical Association; American Medical Women's Association; American Heart Association; American Diabetes Association; steering committee, Women's Health Initiative; Association of American Physicians; Alpha Omega Alpha.

Awards: Hero in women's health, *American Health for Women* magazine, 1997; Mary Horrigan Connors Award for outstanding leadership in women's health, 1999; Top 10 champions of women's health, *Ladies' Home Journal,* 2000; top docs for women, *Boston Magazine,* 2001; Henry Ingersoll Bowditch Award for excellence in public health, Massachusetts Medical Society, 2002; women in science award, American Medical Women's Association, 2003; women's professional achievement award, Harvard College, 2006.

Sidelights

Harvard Medical School professor JoAnn E. Manson has dedicated her career to the in-depth study of women's health and is considered one of the most knowledgeable physicians on the subject. Manson served as the lead investigator in several landmark women's health studies, including two of the largest women's research projects ever launched—the Harvard Nurses' Health Study and the Women's Health Initiative established by the National Institutes of Health. Each study involved more than 120,000 participants.

Manson used data from the studies to explore the risk factors for major chronic diseases in women. She studied data on diet, hormone replacement therapy, and the use of vitamin supplements to see how they related to cardiovascular disease. In the end, Manson has determined that a fit and active lifestyle is the best medicine. "If someone said there was an elixir that reduces your risk of almost every major disease, wouldn't everyone be clamoring to get ahold of it?" Manson asked *USA Today*'s Nanci Hellmich. "I'm convinced from the research that a sedentary lifestyle kills you, and moderate activity like walking can be a lifesaver."

Manson was born on April 14, 1953, in Cleveland, Ohio. Her father, S. Stanford, worked as an engineer for the National Aeronautics and Space Administration (NASA). Her mother, Therese, was a medical social worker. Growing up, Manson enjoyed science but also had an artistic side—she played the harp, painted, and created sculptures; however, Manson decided to study medicine after being influenced by a high school chemistry teacher who championed the cause of placing more women in medicine.

While Manson's pre-med studies at Harvard University kept her busy with the sciences, she also found time for the arts, working as a dance and theater reviewer for the *Harvard Independent*. After graduating from Harvard in 1975, Manson attended Case Western Reserve University School of Medicine in Cleveland, Ohio. She earned her medical degree in 1979, then chose to focus her residency on internal medicine—specifically endocrinology, which is the study of hormones. She completed her residency in Boston.

Initially, Manson figured she would go into clinical practice but, in 1979, her mother was diagnosed with ovarian cancer. After watching her mother battle with and eventually die of the disease, Manson switched career paths, deciding she would rather study women's health and preventive medicine. Manson enrolled in an epidemiology and biostatistics program at the Harvard School of Public Health, earning a master's degree in 1984 and a doctorate in 1987.

Manson is a methodical scientist. She has spent much of her career scouring data from the Nurses' study. First launched in the 1970s, the study has collected data from more than 120,000 nurses, following some for more than 20 years. Manson also worked with the Women's Health Initiative, which is studying postmenopausal health. Many of the health recommendations made to women today are a result of the studies with which Manson has worked. Data from both studies—culled from detailed questionnaires—showed that fiber prevents heart attacks in women and that adult-onset diabetes risk can be reduced by diet and exercise.

According to an article in the *Boston Globe*, data from the Nurses' study showed that if a woman ate well, exercised regularly, and gave up unhealthy habits like smoking, she could cut her risk of heart disease by 80 percent, her risk of diabetes by 90 percent, and her risk of cancer by 50 percent. Manson used this research to write a book detailing how women can improve their cardiovascular health. The result was *The 30-Minute Fitness Solution: A Four-Step Plan for Women of All Ages,* co-written with Patricia Amend. Published in 2001, the book was aimed at getting inactive women moving. It explains the short- and long-term benefits of exercise, then lays out options for women to get them going.

According to the *Boston Globe*'s Karen Hsu, Manson wrote a 1999 article in the *New England Journal of Medicine*—using findings from the Nurses' study—which reported that just three hours of brisk walking a week could reduce heart attacks in women. Manson encourages everyone to walk for exercise. She also practices what she preaches. During her lunch break, Manson takes a brisk, 20-minute walk and, on weekends, she goes on an hour-long hike with her family. Manson is married with three children.

Over the course of her career, Manson has published some 400 articles, mostly on women's health. The only blip in Manson's career came in 1997 after she wrote an editorial in a medical journal endorsing the use of Redux, a diet pill. After the editorial was printed, it was revealed that she had worked as a paid consultant for the pill's manufacturer. The journal's editors admonished Manson, saying she should have revealed that the company had previously paid her as a consultant.

In 1999, Manson was appointed to a full professorship at the Harvard Medical School, a place where only nine percent of professorships are held by women. That same year, she was made chief of preventive medicine at Brigham and Women's Hospital, which is affiliated with Harvard.

Besides being good with research and data, Manson has an impeccable bedside manner, according to patients. Anna Andrews told the *Boston Globe*'s Hsu, "I have a white coat syndrome. My heart beats harder just at the sight of it, but the first thing she does is give you a big smile, and says 'Let's talk.' She's never rushed me."

In a 2007 health article, the *Boston Globe* consulted Manson, asking for her health tips. She made these suggestions: Wear a pedometer—research shows that those who do walk an extra mile each day; add strength training to exercise regimens—it is crucial for preventing muscle and bone loss; do not rely on vitamins—try to get nutrition from foods; eat two fish meals a week—research shows fish oils are beneficial for the heart and brain; consider aspirin for heart protection—but be sure to discuss this with a doctor because it is not right for everyone.

Sources

Books

Marquis Who's Who, Marquis Who's Who, 2008.

Periodicals

Boston Globe, September 13, 1999, p. C1; December 31, 2007, p. C1.

Boston Herald, September 15, 1997, p. 12.
Case Western Reserve University School of Medicine Alumni News, 10, no. 3, 2004.
Newsweek, January 16, 2006, pp. 64-69.
USA Today, November 13, 2002, p. 9D.

Online

"Changing the Face of Medicine: Dr. JoAnn Elisabeth Manson," U.S. National Library of Medicine, National Institutes of Health, http://www.nlm.nih.gov/changingthefaceofmedicine/physicians/biography_212.html (January 27, 2008).
"JoAnn E. Manson, M.D.," *Time,* http://www.time.com/time/2004/obesity/speakers/manson.html (January 27, 2008).
"JoAnn Manson, Professor in the Department of Epidemiology," Harvard School of Public Health, http://www.hsph.harvard.edu/faculty/joann-manson/ (March 24, 2008).

—Lisa Frick

Maroon 5

Rock group

Group formed c. 1999, in Los Angeles, CA. Members include: James Carmichael (born c. 1979. *Education:* Attended Five Towns College), keyboards, guitars; Ryan Dusick (*Education:* Attended University of California at Los Angeles), drums (left band, 2006); Matt Flynn, drums; Adam Levine (born c. 1979, son of Patsy Noah. *Education:* Attended Five Towns College), vocals; Mickey Madden (born c. 1979. *Education:* Attended University of California at Los Angeles), bass; James Valentine (*Education:* Attended the Berklee School of Music), guitars.

Addresses: *Record company*—Octone Records, 560 Broadway, Ste. 500, New York, NY 10012. *Web site*—http://www.maroon5.com/.

Career

Carmichael, Levine, Madden, and Dusick formed Kara's Flowers, c. 1992; Kara's Flowers signed record deal with Reprise/Warner Bros., 1995, and released debut album, *The Fourth World*, 1997; Kara's Flowers dropped by Warner Bros., 1998; the band re-formed as Maroon 5, 1999; Valentine joined Maroon 5, 2001; signed deal with Octone Records, 2001; released debut album, *Songs About Jane*, 2002; released *It Won't Be Soon Before Long*, 2007.

Awards: Grammy Award for best new artist, Recording Academy, 2005; Grammy Award for best pop performance by a duo or group with vocal, Recording Academy, for "This Love," 2006; Environmental Media Award, 2006.

Sidelights

Though it took several years for their first album to become a hit, Maroon 5 eventually rode the success of *Songs About Jane* to an unexpected Grammy Award for best new artist in 2005. While touring in support of the album, the band drew ever-increasing audiences for their sound: white funk-soul-pop-modern rock with hip-hop influences. Dubbing themselves the Hall and Oates for the twenty-first century, Maroon 5 built on the popularity of *Jane* with its follow-up, 2007's *It Won't Be Soon Before Long* which was certified platinum shortly after its release.

Four of the five original members of Maroon 5 knew each other from childhoods spent together in the Brentwood section of Los Angeles. Lead singer Adam Levine, bassist Mickey Madden, and keyboardist/guitarist Jesse Carmichael befriended each other in middle school. Carmichael had taken classical piano lessons as a small child and focused on the instrument until high school, when he began playing more guitar. They began making music together in the early 1990s, and eventually formed their first band, Kara's Flowers while attending Brentwood High School where Levine was a popular, Ferris Bueller-type student. In this band, Carmichael primarily played guitar. The fourth band member was drummer Ryan Dusick, a former athlete.

An alternative rock band, Kara's Flowers drew its name from a girl the whole band had a crush on. While their sound was heavy rock in the beginning, over the next few years it morphed into a more guitar-pop sound influenced by 1960s bands, especially the Beatles. Kara's Flowers landed a record deal with Reprise/Warner Bros. in 1995 and released a debut album in 1997, *The Fourth World*, which was produced by Green Day producer Rob Cavallo. While the record received some good reviews from critics for its upbeat power pop, *The Fourth World* never caught on with audiences. It was essentially an utter failure and Kara's Flowers was dropped by the label in 1998.

Levine later believed the failure of *The Fourth World* turned out to be a positive. He told Larry Katz of the *Boston Herald*, "I'm so happy we failed. Not doing well with something you're really passionate about makes you much more equipped to deal with things when you're a bit older.... I got signed to a major-label deal when I was 16. Life was beautiful. When I got a little older I realized there is plenty to be sad about. I got my heart broken a couple of times. That did wonders for my songwriting."

Because of the album's failure, Kara's Flowers essentially broke up in 1998 and the band members pursued their educations. While Madden and Dusick attended the University of California at Los Angeles (Dusick was an English major), Levine and Carmichael continued their education at the Long Island-based Five Towns College's music school. There, Levine and Carmichael found a new musical direction led by their new found interest in R&B and hip-hop. Inspired by R&B singer Aaliyah's hit 1998 song "Are You That Somebody?," the band came with a new song, "Not Coming Home." Also drawing influence from artists such as Stevie Wonder, Missy Elliott, and Herbie Hancock, what had been Kara's Flowers reformed and changed its sound as well as its name to Maroon 5 in 1999.

There were other changes as well for the newly christened Maroon 5 over the next few years. As Carmichael re-discovered his love of piano and jazz at Five Towns, he focused on that instrument in the new band. The band also added a fifth member to replace Carmichael on guitar. In 2001, guitarist James Valentine joined Maroon 5. Valentine was a native of Lincoln, Nebraska, where he was part of the indie band scene there. While Maroon 5's newly emerging sound was not exactly his musical ideal, Valentine appreciated Levine's soulful voice and pop background.

Maroon 5 was signed to Octone Records by James Diener later in 2001. The band began recording some of the songs already written as well as new songs, all of which were put down before year's end. The lyrics on what became *Songs About Jane* were inspired by Levine's on-again, off-again, painful romance with a girlfriend named Jane. He refused to talk more about her or their relationship, other than through his music.

Occasionally playing their new songs to audiences in Los Angeles while recording the album, Maroon 5 found themselves out of step with hipsters' expectations. Valentine told Scott Mervis of the *Pittsburgh Post-Gazette*, "When we started to do some of the first songs, people thought we were joking because it was out of line with what you were supposed to do as a young white band in L.A. If you weren't doing the '80s like every hipster band going right now, it was like, 'What are you doing? You're supposed to be doing like New Wave, that's what's in style this week.'"

Maroon 5 released *Songs About Jane* in the summer of 2002. For the first few months of the album's release it only sold a few hundred copies, seemingly proving fickle Los Angles listeners correct. Even the first single, "Harder to Breathe," was not initially popular except on a few modern rock stations. The band then spent most of the next two years on the road in support of the album, playing endless gigs to drive up interest. Singer/songwriter John Mayer gave the band the opening spot on his early 2003 tour because he knew Valentine from their time at the Berklee School of Music in the mid-1990s. Maroon 5 also opened for popular bands like Matchbox 20 and Counting Crows.

The hard work soon began to pay off. The tide began to turn in the fall of 2003 when a re-released "Harder to Breathe" became a chart-topping hit 16 months after its initial release. By October of 2003, the band had sold about 300,000 copies of *Songs About Jane* as well. Maroon 5 also became a headliner in their own right, playing about 200 scheduled dates in 2004 alone. They continued to open for bigger artists as well, including more touring with Mayer.

By the spring of 2004, Maroon 5 was selling about 70,000 copies per week of *Songs About Jane,* and had sold more than two million copies total of the album. That same month the single "This Love" became a number-one hit in the United States, followed by another smash, "She Will Be Loved." Part of their appeal was the ability to attract modern rock, adult contemporary, and top 40 fans. Another was the appeal of Levine, who became something of a sex symbol, especially after his performance in the band's often provocative music videos.

A divide emerged in the band's image because of their popular videos. Carmichael told *Keyboard*'s Peter Kirn, "I don't think a lot of people understand our band right now. I think that when people see the videos that we've made, they have a much popier version of who we are as people. But that leaves out the side of our live show that's much more raw and spontaneous."

In 2005, Maroon 5 shocked many in the music world by winning the Grammy Award for best new artist. Many, including Maroon 5 itself, believed that hip-hop artist Kanye West would nab the honor, but all were surprised at the ceremony when Maroon 5's name was called. Despite such wins, the band still had to defend itself as being more than just the hit-producing pop band of the moment.

During the endless touring which extended through 2004 and into 2005 when the band launched its first major tour, Dusick's physical problems caught up with him. He had suffered from extreme tendonitis for some time, then had a shoulder injury in the summer of 2004 and was forced to step aside temporarily. He was replaced for a time by Matt Flynn, who had previously played with the B-52s, among other bands. Dusick eventually left the band in 2006 due to chronic nerve damage, and Flynn returned to be his permanent replacement.

Maroon 5 took off much of 2006 to write and record the follow-up to the quadruple platinum *Songs About Jane.* The album was written while the band was living in Harry Houdini's mansion in Los Angeles, then recorded in Los Angeles-based studios. Released in May of 2007, *It Won't Be Soon Before Long* was an immediate smash for the band. The first single, the disco-tinged "Make Me Wonder," was a radio hit, reached number one on the *Billboard* Hot 100 chart, and was a number-one-selling single and video on iTunes. *It Won't Be Soon Before Long* itself debuted at number one on the *Billboard* 200 the first week of its release. By June of 2007, the album had reached platinum status, less than three weeks after it hit the market.

Maroon 5 deliberately sought to make their recorded sound harder and more reminiscent of the energy of their live shows while adding a slick production influenced by Michael Jackson's *Off the Wall* and Prince's *Controversy*. Lyrically, *It Won't Be Soon Before Long* featured some underlying angst reflective of concerns about the world, but, for the most part, Levine's songs again focused on heartbreak and the sometimes bitterness of love. Writing in the *Los Angeles Times*, Ann Powers called the album "an icy-hot blend of electro-funk and blue-eyed soul that works its cruel streak with the confidence of Daniel Craig's James Bond."

As soon as *It Won't Be Soon Before Long* was released, Maroon 5 began touring again. The band believed playing to live audiences was important to their success as a band, and helped boost their still-problematic credibility among some listeners. However, some still considered them no better than a boy band or a studio contrivance. Levine told Edna Gunderson of *USA Today,* "There are people who love our band, but there are people who don't know what we're about, and they might get turned on by this record. And then there are the haters. I hope by this point they'll realize we're a good band and that we're for real. We're not a straight-up rock'n'roll band, but I think it's cool to redefine what rock is."

While Levine was content with Maroon 5's success, he could also see past his life in the band. Unlike other band members, he regularly participated in outside projects with rap, hip-hop, and soul artists. Levine was also regularly in the gossip pages for his romantic dalliances with a number of celebrity women. Speaking about post-Maroon 5 plans, Levine told Linda Laban of the *Boston Herald,* "Life is so fascinating. I like to experience it from different angles. If you have the luxury to move on gracefully from something, you should do that. A lot of people get stuck with what they do, not necessarily because they want to do it. Which is a really [lousy] reality for a lot of people."

Selected discography

As Kara's Flowers

The Fourth World, Reprise/Warner Bros., 1997.

As Maroon 5

Songs About Jane, Octone Records, 2002.
1.22.03.Acoustic, Octone Records, 2004.
Live—Friday the 13th, Octone Records, 2005.
It Won't Be Soon Before Long, Octone Records, 2007.

Sources

Periodicals

Associated Press, May 21, 2007.
Boston Herald, October 29, 2003, p. 52; August 19, 2004, p. 61.
Columbus Dispatch (Columbus, OH), July 29, 2004, p. 8.
Keyboard, January 1, 2005, p. 20.
Los Angeles Times, May 22, 2007, p. E2; May 31, 2007, p. E12.
New York Times, May 21, 2007, p. E1.
Pittsburgh Post-Gazette, April 15, 2005, p. W22.
PR Newswire US, April 26, 2007; June 27, 2007.
San Diego Union-Tribune, June 17, 2004, p. NC1.
USA Today, May 23, 2007, p. 1D.

Online

"Maroon 5's White Funk," *Rolling Stone,* http://www.rollingstone.com/artists/maroon5/articles/story/6053686/maroon_5s_white_funk (August 18, 2007).

—A. Petruso

Manny Mashouf

Founder of Bebe

Born Manoucher Mashouf, c. 1938, in Iran; married Neda; children: Karim (son). *Education:* Earned degree in political science from San Francisco State University, 1966.

Addresses: *Office*—Bebe Stores Inc., 400 Valley Dr., Brisbane, CA 94005.

Career

Owner-operator of a chain of San Francisco-area steakhouses, early 1970s; opened first women's clothing store, Caspian Corner, San Francisco, 1976, followed by second, called "bebe," 1977; took Bebe Stores, Inc. public with an initial public offering (IPO) of stock, 1998.

Awards: San Francisco State University Alumnus of the Year, 2005.

Sidelights

Manny Mashouf founded the phenomenally successful women's apparel chain Bebe Stores, Inc. back in 1976 with a single San Francisco boutique. Over the next three decades, the company grew into a powerhouse with a presence in nearly every major American mall or shopping district, and its lowercase "bebe" logo on T-shirts became a ubiquitous must-have for a certain demographic of fashionable young women. "Financial success is the reward for excellence," Mashouf said of his busi-

ness strategy in an interview with Kristin Young in *WWD*. "We need to keep giving Bebe customers what they get excited about every day of the week."

Mashouf was born in Iran in the late 1930s, and spent his earliest years in its capital city, Tehran, where his first shopping experiences came when he accompanied his older sister on her clothes-buying jaunts. The family emigrated to the United States, and Mashouf eventually earned a degree in political science from San Francisco State University in 1966. Over the next decade, he opened a steakhouse that expanded to three more locations in the San Francisco area, but came upon an empty storefront on Polk Street in the city one day in 1976, and decided it would be an ideal place to start the clothing business he had been thinking of launching. "My first inclination was to make men's clothing in the basement of the store," he recalled in an interview with Joanna Ramey in *WWD*. "I bought three machines, hired a master tailor and patternmaker. Then I realized by the time I'd make enough clothing to fill the store, it would be out of fashion."

Instead Mashouf decided to sell clothing lines from established brands such as Esprit while also offering goods from a house label. With both, he hoped to tap into an as-yet-underserved niche market somewhere between teen and mature, aiming to lure the young, single woman with a good job who sought out apparel that made her "look vivacious, sexy, but not junior and cheap," he explained to Ramey in the *WWD* article. The original name of his store was Caspian Corner but Mashouf decided to call a second store he opened on Union Street in 1977 "Bebe," which he borrowed from the famous soliloquy in Shakespeare's *Hamlet:* "to be or not to be."

In 1990, Mashouf came up with a novel way of boosting his company's profile by offering to give free clothes to aspiring young actors in exchange for appearing in ads for Bebe Stores. Charlize Theron was an early recruit, and the strategy worked out well for both parties. "They liked the clothes and they liked the exposure," he said in a 1999 interview that appeared on Forbes.com. With eight Bebe stores in California by 1991 and total sales of $8 million annually, Mashouf announced an ambitious expansion plan that set the goal of 20 new Bebe stores across the United States by 1993, which it met and then surpassed.

Bebe's Hollywood connections helped Mashouf land an invaluable promotional opportunity when wardrobe associates for the top-rated FOX television show *Melrose Place* began using Bebe outfits to costume the show's star, Heather Locklear, in her role as a vixenish villain/advertising executive on the campy cult-favorite series. Locklear's Amanda Burns committed her most heinous interpersonal crimes wearing tight, form-fitting miniskirted business suits in eye-catching colors. Similar successes in costuming Calista Flockhart in *Ally McBeal* and Sarah Michelle Gellar in *Buffy the Vampire Slayer* further boosted profits for Bebe, but Mashouf was adamant there were no more free clothes giveaways to starlets—though some names did receive store discounts. "If the merchandise is good enough, it should be paid for," he said in the Forbes.com interview.

In June of 1998, Mashouf took his company public with an initial public offering (IPO) of stock on the National Association of Securities Dealers Automated Quotations (NASDAQ) that raised several million dollars and served to underwrite the opening of more stores as well as lucrative footwear, eyewear, swimwear, and fragrance licensing agreements. By 2000, there were 135 Bebe stores, and plans continued to open 25 to 35 new addresses every year. Sales flattened for the next few years in a recession period, but the company continued to be a dominant player in the women's contemporary sector of mass-market retailing. In 2006, with 228

Bebe stores, Mashouf presided over an empire whose growth had put his family at the No. 242 spot on *Forbes* magazine's annual "400 Richest Americans" list, with a net worth estimated at $1.5 billion. By then Bebe had branched out into a limited-edition luxury line that debuted on the runway during the Los Angeles Fashion Week 2006 as Collection Bebe, and had opened a freestanding accessories store called "Neda by Bebe."

The new division's name came from Mashouf's wife and business partner, Neda, whom he met in 1984 when she came into one of his stores to make a layaway payment on a leather coat. She was several years his junior, but also of Iranian heritage and at the time enrolled at San Francisco State University as a computer science major. Neda Mashouf went from being the Bebe target customer to a designer of much of its house label, and together she and her husband came to own 73 percent of the company's stock. In 2005, the Mashoufs gave their alma mater the largest private individual donation in the history of San Francisco State University, bestowing $10 million for a new College of Creative Arts building and performance venue that would bear the family name when completed in 2012. Mashouf's son, Karim, was also a graduate of the school, and went to work as a Bebe executive. Commenting on the wealth accrued from his immensely successful business, Mashouf told *WWD*'s Ramey that "it hasn't changed me and I don't think money will ever change me, no matter how much it is. I'm still the same person I was … when I was in college."

Sources

Periodicals

San Francisco Business Times, April 30, 1999, p. 23.
WWD, December 18, 2000, p. 18; November 29, 2006, p. 9.

Online

"Bebe Stores Inc.: This Is No Fashion Victim," *BusinessWeek,* http://www.businessweek.com/1999/99_22/b3631025.htm (July 11, 2007).
"Entrepreneur as Stunt Man," Forbes.com, http://members.forbes.com/forbes/1999/1101/6411228a_print.html (July 17, 2007).
"SF State Receives Largest Individual Gift in Its History: $10 Million," San Francisco State University, http://www.sfsu.edu/~news/prsrelea/fy04/070.htm (July 11, 2007).

—*Carol Brennan*

Dietrich Mateschitz

Founder of Red Bull International

Born May 20, 1944, in St. Marein im Mürtzal, Styria, Austria; son of two teachers; children: one son. *Education:* Earned degree in marketing from the University of Commerce, Vienna, Austria, c. 1972.

Addresses: *Office*—Red Bull North America, Inc., 1740 Stewart St., Santa Monica, CA 90404.

Career

Worked as a tour guide and skiing instructor in Austria, late 1960s; joined Unilever as a marketing associate, c. 1972; also worked for Jacobs Coffee; director of international marketing for Blendax, 1979-84; founded Red Bull International, 1984.

Sidelights

Dietrich Mateschitz founded the company that makes and sells the immensely popular energy drink Red Bull. An Austrian marketing whiz and extreme-sports enthusiast, Mateschitz has managed to meld his love of daredevil endeavor with his company's publicity/promotional machine by sponsoring parachute-skiing events and other sporting challenges, nearly all of which seem to fit neatly with the company's slogan: "Red Bull Gives You Wings." "The most important thing in life is to find fulfillment," he enthused in an interview with Franz Lidz for *Sports Illustrated*. "There are many possible paths that lead to dead ends or put you in the wrong direction. You keep moving for stability and happiness. For me Red Bull was the perfect path."

Fittingly, Mateschitz was born a Taurus, or sign of the bull, on May 20, 1944, in St. Marein im Mürtzal, a town in the province of Styria, Austria. Both of his parents were schoolteachers, but separated when he was still quite young. He was an avid athlete as a child, drawn first to soccer and later to downhill skiing, which offered his first job opportunity when he became an instructor during his college years. Like many Europeans of the postwar generation who benefited from a near-absence of university tuition fees, Mateschitz took a leisurely path through higher education, stretching out his semesters over a full decade before he earned his degree in marketing from Vienna's University of Commerce. "I changed universities a lot of times," he said by way of explanation in an interview with Sholto Byrnes for London's *Independent*. "You know, it's a good time, so you shouldn't shorten it unnecessarily." Only in his last years did he begin accelerating his coursework, pointing out to Byrnes that "when you are a student and you are a tour guide in the summer and a skiing instructor [in winter], this is OK when you are 23, 24, 25. But a student ski instructor at 28, 30? It's not so funny any more."

After graduating from college in the early 1970s, Mateschitz worked for Unilever, the British-Dutch soap maker and personal-products giant before moving over to a well-known German coffee company for a similar marketing job. In 1979, he joined Blendax—another German company that sold toothpaste and shampoo at the time—as its director of international marketing. He began traveling to Asia regularly for his job, and discovered he could alleviate jet lag after the long flights by quaffing the energy drinks that were popular in Southeast Asia and Japan at the time. One of his business contacts in Bangkok was a Thai entrepreneur named Chaleo Yoovidhya, whose family business included a division that made one of these tonic drinks. In 1984, Mateschitz left Blendax and partnered with Yoovidhya to perfect and market what became Red Bull, whose original incarnation was the beverage Krating Daeng (Thai for red water buffalo). The ingredients were essentially the same in both the original and international-bestselling version—citrus and herb flavorings mixed with lots of sugar, plus taurine, an amino acid, and doses of caffeine and glucuronolactone, a carbohydrate—except the new Red Bull in a distinctive silver and blue aluminum can would be carbonated.

Red Bull took three years to reach Austrian consumers, with Mateschitz needing first to win the approval of both government regulators as well as skeptics who asserted that he and Yoovidhya were about to see their half-million-dollar investment disappear down the drain. The first focus-group tests on Red Bull were not a good harbinger of success, Mateschitz recalled in an interview with Kerry A. Dolan in *Forbes*. "People didn't believe the taste, the logo, the brand name. I'd never before experienced such a disaster." When the product did arrive in stores, however, it began selling well enough, and that success was repeated in Hungary and then Britain. A 1994 launch in Germany had mixed results: Red Bull sold out so quickly that Mateschitz's production line could not meet the huge demand when the factory ran out of aluminum for the cans.

Red Bull was a novelty when it began appearing in U.S. stores in 1997, but Mateschitz's clever marketing strategy positioning it as a renegade product with no big corporate ties helped it catch on with teens and young adults. It also was hyped as an ideal mixer for alcoholic drinks, especially vodka, and developed a reputation for moderating the negative effects of a night of drinking; rumors occasionally surfaced that Red Bull contained a secret ingredient, which the company did little to dispel. A decade later, Red Bull no longer dominated the

beverage niche sector it had single-handedly developed, after new competition from Monster, Crunk, and Diesel began cutting into its once-mighty 75 percent share of the energy-drink market.

Early on in his company's history, Mateschitz strove to make Red Bull a presence in the more riskier forms of sports entertainment. One of his first coups came just when Red Bull arrived on the Austrian market, when he persuaded a well-known Formula One auto racing star, Gerhard Berger, to hold one when the television cameras were rolling. Since then, Mateschitz has sponsored numerous extreme-sports athletes and events, such as the Red Bull Air Race World Series, an international aerobatics competition, and the Red Bull Flugtag, an annual contest for homemade flying machines. He also owns a pair of European Grand Prix racing teams, sponsors and owns a NASCAR team, and acquired the New York MetroStars, a Major League Soccer team, in 2006, which he promptly renamed the New York Red Bulls.

Mateschitz has never married, but is the father of a teenaged son from a past relationship. Intensely private, he rarely sits for interviews and often bristles at questions regarding his personal life. When an Austrian gossip magazine proved too interested in his lifestyle, the publicity-shy mogul managed to purchase the publication, which promptly halted coverage of the new boss. At his company headquarters in Fuschl, near Salzburg, he runs an organization infused with a similarly iconoclastic spirit. "Instead of having presidents, directors and chairmen, we had a defensive line, an offensive line, coaches and quarterbacks," he explained to Byrnes in the *Independent* interview. "All this sounds better than directors and a board. In our company, we have almost no control system because we believe in self-motivation and responsibility. Of course, you have to be able to handle this freedom."

Sources

Beverage World, June 15, 2006, p. 14.
Brandweek, May 28, 2001, p. 21.
Economist, May 11, 2002.
Forbes, March 28, 2005, p. 126.
Independent (London, England), January 6, 2005, p. 2.
New York Times, October 29, 2006.
Sports Illustrated, August 4, 2003, p. A8.

—*Carol Brennan*

Cormac McCarthy

Author

Born Charles Joseph McCarthy, Jr., July 20, 1933, in Providence, RI; son of Charles Joseph, Sr. (an attorney) and Gladys (McGrail) McCarthy; married Lee Holleman, 1961 (divorced); married Anne DeLisle (a pop singer and restaurateur), 1967 (divorced); married Jennifer Winkley, 1998; children: Cullen (from first marriage), John Francis (from third marriage). *Education:* Attended the University of Tennessee.

Addresses: *Agent*—International Creative Management, 40 W. 57th St., New York, NY 10019. *Office*—c/o Alfred A. Knopf, 201 E. 50th St., New York, NY 10022.

Career

Served in United States Air Force, 1953-57; began writing novels, 1959; worked in an auto-parts warehouse, Chicago, IL, c. early 1960s; published first novel, *The Orchard Garden,* 1965; wrote teleplay, *The Gardener's Son,* PBS, 1977; joined the Santa Fe Institute, Santa Fe, New Mexico, c. 2001; *The Road* chosen for the Oprah Winfrey Book Club, made appearance on the *Oprah Winfrey Show,* 2007.

Awards: Ingram-Merrill Foundation grant for creative writing, 1960; American Academy of Arts and Letters traveling fellowship to Europe, 1965-66; William Faulkner Foundation Award for *The Orchard Keeper,* 1965; Rockefeller Foundation grant, 1966; Guggenheim Fellowship, 1976; MacArthur Foundation grant, 1981; Jean Stein Award, American Academy and Institution of Arts and Letters, 1991; National Book Award for fiction, for *All the Pretty Horses,* 1992; National Book Critics Award for fiction, for *All the Pretty Horses,* 1992; Pulitzer Prize for fiction, for *The Road,* 2007; Institute of Arts and Letters Award; Lyndhurst Foundation grant.

Sidelights

Though intensely private author Cormac McCarthy generally eschews publicity, interviews, and the expected literary lifestyle, he is widely recognized as a significant American author, producing classic works of fiction written in amazingly effective language. His novels nearly always avoid domestic issues to focus on characters, primarily male and often illiterate, who are usually outcasts and whose lives are explored through what the *New York Times'* Richard B. Woodward described as an "intense natural observation, a kind of morbid realism." Despite low sales for much of his career until the novels that made up the "Border Trilogy" were published in the 1990s, McCarthy was a writer's writer whose books were highly regarded by other writers and academics.

Born Charles Joseph McCarthy, Jr. on July 20, 1933, in Providence, Rhode Island, he was the son of Charles Joseph, Sr., an attorney, and his wife, Gladys. Of Celtic Irish decent, Cormac was a family nickname first given to his father by Irish aunts. McCarthy and his five brothers and sisters were raised in relative wealth outside of Knoxville, Tennessee, while their father worked for the Tennessee Valley Authority. Around the large family house were woods and people living in small shacks. Mc-

Carthy was intrigued by the lives being lived in the impoverished homes as well as Knoxville's underworld, and such interests later informed his novels.

McCarthy received his education at parochial schools, though he hated school and enjoyed a number of hobbies. Despite his intense dislike of educational institutions, he attended the University of Tennessee for a few years studying engineering, business, and liberal arts. He left college to join the U.S. Air Force in 1953. After four years in the Air Force, McCarthy returned to the University of Tennessee. Having become a voracious reader of literature while stationed in Alaska, he began focusing on the subject at college, writing several stories for a school literary magazine, and began writing novels himself in 1959. After a total of four years at the University of Tennessee, McCarthy dropped out again without receiving a degree in 1960.

McCarthy's creative efforts were aided by winning an Ingram-Merrill Foundation grant for creative writing in 1960. As he focused his energies on writing, McCarthy married his first wife, Lee Holleman, in 1961, with whom he had a son named Cullen the following year. The couple's marriage was short-lived, and they soon divorced. McCarthy was already working on what would become his first novel, *The Orchard Keeper*, as he had been since college, living in cities such as Asheville, North Carolina, and New Orleans, Louisiana. He finished it while working at an auto parts warehouse part-time in Chicago.

McCarthy then sent the manuscript for *The Orchard Keeper* to Random House, where it reached the hands of respected editor Albert Erskine. Understanding McCarthy's talent, Erskine became the author's long-time editor and helped get the novel in print. Published in 1965, *The Orchard Keeper* is set in the hills of Tennessee where a way of life in the woods is vanishing. The story focuses on the life of a young boy, two older men who come in and out of it, and their shared love for coon hounds. The novel won the William Faulkner Foundation Award in 1965. Comparing McCarthy to such storied authors as Faulkner and explaining his appeal as a writer, Woodward explained in the *New York Times*, "McCarthy's prose restores the terror and grandeur of the physical world with a biblical gravity that can shatter a reader. A page from any of his books—minimally punctuated, without quotation marks, avoiding apostrophes, colons or semicolons—has a stylized spareness that magnifies the force and precision of his words. Unimaginable cruelty and the simplest things, the sound of a tap on a door, exist side by side...."

In 1965, McCarthy also won the American Academy of Arts and Letters traveling fellowship to Europe, which he held through 1966 and resulted in travel in 1967. Writing was McCarthy's primary life focus, and he never held a steady job, including the teaching of writing, at any time, which led to problematic personal relationships. He married his second wife, Anne DeLisle, whom he met in Europe, in 1967. For most of their eight-year relationship, they lived in a converted barn on a dairy farm in poverty, bathng in a nearby lake. Despite limited to nonexistent income save from awards, McCarthy would turn down offers of thousands of dollars to speak at universities about books. McCarthy and DeLisle eventually divorced.

Early in the couple's marriage, they lived on the Mediterranean island of Ibiza where McCarthy wrote his second novel *Outer Dark*. Published in 1968, the book was set in the South and focused on a young girl's wandering search for her baby who had been created by an incestuous relationship with her brother. The brother also travels throughout the South, witnessing horrific acts of violence including the murder of a child by three men. McCarthy followed *Outer Dark* with 1974's *Child of God*, which focused unflinchingly on the Lester Ballard, a necrophiliac and mass murderer who resides with his many victims in underground caves. In the book, McCarthy does not explore why Ballard is the way he is, but depicts him with some sympathy and humor.

Occasionally, McCarthy worked in a different genre. In 1974, director Richard Pearce contacted McCarthy to asked him to write the teleplay for *The Gardener's Son*. McCarthy agreed to the assignment and the production aired on PBS in 1977. The drama was set in the 1870s in South Carolina and focused on the murder of a mill owner by an unstable boy who had a wooden leg. The boy is hung for his crime. A young male child is also at the heart of his 1979 novel, *Suttree*, which was one of his only books to deal directly with family and autobiographical issues. A difficult conflict between a father and a son sits at the novel's heart, as the adult son defies his successful father by living on a houseboat and fishing on a polluted river. The son seemed to be based on McCarthy, who based many of the drunks and fighters on friends and acquaintances he knew long ago from Knoxville's bar scene.

By this time, McCarthy was living in the Southwest. He did not write about areas he had not visited and had been making scouting trips there by the mid-1970s. McCarthy moved to the Southwest in 1974, and began making his primary residence El Paso,

Texas, in 1976. He still regularly returned to Tennessee, and was temporarily living in a Knoxville motel room when he learned he won one of the so-called "genius grants" from the MacArthur Foundation in 1981. The following year, McCarthy bought a small stone cottage in El Paso, which remained his home for some time.

McCarthy's next novel, 1985's *Blood Meridian; or, The Evening Redness in the West,* was the result of his research in the Southwest. Full of violence and nihilism, it was based on historical events there in 1849 to 1850 to explore evil on the American frontier. McCarthy accomplishes this through the eyes of a character called "the kid" who falls in with a scalp-hunting gang.

While more recognition was coming McCarthy's way because of the literary prowess of his novels, he still lived a relatively simple lifestyle through the 1990s. He renovated his cottage until funds dried up, and saved money by cutting his own hair and doing his laundry at a nearby Laundromat. He also ate meals cooked on a hot plate or at a cafeteria. His collection of 7,000 books was primarily housed in storage facilities. By this time, he began what became his most ambitious literary work, a trio of novels known as the "Border Trilogy."

In 1992, McCarthy published the first of the three, *All the Pretty Horses,* Unlike previous novels, the novel was more accessible to the average reader and less dark as it focuses on a teenager from Texas, John Grady Cole, in 1950, and his adventures in Mexico. Cole convinces a friend, Lacey Rawlins, to ride off on horseback there after the death of Cole's grandfather and amidst his parents' divorce. In Mexico, Cole discovers a gift for breaking horses on a ranch where he and Rawlins work as vaqueros. At the ranch, he also has an affair with the owner's daughter which ends badly and with arrests on trumped-up charges for the Americans. While description remained important in *All the Pretty Horses,* dialogue, often comical but austere, takes precedence sometimes. The novel won several awards, including the National Book Award, and was a best seller.

The success of *All the Pretty Horses* brought McCarthy a wider audience, which grew with the other two volumes of the trilogy, 1994's *The Crossing* and 1998's *Cities of the Plain.* Like *Horses, The Crossing* also focuses on Americans crossing over the Mexican border and was a best seller. Set in 1941, *The Crossing* draws on Mexican history to tell the story of the Parham brothers who go there looking for

work, encounter such characters as a she-wolf and an Indian, and how one sibling loses his life. McCarthy ties the novels together in *Cities on the Plain,* where John Grady Cole and Billy Parham meet in 1951. They work on the same ranch in Orogrande, New Mexico, and must deal with the end of the ranch life as a military base will soon replace it and their way of life. Love also plays a role in the novel as Cole sells his horse to buy a 16-year-old Mexican prostitute from nearby Juarez and marry her.

With the success of the "Border Trilogy," McCarthy bought a new home in the El Paso area, married his third wife, Jennifer Winkley, in 1998, and had a son with her, John Francis. He continued his hobby of playing pool and was also a devoted golfer and working out enthusiast. The family soon moved to Santa Fe, where around 2001 McCarthy began working at a scientific think tank called the Santa Fe Institute. He was the only fiction writer among scientists meeting to offer analysis of interdisciplinary problems from a variety of scientific areas. He still remained reclusive and generally refused to grant media interviews or appear at literary events. He continued to write, however, though it took seven years for him to produce his next novel. When he did and *No Country for Old Men* was published in 2005, McCarthy's media appearances increased to one in support of the novel.

In *No Country for Old Men,* McCarthy returned to the violent themes of his earlier novels as he focuses on the experiences of Llewellyn Moss. While hunting antelope in the desert, Moss steals money from a drug deal gone wrong and is chased across Texas by the dealers and others who want the money back. Unlike previous works, the plot moves quickly and was compared to a screenplay by some critic. A filmed adaptation of the novel was expected in late 2007.

McCarthy continued on darker themes with 2006's *The Road,* which won 2007's Pulitzer Prize for Fiction. Set after a nuclear explosion, the novel focuses on the journey of a father and son as they struggle to survive in a post-apocalyptic winter. Few people survived and they know their own survival will probably be short-lived. Unexpectedly, media icon Oprah Winfrey selected the novel for her book club and even convinced McCarthy to appear on her show in June of 2007 in an interview taped at the Santa Fe Institute.

In the interview, McCarthy admitted his young son was the inspiration for the novel and a new perspective in his life. The *Plain Dealer*'s Karen R. Long quoted McCarthy as saying on *The Oprah Winfrey Show,* "I just had this image of these fires up on a hill ... and I thought a lot about my little boy. You have a child when you are older, and it wrenches you up out of your nap and makes you look at things fresh. It forces the world on you, and I think it's a good thing."

Selected writings

Novels

The Orchard Keeper, Random House (New York, NY), 1965.

Outer Dark, Random House, 1968.

Child of God, Random House, 1974.

Suttree, Random House, 1979.

Blood Meridian; or, The Evening Redness in the West, Random House, 1985.

All the Pretty Horses, Random House, 1992.

The Crossing, Random House, 1994.

Cities of the Plain, Random House, 1998.

No Country for Old Men, Knopf (New York, NY), 2005.

The Road, Knopf, 2006.

Teleplays

The Gardener's Son: A Screenplay, Ecco Press (Hopewell, NJ), 1996.

Sources

Periodicals

Buffalo News (Buffalo, NY), June 26, 1994, p. 7.
Houston Chronicle, June 27, 1999, p. 8.
Independent (London, England), June 13, 1998, p. 11.
Los Angeles Times, April 17, 2007, p. A19; June 4, 2007, p. E3.
New York Times, April 19, 1992, p. 28; May 17, 1992, p. 9; May 17, 1998, p. 16.
Plain Dealer (Cleveland, OH), June 6, 2007, p. E7.
Texas Monthly, July 1998, p. 76.
Vanity Fair, August 2005, p. 98.

Online

Contemporary Authors Online, Gale Group, 2007.

—A. Petruso

Mary McDonnell

Actress

Born April 28, 1952, in Wilkes-Barre, PA; married Randle Mell (an actor); children: Olivia, Michael. *Education:* Attended the State University of New York—Fredonia.

Addresses: *Agent*—William Morris Agency, 151 El Camino Dr., Beverly Hills, CA 90212; The Gersh Agency, 232 North Canon Dr., Beverly Hills, CA 90210.

Career

Actress in films, including: *Garbo Talks*, 1984; *Matewan*, 1987; *Tiger Warsaw*, 1988; *Dances with Wolves*, 1990; *Grand Canyon*, 1991; *Sneakers*, 1992; *Passion Fish*, 1992; *Blue Chips*, 1994; *Independence Day*, 1996; *Mumford*, 1999; *Donnie Darko*, 2001; *Crazy Like a Fox*, 2004. Theater appearances include: *Buried Child*, Theatre de Lys, 1978-79; *Letters Home*, American Place Theatre, New York City, 1979; *Still Life*, American Place Theatre, New York City, 1981; *A Doll's Life*, Hartford Stage Company, Hartford, CT, 1986-87; *National Anthems*, New Haven, CT, 1988; *The Heidi Chronicles*, Plymouth Theatre, New York City, 1990; *O, Pioneers!*, Boston, MA, 1990; *Summer and Smoke*, Criterion Center Stage Right Theatre, New York City, 1996. Television appearances include: *As the World Turns*, CBS, 1980; *E/R*, CBS, 1984-95; *O, Pioneers!* (play), 1991; *The American Clock* (play), 1993; *High Society*, CBS, 1995-96; *Replacing Dad* (movie), CBS, 1999; *Ryan Caulfield: Year One*, Fox, 1999; *ER*, NBC, 2001-02; *Battlestar Galactica* (miniseries), Sci Fi, 2003; *Battlestar Galactica*, Sci Fi, 2004-08. Also worked as an acting teacher with her husband.

Awards: Obie Award, *Village Voice*, for *Still Life*, 1981.

Sidelights

Finding success on stage, screen, and television, Mary McDonnell has had a long, varied acting career. She has been nominated and won numerous awards for her work, including an Academy Award-nominated turn in the western *Dances with Wolves* and an Obie Award-winning performance in *Still Life*. In the early 2000s, McDonnell was receiving acclaim for her television work, including a stint on *ER* and playing the president in the Sci Fi remake of the series *Battlestar Galactica*.

McDonnell was born on April 28, 1952, in Wilkes-Barre, Pennsylvania, the daughter of a consultant for big corporations. Raised in Ithaca, New York, McDonnell had five sisters and one brother. Sports held more interest for her than the arts as a youth. She was a competitive swimmer throughout her childhood. McDonnell also had dramatic moments as a young person, which she believed led her father to understand she might pursue acting.

McDonnell told the Associated Press's Hillel Italie: "I would have an emotional reaction to an imaginary situation that was extraordinary. In seventh grade there was a movie I saw about the sinking of the Titanic, and I projected into it so deeply I ran into the bathroom afterwards and locked the door. I was hysterical. My mother had to open the door with a screwdriver."

McDonnell did not begin acting until college, however. She got the desire to act while a student at the State University of New York at Fredonia. Acting soon came to mean much to McDonnell. She told Candace Burke-Block of the *Chicago Sun-Times*, "Acting gives me the opportunity to contact things that I have inside of myself that I can't necessarily touch in my daily life. It gives me a chance to express it, to open up. For me there is so much going on internally that acting allows me to channel it creatively, so that it doesn't explode inside of me and turn into daily neuroses. It's hard work, but it's a very healthy thing for me to do, a real opportunity to be a healthier person."

After college, McDonnell focused on stage work, both regional productions and in New York City, throughout the late 1970s and the whole of the 1980s. Early notable roles included playing emotionally abused Shelly in Sam Shepard's play *Buried Child* beginning in 1978 in New York City. The appearance marked her New York debut as an actress. In 1981, McDonnell nabbed an Obie Award for her work as Cheryl in *Still Life* at the American Place Theatre. By 1986, she was playing Nora in a production of Henrik Ibsen's *A Doll House* for the Hartford Stage Company. Her work in the role was praised as was her turn as the wife in the 1988 production of *National Anthems* at New Haven, Connecticut's Long Wharf Theatre.

McDonnell also occasionally worked in film in the 1980s. Her first film role came in 1984's *Garbo Talks* as Lady Cauplet. McDonnell followed this film with a more acclaimed turn in *Matewan*. In this film, which was directed by John Sayles and released in 1987, McDonnell played Elma Radnor, a boardinghouse owner in West Virginia in the 1930s. The film focused on a labor dispute in local coal fields.

By 1990, McDonnell was appearing in the title role of the New York City production of *Heidi Chronicles* and as Alexandra Bergson in the classic *Oh Pioneers!* in Boston. The latter production was filmed for television, and critics singled out McDonnell for her performance. John Voorhees of the *Seattle Times* wrote, "While McDonnell is excellent, and makes this production worth watching, the rest of the company seldom achieves her level of emotional involvement."

In 1990, McDonnell had the breakout role of her film career when she played Stands With a Fist in *Dances With Wolves*. The role was challenging for McDonnell as she played a white woman who had been living with Sioux Indians since she was a young child. Her parents had been killed by the Pawnee, but she escaped and was later found and adopted by the Sioux medicine man, Kicking Bird. With the Sioux way of life being encroached upon by whites and an attractive white man, Lt. John Dunbar (played by the film's director, Kevin Costner) showing interest in her, McDonnell's character is forced to recall her English in order to serve as translator between Dunbar and Kicking Bird. This process causes her to confront the trauma and loss she had buried since childhood.

McDonnell found the role complex. She told Peter M. Nichols of the *New York Times*, "She has to set up a duality. As an adult she again has to let in that pain, face up to it and move forward with it. In the process, she wins love and intimacy. That's an interesting lesson of a life well lived." For her sensitive portrayal of Stands With a Fist in *Dances With Wolves*, McDonnell was honored with an Academy Award nomination for best supporting actress as well as a Golden Globe Award nomination.

After *Dances With Wolves*, McDonnell's film career blossomed through much of the 1990s. She told Catherine Dunphy of the *Toronto Star*, "I'm not surprised I'm making movies but I would never have seen myself in these movies." In 1991, she appeared in *Grand Canyon*, which contrasted the lives of upper-middle-class white people and working-class African Americans in Los Angeles. McDonnell played Claire in the film, a married woman who wants to adopt an abandoned baby she finds. After such serious fare, McDonnell was happy to co-star as Liz in a caper comedy, 1992's *Sneakers*, about a long-time group of friends.

While such films brought McDonnell some attention, she received additional Academy Award and Golden Globe Award nominations for her work in the film *Passion Fish*. Also released in 1992 and directed by Sayles, McDonnell starred as May-Alice Culhane, a diva soap opera actress who is left a paraplegic after a taxi accident. McDonnell's Culhane is compelled to leave New York City and return home to Louisiana to live out her days with bitterness. One live-in attendant (played by Alfre Woodard) she hires to take care of her also comes with a set of problems. The Culhane character surmounts the depression caused by her physical disability with the help of her wise and disciplined attendant.

After *Passion Fish*, McDonnell appeared in several films of note in the 1990s, including playing First Lady Marilyn Whitmore in the 1996 sci-fi smash *Independence Day* and empty rich woman Althea Brockett in 1999's *Mumford*. However, a few of her film roles were more questionable. In addition to roles in several independent films, McDonnell played Jenny Bell in 1994's *Blue Chips*, the film showcasing basketball star Shaquille O'Neal. Besides one appearance on stage in 1996, in a production of *Summer and Smoke*, McDonnell soon found herself working more and more in television.

In 1993, McDonnell appeared in a sweeping miniseries adaptation of the Arthur Miller play *The American Clock*. Set during the Great Depression, McDonnell played Rose Baumler, the wife of a successful dress manufacturer. She must cope with the family's financial losses as they move downward socially and economically from Manhattan to Brooklyn.

A few years later, McDonnell made a return to series television. After flirting with the genre in the 1980s—she appeared in a soap, *As the World Turns*, and a comedy, *E/R*, she next appeared in another situation comedy, *High Society*. She played a high-flying, hard-living Manhattan publisher in the short-lived series. After an even shorter stint on the quickly cancelled *Ryan Caulfield: Year One* in 1999, McDonnell was nominated for an Emmy Award for her work on the hit drama *ER*. She took on the role of Eleanor Carter for the 2001 to 2002 season.

Series were not McDonnell's only television work. She appeared in a number of television movies, especially in the mid- to late 1990s and early 2000s. One television movie in which McDonnell received praise for her acting was 1999's *Replacing Dad*. She played Linda Marsh, whose school principal husband, George, leaves her for a younger woman, their daughter's teacher. The *New York Times*' Anita Gates wrote, "Ms. McDonnell is the attraction here. She is a fine actress and is so beautifully directed by Joyce Chopra that her shock, pain, and intelligence mingle to uncommonly powerful effect."

In 2003, McDonnell took a leading role in another science-fiction show. That year, she appeared in the miniseries based on the 1970s series *Battlestar Galactica*. This version with its darker, grittier plot still incorporated the humans running away from their lost civilization and the Cylons who want to continue to control them; it featured many of the same characters and concepts as the 1970s show. The success of the original miniseries justified a full-blown series, which began airing in 2004.

In both the miniseries and series, McDonnell played the president of the colonies, Laura Roslin. In addition to being in conflict with the ship's commander, played by Edward James Olmos, McDonnell's character suffers from breast cancer and experiences drug-induced hallucinations that cause her to believe her actions are the will of the gods. Over the years, the series also shifted from dealing with the conflict with the Cylons to conflicts with the fleet. Because the series also explored complex ideas about religion and conflict, the actress saw parallels to contemporary times.

McDonnell told Rob Owen of the *Pittsburgh Post-Gazette*, "From the outset, I found it extraordinarily relevant to the issues we're facing right now in terms of war and, in particular, in terms of how we perceive ourselves in relation to the concept of the enemy. I think we are in the process of desperately trying to evolve that into a more sophisticated understanding of what that means, and we're not doing a very good job of it." McDonnell also told *Entertainment Weekly* that Roslin meant much to her and had influenced her as well. She stated, "She's released me, in a way.... This part has taken me [and] Laura—we've gone together—into understanding the levels on which a great deal of the powerful people on the planet are thinking and need to be thinking in order to survive this very dark time."

While McDonnell was initially unsure about taking the role on *Battlestar Galactica*, she came to embrace it and enjoy the challenge. Though she had done a few films in the early 2000s, such as 2001's cult hit *Donnie Darko*, it was this science-fiction series that meant so much to her. Scheduled to air its last season in 2008, McDonnell could not imagine life without *Battlestar Galactica*. She told *Entertainment Weekly*, "I feel very satiated. Oh my gosh, how does one move on from *Battlestar*? Because having had the opportunity to delve into these issues and try to articulate them, I don't want to stop."

Sources

Books

Contemporary Theatre, Film, and Television, vol. 60, Thomson Gale, 2005.
Who's Who in America, 56th ed., Marquis Who's Who, 2007.

Periodicals

Associated Press, January 29, 1993.

Calgary Herald (Alberta, Canada), May 20, 1993, p. D10.

Chicago Sun-Times, January 20, 1992, sec. 2, p. 4; October 30, 1995, p. 35.

Daily Variety, August 23, 1993.

Entertainment Weekly, March 30, 2007, pp. 19-20.

Los Angeles Times, June 6, 2007, p. S12.

New York Times, December 2, 1990, sec. 2, p. 26; September 6, 1996, p. C5; March 12, 1999, p. E34.

Pittsburgh Post-Gazette (PA), July 10, 2005, p. E1.

Seattle Times, May 16, 1991, p. D10.

Toronto Star, September 11, 1992, p. C7.

USA Today, September 24, 1999, p. 8E.

Wilkes Barre Times Leader (PA), March 7, 2007, p. D3.

Online

"Mary McDonnell," Internet Movie Database, http://imdb.com/name/nm0001521/ (November 5, 2007).

—*A. Petruso*

Douglas Melton

Robert Pitts/Landov

Professor and research scientist

Born Douglas A. Melton, September 26, 1953, in Chicago, IL; son of A. (a grocery store manager) and Betty (a court reporter) Melton; married Gail O'Keefe; children: Samuel, Emma. *Education:* University of Illinois at Urbana-Champaign, B.S., 1975; Cambridge University, B.A., 1977; Trinity College and MRC Laboratory of Molecular Biology, Cambridge University, Ph.D., 1980.

Addresses: *Office*—7 Divinity Ave., Rm. 465, Cambridge, MA 02138. *E-mail*—dmeltonmcb.harvard. edu.

Career

Assistant professor, Harvard University, 1981-84; associate professor, Harvard University, 1984-87; John L. Loeb Associate Professor of the Natural Sciences, Harvard University, 1987-88; professor of molecular and cellular biology, Harvard University, 1988—; biologist, Massachusetts General Hospital, Boston, 1993—; investigator, Howard Hughes Medical Institute, 1994—; Thomas Dudley Cabot Professor in the Natural Sciences, Harvard University, 1999— co-director of the Harvard Stem Cell Institute, Harvard University, 2004—. His scientific papers appear in such journals as *Science, Development,* and the *New England Journal of Medicine.*

Member: Associate member, Children's Hospital, Boston, 1994—; National Academy of the Sciences, 1995—; American Academy of Arts and Sciences, 1995—; chairman of the scientific advisory board, Stowers Institute for Medical Research, 1999—; Institute of Medicine, 2001—.

Awards: Marshall scholar, Marshall Aid Commemoration Commission (U.K.) 1975-78; Searle scholar, Kinship Foundation, 1983-86; young investigator award, American Society of Biochemistry & Molecular Biology, 1991; George Ledlie Prize, Harvard University, 1991; Richard Lounsberry Award, National Academy of Science, 1995; Eliot P. Joslin medal, Joslin Diabetes Center, 2002; named one of the 100 people who shape our world, *Time* magazine, 2007.

Sidelights

Many American researchers chafed at the restrictions by the federal government put on their efforts to develop new medical technology using embryonic stem cells in 2001. Douglas Melton, a biology professor at Harvard University, was one of them. He testified at hearings before Congress in 1999, discussing the good that could come out of the research. Despite his efforts, laws were enacted to limit the lines of cells that would be available for research in any scientific labs that received government funding. Melton did not give up, continuing his research in a privately funded environment.

Melton earned his bachelor's degree in biology from the University of Illinois long before he became involved in researching stem cells. After finishing his undergraduate work, he traveled to England on a Marshall scholarship and studied the history and philosophy of science at Cambridge University, receiving a second bachelor's degree there. He stayed on for a Ph.D. in molecular biology at Trinity College and MRC Laboratory in Molecular Biology, part of Cambridge University. After graduating, he published several papers on frog development, becoming well known for his research in that area.

In 1993, everything changed. His son, Samuel, then six months old, was diagnosed with type 1 diabetes. (His teenage daughter, Emma, was diagnosed with the same disease in 2001.) The disease requires daily injections of insulin for the diabetic to survive. "Like any parent, I asked myself, What can I do?" Melton recalled to Claudia Dreifus of the *New York Times.* "The answer was to shift my research to an area that might help. I wanted my children to know I was doing everything I could for them." Melton began studying the pancreatic development of frogs in order to focus on the organ that secretes insulin in healthy bodies. He was engaged in these studies when other scientists introduced the possibility of growing human embryonic stem cells in a laboratory environment. Melton began working with human cells, using his previous studies of the pancreas to research how embryonic stem cells could be applied to grow the beta-cells that would create insulin. Unfortunately, stem cell research was still relatively new and there were very few stem cell lines available to work with.

Melton's studies were controversial due to the ethical debate of using embryonic stem cells, harvested from fertilized eggs, in experiments. Many Americans believe that life begins at conception rather than at birth, so using embryonic stem cells, which could only be taken from embryos in "fatal" ways, created a great deal of ethical concern. The debate landed in the U.S. Congress, where hearings took place in order to determine what laws, if any, should govern the research. Melton testified about the hopes he had that he would be able to use the research to find a cure for the type 1 diabetes his son suffered from. Two years later, laws were passed keeping any federally funded labs from working with stem cells and limiting the number of available cell lines that researchers were allowed to work with. The shortage before had been problematic, but the laws made research even more difficult.

To begin with, Melton had a new layer of record-keeping to handle. In 1999, he was made the Thomas Dudley Cabot Professor of Natural Science at Harvard University and, in 2004, he became co-director of Harvard's Stem Cell Institute. In order to keep the Stem Cell Institute in compliance with the laws, new security measures had to be put into place. Graduate student researchers and postdoctoral workers on federal funding were no longer allowed to be on staff. All staff were required to have key cards. Money for mundane purchases, normally handled through the larger budget of Harvard University, had to be handled through the Stem Cell Institute exclusively. "We have an accountant who makes sure that not a penny of federal funds goes to embryonic stem cell research," Melton told Dreifus. "We have [to] separate everything—light bulbs, computers, centrifuges."

Despite these difficulties and restrictions, Melton has persevered. In 2001, he led a team at Harvard researching the connection between blood vessels and the construction of the body: they showed that cells that would become the dorsal aorta—a major blood vessel—directly impacted the levels of insulin in the pancreas. In 2003, Melton's team had developed 17 new lines of stem cells, which they pledged to make available to the scientific community. These lines were cultured from early embryos donated by patients at an infertility clinic in Boston; if they had not been used for research, the embryos would have been discarded. "We made them for our use and to share with the research community," Melton said in *Genomics & Genetics Weekly.* Referring to the small number of lines available to American researchers, which come from ten labs, Melton said, "The ostensibly available lines are too few. And either they don't live long enough to survive shipment or they are very expensive." *The New England Journal* responded to the development by publishing an editorial requesting that the cell lines be added to the registry of lines allowed to be used in the United States. "There is too much suffering that may be remediable through the therapeutic application of this new approach to place stem cell lines off limits," a *USA Today* article quoted the editors as having written.

Since those 17 lines were released in 2003, Melton has continued his work, bringing the number of lines created to more than 100. His team has also worked toward ways of creating embryonic stem cells without using human ova. One of these projects fuses adult skin cells with an already existing embryonic line. Not only does this help in avoiding controversy, there is a much greater chance that a body would accept transplants because the adult cells would match the DNA of the patient. The federal government applauded the steps, implying that the ban on using stem cells had pushed the scientists toward finding new ways to use the technology. Alan Leshner and James Thomson, in their commentary published by the *Washington Post,* wrote, "Far from vindicating the current U.S. policy of withholding federal funds from many of those working to develop potentially lifesaving embryonic stem cells, recent papers in the journals *Science* and *Cell* described a breakthrough achieved despite political reasons." On Melton's profile on the Howard Hughes Medical Institute Web site, the contributor expressed the hopes of the team that this approach would reduce controversy.

Melton himself, who was named one of the 100 people who shape our world by *Time* magazine in 2007, remains active about speaking out against the restrictions, which he feels limits the young minds that would otherwise be working in the field. He also feels that explaining scientific developments to the public would open up a conversation that might lessen controversy. As he said on the Howard Hughes Medical Institute Web site, "Among the many lessons I've learned is that we, as scientists, should make greater efforts to explain what we are doing and why we are doing it. For better or worse, this needs to be done in newspapers and on TV, not just in scientific journals."

Sources

Periodicals

Applied Genetics News, October, 2001.
BioWorld Week, March 8, 2004, p. 4.
Genomics & Genetics Weekly, November 28, 2003, p. 75.
M2 Presswire, May 2, 2005.
National Right to Life News, September 2005, p. 7.
New York Times, January 24, 2005, p. F2.
Roanoke Times, December 9, 2007, p. 2.
Science, September 28, 2001, p. 2365.
Time, May 2, 2007.
USA Today, March 4, 2004, p. 2D.
U.S. News & World Report, March 15, 2004, p. 70.
Washington Post, December 3, 2007, p. A17.

Online

"Douglas A. Melton," Harvard Stem Cell Institute, http://www.hsci.harvard.edu/pri-fac-profile/271 (February 18, 2008).
"Douglas A. Melton," Harvard University Department of Molecular and Cellular Biology, http://www.mcb.harvard.edu/Faculty/Melton.html (February 18, 2008).
"Douglas A. Melton, Ph.D.," Howard Hughes Medical Institute, http://www.hhmi.org/research/investigators/melton_bio.html (February 18, 2008).
"Douglas A. Melton, Ph.D.," Stowers Institute for Medical Research, http://www.stowers-institute.org/Public/ScientificAdvisoryBoard.asp (February 18, 2008).
"Scholar Profile: Douglas A. Melton," Searle Scholars Program, http://www.searlescholars.net/people/1983/melton.html (February 18, 2008).

—Alana Joli Abbott

Frank Miller

Comic book author, screenwriter, and film director

Born January 27, 1957, in Olney, Maryland; son of Marjorie Brigham Miller (a retired nurse); married Lynn Varley (a comic colorist) (divorced).

Addresses: *Contact*—Dark Horse Comics, 10956 SE Main St., Milwaukie OR 97222; Troublemaker Studios, 4900 Old Manor Road, Austin, TX 78723.

Career

Began career with Marvel Comics, inking and writing for the character Daredevil, 1979-early 1980s; worked on comic character Wolverine, 1982; created, inked and wrote *Ronin* for DC Comics, 1983-84; created *Batman: The Dark Knight Returns* series, 1986; followed with *Batman: Year One*, 1987; wrote screenplays for *RoboCop 2*, 1990, and *RoboCop 3*, 1993; created *Sin City* graphic novels, 1991-99; released *Batman: The Dark Knight Strikes Again*, 2002; co-directed *Sin City*, 2005.

Member: Comic Book Legal Defense Fund.

Awards: Will Eisner Comic Industry Award (also called an Eisner Award) for best writer/artist, 1993; Eisner Award for best penciler/inker-B&W, 1993; Eisner Award for best graphic album (reprint), for *Sin City*, 1993; Eisner Award for best limited series, for *Sin City: A Dame to Kill For*, 1995; Eisner Award for best short story, for *Sin City: The Babe Wore Red*, 1995; Eisner Award for best limited series, for *Sin City: The Big Fat Kill*, 1996; Eisner Award for best graphic album (reprint), for *Sin City: That Yellow Bastard*, 1998; Eisner Award for best limited series, for *300*, 1999; Eisner Award for best writer/artist, for *300*, 1999; Austin Film Critics Award for best animated film, for *Sin City*, 2006.

Sidelights

In the 1970s, Frank Miller launched a comic-book revolution by adding literary depth and emotional power to comic's costumed heroes. During the late 1970s and early '80s, he thrilled readers with his take on Wolverine and Daredevil and created enduring characters such as the assassin Elektra. In 1986, Miller re-imaged Batman with his psychologically dark and morally complex storylines. In the 1990s, Miller became famous for his violent, yet stylish *Sin City* series of graphic novels, which took the comic-book medium to a new creative level. In 2005, Miller turned to moviemaking, serving as co-director in a visually striking adaptation of his Sin City series. Afterward, he landed more movie projects, including a solo job writing and directing *The Spirit*, an adaptation of Will Eisner's famed comic. Highly successful in the comics industry, Miller stands poised to make his mark in the movies as well.

Miller was born on January 27, 1957, in Olney, Maryland, but was raised in Montpelier, Vermont, in a family of four boys and three girls. He produced his first comic at the age of six and proudly trotted it into the kitchen, handing the stapled mess to his mother. "The paper was all folded over and I'd drawn all over it," Miller told the London *Daily Telegraph*'s Will Lawrence. "That was my first hand-made comic. I held it up and told her that this was what I was going to be doing for the rest of my life. I really was dedicated to creating comics from that age."

Growing up, Miller spent his free time reading comics, including Batman, and watching the family's black and white television. He was infatuated with TV's fictional characters who could perform amazing feats. "In third grade, my friends and I formed a superhero club," Miller told Susan Green in an article for the *Rutland Herald.* "We'd run around with our arms forward, as if flying."

During adolescence, Miller felt restless and dreamed of escaping small-town life for a turn in the big city. A few years after graduating from high school, Miller moved to New York City, home to both Marvel and DC Comics. "It was all or nothing," he told Green. "I felt, 'I have to do this or I'll die.'" With no formal training, Miller realized he had a lot to learn about drawing if he wanted to break into the comic-book world. To practice drawing human physiques, Miller bought muscle magazines to get a feel for how a hero's body might look. He also began hanging out in the studio of comic artist Neal Adams. Adams had broken into the field in the 1960s, making his mark such comic superheroes as Green Lantern and the X-Men. As Miller struggled to get a foothold in the industry, he supported himself through carpentry jobs and intermittent checks from his mother. Occasionally, he was hired to do fill-in work on various comics.

Miller's big break came in 1979 when Marvel Comics enlisted him to draw Daredevil, a comics superhero who had emerged in the 1960s. Daredevil is unique among crime fighters: He is blind, having lost his sight in a childhood accident. Because Daredevil was unable to see, his other senses evolved, and he gained the unique ability to perceive his surroundings with a "radar-sense." Though many comic artists have worked on the character, Miller's adaptations are the most celebrated. Miller started as a mere artist for the series then began writing the storylines. He revamped the series, introducing elements to mimic Hollywood's dark and shadowy film noir crime flicks of the 1940s and '50s. Miller also created Elektra, a ninja assassin with romantic ties to Daredevil. Elektra first appeared in "Daredevil No. 168" in January of 1981.

In 1982, Miller collaborated with X-Men writer Chris Claremont to produce a four-issue series featuring the X-Man character Wolverine, a superhero with animal-like mutations and a supernatural ability to heal himself. Miller's next big project involved the creation of his own series, *Ronin,* for DC Comics. In ancient Japan, a ronin was a samurai who had lost his master. In the series, a thirteenth-century ronin is transported to the twenty-first century, where lawlessness and depravity reign. Action-packed and filled with pulpy dialogue, *Ronin* debuted in 1984.

Next, Miller breathed new life into comics superhero Batman, whose popularity had waned. Released in 1986, Miller's *Batman: The Dark Knight Returns* series dealt with the latter portion of Batman's career. *Dark Knight* featured a ruthless, quasimystical Batman more reminiscent of the original 1930s Batman who was gritty and psychologically dark. By the time Miller began writing *Dark Knight,* Batman was no longer seen as a shadowy figure in his own right—the 1960s Batman television series, starring Adam West and filled with campy humor, had given Batman a lighter persona.

Miller redefined the character and introduced more melodramatic storylines. This Batman is tortured, filled with as many flaws as his enemies. Miller also turned some of the characters into metaphors for commenting on the politics of the day. Miller followed with a *Batman: Year One* series, which revisited Batman's childhood and delved into the beginning of Batman's career as a crime-fighting vigilante. The series pushed the limit of what people thought was possible in the genre, proving comics could be used as real literary vehicles to entertain adults—not children.

Dark Knight drew a more mainstream audience than most comics. It was featured in *Rolling Stone* magazine and landed on the *New York Times* best-seller list. It became a new standard by which comics were judged and ushered in an era of darker, more realistic comic-book characters. Miller's *Dark Knight* series also triggered a resurgence of interest in the character, prompting filmmaker Tim Burton to resurrect the crime fighter in his 1989 rendition of *Batman,* starring Michael Keaton as the caped crusader and Jack Nicholson as the Joker.

Miller's success as a storyteller prompted Hollywood to come calling. In the late 1980s, he was asked to write the screenplay for the two live-action *RoboCop* sequels. In the end, Miller was unsatisfied with the process and disturbed with all the finagling over the writing. The experience soured his view of Hollywood. Speaking to *Esquire,* Miller put it this way, "What I learned there is that your screenplay is a fire hydrant with an awful lot of dogs lined up behind it." After the *RoboCop* screenwriting venture, Miller returned to comics, beginning work on his bleak *Sin City* collection, published by Dark Horse Comics beginning in 1991.

Sin City is short for Basin City. Miller's Sin City is a fictional crime-riddled metropolis inhabited by snaky, trench-coated villains and sexy, armed hookers. The men are hard-drinking barbarians and the women are stunning. Miller rendered the panels using only black ink, avoiding outlines and shading. As a result, some figures are reduced to black silhouettes, while others appear as white images against a panel of inky black. The highly acclaimed seven-volume series made Miller a cult comic hero.

In 2001, Miller returned to Batman, releasing *Batman: The Dark Knight Strikes Again* series, published as a graphic novel in 2002. This tale takes place in a dystopian future where Batman has retired and decides to return to his work to save the world from itself. Once again, Miller used satire in the storylines to comment on the political climate. In this series, the U.S. president is really a computer-generated puppet controlled by corporate interests.

As Miller quietly went about his work, moviemakers continually courted him, seeking rights to turn his legendary *Sin City* graphic novels into a movie. He turned down more than ten offers, fearing no one would be faithful to the material. In 2003, director Robert Rodriguez of *Spy Kids* fame tracked down Miller with another proposal to take *Sin City* to the big screen. Miller said no. A few weeks later, Rodriguez contacted Miller again and asked him to fly to Austin, Texas, where Rodriguez is based, to shoot a test. Rodriguez told Miller that if he did not like the outcome, at least he would have a fun *Sin City* DVD to take home. Miller arrived to find actor Josh Hartnett ready to go. "This was no damn test," Miller told *Newsweek*'s Devin Gordon. "This was the first day of principal photography."

Rodriguez baited Miller with another incentive—an offer to co-direct the film, which would give him creative input. Miller agreed to take on the task. The deal caused trouble for Rodriquez, putting him in violation of strict Directors Guild of America rules by offering a co-director credit to someone with no film experience. Undaunted, Rodriguez quit the Guild and went ahead with the film. As production got under way, Quentin Tarantino joined the fray and guest-directed one scene. The trio worked well together. "They all got along like little boys in the sandbox, playing with their Ninja Turtles and having a great time," actress Brittany Murphy told *Newsday*'s Tom Beer.

Besides Murphy, who made her debut with 1995's *Clueless,* the 2005 movie featured a star-studded cast that included Jessica Alba, Rosario Dawson, Benicio Del Toro, Clive Owen, Mickey Rourke, Bruce Willis, and Elijah Wood. For the actors, the experience was unique because instead of filming on a set, they had to run their scenes against a plain, green screen. The backdrops—consisting of bulky buildings and poorly lit interiors—were created digitally and then "inserted" behind the actors. As a result, the movie itself resembles a comic book more than a film. In fact, the frames match up nearly panel for panel with the original comic, as does the dialogue. Just like the original comic, the film is composed of bleak blacks and barren whites. Color is reserved for accents—blood-red lips or the green eyes of a damsel.

As with Miller's original panels, the movie is ultra-violent. Writing in *Newsweek,* Gordon said the "movie seeks out the line between an R rating and an NC-17, then toe-tickles it for 135 minutes. It's gory stuff, but it's also a visually arresting blitzkrieg with action so bare-knuckled you'll leave the theater spitting teeth." Moviegoers flocked to theaters to see this comic-book-come-to-life. The movie, which cost $45 million to make, led the box office its opening weekend by taking in $28.1 million.

The movie mingles three of Miller's seven Sin City volumes. One tale involves a thug named Marv, as played by Rourke, who goes on a killing rampage while looking for the people responsible for murdering a prostitute whose company he enjoyed. Another storyline involves a man named Dwight, played by Owen, who works to dispose of a cop who was killed in the prostitute's quarters. In the third tale, a jaded cop, as played by Willis, tries to rescue a kidnapped girl from a psychopath.

The positive experience shifted Miller's view of Hollywood, and he allowed director Zack Snyder to adapt his historically inspired graphic novel *300* for the big screen. Released in 2006, it grossed $70 million its first weekend. *300* is an epic tale that deals with the Spartans and a retelling of the Greek war. Miller had created the *300* series in the late 1990s. His ex-wife, comic colorist Lynn Varley, worked on the series with him. She also colored *Ronin* and *Dark Knight Returns.*

As for the future, Miller's fans were eagerly awaiting another Dark Knight graphic novel. Miller began *Holy Terror, Batman* after 9/11—a book that pits

Batman against Al Qaeda. As of the end of 2007, Miller had yet to finish it because film projects were taking up most of his time. As 2008 got under way, Miller was busy with his movie adaptation of *The Spirit* and talks of *Sin City* sequels were in the works. Much to his comic fans' chagrin, Miller seems happy with the change of entertainment media. Speaking to Geoff Boucher of the *Los Angeles Times*, Miller noted his infatuation with the movie industry. "It's gone from being an abusive relationship to a torrid affair," he said. "And it is very satisfying."

Selected writings

Graphic novel collections

Sin City: The Hard Goodbye, Dark Horse Comics, 1993.

Sin City: A Dame to Kill For, Dark Horse Comics, 1994.

Sin City: The Big Fat Kill, Dark Horse Comics, 1994.

Ronin, DC Comics, 1995.

Batman: The Dark Knight Returns, Titan Books, Ltd., 1996.

Sin City: That Yellow Bastard, Dark Horse Comics, 1997.

Sin City: Family Values, Dark Horse Comics, 1997.

Sin City: Booze, Broads, and Bullets, Dark Horse Comics, 1998.

300, Dark Horse Comics, 1999.

Hell and Back: A Sin City Love Story, Dark Horse Comics, c. 2000.

Batman: The Dark Knight Strikes Again, DC Comics, 2002.

Daredevil/Elektra: Love and War, Marvel Entertainment Group, 2003.

Sources

Periodicals

Burlington Free Press, January 15, 2005, p. 1C.

Daily Telegraph (London, England), March 9, 2007, p. 31.

Guardian (London, England), May 27, 2005, p. 14.

Los Angeles Times, April 29, 2007, p. E1.

Newsday, March 23, 2005, p. C8.

Newsweek, March 28, 2005, p. 52.

Rutland Herald (VT), May 1, 2005.

Times Argus (Montpelier-Barre, VT), April 4, 2005.

Online

"Frank Miller: Sin City," BBC, http://www.bbc.co.uk/films/2005/05/25/frank_miller_sin_city_interview.shtml (October 1, 2007).

"Q&A with Frank Miller," *Esquire*, http://www.esquire.com/print-this/ESQ0407-APR_SCREEN_MILLER (October 1, 2007).

—Lisa Frick

Mike Modano

AP Images

Professional hockey player

Born June 7, 1970, in Livonia, MI; son of Mike (a construction foreman) and Karen Modano; married Willa Ford (a singer and actress), August 25, 2007.

Addresses: *Contact*—Dallas Stars, 2601 Avenue of the Stars, Frisco, TX 75034. *E-mail*—infomike modano.com. *Home*—Dallas, TX. *Web site*—http://www.mikemodano.com.

Career

Began career with the Prince Albert, Saskatchewan, Raiders of Canada's Western Hockey League, 1986-88; drafted by the NHL Minnesota North Stars as No. 1 pick, 1988; center for Minnesota/Dallas North Stars, 1989—.

Awards: Western Hockey League East First All-Star Team, 1989; NHL All-Rookie Team, 1990; NHL All-Star Game, 1993, 1998, 1999, 2000, 2003, 2004; Dallas North Stars MVP, 1994; United Cerebral Palsy Tom Landry Award of Excellence in Volunteerism, 1998; USA Hockey Bob Johnson Award, 2002; Dallas All Sports Association's Children's Medical Center/Athlete Role Model Award, 2003; NHL Good Guy Award, *Sporting News*, 2004; Texas Sports Hall of Fame, 2007.

Sidelights

Mike Modano was barely 18 when the Minnesota North Stars selected him as the No. 1 pick in the 1988 National Hockey League (NHL) draft,

making him the second U.S.-born player ever chosen first. Considered an up-and-coming star, Modano had a puck-shooting speed of 100 mph and he had an uncanny ability to thread his way through the defense. Over the course of the next two decades, Modano remained a steady, reliable presence on the ice and in 2007 became the leading U.S.-born goal-scorer of all time, besting Joe Mullen's career record of 502 regular-season goals. Modano also holds the notoriety of being the top all-time point-producing U.S.-born player. "You look at his consistency, and that says a lot about him," teammate Stu Barnes told the *Dallas Morning News'* Mike Heika. "You know what you're going to get from him. He has maintained a really high level for a really long time."

The youngest of three, Modano (pronounced moh-DA-noh) was born on June 7, 1970, in the Detroit suburb of Livonia, Michigan, to Mike and Karen Modano. His father worked as a construction foreman. Modano was a lively youngster so his parents introduced him to hockey, hoping he could vent his energy that way. "Hockey was just one of those things we thought could get out his aggressions," Modano's father told David Tarrant of the *Dallas Morning News*. "He was just rambunctious." On Modano's first outing, his parents were cautious, pushing him around the ice while he held on to the back of a chair. By the end of their next skating session, Modano had ditched the chair altogether and was skating on his own.

Soon, Modano was playing hockey in the Detroit-based Little Caesars youth program. When he could not get to the rink, Modano practiced in the basement, taking shots against his mother. She would slip on a catcher's mask and clutch a garbage-can lid for a target, while he whacked away, sending hundreds of shots speeding in her direction. Modano dented the duct work and busted a number of basement windows. During the winter, the family flooded the back yard, forming a makeshift rink on which Modano skated both before and after school.

While Modano enjoyed hockey, he also played baseball, football, and tennis. At the age of eight, he made it to the national semifinals of the Punt, Pass, and Kick tournament after winning the event in Michigan. During his freshman year of high school, Modano lettered in tennis. By his early teens, though, he decided to focus on hockey and take his game to the next level. At 16, Modano left home, heading north to Saskatchewan, Canada, to play in the Western Hockey League (WHL), a preeminent junior ice hockey league known for grooming future NHL players. Modano was picked up by the Prince Albert Raiders. Speaking to the *Detroit Free Press'* Steve Crowe, Modano's mother recalled the move. "It was a hard decision to make, but we said, 'This is your life. If you really want to play your hockey, it's up to you.' So he packed his bags and left. Hockey has been Mike's life. It's all he's wanted to do since he was seven."

When the Raiders coaches first met the lanky teen in 1986, they did not figure he would last long. "He came walking in, about 6-foot-1 and weighed about 145 pounds, if he had about $15 worth of quarters in his pockets. He had braces and bleached blond hair," former coach Brad Tippett noted in a *Chicago Tribune* article. "We looked at each other and said he's going to get killed." Then Modano got on the ice. "After about three minutes, we picked up our jaws and he was given the name 'Magic.'"

Modano became an instant celebrity in hockey-crazed Prince Albert, a small secluded town in the upper reaches of Canada. In his first season with the Raiders, Modano smacked in 30 goals and had 32 assists in 68 games, becoming the runner-up for the WHL Eastern Division rookie of the year award. During his second season, Modano scored 47 goals and had 80 assists in 65 games. Reporters from all over Canada flocked to Prince Albert to watch him play.

While in Prince Albert, Modano lived with a surrogate family— Carol and Ralph Ring—a couple who had boarded many Raiders players before. They described Modano as a typical teenager who liked to go to the movies and golf. He was also kind enough to oblige the neighborhood youth in games of street hockey. "The kids would come to the door and say, 'Mike, would you come play with us?' These were 10-, 12-year-old kids. He'd play with them. He was real good with the kids," Carol Ring recalled to the *Dallas Morning News'* Tarrant.

As the 1988 NHL amateur entry draft approached, scouts zeroed in on Modano, and he was selected by the Minnesota North Stars as the No. 1 pick. He reported to training camp in the fall of 1988, but left shortly thereafter because he could not come to a contact agreement. During the lockout, Modano returned to Prince Albert to play for the Raiders and finally reached a deal with the North Stars in January. League rules, however, prevented Modano from joining the team until he completed the season with the Raiders. Modano finally joined the North Stars on the ice during the 1989 spring playoffs.

During his first game of his first full season (on October 5, 1989), Modano scored a goal on his first shot. Over the course of that season, Modano tallied 29 goals and 46 assists, finishing second in rookie of the year voting. He also scored his first hat trick that season, in March of 1990. A hat trick occurs when a player scores three goals in one game. Modano helped the team to the Stanley Cup Finals in 1991, notching 20 points in the playoffs, though the team lost to the Pittsburgh Penguins.

At the start of the 1993-94 season, the North Stars relocated to Dallas and in an effort to drum up support for the new sports franchise in town, the North Stars made Modano its poster boy, touting him as the good-boy celebrity next door. The move had a positive effect on Modano, and that first year in Dallas he scored a career-best 50 goals and was voted the team's MVP. With his curly blond locks, the 6-foot-3-inch, 205-pound Modano became an instant, much-celebrated public figure in Dallas. When he left the arena, he often found women had slipped their business cards under the wipers of his BMW. Roses appeared in his locker. His No. 9 jersey remains the franchise's bestseller.

Just as Modano seemed to be coming into his own, a lockout shortened the 1994-95 season. In 1995-96, Modano scored a career-high four goals in one game during a February outing against the Edmonton Oilers; his 500th career NHL point followed in

March. A coaching change in 1996 further invigorated Modano, and he ended the 1996-97 season leading the Stars with the most goals and assists, scoring 35 and 48, respectively. In 1996, Modano was a member of the inaugural U.S. World Cup Champion Team that upset Canada.

In 1999, the Stars made it to the Stanley Cup Finals, where they faced off against the Buffalo Sabres. During triple overtime in Game 6, Modano, playing with a broken wrist, got control of the puck, protected it, and passed it off to Brett Hull for the title-winning goal. He calls that assist one of the highlights of his career. "Having that moment when we were on the ice scoring that goal and being next to each other seeing it go in, that's a vision in my mind that I will never forget," Modano told Stephen Hawkins in an article for the *Chicago Tribune.* In the Stars' 2-1 Finals victory, Modano had both assists. During the Finals, Modano led all players with seven goals scored.

Modano kept up the steady work, remaining a consistent player over the next few years. In 2002-03, Modano nabbed 57 assists, the most since relocating to Dallas, and finished with 85 points, the third-highest point total of his career. In 2003-04, his 15th season with the Stars, Modano scored his 1,100th NHL point, becoming the third U.S.-born player to reach that milestone. On March 17, 2007, Modano scored his 503rd regular-season goal, breaking Joe Mullen's career record of 502 regular-season goals, making Modano the top U.S.-born goal-scorer of all time. He was the 39th player to reach the 500 mark.

Despite his steady play, Modano has never put up megastar numbers—he has never led the league in points or goals scored in a season. Instead, his longevity and steadiness have combined to give him an honorable career. Speaking to the *Dallas Morning News'* Heika, former teammate Hull played down the numbers: "He's one of the greatest players I've ever played with, and I don't think his numbers tell the whole story. He has played in a system for most of his career where he's been asked to sacrifice scoring to play team defense. There's no telling what kind of numbers he could have put up in a different system." Though Modano is a forward, he has been asked to focus on defense, making him more than just a scoring machine. Modano is more adept than most forwards at preventing the opposition from scoring.

Over the course of his career, Modano has played on his share of star-studded teams. As of 2007, he had been selected for the NHL All-Star team six times. Modano also played for Team USA at the 1998, 2002, and 2006 Olympics. At the 2002 games in Salt Lake City, Modano helped Team USA to the gold medal game, where they lost in a grueling match to Canada, earning silver. At the Torino, Italy, games in 2006, Modano was chosen team captain.

Besides hockey, Modano focuses on charity work. In 2000, he established the Mike Modano Foundation, which works to combat child abuse and neglect. He was also instrumental in getting the Dallas-based Mike Modano Infant and Toddler Cottage opened in 2003. The facility is used on an emergency basis to house children who have been taken into protective custody. From 1998 to 2001, Modano supported United Cerebral Palsy by donating $100 per point he scored to the charity. When Modano is not busy with his charity work or playing hockey, he spends time with his wife, actress and pop singer Willa Ford. The two met on a set-up by a mutual friend and dated about four years before marrying on August 25, 2007. Ford is best known for competing on ABC-TV's *Dancing with the Stars* in 2006.

As the 2007-08 season began, all eyes focused on Modano as he neared Phil Housley's career-points record of 1,232. Housley, who retired in 2003, held the record for most career points by a U.S.-born player. Modano made history on November 7, 2007, when he scored his 1,233rd career point, surpassing Housley's record. As the 2007-08 season continued, fans stayed behind Modano, wondering just how high he would drive the record. Modano averages just less than one point per game, and it is unclear how many more seasons he will have to add to that record. At 37, Modano could be nearing retirement. Though his contract expires in 2010, Modano has noted that he has more trouble getting ready for each upcoming season. As Modano told *USA Today*'s Kevin Allen, "It's year-to-year at this point."

Sources

Periodicals

Chicago Tribune, March 2, 2003, p. 7 (Sports); February 25, 2007, p. 12 (Sports).
Dallas Morning News, March 21, 1993, p. 1B; February 26, 1995, p. 1E; March 13, 2007, p. 10C.
Detroit Free Press, January 15, 1988, p. 1D; October 19, 1989, p. 1D.
USA Today, November 9, 2007, p. 6C.

Online

"Awards & Honors," Mike Modano.com, http://www.mikemodano.com/player.php?cat=2000&cid=2002 (October 13, 2007).

"Mike Modano: Bio/News," Dallas Stars, http://
stars.nhl.com/team/app?page=PlayerDetail&
playerId=8449645&service=page&tab=bio
(October 13, 2007).

"Mike Modano's Biography," Mike Modano.com,
http://www.mikemodano.com/player.php?cat=
2000&cid=20027 (October 13, 2007).

—Lisa Frick

Mo'Nique

Actress and comedian

Born Monique Imes, December 11, 1967, in Wood-lawn, MD; daughter of Steven, Jr., and Alice Imes; married Shalon Watkins (divorced); married Mark Jackson, December 25, 1997 (divorced, 2001); married Sidney Hicks, May 20, 2006; children: Shalon, Jr. (first marriage), Mark Jr. (second marriage), Jonathan and David (twins, from third marriage).

Addresses: *Management*—The Collective, 9100 Wilshire Blvd., Ste. 700 West, Beverly Hills, CA 91202.

Career

Customer service representative, MCI, through 1989; launched stand-up career, 1987; began acting career, c. 1999; founder and designer, Mo'Nique's Big Beautiful and Loving It, 2000-02; morning show co-host, WHUR Radio, Washington, D.C., through 2002; published first book *Skinny Women Are Evil: Notes of a Big-Girl in a Small-Minded World*, 2003; signed on as spokesperson and model for Just My Size, 2005. Television appearances include: *Showtime at the Apollo*, 1989; *Russell Simmons Def Comedy Jam*; *BET Comic View*; *Moesha*, UPN, 1999-2000; *The Parkers*, UPN, 1999-2004; *The Queens of Comedy* (special), Showtime, 2001; *It's Showtime at the Apollo* (host), 2002; *Good Fences* (movie), 2003; *The 4th Annual BET Awards* (host), BET, 2004; *Mo'Nique's Fat Chance* (special), Oxygen, 2005; *Mo'Nique: I Coulda Been Your Cellmate* (special), Showtime, 2007; *Flavor of Love: Charm School*, VH1, 2007. Television work includes: executive producer, *Mo'Nique's Fat Chance* (special), 2005. Film appearances include: *3 Strikes*, 2000; *Baby Boy*, 2001; *Two Can Play That Game*, 2001; *Half Past Dead*, 2002; *Soul Plane*, 2004; *Hair Show*, 2004; *Shadowboxer*, 2005; *Domino*, 2005; *Farce of the Penguins*, 2006; *Phat Girlz*, 2006; *Beerfest*, 2006. Film work includes: executive producer, *Phat Girlz*, 2006.

Awards: Image Award for best comedy actress, National Association for the Advancement of Colored People, for *The Parkers*, 2001, 2002.

Sidelights

A star of the hit UPN comedy series *The Parkers* and several stand-up specials, full-figured, African-American actress/comedian Mo'Nique also had a solid film career. In all she did, Mo'Nique promoted plus-sized womanhood as acceptable, and looked at her size as a gift. She told Bob Longino of the *Atlanta Journal-Constitution*, "I always said that when God put me in position, I would change the way people view beauty. You don't have to be a size zero to be beautiful."

Born Monique Imes on December 11, 1967, in Maryland, she was one of four children of Steven Imes, Jr., and his wife, Alice. Mo'Nique claimed she was heavy as a baby and continued to be so throughout her childhood and adult life. With her family's support, she always accepted her physical appearance and never let it affect her self-esteem.

Raised in Baltimore, Mo'Nique was interested in performing by the time she was a toddler. Inspired by television situation comedies, she could see herself in certain characters like Thelma on *Good Times* and Ginger on *Gilligan's Island*. By the time she reached adulthood, Mo'Nique was working as a customer service representative for MCI.

Mo'Nique began her comedy career on a dare in 1987. One of her brothers, Steve, tried his hand at stand-up comedy. He was, according to his sister, very bad and a poor representative of the family. He bet his sister to go on stage herself at Baltimore's Comedy Factory Outlet, so she came up with an hour's worth of material and performed it. Mo'Nique received a standing ovation and a new career focus. She spent two years building up her comedy career and was able to leave MCI to concentrate on comedy full time by 1989.

Mo'Nique loved the rush of performing as a stand-up comedian, telling Steve Hedgpeth of the *Star-Ledger*, "I get instant gratification. I get to be selfish. When you do standup, it's just you. When you hit the stage, it's just you, and I love the fact that you know within five seconds if they like you.... I love for people to touch me, that I'm right here in your face."

In her obscenity-filled stand-up, Mo'Nique did not tell jokes per se but talked about family, sex, and her own life as a plus-sized woman in a funny way. Some of her comedy was extremely personal. Her first husband, Shalon Watkins, was physically abusive, and Mo'Nique drew on this experience for her comedy act. She did so not only for the comic value she could get out of it but also to reach out and affect those in her audience going through the same thing.

Within a few years, Mo'Nique began appearing on a number of television shows which showcased comedians. She made her television debut in 1989 on *Showtime at the Apollo*. Mo'Nique also appeared on *Russell Simmons Def Comedy Jam* and *BET Comic View*.

A 1997 appearance at the Montreal comedy festival led to Mo'Nique appearing on television not just a comedian, but also an actress. At the festival, she impressed talent scouts with her wit and sense of humor. She was soon being considered for acting roles. Within two years, Mo'Nique landed a role on a television situation comedy *The Parkers*.

The origins of the show lay in *Moesha*, a popular UPN situation comedy in the late 1990s. One character on *Moesha*, Kim Parker (played by Countess Vaughn), was given her own spin-off series in 1999: *The Parkers*. Mo'Nique was cast as Kim Parker's flamboyant, man-hungry mother, Nikki, on the series. Of Mo'Nique, series co-creator Sara Finney-Johnson told Nicholas Fonseca of *Entertainment Weekly*, "Her weight was never an issue. The execs at UPN were just excited that this woman was actually funny."

The mother-daughter duo at the heart of *The Parkers* were both students at Santa Monica College, and Nikki Parker also was an important employee at a cosmetics firm. Emphasizing both physical comedy and sharp one-liners, the show proved instantly popular with black viewers. *The Parkers* soon posted better ratings than *Moesha*. By 2001, it was the number-one show among African-American viewers and remained so for most of the time it was on the air. Most critics and white audiences dismissed *The Parkers*, however.

During the run of *The Parkers*, Mo'Nique continued her comedy career. In the summers of 2001 and 2003, she toured with female comedians Laura Hayes, Sommore, and Adele Givens as the "Queens of Comedy." The tour was filmed for a popular Showtime special. Mo'Nique also regularly toured on her own every year to enthusiastic, loyal audiences. She built her career up in other ways as well. Mo'Nique served as the host of the 2002 season of *It's Showtime at the Apollo* and the 2004 BET Awards. Through 2002, she also hosted a radio show on WHUR in Washington D.C. from her home in California.

In addition, Mo'Nique launched a film acting career as *The Parkers* and her comedy tours brought her more attention. She appeared in her first film in 2000, *3 Strikes*, and two more in 2001, *Baby Boy* and *Two Can Play That Game*. The latter was a dating comedy starting Vivica A. Fox. Mo'Nique played a female friend of Fox's character.

Outside of show business, Mo'Nique also expanded her interests. She founded a plus-sized clothing company, Mo'Nique's Big Beautiful and Loving It (BBLI) in 2000. Mo'Nique designed some of the line's pieces, which included business, casual, dressy, and evening wear, before the company folded in 2002. She published a book in 2003, *Skinny Women Are Evil: Notes of a Big Girl in a Small-Minded World*, written with Sherri A. McGee. *Entertainment Weekly*'s Fonseca wrote of the best-selling tome, "The book—in which she hilariously riffs on business dinners with vegetarians and the perils of plus-sized togs—is a fluffy read. But it's also filled with the staunch determination that's been vital to her success in Hollywood...."

The Parkers ended its run in May of 2004, with Mo'Nique's character marrying one of her love interests. The actress was philosophical about the show's end. She told *Jet*, "It was just time.... *The Parkers* went out at the top of the game. We don't want nobody to send us away 'like we are tired of them.' I think we did what we were supposed to do. For five years, we made you laugh and now you can laugh for 50 years."

After the end of *The Parkers*, Mo'Nique continued to tour as a comedian as well as take on more film roles. In 2004 alone, she had significant roles in *Soul Plane* and *Hair Show*. In the latter film, an independent production, Mo'Nique played a forthright hairstylist named Peaches Whitaker who is estranged from her more successful sister because of a disagreement over an inheritance. The sisters reconcile amidst the humorous action of the film which culminates at a hair show. Mo'Nique drew on her own experience hosting hair shows in Baltimore early in her career for the film.

Mo'Nique's ventures outside of television and film also played into her career. Though her own BBLI line had failed, she returned to fashion in 2005 as the Just My Size spokesperson and the brand's face. As part of this collaboration, she had a special on Oxygen, *Mo'Nique's Fat Chance*. This program focused on a beauty pageant, hosted by Mo'Nique, for full-figured women. The point of *Mo'Nique's Fat Chance* was to celebrate women as they are.

Expanding her own acting career in 2005, both of her films that year displayed Mo'Nique's acting chops. In *Shadowboxer*, she played a junkie named Precious. Mo'Nique also had a dramatic role in the thriller *Domino* as Lateesha Rodriguez.

Mo'Nique's family also expanded in this time period. The mother of two sons, one from each of her first two marriages, Mo'Nique gave birth to twins in late 2005. Their father was Sidney Hicks, a childhood friend whom she married in May of 2006. Taking some time off from her acting career,

Mo'Nique continued to tour as a comedian. She and her co-author also collaborated on a second publishing venture, a cookbook. Published in 2006, *Skinny Cooks Can't Be Trusted* emphasized cooking with hearty ingredients such as whole milk, butter, cream, and sugar. Mo'Nique also included her own childhood food memories in addition to recipes.

Returning to the big screen in 2006, Mo'Nique lent her voice to the animated *Farce of the Penguins* and appeared in the comedy *Beerfest*. She also was both the star and executive producer of *Phat Girlz*. In the comedy, she played Jazmin Biltmore, a department store worker who comes to fully embrace her plus-sized status though American society does not. The film is ultimately a celebration of accepting who you are, especially if you are full-figured. Reviewing *Phat Girlz* in the *San Francisco Chronicle*, Peter Hartlaub commented that "Mo'Nique, whose previous film roles have been mostly loud, over-the-top cameos, shows more range here, and her likeability in the quieter moments makes her violent outbursts that much more funny."

In 2007, Mo'Nique came back to television with two off-beat projects. The Showtime special *Mo'Nique: I Coulda Been Your Cellmate* chronicled her stand-up performance at the Ohio Reformatory for Women on Mother's Day 2006. The program also featured the comedian talking with some of the inmates about their lives. Of the affecting experience, Mo'Nique told the *Star-Ledger*, "When you hear their stories, it allows you to quit being judgmental. You can see through it all, they could smile. It was incredible.... As much as I thought I was going in there to do something for those women, they did so much for me."

Later that year, Mo'Nique played a key role in *Flavor of Love Girls: Charm School*, a reality transformation show on VH1. Taking contestants rejected on previous editions of the popular reality show *Flavor of Love*, Mo'Nique guided the often indelicate women through etiquette and manners training as well as other areas of self-improvement. Highlighting the women's infighting as well, *Flavor of Love Girls: Charm School* was also a competition with a contestant eliminated every week. When the program began airing in April of 2007, it instantly became VH1's most popular program. Mo'Nique also began filming roles in two films that were scheduled for release in 2007 or 2008: *Steppin: The Movie*, and *The Better Man*.

In all that she did, Mo'Nique remained committed to being true to herself and not an unreachable "star." She told Marti Yarbrough of *Jet*, "I thank

God for the blessings, for the talent and for using me to make people laugh. I never want to be a 'celebrity' where people feel like I'm untouchable. I want people to know that I'm just like you are."

Selected writings

Nonfiction

(With Sherri A. McGee) *Skinny Women Are Evil: Notes of a Big-Girl in a Small-Minded World*, Atria, 2003.

(As Mo'Nique Imes Jackson; with Sherri A. McGee McCovey) *Skinny Cooks Can't Be Trusted*, Amistad, 2006.

Sources

Periodicals

Atlanta Journal-Constitution, September 2, 2001, p. 1L; August 6, 2005, p. 3C.

Brandweek, May 16, 2005.

Grand Rapids Press (Grand Rapids, MI), January 6, 2007, p. E6.

Entertainment Weekly, May 2, 2003, pp. 34-35.

Jet, November 11, 2002, p. 58; May 10, 2004, p. 54; October 25, 2004, p. 56; August 8, 2005, p. 60.

New York Times, May 12, 2007, p. B14.

Plain Dealer (Cleveland, OH), January 13, 2006, p. 33; November 1, 2006, p. F1.

San Francisco Chronicle, April 8, 2006, p. E1.

Star-Ledger (Newark, NJ), April 29, 2001, p. 5; March 30, 2007, p. 43.

USA Today, April 27, 2007, p. 7E.

Online

"Mo'Nique," Internet Movie Database, http://www.imdb.com/name/nm0594898/ (August 1, 2007).

—A. Petruso

Rachel Moore

Dance company executive

Born Rachel Suzanne Moore, February 19, 1965, in Davis, CA; daughter of Charles Vincent and Patricia (Dudley) Moore; married Robert Ryan (a business consultant and executive). *Education:* Brown University, B.A. (with honors), 1992; Columbia University, M.A., 1994.

Addresses: *Office*—American Ballet Theatre, 890 Broadway Fl. 3D, New York, NY 10003-1211.

Career

Dancer, American Ballet Theatre II, New York City, 1982-84; dancer, American Ballet Theatre, New York City, 1984-88; development officer, National Cultural Alliance, Washington, D.C., 1994-95; director and coordinator, Center for Community Development and the Arts, Americans for the Arts, Washington, D.C., 1995-97; managing director, Ballet Theatre of Boston, Boston, MA, 1998; executive director, Project STEP, Boston, MA, 1998-2001; director, Boston Ballet Center for Dance Education, Boston, MA, 2001-04; executive director, American Ballet Theatre, 2004—.

Awards: Presidential Scholar, U.S. Department of Education, 1982; National Foundation for the Advancement of the Arts Distinguished Alumni Award, 2008; Teacher's College Distinguished Alumni Award, 2007.

Photograph by Jerry Ruotolo. Courtesy of Rachel Moore, ABT.

Sidelights

After a career as a dancer with American Ballet Theatre, Rachel Moore began working on the other side of the arts business as an administrator and advocate. After a post at the National Cultural Alliance, she held a series of positions at such institutions as Ballet Theatre of Boston and Boston Ballet Center for Dance Education. In 2004, Moore returned to New York City to become the executive director of American Ballet Theatre.

Born Rachel Suzanne Moore on February 19, 1965, in Davis, California, she was the daughter of Charles and Patricia Moore. Both her parents were economists, and raised their daughter in the city of her birth. Moore did not begin studying ballet until the age of eleven when she began taking classes at the Davis Arts Center. Moore quickly progressed by working harder than all her classmates. Within a year of graduating from high school, she became a professional ballet dancer.

Moore began her career in 1982 as a dancer in New York City with American Ballet Theatre II, the young touring wing of American Ballet Theatre. She spent two years with the company before joining the main American Ballet Theatre company in 1984. After four more years as a dancer, long-term foot and ankle problems compelled Moore to end her dance career and focus on her education.

Moore's career path was influenced by her experiences as a member of the Dancers' Union Committee and chair of the Dancers' Emergency Fund for American Ballet Theatre. She decided to pursue a career in arts administration. Moore first entered Brown University in 1988, and she earned her B.A. with honors in political philosophy from the school in 1992. Moore then moved back to New York City to do graduate work at Columbia University. She was awarded her M.A. in arts administration in 1994.

Degrees in hand, Moore began working in arts administration in Washington, D.C. She moved there to work as a development officer for the National Cultural Alliance in 1994. Leaving the position in 1995, Moore became the director and coordinator for the Washington-based Center for Community Development and the Arts, part of the nation service organization Americans for the Arts. She spent two years in the posts before moving to Boston and focusing again on dance as an administrator.

In 1998, Moore became the managing director of Ballet Theatre of Boston. In this newly created position, she was responsible for many administrative and operational duties for the company and its school. Moore was happy to be back working in dance again. She told Karen Campbell of the *Boston Herald* upon taking the job, "Having been a dancer with an understanding of the dance world, I had been working in arts advocacy for a long time. I was feeling a little distant from the actual art form, and I felt a strong need to get closer to artists and the production of art. Ballet was my first love, so this is a perfect fit. It's like coming home."

However, Moore left the post after less than a year to become the executive director of Project STEP in Boston. Moore remained at the classical music school for low-income students until 2001 and learned much about the art of fund-raising and arts outreach there. In 2001, she took another education-related and dance-related position by becoming the director of Boston Ballet Center for Dance Education.

The first to be named director of the center, Moore's position was heading the $3 million educational arm of Boston Ballet and its more than 2,000 students learning in various locations around the city and its suburbs. Soon after taking the post, Moore told Ellen Pigott of *Dance Magazine*, "I can speak the [languages of the] world of business and dance, and help communication between the two." Upon taking the post, Moore worked to better link the center's various programs and locations around the city, which had previously been working at odds with one another. She also began implementing her own five-year plan for the center, emphasizing a populist philosophy to dance education and the future of center.

After three years of leading the center, however, Moore left Boston in 2004 for a more prestigious position in New York City. That year, she returned to American Ballet Theatre to become its executive director. At the time, American Ballet Theatre had experienced much turnover among its executive directors—Moore was the fourth in four years—and there were concerns about its financial stability. Among her immediate concerns were creating a balanced budget, despite previous significant budget deficits, and a strategy for the ballet.

Upon taking the job, Moore expressed her happiness at being back at American Ballet Theatre. She told Jennifer Dunning of the *New York Times*, "I've known a lot of these people for a long time, and I know the culture of the organization. I have a common artistic language with Kevin [McKenzie, artistic director] and the artistic staff. I'm never going to second-guess that we need 24 swans. And I think that having a business background I'm able to communicate with people outside the dance world why it's so important to do what we do."

Moore embraced the challenges presented by American Ballet Theatre and promoted the ideas of long-range planning, building an endowment, restructuring the senior staff, and economizing to maximize the ballet's funding. She was successful in changing the business environment around American Ballet Theatre, and in just over a year, she was able to nearly double its endowment and have a budget surplus as well as increased box-office receipts. While Moore no longer danced herself, she was still drawn to the experience when she watched her company perform. She told *Vogue*'s Rebecca Johnson, "I dance in my seat. I can't help it; I still feel the music."

Sources

Books

Who's Who in the East, 35th ed., Marquis Who's Who, 2007.

Periodicals

Boston Globe, January 11, 2001, p. D5.

Boston Herald, January 30, 1998, p. S15.

Dance Magazine, September 1, 2001, p. 80; May 1, 2005, p. 24.

New York Times, March 19, 1984, p. C13; February 27, 2004, p. E3; July 2, 2004, p. B2; December 27, 2005, p. E1; August 5, 2007, p. AR29.

Vogue, August 2006, p. 266.

WWD, June 24, 2004, p. 4.

—*A. Petruso*

Ron Mueck

Sculptor

Born in 1958 in Melbourne, Australia; son of toy-makers; married to Caroline Willing (a scriptwriter); children: two daughters. *Education:* Apprenticed to puppeteer Jim Henson.

Addresses: *Agent*—James Cohan Gallery, 533 West 26th St., New York, NY 10001. *Home*—London, England.

Career

Worked as a window-display artist, puppet-maker, puppeteer, and modelmaker before 1996; film credits include *Labyrinth*, 1986, and the British children's television series *Gophers*, 1990; included in the 1997 art exhibit *Sensation: Young British Artists From the Saatchi Collection*; first solo gallery show at the Anthony d'Offay Gallery, London, 1998; National Gallery of Britain, artist-in-residence, c. 2001-03; made New York debut with solo show at the James Cohan Gallery, 2001; subject of retrospectives at the Brooklyn Museum, 2006, and The Andy Warhol Museum, 2007; works have been acquired by the National Gallery of Australia, ARoS Museum (Denmark), and the Hirshhorn Museum and Sculpture Garden, Washington, DC.

Sidelights

Ron Mueck is an Australian-born sculptor based in Britain whose lifelike human forms have made him one of the most acclaimed creative talents to emerge from the much-hyped Young British Artists movement in the mid-1990s. Mueck crafts his hyperrealistic figures from silicone or fiberglass, and spends months painstaking creating details like hair, wrinkles, and even blood. The incredibly life-like results have made the artist's works a favorite of both museum visitors and art critics alike. One from the latter group, the *Observer*'s Sean O'Hagan, asserted that "Mueck's epic and tiny human figures, in all their exaggerated realism and mysterious otherworldliness ... hark back to a time when art pertained to the sacred."

Mueck—whose surname is pronounced "MEW-eck"—was born in 1958 in Melbourne, Australia, to parents who were German émigré toymakers. They moved the family, which included a brother, to Britain in the early 1960s, and Mueck grew into a shy, awkward adolescent. "I was really self-conscious as a teenager," he told Judith Palmer in an interview that appeared in the *Independent*. "I wanted to be invisible. I wasn't very sociable, and I'd just stare at the other groups of kids, unable to imagine what they might be talking about."

After working first as a window-display artist, Mueck became a model maker and puppeteer, and apprenticed with Jim Henson of *The Muppet Show* and *Sesame Street* fame. He worked on children's television shows, and moved into film in the mid-1980s, creating the goblins in *Labyrinth*, the 1986 fantasy movie starring David Bowie. Mueck went on to launch his own company that made props and animated figures for advertising; however, he grew dissatisfied with the work, as he told Palmer in the *Independent*. "Everything I was doing was geared towards that final flat image, the piece of print. It felt like I was just a step in the process, a tradesman doing one portion of the finished thing."

By the mid-1990s, Mueck was married to Caroline Willing, a scriptwriter, with whom he had two young daughters. Willing's mother was the artist Paula Rego, who asked him to make a Pinocchio figure for one of her tableaux. The figure was included in a 1995 exhibition of Rego's paintings at the Hayward Gallery in London, and "so eerily life-like was the quizzical little figure that a gallery security guard used to turn the boy to face the wall every night," wrote Palmer in the *Independent*.

Rego introduced Mueck to Charles Saatchi, the well-known British art collector, famous for his support of young, often daring new artists. Saatchi bought the second piece Mueck made after Pinocchio, called *Dead Dad*. It would become one of the most talked-about pieces included in *Sensation: Young British Artists from the Saatchi Collection*, an exhibition at the Royal Academy of Art in London that launched the careers of several new artists, among them Damien Hirst and Tracey Emin. *Dead Dad* commemorates Mueck's late father, and is about two-thirds the size of a normal human figure. Telling Palmer he wanted to make something he could cradle in his arms, he began the work as a way of dealing with the loss of his parent. "He died in Australia, and I never saw the body," he said in the *Independent* interview. "This was a way of saying goodbye to him and creating something to fill the space of that empty experience."

Dead Dad was made by the same process that Mueck used to create his puppets, using fiberglass or silicone molds, then painting all the surface details. He then drills or punches holes in the "skin" to hold hair. At the *Sensation* show, Mueck's work "drew gasps of wonder from both the curious and the jaded," wrote O'Hagan in London's *Observer* newspaper. "A slightly smaller-than-lifesize sculpture of a male corpse, naked, alabaster pale and laid out as if awaiting the mortician's blade, *Dead Dad* was that rare thing, a contemporary artwork that was both genuinely humble and genuinely heart-stopping."

Mueck had his first solo show at the prestigious Anthony d'Offay Gallery in London in 1998, and made his New York solo debut at the James Cohan Gallery in 2001. The latter show consisted of just two pieces, but *New York Times* critic Michael Kimmelman asserted "this is one of the most memorable little shows in years." One of the pair was a giant head that was a self-portrait, called *Mask II*,

and the other a 35-inch-long *Mother and Child*—a figure of a woman who has just given birth and is looking at the newborn placed on her stomach. "Tension runs through straightened arms and raised neck, the woman straining to see the baby," Kimmelman wrote. "A single strand of the woman's hair catches in the corner of her mouth .... The expression conveys exhaustion and dumbstruck wonderment, a lightly comic, ultimately grave miracle of minutely reproduced observation."

At Britain's Millennium Dome exhibition in 2000, Mueck submitted a 15-foot-high figure called *Boy*, which went on to appear in the important Venice Biennale art event and was later acquired by the ARoS Museum of Aarhus, Denmark. In 2001, Mueck was invited to become artist-in-residence at London's National Gallery, a stint that ended with a 2003 exhibition of new work based on Old Masters paintings and sculptures in the museum's collection. The aforementioned *Mother and Child* came from this period, as did a new one, *Pregnant Woman* (2002), which became part of the permanent collection of the National Gallery of Australia.

In 2006, the Brooklyn Museum feted Mueck with a solo exhibition, and the dozen works shown included *Dead Dad* plus several new ones, including a 16-foot-long newborn baby with its umbilical cord still attached which was titled *A Girl*. Reviewing the Brooklyn show for the *New York Times*, Grace Glueck wrote that Mueck's artistry evokes the paintings of British artist Lucian Freud. She singled out a piece called *Big Man*, describing it as "an anonymous seven-foot hulk—totally nude, including his bald head—that squats in a corner regarding the world with saturnine displeasure, [and] invokes Mr. Freud's paintings of his vast, fleshy model Leigh Bowery," Glueck wrote. "Mueck differs from such artists, however, in his empathetic involvement with his subjects, who seem to embody, in one way or another, the challenges and perils of the human condition."

Sources

Independent (London, England), June 2, 1998, p. 2.
New York Times, June 1, 2001; November 10, 2006.
Observer (London, England), August 6, 2006, p. 35.
Sunday Times (London, England), March 23, 2003, p. 6.

—*Carol Brennan*

Haruki Murakami

Author

Born January 12, 1949, in Kyoto, Japan; son of teachers; married Yoko Takahashi, 1971. *Education:* Waseda University, Tokyo, Japan, 1975.

Addresses: *Contact*—c/o Knopf Publishing Group, Random House, 1745 Broadway, New York, NY 10019. *Home*—Tokyo, Japan.

Career

Owner/operator, Peter Cat jazz club, Tokyo, 1974-82; published first book, *Kaze no uta o kike* (Hear the Wind Sing), 1979; visiting scholar, Princeton University, 1991-93; writer-in-residence, Tufts University, Medford, MA, 1993-95.

Awards: New Writer's Award, *Gunzo* journal, for *Kaze no uta o kike* (Hear the Wind Song), 1979; Noma Literary Newcomer's Prize, for *A Wild Sheep Chase,* 1982; Tanizaki Literary Prize, for *Hard-Boiled Wonderland and the End of the World,* 1985; Yomiuri Literary Prize, for *The Wind-Up Bird Chronicle,* 1995; Kuwabara Takeo Academic Award, for *Underground,* 1999; Franz Kafka Prize, 2006; World Fantasy Award for best novel, for *Kafka on the Shore,* 2006.

Sidelights

For more than 25 years, Japanese author Haruki Murakami has been spinning out quirky, yet strangely compelling surrealist fiction that has made him popular both at home and overseas. Embraced abroad, Murakami's novels have been translated into 40 languages. He is well-read in China, South Korea, and Germany. *Kafka on the Shore,* translated to English in 2005, was a best-seller in both the United States and Russia. In 2006, he received the Franz Kafka Prize, an international literary award given annually to an author whose work appeals to readers across the globe. Many winners of the prize have gone on to win the Nobel Prize in Literature— and fans hope that Murakami will be among them. Of all contemporary Japanese writers, he is the most well-known and read.

Murakami was born on January 12, 1949, in Kyoto, Japan, though he grew up in Kobe. Murakami's grandfather was a Buddhist priest, while his mother and father both taught Japanese literature. Murakami's parents raised him in a household with strong cultural traditions and a reverence for the past, which he questioned early on. His parents also exposed him to Japanese writers, but Murakami never felt a connection to their work. "My parents were always talking about Japanese literature and I hated it," Murakami told the *Guardian*'s Richard Williams. Murakami was fascinated with books, though, and loved to travel into distant lands on the backs of words.

"So I read foreign literature, mostly European writers of the 19th century—Chekhov, Dostoyevsky,

Flaubert, Dickens," Murakami told the *Guardian.* "They were my favorite authors. Then I took up American paperbacks. Hardboiled detective stories. Science fiction. Kurt Vonnegut, Richard Brautigan, Truman Capote. After I studied English, I began to read those books in English. That was quite an experience. It was like a door was opening to another world." Fascinated with American culture, Murakami received further indoctrination through his transistor radio, which introduced him to tunes from Elvis, the Beach Boys, and the Beatles.

A defining moment occurred in 1964 when Murakami received a ticket to see Art Blakey and the Jazz Messengers for his birthday. Blakey was a popular post-World War II American jazz drummer. Murakami was taken with the group's blissful bebop style set against a backdrop of laid-back indifference. It was the most amazing music he had ever heard and from that moment on, Murakami was hooked on jazz.

In 1968, Murakami enrolled at Waseda University in Tokyo, where he met Yoko Takahashi. They married in 1971. Murakami loved literature, but he did not think he had enough talent to make it as a writer. Instead, he turned to music and dreamed of opening a jazz club, quitting college to pursue that dream. Both he and his wife spent the next few years working—days at record companies and nights at coffee bars. They scraped and saved, borrowed money from friends and relatives and, in 1974, opened a small jazz bar in Tokyo called Peter Cat, named after Murakami's pet.

Peter Cat was located in a basement rental. During the day, Peter Cat served coffee and at night it served jazz, with young musicians performing live. It was a small operation. Murakami made the drinks, washed the dishes, spun the records, and booked the acts. When business was slow, he read and worked toward finishing his degree, which he completed in 1975.

One day in 1978, Murakami felt the urge to write. In an essay he penned for the *New York Times Book Review,* Murakami described the epiphany. "When I turned 29, all of a sudden out of nowhere I got this feeling that I wanted to write a novel—that I could do it. I couldn't write anything that measured up to Dostoyevsky or Balzac, of course, but I told myself it didn't matter. I didn't have to become a literary giant. Still, I had no idea how to go about writing a novel or what to write about."

Murakami bought a fountain pen and some paper and started writing. For the next six months, he wrote late into the night, sharing passages and ideas with his wife. The work resulted in 1979's *Kaze no uta o kike* or *Hear the Wind Song,* which won the *Gunzo* journal's new writer's award. The book—its title borrowed from a Truman Capote short story and featuring Beach Boys lyrics on the back cover—became an instant success among the average young Japanese reader. With an oddball sense of humor and impassive tone, the book covered student dissent and coming-of-age through the eyes of an unnamed narrator.

Murakami credits music with inspiring his writing. In a *New York Times Book Review* essay, Murakami described how he always felt there was music swirling around in his head so he decided to see if he could transfer that into words. "Whether in music or in fiction, the most basic thing is rhythm. Your style needs to have good, natural, steady rhythm, or people won't keep reading your work. I learned the importance of rhythm from music—and mainly from jazz. Next comes melody—which, in literature, means the appropriate arrangement of the words to match the rhythm.... Next is harmony—the internal mental sounds that support the words. Then comes the part I like best: free improvisation. Through some special channel, the story comes welling out freely from inside."

In 1980, Murakami's second novel, *Pinball, 1973,* hit the shelves in Japan. Around this time, Murakami decided to close the jazz club to concentrate on writing. *A Wild Sheep Chase* followed in 1982. A standout, this novel revealed the depth of Murakami's unique style. The fantasy-mystery-comedy follows the exploits of a divorced Japanese yuppie on the hunt for a mystical sheep. The book's translations garnered international attention and sold more than a million copies worldwide.

Murakami wrote *A Wild Sheep Chase* without any predetermined plot. He simply sat down and his unique, off-the-cuff style emerged. Murakami prefers to write this way. "It's kind of a free improvisation," he told the *Guardian.* "I never plan. I never know what the next page is going to be. Many people don't believe me. But that's the fun of writing ... because I don't know what's going to happen next. I'm searching for melody after melody. Sometimes once I start, I can't stop. It's just like spring water. It comes out so naturally, so easily."

During his free time, Murakami translates English novels into Japanese. He often works with Motoyuki Shibata, a professor of American literature at the University of Tokyo. Over the years, Murakami has translated Capote, F. Scott Fitzgerald, J. D. Salinger,

Tim O'Brien, and Grace Paley so his fellow Japanese readers can enjoy the works that so inspired him. As Murakami's fame grew, demand for his translated books grew as well and the authors he translated gained popularity in Japan.

By the late 1980s, Murakami was living in Rome and working on *Norwegian Wood*. Published in Japan in 1987, the book sold approximately two million copies its first year and catapulted Murakami into pop-icon status. *Norwegian Wood* diverged from Murakami's previous efforts. The novel was written in a more straightforward, sentimental style and attracted a new demographic of readers—teens and women in their 20s.

Norwegian Wood delves into the life and psyche of an emotionally detached 37-year-old who is delivered back to his college days when he hears a Muzak version of the Beatles song this book is named for. The book covers his journey toward adulthood and the women he loved and lost. Like many of Murakami's works, the book references American culture, conjuring up everything from *The Great Gatsby* to Thelonious Monk. While the book proved to be a hot seller, Japanese critics dismissed it because it bucked many literary conventions and contained what they thought was too much sex.

Murakami became so popular he decided to leave Japan again because he did not like the attention. In the early 1990s, he lived in the United States, serving as a visiting scholar at Princeton University from 1991-93 and as a writer-in-residence at Tufts University in Medford, Massachusetts from 1993-95. During the time Murakami was away from Japan, the country experienced enormous change. In the early 1990s, Japan's economic bubble burst and a recession hit. In 1995, an earthquake in Kobe killed thousands. That same year, the country witnessed its first act of domestic terrorism when a dissident group attacked the Tokyo subway system by releasing sarin gas. Twelve people died and more than 1,000 were injured.

After these events, Murakami felt an urge to do something for his own country, for his own people. He returned to Japan and began work on 1997's *Underground: The Tokyo Gas Attack and the Japanese Psyche*, a journalistic look at the sarin gas attacks. Murakami spent a year interviewing 63 victims who were on the train that day. In an interview with *Salon*, Murakami discussed the project. He said the victims were "very hard-working people, ordinary people, ordinary Japanese, and they were attacked with poison gas for no reason at all. It was ridiculous. I just wanted to know what happened to them. Who are those people? So I interviewed them one by one. It took one year, but I was impressed to find who those people are."

The experience changed Murakami's perceptions of his fellow Japanese and he felt compassion toward them for the first time. Murakami never could understand business people and why they worked so hard for corporate entities, but once he heard their stories, he understood their humanity. "They come home at 10 p.m. and their kids are sleeping," he told *Salon*. "The only day they see their children is Sunday. It's horrible. But they don't complain. So I asked them why not and they said it's no use. It's what all the people are doing, so there's no reason to complain." In the end, Murakami realized that the businessmen and the Aum Shinrikyo cult members who launched the attack were more alike than different. He believes they all did what they did because they saw no alternative.

Murakami continued writing fiction. He scored another hit with *Ubime no Kafka*, or *Kafka on the Shore*, published in Japan in 2002. The book simultaneously follows the journeys of a teenager named Kafka who runs away from home and an elderly man named Satoru Nakata who lost his ability to read after a bizarre childhood accident. He can, however, communicate with cats. The book's English translation was released in 2005 to rave reviews and, in 2006, won the World Fantasy Award for best novel.

Murakami wrote the book in six months and spent a year on revisions. When he is writing, Murakami follows a strict regimen. He goes to bed at 9 p.m. then wakes up at 4 a.m.—without the aid of an alarm—to start writing. He works until around 11 a.m., producing about 4,000 characters a day, which is equivalent to about two or three pages of English. In the afternoons, he writes a little more or works on translations. He also runs every day and says the physical workouts fuel his writing mind. For more than 20 years, Murakami has run at least one marathon annually.

In 2007, *After Dark* was released in English. The book, with dark undertones, takes place over the course of a single night and explores loneliness and alienation—two common themes for Murakami. While Murakami's international popularity among young readers has seen tremendous growth the past few years, older Japanese readers have been slow to accept his style. Some Japanese critics believe

Murakami's popular appeal and continual references to Western culture detract from his work. They say his postmodernist books are devoid of the richness of language and style that traditional Japanese literature offers.

Selected writings

Kaze no uta o kike, 1979; *Hear the Wind Song* (first in the "Trilogy of the Rat"), translated by Alfred Birnbaum, Kodansha, 1987.

Pinball, 1973 (second in the "Trilogy of the Rat"), 1980; translated by Alfred Birnbaum, Kodansha, 1985.

Hitsuji o meguru boken, 1982; *A Wild Sheep Chase* (third in the "Trilogy of the Rat"), translated by Alfred Birnbaum, Kodansha, 1989.

Sekai no owari to hadoboirudo wandarando, 1985; *Hard-Boiled Wonderland and the End of the World*, translated by Alfred Birnbaum, Kodansha, 1991.

Noruwei no mori, 1987; *Norwegian Wood*, translated by Alfred Birnbaum, Kodansha, 1989; translated by Jay Rubin, Vintage International, 2000.

Dansu, dansu, dansu, 1988; *Dance Dance Dance*, translated by Alfred Birnbaum, Vintage Books, 1994.

South of the Border, West of the Sun, 1992; translated by Philip Gabriel, Vintage, 2000.

The Wind-Up Bird Chronicle, 1994; translated by Jay Rubin, Knopf, 1997.

Underground: The Tokyo Gas Attack and the Japanese Psyche, 1997-98 (issued in two volumes); translated by Alfred Birnbaum and Philip Gabriel, Vintage, 2001.

Sputnik Sweetheart, 1999; translated by Philip Gabriel, Knopf, 2001.

Ubime no Kafka, 2002; *Kafka on the Shore*, translated by Philip Gabriel, Knopf, 2005.

After Dark, 2004; translated by Jay Rubin, Knopf, 2007.

Sources

Periodicals

Daily Yomiuri (Tokyo, Japan), June 16, 2002, p. 9.
Guardian (London, England), May 17, 2003, p. 20.
Newsweek, April 30, 2001, p. 78.
New York Times, June 14, 2005, p. E1.
New York Times Book Review, July 8, 2007, p. 27.
Washington Post, May 20, 2007, p. BW10.

Online

"Haruki Murakami," Random House, http://www.randomhouse.com/features/murakami/site.php (January 27, 2008).

"Nobel Prize Winner in Waiting?" *Guardian*, http://books.guardian.co.uk/departments/generalfiction/story/0,,496599,00.html (February 21, 2008).

"The Outsider," *Salon*, http://www.salon.com/books/int/1997/12/cov_si_16int.html (January 27, 2008).

—Lisa Frick

Robert Nardelli

Chief Executive Officer of Chrysler

Norm Betts/Bloomberg News/Landov

Born Robert Louis Nardelli, May 17, 1948, in Old Forge, PA; son of a plant manager and a homemaker; married Susan, 1971; children: three sons, one daughter. *Education:* Western Illinois University, B.S., 1971; University of Louisville, M.B.A., 1975

Addresses: *Office*—Chrysler LLC, 1000 Chrysler Dr., Auburn Hills, MI 48236.

Career

Various positions, General Electric (GE), 1971-88; executive vice president and general manager of worldwide parts and components, Case Corp., Racine, WI, 1988-89, executive vice president and general manager of construction equipment group, 1989-91; president and chief executive officer of Canadian Appliance Manufacturing Company, Toronto, Ontario, Canada, GE, 1991-92, president and chief executive officer of GE Transportation Systems, Erie, PA, 1992-95, president and chief executive officer of GE Power Systems, Schenectady, NY, 1995-2000; president and chief executive officer, The Home Depot, Inc., 2000-02, then chairman, president, and chief executive officer, 2002-07; chairman and chief executive officer, Chrysler LLC, Auburn Hills, MI, 2007—.

Member: Board of directors, the Coca-Cola Company, 2002-05; President's Council on Service and Civic Participation, 2003-c. 2007.

Awards: Distinguished Pennsylvanian Award, Gannon University, 1995; Distinguished Alumni Award, Western Illinois College of Business & Technology,

1997; executive of the year, Schenectady County Chamber of Commerce, 2000; Alumnus of the Year Award, University of Louisville, 2001; honorary degrees from the University of Louisville, 2001, Sienna College, 2001, and Western Illinois University, 2002.

Sidelights

After spending most of three decades in various positions within General Electric (GE), Robert Nardelli was passed over to become chairman of the company, so he left to become the controversial head of Home Depot. Forced to resign as Home Depot chief executive officer (CEO) seven years later, he negotiated a settlement package, which became the hallmark of executive excess. Late in 2007, Nardelli took on new challenges when he became the head of Chrysler, the struggling American automaker.

Nardelli was born on May 17, 1948, in Old Forge, Pennsylvania. His father worked at GE, first as an hourly employee and later as a plant manager. His mother was a homemaker who raised Nardelli and his sibling. Nardelli entered Western Illinois University on a football scholarship in the late 1960s, and worked summers paving highways. He majored in business, and earned his B.S. in the subject in 1971.

After earning his undergraduate degree, Nardelli joined General Electric, where he spent the next 17 years. He primarily worked in manufacturing management. His positions in GE included general manager of manufacturing for the lighting systems products division and general manager of the transportation systems division. Nardelli also worked in the appliances and lighting system business units, completing his M.B.A. at the University of Louisville in 1975.

Nardelli left GE in 1988 to take a job with the Wisconsin-based Case Corp. He began his tenure with the company in the parts and components group as executive vice president and general manager of the group. About a year later, Nardelli was given a new position within Case. In November of 1989, he was named executive vice president and general manager of the construction equipment group, including responsibilities in manufacturing, engineering, marketing, and sales. In this post, Nardelli oversaw 9,000 employees as well as manufacturing plants in the United States and Europe.

In 1991, Nardelli returned to GE. He took a job with a subsidiary, Canadian Appliance Manufacturing Company (CAMCO), in Toronto. Nardelli was the company's president and chief executive officer. In 1992, Nardelli returned to the United States to become the president and chief executive officer of GE Transportation Systems, based in Erie, Pennsylvania. This division made locomotives. During his tenure, the business changed its basic technology from DC to AC. GE Transportation Systems also doubled in size and became more global in scope by cutting jobs and outsourcing some work.

Nardelli was given the same titles at a different GE subsidiary, GE Power Systems, based in Schenectady, New York, in 1995. When he took over the division, it was turning a profit but did not have a solid long-term outlook as the market for turbines and generators from utilities in the United States was limited. Within five years, Nardelli turned GE Power Systems around. Sales increased from $6.4 billion in 1995 to $9.7 billion in 1999. Profits in the same time period jumped from $700 million to $1.7 billion. Nardelli was able to increase these numbers by expanding the kind of equipment the division sold as well as adding a global service business to operate the equipment for customers. Major job cuts and outsourcing also contributed to the division's turnaround. In addition, Nardelli transformed GE Power Systems through acquisitions and other deals, making 90 such transactions over the course of his tenure.

Nardelli's success with the Power Systems unit did not go unnoticed at GE headquarters. Legendary GE chairman Jack Walsh planned on retiring in the early 2000s, and Nardelli became one of three internal candidates—along with Jeffrey R. Immelt and W. James McNerney, Jr.—to take over his job. Walsh had mentored Nardelli throughout his career as well. As the powers that be were closing in on their decision in 2000, Nardelli was seen as the strongest candidate. Edward Jones & Company analyst Bill Fiala told Beth Piskora of the *New York Post*, "Nardelli has probably stood out the most in the past six months. He's managed a huge boom in his business without a stumble. He's seen revenues double in the last 12 months." However, Nardelli was not selected to replace Walsh, Immelt was.

After being passed over for the post, Nardelli decided to leave GE and look for new opportunities. By the end of 2000, he had taken a job at the Home Depot, a home improvement retailer. Nardelli was hired as that company's president and chief executive officer, replacing Home Depot's co-founder Arthur Blank, despite having no real retail experience. Given a multi-million dollar deal of stock and compensation, he also took a position on the board. In 2002, Nardelli became the chairman of Home Depot while remaining in his other posts.

When Nardelli took over Home Depot in 2000, it was a highly regarded company and the largest home improvement retailer in the world, with 1,087 stores in North and South America. Sales and reputation, especially for customer service, were strong, and there were plans to double the number of stores. Finding enough employees for these stores was a difficult task, and there were also fears about the company's long-term health because of economic concerns, lower consumer spending, a slower home building market, and competition from rival retailer Lowe's. By 2000, profits had only increased eleven percent from the previous year, while, in 1999, profits had increased 40 percent from the previous year.

Nardelli was charged with making the business run better in the face of these challenges. He imposed a sense of efficiency and discipline on Home Depot, something the company had sorely lacked since its founding in 1979. Other changes included trimming the number of new stores Home Depot opened in 2000 and 2001, centralized purchasing, better inventory controls, cutting costs, and transforming the management structure.

In the first three years of Nardelli's tenure, Home Depot's stock price fell rapidly despite modest annual increases in sales and profits. The company's reputation for excellent customer service also took a hit as lauded full-time, well-informed personnel were replaced by fewer part-timers with less knowledge. By 2006, stockholders were increasingly unhappy with the direction Nardelli had taken the company, with falling stock prices even as sales increased, and with what was perceived as an excessive compensation for sometimes abrasive leadership. Between 2000 and 2006, he had been paid $123.7 million in compensation, not including stock options.

With the agreement of and pressure from the company's board, Nardelli resigned abruptly in January of 2007 and was replaced by Frank Blake. Upon resigning, the Associated Press quoted Nardelli as saying, "I am extremely proud of what we have accomplished at The Home Depot since 2000 and I believe that I leave a stronger and more resilient company than when I arrived, and one that is well positioned to capitalize on the substantial opportunities ahead of it."

Nardelli had negotiated a large severance package when he signed with the company in 2000, one of the most expensive among Fortune 500 CEOs. He received a package worth at least $210 million when he resigned, including $20 million in the form of a cash severance payment and $32 million in retirement benefits. Nardelli's package was widely criticized as a prime example of extravagance of American executives, especially at underperforming companies. Amidst promises to investigate such situations, Congressman Barney Frank, then the incoming chairman of the House Financial Services Committee, told Ylan Q. Mui of the *Washington Post*, "Mr. Nardelli's contribution to raising Home Depot's stock value consists of quitting and receiving hundreds of millions of dollars to do so."

It was unclear what Nardelli's next move would be after his resignation as he was not allowed to sign with a competing company for one year. He left home improvement retail behind and signed with the new Chrysler Corporation. After a merger with a German automaker to form DaimlerChrysler failed to be profitable, the German arm decided to sell off most of the American automaker. About 80 percent of Chrysler was purchased by a private investment firm, Cerberus Capital Management. This group hired Nardelli to run the company.

As with Home Depot in 2000, Nardelli's hiring was seen as both contentious—he had no automotive experience—and a surprise—observers believed Cerberus advisor Wolfgang Bernhard would get the job. By taking the post, Nardelli was presented with a chance for redemption as he was charged with returning the company to profitability. He was confident as he took over at the automaker, despite naysayers. Nardelli told the *New York Times'* Micheline Maynard, "While I'm new to Chrysler, and new to the car industry, manufacturing and transportation is a business I know, I like, and I grew up in."

When Nardelli began as chairman and chief executive officer in August of 2007, he vowed to initially only speed up restructuring plans already in motion—which included the importation of small Chinese cars and investing in fuel-efficient technology—and not to cut any further into the labor force or factory capacity beyond what was already planned. Nardelli also intended on increasing attention on international markets. In addition, Cerberus charged him with improving productivity at factories and increasing quality as well as discipline to sales.

Within a few months, Nardelli began making moves which were expected to have a long-term impact. For example, he hired James E. Press, the top North American executive of Toyota, and Philip E. Murtagh, a General Motors executive who helped build the company's interests in China. The pair took on top executive positions, and more such hirings followed, including naming a chief customer officer, Douglas Betts who was hired away from Nissan. Cerberus also invested $500 million, making 500 improvements to Chrysler's vehicles after Nardelli took over. While Chrysler was improving its executive ranks and its vehicles, Nardelli announced to employees that the company would lose $1.6 billion in 2007.

The situation at Chrysler remained challenging for Nardelli in 2008, although the company was on track to meet Cerberus's goals in the first quarter. In March, he sent a memo to employees, informing them that the company would impose a vacation shut down for two weeks in July of 2008 as a cost-cutting measure. Also in March, Nardelli was the keynote speaker at the prestigious New York Auto Show. There, he stated that Chrysler would be following a plan expected to return the company to profitability in 2008 by restructuring operations and downsizing its pool of dealers. He also cut hundreds of models from the Chrysler line-up. By April 2008, Nardelli was expanding Chrysler's car and truck building alliance with Nissan Motor Company, as part of the company's quest to expand internationally.

Despite difficulties and doubters, Nardelli believed in himself and the company he headed. He told *Fortune*'s Geoff Colvin, "Chrysler has been knocked down but never knocked out. It's always been able to come back tougher and more aggressive. That's what gives me hope about our ability to do this again and reposition Chrysler for America, for the auto industry, and certainly for Detroit."

Sources

Books

Complete Marquis Who's Who, Marquis Who's Who, 2008.

Periodicals

Associated Press, May 25, 2006; January 3, 2007; August 6, 2007; December 5, 2007; April 18, 2008.

Associated Press State & Local Wire, November 27, 2000; December 5, 2000.

Atlanta Business Chronicle, May 23, 2003, p. A3.

BusinessWeek, November 26, 2001, p. 102; January 15, 2007, p. 56; August 20, 2007, p. 35; September 24, 2007, p. 42.

Daily Telegraph (London, England), August 7, 2007, p. 3.

Fortune, April 14, 2008, p. 49.

Guardian (London, England), March 14, 2008, p. 34.

New York Post, June 6, 2000, p. 36.

New York Times, January 4, 2007, p. C1; August 7, 2007, p. A1.

Plain Dealer (Cleveland, OH), September 26, 1999, p. 1H.

PR Newswire, November 15, 1989; May 30, 1995; December 5, 2000; November 20, 2001; January 3, 2007; February 14, 2008.

Retail Merchandiser, May 1, 2001, p. 18.

Ward's Auto World, April 1, 2008, p. 8.

Washington Post, January 4, 2007, p. D1; August 6, 2007, p. A8; August 7, 2007, p. D1.

Windsor Star (Windsor, Ontario, Canada), April 18, 2008, p. A7.

—A. Petruso

Daniel Ortega

AP Images

President of Nicaragua

Born Jose Daniel Ortega Saavedra, November 11, 1945, in La Libertad, Nicaragua; married Rosario Murillo; children: five children, two stepchildren. *Education:* Attended the Central American University, Managua, Nicaragua, early 1960s.

Addresses: *Office*—Presidente, Casa de la Presidencia, Managua, Nicaragua. *Web site*—http://www.presidencia.gob.ni.

Career

Guerrilla leader, 1967-79; member of Nicaragua's ruling military junta, 1979-84; coordinator of the junta, 1981-84; elected president of Nicaragua, 1984; lost reelection campaign, 1990; ran unsuccessfully for president, 1996 and 2001; elected president, 2006; sworn in as president, 2007.

Sidelights

Daniel Ortega, a key Latin American figure of the cold war, helped lead the 1979 Nicaraguan revolution and then governed his impoverished nation for eleven years. An ally of Cuban dictator Fidel Castro and the Soviet Union, a nemesis of U.S. president Ronald Reagan, Ortega and his Sandinista party pursued a socialist economic program and frequently restricted their political opponents' civil liberties. Under Ortega, the Sandinistas fought a long civil war that cost 50,000 lives against the Contras, a rebel group funded by the United States. Voted out of office in 1990, Ortega remained the leader of the Sandinista party and ran for president

again three more times, finally winning in 2006. Promising a more moderate political course than in his past, including respect for the free market and civil liberties, Ortega took office in early 2007. He immediately forged closer ties with the socialist governments of Cuba and Venezuela, seeking economic aid.

Jose Daniel Ortega Saavedra was born in La Libertad, Nicaragua, on November 11, 1945. His father had fought in Cesar Augusto Sandino's army of peasants against U.S. occupation in the 1920s, and his parents both opposed the rule of Nicaraguan dictator Anastasio Somoza, son of the dictator whose National Guard shot Sandino to death in 1934. Ortega and his family moved to the Nicaraguan capital, Managua, in the mid-1950s. Ortega embraced his parents' views and was first arrested for his political activity at age 15.

In 1963, after spending a few months in college, Ortega joined the Sandinista National Liberation Front, a guerrilla group named after Sandino. In 1967, he was named the leader of the Sandinistas' urban guerrilla campaign. That same year, the National Guard arrested him for taking part in a bank robbery, and he spent the next seven years in jail. He was released in 1974 as part of a prisoner exchange.

After his release, Ortega traveled to Cuba, where he reportedly received several months of guerrilla training. When he returned to Nicaragua, he worked to unite the Sandinistas' many factions and form alliances with business groups and political organizations also opposed to Somoza. The Sandinistas' guerrilla campaign became a full-fledged civil war with a late 1977 battle against the National Guard and an attack on the National Palace in Managua in August of 1978. Ortega and his brother, Humberto, led a powerful Sandinista faction called the Insurrectionists, and Ortega became a top Sandinista military commander.

Conservatives in the United States were suspicious of the Sandinistas because they took inspiration from the Cuban Revolution of 1959, which had led to a communist dictatorship. Ortega told Karen DeYoung of the *Washington Post* that he was not fighting for a Marxist revolution, but for a democratically elected government—a point that would be hotly disputed for years. "We are, and have always been, for one very calculated goal—the fall of the Somoza dictatorship," Ortega said. "We want the installation of a popular, democratic government that responds to the people's needs, that gives the people work, that gives land to the peasants, and health services."

The Sandinistas defeated Somoza's forces in July of 1979. Ortega was part of a five-member military junta that took over the country. The junta seized all of Somoza's vast landholdings and ordered the National Guard and Congress dissolved. "When Somoza was the owner of this country, he gave us the crumbs that he wanted to," Ortega told a rally of supporters in August, as quoted by Charles A. Krause of the *Washington Post*. "When he saw the imminence of his defeat, he took the economy with him in such a way that we found ourselves with an empty house but with a great spirit." The metaphor ended up being ironic. Despite his status as a leader of a poor people's revolt, Ortega seized a mansion in Managua owned by banker Jaime Morales and moved in.

That September, Ortega gave a speech at a meeting of nonaligned nations, or developing countries, in Cuba. He asserted that Nicaragua "wants to invest in tractors and plows instead of weapons" (according to Karen DeYoung of the *Washington Post*). Later that month, he and other members of the junta traveled to Washington, where U.S. president Jimmy Carter welcomed them and U.S. officials discussed aiding Nicaragua economically. The Carter administration hoped to encourage the Sandinistas to choose a moderate political path, but American conservatives feared they would form a dictatorship and export revolution throughout Latin America, as Cuba had. Ortega dismissed such fears as a "provocation" meant "to provide a pretext for intervening in Nicaragua" (according to John M. Goshko of the *Washington Post*).

Ortega and the junta began efforts to reduce poverty in Nicaragua, including better education to promote literacy and new efforts to break up large parcels of land owned by a few families. In 1981, Ortega announced plans for government takeovers of privately owned farms the government considered unproductive. He also pledged to seize businesses whose owners were trying to illegally move money out of the country.

The Sandinistas allowed only limited political freedoms. Soon after taking power, the junta passed a media law that banned privately owned television stations and gave the government the power to fine newspapers and radio stations and order them to temporarily halt publishing or broadcasting. In 1981, after members of a business group published an open letter criticizing some statements by Ortega and Nicaragua's growing alignment with the Soviet Union, the Sandinistas jailed them. The opposition newspaper *La Prensa* was sometimes censored and attacked by mobs on a few occasions, though it continued publication.

In November of 1980, Carter lost the U.S. presidential election to Ronald Reagan, who had criticized Carter for his willingness to reach out to the Sandinistas. The United States cut off most of its aid to Nicaragua in 1981, accusing the country of obtaining weapons from Cuba and expressing suspicion that its military buildup was part of an offensive, not defensive, strategy. Ortega, meanwhile, repeatedly warned Nicaraguans that the United States would invade. Instead, in 1982, the United States threw its support behind the Contras, a rebel group that included Somoza loyalists and began attacking Sandinista forces from bases in neighboring Honduras. The Sandinistas responded by declaring a state of emergency, censoring the news, and restricting political activity.

Ortega and the other junta members began making more radical statements in favor of socialism. In May of 1982, Ortega visited Moscow, where Soviet leaders greeted him warmly with a ceremonial ride into the city. He met with Soviet premier Leonid Brezhnev and asked for expanded economic assistance to Nicaragua and military aid.

In November of 1984, during the war with the Contras, the Sandinista government held national elections. Ortega ran for president. The conditions and results of the election were hotly disputed. Several opposition groups boycotted the vote, saying they could not compete effectively because the Sandinistas were restricting civil liberties, including press freedom. Pro-Sandinista mobs disrupted some opposition rallies, but the government eased its censorship of *La Prensa* and allowed limited radio and television time to opposition parties. Ortega and the Sandinistas won 67 percent of the vote and a majority in a new National Assembly. The Reagan administration, arguing that the elections were meaningless because the Sandinistas dominated Nicaraguan society, increased its support for the Contra rebels and imposed a trade embargo on Nicaragua. It lasted five years, hobbling the Nicaraguan economy.

The civil war cost more than 50,000 lives. It ended in the late 1980s, when the Sandinistas and Contras signed a peace agreement negotiated by Oscar Arias Sanchez, president of Costa Rica. The agreement included a promise of free elections, which were held in February of 1990.

Ortega ran for re-election as president on his record of fighting U.S. influence and instituting land reform and literacy programs. But voters were angry at the Sandinistas over very high food prices, farming laws that forced farmers to sell their crops at low government-set rates, and Cuban-style Sandinista block committees that often intruded in people's private lives. In early 1990, just before the election, Ortega promised to free more than 1,000 political prisoners, including captured Contras. He also loosened the requirements for getting an exit visa to leave Nicaragua, one of only three governments in the Western Hemisphere that required its citizens to get permission to leave the country. The opposition argued that the moves were merely attempts to win votes.

In February, Ortega lost the election to Violeta Barrios de Chamorro of the National Opposition Union, attracting about 41 percent of the vote to her 55 percent. His concession speech promised a peaceful transition of power. It was one of the few times that a revolutionary government had ceded power in free elections. Ortega's term ended in April of 1990.

After his defeat, Ortega remained the leader of the Sandinistas, who became the main opposition party in the National Assembly. In May of 1996, Ortega ran as the Sandinista candidate for president. He lost to Arnoldo Aleman Lacayo, head of the conservative Liberal Constitutional Party, formerly the dictator Somoza's party.

As the 1990s ended, Ortega's reputation suffered two serious blows. In 1998, Ortega's stepdaughter, Zoilamerica Narvaez, accused him of sexually abusing her during the entire time he was Nicaragua's leader, starting when he was 34 and she was eleven. Ortega used his immunity as a member of the national legislature to avoid facing criminal charges related to the allegation. His wife, Rosario Murillo, Narvaez's mother, defended her husband and viciously attacked her daughter for her accusations.

A year later, Ortega signed a controversial political pact with his political archrival, Aleman. It changed the election laws so that presidential candidates could win election with only 35 percent of the vote. The deal gave Ortega control of several government appointments and gave both men immunity from prosecution. To protest the pact and Ortega's tight control over the party, several prominent Sandinistas left and formed their own party. Ortega ran for president again in 2001 and lost to Liberal Constitutional Party candidate Enrique Bolanos, but finished with a strong 42 percent of the vote. In 2005, when Sandinistas in the National Assembly attempted to impeach Bolanos, Ortega, responding to international pressure to preserve Nicaragua's political stability, told the Sandinistas to stop the impeachment.

In the 2006 elections, Ortega ran for president once again. His political style had changed greatly since the 1980s, when he often traveled the country in a military jeep, wearing combat fatigues and sporting a machine gun. In 2006, he traveled in a silver Range Rover or a Mercedes SUV and campaigned in white button-down shirts and jeans, with a Nicaraguan flag around his shoulders. Ortega repeatedly promised to pursue political reconciliation. His campaign song was a Spanish hip-hop version of John Lennon's "Give Peace a Chance," with a chorus promising reconciliation and unity. For a running mate, he chose Morales, the ex-banker and Contra supporter whose mansion Ortega seized after the revolution. (A land swap had reportedly settled their long dispute over the mansion.)

Ortega said that he would respect civil liberties and the economic policies enacted in the 1990s and 2000s, such as a free-trade pact with the United States and the privatization of formerly state-owned businesses. He said he would work to attract foreign investment to deal with Nicaragua's enduring poverty (four out of five Nicaraguans earn $2 a day or less). In the 1980s, Ortega had distanced himself from the Church and often fought with it. But by 2006, he had become a devout Roman Catholic who regularly attended mass, asked the Church to forgive past Sandinista excesses, and befriended Nicaragua's Catholic Cardinal Miguel Obando y Bravo, who had opposed Ortega's 1980s government.

Ortega won the five-way election with about 38 percent of the vote, ahead of Eduardo Montealegre, who was second with about 29 percent. He was sworn in as president in January of 2007. His inaugural ceremony was filled with the sort of populist rhetoric he had embraced in the past but avoided during the campaign. A recording of an angry Ortega speech from the 1980s played over loudspeakers, and Ortega appeared with two other leftist Latin American presidents, Hugo Chavez of Venezuela and Evo Morales of Bolivia, who gave speeches supporting him. Ortega laid out his governing agenda in an extremely long speech. He promised to forge economic ties with other left-wing governments in South and Central America and pledged to provide electricity to impoverished areas of Nicaragua. "Our agenda is unfinished," he said (as quoted by Max Blumenthal on TheNation.com). "When we left the illiteracy rate was 13 percent. Today it is 35 percent."

The next day, Ortega, Chavez, Morales, and Cuban vice president Jose Ramon Machado Ventura signed a pact implementing Chavez's economic cooperation project, which included $30 million in debt forgiveness and low-interest loans for Nicaragua, 100,000 barrels of low-cost oil, and more than two dozen new electric plants. In August, Ortega reached out to another developing nation estranged from the United States: Iran agreed to finance a $350 million port on Nicaragua's Caribbean coast, construct 10,000 new houses in the country, and help build a $120 million electrical plant. The power plants were meant to help alleviate an electrical crisis in Nicaragua, which suffered daily blackouts during much of 2007. Ortega also planned to ask the center-left leader of Brazil, Luis Inacio Lula de Silva, for help combating the power crisis.

Sources

Periodicals

Chicago Tribune, February 1, 1990, News section, p. 18; February 27, 1990, News section, p. 1.
Christian Science Monitor, September 15, 2005.
New York Times, November 12, 2006; February 24, 2007; August 6, 2007.
Washington Post, October 16, 1978, p. A2; July 22, 1979, p. A14; August 4, 1979, p. A15; September 7, 1979, p. A12; September 25, 1979, p. A6; June 3, 1981, p. A17; July 20, 1981, p. A21; November 25, 1981, p. A1; May 5, 1982, p. A18; November 6, 1984, p. A1; December 28, 1984, p. A1; February 27, 1990, p. A1; March 7, 1990, p. A31; October 9, 2006; October 29, 2006, p. B2.

Online

"The Kinder, Gentler Daniel Ortega," TheNation. com, http://www.thenation.com/doc/20070205. tif/blumenthal (November 23, 2007).
"Ortega, Daniel," Encyclopedia Britannica Online Library Edition, http://library.eb.com/eb/article-9057473 (November 23, 2007).
"Ortega Wins Nicaraguan Election," BBC.com, http://news.bbc.co.uk/go/pr/fr/-/2/hi/americas/6117704.stm (November 23, 2007).
"Profile: Daniel Ortega Saavedra," CNN.com, http://news.cnn.com/SPECIALS/cold.war/kbank/profiles/Ortega (November 23, 2007).
"The Return of Daniel Ortega," TheNation.com, http://www.thenation.com/doc/20061120.tif/Ortega (November 23, 2007).

—*Erick Trickey*

Brad Paisley

AP Images

Country singer

Born October 28, 1972, in Glen Dale, WV; son of Doug (a department of transportation worker) and Sandy (a teacher) Paisley; married Kimberly Williams (an actress), March 15, 2003; children: William Huckleberry. *Education:* Studied guitar with Clarence "Hank" Goddard; attended West Liberty State College, WV, 1991-93; Belmont University, Nashville, TN, B.B.A., 1995.

Addresses: *Management*—JAG Management, Jimmy Gilmer, 41 Music Square East, Nashville, TN 37203. *Record company*—Arista Nashville, 1540 Broadway, New York, NY 10036. *Web site*—http://www.bradpaisley.com.

Career

Played on WWVA's Jamboree USA radio program, 1980s; intern, American Society of Composers, Authors, and Publishers, Atlantic Records, and Fitzgerald-Hartley Management, 1990s; signed songwriting contract with EMI, 1995; signed with Arista Nashville, 1998; released debut album, *Who Needs Pictures,* 1999; Grand Ole Opry debut, 1999; inducted as a regular cast member, Grand Ole Opry, 2001; has appeared at international festivals in England, Scotland, Ireland, Canada, and Japan; "Bonfires and Amplifiers" tour for album *5th Gear,* 2007.

Awards: Top new male vocalist, Academy of Country Music, 1999; song of the year, for "He Didn't Have to Be," TNN Music Awards, 2000; video of the year, for "He Didn't Have to Be," TNN Music Awards, 2000; Discovery Award for "He Didn't Have to Be," TNN Music Awards, 2000; Horizon Award, Country Music Association, 2000; vocal event of the year award for "Too Country," Country Music Association, 2001; international songwriter of the year, Nashville Songwriters Association, 2000-01; Connie B. Gay Award, Country Music Association, 2002; album of the year, for *Time Well Wasted,* Academy of Country Music, 2005; musical event of the year for "When I Get Where I'm Going," Country Music Association, 2006; album of the year, for *Time Well Wasted,* Country Music Association, 2006; top male vocalist, Academy of Country Music, 2006; male vocalist of the year, Country Music Association, 2007; music video of the year, for "Online," Country Music Association, 2007; Grammy Award for best country instrumental performance, for "Throttleneck," National Academy of Recording Arts and Sciences, 2008.

Sidelights

Country music star Brad Paisley is well known for bring traditional styles back to country. Instead of following the trend where many stars in the country world record their songs as cross-over numbers for pop radio stations, Paisley sticks to his originals. Not only a singer, Paisley excels at guitar, and has also worked as a songwriter, writing many of the numbers he and his band—most of whom have been together for 12 years—perform.

But despite his seeming rapid rise from obscurity to stardom at his first album's release in 1999, Paisley has been in the industry for a long time. It all started with his grandfather. "I got my first guitar when I was eight years old," Paisley told an interviewer for the *Virginian Pilot*. "My grandfather, who died in 1987, gave it to me. He was the best friend I ever had. Two months before he died, I opened for the Judds—he got to see that.... It was like giving Moses a look at the Promised Land. He knew that guitar was the best gift I ever received." The two spent hours together as Paisley was growing up: His grandfather, Warren Jarvis, was a railroad worker who worked the night shift, giving him time to spend with his grandson during the day. They listened to country music, and Jarvis began teaching him how to play guitar. Though at first Paisley was reluctant, preferring sports and more active endeavors, he took to the instrument. "I kind of fought it for a while, 'cause at eight you'd rather play sports or do anything other than something that hurts your hand," Paisley told Melissa Block on *All Things Considered*. "But the thing that kept me going was knowing how bad he wanted me to do that. I think he enjoyed it so much he wanted me to be able to have that in my life. He changed my life in a way no one ever will again." Soon he and Jarvis were playing everywhere they could, "anywhere the relatives wouldn't complain," Paisley quipped in *People*.

Jarvis gave him a love of country music, teaching him all of the old Buck Owens numbers. "I had to do the opposite of any other kid," Paisley explained in *Entertainment Weekly*, "I had to go study rock and roll. I'd go 'Oh yeah, I love AC/DC'—and then I would go buy it." While country music remained his love, he also practiced songs by U2 to perform for his friends, and he enjoyed jazz and sang gospel in church with his family. His first song, written when he was 12, was "Born on Christmas Day." According to a contributor for the Country Music Television Web site, "His junior high school principal heard it and asked him to do it at the next Rotary Club meeting." Paisley, always eager to perform—he quipped in *People* that one of the nice things about coming from a small town was, "If you wanna be a star, they'll make you one"—accepted, and in the audience was a radio programming director, who then invited him to perform on Jamboree USA, a popular country radio program. The performance was a success, and Paisley was invited to become a regular on the program, where he appeared steadily for eight years, often opening for such country stars as Little Jimmy Dickens and Roy Clark. He became the youngest member elected to Jamboree USA's Hall of Fame.

Along with performing on the radio, Paisley studied guitar with local musician Clarence "Hank" Goddard, who invited Paisley to perform with his band. "Hank would let me play a solo, and I'd butcher it, but he'd smile and give me encouragement," Paisley recounted in *Guitar Player*. "He made me work on my scales, and play solos.... That's when I really started working on my lead playing." His formal education began at West Liberty College, a local school, but a professor encouraged him to follow his interests to Belmont University in Nashville, where he could study music business. At first, Paisley was reluctant to leave his small town, but once in Nashville, he settled in, meeting fellow students Frank Rogers (who would produce his first album), Chris DuBois, and Kelley Lovelace, who have both co-written songs on Paisley's albums.

During college, Paisley played on demos and worked as a songwriter, earning money and starting to make inroads in the industry. His work was noticed, and he was signed by Arista Nashville in 1998. A year later, he released his first album, *Who Needs Pictures*, bringing on Rogers as his producer despite the fact that Rogers had never produced an album, and playing with his stage band, a trend uncommon in country music, when most singers work with a band more familiar with recording in a studio. "He Didn't Have to Be," a single he co-wrote with Lovelace, topped the Billboard charts, and the album went platinum. A series of awards thrust Paisley into the spotlight—a light he made a point to share with his band. The humble entertainer was overwhelmed by his sudden celebrity: "It's a good kind of feeling, but it's also a whirlwind to some extent, but it's fun," he told the Los Angeles *Daily News*. "It beats working, that's for sure."

In 1999, Paisley was also invited to sing at the Grand Ole Opry, and he began doing as many shows there as his schedule would allow—a trend that echoed his more traditional sound. "Many Hot Country performers have been criticized for not playing the Opry, and there's some concern for its future," wrote S. Renee Dechert in *Popular Music and Society*. "Paisley, however, is a regular." So regular, in fact, that his second album, *Part II*, featured a track of Paisley performing "The Old Rugged Cross" at the Opry, introduced by Little Jimmy Dickens. His performances there in 1999 also made him, at 27, the youngest cast member.

Part II, released in 2001, also featured Paisley's third No. 1 hit, "I'm Gonna Miss Her (The Fishing Song)." The song tells the story of a woman who gives her boyfriend an ultimatum: her or the fish. After choosing the fish, he says he is sure he will miss her, but is easily distracted by the fish biting his line. Not only did the song capture Paisley's sense of humor, which helped him earn a reputation as a comedic songwriter, the music video also featured actress Kimberly Williams, who Paisley married in 2003.

Part II did not capture any awards, nor did Paisley's third album, *Mud on the Tires*, though he earned several nominations. "I'm enjoying this losing streak," Paisley said in the *St. Louis Post-Dispatch* in 2006. "Nobody dislikes you when you lose, and nobody's looking to pick you off." Paisley was the most-nominated male country artist at that year's Grammy awards, but he took no awards home. That trend changed with his fourth album, *Time Well Wasted*, which was named Album of the Year by both the Academy of Country Music and the Country Music Association. Paisley's serious numbers and comedic hits both won praise, and *Entertainment Weekly* contributor Chris Willman noted, "he's had more successfully comic songs than anyone in country since the 1970s."

In 2007, Paisley hit the road on his "Bonfires and Amplifiers" tour, and his fifth full album (not including a Christmas album) went gold, producing another two No. 1 hits. He returned home as often as he could to spend time with his family's newest addition, William Huckleberry Paisley, in either the Paisleys' Los Angeles home or his preferred home of Franklin, Tennessee. "Brad's a great dad," said wife Kimberly Williams-Paisley in *People*. "It's really fun to leave him with Huck. No matter what happens, when I ask how it went, the first thing Brad says is, 'Oh, we had a ball.'"

Friends have said that they would call Paisley a workaholic if he were not having so much fun. "He's extremely intelligent and a very quick learner," said Paisley's tour designer Scott Scovill in the Minneapolis *Star Tribune*. "He can grab animation software and start doing animation.... For fun, he'll sit down and edit his videos or his TV special." Critics have noted this sense of fun in his music as well. "If Brad Paisley weren't a country superstar, he could be a comedian," a critic for *Blender* magazine was quoted as having said in the Minneapolis *Star Tribune*. Along with his comedy, country veteran Buck Owens praised Paisley's nostalgic sound. "Brad's the real thing," he said in *People*. "There's no pretense."

Paisley attributes some of his success to being able to combine traditional country styles and themes with rock and jazz inspirations, as well as not taking his music too seriously. "I think levity is very necessary in our modern world," he said in *Entertainment Weekly*. For Paisley, "it probably comes from a love of the old country music, because this was such a big part of our format at one time." He also remembers his roots. "I've spent many years with my band playing little fairs on flatbed trailers," he said in *Guitar Player*. "We'd show up, and no one knew who we were, so we'd work the whole time to try to convince people not to leave." Despite, or perhaps because of, his fame, he keeps that same attitude in his live performances: dedication to giving people a good show. He told *People*, "I feel more nervous than I've been in my career. There still isn't a night when I don't worry if people will come [to a show]." But despite his nerves, he and his band continue to love their jobs. "There isn't a single night when we walk out there and hate our job," Paisley said in *Guitar Player*. "I am so thankful we've gotten to this level. It's ridiculous we get paid for this.... It still blows my mind."

Selected discography

Who Needs Pictures, Arista Nashville, 1999.
Part II, Arista Nashville, 2001.
Mud on the Tires, Arista Nashville, 2003.
Time Well Wasted, Arista Nashville, 2005.
A Brad Paisley Christmas, Arista Nashville, 2006.
5th Gear, Arista Nashville, 2007.

Sources

Books

Contemporary Musicians, vol. 42, Gale Group (Farmington Hills, MI), 2003.

Periodicals

Daily News (Los Angeles, CA), May 3, 2000, p. L3.
Entertainment Weekly, August 24, 2007, p. 27.
Guitar Player, October 1999, p. 39; December 2007, pp. 78(13).
People, October 9, 2000, p. 87; November 14, 2005, p. 91; November 2006, p. 52; Fall 2007, p. 38.
Popular Music and Society, October 2003, pp. 412-13.
Star Tribune (Minneapolis, MN), August 19, 2007, p. 1F.
St. Louis Post-Dispatch, March 23, 2006, p. 5.

Teen People, August 1, 2001, p. 117.
Virginian Pilot, February 3, 2000, p. W5.

Online

"Biography: Brad Paisley," Country Music Television, http://www.cmt.com/artists/az/paisley_brad/bio.jhtml (February 22, 2008).
"Brad Paisley," *Biography Resource Center Online,* Gale Group, 2002.

"Brad's Biography," Brad Paisley's Web site, http://www.bradpaisley.com/site.php?content=bio (February 22, 2008).

Transcripts

All Things Considered, #4930009, National Public Radio, September 29, 2005.

—*Alana Joli Abbott*

Hayden Panettiere

Actress

Born Hayden Leslie Panettiere, August 21, 1989, in Palisades, NY; daughter of Skip (a firefighter) and Lesley (an actress) Panettiere.

Addresses: *Office*—c/o NBC-TV, 30 Rockefeller Plaza, New York, NY 10112.

Career

Actress on television, including: *One Life to Live,* ABC, 1994-97; *How Do You Spell God?* (movie), 1996; *Guiding Light,* 1996-2000; *A Will of Their Own* (miniseries), 1998; *Too Rich: The Secret Life of Doris Duke* (movie), 1999; *If You Believe* (movie), 1999; *Chestnut Hill* (movie), 2001; *Ally McBeal,* 2002; *Normal* (movie), 2003; *Malcolm in the Middle,* 2003-05; *Tiger Cruise* (movie), 2004; *Lies My Mother Told Me* (movie), 2005; *Heroes,* 2006—. Film appearances include: *The Object of My Affection,* 1998; *A Bug's Life* (voice), 1998; *Message in a Bottle,* 1999; *Dinosaur,* 2000; *Remember the Titans,* 2000; *The Affair of the Necklace,* 2001; *Joe Somebody,* 2001; *Raising Helen,* 2004; *The Dust Factory,* 2004; *Racing Stripes,* 2005; *Ice Princess,* 2005; *Mr. Gibb,* 2006; *The Architect,* 2006; *Bring It On: All or Nothing,* 2006; *Shanghai Kiss,* 2007; *Fireflies in the Garden,* 2008. Created bag for Dooney & Bourke, 2007; spokesperson, SaveTheWhalesAgain. org.

Awards: Young Artist Award for best performance in a feature film—supporting young actress, Young Artist Foundation, for *Remember the Titans,* 2001; Young Artist Award for best performance in a TV

Kevin Mazur/WireImage/Getty Images

series—supporting young actress, Young Artist Foundation, for *Heroes,* 2007; Saturn Award for best supporting actress in a television program, Academy of Science Fiction, Fantasy, and Horror Films, for *Heroes,* 2007; Teen Choice Award for choice TV actress: drama, FOX, for *Heroes,* 2007; Feature Film Award for acting, Newport Beach Film Festival, for *Shanghai Kiss,* 2007; Rising Star Award, Vail Film Festival, 2007; Gretchen Wyler Award, Hollywood Office of the Humane Society of the United States, 2008.

Sidelights

A young actress best known for her role as the indestructible cheerleader on the hit NBC drama *Heroes,* Hayden Panettiere is also an activist who had an arrest warrant issued in Japan in 2007 for participating in a protest against the slaughter of dolphins. Panettiere began her acting career in commercials and soap operas before moving into film and other television roles. Film highlights include roles in the films *Remember the Titans, Raising Helen,* and *Bring It On: All or Nothing.*

Born on August 21, 1989, in Palisades, New York, Panettiere is the daughter of Skip and Lesley Panettiere. Her father worked as a firefighter in

New York City. He reached the rank of lieutenant and retired six months before the September 11, 2001, terrorist attacks on New York City and Washington, D.C. Her mother was an actress who appeared on soaps such as *All My Children* and *Loving*.

Panettiere began modeling as an infant, and launched her acting career at eleven months with appearances in television commercials. One of her first memories of acting was a mistake she made. Panettiere told the *Washington Post*'s Bridget Byrne, "I was holding this Christmas tree ball and I broke it.... I remember being so embarrassed."

When Panettiere was five years old, she moved on to a regular role on the soap opera *One Life to Live*. She played Sarah Victoria Roberts for three years until 1997. Panettiere then was cast in another soap, *Guiding Light*, in 1996. On this program, she faced new challenges playing Lizzie Spaulding, a character who gets leukemia, is kidnapped, and shoots her mother's lover. She remained on *Guiding Light* until 2000.

While appearing on *Guiding Light*, Panettiere began her film acting career with roles in two films in 1998. In addition to appearing in *The Object of My Affection*, she provided the voice of Princess Dot in the animated feature *A Bug's Life*. She was nominated for a Grammy Award for best spoken works album for children for her reading of the related *A Bug's Life Read-Along*.

In 2000, Panettiere garnered more critical notice for her work as Sheryl in the film *Remember the Titans*. Her character was the tomboy daughter of a white football coach who loses his position to a black coach when high schools are combined in 1971 Virginia. Panettiere's Sheryl is rude to and yells at the new coach, played by Denzel Washington, but her already extensive background in acting meant that Panetierre was not daunted to work opposite the Oscar winner.

While *Remember the Titans* received much praise for handling its sensitive subject matter, not all of Panettiere's film roles were so highly regarded. In the roundly panned revenge comedy *Joe Somebody*, she played the daughter of a newly divorced single dad played by Tim Allen.

Critics still took note of Panettiere's talent. Reviewing *Joe Somebody* in the *San Diego Union-Tribune*, Jerry McCormick wrote, "Panettiere, so brilliant as the coach's daughter in *Remember the Titans*, continues her little-girl-who-knows-more-than-the-adults routine and once again, it works. She's truly the brightest spot in the film."

In addition to films, Panettiere appeared in a number of television movies and a miniseries in the late 1990s and early 2000s. One praised role was in the 1999 television movie *Too Rich: The Secret Life of Doris Duke* in which she played a lonely heiress. Panettiere returned to series television in 2002 when she joined the cast of the hit show *Ally McBeal*. Panettiere played the titular character's long-lost ten-year-old daughter, Maddie, the result of a fertility mess.

Though Panettiere was 12 years old, she found it somewhat difficult to play someone only two years younger. She told Kathryn Shattuck of *New York Times*, "It's always really challenging to play someone younger than you are. Maddie is very sophisticated, and she acts like a 12-year-old. But she looks and dresses like the 10-year-old that she is."

While spending a year playing Maddie on *Ally McBeal*'s last season then performing in a recurring role as a geeky but powerful girl on *Malcolm in the Middle* from 2003 to 2005, Panettiere continued to act in films. In 2004, she played teen rebel Audrey in the romantic comedy *Raising Helen*. Her character was one of three recently orphaned siblings who are being raised by their somewhat clueless aunt.

Panettiere sometimes suffered for her career choice in school. She attended schools in New York until the age of 14, and was often a reluctant part of the popular group. By this time, her peers were tormenting the young performer because of her career. She told the *Daily Record*'s Terry Gilfillan, "At school I was teased a lot because I was an actor. They used to be awful. I went through a big period where I was tortured at school. Absolutely just ripped apart. It was very hard for me but I think it made me a stronger person and I'm glad that it happened." Because of this situation, as well as her career, Panettiere was home schooled to complete her high school education.

Not letting personal problems deter her, Panettiere took on a very different role in 2005 when she played a young girl living on a horse-racing farm in the family oriented comedy *Racing Stripes*. Her character's life is changed when a zebra who thinks he is a race horse comes to the farm, and she trains him to race despite her father's objections to riding any animal. Panettiere had to ride both horses and zebras for the film, and enjoyed the experience. She told Stephen Schaefer of the *Boston Herald*, "Definitely, this was the strangest movie I've ever made. I loved it and it was amazing to work on because I'm an animal fanatic and I could take care of the baby zebras."

Also in 2005, Panettiere was in a very different type of sports movie. In *Ice Princess*, she played the unhappy daughter of an ice skating coach mother who is living her skating dream through her. While the film was panned as appealing only to its target preteen audience, some critics noted Panettiere's performance took the film to a different level. In the *San Francisco Chronicle*, Mick LaSalle commented, "The best thing about *Ice Princess* is the performance of Hayden Panettiere.... She's only 16, but she has a way of thinking on camera and conveying a mix of emotions simultaneously that jumps off the screen."

While critics were noticing Panettiere and her acting ability, she had not broken out into the general public's consciousness yet. This situation changed in 2006 when she was cast in a featured role in the ensemble science fiction drama *Heroes*, about superhero characters who are learning to deal with their powers and place in a troubled world. Panettiere explained the show to Dave Walker of the *Times-Picayune*: "The show is about people crossing paths and how small the world really is. It's not just about our powers. It's about mankind. It's about the world. If we don't succeed [in saving it], the world will be completely changed and pointed in a different direction, and for the most part it's not for the good.... It's about doing what's right and what we're kind of meant to do."

On *Heroes*, Panettiere played Claire Bennett, a cheerleader who can instantly recover from any injury. She joked about her often-killed but self-healing character to Alex Strachan of the *Ottawa Citizen*, "I die all the time. So it's no big deal. I feel like Kenny in South Park. Like 'Oh my God, they killed Claire.'" *Heroes* became a number-one show for NBC, and was soon extremely popular worldwide.

Panettiere used the popularity of *Heroes* to build her film career. She hoped the television role would help her land better films, telling the New York *Daily News*' Marisa Guthrie, "It's definitely changed things. That's one of the reasons I did the show, because all of the movies I wanted to do went to ac-

tors who had that following from a TV show." Among the films she chose to do was the 2006 indie *The Architect* in which she played the insightful daughter of an idealistic designer living in Chicago. In 2008, she appeared in *Fireflies in the Garden*, which co-starred Julia Roberts and Emily Watson.

In addition to acting, Panettiere also launched a singing career. Signing a deal with Hollywood Records, she spent three years working on her debut album, set to drop in late 2008, and co-wrote most of the songs on the release. She contributed songs to various movie soundtracks as well. Panettiere also agreed to star in the Dooney & Bourke 2007 holiday ad campaign, and designed a bag for the company. She told *People*, "I wanted to do something people haven't seen from Dooney & Bourke before, so my bag is red patent leather. It's funky and fun and it looks squeaky clean, sort of like a brand-new car."

Panettiere also used her newfound fame to draw attention to causes which were important to her, including animal charities such as ICUN Wildlife Foundation and the Whaleman Foundation. To that end, Panettiere participated in a Save the Whales protest in Japan in October 2007. The activists confronted Japanese commercial fishing boats on a dolphin hunt in Taiji Wakayama. The group swam towards dolphins being herded into a cove by the fisherman so they could be killed.

For her participation in the event, an arrest warrant was issued for the actress. Despite the warrant, Panettiere vowed she would participate in such protests again. She was also surprised by the media attention she received in the States. She told Monica Corcoran of the *Los Angeles Times*, "In Hollywood, you have to wear no underwear to get any publicity. So I didn't expect it to get so much attention. Even [gossip blogger] Perez Hilton blogged about it!" Early in 2008, Panettiere was given an activism award from the Hollywood Office of the Humane Society of the United States, the Gretchen Wyler Award.

Panettiere became a favorite of paparazzi as her fame increased (in part because she was dating actor Stephen Colletti for some time), but she vowed not to become like other young Hollywood starlets who lived fast and ended up in rehab. She told Cindy Pearlman in the *Chicago Sun Times*, "Unfortunately in this business when people start getting those [celebrity] perks, they sort of head down the wrong road. They lose track of what's important. They forget about their craft. They forget about the love of it and sometimes it causes people to slack off and lose focus. I love my craft and what I do. I want to mature in it and get better every time I do it. In the future, I want to be looked at as a respected actress."

Sources

Books

Complete Marquis Who's Who, Marquis Who's Who, 2008.

Periodicals

Boston Globe, May 28, 2004, p. C5.
Boston Herald, January 9, 2005, p. 35.
Chicago Sun Times, August 26, 2007, p. D3; November 16, 2007, sec. Features, p. 50.
Daily News (New York, NY), December 3, 2006, p. 10.
Daily Record, April 19, 2008, p. 4.
Herald News (Passaic County, NJ), February 24, 2005, p. E12.
Hindustan Times, March 31, 2008.
Independent Extra, April 24, 2008, sec. Extra, p. 10.
London Free Press (London, Ontario, Canada), May 3, 2007, p. T3.
Los Angeles Times, November 25, 2007, p. P10.
New York Times, April 21, 2002, sec. 13, p. 55.
Ottawa Citizen, February 3, 2007, p. K3.
People, October 29, 2007, p. 112.
Philadelphia Daily News, January 14, 2005, sec. Features, p. 36.
San Diego Union-Tribune, December 20, 2001, sec. Entertainment, p. 20.
San Francisco Chronicle, March 18, 2005, p. E5.
Soaps on ABC, April 3, 2008.
St. Louis Post-Dispatch (St. Louis, MO), December 21, 2001, p. E1.
Times-Picayune (New Orleans, LA), May 11, 2007, p. 17.
USA Today, April 30, 2007, p. 3D.
Vanity Fair, February 2007, p. 125.
Washington Post, October 12, 2000, p. C15.
West Australian (Perth, Australia), September 15, 2007, p. 14.

—*A. Petruso*

Tony Parker

Gary Gershoff/WireImage/Getty Images

Professional basketball player

Born William Tony Parker, May 17, 1982, in Bruges, Belgium; son of Tony Parker Sr. (a professional basketball player) and Pamela Firestone (a model); married Eva Longoria (an actress), July 7, 2007.

Addresses: *Contact*—San Antonio Spurs, One AT&T Center, San Antonio, TX 78219. *Home*—San Antonio, TX. *Web site*—http://www.tp9.net.

Career

Signed with Paris Saint-Germain Racing, of the French Pro A League, c. 1999; entered NBA draft, 2001; played for the San Antonio Spurs, 2001—.

Awards: Junior (Under-18) European Championships, MVP, 2000; NBA All-Rookie First Team, 2001-02; NBA All-Star Team, 2006, 2007; named NBA Championship Finals MVP, 2007.

Sidelights

With his no-look passes, incredible speed, and dead-eye jumpers, point guard Tony Parker led the San Antonio Spurs to the National Basketball Association (NBA) championship in 2003, 2005 and 2007. During the 2007 NBA Finals, the Belgian-born, French-raised Parker averaged 24.5 points per game. Parker's stellar post-season performance earned him Most Valuable Player (MVP) honors, making him the first European in league history to win the NBA Finals MVP award. Though Parker is always in the spotlight on the court, when he walks off the court all eyes focus on his wife—*Desperate Housewives* star Eva Longoria, whom he married in 2007.

Parker was born on May 17, 1982, in Bruges, Belgium, though he was raised in France where his American father, Tony Parker Sr., played basketball professionally. The elder Parker honed his basketball skills at Loyola University in Chicago, then headed to Europe to play. While there, he met Dutch model Pamela Firestone. The two married and had three sons—Tony Jr., Terence, and Pierre. They eventually divorced.

Given his father's occupation, Parker naturally took an early interest in basketball. The family photo album contains pictures of Parker, just 18 months old, holding a basketball. However, as a child Parker initially preferred soccer. With his speed and coordination, he showed potential to become a soccer star. Parker's sports focus changed during a 1991 visit to Chicago, Illinois. Parker, just nine, was visiting his grandparents in the Windy City and got swept up in the NBA playoffs, which featured Michael Jordan and the Chicago Bulls. Glued to the television, Parker watched the slam-dunking Jordan lead the Bulls to their first championship. Mesmerized by the NBA—and Jordan in particular—Parker decided he wanted to become a professional basketball player. He gave up soccer and his father began teaching him everything he knew.

In 1994, Parker began playing for a basketball team in Deville-les-Rouen, France. At 15, he enrolled at the Institut National du Sport et de l'Education Physique (National Institute of Physical Education), a Paris-based sporting academy for the country's top athletes. During this time, Parker continued to follow Jordan's career and spent his free time watching tapes of Jordan and other top NBA guards. During a 1996 visit to Chicago, Parker got to meet his hero when his uncle arranged for him to attend a Bulls practice session. Parker met Bulls standout Scottie Pippen and got his picture taken with Jordan. Speaking to the *Austin American-Statesman's* Mark Rosner, Parker described his admiration for Jordan this way: "I followed Michael because I like his mentality, [because] he never wants to lose, [because of] his leadership. I like to watch [point guards] Gary Payton and Jason Kidd, Magic [Johnson]. I'm a student of it."

What Parker watched on television, he tried to transfer to the court. At 17, he signed with Paris Saint-Germain Racing, a basketball team that competed in the French Pro A League. "Most of the guys I played with and against were 29, 30 years old," Parker told *Sports Illustrated Kids* writer Mike Monroe. "I got banged around quite a bit, but it was a great learning experience and made me mature." In 2000, Parker led the French national under-18 team to victory in the junior European Championships, earning MVP honors.

While Parker was well-known in his own country, he did not grab the attention of the U.S.-based NBA until the 2000 Nike Hoop Summit, held in Indianapolis, Indiana. Playing for the European junior team, Parker showed off his talents against some of the United States' top high school prospects. In a game that pitted the European All-Stars against the U.S. All-Stars, Parker managed 20 points, seven assists, and four rebounds in a 98-97 loss to Team USA, piquing the interest of NBA scouts.

In 2001, the 6-foot-2, 180-pound Parker entered the NBA draft and was chosen by the Spurs as the 28th pick. Initially, Spurs coach Gregg Popovich intended to use Parker as a backup to Antonio Daniels. The Spurs started the season sluggishly and after just five games, Popovich inserted 19-year-old Parker into the starting lineup. Parker ended the season being named to the All-Rookie First Team. In the 2002-03 season, his second on the team, Parker's steady play helped lead the Spurs to an NBA title. The Spurs captured another in 2005.

Though Parker was playing consistently, he still had a lot of maturing to do. He continued to work on his offense, improving his range and accuracy, though he lived in the shadow of his teammate, power forward and scoring machine Tim Duncan. During the 2005-06 season, Duncan was sidelined with an injury and Parker came alive, leading his team in scoring. He averaged 18.9 points per game and was named to the NBA All-Star team. Parker continued to be a playmaker during the 2006-07 season and in April of 2007 scored a career-high 35 points in a game against the Phoenix Suns. He led his team to the championships, where the Spurs beat the Cleveland Cavaliers. During the NBA Finals, Parker averaged 24.5 points and 3.3 assists per game. He was named Finals MVP, becoming the first European to win such honors.

Besides winning the NBA championship in 2007, Parker wed Longoria, famous for her role as Gabrielle on the ABC hit *Desperate Housewives*. The two met in November of 2004 when Longoria, a Texas native, attended a Spurs basketball game with her father, a huge fan of the team. Sitting in the stands, Longoria was approached by a Spurs official who asked if she and her father wanted to meet the team. When Longoria was introduced to Parker, she spoke to him in his native language because she remembered reading in the program that he was from France. Intrigued, Parker invited Longoria to dinner. They married in a lavish July 7, 2007, wedding in a castle outside Paris.

The newlyweds planned to settle down in San Antonio, where they built a new house on a 23-acre compound that included an indoor basketball court and small-scale water park. When Parker is not hanging out at home or playing basketball, he dabbles in music. In 2007, Parker released a hip-hop album in France, titled *Balance-Toi,* or Bounce. Longoria made a cameo appearance in one of Parker's videos, but the album never really took off.

While Parker's fame continues to rise in the United States, he has yet to achieve superstar status back in France. After winning the 2007 NBA championship, Parker wrapped a French flag around his shoulders for post-game festivities to honor those fans who wake at 3 a.m. to watch him play. Speaking to Insidehoops.com after being named the NBA Finals MVP, Parker acknowledged that in France, his fame has yet to eclipse that of French soccer star and

World Cup champion Zinedine Zidane. "Zidane is always going to be the man in France because soccer is so popular, but hopefully French people can realize what I just accomplished, three championships in five years, that's not bad."

Sources

Periodicals

Austin American-Statesman (Austin, TX), November 25, 2001.
Jet, July 2, 2007, pp. 50-52.
Sports Illustrated, August 14, 2006, p. 54; June 27, 2007, pp. 56-60.
Sports Illustrated Kids, March 2007, p. 27.

Online

"Basketball, a Destiny," Tony Parker's Official Website, http://www.tp9.net/en/viebio1.htm (July 30, 2007).
"Tony Parker," NBA.com, http://www.nba.com/playerfile/tony_parker/career_stats.html (July 30, 2007).
"Tony Parker interview after winning finals MVP," InsideHoops.com, http://www.insidehoops.com/parker-interview-061507.shtml (July 30, 2007).

—Lisa Frick

Mary E. Peters

U.S. Secretary of Transportation

Born December 4, 1948, in Phoenix, AZ; married Terry Peters, July, 1966; children: Tammy, Terry, Tina. *Education:* University of Phoenix, B.A.; attended Harvard University's John F. Kennedy School of Government Program for State and Local Government Executives.

Addresses: *Contact*—U.S. Department of Transportation, 1200 New Jersey Ave. SE, Washington, DC 20590.

Career

Contract administrator, then deputy director for administration, Arizona Department of Transportation, 1985-98; director, Arizona Department of Transportation, 1998-2001; administrator, Federal Highway Administration, 2001-05; national director of transportation policy for HDR, Inc., Phoenix, AZ, 2005-06; Secretary of Transportation, U.S. government, 2006—.

Member: Chair, Highway Expansion Loan Program Advisory Board, c. 1998-2001; reauthorization steering committee, American Association of State Highway and Transportation Officials (AASHTO), 2001; co-vice chairwoman, National Surface Transportation Policy and Revenue Study Commission, 2006; chair, Standing Committee on Planning and the Asset Management Task Force for the AASHTO; board of directors, Arizona Quality Alliance; board of directors, Intelligent Transportation Society of America; board of directors, Project Challenge; board of directors, Women Executives in State Gov-

ernment; Governer's Diversity Advisory Council; Greater Arizona Development Authority; Women's Transportation Seminar.

Awards: Top 100 Who's Who of Arizona Women in Business; most influential person in Arizon transportation, *Arizona Business Journal*; person of the year award, Women's Transportation Seminar—Phoenix Chapter, 1994; national woman of the year, Women's Transportation Seminar, 2004; ARTBA award, American Road and Transportation Builders Association, 2005.

Sidelights

After serving as the Director of the Arizona Department of Transportation and as the 15th Federal Highway Administrator, Mary E. Peters was confirmed as the 15th Secretary of Transportation in 2006. As a member of President George W. Bush's Cabinet, Peters is responsible for transportation in the United States, from maritime and air to surface transit. Along with the goal of making travel safer, in whatever venue, Peters and her department are responsible for allocating taxpayer dollars to create reliable and efficient transportation structure.

A fourth-generation Arizona native, Peters attended the University of Phoenix for her bachelor's degree.

From 1985 through 2001, she worked in the Arizona Department of Transportation (ADOT). She began her career as a contract administrator, but climbed the ranks, moving to deputy director for administration, then deputy director. She was appointed director of the agency by then Arizona Governor Jane Hull in 1998. While in that position, she managed to accelerate work on the freeway system in Arizona's Valley, and the project was completed seven years ahead of schedule. "At ADOT she established a reputation as an effective manager, working collaboratively with local governments and other partners," wrote a contributor to M2 Presswire. During her tenure as Director, *Arizona Business Journal* recognized Peters as the Most Influential Person in Arizona Transportation.

In 2001, Peters was appointed the 15th Federal Highway Administrator, making her the first woman to hold that position. Peters focused her vision on making highways safer, enhancing crash prevention technologies and providing support for community-based programs. Peters also made inroads in finding more efficient methods of funding bridge and highway projects, seeking out private sector investment to supplement taxpayer funds. M2 Presswire quoted Mary Jane O'Meara, president of the Women's Transportation Seminar, describing Peters as "a consummate professional who has achieved great success and yet is extremely gracious and generous with her time." Peters received the Women's Transportation Seminar's 2004 National Woman of the Year Award. Then Secretary of Transportation Norman Y. Mineta said of her work in M2 Presswire, "Mary has left a lasting impression on the history of surface transportation. She has made us all think about the future of surface transportation in ways we might not have otherwise."

Peters left the Federal Highway Administration in July of 2005 to pursue work in the private sector, taking a position with HDR, Inc., an engineering firm based out of Phoenix, Arizona. It was not long, however, before she would make a return to Washington, D.C., when Bush nominated her to fill the position of Secretary of Transportation. "Mary Peters is the right person for this job," Bush was quoted as saying by the *Washington Times*. "She brings a lifetime of experience on transportation issues, from both the private and public sectors." When she was confirmed into the position by the Senate, Peters became the second woman to hold the position, and she pledged to update the transportation system. "The top of the list always is making travel safer," she said during her speech after she was sworn into office. "But we also want to work to improve the system performance and reli-

ability and to find 21st-century solutions for 21st-century transportation challenges." She continued, "I am committed to making sure that all the resources of the department are used to deliver: to make our roads safer, to do everything we can to ensure that our skies, highways, ports and rails are free of traffic congestion."

As the Secretary of Transportation, Peters sought to improve spending, much like she had at the Federal Highway Administration. She proposed public-private partnerships to more than 150 business executives in a transportation symposium in early 2007. This idea would be a change from the typical state-federal collaboration for most transportation funding, removing some of the burden from taxpayers. Peters argued that government funds could no longer handle the transportation demands. "For many years, transportation was government-planned and government-made," she was quoted as having said in *Logistics Management*. "Transportation is a business. If we treat it as a business, maybe it can become a source of growth in America, rather than a source of irritation."

Though Peters is known for her work improving the safety of highways and bridges, she did not foresee the tragedy that struck Minnesota when the I-35 bridge collapsed in Minneapolis on August 1, 2007. Peters responded with funding and with a call out to all states to inspect all steel arch truss bridges similar in construction to the I-35 bridge, but could offer no explanation as to why the collapse occurred. Peters also became the center of controversy when she was criticized by the Teamsters Union for allowing unsafe Mexican trucks to cross over the U.S. border. Though the cross-border strategy was intended to allow American truckers to compete in a Mexican market, the safety hazards brought by the Mexican vehicles, which are not subject to the same inspections as American vehicles, gave critics a cause for concern. "The public has a right to know exactly how the DOT plans to ensure the safety and security of those who drive on our highways," Todd Spencer, executive vice president of the Owner-Operator Independent Drivers Association, stated in the *Journal of Commerce*.

Beyond these difficulties, Peters alienated bicyclists by not considering bicycling under the jurisdiction of transportation. In an interview on PBS's *NewsHour*, Peters said that much of the earmarked money intended to go toward transportation improvements instead went to other causes. "There are museums that are being built with that money, bike paths, trails, repairing lighthouses. Those are some of the kind of things that that money is being spent on, as opposed to our infrastructure." Those who argue that bike paths and lanes help to ease traffic congestion were frustrated with Peters' remarks.

Along with her work on the President's Cabinet, Peters is interested in transportation for another reason: She is an avid motorcyclist. As Secretary of Transportation, Peters visited the Harley-Davidson plant in Malwaukee, Wisconsin, and discussed the rise in fatalities in motorcycle accidents: deaths that could have been prevented had the riders been wearing helmets. While clear that the federal government would not mandate helmet laws, as that was under the jurisdiction of the individual states, she implored motorcyclists to wear helmets. Peters was in an accident herself in 2005, and she credits wearing her helmet with keeping her from sustaining serious injuries.

Peters has also been known to have fun with her position. In December of 2006, she released a statement that Santa, who was making an effort to be more environmentally friendly, would be flying in a hydrogen-powered sleigh that year. The release stated that Peters and members of the Department's Research and Innovative Administration Holiday Team had inspected the sleigh and signed a Hydrogen Prototype Vehicle Waiver authorizing Santa to make his deliveries through U.S. airspace. "Santa's new sleigh guarantees on-time delivery of toys to millions of good girls and boys," a contributor reported in M2 Presswire.

Sources

Books

Carroll's Federal Directory, Carroll Publishing, 2007.

Periodicals

Journal of Commerce, May 7, 2007, p. 30.
Logistics Management (Highlands Ranch, CO), March 1, 2007, p. 20
M2 Presswire, December 24, 2003; May 28, 2004; December 21, 2006; August 3, 2007.
Milwaukee Journal Sentinel, October 27, 2006.
Nation's Cities Weekly, February 19, 2007, pp. 1-2.
Political/Congressional Transcript Wire, October 17, 2006.
Washington Post, September 6, 2006, p. A13.
Washington Times, September 6, 2006, p. A6.

Online

"Mary E. Peters," Federal Highway Administration, http://www.fhwa.dot.gov/administrators/mpeters.htm (February 22, 2008).
"Mary E. Peters, Secretary of Transportation," U.S. Department of Transportation, http://www.dot.gov/bios/peters.htm (February 22, 2008).
"Transportation Secretary Discusses Concerns about National Infrastructure," PBS: Online NewsHour, http://www.pbs.org/newshour/bb/transportation/july-dec07/infrastructure_08-15.html/ (February 22, 2008).

—*Alana Joli Abbott*

Jodi Picoult

David Levenson/Getty Images

Author

Born Jodi Lynn Picoult, May 19, 1966, in Long Island, New York; daughter of Myron (a securities analyst) and Jane (a preschool teacher) Picoult; married Timothy Warren Van Leer (an antiques dealer), November 18, 1989; children: Kyle, Jake, Samantha. *Education:* Princeton University, bachelor's degree in creative writing/English, 1987; Harvard University, master's degree in education, 1990.

Addresses: *Contact*—Atria Books, 11th Flr., 1230 Avenue of the Americas, New York, NY 10020. *Home*—Hanover, New Hampshire. *Web site*—http:// www.jodipicoult.com.

Career

Began career on Wall Street writing bond portfolios, 1987; wrote copy for an ad agency and taught eighth-grade English, late 1980s; published first novel, 1992; became full-time writer, 1992.

Awards: New England Bookseller Award for Fiction, 2003; best fiction books of the year list, *Washington Post*, 2004; Margaret Alexander Edwards Award, American Library Association, for *My Sister's Keeper*, 2004; Alex Award, Young Adult Library Services Association, for *My Sister's Keeper*, 2005; Bookbrowse Diamond Award for novel of the year, for *My Sister's Keeper*, 2005; Vermont Green Mountain Book Award, for *My Sister's Keeper*, 2005; Abraham Lincoln Illinois High School Book Award, Illinois School Library Media Association, for *My Sister's Keeper*, 2006; "Fearless Fiction" Award, *Cosmopolitan*, 2007.

Sidelights

Since 1992, Jodi Picoult has been churning out best-selling novels at a rate of nearly one per year. While each novel is unique, most include the same ingredients—a clever plot, a juicy topic, and a heart-rending family dilemma that forces her characters into a moral quagmire. Picoult takes on hot-button issues, writing about school killings, child molestation, date rape, euthanasia, infidelity, and teen suicide. Over the years, she has developed an ever-widening fan base that includes multiple generations of both male and female readers. In 2007, Picoult's 14th novel, *Nineteen Minutes,* debuted at No. 1 on the *New York Times* best-seller list. Along the way, Picoult caught the eye of DC Comics, which hired her to write some plotlines for its Wonder Woman series. The first of her five-series superhero epic hit bookstores in 2007.

Jodi Lynn Picoult was born on May 19, 1966, on Long Island, New York, to Myron and Jane Picoult. Her father worked as a securities analyst, while her mother taught preschool. Picoult grew up in the Long Island hamlet of Nesconset in an upmarket housing development where streets bore names like Prince Charming Lane. Picoult once told the *New Hampshire Sunday News* that her childhood was so idyllic she had no business becoming a writer.

Picoult composed her first tale at the age of five, a short story titled "The Lobster Which Misunderstood." In fourth grade, Picoult decided to become a writer after she received a failing grade on a paper she wrote about her summer vacation. "I wrote from the point of view of a piano I'd practiced on and she said she didn't assign fiction," Picoult recalled to *Teen Ink*. "Of course, she hadn't assigned nonfiction, either."

Picoult studied writing at Princeton University under the guidance of memoirist Mary Morris. "She basically ripped me to shreds and showed me I wasn't as good as I thought I was," Picoult told *Publishers Weekly*. "But she also believed in me in a way that made me fight back and realize I could be better.... I think the most important thing that she taught me is that a good novel functions as if every chapter is a short story. She taught me that a novel is really just a bunch of connected short stories."

In 1987, Picoult graduated magna cum laude from Princeton. During college, she had published two stories in *Seventeen* magazine. Despite this early success, Picoult realized it would be hard to earn a steady income as a writer, so she turned to more solid pursuits and took a job writing bond portfolios for a Wall Street brokerage firm. Picoult also wrote copy for an ad agency and taught eighth-grade English. By 1989, Picoult had married her college sweetheart, Timothy Van Leer, and returned to school, studying for a master's degree in education at Harvard University.

Around this time, Picoult began working on her first novel, *Songs of the Humpback Whale*, which concerns an oceanographer who studies whales. Picoult used a unique construction for the book—the story is told by five different characters, each reporting their account of what took place one disastrous summer. Determined to get the book in print, Picoult worked tirelessly to find a publisher. "I wouldn't let it go at a rejection," she told Stephen Seitz of the *New Hampshire Sunday News*. "I'd keep calling until they'd take my calls just to get rid of me. If they told me the book wasn't right for them, I'd ask who it was right for. Then I'd call that person."

Songs of the Humpback Whale was published in 1992. Shortly after it came out, Picoult gave birth to a son, Kyle. Just as she thought her writing career might take off, Picoult found herself immersed in motherhood and struggled to find balance between work and family. Picoult explored this theme in her next book, 1994's *Harvesting the Heart*, which tells the story of a young mother so torn with her identity that she abandons her husband and son. Picoult considers this her most biographical novel. She followed with 1995's *Picture Perfect*, another novel exploring family and relationships. In 1996, she published *Mercy*, which examines love and loyalty.

Picoult points to her husband's support as being key to helping her turn out novels at such a fast pace. In a biographical sketch posted on her Web site, Picoult wrote, "My husband, who is half antiques dealer/half stay-at-home-dad, is fully responsible for making my life run smoothly." He drives the carpool, packs the kids' lunches, and brings her meals so she can concentrate on her work. Picoult begins her days with a 5:30 a.m. walk with friends. After the kids leave for school, she begins writing and researching, working until about 4 p.m.

In 1998, Picoult published *The Pact*, a heart-rending tale about two teens and a suicide pact gone awry. Lifetime picked up the novel and turned it into a 2002 movie starring Megan Mullally as a grieving mother. Fans tuned in hoping to catch a glimpse of Picoult—she made a brief appearance in the film as a mourner at the funeral of one of her characters. Lifetime also turned Picoult's *Plain Truth* into a movie in which she made a similar, brief appearance.

Published in 2000, *Plain Truth* is a book about an adolescent Amish girl accused of hiding a pregnancy and letting her newborn die. Big-city attorney Ellie Harrison is called in to defend the girl and ends up living among the Amish while she builds her case. In *Plain Truth*, Picoult is a slave to detail. A conscientious researcher, Picoult spent a week living in an Amish community before writing the novel, waking at 4:30 a.m. to milk cows, attend morning Bible study, and prepare meals. While she was writing *Perfect Match*, published in 2002, Picoult consulted a district attorney to help her script the dialogue for the trial scenes. In *Perfect Match*, a district attorney struggles to find justice after her son has been sexually abused, allegedly by a priest.

A real page-turner, 2004's *My Sister's Keeper*, was named to the *Washington Post*'s best fiction books of the year list. The book is about a 13-year-old girl named Anna who was brought into the world to be a bone marrow match for her older sister, Kate, who has leukemia. Anna spends her life undergoing surgeries and transfusions in the name of saving her sister. When Anna's parents tell her she must donate a kidney to Kate, Anna hires an attorney, hoping to gain the freedom to make her own decisions.

In 2005, Picoult published *Vanishing Acts,* the story of Delia Hopkins, a woman who makes her living tracking down missing people with the help of a bloodhound. On the eve of her wedding, Delia is haunted by a fleeting childhood memory that seems suspiciously out of place with what she knows to be her life. Then, her father is arrested, charged with kidnapping her 28 years before.

The father is sent to an Arizona jail to await trial and readers get a real glimpse of life behind bars, as well as an introduction to running a crystal meth operation. Picoult prides herself in the research she conducted. "I went to a jail in Arizona," Picoult told *Publishers Weekly.* "Every detail about jail in that book is real. One of the detention officers set up interviews with inmates for me. The recipe for crystal meth came from an inmate named Corvette Steve. The good news is that I left out some very important steps. Don't try this at home. It will blow up in your face."

Picoult is especially proud of 2006's *The Tenth Circle.* The book veers from traditional fiction in that it contains traditional narrative passages as well as comic-book panels. *The Tenth Circle* centers around Daniel Stone, a comic-book artist and father. Daniel is struggling to deny the past, a horrible childhood spent in an Alaskan village where he grew up a loner, the only non-Inuit boy around. After his daughter accuses her boyfriend of date rape, she runs away to the remote village where her father was raised. Daniel follows and is forced to confront his history.

The book contains what is supposed to be one of Daniel's comic books—this one about a father who literally has to rescue his daughter from hell. Picoult worked with San Diego artist Dustin Weaver, who rendered the drawings. The comic panels run between every chapter. The comic can be read by itself as a stand-alone; likewise, the narrative can stand by itself. Or, people can read them simultaneously as they appear in the book. Before writing the novel, Picoult visited the Yup'ik Inuit village on the Alaskan tundra.

Executives at DC Comics took note of Picoult's graphic novel and approached her about writing some storylines for its Wonder Woman series. Initially, Picoult was leery but her children egged her on. As with any project, Picoult did a lot of prep work before starting. She studied Wonder Woman's foes and read old Wonder Woman comics, dating back to the 1940s when the superhero fought Nazis.

Picoult enjoyed the project, although she found the genre more difficult than fiction since she was used to telling stories as scenes, not panels. Picoult also takes pride in being one of only two women to write for Wonder Woman in the character's 60-year history. Picoult's first Wonder Woman comic was released in March of 2007.

"It was one of those once in a lifetime opportunities," Picoult told *New Hampshire Magazine*'s Rick Broussard. "Who doesn't want to *be* Wonder Woman. In a way, the whole juggling of family and real job and sideline jobs and all of that is exactly what Wonder Woman is all about." Picoult also took the opportunity to personalize the comic. In Picoult's series, readers will meet Agent Kyle and Agent Jake, who are named after her sons. In one panel, her husband's name appears on a name plate that sits atop a desk.

Picoult's 2007 book, *Nineteen Minutes,* debuted at No. 1 on the *New York Times* best-seller list. The novel, which takes place in a fictional New Hampshire town, focuses on a 17-year-old boy who kills ten classmates during a 19-minute rampage, then has to face the consequences. Picoult used the book to explore today's cultural conditions and how they might contribute to the problem of school violence. The killer, Peter, is an outcast, small for his age, and taunted for speaking "Martian." He has been bullied since kindergarten.

The book caused a stir in Picoult's hometown of Hanover, New Hampshire, and was removed from the high school's reading list because administrators thought the setting resembled the town too closely and feared a copycat crime. Before beginning the novel, Picoult researched the 1999 Columbine killings, receiving detailed information from a sheriff's deputy. She wound up with a DVD of Columbine shooters Dylan Klebold and Eric Harris and got to watch them take target practice at a tree, shouting out the names of classmates they despised.

While Picoult's books have won numerous awards and landed atop best-seller lists, there are critics who say her intricate plots lack credibility because of their soap opera nature. Others accuse her of simply latching on to the day's hottest issues. Picoult shakes off such criticism and told *Writer*'s Leslie Garisto Pfaff that many of her ideas come from exploring moral issues she is unsure about. Other times, she starts thinking about some tragedy that could befall her family and goes from there. "I start with the 'What if?' question—what if this were to happen? And then it almost feels like the idea is percolating. I just have to let it sit in my brain and, eventually, little things jump out, and when they do, it's almost like popcorn in a Jiffy Pop bag—the idea broadens in scope until it's not just about one narrow, little 'What if?' question, but a bigger, more universal moral question."

Selected writings

Songs of the Humpback Whale, Washington Square Press, 1992.

Harvesting the Heart, Penguin, 1994.

Picture Perfect, Putnam, 1995.

Mercy, Putnam, 1996.

The Pact, William Morrow & Co., 1998.

Keeping Faith, William Morrow & Co., 1999.

Plain Truth, Pocket Books, 2000.

Salem Falls, Pocket Books, 2001.

Perfect Match, Pocket Books, 2002.

Second Glance, Atria Books, 2003.

My Sister's Keeper, Atria Books, 2004.

Vanishing Acts, Atria Books, 2005.

The Tenth Circle, Atria Books, 2006.

Nineteen Minutes, Atria Books, 2007.

Sources

Periodicals

Concord Monitor, February 25, 2007, p. D4.
Marie Claire, March 2007, p. 80.
New Hampshire Sunday News (Manchester, NH), December 24, 2000, p. B7; April 8, 2001, p. E1; October 3, 2004, p. A1; September 25, 2005, p. A1.
People, March 12, 2007, p. 53.
Publishers Weekly, February 14, 2005, p. 22.
Writer, December 2006, pp. 20-23.

Online

"About Jodi Picoult," Jodi Picoult Website, http://www.jodipicoult.com (July 30, 2007).
"Author—Jodi Picoult," *Teen Ink,* http://teenink.com/Past/2006/November/20683.html (July 30, 2007).
"Interview with Jodi Picoult," *New Hampshire Magazine,* http://www.nh.com/apps/pbcs.dll/article?AID=/20070301.tif/NHM01/70301040.tif/-1/NHM (July 30, 2007).
"New Hampshire People," NewHampshire.com, http://www.newhampshire.com/nh-people/jodi-picoult-biography.aspx (July 30, 2007).

—Lisa Frick

Gordon Ramsay

Jon Furniss/WireImage/Getty Images

Chef and television personality

Born Gordon James Ramsay, November 8, 1966, in Elderslie, Renfrewshire, Scotland; son of Gordon (a physical-education teacher and musician) and Helen (a nurse) Ramsay; married Cayetana (Tana) Hutcheson (a teacher); children: Megan, twins Jack and Holly, Matilda. *Education:* Studied hotel and catering management at Oxford Technical College, 1983-85.

Addresses: *Office*—1 Catherine Pl., London SW1E 6DX, England.

Career

Apprentice footballer with the Glasgow Rangers Football Club until 1983; held chef positions at London's Mayfair Intercontinental Hotel, 1985, Harvey's Restaurant, 1985-87, and Le Gavroche, 1987-89; also worked in France at Hotel Diva Isola 2000, 1989-91, Guy Savoy, 1991-93, and Le Jamin, 1993; chef and proprietor, Aubergine Restaurant, London, 1993-98; co-founder and joint proprietor, Gordon Ramsay Holdings, Ltd., 1997—; L'Oranger, 1997; London restaurants include: Gordon Ramsay, 1998—, Pétrus, 1999—, Gordon Ramsay at Claridge's, 2001—, The Savoy Grill, 2003—, Banquette, 2003—, Boxwood Café, 2004—, Maze, 2005—, and La Noisette, 2006—; opened Verre at Hilton Dubai Creek, 2001, Gordon Ramsay at The Conrad Tokyo, Japan, 2005, and Gordon Ramsay at The London, New York City, 2006; star of television series *Ramsay's Boiling Point,* London Weekend Television, 1998; *Ramsay's Kitchen Nightmares,* Channel 4, 2004-06; *Hell's Kitchen,* ITV, 2004—, FOX Network (USA), 2005—; *The F-Word,* Channel 4, 2005—; *Kitchen Nightmares,* FOX, 2007—.

Awards: Newcomer of the Year award, 1995, Chef of the Year award, 2000, and Independent Restaurateur of the Year award, 2006, all from *Caterer & Hotelkeeper* magazine; Order of the British Empire, 2006.

Sidelights

Brash British chef Gordon Ramsay oversees eight restaurants in London alone, plus outposts of his fine-dining empire in New York City, Tokyo, and even Dubai in the Middle East. The fiery-tempered Scottish chef has been making waves in the world of London haute cuisine since the early 1990s and parleyed his fame into several reality television shows in which he became famous for unleashing torrents of verbal wrath on hapless kitchen employees or chef-hopefuls. His most talked-about British series, *Kitchen Nightmares,* debuted in its U.S. version on the FOX network in September of 2007 and features restaurant makeovers of second-rate establishments. Outside the kitchen, however, Ramsay is known as exceedingly polite, and even he admitted that his personality is a "Jekyll and Hyde" one. He told *Entertainment Weekly*'s Michael Endelman. "I put my chef's jacket on and it just happens!"

Born in 1966, Ramsay spent the first four years of his life in Elderslie, a town near Glasgow, Scotland. The family, which included his intermittently employed father, whose preoccupation with playing in bands in bars only fueled a drinking habit, moved to Stratford-upon-Avon, England, where they lived in public housing. His mother, Helen, had trained as a nurse, and there was also a younger brother, Ronald, whose battles with heroin addiction would occasionally turn up in newspaper reports when Ramsay gained fame in Britain. The family returned to Scotland when Ramsay's burgeoning soccer talent led to his signing with the Glasgow Rangers Football Club, one of Scotland's top professional teams, as an apprentice footballer. His knee gave out, however, during his first season, and he was cut from the team. He later described this as a turning point in his life. "When I got told by my manager, 'Thanks, but no thanks,' I bawled my eyes out—for hours," he told Endelman in *Entertainment Weekly*. "It just got pulled away from me with no choice. Because I was that close, to be honest. I wasn't brilliant, but I wasn't bad as a pro player."

Ramsay visited a career counselor, who suggested three options ideally suited for his aptitude: enlisting in the Royal Navy, enrolling in the police academy, or taking a hospitality-industry training course. He chose the third, and studied at Oxford Technical College between 1983 and 1985. It was a work-study course, and he signed on with a restaurant in Stratford-upon-Avon for a time, but realized he was uninterested in learning the nuances of the bland fare they served, and quit both the job and school. Heading to London, he found a place in the kitchen of the Mayfair Intercontinental Hotel, but soon talked his way into a job with a famous young chef just a few years his senior, Marco Pierre White, at White's new eatery in South London, Harvey's. He spent two years there before moving on to Le Gavroche, another London restaurant, and then he trained at several places in France, including the Hotel Diva Isola 2000 in the Côte d'Azur.

Returning to London, Ramsay was invited by a group of Italian investors to take over a newly purchased property and run his own kitchen. The Aubergine Restaurant Chelsea opened in 1993 and within two years had received a coveted star in the *Michelin Guide,* a renowned restaurant and hotel ratings handbook published annually that critiques venues across western Europe. Aubergine earned its second Michelin star in 1997, and its success led to a second restaurant that Ramsay opened with the help of the Italians called L'Oranger. It was not as successful as Aubergine, however, and Ramsay began to dream of opening his own place as a sole proprietor.

In March of 1998, Ramsay was secretly negotiating for a leased space in London, while worrying over rumors that the Italians were about to fire him and replace him with his former mentor, White. One day, a motorbike pulled up in front of Aubergine, and its rider strode in and swiped the reservation book from the front desk. Ramsay went to the press and blamed White for the theft, which was serious enough to bring a top restaurant to quick financial ruin in an era before computerized booking systems became commonplace, but White denied the charges. Mysteriously, pages from the book would be faxed in intermittently, which helped Aubergine stay in operation. Years later, Ramsay admitted to Bill Buford in a lengthy profile that appeared in the *New Yorker* that he had paid someone to steal the book in order to thwart White's chances at taking over Aubergine. "You're the first person I ever told," he said to Buford, adding, "I still have the book in a safe at home." He conceded it had been a risky move, but it had been personally gratifying to unsettle White and cause the Italian backers to reconsider hiring the rival. "Even now it sends a chill down my spine. Because it would have been all over if I'd been caught. But that's the risk you take, isn't it?"

Ramsay was fired by the investors four months later anyway, but by then he had closed on the new space. The doors of Restaurant Gordon Ramsay opened in 1998. It won two Michelin stars in the 1999 guide, but Ramsay's attempt to earn a third one was part of the drama chronicled in a reality documentary series, *Ramsay's Boiling Point*, that ran on the London Weekend Television network in 1998. He did not succeed, but the behind-the-scenes look at the madness that occurs behind the kitchen doors of a top London restaurant—along with some candid displays of Ramsay's already-famous temper—made for captivating viewing, especially one incident in which Ramsay smacked a waiter in the head when he caught him putting a roll back in the breadbasket after it had been on the floor.

Pétrus, Ramsay's next venue, opened its doors on St. James Street in March of 1999, and earned its first Michelin star that same year. Like his other dining rooms, there was a lengthy waiting list for a table at Pétrus, and astronomical prices. In July of 2001, the restaurant and the namesake vintage became fodder for tabloid reports and more sober accounts in London's financial media that chronicled a minor scandal. Six Barclays Bank investment bankers ran up a $62,000 dinner tab, including a $17,000 bottle of 1947 Château Pétrus and were fired when they tried to expense the meal with the company.

Ramsay was skilled at cultivating this kind of press and turned up regularly in London newspapers for his antics, which included ejecting a famously picky London critic. Profits remained high, however, and he began opening up a slew of new eateries, including Gordon Ramsay at Claridge's, the Savoy Grill, Banquette, and the Boxwood Café, all by 2004, along with his first Middle East outpost, Verre at the Hilton Dubai Creek. His television career had taken off in earnest, too, thanks to a pair of terrifically high-rated series that captivated British foodies. The first of these was *Ramsay's Kitchen Nightmares* which ran on Channel 4 in Britain and featured his one-week turnaround of a flagging restaurant somewhere in Britain. At the Glass House in Ambleside, Cumbria, he nearly came to blows with the owner over a Caesar salad, but "Ramsay's biggest roasting, however, was reserved for head chef Richard Collins," noted an article on the show that appeared in *Caterer & Hotelkeeper*, "with his culinary novelties such as garlic popcorn, duck cakes with chilli jam and a much-derided pomegranate risotto, a dish Ramsay blasted as 'revolting.'" He streamlined the menu, convinced the owner to take a more active role, and then hired away two of the more able members of kitchen staff for one of his London restaurants.

Ramsay gained further fame for the other series that launched in Britain in 2004, *Hell's Kitchen.* This one, which ran on the ITV network, featured a talent-elimination contest for chefs in training. Viewers turned in each week to watch the imposing Ramsay—towering well over six feet, with wild blond hair and a fearsome Scottish baritone—berate the young hopefuls and weed out the weaker-willed among them. *The F-Word,* which premiered on Channel 4 in 2005, was his third series, and Ramsay co-hosted it along with a restaurant critic, Giles Coren. The show featured Ramsay's cooking demonstrations, with audience members joining him in front of the cameras, and various remote reports, such as visits to a farm where he was raising pigs in preparation for holiday-feast slaughter.

The New Year's Eve Honors issued from Buckingham Palace in 2005 awarded Ramsay an OBE, or Order of the British Empire. "I'm humbled and delighted to accept this honour, which is the most wonderful way to round off an extraordinary year," a report in London's *Independent* by Arifa Akbar quoted him as saying. That event-filled year included the opening of two more restaurants: Maze on Grosvenor Square in London, with a new young chef named Jason Atherton in charge, and Gordon Ramsay at The Conrad Tokyo, his first foray in Japan. His company, Gordon Ramsay Holdings, continued to open new restaurants, some even in the mid-price range, such as La Noisette on Sloane Square in 2006, which won its Michelin star a year later. In 2006 he also published his autobiography, *Humble Pie,* after issuing eight separate cookbooks.

Ramsay's mini-empire of restaurants won him the Independent Restaurateur of the Year award from *Caterer & Hotelkeeper* magazine in 2006, making him one of a small handful of chefs ever to have won three of the British-industry honors during his career; the first "Catey," as the awards are known, came in 1995 when he was named Newcomer of the Year, followed five years later with a Chef of the Year honor. Though having said in prior interviews that he was uninterested in conquering New York City, in 2006 he opened his first venture there, Gordon Ramsay at The London. The recently renovated hotel—formerly the Rihga Royal—inked a deal with Ramsay to replicate his original London restaurant, Restaurant Gordon Ramsay. Not surprisingly, he began carrying out a minor press war with one of the city's most powerful restaurant critics, Frank Bruni of the *New York Times*. Bruni's critique, published in January of 2007, gave the new place a mere two stars in his paper's rating system, deriding its "cautious menu, as reliant on default luxuries and flourishes like foie gras and black truffles as on real imagination."

Interviewers who profile Ramsay usually note that his famous bluster seems to come forth only when television cameras are rolling, but he is known as a demanding boss. When Buford trailed him at The London, Ramsay excoriated several members of his kitchen staff, then told the writer, "Tomorrow I'm making them run round Central Park to insure that they hate me more—that'll help them focus." Employees elsewhere in his kitchens submit to regular substance-abuse tests and monthly weigh-ins, telling Elisa Lipsky-Karasz in *W*, "I hate fat chefs. The days of the chain-smoking, ... maniac, 250-pound chef are gone."

In September of 2007, an American version of Ramsay's restaurant-makeover series, *Kitchen Nightmares*, debuted on the FOX Network. Its first victims were two establishments on Long Island, and it was compelling viewing, noted *New York Times* journalist Ginia Bellafante. "The subtext of *Kitchen Nightmares* is that ordinary middle-class business owners need brash and brilliant moguls to save them from a sad reliance on their own mediocrity," she wrote. "It is an ugly message that Mr. Ramsay makes undeniably hypnotic."

Ramsay lives in London with his wife, Tana Hutcheson, and their four children. Their home in the Spencer Park neighborhood of London features separate his-and-her kitchens. His interest in the health of his staff is not merely a quirk, and he has found time to run marathons regularly, even completing a few double marathons. "It's a bit, like, kamikaze, you know, but chefs are that mental," he told Lipsky-Karasz in the *W* interview. "I thrive on pressure. I am an adrenaline junkie."

Selected writings

Gordon Ramsay's Passion for Seafood, Conran Octopus (London), 1999.

Gordon Ramsay's Passion for Flavour, Conran Octopus, 2000.

A Chef for All Seasons, Quadrille (London), 2000.

Gordon Ramsay's Just Desserts, Laurel Glen (San Diego, CA), 2001.

Gordon Ramsay's Secrets, Quadrille, 2003.

Kitchen Heaven, Michael Joseph Ltd., 2004.

Gordon Ramsay Makes It Easy, John Wiley (Hoboken, NJ), 2005.

Humble Pie: My Autobiography, HarperCollins Entertainment (New York City), 2006.

Gordon Ramsay's Fast Food: Recipes from "The F Word," Key Porter Books, 2007.

Sources

Caterer & Hotelkeeper, December 9, 2004, p. 38; July 13, 2006, p. 75.

Entertainment Weekly, June 22, 2007, p. 19.

Independent (London, England), December 31, 2005, p. 28.

New Yorker, April 2, 2007.

New York Times, January 31, 2007; September 19, 2007.

People, July 24, 2006, p. 67.

Scotsman (Edinburgh, Scotland), January 19, 2002, p. 12.

W, August 2006, p. 149.

—Carol Brennan

Tim Redmond

President of Blue Horizon Organic Seafood Co.

Born May 27, 1947, in Highland Park, MI; married Pattie; children: four. *Education:* Attended Michigan State University, East Lansing, MI; University of Michigan, Ann Arbor, MI, bachelor's degree in English, 1970.

Addresses: *Contact*—Blue Horizon Organic Seafood Co., Inc., 804 Estates Dr., Ste. 200, Aptos, CA 95003; PO Box 1385, Soquel, CA 95073. *Home*—Michigan. *Web site*—http://www.bluehorizonseafood.com.

Career

Co-founder, principal, Eden Foods, 1968-early 1980s; founding director, executive vice president and vice president of sales and marketing, American Soy Products, Inc., 1985-c. 2003; president, Blue Horizon Organic Seafood Co., 2005—.

Sidelights

A pioneer of the natural-foods industry, Tim Redmond has spent 40 years working to bring organic, minimally processed foods to the American dinner table. In the late 1960s, Redmond helped found a natural-foods co-op in Ann Arbor, Michigan, which morphed into Eden Foods, now a major U.S. organic-foods producer. Redmond also played a leading role in the formation of American Soy Products, which built the first soymilk factory in the United States. In 2005, he co-founded Blue Horizon Organic Seafood Co., with the intent of providing sustainable, wild-caught, and organically farmed seafood to the everyday consumer.

Redmond was born on May 27, 1947, at Michigan's Highland Park General Hospital, the same facility where his grandfather worked as a surgeon. He spent his childhood not far from there, in the Detroit suburb of Birmingham, growing up in a middle-class family with parents who were members of the country club. In a telephone interview with *Newsmakers*, Redmond described himself as a "typical high school goofball" who participated in a lot of sports. Redmond began college at Michigan State University in East Lansing, where he played on the golf team. In 1967, his junior year, he transferred to the University of Michigan in Ann Arbor.

An English major, Redmond wrote a lot of poetry during this time, grew his hair long, and explored different philosophies. He says he began transitioning from a kid filled with indifference to a young man who was becoming more engaged and serious about life. This was during the 1960s, a time when the hippie counterculture was sweeping college campuses. Redmond started living a more natural lifestyle, he told *Newsmakers*, and moved away from "eating Twinkies and hot dogs and soda pop and thinking that was a good way to fuel your engine."

In 1968, Redmond formed a co-op with a group of like-minded folks who were looking to eat more organic, less-processed foods. The co-op members pooled their money and gave it to a middleman who used it to procure bags of brown rice, miso, and whole wheatberries from a natural-foods store in New York. They called their co-op Eden, which stands for Environmental Defense Energy Network. At first, members simply got food for themselves, but in a short amount of time, the co-op became more formalized—members rented an apartment above a bicycle shop on East William Street in Ann Arbor, installed a stone grinder and began an operation of bagging up flour, dried fruit, grains, nuts, and beans under their own label and putting them on the shelf to sell. Soon, Eden was ordering whole truckloads of natural foods to meet the demand. At times, their order included up to 2,000 pounds of brown rice, which Redmond and his friends had to lug upstairs to the store.

In 1970, Redmond earned his English degree. "I thought I might want to teach or write," he told *Newsmakers*, "but I got more interested in food and food production." After college, Redmond moved to Boston to work in a macrobiotic restaurant, intending to return to Ann Arbor and open his own such eatery. He gave up on that idea, however, and in late 1970, he formed a 50-50 partnership with Bill Bolduc to create Eden Foods Inc. They took out a bank loan and built a larger store on State Street in Ann Arbor.

Over the next decade, Redmond helped oversee Eden's transformation from a simple retail store into a regional natural-foods distributor with manufacturing, importing, and retailing arms. By the mid-1970s, Eden products could be found at stores and co-ops throughout the Midwest. Eden continued to grow, sourcing its own organic farmers and manufacturing more and more of its own products, relying less and less on third-party brands. Redmond said the company was built on the backs of people who worked hard because they had a passionate desire to change the quality of the nation's food supply. "When we first started, we had a lot of people with advanced degrees from college out in the warehouse pulling products just because they believed in the mission we had. The company grew out of positive energy. We worked our butts off, but nobody minded much," he told *Newsmakers*.

Redmond left Eden Foods in the early 1980s but continued to run the local Eden grocery and deli in downtown Ann Arbor. In 1985, he became the founding director of a new food company, American Soy Products, Inc., which manufactured soymilk for Eden Foods under the label Edensoy. In 1986, American Soy Products opened the first U.S.-based soymilk plant and became the first company to market soymilk to supermarkets. As executive vice president and vice president of sales and marketing, this work fell to Redmond, who said it was a hard sell at first, trying to get retailers to see soy as a human food and not just an animal food. Eventually, the lactose-free, low-sodium, high-protein drink began to sell, with Edensoy becoming the market leader.

Along with Ron Roller, president of American Soy Products, Redmond helped formulate another natural-foods beverage—Vruit. Aimed at health-conscious consumers, the non-sugared, non-carbonated, non-caffeinated beverage hit the market in 1995 and is still nationally distributed. As the name suggests, the product is a blend of fruit and vegetable juices. The popular orange-veggie blend includes apple, orange, peach, carrot, cucumber, celery, and spinach juice. "It's not a substitute for fresh vegetables and fruit," Redmond told the *Detroit Free Press'* Rachel Konrad shortly after the product arrived on the market. "But it's better than nothing. And popping a straw into a box is more convenient than taking time to peel, wash, and cook." Roller and Redmond also created the Soy Fusion drink.

Around 2003, Redmond left American Soy Products and became a food industry consultant. He worked with some organic shrimp farmers in Ecuador, which piqued his interest in the seafood industry. In 2005, Redmond joined forces with John Battendieri to found Blue Horizon Organic Seafood Co., which offers consumers a broad range of seafoods, some sustainably harvested and others organically farmed. Besides supplying private label seafood, Blue Horizon rolled out its own brand of skillet meals, as well as a frozen line of Last Minute Chef microwaveable entrees and appetizers.

Redmond sees a bright future for Blue Horizon because consumers, recognizing the benefits of omega 3 fatty acids, are adding sea protein to their diets at an increasing rate. The world's fish supply cannot sustainably handle the demand, Redmond says, noting that 55 percent of the shrimp consumed today comes from on-shore aquaculture operations. Blue Horizon relies on aquaculture, Redmond told *Newsmakers*, but sources only from clean operations where no synthetic chemicals are used and where workers are treated fairly and given health insurance.

Blue Horizon uses only farmers who protect the aquatic ecosystems where they farm. While the U.S. Department of Agriculture has yet to adopt organic standards for aquaculture, Blue Horizon relies on farms that comply with European standards and is working to help formulate U.S. rules. As with land-based agriculture, the difference comes down to chemicals. For instance, an organic aquaculture farm may have 10,000 shrimp in a ten-acre pond, whereas a conventional aquaculture farm may place 100,000 shrimp in the same space. "The shrimp get stressed out," Redmond told *Newsmakers*, requiring antibiotics to stay alive. These shrimp also get hormones to grow faster and preservatives after harvesting so they retain their water and remain plumper. "With organic farming, it's an environmental positive out and out," Redmond told *Newsmakers.* "It keeps the water cleaner, keeps the food cleaner."

Along with his wife, Pattie, Redmond raised four eco-conscious kids in a passive-solar house, growing much of their food in their own organic garden. Redmond's wife was involved with Eden in the early days, keeping books and working at the State Street store. In the early 1970s, she was a grower and wholesaler of sprouts, the first in Ann Arbor. Most of all, Redmond says, she has been his best advisor and weathervane. The Redmond children have taken their parents' healthy living message to heart: Redmond's youngest son works for Whole Foods, his youngest daughter does sustainable design projects, and his oldest daughter, Sara Snow, hosts *Living Fresh* on the Discovery Home Channel, a show aimed at providing viewers with the tools for living healthier.

"My dad could have done a great many things when he left college, a young idealistic hippie with a college education and a successful father to help tow him along," Snow wrote on her Discovery Health blog. "But he didn't do many things. He did one extremely important thing. He set out to help change America through the foods we eat. He grew up eating his share of white bread and canned vegetables and was frightened for the future ... if these were the foods that Americans would continue to consume. So, instead of wasting his time soapboxing or complaining, he did something about it."

As for the future, Redmond told *Newsmakers* that he is "raring to go for another 40 years. I like working. Sixty is not old." He wants to continue making a difference and hopes others see that they, too, can make a difference. "What you do every day matters—what you buy, how you buy things, where you buy them, they matter. They are as much a vote as pulling the lever at the polling booth."

Sources

Periodicals

Detroit Free Press, June 10, 1996, p. 8F.
Detroit News, May 25, 1999, p. 2B.
Indianapolis Business Journal, September 11, 2006, p. 1.
PR Newswire, January 31, 2007; March 30, 2007.

Online

"About Blue Horizon Seafood," Blue Horizon Organic Seafood Co., http://www.bluehorizon-seafood.com/about.html (August 3, 2007).
"A Little About Me ... and Where I Come From," Sara Snow's Get Fresh Blog, http://discovery.blogs.com/snow/2007/07/a-little-abou-1.html (August 3, 2007).
"Unified Western Grocers and Nature's Best 'Catch' Blue Horizon Organic Seafood Products for Expanded Distribution," *Forbes,* http://www.forbes.com (August 3, 2007).

Other

Personal interview with Tim Redmond, August 24, 2007.

—Lisa Frick

Paula Rosput Reynolds

Chief Executive Officer of Safeco

Born Paula Gail Rosput, October 2, 1956, in Newport, RI; divorced first husband; married Stephen P. Reynolds (a utility executive), October 2004; children: one (from first marriage). *Education:* Wellesley College, B.A., 1978.

Addresses: *Office*—Safeco Corporation, 1001 Fourth Ave., Seattle, WA 98154.

Career

Economist, consulting firm in Boston, 1978-79; economist, Pacific Gas Transmission Company, 1979, rose to the post of senior vice president; unit president, Panhandle Eastern Corporation, c. 1995, which was acquired by Duke Energy North America of Houston, TX; president and chief executive officer, Duke Energy Power Services, late 1990s; president and chief operating officer, AGL Resources, Atlanta, GA, late 1998, then president and chief executive officer, 2000-05, and board chair, 2002-05; named president and chief executive officer, Safeco Corporation, January 2006; named board chair, May 2008.

Member: Board of directors, American Gas Association; board of directors, United Way of Metropolitan Atlanta, c. 2000-2006; board of directors, Coca-Cola Enterprises, 2001—; board of directors, Delta Air Lines, 2004—.

Awards: Ten Leading Innovators in Energy, Public Utilities Fortnightly, 1999; Shattered Ceiling Award, Atlanta Women's Foundation, c. 2000; inducted into business hall of fame, Georgia State University, 2004; 50 most powerful women in business, *Fortune* magazine, 2006; 100 most powerful women, *Forbes* magazine, 2006-07.

Sidelights

Paula Rosput Reynolds became chief executive of the Safeco Corporation, a Seattle-based property and casualty insurance company, in 2006 after a long career in the energy and utility industry. A year later, she was the only woman to rank among a *Wall Street Journal* survey of the top 50 highest-paid financial-services executives in the United States. One of the reasons she moved cross-country to take the job, she told *Atlanta Journal-Constitution* writers Maria Saporta and Robert Luke, was to be able to cohabitate with her husband, an executive with Puget Energy in Bellevue, Washington. "How many times will a Fortune 500 job come up in Seattle, Washington, where my husband and I could be in the same city?"

A native of Rhode Island, Reynolds was born in 1956, and described herself as "the short, fat girl with glasses" to Patricia R. Olsen in the *New York Times* interview. "My parents tried to teach me that being smart and being nice would ultimately make up for the shortcomings of childhood." She went on to Wellesley College in Wellesley, Massachusetts, a women's liberal arts college whose alumnae include U.S. Senator Hillary Rodham Clinton. After graduating in 1978 with a degree in economics, Reynolds took a job with a Boston consulting firm.

A year later, in 1979, Reynolds was hired as an economist with the Pacific Gas Transmission Company, or PGT, and by the mid-1990s had reached the position of senior vice president with the San Francisco-based division of the larger Pacific Gas & Electric, which is the main provider of natural gas and electricity to residents of northern California. One of her job duties was to supervise construction of a controversial natural-gas pipeline from Alberta, Canada, into northern California. Her involvement in this sector of the energy industry led to a new job as president of a unit of Panhandle Eastern Corporation, which also built and ran natural gas pipelines. The Houston, Texas, company was acquired by Duke Energy North America, and Reynolds was given a new title as president and chief executive officer of Duke Energy Power Services, the non-regulated division of Duke Energy.

In late 1998, Reynolds joined AGL Resources of Atlanta as chief operating officer. This was a division of the Atlanta Gas Light Company, founded in 1856 to light the gaslamps on the streets of pre-Civil War Atlanta. The AGL division was a holding company for several other businesses, including a half-dozen natural-gas utility companies spread across six states. Reynolds became president and chief executive officer of AGL in 2000 when her immediate boss resigned; two years later AGL's board named her chair, too, which made her the highest ranking female executive in Georgia. During her five years on the job, she oversaw a period of increased growth and profitability for AGL, whose stock was a favorite of Wall Street analysts.

Reynolds kept AGL on course and managed to double the price of its shares after reducing the workforce by 25 percent, which became a necessary task at a time when the company was suffering heavy financial losses. "Laying people off weighs on you because you know how much you're affecting their lives," she told Olsen, the *New York Times* journalist. "I was plagued with doubt. I'd go home every day and ask myself, 'Did I do any good today?'"

After more than a quarter-century in the energy sector, Reynolds surprised many of her colleagues when she accepted an offer from Seattle-based Safeco Corporation, an insurance provider, to become its next president and chief executive officer in late 2005. This was just a year after her marriage to Stephen Reynolds, the man who had hired her at PGT back in 1979. Both had first marriages that ended in divorce, and had remained in professional

contact over the years. They wed in 2004, when she was still living in Atlanta, where she cared for her teenaged son and an ailing father, and had agreed to a commuter marriage that involved her new husband—by then the CEO of Puget Energy in Bellevue, Washington—flying to Atlanta each weekend. Fortuitously, Reynolds was on the board of Delta Airlines, and because of this her new husband enjoyed one of the perks of being married to a Delta board member—free airfare anywhere Delta flies.

Safeco presented an unusual challenge for Reynolds, in part because it was three times larger than AGL, with 7,600 employees and $6.2 billion in revenues in 2006, but also because she was unfamiliar with the property and casualty insurance-business. In contrast to the energy and natural-gas industry, she told Meg Green of *Best's Review,* insurance was "a very high-margin business compared to the business I came over from. There, we made a lot of long-term capital investments, and had to hope it worked out. Here, if I make a judgment on price, I can fix it any time I want. I am not locked in for 30 years on decisions I make."

Shortly after taking over at Safeco, Reynolds was the subject of a *Wall Street Journal* profile by Joann Lublin with a rather unusual angle—her marriage to Stephen Reynolds, who still chaired Puget Energy. In the article headlined "CEOs Juggle Love, Power," Lublin pointed out that the couple had an unusual distinction as the only married CEO pair of two publicly traded U.S. companies. When Reynolds took the job with Safeco, it meant that she and her husband could live together permanently for the first time in their marriage. Lublin interviewed her in early 2006, and Reynolds said that though her 92-year-old father had a caregiver who came to the house on a part-time basis, she preferred to clean the house herself instead of hiring a service. "It's part of how I keep myself grounded."

Sources

Atlanta Journal-Constitution, December 8, 2005.
Best's Review, October 2007, p. 56.
New York Times, March 6, 2005.
Seattle Times, December 8, 2005.
US Banker, October 2007, p. 93.
Wall Street Journal, March 7, 2006, p. B1.

—*Carol Brennan*

Rihanna

Francis Specker/Landov

Singer

Born Robyn Rihanna Fenty, February 20, 1988, in St. Michael's Parish, Barbados; daughter of Ronald (a warehouse supervisor) and Monica (an accountant and boutique owner) Fenty.

Addresses: *Contact*—Def Jam Recordings, 825 8th Ave., New York, NY 10019. *Home*—Los Angeles, CA.

Career

Signed with Def Jam Recordings, c. 2004; released first album, *Music of the Sun,* 2005; made first film appearance, a cameo in *Bring It On: All or Nothing,* 2006; released second album, *A Girl Like Me,* 2006; released third album, *Good Girl Gone Bad,* 2007.

Awards: Female breakout artist and choice R&B artist, Teen Choice Awards, 2006; female artist of the year, female Hot 100 artist of the year, and pop 100 artist of the year, Billboard Music Awards, 2006; best R&B artist, MTV Europe Music Awards, 2006; best new artist, song of the year for "Pon de Replay," best dance single for "Pon de Replay," album of the year for *Music of the Sun,* entertainer of the year, Barbados Music Awards, 2006; best new video artist, MTV Video Music Awards Japan, 2006; album of the year for *A Girl Like Me,* best entertainer of the year, best female entertainer of the year, best selling recording artist, Barbados Music Awards, 2007; top 25 entertainers of the year, *Entertainment Weekly,* 2007; favorite female artist, soul/R&B, American Music Awards, 2007; best-selling pop female artist, world's best-selling R&B artist, World Music Awards, 2007; monster single of the year, for

"Umbrella" with Jay-Z, MTV Video Music Awards, 2007; soul video of the year, VH1, 2007; pop/R&B artist of the year, best pop/R&B single for "Don't Stop the Music," best female music video for "Shut Up and Drive," song of the year for "Umbrella," album of the year for *Good Girl Gone Bad,* female entertainer of the year, people's choice entertainer of the year, Barbados Music Awards, 2008; Grammy Award for best rap/sung collaboration, Recording Academy, for "Umbrella," shared with Jay-Z, 2008; favorite R&B song, for "Shut up and Drive," People's Choice Awards, 2008.

Sidelights

Barbados-born songstress Rihanna hit the airwaves in 2005 with her debut album, *Music of the Sun,* which spawned the reggae-tinged dancehall hit "Pon de Replay." Some industry insiders dismissed her as a one-hit wonder, but Rihanna proved them wrong. Her second album, released eight months after the first, included the No. 1 hit "S.O.S." In 2007, she followed with the hit single "Umbrella," which spent seven weeks atop the Billboard Hot 100 and a record-setting ten weeks atop the United Kingdom (U.K.) singles charts. Rihanna went on to win a Grammy for the song, making her the first woman from Barbados to earn such an honor. Having released three albums and a handful of top 10 hits by the age of 19, Rihanna has proved she is well on her way to becoming the new reigning diva of R&B.

Rihanna was born Robyn Rihanna Fenty on February 20, 1988, in St. Michael's Parish, Barbados. Her mother, Monica, hails from Guyana and is an accountant-turned-boutique owner. Her father, Ronald, is a Barbadian and has worked as a warehouse supervisor. Growing up, Rihanna watched her father struggle with addiction as he battled crack, marijuana, and alcohol. Her parents were separated for long periods of time and finally divorced when Rihanna was a teen. "My mom would take us to see him, and he would be in the worst condition," Rihanna told *Allure*'s Brooke Hauser. "She stopped taking us because she didn't want us to see him like that." Rihanna's mother worked long hours to support the family, leaving Rihanna, the oldest, in charge of the household and responsible for her brothers Rajad and Rorrey. Rihanna's father has since beaten his addictions and has accompanied Rihanna on tour.

Rihanna has been singing nearly all of her life. As a child she honed her skills in the shower, crooning Whitney Houston, Mariah Carey, and Celine Dion ballads from the steamy comfort of the bathroom. Rihanna sang so loud and enthusiastically that the neighbors complained. By her early teens, Rihanna had joined an all-girl music group. "Growing up, I always sang," Rihanna told Derek Paiva, an entertainment writer for the *Honolulu Advertiser*. "But no one ever was really pushing me to do it. It was something that I wanted to do. So I developed a personal passion for it, fell in love with music, and developed my own taste and style." Rihanna won a high school talent show with a rendition of Mariah Carey's "Hero."

These days, Rihanna enjoys dressing like a sleek and sexy model. She is also a spokeswoman for CoverGirl cosmetics. Growing up, though, she described herself as a tomboy. With 13 male cousins and two younger brothers, Rihanna and a lone female cousin worked hard to be accepted among the boys, who continually tried to run them off. "We wanted to do what they did," Rihanna told the *Advertiser*. "We wanted to climb trees. We wanted to fight. We wanted to catch animals.... We had to defend ourselves a lot!"

Rihanna had trouble at school, where kids shunned her and teased her because her brown skin was lighter than theirs. Rihanna inherited a lighter, West Indian complexion from her Barbadian father—she also has a set of glass-green eyes. "People hated me because I'm fair in complexion," she told *Entertainment Weekly*'s Margeaux Watson. "I had to develop a thick skin because they would call me white."

Rihanna's career enjoyed a jump start in 2003 when a friend helped orchestrate a meeting with U.S. songwriter and producer Evan Rogers, who was vacationing in Barbados. Rogers has worked with such stars as Christina Aguilera, Kelly Clarkson, and Donny Osmond. After hearing about Rihanna, Rogers summoned her to come sing in his hotel room. She chose to perform the Destiny's Child's hit "Emotion." Speaking to *Entertainment Weekly*, Rogers described how Rihanna captured his attention the moment she walked into the room. "She carried herself like a star even when she was 15. But the killer was when she opened her mouth to sing. She was a little rough around the edges, but she had this edge to her voice." Impressed, Rogers invited Rihanna to fly to the United States to make a demo with him.

They recorded a four-track demo, which included a version of "Pon de Replay." Rogers distributed the demo and it fell into the hands of Jay-Z, head of Def Jam Recordings. After hearing the demo, Jay-Z called Rihanna in Barbados and summoned her for an audition. After arriving in the United States, Rihanna went into Jay-Z's office and belted out a few tunes a cappella. Within 12 hours, she had signed a deal with the label.

Soon, Rihanna began working on her first album, which was produced by Rogers and his longtime business partner Carl Sturken. In August of 2005, 17-year-old Rihanna released *Music of the Sun*, which featured a set of strong dance tunes highlighting her vocals. The album peaked at No. 10 on the Billboard Top 200 chart, buoyed by the success of the hypnotically catchy dance tune "Pon de Replay," the first single Rihanna released. "Pon de Replay" spent 27 weeks on the Billboard Hot 100 chart, peaking at No. 2. Speaking to the *Honolulu Advertiser*, Rihanna noted that she initially shied away from recording the song. "I thought it sounded like a nursery rhyme," she said. "It didn't sound like singing." Rihanna said it was such a different style she was not immediately drawn to it, but once she started recording she realized the song had an incredible vibe.

In April of 2006—just eight months after the release of her debut album—Rihanna rolled out a second, titled *A Girl Like Me*. The album included the electro-funk breakout hit "S.O.S.," which topped both the

U.S. and Australian charts. The song borrowed the drum beat, bass line, and synthesizer loop from the 1980s hit "Tainted Love." Christina Milian was supposed to record the song, but she turned it down because she thought the song had too much of a pop flare for a true R&B singer; however, Rihanna liked the song, particularly because it expressed more mature emotions than she had explored in her previous album. "'S.O.S.' talks about being rescued from a crazy feeling, calling out for help," Rihanna told *Jet*. "You know like when you have a huge crush on a guy, come rescue me from feeling this crazy."

The album also included a slow, piano-driven ballad, "Unfaithful," which hit No. 6 on the Billboard Hot 100. Following the album's release, Rihanna embarked on a promotional tour through the United States, Europe, and Canada. The album peaked at No. 5 on the Billboard Top 200, was certified platinum and earned Rihanna a bevy of awards in 2006, including female artist of the year at the Billboard Music Awards.

True to form, Rihanna did not take much of a break between albums and in June of 2007 released a third, *Good Girl Gone Bad*. Speaking to Margeaux Watson of EW.com, Rihanna said that she inherited a strong work ethic from her mother, whom she described as a workaholic: "If she took a week off from work, she got so miserable at home." Rihanna said that she is the same way—she gets antsy whenever she has free time. "When I take a break I get really fidgety and restless and I wanna get back to work.... But also, I am very passionate about what I do. I love making music. I love the process of it. And every time, I like to switch it up a little bit and make it different."

For certain, *Good Girl Gone Bad* makes a departure from the youthful, party-girl innocence articulated on her first two albums. Rihanna was quite young when the first two albums came out and she relied on Rogers and Def Jam executives to make most of the decisions. With this third album, Rihanna took more ownership and sought to leave her innocent, good-girl image behind. Rihanna recorded more adult-themed songs and reworked her image in an effort to separate herself from the pack. The night before the photo shoot for the cover of *Good Girl Gone Bad*, Rihanna persuaded her hairstylist to come to her Los Angeles hotel room and chop off her long, brown locks to create a blunt, inverted bob, which she dyed jet black.

The changes went beyond looks. For this album, Rihanna tapped a large number of established producers and songwriters. Justin Timberlake and Ne-Yo earned songwriting credits, while Timbaland, Stargate, and Christopher "Tricky" Stewart all earned producer credits, along with Rogers and Sturken. The album's lead single, "Umbrella," features Jay-Z on accompanying vocals. The song simultaneously topped the Hot 100, Pop 100, and Hot Digital Songs charts. In sum, more than 2.2 million music listeners have downloaded the song, which set a record for digital downloads in a debut week. The song—about the strength of enduring relationships—was a hit around the globe, spending 595 weeks on 20 different charts. During the 17th week of 2007, it entered the Billboard Hot 100 and stayed upon charts around the world, exiting after the 22nd week of 2008 when it sat atop the Germany Singles Top 100 before slipping off the charts. The single received rave reviews in Europe. It topped the U.K. singles charts for ten consecutive weeks, making it the longest-running U.K. chart-topper of the 21st century. The album included several other hits, such as "Shut Up and Drive," "Hate That I Love You," and "Take a Bow," the latter of which topped the Billboard Hot 100.

Despite Rihanna's string of successes, she did not realize her stardom potential until after "Umbrella" created such a buzz. "It really overwhelmed me when 'Umbrella' was No. 1 for so many weeks all over the world, not only in America, and broke records and made history," she told *Entertainment Weekly*. "'Umbrella' just went way ahead of me and where my mind was a lot quicker and earlier than I expected it to." Rihanna went on to win a Grammy for the song.

Jay-Z told *Entertainment Weekly* that he was thrilled with Rihanna's third album and the control she exerted over its creation. "She's found her voice. That's the best thing for any label—to have an artist step in and take control of their own career. She's left the nest."

With two platinum albums under her belt, Rihanna has traveled a long way from her working-class island origins. As her star continues to rise, advertisers are knocking on her door, hoping to sign her for promotions. Rihanna became the spokeswoman for Gillette's Venus Breeze razors, with Gillette insuring her legs for $1 million. In addition, she has a partnership with CoverGirl. When *Good Girl Gone Bad* was released, the first 800,000 copies included coupons for Wetslicks Fruit Spritzers.

When Rihanna is not busy working, the tattooed beauty enjoys playing Guitar Hero on her Xbox. Rihanna has a set of tiny star tattoos on her neck, a treble clef on her ankle, and a Sanskrit prayer on her hip. Among her circle of friends, Rihanna is known as the mischievous prankster. One favorite trick includes squeezing lemon juice into friends' mouths as they sleep. Most friends still call her Robyn, the name she used while growing up.

As for the future, Rihanna hopes to break into film. She made a cameo in 2006's *Bring It On: All or Nothing*. Whether that happens or not, Rihanna is sure that a bright future awaits her. She said she believes her success is due to becoming more comfortable with expressing her true self. "Some people never figure themselves out, and that's sad," she told *Cosmopolitan*'s Monica Corcoran. "I'm still learning who I am, but I'm not scared to be myself anymore."

Selected recordings

Albums

Music of the Sun, Def Jam, 2005.
A Girl Like Me, Def Jam, 2006.
Good Girl Gone Bad, Def Jam, 2007.

Singles

"If It's Lovin' That You Want," Def Jam, 2005.
"Pon de Replay," Def Jam, 2005.
"S.O.S.," Def Jam, 2006.
"Unfaithful," Def Jam, 2006.
"Don't Stop the Music," Def Jam, 2007.
"Hate That I Love You," Def Jam, 2007.
"Shut Up and Drive," Def Jam, 2007.
(Featuring Jay-Z) "Umbrella," Def Jam, 2007.
"Take A Bow," Def Jam, 2008.

Sources

Periodicals

Allure, January 1, 2008, p. 146.
Billboard, May 12, 2007, pp. 24-27.
Cosmopolitan, March 2008, pp. 46-49.
Entertainment Weekly, June 29, 2007, pp. 81-83; November 30, 2007, pp. 82-83.
Jet, May 22, 2006, p. 35.
Music Week, July 28, 2007, p. 4.

Online

"Caribbean Queen," *Entertainment Weekly*, http://www.ew.com/ew/article/0,,20043298.tif,00.html (May 9, 2008).
"18 Things You Need to Know About Rihanna," *Honolulu Advertiser*, http://the.honoluluadvertiser.com/article/2006/Sep/15/en/FP60915030.tif3.html (April 13, 2008).
"Rihanna Has Her Day in the Sun," *USA Today*, http://www.usatoday.com/life/music/news/2005-08-01-otv-rihanna_x.htm (May 18, 2008).

—Lisa Frick

Tony Romo

Professional football player

Born Antonio Ramiro Romo, April 21, 1980, in San Diego, CA; son of Ramiro Jr. and Joan Romo. *Education:* Eastern Illinois University, B.B.A., 2003.

Addresses: *Office*—c/o Dallas Cowboys, Cowboys Center, One Cowboys Parkway, Irving, TX 75063-4727.

Career

Signed as a free agent by the Dallas Cowboys, 2003; starting quarterback for the Dallas Cowboys, 2006; co-hosted radio show *Inside the Huddle*, 2006.

Awards: First team, All-Ohio Valley Conference; third team, All-America honors, Associated Press; player of the year award, Ohio Valley Conference, 2000, 2001; Walter Payton Award, Ohio Valley Conference, 2002.

Sidelights

Tony Romo went undrafted by a National Football League (NFL) team in 2003 after an impressive college career at Division I-AA powerhouse Eastern Illinois University, but he soon proved himself to be a talented quarterback when he became a starter for the Dallas Cowboys in 2006. Romo led the Cowboys to the playoffs at end of the 2006 and 2007 seasons. The star player had only begun playing football while a high school junior.

Romo was born on April 21, 1980, in San Diego, California, the son of Ramiro Romo, Jr., and his wife, Joan. His father had once played college soccer in Wisconsin. Romo was raised in the small town of Burlington, Wisconsin. As a child, basketball was his favorite sport and he told his grandparents that he would play for the Chicago Bulls someday.

Romo attended Burlington High School, where he focused on basketball—what he still thought was his best sport—and golf. It was not until his junior year at Burlington that Romo began playing football. In his first high school game, he demonstrated his potential by throwing for 300 yards. Romo continued to put up impressive numbers as he remained the team's primary quarterback in his junior and senior seasons. At the end of his high school football career, he had thrown for 4,000 yards and 42 touchdowns. In all sports that he played, Romo demonstrated a competitiveness and an ability to quickly make decisions.

After being discovered by Eastern Illinois University's assistant head coach Roy Wittke, Romo entered the prominent Division I-AA school with a solid football history on a partial scholarship. After being redshirted in 1998, he spent much of his freshman year on the bench, only playing limited minutes, but worked hard to improve his game. By his sophomore year, Romo's talent at the quarterback position truly emerged.

In 2000, Romo was the team's number-one quarterback after spring practice, and blossomed during the season. His Panthers had an 8-4 record, set a school record by averaging 39.1 points per game, and made the I-AA playoffs. Romo contributed by throwing for 2,583 yards and 27 touchdowns. He completed 59 percent of his passes and was second nationally in throwing efficiency. Of his coming out, Romo told *USA Today*'s Jack Carey, "I wanted to show everybody I could take the position and do well. I thought I had a good head on my shoulders and tried to use it, and things worked out for the best."

Romo continued to dominate the Ohio Valley Conference during his junior and senior seasons. By the time he reached his senior year, he was able to break Eastern Illinois' record for most touchdown passes. Romo ended his 2002 senior season by throwing for 3,165 yards and 34 touchdowns, while leading Eastern Illinois to another 8-4 season. At the end of his career with the Panthers, Romo had thrown for a total of 8,212 yards and 85 touchdowns.

Romo's success at Eastern Illinois attracted the attention of NFL scouts, many of whom came to watch him in person. Though several teams considered drafting him in the 2003 NFL entry draft—including the Dallas Cowboys—Romo's name was not called; however, Dallas beat out other teams to sign Romo as a free agent. He then spent most of the next three-and-a-half seasons on the bench, observing and learning the quarterback position on a professional level. Romo made brief appearances in six games in 2004 and 16 games in 2005, but unexpectedly became Dallas' savior in 2006.

That season, Romo impressed in his preseason appearances, but Cowboy's coach Bill Parcells named the more experienced Drew Bledsoe his quarterback. Parcells, however, gave Romo his chance in week seven. Bledsoe had been erratic and mistake prone throughout the season, so Parcells put Romo in as quarterback at half-time of the game against the New York Giants. While the Cowboys still lost 36-22, Romo threw for 227 yards and two touchdowns. Showing his inexperience, Romo also threw three interceptions.

Romo was Dallas' starter for the rest of the 2006 season. In his next four games, Romo threw for 1,088 yards and five touchdowns, but only two interceptions. The Cowboys won three of the four games. His teammates lauded Romo's rise, with linebacker Kevin Burnett telling Mike Rainey of the *St. Louis Post-Dispatch*, "Romo is having one of those Cinderella seasons. He's the type of quarterback who is cool. He extends the play, he gets himself out of bad situations. If we go to the Super Bowl, he's going to be the guy who takes us there."

Romo continued to impress for much of the rest of the 2006 season, and even held the league's leading passer rating for a time. As his star rose on the field, he began being linked with starlets like country singer Carrie Underwood and singer/actress Jessica Simpson. While Romo was able to imbue the Cowboys with a newfound swagger and confidence, he was unable to lead them to the Super Bowl. He ended the season with at least two blowout losses in his last few games. While Dallas made the playoffs, the team lost in the wild card game to the Seattle Seahawks 21-20 after Romo bobbled the snap on the potential winning field goal near the end of the game.

Shaking off the non-fairy tale ending to his 2006 season, Romo emerged a better, more experienced quarterback in 2007. He remained the starter for new coach Wade Phillips, who praised Romo's dedicated work ethic and intense preparation. Phillips told Kathleen Nelson in the San Luis Obispo, California, *Tribune*, "He's really worked at the game. He's worked at his craft." Romo started the 2007 season strong, with a high quarterback rating and Dallas posting a 10-1 record. Because of his success, Romo was given a new long-term contract extension with the Cowboys for six years and $67.5 million, including $30 million in guaranteed money during the season.

Romo ended the 2007 regular season with strong numbers—he threw for 4,211 yards and 36 touchdowns with only 19 interceptions—but he again struggled at the end of the season and in the playoffs. The Cowboys earned a first-round bye, and Romo spent part of the week off with Simpson on a vacation in Mexico. In Dallas' play-off game with the New York Giants, the Cowboys played poorly in their 21-17 loss. Romo passed for 201 yards, but only completed 18 of 36 passes. He threw for one touchdown as well as one interception, on his final play of the game. Many observers blamed Romo's getaway for the loss, though his teammates defended him.

After the game, Romo said he would take responsibility for the Cowboys' continued struggles in the playoffs. ESPN.com quoted him as saying, "I know how hard everyone in that locker room worked to get themselves in position to win that game today and for it to end like that, and for me to be the cause is very tough to swallow right now. I take responsibility for messing up at the end there. That's my fault. I cost the Dallas Cowboys a playoff win, and it's going to sit with me a long time." He hoped to do better in 2008 and beyond.

In his time off from football, Romo reads sports books and has pursued his love of golf. In 2004 and 2005, he tried to qualify for both the Byron Nelson and the U.S. Open golf tournaments. Romo insisted that he lives a simple life, telling Ohm Youngmisuk of New York's *Daily News,* "My life … there really isn't too much to it. You guys would be pretty bored if you hung out with me all the time."

Sources

Books

Marquis Who's Who, Marquis Who's Who, 2008.

Periodicals

Capital Times (Madison, WI), November 29, 2007, p. D1.

Chicago Sun-Times, November 1, 2002, p. 138.

Daily News (New York, NY), December 1, 2006, p. 105.

Fort Worth Star-Telegram (TX), December 31, 2006; January 7, 2007; January 14, 2008.

New York Post, January 10, 2008, p. 85.

New York Times, November 11, 2007, sec. 8, p. 1.

Seattle Times, January 3, 2007, p. D1.

St. Louis Post-Dispatch, November 23, 2006, p. B11.

Tribune (San Luis Obispo, CA), September 28, 2007.

USA Today, August 24, 2001, p. 3F.

Online

"Cowboys coach says Romo reinjured thumb in loss to Giants," ESPN.com, http://sports.espn.go.com/nfl/playoffs07/news/story?id=3199765 (February 25, 2008).

"Tony Romo," NFL.com, http://www.nfl.com/players/tonoyromo/profile?id=ROM787981 (February 25, 2008).

—A. Petruso

Irene Rosenfeld

Chief Executive Officer of Kraft Foods

Born Irene Blecker in 1953 in New York, NY; daughter of Seymour and Joan Blecker; married Philip L. Rosenfeld (deceased); married Richard Illgen (a mergers and acquisitions specialist); children: Carol, Allison (from first marriage). *Education:* Cornell University, Ithaca, NY, B.A., 1975; M.S., 1977; Ph.D., 1980.

Addresses: *Office*—Kraft Foods Inc., 3 Lakes Dr., Northfield, IL 60093.

Career

Worked at Dancer Fitzgerald Sample advertising agency, New York City, 1979-81; associate market research manager, General Foods, 1981; executive vice president and general manager of the beverages division, Kraft Foods Inc., 1991-94; executive vice president and general manager of the desserts and snacks division, Kraft Foods Inc., 1994-96; president, Kraft Foods Canada, 1996-2004; group vice president, Kraft Foods Inc., 2000-04; president, Kraft Foods North America, 2003-04; chair and CEO, Frito-Lay Inc., 2004-06; CEO, Kraft Foods Inc., 2006-07; chair and CEO, Kraft Foods Inc., 2007—.

Member: Economic Club of Chicago; board of directors, Grocery Manufacturers Association and AutoNation Inc.; trustee, Cornell University, Ithaca, NY; former trustee, Steppenwolf Theatre Co., Chicago.

Awards: Masters in excellence award, Cornell University's Center for Jewish Living, 2005; 50 most powerful women in business, *Fortune* magazine,

Jacques DeMarthon/AFP/Getty Images

2006; 50 women to watch, *Wall Street Journal*, 2006; Next 20 female CEOs, *Pink* magazine and the Forté Foundation, 2006; 100 most powerful women, *Forbes*, 2006-07.

Sidelights

As chief executive officer of Kraft Foods Inc., Irene Rosenfeld oversees the world's second-largest food company. Kraft—the maker of Jell-O, Velveeta cheese, Oscar Mayer hot dogs, and the famed blue-box macaroni—nets $34 billion in annual sales and has a workforce 90,000 strong. As the head of Kraft, Rosenfeld is one of the top female executives in the United States. A 25-year veteran of the food and beverage industry, Rosenfeld took over Kraft in 2006 after falling stock prices, rising operating costs, and a lackluster growth in sales forced the ouster of the former CEO. Known as a gifted marketer with a knack for turning around troubled brands, Rosenfeld is consistently named to lists of the most powerful women in business.

Rosenfeld was born in 1953 in the borough of Brooklyn in New York City to Seymour and Joan Blecker. She grew up in Long Island and played basketball in high school. When it came time for college,

Rosenfeld stayed close to home, choosing Cornell University, which is located in Ithaca, New York. Rosenfeld earned three degrees from Cornell—a bachelor's degree in psychology, 1975; a master's in business, 1977; and a doctorate in marketing and statistics, 1980. As an undergraduate at Cornell, Rosenfeld ate her meals at the kosher dining hall because that is where her boyfriend dined, though she discovered the practice rooted her deeper in her Jewish faith and prompted her to keep a kosher home herself.

In 1979, Rosenfeld landed a job at the exclusive New York City ad agency Dancer Fitzgerald Sample, later known as Saatchi and Saatchi. In 1981, Rosenfeld joined General Foods, starting in the market research division. At the time, sales of Kool-Aid were slowing due to conscientious parents seeking less sugary drinks. Rosenfeld boosted sales, though, through a marketing campaign that repositioned the drink as a healthier alternative to soda pop.

By 1991, Rosenfeld had been promoted to vice president and general manager of the company's beverages division. With an ability to spot market trends, Rosenfeld realized prepackaged drinks were gaining in popularity. She urged the company to purchase the foil-pouched drink-maker Capri Sun Inc. After Kraft acquired Capri Sun, the beverages division became Kraft's fastest-growing unit. "Irene recognized the growing ready-to-drink business opportunity and recognized that we at Kraft were not in it in a meaningful way," Kraft executive vice president Paula Sneed recalled in an article in the Montreal *Gazette*. Rosenfeld also brought religious tolerance to the company, setting up Hanukkah candles in the lobby next to the Christmas tree during the holiday season.

In 1994, Rosenfeld was named vice president and general manager of the desserts and snacks division. Under Rosenfeld's direction, the company introduced sugar-free Jell-O snack cups, which reversed the slide in Jell-O sales. In the early 1990s, Kraft and General Foods merged and in 1996, Rosenfeld became president of Kraft Foods Canada. In an effort to reach consumers, Rosenfeld had the company mail out a free magazine filled with recipes and cooking tips to one million households, thus creating interest in Kraft products. By 2000, Rosenfeld was group vice president of Kraft Foods Inc. Her major accomplishment in this position included the successful integration of Nabisco, the maker of Oreos and Ritz crackers, which Kraft purchased for $18.9 billion in 2000. In 2003, Rosenfeld was named president of Kraft Foods North America.

After 20-plus years with the company, Rosenfeld left in 2004 to become chairman and CEO of Frito-Lay—a snack division of PepsiCo—which includes brands like Lay's, Doritos, Fritos, Rold Gold, Tostitos, and Quaker. Once again, Rosenfeld spotted an emerging trend in consumers desiring healthier snacks. She persuaded Frito-Lay to make a switch to using heart-healthier sunflower oil, which is low in saturated fat. She also oversaw the rollout of the 90-calorie Quaker chewy granola bar, which boasted 30 percent fewer calories than the original. She urged the company to acquire Stacy's Pita Chips. In 2005, the healthier snacks unit of Frito-Lay enjoyed double-digit growth, as compared to the single-digit growth of Frito-Lay's traditional products. Frito-Lay's net revenues grew eight percent—to $10.3 billion—in 2005, making the snacks division the most profitable unit of PepsiCo.

In 2006, a troubled Kraft lured Rosenfeld back to its headquarters in Northfield, Illinois, naming her CEO. The situation at Kraft was unstable with stagnant sales and growing operating costs. In 2005, costs for packaging, fuel, and other commodities soared by $800 million. Kraft passed the cost along to consumers, who balked at the higher prices and turned to private-label products that sold for less. In addition, stock prices had dipped 21 percent in 2005 amidst declining profits and a loss of market share.

After taking over and studying the product lines, Rosenfeld announced that she planned to revive the company by developing healthier, more convenient, and improved products. "We have to stop apologizing for our categories and start reinventing them," Rosenfeld told *Fortune*'s Matthew Boyle. Under Rosenfeld's direction, Kraft upgraded beans for Maxwell House coffee, tried new versions of DiGiorno pizza, and changed the shape of the Oreo—for a limited time only. Kraft also rolled out a new Singles Select cheese with a sharper, more robust taste. The cheese was targeted at adult consumers nostalgic for the individually wrapped singles they grew up with but preferring more adult tastes. Rosenfeld also increased sales of macaroni-and-cheese by introducing a more convenient, snack-sized microwavable version called Easy Mac. Kraft introduced organic and 50 percent whole grain lines of macaroni, as well as a deluxe line that features sun-dried tomato.

As 2007 rolled to a close, the numbers were looking better at Kraft. The innovations in the mac-and-cheese line led to a six percent increase in macaroni sales in 2007, reversing what had been a four-year decline. Some analysts hailed the increase as a sign that Rosenfeld's plan to revitalize tried-and-true products just might work. Some insiders were less optimistic. As Morningstar Inc. analyst Gregg Warren told David Sterrett of *Crain's Chicago Business,* "Macaroni and cheese shows how Kraft can turn around some brands. That said, there are limitations to what they can do, because when you have $34 billion in sales, you have to do lots of things to make a difference."

Sources

Books

Marquis Who's Who, Marquis Who's Who, 2008.

Periodicals

Crain's Chicago Business, July 9, 2007, p. 1; December 24, 2007, p. 1.
Fortune, April 30, 2007, p. 108.
Gazette (Montreal, Canada), June 28, 2006, p. B7.
International Herald Tribune, February 19, 2007, p. 13.
Times (London, England), June 27, 2006, p. 39.

Online

"At Kraft, a Fresh Big Cheese," *BusinessWeek,* http://www.businessweek.com/print/investor/content/jun2006/pi20060626.tif_973843.htm (January 27, 2008).
"Irene Rosenfeld," Kraft, http://www.kraft.com/Investor/corporate-governance/board-of-directors/bios_rosenfeld.htm (January 27, 2008).
"It's the Best of Times for Women in Corporate America," *15 Minutes* magazine, http://www.15minutesmagazine.com/archives/Issue_67/front_page.htm (February 14, 2008).
"The 100 Most Powerful Women: #9 Irene Rosenfeld," *Forbes,* http://www.forbes.com/lists/2007/11/biz-07women_Irene-Rosenfeld_DQ2V.html (January 27, 2008).

—*Lisa Frick*

Patricia Russo

AP Images

Chief Executive Officer of Alcatel-Lucent

Born Patricia Fiorello, June 12, 1952, in Trenton, NJ; daughter of a doctor and a homemaker; married Frank Russo, 1983; children: two stepchildren. *Education:* Georgetown University, B.A., 1973; Harvard University, completed Advanced Management Program, 1989.

Addresses: *Office*—Alcatel-Lucent Executive Offices, 54 rue de la Boétie, 75008 Paris, France.

Career

Sales and marketing management, IBM Corporation, 1973-81; management and executive positions in strategic planning, marketing, human resources, and operations, AT&T, 1981-92, president of Business Communications Systems, 1992-96; executive vice president of corporate operations, Lucent Technologies, 1997-99; executive vice president and chief executive officer of Service Provider Networks Group, 1999-2000; president and chief operations officer, Eastman Kodak, 2001; chairwoman and chief executive officer, Lucent Technologies, 2002-06; chief executive officer, Alcatel-Lucent, 2006—.

Awards: 50 Most Powerful Women in American Business, *Fortune*, 1998, 1999, 2001; tenth most powerful woman in the world, *Forbes*, 2007.

Sidelights

Patricia Russo successfully moved up the corporate ladder from her positions in sales and marketing at IBM to become the CEO of international corporation Alcatel-Lucent. Listed three times as one of the 50 Most Powerful Women in Business by *Fortune* magazine, *Forbes* magazine declared her the tenth most powerful woman in the world in 2007. When she joined AT&T in 1981, she was responsible for turning around a telecommunication department, and that beginning of her career with the company allowed her to help launch and lead spinoff corporation Lucent Technologies. When Lucent suffered in the market of the late 1990s, Russo took a job with Eastman Kodak, becoming number two in that company, only to return to Lucent a year later as CEO. She has been responsible for guiding Lucent through its merger with French telecommunications company Alcatel since 2006.

On her success as a woman in business, Russo told *Institutional Investor*, "The landscape certainly looks a lot different today from when I started out. We have made a lot of progress. But if you just look at the raw numbers, it's hard to argue that there's full representation of women in senior jobs. We've always been a pretty diverse company. So quite frankly, it's not as much on my radar screen as it is in some other companies. I have women running my wireless and wireline businesses. I believe that the more views you have attacking a problem, the better the answer."

Born on June 12, 1952, Russo grew up as the second oldest in a family of seven children. The daughter of a doctor and a homemaker, she was a natural athlete, and in high school she was the co-captain of her basketball team and captain of the cheerleading squad. Two of her siblings, however, grew up physically challenged, which shaped Russo's understanding of family. In 1983, she married Frank Russo and became the stepmother of two children.

A graduate of Georgetown University with a degree in political science and history, Russo spent eight years in the sales and marketing department at IBM. She was one of the few woman in her department, as the attitude at the time was that women were not cut out for careers in sales. In 1981, she was hired by AT&T, where she moved up in the company's sales and marketing departments. In 1992, Russo was moved into the Global Business Communications Systems area, which was floundering and required an overhaul. Russo turned the division around, cutting costs and expanding overseas, focusing efforts on their core products. The division transformed from a failing arm of the company to a profitable unit.

In 1996, Russo moved into AT&T's equipment spin-off, Lucent Technologies. In 1999, Russo became the vice president and chairwoman of the Service Provider Networks Group, a division worth $24 billion that employed 80,000 workers. But as Russo's career reached this height, the telecommunications industry suffered a blow. Many companies began failing, and Lucent was among them, its sales and stock dropping drastically. Russo's division was reduced, and Russo soon left the company for a position at Eastman Kodak.

Hired for the number-two position at Eastman Kodak, she focused on helping to modernize Kodak from film to digital imaging. They also knew of her track record for reorganizing and divesting businesses. She helped the company with a plan to spin-off a new company called Appairent in order to reduce their losses. "Russo's reputation is for skill in motivating people," Gale Morrison wrote in *Electronic News.*

While Russo worked at Kodak, Lucent continued to falter. At the end of 2000, CEO Richard McGinn was let go, and in January of 2002, Russo was invited back to Lucent, this time in the head position. When she accepted the job, which came with a healthy compensation package, she became one of six female CEOs running Fortune 500 companies. The return was like a homecoming for Russo despite the

work that stretched ahead of her. Lucent was drowning in debt, and demand for Lucent's services was very low. Russo announced her goal to turn a profit by early 2003. "The strategy and the product plan are right," she said in *BusinessWeek.* "And I can accelerate them."

Although many of Lucent's employees had been let go before Russo came back on board, the company was still employing more staff than could be afforded. Russo laid off thousands of workers, and focused on reducing operating expenses, working capital, and vendor-financing commitments. She developed a tighter focus for the company, changing Lucent's goal from providing equipment to offering customer services, then sold off businesses that did not support this new direction. Russo also enhanced the sales department, which had always been one of Lucent's strengths. But by the end of 2002, things still looked bleak. Russo was named chairwoman of Lucent in 2003, and shortly thereafter, her changes began to show in their profit margin. In 2004, Lucent showed its first profit since 2000. "Nobody likes to make decisions that affect people in the business," Russo said in *Institutional Investor.* "But it's my responsibility. I and the senior leadership team had to be proactive and aggressive about taking action so that this company would weather that storm. And we did. But it was not a fun time, for sure."

The new profitability of Lucent made it an appealing acquisition, and in 2006, Alcatel in France bought the company, merging the two into Alcatel-Lucent and keeping Russo as the CEO. The deal was one of the largest in the industry, and Russo was shown in pictures of the Paris press conference looking ecstatic. But the merger was a challenge, and integration took time—which cost money, leading Russo to suggest further lay offs. By October of 2007, the company had missed its financial forecasts three times since the initial acquisition. These difficulties led some critics, particularly in Parisian businesses, to suspect that Russo's stay with the company would not last. Other industry commentators suggested that the merger itself was a mistake. "It's easy to sit on the sidelines and make strategic judgments," Russo commented in *BusinessWeek* Online. But she defended her strategy and said that the troubles came from "problems that we're going to work our way out of." She continued to push Alcatel-Lucent into service and support, and under her, it ranked second, behind Ericsson, in that field. While the changes continued, Russo gave the press little reason to increase their faith in the company, acknowledging that the outlook for the next year was uncertain. In other interviews, however, she has kept a positive attitude. "We're not done. We will execute on what we've started," she was quoted as having said on the *Wall Street Journal* Blog. "We believe in what we can create."

Sources

Books

Almanac of Famous People, 9th ed., Gale (Detroit, MI), 2007.
International Directory of Business Biographies, 4 vols., St. James Press (Detroit, MI), 2005.

Periodicals

America's Network, February 1, 2002, p. 46.
BusinessWeek, January 21, 2002, p. 34.
Economist, October 27, 2007, p. 74.
Electronic News, January 14, 2002, p. 24.
eWeek, September 29, 2007.
Forbes, May 14, 2001, p. 32.
Information Week, October 3, 2007.
Institutional Investor, February 2005, p. 20.
Lightwave, July, 2003, "National Security Telecommunications Advisory Committee," p. 41.
RCR Wireless News, February 18, 2008, p. 9.
Telecom Asia, October 2006, p. 40.
TelecomWeb News Digest, April 30, 2008, "Rumor Du Jour: CEO Endangered as Alcatel-Lucent Fumbles Again."

Online

"Alcatel Rules Change Threatens Russo," *BusinessWeek* Online, http://www.businessweek.com/globalbiz/content/may2008/gb20080516.tif_848053.htm (May 19, 2008).
Biography Resource Center Online, Gale Group, 2002.
"Is the Worst Over at Alcatel-Lucent?," *BusinessWeek* Online, http://www.businessweek.com/globalbiz/content/nov2007/gb20071128.tif_204292.htm (May 10, 2008).
"Lucent Technologies CEO Patricia Russo," Public Radio Marketplace Online, http://marketplace.publicradio.org/segments/corneroffice/corner_russo_bio.html (May 18, 2008).
"Mean Street: What Alcatel-Lucent's Pat Russo Can Learn from Spock," *Wall Street Journal* Blog, http://blogs.wsj.com/deals/2008/050/05/mean-street-what-alcatel-lucents-pat-russo-can-learn-from-spock/?mod=WSJBlogprint/ (May 5, 2008).
"The 100 Most Powerful Women: Number 10: Patricia Russo," *Forbes Online,* http://www.forbes.com/lists/2007/11/biz-07women_Patricia-Russo_ZE1Y.html (May 18, 2007).
"Patricia Russo," InfoPlease, http://www.infoplease.com/spot/womenceo1.html (May 18, 2008).
"Patricia Russo, Chief Executive Officer," Alcatel-Lucent, http://www.alcatel-lucent.com/ (May 18, 2008).

—*Alana Joli Abbott*

Mikhail Saakashvili

AP Images

President of the Republic of Georgia

Born December 21, 1967, in Tbilisi, Georgia; son of Nikoloz Saakashvili (a doctor) and Giuli Alasania (a professor); married Sandra Roelofs; children: Eduard, Nikoloz. *Education:* Kiev University Institute of International Relations, undergraduate degree, 1987; Strasbourg Human Rights International Institute, law degree, early 1990s; Columbia University, J.D., mid-1990s; studied law at the George Washington University National Center of Law, mid-1990s.

Addresses: *Office*—Administration of the President, 7 Ingorokova St. Index 0134, Tbilisi, Republic of Georgia.

Career

Worked for Norwegian Institute of Human Rights, 1992; worked for Human Rights Committee of Georgia, 1992-93; lawyer, Patterson, Belknap, Webb, and Tyler in New York City, mid-1990s; elected to parliament, Republic of Georgia, 1995, then named majority leader in parliament, 1998; leader of Georgian delegation and assembly vice-president, Parliamentary Assembly of the Council of Europe, 2000; minister of justice, Republic of Georgia, 2000-01; elected to parliament, Republic of Georgia, 2001; chair of Tbilisi city council, Republic of Georgia, 2002-03; president of Georgia, 2004-07, 2008—.

Sidelights

Mikheil Saakashvili, a young, brilliant, but brash politician, became president of Georgia, the former Soviet republic between Russia and Turkey, in 2004, after leading a dramatic and peaceful revolution that forced former Soviet official Edward Shevardnadze out of the presidency. He quickly and dramatically moved Georgia toward a free-market economy and a closer alliance with Western countries, all while sparring with Russia and breakaway regions of his own country. Georgia's economy boomed under Saakashvili's leadership, but he grew intolerant of increasing opposition to his policies. His suppression of protests in the fall of 2007 wounded his image as a democratic reformer, but he won re-election as president in January of 2008 and continued his pro-Western, pro-capitalist, anti-Russian policies.

Saakashvili was born in Georgia's capital, Tbilisi, in December of 1967 to Nikoloz Saakashvili, a doctor, and Giuli Alasania, a professor who has studied Georgian history. After graduating from secondary school, Saakashvili attended the Kiev University Institute of International Relations, a prestigious Soviet school in Ukraine (which, like Georgia, was then part of the Soviet Union and is now an independent country). He studied human rights law at the Strasbourg Human Rights International Institute in Strasbourg, France, where he met his wife, Sandra Roelofs, who is Dutch.

Despite his youth, Saakashvili quickly became a key player in negotiations to settle ethnic and separatist tensions unleashed in Georgia by the breakup of the Soviet Union. Two regions of Georgia, South Ossetia and Abkazia, fought civil wars with the Georgian government in the early 1990s because they wanted to be connected to Russia, not Georgia. In 1992, while working at the Norwegian Institute of Human Rights, Saakashvili organized a peace conference that led to a cease-fire between the Georgian government and South Ossetian insurgents. In 1992 and 1993, while working for the Human Rights Committee of Georgia, he helped negotiate prisoner exchanges between Georgia and separatists in Abkhazia and between Armenians and Azeris, who had fought over Nagorno-Karabakh, a breakaway region of Azerbaijan.

In the mid-1990s, Saakashvili studied law in the United States. He earned a master's degree in law at Columbia University and studied for a year at the George Washington University National Center of Law, then practiced commercial law in New York City for about a year; however, when Zurab Zhvania, a leading politician in Georgia, visited him in New York and asked him to come home and join the government, he accepted the invitation.

Elected to Georgia's parliament in 1995, Saakashvili became chair of a committee on legal and constitutional issues. He and the committee successfully pushed for major legal and judicial reforms, such as merit-based selection of judges and making the courts more open and transparent. Saakashvili's reform work made him a popular figure in Georgia. He became majority leader in parliament in 1998. About a year later, he was elected to lead Georgia's delegation to the Parliamentary Assembly of the Council of Europe, which elected him to the position of assembly vice-president in January of 2000.

In October of 2000, Georgia's president, Edward Shevardnadze, a former foreign minister for the Soviet Union, named Saakashvili minister of justice. In his new job, he pushed for prison reform, visiting prisons as part of his work. Saakashvili also displayed a populist streak that impressed many Georgians. Unlike most of the country's leaders, he walked and took public transportation to work; citizens often stopped him on the street to tell him their complaints about the government.

Saakashvili launched several investigations of corruption in the government, but Shevardnadze and other officials did not follow through with prosecutions. In one dramatic moment at a cabinet meeting, Saakashvili confronted several other ministers with photos of their lavish vacation homes. He asked how they could afford them on their official salaries of $100 a month and accused them of acquiring them through corrupt land deals. In September of 2001, Saakashvili resigned from the cabinet, complaining that he could not serve in a government that tolerated corruption.

Saakashvili was elected to parliament as an independent a month later, and he soon founded a new political party, the United National Movement, with an anti-corruption platform. He left parliament to run successfully for city council in Tbilisi, the capital, where one-third of all Georgians live. He was elected council chair. Under his leadership, the council improved city services and rooted out corruption in the city government.

In November of 2003, Saakashvili ran for parliament again, with the slogan "Georgia Without Shevardnadze." Observers and pollsters forecast that his National Movement would win the elections, but officially released totals showed Shevardnadze's coalition winning. International observers called the elections deeply flawed, and a Georgian human rights group reported ballot stuffing, beatings of election officials, and the burning of an opposition party office. Saakashvili and two other Georgian leaders, Nino Burjanadze, speaker of parliament, and Zhvania, leader of the United Democrats party, accused the government of rigging the election and called for national protests. Saakashvili (according to Owen Matthews and Frank Brown of *Newsweek*) asked Georgians to "declare civil disobedience to the Shevardnadze regime."

The protests, which became known as the Rose Revolution, lasted 19 days and attracted up to 40,000 people. Saakashvili traveled across Georgia to convince supporters to come to Tbilisi to join the demonstrations. On November 22, when the parliament was scheduled to meet to certify the election results, Saakashvili, Burjanadze, Zhvania, and other protesters flooded the parliament session to stop the vote. As Saakashvili entered, he held a red rose in one hand to show he was leading a peaceful protest. Guards, whom the protesters had fed during the long siege, stepped aside and let the protesters in. Shevardnadze and other legislators fled. The next morning, after an overnight negotiating session with Saakashvili and other members of the opposition, Shevardnadze resigned.

"We were afraid all the way through," Saakashvili told *Newsweek* writer Ken Stier. "To the superficial observer, it looked like a music festival, but it was not. It was very close to violence. It could have gone very, very badly. When we went into the Parliament, there were a lot of armed people there, and when we entered the square in front of Parliament, there were a lot of arms, busloads of weapons."

New elections were held in January of 2004, and Saakashvili ran practically unopposed for president, winning in an enormous landslide. He said he looked to American political figures such as former president John F. Kennedy and U.S. Senator John McCain as role models. "I was really raised on American democracy," he told Peter Baker of the *Washington Post.*

To many in the West, the Rose Revolution and Saakashvili's electoral victory were signs that democracy was advancing in the former Soviet republics. "Saakashvili is bright, charismatic, energetic, and very honest," Georgian political analyst Dodona Kiziria of Indiana University told Anna Kuchment of *Newsweek.* Standing up to the government's corruption "really took courage, because Shevardnadze was a giant," Kiziria added. At the same time, she noted, Saakashvili's brash, populist personality had a downside. "The only problem with Saakashvili is that he must be restrained once in a while and taught to be more subtle and diplomatic," she said.

That was the polite way of putting it. "If he becomes president, it will be an economic and political disaster for Georgia. Saakashvili is not very sane," Irina Sarishvili-Chanturia, a Shevardnadze supporter, told Baker of the *Washington Post.* "He's absolutely uncontrolled…. He's really dangerous."

As president, Saakashvili pushed for Western-style free-market economic reforms and promised to create elite investigative units to tackle corruption. His government abolished dozens of permit rules that restricted business. It laid off almost half of its civil servants and disbanded the traffic police, infamous for taking bribes. It also privatized many state-run institutions, such as the country's hospitals. The moves succeeded in stimulating the impoverished Georgian economy; its gross domestic product tripled during his first term.

Saakashvili declared that he wanted Georgia to become a member of the North Atlantic Treaty Organization (NATO), the Western military alliance. United States President George W. Bush showed his support of Saakashvili with a visit to Georgia in the spring of 2005. Bush praised him for "building a democratic society … where a free press flourishes, a vigorous opposition is welcome, and unity is achieved through peace," according to Anne Applebaum of the *Washington Post.* The U.S. also helped train Georgian troops and awarded the country a $300 million grant from its Millennium Challenge program, designed to help the economies of small democracies.

Saakashvili also tried to exert greater control over the still defiant South Ossetia and Abkhazia regions. That increased tensions with Russia, which supports the separatist movements there. Like other former Soviet republics, Georgia has also quarreled with Russia over the high prices Russia charges for natural gas exports. The tensions became especially strong in 2006, when Russia embargoed imports from Georgia, expelled many Georgians from Russia, and slowed its approval of visas for Georgians who wanted to visit Russia.

Saakashvili defiantly proclaimed that Georgia would find new markets. "We've been thrown into the open sea. The time has come for us to learn to swim," he said, according to Owen Matthews and Anna Nemtsova of *Newsweek International.* To lessen its dependence on Russian natural gas, Georgia signed gas deals with Iran. In September of 2006, tensions escalated further, as Georgian authorities arrested four Russian military officials. Saakashvili accused them of plotting to overthrow him. Russian President Vladimir Putin threatened to formally recognize South Ossetia and Abkhazia as independent countries if Western nations did the same for Kosovo, the breakaway province of Serbia.

During his first term, critics of Saakashvili argued that he had an authoritarian streak, did not always respect the law and free speech, and was inflaming tensions with Russia with rash actions. Laid-off police, civil servants, and residents of rural areas that had not experienced much economic growth also opposed the government. In November of 2007, after protesters staged five days of peaceful protests outside the parliament, Saakashvili sent riot police to break up the crowd with rubber bullets and tear gas. Next, he declared a two-week state of emergency, banned public protests, and shut down most news outlets, including two opposition television stations and cable broadcasts of foreign news channels. He defended his actions, accusing the protesters of being manipulated by Russian agents. But Saakashvili had injured his democratic reputation. Faced with extreme criticism from his international allies, he announced that he would move up the presidential election from the fall of 2008 to January 5.

Saakashvili stepped down from the presidency for two months in order to run for re-election. He spent the end of 2007 campaigning across the country, promising to fight unemployment and poverty and change his cabinet. Before the vote, international observers complained the government was engaged in voter intimidation and had padded the voting rolls with untraceable names.

In January, Saakashvili was declared the winner of the election with 53 percent of the vote, enough to avoid a runoff election and far ahead of his closest rival, who got 26 percent. In an ironic echo of the Rose Revolution protests, opponents of Saakashvili organized protests, claiming that Saakashvili had not actually won more than 50 percent and was obligated to participate in a runoff. But European election observers called the vote a major step forward for democracy, while also pointing to some violations of election law.

On January 20, Saakashvili was sworn in for a second term as president. "This election proved that our democracy is blossoming, and that we can build democratic institutions that will endure far longer than any single individual," he said in his inaugural speech, according to a transcript on his presidential Web site. He promised that the opposition would have a more influential role in government institutions. He also pledged to make the fight against poverty the central goal of his new term, through improved social benefit programs, credit programs, and aid to rural areas.

In March of 2008, Saakashvili visited the United States and won Bush's endorsement of Georgia's request to join NATO. Acceptance into the military alliance, Saakashvili hoped, would send Russia a strong signal that it could no longer threaten Georgia; however, tensions with Russia escalated in the spring of 2008 when Putin declared he would seek even closer relationships with South Ossetia and Abkhazia and sent more troops to the area. It appeared that the same international issues that Saakashvili confronted in his first four years as president would also dominate his second term.

Sources

Periodicals

Economist, January 12, 2008, p. 43-44.
Newsweek, November 24, 2003, p. 41; November 25, 2003; December 8, 2003, p. 60; May 11, 2005; August 2, 2007.
Newsweek International, May 17, 2004; August 23, 2004; May 8, 2006; October 9, 2006; October 16, 2006; November 19, 2007.
U.S. News & World Report, November 19, 2007, p. 30.
Washington Post, November 26, 2003, p. A1; January 5, 2004, p. A11; February 21, 2004, p. A19; November 9, 2007, p. A16; November 13, 2007, p. A19; January 2, 2008, p. A9; January 6, 2008, p. B6; January 14, 2008, p. A18; March 24, 2008, p. A13; May 1, 2008, p. A10.

Online

"Biography" President of Georgia, http://www.president.gov.ge/?1=E&m=1&sm=3 (May 11, 2008).
"Inauguration" President of Georgia, http://www.president.gov.ge/?1=E&m=1&sm=1 (May 11, 2008).
"Profile: Mikhail Saakashvili" BBC News, http://news.bbc.co.uk/go/pr/fr/-/2/hi/europe/7084480.stm (May 11, 2008).

—*Erick Trickey*

Zainab Salbi

Michael Buckner/Getty Images

Activist and author

Born c. 1969 in Iraq; daughter of Basil and Alia Salbi; married second husband Amjad Atallah (co-founder of Women for Women International). *Education:* George Mason University, B.A., 1996; London School of Economics and Political Science, M.A., 2001.

Addresses: *Office*—Women for Women International, 4455 Connecticut Ave. NW, Ste. 200, Washington, DC 20008.

Career

Worked as a translator, Washington, DC, c. early 1990s; founder and president, Women for Women International (originally Women for Women in Bosnia), Washington, DC, 1993—.

Awards: Trailblazer award, *Forbes* magazine, 2005; Washingtonian of the Year, *Washingtonian*, 2006; John F. Kennedy New Frontier Award, 2007; Young Global Leader, World Economic Forum, 2007.

Sidelights

The co-founder of Women for Women International, Zainab Salbi affected world change by helping women in war-torn countries connect with and find economic support from women in the West. She has served as president of the group from its launch in 1993. A native of Iraq, Salbi also offered insight into the person and regime of Saddam

Hussein with her 2005 autobiography *Between Two Worlds: Escape from Tyranny: Growing Up in the Shadow of Saddam.*

Born in Iraq during the late 1960s, she is the daughter of Basil and Alia Salbi. Her father was a skilled pilot for Iraqi Airlines; she grew up in a life of privilege, since her parents were part of the social elite in Baghdad. They knew Saddam Hussein before he came to power, but her parents were not impressed with him. He cultivated their friendship after he took charge of Iraq, though they did not want it. When Salbi was eleven years old, her father reluctantly became Saddam's personal pilot because to refuse him could mean dire consequences. The family spent much time with Saddam and his cronies, where they were watched, controlled, and lived in fear.

Of her early years, Salbi told *body+soul*, "Growing up in Iraq, I saw all kinds of injustice—my best friend's father getting executed, my mother on the verge of deportation simply because she was a Shia. As a child, I could do nothing about these things. I feared even showing my tears."

While Salbi was studying languages at an Iraqi university, her mother feared for her safety. In an attempt to protect her daughter, Salbi's mother sent her to the United States in 1990 where an arranged marriage awaited her. The marriage was abusive and she soon left her husband after he raped her. While Salbi was in the United States, Iraq invaded Kuwait, which led to the Gulf War of the early 1990s. Salbi waited to return to Iraq because of the war, but after it ended she decided to remain in the United States.

Moving to Washington, D.C., Salbi took a job as a translator. She also began working on her bachelor's degree at George Mason University in Virginia. While a student there, international events inspired her to become an activist. Salbi, her second husband Amjad Atallah, and her friends were moved by the plight of women during the Yugoslavian civil war. Because of the Bosnian Serb policy of ethnic cleansing, many women were forced out of their homes and raped, tortured, or otherwise physically harmed.

Amidst her anger and her desire for the United States to do something about the situation in Yugoslavia, Salbi realized she could affect change. She founded what was then known as Women for Women in Bosnia (later known as Women for Women International) in 1993 to aid women in Bosnia-Herzegovina and Croatia on a shoestring budget. The grassroots nonprofit found female volunteers in the United States and other Western countries to give financial and emotional support to women in the war-torn region.

Each volunteer was matched with a woman in need of help in Bosnia or Croatia. The Western sponsor sent $20 and a letter each month to their "sister" (in Women to Women terms) in a refugee camp. The money was used for food and personal items. The correspondence was just as important. Salbi explained to Bill Sizemore of the *Virginian-Pilot*, "The letters have an impact both ways. The women over there were completely isolated, in refugee camps. A lot of them felt very embittered and abandoned. So the letters acted as a connection to the outside world. To a lot of them, it restored the hope that there are still good people out there—there are still people who care." After a sponsored woman was able to work and take care of herself, she left the program.

While the work Women for Women was doing was important, the group struggled in its early days. For the first six months of the group's existence, operations were done out of the basement of Atallah's parents' home in Fairfax, Virginia. After getting a grant from Working Assets, Women for Women rented an office in Washington, D.C., and hired staff members. Within the first three years of the group's existence, more than 1,000 women received $250,000 in aid. By 1996, Women for Women started a microlending program to help survivors start their own businesses. Job and life skill programs were also added to help women further improve their lives.

While Salbi served as president of Women for Women, she also continued working on her degree as much as she could. Though she remained in charge of the group, she cut back on her responsibilities so she could finally earn her bachelor's degree from George Mason University in 1996. Salbi later returned to school, and she earned her master's degree from the London School of Economics and Political Science in 2001.

Over the years, Salbi expanded the Women for Women program. By the late 1990s, women in Rwanda joined the program to get help, as did women in Nigeria and Bangladesh. In the early 2000s, Women for Women also reached Columbia, the Congo, Sudan, and Afghanistan. Over the years, the basic sponsorship program of Women to Women remained the same, though the amount sent each month increased slightly. By 2005, it was estimated that the group had helped 52,000 women.

In 1997, Salbi had talked of returning to Iraq when Saddam was no longer in control of the country. After the United States invasion of Iraq and removal of Saddam from power in 2003, she went back to her native country to visit several times. She also expanded the scope of Women for Women to include Iraq after the initial war ended; however, because of safety concerns for women and staff in Iraq, the sponsorship program cannot operate there. In a 2005 *Washington Post* online chat, Salbi explained about the group's presence in Iraq, "We work with women across the country to both work on giving them job opportunities and to raising their awareness about the importance of their role and contribution to society, economy, politics and health.... [W]e believe that we cannot have a strong country if we do not have strong women. Strong women do lead to strong nations, and that is what we work on."

As Iraq became international news, Salbi decided to write a book about Iraqi women because she perceived the international reputation of them was incomplete. As she worked on the book with the guidance of her agent, she began including her own stories, which soon became the focus of the project. Salbi ultimately wrote a memoir, with co-author

Laurie Becklund, of her childhood in Iraq. Published in 2005, *Between Two Worlds: Escape from Tyranny: Growing Up in the Shadow of Saddam* was generally well-received. Writing in *Vogue*, Kate Bolick noted, "Her book, a torrent of vividly recalled memories, reads with the sort of artless verve that can come only from one who's been unshackled from a lifetime of repression."

Salbi's memoir was popular, but her primary focus was ensuring Women for Women continued to grow and affect lives worldwide. By 2006, about 30,000 women worldwide were using its programs. Thus, 5.3 million people, including family and community members, were being affected by Women for Women's work. Because of Salbi's vision, the group received the 2006 Conrad N. Hilton Humanitarian Prize. With an award of $1.5 million, the prize is the world's largest humanitarian honor. Salbi earmarked the funds to start a new project within Women for Women to construct permanent "opportunity centers" in regions where the group operates, to help women gain access to economic, social, and political programs in their communities.

Ultimately, Salbi knew her work with Women for Women had a contradictory element to it. She told *Radio Free Europe*, "I really believe war is like a flashlight on humanity. It shows us the worst of it, and it shows us the best of it. And part of the success for me comes from the best of humanity. Because every time I go and visit women in Bosnia or in Iraq or in Afghanistan or the Congo or other countries, I am in awe of the strength of these women, and the strength of humanity, and the beauty of humanity—as much as I am in awe of its ugliness."

Selected writings

Strategic Planning and Institutional Development, Palestinian Academic Society for the Study of International Affairs, 1999.

(With Laurie Becklund) *Between Two Worlds: Escape from Tyranny: Growing Up in the Shadow of Saddam*, Gotham, 2005.

The Other Side of War: Women's Stories of Survival and Hope, National Geographic, 2006.

Sources

Periodicals

Africa News, October 22, 2006.

Associated Press Worldstream, November 7, 2007.

body+soul, May 2007, p. 25.

Milwaukee Journal Sentinel, October 6, 2005, p. A2.

News Tribune (Tacoma, WA), November 20, 2005, p. E7.

Radio Free Europe, April 19, 2007.

San Francisco Chronicle, January 27, 2002, p. E1.

State Department Documents and Publications, November 20, 2006.

Times (London, England), November 1, 2005, p. 4.

Virginian-Pilot (Norfolk, VA), February 28, 1997, p. B7.

Vogue, November 2005, p. 244.

Online

"Between Two Worlds," *Washington Post,* http://www.washingtonpost.com/wp-dyn/content/discussion/2005/09/30/DI2005093000803.tif.html (October 12, 2005).

Contemporary Authors Online, Thomson Gale, 2006.

—A. Petruso

Johan Santana

Professional baseball player

Born March 13, 1979, in Tovar, Venezuela; son of Jesus (a power company repairman) and Hilda; married to Yasmile; children: Jasmily, Jasmine.

Addresses: *Office*—Minnesota Twins, Hubert H. Humphrey Metrodome, 900 South 5th St., Minneapolis, MN 55415.

Career

Pitcher for minor-league teams in the Houston Astros organization, 1996-99; pitcher for Minnesota Twins, 2000-02, 2003—; pitcher for minor-league Edmonton Trappers, 2002.

Awards: Cy Young Award for best American League pitcher, Baseball Writers' Association of America, 2004 and 2006; Best American League pitcher, *Sports Illustrated* players' poll, 2005.

Sidelights

Johan Santana, arguably the premier baseball pitcher of his generation, a hero in his native Venezuela, dominated American League hitters in the mid-2000s. In 2004 and 2006, he unanimously won the Cy Young Award, acknowledging him as the best pitcher in the American League. He had learned to tame his sometimes wild, erratic pitching and had developed three pitches that baffled hitters: a speedy fastball, a low-hanging slider, and a deceptive change-up. In 2005, *Sports Illustrated*'s S. L. Price wrote that Santana was "becoming increasingly known as the best pitcher in the world."

Santana grew up in Tovar, a town of 33,000 people in Merida, the mountainous, rural region of Venezuela that the rest of the country often considers a backwater. His Venezuelan nickname is El Gocho, a reference to people from the Merida area that means either cowboy or hillbilly, depending on how the word is translated or used. His father, Jesus, was a gifted baseball infielder on teams in the Andean mountains, but he never played professionally; he worked as a repairman for Venezuela's national power company.

Santana began playing baseball as a kid with his older brother, Franklin. In 1994, when Santana was 15, a baseball scout saw him play outfield in the national championship and, impressed with his speed, invited him to the Houston Astros' baseball academy in Guacara, Venezuela. Santana enrolled at the academy in January of 1995 and quickly converted to pitching after coaches noticed his strong throwing.

Santana spent four years with the Houston Astros' minor league teams, developing a reputation as a powerful but erratic pitcher. The Astros left him unprotected in a 1999 draft, and the Minnesota Twins picked him up in a draft-and-trade deal. The team brought him to the major leagues for the 2000 season, but his pitching was mediocre; he earned a 5.34 earned run average in 25 relief appearances and a 9.82 ERA in five starts. He posted a 4.74 ERA in 2001, but only pitched 15 times because of an elbow injury.

When the 2002 season began, the Twins sent Santana to Edmonton, the Twins' triple-A club, so he could work with pitching coach Bobby Cuellar on perfecting a change-up pitch and converting from a relief pitcher to a starting pitcher. "Bobby told me about throwing different pitches as a starter and having confidence in your changeup," Santana told *Sports Illustrated* writer Ben Reiter. The conversion worked. Santana excelled at Edmonton, posting a 3.14 ERA, and he was called up to the Twins in May. There, alternating between starter and reliever, he posted an 8-6 record and a 2.99 ERA. However, in Game 5 of that year's American League Championship Series, Santana gave up a key home run to Adam Kennedy, putting the Anaheim Angels ahead 6-5 on the way to a blowout that sent the Angels to the World Series.

Santana came into the 2003 season expecting to be a starter, but the Twins signed veteran starter Kenny Rogers, so Santana found himself in the bullpen again. Furious at first, Santana channeled his frustration into strong pitching, compiling a 2.41 era by the end of June. The Twins added him to the starting rotation in July, and he finished the year with a 12-3 record. With 96 walks and 21 wild pitches between 2002 and 2003, he had not quite shaken his reputation as powerful but erratic. "I used to be hyper, throw crazy, and not think about what I wanted to do with each pitch," he told Albert Chen of *Sports Illustrated,* His performance in the 2003 playoffs was disappointing: He left his first game after four innings with leg cramps, posting a 7.04 ERA in two appearances.

In 2004, Santana established himself as a star. Though he started the year slowly because of elbow surgery, he ended up winning 20 games against only 6 losses and struck out 265 batters. After the All-Star break, he was nearly perfect: He went 13-0 with an astonishing 1.21 ERA. He led the Twins to the AL Central title, nine games ahead of second-place Chicago. At the end of the season, by a unanimous vote of the baseball writer's association, Santana won the American League Cy Young Award for best pitcher. His opponents agreed: In August of 2005, major-league players polled by *Sports Illustrated* also chose Santana as the league's best pitcher.

"He's unhittable," Rondell White of the Detroit Tigers told *Sports Illustrated*'s Price. "I mean, no one is unhittable, but he's pretty close." Santana regularly threw three overpowering pitches for strikes, Price explained: "A 95-mph fastball, a knee-buckling slider, and the changeup that, because it is delivered with exactly the same motion as his fastball but travels 15 mph slower, is breathtaking." Santana also revealed an unusual habit that he said contributed to his success: Before his starts, he looks at the lineup of the team he will face, then turns to his PlayStation Portable game and pitches against virtual versions of his opponents. "Believe it or not, sometimes I see things in video games that will come true," Santana told Price. "It gives you ideas. I see the scouting reports, though I don't go by that, and in these video games you can see what the hitters have, how to approach them. It's pretty cool."

In 2005, Santana signed a four-year, $40-million contract, the most the Twins had ever paid a player. Fans waved Venezuelan flags in the stands when he pitched, his starts were regularly shown on Venezuelan television, and television crews from Venezuela followed him around most of the year. He won 17 straight games during 2005, almost reaching Roger Clemens' American League record of 18 straight. He finished the year with a 16-7 record and a 2.87 ERA. In 2006, he led the Twins to their fourth AL Central title in five years while leading the major leagues with 19 wins, 245 strikeouts, and a 2.77 ERA. He won his second Cy Young award, again by a unanimous vote, only the fourth pitcher in baseball history to win multiple Cy Youngs unanimously. "Last time, after winning the Cy Young, I was trying to prove that what happened in 2004 wasn't a fluke," Santana told reporters, as quoted by Dave Sheinin in the *Washington Post*.

As usual, Santana started off the 2007 season slowly, with a 6-6 record. By now, baseball fans expected Santana to heat up in the second half of the year, and he did. He compiled a 1.29 ERA between June 19 and July 16, and by mid-August he had a 12-9 record. However, the Twins were stuck in third place, behind the Detroit Tigers and Cleveland Indians, and Santana's future with the team was uncertain. He broke off contract negotiations with the Twins in April and said he would not talk with them again until he became a free agent at the end of 2008. The Twins had reportedly offered him a contract extension of two or three years, fewer years than comparable players had signed to as free agents. The press speculated that Santana would leave the Twins after 2008, becoming the most sought-after player in the free agent market.

Sources

Periodicals

Sports Illustrated, October 21, 2002, p. 50; July 14, 2003, p. 119; August 30, 2004, p. 103; May 23, 2005, p. 42; August 22, 2005, p. 37; April 16, 2007, p. 70; July 16, 2007, p. 26.

Sports Illustrated for Kids, July 2007, p. 20.
Washington Post, November 17, 2006, p. E10.

Online

"MLB: Johan Santana Player Page," SI.com; http://www.sportsillustrated.cnn.com/baseball/mlb/players/6441/ (August 18, 2007).

—*Erick Trickey*

Nicolas Sarkozy

President of France

Born Nicolas Paul Stéphane Sarkozy de Nagy-Bocsa, January 28, 1955, in Paris, France; son of Paul and Andrée (Mallah) Sarkozy de Nagy Bosca; married Marie-Dominique Culioli, September 23, 1982 (divorced, 1996); married Cécilia Ciganer-Albéniz, October 1996 (divorced, October 2007); married Carla Bruni (a model and singer), February 2, 2008; children: Pierre, Jean (from first marriage), Louis (from second marriage). *Education:* Institute d'Edudes Politiques de Paris, postgraduate diploma in political science, 1969; Nanterre University, master's degree, 1978; postgraduate studies, Institute d'Edudes Politiques de Paris, 1979-81.

Addresses: *Office*—Palais de l'Elysee, 55-57 rue du Faubourg, Saint-Honoré 75008 Paris, France.

Career

Town councilor, Neuilly-sur-Seine, France, 1977, then mayor, 1983-2002; called to the Paris bar, 1981; vice chairman, Hauts-de-Seine General Council, 1986-88; national assembly deputy, Hauts-de-Seine, 1988-2002; minister of budget, Government of France, 1993, then spokesman, 1993-94, acting minister of communications, 1995, secretary general, 1998-99, minister of interior, internal security, and local freedoms, 2002-04, minister of economic affairs, finance, and industry, 2004, minister of interior, internal security, and local freedoms, 2005-07, president, 2007—.

Member: President, Union for a Popular Movement (a political party), 2004—.

Awards: Chevalier de la Legion d'honneur, French government.

Sidelights

Elected the president of France in 2007, the energetic Nicholas Sarkozy had an extensive career in French politics including a position as the long-time mayor of Neuilly-sur-Seine and ministry positions in several French governments. While often controversial, the modernizing Sarkozy also made headlines for his love life. His second wife, Cécilia Ciganer-Albéniz, supported his political career until he was elected president. After their divorce, Sarkozy quickly became involved with model/singer Carla Bruni, and married her a few months after they met.

Sarkozy was born on January 28, 1955, in Paris, France, the son of Paul Sarkozy de Nagy Bosca and his wife, Andrée. His father was a Jewish native of Hungary and a minor aristocrat who immigrated to France after World War II to escape Communism. His father later converted to Roman Catholicism. His mother was the granddaughter of a Greek immigrant and a law student. The couple had three sons—Sarkozy was the middle child—before Paul abandoned the family when Sarkozy was five years old. (His father later remarried twice and had two more children.)

The scars of the abandonment deeply affected Sarkozy and his family, as his maternal grandfather took responsibility for their welfare while his mother completed her law degree and took a job. Educated at a private Catholic high school with his siblings, the family eventually moved to the upscale Paris suburb of Neuilly-sur-Seine. Sarkozy's political career began at the age of 22, when he became a town councilor in Neuilly. He then focused on his education, earning a law degree from Nanterre University in 1978, then doing postgraduate studies at the Paris Institute for Political Studies from 1979 to 1981. Sarkozy was called to the Paris bar in 1981.

Returning to politics in 1983, Sarkozy was elected mayor of Neuilly by unexpectedly defeating Charles Pasqua. When Sarkozy won, he was the youngest mayor of a city in France. He remained in the post until 2002, though he often held other positions in his political party and various national governments. In 1993, Sarkozy came to national attention in France when he oversaw a hostage negotiation with a mentally ill gunman who was holding school children. The children were freed and the man was later killed by the police.

In the government of Prime Minister Edouard Balladur, Sarkozy was named budget minister in 1993. He later became spokesman for the government from 1993 to 1994. Balladur was a rival of Jacques Chirac, the head of Sarkozy's conservative political party, but Sarkozy endorsed Balladur's candidacy for presidency over Chirac's in 1995. This decision laid the seeds for a strained relationship between Sarkozy and Chirac, which would continue into the next decade.

Chirac won the 1995 election for president, and Sarkozy was not named to any position of importance in his administration. Sarkozy briefly served as acting minister of communications in 1995, then secretary general from 1998 to 1999. While he was essentially shut out of Chirac's governments, Sarkozy built up his political skills and importance to the party through his mayoral position.

In 2002, Sarkozy was selected to become the head of the interior ministry in the newly re-elected government of Chirac. Because of rising crime in France, Sarkozy not only took the traditional duties of a minister of the interior but was also in charge

of emphasizing domestic security. He implemented a law-and-order campaign. Thus his full title was minister of the interior, internal security, and local freedoms.

Sarkozy left the interior ministry behind in 2004 to become Chirac's minister of economic affairs, finance, and industry. During his time in the post, he oversaw the government bailout of the engineering company, Alstom, which was bankrupt and failing. Not everyone in his party agreed with this move, dubbing it interventionist.

During his nearly two years in charge of the interior ministry and few months as finance minister, Sarkozy emerged as Chirac's chief rival and gained much support from the people. While Chirac wanted his one-time prime minister Alain Juppé to be his successor, Juppé was convicted for corrupt funding practices. Sarkozy emerged as Chirac's ambitious successor to the presidency. Polls also showed that Chirac was falling in popularity, while Sarkozy was on the rise because of his work in the post, adding to the tension between the two.

Juppé's fall also compelled him to resign as the head of their political party, the Union for a Popular Movement (UMP). Sarkozy made a run for the head of the UMP to ensure his presidential candidacy in 2007, and was easily elected to the position in November of 2004. Chirac would not allow Sarkozy to be both the head of the party and hold a ministry position in his government, therefore, Sarkozy stepped down as finance minister to focus on running the UMP.

Conceding to Sarkozy's popularity and political skill, however, Chirac asked him to return as interior minister in 2005. Sarkozy continued his tough talk on immigration and crime, a widely held stance in France, and remained popular. He said he would clean up neighborhoods troubled by petty crimes as well as deport illegal immigrants. This stance was believed to have contributed to the second-generation immigrant youth riots and arson activities which plagued France in the summer of 2005. Yet Sarkozy moved to immediately address the rioter's concerns and worked to subdue the rioters when other government officials did little. Sarkozy's actions only increased his power.

By January of 2007, Chirac declined to seek another term as French president, conceding to the popularity of his rival, Sarkozy. Sarkozy ran unopposed in the January elections to determine the candidate for UMP, gaining the support of former rivals such as

Juppé. As the UMP candidate, he promised to bring more radical change to France. Sarkozy wanted to reform the welfare system and pensions as well as protect France from the effects of globalization.

In March of 2007, Sarkozy resigned from his position as interior minister in Chirac's government to focus on his presidential bid. He held only a narrow lead over Socialist Ségolène Royal and center-right nominee Francois Bayrou, and a greater one over the other nine candidates, ahead of the first election date, April 22. After the first round of voting, Sarkozy and Royal remained in the race for the May 6 second round of elections. Sarkozy again held the lead.

Ahead of the May of 2007 elections, Sarkozy worked to gain centrist voters by proving he was more than a tough ball of energy but also sympathetic in that he wanted to protect as well as unite the French people. Yet he made no secret of his plans to make the French work more and make it much easier for companies to hire and fire employees. Royal played up Sarkozy's divisiveness and problematic personality in her campaign, but to no avail. Sarkozy easily won with 53 percent of the vote in what was an unusually high voter turnout for the French presidential election. By winning the election, Sarkozy became the first son of an immigrant to become France's president.

As soon as he took office, Sarkozy began implementing significant changes. He cut the number of Cabinet positions to 15 and appointed seven women to posts. Sarkozy also created a new ministry of immigration, integration, and national identity to handle related issues. In addition, he appointed several people from other political parties to his government, including Socialist Bernard Kouchner as France's top diplomat, to make good on his promises for better human rights and an improved relationship with the United States. Sarkozy made moves to implement his campaign promises related to economic reform as well, including cutting taxes on overtime and limiting the power of unions.

Sarkozy's political stance was soon confirmed in parliamentary elections, held on June 10, 2007. His UMP party did well, gained seats, and was expected to carry a vast parliamentary majority. The parliamentary elections were seen as popular confirmation of Sarkozy's desire to implement reform, including the economic reform of a longer work week, and perhaps reform the French constitution.

Within a few months of taking office, Sarkozy's personal life seemed to overshadow his political work. His second wife, Cécilia Ciganer-Albéniz, had been his most reliable aide for much of their marriage, which began in 1996; however, she did not hide the affair she had with another man in 2005. Though the couple eventually reconciled, Ciganer-Albéniz did not play a role in her husband's presidential campaign and the couple divorced in October of 2007.

Shortly after the divorce, Sarkozy became involved with Carla Bruni, an heiress/supermodel of the 1990s who later had a singing career in France and was known for dating such celebrities as Mick Jagger and Eric Clapton. The pair made front page news in France by taking high-profile vacations to Egypt and Jordan, and bringing their children to France's EuroDisney. While it was commonly believed the couple married in January of 2008 after a whirlwind romance, they actually tied the knot on February 2, 2008.

While many in France focused on his personal life, Sarkozy continued to run the French government in a manner different from his predecessor. In February of 2008, he announced a three-year plan to improve and revive the suburban ghettos where Arab and African immigrants often lived in squalor as second-class citizens. Sarkozy promised an increased police presence to quell drug dealers and other social issues, better access to education and job training, and improved bus, train, and tram transportation to aid work prospects.

Such a plan was intended to give hope to immigrant residents, but was also seen as too hard-line by some residents and costly by observers who noted the government already faced a huge deficit. Despite naysayers, Sarkozy believed in his vision and what it meant for France. Geraldine Braum of the *Los Angeles Times* quoted him as saying "I want to tell these kids, who are French, nobody will be judged by their skin color or by the address of their district. France is all of you, in the diversity of what you are and want you believe in."

Despite such measures, Sarkozy faced dropping poll numbers at the end of 2007 and early 2008. The reasons for his double-digit drop in popularity were France's failing economy despite reforms, as well as his high-profile, showy lifestyle. Even his son, Jean, broke ranks with his father's UMP party by not supporting the candidacy of David Martinon for mayor of Neuilly in March of 2008 local elections. Such declining support was putting Sarkozy's reforms in jeopardy, and the Socialist gained a small majority of the votes in the first round. The defeat did not deter Sarkozy, who took it as a challenge to implement more reform faster.

Sarkozy believed in himself and his vision for France, despite these growing problems. Of his political style, ally Brice Hortefeux told Craig S. Smith of the *New York Times*, "Other politicians don't want to take risks, but he will take any risk."

Selected writings

Nonfiction

Testimony: France in the Twenty-first Century, Pantheon (New York City), 2007.

Sources

Books

Complete Marquis Who's Who Biographies, Marquis Who's Who, 2008.

Periodicals

Associated Press, May 7, 2002; November 29, 2004; March 27, 2007; May 6, 2007; May 18, 2007; February 10, 2008.

Economist, January 13, 2007; April 28, 2007; June 16, 2007; March 22, 2008.

Guardian (London, England), July 17, 2004, p. 15.

Los Angeles Times, January 9, 2008, p. A4; January 16, 2008, p. A7; February 9, 2008, p. A3; March 2, 2008, p. I94; March 14, 2008, p. A3; March 17, 2008, p. A3; April 17, 2008, p. A3.

New York Times, May 7, 2007, p. A16; May 19, 2007, p. A4.

Sunday Telegraph (London, England), July 15, 2007, p. 33.

Online

"Sarkozy: I have mandate for change," CNN.com, http://www.cnn.com/2007/WORLD/europe/05/07/france.election/index.html (May 7, 2007).

—A. Petruso

Allen Schwartz

Founder of A.B.S. by Allen Schwartz

Born Allen Bruce Schwartz, c. 1945, in NY; son of Daniel (a garment salesperson) and Sue (a boutique owner) Schwartz; married Pam (a homemaker); children: Danielle, John.

Addresses: *Office*—A.B.S. Corporate, 1231 Long Beach Ave., Los Angeles, CA 90021.

Career

Worked in the mailroom of a lingerie company, early 1960s; sales associate, Russ Togs, c. 1964-68; sales executive, Esprit de Corp, 1968-77; East Side Clothing Company, New York City, co-founder, 1977, and executive, 1977-81; founded A.B.S by Allen Schwartz, 1982; launched "Oscar Watch" line, 1996; company acquired by Warnaco, Inc., 2000, and Schwartz became design director.

Sidelights

Allen Schwartz is design director of A.B.S by Allen Schwartz, a clothing company that surged to fame in the 1990s with its clever copies of designer originals. Based in Los Angeles, Schwartz's company has been scorned by the fashion establishment, but it consistently racks up impressive sales figures year after year. The founder is impervious to his critics, once telling *Forbes* journalist Nina Munk that "when something costs $1,400 they call it an original; at $400 it's a knockoff. I'm doing nothing different than Calvin [Klein], except he's probably at La Grenouille for lunch for three hours, shaking hands with the [fashion magazine] editors. I don't have time for that crap."

Schwartz was born in the mid-1940s and grew up in the New York City borough of Brooklyn. His parents were involved in the fashion business—his father, Daniel, was a dress sales executive, while his mother, Sue, had a clothing boutique in Long Beach, New York. Early on, Schwartz began looking for a job in the field on his own, and he started off in the mailroom of a lingerie company before moving on to Russ Togs, an apparel manufacturer, where he spent four years in sales. In 1968, he joined the company that became juniors-apparel manufacturer Esprit de Corp as a sales executive, and he left nine years later after selling his 20 percent stake in order to strike out on his own.

Schwartz had moved to San Francisco to work at Esprit. After leaving the company he returned to New York City, and with two business partners in 1977 he launched the East Side Clothing Company, a junior-apparel maker. Four years later, he sold his share of the company to his partners, and by 1982, he was living back in California, this time in the Los Angeles area. That same year he founded "A. B.S. by Allen Schwartz" and began designing and making women's apparel to fill what he saw as an underserved niche in the market. "Our target was to be a designer line in the contemporary department," he explained in an interview with Mary Lynn Richmond in *WWD*. "It was risky because I didn't know if that customer was there but I felt that somebody would appreciate its value. It was kind of the beer pocketbook, champagne taste theory."

Schwartz's first few years in business were uneven financially, but around 1985 he began using some new, cheaper but more sophisticated fabrics in his line, and sales soared. The company's first store opened in Santa Monica, California, in 1988, followed four years later by one in Wheatley Heights on New York's Long Island. A.B.S. became known for its knock-offs of top designer clothing—a practice that had gone on in the apparel industry for generations, but Schwartz's ability to get the look to the stores with such a quick turnaround time ushered in a new era of copycatting. Most designers banned him from their runway shows, especially after imitations of the new, athletic gear-inspired line from DKNY—shown in New York City the fall of 1993 for the coming spring—actually turned up in stores before the DKNY goods arrived. In his opinion, he was simply meeting the demands of the market. "I'm not here to have someone hand-cut a garment for 12 hours," he told Munk in the *Forbes* interview. "I live in the real world. I'm not in the business of selling 60 dresses. I'm in the business of selling 10,000 dresses."

By 1995 Schwartz had opened several more A.B.S. stores, and his clothing was also sold at major U.S. department stores, including Nordstrom, Saks Fifth Avenue, Neiman Marcus, and Bloomingdale's—but the company teetered perilously close to failure when Schwartz discovered an embezzler at his headquarters who absconded with $2 million. He began thinking about new business strategies that could rescue A.B.S.'s fortunes and had an epiphany while watching the Academy Awards telecast and realizing that many viewers tuned in just to see what the stars were wearing. Under a new division he dubbed "Oscar Watch," A.B.S. began turning out affordable copies of the most popular red-carpet gowns, with its first hit a facsimile of the wedding dress worn by Carolyn Bessette at her 1996 marriage to John F. Kennedy Jr., which sold 28,000 copies.

That dress had been made for the bride by Narciso Rodriguez for Cerruti, and soon Schwartz set his sights on other designers. He created versions of the chartreuse Asian-style number from Dior worn by Nicole Kidman at the 1997 Academy Awards,

and then the greenish-brown ball gown worn by Hilary Swank in 2000 when she won the Oscar for *Boys Don't Cry*. By using cheaper synthetic fabrics, Schwartz and his team could churn out the most-photographed dresses at a fraction of the cost of an original and have it available at department stores in just a few short weeks. Schwartz was dismissive of his critics in the designer-realm of the fashion industry. "My dresses are better than the originals," he told *New York Times* writer Elizabeth Hayt. "They're more forgiving, less risky. They're a good fit at a good price. Movie stars and suburban housewives buy our clothes. Nobody in the real world wears the real dresses."

In 2000, A.B.S. was bought by Warnaco, a company that owns several well-known labels, including Calvin Klein Jeans and Speedo. The price tag was rumored to be in the ballpark of $20 to $30 million, and apart from the financial windfall, little changed for Schwartz at the office, where he continued to oversee design. Married and the father of two children, he forecasted enduring success for A.B.S., theorizing that fashion designers and other companies often fail because they are too focused on defining themselves by a certain image. "They can run a look for one year, two, maybe five," he reflected in the interview with Richmond for *WWD*. "But when that look slows—and it always does—or when it stops, they've made their mark in the industry and they live and die and struggle with that."

Sources

Periodicals

Forbes, June 19, 1995, p. 48.
Los Angeles Magazine, February 2001, p. 44.
New York Times, April 23, 2000; March 9, 2006.
People, August 11, 1997, p. 142.
WWD, March 30, 1988, p. 12.

Online

"About A.B.S.," A.B.S., http://www.absstyle.com/asstd_pages.php?temp=company (October 9, 2007).

—*Carol Brennan*

H. Lee Scott, Jr.

Chief Executive Officer of Wal-Mart

Born Harold Lee Scott Jr., March 14, 1949, in Joplin, MO; son of Harold (a gas station owner) and an elementary school music teacher; married Linda Gail Aldridge; children: Eric Sean, Wyatt Parson. *Education:* Pittsburg State University, B.A., 1971; completed executive-development programs at Pennsylvania State University and Columbia University.

Addresses: *Office*—Wal-Mart Stores Inc., 702 SW 8th St., Bentonville, AR 72716-8611.

Career

Employed by McNally's (a tire-mold manufacturer), 1970s; terminal manager, Yellow Freight System, 1977-79; employed by Queen City Warehouse, Springfield, MO, 1979; assistant director, transportation department, Wal-Mart, 1979; director of transportation, vice president of transportation, vice president of distribution, senior vice president of logistics, Wal-Mart, 1980s through early 1990s; executive vice president of logistics, Wal-Mart, 1993-95; executive vice president of merchandising, Wal-Mart, 1995-98; chief executive of Wal-Mart Stores Division, 1998-99; chief operating officer and vice chairman, Wal-Mart, 1999-2000; president and chief executive officer, Wal-Mart, 2000—.

Sidelights

Someone meeting H. Lee Scott, Jr. in person might be surprised to know that he was the chief executive officer (CEO) of Wal-Mart, the largest com-

Richard Sheinwald/Bloomberg News/Landov

pany in the world. Not only does Scott have an unassuming demeanor and folksy manner of speech, he appears at local Wal-Marts, unannounced, once every week, just to touch base with associates who work on the floor and make sure that the company is running the way it should in person as well as on paper.

Born on March 14, 1949, in Joplin, Missouri, Scott grew up in Baxter Springs, Kansas, with two brothers. His father owned a gas station and his mother taught music at an elementary school. He was active in both music and sports during his school career, and attended Pittsburg State University in Pittsburg, Kansas, for his undergraduate degree. He met his wife Linda during college and, in order to pay for both college and executive development courses at Pennsylvania State University and Columbia, they lived in a rented trailer, raising their son. "I worked at McNally's [a tire-mold manufacturer] from about 3:30 p.m. to midnight, and studied between midnight and 2 a.m.," Scott told Paul Harris of the London *Observer*. "At the time, it didn't seem difficult, it just seemed cold, because the heater in the trailer didn't work."

Despite his education, Scott had trouble finding a position in his field. He applied at the trucking company Yellow Freight System, but was turned down for a job until a friend intervened. Once employed, Scott quickly climbed into a management position, showing his skill at negotiation and collection of outstanding bills. It was in this position that he first encountered David Glass, former CEO of Wal-Mart, who, at the time, was head of finance. Scott tried to collect an outstanding $7,000 Yellow Freight System was owed; Glass denied the claim and refused to pay. But Scott's handling of the interaction so impressed Glass that he offered Scott a job. "I'm not the smartest guy that's ever been in your office, but I'm not going to leave the fastest-growing trucking company in America to go to work for a company that can't pay a $7,000 bill," Scott remembered telling Glass, recalling their conversation in an interview with *BusinessWeek*'s Wendy Zellner.

Though he had claimed loyalty to his position, Scott left Yellow Freight System to work for Queen City Warehouse in Springfield, Missouri, in 1979. Offered the position of assistant director in the transportation department of Wal-Mart in 1979, Scott accepted, beginning his long career inside the company. Though he thought he would be the head of the department, upon his arrival, he discovered that the person he had been told he was replacing had not yet left the company, and Glass asked him to work as the second in command. Showing a lack of ego that has been notable throughout his career at Wal-Mart, Scott acquiesced, and waited to move up into the position until it was right for the company.

The beginning of his career was off to a rocky start, however. He was a stickler for the rules, and became known as extremely stern and, at the time, inflexible. When the truckers under him committed infractions, he wrote a letter to all of the truck drivers on staff, threatening to fire those whose performance was hindered. This alienated the workers under him who followed the rules, and they approached Sam Walton, founder of Wal-Mart, asking that Scott be fired. Instead, Walton encouraged Scott to open his door and listen to the workers individually. These instructions humbled Scott and he learned part of the culture that Walton was trying to embrace. "You couldn't be around Sam Walton and not fully understand the culture of the company," Joseph S. Hardin Jr., a former Wal-Mart executive who is now the CEO of Kinko's Inc., told *BusinessWeek*. "That's one of the things that has helped Lee so much."

The lesson served Scott well, and he was promoted several times in the next few years, moving into leadership positions inside transportation, distribution, and logistics. He worked with distributors to develop innovative technology, including the uni-

versal barcode that allows retailers to track their merchandise at all stages of the distribution process. In 1995, he was assigned to merchandising, an area outside his expertise, because the company was lagging and wanted new ideas on how to promote itself. Using the same techniques he had developed in logistics, Scott listened to vendors and distributors to develop a way to grow sales. From slashing inventory to changing displays and presentation, Scott's efforts made a big impact on Wal-Mart, and, in 1998, three years after becoming head of merchandising, Scott was promoted to CEO of the Wal-Mart Stores Division.

The appointment to CEO of Wal-Mart Stores was a solid indication that Scott would be chosen as then-CEO Glass's successor. "It's his to lose," Glass commented in *BusinessWeek* in 1999. Walter Loeb of Loeb Associates consultants noted of the promotion in a 1998 article in *WWD*, "[W]ithin the past year he has risen because of his business leadership as well as the capabilities he has developed as a merchant." Loeb, a year later, said in the same periodical, "[Scott] is one of the most important, dynamic people Wal-Mart has." Scott's appointment was also notable given the number of competitors, including Kmart and Saks Fifth Avenue, that hired outsiders into key positions that same year, rather than hiring from within. In 2000, the predictions were fulfilled as Glass retired, promoting Scott to head of the company. He had big dreams for the company, always hoping for improvement no matter what the sales increases looked like. "If you consider the workers inside this company, and if we could accelerate our improvement, we could really be a successful company some day," he said in *WWD*. "I mean that."

Scott's years at the top have not been easy as he has faced some of the biggest challenges the retailer has encountered since its founding. After the United States government, Wal-Mart was, as of 2004, the most-sued entity in the world. In 2004, current and former female employees, numbering approximately 1.6 million, filed a class-action law suit accusing the company of sex-discrimination. Wal-Mart has been criticized for using foreign labor dependant on sweatshops, has been called anti-union, and has been accused of paying unfair wages with poor health-care benefits. As late as 2007, statements from activist groups including the Service Employees International Union, came down on Wal-Mart's policies: "No one, in good conscience or without a real commitment from Wal-Mart to make substantive changes, could look the other way and ignore the awful fact that Wal-Mart still fails to provide company health care to [more than] half of its employees," read a statement by the union-run Web site, WakeUpWalMart.com, reprinted in the *New York Times.*

Even before becoming the CEO, Scott made efforts to combat criticism of the company, meeting with politicians and engaging in conversations, as well as putting forward a positive image in the media. "For the most part [I was] listening," he said of his lunches with politicians during the Clinton administration in *BusinessWeek.* "I already know what I think. I want to hear what they think." Scott also made diversity a priority in hiring, given equally qualified applicants, and made his own salary dependent upon meeting diversity goals. In response to criticism about environmental concerns, Scott researched ways that Wal-Mart could become more environmentally friendly and still save money. He increased the efforts of the company to communicate with the public, launching a Web site to answer questions and making appearances on television shows. Commenting in *USA Today*, Scott noted that he wanted to combat Wal-Mart's negative reputation and address concerns of wealthy individuals who neither worked at nor shopped at his stores. "One of the things that strikes me is so many of the critics are people whose lifestyle doesn't change when the price of fuel changes," he said. "In some ways, people forget about average working people, and how they live their lives." His hopes with the public relations campaign was to give associates at Wal-Mart back some of their pride in their work.

Scott has long viewed himself as part of the team, going so far as to refuse to pose for *Fortune* magazine's 2003 Most Admired Company cover, as he felt it would give him too much credit for the company's success. In order to set a good example for his employees, he sold his BMW in favor of a Volkswagon Bug, and makes far less in salary than CEOs of comparable companies. In keeping with Walton's open door policy, Scott launched an employee Web site, Lee's Garage, where employees can ask questions ranging from local to company-wide concerns. As for his own goals, senior vice president of corporate affairs Jay Allen told *Supermarket News*, "He's always answered the same way, that when he walks out the door, he wants to know if Sam Walton were standing there that he'd say, 'You did a good job.'"

Sources

BusinessWeek, November 15, 1999, p. 84; January 14, 2002, p. 71; October 3, 2005, p. 94; April 16, 2007, p. 12.

Daily News Record, July 12, 2004, p. 4.

New York Times, February 17, 2006, p. C1; February 7, 2007, p. C2; April 20, 2007, p. C5.

Observer (London, England) September 12, 2004, p. 27.

Supermarket News, July 21, 2003, p. 22; June 6, 2005, p. 28.

Time, November 1, 2004, p. 8.

USA Today, January 13, 2005, p. 1B; January 13, 2005, p. 5B.

WWD, January 20, 1998, pp. 2(2); January 11, 1999, p. 2; May 22, 2002, p. 2; July 26, 2007, p. 12.

—*Alana Joli Abbott*

Kathleen Sebelius

Governor of Kansas

Born Kathleen Gilligan, May 15, 1948, in Cincinnati, OH; daughter of John J. and Mary K. (Dixon) Gilligan; married Keith Gary Sebelius (an attorney and judge), 1974; children: Edward Keith, John McCall. *Education:* Trinity Washington University, B.A., 1970; University of Kansas, M.P.A., 1977.

Addresses: *Office*—Office of the Governor, State Capitol, 300 SW 10th Ave., Ste. 212S, Topeka, KS 66612-1590.

Career

Director of planning, Center for Community Justice, Washington, DC, 1971-74; special assistant, Kansas Department of Corrections, 1975-78; executive director, Kansas Trial Lawyers Association, 1978-86; elected to the Kansas State House of Representatives, 1986, 1988, 1990, 1992; elected insurance commissioner, State of Kansas, 1994, 1998; elected governor of Kansas, 2002, reelected, 2006. Also elected president of the National Association of Insurance Commissioners, 2001, and chair of the Democratic Governors Association, 2007.

Awards: Public Official of the Year, Governing Magazine, 2001.

Sidelights

In 2002, Kansas Democrat Kathleen Sebelius won election as governor of Kansas, marking a major shift in the politics of what had been an unassail-ably Republican state. She was reelected by a landslide four years later, and, in the interim, advanced to a position of national prominence in the Democratic Party. During the 2008 campaign season, she was often asked what her party needed to do to win over undecided voters, especially in the race for the White House. "There is clearly a pathway to putting together a coalition in each of our states where people will vote for a Democrat," Sebelius told John Powers and Rebecca Johnson, both of whom profiled her for the February 2008 issue of *Vogue.* "But it has to get beyond party identification. It has to do with leadership and vision and values identification. You don't get up and say, 'I'm a Democrat, and I support X, Y, and Z.' You say, 'I'm an American.'"

Sebelius was born on May 15, 1948, in Cincinnati, Ohio. Her father, John J. Gilligan, served as governor of Ohio in the 1970s, making them the only father-daughter set of governors in U.S. history. She was one of four children in a Roman Catholic family, all of whom were schooled in national and local affairs at an early age. "My father had a habit of reading the paper to us in the morning, which frankly drove all of us stark raving mad," Sebelius recalled in an interview with *Cincinnati Post* writer

Michael Collins. "But he was very interested in issues and current events and felt that it was important for us to follow and know something about them."

For much of her childhood, Sebelius' father served on the Cincinnati City Council, and in 1964, when she was 16 and a junior at the all-female, Roman Catholic Summit Country Day School in the city, he was elected to Congress. He served two years in Washington, and in 1970, was elected governor of Ohio. That same year, Sebelius graduated from Trinity Washington University in Washington, D.C., another single-sex Roman Catholic institution. Located in one of the city's less prestigious neighborhoods, the school helped shape Sebelius' future political career as much as her father's achievements had. She played on the basketball team and held several internships as part of her political science degree work, including one "at a school on North Capitol Street and we used to do basketball clinics with the kids," she told Elizabeth Palmer, a writer for the school's alumni magazine. "I think there was a sense at Trinity, living in northeast Washington, that you were very much a part of that community and to open your eyes and get involved was a message that a lot of people gave us."

Sebelius' father lost his 1974 gubernatorial reelection bid, but not before the Ohio governor's mansion in Columbus hosted her wedding to Keith Gary Sebelius, whom she had met during her years at Trinity. Known by his middle name to distinguish him from his prominent father, Gary Sebelius was a Georgetown University law student who hailed from western Kansas, which his father Keith Sebelius represented in the U.S. House of Representatives from 1969 to 1981. The elder Sebelius took over the seat vacated by another prominent Kansas Republican, U.S. Senator Bob Dole.

Prior to her 1974 marriage, Sebelius worked in Washington for three years as the director of planning for the Center for Community Justice, and following her wedding, moved to Kansas where her husband began his law practice. She enrolled at the University of Kansas to earn a master's degree in public administration while also working for the state department of corrections. In 1978, she became executive director of the Kansas Trial Lawyers Association, a lobbying group, and her involvement in the state's Democratic Party organization eventually led to a concerted effort to draft her as a candidate for office. She had the qualifications and the commitment to do so, but as she noted in the *Cincinnati*

Post interview, she also possessed an extraordinarily valuable asset. "For Kansas Democrats, having a Democrat show up on the scene whose last name was Sebelius was sort of delicious," she told Collins.

In 1986, Sebelius won election to the Kansas State House of Representatives from the district that included her historic Potwin neighborhood of Topeka, the state capital. She had two small sons at the time, ages two and five, and the three-month legislative sessions offered her the opportunity to have a meaningful job that did not intrude too seriously on her family's schedule. She was reelected three times, and in 1994, decided to make her first bid for statewide office as insurance commissioner. This could be considered a risky move for someone with future political aspirations, because once Sebelius took office she had to please two constituencies: the powerful insurance industry and consumers. Despite that, Sebelius overhauled the state regulatory agency that oversaw the industry, ridding it of some of its long-entrenched rules and making it a more consumer-oriented entity.

Sebelius won election as the state's newest insurance commissioner, an office established in 1871. She was the first Democrat to hold the office in more than 100 years, a reflection of Kansas' long history as a staunchly Republican state. In addition to producing a number of notable Republicans who moved to the national political stage, such as Dole—who made an unsuccessful run for the White House in 1996—and President Dwight D. Eisenhower, Kansas was also the subject of a 2004 book, *What's the Matter with Kansas? How Conservatives Won the Heart of America,* in which journalist Thomas Frank examined the shift in Republican Party politics over the past 20 years. A state like Kansas, Frank argued, had suffered greatly under Republican economic policies in the last two decades of the twentieth century, yet continued to be an overwhelmingly "red" state, the informal political tag given to Republican states to distinguish them from the more socially liberal—and often more prosperous—"blue" states of the East and West coasts. GOP strategists, Frank argues, won over formerly Democratic voters by fomenting a cultural war over social issues like women's reproductive rights and school prayer.

Kansas statehood dated back to 1861, just a few months before the start of the U.S. Civil War. That conflict's prevailing issue, slavery, had played out in the state in the prior decade to such a degree that it was known as "Bleeding Kansas," as pro-slavery and abolitionist settlers rushed there to establish it as either a free state or a slave state and engaged in violent clashes with one another. In the end, the abolitionists won out, and the party founded on the abolition of slavery, the Republican Party, would dominate state politics for the next 140 years. By the 1990s, however, the cultural wars fomented by national GOP strategists had effectively divided the state's Republican Party into moderates and their more extremist counterparts.

This division played a crucial role in Sebelius' victory in the 2002 Kansas governor's race. Republicans of a more conservative Christian outlook objected to Sebelius' pro-choice views on abortion, while moderates distanced themselves from their fellow GOP lawmakers and in a few cases even switched party allegiance. This was the case with Sebelius' running mate for lieutenant governor, John Moore, a former aviation executive. Their ticket won with 53 percent of the vote, though the Republican challenger and the more conservative wing of the party "would have liked it to be issue-by-issue— you know, let's make this a divisive conversation," she told Powers in the *Vogue* interview. "There were attempts to say I was soft on crime, I was too liberal, I was this, I was that."

Sebelius was not the first female Democrat to be elected governor of Kansas—that honor went to Joan Finney, who served from 1991 to 1995. Sebelius did, however, earn a unique place in U.S. history thanks to her father, when they became the first father-daughter pair of governors in the annals of American politics. John Gilligan was 81 years old at the time of her electoral victory and told Collins in the *Cincinnati Post* article that he was "enormously impressed by the way she did it. I'm really glad I never had to run against her."

Sebelius' main challenge was a looming fiscal crisis tied to two separate issues: the first was an estimated of budget deficit of $1.1 billion, which was already problematic before the Kansas Supreme Court ordered that the state needed to provide more public-school funding to the tune of $150 million a year. To find the funds, Sebelius created BEST, or budget efficiency savings teams, in the spring of 2003, which went to work over the next several months looking for ways to cut costs. Under Sebelius' orders, they renegotiated contracts for scores of products that the state purchased on a regular basis, from paper-towel dispensers to printer toner cartridges, sold unused vehicles, and ordered thermostats adjusted in all government buildings to save on energy costs.

Sebelius also tried to build bridges and win support from a Republican-dominated state legislature by appointing Republicans to her cabinet. Her success after barely a year on the job was so impressive that her name even began to come up as a potential running mate for John Kerry, the Democratic hopeful for the White House in 2004. In 2005, *Time* magazine named her of the nation's top five governors, and she was reelected to a second term a year later with a stunning 58 percent of the vote. Statistics for that same year showed that among Kansas's 1.6 million voters, 46 percent were registered Republicans and just 27 percent were registered as Democrats. Sebelius's second win even prompted a *New York Times* editorial that bore the headline "What's Right with Kansas," a nod to Frank's book title. Citing her victory and other electoral wins in the state by either moderate Republican candidates or those who had switched party allegiance to Democrat, the newspaper's editorial writers termed it a "major shift in the nation's heartland. Kansas—lately considered the reddest of red states—emerged from the election as a bastion of moderation."

Fellow Democratic state executives elected Sebelius to chair the Democratic Governors Association (DGA) for 2007. During her tenure she led the DGA on an impressive fundraising campaign that proved vital to the 2008 national elections. That year's race for the Democratic Party presidential nomination was bitterly fought between Illinois senator Barack Obama and New York senator Hillary Clinton, and political analysts dismissed the idea that either would select a female running mate. Sebelius' name, however, was often mentioned as a potential cabinet nominee should a Democrat return to the White House in 2009. Limited to two terms as Kansas governor, she was also rumored to have an eye on one of Kansas' two seats in the U.S. Senate in 2010.

Sebelius' two sons are adults and have actively participated in her campaigns, making them the third generation of political activists on both sides of their family tree. Her husband, a federal judge, preferred the term "First Dude" as opposed to "First Gentleman," used in reference to the husbands of female governors, and good-naturedly fulfills official duties that include supervising the annual Easter egg hunt at the governor's mansion. Her father finally retired from public office in 2007 at the age of 86 after serving two terms on the Cincinnati Board of Education. "My father took huge political risks," she told *Vogue* late in 2007. "He won some elections and he lost some elections. But I learned that losing is not the end of the world. You have to be willing to fight for something and risk taking the loss."

Sources

Periodicals

American Prospect, March 2008, p. 18.

Cincinnati Post, December 14, 2002, p. A1; January 30, 2007, p. A1.

New York Times, November 15, 2006; May 9, 2007.

Time, November 21, 2005, p. 36.

USA Today, June 6, 2006. p. 11A.

Vogue, February 2008, p. 244.

Wichita Eagle (Wichita, KS), October 22, 2006.

Online

"Profile: Kathleen Sebelius '70, Governor of Kansas," Trinity Washington University Web site, http://www.trinitydc.edu/admissions/profiles/profile_sebelius.php (May 11, 2008).

—*Carol Brennan*

Danny Seo

Environmentalist, television host, and author

Born April 22, 1977 in Pennsylvania; son of an anesthesiologist and a homemaker.

Addresses: *Home*—Bucks County, PA. *Office*—Lime TV, c/o GAIAM, 350 Madison Ave., 17th Fl., New York, NY 10017.

Career

Founded the activist group Earth 2000, 1989; published first book, *Generation React: Activism for Beginners,* 1997; writer for *Vegetarian Times,* c. 1998-2002; columnist for *Organic Style* magazine, 2001-05, and *Country Home* magazine, 2006—; host of *Simply Green With Danny Seo* on Lime TV, 2006—.

Sidelights

Danny Seo promotes environmentally friendly home-décor products and clothing via his growing media empire. The author of several how-to books on using building and design materials that are either less chemically toxic than their standard counterparts or come from renewable-source materials, Seo also hosts a series for Lime TV, the Internet lifestyle network. "There's a stereotype that the average American is too lazy to be socially responsible, but I don't believe it," he told Macon Morehouse in *People.* "I think they just don't know how to get started."

Seo was born on April 22, 1977, which is also Earth Day. His parents were Korean immigrants who raised their three children in Reading, Pennsylvania.

Jon Kopaloff/Getty Images

As the youngest son of an anesthesiologist-father, Seo sensed pressure to succeed from an early age in his achievement-oriented family. He first became interested in social issues in 1989, when he stayed up late to watch an episode of the *Morton Downey Jr. Show,* whose guest that night was Ingrid Newkirk, president of People for the Ethical Treatment of Animals (PETA). When Seo heard Newkirk explain how chickens are raised on factory farms for American dinner tables, he was sickened and announced the following day—his 12th birthday—that he was now a vegetarian.

Inspired by the Earth Day activities, Seo went on to found the group Earth 2000, whose first members were seven of his closest friends. "At 12, I was naive enough to think the world was coming to an end but idealistic enough to think, 'Perhaps I can change that,'" he wrote in *Career World.* "I figured within eleven years, I could change the world. My goal was to save the planet by the year 2000." Earth 2000's first official action was a tree-planting event, but the youth group eventually swelled to 20,000 members and brought its founder acclaim as a savvy teenage activist. Eschewing college, Seo moved to Washington, D.C., and launched a series of new ventures.

Seo's youthful energy landed him a $33,000 publishing deal, and he shared tips on staging protests and dealing with the media in his first book, *Generation React: Activism for Beginners,* which appeared in 1998. That same year, his increasing public profile landed him on *People* magazine's annual ranking of the "50 Most Beautiful People." He was also invited to participate in a challenge by television talk-show host Oprah Winfrey, and succeeded in raising $30,000 in 30 days to build a Habitat for Humanity house. He declined to appear at the ribbon-cutting ceremony to meet the new homeowners, explaining to *Seattle Times* journalist Ann Gerhart that such staged events unnerve him. The beneficiaries "shouldn't have to show up and give praise.... The whole point of being selfless is not to get something in return. I know that's bizarre to a lot of people—a self-improvement guru telling them to be more selfless and you'll be a better person."

Seo's next book, *Heaven on Earth: 15-Minute Miracles to Change the World,* was published in 1999. He also began to develop his theory of "Conscious Style," a term that he trademarked. It centered on the idea that consumers could make choices that were both aesthetically cutting-edge but also earth-friendly, and he elaborated this theory in more detail in a 2001 book, *Conscious Style Home: Eco-Friendly Living for the 21st Century.* Its pages chronicled the renovation project he undertook at his parents' Pennsylvania home to rid it of toxic materials used in most residential construction. "My job isn't to convince you to protect the environment," Seo explained in an interview with *USA Today* writer Marco R. della Cava. "I'm also not here to tell you this is cool. But I am here to tell you that it's just an easier way to live, and it helps the environment."

By 2003, Seo was living in New York City and serving as editor-at-large for *Organic Style* magazine, writing its "Green Buzz" column that featured celebrities who were committed to following an environmentally friendly lifestyle. A public-relations expert, Seo was determined to bring his ideas to a wider audience, and knew that celebrities were an excellent medium for his message. One year, he was attending the Sundance Film Festival and wore an anti-fur t-shirt with the slogan, "Club Sandwiches, Not Seals." Paris Hilton was so intrigued by it that he gave her one, and after she was photographed wearing it, the retailer Abercrombie & Fitch began selling the line. "At the end of the day, if a celebrity can bring something into the mainstream as unsexy as solar electricity or electric cars, I don't see what the harm is," he told Michael Learmonth in *Folio.* "It can only help the cause."

Seo launched a decorating venture that sourced nontoxic paints and wood from renewable sources. He also participated in an annual *W* magazine event in which celebrities donate their goodie-bag freebies—a generous perk for the famous and already-rich—to a yard sale whose proceeds went to a specific charity every year. Oddly, Seo himself was a minor celebrity in South Korea thanks in part to his appearance in television commercials for Samsung. For one spot that aired during the 2002 World Cup soccer tournament, Seo convinced Samsung to make a donation to an organization that was battling human consumption of dog meat in South Korea. With that largesse, the organization was able to open a dog adoption shelter, which was first of its kind in the country.

Seo renovated his own Pennsylvania property, an old farmhouse in Bucks County. He also delivered tips for environmentally responsible living on his series for Lime TV, *Simply Green With Danny Seo.* Lime TV began as a cable channel aimed at healthy and earth-friendly living, and switched to Internet-only content in early 2007. In interviews, Seo often claims that his biggest single influence is "MacGyver." He told *New York Times* journalist Julia Szabo that the fictional hero of the 1980s television drama "is a huge influence on everything I do. MacGyver would be in, say, a Turkish prison, and he'd go through his pockets and find a piece of gum and some lint, then use the rays of the sun through his cell window to make a bomb. That's what I like: being creative and thinking outside the box."

Selected writings

Generation React: Activism for Beginners, Braille International, 1998.
Heaven on Earth: 15-Minute Miracles to Change the World, Atria, 1999.
Be the Difference: A Beginner's Guide to Changing the World, New Society Publishers, 2001.
Conscious Style Home: Eco-Friendly Living for the 21st Century, St. Martin's Press, 2001.
Simply Green Parties: Simple and resourceful ideas for throwing the perfect celebration, event, or get-together, Collins, 2006.
Simply Green Giving: Create Beautiful and Organic Wrappings, Tags, and Gifts from Everyday Materials, Collins, 2006.

Sources

Career World, April-May 2006, p. 17.
Financial Times, October 15, 2005, p. 2.
Folio, September 1, 2003.
New York Times, August 30, 2001.
People, October 11, 1999, p. 93.
Publishers Weekly, July 31, 2006, p. 4.

Seattle Times, September 19, 1999, p. L2.

Sunday Times (London, England), January 26, 2003, p. 12.

USA Today, August 31, 2004, p. 1D; October 27, 2006, p. 5D.

—Carol Brennan

Michele Serros

Author

Photograph by Marie Gregorio-Ouiedo. Courtesy of Michele Serros.

Born c. 1967, in Oxnard, CA; daughter of Beatrice Serros; married Gene Trautman (a drummer; divorced). *Education:* Santa Monica City College, A.A.; University of California, B.A. (with honors), 1996.

Addresses: *Office*—c/o Simon Pulse Publicity Department, Simon & Schuster, 1230 Avenue of the Americas, New York, NY 10020.

Career

Published first book, *Chicana Falsa, and Other Stories of Death, Identity, and Oxnard,* 1994; road poet for Lollapalooza, 1994; writer for *The George Lopez Show,* ABC, 2002. Also worked as a commentator for *Morning Edition* and host of *Along for the Ride,* both on National Public Radio; was a freelancer for *Latino USA;* taught poetry at inner-city schools and women's prisons.

Awards: Latino Spirit Award, California Latino Legislative Caucus.

Sidelights

Chicana author Michele Serros uses humor and wit to chronicle her experiences as a brown-skinned woman in the United States. Beginning with her acclaimed collection, *Chicana Falsa, and Other Stories of Death, Identity, and Oxnard,* which was written while she was still a college student,

Serros reluctantly embraced her position as a Hispanic role model. Serros also used her writing skills on radio and television productions.

Born around 1967 in Oxnard, California, Serros is a fourth-generation Mexican American who was discouraged from learning Spanish by her parents. She was raised in Oxnard, and her parents were both hard workers who held two jobs each to support their family. Though her mother, Beatrice, had unfulfilled artistic ambitions, she and her husband found their role models on television.

Serros told the *Dallas Morning News'* Beatriz Terrazas, "They wanted to make a home as close to *The Brady Bunch* as possible for us. Every payday my mom would buy Kentucky Fried Chicken and we would wheel the TV out to the patio to watch *The Brady Bunch.* That was the life we wanted."

Interested in books and writing since her youth, young Serros believed that all writers were men from the East Coast chronicling the lives of well-off people who lived in big cities. On her sister's suggestion, Serros considered adopting an appropriate pseudonym, Michael Hill. Yet her favorite authors were Judy Blume, Beverly Cleary, and Louise

Fitzhugh. Over time, she learned she did not need to change her name to be accepted as a writer, and she could be herself to write. Serros moved to Los Angeles when she was 19 years old to explore the writing scene there and go to college, first at Santa Monica City College.

Triggered by the death of her mother in 1991 and a class at Santa Monica City College, Serros began to see she could be a published author, too. The class was on Mexican-American literature and featured far more Spanish-surnamed authors than she expected were out there. The experience led her to craft her poems, short stories, and vignettes into a short book.

In 1994, Serros was able to publish the collection, titled *Chicana Falsa, and Other Stories of Death, Identity, and Oxnard.* The original publisher, Lalo Press, went out of business soon after the book came out, and Serros herself hocked the books out of her trunk and garage for several years. Though the volume lacked the usual ISBN (Industry Standard Book Number), she was able to convince a few book stores to carry it.

Despite this setback, Serros found an audience for the book, which was eventually added to high school and college curriculums throughout the United States over the next few years. During this time, Serros completed her degree with honors from the University of California at Los Angeles in 1996. While she was a student there, professors began using her book in their classes. Fellow students would track her down to help with their assignments on it.

A new edition of *Chicana Falsa, and Other Stories of Death, Identity, and Oxnard* was published in 1998 by Riverhead Press. The collection struck a chord with critics who praised it for its racial honesty, wisdom, and wit. Some critics especially singled out the short story, "Attention Shoppers," which uses the frozen food section at an Oxnard grocery story to illustrate racist concepts through frozen vegetables. The poems, too, were acknowledged for their powerful statements on racial attitudes and language, primarily concerning Hispanic Americans. In addition, universal themes explored such issues as conformity, identity, and loneliness.

Reviewing the new edition in the *San Francisco Chronicle,* Patricia Holt wrote, "Michele Serros brings a rare authority and confidence to these pages. Like Sandra Cisneros, Gary Soto, Ana Castillo, and others, she has a gift for the conversational aesthetic." Along similar lines, Christine Gra-

nados of the *Austin American-Statesman* commented, "Serros is one of the first Mexican-American writers since Dagoberto Gilb to capture the irony and, more important, the humor in the culture. She has been described as a spoken-word artist, writer, and poet, but I consider her a comedian."

Yet Serros was also told her writing in the book was not as Mexican-American as it should be. She informed Cheryl Klein of the *University Wire,* "It didn't capture that quote-unquote 'essence' of Chicano lit. I'm fourth-generation Mexican. [My book has] references that aren't familiar to them. There's a lot of pop culture references. They might see it as very white-washed."

Two years later, Serros published a second collection of mostly stories and vignettes, *How to Be a Chicana Role Model.* Influenced by her own experiences as a writer who is now expected to be a role model, she wrote about people's expectations of her and the effect these had on her life. The racism Serros encountered also informed the text. Regrettably, some academics assumed all Latina writers were the same, while others ignored her or regarded her as a domestic worker. Serros emphasized that the book was fiction, but she also admitted most of the incidents actually happened to her. She added embellishments to the events, however.

Given that her dark sense of humor was still on display, critics generally embraced *How to Be a Chicana Role Model. Publishers Weekly* wrote, "Though this outing lacks some of the fizz of *Chicana Falsa,* Serros turns out a funny yet poignant defense of her craft." The book became a bestseller in certain markets, such as Los Angeles.

While working as an author, Serros also made a living with words in other venues. By the early 2000s, she had worked for National Public Radio as a commentator for *Morning Edition* and host of *Along for the Ride.* After living in New York City for several years, Serros returned to the West Coast to take a job writing for the ABC situation comedy, *The George Lopez Show.*

Serros was happy to be writing for a show that emphasized a middle-class Hispanic family. She told Cecilia M. Gomez-Gonzalez of the *Press Enterprise,* "Some of the other Latino programs were so stereotypical. There's no way I would have worked on any of those. I could not have been prouder to work on this. This show, it's about a funny family who have a suburban lifestyle and, hey, they happen to be Latino."

After her stint on *The George Lopez Show* ended, Serros returned to New York City and again focused on her writing. She also continued to freelance for National Public Radio as well as Latino USA. In 2006, she published her first novel, a young adult work titled *Honey Blonde Chica.*

The novel focuses on upper-class Hispanic Evie Gomez, who has an identity crisis despite her life of wealth and privilege. She and her teen clique friends face a number of adolescent problems that the author explores in a tone similar to popular *Gossip Girl* books. Serros told Maricella Miranda of the *St. Paul Pioneer Press,* "I liked the idea of writing about well-to-do Latinos.... I was sort of getting tired of the poor Mexican."

For her next project, Serros planned on writing a novel for an adult audience. No matter what she wrote, Serros wanted to help her audience. She told Terrazas of *Dallas Morning News,* "When I was younger, books allowed not only an escape for me but a chance to use my imagination—more so than a TV show or a movie. There was a lot of chaos in my home. My parents would fight a lot. In school I had the typical problems wanting to be accepted ... every time I opened a book I had a whole new set of friends. I would like to give this gift of escape to someone else."

Selected writings

Story and poetry collections

Chicana Falsa, and Other Stories of Death, Identity, and Oxnard, Lalo Press, 1994; new ed., Riverhead Books, 1998.

How to Be a Chicana Role Model, Riverhead Books, 2000.

Novels

Honey Blonde Chica, Simon Pulse, 2006.

Sources

Periodicals

Austin American-Statesman (TX), June 7, 1998, p. D6.
Dallas Morning News, August 15, 2000.
Press Enterprise (Riverside, CA), October 8, 2002, p. E6.
Publishers Weekly, June 19, 2000, p. 61.
San Antonio Express-News (TX), July 25, 2000, p. 1D.
San Diego Union-Tribune, August 24, 2000, p. E1.
San Francisco Chronicle, June 3, 1998, p. E3.
School Library Journal, August 2006, p. 128.
St. Paul Pioneer Press (MN), October 25, 2007.
University Wire, August 24, 1998.
Whittier Daily News (CA), April 24, 2005.

Online

Contemporary Authors Online, Thomson Gale, 2007.

—A. Petruso

Simran Sethi

Marsaili McGrath/Getty Images for Sundance

Television producer and journalist

Born Preti Simran Sethi, c. 1971; daughter of Hema Sethi (a restaurant owner). *Education:* Smith College, B.A., 1992; graduate studies at Università degli Studi di Urbino, 1992; Presidio School of Management, M.B.A., 2005.

Addresses: *Office*—Treehugger c/o Jessica Root, 320 13th St., Brooklyn, NY 11215.

Career

Segment producer, MTV, New York, NY, 1993-94; news anchor and producer, MTV Asia, Singapore, 1994-96; co-creator of news division, senior news correspondent, and senior producer, MTV India, Bombay, India, 1996-98; founder and president, SHE TV, 1998-99; volunteer and intern manager, New York Open Center, 1999-2000; communications director, Pangeea, 2000; host, writer, and anchor for *Daily Remix*, Oxygen Media, 2000-01; host and writer, *Ethical Markets*, 2003-06; TreeHugger.com, executive director of TreeHuggerTV and TreeHugger Radio, 2006-07, then freelance host and writer of audio and video content, 2007—; ecology expert, *The EcoZone Project*, 2007—; co-host and writer, The Green, 2007—; freelance sustainability journalist, 2007—.

Awards: Vloggie Award for best green vlog for Treehugger.com, 2006; CableACE Award for *Hate Rock*; New York International Film and Television Award for *Help Not Wanted*; New York International Film and Television Award for *24 Hours in Rock and Roll*; New York International Film and Television Award for *Freaks, Nerds, and Weirdos*; Houston Worldfest Award for *Sex in the '90s*; Houston Worldfest Award for *Help Not Wanted*.

Sidelights

Producer and journalist Simran Sethi is a well-known expert and commentator on environmental and sustainability issues. Beginning her media career working for MTV News, she eventually moved toward social responsibility-related journalism. To that end, Sethi created the *Ethical Markets* television program and played a significant role in the audio and video ventures of TreeHugger. com. By 2007, Sethi was serving as a co-host for a block of environmental programming for the Sundance Channel. *Vanity Fair* wrote of Sethi, "In an era beset by apathy and cynicism, she exudes on-the-ball spunk and has an optimism so infectious you'll want to pick up a drum beside her."

Born around 1971 in Germany, Sethi moved to Winston-Salem, North Carolina, when she was six years old. There, her mother, Hema Sethi, co-owned Kababs Indian Bar and Grill. Sethi graduated from the local Mount Tabor High School, then left Winston-Salem to enter Smith College. Sethi eventually earned her B.A. in sociology and women's studies, graduating cum laude in 1992.

While still in college, Sethi was offered a job with MTV. Upon graduation and completion of some graduate work at Italy's Università degli Studi di Urbino in Italian culture, she accepted MTV's offer. She then began working as a segment producer for MTV News. Between 1993 and 1994, Sethi was involved in the production of documentaries for the network including *Hate Rock, Sex in the '90s,* and *Help Not Wanted.* All of these documentaries won awards for the network.

In 1994, Sethi headed to Asia to work for MTV's outlet there. For MTV Asia, based in Singapore, she worked as a producer and news anchor. Moving on to MTV India in 1996, she was the co-creator of that network's news division. While popular culture was the focus of much of what she did for MTV, Sethi had deeper awareness of issues in the world and incorporated them into her work whenever possible. Leaving MTV in 1998, Sethi founded her own production company, SHE TV. Through this company, she served as a consultant for the BBC and worked on projects in India.

By 1999, Sethi was again living in the United States, where she spent a year as a volunteer intern manager at New York Open Center. This non-profit was a large holistic healing center. In the spring of 2000, she began working as the communications director of Pangeea, handling communications strategies for volunteerism-related Web sites. Later that year, Sethi took a job with Oxygen Media as an anchor and writer for *Daily Remix,* a music program on the Oxygen network which ran until the fall of 2001.

Over the years, Sethi had become more interested in issues of sustainability. Explaining this evolution to Rebecca Roussell of the Raleigh, North Carolina *News & Observer,* Sethi said, "It was really looking at the idea of myself and looking at the kinds of stories in the media that I felt needed to be out there. And that was sort of the evolution of my work even at MTV. I was the one who always focused on the stories about HIV and AIDS, voter empowerment for young people, and the ways in which young adults were making a difference." To that end, Sethi also continued her education by entering the Presidio School of Management in 2003. She earned an M.B.A. in sustainable management there in 2005.

While an M.B.A. student, Sethi continued to work on television. She created and served as the host and writer of *Ethical Markets.* This show aired on digital cable, Lime TV, and various PBS markets across the United States beginning in 2003. *Ethical Markets* emphasized the positive actions and activities of socially and environmentally responsible people, businesses (both for-profit and non-profit), and government entities. Sethi's program touched on such topics as "green" building design, renewable energy sources like solar power and wind energy, and organic food. The show aired through December of 2006. In 2007, she co-authored a companion book to the series. Written with Hazel Henderson, *Ethical Markets: Growing the Green Economy* offered biographical sketches of leaders—both individuals and companies—active in the environmental movement.

By this time, Sethi was living in the heartland. In August of 2006, Sethi had moved to Lawrence, Kansas, because her boyfriend, Daniel Goldstein, began attending Kansas University. She had a new job as well, working as the television director and head of new media operations for the environmental Web site TreeHugger.com. As the executive director of TreeHuggerTV, she created video segments for the Web site and also appeared on camera as the anchor for some videos. While much of her work for the site focused on national issues, Sethi found some stories in Lawrence as well. For example, she did a segment about Local Burger, a burger place in the area which used sustainable resources.

Sethi also branched out into radio, working with Stacey Fox to produce a series about making environmental issues relevant. It was produced for *Eco Talk,* an Air America radio show. The resulting episodes also aired on TreeHugger.com, where Sethi was also in charge of radio operations and other audio content. Sethi created other radio podcasts as well for the Web site.

Sethi's work led to more media exposure. Late in 2006, she was featured on both Martha Stewart's show and *The Oprah Winfrey Show.* For the former, Sethi offered advice on how to incorporate environmental awareness into home life. For the latter, Sethi was featured in a segment about how to create an environmentally aware Christmas. By 2007, Sethi was working for TreeHugger.com on a freelance basis, and had another position offering environmental home advice. She served as the ecology expert for *The EcoZone Project.* On this syndicated home makeover series, green solutions were the focus of the rebuilding projects.

In 2007, Sethi also began serving as the co-host of The Green, a weekly programming block on the Sundance Channel which focused on environmental issues. This marked the first time an American network had regularly scheduled programming focused solely on the environment. Included in the block were the documentary series *Big Ideas for a Small Planet* and *Crude Awakening—The Oil Crash* as well as longer documentaries, profiles of people living an environmentally conscious lifestyle, and ideas for how viewers could do the same.

For Sethi, her environmental work was all-encompassing. She told Eliza Thomas of *Common Ground*, "I work really hard, and I care deeply about the work I do so it's not just 'oh, I just do that job and when I'm home I disconnect from it.' My work never ends because it flows through to my life."

Selected writings

Nonfiction

(With Hazel Henderson) *Ethical Markets: Growing the Green Economy*, Chelsea Green Publishing Company, 2007.

Sources

Periodicals

Baltimore Sun, April 16, 2007, p. 6C.
Journal-World (Lawrence, KS), October 3, 2006; December 1, 2006.
Library Journal Reviews, February 15, 2007, p. 128.
News & Observer (Raleigh, NC), July 3, 2005, p. E1.
U.S. Newswire, January 12, 2007.
Vanity Fair, May 2007, p. 240.
Winston-Salem Journal (Winston-Salem, NC), July 1, 2005, p. E7.

Online

"Conversations: Simran Sethi," *Common Ground,* http://commongroundmag.com/2007/3/simransethi.html (August 2, 2007).
"Simran Sethi," LinkedIn, http://www.linkedin.com/in/simransethi (August 2, 2007).

—A. Petruso

Lionel Shriver

Author and journalist

Born Margaret Ann Shriver, May 18, 1957, in Gastonia, NC; daughter of Donald W. (a Presbyterian minister and seminary president) and Peggy (an administrator for the National Council of Churches) Shriver; married Jeff Williams (a jazz drummer). *Education:* Columbia University, B.A., 1978, M.F.A., 1982.

Addresses: *Office*—c/o Author mail, 7th fl., HarperCollins Publishers, 10 E. 53rd St., New York, NY 10022.

Career

First novel, *The Female of the Species,* published by Farrar, Straus & Giroux, 1987. Instructor in English and writing at the college level; contributor to the *Wall Street Journal, Guardian, Daily Telegraph,* and *Independent.*

Awards: Orange Prize for Fiction, for *We Need to Talk about Kevin,* 2005.

Sidelights

Novelist Lionel Shriver divides her time between New York City and London, England, which became her adopted home in the late 1980s. For much of that decade and the next, Shriver produced several novels that earned terrific reviews but failed to catch on with the reading public. That changed in 2003 with the publication of *We Need to Talk about Kevin,* which won the prestigious Orange Prize for

Fiction in Britain two years later. Discussing her career trajectory with *New York Times* writer Sarah Lyall, Shriver said she was content with how things turned out in the end. "I paid my dues. I did not write a novel at 21 and it sells a million copies and everybody thinks I'm brilliant and I'm on TV," she reflected. "I'm glad. Looking back I didn't feel glad all those years. But if I was going to pick my own story, I might have picked this one."

Shriver's traditionally masculine first name is one she adopted herself as a teenager. Her given name is Margaret Ann, and she was born in May of 1957, in Gastonia, North Carolina, and spent a large part of her formative years in Raleigh, North Carolina. Her father, Donald, was a Presbyterian minister who moved his family to Atlanta, Georgia, in the early 1970s to take a job at Emory University. Shriver attended a progressive high school in Atlanta, whose courses permitted her creative-writing talents to flourish. These had become apparent as far back as her elementary school days, where early on she found herself "intoxicated by my capacity to use words," she told a writer for the *Independent,* a London newspaper. "When I was given assignments that had a creative element, I really went to town. I used to write ridiculously long—my stories would run to 30 pages."

The new high school in Atlanta offered independent study, and Shriver jumped at the chance to design her own learning project. Her first completed assignment she turned in was a treatise on overpopulation that stretched to 100 pages. She also took the Scholastic Aptitude Test early so that she could begin taking Russian-language classes at Emory; after graduating from high school she enrolled full-time at Emory at age 17 but then transferred to Barnard College in New York City, the liberal arts college for women affiliated with Columbia University. She earned her undergraduate degree in creative writing, a process she described in the *Independent* interview as "mostly workshops with a bunch of other people who probably couldn't write either, ripping each other's stories to pieces."

Shriver went on to earn her graduate degree from Columbia, too, in 1982, and then embarked on a years-long global jaunt that included stops in Kenya, Thailand, Israel, and Northern Ireland. Her first novel seemed to draw upon her experiences in far-flung lands and her stint at Columbia, where she studied under famed anthropologist Margaret Mead. Published in 1987, *The Female of the Species,* featured a well-known anthropologist, Gray Kaiser, as its protagonist. Kaiser, who gained fame earlier in her career with a study of a village in East Africa that, during World War II, was the site of a crash-landing by an American pilot; the locals were initially hostile, and so the pilot convinced them that he was a god. Kaiser is now nearing 60, lives with a fellow anthropologist but has a platonic relationship, and suddenly falls passionately in love with a new graduate student she is assigned to mentor. Shriver's debut was reviewed in *People* magazine by Ralph Novak, who called it a "terrific first novel.... Shriver's tale is about emotional neediness, about masochism, and it all too often seems all too true."

Subsequent novels by Shriver also earned favorable notices in *People* and other mainstream magazines, but failed to catch on with readers. The second book, *Checker and the Derailleurs,* featured a charismatic New York City rocker, while *The Bleeding Heart,* published in 1992, centered around an expatriate American living in Northern Ireland. Population-control strategies drove forward the plot of Shriver's 1994 novel *Game Control,* set among the international community in Kenya, and in *A Perfectly Good Family,* artist Corlis McCrea returns to the North Carolina mansion where she was raised after years abroad. She finds herself caught in the middle of a financial quandary between the other heirs—her diametrically opposite brothers and her late parents' pet cause, the American Civil Liberties Union. "Shriver sets up and controls this tense tri-

umvirate with admirable precision and a keen understanding of the hastily formed alliances and subtly accorded trade-offs involved in family exchanges," declared Alex Clark, a critic for the London *Guardian.* "Choice, Shriver underlines, is enslavement as well as liberation."

Shriver's sixth novel, *Double Fault,* appeared in 1997 and centered on Wilhemena (Willy) Novinsky, a professional tennis player in her twenties who is unwisely obsessed with her ranking in the sport. This gives her a necessary competitiveness, but plays havoc with her personal life when her new husband's star begins to rise to the very top of the sport. "Never completely comfortable with her competitiveness, Willy turns her rage against herself, and inevitably it splashes onto Eric," wrote *New York Times* book reviewer Michael Mewshaw. "She roots for his opponents, refuses to applaud his victories, cuts his strings, and even cracks his head open with a racquet.... Shriver shows in a masterstroke why character is fate and how sport reveals it."

Six years passed before Shriver's next work of fiction appeared in print. By then a denizen of London, she was fascinated with the spate of school shootings in the United States in the late 1990s, some of the most notorious ones committed by white male teens from seemingly happy middle-class families. She began writing a story from the perspective of the mother of a fictional school shooter, but the topic was incendiary enough—as were Shriver's hints about bad parenting—that the manuscript was turned down by dozens of publishers, and even Shriver's literary agent declined to represent it. Finally, in 2003 a British house, Serpent's Tail, published *We Need to Talk about Kevin,* and a New York City house, Counterpoint Press, issued its U.S. edition.

We Need to Talk about Kevin is told in flashback via letters written by Eva, an erudite publisher of travel guides who put aside her qualms about motherhood when she fell in love with her husband, Franklin. Their first child, Kevin, proved a difficult baby, unmanageable toddler, gloomy adolescent, and finally the boy who brings a cross-bow to school one day, takes several students and employees hostage, and kills them one by one. Eva's letters, written to Franklin a year after the incident, reveal her initial ambivalence about motherhood and her fear that this is what caused Kevin to turn out so badly. On the other hand, Eva realizes that she enjoyed a healthy and loving bond with Celia, their second child, whom she clearly adores—as much as Franklin once doted on Kevin.

It earned just a few cursory reviews from the *New York Times, Publishers Weekly,* and *Booklist,* but soon became a word-of-mouth hit—the first of Shriver's career. A journalist with the *New York Observer,* Philip Weiss, wrote that the book initially caught on among a small substrata of female fiction writers in New York City, who were intensely enthusiastic in recommending it to friends. One of them was Pearson Marx, who told Weiss that Shriver's book was a welcome antidote to the so-called "mommy lit" trend, "about women balancing home, children and husband, and it always has to end on an upbeat note and the women realize, blah blah blah.... Well, this book breaks through that piety, and it is being ignored and almost punished for doing so."

Shriver wrote *We Need to Talk about Kevin* when she was in her early 40s, and still struggling with the decision to have a child herself, Eventually she decided that she was not cut out for the role of mother, and in an interview with Suzy Hansen for Salon.com cited the visits that Eva makes to Kevin in prison part of what she described as "the burdens of parenthood: Oh my god, my kid can do anything—including not just doing things to other people, but doing things to you—and I'm expected to stay in there with them." Her novel enjoyed terrific sales in Britain, too, and was also honored with the 2005 Orange Prize for Fiction, awarded to a work of contemporary fiction by a female writer.

For her next work, Shriver resumed writing about the more prosaic topic of conventional relationships fraught with angst and miscommunication. *The Post-Birthday World,* published in 2007, centered on American children's book illustrator Irina McGovern, who shares a London home with her intellectual policy-analyst boyfriend Lawrence. Once a year, they dine out with an old friend of his, a professional snooker player named Ramsey, whose penchant for wild living marks him as the direct opposite of Lawrence. He is also somewhat famous in the pub sport, which is similar to billiards. Lawrence is out of town when the newly divorced Ramsey's birthday dinner looms, so Irina takes him out, and is shocked by both his attempt to seduce her and what seems to be her growing acquiescence.

After the first chapter, however, Shriver begins dual narratives—one in which Irina succumbs to Ramsay, and another in which her life with Lawrence remains undisturbed. "Lawrence is kind, abstemious, and seemingly reliable," wrote *New York Times* reviewer Michiko Kakutani—but also a bit of a prig. Ramsey, on the other hand, "is raffish and impulsive. But what Irina initially takes to be simple animal attraction soon turns into something more complicated and harder to dismiss."

For the first time in Shriver's two-decade-long literary career, *The Post-Birthday World* collected scores of positive reviews and even spent a couple of weeks on the *New York Times* best-seller list in the spring of 2007. "The well-worn fork-in-the-road concept could easily have yielded a sterile exercise," asserted *Entertainment Weekly*'s Jennifer Reese, "but Shriver, a brilliant and versatile writer, allows these competing stories to unfold organically, each a fully rounded drama, rich with irony, ambiguity, and unforeseeable human complications." Critiquing it for the *New Statesman,* Sophie Ratcliffe conceded that the alternating storylines might "sound gimmicky—which it isn't.... [T]he writing is continually engaging, the 1990s period detail rich, and the novel itself is a compelling take on the desire to have more than one opinion, or passion, at a time."

Once again, Shriver admitted that the origins of the plot had some echoes in her own life. She had been involved with a fellow writer for a number of years, who shared her passion for tennis, before meeting a jazz musician whom she eventually married. As she explained to Lynn Andriani in a *Publishers Weekly* interview, her dilemma was much like Irina's, but once she made her decision, "the other life in which I had made the opposite decision had a funny kind of reality to it. Even years later, there is a parallel universe in my head, of if I hadn't left, and what would that be like?"

Selected writings

Novels

The Female of the Species, Farrar, Straus, & Giroux (New York City), 1987.
Checker and the Derailleurs, self-illustrated, Farrar, Straus, & Giroux, 1988.
The Bleeding Heart, Farrar, Straus, & Giroux, 1990; published in Britain as *Ordinary Decent Criminals,* HarperCollins (London), 1992.
Game Control, Faber & Faber (London), 1994.
A Perfectly Good Family, Faber & Faber, 1996.
Double Fault, Doubleday (New York City), 1997.
We Need to Talk about Kevin, Counterpoint (New York City), 2003.
The Post-Birthday World, HarperCollins (New York City), 2007.

Sources

Periodicals

Bookseller, October 22, 2004, p. 25.
Entertainment Weekly, March 16, 2007, p. 71.
Guardian (London, England), March 29, 1996, p. 17.

Independent (London, England), April 3, 2008, p. 6.

New Statesman, May 7, 2007, p. 72.

New York Observer, June 30, 2003, p. 1.

New York Times, September 14, 1997; August 27, 2006; March 9, 2007; March 19, 2007.

People, April 27, 1987, p. 10.

Publishers Weekly, January 29, 2007, p. 27.

Online

"The Sins of the Mother," Salon.com, http://dir.salon.com/story/books/int/2003/05/08/kevin/index.html (May 8, 2008).

—Carol Brennan

Sarah Silverman

Actress and comedian

Born December 1, 1970, in Bedford, NH; daughter of Donald (a clothing store owner) and Beth Ann (a college theater director) Silverman. *Education:* Attended New York University, c. 1988-89.

Addresses: *Agent*—Creative Artists Agency, Inc., 9830 Wilshire Blvd., Beverly Hills, CA 90212. *Home*—Los Angeles, CA.

Career

Began career as a stand-up comic in New York City, late 1980s. Actress on television, including: *Comic Strip Live,* early 1990s; *Saturday Night Live,* NBC, 1993-94; *Mr. Show with Bob and David,* HBO, 1995-97; *Star Trek: Voyager,* 1996; *The Larry Sanders Show,* 1996; *Seinfeld,* 1997; *Brotherly Love,* 1997; *JAG,* 1997; *The Naked Truth,* 1997; *Futurama,* 2000; *V.I.P.,* 2002; *Greg the Bunny,* FOX, 2002-04; *Frasier,* 2003; *Monk,* 2004, 2007; *Entourage,* 2004; *American Dad,* 2005; *The Sarah Silverman Program,* Comedy Central, 2007—. Film appearances include: *Overnight Delivery,* 1998; *Bulworth,* 1998; *There's Something About Mary,* 1998; *The Bachelor,* 1999; *The Way of the Gun,* 2000; *Black Days,* 2001; *Say It Isn't So,* 2001; *Heartbreakers,* 2001; *Evolution,* 2001; *Run Ronnie Run,* 2002; *The School of Rock,* 2003; *Nobody's Perfect,* 2004; *Rent,* 2005; *I Want Someone to Eat Cheese With,* 2005; *Jesus is Magic* (also writer) 2005; *School for Scoundrels,* 2006; *The Aristocrats,* 2006.

Sidelights

Sarah Silverman belongs to a rarified club of female comedians who have achieved certain milestones of success in mainstream entertainment.

In 2005, her one-woman, off-Broadway show *Jesus Is Magic* was turned into feature film, and in 2007 her eponymous sitcom-like series began airing on Comedy Central. A favorite among male comedians for the risqué nature of her jokes, some of which have landed her in trouble in the media, Silverman delivers her self-deprecating or cutting commentary with a straight face that belies her irreverent attitude, but much media attention has focused on her appearance. "Silverman would be a singular talent even if she wasn't beautiful," noted Owen Gleiberman in *Entertainment Weekly,* "but it would be foolish to deny that watching a stand-up comedian who resembles the world's sexiest art-history major" did not have its appeal. Silverman, Gleiberman continued, "makes her attractiveness relevant by delivering each scathing, oooo-did-she-really-say-that? joke as if it were a come-on."

Born in 1970, Silverman was the last of Donald and Beth Ann Silverman's four daughters. The family lived in Bedford, New Hampshire, an affluent suburb of Manchester, and were an exuberant, somewhat nontraditional clan. Beth Ann headed the theater department at a local college, while Silverman's father owned a chain of local clothing stores and delighted in such pranks as teaching his youngest daughter to swear when she was still a toddler. "I was raised by parents who had no boundaries in terms of what a child should or shouldn't hear or see," Silverman said in an interview with *New York Times* writer Marcelle Clements. "I didn't have much idea of what was not to be talked about."

Silverman's parents divorced around the time she entered first grade, and the resulting emotional upheaval provoked a bed-wetting habit that endured until she was in her teens; after that, she began to suffer from occasional panic attacks. In interviews, the comedian has said that psychotherapy alleviated her clinical depression, as did anti-depressant drugs, but she has also noted that despair seems to breeds comic gold in her industry. "I had an unhappy childhood and, sadly, I think that that really helps," she told *Back Stage West* journalist Jamie Painter Young. "I think a lot of humiliation and living through it and coming out the other side puts a perspective on how silly things are."

Known as the outrageous one in a family of extroverts, Silverman gravitated toward musical theater in her teens, playing the title role in a production of *Annie* at the age of 12. Her first stand-up appearance came during a summer school stint in Boston, where she visited a comedy club with friends and signed up for the open mic slot. For college, she chose New York University and its drama program, but began spending far more time hanging around comedy clubs in the city, often distributing flyers in exchange for a chance onstage at the end of the night. Exasperated by her failure to take her studies seriously, her father told her, "'I'll make a deal with you. If you quit college, I'll pay your rent and utilities for what would be your sophomore, junior, and senior years,'," she recalled in a later interview with *Back Stage West*, this time with Jenelle Riley. "It saved him a ton of money."

Moving through the comedy club circuit, Silverman eventually made it onto an episode of *Comic Strip Live*, a late-night FOX television series that aired between 1989 and 1994. Producers for *Saturday Night Live* (*SNL*) saw the performance, and she won a highly coveted slot as a writer and performer on the legendary NBC sketch comedy series for its 1993-94 season. She appeared only briefly in a few skits, however, and much of her written material was rejected; at the end of the season, she learned that *SNL*'s executives had fired her when her agent called to tell her he had received a faxed letter notifying him of her dismissal. The entire experience was traumatic, to say the least, she told Riley in the *Back Stage West* interview. "It didn't occur to me that I wouldn't be asked back," she recalled, and said that being fired devastated her. Accordingly, she faltered for nearly a year in her stand-up routine, hampered by a palpable lack of confidence on

stage. In the end, she realized that the worst had already happened to her, which ultimately freed her from fear. "It was like a broken bone; it just healed stronger. Nothing in terms of a downfall in my career could raze me after that," she told Riley.

In the mid-1990s, Silverman moved cross-country to Los Angeles, and began landing small parts on television, including a role as Rain Robinson in two episodes of *Star Trek: Voyager*. The irreverent comedy duo of Bob Odenkirk and David Cross hired her for their HBO sketch comedy series, *Mr. Show with Bob and David*, which achieved cult status, and she spoofed her *SNL* stint on another much-loved HBO series, *The Larry Sanders Show*, as a television writer whose jokes never make it to the air. From this point, she began to win small roles in films, beginning with the 1998 romantic comedy *Overnight Delivery*, which also featured two relative unknowns, Paul Rudd and Reese Witherspoon. She also had a part in one of that year's top-grossing films, *There's Something About Mary*, but soon realized that she was being typecast as the mean female character.

Silverman's acerbic wit landed her in some trouble in July of 2001 when she appeared on *Late Night With Conan O'Brien* and used a derogatory term for Asian Americans while discussing tactics for evading jury duty. The head of a watchdog group, Guy Aoki of the Media Action Network for Asian Americans, mounted a campaign against *Late Night*'s network, NBC, and Silverman. NBC was forced to issue an apology, but Silverman refused; instead, she wrote to Aoki and suggested they meet in person to discuss what she maintained was a joke about racism, not a racist joke. Aoki divulged her e-mail address in the media and she was inundated with hate mail, some of it virulently anti-Semitic. A few weeks later, she defended her joke at the invitation of talk show host Bill Maher on his show *Politically Incorrect*, and a month later reappeared on Maher's chatfest, this time with Aoki. Their verbal sparring devolved into name-calling. "The truth of the matter is, it's not a moral issue in terms of the network," she reflected in the midst of the controversy when interviewed by the *New York Observer*'s Alexander Jacobs, noting that NBC "may put this facade on that it is, but it's about advertisers and the F.C.C. and pleasing them. It has nothing to do with morals; they are void of morals. It's all about money."

That same August, Silverman began performing a one-woman show called *Jesus Is Magic* in New York City's off-Broadway venues, and the routine was eventually filmed and released as the concert film *Jesus Is Magic* in 2005. In it, she mentions the battle with Aoki, telling her audience that the activist "put my name in the papers calling me a racist, and it hurt," she said, according to Dana Goodyear in a lengthy *New Yorker* profile. "As a Jew—as a member of the Jewish community—I was really concerned that we were losing control of the media." Silverman's Jewish heritage has proved rich comic fodder for her over the years, with many of her quips classifying her as the stereotypical Jewish American Princess, but on a more serious note she believes it has also hampered her career. "Whenever I talk to a suit, or if I am on a friendly level with someone networky, I always ask them the same question, which is: 'If Winona Ryder kept her name Winona Horowitz, would she have all these leading-actress roles under her belt?'," she told Jacobs in the *New York Observer* interview. "And 100 percent of them said, 'No.' I couldn't believe they would be that honest! Isn't that weird? You know, I mean, it's not because there are non-Jews running Hollywood!"

In 2005 Silverman also appeared in *The Aristocrats*, a documentary film about a notorious joke that for decades had been a secret career touchstone among comedians, who privately regaled one another in a retelling of a raunchy tale about a vaudeville family act, with each attempting to give it an even cruder twist. Silverman's version included her deadpan assertion that veteran New York City talk show host Joe Franklin had sexually assaulted her, and subsequent footage of Franklin shows him fuming over the remark. Meanwhile, her feature film career was still relegated to supporting roles in such films as *The School of Rock* and *School for Scoundrels*. In 2006, however, she landed her own series on Comedy Central, and the first six episodes of *The Sarah Silverman Program* began airing in early 2007. Her show was a mix of reality and fiction, originally filmed right in her Los Angeles apartment and starring her sister, actress Laura Silverman, as her on-screen sister, Laura. Silverman played Sarah, a deeply self-absorbed young woman who makes near-constant offensive remarks—about African Americans, the homeless, and nearly all population groups—in what appeared to be a parody of a quirky, single-girl sitcom. "I'm just like you," she burbles in the voice-over introduction. "I live in Valley Village, I don't have a job, and my sister pays the rent."

Like Silverman's comic routine, her series was either loved or loathed by critics and audiences alike. Critiquing it for *Daily Variety*, Brian Lowrey de-scribed it as "a juvenile, crude, and wholly irreverent exercise that, in its energy and penchant for the absurd, resembles a latter-day version of 'Pee-wee's Playhouse' pitched to the college-frat set. Although Silverman's shtick won't be everyone's overcaffeinated cup of tea, the series seems destined to gain a well-deserved cult following." The series did well enough that Comedy Central ordered 14 more episodes for 2007-08, which made Silverman one of a small but notable list of female comedians who garnered their own show on the highly watched, but male-dominated cable network.

Silverman has been romantically linked with ABC late-night television talk show host Jimmy Kimmel since 2003. The pair first crossed paths at a Friars Club roast for Hugh Hefner two years earlier which was emceed by Kimmel; Silverman was the only female to take the dais that night, and kicked off her act with a dig at Kimmel. "I introduced her," Kimmel told James Poniewozik in *Time*, "and she said, 'Jimmy Kimmel: he's fat and has no charisma. Watch your back, Danny Aiello.'" The pair sometimes do joint interviews, such as one that appeared in a January 2007 issue of *Esquire* in which they made jokes about their relationship's most intimate aspects, and Silverman proved once again she never retreated from poking fun at everyone, including herself. "I'm always in those tabloids where they show who's badly dressed," she told the writer, Mike Sager. "It's funny, because each time I'm getting my picture taken, I'm thinking, This is a nice outfit. There's no way this will make the badly dressed list. I'm matching and everything." Kimmel pointed out that once she sees the published result, she concurs with the assessment. "I'm like, They're right. It's not so good. I just look like a transvestite when I try to dress up."

Sources

Back Stage West, October 31, 2002, p. 8; November 10, 2005, p. 1.
Daily Variety, January 31, 2007, p. 14.
Entertainment Weekly, November 18, 2005, p. 106.
Esquire, January 2007, p. 86.
New Yorker, October 24, 2005, p. 50.
New York Observer, August 6, 2001, p. 11.
New York Times, November 9, 2005; January 31, 2007; February 1, 2007.
Time, February 5, 2007, p. 64.

—*Carol Brennan*

Lorna Simpson

Artist and photographer

Born August 13, 1960, in New York, NY; daughter of Elian and Eleanor Simpson; divorced; children: Zora Simpson Casebere (with artist James Casebere). *Education:* New York School of Visual Arts, B.F.A., 1982; University of California at San Diego, M.F.A., 1985.

Addresses: *Home*—Brooklyn, NY.

Career

Photographer, video artist, and mixed-media artist, New York City, 1985—; invited to participate in the Venice Biennale, 1990; works acquired by several major museums, including the Boston Museum of Fine Arts, San Francisco Museum of Modern Art, Corcoran Gallery of Art in Washington, DC, Museum of Contemporary Art in Chicago, and Walker Art Center of Minneapolis; a 20-year retrospective of her work was mounted by the American Federation of Arts and toured several North American cities before arriving at the Whitney Museum of American Art, 2007.

Awards: NEA Fellowship, 1985; Louis Comfort Tiffany Award, 1990; College Art Association grant, 1994; American Art Award, Whitney Museum, 2001; Joyce Alexander Wein Artist Prize, Studio Museum in Harlem, 2006.

Sidelights

Multimedia artist Lorna Simpson was feted with a career retrospective at the Whitney Museum of American Art in 2007 that also brought her compelling photographs and video installations to several major American cities. Simpson's newest works often premiere at the Studio Museum in Harlem, which in 2006 made her the inaugural recipient of its new Joyce Alexander Wein Artist Prize. "Simpson's photography is provocative and confrontational," declared *Essence* writer Jorge Arango. "It deals with the way society treats Black women—ignoring them, refusing them credibility, despising their hair. Her videos grapple with people's tendency to lie about their identity to lovers, friends, and acquaintances, and with the less-than-noble impulses that motivate those lies."

Simpson was born in 1960 in the borough of Brooklyn in New York City, and spent her early years there and in California. She earned her undergraduate degree from the New York School of Visual Arts in 1982, and was drawn to the medium of photography thanks in part to her interest in the work of Harlem photographer Roy DeCarava, whose work captured African-American life in New York City from the 1950s onward. Simpson went on to the University of California at San Diego for her graduate degree in fine arts, and returned to New York after graduating in 1985. Just five years later, she earned a place in art history as the first African-American woman whose work was selected for inclusion in the prestigious Venice Biennale, a contemporary art exhibition held every two years in Venice, Italy.

Early in her career Simpson worked almost exclusively in still photography, and for a time used only an African-American female model, clothed in a white shift, for many of her images, which were combined with text to prompt the viewer into examining his or her assumptions about race and gender. One of these works is the four circular portraits, all identical, in *Twenty Questions (A Sampler)*, which dates from 1986. The quartet of photographs, which depict the model from behind, pose the questions: "Is she as pretty as a picture"; "or clear as crystal"; "or pure as a lily"; "or black as coal"; "or sharp as a razor?"

Simpson also created large-scale works with the help of the Land camera developed by Polaroid, which weighed more than 200 pounds and was able to make 4' x 5' prints of exceptional quality. One of these is *Waterbearer*, also from 1986, which depicts a woman, shown from behind, with both arms outstretched pouring water out of two different vessels. The accompanying text reads: "She saw him disappear by the river, they asked her to tell what happened, only to discount her memory." *Wigs*, which dates from 1994, is a series of lithographs of women's hairpieces of varying colors and styles, which "prompt us to speculate about the women who might have worn these hairpieces," explained Sarah Valdez in *Art in America*. "Simpson thus teases out the pernicious reality of stereotyping according to genetic traits. The work makes viewers realize that racial profiling goes on all the time."

In the 1990s, Simpson began a photography series depicting a woman wearing a traditional man's suit. Later in the decade, she showed photographs under the collective title "Public Sex," which were devoid of figures and instead depicted dark cityscapes, with text that seemed to hint at illicit liaisons. She also began working in short film and video, and one acclaimed work in this genre was *Call Waiting* from 1997, shown in exhibitions as a DVD projection. It consists of multiple and simultaneous phone conversations carried on by several different actors. "Romantic intrigue connects the entire lot with an eerie prescience," noted Valdez in the *Art in America* article, "evoking at once the way electronic communication allows people to connect with one another, all the while driving them apart and encouraging deception."

Simpson used the same video medium for 2002's *31*, which featured 31 different television screens showing footage of one woman during the routine of her day. It premiered at Documenta 11, the prestigious art event in Kassel, Germany. "As usual in Simpson's work, we can't see the woman's face straight on, but we clearly see that her reality is made up of many moments, none of which defines her existence," wrote Valdez in *Art in America*. "Simpson upsets the very notion of a portrait and once more points up subjectivity. She gives us a sense that identity is something performed rather than fixed."

Around this same period Simpson began to add music to her video works, such as *Easy to Remember* in 2001, which *New York Times* art critic Holland Cotter described as footage of "15 pairs of lips [which] collectively hum a Rodgers and Hart song that Ms. Simpson remembers, in a John Coltrane version, from her childhood," Cotter wrote, and likened the melody to Beethoven's enduring "Ode to Joy. " "When the film made its debut in the 2002 Whitney Biennial a few months after Sept. 11, its poignancy was almost unbearable."

Simpson's works have been acquired for the permanent collections of several major institutions, including the Boston Museum of Fine Arts, San Francisco Museum of Modern Art, Corcoran Gallery of Art in Washington, DC, Museum of Contemporary Art in Chicago, and Walker Art Center of Minneapolis. The traveling retrospective *Lorna Simpson*, showed 20 years of her work and was organized by the American Federation of Arts. She lives in a restored brownstone home in the Clinton Hill section of Brooklyn with her partner, the artist Jim Casebere, and a daughter born to them in 1999, Zora, but each work out of separate studios housed in a four-story loft designed by British architect David Adjaye. Reviewing the works shown in the two-decade retrospective at the Whitney, the *New York Times'* Cotter noted that despite the inclusion of music in her later works, which seem to add a bit of whimsy, he had already previewed a newer work not included in the exhibition in which the artist "returns to themes—race and control, blackness and whiteness as equally problematic conditions—that she has been exploring with persistent, quiet rigor for more than two decades."

Selected solo exhibitions

Alternative Gallery, 5th Street Market, San Diego, California, 1985.
Just Above Midtown, New York, New York, 1986.
Jamaica Arts Center, Queens, New York, 1988.
Mercer Union, Toronto, Ontario, Canada, 1988.
Wadsworth Atheneum, Hartford, Connecticut, 1989.
Denver Art Museum, Denver, Colorado, 1990.

Portland Art Museum, Portland, Oregon, 1990.

Museum of Modern Art, New York, New York, 1990.

University Art Museum, California State University, Long Beach, California, 1990.

Josh Baer Gallery, New York, New York, 1991.

Center for Exploratory and Perceptual Art, Buffalo, New York, 1991.

John Berggruen Gallery, San Francisco, California, 1993.

Shoshana Wayne Gallery, Santa Monica, California, 1993.

Josh Baer Gallery, New York, New York, 1993.

Contemporary Arts Museum, Houston, Texas, 1993.

Whitney Museum of American Art at Phillip Morris, New York, New York, 1994.

Fabric Workshop, Philadelphia, Pennsylvania, 1994.

Rhona Hoffman Gallery, Chicago, Illinois, 1994.

Sean Kelly Gallery, New York, New York, 1995.

Albrecht Kemper Museum of Art, St. Joseph, Missouri, 1995.

Cohen/Berkowitz Gallery, Kansas City, Missouri, 1995.

Karen McCready Fine Art, New York, New York, 1996.

Galerie Wohnmaschine, Berlin, Germany, 1996.

Miami Art Museum of Dade County, Miami, Florida, 1997.

Scenarios: Recent Work by Lorna Simpson, Walker Art Center, Minneapolis, MN, 1999.

Scenarios: Recent Work by Lorna Simpson, Addison Gallery of American Art, Andover, MA, 2000.

Lorna Simpson, Cameos and Appearances, Whitney Museum of American Art, New York, New York, 2002.

Lorna Simpson: 31, Whitney Museum of American Art, New York, New York, 2002.

Lorna Simpson, The Studio Museum of Harlem, New York, 2002.

Lorna Simpson, Centro de Arte Contemporaneo, Salamanca, Spain, 2002.

Lorna Simpson: Easy to Remember, Weatherspoon Art Museum, University of North Carolina, Greensboro, NC, 2002.

Lorna Simpson, Irish Museum of Modern Art, Dublin, Ireland, 2003.

Lorna Simpson, Consejo Nacional Para la Cultura y las Artes, Mexico City, Mexico, 2003.

Lorna Simpson: Corridor, Wohnmaschine, Berlin, Germany, 2004.

Lorna Simpson, Sean Kelly Gallery, New York, New York, 2004.

Lorna Simpson: 31, Mary & Leigh Block Museum of Art, Northwestern University, Evanston, Illinois, 2004.

Lorna Simpson, The College of Wooster Art Museum, Wooster, Ohio, 2004.

Lorna Simpson: Videos and Photographs, Galerie Obadia, Paris, France, 2004.

Lorna Simpson, Walter E. Terhune Gallery, Owens Community College, Toledo, Ohio, 2004.

Lorna Simpson, American Federation of the Arts traveling show, Museum of Contemporary Art, Los Angeles, California; Miami Art Museum, Miami, Florida; Whitney Museum of American Art, New York, New York; Kalamazoo Institute of Art, Kalamazoo, Michigan; Gibbes Museum, Charleston, South Carolina, 2006-07.

Lorna Simpson: Duet, The Studio Museum of Harlem, New York, 2007.

Sources

Art in America, December 2006, p. 106.

Essence, May 2002, p. 172.

New York Times, July 20, 1990; March 2, 2007; April 1, 2007.

—Carol Brennan

Alfonso Soriano

Professional baseball player

Born Alfonso Guilleard Soriano, January 7, 1976, in San Pedro de Macoris, Dominican Republic; son of Andrea Soriano; married Angelica; children: Alisis, Angeline, Alfonso Jr.

Addresses: *Contact*—Chicago Cubs, Wrigley Field, 1060 West Addison, Chicago, IL 60613.

Career

Signed with the Hiroshima Toyo Carp of the Japanese baseball league, 1994; played baseball in Japan, 1995-97; signed with the New York Yankees, 1998; made major league debut with Yankees, 1999; traded to Texas Rangers, 2004; traded to Washington Nationals, 2005; traded to Chicago Cubs, 2006.

Awards: All-Star Team, 2002, 2003, 2004, 2005, 2006, 2007; Major League Baseball All-Star Game, Most Valuable Player, 2004; American League Silver Slugger Award, 2002, 2004, 2005; National League Silver Slugger Award, 2006.

Sidelights

Alfonso Soriano is the only major league baseball player in the "40-40-40" club. In 2006, while playing for the Washington Nationals, Soriano smacked 46 homers, stole 41 bases, and slapped 41 doubles, becoming the first player to put up numbers in the 40s in all three categories in a single season. During the off-season, Soriano's offensive skills garnered him an eight-year, $136 million free-

agent contract with the Chicago Cubs, the biggest deal in the club's history. By the start of the 2007 season, there was speculation that Soriano could become baseball's first 50-50 player—no one has ever stolen 50 bases and hit 50 homers the same season. "He has a great combination of speed and power," Cubs manager Lou Piniella told *Sports Illustrated Kids* writer Ted Keith. "Those are pretty good numbers to shoot for."

Soriano was born on January 7, 1976, in San Pedro de Macoris, Dominican Republic. He was raised by his grandfather, a chicken farmer, and his mother, Andrea Soriano, in the tiny Caribbean town of Ingenio Quisqueya. The youngest of four, Soriano spent many days tagging along beside his brothers as they headed to the baseball field. He was playing ball by the age of six. Growing up, Soriano's baseball hero was Golden Glover Tony Fernandez, who was also from the Dominican Republic. As Soriano grew older, he dreamed of a future playing professional baseball. When he batted, he tried to emulate the stances of the major leaguers he watched on television. "I would be Cal Ripken," Soriano told the *Washington Post*'s Barry Svrluga. "Then I would be Tony Fernandez. I had heroes. I wanted to be like them." At the time, Soriano was small and skinny, giving off no hints he would grow into a 180-pound, 6-foot-1-inch power hitter.

When Soriano was a teenager, many of his friends cut school so they could play baseball at the local academies sponsored by major league teams scouting for young talent. Soriano stayed in school, though, on his mother's orders, so U.S. scouts never got a chance to see him play. Instead, Soriano played baseball after school in a community league that faced off against the teams from the Japanese academies. The Japanese scouts saw potential in Soriano, a shortstop at the time. In 1994, Soriano signed with the Hiroshima Toyo Carp and by 1995 he was playing ball in Japan. "At first my mother didn't want me to drop my studies when I signed with the Japanese [league], but thanks to family members who convinced her I was old enough to make that decision, I was allowed to take the opportunity and go to Japan," he told *Latino Leaders*.

Living in Japan made Soriano homesick. He struggled with the language and with the food, which was so different from his Caribbean homeland. Fellow Dominican players had to talk him into staying. In 1996, playing in the Japanese minor leagues, Soriano hit .214. His batting average hit .252 the next year and by 1997, he was playing in the Japanese majors. Shortly thereafter, the team released Soriano over a contract dispute.

In May of 1998, Soriano traveled to the United States and played in a semi-professional league in Los Angeles, trying to grab the attention of major league scouts. He signed as a free agent with the Yankees in 1998. Soon, he was working out at the club's facilities in Tampa, Florida, and began studying English. In Tampa, Soriano frequented a Latin restaurant that reminded him of home. There, he met a waitress from Panama named Angelica, who later became his wife.

Though Soriano had already played in the major leagues—in Japan—the Yankees assigned him to a Class AA minor league team in 1999, where he hit .305. By the end of the season, the Yankees had called Soriano up and he made his major league debut on September 14, 1999, pinch-running for Darryl Strawberry. Ten days later, Soriano hit his first major league homer.

During 2000, Soriano made just 22 appearances with the Yankees, who already had a star shortstop in Derek Jeter, leaving Soriano out of the lineup. In 2001, Soriano garnered more playing time after Yankees All-Star infielder Chuck Knoblauch suffered an arm problem and Soriano stepped in to fill his position at second base. That season, Soriano stole 43 bases, breaking the Yankees' single-season rookie stolen base record set in 1910.

In 2002, the Yankees made Soriano their leadoff hitter and his offensive skills began to attract attention. He hit .300 that season and made his first All-Star team. Soriano also had 39 homers and smacked in 102 runs. He led the American League with 209 hits and 41 stolen bases. In 2003, Soriano hit 13 leadoff homers, a single-season major league record. That year, the Yankees beat the Boston Red Sox to win the American League pennant, but lost the World Series to the Florida Marlins.

In February of 2004, Soriano was traded to the Texas Rangers. By now, the bat-whacking speedster had become a fan favorite and he garnered the most votes of any player during that year's All-Star balloting. He rewarded voters during the All-Star game by smacking a first-inning, three-run homer off National League starter Roger Clemens. After the game, Soriano was crowned All-Star Most Valuable Player.

In December of 2005, Soriano was acquired by the Washington Nationals, who desperately wanted Soriano's offensive power but already had an All-Star second baseman—Jose Vidro. The Nationals wanted Soriano to play left field but he refused and was yanked from the starting lineup during spring season play. Eventually, Soriano agreed to the position change. Soriano grew into the position, contributing to double plays and tallying 22 outfield assists that season.

Though Soriano struggled at times adapting to the outfield, he remained steady behind the plate. During 2006, Soriano hit 46 homers and stole 41 bases, making him the fourth 40-40 player in history behind Jose Canseco, Barry Bonds, and Alex Rodriguez. At the end of the season, Soriano became a free agent and was scooped up by the Chicago Cubs, who, as of 2007, had not won a World Series in nearly 100 years. The Cubs moved Soriano again, this time to center field.

During the off-season, the bat-slapping, base-stealing Soriano often returns to the Dominican Republic. He brings countless baseballs and other equipment, which he distributes to the kids playing on the streets, hoping some of them will one day realize their dream, just like he has.

Sources

Periodicals

Baseball Digest, October 2002, p. 46; November 2006, p. 54.

Chicago Sun-Times, November 21, 2006, sec. Sports, p. 100.

Latino Leaders, October/November 2004, p. 32.

Sports Illustrated, May 1, 2006, p. 73.

Sports Illustrated Kids, June 2007, p. 22.

USA Today, April 2, 2007.

Washington Post, July 11, 2006, p. E1.

Online

"Alfonso Soriano," Baseball-Reference.com, http://www.baseball-reference.com/s/soriaa101.shtml (July 30 2007).

"Alfonso Soriano," ESPN, http://sports.espn.go.com/mlb/players/profile?statsId=6154 (July 30, 2007).

—*Lisa Frick*

Tori Spelling

Actress

Born Victoria Davey Spelling, May 16, 1973, in Los Angeles, CA; daughter of Aaron (a television producer) and Candy (an actress) Spelling; married Charlie Shanian (an actor), July 3, 2004 (divorced, April, 2006); married Dean McDermott (an actor), May 7, 2006; children: Liam (from second marriage).

Addresses: *Office*—c/o Oxygen Media, LLC, 75 9th Ave., New York, NY 10011.

Career

Actress on television, including: *Saved by the Bell,* NBC, 1990-91; *Beverly Hills, 90210,* FOX, 1990-2000; *So Downtown,* WB, 2003; *So NoTORIous,* VH1, 2006; *Tori & Dean: Inn Love,* Oxygen, 2007—. Has also appeared in television movies, including: *Shooting Stars,* 1983; *The Three Kings,* 1987; *A Friend to Die For,* 1994; *Awake to Danger,* 1995; *Deadly Pursuits,* 1996; *Co-Ed Call Girl,* 1996; *Mother, May I Sleep with Danger?,* 1996; *Alibi,* 1997; *Way Downtown,* 2002; *A Carol Christmas,* 2003; *Family Plan,* 2005; *Hush,* 2005; *Mind Over Murder,* 2006; *Housesitter,* 2007. Film appearances include: *Troop Beverly Hills,* 1989; *The House of Yes,* 1997; *Scream 2,* 1997; *Trick,* 1999; *Scary Movie 2,* 2001; *Sol Goode,* 2001; *Evil Alien Conquerors,* 2002; *Naked Movie,* 2002; *Starring,* 2003; *50 Ways to Leave Your Lover,* 2004; *Cthulhu,* 2007; *Kiss the Bride,* 2008.

Mark Mainz/Getty Images for TV Guide Channel Studios

Sidelights

Tori Spelling grew up in the public eye as the daughter of the most prolific producer in television history, Aaron Spelling. Spelling followed her father into the business, but endured the barbs of critics who claimed she won her role on the long-running FOX series *Beverly Hills, 90210* simply because her father was the show's producer. Once she reached her thirties, Spelling found her niche as a reality-television personality who proved confident enough to mock her status as the quintessential spoiled California blonde. She appeared in a VH1 series called *So NoTORIous,* and then on an Oxygen cable channel series that followed her and her new husband, Dean McDermott, as they struggled to renovate a California bed & breakfast.

Spelling was born Victoria Davey Spelling on May 16, 1973, in Los Angeles, the first child of television producer Aaron Spelling and his wife, Candy. Aaron Spelling had been working in the entertainment industry since the early 1950s, moving from acting to writing to producing, and during Spelling's childhood his talent for creating hit shows began to pay off. Series produced by his company would come to dominate the prime-time television line-up for much of the 1970s and '80s. They included *Charlie's Angels, The Love Boat,* and *Dynasty,* all of which made Spelling's father one of the most powerful—and wealthiest—figures in American network television. The family, which included her younger brother Randy, lived in a palatial estate that was the largest private residence in the state of California, at 56,000 square feet and 123 rooms.

The Spellings were Jewish, but also celebrated Christmas, and their father—who had grown up in desperately poor circumstances—lavished attention and luxuries on them, including having snow brought in from the mountains via refrigerated trucks so that they could build snowmen on their lawn on Christmas morning. As an adult, Spelling admitted she was embarrassed by her family's affluence, and said that even in affluent Beverly Hills she was teased at school. A bashful child, she was known to hide behind her mother's skirts when company came, but found she had no fear when she performed impromptu numbers at her parents' extravagant soirees.

Spelling told her father that she wanted to act, and she landed her first part in one of his series, *Vega$,* at the age of seven. She went on to small parts in other Spelling productions, including *Fantasy Island* and *The Love Boat,* and at age ten appeared in the first of several television movies that would become the mainstay of her career. As a teen, she attended Beverly Hills High School for a time, but graduated from a private academy, the Harvard-Westlake School in North Hollywood. She made her feature-film debut in *Troop Beverly Hills* in 1989, a Shelley Long comedy. A year later, she was cast in a few episodes of the NBC sitcom *Saved by the Bell.*

Spelling wrote poetry and even a play during her teen years, and planned on studying English and theater in college; however, before she began classes, she auditioned for the pilot episode of a new series her father was producing, *Beverly Hills, 90210,* and was given a small part. When the pilot was picked up by the FOX Network, Spelling put her college plans on hold. The hour-long drama initially began as a satire of wealthy high schoolers much like Spelling and her friends, but quickly abandoned its tongue-in-cheek humor for more straightforward drama. Spelling was cast as Donna Martin, a dim, rich teenager whose careful safeguarding of her virginity became a major story arc over the first few seasons.

Critics savaged *Beverly Hills, 90210*—along with Spelling's acting abilities—but the series was a hit with teens and young adults alike, and she and her fellow castmates all became household names in the early 1990s. The show ran for a decade, and followed the characters through their college years, with typically over-the-top storylines that were a hallmark of her father's television hits. Spelling was happy to be earning her own money from the successful series, and moved out of her parents' immense house to her own apartment, telling Andrew Billen in Britain's *Observer* newspaper that she enjoyed "being somewhere where I can see the whole place from a chair."

Spelling's real-life romantic foibles were well-documented by the tabloid press. For a two-year period she was linked with Nick Savalas, son of actor Telly Savalas, a relationship she later characterized as detrimental to her self-image. "He was never physically abusive, but he was verbally abusive, telling me ten times a day how ugly I was," she told *Entertainment Weekly*'s Dana Kennedy a few years later. "I cried all the time. " Spelling's self-image issues were further exacerbated by fan sites for *Beverly Hills, 90210* in the earliest years of the Internet, where devotees of the series speculated about her fluctuating weight and whether or not she had undergone breast-augmentation surgery.

Beverly Hills, 90210 ended its run in 2000, but by then Spelling had already become a staple of the made-for-television drama, starring in small-screen movies with titles like *Mother, May I Sleep with Danger?* and *Co-Ed Call Girl.* She scored surprisingly good reviews for two independent films, one called the *The House of Yes* in 1997 that starred Parker Posey as a Jacqueline Kennedy Onassis-obsessed young woman from a wealthy Virginia family. Spelling's character was a donut-shop waitress whose visit to her new fiancé's home showcases the family's rather unwholesome relationships. "Casting Spelling as the fiancée was an inspired stroke, as [audiences] already associate her with a certain cluelessness," wrote Dennis Harvey in *Variety,* "but she's quite good, as Lesly gradually reveals a surprising determination beneath her squarer-than-square surface." She also earned good reviews for a role in *Trick* in 1999, a gay comedy that bolstered her already-substantial fan base among gay men.

Spelling had a difficult time moving forward with her career, however, and seemed to be relegated to parts in the television movies she had once claimed to be avoiding. She was told her face was too recognizable for sitcoms, explaining in one interview that "on network pilots, they can't picture me being hard up and being a waitress," she joked with Kate Aurthur of the *New York Times,* "but Lifetime viewers are totally O.K. with me being an Olympian skier."

On July 3, 2004, Spelling married actor Charlie Shanian in a lavish wedding at her parents' estate that cost an estimated $1 million; however, the following summer she met Canadian-born actor Dean McDermott in Ottawa when both were cast in the television movie *Mind Over Murder,* and the two fell in love. Three weeks later, both flew back to Los Angeles and shortly thereafter announced their separation from their respective spouses. The fact that McDermott was the father of one son and in the process of adopting a second child further fueled the tabloid coverage of the romance, but as Spelling told Michelle Tauber in *People,* "I feel sorry for people who meet The One and let it pass them by. You're doing not just yourself an injustice, but you're doing the person you're with an injustice. We knew we were meant to be together."

Her divorce from Shanian finalized in April of 2006. Weeks later, Spelling married McDermott in a ceremony that was in marked contrast to her first wedding—on a beach in Fiji, with no friends or family members present. Spelling had been estranged from her mother for several months by then in another facet of her life that was faithfully chronicled in the tabloid press. In some media reports, the rift was linked to a friendship her mother had with the man who had once introduced Aaron and Candy, but in other accounts the difficulties were said to stem from Spelling's new reality show on VH1, *So NoTORIous,* which began airing in the spring of 2006.

So NoTORIous was a send-up of the reality-television genre and of Spelling's own celebrity, with television cameras following her on a daily routine in Los Angeles. Some aspects of the portrayal were close to her actual life, but the series was actually scripted. Her father was represented by a voice over a speakerphone—much like the famous Charlie of *Charlie's Angels,* the boss who was never seen on the series—while her television mother, called Kiki, was played by Loni Anderson; Candy Spelling was said to have been irate about the character, who was obsessed with shopping. That relationship was one of the reasons *So NoTORIous* landed on VH1, though it had been originally filmed as an NBC pilot. "Networks want them to have this contentious relationship, and then at the end, tie it up in a neat bow," she explained to Aurthur in the *New York Times* interview. "But that's not reality. Reality is that a lot of mother-daughters have a relationship where they love each other, of course, but they just can't get there."

Reality television seemed to suit Spelling much better than any other format, giving her a chance to display her comedic talents and hone her skills as a producer. Making fun of herself, she enthused, was "really freeing. I've been a target my entire life. At this point, there's nothing anyone can say that will faze me," she told Ulrica Wihlborg in *People,* adding that for the *So NoTORIous* launch party, the planners told her they wanted to hire drag queens who modeled themselves after her. "They were like, 'Does that offend you?'" she told Wihlborg. "Of course it doesn't offend me! There's this famous drag queen called Suppositori Spelling. I'm like, 'You have to find her!'"

In June of 2006, Aaron Spelling died of complications following a stroke. Spelling was in Toronto on location at the time, and learned of his death from a text message sent to her by a friend, who had heard it on the news. Once again, the tabloid press wondered why Spelling had not been at her father's bedside, but she said she had not been warned that her father was so close to death. The real-life drama intensified when Candy Spelling, the executor of her late husband's $300 million estate, gave both Spelling and her son just $800,000 each as their inheritance. However, the pair were reconciled a year later when Spelling's first child, Liam Aaron McDermott, was born, and Candy Spelling established a multimillion-dollar trust in her grandson's name.

By that point, Spelling and McDermott were starring in their own reality series, *Tori & Dean: Inn Love,* which began airing on the Oxygen cable channel in March of 2007. The first season followed them as they struggled to renovate a bed & breakfast inn they had leased in Fallbrook, California, about two hours south of Los Angeles. The second season introduced their infant son as Spelling and McDermott began to tire of innkeeping and sought new sources of income. In early 2008, the couple announced they were expecting a second child. Spelling was busy writing an autobiography, also expected later in 2008. Interviewed by Hadley Freeman in London's *Guardian* a few months after becoming a mother, Spelling reflected on her own storied childhood and the fact that she—unlike so many among a newer generation of moneyed starlets—had avoided trouble with the law or well-publicized substance abuse travails. "My parents instilled great values in us," she told Freeman. "I mean, yeah, we had an extravagant lifestyle, but they taught us to be nice, be honest, work hard, and that always stayed with us."

Sources

Entertainment Weekly, January 26, 1996, p. 34.
Guardian (London, England), June 11, 2007, p. 14.
Harper's Bazaar, August 1999, p. 30.

Newsweek, April 23, 2007, p. 70.

New York Times, October 10, 1997; March 30, 2006.

Observer (London, England), May 4, 1997, p. 6.

People, August 24, 1992, p. 44; April 10, 2006, p. 69; May 22, 2006, p. 120; July 10, 2006, p. 69.

Variety, January 27, 1997, p. 73.

—*Carol Brennan*

Spice Girls

Pop group

Group formed in London in 1994; members include Victoria Beckham (born Victoria Adams, April 17, 1974; Posh Spice); Melanie Brown (born May 29, 1975; Scary Spice); Emma Bunton (born January 21, 1976; Baby Spice); Melanie Chisholm (born January 12, 1974; Sporty Spice); Geri Halliwell (born Geraldine Halliwell, August 6, 1972; Ginger Spice; left group May 31, 1998); group separated in 2001, and reunited in 2007.

Addresses: *Record company*—Virgin, 5757 Wilshire Blvd., Ste. 300, Los Angeles, CA 90036. *Web site*—http://www.thespicegirls.com.

Fitzroy Barrett/MCT/Landov

Career

Group formed in London, 1994; signed to Virgin and released first album, *Spice*, 1996; released *Spiceworld*, 1997; released movie *Spiceworld*, 1997; disbanded, 2001; reunited for tour in 2007.

Awards: Best new act, best British group, and best pop video, for "Say You'll Be There," Smash Hits!, 1996; platinum status for *Spice*, British Phonographic Industry Sales award, 1997; international hit of the year and best British-written single, both for "Wannabe," British Academy of Composers and Songwriters, 1997; London's Favorite Female Group, Capital FM Awards, 1997; album of the year for *Spice*, Billboard Music Awards, 1997; new artist, Billboard Music Awards, 1997; best dance video for "Wannabe," MTV Video Music Awards, 1997; favorite band, duet, or group, favorite new artist, and favorite album, for *Spice*, American Music Awards, 1998; platinum status for *Spiceworld*, British Phonographic Industry Sales award, 1998; outstanding contribution to the British music industry, Brit Awards, 2000.

Sidelights

Their name was synonymous with girl power. When the Spice Girls exploded onto the pop scene, their dance-pop base shook up an independent pop-driven music scene. The Spice Girls demanded attention, and, according to a contributor for the *St. James Encyclopedia of Popular Culture*, "left a noticeable crater in the pop culture landscape that was still evident by the turn of the century.... [T]he Spice Girls made being shallow and fun cool again." Stephen Thomas Erlewine described the group's appeal in a biography for AllMusic.com: "Spice Girls use dance-pop as a musical base, but they infused the music with a fiercely independent, feminist stance that was equal parts Madonna, post-riot grrrl alternative rock feminism, and a co-opting of the good-times-all-the-time stance of England's new lad culture." From 1996 to 1998, the Spice Girls were a force in the music scene; their presence slowed through 2000, after which the members produced various solo albums. They announced a reunion tour in 2007—the first time all five Spice Girls would be on stage together in nine years.

The brainchild of manager Chris Herbert, the Spice Girls was a "manufactured" group in the vein of the British boy-band Take That. Herbert thought if the concept worked for men, it might work for women, and so he held auditions in 1993 for "streetwise, outgoing, ambitious, and dedicated" young women. Four hundred girls showed up, and each was given one minute to sing and dance. Melanie Brown, Melanie Chisholm, and Victoria Beckham (then Adams) attended the auditions, all three passing onto the second and final audition. Geri Halliwell missed the first audition, but begged Herbert for a shot; she, along with the other three girls and Michelle Stephenson, were selected to be the five girls for a band called Touch. The five met in June of 1993, and it became clear early on that Stephenson did not gel with the other girls; she left, and Emma Bunton took her place, becoming the fifth and final member of the band that would become the Spice Girls. The name Touch only lasted until August, when Halliwell came up with the name Spice, based on the song "Sugar and Spice" that they had already recorded.

Despite Herbert's early control and his funding of the work, the girls had different ideas of how the group should go. Given their differing personalities, they wanted to emphasize those differences rather than dress in identical clothing as Herbert suggested. Determined to strike off on their own, in 1994 they took their recordings and headed out, looking for a new manager. They did not find one until 1995, when they signed with Simon Fuller, who helped them get in touch with songwriters and start planning their debut album. Fuller also arranged a number of media interviews for the girls. During a meeting with British teen magazine editor for *Top of the Pops*, the girls acquired nicknames that would define their role in the group. Halliwell became Sexy Spice, due to her history having done work as a nude model. She later changed to Ginger Spice, for her red hair. Beckham, who had grown up in an affluent family, became Posh Spice. Chisholm was known as both Melanie C and Sporty Spice due to her interest in athletics. Brown, or Mel B, was dubbed Scary Spice due to her tongue ring and interest in hip-hop music. Bunton, the youngest of the group and the latecomer, became Baby Spice. With both a manager and a contract with Virgin Records, the girls launched into the pop scene with their single "Wannabe." According to Erlewine, "[I]t became the first debut single by an all-female band to enter the charts at number one in England."

"We're as shocked as everyone else by the success of 'Wannabe,'" Beckham was quoted on the Spice Girls Web site as having said in July of 1996. "It doesn't put us under any pressure to follow it up. If it's the only number one we have, at least it proves what we're capable of." But "Wannabe" was not their only hit on their first album. The girls recorded *Spice*, which released at the end of that year, and featured "Say You'll Be There," and the ballad "2 Become 1," both of which also entered the charts at number one. Two million copies of the album sold in the first two weeks and, as sales continued, the album became the biggest album of the year in both the United Kingdom and the United States. The sales continued, climbing to nearly 20 million worldwide. Fuller arranged sponsorships for the group, and products including Pepsi, Polaroid, and the Sony Playstation received the "spice seal of approval." According to a contributor for *Contemporary Musicians*, "The extremely lucrative marketing franchise known as the Spice Girls showed no signs of slowing the rather frenetic pace of goods and services" they sponsored.

The phenomenal successes encouraged the girls to move to the big screen. Fuller planned their second album, *Spiceworld*, to release alongside a feature film bearing the same name, in 1997. In the meantime, the girls launched a book and manifesto, *Girl Power!*, which sold 200,000 copies its first day on the market. Between filming and recording, the girls attended a number of public events, including a Chelsea vs. Manchester United soccer game where Beckham met her future husband, soccer star David Beckham, and a concert for the Prince's Trust, where Halliwell famously pinched Prince Charles's bottom. Their first live concert did not happen until October of 1997, when the girls sang for 40,000 fans in Istanbul, Turkey. Their international appearances continued with a South African appearance where they met Nelson Mandela, then-president of South Africa.

Neither *Spiceworld* the album nor the movie lived up to the expectations set by their initial album. Though the album entered the British charts at number one, the contributor to *Contemporary Musicians* wrote, it "was viewed as a disappointment in light of its predecessor's phenomenal sales record." Some critics saw this as backlash against the too-present appearance the Spice Girls had in the media. The movie, which featured cameos from Roger Moore and Sir Elton John, also had disappointing sales. According to *Contemporary Authors*, "The biggest impact of the movie was that it managed to somewhat bolster the rather lackluster sales of *Spiceworld*, the album, which helped to keep the group firmly in the eye of the media and the public." Shortly after Beckham announced her engagement to soccer player David Beckham, the girls began the Spiceworld tour.

Despite healthy tour sales, not all was happy behind the scenes. The girls fired Fuller, and the media published several alternating reasons why. Some reported that he and Bunton had had an affair that ended badly. Others blamed money problems, claiming he took a larger cut of merchandising than was his due. Halliwell took over managerial duties throughout their sold-out world tour. But in May of 1998, when the girls appeared in Norway, Halliwell missed two concerts, and the group publicly announced that the five Spice Girls were down to four. "Sadly I would like to confirm that I have left the Spice Girls," Halliwell announced, as quoted on the Spice Girls Web site. "This is because of differences between us. I'm sure the group will continue to be successful and I wish them all the best.... PS, I'll be back." The tour continued, though the shift was hard on the remaining Spice Girls. "The first few times on stage without Geri were strange," Brown said on the Spice Girls Web site. "Obviously we had to share out the lines she sang between us and sometimes I'd forget to sing her lines." Chisholm commented, "[I]t really hit home when we had a few days off. We were just gutted, we couldn't even get out of bed. You know, when you feel just so deflated, absolutely deflated."

But like the girl power they advertised, the Spice Girls persevered. "The departure of Halliwell at the beginning of the American leg of their world tour ... did not keep the group down and certainly did not discourage Spice Girls fans from attending their concerts," wrote a contributor to the *St. James Encyclopedia of Popular Culture*. After the end of the tour, Brown recorded a duet single with Missy Elliot, and the girls together recorded a Christmas single, "Goodbye," which hit number one. Their personal lives also moved in a positive direction, with both Brown and Beckham getting married and having children. They maintained an aura of celebrity but cut back on their group work, taking some time off from the music scene. Chisholm and Halliwell both released solo albums in 1999 and, in 2000, Chisholm headed back to the studio with the remaining Spice Girls to record *Forever*. The album had more of a rhythm and blues sound than their previous hits, and only one single from the album topped the British charts.

Whether motivated by disappointing sales for their third album or because the Spice Girls had moved on to other pursuits in their personal lives, the group announced their separation in 2001, three months after *Forever* was released. Despite the split, all of the members stayed active in the media spotlight, and stayed friends. Bunton told an interviewer for *People* magazine, "We are always on the phone, checking everyone's all right. We talk about boys and what we're wearing. Girly stuff." Bunton, like Halliwell and Chisholm, released a solo album, *A Girl Like Me* in 2001, which featured a more acoustic sound than anything the Spice Girls had done together. She released two subsequent albums, joined BBC1's *Strictly Come Dancing* television program and, in 2007, she and boyfriend Jade Jones had a child. Beckham released an album, *Victoria Beckham,* and an autobiography, *Learning to Fly.* She also had her second son and started working in fashion, developing the VBRocks line for Rock and Republic, and her own independent label, dVb. Chisholm released several solo albums, forming her own independent music label. She loved performing live, so Chisholm toured internationally, playing at 200 live shows throughout her career. Halliwell began raising funds for cancer charities, and she took a position as a goodwill ambassador for the United Nations Population Fund, raising awareness about reproductive health. She published an autobiography, *If Only,* in 1999, and has written a series of children's books to be published in 2008. She gave birth to a daughter in 2006. Brown became involved in a difficult custody battle when she divorced, then had a relationship with actor Eddie Murphy, which resulted in a second child. Later, she married movie producer Stephen Belafonte. She acted on several British television programs, played the role of Mimi in the musical *Rent,* and released several solo albums. Brown performed on *Dancing with the Stars* in the fall 2007 season.

In 2007, the Spice Girls announced their reunion tour, which would begin on the second of December and coincide with the release of their *Greatest Hits* album. "We're kind of the same, except we're 10 years older," Brown told Ramin Setoodeh of *Newsweek.* "We're more classy. Between the five of us, we've got seven kids." Brown revealed in the same interview that all of the children were expected to come on tour with their mothers. The response to the news of the reunion tour was mixed. Jude Rogers wrote in the *New Statesman* that critics had labeled the Spice Girls as "washed-up old crones, backbiting bitches, merciless money-grubbers, Top 40 turkeys ... and a short-frocked, sloganeering riot squad who destroyed feminism forever." Rogers was inclined to buy into the negative image, but after he saw the show he changed his mind. "You were reminded of what was good about the Spice Girls," he wrote. "While other mid-Nineties pop girls were like processed meat, plastic-wrapped and sealed, the Spice Girls came across as individuals with a real, tangible sense of humour." Concerts sold out in the United States and United Kingdom. Reviewer Brian Mccollum of the *Detroit Free Press* wrote of the concert, "The show was a reminder of a gentler age, before the squiggly sounds of pitch-corrected voices filled the radio, before the gossip exploits at PerezHilton.com got more attention than the music that's supposed to make any of it matter in the first place." Despite the tour's success, the last leg was cancelled, ending the tour before the Spice Girls were to perform in China, South Africa, Australia, and Argentina. Some critics believed that Beckham was the source of the split, given her comments to the *World Entertainment News Network*: "I'm not in the music industry any more. I'm in the fashion industry."

Assessing the Spice Girls' career in the *St. James Encyclopedia of Popular Culture,* the contributor wrote, "[A]t their best, they provided a self-esteem boost for thousands of young girls and, at their worst, may have only been 'mere' entertainment." Paul Conroy, head of Virgin Records, told *Music Week,* "I have never known an act that had to work as hard as those girls did for everything that they got and have always thought they deserved every bit of their success because of it." In the same article, Alan Edwards, who worked public relations for the band in the 1990s, said, "Although [the media] might knock them, the Spice Girls are very loveable and British. Like anything from the Beatles, Carry On Films and the Queen Mother to Michael Caine, they have become part of our culture."

Selected discography

As the Spice Girls

Spice Girls, Virgin, 1996.
Spiceworld, Virgin, 1997.
(Without Geri Halliwell) *Forever,* Virgin, 2000.
Greatest Hits, Virgin, 2007.

Melanie Brown

Hot, Virgin, 2000.
L.A. State of Mind, Amber Café, 2005.

Emma Bunton

A Girl Like Me, Virgin, 2001.
Free Me, 19 Recordings/Universal, 2004.
Life in Mono, Universal, 2006.

Melanie Chisholm

Northern Star, Virgin, 1999.
Reason, EMI, 2003.
This Time, 2007.

Geri Halliwell

Schizophrenic, EMI, 1999.
Scream If You Wanna Go Faster, EMI, 2001.

Sources

Books

Contemporary Musicians, Gale (Farmington Hills, MI), vol. 22, 1998; vol. 54, 2005.
St. James Encyclopedia of Popular Culture, St. James Press (Farmington Hills, MI), 2000.

Periodicals

Detroit Free Press, February 17, 2008.
Music Week, November 10, 2007, p. 13.
New Statesman, January 7, 2008, p. 40.
Newsweek, November 12, 2007, p. 89.
People, February 7, 2005; February 14, 2005, p. 56.
World Entertainment News Network, February 1, 2008; February 3, 2008.

Online

Biography Resource Center Online, Thomson Gale, 1999, 2003.
Contemporary Authors Online, Thomson Gale, 2005.
"Spice Girls: Biography," AllMusic.com, http://www.allmusic.com/ (February 22, 2008).
"Timeline," Spice Girls, http://www.thespicegirls.com/facts/timeline/ (February 22, 2008).

—*Alana Joli Abbott*

John Stamos

Actor

Born John Phillip Stamos, August 19, 1963, in Cypress, CA; son of William (a restaurateur) and Loretta Stamos; married Rebecca Romijn (a model and actress), September 19, 1998 (divorced, 2005).

Addresses: *Contact*—NBC Studios, 3000 W. Alameda Ave., Burbank, CA 91523. *Contact*—William Morris Agency, 151 El Camino Drive, Beverly Hills, CA 90212-2775. *Home*—Los Angeles, CA.

Career

Actor on television, including: *General Hospital*, 1981-83; *Dreams*, 1984; *Alice in Wonderland* (movie), 1985; *You Again?*, 1986; *Full House*, 1987-1995; *The Disappearance of Christina* (movie), 1993; *Fatal Vows: The Alexandra O'Hara Story* (movie), 1994; *A Match Made in Heaven* (movie), 1997; *The Marriage Fool* (movie), 1998; *Thieves*, 2001; *Jake in Progress*, 2005-06; *ER*, 2005—; *Wedding Wars* (movie), 2006. Film appearances include: *Never Too Young To Die*, 1986; *Born to Ride*, 1991; *Dropping Out*, 2000; *My Best Friend's Wife*, 2001; *Knots*, 2004. Stage appearances include: *How to Succeed in Business Without Really Trying*, 1995; *Cabaret*, 2002. Producer credits include: *Beach Boys: An American Family*, 2000; *Martin and Lewis*, 2002; *The Virgin Chronicles*, 2002; *Jake in Progress*, 2005.

Awards: Soapy Award for most exciting new actor, 1983; best young actor in a daytime soap, Young Artist Awards, 1984.

Jim Spellman/WireImage/Getty Images

Sidelights

Playing the fun-loving Uncle Jesse on the wholesome 1980s sitcom *Full House*, John Stamos became a celebrity and Hollywood pinup boy. However, when the show ended its eight-season run in 1995, Stamos struggled to find his place in the acting world. Over the next decade, he appeared in several films and a few failed sitcoms before gaining a new lease on his acting life with an appearance on *ER* in 2005. Stamos was supposed to stay for only two episodes, but his machismo played so well with the cast that he was offered a permanent spot on the show and helped revive its ratings.

NBC Entertainment president Kevin Reilly credited Stamos with helping breathe new life into *ER*. "John is definitely a draw," Reilly told *Entertainment Weekly*'s Lynette Rice. "After Noah [Wyle] left we were down a man, so there was room for another male character. John has the right amount of chemistry and charisma."

Stamos was born on August 19, 1963, in Cypress, California, to Bill and Loretta Stamos. His grandfather, a Greek immigrant, shortened the family name from Stamotopoulos. Stamos had two little sisters. As a child, he was interested in acting and snuck into the recording studios at Paramount to watch the filming of shows like *Laverne & Shirley* and *Happy Days.* When Stamos was 15, he began taking acting classes and auditioned for commercials and other roles. Growing up, Stamos was required to help out at his father's three fast-food restaurants, located in Orange County. Stamos told the *Fresno Bee's* Kathy Barberich that he spent his childhood "flipping burgers and eggs and anything else that could be flipped."

Stamos attended Kennedy High School in La Palma, California, and played the drums in the school's marching band. "I was lame in high school," Stamos told the *Orange County Register's* Barry Koltnow. "I wasn't an athlete or popular or anything like that. I was a band geek." The highlight of his high school years was a trip to Ireland to march in the St. Patrick's Day parade. When he was not busy pursuing his acting career, Stamos played in various local rock bands and was popular on the prom circuit.

After high school, Stamos was going to attend Cypress College but in 1981 landed a role on the long-running ABC soap *General Hospital,* playing a tough, street-smart boy named Blackie Parrish. Slated for just five episodes, Stamos became an instant heart-throb and ended up staying on the show for two years. In 1983, he earned a Daytime Emmy nomination for best supporting actor, becoming the youngest actor ever nominated in that category. He did not win, but he did get a 1983 Soapy Award for most exciting new actor. Though Stamos was well on his way to an acting career, his father continued to make him work at the family restaurants on weekends. Customers began to recognize him. Finally, Stamos told the *Fresno Bee's* Barberich, he confronted his father. "I said, 'Dad, I'm on national television. This is embarrassing.' Finally, he didn't make me [help] anymore."

After leaving *General Hospital*—his character went to jail for manslaughter—Stamos, in 1984, landed on the CBS drama *Dreams.* This show followed the exploits of some young rockers struggling to make it in the music world. Stamos, who in real life plays the drums, piano, and guitar, wrote several songs for the show and recorded an accompanying album. It was canceled after one season.

Over the next few years, Stamos was more successful with music than with acting. Growing up, Stamos was a die-hard Beach Boys fan. He attended his first concert in 1976 and later befriended the

band members. In 1985, the Beach Boys invited Stamos to fill in on drums during a Fourth of July gig in Washington, D.C., to play in front of 1.5 million people. The Beach Boys, impressed with Stamos' beat-keeping abilities, invited him to tour with them in the late 1980s. Stamos also played the drums in the Beach Boys' video for the 1988 hit song "Kokomo," which topped the singles charts. Stamos has guest-toured with the band on and off ever since and has played alongside John Fogerty, Bruce Springsteen, Little Richard, and B.B. King.

In 1986, Stamos tried to break into feature films with a leading role in *Never Too Young to Die.* The film, which flopped at the box office, featured Stamos as the avenging son of a secret agent who gets killed. Stamos also failed with 1986's *You Again?*, an ABC show where he played an irresponsible young adult who moves back in with his father, played by Jack Klugman. *You Again?* lasted only one season and folded about the same time ABC executives were putting together a new sitcom about a widowed father raising his young daughters with the help of his extended family. With Bob Saget cast as the father and Stamos as Uncle Jesse, *Full House* was born. The show helped launch the careers of the Olsen twins—Mary-Kate and Ashley. With his face splashed on television screens weekly, Stamos rose to fame quickly playing the leather-jacketed, motorcycle-riding, guitar-wielding Uncle Jesse. After getting off to a slow start in 1987, the show hit the Top 20 its second season. *Full House* ran eight seasons and was canceled in 1995. After the show ended, it aired in syndication, although this did not help Stamos' career. Forever immortalized onscreen with his sky-high 1980s mullet hairstyle and leather jacket, Stamos struggled to find other roles.

Stamos worked on a few other projects during his sitcom years, but the characters he played were not very memorable. In 1991, he starred in *Born to Ride,* a World War II motorcycle flick. The failed film featured Stamos as Grady Westfall, a racer who is recruited to join the Army and train troops to ride motorcycles. In 1993, Stamos played a successful businessman accused of killing his wife in the USA Network feature *The Disappearance of Christina.* He played a serial killer in the 1994 CBS production of *Fatal Vows: The Alexandra O'Hara Story.* None of these features did much to boost his career. Struggling for acting jobs, Stamos formed his own production company, St. Amos Productions. He produced the ABC miniseries *Beach Boys: An American Family* in 2000, which earned an Emmy nomination. In 2002, he produced *The Virgin Chronicles* for MTV. That same year, Stamos also produced *Martin and Lewis* for CBS, a telefilm that explored the relationship between actors Dean Martin and Jerry Lewis.

Stamos' acting career got a much-needed boost in 1995 when he tried his hand at stage acting. After a grueling audition that lasted more than an hour, Stamos won the role of J. Pierrepont Finch in the Broadway musical *How to Succeed in Business Without Really Trying*. Stamos replaced Matthew Broderick in the starring role. According to the *San Jose Mercury News*, Stamos took the audition very seriously. "I studied a lot before. I worked on it night and day. I knew I really wanted it. I worked very, very hard. I knew it was the thing I needed to do in my life...." Playing the singing and dancing entrepreneur Finch stretched Stamos and showed the acting world he had more depth to him than Uncle Jesse. In 2002, Stamos returned to Broadway, playing the show-stealing Emcee in the musical *Cabaret* and was credited with boosting ticket sales.

Along the way, Stamos met *Sports Illustrated* supermodel Rebecca Romijn at a Victoria's Secret fashion show. Within a few months, they were dating and married in September of 1998. Romijn later became famous for her role as the shape-shifting comic book heroine Mystique in the *X-Men* movies. The couple filed for divorce in 2004. Rumors flew through Hollywood that Stamos was jealous his wife's career was taking off while his stalled, but he told *People*'s Ulrica Wihlborg that was not the case. "We weren't exactly up for the same jobs, so what's there to be jealous of? We both weren't getting everything we needed out of our marriage, and it was time to move on for both of us."

In 2001, Stamos appeared in the ABC-TV crime caper *Thieves*, playing a career criminal who becomes a covert government agent. It was canceled after just 13 episodes. In 2005, Stamos earned the title role on the ABC comedy *Jake in Progress*, hoping this would be the role to revive his television career. He played Jake Phillips, a womanizing New York City publicist who is trying to change his ways. Though the show intrigued viewers at first, the romantic comedy never really took off and was canceled after 21 episodes.

In 2005, Stamos appeared on *ER*, portraying a flirty Gulf War vet named Tony Gates. It was supposed to be a two-episode stint, but Stamos' character hit a nerve and got to stay. Playing a paramedic-turned medical intern, Stamos provided a much-needed lift to the show, bringing viewership up to 13.9 million in 2006. Most of Stamos' character's storyline involves his romance with surgeon Neela Rasgotra, played by Parminder Nagra. Though the show was contracted to end after the 2007-08 season, there were rumors it might be kept on the air for a 15th season.

Speaking to *TV Guide*, Stamos said being successful on television again is a dream come true. "Joining *ER*, I feel like that kid who got the golden ticket in *Charlie and the Chocolate Factory*. I've been offered chocolate bars all these years, but there had been no golden ticket." While Stamos was happy about his life career-wise, he noted the irony that his acting career had turned around about the same time his divorce became final. "It's like I can't have it all at one time," he told *Entertainment Weekly*. "Like your career and whatever can be good, but then you have no relationship. Or your relationship is good, but you have no career."

Around the time Stamos became a regular on *ER*, he was also cast in the 2006 A&E romantic comedy *Wedding Wars*. In this television movie, Stamos played a gay party planner hired to arrange his brother's wedding. However, when he finds out his brother's negative stance on gay marriage, he goes on strike. Stamos said he took the role because he supports gay marriage and wanted to find a way to speak out on the issue. "I believe that nobody should be denied equal rights because of who they love," he told the *New York Post*'s Joel Keller.

Though busy with *ER*, Stamos still found time to work as a producer. In 2007, he began working on a feature film about the famous television family *The Jeffersons* and was also developing a Western for TNT. Stamos also acted alongside Sean "P. Diddy" Combs in an ABC television adaptation of the Tony Award-winning play *A Raisin in the Sun*. The play delves into the struggles of an African-American family living in 1950s Chicago. It was scheduled to air in 2008. While Stamos relishes the fact that he has plenty of work right now, he also has plans for the future and what he might do after he retires. "Maybe I'll go to Australia to open my own restaurant, a little fast-food place on the beach," he told *People*'s Wihlborg. "I'll play in a crappy old rock and roll band ... and hang out on the beach. I like acting, but I won't be doing it until I'm 90."

Sources

Periodicals

Entertainment Weekly, January 28, 2005, pp. 36-38; December 8, 2006, pp. 21-22.
Fresno Bee, May 9, 1991, p. F1.
Newsday, February 12, 1989, sec. Part II, p. 2.
Orange County Register, April 3, 1989, p. F1; March 14, 2002, p. E.
People, March 21, 2005, p. 97.
San Jose Mercury News, January 7, 1996, sec. Arts, p. 15; August 23, 2004, p. 2A.
TV Guide, December 18-24, 2006, p. 28.

Online

"Gay for a Day: Studly Stamos is a Wedding Planner at 'War,'" *New York Post,* http://www.nypost. com/seven/12072006.tif/tv/gay_for_a_day_tv_ joel_keller.htm (June 27, 2007).

—*Lisa Frick*

Arran and Ratana Stephens

Founders of Nature's Path

Born Arran Stephens on January 6, 1944, on Vancouver Island, British Columbia, Canada; son of Rupert and Gwen Stephens; married Ratana Stephens, a native of India, in 1969; children: Shanti, Gurdeep, Jyoti, Arjan. *Education:* Ratana Stephens holds a BA in psychology and an MA in English literature.

Addresses: *Home*—Richmond, British Columbia, Canada. *Office*—9100 Van Horne Way, Richmond, BC V6X 1W3 Canada. *Web site*—http://www. naturespath.com. *Web site*—http://www. arranstephens.com.

Career

Arran Stephens founded the Golden Lotus vegetarian restaurant, Vancouver, British Columbia, Canada, 1967; co-founder/operator of LifeStream, 1971-1981; co-founder of Nature's Path, 1985; president and CEO of Nature's Path, 1985—. Ratana Stephens worked as a college lecturer in India in the late 1960s; after moving to the United States in 1969, she helped her husband run LifeStream; co-founder of Nature's Path, 1985; managed the couple's Woodlands Natural Foods Restaurants through the 1980s and into 1995; chief operating officer, Nature's Path, 1995—.

Member: Organic Trade Association, Whole Grains Council, International Federation of Organic Agriculture Movements, Canadian Health Food Association.

Awards: Together (awarded to Nature's Path): People's Choice Award, National Natural Foods Association, 1994; President's Award, Natural Foods Expo West, 2003; Top 100 Employers (Canada), *Maclean's* magazine, 2003, 2004, 2005; Organic Foods Award, Soil Association, 2004; British Columbia Export Award, Canadian Manufacturers & Exporters/Ministry of Economic Development, 2005; E. F. Schumacher Award for Greenest Business, Green Party of British Columbia, 2007. Arran Stephens: Ernst & Young Entrepreneur of the Year Award (Pacific Region), 2002; Organics Award of Excellence for lifetime achievement, Canadian Health Food Association, 2002; CEO of the Year, Canadian Institute of Food Science and Technology, 2003; inducted into the Canadian Health Food Association's Hall of Fame, 2005.

Sidelights

As pioneers of the natural-foods movement, Arran and Ratana Stephens operated one of Canada's first vegetarian restaurants in the late 1960s. In 1985, they founded Nature's Path, intent on providing consumers with healthy, wholesome, sustainably grown foods. Since then, the Canadian foods company has become North America's leading producer of organic breakfast foods. Nature's Path owns 30 percent of the organic cereal market, thanks in part to its highly popular EnviroKidz line. The company, which manufactures hot and cold cereals, energy bars, whole-grain breads and pastas, waffles, snack foods, and baking mixes, distributes its products in 40 countries.

Nature's Path is the only family owned independent business successfully competing in the organic-foods sector. Company president and CEO Arran

Stephens says he is not surprised his company does well against giants like General Mills, Kellogg's, and Kraft. Speaking to Susan McClelland of *Maclean's*, he told this story: "I once was asked how a pipsqueak company like mine could ever compete against the giant cereal producers. I responded with, 'Have you ever heard of David and Goliath?' In my case, David has a product the public wants."

Arran Stephens was born January 6, 1944, in Canada on Vancouver Island. He was the youngest child of Rupert and Gwen Stephens. Arran grew up on the Vancouver Island family farm—an 89-acre expanse dedicated to berry- and vegetable-growing. By the day's standards, Rupert was an unconventional farmer. He experimented with organic farming, using sawdust for mulch and relying on manure and seaweed instead of chemical additives. In 1957, Rupert gave up farming and moved the family to Los Angeles so he could pursue a career in songwriting. Used to farm life, the teenage Arran struggled in the bustling city. Eventually, he found his place among the hippie counterculture of the 1960s and lived on the streets, struggling to survive as an artist and poet.

In January of 1967, Arran traveled to India seeking spiritual enlightenment. He spent seven months there, studying under many mystics, including a notable Indian guru named Sant Kirpal Singh, author of *Man, Know Thyself*. In India, Arran studied the Buddhist notion of "right livelihood," the idea that one ought to find an occupation that uplifts and supports all living beings. Keeping this in mind, Arran returned to Vancouver and opened the Golden Lotus. It was one of Canada's first vegetarian restaurants.

In 1969, he returned to India and was asked if he would be interested in an arranged marriage. Arran consulted his guru before saying yes. After a one-day engagement, he married Ratana, who at the time worked as a college lecturer. "I'd say our marriage was divinely arranged," Arran told *Conscious Choice* writer James Faber. "At one point I was scared, but surrendered and trusted the judgment of my teacher. It was an absolutely sublime experience for me, and we fell in love."

The newlyweds settled in Canada and continued running the restaurant. Later, Arran wrote a book about his experiences in India. In 1971, the Stephenses helped found a natural-foods supermarket called LifeStream. "Back then," Arran told *Maclean's*, "there were no tofu or soy products around. We had to make them ourselves."

Bickering among partners forced them to sell the company in 1981, though they later reacquired it from Kraft in 1995. Meanwhile, the couple continued to operate their vegetarian restaurant, now called Woodlands. In 1985, Arran and Ratana founded Nature's Path and began selling its products from the back of the restaurant. One early favorite included organic manna bread made from a recipe they discovered in *The Essence Gospel of Peace,* an ancient Aramaic text.

Nature's Path added breakfast cereals and, in 1990, opened the first certified-organic cereal-manufacturing facility in North America. It was located in Delta, British Columbia. At this point, the company struggled and the Stephenses found themselves short on capital, wondering if they could make payroll. To stay afloat, they negotiated payment plans with suppliers after getting behind on their bills. While Arran concentrated on Nature's Path, Ratana managed the Woodlands Natural Foods Restaurants, which had grown to four locations. They sold the restaurants in 1995 after Nature's Path was back on solid footing. Ratana then joined the company and became chief operating officer.

Arran credits his wife's business acumen with getting them through the tough times. Ratana had grown up in the confectionery business. As a child, she watched her family lose its house and business after the venture failed. She did not want her kids to have the same experience. In an interview with former University of British Columbia history professor Catherine Carstairs, posted to the Nature's Path Web site, Arran discussed his wife's management style: "In any business, everything boils down to good management and good PR with your customers and staff. Ratana brought that personableness, charm, and heart into Nature's Path. She's also very bottom-line oriented. She can make a nickel scream!"

During the 2000s, Nature's Path enjoyed steady growth at an annual rate of 25 to 30 percent. The company added another cereal plant in Blaine, Washington, and opened a factory in Mississauga, Ontario, which makes toaster pastries. Arran and Ratana make a point to know each employee's name—there are about 300. Each day, they visit one of the plants to check on the workers. The Stephenses also focus on social responsibility and environmental sustainability. Nature's Path uses recycled paperboard and vegetable-based inks for packaging. The head office features a green roof and an organic garden for the staff. In addition, one percent of sales from EnviroKidz is donated to species and habitat conservation and education programs.

As larger corporations try to gain a foothold in the organic market, Nature's Path works to stay ahead of the pack. Offers to buy the company come in all the time, but instead of selling, the Stephenses wish to compete. Arran says product development is key. Nature's Path likes to take traditionally unhealthy but popular foods and re-create them. One example is the toaster pastry. Nature's Path created one with less sugar and devoid of the white flour and trans fats that are prevalent in most toaster pastries. The product sells well.

"We try to be quite strategic in coming out with something that is better than our competition's," Arran told Nick Roskelly of *Stagnito's New Products Magazine.* "Our goal is be No. 1 or No. 2 in a category. If we can't do that, then I think we should be looking at developing another product." As for the future, Arran plans to expand Nature's Path reach by venturing into the food-service market. He is especially interested in working with airlines and the military.

Selected writings

Journey to the Luminous: Encounters with Mystic Adepts of Our Century. Elton Wolf Publishing (Seattle, WA), 1999.

Sources

Periodicals

Food in Canada, January/February 2006, p. 62; January/February 2007, p. 42.
Maclean's, October 27, 2003, p. 70.
Stagnito's New Products Magazine, March 2004, p. 36, p. 38.

Online

"A Lifelong Journey," *Conscious Choice,* http://www.consciouschoice.com/2000/cc1303/alifelongjourney1303.html (May 21, 2008).
"Enjoying the Fruits of His Labor," *Bellingham Herald,* http://www.bellinghamherald.com/business/v-print/story/147567.html (March 31, 2008).
"Interview with Arran Stephens: President & Founder of Nature's Path Foods," Nature's Path, www.naturespath.com/index.php/plain/content/download/959/5916/file/Arran_Interview_DrCarstairs.pdf (March 31, 2008).
"Our People," Nature's Path, http://www.naturespath.com/about_us/our_people (March 31, 2008).
"Our Roots," Nature's Path, http://www.naturespath.com/about_us/our_roots (March 31, 2008).

—*Lisa Frick*

Julia Stewart

Frank Polich/Reuters/Landov

Chief Executive Officer of International House of Pancakes

Born Julia A. Stewart in 1955 in Visalia, CA; daughter of Dan Stewart (a history and civics teacher) and a physical education teacher; married Jon Greenawalt (divorced); married Tim Ortman (a filmmaker), August, 2007; children: Alec, Aubrey (from first marriage). *Education:* Attended the University of California—Santa Barbara, c. 1973-74; San Diego State University, B.A., 1977.

Addresses: *Office*—IHOP, 450 N. Brand Blvd., Glendale, CA 91203-1903.

Career

Regional marketing director, Carl's Jr. Restaurant, 1978-80; regional marketing manager, Burger King Corporation, 1980-84; marketing director, Spoons Grill & Bar/Stuart Anderson's Black Angus/Cattle Co. Restaurants, 1985, vice president for marketing, 1986-91; assistant general manager, Taco Bell/Yum! Brands, 1991, became western region vice president for operations, then national vice president for franchising and licensing, 1997-98; president of domestic division, Applebee's International, Inc., 1998-2001; president and chief operating officer, International House of Pancakes (IHOP), 2001, chief executive officer, 2002, board chair, 2006.

Sidelights

Julia Stewart has served as president and chief executive officer of International House of Pancakes (IHOP) since 2001. Her tenure has been one of tre-

mendous success for the U.S. casual-dining chain, almost all of whose 1,328 restaurants operate under the franchise model. Though she had spent much of her career with other players in the restaurant business, including Taco Bell and Applebee's, Stewart actually began her career at an IHOP restaurant back in the early 1970s as a teenaged waitress. When she was offered the top job in 2001, she told *Los Angeles Business Journal* writer Emily Bryson York, she felt "that little tug on my heart saying, 'Oh my God, I started there as a food server, I get to go home.'"

Stewart was born in 1955 in Visalia, California, a farming community in the San Joaquin Valley, the agricultural center of the state. Her mother taught physical education, and her father taught American history and civics. Both viewed teaching as one of the most honorable of professions, and hoped their only child would follow them into it. "I remember going to class with my mom, seeing how unruly the kids were and thinking, 'This is so much effort for so little money,'" she recalled in an interview with *New York Times* journalist Claudia H. Deutsch.

Stewart landed her first job as an IHOP waitress when she was around 15 years old. She was immediately entranced by the food service business. "I loved that you got feedback everyday," she explained to York in the *Los Angeles Business Journal* interview. "You didn't work a shift without learning what you did and didn't do. How it worked, how many re-fires, how many tips. There was always some mechanism for knowing how you delivered upon their expectations and I loved that."

Stewart won a scholarship to the University of California, but disliked the radical atmosphere of its Santa Barbara campus. She transferred to San Diego State University and planned to major in speech therapy, but some marketing communications classes she took ignited a desire to study business instead; she theorized that being a manager would be a form of teaching, because she would be imparting knowledge and serving as a mentor. Nevertheless, her decision was a rebuke of sorts back home. "My parents were incredibly disappointed," she recalled in the *New York Times* interview with Deutsch. "My father kept shaking his head, saying, 'We raised you to believe that money isn't the most important thing.'"

After graduating from San Diego State University in 1977, Stewart became a regional marketing director for Carl's Jr. Restaurants, a popular Southern California fast-food chain. In 1980, she went to work for the Burger King Corporation as a regional marketing manager, and after four years moved on to Stuart Anderson's Black Angus steakhouse chain, where she had noticeable results in reinvigorating the brand and bringing new customers into its dining rooms. She had long harbored a dream to some day run a company on her own, but knew she needed more than just marketing expertise to rise to the top of the executive ladder. To gain the required skills in balance sheets and profit and loss, in 1991 Stewart signed on with a management training program run by Taco Bell, which was owned by PepsiCo Inc. at the time. She spent her first six months as the assistant general manager at a Taco Bell—a move that her friends and family saw as a step down.

But Stewart's management skills were quickly recognized by her mentors in the training program, and she rose rapidly through Taco Bell's ranks to become its western regional vice president for operations, overseeing 1,000 restaurants and, in 1997, its national vice president for franchising and licensing. In 1998, she was hired by Applebee's International, Inc. to run its U.S. division. She improved the bar and grill chain's numbers with a new ad campaign under the slogan, "Eating Good in the Neighborhood." She had been hired at Applebee's, however, with the assumption that her position was a stepping stone to eventually running it altogether. She went to see its chief executive officer, Lloyd Hill, and said, "'It's been three years. It's time,'" she told David Farkas in *Chain Leader*. "He said, 'Nah, I don't think so.' And I said, 'Then it was probably best to leave.'"

Stewart, the mother of two, spent a few months out of work before IHOP invited her to become its president and chief operating officer in December of 2001. At the time, she was the only woman who was running a publicly traded restaurant company in the United States. Within a year, she advanced to the post of chief executive officer, and in 2006, added board chair to her list of job duties. IHOP's recognizable A-frame restaurants, topped by distinctive bright-blue roofs, had been an American landmark for decades, but had struggled to hang on to customers in the 1990s in a much more crowded field. Stewart went to work revising the franchise model, and changed it so that IHOP now helped its franchisers secure credit to build their own restaurants, rather than the previous method in which IHOP bore the construction costs for new units.

As Stewart had predicted, franchisees now had more of a personal stake in seeing their businesses succeed, and the numbers improved. The stock price for IHOP also rose, doubling between 2002 and 2006. In August of 2007, Stewart led a bid to take over her former employer, Applebee's, which was now in serious financial trouble. The $2.1 billion deal went forward, and IHOP acquired the 508 company-owned Applebee's restaurants, the largest casual-dining chain in the United States. Her plan involved turning them into franchise units.

Some IHOP franchisees refer to Stewart as "the Velvet Hammer" for her management style. Even her parents came to view her choice of career as a positive one in which she could contribute to society. Her father once came along one day on her Taco Bell job as she visited several restaurants. Seeing how she served as a mentor to her staff, who were mostly teenagers, he apologized for doubting her choices so many years before. "He said, 'You do teach, you do coach, and I really am proud of you,'" Stewart recalled in *New York Times* interview with Deutsch. "I still tear up when I talk about this."

Sources

Chain Leader, November 2007, p. 36.
Fortune, October 15, 2007, p. 48.
Los Angeles Business Journal, July 9, 2007, p. 23.
Nation's Restaurant News, July 30, 2007, p. 94.
New York Times, January 7, 2007; August 11, 2007.

—*Carol Brennan*

Tilda Swinton

Francis Specker/Landov

Actress

Born Katherine Matilda Swinton, November 5, 1960, in London, England; daughter of John (a military officer) and Judith Balfour (maiden name, Killen) Swinton; children: twins Xavier and Honor (with John Byrne, a writer and artist). *Education:* New Hall College, Cambridge University, B.A., 1983.

Addresses: *Agent*—Endeavor, 9601 Wilshire Blvd., 3rd Fl., Beverly Hills, CA 90210. *Home*—Nairn, Scotland.

Career

Actress in films, including: *Caravaggio*, 1986; *Aria*, 1987; *The Last of England*, 1988; *War Requiem*, 1989; *Edward II*, 1991; *Orlando*, 1992; *Wittgenstein*, 1993; *Female Perversions*, 1996; *Conceiving Ada*, 1997; *Love Is the Devil: Study for a Portrait of Francis Bacon*, 1998; *The War Zone*, 1999; *The Beach*, 2000; *The Deep End*, 2001; *Vanilla Sky*, 2001; *Adaptation*, 2002; *The Statement*, 2003; *Young Adam*, 2003; *Thumbsucker*, 2005 (also executive producer); *Constantine*, 2005; *The Chronicles of Narnia: The Lion, the Witch and the Wardrobe*, 2005; *Stephanie Daley*, 2006 (also executive producer); *Julia*, 2007; *Michael Clayton*, 2007; *The Man from London*, 2007; *Synecdoche*, 2007; *Come Like Shadows* (also known as *Dunsinane*), 2008; *The Curious Case of Benjamin Button*, 2008. Stage appearances include: *Mother Courage*, Royal Shakespeare Company, Barbican Theatre, London, 1984; *Measure for Measure*, Royal Shakespeare Company, Barbican Theatre, London, 1984; *Man to Man* (solo show), Traverse Theatre, Edinburgh, and Royal Court Theatre, London, c. 1987; *Mozart and Salieri*, Vienna,

Berlin, and London, c. 1989. Television appearances include: *Zastrozzi: A Romance* (miniseries), Channel 4, 1986; *Your Cheatin' Heart*, British Broadcasting Corporation, 1990.

Awards: Best actress award, Venice Film Festival, for *Edward II*, 1991; Academy Award for best supporting actress, Academy of Motion Picture Arts and Sciences, for *Michael Clayton*, 2008.

Sidelights

With ethereal looks and a steely intensity on screen, Tilda Swinton has been called "the most unique British actress of the past 20 years" by the London newspaper the *Observer*. Known by her flaming red hair and alabaster complexion, the Scot has proven to be a versatile, chameleon-like performer with a particular talent for vaguely androgynous characters thanks to her breakout performance in the 1992 period film *Orlando*. Swinton's career has swung from arty British films of the late 1980s to the Hollywood tale of corporate evil, *Michael Clayton*, for which Swinton won her first Academy Award.

Born Katherine Matilda Swinton in November of 1960, Swinton is the only daughter of a Scottish military officer who reached the rank of major-general in the Queen's Household Guards. Her parents were living in London at the time of her birth but the family seat was a castle in Scotland called Kimmerghame located on land that had been in the family for more than 30 generations. The Swinton lineage is traceable back to C. E. 886, when an ancestor of hers is on record as having sworn allegiance to Alfred the Great. In interviews, Swinton has downplayed this, and remains resolutely leftist in her political orientation. "All families are old," she told Suzie Mackenzie in the *Guardian.* "It's just that mine have lived in the same place a long time and happened to write things down."

Like her three brothers, Swinton was sent to boarding school at a young age. She was ten when she entered the West Heath School near London, where she was in the same class as a young Diana Spencer, the future Princess of Wales. West Heath was an elite school, but not considered the best place for a young women to prepare for a college degree; instead the well-heeled young women were expected to marry well and produce another generation of what Swinton has sometimes referred to as the "owning classes," according to the *Guardian's* Mackenzie. She defied expectations, however, by earning top marks, and even became the only member of her class to win four A-levels, the subject-based certificates that serve as college-entrance exams in the British educational system.

Entering New Hall, a women's college at Cambridge University, Swinton originally intended to study literature with the goal of becoming a writer, but became involved in the theater scene and switched her course of study to social and political sciences. After graduating in 1983, she won a place in the prestigious Royal Shakespeare Company of London, but soon realized that even in this artistic atmosphere she was expected to conform to certain conventions. In 1986, she made her film debut in *Caravaggio,* an early work from a stage-set designer-turned-filmmaker, Derek Jarman, about the Italian Renaissance painter of the same name. Openly gay, Jarman introduced some of the first positive gay imagery in the history of British filmmaking, and Swinton's debut as a woman in late sixteenth-century Italy who becomes enmeshed in a romantic triangle is the best-known film of Jarman's career.

Swinton made her next eight films with Jarman before his death from AIDS-related complications in 1994. These credits include 1987's *Aria* and *War Requiem,* a 1989 work that was the last screen appearance of Laurence Olivier. For her role as Isabella of France in the writer-director's 1991 adaptation of the late sixteenth-century drama *Edward II,* she

picked up the Best Actress award at the Venice Film Festival. She described Jarman as "the first person I ever met that lived as an artist," she told *New York Times* writer Lynn Hirschberg. "He was a person who found a way to make movies without any studio. Through him, I saw that I could live in a pre-industrial way."

Swinton first gained serious attention in the mainstream media for her title role in *Orlando* in 1992. Writing in the *Guardian,* Mackenzie called it "easily her best. Based on Virginia Woolf's novel, it is about a boy who becomes a man who becomes a woman. Spanning 400 years, it is a filmed essay about escape.... Girls don't inherit, so when Orlando becomes a woman she is told she may as well be dead. To all presiding purposes, she does not exist." The lavish period film from filmmaker Sally Potter was nominated for two Academy Awards in the costume and design categories.

In 1995 Swinton was the subject of bemused press reports for her participation in a conceptual art project at London's Serpentine Gallery. For seven days in a row she climbed into a glass box and slept—or appeared to sleep—for eight hours a day. When another *Guardian* journalist asked why she did it, she cited "idleness," as the reason. "I'm very tired at the moment, I've been working hard.... And I am fascinated that people in this country tend to be much more attentive to people when they're asleep or stricken or dying or dead." She noted further that there was also the idea that, "lying down in public [is] an aggressive act," she told the same interviewer, Simon Hattenstone. "You walk through London and see people lying down in doorways and you see people get so angry."

In the late 1990s Swinton appeared in some roles that other female thespians might have avoided altogether. She played a bisexual attorney in *Female Perversions,* a clueless mother in an incest-themed drama, *The War Zone,* and a bar hostess in the portrayal of real-life artistic debauchery in *Love Is the Devil: Study for a Portrait of Francis Bacon.* The last work dealt with the period in Irish painter Francis Bacon's life when he took a man who had burgled his London house as his lover; a future James Bond, Daniel Craig, played the petty thief. In a more conventional role, Swinton appeared in 1997's *Conceiving Ada* as Ada Lovelace, the mathematically gifted daughter of the poet Lord Byron who was involved in the development of what is usually termed the world's first computer, called the "Difference Engine," in the early 1840s.

Swinton began appearing in American-made fare early the next decade. She had been urged to try her luck in Hollywood by her agent, and recalled that she acquiesced only against her better judgment. "I remember saying there was really no point," she told *Entertainment Weekly*'s Karen Valby. "What was there being made that could ever accommodate me?" To her surprise, Swinton was offered a juicy role as an unbalanced leader of a commune in *The Beach,* which starred Leonardo DiCaprio as the tourist who seeks out the Thai beach compound. She earned a Golden Globe nomination for *The Deep End* in 2001, in which she was cast as Margaret, the wife of a Navy officer at sea. Her character struggles to cover up the death of her gay teenage son's menacing lover at their waterfront Lake Tahoe home, then finds herself involved in a blackmail plot. "As we see Margaret first, we think her weak," wrote Mackenzie in the *Guardian.* "But she is, under duress, steel. What was remarkable in Swinton's performance was her avoidance of climaxes of emotion. She insists on the ordinariness of her action, as she goes about, with a ceremonial informality, covering up for her child."

Next, Swinton had a small role in *Vanilla Sky,* and appeared in Spike Jonze's *Adaptation* with Nicolas Cage and Meryl Streep. In 2003, she starred in *Young Adam,* a tale of murder and sexual intrigue set in 1950s Scotland. *Thumbsucker,* released in 2005, was an unconventional film about a teenager who still retains the infantile habit. Most studios turned it down; Swinton signed on as the title character's mother and the movie's executive producer. Keanu Reeves had a role in it, as he did in a subsequent project for Swinton, *Constantine.* This 2005 big-budget movie was based on the graphic novel series "Hellblazer" and featured Swinton as the angel Gabriel, who in biblical lore served as God's messenger.

Swinton's pale skin made her an ideal choice for the part of the villainous White Witch in *The Chronicles of Narnia: The Lion, the Witch and the Wardrobe,* also released in 2005. Still determined to upend convention whenever possible, Swinton had to convince the film's producers that it was perfectly acceptable for a bad witch to have light-colored hair. In 2006, she played a pregnant forensic psychologist given the task of analyzing the motives of a teenager accused of hiding her pregnancy and killing the newborn in *Stephanie Daley.* A year later she took on the title role in *Julia* as a con artist and child kidnapper.

Another release from 2007 which earned Swinton terrific reviews was as an unbalanced lawyer in *Michael Clayton.* The title character is played by George Clooney and is a corporate "fixer" hired to clean up potentially embarrassing situations. Swinton was cast as Karen Crowder, the corporate counsel for a major agribusiness corporation. "A Lady Macbeth in pumps and discreet pearls, Karen has pledged her troth to her corporate masters," declared *New York Times* film critic Manohla Dargis. "She's a cliché—brittle, sexless, friendless, cheerless and all the rest—but what makes her work is her unnerving banality, visible in the blank canvas of a face that looks untouched by gentleness or empathy. This is a pitiful creature, as unloved by her writer-director creator as by the genius actress who plays her." Swinton won her first Oscar for the role in early 2008.

At the BAFTA Awards, Swinton was accompanied by a 30-year-old German-born artist named Sandro Kopp, who worked on the *Narnia* film with Swinton. Kopp was also with her at the Academy Awards later that winter, which prompted a minor flurry of tabloid gossip. When she and Kopp arrived at the house that Swinton shares with John Byrne, the father of her son-and-daughter twins born in 1998, she was confronted by a phalanx of journalists and photographers. "What is true is that John and I live here with our children and Sandro is sometimes here with us and we travel the world together," the perennially unflappable Swinton told the press, according to the *Sunday Times.* "We are all a family. What you must also know is that we are all very happy. Sandro is visiting now. As you can see, we are all putting our luggage into the house together."

Swinton's apparent aversion to more conventional roles, both on film and in real life, was well-documented before the reports of the "love triangle" appeared in the tabloids, but a 2001 interview she gave to a journalist for the Edinburgh-based *Scotsman,* Alastair McKay, seemed eerily prophetic. She said that even as a very young child she knew she was different from her family and peers, and told McKay that indeed, she had forged her own path—but the alternative would have been equally challenging to her, which she explained would have been "to make sure that you are following the script, that you are wearing the right things and you are marrying the right person, and buying the right car, and doing the right job and eating at the right restaurant. Or whatever those things are: having the right amount of children at exactly the right time, and the right relationships with everybody. That must be a hell of an effort."

Sources

Cineaste, Winter 1993, p. 18.
Entertainment Weekly, October 12, 2007, p. 38.

Guardian (London, England), August 24, 1995, p. 8; September 20, 2003, p. 24; March 11, 2005.

New York Times, August 28, 2005; October 5, 2007.

Observer (London, England), October 9, 2005, p. 14.

Scotsman (Edinburgh, Scotland), December 1, 2001, p. 4.

Sunday Times (London, England), August 17, 2003, p. 4; February 17, 2008, p. 3.

—*Carol Brennan*

Alice Temperley

Fashion designer

Born in 1975, in England; daughter of Julian (a former journalist and orchard owner) and Di (an orchard owner) Temperley; married Lars von Bennigsen (a banker), 2002. *Education:* Graduated from Central St. Martin's College of Art; earned M.A. from Royal College of Art, c. 1999.

Addresses: *Home*—London, England. *Office*—Temperley London, 6-10 Colville Mews, Lonsdale Road, London W11 2DA, England.

Career

Launched clothing label, Temperley London, in 2000; opened London boutique, 2002; opened New York City store, 2003.

Sidelights

In 2007, British fashion designer Alice Temperley became the newest young talent selected by mass retailer Target for its Go International limited-edition line of women's clothing. Temperley's appealingly feminine designs began selling at Target stores in September of 2007 and, like her standard collections, captured an often overlooked niche in fashion for pretty, wearable clothes that avoid trendiness. Writing in the London *Observer*, Chloe Fox called Temperley "this decade's most PR-perfect British fashion success story: she's a Somerset-born beauty whose designs make girls feel like women, whose barefoot Gatsby-esque gatherings can bring out the child in even the most sophisticated fashion cat."

Born in 1975 and the first of four children in her family, Temperley grew up on a cider farm in Somerset that her parents had bought as newlyweds. Her father, Julian, had been a journalist in South Africa and other places before marrying her mother, Di. The Temperleys added adjacent land in Somerset to their original parcel over the years, and their business grew it into one of the largest apple orchards in Europe.

Displaying a creative streak at a very early age, Temperley inherited her interest in fashion from her mother, who had worn a handmade gown with a train of real peacock feathers for her wedding. Once, when Temperley was four, she took scissors to a prized antique lampshade of her mother's. "Mum walked in, and beads were all over the floor," she recalled in an interview with *People*. "She wanted to be cross, but said it was just so sweet because all I said was, 'I want to make myself a necklace.'" After her parents bought her a proper supply of beads, Temperley began making earrings and within a few years was selling them at the cider stall on weekends. During her teen years, she made elaborate wall hangings and sewed fanciful costumes for her two sisters and brother.

Temperley entered one of the top art colleges in Britain, Central St. Martin's College of Art, where she studied textile arts. When she finished in the late 1990s, she was offered a job by Donna Karan, the American fashion designer, but turned it down and took a job at a textile company instead, while working toward a master's degree from the Royal College of Art. She began dating the German-born banker Lars von Bennigsen, and when he was transferred to a Hong Kong office, Temperley went with him and used the opportunity to travel across Asia to learn more about fabrics. "I wanted to find where all the best silks are made, all the best finishings," she told *People*. Von Bennigsen was supportive of her idea to launch her own clothing label, which she did when they returned to London.

Temperley's dresses quickly gained a cult following among style-setters in London, and in 2002, two years after launching Temperley London, Temperley and her husband opened a boutique in the Notting Hill area. The property also doubled as living quarters for Temperley and von Bennigsen, who eventually quit his job in finance in order to oversee her business. Her designs were a hit with high-end fashion retailers in the United States, selling at Henri Bendel in New York City and on the West Coast at Fred Segal. In late 2003, Temperley opened a New York City store, a nearly 5,000-square-foot space at the intersection of Broome and Mercer streets in SoHo. The appeal of her designs was transatlantic, she realized, and had more to do with generation than geography. "A lot of women my age have grown up shopping at thrift stores and market stalls, and they've learned to appreciate clothes of lasting quality," she theorized in an interview with *Vogue*'s Mark Holgate. "They don't need to have the latest thing. They're not interested in being part of the throwaway, trend-obsessed culture we live in."

Feminine and flattering are the two most-oft used words to describe Temperley's designs, which began with a dress line but expanded to include a full range of garments, including knitwear and trousers. "I design what I want to wear," Temperley explained about her design philosophy to *Financial Times* writer Edwina Ings-Chambers. She was still intensely focused on textiles and created her collections around prints she had designed herself and then had made into bolts of fabric. She then worked out next season's look with the help of her staff. "We look at what would work well on someone with a bust and what would work on someone with bigger hips and what would work on someone with a less-defined waist," she explained to Emily Davies in the *Times* of London.

Temperley continued to expand, launching a bridal division in 2005 and opening her second, antiques-filled U.S. outpost, this one off Melrose Avenue in Los Angeles. Despite the growing number of high-profile clients—Sarah Jessica Parker, Mischa Barton, Scarlett Johansson, and Gwyneth Paltrow were fans, and Hollywood stylist Rachel Zoe frequently used Temperley's clothes for her celebrity clients—Temperley avoided courting too much press for her business. She also preferred to remain out of the fashion-world orbit, which helped her avoid "feeling like I have to sell myself," she told Davies in the *Times* of London interview. "I don't go to every industry party. In a way the fashion industry terrifies me—the shallowness, the fickleness."

Instead Temperley and von Bennigsen carry on a fun, jet-set lifestyle with several high-profile or tastemaking pals, including the model Jacquetta Wheeler and *Top Chef* personality Padma Lakshmi. Temperley's sister, Mary, serves as director of sales for the company, which von Bennigsen plans to grow into a global lifestyles brand, with accessories, cosmetics, and even a home furnishings line in the works. They return to Somerset every year for England's National Apple Day in October, where her parents host an annual event for friends and neighbors. She and her husband also host an annual themed bash at the farm every summer for her birthday, which has become one of the most coveted invitations of the season. "I couldn't have done any of it without him," Temperley stressed in the interview with Fox for the *Observer*. "There have been so many times over the past five years that I have been broken, literally sobbing in a corner. Every time Lars has picked me up and told me it's going to be OK and that I have to carry on. He's the one who keeps the wheels turning."

Sources

Financial Times, September 10, 2002, p. 9.
New York Times, November 6, 2005.
Observer (London, England), April 30, 2006, p. 12.
People, August 16, 2004, p. 101.
Sunday Times (London, England), September 24, 2006, p. 14.
Times (London, England), July 5, 2004, p. 10.
Vanity Fair, September 2005, p. 208.
Vogue, August 2004, p. 192; May 2006, p. 128.
WWD, November 2, 2005, p. 14.

—*Carol Brennan*

T. I.

Rap musician

Dennis Van Tine/Landov

B orn Clifford Joseph Harris Jr., September 25, 1980; son of Violeta Morgan; children: Messiah, Domani, King, Deyjah.

Addresses: *Contact*—Atlantic Records, 1290 Avenue of the Americas, New York, NY 10104. *Web site*—http://www.grandhustle.com.

Career

B egan music career after signing with Arista at age 18; released first album, 2001; co-CEO and founder of Grand Hustle Records, 2003—. Film appearances include: *ATL*, 2006; *American Gangster*, 2007.

Awards: Vibe Award, best street anthem, for "Rubber Band Man," 2004; Vibe Award, best street anthem, for "U Don't Know Me," 2005; Billboard Music Awards, rap artist of the year and rap album of the year, for *King*, 2006; Billboard Music Awards, rap album artist of the year, rap song artist of the year, and video clip artist of the year, 2006; BET (Black Entertainment Television) Awards, best male hip hop artist, 2006 and 2007; Grammy Award, best rap solo performance, Recording Academy, for "What You Know," 2007; Grammy Award, best rap/sung collaboration, with Justin Timberlake, Recording Academy, for "My Love," 2007; BET Hip-Hop Awards, CD of the year, for *T. I. vs. T. I. P.*, 2007; BET Hip-Hop Awards, ringtone of the year, for "Big Things Poppin' (Do It)," 2007.

Sidelights

A tlanta-reared rapper T. I. never hides his street-thug past. The Grammy-winning lyricist used to sell crack cocaine before he began peddling CDs in the early 2000s. In 2006, T. I.'s mainstream appeal skyrocketed following the release of his fourth album, *King*, which was the top-selling hip-hop album of the year. In 2007, he starred opposite Academy Award-winner Denzel Washington in *American Gangster* and was also featured in a Chevrolet commercial with NASCAR's Dale Earnhardt Jr. T. I.'s rising fame also made him popular in the cellular world, with his voice anchoring top-selling ringtones.

Born Clifford Joseph Harris Jr. on September 25, 1980, T. I. was raised in the poor Bankhead area of Atlanta by his grandmother. As a child, he earned the nickname Tip, which later morphed into T. I. P. when he started rapping and to T. I. after he secured his first record deal. Early on, T. I. was a budding entrepreneur. In elementary school, he sold candy bars to classmates to generate cash. By junior high, T. I. switched to selling crack. As a teen, T. I. rapped semi-regularly with a group of school buddies. After a friend was killed, the boys recorded a song, "I Miss You." Cutting the track prompted T. I. to consider a career in music.

In 1999, T. I. met Kawan "K.P." Prather, an executive with LaFace Records, a subsidiary of Arista. Instantly, Prather knew he wanted to give the 18 year old a chance. Speaking to Sonia Murray of the *Atlanta Journal-Constitution*, Prather said, "I believed him before I even heard him rap," Prather said. "He had the same kind of look in his eye that he has now. Like, 'I hope you get this because I'm special. Now you can either come along with me, or you can say, "I had a chance to be a part of that."'"

Prather signed T. I. to a record deal and seeing another way to make it in life, T. I. stopped selling drugs. At this time, he also changed his name from T. I. P. to T. I. to avoid confusion with another Arista artist, Q-Tip. Ready for a fresh start, T. I. was disappointed when he released 2001's *I'm Serious* and it failed to generate much interest. The disc was created with the help of the hit-making production duo Pharrell Williams and Chad Hugo, who produce under the name the Neptunes. "When it didn't blow up, it was like, whoa, we weren't expecting this," T. I. told *New York Times* reporter Lola Ogunnaike.

T. I.'s music, however, gained a small following in the South, so he toured there relentlessly trying to drum up support. T. I. began releasing mixtapes, which are small compilations of songs, and little by little, the crowds grew at the small clubs where he played. T. I. wanted to produce another album, but was dropped by Arista. He courted the hip-hop label Def Jam, which also turned him down. In the end, Atlantic Records signed him to a joint recording venture with his own newly formed imprint, Grand Hustle.

In 2003, T. I. released *Trap Muzik*. Filled with sing-song chants about street life and the drug game, the album sold a half-million copies and was certified gold. It spawned two well-known hits: "24's" and "Rubber Band Man." T. I.'s star was rising but he hit a snag in 2004 when he was jailed for a few months for violating probation stemming from a late 1990s drug charge. Stuck behind bars, T. I. was unable to promote the album to its fullest potential.

T. I.'s next album, 2004's *Urban Legend*, sold even better. With hits like "Bring 'Em Out" and "U Don't Know Me," the album went platinum, selling more than a million copies. The next year, 2005, was a busy one for T. I. He toured with Nelly and also

contributed his voice to the Destiny's Child hit "Soldier." In addition, T. I. became the first rapper to appear on the television hit *The O.C.*, which was known for showcasing hot, new talent.

In 2006, T. I. released *King*, which sold a half-million copies its first week. Sales were rapid due in part to T. I.'s rising popularity, but also because of a marketing ploy. "What You Know," the album's first single, was not made available though iTunes or sold in stores as a single. Sprint cell phone users could acquire the song, but everyone else had to buy the album to get a copy of the song. Filled with club anthems, street stories, and contemplative cuts, *King* was the top-selling rap album of the year, outselling the likes of Jay-Z and Ludacris. The album also showcased T. I.'s poetic side, featuring verses constructed as quatrains (four lines of verse).

Just weeks after *King* was released, T. I. was riding in his van with his entourage when they became the target of a highway shootout. King's personal assistant and childhood friend Philant Johnson was killed. The shooting reportedly happened following a nightclub spat earlier in the evening and was also one of a number of gunfire attacks in recent weeks involving hip-hop singers, which served to dampen respect for the genre.

King generated many awards for T. I., including Billboard Music Awards for Rap Artist of the Year and Rap Album of the Year. The hit single "What You Know" won T. I. a Grammy for Best Rap Solo Performance. T. I. was disappointed, however, when Ludacris won the Grammy for best hip-hop album for *Release Therapy*. Tension between the two rappers mounted as T. I. spoke out in public, insisting *King* was the better album.

Around the same time *King* was released, T. I. made his acting debut in *ATL*. The movie follows the lives of four Atlanta teens as they try to escape the hood. In 2007, he took a turn alongside Denzel Washington in the Harlem drug movie *American Gangster*.

In 2007, T. I. released his fifth album, *T. I. vs. T. I. P.* As the title suggests, the album explores his alter egos—the street-hardened T. I. P. and the celebrity entertainer T. I. "I think T. I. P. thinks T. I. is a little too concerned with fame and stardom," T. I. told Rebecca Louie of the *New York Daily News*. "And T. I. thinks T. I. P. is too concerned with the way we used to live rather than the way we need to live right now. Both of these individuals reside within Clifford Harris. He just pretty much sits back and watches the show."

The album was divided into three acts. The first, laden with gritty verses, features T. I. P.-heavy songs like "Watch What You Say To Me" and "Da Dopeman." The second act is all T. I., with smooth-sounding woman-wooing songs, such as "Show It to Me." In the third act, the two sides fight with each other. The album, with guest appearances by Eminem, Jay-Z, Justin Timberlake, Ciara, and Wyclef Jean, did not create as much of a buzz as *King*.

On October 13, 2007, his alter ego, T. I. P., seemed to rise to the surface again when the rapper was jailed on several weapons-related charges. T. I. was arrested by agents from the U.S. Bureau of Alcohol, Tobacco, Firearms and Explosives (ATF) after picking up three machine guns, two silencers, and a pistol from an undercover ATF officer. According to authorities, his bodyguard had purchased them on his behalf. A search of T. I.'s home turned up several more weapons. He entered a plea of not guilty on October 19, 2007. The same day T. I. was arrested, he won two awards from the BET Hip-Hop Awards: CD of the Year (tied with Common's *Finding Forever*) and Ringtone of the Year for his song "Big Things Poppin' (Do It)".

Besides his record imprint Grand Hustle Records, T. I. is involved in several entrepreneurial ventures. He owns New Finish, a construction company; Elite Auto Concierge, a car customization shop; and Club Crucial, an Atlanta nightspot. He also started his own clothing line, AKOO, which is short for "A King of Oneself." T. I. has four children—Messiah, Domani, King, and Deyjah. He also considers one of girlfriend Tameka "Tiny" Cottle's daughters his, though he is not her biological father.

Selected discography

I'm Serious, Arista, 2001.
Trap Muzik, Atlantic, 2003.
Urban Legend, Atlantic, 2004.
King, Atlantic, 2006.
T. I. vs. T. I. P., Atlantic, 2007.

Sources

Periodicals

Atlanta Journal-Constitution, May 4, 2006, p. D1; June 24, 2007, p. K1.
Billboard, May 5, 2007.
New York Times, April 12, 2006, sec. Arts, p. 3.
People, April 24, 2006, p. 94.
Plain Dealer (Cleveland, OH), August 3, 2007, p. T16.
St. Louis Post-Dispatch, June 22, 2006, sec. Get Out, p. 9.

Online

"A rapper sees 'big things' happen when his persona pulls double duty," *New York Daily News*, http://www.nydailynews.com/entertainment/music/2007/07/02/2007-07- 02_artist_has_hot_tip-1.html (August 14, 2007).
"MIA T. I. Upstages BETs," E! Online, http://www.eonline.com/print/index.jsp?uuid=63096652.tife555-417e&hyph en;beb0-2ea189d3fcd4 (October 19, 2007).
"T. I.; In rap, inner war can be a trap," *New York Times*, http://www.nytimes.com/2007/07/03/arts/music/03sann.html?ex=13411152.tif00&en=15de6cf8ae9fae69&ei=5088&partner=rssnyt&emc=rss (August 14, 2007).
" T. I.'s lawyers ask for bond, home confinement ," CNN.com, http://www.cnn.com/2007/SHOWBIZ/Music/10/19/ti.hearing/index.html?iref=newssearch (October 19, 2007).
"T. I.'s new music pits him against his younger self," *Chicago Tribune*, http://www.chicagotribune.com/features/chi-0708_tijul08,1,325300.story?coll=chi-entertainment-utl&ctrack=2&cset=true (August 14, 2007).

—*Lisa Frick*

Justin Timberlake

Ian West/PA Photos/Landov

Singer and actor

Born Justin Randall Timberlake, January 31, 1981, in Memphis, TN; son of Randy Timberlake and Lynn Harless (maiden name, Bomar).

Addresses: *Office*—Tennman Records, PO Box 18765, Beverly Hills, CA 90209.

Career

Appeared on *All-New Mickey Mouse Club,* Disney Channel, 1989-94; member, 'N Sync (pop group), 1996-2002; launched film acting career with *Longshot,* 2000; began solo singing career, 2002; signed deal with Turner Broadcasting to be special sports correspondent, 2003; signed agreement to become spokesman for McDonald's, 2003; appeared in film *Edison,* 2005; founded William Rast clothing line (with Trace Ayala), 2005; appeared in films *Alpha Dog, Southland Tales,* and *Black Snake Moan,* all 2006; appeared on *Saturday Night Live,* 2006; co-founded (with Eytan Sugerman) first restaurant, Destino's, 2006; chairman and chief executive officer, Tennman Records, Beverly Hills, CA, 2007—; provided voice for *Shrek the Third,* 2007; songwriter, producer, and singer for tracks on Duran Duran's album *Red Carpet Massacre,* 2007; served as co-executive producer for television series *My Problem with Women,* 2008; songwriter and producer for tracks on Madonna's album *Hard Candy,* 2008; hosted the ESPYs, 2008.

Awards: Grammy Award for best pop vocal album, National Academy of Recording Arts and Sciences, for *Justified,* 2003; Grammy Award for best male pop vocal performance, National Academy of Recording Arts and Sciences, for "Cry Me a River," 2003; MTV Europe Music Award for best pop artist, 2006; MTV Europe Music Award for best male artist, 2006; Grammy Award for best dance recording, National Academy of Recording Arts and Sciences, for "Sexy-Back," 2006; Grammy Award for best rap/sung collaboration, National Academy of Recording Arts and Sciences, for "My Love," 2006; People's Choice Award for favorite R&B song, for "SexyBack," 2007; MTV Video Music Award for best choreography for "My Love," 2007; MTV Video Music Award for best direction for "What Goes Around ... Comes Around," 2007; BRIT Award for international male solo artist, British Phonographic Industry, 2007; MTV Video Music Award for quadruple threat of the year, 2007; American Music Award for male artist of the year, 2007; American Music Award for favorite male pop artist, 2007; World Music Award for best male pop artist, International Federation of the Phonographic Industry, 2007; Grammy Award for best male pop vocal performance, National Academy of Recording Arts and Sciences, for "What Goes Around ... Comes Around," 2007; Grammy Award for best dance recording, National Academy of Recording Arts and Sciences, for "LoveStoned/I Think She Knows," 2007; People's Choice Award for favorite male singer, 2008; People's Choice Award for favorite pop song, 2008.

Sidelights

Moving from being a member of international boy band phenomenon 'N Sync to an accomplished solo artist, Justin Timberlake became an internationally respected singer on the strength of two solo albums, *Justified* and *FutureSex/LoveSounds*. He used his musical success to launch a number of other enterprises including a record label, clothing line, and numerous product endorsements. Timberlake began his career on the *All-New Mickey Mouse Club*, and became a serious film actor in the early 2000s by appearing in films such as *Alpha Dog*.

Born on January 31, 1981, in Memphis, Tennessee, Timberlake is the son of Randy Timberlake and Lynn Harless. Raised in a small Tennessee town, he was a shy child until the age of eight or nine. Around that time, the young Timberlake had a realization that performing would bring him attention and that he enjoyed it. He discovered he had natural talent, and soon began working professionally, with an appearance on *Star Search*.

Timberlake's performing career began in earnest when he was cast on the Disney Channel's *All-New Mickey Mouse Club*. Appearing on the show from 1989 to 1994, he was not the only cast member to achieve success. His co-stars included J. C. Chasez, who also became a member of 'N Sync, actress Keri Russell, and singers Britney Spears and Christina Aguilera. Timberlake and Spears later became romantically involved during his 'N Sync days.

After *All-New Mickey Mouse Club* was cancelled, Timberlake found success again. Within two years, he had joined the singing group 'N Sync. Initially guided by boy-band guru Lou Pearlman, five members—Timberlake, Chasez, Lance Bass, Joey Fatone, and Chris Kirkpatrick—quickly established themselves as a pop singing powerhouse with their self-titled 1998 debut album and a large teen following. Following a 1998 Christmas album, 'N Sync released two more albums, 2000's *No Strings Attached* and 2001's *Celebrity*. The group sold more than 26 million albums total in the United States alone over the course of their career.

During his time with 'N Sync, Timberlake went from being the baby of the group to its front man and a sex symbol, seemingly outgrowing his teen following by the early 2000s. He emerged as the stand-out among the five, creating tension between the members. Questions swirled over whether the group would last. *Celebrity* sold only 4.8 million copies, millions less than previous releases. Even before the "Celebrity 2002" tour in support of 'N Sync's last album, Timberlake began recording what became his first solo album and would change the course of his career.

Released in November of 2002, Timberlake co-wrote all 13 tracks on *Justified* with the leading writers and producers in hip-hop and R&B including Timbaland, the Neptunes, and Bryan McKnight. The sound was far more mature, sophisticated, and sexually raw than anything released by 'N Sync, and was influenced by a variety of musical styles. Critics were somewhat surprised by the change, but generally praised the direction the multi-talented Timberlake took. The New York *Daily News*'s Jim Farber called the record, "a sexy, funny, and surprisingly bold work that ultimately has a lot more to say about this 21-year-old's current creativity than his musical or romantic past."

Explaining *Justified*'s origins to Elysa Gardner of *USA Today*, Timberlake says, "I grew up listening to Stevie Wonder, Marvin Gaye, Donny Hathaway, Al Green, Michael Jackson, Prince. If you know that, then this album makes perfect sense. It's not a departure from anything I've done, because I haven't done anything on my own. 'N Sync is great, but this is different—not only from 'N Sync, but from anything out there.... People aren't used to hearing me in this way, and it may take them a few listens to get it."

Fans embraced the new Timberlake as well, sending singles "Like I Love You," "Cry Me a River," and "Rock Your Body" to the top of the charts. Within two months of the release of *Justified*, more than 2.2 million copies were sold in the United States alone. The album later went at least triple platinum, and sold seven million copies worldwide by mid-2006. With the success of *Justified*, Timberlake left 'N Sync behind and the group went on what was assumed to be a permanent hiatus.

In between tours in support of his solo album—including a co-headlining outing with Aguilara—Timberlake pursued other interests. In 2003, he inked a one-year agreement with Turner Broadcasting to serve as a special correspondent for TBS and TNT sports programming. Timberlake contributed segments and features, which aired during NBA games, as well as stock car racing, golf, and college football. That same year, he also signed a two-year deal to become a spokesman for McDonald's worldwide. As part of the agreement, he recorded vocals for the company's signature "I'm Lovin' It" commercials.

While Timberlake was sitting on top of the world, he became caught up in a controversial event. Singing at the half-time show of the 2004 Super Bowl, he accidentally tore part of the costume of co-star Janet Jackson and revealed much of one of her breasts on national television. While Timberlake was supposed to tear off part of the outfit at that time, both the inner and outer pieces were unintentionally removed in what came to be known as a "wardrobe malfunction." The incident caused an uproar, and the network broadcasting the Super Bowl, CBS, potentially faced fines.

The storm surrounding the Super Bowl incident did not greatly affect Timberlake's career or outside projects. Thus, in 2005, he launched his own clothing line, William Rast, with his best friend from childhood, Trace Ayala. Inspired by Timberlake's distinctive style, Ayala did most of the designing while Timberlake oversaw fashion shows and other details. To avoid the celebrity clothing line trap, it was not even publicly announced that Timberlake was part of the project until shortly before an October of 2006 fashion show. That same year, Timberlake also co-founded his first restaurant, Destino's, with Eytan Sugarman.

Though Timberlake's outside projects were satisfying, his primary focus remained music. In September 2006, he released his second album, *FutureSex/LoveSounds*. As with *Justified*, Timberlake co-wrote the tracks with leading artists like Timbaland, and also co-produced the record. Building on the dance/hip-hop sound he created for *Justified*, *FutureSex/LoveSounds'* first single "SexyBack" was a number-one hit as was "My Love." *FutureSex/LoveSounds* debuted as the number-one album in the United States the first week of release as well as in multiple other countries, and sold six million copies worldwide by May of 2007.

Critics praised both the album and how Timberlake was managing his singing career, with Andrew Dansby of the *Houston Chronicle* noting "he's successfully reinvented himself as a modernized pop practioner." Writing in the *New York Times*, Jon Pareles commented "Mr. Timberlake has suavely made a rare kind of transition: from boy-band trouper to self-determined songwriter and bandleader. He doesn't hide who his mentors are.... To compensate for what he lacks in grit and wildness, Mr. Timberlake makes smart choices for producers and brings rappers into his songs."

As *FutureSex/LoveSounds* was becoming Timberlake's second major hit, his acting career was also growing. He made a well-regarded appearance as a guest host on *Saturday Night Live* in December of 2006. Among the show's highlights was a digital short he made with Andy Samberg which parodied R&B sex songs. The short, "D*** in a Box," became a YouTube hit, viewed more than ten million times in December of 2006.

While that short brought Timberlake a wide audience, he wanted to be taken seriously as an actor. After launching his film career with *Longshot* in 2000 and playing a reporter in the 2005 direct-to-video release *Edison Force*, he had three meaty film roles in 2006. One was *Alpha Dog*, based on a true story. In the film, Timberlake played a member of a Los Angles gang of bored teens who helped kidnap and kill the brother of another teenager who had betrayed them in a drug deal. His character, Frankie Ballenbacher, tries to prevent the killing of the young hostage.

Of his secondary career and *Alpha Dog*, Timberlake told John Hiscock of the *Toronto Star*, "To me, acting is a hobby. I've been lucky enough to have a musical career that has gone pretty good and acting is something I have always wanted to do. I've been offered a lot of different things I have turned down without thinking twice about, but *Alpha Dog* was an opportunity for me to sink my teeth into something. It just spoke volumes to me."

In addition to *Alpha Dog*, Timberlake also appeared in *Southland Tales* and *Black Snake Moan* in 2006. In the latter film, he had a small role as a troubled soldier and impressed his director, Craig Brewer, with his work in the film. Brewer told Reed Tucker of the *New York Post*, "When I see him in other movies and on *SNL*, I really respect how he's handling himself. Even his critics and detractors are looking at him, shrugging their shoulders and saying 'God, am I really loving Justin Timberlake?' It's about time."

While Timberlake appeared in another film in 2007—providing the voice for Artie in the animated *Shrek the Third*—he spent much of the year focusing on music again. He toured in support of *FutureSex/LoveSounds* several times and filmed his stop at New York City's Madison Square Garden for an HBO music special. Timberlake also launched his own record label. A joint venture with Interscope Records, Timberlake served as the chairman and chief executive officer of Tennman Records. In addition, Timberlake's musical career took a different turn when he began contributing to other artists' works as a songwriter, producer, and performer. In 2007, he helped write, produce, appeared on one track, and co-wrote and co-produced two others tracks on the Duran Duran release *Red Carpet Massacre*.

Timberlake's career continued to remain diverse in 2008. He co-wrote and co-produced five songs on Madonna's album *Hard Candy.* Timberlake also sang on one track, "4 Minutes," which was a number-one hit in the United Kingdom. His producing career also extended to acts signed to his label, as he worked with songwriter Matt Morris on his first album for Tennman Records. In addition, Timberlake acted in two films scheduled for release in 2008, the Mike Myers comedy *The Guru* and *The Open Road.* Timberlake added executive producer to his list of accomplishments as he acted in that capacity for a television series scheduled to air on NBC, *My Problem with Women.* He continued to capitalize on his celebrity by endorsing products such as a new line of men's fragrances put out by Parfums Givenchy.

Describing the appeal of Timberlake as a singer and larger cultural symbol, producer/songwriter Jimmy Jam told Jon Bream in the *Vancouver Province,* "He's got It—whatever It is. Whatever Eminem has. Whatever the Elvises had back in their day. Whatever It is for this generation, Justin has got It."

Selected discography

(With 'N Sync) *'N Sync,* Jive, 1998.
(With 'N Sync) *Home for Christmas,* Jive, 1998.
(With 'N Sync) *No Strings Attached,* Jive, 2000.
(With 'N Sync) *Celebrity,* Jive, 2001.
Justified, Jive, 2002.
FutureSex/LoveSounds, Jive, 2006.

Sources

Books

Complete Marquis Who's Who Biographies, Marquis Who's Who, 2008.

Periodicals

Associated Press, September 8, 2006.
Birmingham Evening Mail (Birmingham, England), November 2, 2007, p. 42.
Business Wire, March 28, 2003.
Canada NewsWire, October 25, 2007.
Chicago Sun-Times, November 10, 2002, p. 1.
Daily News (New York, NY), October 30, 2000, p. 38; October 28, 2002, p. 41; May 8, 2003, p. 105.
Entertainment Weekly, March 28, 2008, p. 15; April 25, 2008, p. 58.
Fresno Bee (Fresno, CA), January 18, 2007, p. A1.
Houston Chronicle (Houston, TX), September 12, 2006, p. 1.
Music Week, May 10, 2008, p. 28.
New York Post, January 7, 2007, p. 36.
New York Times, September 2, 2006, p. B7; October 22, 2006, sec. 9, p. 1; December 23, 2006, p. B11.
PR Newswire, June 19, 2006; September 20, 2006; May 28, 2007; February 22, 2008.
San Diego Union-Tribune, September 5, 2003, p. E3.
San Francisco Chronicle, March 6, 2002, p. D1; February 3, 2004, p. A1.
Toronto Star, January 5, 2007, p. D3.
Toronto Sun, December 23, 2002, p. 38.
USA Today, October 28, 2002, p. 1D.
Vancouver Province (Vancouver, British Columbia, Canada), September 2, 2003, p. B3.
Village Voice, February 14, 2007.
Winnipeg Sun (Winnipeg, Manitoba, Canada), January 7, 2007, p. C4.

—A. Petruso

Jean Touitou

Founder of A.P.C. and fashion designer

Born c. 1952, in Tunisia; son of Odette; married Judith; children: Lily. *Education:* Studied linguistics and history at the University of Paris (Sorbonne).

Addresses: *Home*—Paris, France. *Office*—A.P.C., 45 Rue Madame, 75006 Paris, France.

Career

Worked as a teacher and as a chef before taking a job with a leather manufacturer; with the fashion designer and retailer Kenzo, c. late 1970s, and another fashion company called Irie; held then key position in the menswear design department of Agnès B; founded Atelier de Production et de Creation (A.P.C.), 1986; opened first store, 1988; founder of a private preschool in Paris, 2008.

Sidelights

Jean Touitou conceived his French clothing label, A.P.C., back in the mid-1980s as a kind of anti-fashion statement. Determined to design and sell well-made items of apparel that would last their wearer at least five years, Touitou launched the company, whose French-language acronym stands for Atelier de Production et de Création or "Studio of Production and Creation," as a design collective that drew upon past as well as current trends. "The thing about fashion that bothers me is that it's not about clothes, but more about image and noise, which is nonsense," the characteristically outspoken Touitou told *WWD* writer Eric Wilson. "At the end of the day, it's only scarves for tourists at the airport."

Touitou was in his mid-thirties when he founded A.P.C. in 1986 with a menswear line. He was born in Tunisia into a family of Tunisian Jews—a religious community whose presence in the North African country dates back to Roman times—but the Touitous emigrated to France—Tunisia's colonial ruler until 1956—when he was nine years old. He went on to study linguistics and history at the Sorbonne, and became involved in leftist political causes as a young man. With his varied ambitions, Touitou had a difficult time settling on one career: He taught school for a time, tried out life as a chef, and then worked for a leather manufacturer. He finally found his calling when he took a job in the stockroom of the Paris fashion emporium Kenzo. Named after the Japanese-born designer whose wares had a strong following among fashion cognoscenti in the 1970s, Kenzo was an exciting place to work, Touitou recalled in an interview with Christy de Raimond of the *Daily News Record.* "There was an international feeling. A lot was going on, the punk movement, the music and art scene. We worked hard at Kenzo but we had a great time."

After Kenzo, Touitou went on to other jobs in the French fashion industry, including a key position in the menswear department of designer Agnès B. He founded A.P.C. in 1986 with a collection of menswear, but realized that women were buying the well-fitted shirts for themselves and launched a separate women's line in 1990. He opened the first A.P.C. store in Paris in 1988, locating it on the less fashionable side of the Latin Quarter, which is the traditional students' neighborhood near the Sorbonne. It was a family-run operation, and remained so years later: Touitou's father assumed responsibility for the finances, and his sister handled the occasional public relations task.

Touitou was adamant, however, that his company could succeed without spending precious resources on advertising or, as many start-up labels do, by giving clothes away to celebrities. A.P.C. declined to participate in Paris's twice-yearly Fashion Week extravaganzas, at which store buyers and journalists assemble to preview the new collections. Instead he simply hired two models and presented the new lines to a select group in an informal party atmosphere; however, fashion writers were among some of A.P.C.'s most devoted customers, with the *Independent*'s Lucy Ryder Richardson noting that "A.P.C.'s product is fairly priced and looks both unisex and anonymous. What seems quite ordinary hanging from the rails, however, has something about it that pulls the aficionado closer.... There's the perfect pair of needlecords, the kind you designed in your mind but could never quite find, the V-neck jumper with that little bit of extra volume at the cuffs, or the neat plastic mac that comes cut like a duffel coat."

Keenly interested in other forms of creative expression besides fashion, Touitou began branching out into art and music in the 1990s. He built a recording studio inside A.P.C.'s Paris headquarters, which all employees are free to use on the weekends, and also created an in-house record label. Its releases include *Abstract Depressionism,* for which several musicians contributed what they considered the saddest song ever. He has also collaborated on various projects with filmmakers Wes Anderson and Zoe Cassevetes, and told several journalists about a plan to import coca leaves from South America to make what he liked to call "cocaine tea," but quickly asserted "it has nothing to do with the drug," as he told *W*'s Venessa Lau. "It's legal to buy coca leaves in South America, and it's legal to have tea made of it. It's very energizing and not as bad as coffee."

A.P.C. sells its wares through a well-designed catalog, a few select store accounts such as Barneys New York, and in 29 separate A.P.C. stores. Occasionally the collections feature limited-edition pieces by well-known designers such as Martin Margiela. For the most part, however, Touitou steers clear of those in the fashion world who do not share his interests in music, art, and philosophy, dismissing what he described as those who "have nothing to say except 'this embroidery took Mr. Schmuck and his atelier 1,328 hours of insane work,'" as he told Richardson in the *Independent*. In 2007, he bought out his business partner because the other wanted to move forward with A.P.C., but Touitou was firmly opposed to adding non-apparel items like fragrance under A.P.C.'s name. "If it's overexposed, it just dies," he asserted in an interview with Christine Muhlke in the *New York Times Magazine.*

In January of 2008, Touitou ventured into distinctly non-fashion territory when he and his wife founded a private preschool in Paris called A.P.E., or Ateliers de la Petite Enfance. They launched it after Touitou was dissatisfied with the regimented style of learning that state-run schools offer preschoolers and the corresponding lack of any imagination-developing curricula at expensive private nursery schools. Students, who include his young daughter Lily, wear stylish little smocks and sit in child-sized chairs based on a design by Alvar Aalto, the Finnish architect often hailed as the father of modernism. Touitou hopes to replicate the A.P.E. schools elsewhere in Paris, telling *W*'s Christopher Bagley that he had finally seized upon the "way to build something solid that might last longer than fashion."

Sources

Daily News Record, June 29, 1990, p. 3.

Independent (London, England) October 25, 2001, p. 8.

New York Times Magazine, March 9, 2008, p. 168.

W, December 2005, p. 107; April 2008, p. 190.

WWD, July 18, 2001, p. 5; September 14, 2005, p. 50.

—*Carol Brennan*

Natasha Tretheway

Logan Mock-Bunting/Getty Images

Poet and professor

Born in 1966 in Gulfport, MS; daughter of Eric (a poet and professor) and Gwendolyn Ann (Turnbough; a social worker) Trethewey; married Brett Gadsden (a history professor), 1998. *Education:* University of Georgia, B.A., 1989; Hollins University, Roanoke, VA, M.A., 1991; University of Massachusetts at Amherst, M.F.A., 1995.

Addresses: *E-mail*—ntrethe@emory.edu. *Office*—N209 Callaway Center, Creative Writing Program, Emory University, 537 Kilgo Circle, Atlanta, GA 30322.

Career

Welfare caseworker, Augusta, GA, c. 1989-90; assistant professor of poetry, Auburn University, Auburn, AL, c. 1998-2001; assistant professor of English and creative writing, then Phillis Wheatley distinguished chair professor of poetry, Emory University, Atlanta, GA, c. 2001—; Lehman Brady Joint Chair Professor of Documentary and American Studies, Duke University, Durham, NC, 2005-06; also taught at the University of North Carolina-Chapel Hill. Contributor to periodicals, including *Agni, American Poetry Review, Callaloo, Kenyon Review, New England Review,* and *Southern Review.*

Awards: Grolier Poetry Prize, for "Storyville Diary," Grolier Poetry Book Shop, 1999; Cave Canem Poetry Prize, for *Domestic Work,* 1999; Mississippi Institute Arts and Letters Book Prize, for *Domestic Work,* 2001; Lillian Smith Book Award, for *Domestic Work,* 2001; Pushcart Prize, for "Labor," 2002; Guggenheim Fellowship, John Simon Guggenheim

Memorial Foundation, 2003; Mississippi Institute of Arts and Letters Book Prize, for *Bellocq's Ophelia,* 2003; Pulitzer Prize for Poetry, for *Native Guard,* 2007; honorary doctorate of letters, Delta State University, 2007; Jessica Nobel-Maxwell Memorial Award for Poetry; Julia Peterkin Award, Converse College; Money for Women/Barbara Deming Memorial Fund Award; Margaret Walker Award for poetry; Distinguished Young Alumna Award, University of Massachusetts at Amherst.

Sidelights

The winner of the 2007 Pulitzer Prize for poetry, Natasha Trethewey has published three lauded collections of poems and also works as a professor of English and creative writing at Emory University. Often influenced in her writing by growing up biracial in the Southern United States, the author was considered gifted by many critics. Reviewing her third collection of poetry, *Native Guard,* in *Washington Post Book World,* Darryl Lorenzo Wellington commented, "Given her material, she could easily write essays or a memoir. But she has a genuine gift for verse forms, and the depth of her engagement in language marks her as a true poet."

Born in 1966, in Gulfport, Mississippi, Trethewey is the daughter of Eric Trethewey and his then-wife Gwendolyn. Her white father was a native of

Canada, a poet and professor who came to work at Hollins University, and her African-American mother was a social worker. Trethewey spent six years living in Gulfport, where her family experienced acts of racism because her parents' marriage was illegal in Mississippi; the Klu Klux Klan once burned a cross on their lawn. After her parents divorced when she was in first grade, she moved to Decatur, Georgia, with her mother, and lived primarily in Georgia until 1990.

Always an enthusiastic reader, Trethewey showed signs of being a gifted writer from an early age. She wrote poems about Martin Luther King, Jr. in third grade which were bound and added to her school's library. By fifth grade, Trethewey was writing a 60-page Victorian murder mystery. Indeed, the young Trethewey favored fiction as a child. She told Kathy Janich of the *Atlanta Journal-Constitution*, "I don't know if I ever set out to be a poet. I do know that at one point in my life I set out to be a fiction writer. I wrote little things like a lot of kids do. And that's the kind of thing my father would encourage me to do on long trips: 'Why don't you write a poem about these trees that we're passing?'"

Trethewey's biracial background, as well as her parents, influenced her writing in other ways as she grew older. Trethewey's father nearly derailed her early poetry career when the young Trethewey showed him one of her poems and he critiqued it harshly. Upset, she tore up the piece and vowed she would never write again. Later in life, Trethewey realized her father was taking her writing seriously by offering such criticism.

Another important incident which drove Trethewey to write was her mother's death. After her parents' divorce, her mother remarried. She was murdered by her second husband in 1985, an event that left Trethewey—then a freshman at the University of Georgia—devastated. Trethewey told Teresa K. Weaver of the *Atlanta Journal-Constitution*, "I immediately turned to poetry to make sense of it and grapple with it and just to articulate some of those feelings."

Trethewey made literature and poetry her focus as a college student. She studied English at the University of Georgia, and was also the head cheerleader during her senior year. Trethewey earned her bachelor's degree in English in 1989, but never took a creative writing class. After spending 16 months as a welfare caseworker in Augusta, Georgia, Trethewey entered the college where her father taught, Hollins, and studied English and creative writing there. She was granted her M.A. in 1991. Finally, Trethewey went north to the University of Massachusetts at Amherst where she earned her M.F.A. in poetry in 1995.

In 2000, Trethewey published her first book of poetry, *Domestic Work*. She won several awards, including the Lillian Smith Book Award, for the collection. In the book, Trethewey writes about the work of everyday life for women, especially African-American women, from actual jobs, to relationships, to raising children, through the life of one woman. She was inspired in part by her black grandmother, Leretta Turnbough, who lived in segregated Gulfport, worked as a domestic servant, elevator operator, beautician, factory worker, and seamstress. Trethewey dedicated the book to her. Trethewey also included several poems inspired by her own mixed race background, including "White Lies," which focuses on how she tried to pass for white when very young.

Reviewing *Domestic Work* in *Ploughshares*, Kevin Young praised Trethewey and her poems. Young wrote, "In a voice confident, diverse, and directed, Natasha Trethewey's *Domestic Work* does what a first book should, and more, all while avoiding what first books often do—either borrowing themes from other poets or recycling a narrow vision of family life. Here, Trethewey brilliantly discusses family not for its extremes or its small hurts, but rather for the small intimacies that symbolize larger sufferings of history, both personal and public."

Trethewey began teaching at Emory University in Atlanta in 2001, as a professor of English and creative writing. The following year, she published her second poetry collection, *Bellocq's Ophelia*. More focused in theme than *Domestic Work*, this collection explores the life of fictional prostitutes in New Orleans in the early 1900s. She was inspired to write the poems based on photographs of such women shot by well-known New York City photographer E. J. Bellocq. The poems are written from the women's points of view, and one of the primary voices is a light-skinned African American. Most of the poems were written as letters home or journal entries.

Like *Domestic Work*, *Bellocq's Ophelia* was also well received. *Publishers Weekly* commented, "Trethewey goes two-for-two by successfully taking on the poetically dubious task of working from art and making it signify anew." Adrian Oktenberg of the *Women's Review of Books* noted, "Trethewey's language throughout is calm, fluid, one line moving into the next as a fish moves through water, language borne in its natural element.... In all, the book is finely crafted, elegantly played out—but not finished!"

It took five years before Tretheway published her next collection, *Native Guard*, which was dedicated to her mother. She began working on it as early as 2002, and used her 2003 Guggenheim Fellowship to help fund the related research in the Southeast. Like *Bellocq's Ophelia*, many the poems are a first-person imagined history, in this case, a former slave serving in the Native Guard of Louisiana during the Civil War. The Native Guard was the first legitimately sanctioned regiment of African-American soldiers, and they guarded Confederate soldiers at Fort Massachusetts on Ship Island, off the coast of Mississippi. Her primary character had to write letters home for the illiterate Confederate prisoners of war as well as for his fellow soldiers.

Tretheway also touched on her family background in *Native Guard*, as she relates her personal struggles to the lost past of the South. Several poems, including "Miscegenation" and "My Mother Dreams of Another Country," talk about her parents' marriage, her subsequent birth, and her mother's death. Much of the first section of *Native Guard* focuses on bereavement, especially the loss of a mother as Tretheway experienced it. The poet related this experience to the loss of self and the history of a people, as the essentially forgotten story of the Native Guard showed. Tretheway admitted her mother and her violent death were important to the book. She told the *New York Times'* Deborah Solomon, "I can't go back and save her. I can only save her memory. Figuratively, the title represents the idea that I am a native guardian to the memory of my mother's life."

Reviewing the collection of 30 poems in the *Washington Post Book World*, Wellington noted, "Tretheway has a gift for squeezing the contradictions of the South into very tightly controlled lines." Similarly, Carrie Shipers of *Prairie Schooner* noted of *Native Guard*, "The major strength of these poems is the compelling connections Tretheway makes between personal experience and cultural memory."

The strength of *Native Guard* led to more awards for Tretheway. She was surprised to learn that she won the 2007 Pulitzer Prize for poetry for the collection. Emory University officials informed her about the award while she was teaching a workshop class, and she ended the class early to celebrate. Tretheway was only the fourth African American to win the Pulitzer Prize for poetry.

Winning the Pulitzer had deep personal meaning for Tretheway. She told Bill Thompson of Charleston, South Carolina's *Post and Courier*, "I wanted to write this book to remember my mother, to really make a monument to her and her life. I started really putting together the book as the 20th anniversary of her death approached. She died just shy of her 41st birthday. I'll turn 41 while I'm in Charleston. I wanted this book in hardcover because I wanted it to feel more real, more enduring. For the Pulitzer committee to put this stamp on it will make it endure ever more."

After the win, Tretheway planned on continuing to write, but was not going to let such a prestigious prize affect her work. She told Weaver of the *Atlanta Journal-Constitution*, "Writing a poem is a terribly, terribly difficult and terribly wonderful thing. And I wouldn't want past successes or past failures to join me when I sit down to write. I hope I can banish all those things."

Selected writings

Poetry collections

Domestic Work, Graywolf Press (St. Paul, MN), 2000.
Bellocq's Ophelia, Graywolf Press, 2002.
Native Guard, Houghton Mifflin (Boston), 2007.

Sources

Periodicals

Associated Press State & Local Wire, April 17, 2007; December 7, 2007.
Atlanta Journal-Constitution (Atlanta, GA), September 15, 2002, p. 8L; April 17, 2007, p. 7A; April 29, 2007, p. 1B.
Georgia Trend, October 1, 2003, p. 42.
New York Times, May 13, 2007, p. 15.
Ploughshares, Winter 2000, p. 205.
Post and Courier (Charleston, SC), April 22, 2007, p. H3.
Prairie Schooner, December 22, 2006, pp. 199(3).
Publishers Weekly, February 25, 2002, p. 57.
Roanoke Times (Roanoke, VA), October 3, 2001, p. 1.
Sun Herald (Biloxi, MS), April 19, 2007.
U.S. States News, May 23, 2007.
Washington Post Book World, April 16, 2006, p. T4.
Women's Review of Books, October 2003, pp. 20(3).

Online

Contemporary Authors Online, Gale, 2007.

—A. Petruso

Spencer Tunick

Lluis Gene/AFP/Getty Images

Photographer

Born January 1, 1967, in Middletown, NY; son of a hotel photographer. *Education:* Emerson College, B.A., 1988; attended the International Center for Photography.

Addresses: *Home*—New York, NY. *Office*—c/o I-20 Gallery, 557 W. 23rd St., New York, NY 10011.

Career

Music photographer for *Paper* magazine, 1990s; began photographing nude figures in New York City, 1992; solo gallery exhibitions hosted by Thicket, New York City, 1995; cross-country project profiled in the documentary *Naked States,* 2000; launched "Nude Adrift" project, 2001, which was chronicled in the 2003 documentary *Naked World.*

Sidelights

Spencer Tunick is a photographer and artist who works in a unique medium: large-scale nude "sculptures," which he assembles with the help of dozens, or even thousands, of live participants. When he began taking such photographs in the early 1990s, Tunick often faced arrest, but as his reputation and artistic credibility have grown over the years the harassment has abated. His subjects receive no payment for their participation except for a signed photo of the final image. Though shedding one's clothes in front of hundreds of strangers for a photograph has a somewhat mischievous air about it, Tunick theorizes that "for some of the participants, it's disappointingly not as erotic as they would like it to be. I work fast and you are naked for short amounts of time," he explained to Sharon Krum in the *Times* of London.

Tunick was born on the first day of 1967 in Middletown, New York. He grew up in the nearby town of South Fallsburg as the son of a hotel photographer; his grandfather and great-grandfather were also in the business, having worked as photojournalists earlier in the century. At Emerson College in Boston, however, Tunick majored in film and speech, and did not take up the camera in earnest until living in New York City in the early 1990s. While working as a photographer for the New York City magazine *Paper,* he began photographing nudes on the street in 1992. "My first was a woman crouching in the street holding a live white rat," he recalled in an interview with Joyce Wadler of the *New York Times.* "I attached an African root—a big long root that looks like a giant tail—to her back and strung it across Third Street.... I also did a naked woman holding a swordfish. Then I couldn't afford the props."

Tunick's friends began clamoring to be furtively photographed in and around New York City, and one of his first full-scale pieces came when he gathered several dozen people to strip at the United Nations Plaza in Manhattan later in 1992. His work began gaining fame in countercultural circles, and he signed on with a gallery. Reviewing a 1995 exhibition of Tunick's work at Thicket in New York City, *Art in America* critic Richard Vine asserted that Tunick "clearly has an exceptional eye and a compelling sense of implicit drama.... Even in group shots, the tension lies not so much in the interrelationships of the participants as in the isolation of each figure within the surrealistically impersonal environs."

Tunick and his mission also gained some press because New York City police habitually arrested him, which began in December of 1994 at Rockefeller Plaza when he staged a shot of a naked man draped over one of the Plaza's enormous Christmas bulbs. The criminal charges varied in each, but usually involved misdemeanor violations for unlawful assembly, disorderly conduct, and reckless endangerment. Finally, Tunick took the city to court, claiming that his works were protected under the First Amendment's freedom of speech clause. A higher court agreed that his civil rights had been violated—tellingly, police rarely arrested the naked people, only Tunick—and that decision was appealed all the way to the U.S. Supreme Court, which declined to hear the case.

Tunick's reputation was further boosted by a 2000 documentary film, *Naked States*, that chronicled his quest to photograph people in each of the 50 American states. A year later, he launched his "Nude Adrift" project, which was aimed at taking photographs on every continent. More and more bodies began turning up in each of Tunick's increasingly orchestrated shoots, often staged at well-known landmarks. His subjects were recruited via newspaper ads or flyers handed out on the streets of major cities. There was usually an even split of genders in each, and Tunick soon became skilled in sensing which of the interested strangers would show up at the appointed, often pre-dawn hour for the photo shoot. "When I hand out flyers inviting people to participate I don't give them to women who wear gold jewellery or pearls, or men who wear business suits," he told Krum, the *Times* of London journalist. "You know that they don't take risks with their bodies. Once I handed a flyer to a guy in a serious suit and he marched right over to a policeman and gave it to him."

Tunick set a new record in Barcelona, Spain, in 2003 with 7,000 participants, and a new documentary film, *Naked World*, chronicled similar shoots in Melbourne, Australia; Cape Town, South Africa; São Paulo, Brazil; and Tokyo, Japan. A year later, Tunick assembled 2,754 people in Cleveland, Ohio, which surpassed his previous North American record of 2,500 disrobed citizens of Montreal, Canada. Rivers featured prominently in some memorable images from Tunick's camera in 2005, with roughly 2,000 subjects turning up for a shoot on the River Tyne quays of Newcastle, England in July of 2005, and 1,493 people lining up across the Rhone River in Lyon, France two months later. In May of 2007, Tunick set a new record with an estimated 18,000 naked bodies assembled at Mexico City's famous Constitution Plaza.

In the second decade of his career, Tunick has gained some artistic clout, with his immense photographs often commissioned or sponsored by legitimate museums and arts foundations. The Cleveland shoot, for example, was done under the aegis of the city's Museum of Contemporary Art. In 2007, the Dream Amsterdam Foundation in the Netherlands commissioned several works as part of an annual performance-art project in and around the famously liberal Dutch city. Later that summer, Tunick traveled to Switzerland at the behest of Greenpeace to photograph participants on an Alpine glacier to call attention to global warming.

Tunick also prefers to stage his photo shoots at dawn, in part because of the ideal light it affords, and also because "people are less confrontational, less violent in the morning," he told a writer for London's *Independent*, Maggie O'Farrell. Early in his career, the small number of people who appeared in his works were often young and had impressive physiques, but as Tunick's reputation grew a more diverse array of participants became part of his projects. "When people pose I think it heightens their awareness of their own bodies," he told Krum in the *Times* of London profile, "how precious life is, and how connected you really are to your neighbor."

Sources

Art Business News, September 2004, p. 12.
Art in America, October 1995, p. 122.
Independent (London, England), February 17, 2001, p. 10; October 9, 2004, p. 24.
New Statesman, April 28, 2003, p. 41.
New York Times, April 30, 1999.
Observer (London, England), January 22, 2006, p. 20.
Psychology Today, September-October 2003, p. 79.
Times (London, England), July 9, 2005, p. 6.

—*Carol Brennan*

Carrie Underwood

Francis Specker/Bloomberg News/Landov

Singer

Born March 10, 1983, in Muskogee, OK; daughter of Stephen (a paper mill worker) and Carole (a teacher) Underwood. *Education:* Graduated from Northeastern State University, Tahlequah, OK, 2006.

Addresses: *Record company*—Arista Records, 745 5th Ave., 6th Flr., New York, NY 10151. *Web site*—http://www.carrieunderwoodofficial.com.

Career

Winner of *American Idol* singing contest, 2005; released first single, "Inside Your Heaven," 2005; released first album, *Some Hearts,* 2005.

Awards: World's sexiest vegetarian, People for the Ethical Treatment of Animals, 2005; CMT Music Awards, female video of the year and breakthrough video of the year, for "Jesus, Take the Wheel," CMT, 2006; album of the year and country album of the year, for *Some Hearts,* and new country artist of the year, female country artist of the year, and female *Billboard* 200 album artist of the year, *Billboard,* 2006; top female vocalist, album of the year for *Some Hearts,* and best music video for "Before He Cheats," Academy of Country Music, 2006; Dove Award for country recorded song of the year, for "Jesus, Take the Wheel," Gospel Music Association, 2006; CMA Horizon Award and female vocalist of the year award, Country Music Association, 2006; Grammy Awards for best new artist and best female country vocal performance, Recording Academy, for "Jesus, Take the Wheel," 2007; video of the year and female video of the year, for "Before He Cheats," Country Music Television, 2007.

Sidelights

Of all the singers who have appeared on the ultra-popular television show *American Idol,* country singer Carrie Underwood has become the most popular and successful. Her debut album, *Some Hearts,* had sold six million copies by 2007, sustaining its popularity more than a year and a half after its release in late 2005. When Underwood debuted on the show, her strong voice was undercut by an awkward stage presence. But by the end of the 2005 season, she won over the judges—as well as pop and country fans nationwide—with her vocals, her disarming beauty, her innocent personality, and a musical style that fits in well on contemporary country radio.

Underwood, born in 1983 in Muskogee, Oklahoma, grew up on a farm on the edge of Checotah, Oklahoma, a small town of only 3,400 people. She started singing at her church when she was only three years old. "She always sang—always," her mother, Carole, told Mike Lipton and Darla Atlas of *People.* "She'd be riding in the car and one of her sisters would say, 'Mama, make her quit singing in my ear!'" As she grew up, Underwood began performing at various small-town events, then at festivals in states near Oklahoma.

The class salutatorian at her high school, Underwood went on to Northeastern State University in Tahlequah, Oklahoma, where she studied broadcast journalism. During college, she continued singing. She was also runner-up in the college's 2003 beauty pageant and quarterback of her sorority's touch football team. During her senior year in college she tried out for *American Idol* at an audition in St. Louis, Missouri. She was one of 12 finalists chosen for the show. Before that, she had never ventured very far from Oklahoma or traveled by plane.

For the first few weeks of the 2005 *American Idol* season, *Entertainment Weekly* later recounted, Underwood got by with "sweet country songs and homely fashion choices." The unpretentious small-town girl was more used to blue jeans than high style. Her turning point came in the March 22 episode, when she perfomed "Alone," a ballad by the classic-rock band Heart. She came on stage wearing a flashy jacket, with her hair done up in a frizzy 1980s style, and sang the melodramatic song with "an almost ominous power." Soon, it became clear that the contest was coming down to her and Southern rocker Bo Bice. Just before the season finale, Nicholas Fonseca of *Entertainment Weekly* placed the odds on Bice. He praised Underwood's singing, prettiness, and sweet persona, but said she had a "woeful" stage presence: "Sometimes she looks like she's going to break out a robot dance." However, Fonseca guessed wrong: Underwood won the contest on May 25 with her performance of "Inside Your Heaven," a song written for the show.

Underwood celebrated her victory with a party at Skybar in Los Angeles. After a quick trip home to Oklahoma, where she picked out the new Ford Mustang she won from the show, she returned to Los Angeles to rehearse for a tour and record her debut album. Her first single, her version of "Inside Your Heaven," was rushed into stores. Underwood and Bice both appeared on the American Idols Live! tour that summer, which began in July in Sunrise, Florida, and included 43 dates nationwide. "This is my time to see the world," she told *People.* "Home will be there when I get back." That year, she signed endorsement deals with Hershey's chocolate and Skechers shoes. Meanwhile, People for the Ethical Treatment of Animals (PETA) named her the World's Sexiest Vegetarian for 2005.

Some Hearts, Underwood's first album, was released in November of 2005 and sold 300,000 copies within a week. Its first single, "Jesus, Take the Wheel," co-written by accomplished Nashville songwriter Hillary Lindsey, spent six weeks at the top of *Billboard's* country singles chart. Reviews were lukewarm.

Chris Willman of *Entertainment Weekly* called the album slick and too serious, aimed at "young people who want to feel middle-aged," and said even its best songs were not as good as the weakest tracks on an album by fellow country crooner LeAnn Rimes. *People* reviewer Chuck Arnold gave the album two and a half stars, complaining that Underwood "oversings on overproduced ballads" but that her "southern charm shines through" on other songs.

Country radio was much more impressed with the album, playing it frequently. At first, recalled Tom Baldrica, Sony BMG Nashville's vice president of marketing, radio programmers were divided, with some excited to play an artist with so much national publicity and others unsure they wanted to add a talent contest winner to their playlists. But "when 'Jesus, Take the Wheel' came along, everybody in country radio heard that and said, 'It doesn't matter where this came from,'" Baldrica told Brian Mansfield of *USA Today.* Underwood promoted herself heavily during 2006, touring that summer with country star Kenny Chesney, who gave her tips on performing, and appearing in the finale of *American Idol's* 2006 season.

That same year, Underwood finished her college degree and became a spokesperson for PETA. Another single, "Before He Cheats," released late in 2006, eventually became a number-one hit. Awards poured in. She won five *Billboard* Music Awards in December of that year. "Jesus, Take the Wheel" won awards from the Gospel Music Association and the country video channel CMT. She also won the Country Music Association's female vocalist of the year award. Though most of the country establishment seemed to be accepting her, there were exceptions. Singer LeAnn Rimes wrote on her Web site, according to *USA Today's* Mansfield, that Underwood's CMA award was "disheartening" because she had not "paid her dues long enough to fully deserve that award."

That fall, Underwood told *People* how much her life had accelerated. "Before *American Idol,* I was your typical college student. I was in a sorority. I'd never been to New York. When I sang, it was before about 15 people." Because of her touring schedule, she said, she had not had much time to enjoy her new house in Nashville, and found it hard to be away from her parents for a long time. She said she kept a Bible next to her bed for spiritual comfort.

During 2007, Underwood began recording her second album, but her first album remained very popular. By January of 2007, it had spent 20 weeks at the top of the *Billboard* country albums chart. It was far outselling albums by other *American Idol* winners Fantasia, Ruben Studdard, and Taylor Hicks. Her song, "Wasted," hit number one on the *Billboard* country chart after she performed it on an *American Idol* episode. "When country thrives, it's because there's a voice that speaks to young women, and Carrie is that," CMT executive vice-president Brian Philips explained to *Entertainment Weekly*'s Leah Greenblatt.

By 2007, Underwood was appearing in gossip columns, thanks to a new romance. She had broken up with her college boyfriend in 2005 after going to Los Angeles for *American Idol*, and later complained to interviewers that it was hard to meet men to date while famous, because she was often traveling and unsure whether the men who asked her out mostly wanted to get their picture in magazines. But by early 2007, she was reportedly dating British pop singer Oliver Trevena. He accompanied her to the Grammy Awards, where she won Best New Artist.

On the 2007 season finale of *American Idol*, Underwood sang "I'll Stand By You" by the Pretenders. She was also recognized for *Some Hearts'* sales of more than six million copies; it was the first country album to sell that well in ten years. Industry executives predicted similar success for Underwood's new album, *Carnival Ride*, which was released in October of 2007.

Selected discography

"Inside Your Heaven" (single), Arista, 2005.
Some Hearts, Arista, 2005.
Carnival Ride, Arista, 2007.

Sources

Periodicals

Cosmopolitan, May 2007, pp. 48-51.
Entertainment Weekly, May 20, 2005, p. 34; December 2, 2005, p. 81; January 26, 2007, p. 14; June 2007 (Idol Yearbook special issue), p. 70.
People, June 6, 2005, p. 60; June 13, 2005, p. 79; November 14, 2005, p. 147; December 5, 2005, p. 47; November 2006 (Country special issue), p. 38; February 26, 2007, p. 58.
USA Today, April 17, 2007, p. 1D.

Online

"Carrie Underwood: Biography," *All Music Guide*, http://wc06.allmusic.com/cg/amg.dll?p=amg&sql=11:3ifqxqwsldke~T1 (August 18, 2007).
"Carrie Underwood: Biography," CMT.com; http://www.cmt.com/artists/az/underwood__carrie/bio.jhtml (August 19, 2007).

—*Erick Trickey*

Giambattista Valli

Fashion designer

Born in 1966 in Rome, Italy. *Education:* Attended the European Design Institute, mid-1980s; earned degree from Central Saint Martins College of Art and Design, 1987.

Addresses: *Office*—c/o Gilmar USA, 57 E. 64th St., New York, NY 10021-7066.

Career

Began career in public-relations for Rome's Fashion Week events; public relations associate for Roberto Capucci, c. 1988; later became member of design staff; senior designer of Fendissime line, Fendi, c. 1990; senior designer for women's ready-to-wear, Krizia, c. 1995; designer of ready-to-wear line for Emanuel Ungaro, 1997; creative director for Emanuel Ungaro, 1998; creative director of Ungaro Fever, 2001, creative director of ready-to-wear, diffusion lines, and accessories, 2001-04; launched eponymous label, March 2005.

Sidelights

Italian fashion designer Giambattista Valli first rose to prominence as the up-and-coming new designer at Emanuel Ungaro, the Paris-based ready-to-wear and haute couture house. In 2005, Valli launched his own line, which earned enthusiastic reviews for its ultra-feminine silhouettes. "At some point you have to decide what you want to be: a translator all your life, or yourself," he told Katya Foreman in *WWD*, after launching his own label. "If I look back then I think I was totally crazy, but at the time, all I was thinking was next, next, next."

Valli was born in Italy's capital, Rome, in 1966, and in his youth was sent to Roman Catholic schools located inside the Vatican, the papal enclave in the city. He keeps in his office a photograph of him with John Paul I, the pope who reigned for just 33 days in 1978, and his interest in fashion is on display in the image, as Valli is sporting turquoise shorts. He loved fashion as a child, he told *WWD*. "Even as young as five, I would sketch everything" he saw on awards shows broadcast on Italian television—broadcasts that were still in black and white at the time, he told Foreman. "I would draw their outfits and try to guess what colors."

Valli studied at the School of Art in Rome as a teenager, went on to the European Design Institute in 1986, and then to Central Saint Martins College of Art and Design in London, from which he graduated with a degree in illustration. His first job was with Cecilia Fanfani, a planner of Rome's Fashion Week events, and that led to a stint in public relations with Roberto Capucci, an avant-garde designer based in Rome. He eventually moved up to a position on Capucci's design staff before moving on to the house of Fendi, one of Italy's biggest names in fashion, as senior designer for its Fendissime line, which is aimed at younger women.

Valli then went to Krizia, the Milan label founded by Mariuccia Mandelli, where he was senior designer for women's ready-to-wear. He was lured away when Emanuel Ungaro asked him to submit some sketches after hearing about the young designer's talents from a mutual colleague. Valli duly turned in some ideas, then went to India for a vacation; he was forced to cut the trip short when Ungaro liked the sketches so much that he asked to meet with Valli immediately. Ungaro founded his own label in 1965 after serving a long apprenticeship with legendary Spanish couturier Cristobal Balenciaga. Ungaro's "career high came in the taffeta-heavy '80s," noted a writer for London's *Guardian* newspaper, Charlie Porter. "His highly decorated, ruched, starchy dresses-with-a-sense-of-occasion suited the times."

Like many designers, Ungaro struggled through the early 1990s, and, in 1996, he entered into a financial partnership with the large Italian fashion house of Salvatore Ferragamo. That deal precipitated the decision to bring in Valli as the new designer for the ready-to-wear line in 1997. A year later, he was named creative director and, in 2001, took over Ungaro Fever, a clothing line aimed at younger customers. Both he and Ungaro said in interviews that the fit was a good one. "You know, in most of the houses, they bring in somebody new who doesn't think about what is the real story," Valli told Porter in the *Guardian*. "They build up their own, but it doesn't fit with the style of the house. But with Mr. Ungaro there is never a case of me or you. I always propose what I think is right for Ungaro. I never propose the trend of the moment."

Ungaro delivered strong praise for Valli later in 2001, when the younger designer took over the ready-to-wear, diffusion lines, and accessories, and premiered his first collection at the Paris spring/summer collections in October. It was a rare occurrence in the fashion world for a living designer to pass on the reins to a successor. "It was my personal duty to give to him what I received," Ungaro explained to Miles Socha in *WWD* about his protégé. "Season after season, he has shown that he understands the spirit of the house. He's clever; he's young. And of course, after so many years, he understands the culture of Ungaro. He's gathered the power and the knowledge."

Over the next few seasons, however, there were reports of problems at Ungaro with the Ferragamo bosses, and perhaps even between Valli and Ungaro. "Insiders describe their working relationship as estranged," wrote Socha in a 2004 *WWD* report. "Valli gave the brand a new currency among the celebrity and social set, but reviews have been uneven and his sexed-up styles often chafed with the house's couture roots." The *WWD* article mentioned that Vincent Darre from Moschino had been named the new designer at Ungaro, but Socha also noted that Valli was planning to launch his own line.

Valli debuted his first collection under his own name in March of 2005 at the Paris fall/winter collections. His financial backing was provided by Gilmar, an Italian apparel manufacturer, but he remained a Paris-based designer. The frilly, flirty looks he had perfected at Ungaro remained a strong part of his creative output. Writing in early 2006 about his second collection, *Vogue*'s Hamish Bowles asserted that "Valli has begun to evolve a signature style that draws on the dynamic chic of late-fifties Italian style icons (Marella Agnelli, Silvana Mangano, Monica Vitti) and the exaggerated proportions and silhouettes of that period's couture clothing—but executed with a light, modern hand."

Valli launched a footwear line in the spring of 2008, and was readying his first boutique in the United States in New York City. A high-profile celebrity clientele has regularly been photographed in his clothes, including Victoria Beckham, Penelope Cruz, and Mischa Barton. Occasionally rumors arose that he was in line for another top job at an established house, such as Valentino. He professed to be uninterested in any more arrangements of the kind, he told a writer for London's *Independent*. "It's almost like someone who gets his freedom and then doesn't want to marry again. I want to taste it a little bit."

Sources

Guardian (London, England), April 7, 2001, p. 26.
Independent (London, England), December 17, 2007, p. 6.
Vogue, March 2006, p. 350.
WWD, October 9, 2001, p. 9; October 25, 2004, p. 2; October 3, 2007, p. 12.

—*Carol Brennan*

Kat Von D

Tattoo artist and television personality

Born Katherine Von Drachenberg, March 8, 1982, in Monterrey, Nuevo León, Mexico; daughter of René Drachenberg and Sylvia Galeano (both missionaries); married Oliver Peck (a tattoo artist), 2004 (divorced, c. 2007).

Addresses: *Home*—Los Angeles, CA. *Office*—High Voltage Tattoo, 1259 N. La Brea Ave., West Hollywood, CA 90038. *Publicist*—42 West, 11400 W. Olympic Blvd., Ste. 1100, Los Angeles, CA 90064.

Career

Tattoo artist, Sin City Tattoo, Los Angeles, 1998-2000; tattoo artist at Blue Bird Tattoo, Pasadena, CA, Red Hot Tattoo, Arcadia, CA, Inflictions, Covina, CA, True Tattoo, Los Angeles, c. 2000-05; appeared on TLC's *Miami Ink,* 2005-06; star of TLC's *LA Ink,* 2007—; owner, High Voltage Tattoo, 2007—.

Sidelights

Tattoo artist Kat Von D inked her way into stardom in 2005 as a featured artist on the cable television program *Miami Ink.* After two seasons, she returned to her hometown of Los Angeles and opened High Voltage Tattoo, which serves as home base for a spinoff show called *LA Ink.* Highly popular, *LA Ink* captured 2.9 million viewers during its 2007 premiere, making it TLC's most-watched premiere since *What Not to Wear* debuted in 2003. For Von D, a twentysomething who began tattooing friends at 14, the show represents an opportunity to share her art medium with the world and improve the image of the industry.

Like many of the people she tattoos, Von D is a living, walking canvas; she is covered in ink that stretches from her face to her ankles. Roses circle her neck, Beethoven graces her hip and portraits of Mexican actresses Maria Victoria and Elsa Aguirre round out her shins. A piano sits on her ankle. Von D's favorite tattoo is a series of stars on her left temple, including one on her eyelid, inspired by the Motley Crüe song *Starry Eyes.* "I think people should just get a tattoo that they want to look at forever," Von D told the *Los Angeles Times'* Amy Kaufman. "People read into the meaning behind every tattoo, but in reality it's just aesthetics. It's something you do because you have the power to alter your body."

The future body inker was born Katherine Von Drachenberg on March 8, 1982, in Monterrey, Nuevo León, Mexico. Her parents, René Drachenberg and Sylvia Galeano, both hailed from Argentina but were busy with missionary work in Mexico when Von D was born. Her father was part German, while her mother was of Spanish-Italian descent. She has an older sister and younger brother. When Von D was four, the family moved to Colton, California. She is fluent in English and Spanish.

Von D drew incessantly as a child, inspired by her grandparents who were painters. "I've been drawing ever since I can remember," she noted on an "Artist Q&A" posted to the TLC Web site. "My mom actually saved all my drawing and sketches since before I can remember." Besides sketching, Von D took an early interest in music. Her father's mother, once a professional pianist in Germany, introduced her to music by Beethoven and Chopin. By age seven, Von D was taking piano lessons. Fascinated by Beethoven, she studied historic composers, painters and sculptors. She counts da Vinci, Michelangelo, and Caravaggio amongst those who inspire her.

As a preteen, Von D discovered punk rock. Many of the punk rockers she befriended had tattoos and, at age 14, Von D decided to get one. Her first tattoo was an old English "J" inked on her ankle—it stands for James, her first love. Around this time, a friend asked Von D for a tattoo. After procuring a crude, homemade tattoo gun, Von D inked a Misfits skull into her friend's skin. The Misfits were a popular punk rock band.

As a teenager, Von D ran away from home. Speaking to *People*'s Jessica Herndon, Von D said it was hard for her "really strict" parents to understand her behavior. "For their daughter to be tattooed, drop out of high school, and be rock and roll—they thought I was possessed by Satan." At 16, she landed a job at a professional tattoo shop called Sin City Tattoo. "This gnarly biker dude hired me, and he knew I was underage but he didn't care," she told the *Los Angeles Times*. "There was a lot of trial and error, because the art was there but the skill definitely wasn't."

Over the next several years, Von D worked at various Los Angeles area shops, eventually landing at True Tattoo in Hollywood where she met tattoo artist Chris Garver, an accomplished and well-known inker. The opportunity of a lifetime came along in 2005 when the two were asked to appear on *Miami Ink,* a new reality television program on TLC aimed at following the lives of a troupe of tattoo artists as they opened a shop in Miami. The only woman among the group, Von D garnered attention for her unique tattooing style—she leans toward realism, inking intricate, fine-lined black and grey portrait-type tattoos. Outspoken, and often sporting glittery blue eye shadow and cherry red lips, Von D reeled in viewers; however, after two seasons and a falling out with a co-star, she left.

Von D was not off the air for long. She set up her own West Hollywood shop, High Voltage Tattoo, and was back in business with a spinoff called *LA Ink,* which debuted in 2007 on TLC. When the show is in production, the shop is closed during the day for filming. In the evenings, it opens for walk-ins. As a prominent LA inker, Von D has tattooed many celebrities, including actress Jenna Jameson, actor Jared Leto, comedian Margaret Cho, as well as band members from Metallica, Slayer, and Incubus.

In 2004, she married tattoo artist Oliver Peck but was separated from him by the time *LA Ink* aired. Following the breakup of her marriage, Von D dated a number of men, including Whitestarr drummer Alex "Orbi" Orbison, son of rock pioneer Roy Orbison. Von D has two sphinx cats and drives a 1951 Chevrolet Deluxe, which she purchased at the age of 18. It is the same car her father had as a young adult. She often skateboards to work, though.

In December of 2007, Von D set a *Guinness World Record* for most tattoos in a day. In one 24-hour period, she inked 400 people as part of a fund-raiser for Vitamin Angels, a not-for-profit agency that works to eliminate childhood blindness caused by Vitamin A deficiency. During the event, everyone got the same tattoo—an "LA" logo—for which they paid $20. The event was featured in an episode of *LA Ink.*

The television exposure has brought Von D a ton of new clients, many of whom come for memorial portraits of loved ones. Speaking to *Garage* magazine, Von D summed up the experience. "I think that some of my new clientele is searching for some closure to help them deal with the loss of someone and they truly believe in me.... I mean, nothing beats the way someone thanks you and hugs you the way these people do when I'm done with their tattoos. People are so appreciative and it's made me realize my role in tattooing and I'm cool with that!"

Sources

Periodicals

Bust, October/November 2007, p. 18.
Chicago Tribune, October 29, 2006, p. 1 (Home & Garden).
Garage, May 3, 2007.
Los Angeles Times, January 8, 2008, p. 1E.
People, September 3, 2007, p. 136.
Straits Times (Singapore), January 9, 2008.

Online

"Kat's Press Kit Biography," Kat Von D, http://www.katvond.net/bio.html (January 27, 2008).

"Kat Von D Tattoos 400 People to Save 32,000 Children in 24 Hours for Vitamin Angels," Reuters, http://www.reuters.com/article/pressRelease/idUS196282+08-Jan-2008+MW20080108.tif (February 16, 2008).

"LA Ink: Q&A with Kat," TLC, http://tlc.discovery.com/tv/la-ink/qanda/kat.html (January 27, 2008).

"Miami Ink: Meet Kat Von D," TLC, http://tlc.discovery.com/fansites/miami-ink/bio/kat.html (January 27, 2008).

"Miami Ink: The Kat Corner," TLC, http://tlc.discovery.com/fansites/miami-ink/kat_corner/facts_print.html (January 27, 2008).

—Lisa Frick

Julie White

Actress

Born June 4, 1961, in San Diego, CA; daughter of Edwin (a dentist) and Sue Jane (a therapist) White; married Carl Pandel (a restaurateur), 1984 (divorced, 1990); married Christopher Conner (an actor), c. 2002; children: Alexandra (first marriage). *Education:* Attended Southwest Texas State University and Fordham University.

Addresses: *Office*—c/o Cavemen, Sony Studios, 10202 West Washington Blvd., Myrna Loy Bldg., Culver City, CA 90232.

Career

Actress on stage, including: *Dark of the Moon,* Studio Arena Theatre, Buffalo, NY, 1984-85; *On the Verge, or The Geography of Yearning,* Huntington Theatre Company, Boston, MA, 1985-86; *Lucky Stiff,* Playwrights Horizons Theater, New York City, 1988; *Early One Evening at the Rainbow Bar and Grille,* Workshop of the Players Art Theater, New York City, 1989; *The Heidi Chronicles,* Plymouth Theatre, New York City, 1989-90; *Largo Desolato,* Yale Repertory Theatre, New Haven, CT, 1990-91; *The Stick Wife,* Manhattan Theatre Club, New York City, 1991; *Spike Heels,* Second Stage Theatre, New York City, 1992; *Money and Friends,* Center Theatre Group, Ahmanson Theatre, Los Angeles, CA, 1992-93; *Absurd Person Singular,* Long Wharf Theatre, New Haven, CT, 1992-93; *The Family of Mann,* Second Stage Theater, New York City, 1994; *Dreading Thekla,* Williamstown Theatre Festival, Williamstown, MA, 1997; *Dinner with Friends,* South Coast Repertory, Costa Mesa, CA, 1998, Variety Arts Theatre, New York City, 1999-2000; *Bad Dates,* Playwrights Horizons

Theater, New York City, 2003, Huntington Theatre Company, Boston, MA, 2004; *The Little Dog Laughed,* Second Stage Theater, the Cort Theatre, New York City, 2005-06. Television appearances include: *Grace Under Fire,* ABC, 1993-97; *Six Feet Under,* HBO, 2001-03; *Cavemen,* ABC, 2007—. Film appearances include: *Flypaper,* 1997; *Say It Isn't So,* 2001; *Slap Her ... She's French,* 2002; *War of the Worlds,* 2005; *The Astronaut Farmer,* 2007; *Transformers,* 2007; *The Nanny Diaries,* 2007; *Michael Clayton,* 2007.

Awards: OBIE Award for best leading actress in a play, *Village Voice,* for *The Little Dog Laughed,* 2006; Tony Award for best performance by a leading actress in a play, League of American Theaters and Producers and the American Theatre Wing, for *The Little Dog Laughed,* 2007.

Sidelights

Actress Julie White has triumphed on television and stage. She has won a Tony Award, and her work in such New York hits as *Bad Dates* and *The Little Dog Laughed* was praised by critics and audiences alike. Television viewers knew White first from her role as the sidekick on *Grace Under Fire.* She later had acclaimed work in *Six Feet Under* and was added to the cast of the questionable *Cavemen* situation comedy in 2007. White appeared in small film roles as well, including parts in *War of the Worlds* and *Transformers*.

Born on June 4, 1961, at a naval hospital in San Diego, California, White was the second of three daughters of a dentist, Edwin White, and his therapist wife, Sue Jane. The family moved to Austin, Texas, when White was small, and she spent her childhood there. As a child, White was outgoing and loved to be the center of attention. She was also addicted to movie musicals that she watched on television while home with a stomach ulcer through much of third grade.

White began acting in local productions in Austin during her childhood and, by her teen years, was driving herself to auditions. In addition to appearing with the Center Stage Theatre Group, she was cast in community theater productions of *Two Gentleman of Verona* and *Company*. After graduating from Austin's Anderson High School, White attended nearby Southwest Texas State University. There, she starred in the musical *The Baker's Wife*. The creators of the show, Joseph Stein and Stephen Schwartz, saw her performance and told her to move to New York City to further her career.

Taking their advice, White entered Fordham University and continued her acting studies there. When her auditioning led to paying work, she dropped out and never completed her degree. She was also married during this period to restaurateur Carl Pandel. The couple had their only child, Alexandra, in 1986, and divorced in 1990. Throughout her marriage, pregnancy, motherhood, and divorce, White continued to work, primarily on stage. She made her New York debut in 1988 in the Off-Broadway musical *Lucky Stiff*. She followed this with a co-starring role in the hit Broadway play *The Heidi Chronicles*, and she appearanced in *Spike Heels* and *Dinner with Friends*.

In 1993, White moved from primarily stage work to her first significant role on television. She was cast as the female sidekick/best friend, Nadine, to Brett Butler's lead in the situation comedy *Grace Under Fire*. The chemistry between Butler and White was evident from the various auditions in Los Angeles, including one in which the women just talked about a man White had met on the plane. White never read with Butler but was given the role on the spot by the casting director. Executive producer Marc Flanagan told *People*, "What sets Julie apart is her unique personality. She's spunky. She's passionate. She's a good ol' girl."

By the end of the first season, *Grace* was the number-one new comedy on television, with the ad-libbing and interplay between White and Butler a key part of the show. Starring in a play written by friend Theresa Rebeck reflected the unexpected shift in career focus for White in the summer after that first season. The actress had the lead in Rebeck's play *The Family of Mann*, which chronicled the soul-sucking work of producing situation comedies for television in Los Angeles. White played Belinda in the comedy, who remains idealistic despite self-deception involved in the creative process.

Her high-minded Belinda has a Ph.D. but goes west to write scripts with meaning for the titular "quality" television series. She learned that power was all that matters in Los Angeles, tarnishing her beliefs. While generally praising the Off-Broadway production, *New York Times* critic David Richards singled out White's performance. He wrote, "If Ms. White were not such an appealing actress, Belinda would be a bit of a dope.... The persistent naivete proves endearing."

After *Grace Under Fire* was cancelled in 1997, White worked in a variety of genres, appearing in stage, television, and film productions. Of particular note was her recurring role on the hit HBO drama *Six Feet Under*. From 2001 to 2003, White memorably played Mitzi Dalton-Huntley, a funeral home owner. White's stage appearances garnered more attention, especially after she moved back to New York City in 2002.

In 2003, White starred in a new play by Rebeck, *Bad Dates*, first in its original Off-Broadway run, then in the 2004 Boston production as well. The comic play was written specifically by Rebeck for White and featured her musings on the meaning of life through White's shoe-obsessed Haley Walker. The one-woman show displayed all of White's talents and was a big triumph in her career. Reviewing the Boston version, the *Boston Globe*'s Louise Kennedy wrote, "the greatest glory belong to White.... She brings to Haley a rich sense of life's complications and disappointments, an infectiously animated physical presence, and the effortlessly calibrated balance between drollery and depth of a born storyteller."

By 2005, White was garnering even more praiseworthy reviews for another stage comedy which poked fun at Hollywood, *The Little Dog Laughed*. White was a success as Diane, the hard-driving, clothes-obsessed talent agent who controlled her closeted gay client, Mitchell. Diane's primary goal was preventing him from revealing his sexual orientation and damaging his burgeoning career. Of her performance, Anita Gates of the *New York Times* wrote, "From the first minute of Douglas Carter Beane's delicious comedy *The Little Dog Laughed* at Second Stage Theater, Ms. [White] owns the stage." For her work in the role, White was honored with both an Obie and a Tony Award.

Though *The Little Dog Laughed* ran through most of 2006, White eventually returned to Los Angeles with her second husband, actor Christopher Conner, and began auditioning for film and television roles again. While she had small parts in films such as 2005's *War of the Worlds,* television offered a chance at something more. Still, White refused television parts in favor of the stage. She was offered a recurring role on the hit ABC drama *Desperate Housewives* as a woman who faked being catatonic, but turned it down to stay with *The Little Dog Laughed* after it moved to Broadway.

White took a role in the 2007 summer box-office smash *Transformers,* playing the mother of the male lead. The $180 million film was a hit. Later that year, White finally returned to television when she was added to the cast of the ABC sitcom *Cavemen.* Based on the popular series of Geico Auto Insurance commercials, the show was a failure among most critics, and White was added to pump up its comic value.

No matter what genre White was acting in, people liked to work with her. *Six Feet Under* creator Alan Ball told Michael Kuchwara of the Associated Press, "Julie's a down-home Texas girl. She's smart as a whip, fun to party with, and she has a very wicked sense of humor. She doesn't have any of the baggage of pretentiousness and entitlement that a lot of people who are world-class actors bring with them. And yet at the same time, she is the kind of actor you can trust with just about anything."

Sources

Books

Complete Marquis Who's Who Biographies, Marquis Who's Who, 2007.
Contemporary Theatre, Film, and Television, vol. 46, Gale Group, 2003.

Periodicals

American Theatre, February 2007, p. 96.
Associated Press, November 14, 2006.
Austin American-Statesman (TX), June 10, 2007, p. J1.
Boston Globe, January 2, 2004, p. C15; January 9, 2004, p. D17.
News Review Messenger (Australia), July 4, 2007.
New Yorker, January 23, 2006, p. 33.
New York Magazine, November 13, 2006.
New York Times, June 29, 1994, p. C15; January 20, 2006, p. E2; June 11, 2007, p. E1.
People, March 27, 1995, p. 57.
Pittsburgh Post-Gazette (PA), July 27, 2007, p. F1.
The Record (Bergen County, NJ), November 14, 2006, p. F9.
USA Today, July 13, 1994, p. 3D.

—*A. Petruso*

Amy Winehouse

Singer and songwriter

Born Amy Jade Winehouse, September 14, 1983, in London, England; daughter of Mitch (a cab driver) and Janis (a pharmacist) Winehouse; married Blake Fielder-Civil (a video director), May 18, 2007. *Education:* Attended the BRIT School for Performing Arts and Technology, London, late 1990s.

Addresses: *Record company*—Island Records, 825 Eighth Ave., New York, NY 10019.

Career

Sang with the British National Youth Jazz Orchestra, late 1990s; music reporter for the World Entertainment News Network Ltd. (WENN), late 1990s; signed to Island Records, c. 2001, and to Brilliant/19 Management following that; released first LP in United Kingdom, *Frank,* 2003.

Awards: Ivor Novello Award for best contemporary song, British Academy of Composers and Songwriters, for "Stronger Than Me," 2004; Ivor Novello Award for best contemporary song, British Academy of Composers and Songwriters, for "Rehab," 2006; BRIT (British Record Industry Trust) Award, British Phonographic Industry, for best British female artist, 2007.

Sidelights

London-born singer Amy Winehouse became Britain's newest soul sensation with the first of her critically acclaimed records, *Frank,* in 2003.

Shortly after the release of its follow-up, *Back to Black,* in the fall of 2006 Winehouse began captivating American listeners as well, thanks to her distinctively torchy, soulful vocal style. Her distinctly retro look—complete with tattoos, heavy eyeliner, and massive beehive hairdo—also made Winehouse a refreshing change from the majority of blandly glamorous pop songstresses who were her contemporaries. *New York Times* music critic Jon Pareles caught one of her live shows in the spring of 2007 and asserted that were the inimitable new star "a purely old-fashioned soul singer, she'd just be a nostalgia act, though one with some telling songs. Her self-consciousness, and the bluntness she has learned from hip-hop, could help lead soul into 21st-century territory."

Winehouse was born on September 14, 1983, in London, England, to parents who were both from Jewish families of the city's once predominantly Jewish area in the East End. Winehouse and her older brother grew up in Southgate, an area of north London, largely in the home of their mother Janis, a pharmacist, whose marriage to cab driver Mitch ended when their daughter was nine years old. Winehouse, however, would remain close to her father, and later in life would sport a tattoo that read "Daddy's Girl."

An extrovert at an early age, Winehouse won a scholarship to the Sylvia Young Theatre School, a prestigious London training ground for students aged ten to 16 with entrance by audition. She was kicked out after two years, for reasons that included her new nose piercing, which she had done herself, and an independence of mind. "All the teachers at school hated me," she told Dan Cairns in a *Sunday Times* interview, a situation that was repeated at two other schools she attended. She had better luck at one of the London city colleges, the BRIT School for Performing Arts and Technology, and after that she worked for a time as a music reporter for the World Entertainment News Network Ltd., known as WENN.

Winehouse sang at an early age with an eye toward a career. When she was ten, she and two friends formed a Salt 'N' Pepa-copycat group, and she grew up listening to a range of jazz, soul, R&B, and disco-era divas, from Dinah Washington to Teena Marie. Her all-time favorite group, however, were the 1960s hitmakers the Shangri-Las from the New York City area, best known for their hit "Leader of the Pack" and other lushly produced melodramatic songs. "The Shangri-La's have pretty much got a song for every stage of a relationship," Winehouse was quoted as saying by Ed Caesar of London's *Independent*, and she enumerated: "When you see a boy and you don't even know his name. When you start talking to him. When you start going out with him. And then when you're in love with him. And then when he [breaks up with] you and then you want to kill yourself."

Winehouse began singing with the National Youth Jazz Orchestra on weekends, and a friend who had access to a recording studio offered to help her make a few demo tapes. She agreed, but had little faith that a recorded version of her torchy style would actually land her a record deal. "I didn't go knocking on people's doors," she said in an interview with *Independent* journalist Charlotte Cripps. "I wouldn't bother sending anybody your tape—people get tapes by the sackload and a lot of the time they don't care." But Winehouse's demo did find the right person, and at the age of 17 she was signed to Island Records, the legendary British label founded in 1959 that brought Jamaican reggae to a world audience and then scored a major coup by signing Irish rockers U2 early in their career. Winehouse also signed with Brilliant/19 Management, the artists' management company run by Simon Fuller, the man credited with bringing the Spice Girls to fame.

Winehouse's debut album, *Frank,* was released in Britain in October of 2003. She had written the lyrics for nearly all of its tracks, and collaborated with hip-hop producer and songwriter Salaam Remi, who made top-selling records for the Fugees and Nas and also produced *Frank.* Her debut reached platinum certification with sales of 300,000, was nominated for two BRIT Awards (the U.K. equivalent of the Grammy Awards), and also made the shortlist for the prestigious Mercury Music Prize, awarded to the best LP of the year from a British or Irish act.

The twin debuts of both Winehouse and *Frank* caused somewhat of a media sensation in Britain: The record was hailed as an elegant throwback to the jazz era but with lyrics updated for a post-feminist world, and Winehouse's arresting vocal style praised as the next big thing to come out of the Isles. Writing about her voice for the *Sunday Times,* Cairns called it "one of the most extraordinary to be heard in pop music for years. A cracked, racked husk that will one moment coo at the object of her affection, the next emit a caustic rasp at the target of her scorn, it harks back to Billie Holiday in its emotional vulnerability, to Joni Mitchell when it eases through the octaves, and to Macy Gray as it lays bare its owner's feelings."

Yet Winehouse was also causing a stir for her provocative statements to the press, which were often delivered amidst a colorful torrent of profanity. She criticized Island and its parent company, Universal, for inserting two songs she did not want on *Frank,* and became known to paparazzi around London for extravagant drinking habits and general carousing. After performing live around Britain for a time, she was plagued by a case of writer's block when it came time to write new songs for a second album. Finally she met DJ/producer Mark Ronson, who had worked with Christina Aguilera, Kanye West, and another newcomer Brit, Lily Allen, and the pair clicked—especially after Ronson heard what Winehouse wanted for her new record in the trove of Shangri-Las records she passed along to him.

Back to Black was released nearly three years after *Frank,* in October of 2006, and immediately became one of the U.K.'s top-selling records of the entire year; nine months later it had sold more than a million copies. It was released in the United States in March of 2007 after advance buzz surrounded the single "Rehab," reportedly a true story of Island and Fuller's attempts to get Winehouse into an alcohol-treatment program. "Things got so bad for me at one point that I was told: 'We're taking you to rehab and, if you don't come today, we're taking you tomorrow,'" the singer admitted in an interview with journalist Eva Simpson for the *Mirror,* a

British tabloid. She acquiesced, she said, but upon arriving was confronted by a long questionnaire they told her to complete. "So I was like, how long it is going to take? He said about half an hour and that was too much." She walked out, and decided to fire the management instead.

The catchy "Rehab," like the rest of the tracks on Winehouse's follow-up, won enthusiastic praise from critics. Writing for *Entertainment Weekly*, Chris Willman asserted that the LP's "modern spin on soul, Motown, doo-wop, and the girl-group sound is timelessly engineered to sound slightly spooky, as if coming out of a radio.... Winehouse is retro enough to be on repeat play at your local Starbucks and badass enough to be the queen of Coachella. They might as well hand her next year's Best New Artist Grammy right now."

During the weeks of media promotion that followed the U.K. release of *Back to Black*, Winehouse continued to display the somewhat reckless behavior that had caused the British tabloids to dub her "Amy Wino." She heckled U2 singer Bono during an awards ceremony, twice appeared to be intoxicated during television appearances, and left the stage after just one song at a London gig when she became sick to her stomach—which she later attributed to food poisoning. She capped off her first U.S. tour by marrying an off-again, on-again boyfriend, Blake Fielder-Civil, in Miami, Florida. The two had dated briefly but then split, with Fielder-Civil returning to his girlfriend and leaving Winehouse heartbroken. They reconciled in April of 2007 and wed just a few weeks later. Meanwhile Alex Claire, the London chef who had been Winehouse's boyfriend until early 2007, sold his story to a British tabloid, in which he claimed she once held his head underwater in the bathtub.

Winehouse's devastation over the breakup with Fielder-Civil inspired several songs on *Back to Black*, she later said. "The songs literally did write themselves," she told *Rolling Stone* interviewer Jenny Eliscu. "All the songs are about the state of my relationship at the time with Blake.... I thought we'd never see each other again. He laughs about it now. He's like, 'What do you mean, you thought we'd never see each other again? We love each other. We've always loved each other.' But I don't think it's funny. I wanted to die."

Even Winehouse's weight became fodder for media speculation. She suddenly dropped several dress sizes in 2006, prompting speculation that she suffered from an eating disorder or recently acquired drug habit. She confessed that it was simply a case of feeling uneasy with comments in the press about her voluptuous figure and a decision to replace a pot-smoking habit with visits to the gym. Marijuana, she told *Mirror* journalist Simpson, "made me eat junk. Now I think that going to the gym is the best drug. I go four times a week and it gives me the buzz I need." She also told Simpson that she's fielded "offers to do modelling and stuff. But I'm like, are they mad?! I'm not exactly an oil painting, am I?"

Winehouse was hailed as a much-needed jolt of audacity and raw talent for an increasingly moribund music business. She was one of the best-selling artists of 2006 and 2007 on both sides of the Atlantic, at a time when record sales seemed to be bottoming out and the public was losing faith in the industry's ability to discover genuine artistic ability and bring it to market. Her lack of inhibition was also part of her appeal, with *Newsweek* writer Joshua Alston describing her as "a perfect storm of sex kitten, raw talent, and poor impulse control. She's compulsively honest and, unlike celebrities who keep their publicists on speed dial, she embraces her dark side and pours it into guileless, confessional lyrics."

Winehouse won her first BRIT Award for Best British Female Solo Artist in 2007, and performed "Rehab" live at the perennially controversy-marred ceremony. Her first record, *Frank*, was released in the United States in September of 2007. When *Rolling Stone* journalist Eliscu asked her if it would bother her if she never made a third record—an unlikely scenario, given her immense success—she replied, "Not really. I've done a record I'm really proud of. And that's about it. It's just that I'm a caretaker and I want to enjoy myself and spend time with my husband.... I don't want to be ungrateful. I know I'm talented, but I wasn't put here to sing. I was put here to be a wife and a mom and to look after my family. I love what I do, but it's not where it begins and ends."

Selected discography

Frank, Island Records, 2003.
Back to Black, Island Records, 2006.

Sources

Entertainment Weekly, May 25, 2007, p. 46.

Independent (London, England), April 21, 2004, p. 14; February 20, 2007, p. 24; June 2, 2007.

Mirror (London, England), February 13, 2007, p. 20.

Newsweek, March 12, 2007, p. 60.

New York Times, May 10, 2007.

Rolling Stone, May 30, 2007.

Sunday Times (London, England), October 5, 2003, p. 12.

—*Carol Brennan*

Len Wiseman

Film director

Born March 4, 1973, in Fremont, CA; son of Loren and Janice Wiseman; married Kate Beckinsale (an actress), May 9, 2004.

Addresses: *Contact*—ICM (International Creative Management), 10250 Constellation Blvd., Los Angeles, CA 90067. *Home*—Los Angeles, CA.

Career

Began career in film industry art departments, working on props for *Stargate,* 1994, *Independence Day,* 1996, *Men in Black,* 1997, and *Godzilla,* 1998; directed television commercials and music videos, c. 1990s; made film directing debut with *Underworld,* 2003, and followed with *Underworld: Revolution,* 2006, and *Live Free or Die Hard,* 2007.

Sidelights

As a child, Len Wiseman dreamed of directing motion pictures. *"Die Hard, Indiana Jones,* and *Lethal Weapon* were the movies that really kicked it off for me in high school," Wiseman told the *Evening Standard*'s Nick Curtis. "I saw a making of *Raiders of the Lost Ark* documentary and thought: 'Man, that's the job I want to do.'" Wiseman's dream came true in 2003 when he made his directing debut with the Gothic action-horror-flick *Underworld.* The film proved moderately successful and Wiseman was tapped to direct 2007's *Live Free or Die Hard,* the fourth installment of the fan-favorite Bruce Willis action-hero franchise.

Born March 4, 1973, in Fremont, California, to Loren and Janice Wiseman, the future film director spent his childhood attached to the family's video camera, filming the neighborhood kids in various plot scenarios he invented. "He would videotape himself jumping off the roof or direct his friends in some play," Wiseman's mother told the *Tri-Valley Herald*'s Tom Anderson. Wiseman's other childhood passion involved art, and he ended up drawing storyboards for films before earning a spot in the director's chair.

In 1988, Wiseman was just a teenager when the first *Die Hard* movie hit theaters. It featured Willis in the role of John McClane, a policeman who becomes a reluctant hero when he is forced to deal with a hostage situation on the 30th floor of a Los Angeles office building. "I was obsessed with *Die Hard* in high school," Wiseman told Susan King of the *Los Angeles Times.* "The action was amazing, and the relationship between the good guys was like nothing else I had seen before." The teenage Wiseman could not get the action-packed thriller out of his head. After seeing the film, he shot his own backyard version starring his friends. With the help of his father, Wiseman even made a battery-powered, blood-squirting explosive vest to enhance the project.

At 18, Wiseman helped with props for a movie filmed at the Marin County Renaissance Festival.

Afterward, he was asked to help the art department with props for 1994's *Stargate*. Wiseman did similar work for the 1996 blockbuster *Independence Day* and also appeared briefly as an extra in the film's final battle scene. More prop work followed with 1997's *Men in Black* and 1998's *Godzilla*. Despite the steady work, Wiseman really wanted to direct films—not make props for them. To gain some directing experience, Wiseman left the movie world and began working with television commercials and music videos. He directed a number of videos, including some for heavy metal rockers Megadeth and the R&B group En Vogue.

Meanwhile, Wiseman continued courting Hollywood, hoping to break into the industry as a director. To market himself, Wiseman had his agent solicit reels of his work. Eventually, Wiseman's work caught the eye of Dimension Films, which pitched a proposal to Wiseman, asking him to create a werewolf film. "I wasn't too thrilled about a werewolf film in general," Wiseman told Patrick Day in an article for the *Chicago Tribune*. "It had a bit of a B movie sounding quality to it. We didn't want it to be a local sheriff in some forest hunting down mysterious killings and that kind of thing." Wiseman bounced the idea off his friends—actor-screenwriter Danny McBride and actor-stuntman Kevin Grevioux. Grevioux suggested it might be possible to make a werewolf film that was a mix of action-thriller *Blade Runner* and the fantasy-horror *The Howling*. Grevioux also suggested a Romeo and Juliet caveat—except it would involve a werewolf and a vampire.

Dimension eventually dropped the idea after hiring another director, Wes Craven, to create a horror flick. Wiseman, Grevioux, and McBride, however, continued working on the concept and pitched it to Lakeshore Entertainment. The company's president, Gary Lucchesi, told Day that the detailed artwork that accompanied the proposal helped cement the deal. "The script arrived with drawings of what the werewolves and vampires were going to look like," Lucchesi said. "So we already saw there was a world that was unique that was going to be created along with the story. You never thought cheesy. You thought, 'This is really cool. This is artistic.'" Wiseman himself had rendered the 12 production drawings that went along with the script.

McBride penned the screenplay, and Wiseman directed the eventual film, which they titled *Underworld*. It opened in 2003. The story focused on a vampire warrior named Selene, played by British actress Kate Beckinsale, who had made a name for herself playing a nurse in 2001's *Pearl Harbor*. Selene hunts—and kills—werewolves, believing they are responsible for the death of her family members. Over the course of *Underworld*, Selene falls for a wereman, played by Scott Speedman of *Felicity* fame.

The movie received fairly mediocre reviews. Film critics did not care for it, although it gained a bit of a following among fans of the horror genre. Writing in the *Orange County Register*, film critic Craig Outhier complained about the actors' performances. "We feel the suspense and tension in *Underworld* but miss the more delicate emotions, especially in regard to the central love story, which ends more like a chaste business arrangement than a taboo-shattering romance." Though not a box-office smash, the movie proved moderately successful. It took in $51.9 million at the domestic box office, but only cost $22 million to make.

In May of 2004—less than a year after the film was released—Wiseman married Beckinsale, the leather-clad star of the film. Beckinsale already had a five-year-old daughter, Lily, with actor Michael Sheen, who also starred in the film. When Wiseman followed with a sequel, 2006's *Underworld: Evolution*, he cast Lily in the role of playing Selene as a child.

Underworld: Evolution included more action shots than the original and was the top box-office draw its opening weekend, taking in $27.6 million in ticket sales. After the opening-weekend hype, however, the movie faded to the background. Writing in *Film Journal International*, Ethan Alter rebuked the film for its murky, hard-to-follow plotline. He also criticized Wiseman and screenwriter McBride for their inability to get a handle on the various characters and conflicts involved in the story. "The history of this universe is constantly changing, which means that the narrative often comes to a dead stop as the characters stand around trying and failing to make sense of each new revelation."

Although his *Underworld* flicks failed to garner the attention Wiseman hoped for, 20th Century Fox sensed his potential and asked Wiseman to direct 2007's *Live Free or Die Hard* sequel. Wiseman was a relative newcomer to the field of directing, yet veteran actor Willis felt comfortable working with him. "Even before I met Len, before we sat down to talk about doing the film, my daughter, Scout, turned me on to *Underworld*," Willis told the *New York Post's* Reed Tucker. "We sat up one night watching it and I thought it was great."

For Wiseman, it was a dream come true. Twenty years earlier, he had mimicked the original film's action sequences in his own yard, filming them with a camcorder. Now, he was being offered the chance to adapt it for the big screen. When *Baltimore Sun* writer Chris Kaltenbach asked Wiseman if he was nervous about taking on the project, he replied, "Of course. It's a huge franchise, and the first film was such a classic to so many people. But, you've only got one life. It was like, 'What am I in this industry for, anyway, if not to try to have some fun and just be part of a franchise that was so important to me growing up?' I thought, 'I can't pass that up. It's *Die Hard.* How many times does an opportunity like that come along?'"

Live Free or Die Hard finds the reluctant hero John McClane battling a vengeful computer hacker named Thomas Gabriel—played by Timothy Olyphant. Olyphant's character is trying to cripple the United States by taking over various computer systems that control important infrastructures, such as those that control power, defense, and banking systems. Besides dealing with hackers, McClane is also involved in a secondary storyline that involves a spat with his college-age daughter, Lucy.

Instead of relying on digital graphics, Wiseman chose to shoot the film old-school style, using live-action shots instead of special effects. In one scene, McClane's car flies across the roadway and smacks a concrete divider, which in turn launches the car into the air, where it hits a hovering helicopter. McClane bails along the way. Instead of using computers, Wiseman insisted on shooting the sequence in real time, with real props, so the flavor of the excitement would not be lost.

"As complicated as that scene looks, it was more about testing and timing," Wiseman told the *New York Post.* "We tested it out in a parking lot. We suspended another car by a crane (because we didn't have another helicopter), then measured out the distance of the jump. Then we lined it up on set. We got it in one take." Another scene finds Willis involved in a fistfight inside an SUV that has crashed into an elevator shaft, dangling by cables. To shoot the scene, a five-story elevator shaft was constructed. Despite all of the stunt work, Willis got by with just 43 stitches to his head over the course of making the film.

Unlike the previous installments, *Live Free or Die Hard* was rated PG-13 instead of R. Some fans did not like the change and missed McClane's sharp, foul-mouthed tongue. Overall, though, the film was warmly received. Writing in *Cinematical,* Erik Davis praised Wiseman for knowing how to shoot an action sequence. He called the movie a "fun ride," but lamented the overuse of explosive set pieces and the fact that the aging McClane was able to survive such an implausible number of explosions and blows to the body. Despite his criticism, Davis said the movie "is not a bad film; it's the film we expected—a sequel punched up to appeal to our Costco-sized addictions."

Live Free or Die Hard, produced on a budget of $110 million, brought in $378 million worldwide. Each of Wiseman's films has earned more than it cost to make. As such, Wiseman should have no trouble getting studios to finance his future projects. After Wiseman's *Die Hard* sequel was released, he was thinking about directing a superhero movie. He was also reviewing a sci-fi script called *Shell Game,* which he had started on before *Underworld.*

Sources

Periodicals

Baltimore Sun, June 29, 2007, p. 3C.
Chicago Tribune, September 15, 2003, p. 3 (Tempo).
Evening Standard (London, England), July 5, 2007, p. 32A.
Film Journal International, March 2006, p. 41.
Los Angeles Times, June 25, 2007, p. E3.
New York Post, June 24, 2007, p. 40.
Orange County Register, September 19, 2003, p. D (Show).
Tri-Valley Herald (Pleasanton, CA), September 7, 2003.

Online

"Review: Live Free or Die Hard—Erik's Review," *Cinematical,* http://www.cinematical.com/2007/06/27/review-live-free-or-die-hard-eriks-review/ (November 19, 2007).

—Lisa Frick

Umaru Yar'Adua

Afolabi Sotunde/Reuters/Landov

President of Nigeria

Born Umaru Musa Yar'Adua, July 9, 1951, in Katsina, Katsina State, Nigeria; son of Musa (a government minister); married Turai, 1975; married Hauwa Umar Radda, 1992 (divorced, 1997); children: seven (from first marriage), Ibrahim, Musa (from second marriage). *Education:* Attended Keffi Government College, 1965-69; Barewa College, certificate, 1971; Ahmadu Bello University, B.S., 1975, and M.Sc., 1978.

Addresses: *Office*—c/o Embassy of the Federal Republic of Nigeria, 3519 International Ct. NW, Washington, D.C. 20008.

Career

Lecturer in chemistry at Holy Child College, 1975-76, Katsina College of Arts, Science and Technology, 1976-79, and Katsina Polytechnic, 1979-83; general manager, Sambo Farms Ltd., 1983-89; company director or board member for several private-sector firms, 1983-99; elected governor of Katsina State, 1999, reelected, 2003; inherited the title of *Mutawalli*, or custodian of the treasury, for Katsina state, from his father, 2002; elected president of Nigeria, April 2007.

Sidelights

Umaru Yar'Adua was elected president of Nigeria in a controversial 2007 election that was marred by accusations of widespread vote fraud. Nevertheless, he was sworn into office in May and immediately began implementing several new re-

forms and measures aimed at winning the public trust of Africa's most populous nation. "This office is just a responsibility," he told journalist Robyn Dixon in an interview for the *Sunday Independent* of South Africa. "It's routine work. When people talk about power, I don't see where the power lies. If you are honest with yourself, the power lies with the law."

Born in 1951, Yar'Adua hails from a politically active, aristocratic family of Fulani heritage, one of Nigeria's largest ethnic groups. He was born in the city of Katsina, the capital for the state of the same name in northwestern Nigeria. After Nigeria achieved its full independence from Britain in 1963, Yar'Adua's father became the minister for Lagos, the capital city at the time. His father also served as the *Mutawalli*, or custodian of the treasury, for Katsina state, which was a title that Yar'Adua later inherited.

Yar'Adua entered the Dutsinma Boarding Primary School in 1962, and went on to the Government College in Keffi in the late 1960s. He earned a certificate from Barewa College in 1971, a bachelor of science degree in education and chemistry from Ahmadu Bello University in the city of Zaria in 1975, and three years later earned a graduate degree in analytical chemistry from the same university. He spent the next five years as a chemistry instructor at various colleges in Nigeria, including Holy Child College in Lagos and the Katsina College of Arts, Science and Technology. In 1983, he took a job as general manager of Sambo Farms Ltd. and, after 1989, served as a company director or board member for several private-sector firms.

In the early 1980s, Yar'Adua was a member of the left-leaning People's Redemption Party, and then co-founded another organization called the People's Front with his brother, a major-general in the Nigerian army. This merged with another group to become the Social Democratic Party. Yar'Adua participated in the 1988 Constituent Assembly, though the country remained under rule of a military junta. He first ran for office in the Katsina gubernatorial race of 1991, but lost. Democracy was fully restored in Nigeria by 1999, and that year he ran again for the post and won.

Corruption had long been a serious problem in Nigeria, with a seeming majority of elected and appointed officials using their position to enrich their own coffers. Yar'Adua was one of the few politicians with an untarnished reputation: Though he had inherited a state government with crushing debt, during his two terms in office he managed the budget so effectively that a fiscal surplus grew. This came despite an intensive, much-needed infrastructure improvement campaign in Katsina State, including the construction of new roads and several new clinics and schools. Yar'Adua was also believed to suffer from a kidney ailment, and some speculated that this may have been the reason that his name was announced in December of 2006 as the candidate for the People's Democratic Party (PDP) in the coming presidential elections. The PDP's chair was the incumbent president, Olusegun Obasanjo, whose record had been blemished by charges of corruption. It was thought that because Yar'Adua was ill, he would prove a weak, easily manipulated leader—in other words, a puppet of Obasanjo. Others noted that years before, Yar'Adua's brother—who had since died—and Obasanjo had been jailed together as political prisoners during the military junta era, and Yar'Adua's nomination may have been a gesture of respect.

In March of 2007, Yar'Adua collapsed at a campaign rally, and subsequently flew to Germany for unspecified medical treatment. There were even rumors in Nigeria that he was close to death, but Yar'Adua returned and renewed his campaign commitments, and even challenged naysayers who claimed he was unfit to hold office to meet him for a squash tournament. Even without such worries, Yar'Adua was not expected to win. He was viewed as Obasanjo's handpicked successor, and there was tremendous dissatisfaction with the outgoing president because of the notorious and highly publicized episodes of corruption. Nigerians went to the polls on April 21, and the election was marred by charges of ballot stuffing, voter intimidation, missing ballot boxes, and general chaos that erupted into violence in some cities. Two days later, the official tally was announced and Yar'Adua was the winner with 70 percent of the vote.

Nigerians protested vehemently at what many believed to have been a blatantly rigged election, with international observers and Yar'Adua's two leading opponents—Muhammadu Buhari of the All Nigeria People's Party (ANPP) and Atiku Abubakar of the Action Congress (AC)—voicing concern about the legitimacy of the official results. Yar'Adua quickly moved to dispel doubts, saying, "the contest has come and gone," according to a report by *New York Times* journalist Lydia Polgreen. "So must our differences dissipate in the cause of the greater good of moving our dear nation ahead."

Yar'Adua was sworn into office on May 29, 2007, and quickly began to move to restore the public's trust in the federal government. Declaring himself a servant of the people, he sought and won a government of national unity with the ANPP and the Progressive People's Alliance, another leading party. Setting an example of transparency for his administration, he also divulged his personal wealth, a figure of about $5 million, much of it inherited. He became the first Nigerian leader ever to provide a financial disclosure statement.

Yar'Adua is also the first Nigerian leader in nearly three decades to hold a college degree. He has seven children with his wife Turai, whom he married in 1975, and two children with a second wife he took—an Islamic custom permitted in Nigeria—in the 1990s, but that marriage ended after five years. Despite his wealth, Yar'Adua is known for his spartan lifestyle. "I go to the mosque and I pray as an ordinary person would pray, because I don't want to have problems when I leave office," he told Dixon, the *Sunday Independent* reporter. "The less you allow power to get to you, the more you are able to adjust when leaving office."

Sources

African Business, June 2007, p. 12.
Financial Times, July 12, 2007, p. 3.

New York Times, March 8, 2007; April 24, 2007; October 4, 2007.

Sunday Independent (South Africa), May 20, 2007, p. 16.

Time International, June 11, 2007, p. 29.

—*Carol Brennan*

Ken Yeang

Courtesy of Dr. Ken Yeang

Architect and author

Born in 1948, in Penang, Malaysia; son of a physician father; children: four. *Education:* Architectural Association School, architecture degree, London, 1971; attended the University of Pennsylvannia, 1973; Cambridge University, Ph.D., 1975; also attended Harvard University and the Malaysian Institute of Management.

Addresses: *Office*—Llweleyn Davis Yeang, Brook House, Torrington Place, London WC1E 7HN United Kingdom.

Career

Principle, T. R. Hamzah and Yeang Senderian Berhad (later known as T. R. Hamzah and Yeang International), Malaysia, 1976—; designed Plaza Atrium, Kuala Lumpur, Malaysia, 1986; designed IBM Plaza, Malaysia, 1990; lecturer, Nottingham University, U.K., 2003-05; partner, MPR Ken Yeang International, 2004—; director, Llweleyn Davis Yeang (an architecture firm), London, 2005—.

Member: Royal Institute of British Architects; advisory committee, ARCHIVE Institute; advisory committee, Skyscraper Museum.

Awards: PAM Architecture Award (Malaysia) for the IBM Plaza, 1989; PAM Architecture Award for The Weld Interior, 1989; PAM Architecture Award for commercial building, 1991; PAM Architecture Award for single residential building, 1991; Norway Award for outstanding contribution to quality in the field of architecture, 1992; PAM Architecture Award for the Menara Mesiniaga, 1993; merit award, Kenneth F. Brown Asia Pacific Culture and Architecture design award, for the Roof-Roof House, 1995; IAKS Award, International Association for Sports and Leisure Facilities, for the Selangor Turf Club Grandstand, 1995; AGA Khan Award for architecture, for the Menara Mesiniaga, 1996; international architecture award, Royal Australian Institute of Architects (RAIA), for the Menara Mesiniaga, 1996; PAM Architecture Award for the Central Plaza, 1997; design excellence award, Malaysian Institute of Interior Designers, for Conoco Asia Pacific Ltd., 1997; international architecture award, RAIA, 1998; UIA Auguste Perret Prize for Applied Technology in Architecture, 1999; Prince Claus Award, Prince Claus Fund, 2000.

Sidelights

The pioneer behind the bioclimatic skyscraper and a designer of many green (environmentally conscious) large buildings, architect Ken Yeang has designed such buildings as Kuala Lumpur's Menara Mesiniaga and Penang's UMNO Tower. His ecologically sensitive buildings feature both organic and inorganic elements. In addition to designing more than 200 projects, Yeang also wrote numerous books on and lectured about eco-design. As Texas A&M College of Architecture dean J. Thomas Regan told the U.S. States News, "Yeang's work challenges society and environmental design—philosophically, psychologically, technically, aesthetically, politically, and culturally. He is an inventive and prolific architect who is radically changing not only the face of architecture, but environmentalism as well."

Born in Penang, Malaysia, in 1948, Yeang is the son of a doctor. After attending the Penang Free School, Yeang received much of his education in England. He attended a boys school, Cheltenham College, from 1962 to 1966, then studied architecture at London's Architectural Association beginning in 1966. From 1971 to 1974, Yeang worked on his Ph.D. at Cambridge University, and was influenced in his career course by the times. He told Nadia Elghamry of *Estates Gazette*, "When I was a student, it was the time of the hippy movement. I was looking at solar energy and I decided that eco-design needed to be sorted. The theory was not right, so I went to my supervisor and asked if I could do a Ph.D."

Yeang's Cambridge doctorate, "A Theoretical Framework for the Incorporation of Ecological Considerations in the Design and Planning of the Built Enivronment," included his early theories about green design. Yeang later continued his education in the United States, taking graduate courses at Harvard and the University of Pennsylvania, and business classes at the Malaysian Institute of Management.

While Yeang planned on a career in academia, his father asked him to move back to Malaysia. In 1976, he co-founded T. R. Hamzah and Yeang Senderian Berhad (later known as T. R. Hamzah and Yeang International) with Tengku Robert Hamzah, a member of a Malaysian royal family and a fellow student at the Architectural Association. As a professional, Yeang began designing projects which brought architecture and ecology together, and were sensitive to the area in which they were located. Yeang told CNN.com of his holistic view, "In my heart I believe that biology is the beginning and end of everything. It's the biggest source of ideas, the biggest source of invention. Nobody can invent better than nature ... nature is my biggest source of inspiration."

With T. R. Hamzah and Yeang Senderian Berhad, Yeang began doing research into bioclimatic design in the 1970s and 1980s. He and his colleagues collected data and produced papers on the subject. Yeang was also testing his theories in some

buildings. Yeang built his first high-rise, Kuala Lumpur's Plaza Atrium, in 1986, under many of these principles. Yeang kept in mind the tropical area in which it was built, and put the atrium in an unusual place—between the inside and outside like a colonnade. In this high-spaced atrium, sunlight was diffused and the hot air was allowed to escape through louvers.

By the early 1990s, Yeang had developed the principals behind bioclimatic skyscrapers. His bioclimatic skyscrapers defied the conventional idea that such tall buildings could not be completely green. This type of tall building was built with an ecological conscience, often with plants or other greenery, and features to encourage low energy consumption. Many of his buildings had heating and air conditioning systems, but he worked to make them self-sufficient. Yeang was initially designing these buildings in Malaysia, then other countries in Southeast Asia.

One of Yeang's first bioclimatic skyscrapers was the Menara Mesiniaga IBM Tower in Kuala Lumpur. This building, built in 1992, featured creative ways of processing the air. As Clifford A. Pearson explained in the *Architectural Record*, "Instead of relying solely on mechanical systems to condition, circulate, and ventilate air, the building supplements such systems with operable windows, natural ventilation, shaded outdoor spaces, and proper orientation to the sun." Other bioclimatic skyscrapers designed by Yeang included the conceptual Tokyo Nara Tower in 1992, Penang-based MBF Tower in 1993, and the Guthrie Pavilion outside of Kuala Lumpur and the UMNO Tower, both in 1998.

Yeang began regularly working in England by the early 2000s. He became partners with MRP (Mason Richards Partnership), which became known as MRP Ken Yeang International in 2004, and joined a British-based architectural firm, Llweleyn Davis Yeang, as a director in 2005. In England, he continued to focus on designing large buildings and masterplans that were green. In the latter, he often incorporated his ideas about high-rise buildings as vertical urban design. Through his British companies, Yeang designed two high-rise residential towers around a 15-acre park in the Elephant and Castle area of Southwark, London, in the early 2000s. He also worked on international projects like the 43-story Al Ghofa Tower in Kuwait City, Kuwait, as well.

Yeang was also concerned with furthering the education of other architects. To that end, he served as a lecturer at Nottingham University in Nottingham,

England, between 2003 and 2005. There, he was involved as a reviewer in the 2003-04 Minerva Tower educational design project. In addition, Yeang wrote or co-wrote a number of books on the focus of his design work—tall buildings—including *Bioclimatic Skyscrapers*, published in 1994, *The Green Skyscraper*, published in 1999, *Reinventing the Skyscraper: A Vertical Theory of Urban Design*, published in 2002, and *Ecodesign: A Manual for Ecological Design*, published in 2006.

While Yeang believed that his eco-conscious designs helped the environment, he saw green buildings as only the tip of the iceberg. He told CNN.com, "A lot of people think that if I put [in] a green building everything is going to be fine, but actually it's not just the green buildings we need, but green businesses, green governments, green economics. We have to extend the greening of buildings to our business and our lifestyles—that is the most important thing to do next."

Selected writings

Tropical Verandah City, Longman (Malaysia), 1986.
Bioclimatic Skyscrapers, Artemis (London), 1994.
Designing With Nature, McGraw-Hill (New York City), 1995.
The Skyscraper Bioclimatically Considered: A Design Primer, Academy Group (London), 1996.
The Green Skyscraper: The Basis for Designing Sustainable, Intensive Buildings, Prestel Publishing (Munich, Germany), 1999.
(With Robert Powell) *Rethinking the Skyscraper: The Complete Architecture of Ken Yeang*, Thames & Hudson (London), 1999.
Reinventing the Skyscraper: A Vertical Theory of Urban Design, Academy Press, 2002.
Ecodesign: Instruction Manual, Academy-Wiley (London), 2005.

Ecodesign: A Manual for Ecological Design, Academy-Wiley, 2006.
Eco Skyscrapers, Images Publishing Group (Mulgrave, Australia), 2007.
The Mutiara Masterplan, Images Publishing Group, 2007.

Sources

Periodicals

Age (Melbourne, Australia), August 14, 1993, p. 12.
Architectural Record, March 1993, p. PR26; August 1998, p. 81; July 2001, p. 30; January 1, 2008, p. 52.
Architectural Review, February 2000, p. 23.
Building, July 6, 2001, p. 50.
Building Design, May 28, 2004, p. 1.
Estates Gazette, August 13, 2005, p. 44.
Financial Times (London), June 4, 1990, p. I13.
New Scientist, September 3, 1994, p. 4242.
Planning, August 5, 2005.
Straits Times (Singapore), December 12, 2001.
U.S. States News, November 1, 2006.

Online

"Biography: Ken Yeang," CNN.com, http://www.cnn.com/2007/TECH/science/07/18/yeang.bio/ (October 12, 2007).
"Dr. Ken Yeang," University of Nottingham, http://www.nottingham.co.uk/sbe/tallbuildings/KenYeangTop.htm (February 25, 2008).
"Q&A: Ken Yeang Interview" CNN.com, http://www.cnn.com/2007/TECH/science/07/16/yeang.qa/index.html (October 12, 2007).

—*A. Petruso*

Laura Ziskin

Stephen Shugerman/Getty Images

Director and producer

Born March 3, 1950, in San Fernando Valley, CA; daughter of Jay Ziskin (a psychologist); married Julian Barry (divorced); partner of Alvin Sargent, 1991—; children: Julia Barry. *Education:* Graduated from University of Southern California film school, 1973.

Addresses: *Office*—Laura Ziskin Productions, 10202 W. Washington Blvd., Astaire Building, Culver City, CA 90232.

Career

Began writing screenplays for game shows and became a development executive; associate-producer, *The Eyes of Laura Mars*, 1978; produced *Murphy's Romance*, 1985; served as executive producer for *Pretty Woman*, 1990; president, Fox 2000, 1994-99; formed Laura Ziskin Productions, 1999; produced 74th annual Academy Awards, 2002; produced 79th annual Academy Awards, 2007. Worked as producer or executive producer on various films, including *What about Bob?* 1991, *As Good as It Gets*, 1997, and the *Spider-Man* series, 2002, 2004, 2007.

Awards: Saturn Award for best single television presentation, for "Fail Safe" 2001; Israel Film Fest Visionary Award, 2003; David O. Selznick Award Achievement in theatrical motion pictures, the Producers Guild of America, 2005.

Sidelights

Producer Laura Ziskin is best known for her romantic comedy *Pretty Woman,* which was her first film as an executive producer, and for the superhero movie *Spider-Man* and its sequels. Ziskin headed 20th Century-Fox's new division Fox 2000 from 1994 to 1999, when she left to form her own company, Laura Ziskin Productions. In 2002, she became the first solo female producer of the Academy Awards.

A native Californian, Ziskin studied film at the University of Southern California, graduating in 1973. Her early career in Hollywood included writing scripts for *The Dating Game,* working as a typist, being an assistant to Barbra Streisand, and screening scripts for another producer. She worked as the associate-producer for her first film, *The Eyes of Laura Mars,* in 1978. In 1980, she tired of being an assistant. "I'm as smart as he is. Why am I not doing this for myself?" she quipped to an interviewer for *People.* Focusing on both career and family, she married Julian Barry and the couple had a child. Her devotion to raising her daughter convinced her to take some time off from her work, and compromise in both career and family allowed her to have both successfully. "When I made the decision to be a studio executive … I was trying to decide whether to be a director. My decision ultimately was dictated by my role as a mother," she explained in a *Newsweek* roundtable. "I directed a short film. I shot for six days. I left before my daughter got up in the morning, and I came home after she had gone to sleep. If I multiplied that by three months or five months of making a movie, I would miss five months of my child's life, and I wasn't willing to do that."

When she started producing on her own, conventional wisdom was to aim movies at 17-year-old boys, but Ziskin was determined to produce movies she wanted to watch. In 1990, she was the executive producer on the movie *Pretty Woman*, a romantic comedy about a corporate raider and a prostitute, which became the second-highest grossing film of the year. "You can make a movie that appeals to women and still do gigantic business," she told *People*.

Studios noticed the successes of her movies. In 1994, she became the president of Fox 2000, a new movie division, and she chose to draw on novels for her inspiration. By 1996, the studio had optioned 30 novels. "People who write books generally spend years working out characters and plots. And when you start with good material you can attract the best talent for your picture," she explained to Paul Nathan of *Publishers Weekly*.

In 1999, she left Fox to form her own production company. She was quickly offered a three-year contract with Columbia to produce pictures there. Under the new contract, she was the producer for all three *Spider-Man* movies, based on the Marvel Comics superhero. Producing *Spider-Man* was a turning point in her career; the concept for the story did not originate with Ziskin, as many of her films have. "I'd never tried anything with such big special effects or that overtly pop culture before," she said in an interview in *Hollywood Reporter*. Working on that scale was career changing, but Ziskin acknowledged that the struggles a film goes through in production are the same whether the film has a million dollar budget or a hundred million.

In 2002, she produced the 74th Annual Academy Awards, which was fitting as her own films had landed ten Oscar nominations and won two Oscars. Directing the Oscars had been a life-long dream. "They're about honoring the best in our industry and giving those awards. That's what's important,"

she told Barry Garron of *Hollywood Reporter*, noting that while she wanted to keep the program traditional, she intended to give it her own spin. The broadcast earned eight Emmy nominations, including one for best producer. But that she was the first woman to be a sole producer of the Academy Awards seemed unimportant to Ziskin. "I don't think it's a big deal. I think the fact that I'm a woman affects what I do in every way possible," she quipped in *Hollywood Reporter*. "I think it's for other people to say whether it means anything. If it means something to other women, then great."

But the role of women in Hollywood is not a topic Ziskin neglects. She told Kathy A. McDonald of *Daily Variety*, "Women are now culture-makers. We make movies, which are arguably the most powerful medium ever known in the history of civilization." She also expressed her concerns that women in Hollywood are not paid the same wages that men in similar positions receive. "I'm a card-carrying feminist, but I found [it] hard to be heard," she explained in an interview for *Hollywood Reporter*. "I'd need to say something five times. We just have to be persistent."

Ziskin herself has received many of the honors her male peers have earned over the years. In 2003, she was awarded the Israel Film Fest Visionary Award. The next year, she was honored with the Producers Guild of America's David O. Selznick Award for her body of work in feature films, placing her among previous recipients, including Stanley Kramer and Jerry Bruckheimer. In 2006, she was asked to repeat her role as producer for the 79th Annual Academy Awards.

Along with her many achievements in film, Ziskin is also a survivor of cancer. Her experiences with cancer have caused her to work toward demystifying the disease. "we have to … talk about it, challenge it, fight it in every arena," she said in her award speech at the Tribute to the Human Spirit Awards Dinner. Ziskin continues to strive for success in her career and her family. She lives with partner Alvin Sargent and works out of her offices in Culver City, California.

Sources

Periodicals

Daily Variety, September 20, 2002, p. A6; November 18, 2004, p. 21.

Hollywood Reporter, March 22, 2002, p. S-3; January 21, 2005, p. S-4; July 24, 2006, p. 8; December, 2006, p. 76; June 5, 2007, p. 18.

Newsweek, Summer 1998, p. 116.
People, Spring 1991, p. 47.
Publishers Weekly, March 11, 1996, p. 24.
Variety, June 9, 2003, p. 59.

Online

Hollywood.com, http://www.hollywood.com/celebrity/Laura_Ziskin/188847#fullBio (November 14, 2007).

—*Alana Joli Abbott*

Mark Zuckerberg

Founder of Facebook.com

Born Mark Elliott Zuckerberg, May 14, 1984, in Dobbs Ferry, NY. *Education:* Attended Harvard University, 2002-04.

Addresses: *Office*—Facebook, 156 University Ave., Palo Alto, CA 94301.

Career

Founded Facebook.com, February, 2004, in Cambridge, MA; moved company to Palo Alto, CA, June, 2004.

Sidelights

Mark Zuckerberg serves as chief executive officer of Facebook.com, the social networking Web site he started in his college dormitory room at Harvard University. A phenomenal success following its debut in early 2004, Facebook.com eventually grew to 42 million active members and has become a global Internet presence on par with Myspace.com and Google. Zuckerberg abandoned his studies soon after Facebook gained momentum and moved his fledgling company to Palo Alto, California. He became a millionaire several times over when Microsoft acquired a small stake in the company in October of 2007.

Zuckerberg was born in 1984 and grew up in Dobbs Ferry, a suburb of New York City in nearby Westchester County. An early computer enthusiast, he was writing his own programs by the time he was in sixth grade and proved so talented that he transferred out of the local public school, Ardsley High, after his sophomore year to Philips Exeter Academy. He chose the private boarding school in New Hampshire because his public school "didn't have a lot of computer courses or a lot of the higher math courses," he told Michael M. Grynbaum in an interview that appeared in the *Harvard Crimson.* Philips Exeter also had an excellent Latin program, and Zuckerberg initially hoped to study classics at Harvard.

Zuckerberg's first foray into commercial software development came inadvertently. For his senior-year independent project at Philips Exeter, he designed a media player that had the ability to search for and recommend new songs based on its users' musical tastes. He came up with the idea, he explained to Grynbaum in the *Harvard Crimson* interview, when "the playlist ran out on my computer, and I thought, 'You know, there's really no reason why my computer shouldn't just know what I want to learn next.'" He and the friend who helped create it, Adam D'Angelo, called it the Synapse Media Player, and after they put it out for free on the Internet, it began racking up an impressive number of downloads. Offers to acquire Synapse came pouring in from established companies, but Zuckerberg and D'Angelo hesitated, and when they finally decided to explore a commercial license, the $2 million offer had expired.

Zuckerberg entered Harvard University in the fall of 2002 but ran into trouble during his two years there for various programs he wrote and put up on the student computer network at the school. The first, Coursematch, was innocent enough—this merely listed the other students who were enrolled in a class, according to a query search—but the second one, Facemash.com, offered users a chance to rate the attractiveness of fellow students by photo. Facemash lasted just four hours before it was shut down and Zuckerberg was officially reprimanded by the school's administration for unlawfully accessing the Harvard computer system.

Zuckerberg's next brainstorm proved to be the ultimate end of his college career, though not because of its illicit nature: He decided to make an online version of the "facebook," which Ivy League and elite East Coast colleges typically hand out to incoming freshmen. It serves as sort of a reverse yearbook, with photos and personal details for each member of the incoming class. After another period in which he holed up in his dormitory room for several days to write code, Zuckerberg launched thefacebook.com on February 4, 2004, and it was an instant success. Within two weeks, there were more than 4,000 registered users among Harvard students, faculty members, and alumni. The site had a certain cache because it was accessible only to those registered with a harvard.edu email address. Soon students at other top-tier schools were requesting their own version of Facebook, and by early April Zuckerberg had created similar sites for the Yale, Columbia, and Stanford computer networks.

Zuckerberg never returned to Harvard after taking a leave of absence in the spring of 2004. Instead he headed to Palo Alto, California, located in what is known as Silicon Valley, the longtime center of the computer software and information technology industry in the United States, and established a corporate office. Over the next three years he allowed Facebook.com, as it became known in August of 2005, to grow slowly. It permitted high school students to join the site in 2005, and a year later offered open enrollment to anyone over the age of 13, which caused a sharp spike in membership. By late 2007, an estimated 150,000 new users were joining Facebook every day.

Zuckerberg expected Facebook to begin turning a profit in 2008. The site's revenue came from ad space it sold, but those dollars were not enough to meet the costs of maintaining and improving the site. He sold his first stake in the privately held company in 2005 to Accel Partners, giving up a 13 percent share in return for an investment of $12.7 million. In October of 2007, Zuckerberg and his site made headlines in the business media when the Microsoft Corporation acquired a mere 1.6 percent stake in Facebook for $240 million; that was based on a valuation of the company at a stunning $15 billion. That number, however, reflected an already-in-place agreement that allowed Microsoft to serve as broker for ads that will run on Facebook's U.S. site until 2011. The $15 billion figure, explained *Wall Street Journal* writers Robert A. Guth, Vauhini Vara, and Kevin J. Delaney, was tied to the fact that "Facebook presents a big opportunity for online advertising, in part because it collects detailed information about its users—such as their hobbies, favorite music, location, age, and gender—that can be used to place highly targeted ads."

Zuckerberg explains that Facebook's unique appeal is that it provides a way to connect people who already have some actual personal, professional, or family link to one another in the real world. In interviews, he described this already-existing network as the "social graph," and as he explained to Steven Levy for a *Newsweek* cover story in August of 2007, "The social graph is this thing that exists in the world, and it always has and it always will. It's really most natural for people to communicate through it, because it's with the people around you, friends, and business connections or whatever. What [Facebook] needed to do was construct as accurate of a model as possible of the way the social graph looks in the world."

Sources

Financial Times, October 27, 2007, p. 8.
Fortune, June 11, 2007, p. 127.
Guardian (London, England), July 27, 2007, p. 17.
Harvard Crimson, June 10, 2004.
Newsweek, August 20, 2007, p. 41.
Wall Street Journal, October 25, 2007, p. B1.

—*Carol Brennan*

Obituaries

Brooke Astor

Born Roberta Brooke Russell, March 30, 1902, in Portsmouth, NH; died of pneumonia, August 13, 2007, in Briarcliff Manor, NY. Philanthropist. Brooke Astor was often referred to as the last of the grand dames of American society. A noted philanthropist who came into an immense fortune upon the 1959 death of her third husband, Astor spent the next four decades giving away nearly $200 million to various New York City-based charities, social causes, and cultural institutions. When her remarkable life ended at the age of 105, she was lauded by the *New York Times* as an "Aristocrat of the People" in the headline of her obituary. That article also quoted an oft-repeated aphorism of hers borrowed from a Thornton Wilder play: "Money is like manure; it's not worth a thing unless it's spread around."

Roberta Brooke Russell was born on March 30, 1902, before the Wright Brothers made the world's first successful airplane flight. Her father was a high-ranking Marine Corps officer who served as commander of the armed-forces branch during the 1930s, and Astor's early life included stays in several exotic locales, such as China, Haiti, Panama, and other places where her father was stationed. An only child, she was often alone, and occupied her time by writing short stories. In her teens she attended the Madeira School in Virginia, and was married at age 17 to Princeton graduate J. Dryden Kuser, son of one of the original investors in the Fox Movie Studios, which later lent its name to the news and entertainment empire. The union produced one son, Anthony, but was an unhappy one; Astor later revealed that her husband drank, gambled, and was physically abusive to the point of breaking her jaw when she was pregnant. After a decade, they divorced, and Astor moved to New York City as a single parent.

Astor's second marriage to stockbroker Charles "Buddie" Marshall was a much happier one, and her son Anthony would later take his stepfather's surname. She remained active on New York's social circuit and in a number of charitable and cultural organizations, even working as a volunteer nurse at a veterans' hospital during World War II. For a time she served as features editor at *House & Garden*, but, with her characteristic humor, claimed that "my value to" its editor in chief—according to her *Washington Post* tribute by Adam Bernstein—"was that I could get people to let me photograph their houses, their gardens, their children, their stables, their linen closets, dress closets, and kitchen cupboards."

Widowed in 1952, Astor was soon courted by Vincent Astor, scion of one America's oldest fortunes founded by fur trader John Jacob Astor, believed to be the first U.S. millionaire. Vincent's father died during the sinking of the *Titanic* in 1912, and he was immensely wealthy. They wed in 1953, but he died just six years later. In his will he left her in charge of the Vincent Astor Foundation, which handed out almost $200 million in grants until she closed it in 1997. Unlike other charitable foundation executives, Astor reviewed all grant applications and often visited the numerous organizations that requested funds. These included homeless shelters, after-school programs for low-income students, and scores of other good-works programs. She also donated generously to New York's major cultural institutions or landmarks, among them the New York Public Library, Carnegie Hall, Metropolitan Museum of Art, the Bronx Zoo, and the Apollo Theater.

Astor was 95 years old when she closed the Foundation, stating that her age was the sole reason for her decision, but she remained in remarkably good health well into her nineties. Long a fixture at parties and other social events on New York's social scene, she had homes on Park Avenue, on the coast of Maine, and in Westchester County. After her

100th birthday fete, thrown by a Rockefeller, she was rarely seen in public, and rumors of her declining health circulated. Her plight became front-page news in July of 2006 when her grandson accused his father, Anthony Marshall, of elder abuse and financial mismanagement of her assets. A judge found no evidence of actual abuse, but Astor's legal guardianship was transferred to her longtime friend Annette de la Renta, wife of the fashion designer Oscar de la Renta, who moved her to the 65-acre Westchester County home, Holly Hill, in Briarcliff Manor, New York. She died there on August 13, 2007, from pneumonia. Three months later her 83-year-old son was charged with several criminal counts of embezzlement and fraud, including persuading his mother to change her will when she was of diminished mental capacity. He was even accused, in the press, of delaying the installation of her tombstone at her grave in Sleepy Hollow Cemetery, which according to her wishes read, "I had a wonderful life."

Astor's legacy remains the numerous programs and institutions that benefited from her generosity, few of which bear her famous name. She once defined power in an interview as "the ability to do good things for others," according to the *Washington Post.* "The act of giving makes me powerful inside. I would tell anyone, if you have enough money for three meals a day and you're not too busy, you ought to do something for others."

At the time of her death, Astor was 105 years old. She is survived by her son, Anthony; grandsons Philip and Alec, and three great-grandchildren. **Sources:** *Chicago Tribune,* August 14, 2007, sec. 3, p. 6; CNN.com, http://www.cnn.com/2007/US/08/13/astor.obit.ap/index.html (August 14, 2007); *Los Angeles Times,* August 14, 2007, p. B8; *New York Times,* August 14, 2007, p. A1, p. C16; *People,* August 27, 2007, p. 76; *Times* (London), August 15, 2007, p. 46; *Washington Post,* August 14, 2007, p. B6.

—*Carol Brennan*

Red Auerbach

Born Arnold Jacob Auerbach, September 20, 1917, in New York, NY; died of a heart attack, October 28, 2006, in Washington, DC. Basketball coach. Red Auerbach, perhaps the greatest coach in professional basketball history, made the Boston Celtics into a dynasty with his aggressive personality, ground-breaking coaching, and shrewd deal-making. "He was a combative figure who always sought an edge, whether taunting his foes by lighting premature victory cigars on the bench or going jaw to jaw with the referees," wrote Richard Goldstein in the *New York Times.* Auerbach led the Celtics to nine championships as coach in the 1950s and 1960s, a record, and another nine as general manager and as club president in the 1970s and 1980s. He spent 60 years in pro basketball, including 55 years with the Celtics, coaching eleven future Hall of Famers.

By the time he died in 2006, Auerbach had grown more important to basketball than statistics and championship rings could show. "Beyond his incomparable achievements, Red had come to be our basketball soul and our basketball conscience," said David Stern, commissioner of the National Basketball Association (as quoted on SI.com). "The void left by his death will never be filled."

Though almost everyone called him Red, he was born Arnold Jacob Auerbach, in the New York borough of Brooklyn in 1917, to Hyman Auerbach, a Jewish immigrant from Russia who owned a dry-cleaning business, and his wife, Mary Thompson, an office clerk. He got the name Red while working at the dry cleaner. Auerbach played basketball as a guard at Eastern District High School in Brooklyn and at George Washington University in Washington, D.C., where he earned bachelor's and master's degrees in education. After graduating, he coached high school basketball and taught physical education and history. He joined the Navy during World War II.

Auerbach became a professional coach in 1946, taking over the Washington Capitols of the new Basketball Association of America. The Capitols won the Eastern Division title that year with a 49-11 record. He coached the team for three years, then spent one as coach of the Tri-Cities Blackhawks in Illinois.

In 1950, Boston Celtics founder and owner Walter Brown hired Auerbach as coach and gave him full control over personnel decisions. He hoped Auerbach would turn around the team's poor record and meager popularity in Boston compared to baseball's Red Sox and hockey's Bruins. Auerbach did just that, coaching young guard Bob Cousy to become a popular rookie of the year and picking up talented front-court shooter Ed Macauley. The Celtics made the playoffs for six straight seasons. In 1956, he drafted center Bill Russell, whose speed and athleticism far exceeded other centers of the time. Russell was the final player the team needed to become a dynasty. They won the 1957 NBA championship, lost in the 1958 finals, and then won eight championships in a row.

Though Auerbach had a gift for spotting prospects who would grow to be stars, teamwork was central to the Celtics' approach to the game. Auerbach said he would rather work with a good team player than someone more talented but selfish. "He'd bark and growl at his players, but there was always a reason for it, and they got the message," former Celtic and NBA coach Wayne Embry once told the *Chicago Tribune* (as quoted by Goldstein in the *New York Times*). "On the Celtics, you accepted your role and took pride in being the best."

Another ex-Celtic, John Havlicek, agreed. "His greatest talent was knowing how to handle men and how to react to any game situation," he wrote in the foreword to Auerbach's autobiography, according to the *New York Times'* Goldstein. "He would curse us, coddle us, maybe even enrage us. Anything he thought would make us perform better."

As he filled the Celtics with talent, Auerbach paid no attention to race. That made him a pioneer. In his first year, 1950, he drafted Chuck Cooper, the first black player ever picked in an NBA draft. He was the first coach to introduce an all-black starting lineup, in 1964. And when he moved from coach to general manager in 1966, after his eighth straight championship, he made Russell the NBA's first black head coach.

For his work as a coach, Auerbach was inducted into the Basketball Hall of Fame in 1969. The Professional Basketball Writers Association of America named him the greatest NBA coach of all time in 1980. It took four decades for another NBA coach to equal Auerbach's record of nine championships. Los Angeles Lakers coach Phil Jackson finally matched the feat in 2002.

While general manager, Auerbach continued to work sharp deals to bring new talent to the Celtics. The team won the 1968, 1969, 1974, 1976, 1981, and 1984 championships while he held the position. In 1978, he made his most brilliant move as GM, drafting Larry Bird while he was still a junior at Indiana State. Bird went on to lead the Celtics to three championships. After the triumphant 1983-84 season, Auerbach turned over day-to-day control of the team to new general manager Jon Volk, his former assistant. The team honored Auerbach with a ceremony at Boston Garden, then the Celtics' arena, in January of 1985, with 40 current and former Celtics surrounding Auerbach on the court as a banner commemorating his work was lifted into the rafters. In 1986, the team won the NBA championship again.

Auerbach retained the title of president of the Celtics until his death on October 28, 2006. He died of a heart attack near his home in Washington, D.C. He was 89. His wife of 59 years, Dorothy, died in 2000. He is survived by his daughters, Nancy and Randy, a granddaughter, and three great-grandchildren. **Sources:** *Los Angeles Times,* October 29, 2006, p. B12; *New York Times,* October 30, 2006, p. A23; *SI.com,* http://sportsillustrated.cnn.com/2006/basketball/nba/10/29/auerbach.reaction.ap/i ndex.html (October 30, 2006); *SI.com,* http://sportsillustrated.cnn.com/2006/basketball/nba/10/29/obit.auerbach.ap/index .html (October 30, 2006).

—*Erick Trickey*

John W. Backus

Born December 3, 1924, in Philadelphia, PA; died March 17, 2007, in Ashland, OR. Computer programmer. As a programmer in the 1950s, John Backus felt there must be an easier way to complete his daily work duties. Looking for a way to avoid the tedious task of hand coding individual machines, which was how computer programming was done at the time, he formed a team to create Fortran. This was the first computer language that combined algebra and English, and it allowed programmers to do in 47 statements what had previously taken 1,000 instructions. It was essentially the first piece of software, as it could be used on multiple machines rather than each machine having to be coded by hand.

The development of Fortran, which stood for Formula Translator, was groundbreaking, a "turning point" according to computer historian J. A. N. Lee, commenting in the *New York Times.* Though it was developed in 1957, versions of Fortran are still in use, and it has become the basis for a wide variety of programming languages and software created after its release. Dag Spicer, the senior curator at the Computer History Museum in Mountain View, California, told Michelle Quinn of the *Los Angeles Times,* "Fortran is really the defacto language for scientific computing. It had to happen for computers to propagate."

Born in 1924, Backus grew up in Wilmington, Delaware. His father, who had been a chemist, worked as a stockbroker. High school was a trial for Backus, and though he did not excel as a student, he went on to study chemistry at the University of

Virginia. His academics there also faltered, and he was failing out of his classes when he was drafted into the Army in 1943.

Though Backus struggled as a student, he tested well, and the Army sponsored him in programs at three universities, from medicine to engineering. His medical studies stalled when a tumor was found on his skull, and though he received successful treatment, his return to medical school was lackluster. Intrigued by mathematics and radio technology, he enrolled at Columbia University, from which he received his Master's degree in 1949.

It was almost by chance that he received his first position with IBM. While taking a tour of the company's headquarters in New York, Backus acknowledged that he was seeking a job and was near completing his graduate degree in math. This offhand comment led to an informal interview with Rex Seeber, the inventor of the Selective Sequence Electronic Calculator (SSEC), who would become Backus' first employer. His first job involved calculating lunar positions on the SSEC for the National Aeronautics and Space Administration's Apollo program.

In 1952, Backus moved on to work on the IBM 701 computer, a bulky machine that was state of the art for its time. Instead of finding lunar positions, Backus's work now involved calculating missile trajectories. Frustrated by the amount of time he spent coding each task, Backus developed a system called speedcoding, a process that made programming the 701 much faster. When he was asked to transfer to the new 704 in 1954, Backus asked if he could instead develop a programming team to make the task even easier. "Much of my work has come from being lazy," Backus was quoted as having said in the *Los Angeles Times*. "So when I was writing programs for computing missile trajectories, I started work on a programming system to make it easier to write programs."

Backus' team was just as unconventional as his project. The group included a chess wizard, an expert at the game of bridge, a crystallographer, a cryptographer, a researcher from the Massachusetts Institute of Technology, a young woman who had just graduated from Vassar College, and an employee borrowed from United Aircraft. Backus led his team through long hours broken up by snowball fights and other types of group camaraderie. In 1957, the team released Fortran, a program that opened doors to future computer technicians. "95 percent of the people who programmed in the early years would never have done it without Fortran,"

Ken Thompson, developer of the Unix operating system, was quoted as having said in the *Chicago Tribune*. For his work, Backus received the W. W. McDowell Award in 1967. In 1975, Backus was awarded the National Medal of Science, and in 1977, he received the Turing Award from the Association for Computing Machinery. His contributions to the field were also honored in 1993 with the highest award from the National Academy of Engineering, the Charles Stark Draper Prize.

After Fortran, Backus continued to work at IBM, finding ways to make using computers easier. He worked with Danish programmer Peter Naur to develop mathematical notation to describe the structure of programming languages, released as the Backus-Naur form. In 1963, he became one of the first IBM fellows and moved to California to work in the research laboratories there. He continued to work with ideas in functional programming, which would allow users to describe the problem they wanted solved, rather than giving the computer step-by-step instructions on how to solve it. He stayed with IBM until his retirement in 1991.

After his wife died in 2004, Backus moved to Ashland, Oregon, to live near his daughters. He died in his home from age-related causes on March 17, 2007. **Sources:** *Chicago Tribune*, March 20, 2007, pp. 2-12; CNN.com, http://www.cnn.com/2007/TECH/03/20/obit.backus.asp/index.html (March 20, 2007); *Los Angeles Times*, March 21, 2007, p. B10; *New York Times*, March 20, 2007, p. C12; *Times* (London), April 3, 2007, p. 54; *Washington Post*, March 21, 2007, p. B7.

—*Alana Joli Abbott*

Joey Bishop

Born Joseph Abraham Gottlieb, February 3, 1918, in the Bronx, NY; died of multiple organ failure, October 17, 2007, in Newport Beach, CA. Comedian. Joey Bishop, a member of the Rat Pack and sometimes known as Frank Sinatra's comic, was known for his understated style and his penchant for ad-libbing. Among the singers and actors of the Rat Pack, a group that originally formed around Humphrey Bogart and at its height included Frank Sinatra, Sammy Davis, Jr., Dean Martin, and Peter Lawford, Bishop was the sole comedian, and was responsible for writing much of their nightclub act during the 1960s.

Though best known for his years with the Rat Pack, Bishop's career bridged stage and screen. From nightclub performances to films to television,

Bishop appeared in all the mediums available for a comedian during his career. He was the star of a sitcom and was a night talk-show host and rival of Johnny Carson. A rarity in Hollywood, he was a faithful husband who was devoted to his wife, Sylvia Ruzga, until her death in 1999.

Bishop, born Joseph Abraham Gottlieb, was the youngest of five children, the son of Jewish immigrants. Never accomplished at school (according to CNN.com, Bishop once remarked, "In kindergarten, I flunked sand pile"), Bishop used school to test audiences, performing impersonations of actors including Edward G. Robinson and Jimmy Durante for his peers. He also learned how to play the banjo and tap-danced. By the time he was a teenager, he had appeared on the radio and had won amateur competitions in entertainment.

After dropping out of high school, Bishop and two friends formed a vaudeville-style music and comedy act. Calling themselves the "Bishop Brothers" after the member of the group who had the car and drove them to their performances, the three worked clubs in New Jersey, Pennsylvania, and the Catskill Mountains. When Bishop's partners were drafted into military service in 1941, the year Bishop married Sylvia Ruzga, he kept the name and went solo.

Bishop had some success as a solo comedian, performing regular gigs in Cleveland, Ohio, before he, too, was drafted in 1942. When he returned to show-business in 1945, his sarcastic style and ad-libbed performances caught the attention of critics. His career changed entirely in 1952 when he was noticed by Frank Sinatra at one of Bishop's performances. At Sinatra's invitation, Bishop began opening for the singer, and gained a reputation as "Sinatra's Comic." Soon, Bishop was getting higher profile jobs even when Sinatra was not also performing. He began making regular appearances as a guest on television programs, including Johnny Carson's *Tonight Show* and the game show *What's My Line?*

In 1960, Bishop served as the emcee at the inaugural ball of then President-elect John F. Kennedy, whom the Rat Pack had made an honorary member. Bishop's usual candid and casual sense of humor accompanied him there, as well: According to the *Los Angeles Times*, Bishop quipped to the Kennedys, "I told you I'd get you a good seat."

Along with that high-profile event, Bishop began performing regularly with the entire Rat Pack in their stage-show at the Sands hotel in Las Vegas. The show and the first Rat Pack movie, *Ocean's*

Eleven, both premiered in 1960. Though Bishop received last billing in the stage show, he was known to have written most of the material used by the performers. According to an article in the *Los Angeles Times*, Sinatra himself told *Time* that year, "meetings could not have come off without the speaker of the house, Joey Bishop, at the hub of the big wheel." Bishop had a reputation for being the only member of the Rat Pack who could tease or put-down Sinatra, both in front of an audience and in private, and find himself further in Sinatra's good graces.

As a popular guest on talk shows, including being the most popular guest host on Johnny Carson's *Tonight Show* through most of the 1960s, it was only a short time before Bishop was offered his own television program. The original *Joey Bishop Show*, a sitcom, aired from 1961 to 1965, and Bishop played first a public relations assistant, then a talk show host. In 1967, hoping to compete with Carson, ABC asked Bishop to host his own talk show, also called *The Joey Bishop Show*. Bishop's sidekick was the then little-known Regis Philbin, who has become well-known for his own modern talk shows. Bishop's talk show lasted two-and-a-half years.

Bishop appeared in several movies, including *The Naked and the Dead*, in which he quipped he "played both roles.' He also performed on Broadway in *Sugar Babies*. But after the cancellation of his talk show in 1965, he fell out of the spotlight. Sinatra's death in the late 1990s rekindled interest in the Rat Pack. Bishop, as the group's last surviving member, was contacted for a number of interviews and was depicted in television movies. "The secret of comedy is when the audience can't wait to hear what you're gonna say," Bishop said in a 1998 interview with the *Dallas Morning News*, quoted in the *Washington Post*. "I see them doing comedy now so loud. My conception of true comedy is to be overheard, not heard. That's what made the Rat Pack so great."

"Joey has something going for him that a lot of others don't," Carson once said. "He's likable." His likeability, talent, and style, though it included a nickname "The Frown Prince" in reference to his dour expressions, earned Bishop praise from comedians including Carson and Stan Laurel of Laurel and Hardy. In a statement after Bishop's death, Philbin said of working under Bishop, "I learned a lot about the business of making people laugh. He was a master comedian and a great teacher and I will never forget those days or him."

After years of failing health, Bishop died of multiple organ failure in his home in Newport Beach, California, on October 17, 2007. Bishop is survived by his son, Larry, two grandchildren, and companion Nora Garibotti. **Sources:** CNN.com, http://www.cnn.com/2007/SHOWBIZ/Movies/10/18/obit.bishop/index.html (October 18, 2007); *Los Angeles Times*, October 19, 2007, p. B10; *New York Times*, October 19, 2007, p. C13; *Times* (London), October 20, 2007, p. 76; *Washington Post*, October 19, 2007, p. B6.

—*Alana Joli Abbott*

P. W. Botha

Born Pieter Willem Botha, January 12, 1916, in Orange Free State, South Africa; died October 31, 2006, in George, Western Cape Province, South Africa. Politician. P. W. Botha led South Africa during its final, horrific years as the last white-ruled nation on the African continent. The onetime Minister of Defense became prime minister in 1978 and president six years later, and spent the 1980s at the head of a white minority regime that was desperate to maintain political control over the remaining 85 percent of the population. Botha was famously known as the "Groot Krokodil (Great Crocodile)" for his tenacity and determination in maintaining the country's system of apartheid.

Born Pieter Willem Botha in 1916 into a farm family of Afrikaner heritage, the future president and prime minister grew up in Orange Free State, an independent territory established as a separate land for Afrikaners, as white South Africans of Dutch descent became known. As a young man, he studied law at Grey University College, which later became the University of the Orange Free State, but left in 1935 without a degree to work for the National Party (NP), the leading political voice of the Afrikaners, and for a time was even a member of the *Ossewabrandwag*, or "Ox Wagon Fire Guard," a right-wing Afrikaner paramilitary outfit with ideological ties to Germany's Nazi Party. He rose to the post of secretary of the party's National Youth League in the 1940s, and was elected to South Africa's parliament in 1948 as part of a wave of NP electoral victories that year. He represented the district of George in Cape Province.

With a majority in parliament, Botha and other NP legislators began enacting stringent laws that separated South Africa's indigenous black population from the mixed English, German, and Dutch who had been settling in the fertile, gold- and diamond-rich land over the past three centuries. These statutes, collectively termed apartheid, denied blacks any political role and relegated them to substandard status that even denied them most basic citizenship rights. Employment, housing, and education were all segregated, and interracial marriage was outlawed.

Resistance to apartheid remained strong, however, and the ruling National Party countered this with increasingly hostile strategies. It was in this climate that Botha rose to prominence in government, becoming Deputy Minister of Internal Affairs in 1958 and Minister of Community Development and Colored Affairs three years later. From 1966 to 1978 he served as the country's defense minister, and in this capacity oversaw the government's increasing stringent controls over South African society that were carried out with the intention of suppressing dissenting views of apartheid. In foreign policy, this also included the country's attempts to foment unrest or suppress legitimate political movements in neighboring, black-controlled states like Angola, Zimbabwe, and Mozambique. He rose to the post of prime minister in 1978 after a party scandal, but the NP was now dangerously divided, and Botha adopted a more liberal tone in order to heal the rift. This included his support for constitutional reform that permitted South Africa's Coloreds—as its mixed-race residents were called—and Asian some political representation.

Under a new system, Botha became state president as well as prime minister in 1984, but internal violence against NP rule increased that decade, and Botha's government fought back viciously. A state of emergency went into effect, and thousands of blacks—along with white South Africans who called for the end of apartheid—were detained; an estimated 4,000 died as a result of the embattled government's attempt to maintain control over a black majority. Only the threat of economic ruin, thanks in part to international sanctions against the South African government, resulted in a change in strategy and a decision to open negotiations with the long-jailed leaders of the African National Congress (ANC).

In the midst of this shifting climate, Botha suffered a stroke in January of 1989 that his family claimed was a result of poisoning by political foes in the Cabinet. He resigned as prime minister, but kept the title of state president despite widespread criticism from within his party, but was eventually pushed out altogether in September of 1989. He was succeeded by F. W. de Klerk in both roles, who freed Nelson Mandela and other ANC figures in early 1990. Botha himself had even met with Mandela—

the world's most famous political prisoner—in mid-1989, but the visit was more symbolic than productive. Mandela was elected president of South Africa in 1994 in the country's first free and fair elections.

Botha retired to a home called Wilderness, near his former constituency of George in what had become the Western Cape Province, and he died there at the age of 90 on October 31, 2006. His first wife, Anna "Elise" Rossouw Botha, died in 1997, and he is survived by second wife Barbara Robertson, whom he wed in 1998, as well as sons Rossouw and Pieter Willem and daughters Elanza, Amelia, and Rozanne. Unlike many prominent figures of the apartheid era, Botha never appeared before South Africa's Truth and Reconciliation Commission (TRC), the post-apartheid body charged with hearing testimonies concerning abuses and setting restitution amounts, though he was summoned to testify. When he failed to appear he was charged with contempt and given a suspended one-year prison sentence, but even this was overturned on appeal. "I have nothing to apologize for," Botha claimed at the time, according to his *Chicago Tribune* obituary. "I will never ask for amnesty. Not now, not tomorrow, not after tomorrow." **Sources:** *Chicago Tribune*, November 1, 2006, sec. 2, p. 11; *Los Angeles Times*, November 1, 2006, p. B10; *New York Times*, November 1, 2006, p. C20; *Times* (London), November 2, 2006, p. 70.

—*Carol Brennan*

Ed Bradley

Born Edward Rudolph Bradley Jr., June 22, 1941, in Philadelphia, PA; died of complications related to leukemia, November 9, 2006, in New York, NY. CBS News correspondent and anchor. For a quarter of a century, Ed Bradley worked as a roving correspondent for *60 Minutes*, becoming one of the most recognized and well-respected journalists of his time. Over the course of his career, Bradley won nearly every broadcasting award available, including 19 Emmys, a George Foster Peabody Award, and a Lifetime Achievement honor from the National Association of Black Journalists.

Bradley was born in 1941 in Philadelphia, Pennsylvania. His father was an entrepreneur who worked long hours running a vending machine business and a restaurant. Bradley was raised mostly by his mother after his parents divorced but spent his summers in Detroit with his father. Bradley studied education at Cheyney State College, now Cheyney University of Pennsylvania. Here, the 6-foot, 235-pound Bradley played center and defensive end on the football team, earning the nickname "Big Daddy."

Bradley became interested in radio during college after a friend, who worked as a disc jockey, let him read some news on the air one night. After graduating from Cheyney in 1964, Bradley took a job teaching sixth grade. His real passion, however, lay in music and radio so he began moonlighting—without pay—as a DJ for WDAS-FM in Philadelphia. Bradley hosted a jazz show, provided play-by-play announcing for basketball games, and did a little reporting for the station. In the mid-1960s, when race riots broke out in the city, Bradley began covering them and did such a fine job the station took notice and started paying him for his work.

Soon, Bradley gave up teaching and in 1967 secured a job as a reporter with WCBS Radio in New York. He left after four years and in 1971 began working as a stringer for CBS News, joining its Paris bureau. As the Vietnam conflict heated up, CBS dispatched Bradley to Saigon, Vietnam, where he became adept at war zone reporting. In 1973, while he was in Cambodia covering the conflict, Bradley was injured when shrapnel from a mortar attack ripped into his back. Cameras rolled as he was carried off on a stretcher.

After the incident, Bradley returned to the United States to work at the CBS bureau in Washington and was given the high-profile job of covering Jimmy Carter's presidential campaign. Bradley returned to Vietnam, however, to cover the fall of Saigon in 1975, as the South Vietnamese army collapsed and the North Vietnamese Communists captured the city. Bradley was there with U.S. troops during their last hours in Vietnam and was one of the last U.S. citizens to be evacuated from the area.

In 1976, CBS tapped Bradley to be its chief White House correspondent and he began covering Carter's presidency. He also began anchoring the CBS Sunday evening news. Bradley, however, preferred working abroad and in 1978 took a job as a correspondent for *CBS Reports* and was happily dispatched to Cambodia, China, Malaysia, and Saudi Arabia.

One of Bradley's most memorable stories came from this time. Following the fall of Saigon, countless Vietnamese fled the war-torn area in rickety boats.

In 1979, Bradley was covering the story and one day ended up in the waters off Malaysia helping rescue refugees from a sinking craft. Bradley won his first Emmy for the story.

Soon after the poignant report, CBS asked Bradley to join *60 Minutes.* He started during the 1981-82 season and although the news program already showcased the talents of seasoned veterans Mike Wallace and Morley Safer, Bradley found his way into the spotlight.

The key to Bradley's reporting involved his meticulous research and his empathy. He had an uncanny ability to explore any story and look genuine doing it, whether it was politics, human interest, or an expose. During his 25 years on *60 Minutes,* Bradley brought viewers tantalizing interviews with such sports stars as Muhammad Ali and Tiger Woods and music icons Lena Horne and Michael Jackson. He spoke with 9/11 widows, covered stories about sexual abuse in the Catholic Church, and the shortage of AIDs drugs in Africa. Bradley earned an Emmy for a 2000 interview with Oklahoma City bomber Timothy McVeigh; it was the only television interview McVeigh agreed to do.

"He could do a story about anything," *Face the Nation* moderator and former Bradley colleague Bob Schieffer told the *Los Angeles Times'* Matea Gold. "What made him so good was that he had this ability when interviewing people to get them to be themselves. Sometimes that was to their advantage and sometimes it wasn't." Bradley was also a bit rebellious. In the 1980s, he started wearing a gold earring, which caused a stir in the broadcast world. Yet for Bradley, who came across to viewers as a dignified gentleman, the jewelry never took away from his credibility as some feared.

During the early years of his career, Bradley was a rare African American in the news world. He was the first black White House correspondent for CBS News. Bradley, however, worked hard not to let his race define him. He refused to cover only stories related to race—he wanted to cover everything. In the end, Bradley succeeded in his goal of becoming a trailblazer for good journalism, not just one for black journalists.

While Bradley took his work seriously, he also knew there was more to life than reporting. He took vacations to his ski home near Aspen, Colorado, and spent his lunch breaks at the gym. There was also music. Bradley's lifelong interest in jazz led to a friendship with legendary trumpeter Wynton Marsalis, musical director of Jazz at Lincoln Center. Up until his death, Bradley hosted a weekly radio show from Lincoln Center. Bradley also befriended singer Jimmy Buffett and was known to get onstage and play the tambourine alongside Buffett.

Bradley filed his last story less than two weeks before his death. On October 29, 2006, his expose on a Texas oil refinery explosion aired on *60 Minutes.* When he finished taping the segment, Bradley checked himself into a hospital. Most of Bradley's colleagues did not even know he was ill.

Bradley died on November 9, 2006, at Mount Sinai Hospital in New York City of complications due to chronic lymphocytic leukemia. He was 65. Married three times, he is survived by his wife, artist Patricia Blanchet. **Sources:** CNN.com, http://www.cnn.com/2006/SHOWBIZ/TV/11/09/obit.bradley/index.html (November 10, 2006); *Entertainment Weekly,* November 24, 2006, p. 16; *Los Angeles Times,* November 10, 2006, p. B8; *New York Times,* November 10, 2006, p. A1, p. A29; *Times* (London), November 13, 2006, p. 63; *Washington Post,* November 10, 2006, p. A1, p. A18.

—Lisa Frick

Ruth Brown

Born Ruth Alston Weston, January 12, 1928, in Portsmouth, VA; died of a heart attack and a stroke, November 17, 2006, in Henderson, NV. Singer and actress. Ruth Brown's singing career began with her voice marking the transition from blues to rhythm and blues (R&B). Many singles she released not only helped fledgling Atlantic Records become a major player in the industry but also topped the R&B charts, and a few were crossover hits in the 1950s. Brown's career almost ended in the 1960s, but with help from comedian Redd Foxx she was able to establish an acting career that led to a Tony award and a Grammy award. John Waters, director of the 1988 film *Hairspray,* told *Entertainment Weekly,* "Ruth Brown was a ballsy lady and an incredible singer who surprised everybody by being a great actress and a first-rate repo man for rhythm and blues singers everywhere."

Brown was born in Portsmouth, Virginia, in 1928. Her earliest memory of singing was when she sang in a church at four years of age. She continued to sing in the choir but longed to sing secular music. When she was older, Brown won the amateur competition at the famed Apollo Theatre in Harlem, New York.

As a teenager, Brown would tell her parents she was going to choir rehearsal, but would sneak off to sing for the military at USO shows. She would dress like singer Billie Holiday, including wearing a gardenia in her hair, which was Holiday's trademark. At 17, Brown ran away to join trumpeter Jimmy Brown's band. She also married him and used his last name on stage. Later she learned her marriage was not legal as Brown was already married to someone else. She, however, chose to keep the last name.

Brown was unwelcome at her family home, but she found work in Detroit with bandleader Lucky Millinder. She worked with his band for one month. He fired her for serving drinks to the musicians. Brown was stranded in Washington, D.C., but accepted work at the Crystal Caverns club, which was owned by Blanche Calloway, sister of famed Cab Calloway. Voice of America Radio disc jockey Willis Conover heard Brown and helped her get a contract at Atlantic Records.

Brown was on her way to New York to begin recording when she was involved in a car accident that left her hospitalized for close to a year. Her legs were injured so badly she would feel pain for the remainder of her life. Even though she only had a verbal agreement to join Atlantic, the founders, Ahmet Ertegun and Herb Abramson, paid for her hospital stay. When Brown was well enough to travel, she headed to New York and recorded her first single, "So Long," on crutches.

Brown's first single was a hit. She wanted to sing more ballads, but Abramson and Ertegun thought her voice was better suited for up-tempo songs. During the recording of her next single, "Teardrops From My Eyes," her voice cracked into a squeal. Abramson liked what he heard, calling it a tear. She wrote in her autobiography, *Miss Rhythm,* quoted in the London *Times,* "If I was getting ready to go and record and I had a bad throat, they'd say 'Good!'" When the song was released, it reached number one on the R&B chart.

Brown's sound was new. Most songs on the R&B charts were blues records, but Brown's singles would soon change that. She and other new performers, including Etta James, recorded up-tempo songs and the transition from the blues and jazz

was complete. Brown also sang records that helped usher in rock'n'roll and those were a hit with white audiences. Throughout Brown's career, her singles were major hits on the R&B charts. She had limited success with mainstream charts. However, when her songs were covered by white singers such as Patti Page and Frankie Laine, they were instant hits with white music listeners.

Undeterred, Brown would become one of the highest paid female black singers in the 1950s. She released singles, "I'll Wait For You," "5-10-15 Hours," and the hugely popular "(Mama) He Treats Your Daughter Mean." When the 1960s rolled in, R&B experienced a shift and Brown's style was no longer in fashion. She would soon leave Atlantic and faded from the music scene.

As a single mother, Brown struggled to make ends meet. She found work as a teacher's aide, school bus driver, and as a domestic. Atlantic Records, which had been dubbed The House that Ruth Built, claimed she owed them $30,000 in studio fees. Brown and many other black performers found themselves in dire straits while the record companies made millions off of their royalties.

Brown would receive help from comedian Redd Foxx. He paid for her to move to Los Angeles and gave her a role in his musical, *Selma.* Brown began singing again, but also landed a role on the television show *Hello, Larry.*

Brown began her stage career, joining the revue *Black and Blue* in Paris and later she joined the revue on Broadway. Brown won a Tony award for her performance. Although her life was on an upswing, Brown continued working toward receiving royalties owed to her. She and her lawyer, Howard Begle, enlisted the help of Rev. Jesse Jackson and others to help her and the other R&B and jazz singers and musicians. Atlantic Records finally conceded and she received $20,000 and her debt to the company was forgiven. Atlantic also contributed $1.5 million to start the Rhythm & Blues Foundation, an organization dedicated to helping ailing and needy entertainers from the previous decades.

In addition to her work on stage, Brown also released an album, *Blues on Broadway* that earned her a Grammy award in 1990. She later won new fans when she portrayed Motormouth Maybelle in the film, *Hairspray,* released in 1988. Brown also hosted the radio programs "Harlem Hit Parade," and "BluesStage." Brown's influence on various singers and musicians across many genres garnered her an induction into the Rock'N'Roll Hall of Fame.

Brown continued to perform in clubs and concerts until she became seriously ill. She suffered a heart attack and a stroke following surgery in October of 2006. She never regained consciousness and died on November 17, 2006, in Henderson, Nevada. She was 78. Singer Bonnie Raitt told the *Los Angeles Times*, "What always hit me about Ruth was her sass and the force of her spirit. Even though she had a girlish quality, behind it there was no kidding around.... She would sell the song, and the force of her personality was so strong." She is survived by two sons and three grandchildren. **Sources:** *Chicago Tribune*, November 18, 2006, sec. 1A, p. 10; *Entertainment Weekly*, December 1, 2006, p. 25; *Los Angeles Times*, November 18, 2006, p. B13; *New York Times*, November 18, 2006, p. B10; *Times* (London), November 20, 2006, p. 62; *Washington Post*, November 18, 2006, p. B5.

—*Ashyia N. Henderson*

Art Buchwald

Born Arthur Buchwald, October 20, 1925, in Mt. Vernon, NY; died of kidney failure, January 17, 2007, in Washington, D.C. Humor columnist. In syndicated columns that ran for more than 60 years in more than 500 newspapers, Art Buchwald fulfilled one of his goals in life. "I was put on earth to make people laugh," he was quoted in *Entertainment Weekly* as having said. Through his columns, memoirs, four novels, a stage play, a screen play, and a number of radio and television appearances and interviews, Buchwald spent his life doing just that. When he began writing his first column as an American living in Paris, he became part of the daily read for Americans and Europeans alike. "The routine for readers was to scan the front page, check out the sports scores and the funnies, then settle into 600 words from either Buchwald or [fellow satirist] Russell Baker," wrote a columnist for the London *Times*.

Buchwald's career introduced him to world leaders and celebrities, but though he hobnobbed with big names, he never became a snob: His phone number was always listed in the phone book, and he professed to love people. Though his columns showed a savage wit, they also contained optimism on topics from politics to dying. Buchwald received the Pulitzer Prize for Outstanding Commentary in 1982 and the 2006 Ernie Pyle Lifetime Achievement Award from the National Society of Newspaper Columnists. He was also elected into the American Academy and Institute of Arts and Letters in 1986, and was named a Commander of the Order of Arts and Letters in France in 2006.

For someone so well known for his comedy, Buchwald grew up with all the trappings of tragedy. The son of Joseph and Helen Buchwald, he was the fourth child and the only boy in the family. Soon after his birth, his mother was admitted into a mental hospital for depression. Left alone with four children, Joseph Buchwald had no way to support his family during the Depression and shuttled the four off to orphanages and foster homes. When Buchwald began school, he realized he could cope with his loneliness by making others laugh, and he quickly became the class clown.

Buchwald dropped out of two high schools before, at 17, he lied about his age to join the Marine Corps. He spent most of his tour in the Pacific, earning his sergeant stripes and editing his squadron's newsletter. When he returned to the United States, he used the G.I. Bill to attend the University of Southern California in Los Angeles. After three years, he learned he could use the G.I. Bill to study abroad, and so he took what little money he had and left for Paris. "My dream was to follow in the steps of Hemingway, Elliot Paul, and Gertrude Stein," he was quoted as having said in the *New York Times*. "I wanted to stuff myself with baguettes and snails, fill my pillow with rejection slips, and find a French girl named Mimi who believed that I was the greatest writer in the world."

It was in Paris that he first became a columnist. He took a sample to the *Tribune* editor and got a job writing about haute cuisine by claiming that, while serving in the Marines, he had been a wine taster. Though he bluffed his way into the role and through his assignments as a food critic, his column, "Paris after Dark," became a popular enough feature that his editor asked him to write another. His second column became "Europe's Lighter Side," which, by the early 1950s, was syndicated internationally. One 1953 column, written to explain the Thanksgiving holiday to the French, was run annually for years afterward.

But by the early 1960s, Buchwald began to feel he was running out of material, and he began longing for home. In 1962, he and his wife, Ann McGarry, whom he had met in Paris, packed up their three adopted children and left for Washington. There, he wrote for the *Washington Post*, changing his focus from social commentary to political satire. He never revealed his own politics and seemed to have no agenda other than poking fun at Washington insiders. By 1972, his column, published three times a week, was syndicated in more than 400 U.S. newspapers and 100 international periodicals.

Along with his column, Buchwald tried his hand at memoirs, fiction, and playwrighting. Buchwald felt that his two memoirs, *Leaving Home* and *I'll Always Have Paris!* brought him acknowledgement as not just a humorist, but as a writer. In them, he discussed his bouts with mental disorders: Twice, Buchwald was hospitalized for depression and considered suicide. His frank discussion of his illnesses, both in his memoirs and in television appearances, spread a message of hope for others suffering from depression. Two of his novels were adapted into movies, and he tried his hand at screenwriting. A disagreement with Paramount Pictures over an idea he had pitched became the center of a law suit when Buchwald and producer Alain Bernheim received no credit for their development work on the Eddie Murphy film *Coming to America*. When Buchwald and Bernheim won the suit, Hollywood contracts started featuring what became known as the "Buchwald clause" protecting studios from similar cases.

In 2000, Buchwald had a major stroke, and though he continued to write, his health declined. By 2006, he was on kidney dialysis three times per week, and one of his legs had to be amputated below the knee. In February of 2006, he chose to end his dialysis treatment and entered the Washington Home and Community Hospices, prepared to die within three weeks. But the diagnosis of his doctors was proven wrong: Buchwald lived for another five months at the hospice before deciding to summer in the family's summer home in Martha's Vineyard, Massachusetts. His continued life, knowing that death could come at any time, provided him with fodder for new columns, as well as his final book, *Too Soon to Say Goodbye*, and renewed reader interest in his insights.

Throughout his life, Buchwald received praise from fellow writers and world leaders for his work. Andy Rooney of *60 Minutes* wrote in *People*, "He was one of the most genuinely funny guys this country has ever known." Former U.S. Secretary of State Dean Acheson once called Buchwald "the greatest satirist in English since Pope and Swift," and a London *Times* columnist felt, "He represented the US at its best." Richard Severo of the *New York Times* called Buchwald "the most widely read newspaper humorist of his time." Buchwald himself saw the reason behind his popularity: "If you can make people laugh, you get all the love you want," he said in a final video interview with the *New York Times*. Buchwald died in his son's home in Washington, D.C.,

on January 17, 2007 at the age of 81. **Sources:** *Chicago Tribune*, January 19, 2007, p. 1, p. 3; CNN.com, http://www.cnn.com/2007/SHOWBIZ/books/01/18/buchwald.obit/index.html (January 18, 2007); *Entertainment Weekly*, February 2, 2007, p. 16; *New York Times*, January 19, 2007, p. A1, p. A25; January 25, 2007, p. A2; January 27, 2007, p. A2; *People*, February 5, 2007, p. 124; *Times* (London), January 19. 2007; *Washington Post*, January 19, 2007, p. A1, p. A10.

—*Alana Joli Abbott*

Denny Doherty

Born Dennis Gerrard Stephen Doherty, November 29, 1940, in Halifax, Nova Scotia, Canada; died of kidney failure, January 19, 2007, in Mississauga, Ontario, Canada. Singer and songwriter. Denny Doherty was a member of the immensely successful 1960s rock group the Mamas and the Papas, who issued a string of Top Ten hits in the late 1960s that helped define the era musically. Among their best-known songs is the memorable "California Dreamin'," a 1966 hit that came to embody the spirit of the hippie era. "Alongside the work of the Beach Boys and the Byrds," the songs crafted by Doherty and his bandmates, noted the *Times* of London, "helped to create the myth of America's West Coast as an endless playground of sun, eternal youth, and untroubled hedonism."

A native of Halifax, Nova Scotia, Doherty moved in his late teens to the bigger city of Montreal. There, in 1959, he founded a folk act called the Colonials, which eventually became the Halifax Three and cut a record that failed to achieve much chart success. Doherty and a friend then headed south to New York City, where they began playing the Greenwich Village folk circuit, and there he met Cass Elliot, a young woman with a rich voice also working the folk scene. Together they formed a group called the Mugwumps, then teamed with a young married couple, singer-songwriter John Phillips and his wife, Michelle Gilliam Phillips. After several name changes, the quartet finally settled on the Mamas and the Papas after watching a television documentary film about a notorious U.S. motorcycle gang whose girlfriends were called "mamas."

Doherty and the other three eventually made their way to California, where Dunhill Records chief Lou Adler signed them. They originally sang back-up for "California Dreamin'," written by Phillips, when the known star Barry McGuire ("Eve of Destruction") recorded it, but that failed to chart. Even their version, with the soaring harmonies that became their trademark sound, failed to catch on immediately, but began to surge on the charts in February of 1966—especially in parts of the United States still suffering under winter weather. It reached No. 4 and made the Mamas and the Papas instant stars. The group was rather unusual for the time, as a rock act with performers of both genders, and they gave off an air of attractive bohemian camaraderie.

Doherty and his bandmates were later quite candid about the drama and substance abuse behind their free-spirited image and astonishing vocal harmonies. Elliott was in love with Doherty, but he spurned her attentions and instead harbored a crush on Michelle Phillips, which eventually turned into an affair. "I Saw Her Again" was one of the band's hits, which Doherty and John Phillips had written together about Michelle. A period of immense wealth and typical rock 'n' roll excesses of the era ensued as the band racked up hit after hit over the next year; they also organized the famed Monterey Pop Festival in 1967, the first of the era's major rock festivals. Doherty owned a Laurel Canyon mansion once belonging to silent film star Mary Astor. The divorce of John and Michelle Phillips spelled the end for the band in 1968, though they returned to record one more album for their label as a contractual obligation in 1971.

Doherty, John Phillips, and Elliot each had solo careers, but Elliot's was the only one to attain a modicum of success. This was cut short by her sudden death in 1974; John Phillips died, somewhat not unexpectedly, in 2001 after having received a liver transplant some years earlier as a result of his long-time substance abuse. In the 1980s, however, he and his daughter, television actor Mackenzie Phillips, had regrouped with Doherty as a reunited Mamas and the Papas, with a replacement for Elliott, and toured for several years but never recorded. Returning to Canada, Doherty became known to a generation of Canadian children as the host of a long-running series *Theodore Tugboat* that aired on the Canadian Broadcasting Corporation.

In the late 1990s, Doherty wrote and produced a stage work, *Dream a Little Dream: The Nearly True Story of the Mamas and the Papas Musical,* in which he also appeared when it was staged at an off-Broadway venue in 2003. In early 2007 he suffered a ruptured aortic aneurysm in his stomach and underwent surgery for it, but his kidneys failed afterward. He died in Mississauga, Ontario, on January 19, 2007, at the age of 66, survived by only one group member, Michelle Phillips. He was widowed twice and is survived by his son, John, and daughters, Emberly and Jessica.

The hits Doherty recorded with the Mamas and the Papas remain evocative sonic postcards from the long-gone era. The singular blend of their four voices is best exemplified on songs such as their Shirelles cover, "Dedicated to the One I Love" and "California Dreamin'"—a song that seemed to speak to an entire generation of young baby boomers and their desire to break free of convention by heading out West to places such as Los Angeles and San Francisco, where the counterculture was in full swing at the time. In a 2005 *Kansas City Star* newspaper interview quoted by Joal Ryan for E! Online, Doherty is said to have recounted that fans often came up to him and explained the impact of "California Dreamin'" on their lives, saying, "They [would] go … 'I was living in my father's Oldsmobile in Minnesota, and I heard that song and I just went to California.'" **Sources:** *Chicago Tribune,* January 20, 2007, sec. 3, p. 7; *Entertainment Weekly,* February 2, 2007, p. 16; E! Online, http://www.eonline.com/news/article/index.jsp?uuid=10d45de8-fe6a-4b 83-8bf1-3637a9332ae4 (January 22, 2007); *New York Times,* January 20, 2007, p. A11; *Times* (London), January 23, 2007, p. 54; *Washington Post,* January 20, 2007, p. B6.

—Carol Brennan

Bulent Ecevit

Born May 28, 1925, in Istanbul, Turkey; died of circulatory and respiratory failure, November 5, 2006, in Ankara, Turkey. Politician. Bulent Ecevit was one of modern Turkey's most estimable political leaders, a five-time prime minister who was firmly committed to the state secularism established after the end of the Ottoman Empire in the 1920s. A journalist, translator, poet, and essayist who had spent time in both England and the United States early in his career, Ecevit once opposed Turkey's bid to join the European Union, but later reversed his position, asserting "there can be no Europe without Turkey and no Turkey without Europe," according to *New York Times* obituary by Stephen Kinzer.

An only child, Ecevit was born in Turkey's main city, Istanbul, in 1925, to a mother who was one of the first woman in Turkey to earn a living as an artist. The Ecevits were firmly entrenched members of Turkey's secular middle class, who helped bring World War I hero Kemal Ataturk to power in a bid to eradicate Ottoman rule, which stretched back several centuries. Young, educated Turks like Ecevit's parents—his father was a physician—were followers of Ataturk's Republican People's Party (RPP), and the senior Ecevit was elected to the Turkish Grand National Assembly (TGNA) on its ticket.

Ecevit was schooled at Robert College, an English-language academy in Istanbul, and studied in Ankara before departing for England, where he served as the press liaison at the Turkish Embassy in London from 1946 to 1950 while taking courses in Sanskrit and art history at the University of London. He worked as a journalist in Turkey before traveling to the United States in 1954 on a fellowship awarded by the U.S. State Department for a position with a North Carolina newspaper, the *Winston-Salem Journal and Sentinel*. His final byline for the newspaper offered his thoughts on the entrenched racism he witnessed in parts of the South during his reporting, and in that article he wondered how it came to be that the United States had become such an able defender of downtrodden peoples elsewhere in the world, while in places like Winston-Salem its white citizenry was "guilty of refusing to drink from the same fountain as the man who has fought on the same front for the same cause," he wrote, according to Kinzer's *New York Times* article.

Ecevit also spent time at Harvard University, and upon his return ran for and won a seat in the TGNA in 1957. He lost the seat after a 1960 military coup, but then served in a constituent assembly after that, and became labor minister for the country in 1961. He rose within RPP ranks, but after another military coup in the early 1970s surprised many when he led his own internal party coup against the RPP leader and his longtime political mentor, General Ismet Inonu, and then broke all party ties with the military. When elections were held in 1974, Ecevit became the first leftist politician ever to lead Turkey as prime minister.

Ecevit's brief first stint as prime minister was notable, however, for his decision to invade the Mediterranean island of Cyprus that July, which provoked a strong international response. Cyprus was largely Greek, but there was a sizable Turkish minority, and when the centuries-old animosity between the two powers flared up again with Greece's attempt to unite the island with the Greek mainland, Turkey sent troops; United Nations diplomats were still trying to resolve the issue when Ecevit passed away 32 years later.

Ecevit returned to office as prime minister in 1977 and for a third time in 1978, but massive internal unrest eventually forced him out; the instability in-

tensified, however, and following another military coup in September of 1980 Ecevit and his wife, along with another leading Turkish politician and his wife, were detained by the army at a resort area. House arrest followed, and Ecevit was jailed for three months for an article he penned that criticized the junta (a group of military officers who have taken control of a country following a coup d'état), and finally in 1982 he and several other longtime politicians were banned from all political activities for a ten-year period. He formed the Democratic Left Party (DLP), and placed his wife in charge of it in order to subvert the law, which was overturned by national referendum vote in 1987. Ecevit returned to his TGNA seat in 1991, and became prime minister a fifth and final time in 1999 after financial corruption scandals rocked the political landscape. He stepped down in 2002 after November elections brought an Islamist group, the Justice and Development Party, to power.

Throughout his career Ecevit was known as a reformer and a politician with an admirable record as a human-rights advocate, except for his stance on Turkey's minority Kurd population. He published several books of poetry and political science, and lived in a modest apartment in a suburb of Ankara, the capital. After a stroke in May of 2006 he sank into a coma, and never recovered. He died in Ankara on November 5, 2006, of circulatory and respiratory failure, at the age of 81. He is survived by his wife, Rahsan, whom he married in 1946. Crowds of mourners gathered outside the hospital upon news of his death, which prompted an outpouring of official tributes. "Turkey lost a political philosopher," a CNN report quoted a former TGNA president, Husamettin Cindoruk, as saying. "He created a rhythm for the left, gave it color, and always worked to create political parties with concept, thought and philosophy." **Sources:** *Chicago Tribune*, November 6, 2006, sec. 1, p. 13; CNN.com, http://www.cnn.com/2006/WORLD/europe/11/06/ecevit.obit/index.html (November 6, 2006); *Los Angeles Times*, November 6, 2006, p. B13; *New York Times*, November 6, 2006, p. A21; *Times* (London), November 7, 2006, p. 65; *Washington Post*, November 6, 2006, p. B6.

—Carol Brennan

Jerry Falwell

Born Jerry Lamon Falwell, August 11, 1933, in Lynchburg, VA; died of cardiac arrhythmia, May 15, 2007, in Lynchburg, VA. Religious leader and political activist. Heralded as the leader who mobilized the religious right into politics, Jerry Falwell was as often seen as a divisive and polarizing figure as he was an inspired hero. Whether critically acclaimed or denounced, Falwell's accomplishments in the religious arena—from the growth of his church and his television programs, to the founding of Liberty University—and within the political world are undeniable.

Falwell came into political prominence when he founded the activist group Moral Majority, an organization that is often credited with getting Ronald Reagan and many conservative senators and congressmen elected in 1980. Falwell encouraged pastors to preach about politics from their pulpits and encouraged their parishioners to vote, a concept nearly unheard of at the time for groups that were focused on saving souls rather than becoming involved in earthly conflicts. "In 1979, it was a startling vision," wrote Stephanie Simon in the Lost Angeles Times.

Falwell's religious training began young, when his mother would wake up Falwell and his twin brother on Sunday mornings by blaring the "Old Fashioned Revival Hour" on the radio. But despite his mother's faith, Falwell did not consider himself religious. His father, Carey, a bootlegger and an entrepreneur, disdained religion. An alcoholic, Carey Falwell died of liver disease when he was only 55, and his son was 15 years old. On his deathbed, Carey Falwell converted, a moment that had tremendous significance for his son. At 18 years old, Falwell experienced his own quiet moment of conversion; he affirmed his change of faith in public at the Park Avenue Baptist Church. The next day, he bought his first Bible, a concordance, and a Bible dictionary; two months later, he knew he wanted to follow the path of the ministry.

Falwell attended Lynchburg College for mechanical engineering, but he transferred to Baptist Bible College after his second year. After graduating, he started his own church in Lynchburg with only $1,000 and a congregation of 35 people. He knocked on doors, visiting 100 homes a day, and began a daily half-hour radio broadcast. In six months, his program was on cable television, and by the end of his first year, his congregation had grown to 864.

During this part of his career, Falwell held the same ideal as most other fundamentalist churches: the political realm was to be distrusted, and preachers should focus on the important business of faith. He was particularly critical of the preachers who joined the Civil Rights Movement, as he himself felt there

was evidence to support segregation in the Bible. (He later rescinded that belief.) He busied himself supporting education, founding Liberty Baptist College (later Liberty University) in 1971. In 1973, when the Supreme Court legalized abortion, Falwell felt that Americans with traditional values needed to take up arms. The first thing needed was an organization.

Political strategist Paul Weyrich and Falwell had a conversation in 1979 that set the ball rolling. "I said 'Somewhere out there, there is something of a moral majority,'" Weyrich recounted in the Los Angeles Times. The phrase caught Falwell's imagination, and the Moral Majority was born. The group's intentions—banding together groups with similar moral stances—met severe criticism from fundamentalist leaders at the time, who called Falwell's work a corruption of the devil. "It was no small accomplishment for a fundamentalist preacher to come along and say, 'We're going to work with people whom we've always thought were wrong about everything,'" scholar Michael Cromartie of the think tank Ethics and Public Policy Center said in the Los Angeles Times.

Despite criticism, the movement gained momentum. "He had awakened the slumbering giant of evangelical politics and made it a force to be reckoned with," Ralph Reed Jr., the former executive director of the Christian Coalition, was quoted as saying in the Washington Post by staff writer Joe Holley. The 1980 national elections reflected the nearly seven million conservative voters on Falwell's mailing lists. Political scientist Matthew Wilson told the Chicago Tribune, "Jerry Falwell, more than anyone else, was responsible for galvanizing and spearheading the most important mass political movement of the last 30 years. His Moral Majority really catapulted the Republican Party to power."

In 1987, Falwell left Moral Majority to focus on the success of Liberty University. He told interviewers for the Chicago Tribune "The dream was a Christian institution of education providing preschool, kindergarten, elementary, high school, liberal arts university, graduate schools, seminary, law school, engineering school, [and] medical school." The 2007 graduating class was 2,106 students, including 50 graduates from the first graduating law school class. Falwell served as chancellor and president of the university and attended nearly every sports event the school hosted.

Falwell continued to stay actively involved in politics, infamously accusing civil rights organizations, feminists, and secularists of being part of the cause of the September 11, 2001, terrorist attacks. He later stated that he considered the prophet Muhammad to be a terrorist. Falwell was often asked by Republican leaders to tone down his statements and he later apologized for inflammatory phrasing, but Falwell thrived on controversy. Mel White, Falwell's former speechwriter who quit his job when he openly acknowledged that he was gay, was quoted by Holley at *Washington Post* as saying, "He once told me that if he didn't have people protesting him, he'd have to hire them. He felt it was publicity for the kingdom of God." *New York Times* contributor Peter Applebbome wrote, "Behind the controversies was a shrewd, savvy operator with an original vision for effecting political and moral change." Those visions are what Falwell's supporters often remember. "Everything was bigger than life to Falwell," retired pastor Dr. Jerry Vines told *People* magazine reporter, Sandra Sobieraj Westfall. "He didn't have little visions; he had big visions."

At the announcement of Falwell's death of cardiac arrhythmia on May 15, 2007, both Falwell's supporters and his critics took the opportunity to remember his life and honor his passing. "Falwell manipulated a powerful pulpit in exchange for access to political power and promotion of a narrow range of moral concerns.... But there is no denying his impact on American political life," Rev. Barry Lynn of the Americans United for Separation of Church told Westfall in her article for *People*. Senator John McCain, who had once broken with Falwell, calling him one of the "agents of intolerance" in American politics, later reconciled with the leader, writing in a statement quoted by *Chicago Tribune* writers Lisa Anderson and Margaret Ramirez, "Dr. Falwell was a man of distinguished accomplishment who devoted his life to serving his faith and country." Leading reform rabbi Eric Yoffie was cited by the *Los Angeles Times* as saying of Falwell, "We disagreed often and deeply on the application of religious teachings and traditions to the public sphere; too often he used faith to create divisions within our society. Yet his commitment to encouraging Americans to express their faith was genuine." Falwell died in Lynchburg, Virginia, and his funeral was held in the church he founded, which now has 24,000 members and is presided over by his son, Jerry Falwell Jr. He was 73 years old. **Sources:** *Chicago Tribune,* May 16, 2007, p. 1, p. 4; *Los Angeles Times,* May 16, 2007, p. A1, pp. A12–A13; *New York Times,* May 16, 2007, p. A1, p. A15; *People,* May 28, 2007, pp. 99–100; *Times* (London), May 16, 2007, p. 64; *Washington Post,* May 16, 2007, p. A1, p. A6.

—*Alana Joli Abbott*

Gianfranco Ferré

Born August 15, 1944, in Legnano, Italy; died of a brain hemorrhage, June 17, 2007, in Milan, Italy. Fashion designer. As one of the first foreign-born designers to be named artistic director of Christian Dior, a French fashion house, Gianfranco Ferré left a mark on the fashion world. Through his independent designs and his work at Dior and with Mattioli, Ferré created designs noted for their chic and intelligent sophistication.

Ferré began his career as an architect, giving him a reputation as "the Frank Lloyd Wright of Italian fashion," in reference to the American architect, and his shorter title, "L'architteto," as he was known in Italy. Throughout his career, Ferré applied his architectural studies to garments. "To fashion design he brought ... not just the draughtsman's concern for line and structure, but also a sensuous feel for magnificence of color and sumptuousness of fabric," wrote a contributor to the *London Times*.

Born in Legnano, a town near Milan, Italy, in 1944, Ferré was raised by his mother and aunts. His father, who owned a small industrial business, died when he was very young. Growing up among women gave him both a taste for life's luxuries and an appreciation for values such as measure, discipline, and discretion.

Ferré studied architecture at Milan's Polytechnic Institute, qualifying as an architect in 1969. The job market in his field was not supportive when he graduated and, after trying his luck as an interior decorator, Ferré tried his hand designing handmade jewelry. His necklaces, bracelets, and belts used principles of sculpture and were noticed for their unique use of materials. These accessories were the first work to get attention from the fashion world, and Ferré was featured in Italian *Vogue;* shortly thereafter, he began to work for designers Walter Albini and Christine Bailly. His first clothing project was a line of raincoats.

His work was noticed by many in the field. He began designing accessories, including scarves, for top designers such as Karl Lagerfeld. In 1974, he created a line of ready-to-wear clothing for Bolognese designer Franco Mattioli's Baila label. Considered avant garde, the line was a success, and Ferré formed his own fashion company, contracting his work to other labels. In 1978, he began a signature collection, which he marketed under his own name. His clients and customers included such high profile women as Julia Roberts, Barbra Streisand,

Sophia Loren, and Oprah Winfrey. Ferré did not only cater to stars; he licensed lines of affordable products to be more widely available internationally. His creations were noted for combining deep and rich base colors—grays, browns, and creams—with brighter shades of red and orange. His designs often included white dress shirts, manipulated with multiple collars or large cuffs.

In 1989, Ferré was hired as artistic director of the French fashion company, Christian Dior, due to stylistic similarities he had with the company's designs from the 1940s. The appointment was a source of controversy, as both Italian and French designers were shocked that an Italian-born designer had been selected rather than a native French designer. "Back then, the fact that I was Italian created lots of problems," Ferré explained in a February of 2007 interview with *Women's Wear Daily*, quoted by Eric Wilson of the *New York Times*. "Luckily, though, my French wasn't that bad."

Though many of Ferré's designs at Christian Dior were met with a cool reception by the press, his signature nipped-waist silhouette clothing impressed many customers, and Ferré stayed with the company for ten years. During that time, he was featured in a 1994 documentary by Robert Altman, a film in which his difficulties with the press and his disagreements with his peers were spotlighted. Franca Sozzani, editor in chief of Italian *Vogue*, told the *New York Times*, "He never gave up what he thought of as style, in his own way. He has never been an easy designer, or one who was trying to please the press." Despite these troubles, Ferré contributed to the growth of Dior in both size and prestige compared to competitor Yves Saint-Laurent. Ferré's business sense had contributed to the growth of both Mattioli's business and his own independent lines. His cousin and collaborator Rita Airaghi explained in a *Vogue* interview in 1989, quoted by Jon Thurber of the *Los Angeles Times*, "His projects are practical. He goes to work with everything in his head—market requirements, manufacturing schedules, financial limitations, development of themes, advertising."

After leaving Dior in 1996, he moved his own headquarters to Milan and opened two stores in London. In 2000, Ferré and Mattioli sold the company, named after Ferré, but Ferré stayed on as creative director. His 2008 collection appeared in Milan two weeks after his death.

In response to news of Ferré's death, many of Italy's top designers sent their condolences. "When I think of Gianfranco Ferré, the idea that comes immedi-

ately to mind is the dignity, the calm, the sense of responsibility that he brought to his work," Giorgio Armani told the ANSA news agency, as reported by the *Chicago Tribune*. Designer Robert Cavalli was quoted in the *Chicago Tribune* as calling Ferré "a true artist, pure, a beautiful person who will be missed by the whole fashion world." Donatella Versace told the ANSA news agency, according to ABC News, "He was a great couturier who knew how to create an absolute chic with details that I will never get tired of looking at and that will remain in the history of fashion."

"The design of a dress, furniture, a house, a room, a street and a city are all the same process," Ferré once told an interviewer for *Esquire* magazine, according to Thurber. "As an architect, I learned to think and express myself on flat forms, on paper, and to imagine the contour of the lines of a design." Ferré died of a brain hemorrhage in Milan on June 17, 2007. He was 62 years old. **Sources:** ABC News, http://abcnews.go.com/Entertainment/WireStory?id=3288114&page=2 (March 18, 2008); *Chicago Tribune*, June 18, 2007, sec. 3, p. 9; CNN.com, http://www.cnn.com/2007/WORLD/europe/06/17/designer.dead.ap/index.html (June 17, 2007); *Los Angeles Times*, June 18, 2007, p. B7; *New York Times*, June 18, 2007, p. A17; *Times* (London), June 20, 2007, p. 66; *Washington Post*, June 19, 2007, p. B7.

—Alana Joli Abbott

Gerald R. Ford

Born Leslie Lynch King Jr., July 14, 1913, in Omaha, NE; died December 26, 2006, in Rancho Mirage, CA. President. Gerald R. Ford, the 38th president of the United States, won no presidential elections, enacted no major programs, and won no wars. Yet he earned a respected place in U.S. history by providing steady, dependable leadership after President Richard Nixon and Vice President Spiro Agnew resigned amid criminal scandals. "I am a Ford, not a Lincoln," he famously told the nation (according to James M. Naughton and Adam Clymer of the *New York Times*), playing on the names of cars and 1860s president Abraham Lincoln to present himself as a reliable, humble chief executive. Ford's decision to pardon Nixon was his defining act as president. It probably lost him the 1976 election, but he defended it as necessary for national reconciliation. His honest, moderate leadership after the traumas of Nixon's Watergate scandal and the Vietnam War helped restore confidence in the U.S. government.

Ford was born in Omaha, Nebraska, in 1913, to Leslie and Dorothy King. They named their son Leslie Lynch King Jr. but they divorced when he was two years old, and his mother moved to Grand Rapids, Michigan, taking her son with her. She married Gerald Rudolph Ford Sr., a businessman and leader in the local Republican Party, and renamed her son after him when he adopted him.

Ford attended the University of Michigan on a football scholarship, playing center on the 1932 and 1933 teams, which went undefeated and won the national championship. He attended Yale University Law School and established a legal practice after graduation, but gave it up to enlist in the Navy once the United States entered World War II. He served in the Pacific and left the Navy as a lieutenant commander.

Back in Michigan after the war, Ford was working as a lawyer when one of Michigan's U.S. senators, Arthur Vandenburg, recruited him to run for Congress. Vandenburg, a moderate who wanted the United States to play an active role in world affairs, wanted to see the isolationist congressman who represented Grand Rapids, Bartel Jonkman, defeated. Ford, a strong believer in the Marshall Plan, the U.S. effort to help fund the post-war rebuilding of Europe, beat Jonkman in the Republican primary in 1948, then won the general election. Just after his victory, he married Elizabeth Bloomer Warren, a former model, dancer, and fashion coordinator.

In Congress, Ford served on the House Appropriations Committee, helping to shape the federal budget. His easy friendliness led younger Republicans to turn to him as a leader in their battles against older, entrenched leaders. In 1963, Ford became the third-ranking House Republican, and the next year, he was named to the Warren Commission, which investigated the assassination of President John F. Kennedy. In 1965, Ford was elected House Republican leader, pledging to offer a conservative alternative to President Lyndon Johnson's Great Society anti-poverty programs. He voted against founding the Medicare health program for seniors. He often refused to punish wayward Republicans for voting against the party position, arguing that friendly appeals won more loyalty in the long run. He spent election years traveling the country to campaign for Republican congressional candidates, hoping to win a majority and become speaker of the House. He never did. Instead, he was unexpectedly thrust into America's ultimate leadership role.

Ford became president in an unprecedented way. First, Agnew resigned from the vice-presidency in 1973 after pleading guilty to tax evasion. Nixon nominated Ford, who had been a loyal friend and ally for years, to replace Agnew. Both the U.S. House and Senate voted overwhelmingly to approve the nomination, knowing that Ford might well become the next president. By late 1973, when Ford was sworn in, Nixon was embroiled in the Watergate scandal: During the 1972 election season, Republican aides had hired burglars to ransack the Democratic National Committee headquarters in Washington's Watergate complex. In 1974, the U.S. Supreme Court ordered Nixon to turn over tapes of his conversations in the White House. The tapes showed that Nixon had used his powers as president to try to cover up the roles that White House and Nixon campaign employees had played in the break-in. As the House of Representatives considered impeaching him for obstruction of justice, Nixon resigned.

Ford became president on August 9, 1974. "Our long national nightmare is over," he reassured the country (according to the New York Times' Naughton and Clymer). "Our Constitution works. Our great republic is a government of laws and not of men. Here, the people rule." Ford won immense goodwill with his reassuring start to his presidency, but it disappeared quickly a month later when he gave Nixon a presidential pardon for any crimes he may have committed in office. Americans who wanted to see Nixon brought to justice were furious, but Ford insisted that a criminal trial of a former president would have further divided the nation and prevented it from healing and moving on. The pardon was deeply unpopular at the time, but by the time of Ford's death, many Democrats who had opposed the pardon had come to agree with it.

When Ford became president, the U.S. economy was struggling with inflation, unemployment, and an energy crisis. Ford tried to control federal spending by vetoing several budget bills. But voters, still angry over Watergate, gave the Democrats more seats in Congress in the 1974 election, and Congress began overriding Ford's vetoes. Famously, Ford refused to give New York City a $1 billion loan in 1975 to stave off bankruptcy, provoking the New York Daily News to print the headline, "Ford to City: Drop Dead." (The city later got the loan after altering its budget plan.) Unemployment and inflation both fell during Ford's term in office.

In March of 1975, Ford's popularity hit its lowest point, as communists took over South Vietnam and Cambodia in the final act of the Vietnam War. Ford had argued for military aid to the embattled South Vietnamese government, but the war-weary Congress had refused. Instead, Ford helped ensure that

130,000 Vietnamese refugees were allowed into the United States. That May, when Cambodian communists seized an American merchant ship, the *Mayaguez*, Ford sent U.S. military forces to free the ship. Though it was a tiny victory, it helped reassure allies elsewhere of American resolve.

To improve foreign relations after the strains of Watergate, Ford met with several foreign leaders in 1974 and 1975, including the heads of West Germany, Great Britain, Egypt, and France. He reached an arms control agreement with Soviet leader Leonid Brezhnev in 1975. He also signed the Helsinki Accords, which aimed to reduce tensions with the Soviet Union. Because the accord recognized the borders drawn in Europe after World War II, critics accused Ford of selling out Eastern European nations annexed or controlled by the Soviets. But in the 1980s, Soviet dissidents used the human rights provisions of the accords to successfully challenge communist rule.

In July of 1975, Ford announced he would run for president the next year. He began campaigning across the country. After two assassination attempts against him, both by crazed women in California in September of 1975, aides tried to convince him to cut back on his public campaign appearances, but he would not. He defeated Ronald Reagan, the governor of California, for the Republican nomination. But voters still associated Ford with Nixon because of the pardon. He began the general election 25 percentage points behind Democrat Jimmy Carter, the governor of Georgia. Ford adopted a new strategy: mostly staying in the White House to appear a strong leader, and arguing that he had brought peace, prosperity, and trust. He surged in the polls, nearly catching Carter. But in a debate with him just before the election, Ford insisted that the Soviet Union did not dominate Poland or the rest of Eastern Europe. That November, he narrowly lost to Carter, 50 percent to 48 percent.

In retirement, Ford wrote two books, one of which was the 1979 memoir of his presidency, *A Time to Heal*. At the 1980 Republican National Convention in Detroit, Reagan, the party's candidate for president, offered to make Ford his running mate, but talks collapsed over what powers Ford would assume as vice president. In 1982, Ford's wife, Betty, who had beaten addictions to alcohol and painkillers a few years earlier, founded the Betty Ford Clinic for others fighting addiction. Ford often lectured at universities and oversaw a golf tournament named for him. In 1999, he was awarded the Presidential Medal of Freedom and, with his wife, the Congressional Gold Medal.

Ford died on December 26, 2006, at his home in Rancho Mirage, California. He was 93. No cause of death was announced. He is survived by his wife, three sons, and one daughter. **Sources:** *Chicago Tribune*, December 28, 2006, sec. 1, pp. 6-7; *New York Times*, December 28, 2006, pp. A29-A31; *Times* (London), December 28, 2006, p. 58.

—*Erick Trickey*

Milton Friedman

Born July 31, 1912, in New York, NY; died of heart failure, November 16, 2006, in San Francisco, CA. Economist and educator. One of the premiere economists in the late 20th century, Milton Friedman's economic policies were favored by many country leaders, including President Ronald Reagan of the United States, Prime Minister Margaret Thatcher of the United Kingdom, and military dictator Augusto Pinochet of Chile. His 30-year tenure at the University of Chicago ushered in a new school of economic thought that produced several scholars and economic leaders who went on to win Nobel prizes. Friedman himself would win the Nobel Prize in 1976. Allan H. Meltzer, an economic scholar at Carnegie Mellon University, told the *Los Angeles Times*, "He was a great man. It's hard to think of anybody who never held a government position of any importance who influenced our country—and the whole world—as much as he did."

Friedman was born in the borough of Brooklyn in New York City in 1912. He was the youngest of four and the only son born to Jewish parents who immigrated from a region that is now a part of Ukraine. The family moved to Rahway, New Jersey, when Friedman was still a baby. His parents struggled to make ends meet. His father died during Friedman's senior year of high school. He earned a scholarship to Rutgers University, where he worked as a waiter, store clerk, and a tutor to supplement his income.

After graduation, Friedman enrolled at the University of Chicago, where he earned a masters degree in economics in 1933. He also met Rose Director, who would later become his wife. After receiving his masters, Friedman worked with the U.S. government's national Resources Committee. He helped to design the federal withholding tax system. He would later criticize this type of federal agency and programs, believing they imposed on personal choice and freedom. Friedman also worked at the National Bureau of Economics. He briefly taught at the University of Minnesota.

In 1946 Friedman earned a doctorate in economics from Columbia University. That same year, he began his career at the University of Chicago. He and the other professors in the economics program turned the department into one of the leading economics departments in the United States. Friedman also influenced a number of students, including renowned economist Gary Becker, who would later win the Nobel Prize.

Friedman was very personable and could talk in a language easily understood by the common person who had an interest in economics. He was conservative in his policy-making and thinking. The conservative right used him to speak on their issues and he became a popular speaker and lecturer. He advised presidents Lyndon B. Johnson and Richard M. Nixon on economic policies. His popularity with common folk led him to tour around the United States, speaking on economic policy. Friedman would later use his notes from the tour to write a book, *Free to Choose*, and he hosted a PBS television show of the same name in 1980.

While everyone followed the theories and policies of British economist John Maynard Keynes, who believed that government should be involved in the ebb and flow of its economy, Friedman was touting less government involvement. However, the post-World War II boom that the United States and other countries experienced proved Keynes was right. In the 1970s unemployment would reach new highs and oil prices surged upward, and everyone began listening to Friedman. His free-market or laissez-faire policies were put into practice by both the U.K. and U.S. governments. Unfortunately, Friedman's theories failed all expectations and both governments soon implemented other practices in an effort to thwart the recession both countries had entered.

Friedman was unapologetic and stood his ground. His thought of less government involvement reached beyond the economy. He was on the board that recommended the end of using a draft in times of war; Nixon would end the use of the draft in 1973. Friedman wanted to legalize drugs and prostitution. He also spoke against licensing boards, including the issuance of driver's licenses.

Friedman also became a prolific author. His book, *A Monetary History of the United States, 1867-1960*, co-authored with Anna J. Schwartz, became a classic that was used in colleges and universities globally. He also wrote *Capitalism and Freedom*, which expounded on his theories on income tax and airline deregulation. Friedman also wrote several books with his wife, who was also a leading economist. Together they wrote their memoir, *Two Lucky People*, which was released in 1998.

Friedman was not without controversy. He gave several lectures in Chile and made recommendations to dictator Augusto Pinochet. His critics decried his theories; Friedman was not one to step down from his opinion and would engage in debates with many, including his rival and lifelong friend, John Kenneth Galbraith. Robert M. Solow, who was with the Massachusetts Institute of Technology and a fellow Nobel laureate, told the *New York Times* that Friedman was one of "the greatest debaters of all time." Upon receipt of his Nobel Memorial Prize in Economics, Friedman was met with protests outside the ceremony.

After 30 years, Friedman retired from the University of Chicago. He and his family moved to San Francisco, California. He became a senior research fellow at the Hoover Institution at Stanford University. He had begun writing a column for *Newsweek* magazine in the 1960s and he continued until the early 1980s. Friedman, along with his wife, established a foundation that promoted school vouchers, believing that parents should have the opportunity to choose the schools their children attended.

Friedman suffered from heart failure and died on November 16, 2006. He was 94. He is survived by his wife, his son, Daniel; his daughter, Janet; and three grandchildren. Federal Reserve Chairman Ben S. Bernanke told the *Los Angeles Times*, "In his humane and engaging way, Milton conveyed to millions an understanding of the economic benefits of free, competitive markets, as well as the close connection that economic freedoms bear to other types of liberty." **Sources:** *Chicago Tribune*, November 17, 2006, sec. 1, p. 1, p. 4; *Los Angeles Times*, November 17, 2006, p. A1, pp. A26-27; *New York Times*, November 17, 2006, p. A1, p. A28; *Times* (London), November 17, 2006, p. 78; *Washington Post*, November 17, 2006, p. A1, p. A13.

—*Ashyia N. Henderson*

Robert Goulet

Born November 26, 1933, in Lawrence, MA; died of idiopathic pulmonary fibrosis, October 30, 2007, in Los Angeles, CA. Singer and actor. An actor and singer who made his name in the Broadway debut of *Camelot*, Robert Goulet continues to be best remembered for that role. He went on to sing on the Las Vegas stage and worked on both stage and screen throughout his life. Known by both American and Canadian audiences for his baritone voice and his charm and appearance, Goulet received the top awards for television, theater, and music over the course of his career, winning an Emmy, a Tony, and a Grammy.

Over the course of his career, Goulet was always working on stage, screen, or in the recording studio. He released 24 solo albums and was recorded on more than 60, appeared in films including *Scrooged* and *Atlantic City*, performed in theaters from Broadway to regional venues, and on tour in such shows as *Man of La Mancha* and *South Pacific*. During the height of his career, he sang for Presidents Lyndon Johnson and Richard Nixon, and he was a frequent headliner in Las Vegas.

Born in a French-speaking community in Massachusetts to parents with ties to French Canada, Goulet was encouraged early on to sing. "God gave you a voice, and you must sing," Goulet recalled his father instructing him from his deathbed, according to the *Washington Post*. Goulet chose to honor his father's last wish and, at the age of 13, became dedicated to the idea of becoming a singer. During his teens, he performed with the Edmonton Symphony, for which he was paid. This was the encouragement he needed to devote himself to a career as a professional singer.

After his father's death, Goulet's family moved to Canada, where, after dropping out of high school, he received a scholarship to attend the Royal Conservatory of Music and appeared on the Canadian television program *Pick the Stars*. After an attempt at finding work in New York, Goulet returned to Canada and, in Toronto, began making headway in theater. He was cast in the Canadian Broadcasting Corporation (CBC) production of *Little Women* and appeared on variety shows. He became "Canada's first matinee idol," according to the *Los Angeles Times*, though he is said to have disliked the reputation.

Due to his growing reputation, Goulet was encouraged to audition for a new musical, *Camelot*. His audition went so well that it earned him applause—a rarity—and he was cast as Lancelot. Starring with Julie Andrews and Richard Burton, both primarily known only in England at that point, Goulet received complimentary reviews from Broadway critics. *Variety* called Goulet the "perfect Lancelot," according to the *New York Times*. Though critics were lackluster in their response to *Camelot* on the whole, the fans were not. It ran for 873 performances between 1960 and 1963, and when it was reprised in 1993, Goulet was invited back onto the cast, this time as King Arthur.

The performance made the reputations of all three young actors, and Goulet took his signature song, "If Ever I Would Leave You," from the show. "Something in his voice evokes old times and romance," *New York Times Magazine* critic Alex Witchel was quoted as saying in the *New York Times*. Judy Garland is said to have referred to Goulet as a "living 8x10 glossy," according to the *Los Angeles Times*. Despite this, Goulet had trouble in his own private relationships. In 1956, he had married Louise Longmore, with whom he had a daughter, but their relationship dissolved as the run of *Camelot* was ending. That same year, Goulet married actress Carol Lawrence. Their marriage was a rocky one; in 1976, they separated and four years later, they divorced. In 1982, Goulet married writer and artist Vera Novak, who managed all of his business affairs.

Though Goulet did not appear in the film version of *Camelot*, he continued to appear on stage, earning a Tony for his performance in *The Happy Time*. In addition to his continued stage career, he appeared on *The Ed Sullivan Show* and in several movies, performing with Judy Garland, Frank Sinatra, and Bing Crosby. Goulet appeared on variety shows and television movies, including *Brigadoon* and *Kiss Me Kate*, as well as his own television specials. Along with live-action performances, he served as the voice for a cartoon cat in *Gay Pur-ee* and as the singing voice of a cartoon toy in *Toy Story 2*.

Goulet's stage persona gave him the reputation of a campy, old-school performer and led to parodies of his work. He, in turn, parodied his own reputation. Goulet performed the voice of a cartoon version of himself on *The Simpsons* and appeared in commercials for ESPN and Emerald Nuts. "If you can't laugh at yourself, you're a fool," Goulet was quoted as having said in the *Los Angeles Times*. "My job is to entertain, not go out there and be myself."

A survivor of prostate cancer, Goulet was diagnosed with pulmonary fibrosis and was awaiting a lung transplant at the time of his death. While in the hospital, he remained forward thinking, instructing doctors, according to CNN.com, "Just watch my vocal cords" as they inserted a breathing tube. "Just give me a new pair of lungs and I'll hit the high notes until I'm 100," his wife reported him as saying on E! Online.

"Robert Goulet was a monumental presence on the stage and had one of the great voices of all time, which often overshadowed his many other talents," pianist Roger Williams told the *Los Angeles Times*. "He really could do it all—act, dance and was funny as hell, especially when he was making fun of himself. Robert always took his craft seriously, but never took himself seriously. Oh, how we will miss this great guy." Wayne Newton, who was Goulet's best man at his third wedding, told *People*, "His incredible voice will live on in his music." Goulet is survived by his wife, Vera; his daughter by his first marriage, Nicolette; and his sons from his second marriage, Christopher and Michael. He died in a Los Angeles hospital on October 30, 2007. **Sources:** CNN.com, http://www.cnn.com/2007/SHOWBIZ/Music/10/30/obit.robert.goulet.ap/index.html (October 31, 2007); *Entertainment Weekly*, November 9, 2007, p. 24; E! Online, http://www.eonline.com/news/article/index.jsp?uuid=8e059624-55f7-4e53-abaa-df462834b0e1 (October 30, 2007); *Los Angeles Times*, October 31, 2007, p. B8; *New York Times*, October 31, 2007, p. A25; *People*, November 12, 2007, p. 106; *Times* (London), November 1, 2007, p. 69; *Washington Post*, October 31, 2007, p. B7.

—*Alana Joli Abbott*

Merv Griffin

Born Mervyn Edward Griffin, Jr., July 6, 1925, in San Mateo, CA; died of prostate cancer, August 12, 2007, in Los Angeles, CA. Television host and game-show creator. From a hit single to a television career that spanned five decades and business deals that made him a billionaire, Merv Griffin was an unstoppable innovator. Griffin "was like the Energizer bunny," his son, Tony, commented in *People*. Griffin himself was dedicated to continuing to work until the last day of his life. "Retirement is the choice after death," he was quoted as saying in *People*.

A natural entertainer, Griffin's career in movies and television spanned five decades, and his legacy continues to be broadcast in the shows he created: *Jeopardy!* and *Wheel of Fortune*. Before moving from television to investing in casinos, radio stations, and racehorses, Griffin hosted his own, self-titled talk show for 23 years. A singer and pianist, Griffin was also the composer of the theme song to *Jeopardy!*, a tune to which he kept the rights and on which he earned as much as $80 million.

Even as a child, Griffin was an entrepreneur and an entertainer. He began playing the piano at the age of four, and he both published and sold his own newspapers. For fun, Griffin would host weekly shows on his back porch, enlisting neighboring children to perform, act as stagehands, or serve as audience members. "I was the producer, always the producer," Griffin was quoted as remembering in the *New York Times*.

In 1945, upon hearing of an opening for a pianist at a local radio station, Griffin applied. When he discovered that the job was actually for a singer, he auditioned for that instead. The station was impressed with his voice, and after introducing him on a nationally syndicated program, they soon gave Griffin his own 15-minute radio show five days a week. Three years later, he was offered a position in the Freddy Martin Orchestra. The job paid much less, but the promised spotlight had allure, so Griffin went on the road. His performances and vocal quality drew the attention of star Doris Day, who recommended him for a screen test with Warner Brothers. They hired him and Griffin was featured in a number of movies, often miscast. Eventually, he asked to be released from his contract and he moved to New York, where he performed on Broadway and began to be a regular guest on television programs. The first program he was asked to host was the game show *Play Your Hunch*.

Due to his fairly regular appearances serving as a guest host for Jack Paar of *The Tonight Show*, many thought that Griffin would take over the program when Paar retired. When the network chose Johnny Carson, Griffin was offered a daytime chat show, and the *Merv Griffin Show* debuted. The original version of the show only lasted for a season, but Griffin worked with a syndicate to get the program back on the air. By the time Griffin filmed his last performance in 1986, the show had run for 23 years, filmed 5,500 episodes, and featured more than 25,000 guests. The program won eleven Emmys, including two awarded to Griffin as host. "He sang, he danced, he talked," talk-show host Ellen DeGeneres told *People*. "He was brilliant. I want to be as good as Merv." Though critics sometimes commented that Griffin's style was not hard-ball enough, others felt his ability to get people to talk was one of the reasons for his show's success. "Merv was one of the best interviewers in the business because he was a great listener," pianist Roger Williams said in a statement to the *Los Angeles Times*. "He really cared about what you were saying. He wasn't busy thinking of what his next question was going to be."

In 1964, Griffin produced *Jeopardy!*, a game show that turned the quiz show format upside-down by giving contestants the answer and making them choose the correct question. The program ran for eleven years with host Art Fleming, had a brief revival from 1978 to 1979, and was launched with host Alex Trebek in 1984. The success of *Jeopardy!*

paved the way for *Wheel of Fortune,* which first aired in 1975. It has never gone off the air, making it the longest running game show in television. "I have to say that the ongoing success of *Jeopardy!* and *Wheel* is my biggest thrill," Griffin was quoted in the *Los Angeles Times* as having told *Hollywood Reporter.* "I mean, they're still right there at the top of the ratings—they've never slipped. They're timeless and ageless, and in the history of TV there has never been anything like them."

Griffin cited boredom as his reason for expanding his pursuits beyond television and into investing. In 1987, Griffin bought the Beverly Hilton Hotel and began making investments in other properties. He had already purchased a number of radio stations, which he continued to buy and sell, and he became the owner of Teleview Racing Patrol, the closed-circuit broadcasts used by most horse racing venues. His holdings placed him at a net worth of $1.6 billion.

Griffin received the lifetime achievement award from the Academy of Television Arts and Sciences in 2005. "My word, what a career—in a job you love and couldn't wait to get up every day and get to work. And still can't," Griffin said in his acceptance speech, quoted by E! Online. In *Entertainment Weekly* Trebek said of Griffin, "Other executives … don't seem to derive the joy out of life that Merv did. He wasn't somebody who was accumulating wealth just to accumulate wealth. He was enjoying the thrill of the ride." Griffin suffered from prostate cancer, but battled through it until a relapse ended his life on August 12, 2007, in Los Angeles, California. Griffin is survived by his son, Anthony. **Sources:** CNN. com, http://www.cnn.com/2007/SHOWBIZ/TV/08/12/griffin.obit.ap/index.html (August 13, 2007); *Entertainment Weekly,* August 24, 2007, pp. 11-12; E! Online, http://www.eonline.com/news/article/index.jsp?uuid=13f4f15d-d363-4e45-b01f-795cc67a1d55 (August 13, 2007); *Los Angeles Times,* August 13, 2007, pp. A1, A12-A13; *New York Times,* August 13, 2007, p. A20; *People,* August 27, 2007, pp.73-74; *Times* (London), August 14, 2007, p. 48; *Washington Post,* August 13, 2007, p. B4.

—*Alana Joli Abbott*

David Halberstam

Born April 4, 1934, in New York, NY; died of injuries received in an automobile accident, April 23, 2007, in Menlo Park, CA. Journalist. Pulitzer-prize-winning journalist David Halberstam was, characteristically, on his way to conduct an interview when the former *New York Times* reporter died from injuries sustained in an automobile accident. The author of more than 20 books on topics ranging from American foreign policy to major-league sports, Halberstam earned a reputation early in his career for his reporting from the trenches of Southeast Asia during the Vietnam War. "The world has lost one of our greatest journalists," said Arthur O. Sulzberger Jr., chair and publisher of the *New York Times,* told CNN.com upon hearing news of Halberstam's death.

The son of a surgeon, Halberstam was born in 1934 in New York City and went on to Harvard University, where he served as managing editor of the school newspaper, the *Crimson.* Interested in the growing civil rights movement in the South, he landed his first post-college job as a reporter at a small paper in West Point, Mississippi, in 1955, but his bosses there found him too liberal on the question of desegregation. He moved on to the *Tennessean* in Nashville, where he spent the next several years covering the civil rights dramas unfolding in several Southern states. "I couldn't wait to go to work," the *Times* of London quoted him as saying about his reporting. "Even though it was often fairly dangerous. I had an intuitive sense that I was watching history."

In 1964 Halberstam was hired by the *New York Times* and sent to cover the war in Southeast Asia. Communist North Vietnamese were fighting a ground war for control of the Vietnamese nation, with anti-Communist South Vietnamese militias aided by the U.S. military. Halberstam's coverage of the conflict won the newspaper a Pulitzer Prize for journalism that year, and his writing was so frank that reportedly President John F. Kennedy asked the publisher of the newspaper to bring him back home, but Arthur O. Sulzberger Sr. refused. The dispatches later became the basis for a Halberstam's first non-fiction book, *The Making of a Quagmire: America and Vietnam during the Kennedy Era,* published in 1965.

Halberstam quit the *Times* in 1967 to become a full-time writer. His list of nonfiction books include *The Best and the Brightest* (1972), an examination of how the administrations of both President Kennedy and his successor, Lyndon B. Johnson, became so intractably mired in the Vietnam conflict; *The Powers That Be,* a 1979 look at the new media moguls; and *The Reckoning,* a 1986 account that traced the decline of U.S. automobile manufacturing industry. Halberstam was also an avid sports fan, and penned several works on momentous contests, including *Summer of '49*, which chronicled the New York Yankees-Boston Red Sox American League pennant race that year. At the time of his death, Halberstam was writing a book about the 1958 National Football League playoffs. One of its match-ups pitted the Baltimore Colts against the New York Giants, and is considered one of the most important games in the history of the sport, for it was the first playoff game to be televised nationwide, and the first one to end after new sudden-death overtime rules were implemented. When he died on April 23, 2007, Halberstam was being driven by a University of California graduate student to interview retired quarterback Y.A. Tittle. Two days earlier, Halberstam had given a speech at the school's Berkeley campus about journalism and its role in shaping history.

Halberstam was 73 years old, and is survived by his wife, Jean, and their daughter, Julia. Because of his stellar reporting during the Vietnam era, Halberstam was often asked his thoughts on the U.S. war in Iraq that began in 2003. This war, like Vietnam, appeared to be a situation with no possible positive outcome. Journalists' access to the theater of war were now carefully controlled by the U.S. Department of Defense—unlike in Halberstam's era—and even commentators back home were challenged as unpatriotic for questioning the administration. "The crueler the war gets, the crueler the attacks get on anybody who doesn't salute or play the game," Halberstam told a 2006 conference of journalists, according to *Washington Post* reporter Yvonne Shinhoster Lamb. "And then one day, the people who are doing the attacking look around, and they've used up their credibility." **Sources:** *Chicago Tribune*, April 24, 2007, sec. 1, p. 3; CNN.com, http://edition.cnn.com/2007/SHOWBIZ/books/04/24/obit.halberstam/index.html (April 24, 2007); *Los Angeles Times*, April 24, 2007, p. A1, p. A15; *New York Times*, April 24, 2007, p. C13; *Times* (London), April 25 , 2007, p. 68; *Washington Post*, April 24, 2007, p. A1, p. A19.

—Carol Brennan

Johnny Hart

Born John Lewis Hart, February 18, 1931, in Endicott, NY; died of a stroke, April 7, 2007, in Nineveh, NY. Cartoonist. With an audience of more than one hundred million readers over his nearly 50-year career in comics, Johnny Hart created two of the best known syndicated comic strips in the United States.

With fellow cartoonist Brant Parker, he created the medieval world of *The Wizard of Id*, and on his own, he wrote *B.C.*, a comic featuring a hapless caveman bearing the titular name. *B.C.* began in 1958 and continued until his death; *The Wizard of Id*, which started in 1964, is being continued by the Parker and Hart families.

Hart was born in Endicott, New York, in 1931. He grew up doodling, often creating art to share with friends. He was quoted in the *Washington Post* as having described his early art as "funny pictures, which got me in or out of trouble depending on the circumstances." As a teen, Hart met Parker when the latter was working for the *Binghampton Press*, and Parker began to serve as a mentor figure to the young cartoonist. After graduating from high school, Hart enlisted in the Air Force and served in Korea; along with his regular duties, he drew cartoons that were featured in the military newspaper *Pacific Stars and Stripes*. While in the service, he married Bobby Hatcher, and a year after their marriage, he left the Air Force.

Though he worked successfully as a freelance cartoonist, placing his work in such periodicals as the *Saturday Evening Post*, which ran his first freelance cartoon, and *Collier's*, his sales did not bring in enough income. He accepted a job in General Electric's art department and continued to draw cartoons in his spare time. He sought to design a very simple art style, using few words and little "clutter." He was quoted in the *Washington Post* as having said, "The simpler you do things, the more genius is required to do it. I used to take ideas as far back as I could take them—back to their origin. So cave men became my favorite thing to do because they are a combination of simplicity and the origin of ideas." These cavemen developed into the characters from his comic strip, *B.C.*

Hart was turned down by five syndicators before *B.C.* was picked up and began appearing in newspapers in 1958. The comic strip focused on basic issues of humanity as well as contemporary issues through the lens of prehistory. A love-struck dinosaur named Gronk, the peg-legged philosopher and sometimes baseball coach Wiley, and anthropomorphic animals joined B.C., the naive star of the strip, as comic regulars. The strip also featured two women who had labels rather than names: Cute Chick and Fat Broad. Hart "was totally original," novelist and cartoonist Mel Lazarus was quoted as having said in the *New York Times*. "B.C. broke ground and led the way for a number of imitators, none of which ever came close."

In 1964, Hart and Parker created the comic strip *The Wizard of Id*, and Hart was able to move much of his commentary on life into the venue of social commentary. Along with the disgruntled and over-worked wizard of the title, *The Wizard of Id* cast included a despotic tyrant and a melancholy and often-drunk court jester. Hart provided the text for the strips, which featured Parker's cartoons.

After his mother's death to cancer, Hart suffered a crisis of faith and delved into a number of possible religions, including a belief in reincarnation. Hart stumbled into his Christian faith as two born-again Christians, a father and son, were installing his cable television. They tuned in to a religious broadcast, which sparked Hart's conversion. His faith began making regular appearances in *B.C.*, typically around Christmas and Easter, and caused controversy from some Jewish, Muslim, and secular readers. When the strips got particularly controversial, such as the Easter strip in 2001, which showed a menorah transforming into a cross, papers began to judge the strips and publish them on a case-by-case basis. Some papers dropped the comic completely. Hart's reaction from Christian readers, however, was strongly positive, and freedom of rights advocates took up his cause when some papers tried to move his strips to the op-ed pages rather than the comics section.

Hart was the first cartoonist to join the ranks of Creators Syndicate, formed in the late 1980s. Where most strips were owned by the syndicates, Creators Syndicate opened the door for creators to retain rights to all their own work. "It was … Johnny's commitment to this idea that made us a success," founder and president Richard Newcombe was quoted as having said on CNN.com.

Rather than allowing his characters to be used on a large variety of merchandise, Hart chose to allow local organizations to use the images instead. His characters are featured on the public transit system in Broome County, New York, at his local library, and are used by two local hockey teams. The Broome County Open golf tournament was renamed the B.C. Open in 1972, and the event has collected more than seven million dollars for local charities.

Hart continued to work up until the moment of his death on April 7, 2007. "He died at his storyboard," his wife told the *New York Times,* explaining that he had suffered a stroke in their home in Nineveh, New York. Hart was 76. **Sources:** *Chicago Tribune,* April 9, 2007, pp. 1-11; CNN.com, http://www.cnn.com/2007/US/04/08/obit.hart.ap/index.html (April 8, 2007); *Entertainment Weekly,* April 20, 2007, p. 16; *Los Angeles Times,* April 9, 2007, p. B8; *New York Times,* April 9, 2007, p. A14; *Times* (London), April 23, 2007; *Washington Post,* April 9, 2007, p. B5.

—Alana Joli Abbott

Kitty Carlisle Hart

Born Catherine Conn, September 3, 1910, in New Orleans, LA; died of heart failure, April 17, 2007, in New York, NY. Actress and singer. Kitty Carlisle Hart, an American actress of the stage and screen for decades, enjoyed a remarkably long career that began on Broadway in the early 1930s and spanned to 2006 dates for her one-woman cabaret act. Hart was an irrepressible figure and a New York City legend—a style icon with grace and wit, who was not averse to the occasional self-deprecating comment. One of her most famous quips, as quoted in her *Washington Post* obituary, was the reflection that "with a soupcon of courage and a dash of self-discipline, one can make a small talent go a long way," so said the woman who still boasted a remarkably good performing voice at the age of 96.

The daughter of a physician, Hart was born Catherine Conn in New Orleans, Louisiana, in 1910. Her German-Jewish mother, Hortense, had great ambitions for her only child, and Hart began her musical training at an early age on the piano. Following the death of her father in 1920, when she was ten years old, she and her mother traveled through Europe for a few years before settling in Paris. After a stint at a Swiss boarding school, Hart made her debut on the social circuit in Rome, but she failed to secure a husband with a title, as her mother had planned for her. Hortense offered her daughter two choices for a career—modeling or acting, and Hart chose the latter. She studied at the Royal Academy of Dramatic Arts in London, but according to Marilyn Berger, the writer of Hart's *New York Times* tribute, after her first performance her mother told Hart, "My dear, we've made a ghastly mistake."

Heading to New York City, Hart changed her name to "Kitty Carlisle," which she borrowed in part from the telephone directory, and won her first starring role in a 1932 touring production of the Broadway revue *Rio Rita.* She made her official Broadway debut a year later in *Champagne, Sec*—the musical adaptation of *Die Fledermaus,* the Johann Strauss opera—and earned terrific reviews in it. Hollywood took interest, and Hart was signed to Paramount Pictures, for which she made *Murder at the Vanities,* a musical that also featured legendary pianist-composer Duke Ellington. That same year she sang with the young Bing Crosby in 1934's *She Loves Me Not.* Her best-known film role, however, was in the 1935 Marx Brothers' comedy, *A Night at the Opera.*

Paramount seemed to lose interest in developing Hart's career after that point, so she returned to the New York stage, appeared in wartime revues, and even took summer-stock roles when her job prospects dimmed. A number of prominent men wooed her and even proposed marriage—among them novelist Sinclair Lewis, financier Bernard Baruch, and atomic scientist Robert Oppenheimer—but it was not until 1946 that Hart married a noted figure from Broadway, the playwright and director Moss Hart. They had two children together, and her husband directed her in one of her biggest stage successes, a 1954 marital farce called *Anniversary Waltz*.

The Harts lived part of the time on a farm in Pennsylvania, but once the television era began Hart found herself in demand as a panelist or guest star on the newly popular television game shows. An elegant New Yorker with a socialite's appearance but a down-to-earth graciousness, Hart was ideal for the format, and her quick rejoinders and sharp wit helped make her a household name to most Americans of the era. She was a regular on several shows, but she is best remembered for her longtime service on *To Tell the Truth* from 1956 to 1977. On the popular game show, Hart was one of the panelists who tried to determine which of the three contestants was telling the truth and which two were impostors about having a job that seemed improbably interesting—butler to British prime minister Winston Churchill, for example, or gondolier on the canals of Venice.

Hart described the unexpected 1961 death of her husband—from a heart attack, and on the sidewalk, in the same manner as her father had died—as the one genuine tragedy of her life. In her later years, Hart combined her stage career with philanthropy. She chaired the New York State Council on the Arts from 1976 to 1996 and often found herself in Albany deftly sparring with legislators in debates over the artistic merits of certain plays or works of art. She published her memoir, *Kitty: An Autobiography*, in 1988 and enjoyed a long-running solo cabaret act. As late as October of 2006, she was still singing nightly at the age of 96 in her show *Here's to Life*.

Hart fell ill with pneumonia near the end of 2006 and died of heart failure at her New York City apartment on April 17, 2007, at the age of 96. Survivors include her daughter Catherine, a physician; her son Christopher, a film producer; and three grandchildren. Several years earlier, as she neared her eightieth birthday, she asserted, "I'm more optimistic, more enthusiastic, and I have more energy than ever before," the *New York Times* quoted her as saying, and she attributed her legendary stamina to her independent streak, noting, "You get so tired when you do what other people want you to do."

Sources: *Chicago Tribune*, April 19, 2007, sec. 3, p. 8; *Los Angeles Times*, April 19, 2007, p. B6; *New York Times*, April 19, 2007, p. C13; *Washington Post*, April 19, 2007, p. B7.

—Carol Brennan

Don Herbert

Born Donald Jeffrey Herbert, July 10, 1917, in Waconia, MN; died of bone cancer, June 12, 2007, in Los Angeles, CA. Television personality. During the Golden Era of television, three children's shows were must-see TV: *The Lone Ranger*, *The Howdy Doody Show*, and *Watch Mr. Wizard*. Television personality Don Herbert knew he was on to something when Mr. Wizard science clubs began popping up around the country. *Watch Mr. Wizard* aired from 1951 to 1965. Herbert, through his show, taught science fundamentals to masses of children in a way that entertained.

Herbert was born in 1917 in Waconia, Minnesota. He studied English and general science at La Crosse State Normal College; however, Herbert was more interested in the theater, participating in several college productions. After he earned a degree in 1940, he acted in summer stock locally before moving to New York.

Herbert joined the Army Air Forces, and became a B-54 bomber pilot. As a pilot during World War II, he flew in missions over Italy, Germany, and Yugoslavia. He received the Distinguished Flying Cross as well as the Air Medal with three oak-leaf clusters. Herbert had reached the rank of captain by the end of his tour of duty.

Following his stint in the Army Air Forces, Herbert worked as an actor, model, and radio-show writer. He began developing *Watch Mr. Wizard*, and the program debuted in 1951 on WMAQ-TV in Chicago. Speaking in terms easily understood by children and demonstrating use of common household items, *Watch Mr. Wizard* became hugely popular. "If you used scientific equipment that's strange to the child, it's not going to help him or her understand," Herbert told the Voice of America "Our World" program, as recounted in his *New York Times* obituary by Richard Goldstein.

Watch Mr. Wizard soon aired in more than 100 markets and moved to New York. Herbert only had basic scientific knowledge, but he soon accumulated

18 file cabinets of notes and learned new experiments by doing them himself. Unlike the admonitions of many of twenty-first century programs to not try this at home, *Watch Mr. Wizard* encouraged boys and girls to duplicate his experiments. Soon 5,000 Mr. Wizard science clubs operated throughout the nation. In its heyday, club membership had more than 100,000 children.

Using a boy or girl to assist, Herbert sparked an interest in the field of science. George Tressel, who worked with the National Science Foundation, was quoted by Dennis McLellan of the *Los Angeles Times* as saying, "Over the years, [Herbert] has been personally responsible for more people going into the sciences than any other single person in this country."

Watch Mr. Wizard was on the air from 1951 until 1965. It aired for one more season in 1971, and then as *Mr. Wizard's World* on the cable network Nickelodeon from 1983 to 1990. Herbert, after the show's end, began frequenting the couches of such talk shows as *The Tonight Show* and was one of the first guests on *Late Night With David Letterman*. He was also a panelist on the game show *Hollywood Squares*.

In addition to writing for his show, Herbert wrote several science books, including *Mr. Wizard's Supermarket Science*, and *Mr. Wizard's Experiments for Young Scientists*. The show was honored numerous times, including a Peabody Award in 1953 and the Thomas Alva Edison Foundation Award for "Best Science TV Program for Youth." Herbert died on June 12, 2007, in his home in Los Angeles, of complications from bone cancer. He was 89. He is survived by his second wife, Norma, three children, three stepchildren, and 13 grandchildren. **Sources:** *Chicago Tribune*, June 13, 2007, sec. 2, p. 12; *Los Angeles Times*, June 13, 2007, p. B10; MSNBC.com, http://www.msnbc.msn.com/id/19196808.tif/ (March 23, 2008); *New York Times*, June 12, 2007, p. C13; Official Web site of Mr. Wizard Studios, http://www.mrwizardstudios.com (June 13, 2007); *Washington Post*, June 13, 2007, p. B6.

—*Ashyia N. Henderson*

Andrew Hill

Born June 30, 1931, in Chicago, IL; died on April 20, 2007, in Jersey City, NJ. Jazz musician. Groundbreaking jazz pianist Andrew Hill had the type of career that was filled with highs and lows. His in-

novative style, while lauded by critics, failed to give him a lasting impression with the public. Hill persevered, choosing to teach rather than perform when labels and concert invitations ran low. He would have two comebacks during his life, but instead of dwelling on the past, Hill continued to create new adventurous music, never adhering to any one style.

Hill was born in 1931 in Chicago, Illinois. Some records state he was born in 1937 and in Haiti, but, among many other falsehoods that Hill neither confirmed nor denied, this has been disproven by his family. Hill began teaching himself to play the piano at an early age. As a child, he was seen playing the accordion around the Hurricane Lounge by jazz musician Earl Hines.

In his teens, Hill played with Paul Williams, Charlie "Bird" Parker, and Johnny Griffin. He also accompanied Dinah Washington and played with Roland Kirk's band. Hill signed with Blue Note Records and soon moved to New York.

During an eight-month span in the 1960s, Hill recorded five albums that made many think he was the next Thelonious Monk. The albums *Black Fire, Smokestack, Point of Departure, Judgment*, and *Andrew!* were a cross between hard bop and abstract jazz. He told the *Times* of London, "I always want to come up with something different." Those interested with this type of play continued to expand his fan base.

As interest in his music waned in the early 1970s, Hill began teaching at Colgate University in New York. He moved to California to teach anywhere he could, including prisons and public schools before he became an associate professor of music at Portland State University in Oregon. Not a familiar face to the public, Hill continued to perform in string quartets and write chord music and jazz compositions.

Hill experienced a comeback in the 1980s, but returned to anonymity when his first wife, organist LaVerne Gillette, became terminally ill. After her death in 1989, he returned to performing. During the 1960s, Hill had recorded plenty of material that remained unreleased until the beginning of the twenty-first century. An album, recorded in 1969, was released in 2003 and, according to Matt Schudel of the *Washington Post*, the *New York Times* reviewed *Passing Ships* with this quizzical summation: "the best jazz album of 2003 was recorded in 1969." Hill recorded new material and this was met enthusiastically by both fans and critics. His 2006 release, *Time Lines*, was named album of the year by *Down Beat* magazine.

In 2003, Hill received the JAZZPAR award from Denmark. He was named Composer of the Year four times by the Jazz Journalists Association. The National Endowment for the Arts had named him a Jazz Master in 2008 and he also received a honorary doctorate posthumously from the Berklee College of Music.

Not one to create or play the same music twice, Hill remarked about his career to the *Washington Post*, "The thing about having been on the fringe of fame and fortune for so long, is that I continued to create without the constant glare of society, so I didn't have to stick to any formula." Hill was diagnosed with terminal lung cancer in 2004, and died on April 20, 2007, at his home in Jersey City, New Jersey. He was 75. He was preceded in death by his first wife and survived by his second, Joanne Robinson Hill. **Sources:** *Chicago Tribune*, April 22, 2007, sec. 4, p. 6; *Los Angeles Times*, April 22, 2007, p. B14; *New York Times*, April 21, 2007, p. B10; *Times* (London), May 5, 2007, p. 73; *Washington Post*, April 22, 2007, p. C6.

—*Ashyia N. Henderson*

Don Ho

Born Donald Tai Loy Ho, August 13, 1930, in Honolulu, HI; died of heart failure, April 15, 2007, in Honolulu, HI. Musician. Through his long career as a musician and an entertainer, Don Ho became synonymous with Hawaii to many tourists. Though best known for his music in the 1960s and 1970s, Ho continued to perform at night clubs and run a restaurant until his death. Best known for his single "Tiny Bubbles," Ho was a consummate entertainer and was considered a one-man tourist destination and a great salesman in encouraging tourists to visit Hawaii.

Ho's career included not just night club performances, which he kept up regularly throughout his life, but also television appearances and tours. Despite his international appeal, he is strongly associated with Hawaii, which was his life-long home. "Hawaii is my partner," he was quoted as having said on CNN.com. Called the "undisputed king of Waikiki entertainers" by the *Honolulu Advertiser*, Ho also received the honor of being named one of the "50 Coolest Guys Ever" by *Maxim Magazine*.

Born in 1930 to parents who owned a restaurant and lounge in then-rural Koneohe, Hawaii, Ho was one of nine children of mixed ethnic descent: Hawaiian, Chinese, Portuguese, Dutch, and German. He was a star football player in high school and received a scholarship to attend Springfield College in Massachusetts. The college only held him for one year: He was quickly homesick for Hawaii, and he graduated from the University of Hawaii in 1954.

Inspired by the pilots who had flown in and out of Hawaii during World War II, Ho joined the Air Force, earning his certification as a fighter pilot in Texas, but spending most of his time piloting transport planes between Tokyo, Japan, and Hickam Air Force Base in Honolulu. While serving in the Air Force, he began playing the Hammond organ as a hobby. He left the military as a first lieutenant in 1959, the year Hawaii became a state.

Ho returned to Hawaii to run his parents' restaurant and lounge. Though it had been a popular spot for sailors during World War II, the business was having trouble getting by. Ho's father suggested that he perform live music on the Hammond organ, and Ho pulled together a band. The music began bringing in an audience, and Ho met Kui Lee, a song writer, who began writing music specifically for Ho to perform. "I had no intention of being an entertainer," CNN.com quoted Ho as having said. "I just played songs I liked from the radio, and pretty soon that place was jammed. Every weekend, there would be lines down the street."

By 1962, Ho was headlining at Duke Kahanamoku's night club with a five-piece combo called the Aliis. "I loved the *ipu* [traditional Hawaiian percussion] beat, and you hear it a lot in my music," Ho was quoted as having said in the *Los Angeles Times*. "I started to apply it to modern tunes, and guys started coming in with their ukuleles. It got to be a happening. People love live music."

Ho's music brought in tourists and celebrities to Duke's, and he soon drew the attention of recording executives at Reprise Records. They produced a live album, *The Don Ho Show*, in 1965. The second album, *Don Ho—Again!*, also recorded live, brought Ho international attention. When he toured the continental U.S. that year, his appearance in Los Angeles, California, broke attendance records. Ho soon began appearing on television programs, including *The Tonight Show, Charlie's Angels, I Dream of Jeannie, Batman*, and *The Brady Bunch*.

"Tiny Bubbles," arguably Ho's best-known recording, almost did not make it only his second album. Though it topped the charts when it was released, Ho initially had not wanted to record it. His producer pressed him into putting it on the album. "I didn't like it," Ho was quoted as having said in the *Los Angeles Times*. "So, to get away, I sang it once and ran home." The song became Ho's signature opening and closing number in all of his night club performances.

The popular image of Hawaii in the media was challenged in the Hawaiian renaissance movement, which emphasized preservation of culture rather than its commercialization. But even among the artists of the Hawaiian renaissance, there was respect for Ho. He was named "Salesman of the Century" by a Hawaiian business group and was thought of as an ambassador of Hawaiian goodwill. In 1998, he cofounded the restaurant Don Ho's Island Grill, and he continued to draw audiences to Waikiki. He also encouraged the musical career of his daughter Hoku, who had two singles hit the Top 40 lists in 2000.

In 2005, Ho suffered a heart condition, which he had treated in Thailand. He returned to the stage less than seven weeks later and continued his weekly performances at Don Ho's Island Grill. In 2006, Ho had to take another leave of absence, this time to have a new pacemaker installed. Despite his declining health, he continued to perform. "I'm a kinda guy, I like to work seven days a week, all day if I have to, because where I grew up, it kept you out of trouble," Ho commented in 2006, as quoted on E! Online.

"Singing is what keeps me young," Ho once told the *Los Angeles Times*. "Don Ho is one of the last true classics, the free-and-easy, hanging-out-at-the-bar kind of singers," Adrian Demain, steel guitarist for Cheap Leis, a band based out of San Diego, California, told the *Los Angeles Times*. Ho once told CNN.com, "I've had too much fun all these years. I feel real guilty about it." Ho died of heart failure on April 14, 2007 at the age of 76. **Sources:** CNN.com, http://www.cnn.com/2007/SHOWBIZ/music/04/14/don.ho.obit.ap/index.html (April 14, 2007); E! Online, http://www.eonline.com/news/article/index.jsp?uuid=d9e71197-f900-4d1b-aa19-83c91e57f979/ (April 15, 2007); *Los Angeles Times*, April 15, 2007, p. B12; *New York Times*, April 16, 2007, p. A19.

—*Alana Joli Abbott*

Lady Bird Johnson

Born Claudia Alta Taylor, December 22, 1912, in Karnack, TX; died of natural causes, July 11, 2007, in Austin, TX. First Lady, business owner, and

advocate. Married to U.S. President Lyndon Baines Johnson, Lady Bird Johnson carved out her own identity as an active political wife and used her position to encourage conservation and beautification projects in the United States. She was also a formidable businesswoman, who built ownership of one radio station in Austin into a multimillion dollar communications empire.

Johnson was born Claudia Alta Taylor on December 22, 1912, in the family home in Karnack, Texas. She was the youngest of three and only daughter, of Thomas Jefferson Taylor and his wife Minnie Lee (nee Patillo). Her father was a successful businessman, owning two country stores among other interests. Johnson was dubbed Lady Bird by family servant Alice Tittle when she was a toddler because the woman believed Johnson was "purty as a lady bird," according to CNN.com. Her mother died after a fall when she was five years old, and a maiden maternal aunt, Effie Patillo, moved to Texas to help raise her.

After graduating from Marshall High School at 15, Johnson continued her education at St. Mary's Episcopal School for Girls, a Dallas-based junior college. Johnson later transferred to the University of Texas at Austin. Johnson earned her B.A. in history in 1933 and a journalism degree in 1934 as well as a teaching certificate. After completing her education, she wanted to become a newspaper reporter.

However, those plans were put aside when she met Lyndon Johnson, then an aide to Representative Richard M. Kleinberg in Washington. The couple had a swift courtship—he asked her to be his wife the day after they met—and married on November 17, 1934. She left her career aspirations aside and supported her husband's political ambitions. In 1937, Johnson helped fund her husband's first political campaign for a congressional seat with $10,000 against her inheritance from her mother. He won the seat. She later helped manage his Congressional office when he served in active duty in the U.S. Navy during World War II. She became Lyndon Johnson's public face and spoke for him during this time period.

While Johnson became the consummate political wife, she developed her own business opportunities. In 1942, she used more inheritance funds to buy a radio station in Austin, Texas, which was failing. She spent $17,500 for the station, and her husband's influence in Washington to secure FCC (Federal Communications Commission) approval for both power and air time increases were vital to its success. Lyndon Johnson also helped land a CBS affiliation for the station. Johnson used the station to build a vast communications company, which included television stations and cable interests in Austin and elsewhere, as well as other business interests such as real estate and a bank. Motherhood was also important to Johnson. She gave birth to two daughters in Washington, D.C., Lynda Bird and Luci Baines, in the mid-1940s.

As Johnson was constructing her company and her family, her husband's political star was rising. Lyndon Johnson eventually won a seat in the U.S. Senate, and later became the youngest Senate majority leader. By the late 1950s, he wanted to run for the presidency in 1960, but lost the nomination to Kennedy; however, Lyndon Johnson agreed to be Kennedy's running mate, and Johnson helped her husband and Kennedy campaign to victory. After becoming the vice president's wife, she continued to travel throughout the United States and the world to promote the positions and causes of the president and her husband as well her own environmental concerns.

After Kennedy was assassinated on November 22, 1963, Lyndon Johnson became president and Johnson, first lady. When he took office, she began spending an hour a day recording impressions of her life as first lady. The 1.7 million words she produced were condensed into an 800-page nonfiction book, *A White House Diary*, published in 1971.

In 1964, Johnson helped her husband win the presidency outright in a landslide, logging many miles as she campaigned on his behalf. As first lady, Johnson used her position to encourage nation-wide support for her husband's programs, including Head Start, the Job Corps, and the War on Poverty. Johnson herself had long been interested in nature, conservation, and beautification. She used her influence with her husband to get the Highway Beautification Act of 1965 passed, which limited billboards and encouraged the planting of flowers and trees. Johnson was also concerned with improving the nation's capital during her husband's time in office, leading to the founding of the Society for a More Beautiful National Capital.

Johnson declined to seek an elected second term in 1968, and the Johnsons left Washington in 1969. The couple retired to their ranch in Texas, and Johnson helped establish her husband's presidential library at the University of Texas in Austin. The library opened in 1971. Johnson became a widow in 1973, when the former president died of a heart attack.

After her husband's death, Johnson lived primarily in Austin. Natural beauty remained important to Johnson in widowhood as she founded the National Wildflower Research Center near Austin in 1982. The institute was intended to support research and preservation of native plants in the United States. In 1998, the center was re-named the Lady Bird Johnson Wildflower Center in her honor. Johnson also was member of the Board of Regents at the University of Texas and helped her son-in-law, Charles Robb, with his political campaigns. She was awarded the Medal of Freedom in 1977 and the Congressional Gold Medal in 1988.

Late in life Johnson suffered ill health. Suffering a stroke in 1993, she was later declared legally blind because of macular degeneration. In 2002, she suffered another stroke which took away most of her ability to speak. She was able to communicate by writing, however. A month after being hospitalized for a low-grade fever, Johnson died on July 11, 2007, at her home in Austin. She was 94 and had been in declining health in the last few months of her life. Johnson is survived by her daughters, Lynda and Luci; seven grandchildren, and ten great-grandchildren. **Sources:** CNN.com, http://www.cnn.com (July 17, 2007); *Los Angeles Times*, July 12, 2007, pp. A1, A20-A21; *New York Times*, July 12, 2007, pp. A1, C12; *Times* (London), July 13, 2007, p. 60; *Washington Post*, July 12, 2007, pp. A1, A12-A13.

—A. Petruso

Deborah Kerr

Born Deborah Jane Kerr-Trimmer, September 30, 1921, in Helensburgh, Scotland; died of Parkinson's disease, October 16, 2007, in Suffolk, England. Actress. Film star Deborah Kerr came to Hollywood after appearing in a handful of critically acclaimed British movies of the 1940s, but found herself typecast as a prim, well-mannered female lead in her first few major-studio releases. That changed in 1953 when she starred as an adulterous wife in 1953's *From Here to Eternity*. Its torrid beach scenes scandalized audiences and gave Kerr's career an immense boost. "I don't think anyone knew I could act until I put on a bathing suit," she once joked in an interview, according to *New York Times* writer Douglas Martin.

Kerr was a native of Helensburgh, Scotland, where she was born in 1921, and her family later moved to Alford, England. Her father was an architect with the Royal Navy who died when she was 14 from injuries sustained in World War I. Kerr was a talented ballerina and was enrolled for a time at the ballet school of the Sadler's Wells Theatre in London. She made her stage debut in a 1938 production of *Prometheus* while still in her teens, but soon grew too tall for a career in classical dance and began auditioning for acting jobs instead. A walk-on role in a drama staged at London's Regent's Park led to an offer from a film agent to represent her, and she landed a supporting role in a hit comedy of 1941, *Major Barbara,* that was based on a George Bernard Shaw play. She mastered three separate roles in 1943's *The Life and Death of Colonel Blimp,* and won her proverbial ticket to Hollywood with her performance as an Anglican nun in the Himalayan-set *Black Narcissus* in 1947.

Under contract to MGM, Kerr's first Hollywood film was *The Hucksters,* released later in 1947. In that and her next ten works, she starred alongside some of the industry's top leading men—Clark Gable, Spencer Tracy, and Cary Grant—but she was nearly always cast as a devoted female character whose virtue counterbalances the more interesting flaws in the man she loves. "I wore a halo of decorum and was just about as exciting as an oyster," said Kerr of this period of her career, according to the *New York Times.*

That changed for Kerr when she was cast in *From Here to Eternity,* the 1953 adaptation of the bestselling James Jones novel about adulterous liaisons among U.S. military personnel stationed in Hawaii on the eve of World War II. Kerr played Karen Holmes, the wife of an Army officer (played by Philip Ober) who is carrying on a clandestine affair with one of her husband's colleagues (Burt Lancaster). The film's most iconic image is the beach scene which depicts Kerr and Lancaster in a romantic clinch as waves crash against nearby rocks. "Audiences were stunned to see her in a passionate embrace in the sea foam with Lancaster as the muscular sergeant," noted *Washington Post* writer Adam Bernstein about Kerr's transformation into screen siren. "That scene became a defining moment of uninhibited sensuality and was lampooned for decades in TV skits and films."

The beach footage was actually so racy that a few brief scenes were cut at the time of its original release. It looked great, Kerr agreed, but recalled it as difficult to shoot. "We had to time it for the waves, so that at just the right moment a big one would come up and wash over us," she said, according to her *Los Angeles Times* obituary. "Between each take, we had to do a total cleanup. When it was all over, we had four tons of grit in our mouths—and other places." Her performance earned her an Academy Award nomination for Best Actress in a Leading Role, but she lost to Audrey Hepburn that year.

Kerr went on to play Anna in *The King and I,* the 1956 musical that starred Yul Brynner as the King of Siam and Kerr as his children's governess. That same year she had another memorable role that again cast her against type: In the film version of *Tea and Sympathy,* she played the wife of an official at a boys' boarding school who falls into a relationship with one of the older teen students. Kerr had originated the role three years earlier on Broadway. In 1957, she starred opposite Cary Grant again in the tearjerker *An Affair to Remember* about a shipboard romance that remains one of her best-loved performances.

Nominated a total of six times for an Academy Award, Kerr never won, but was awarded a Lifetime Achievement Oscar at the 1994 ceremony. She lived in Klosters, Switzerland, and Marbella, Spain, with her second husband, the writer Peter Viertel, where her career wound down with stage and television work. As her health declined, she moved back to England. She suffered from Parkinson's disease in her final years, and died on October 16, 2007, in Suffolk, England, at the age of 86. She is survived by Viertel, whom she married in 1960, daughters Melanie and Francesca from her 1945 marriage to Anthony Bartley, and three grandchildren. Viertel died of lymphoma less than a month later. **Sources:** *Los Angeles Times,* October 19, 2007, p. B9; *New York Times,* October 19, 2007, p. C14; *Washington Post,* October 19, 2007, p. B7.

—*Carol Brennan*

Jeane Kirkpatrick

Born Jeane Duane Jordan, November 19, 1926, in Duncan, OK; died of congestive heart failure, December 7, 2006, in Bethesda, MD. Government official. Jeane Kirkpatrick was a Georgetown University professor when newly elected U.S. President Ronald Reagan tapped her to become America's envoy to the United Nations in 1981. Kirkpatrick was the first woman ever to serve in that post, and her four-year stint was a controversial one—not because of her lack of diplomatic experience, her critics claimed, but rather from an innate shortage of diplomatic skills. "Combative and confrontational, she symbolized the assertiveness that characterized American foreign policy after Reagan took office," noted the *Times* of London. "She declared at the time: 'I am not a professional diplomat. I've not signed over my conscience and intellect.'"

Born in 1926 in Oklahoma, Kirkpatrick was the daughter of an oil-field prospector, and the family moved several times during her youth. In 1946, she earned her associate's degree from Stephens College of Columbia, Missouri, and four years later completed work for a bachelor's degree from Barnard College in New York City. She also earned a master's degree in political science from Columbia University, and during these years was an ardent supporter of many leftist political causes, but became disillusioned with the world's first Communist state, the Soviet Union, after revelations surfaced following the death of Josef Stalin in 1953 regarding his regime of terror behind what had become known as "the Iron Curtain."

Kirkpatrick worked as a research analyst for the U.S. State Department before marrying Evron Kirkpatrick, a high-ranking official in the State Department's intelligence unit, in 1955. She became a mother to three sons while working on her doctoral dissertation and teaching at Trinity College in Washington. In 1967, a year before she finished her dissertation on the political legacy of Juan Peron in Argentinean politics, she became an associate professor of political science at Georgetown University, reaching full professor status in 1973. Still a committed Democrat, she grew uneasy with her party's foreign policy, which she believed weakened America's standing on an international stage. An article she wrote for the neoconservative journal *Commentary* in 1979 made an impression on the Republican challenger to U.S. President Jimmy Carter, and when Ronald Reagan was elected in 1980 he named Kirkpatrick as the U.S. ambassador to the United Nations.

Kirkpatrick was technically still a registered Democrat, which made her only member of her party with a seat on the National Security Council, and she was also the highest-ranking woman in the first Reagan administration. Before her, noted Tim Weiner of the *New York Times*, "no woman had ever been so close to the center of presidential power without actually residing in the White House." Her four years on the job were marked by a maelstrom of criticism, including her support for Argentina's 1982 invasion of a sleepy coastal archipelago in the Atlantic that remained a British colonial possession that became known as the Falklands War.

Kirkpatrick also took a strong stance on Central American policy, and was present at two key meetings in 1981 and 1984 during which details were arranged for a secret plan involving $19 million in covert aid to a right-wing guerrilla group in Nicaragua; this was in defiance of Congress, which had declined to approve funds for further military aid for the Contras, as the rebels were known. The $19 million was raised by brokering secret deals

with Iran, at the time one of the United States' most ardent foes. Kirkpatrick resigned from office with the end of Reagan's first term in office, and did not face the same amount of public scorn when word of the plan was leaked in 1986.

Rumored to be in line for either a post as Secretary of State or national security advisor, Kirkpatrick left the Reagan team when other high-ranking officials vetoed both possibilities. She was known for her frank language and capacity for playing hardball with those critical of U.S. foreign policy at the United Nations, but later said some of her deadliest enemies were fellow Reagan appointees. The media was of little help, either, she once said, according to *Washington Post* journalist Joe Holley. "I am depicted as a witch or a scold in editorial cartoons—and the speed with which these stereotypes have been used shows how close these feelings are to the surface," she told *Time* magazine in 1982. "It is much worse than I ever dreamed it would be."

Kirkpatrick returned to Georgetown after stepping down, and decided against a run for the White House in 1988 as a Republican, the party to which she finally switched her allegiance in 1985. Widowed in 1995, she suffered from congestive heart failure and died at her home in Bethesda, Maryland, on December 7, 2006, at the age of 80. She was predeceased by her son, Douglas, but his brothers Stuart—a Buddhist lama in Ann Arbor, Michigan, known as Traktung Rinpoche—and John survive their mother. Kirkpatrick's final mission on behalf of U.S. foreign policy was revealed after her death: In March of 2003, President George W. Bush sent her to Geneva, Switzerland, to prevent the foreign ministers of several Arab states from formally condemning a planned U.S. invasion of Iraq as an act of aggression. Kirkpatrick successfully convinced them it was justified on the grounds of Saddam Hussein's violations of earlier U.N resolutions. Regarding her time in the Reagan White House, the president said she "defended the cause of freedom at a pivotal time in world history," according to the *Washington Post*'s Joe Holley, and Bush further asserted that Kirkpatrick's "powerful intellect helped America win the Cold War." **Sources:** *Chicago Tribune*, December 9, 2006, sec. 1A, p. 11; *New York Times*, December 9, 2006, p. A1, p. A15; *Times* (London), December 9, 2006, p. 76; *Washington Post*, December 9, 2006, p. A1, p. A9.

—*Carol Brennan*

R. B. Kitaj

Born Ronald Brooks, October 29, 1932, in Cleveland, OH; died of possible suicide, October 21, 2007, in

Los Angeles, CA. Painter. With work known as much for the controversy surrounding it as for its innovations, R. B. Kitaj was an inarguably influential artist. Though Kitaj was American, his work is best known in Britain, where he was often grouped with the developers of the Pop Art movement. Through use of collage, figurative painting, and text in tandem with his painting, he developed a style and body of work viewed as significant contributions to the art world, with some critics considering him one of the earliest practitioners of Postmodernism.

Kitaj received many honors for his work, including being elected to the American Academy and Institute of Arts and Letters and the Royal Academy of Arts in London. He was also one of the few Americans to be the subject of a retrospective exhibit at the Tate Gallery in London. Despite these accolades, Kitaj was often critically reviewed, and many considered his reference to literature in many of his works to be pretensions. To these criticisms, according to the London *Times*, Kitaj responded, "some books have pictures and some pictures have books."

Born in Cleveland, Kitaj (pronounced kit-EYE) was only two years old when his father abandoned his family. His stepfather became a dominant influence in his life, and Kitaj took on his stepfather's last name. Both his mother and stepfather were non-observant Jews, a cultural identity that would become vital to Kitaj's later work. Kitaj was interested in art at an early age, and used his talents throughout his life, drawing local figures and prostitutes on his travels as a merchant seaman, and becoming an illustrator for military publications when he was drafted into the U.S. Army in 1955.

His time in the military allowed him to utilize the G.I. Bill and attend art schools in Europe. In addition to studying in Vienna and Oxford, Kitaj was accepted into the Royal College of Art. There he was a classmate to David Hockney, Allen Jones, Derek Boshier, and Peter Phillips, who were well known figures in the British Pop Art movement of the 1960s.

Kitaj did not identify himself with the Pop Art movement, however. Despite his friendship with many of the artists of that movement and some of his own stylistic similarities, he instead grouped himself with earlier artists, including Cézanne and Picasso, or contemporaries including Francis Bacon and Jewish artist Lucian Freud. Kitaj's first solo exhibition premiered in 1963 at the Marlborough New London Gallery. Going against the 1960s and '70s trend toward abstraction, Kitaj put "the subject back into painting," according to critic John Russel, as quoted in the *Los Angeles Times*. Kitaj's style evoked an earlier era while also making his work relevant to a modern audience. "He took the major impulses of our time—printed word and moving image—and brought them alive with a sense of history and context that gave additional meaning to his paintings," critic Peter Goulds wrote of a later exhibition in the *Los Angeles Times*.

Working with a variety of different formats, including collage and silk screen, Kitaj eventually turned to drawing as his dominant form of expression, disowning his earlier work as too simplistic. His 1976 exhibition, "The Human Clay," further embraced his commitment to figurative painting rather than abstraction, drawing unkind words from the avant-garde art community. The exhibition was influential, but it was only one of many that received harsh reviews from critics. He was again criticized for his drawings in a 1980 exhibit, and lambasted for his exhibition at the Tate Gallery retrospective in 1994.

By the time of his Tate retrospective, Kitaj had become dedicated to exploring his Jewish identity. Much of his work from the late '70s featured a Jewish every-man, and in addition to his art, he published two manifestos about what it meant to be a Diasporist. He was quoted in the *New York Times* as having said, "I've got Jew on the Brain. Jews are my Tahiti, my Giverny, my Dada, my String Theory, my Lost Horizon." Typical of Kitaj, this statement referenced the work of a writer: Philip Roth.

The work featured at the Tate retrospective was, according to a critic of the *Times*, "too weighted with recent paintings" that were the source of controversy. The exhibition was attacked so violently that the stress inevitably fed into his personal life. When Kitaj's wife died of a ruptured aneurysm, Kitaj blamed the critics for her death. Soon after, he left London for Los Angeles, and much of his later work was dedicated to his late-wife.

Called by a critic for the *Times* "one of the most passionate and committed artists of his time," Kitaj continued to develop his work as he aged, and his last pieces were considered by critics to show a spontaneous and mature quality. Robert Hughes once wrote for *Time* magazine, quoted in the *Los Angeles Times*, that Kitaj "remains an artist of real, sometimes of remarkable interest: a restless omnivore whose way of painting, part personal confession, part syncopated history and part allusive homage to the old and Modernist masters, is quite unlike anybody else today." Predeceased by both of his wives, Kitaj is survived by two children from his first marriage, screenwriter Lem Dobbs and his daughter Dominie; and his son by his second marriage, Max. He died on October 21, 2007, at his home in Los Angeles, a week before his 75th birthday. **Sources:** *Los Angeles Times,* October 24, 2007, p. B6; *New York Times,* October 24, 2007, p. C11; *Times* (London), October 23, 2007, p. 61; *Washington Post,* October 24, 2007, p. B9.

—*Alana Joli Abbott*

Kisho Kurokawa

Born April 8, 1934, in Nagoya, Japan; died of heart failure, October 12, 2007, in Tokyo, Japan. Architect. A leader in the Metabolism movement in architecture and one of the champions of a "symbiotic" style, architect Kisho Kurosawa was possibly Japan's most influential architect. His ideas for buildings that integrated local traditions with modern influences and for creating modular, adaptable structures, won him admiration in his home nation and internationally.

With work appearing in the Netherlands, France, China, Malaysia, and the United States, as well as across Japan, Kurokawa had a far-reaching influence. Along with other members of the Metabolism movement, he strove to find ways to promote renewable architecture, in which buildings could be changed or replaced with less effort than full scale rebuilding. The Metabolists sought to view buildings as living organisms, posing the idea that buildings could grow and change over time. His goal of symbiosis, intended to encourage integrating diverse styles and influences into a complete look, was sometimes considered controversial, but also led him to win high praise from critics.

Kurokawa grew up in Nagoya, Japan, the son of an architect. As a child during World War II, Kurokawa watched as the city where he was raised was destroyed in Allied air raids. Witnessing the event was a powerful influence on the rest of his life, and he became dedicated to developing architecture that would "move from 'the age of the machine' to the 'the age of life,' according to the *Los Angeles Times.* After the attacks, the family moved to the home of Kurokawa's grandfather, where Kurokawa lived in the tea room. That, too, influenced his ideas about architecture, as Kurokawa grew to integrate the styles and ideas of traditional Japanese structures into his more technological, computer-based designs. His education as a boy included Buddhist

theory, which taught Kurokawa to value diversity. "He credited Buddhism's tolerance for promoting the belief that different elements and styles can coexist in architecture while retaining their individual identities," wrote Bruce Wallace for the *Los Angeles Times.*

After attending Kyoto University for his first degree, he studied at Tokyo University under Kenzo Tange, a distinguished Japanese architect, who helped guide Kurokawa to forming his own company. Based out of Tokyo, Kurokawa began his work, and in 1960, at the age of 26, Kurokawa became a founder of the Metabolist movement. Over the next ten years, his company moved from the theoretical to the practical, and in 1970, his work debuted at the Osaka Expo, for which he designed three buildings.

After the success of his buildings at the Osaka Expo, Kurokawa gained several major commissions, including the Nakagin Capsule Tower in Tokyo, which was built from modules that could be separate spaces, or could be combined to form larger areas, an idea taken from traditional Japanese architecture. His Sony Tower was completed in Osaka in 1976, and he was also commissioned to design the National Ethnological Museum in Osaka and the Hiroshima City Museum of Contemporary Art. In addition to his work in Japan, Kurokawa designed several buildings overseas, including the Chinese-Japanese Youth Center in Beijing, the Sports Center in Chicago, Illinois, a wing of the Van Gogh Museum in Amsterdam, and the highly praised Kuala Lumpur International Airport. The spacious building, which won a Green Globe 21 Certificate as an environmentally friendly building, includes a transplanted tropical rainforest and designs based on Islamic domes.

In addition to his architectural work, Kurokawa solidified his philosophies about architecture in several books and essays. In *The Philosophy of Symbiosis,* translated into both English and German, he explained the basic idea of symbiosis. Kurokawa was both a champion of progressive architecture, being among the first of his peers to use computers in developing his designs, and a traditionalist, in that he relied on earlier Japanese design, using natural textures and traditional concepts. His focus on natural appearances sometimes led to designs where pipes or ducts would remain visible. A retrospective exhibit of his work toured European cities in 1982, and further exhibits followed, touring North America and Japan as well.

Despite receiving many honors across the world, Kurokawa had difficulties in his later years. His Sony Tower was demolished in 2006, and his Nakagin Capsule Tower, built to be changeable and long lasting, was scheduled for destruction at the time of his death. He was also spurred into politics, and he ran for governor of Tokyo, seeking to provide affordable housing and build new parks. His bid for the position was soundly defeated, and he also failed to win an election to the upper house of the Japanese Parliament.

Alongside his bid for political office, Kurokawa continued to design in Japan and across Asia until his death from heart failure on October 12, 2007. He is survived by his second wife, actress Ayako Wakao, who also unsuccessfully ran for Parliament, and two children from his first marriage: artist Kako Matsuura and photographer Mikio Kurokawa. **Sources:** *Los Angeles Times,* October 14 2007, p. B13; *New York Times,* October 21, 2007, p. A22; *Times* (London), October 24, 2007, p. 63; *Washington Post,* October 16, 2007, p. B8.

—*Alana Joli Abbott*

Madeleine L'Engle

Born Madeleine L'Engle Camp, November 29, 1918, in New York, NY; died of natural causes, September 6, 2007, in Litchfield, CT. Author. The author of poetry, plays, autobiography, and religious devotionals, Madeleine L'Engle was best known for the young adult novel that made her famous: *A Wrinkle in Time.* The novel was chosen as a Newbery Medal winner, and, although L'Engle wrote more than 60 books, *A Wrinkle in Time* remains the novel that marked her career.

L'Engle gained her reputation as a children's author, but she never liked the boundaries that implied. "I never write for any age group in mind," she was quoted as having said on CNN.com. "When people do, they tend to be tolerant and condescending and they don't write as well as they can write. When you underestimate your audience, you're cutting yourself off from your best work."

Born to aging parents and named for her great grandmother, L'Engle grew up, much like her famous protagonist Meg Murry, feeling out of place. Surrounded by the arts—her mother was a pianist and her father an author—L'Engle began writing stories herself at an early age. In fifth grade, she was accused of cheating on her entry in a poetry contest, and her mother brought piles of L'Engle's work to school in her defense.

But school continued to be an unhappy affair, and L'Engle was sent to boarding schools in such locations as Switzerland and South Carolina. She studied English at Smith College, where she graduated cum laude in 1941. Along with her interest in writing, she was involved in theater, and when she returned home to New York, she took several small roles, as well as wrote plays. Her first novel, *A Small Rain,* was published in 1945.

Despite the positive start, it was several years before she had another work published. In the theater, she met Hugh Franklin; they married in 1946. They had their first child, Josephine, the following year. Their son, Bion, followed in 1952, and they adopted another daughter, Maria, in 1956. Unable to sell another manuscript, L'Engle worked at a grocery shop that she ran with Franklin in Connecticut. Her writing career was so stalled that she considered quitting all together. But when *Meet the Austins* was accepted in 1960, she regained some of her hope. She shopped another novel around, certain it was for adults, but had the manuscript rejected 26 times. It was only when John Farrar of Farrar, Straus, and Giroux suggested it be published as a children's novel did *A Wrinkle in Time* find a home.

A story that blends fantasy, science fiction, religious ideas, and adventure, *A Wrinkle in Time* has sold eight million copies and has the distinction of being heavily censored. The book features three teens, including one of the young adult genre's early female leads in an adventure story, who must travel across the galaxy to combat an entity that forces conformity and represents dark powers. It is only through love that heroine Meg Murry can triumph against the darkness and rescue her father. Accused by religious conservatives of including witches and presenting inaccurate ideas about God, the book was attacked even as it was lauded by critics. "It seems people are willing to damn the book without reading it," L'Engle once told the *New York Times.* "Nonsense about witchcraft and fantasy. First I felt horror, then anger, and finally I said, 'Ah, the hell with it.' It's great publicity, really." The saga of *A Wrinkle in Time* continued in other books featuring the same characters, including *A Wind in the Door, A Swiftly Tilting Planet, Many Waters,* and *An Acceptable Time.*

The series she began with *Meet the Austins* continued as well, telling stories of an affectionate family that some critics felt was too good to be true. But even in that series, L'Engle tackled difficult questions about faith and mortality. The books also integrated the element of fantasy which L'Engle's readers came to expect: In the fourth title, the 16-year-old narrator learns to telepathically communicate with dolphins, who help her deal with the death of a loved one.

Along with her novels for teens, L'Engle wrote memoirs, picture books, and books on religious themes. For many years, she was the librarian and writer-in-residence in New York's Cathedral Church of St. John the Divine. L'Engle was devoted to her Christian faith and promoted a Jungian understanding of the importance of myth. She often felt that her writing was a subconscious or spiritual experience. According to the *New York Times*, she once said of *A Wrinkle in Time*, "I cannot possibly tell you how I came to write it. It simply was a book I had to write. I had no choice. It was only after it was written that I realized what some of it meant."

Along with her Newbery Award, L'Engle received the National Humanities Medal from U.S. President George W. Bush in 2004. L'Engle died of natural causes at a nursing home in Litchfield, Connecticut, where she had been living for three years. Her death on September 6, 2007, came months before her 89th birthday and the release of a previously unpublished young adult novel based on her own life, *The Joys of Love*. She is survived by her daughters, Josephine F. Jones and Maria Rooney, as well as the legacy of her writing. **Sources:** CNN.com, http://www.cnn.com/2007/SHOWBIZ/books/09/07/obit.lengle.ap/index.html (September 10, 2007); *Entertainment Weekly*, http://www.ew.com/ew/article/0,,20056586.tif,00.html (September 25, 2007); *Los Angeles Times*, September 8, 2007, p. B10; *New York Times*, September 8, 2007, p. A13; *People*, September 24, 2007, p. 72; *Times* (London), September 25, 2007, p. 60.

—*Alana Joli Abbott*

John Macquarrie

Born on June 27, 1919, in Renfrew, Scotland; died of stomach cancer on May 28, 2007, in Oxford, England. Theologian. One of the twentieth-century's leading theologians, the Rev. Professor John Macquarrie wrote more than 30 books developing an accessible theology that combined existentialist philosophy with orthodox Christian thought. In addition to writing, Macquarrie also held several teaching posts in England, Scotland, and the United States. Despite his stature in the church, he continued to speak at village parishes in England.

Macquarrie was born in 1919 in Scotland. His father was a shipyard pattern-maker and an elder in the Presbyterian Church; his grandfather was a native Gaelic speaker. He idolized the local Presbyterian minister who helped spark his interest in philosophy. Macquarrie attended Paisley Grammar School and later Glasgow University. He earned a degree in philosophy and turned to theology. He earned another degree in theology and was ordained as a Presbyterian minister in the Church of Scotland, briefly working as an assistant parish minister.

In 1943, Macquarrie joined the British Army and served in the chaplain department until 1948. He became a parish minister but left to earn his doctorate at Glasgow University. He became a lecturer at the university until he joined the faculty of Union Theological Seminary in New York, in 1962.

Macquarrie began his literary career in 1955 with the release of *An Existentialist Theology*, which was a critique of Rudolf Bultman (a German theologian) and philosopher Martin Heidegger. His second release was *The Scope of Demythologizing* in 1960. Macquarrie's interest in German existentialist philosophy brought him to translate Heidegger's *Being and Time* with Edward Robinson. Also among his writings are *Twentieth Century Religious Thought, In Search of Humanity*, and *Paths in Spirituality*.

Macquarrie's *Principles of Christian Theology*, (published in 1966) became a classic textbook used in schools around the world. Each of his books explored a wide variety of subjects including the nature of God, human spirituality, and the potential for change and transformation. N. K. Bruger wrote in the *New York Times* in a 1972 review of *Paths in Spirituality*, "Unlike some modern theologians, John Macquarrie writes about God as though he believes in him." Not one to cater to typical doctrine, Macquarrie appreciated the broad spectrum of Christian thought. He held a belief that other religions do reveal the ultimate truth. Many felt that this view was heretical. He felt that in order to dispute heresy the Church needed to prove it had the better theology.

During his time in New York, Macquarrie was ordained as an Episcopal priest. He was attracted to the Catholic element that was in the Church. He then moved to England and became the Lady Margaret Professor of Divinity at Oxford University and also canon of Christ Church Cathedral. He was a sought-after lecturer but continued to preach at local parishes. According to the *New York Times*, Dr. William L. Sachs, an Episcopal associate rector, likened hearing Macquarrie's lecture to "listening to a fine, fine Beethoven symphony." Macquarrie was also a priest associate of the Order of the Holy Cross. He was the first to lecture on theology at the University of Beijing and was elected a Fellow of the British Academy.

Macquarrie retired in 1986 but continued to lecture and write. In 2006, a volume of 25 essays was presented as a tribute to Macquarrie for working with publisher SCM Press for 50 years. On May 28, 2007, Macquarrie died of stomach cancer in Oxford, England. He was 87. He is survived by his wife of more than 55 years, Jenny, three children, and two grandchildren. **Sources:** *Los Angeles Times,* June 8, 2007, p. B7; *New York Times,* June 3, 2007, p. A29; *Times* (London), June 1, 2007, p. 80; *Washington Post,* June 11, 2007, p. B6.

—*Ashyia N. Henderson*

Theodore Maiman

Born Theodore H. Maiman, July 11, 1927, in Los Angeles, CA; died May 5, 2007, of systemic mastocytosis, in Vancouver, British Columbia, Canada. Physicist and electrical engineer. Physicist Theodore Maiman built the world's first working laser, which many journalists labeled a death ray. Despite the label, Maiman, and many others who followed, found uses for lasers, especially in the medical field. Maiman spent most of his adult life proving that lasers were beneficial to humanity.

Maiman was in 1927 in Los Angeles, California. His father was an electrical engineer who wanted his son to become a doctor. Maiman wanted to be a comedian. He also had a love of math and eventually switched aspirations. Maiman earned a bachelors degree from the University of Colorado, paying for his tuition by fixing radios and other appliances. Maiman went on to earn a masters degree in engineering physics and also a doctorate from Stanford University. His advisor was Willis Lamb, who earned the Nobel Physics Prize in 1955, the same year Maiman earned his Ph.D.

In 1954, physicist Charles Townes changed the scientific world with a device to concentrate and intensify electromagnetic energy. The machine was called a maser because it used microwave energy. Townes alluded that a machine could be built that used light in the same way. This set off a scurry to invent that machine. Maiman and his employer, Hughes Research Laboratories, were among those in the race.

Many believe the invention of the laser was a group effort. Townes and Arthur L. Schawlow held a patent for the theory. Gordon Gould held a patent

that contained important concepts and he also coined the term laser, which is an acronym for light amplification by stimulated emission of radiation. Maiman, however, actually built the device. He was given nine months and $50,000 by Hughes, plus an assistant. "It was almost a bootleg project for me. They tried to pull funding from me twice," he told a Vancouver reporter, the *Washington Post* recounted.

Lasers amplify light waves of atoms stimulated to radiate and then these atoms are concentrated into an intense beam. Maiman used a high-powered flash lamp and a synthetic ruby, all of which fit in the palm of his hand. His first successful test of the laser was on May 16, 1960. He tried to publish his findings in an American scientific journal, but was turned down; however, his paper was accepted by the British journal, *Nature.* A press conference was also held.

At the time, no one had any theoretically good reasons for lasers to be used so journalists called the laser a death ray. Maiman thought the laser could be used in the medical field, but spent much of his time defending his discovery to a fearful public. He thought Hughes would further develop the laser, but that did not go as expected. Maiman was also overlooked for the Nobel Prize in Physics, which was awarded to Townes and Schawlow.

Maiman soon left Hughes and started his own company, the Korad Corporation. He soon found many uses for the laser and his company was later bought out by Union Carbide. Not one to rest on his laurels, Maiman co-founded Laser Video Corporation and followed that with Maiman Associates. In 2000, he published *The Laser Odyssey,* a retelling of the events surrounding his construction of the first laser.

Maiman was awarded many honors and awards for his discovery and its practical uses, including the Oliver E. Buckley Condensed Matter Prize in 1966, the prestigious Wolf Prize in Physics in 1983-84, and the Japan Prize in 1987. He was inducted into the American National Inventors Hall of Fame in 1984 and elected to the National Academy of Sciences and the National Academy of Engineering.

Maiman, who suffered from systemic mastocytosis, succumbed to the disease on May 5, 2007, in Vancouver, British Columbia. He was 79. A daughter preceded him in death, and he is survived by his second wife, a stepdaughter, and a grandchild. Despite early skepticism of lasers, many uses evolved thanks to Maiman's discovery and subsequent work. Laser applications include CD and DVD players, industrial machines for cutting steel, missile guidance systems, and medical tools used for cataract and stomach ulcer surgery. **Sources:** *Chicago Tribune*, May 13, 2007, sec. 4, pg. 6; *Los Angeles Times*, May 11, 2007, p. B10; *New York Times*, May 11, 2007, p. C10; *Times* (London), May 15, 2007, p. 64; *Washington Post*, May 10, 2007, p. B7.

—*Ashyia N. Henderson*

Marcel Marceau

Born Marcel Mangel, March 22, 1923, in Strasbourg, France; died September 22, 2007, in Cahors, France. Mime. For more than 50 years, Marcel Marceau graced the stage with his silent presence, bringing the art of mime back into popularity for audiences in his home country of France and abroad. He toured the world, giving an average of 200 shows per year for a total of more than 15,000 performances before his retirement in 2005.

In addition to being a world-famous performer, Marceau was also the creator of the International School of Mime in Paris, where he taught. Appearing in a number of movies, he was always a silent character, with the exception of his cameo in Mel Brooks's *Silent Movie*, in which he is the only character to have a spoken line. During the 1970s, Marceau appeared as a guest on *The Tonight Show* with Johnny Carson and *Rowan and Martin's Laugh-In*. He had an extensive repertoire, but the best recognized of his characters was Bip, his Don Quixote-like innocent whose adventures were popular on stages in the United States and Europe.

The son of Jewish parents Charles and Anne Mangel, Marceau had a love of physical theater from the time he was a boy. He was captivated by Charlie Chaplin's work, and he would mimic Chaplin's moves and costuming in the streets of Strasbourg. During World War II, Marceau changed his name upon moving to Paris, hiding his Jewish identity from the Gestapo and French police. He and his brother joined the French Resistance, and Marceau discovered that his talent for art allowed him to forge papers for Jewish children. In 1944, he joined the French Army, and, due to his skill at speaking English, he worked as a liaison to the American troops. His first public performance as a mime was in front of an audience of 3,000 American soldiers. The performance was reviewed well by *Stars and Stripes*.

After the war, Marceau attended Charles Dullin's School of Dramatic Art, studying under the mime Étienne Decroux. Marceau had intended to become a spoken-word actor, but he was told he was a natural mime. Marceau joined Jean-Louis Barrault's theater company to work with Barrault, also a noted mime, and, after a few years, Marceau was doing well enough to form his own theater company.

Although his skills were valued in France, it was not until his first tour in the United States that he gained international renown. From 1955 to 1956, Marceau performed at an Off-Broadway theater in a show that was so successful, it was moved to Broadway. Marceau "should be snared with one of his own imaginary butterly nets and trapped inside the proscenium of an American theater for the entire season, and perhaps for the rest of his natural life," wrote a critic of the original New York performance, quoted in the *New York Times*.

For Marceau, being a mime was not only being an actor, but a sculptor, a writer, a painter, and a musician. "It's not dance," he said, quoted in the *Los Angeles Times*. "It's not slapstick. It is essence and restraint." Marceau was an expert at representing all of those aspects. "He was the theater company all wrapped up in one person," Billy the Mime, a student of Marceau's, told *People*. "He was the director, the writer, the actor—he even made the sets appear."

Marceau wrote and designed a number of shows, from *Creation*, which depicted the Biblical tale of the beginning of the world and Adam and Eve's expulsion from the Garden of Eden, to *Youth, Maturity, Old Age, and Death*, a performance of the ages of man, from embryo to death. His easily recognizable and highly imitated *Walking Against the Wind* is said to have been the inspiration for pop singer Michael Jackson's "moonwalk" dance move. A contributor to the *Times* of London credited Marceau's precedent for the high success of Rowan Atkinson's character Mr. Bean. Marceau's impact on theater and the art of mime in particular were discussed by Anna Kisselgoff in the *New York Times*: "Mr. Marceau remains a model, not a fossil. Anyone who has never seen the staples of the repertory with which Mr. Marceau has toured the United States since 1955 should beat a path [to his performances.]"

Despite the silence of his profession, Marceau was always eager to share tales, and he was active as an ambassador of sorts for the French government. In 1970, he was named a Chevalier de la Légion d'Honneur for cultural affairs. In fact, off stage, Marceau was known for his chattiness. "Never get a mime talking. He won't stop," he was quoted on CNN.com as having quipped. In addition to the Légion d'Honneur, Marceau was awarded numerous degrees, and, due to his continued activity as he aged, he was invited to be an ambassador for a 2002 United Nations conference on aging.

Upon receiving word of Marceau's death, President Nicolas Sarkozy of France remarked, as quoted in the *New York Times*, "France loses one of its most eminent ambassadors." Marceau died at his home in Cahors, France, to where he had retired in 2005. He is survived by two sons from his first marriage, Michel and Baptiste, and two daughters from his third marriage, Camille and Aurélia. **Sources:** CNN. com, http://www.cnn.com/2007/SHOWBIZ/09/23/marceau.ap/index.html (September 25, 2007); *Los Angeles Times*, September 24, 2007, p. B9; *New York Times*, September 24, 2007, p. A25; *People*, October 8, 2007, p. 87; *Times* (London), September 24, 2007.

—*Alana Joli Abbott*

Anita O'Day

Born Anita Belle Colton, October 18, 1919, in Chicago, IL; died November 23, 2006, in Los Angeles, CA. Singer. Anita O'Day was considered one of the most phenomenal jazz singers of the 20th century. Her innovative style brought her fame and celebrity during the big-band era in the jazz genre. Her *Los Angeles Times* obituary quoted *Newsweek* writer Charles Michener, "The dynamic range of her voice may be smaller than any other jazz singer's ... but her flexibility with it allows her to scat, slide, and skitter through a song the way a cat's tongue laps up milk." But while her career reached new highs, O'Day's personal life reached new lows until she turned it around and became a phenomenon all over again.

O'Day was born in Chicago, Illinois, in 1919. Her father, a printer, left the family when she was one. Her mother worked in a meat-packing factory. When she was seven, O'Day had her tonsils removed and the doctor accidentally removed her uvula (the small, fleshy lobe of the soft palate that hangs above the tongue). As a result of that, O'Day had no vibrato and was unable to hold notes. But she sang in the church choir when she visited her grandparents during the summer.

O'Day's young life was full of strife and at age 14, with her mother's blessing, she hitchhiked to Mt. Clemens, Michigan, to join a walkathon circuit. A

walkathon was a craze that began during the Depression Era at a time when people would walk for long periods of time to win money and to eat. During this time, she changed her name to O'Day. According to the *New York Times*, O'Day wrote in her memoir, *High Times, Hard Times*, about the name change, "I'd decided O'Day was groovy because in pig latin it meant dough, which is what I hoped to make."

While she was competing, O'Day would sing for money. A truant officer ended her walkathon career and she returned to Chicago to complete her education. O'Day also continued to sing around local clubs and bars. Her popularity around Chicago brought her to the attention of drummer Gene Krupa. After joining Krupa's band, O'Day recorded her first song with Roy Eldridge, "Let Me Off Uptown." It was a hit and one of the first recordings that featured a duet between a black person and white person. The song not only placed O'Day firmly on the map, but it was one of Krupa's biggest hits. O'Day continued recording with Krupa. As a canary or the girl singer in the band, she bucked tradition by donning band shirts and skirts instead of a ball gown. Her debut was rewarded with the Best New Artist award from *Down Beat* magazine, and she made the top five of favorite new artists that same year.

Because of her accidental surgery, O'Day saw herself more as a song stylist than as a singer. Her vocals were playful and at times, her sound was more like a saxophone. She stated to the *New York Times*, quoted in the *Los Angeles Times*, "I'm not a singer because I have no vibrato.... If I want one I have to shake my head to get it. That's why I sing so many notes—so you won't hear that I haven't got one. It's how I got my style." Among the scat singers, she was considered one of the best. Many ranked her with the likes of Ella Fitzgerald, Sarah Vaughan, and Billie Holiday.

After her stint with Krupa, O'Day joined Stan Kenton's band. Her most memorable song from this pairing was "And Her Tears Flowed Like Wine." This song was also one of Kenton's top sellers. O'Day briefly returned to Krupa's band before she struck out on her own. She recorded numerous albums on the Verve label that helped make her a celebrity.

While her career was taking off, O'Day's personal life was beginning to crumble. In 1946 the constant work led to a nervous breakdown. She and her then-husband, golfer Carl Hoff, were arrested for marijuana possession. O'Day served 45 days in jail. She was arrested again for marijuana possession and served another 45 days. O'Day was arrested a third time for alleged heroin possession, serving 90 days in prison; she claimed she was set up because she did not use heroin at the time. It was after her release that she began using the drug, when she was introduced to it by her lifelong collaborator, drummer John Poole. This addiction caused O'Day to lose everything—houses, cars, money. According to the New York Times, the singer said of her life in her autobiography, "Given a choice, I wanted to be where the action was."

Throughout her tumultuous personal life, O'Day continued to record and release albums. Her innovative stylings made her a much-sought-after performer. She consistently headlined every venue and each performance was widely attended. One of her most memorable performances was her appearance at the 1958 Newport Jazz Festival. O'Day sang nine songs and her act was captured on film for Bert Stern's documentary, Jazz on a Summer Day. O'Day's performance at the festival paved the way for her to entertain internationally. She made appearances in Europe and Japan where swing music was hugely popular.

In 1966 O'Day nearly died from a heroin overdose. She quit cold turkey and began to revive what was left of her career. Her career took an upswing in the 1970s. O'Day continued to perform despite failing health in the 1980s and 1990s. She received her first Grammy nomination in 1990 for her album In a Mellow Tone. She later won the American Jazz Masters award from the National Endowment for the Arts in 1997.

O'Day, suffering from Alzheimer's disease, was recovering from a bout with pneumonia when she died of cardiac arrest at a convalescent hospital in West Los Angeles, on November 23, 2006. She was 87. In describing O'Day, band leader Krupa once stated, according to the Los Angeles Times, "She was a wild chick, all right, but how she could sing!" The feisty singer, whose nickname was the Jezebel of Jazz, said, according to Entertainment Weekly, "When I'm singing, I'm happy. I'm doing what I can do, and this is my contribution to life." **Sources:** Chicago Tribune, November 24, 2006, sec. 3, p. 5; Entertainment Weekly, December 8, 2006, p. 18; Los Angeles Times, November 24, 2006, p. B12; New York Times, November 24, 2006, p. A21; Times (London), November 27, 2006, p. 51; Washington Post, November 24, 2006, p. B7.

—Ashyia N. Henderson

Jack Palance

Born Walter Jack Palahnuik, February 18, 1919, in Lattimer, PA; died of natural causes, November 10, 2006, in Montecito, CA. Actor. Jack Palance's acting career stretched over more than 50 years and 100 roles. Early in his career he was best known for playing the villain in such films such as Panic in the Streets (1950), Sudden Fear (1952), and Shane (1953), but to a younger generation he is remembered for his role in 1991's City Slickers, a comedy that parodied his earlier Western villains—and won him his first Oscar at the age of 73. "When it comes to playing hard-bitten cowboys, there could never be anyone better than Jack," Ron Underwood, the director of City Slickers, told the Los Angeles Times.

Palance was born in a Pennsylvania coal-mining town to parents who were immigrants from the Ukraine. As a teenager he followed his father into the mines, but he soon left to attend the University of North Carolina, which had given him a football scholarship. He dropped out of the university before receiving his degree to become a professional boxer. Then, after the United States entered World War II in 1941, Palance joined the Army Air Forces. After he was discharged from the military Palance resumed his education at Stanford University, where he decided to major in journalism. He worked as a sports reporter for the San Francisco Chronicle for a brief time before deciding that he would rather be an actor. He switched his major to drama and graduated in 1947. Palance then moved to New York, and in 1949 he landed his first big theatrical role: Marlon Brando broke his nose, and Palance, his understudy, took over his role as Stanley Kowalski in A Streetcar Named Desire.

The director of A Streetcar Named Desire, Elia Kazan, was also a film director, and he cast Palance as a fugitive who is infected with the bubonic plague in his next film, 1950's Panic in the Streets. Later that year Palance had his first starring role playing a Marine in The Halls of Montezuma. His next two film roles, as a stalker in Sudden Fear and as a gunslinger in the Western Shane, both earned him Oscar nominations for best supporting actor. A few years later he won an Emmy for playing a burnt-out boxer in the 1956 television drama Requiem for a Heavyweight.

Palance's face—which, according to Entertainment Weekly contributor Josh Rottenberg, "looked like it was hammered out of solid rock"—was one of the secrets of his success at playing hard men. For many years people believed that his unusual features resulted from a fiery plane crash during World War II and subsequent reconstructive surgery, but Palance later debunked this myth and said that the story had been made up by a Hollywood publicist.

Palance's career slumped after 1956. He appeared in a few more well-regarded Westerns, including *The Professionals* in 1966, but also in a number of "spaghetti westerns" and widely panned films. Palance returned to playing the villain in popular films in the late 1980s, including *Young Guns* in 1988 and *Batman* in 1989. Then came 1991's *City Slickers,* a comedy in which Palance played a rugged old cowboy who terrifies three city slickers on a cattle drive. When Palance was awarded the Oscar for best supporting actor for this role, he set the record for the longest time between first being nominated for an Oscar and winning one. He also delighted the awards show audience by dropping to the stage and doing several one-armed push-ups to prove that he was still in shape. The stunt provided the host of the Oscars (and the star of *City Slickers*), Billy Crystal, with a running gag for the rest of that year's Oscars. The joke carried over into the next year's show, which opened with Palance pulling Crystal and a giant Oscar statue onto the stage using only his teeth.

In the last years of his life Palance continued to act, but he also indulged in other passions. He published a book of self-illustrated prose poetry, *Forest of Love: A Love Story in Blank Verse,* in 1996, and he continued to tend his cattle ranch in California and a farm that he owned near his birthplace in Pennsylvania. Palance died of natural causes at his home in Montecito, California, on November 10, 2006. He was 87. He is survived by his two daughters from his first marriage, Holly and Brooke; his second wife, Elaine Rogers Palance; and three grandchildren. Palance's third child, a son named Cody from his first marriage, died of melanoma in 1998. **Sources:** *Chicago Tribune,* November 11, 2006, sec. 1, p. 10; CNN.com, http://www.cnn.com/2006/SHOWBIZ/Movies/11/10/palance.death/index.html (November 13, 2006); E! Online, http://www.eonline.com/news/article/index.jsp?uuid=90854b99-ab2f-4eba-adb5-18bc234e3c1d (November 13, 2006); *Entertainment Weekly,* November 24, 2006, p. 18; *Los Angeles Times,* November 11, 2006, p. B12; *New York Times,* November 11, 2006, p. B10; *People,* http://people.aol.com/people/article/0,26334,1558148,00.html (November 13, 2006); *Times* (London), November 13, 2006, p. 62.

—*Julia Bauder*

Wolfgang Panofsky

Born Wolfgang Kurt Hermann Panofsky, April 24, 1919, in Berlin, Germany; died of a heart attack, September 24, 2007, in Los Altos, CA. Physicist. As the scientist largely responsible for the creation of Stanford University's two-mile-long linear electron accelerator, Wolfgang Panofsky was known as a brilliant administrator, a political advisor who opposed the use of nuclear arms, and was instrumental in making discoveries about the neutral pi meson, a type of pion or elementary particle.

The neutral pi meson, a subatomic particle that theorists had predicted was instrumental in binding atomic nuclei, was difficult to isolate due to its short life span. Neutral pions decay quickly into gamma rays. Panofsky and his colleague, Jack Steinberger, were the first scientists to isolate the neutral pi meson. Through this work, and his role as a researcher and administrator in nuclear physics, Panofsky made a great impact on the study of particle physics.

Born in Berlin, Germany, in 1919, Panofsky was the son of a professor of art history who taught in Hamburg. By eight years old, Panofsky showed signs of high intelligence and was a strong chess player. In 1934, the family fled Germany to escape persecution as Jews. They settled in New Jersey, where Panofsky's father took a position teaching art history at Princeton. Both Panofsky and his older brother, Hans, enrolled in Princeton rather than attending high school. At 15, Panofsky chose to study subjects that required little written English and took courses in mathematics, physics, and Latin. He received his first degree in four years, graduating at the age of 19. Panofsky and his brother were voted "most brilliant in their class," according to the *Washington Post*. Desiring to travel away from home, he enrolled in graduate school at the California Institute of Technology, where he received his doctorate in 1942.

At the California Institute of Technology, Panofsky co-wrote a textbook on optics and electricity with classmate Carl Anderson, which was used throughout World War II. He also studied under physicist Jesse DuMond, who had developed an X-ray spectrometer that Panofsky was instrumental in bringing to operation. Panofsky married DuMond's daughter, Adele, after he graduated.

Because of California law, Panofsky was considered an "enemy alien" after his graduation, which meant he had to obey a number of restrictions on his personal freedom. Despite this, he continued to teach at the California Institute of Technology, developing a reputation in electron physics. With the help of professor Robert Millikan, Panofsky became a naturalized citizen, and he worked on a number of war projects, eventually becoming a consultant on the

Manhattan Project, the military project for developing the atomic bomb. These experiences led him to become an activist for peace later in life. "He really believed in disarming the world," his daughter Carol Panofsky told the *Washington Post*.

After working for several years at the University of California—Berkeley's Radiation Laboratory, where he and Jack Steinberger isolated the neutral pi meson, Panofsky left the institution due to the oath of loyalty the university began to require. He was offered positions at Princeton and the Massachusetts Institute of Technology, but Panofsky accepted a position at Stanford, where he began in 1951. Similar to his time with DuMond, Panofsky arrived at Stanford as a machine being developed—here an upgrade to the university's linear accelerator—was not operable. The length of the machine made using it for experiments nearly impossible. Panofsky developed a new way of using the machinery through a separate experimental station, and by 1953, the accelerator was running at full functionality.

Along with his work for Stanford, Panofsky served as a government advisor. He made efforts to establish communication, during the height of the Cold War, between the Soviet Union and the United States. He contacted scientists on both sides, encouraging them to explain to their leaders the horrific consequences of all-out nuclear war. Panofsky provided advice in the U.S. State Department, helping them to develop ways to monitor radioactive fallout. His work was instrumental to the development of the international treaty banning atmospheric testing of nuclear weapons, and from 1961 to 1964, Panofsky served on the President's Science Advisory Committee. He remained active as an advocate for peace throughout his life.

In the late 1950s, Panofsky began lobbying for an electron accelerator, which he helped to design. Due to the great expense of the accelerator, which was planned to run for two miles beneath the campus, it was nearly abandoned, but President John F. Kennedy, who had used Panofsky as a science advisor, became a strong supporter of the project and saw it through. Panofsky became the project leader in 1960, and the project was completed in 1966. Due to his insistence that the facility, called the Stanford Linear Accelerator Center (or SLAC), be opened to all researchers, "Panofsky created not only a physical setting but a community of physicists, engineers, technicians, and support staff," Stanford physicist Sidney Drell told the *Los Angeles Times*. "His patience and energy never seemed exhausted: He led with candor, with an innate ability to resolve conflicts constructively and by being involved in every aspect of the lab's activities." Panofsky served as

the director of SLAC until his retirement in 1984. During his tenure, three experiments run at the facility received Nobel Prizes. Despite his retirement, Panofsky remained active at the facility up until his death.

"The world has lost a truly great man," Persis Drell, the acting director of SLAC, said to the *Los Angeles Times* on the announcement of Panofsky's death. "[Panofsky's] impact on particle physics was enormous but, in addition, everyone will remember him for his unflinching integrity, personal warmth, and desire to fight for the principles he believed in." Panofsky had a heart attack on September 24, 2007, and died at his home in Los Altos, California. He is survived by his wife, Adele, his sons Richard Jacob, Edward Frank, and Steven Thomas; and his daughters Margaret Ann and Carol Eleanor. Panofsky's autobiography, *Panofsky on Physics, Politics, and Peace* was released a week after his death. **Sources:** *Los Angeles Times*, September 27, 2007, p. B8; *New York Times*, September 28, 2007, p. C10; *Times* (London), October 2, 2007; *Washington Post*, September 28, 2007, p. B7.

—*Alana Joli Abbott*

Brant Parker

Born Brant Julian Parker, August 26, 1920, in Los Angeles, CA; died of complications related to Alzheimer's diesase and an earlier stroke, April 15, 2007, in Lynchburg, VA. Cartoonist. For more than 40 years, Brant Parker entertained audiences with the antics of medieval residents in his comic, *The Wizard of Id*. Created with *B.C.* cartoonist Johnny Hart, *The Wizard of Id* earned its team Reuben Awards for Cartoonist of the Year. Parker, who worked on such comics as *Out of Bounds* and *Crock*, also won the National Cartoonist Society's Humor Comic Strip Award five times and received the Elzie Seger Award in 1986. "Humor is a ... very important part of our survival and existence now," Parker was quoted as having said about his work in the *Los Angeles Times*. "There's nothing that eases tension like a good laugh. It can just about solve all the problems if it were used right."

Born in 1920 in Los Angeles, Parker was the son of a magazine illustrator. Cartooning became a "compulsion" for him as a child, and he often went secretly into the local paper's newsroom to watch the editorial cartoonist during his school recesses, according to an article in the *Washington Post.* "I don't know how I got past the guard," he was quoted as having explained. "I guess I was pretty nervy."

Parker studied at the Otis Art Institute from 1939 to 1942, but he often said that his two-year stint working for Walt Disney studios in the late 1940s was his real art education. He worked on various projects, including the thirty-minute feature *Mickey and the Beanstalk* and several Donald Duck shorts. Between school and his work for Disney, Parker served in the Navy and fought in World War II.

After marrying Mary Louise Sweet in 1947, Parker moved to Binghamton, New York, where he took a position as a political cartoonist. It was while he was in that position that he met Johnny Hart. Parker was asked to judge an art competition at a local high school, where he discovered Hart's art work. Parker encouraged Hart to pursue cartooning as a career and served as a mentor as Hart began working in the industry. Parker continued to work in comics, collaborating on projects such as *Goosemeyer* and working with Bill Rechin and Don Wilder on the strips *Out of Bounds* and *Crock,* a strip about the French Foreign Legion.

In 1964, Hart called Parker with an idea for a cartoon set in the Middle Ages. The two met in a New York hotel room, plastered the walls with panels, and invited a syndicate executive to see their work. *The Wizard of Id* launched soon after and was eventually syndicated in more than 1,000 newspapers. "The original premise was built around the Wizard goofing up and everything backfiring on him," Parker was quoted as having said in the *Chicago Tribune.* "Everything kind of grew out of that." The strip was known for poking fun at politics and culture and became a vehicle for the cartoonists to comment on humans in society.

The strip features a tyrant known only as the King, who calls his subjects Idiots; a hapless wizard; Turnkey, a dungeon guard, and his constantly escaping prisoner, Spook; Sir Rodney, the cowardly knight; and others. Parker was quoted in the *Los Angeles Times* as having said his favorite character in the strip—one he invented—was Spook. "I think it's because of the pathos in Spook's situation. He's stuck in there for life, and he keeps trying to get out. I love pathos humor."

Parker drew the strip and credited Hart with coming up with most of the gags, but the final strips were always a collaborative effort. "It's two different kinds of thinking, always," Parker was quoted

as having said about their collaboration in the *Los Angeles Times.* "The trick is to find two people who are basically alike.... We both enjoy the same kind of humor, so it's been a great relationship."

Parker, who had suffered from Alzheimer's disease and a stroke, passed along art duties for *The Wizard of Id* to his son, Jeff, in 1997. He died on April 15, 2007, eight days after his co-creator, Johnny Hart, died of a stroke. In honor of his and Hart's death, Jeff Parker posted a *The Wizard of Id* strip featuring the King and the Wizard looking through a telescope into the sky. The Wizard quips, "Hey! There's cartoons up there!" Parker died at the nursing home in Lynchburg, Virginia, where he had lived. He was 86 years old. **Sources:** *Chicago Tribune,* April 18, 2007, sec. 3, p. 9; *Los Angeles Times,* April 17, 2007, p. B9; *New York Times,* April 18, 2007, p. A25; *Times* (London), April 23, 2007, p. 55; *Washington Post,* April 17, 2007, p. B7.

—*Alana Joli Abbott*

Willie Pep

Born Guglielmo Papaleo, September 19, 1922, in Middletown, CT; died of complications from Alzheimer's disease, November 23, 2006, in Rocky Hill, CT. Professional boxer. Willie Pep was considered one of the greatest boxers of the 20th century. During his career, which spanned more than two decades, he won 230 fights. He was most known to win on points and decisions, but Pep also had his fair share of knockouts.

Pep was in 1922 in Middletown, Connecticut. His parents were Sicilian immigrants. Pep began boxing in his teenage years. In the early part of the 20th century, amateur boxers were allowed to fight for money. Pep's father worked long hours and also worked extra jobs to feed his family. He, however, appreciated that his son could earn the same amount of money sparring. Pep occasionally sparred with Sugar Ray Robinson.

As an amateur, Pep won the Connecticut state championship twice before turning pro in 1940. He fought in the flyweight, featherweight, and bantamweight classes. Pep won 53 consecutive fights and defeated Chalky Wright for the New York State Athletic Commission World Featherweight title in 1942. At the age of 20, he was the youngest to ever win that title.

Pep served in the Navy during World War II. After his tour of duty ended, he continued his winning streak until he lost by decision to Sammy Angott. In 1946 Pep was involved in a plane crash, where he suffered a broken back and broken leg, and a chest injury. He was paralyzed from the waist down. He regained movement, but spent five months in a body cast. Once his cast was removed, Pep returned to boxing, entering the ring in a month's time. Pep unsuccessfully sued the airline; he attributed the legal loss to the fact that he had such a quick recovery.

In 1948 Pep held the first of four title fights with Sandy Saddler. Saddler won the fight in the fourth round when he knocked out Pep. Pep would win the second fight. He suffered a shoulder injury in the third fight, losing again to Saddler and also lost the fourth and final fight. Throughout the final fight, Saddler and Pep wrestled with one another and even caused the referee to fall. Many thought Pep took a dive, but it was not proven. However, the New York State Athletic Commission revoked Pep's license for 17 months for fouling. Saddler was also suspended for two months.

Pep continued to fight, but never fought for a championship again. He retired in 1959. He did not stay away from the ring too long. At age 42 Pep came out of retirement. He won 43 more fights before he retired for the second time. In all he won 230 fights and lost eleven and had one draw in a career that spanned 26 years.

Pep earned the nickname "Will o' the Wisp" because he "[outfoxed] his opponents with superior speed and footwork," according to the New York Times. Throughout his career, he only won 65 by knockout. He mostly won on points or by decision. Pep even boasted during a bout in 1946 that he would not land a single punch but would win the round anyway; he ended up being right. According the New York Times, he said in an interview with In This Corner, "I jabbed him a few times, but most of the round, I was bobbing and weaving and making him miss, and he missed a hundred punches, I guess, making him look so bad they gave me the round." Regarding this match, sportswriter Don Riley, wrote (according to the Los Angeles Times), "It was an amazing display of defensive boxing skill."

After retirement Pep worked as a boxing referee and traveled around with his friend, Rocky Marciano. He also worked with the Connecticut Boxing Commission as a referee. In 1990 Pep was elected to the International Boxing Hall of Fame. The Associated Press also named him as one of the five best boxers of the 20th century. "He was prob-

ably the greatest pure boxer that ever lived," Hank Kaplan, a boxing historian and archivist, told the Washington Post.

In his later years, Pep suffered from Alzheimer's disease. On November 23, 2006, he died at the West Hill Convalescent Home in Rocky Hill, Connecticut. He was 84. He is survived by his wife and four children. **Sources:** Los Angeles Times, November 25, 2006, p. B13; New York Times, November 25, 2006, p. B10; Times (London), November 27, 2006, p. 51; Washington Post, November 25, 2006, p. B6.

—Ashyia N. Henderson

Carlo Ponti

Born December 11, 1912, in Magenta, Italy; died of pulmonary complications, January 9, 2007, in Geneva, Switzerland. Film producer. Italian film producer Carlo Ponti was responsible for an impressive number of cinematic classics of the mid-twentieth century, but he was equally famous as the husband of one of Italy's best-known film stars, screen siren Sophia Loren. Back in the 1950s, the affair between the starlet and the still-married Ponti scandalized the public and endured for several years as one of Europe's leading tabloid stories. The pair were eventually forced to renounce their Italian citizenship in order to legally marry.

Born on December 11, 1912, Ponti spent his early years in the town of Magenta, near Milan, where his father owned a store that sold sheet music. He earned a degree in law from the University of Milan in 1934 and practiced for a few years before becoming involved in the film industry, first as a member of a production company's board of directors. He worked for Lux Film in Rome and scored his first movie success in his debut as a producer with the 1940 historical drama Old-Fashioned World, whose tale of a long-ago Austrian invasion of Italy resonated with Italians uneasy with their country's alliance with Nazi Germany at the time.

Ponti made several more well-received works during the 1940s, and in 1950 he formed a production company with Dino De Laurentiis. Their company made some of the most visually stunning films of the next decade, including one of the great classics of postwar Italian cinema, Federico Fellini's La Strada in 1954, and then an epic adaptation of the Russian novel War and Peace with an international cast that included Henry Fonda and Audrey Hepburn.

Ponti was the married father of two young children in 1951 when he was asked to serve as a judge in the Miss Rome beauty pageant and spotted an attractive teenager in the audience. He invited 15-year-old Sofia Scicolone to become a contestant and soon signed her to his company and changed her name to Sophia Loren. Ponti was largely responsible for shaping her career, placing her in projects that showcased her sultry looks and fiery personality. One of her best-known roles came in 1960's *La Ciocara*, a saga about wartime trauma; its U.S. release was titled *Two Women*, and with it Loren became the first female star ever to win an Academy Award for Best Actress in a Leading Role for a performance in a non-English film.

By then she and Ponti were heavily involved, both professionally and personally. Ponti's wife, Giuliana Fiastri Ponti, accepted that the marriage was over, but there was no divorce law in Italy at the time. In 1957, lawyers hired by Ponti obtained a Mexican divorce for him, then the attorneys stood by proxy before a Mexican judge who "married" Ponti and Loren—making them not actually present at their own wedding—but once the legal machinations became public, the sham was denounced by the Vatican and Italian prosecutors charged Ponti with bigamy and Loren with concubinage. He was convicted in absentia in 1962, making it impossible for him to return to Italy. The couple finally renounced their Italian citizenship and became citizens of France, where Ponti was granted his divorce; he and Loren were wed there in the city of Sevres in 1966.

The late 1960s through the 1970s were the most fruitful years of Ponti's career as a producer. Ponti adapted another classic of Russian literature, *Doctor Zhivago*, in 1965 with David Lean as director and Omar Sharif and Julie Christie in the lead roles, a three-hour-plus saga that is consistently ranked on lists of the best movies in the history of cinema. Ponti also brought Michelangelo Antonioni's *Blow-Up* to the screen in 1966, a groundbreaking thriller about a fashion photographer who may have inadvertently captured a murder. It was one of several films produced by Ponti that were nominated for an Academy Award. In the 1970s, he made *Andy Warhol's Flesh for Frankenstein* and *Andy Warhol's Dracula*, but the 1975 Jack Nicholson thriller *The Passenger* is one of the more enduring films from this period of Ponti's career, along with another all-star, international disaster film *The Cassandra Crossing* in 1977, which featured Loren, Martin Sheen, Ava Gardner, Richard Harris, and O. J. Simpson as a Roman Catholic priest. According to *New York Times* journalist Douglas Martin, Ponti once asserted, "I can make an art film every day of the week. Nothing to it. What's difficult is to combine a commercial film with art."

Ponti and Loren ran into legal problems again in Italy after Ponti was accused of smuggling his art collection out of the country in the late 1970s. He was finally cleared of wrongdoing in 1990, but Ponti was 78 years old by then. In his later years he and Loren lived in Switzerland. He was hospitalized for pulmonary problems just before New Year's Eve of 2006. He died in Geneva on January 9, 2007, at the age of 94. In addition to Loren, survivors include son Alessandro and daughter Guendalina from his first marriage, and sons Carlo Jr. and Eduardo from his union with Loren. Alessandro became a film producer, Eduardo a movie director, and Carlo Jr. became an orchestra conductor. **Sources:** *Chicago Tribune*, January 11, 2007, sec. 2, p. 11; *New York Times*, January 11, 2007, p. C23; *Times* (London), January 11, 2007, p. 61.

—Carol Brennan

Tom Poston

Born Thomas Poston, October 17, 1921, in Columbus, OH; died after a brief illness on April 30, 2007, in Los Angeles, CA. Actor. Known mainly for playing the lovable yet clueless handyman George Utley on *Newhart*, actor Tom Poston made a career out of playing lovable, bumbling idiots. Whether it was the forgetful man on the street or the clown who lived in a closet, Poston found ways to keep the audience laughing. While not one for leading roles, he found continuous work in film, stage, and television.

Poston was born in 1921 in Columbus, Ohio. He began performing at age nine as an acrobat in a troupe called the Flying Zebleys. He attended Bethany College in West Virginia but soon joined the fight during World War II as an Army Air Forces pilot. Poston later attended the American Academy of Dramatic Arts. Soon after he auditioned for—and won—a small role in the stage production of *Cyrano de Bergerac*.

Poston followed his first role with parts on both stage and on television. He soon joined the TV program *Entertainment* as the emcee. Poston was also a panelist on the quiz show *To Tell the Truth* and host of the television show *Split Personality*.

Poston soon came to the attention of comedian Steve Allen. He auditioned and was so frightened he forgot his name when asked. According to the *Los Angeles Times,* citing an interview with Newshouse News Service, Poston admitted, "[Allen] asked me my name and darned if my mind didn't go blank. I sat there like a big dope and held my head. Steve thought I was kidding. He said 'Hey, that's great. We'll use it.' From then on, I was a regular." Poston's portrayal of the man who could not remember his name earned him an Emmy award in 1959.

When *The Steve Allen Show* moved to Los Angeles, Poston chose to stay behind in New York. He continued to find work in film, television, and on stage. He landed roles in Broadway shows such as *Will Success Spoil Rock Hunter, A Funny Thing Happened on the Way to the Forum,* and *Mary, Mary.*

Poston took on few leading roles, preferring to play supporting roles. He had the opportunity to play the lead in the television sitcom, *Get Smart,* but he opted for a guest role instead. According to the *Los Angeles Times,* he stated "I'd rather be working my head off as a supporting actor than be a giant star unable to get a job."

Poston landed a role on comedian Bob Newhart's self-titled show. He played a college friend of Newhart's character. The part was recurring, but it began a long partnership with Newhart that lasted two decades. After *The Bob Newhart Show* ended in 1978, Poston joined the cast of the hugely popular sitcom *Mork & Mindy* as the grumpy Mr. Bickley.

In the 1980s, Poston earned a role on *Newhart.* He played George Utley, the handyman who could not fix anything. Audiences loved him in this role. When the show ended, Poston continued working steadily despite his age. He had guest roles on several highly rated shows, including *That '70s Show, Home Improvement, Murphy Brown, Will & Grace, Alice,* and Disney Channel's *The Suite Life of Zack & Cody.* Poston also continued to win film roles, with his last roles on *Christmas with the Kranks* and *Princess Diaries 2: The Royal Engagement.*

Poston died on April 30, 2007, in his home in Los Angeles, following a brief illness. He was 85. His friend, Bob Newhart, released a statement quoted in the *Chicago Tribune,* describing him as a "versatile and veteran performer and a kind-hearted individual." Poston is survived by three children. His wife, fellow co-star on *The Bob Newhart Show* Suzanne Pleshette, passed away almost a year later

on January 19, 2008. **Sources:** *Chicago Tribune,* May 2, 2007, sec. 3, p. 10; CNN.com, http://www.cnn.com/2007/SHOWBIZ/TV/05/01/tv.obit.poston.ap/index.html (May 2, 2007); *Entertainment Weekly,* May 11, 2007, p. 20; E! Online, http://www.eonline.com/news/article/index.jsp?uuid=68c3003a-71c9-44 76-89d0-375c708451e4 (May 2, 2007); *Los Angeles Times,* May 2, 2007, p. B8; *New York Times,* May 2, 2007, p. A19; *People,* May 14, 2007, p. 106; *Washington Post,* May 2, 2007, p. B7.

—*Ashyia N. Henderson*

Charles Nelson Reilly

Born January 13, 1931, in New York, NY; died of pneumonia, May 25, 2007, in Beverly Hills, CA. Actor, director, and game show panelist. While most people knew actor Charles Nelson Reilly as a game show panelist on *Hollywood Squares* and *Match Game,* he preferred to be known for his stage direction and acting. His guest spots on game shows and appearances on talk and variety shows overshadowed his roles on the stage and television. Reilly appeared on *The Tonight Show Starring Johnny Carson* more than 90 times.

Reilly was born in 1931 in the New York City borough the Bronx. His father, Charles Joseph Reilly, designed outdoor advertising for Paramount Pictures. Reilly's life took a turn for the worse when his mother, Signe Elvera Nelson, forced his father to turn down a job with Walt Disney. His father had a nervous breakdown and was institutionalized. Reilly and his mother moved to live with relatives in Hartford, Connecticut. He won the lead in a school play at nine and at 18, moved to New York and studied with Uta Hagen and Herbert Berghof. Other famous classmates included Jack Lemmon, Charles Grodin, and Hal Holbrook.

Reilly landed roles in stage productions, including a spot in the original production of *How to Succeed in Business Without Really Trying.* He won a Tony Award for his portrayal. He later joined the cast of *Hello, Dolly!* and began directing with *The Belle of Amherst,* of which he was very proud.

Reilly moved to Los Angeles in the late 1960s to star in the television program *The Ghost and Mrs. Muir.* He made guest appearances on a wide variety of programs, and was a regular on the variety show, *Laugh-In.* Reilly appeared on more talk and variety shows, co-starring with Dean Martin or chatting with Johnny Carson. He also began his career on game shows. He was a panelist on *Hollywood Squares*, but his most successful run was on *Match Game*. There he wore oversized glasses, a captain's hat, and an ascot as he exchanged witty banter and thinly veiled double entendres with co-panelists Brett Somers, Richard Dawson, and host Gene Rayburn.

Reilly's acting career continued with guest roles on *The Patty Duke Show, Nanny and the Professor,* and *Family Matters.* He appeared in films, but his fame centered on his game show appearances. Friend Burt Reynolds, with whom he starred in *Cannonball Run II,* and on Reynold's television show, *Evening Shade,* told *Time* in 1991 (as quoted by the *Los Angeles Times*), "We have a thing in this town that if you are enormously witty and gregarious, you can't be very deep…. People just haven't seen him in this arena."

Reilly also taught acting and ran a school in North Hollywood. He later moved to Florida to teach at the Burt Reynolds Institute. His students included Liza Minnelli, Lily Tomlin, Christine Lahti, and Bette Midler. Reilly continued to direct plays including a revival of *The Gin Game*, which starred Julie Harris and Charles Durning. His final work was his autobiographical one-man show, *Save It for the Stage: The Life of Reilly.* The play was made into a television movie in 2006.

Reilly, who had been in failing health, died of complications from pneumonia on May 25, 2007. He was 76. Reilly, who was openly gay throughout his career, was once told he would never make it in television because of his sexual orientation. While Reilly may have wished for a career known for more than game show appearances, it was those game show spots that proved his naysayer wrong. **Sources:** *Chicago Tribune*, May 28, 2007, sec. 3, p. 8; E! Online, http://www.eonline.com/news/article/index.jsp?uuid=4b006742-ac0c-4b e3-b34f-924a61b4069d (December 11, 2007); *Los Angeles Times*, May 29, 2007, p. B9; *New York Times*, May 28, 2007, p. A17; *Washington Post*, May 29, 2007, p. B6.

—*Ashyia N. Henderson*

Eddie Robinson

Born Edward Gay Robinson, February 13, 1919, in Jackson, LA; died April 3, 2007, in Ruston, LA. Foot-

ball coach. As the first football coach in the history of the National Collegiate Athletic Association to win 408 games, Eddie Robinson made his mark not only as a winning coach, but as a role model for many African-American youths. His work with the Grambling State University football team raised the college from a small school to a college that produced more than 200 players in the National Football League (NFL). His successes opened up the walls of segregation when Grambling played at Tulane Stadium, a place where, at one time, African Americans were not allowed entry.

Robinson was a star quarterback at Leland College, where he earned his bachelor's degree and was encouraged to become a coach. He was the son of a sharecropper and a domestic servant, neither of whom had finished high school. After college, Robinson could not find a coaching job, so he took work in a feed mill, making 25 cents an hour. He married his high school sweetheart, Doris Mott, in 1941, the same year there was an opening for a college football coach at Grambling State University, then known as Louisiana Negro Normal and Industrial Institute. He was hired to coach football, basketball, and baseball, as well as to mow the fields, treat minor sports-related injuries, and write accounts of the games for a local newspaper. In his first season, the team had a rough record, but by the second season, it finished with nine wins and zero losses and had not allowed a single point.

The football team did not play from 1943 to 1944, due to World War II, and in 1945 it faced a different challenge. Two of Robinson's star players were needed by their father to pick cotton. Rather than submit to defeat, Robinson organized the whole team to go out and work in the field, and that year Grambling won the championship. During the early 1960s, due to the number of Grambling graduates who had gone on to the NFL, the all-black college became a major recruiting ground for African-American players. When many of the major southern colleges began to integrate, he did not dissuade his players from leaving, torn between wanting the best team and his support for civil rights. Robinson continued to coach until 1997, when he retired.

His players remember him for more than his football knowledge. Robinson also taught his players etiquette and encouraged them to show faith; he required them to dress in suits and ties when they traveled to games and gave them their laundry stipends at church. He was "a great motivator," Super Bowl most valuable player Doug Williams was quoted as having said in the *New York Times*. "He could build you up and make you believe you could do anything." Everson Walls, a Grambling corner-back who went on to the NFL, told the *Los Angeles Times,* "He gave us a way of looking at life. ... He always wanted us to look for a way to succeed, not a reason to fail." Robinson served as a role model beyond those who played for him at Grambling. Chicago Bears coach Lovie Smith, one of the first African-American coaches to take his team to the Superbowl, told the *Chicago Tribune,* "For most young black men coming up, it was Eddie Robinson who we saw. When you would think about becoming a great coach and who you wanted to pattern yourself after and who looked like you, it was Eddie Robinson."

Robinson was a devoted husband and a devoted patriot. During the civil rights era, he insisted that his players stand and respect the flag during the playing of the national anthem. "I don't believe anybody can out-American me," he was quoted as having said in the *Los Angeles Times.* The *Chicago Tribune* quoted a comment he once made: "The best way to enjoy life in America is to first be an American, and I don't think you have to be white to do so. Blacks have had a hard time, but not many Americans haven't." Married for 65 years, Robinson often told his players that "having one job and one wife" were his proudest accomplishments, according to the *Los Angeles Times.* Robinson, who had been suffering from Alzheimer's disease, died on April 3, 2007. He was 88. **Sources:** *Chicago Tribune,* April 5, 2007, sec. 4, p. 1, p. 4; *Los Angeles Times,* April 5, 2007, p. A1, p. A20; *New York Times,* April 5, 2007, p. A17.

—*Alana Joli Abbott*

Mstislav Rostropovich

Born Mstislav Leopoldovich Rostropovich, March 27, 1927, in Baku, Soviet Union; died of intestinal cancer, April 27, 2007, in Moscow, Russia. Cellist, pianist, and conductor. Russian cellist Mstislav Rostropovich was one of leading luminaries in twentieth-century classical music. Renowned for his virtuosity on the cello, Rostropovich played with some of the world's top orchestras and later in life conducted a few of them, too. He was also an outspoken figure during the repressive totalitarian era of Soviet history, who risked his livelihood and indeed his own life to speak out against injustice.

Born in 1927, Rostropovich—called "Slava" by his friends and family—was born in the Azerbaijani city of Baku into a musically gifted family. His mother, Sofia, was a pianist, and her mother had been director of a music school; on his father's side, Rostropovich was a third-generation cellist, taking up the instrument himself at the age of ten after some training on the piano. Rostropovich's talents were nurtured enough to allow him to make his professional debut with an orchestra at the age of 13. From 1943 to 1948 he studied at the Moscow Conservatory, and began writing his own compositions with two of his teachers, Dmitiri Shostakovich and Sergei Prokofiev.

In 1955, Rostropovich married Galina Vishnevskaya, a soprano, and the pair gave well-attended and critically acclaimed concert recitals. His fame reached international proportions, and he was allowed to travel abroad for performances in New York City and London, which required a certain compliance with official Soviet propaganda; however, he ran afoul of authorities in the late 1960s when he gave his support to dissident writer Alexander Solzhenitsyn, who wrote of the Soviet labor camp system that warehoused thousands of political dissidents in *The Gulag Archipelago* and other works. Rostropovich and his wife allowed Solzhenitsyn to stay at their dacha, or country vacation cottage, for four years. Frustrated by the treatment of Solzhenitsyn—who was awarded the Nobel Prize for Literature in 1970—Rostropovich wrote an open letter to *Pravda,* the official state newspaper. He questioned the government's interference in the arts, wondering "why in our literature and art so often people absolutely incompetent in this field have the final word?" *New York Times* writer Allan Kozinn quoted him as writing in the letter, which was not published but brought Rostropovich and his wife years of personal trouble.

Rostropovich was banned from traveling abroad for the next several years, and found that even his Soviet concert engagements were restricted. Finally, in 1974, he and Vishnevskaya were allowed to travel abroad, but comments he made during the trip prompted Soviet officials to revoke their citizenship. The couple spent the next several years in exile in the West, traveling on special Swiss documents because they were technically stateless persons. From 1977 to 1994, he served as music director of the National Symphony Orchestra of Washington D.C., and was an occasional guest conductor with the London Philharmonic and London Symphony orchestras.

The end of the Soviet Union, beginning with the fall of the Berlin Wall in 1989, began the process of homecoming for Rostropovich and his wife, and he became a staunch supporter of Russia's first post-

Communist leader, Boris Yeltsin. The return to his homeland was even the subject of a documentary film, *Soldiers of Music: Rostropovich Returns to Russia.* He and his wife established the Rostropovich Foundation, which provided medical care to children, and he continued to record essential works from the classical repertoire, with his cello interpretations of Bach and Dvorak considered to be definitive recordings of each.

Rostropovich retired from performing in public with his cello in 2005. Two years later, Russian President Vladimir V. Putin honored an 80-year-old Rostropovich in a special birthday ceremony with the Order of Service to the Fatherland medal. He died a month later, on April 27, 2007, at a Moscow hospital, after a long battle with intestinal cancer. Survivors include Vishnevskaya and their daughters, Olga and Elena. In the world of classical music, Rostropovich was a towering figure, respected as much for his talent as for his moral fortitude. He once testified before the U.S. Senate on National Endowment for the Arts, and commented on controversies over funding for the arts. "I have been a victim of censorship—both as a musician and as a person," *Los Angeles Times* writer Chris Pasles quoted him as saying. "The United States, with its great number of diverse ethnic and religious groups, must preserve in an untouchable state the right of each person to express himself." **Sources:** *Chicago Tribune,* April 28, 2007, sec. 3, p. 7; *Los Angeles Times,* April 28, 2007, p. B12; *New York Times,* April 28, 2007, p. A1, p. A13.

—*Carol Brennan*

Wally Schirra

Born Walter Schirra, March 12, 1923, in Hackensack, NJ; died of a heart attack, May 3, 2007, in La Jolla, CA. Astronaut. American astronaut Wally Schirra was a veteran of the first three manned space programs launched by the U.S. National Aeronautics and Space Administration (NASA). One of the original seven astronauts chosen for the first Mercury program, he went on to become the sole Mercury pioneer to participate in both the Gemini and Apollo programs as well. Schirra logged a total of almost 300 hours in space, but described space as "a hostile environment, and it's trying to kill you," *New York Times* Richard Goldstein quoted him as saying. "The outside temperature goes from a minus 450 degrees to a plus 300 degrees. You sit in a flying Thermos bottle."

Born in 1923, Schirra grew up in a family of aviation enthusiasts. His father had been part of the first wave of U.S. military pilots during World War I and, upon returning to civilian life, became a stunt pilot in New Jersey with his wife; Schirra's mother was a "wing walker" who reportedly performed even before she realized she was pregnant with her son. The future astronaut was 13 years old when he first took the controls of his father's plane, and had his own pilot's license by the time he entered the Newark College of Engineering (known today as the New Jersey Science and Technology University) a few years later. When World War II broke out, Schirra enlisted in the naval officers' training program at the U.S. Naval Academy in Annapolis, Maryland.

Schirra flew 90 combat missions during the Korean War in the early 1950s, and spent the rest of the decade as a test pilot for the U.S. Navy. In his 2005 memoir of his space career, *The Real Space Cowboys* (co-authored with Ed Buckbee), he recounted that he had no interest in becoming part of the first U.S. astronaut-training program at NASA. Instead, he recalled, he and a few colleagues were summoned to Washington for a presentation by NASA officials. "We were listening to a pair of engineers and a psychologist describing the feeling when you're on top of a rocket in a capsule and going around the world," he wrote in the book, according to the *New York Times.* "I was immediately looking for the door, and they said, 'Not to worry, we'll send a chimpanzee first!' There's no way a test pilot would volunteer for something like that."

Despite his misgivings that the manned flight program was a circus-style exhibition designed to prove U.S. technical superiority over the Soviet Union, Schirra agreed to enter the Mercury training program in 1959 and began the intense physical training regimen with his Mercury teammates, who included John Glenn and Alan Shepard. Schirra's onboard role was to supervise the astronauts' life-support systems. In May of 1961, Shepard became the first American in space and, in October of the following year, Schirra became the fifth American in space on the Sigma 7 Mercury craft, which orbited the Earth six times in nine hours. In December of 1965, Schirra piloted the Gemini 6 spacecraft, and, on his last mission in October of 1968, he and his colleagues aboard the Apollo 7 sent back the first televised pictures of the Earth from space.

Schirra retired from NASA a year later and became an executive with a number of business ventures. The writer Tom Wolfe chronicled the men of the Mercury program in his 1979 book, *The Right Stuff,* which was adapted in 1983 as a film of the same name and featured Lance Henrikson as Schirra. Viewing the Earth from space had profoundly impacted the reluctant astronaut, and Schirra supported a variety of environmental causes for the rest of his life. In one of the last interviews he ever gave—for Earth Day of 2007, just a few days before his death—he asserted that he "left Earth three times, and found no other place to go," according to the *Washington Post*. "Please take care of Spaceship Earth."

Schirra died of a heart attack on May 3, 2007, at a hospital in La Jolla, California. He was 84 years old and is survived by his wife, Josephine, his son, Walter III, and his daughter, Suzanne. Colleagues remember him for his pranks, such as the December of 1965 mission when he briefly alarmed mission control back at NASA headquarters by announcing he had just seen an unidentified flying object with eight lesser "modules" propelling it from the front; NASA ground-control engineers realized the joke when Schirra further noted that the "pilot" of the command vehicle was wearing a red suit. On another occasion, upon returning to Earth, he was asked by reporters what goes through their minds when he and his fellow astronauts are on the launch pad about to blast into space. "You think," he replied, according to Eric Malnic at the *Los Angeles Times*, that "all these hundreds of thousands of parts were put together by the lowest bidder." **Sources:** *Chicago Tribune*, May 4, 2007, sec. 3, p. 8; *Los Angeles Times*, May 4, 2007, p. B10; *New York Times*, May 4, 2007, p. A25; *Real Space Cowboys*, Apogee, 2005; *Times* (London), May 5, 2007, p. 72; *Washington Post*, May 4, 2007, p. B7.

—*Carol Brennan*

Sidney Sheldon

Born Sidney Schechtel, February 11, 1917, in Chicago, IL; died of complications from pneumonia, January 30, 2007, in Rancho Mirage, CA. Playwright, screenwriter, producer, and author. From Broadway to Hollywood to best-selling novels, Sidney Sheldon was well known as a prolific writer in several fields. Though best known for his novels, which have been published in 51 languages, he was also an award-winning playwright and screenwriter, having received an Oscar, an Emmy, and a Tony. "At his best, Mr. Sheldon was considered a master storyteller whose novels were known for their meticulous research, swift pacing, lush settings and

cliffhanging chapters," wrote columnist Margalit Fox for the *New York Times*. In 1997, the *Guinness Book of World Records* listed Sheldon as the most widely read author in the world. He has been featured on a postage stamp in Guyana, honored with a star on the Hollywood Walk of Fame, and had a day celebrated in his honor in Chicago, Illinois, and Beverly Hills, California.

Born Sidney Schechtel, Sheldon grew up in Chicago during the Great Depression. His father was a salesman, and neither of his parents had gone past the third grade in school. Sheldon once explained that his father proudly boasted to never have read a book and that his own bookishness made him an odd addition to his family. He wrote from an early age, and at ten years of age, he made his first sale, earning ten dollars for a poem. During the Depression, he worked a number of jobs, including making deliveries for a drugstore. He suffered from bipolar disorder and, at age 17, contemplated suicide. His academic skill landed him a scholarship to Northwestern University, making him the first in his family to attend college, but he was forced to drop out in order to make enough money to get by. While working as a hatcheck attendant, he sold a song to the hotel orchestra. With the idea that he might make his fortune as a song writer, he moved to New York to try his luck. When he had no better luck there than he had in Chicago, he moved out to Hollywood.

In Hollywood, he found work at Universal Studios reading prospective films for $22 per week. In the evenings, he wrote screenplays, and though his first five were rejected, the sixth sold for $250. During World War II he was a pilot in the Army Air Corps but was discharged on grounds of a medical condition. Returning to civilian life, Sheldon eventually made a name for himself as a prolific writer of scripts for Broadway plays and musicals, and at one point he had three musicals being performed on Broadway at the same time. His success on Broadway was echoed by his successes in Hollywood: His first screenplay assignment, *The Bachelor and the Bobbysoxer*, which starred Cary Grant and Shirley Temple, won him the 1947 Academy Award for best original screenplay. He followed that movie with two other classics: *Easter Parade* with Judy Garland and Fred Astaire, and *Annie Get Your Gun*, which has also had life as a stage musical.

His prolific work did not go unnoticed. Dore Schary, who was the production head at MGM, looked at the amount of projects Sheldon had completed and decided to promote him to producer. Though Sheldon continued to make movies during the 1950s, the popularity of television was growing, so he decided to try his hand at the new medium. His first television series, *The Patty Duke Show,* ran seven years with Sheldon writing almost every episode himself, something practically unheard of in Hollywood. Sheldon continued with *I Dream of Jeannie,* a sitcom about an astronaut who discovers a genie on a deserted island and later marries her, which lasted five seasons and earned Sheldon an Emmy.

During the last season of *I Dream of Jeannie,* Sheldon had the idea for a story that seemed too psychological to work in film or on stage. According to the *Chicago Times,* he described his work day this way: "Each morning from 9 until noon, I had a secretary at the studio take all calls. I mean every single call. I wrote each morning—or rather, dictated—and then I faced the TV business." The resulting novel, *The Naked Face,* received many scorning reviews, but it also garnered the Edgar Allan Poe Award. It sold reasonably well, but Sheldon, used to the larger audience of television, pressed for more. His second novel, *The Other Side of Midnight,* featured a wronged woman as the heroine and sold more than ten million copies the year it was released. Sheldon was offered a contract for five more books, all of which became bestsellers.

Though he boasted of writing quickly, often dictating 50 pages a day, the entire writing process for Sheldon was not fast. He prided himself on doing extensive research for each of his books, traveling far and wide to the destinations he depicted in each. He interviewed former CIA chief Richard Helms for a novel involving the CIA and read 60 books on Swiss cosmetics for a novel set in the pharmaceutical industry. Sheldon also strove to keep readers turning pages, using serial techniques such as cliff hangers to move from one chapter to the next. "I love writing books," Sheldon was quoted as having said by CNN.com. "Movies are a collaborative medium, and everyone is second-guessing you. When you do a novel, you're on your own. It's a freedom that doesn't exist in any other medium."

Sheldon's two dozen novels have sold more than 300 million copies worldwide. Sheldon died of complications from pneumonia at Eisenhower Medical Center in Rancho Mirage, California. He was 89. **Sources:** *Chicago Tribune,* January 31, 2007, sec. 1, p. 11; CNN.com, http://www.cnn.com/2007/SHOWBIZ/01/30/sheldon.obit.ap/index.html (January 30, 2007); *Entertainment Weekly,* February 9, 2007, p. 20; *New York Times,* February 1, 2007, p. A21; *Times* (London), February 1, 2007, p. 61.

—Alana Joli Abbott

Anna Nicole Smith

Born Vickie Lynn Hogan, November 28, 1967, in Houston, TX; died of an accidental overdose of prescription medication, February 8, 2007, in Hollywood, FL. Model and actress. Anna Nicole Smith, who began her career as a topless dancer, pushed the boundaries of what fame meant. "It was almost like she was this explorer who went out to the edges of celebrity," Robert Thompson, director of the Center for the Study of Popular Television at Syracuse University, was quoted as saying in the *Washington Post.* "By watching what she was able to achieve, we know more about the nature of celebrity."

From dancer to model to reality-television star, Smith had a way of staying in the spotlight. She moved in and out of lawsuits, the best known based on the inheritance of J. Howard Marshall II, her husband who was 63 years her senior. Smith's life was never far from the tabloids, from her weight fluctuations to the birth of her daughter and the death of her son within a week of each other.

Born Vicki Lynn Hogan in 1967, Smith was the daughter of Donald Hogan, an itinerant laborer, and 16-year-old Virgie Tabers, who later became a deputy sheriff. Marriage between Hogan and Tabers dissolved quickly, and Smith grew up in the small town of Mexica, Texas. She idolized Marilyn Monroe and longed to leave behind small-town life but dropped out of school in ninth grade. At 17, Smith married her fellow Krispy Fried Chicken worker, 16-year-old Billy Wayne Smith. The two had a child, Daniel, but their marriage did not last.

Smith left the Krispy Fried Chicken restaurant to work at Wal-Mart, as a waitress at Red Lobster, and finally to become an exotic dancer in Houston. Already blonde and buxom, she got breast enlargement surgery to enhance her career opportunities. In Houston, she met J. Howard Marshall II, who was immediately taken with her. With encouragement from a friend, Smith submitted photos of herself to *Playboy* magazine. She appeared on the March 1992 cover and was named 1993 Playmate of the Year. Her success in *Playboy* launched her modeling career. She became the spokesperson for Guess! Jeans, and at an agent's suggestion she changed her name from Vicki to Anna Nicole. In 1994, she and Marshall, then 89 to her 26, were married.

When Marshall died 14 months later, Smith was launched into a legal battle for her husband's inheritance, fighting her stepson, E. Pierce Marshall, for a percentage of the estate. Dragged through several court systems, the suit in 2006 was finally brought, through appeal, to the Supreme Court. The case rocketed Smith into the tabloids and into the public eye.

After the successful ratings of a celebrity biography special on E! Entertainment Television, the network approached her about filming a reality television show. "I was like, 'Hmm, I love cameras.' So why not?" Smith was quoted as having said in *Entertainment Weekly*. Her life was featured in all its ups and downs for two seasons as one of the highest rated shows in the history of E!, though it was panned by critics. In the *Washington Post*, Smith was quoted as having promoted the show: "People won't be able to stop watching once they tune in. My life is a roller coaster, so hold on and enjoy the ride."

Smith's life was no less tumultuous after the television show ended. She faced a court case against TrimSpa, a weight-loss service for which she served as a spokesperson, for false advertising. She had a daughter, whose paternity was immediately questioned and taken to court, and lost her son from her first marriage to a drug overdose in the same week.

Throughout her life, Smith loved the attention she received. "I love the paparazzi," she was quoted as having said in the *New York Times*. "They take pictures and I just smile away. I've always liked attention. I didn't get it very much growing up, and I always wanted to be, you know, noticed." According to CNN.com, her estranged sister, Donna Hogan, commented, "She was a woman who was determined to get out of her small town in Texas and make a name for herself." Smith herself once told *Entertainment Weekly*, "I've made my goals. I've done everything I wanted to do." She was labeled a "postmodern pinup for a tabloid age" by Adam Bernstein and Tamara Jones of the *Washington Post*, and American Studies lecturer of the University of California at Berkeley Kathleen Moran commented in the *Chicago Tribune*, "We'd like to be able to come from nowhere like she did, and organize a coup and get it and win."

Smith had often stated that she expected to die like her idol, Marilyn Monroe, through an overdose. Tragically, that was not far from the truth. After the death of her son, she suffered severe depression and was on several medications. On February 8, 2007, she died of an accidental overdose of a sleeping medication that combined badly with her other prescriptions; she was 39. "For those of us who worked closely with Anna Nicole and got to know the woman behind the public persona, this is devastat-

ing news," senior vice president of E! Networks Jeff Shore commented on E! Online. "She was a sweet person who adored her son, made us laugh and cry with her, and who was never afraid of what others may have thought of her. There will never be another like her, and I already miss her." **Sources:** *Chicago Tribune*, February 9, 2007, sec. 1, p. 1, p. 8; CNN.com, http://www.cnn.com/2007/SHOWBIZ/ TV/02/08/anna.nicole.collapses/index.html (February 8, 2007); E! Online, http://www.eonline. com/news/article/index.jsp?uuid=692afa25-abe-423e-b051- 96a001934dfb/ (February 7, 2007), http://www.eonline.com/news/article/index. jsp?uuid=731d70ff-4c4f-4bbl-ab7c- 17498a333134/ (February 8, 2007); *Entertainment Weekly*, February 23, 2007, p. 27, p. 106; Fox.com, http://www. foxnews.com/story/0,2933,261160,00.html (March 26, 2007); *New York Times*, February 9, 2007, p. A12; *People*, February 26, 2007, pp. 102-12; *Times* (London), February 10, 2007, p. 82; *Washington Post*, February 9, 2007, p. A1, p. A9.

—*Alana Joli Abbott*

William Styron

Born June 11, 1925, in Newport News, VA; died of pneumonia, November 1, 2006, in Martha's Vineyard, MA. Author. Though William Styron won acclaim for his 1951 literary debut and several other works, including the 1979 novel *Sophie's Choice*, in his later years he was best known for chronicling his own experience with clinical depression with characteristic literary polish in *Darkness Visible: A Memoir of Madness*. In it he recounted the depths of desolation and gloom he occasionally experienced, but concluded that "whoever has been restored to health has almost always been restored to the capacity for serenity and joy, and this may be indemnity enough for having endured the despair beyond despair," he asserted in it, according to his *New York Times* obituary by Christopher Lehmann-Haupt.

Styron was born in 1925 in Newport News, Virginia, a city whose shipbuilding industry employed his engineer-father. Styron's mother was a Pennsylvania native who died when he was 13—a tragedy that shaped his life and writing—but his father hailed from an old Southern family and Styron's grandmother had even owned two slaves as a child. After completing his high school education at a private academy in Christchurch, Virginia, Styron enrolled in the Marine Corps' officers training school in the midst of World War II, studying at Duke University and being sent to war only in its final days as the United States planned for an invasion of Japan that never happened. After his return, he completed his degree at Duke in 1947 and moved to New York City, where he briefly held a job as a copy editor at a publishing house before being unceremoniously fired for reasons that included, he later said, his slovenly attire and a penchant for reading the *New York Post* at his desk.

With financial support from his father, Styron finished his first novel, *Lie Down in Darkness,* which earned a raft of critical accolades when it was published in 1951. Its story recounts the unhappy life of a young woman, Peyton Loftis, her dysfunctional Southern family, and the series of events that bring on her suicide. Styron was immediately hailed as the new literary voice of the South and the successor to novelist William Faulkner. It also earned international acclaim and led to his being awarded the Prix de Rome, a prestigious literary honor. With the award came a fellowship at the American Academy in Rome, which he took up once he finished a second stint in the Marines during the Korean War. Following that he moved to Paris and wrote his second work, *The Long March,* while joining with other American literary talents living in the city to found the *Paris Review.*

Styron married a poet he began dating while in Rome, the American Rose Burgunder, and the pair eventually returned to the United States, settled in Connecticut, and began a family. *Set This House on Fire,* his next novel, followed the travails of a set of American expatriates in Italy, but critics panned it as ponderous and bleak when it appeared in 1960. It took several more years to write a follow-up—not atypical for Styron, who spent about four hours a day at his desk—but *The Confessions of Nat Turner* returned him to literary fame when it was published in 1967. Its story was a fictionalized account of a real-life event, the 1831 slave revolt that took place near Styron's childhood home, and even won him the Pulitzer Prize for Literature in 1968, but then became the target of criticism from by prominent scholars as inauthentic and an unfair appropriation of a seminal event in African-American history.

Styron stood by his work despite the critics, an unapologetic commitment to creative license that he continued when some faulted his next work, the 1979 novel *Sophie's Choice.* Here he tackled the topic of a Polish woman struggling with her experiences as a Roman Catholic who survived a Nazi concentration camp during World War II, but at great psychic cost. It won the American Book Award for 1980 and was made into a Hollywood movie two years later that won Meryl Streep an Academy Award for the title role.

A father of four, Styron lived in Roxbury, Connecticut, and took his family to a summer home on Martha's Vineyard every year, where he became one of the Massachusetts's community's many literary celebrities. He was a social drinker for many years, but later admitted he overindulged as a way to stave off his darker moods. Once he stopped drinking altogether in the mid-1980s, his brain chemistry was thrown off-balance, and he was diagnosed as clinically depressed. He was hospitalized for a time, but recovered and became an advocate for mental-health treatment on both the lecture circuit and in his best-selling 1990 memoir *Darkness Visible.*

Styron died at the age of 81 on Martha's Vineyard, ostensibly from a bout with pneumonia, on November 1, 2006, but friends and family noted his health had been in decline for some time before that. Survivors include his wife, Rose; his son, Thomas; his daughters Alexandra, Susanna, and Paola; and eight grandchildren. Though he was not as prolific a writer as some of his contemporaries, he left behind a body of work that was unparalleled in its near-perfection as literary legacies. "No other American writer of my generation," fellow Pulitzer recipient Norman Mailer told Lehmann-Haupt in the *New York Times,* "has had so omnipresent and exquisite a sense of the elegiac." **Sources:** *Chicago Tribune,* November 2, 2006, sec. 3, p. 7; CNN.com, http://www.cnn.com/2006/SHOWBIZ/books/11/01/styron.obit.ap/index.html (November 2, 2006); *Entertainment Weekly,* November 17, 2006, p. 18; *Los Angeles Times,* November 2, 2006, p. A1, p. A17; *New York Times,* November 2, 2006, p. C17; *People,* November 20, 2006, p. 53; *Times* (London), November 3, 2006, p. 78.

—Carol Brennan

Miyoshi Umeki

Born May 8, 1929, in Otaru, Hokkaido, Japan; died of complications from cancer, August 28, 2007, in Licking, MO. Actress. Miyoshi Umeki's tragic role in the 1957 film *Sayonara* earned her an Academy Award for Best Supporting Actress, making her the first Asian performer ever to win an Oscar. Her career included stints on Broadway and on the hit ABC sitcom *The Courtship of Eddie's Father* from 1969 to 1972, but Umeki left show business for good when she became a wife and mother.

Born in 1929, Umeki came from an affluent family in Otaru, Hokkaido, Japan, where her father owned an iron factory. She was the youngest of nine children, and was rarely missed by the bustling household when she snuck off to catch performances at the local Kabuki theatre. A talented musician on several instruments, she played the harmonica, mandolin, and piano. "I just loved any sound that you could do it with instrument," as she told an interviewer for *Time* in the 1950s. She also taught herself American pop songs from imported records and, when U.S. forces occupied Japan in the aftermath of World War II, from Armed Forces Radio broadcasts.

Umeki's performing career began when her brother invited three U.S. sailors to the family home, and they began returning to spend evenings playing music together. The Americans encouraged her to sing with them, which led to a gig with a U.S. Army jazz band, and from there she was signed by RCA Japan. Her album of cover songs was recorded under the name Nancy Umeki, and she is thought to be the first Japanese singer ever to record American music. During this period of the early 1950s, Umeki spent three years either recording, giving concerts, or promoting her records.

A talent scout convinced Umeki to try her luck in the United States, and she arrived in New York City in 1955. Signed to Mercury Records, she appeared on a number of television variety programs, including *Arthur Godfrey and His Friends,* and that episode was seen by film director Joshua Logan, who offered her a role in his upcoming project. *Sayonara* was the title of a best-selling novel by James A. Michener about American military personnel in Japan. Umeki was cast as Katsumi, who falls in love with a U.S. Air Force sergeant named Joe Kelly, who was played by Red Buttons. The newlyweds encounter racism from both sides, with U.S. military officials uneasy with such unions and Japanese families vehemently opposed to their daughters' romances with foreigners. Marlon Brando also starred in the film as another Air Force member who falls in love with a Japanese woman. When Buttons' character receives orders to return to the United States and is told he is not permitted to bring his bride him, the couple come to a devastating decision. "In the film's most heartrending moment Brando discovers Buttons and Umeki's bodies entwined on a bed, after they have gone through with a suicide pact," noted Umeki's *Times* of London obituary.

Umeki won the Academy Award for Best Supporting Actress at the Oscars in March of 1958 for *Sayonara,* and appeared visibly shocked when she took the stage to accept it. "I wish somebody would help me right now," she told the audience, according to

USA Today. "I didn't expect and have nothing in my mind." Later that year she appeared on Broadway in *The Flower Drum Song,* the hit Broadway musical from Rodgers and Hammerstein. She originated the role of Mei Li, a mail-order bride, and reprised the role for the 1961 film version.

In the early 1960s Umeki had roles in the films *Cry for Happy, The Horizontal Lieutenant,* and *A Girl Named Tamiko.* From 1958 to 1967 she was married to television director Frederick "Wynn" Opie, and after they divorced she wed documentary producer and director Randall Hood. Her final role was as the housekeeper Mrs. Livingston on the sitcom *The Courtship of Eddie's Father,* which ran on ABC from 1969 to 1972. Bill Bixby played the title character, a widower with a young son (Brandon Cruz) who takes an active role in trying to find his father a new wife.

For a time, Umeki and Hood ran a film equipment rental business in the Los Angeles area, but he died in 1976. A quarter-century later, she moved from her longtime North Hollywood neighborhood to Missouri, where her son, Michael, lived with his family. She died of cancer in a nursing home in the city of Licking on August 28, 2007, at the age of 78. Survivors include her son, two grandchildren, and numerous relatives in Japan. "She was quite proud of her accomplishments," Michael Hood said, according to Umeki's *Los Angeles Times* obituary by Dennis McLellan. "She loved performing, loved what she did, but she simply wanted to retire.... She was done with show business. She wanted to get out and just lead a nice, quiet family life." **Sources:** *Los Angeles Times,* September 6, 2007, p. B8; *New York Times,* September 6, 2007, p. C16; *Time,* December 22, 1958; *Times* (London), September 20, 2007, p. 66; *USA Today,* September 5, 2007.

—Carol Brennan

Jack Valenti

Born Jack Joseph Valenti, September 5, 1921, in Houston, TX; died of complications after a stroke, April 26, 2007, in Washington, DC. Motion-picture industry executive. Jack Valenti is credited with devising the motion-picture ratings system that determines whether a film is released in American theaters as G, PG, PG-13, R, or NC-17. As the longtime president of the Motion Picture Association of America, Valenti convinced the film studios to adopt a system of ratings that would be acceptable to government authorities and sidestep a possible government regulation of content.

Of Sicilian heritage, Valenti was born in 1921 and grew up in Houston, Texas. In his late teens, he worked as an usher at a movie theater but eventually went to work in the marketing department of the Humble Oil Company, the forerunner of Exxon-Mobil, while taking night-school classes at the University of Houston. During World War II, he piloted a B-25 bomber for the U.S. Army Air Corps, and, upon returning to civilian life, earned a graduate business degree from Harvard University in 1948. In the early 1950s, he became a co-founder of a Texas advertising agency, and one of his firm's clients was the Texas Democratic Party. Through this, he came to know Lyndon B. Johnson, a Texan who was also the Senate majority leader. Johnson would soon become the running-mate for Democratic White House hopeful John F. Kennedy in 1960.

Valenti and Johnson became close friends, and, when Kennedy was elected to the White House, Valenti served as a special liaison for the vice president. He was in charge of the Texas press schedule, for example, when Kennedy and Johnson visited Dallas in November of 1963. Valenti was in the same motorcade—albeit several cars back—when Kennedy was killed by sniper fire, and is seen in photographs taken aboard Air Force One near an ashen-faced Johnson as the vice president is sworn into office as Kennedy's successor. Johnson made Valenti his special assistant, a capacity in which he served for the next three years. In 1966, Valenti became president of the Motion Picture Association of America (MPAA), a powerful consortium of studio owners in Hollywood. An influx of racy European films were prompting calls for some form of a ratings system and possibly even supervision of film content by a government agency.

Valenti hammered out a plan that was acceptable to all sides: moviegoers, the government, cinema owners, and the studios. This would become known as the MPAA's voluntary ratings code, with G denoting a general admission film—with no objectionable language nor scenes of violence or sex; followed by PG, R and X; the X rating was replaced by NC-17 some years later, for "no one under 17 admitted," and a PG-13 category was introduced in 1984. Valenti and the MPAA established a ratings board made up of a cross-section of Americans that remained, even after his death, one of the most secretive groups in American society; neither the names of its members nor their guidelines for rating films are known to anyone outside of the MPAA committee that pays them. Studios are often forced to comply with suggested edits or risk losing thousands of dollars at the box office with an NC-17 rating.

Valenti remained head of the MPAA until 2004, and was a familiar public face representing the axis of Hollywood and Washington. Known for his impeccable silver coif, custom-made suits, and eloquent turns of phrase, Valenti was a powerful figure and delivered an annual address at the Academy Awards. In addition to his ratings system, his long tenure at the MPAA was marked by several little-known lobbying coups that protected the rights of the studios. After suffering a stroke, Valenti died on April 26, 2007, at his Washington, D.C. home. Survivors include his daughters, Courtenay Lynda and Alexandra Alice, and his son, John Lyndon; all three were from his 1962 marriage to Mary Margaret Wiley, whom he had met when she worked as Johnson's secretary. Known for his admiration of the president that sometimes bordered on the extreme, Valenti was teased for a speech he gave in 1965 before the Advertising Federation of America in which he asserted, "I sleep each night a little better, a little more confidently because Lyndon Johnson is my president," according to *New York Times* David M. Halbfinger. Complaining to Johnson later about the derision he earned from that remark, the president remarked, "I don't know what you're fretting about, Jack," *Los Angeles Times* journalist James Bates quoted Johnson as telling Valenti. "Do you know how few presidential assistants say anything memorable?" **Sources:** *Chicago Tribune*, April 27, 2007, sec. 1, p. 15; CNN.com, http://www.cnn.com/2007/SHOWBIZ/Movies/04/26/valenti.obit/index.html (April 27, 2007); *Entertainment Weekly*, May 11, 2007, p. 12; *Los Angeles Times*, April 27, 2007, p. A1, p. A16; *New York Times*, April 27, 2007, p. C10.

—Carol Brennan

Porter Wagoner

Born Porter Wayne Wagoner, August 12, 1927, in South Fork, MO; died of cancer, October 28, 2007, in Nashville, TN. Musician. Country-music legend Porter Wagoner recorded dozens of songs over a 50-year career and hosted one of the longest-running country-music series in the history of television. He was also known for his duets with Dolly Parton, who was an unknown Tennessee singer when she began appearing regularly on *The Porter Wagoner Show* in 1967.

Wagoner was born in 1927 on a Missouri farm, and grew up a devotee of the Saturday-night broadcasts originating from Nashville's Grand Ole Opry. His older brother, Glenn, encouraged his burgeoning musical talents, but the month that Wagoner turned 12 his brother died of myocarditis, an inflammation of the heart. The family's tragedy was further exacerbated by their deepening financial crisis, which began during the economic downturn of the 1930s known as the Great Depression. Wagoner left school after the seventh grade to help out with the farm chores, but also managed to save $8 to buy his first guitar from Montgomery Ward department store by trapping and skinning rabbits, then selling the pelts.

In 1943, Wagoner's family was forced to sell their farm. Everything went on the auction block, including the family mule, and the funds financed a move to the city of West Plains, Missouri, where the 16 year old found a job with a local butcher. He played guitar when business was slow, and his boss liked his singing so much that he gave him the chance to perform on the local radio station as a way to advertise for the shop. Wagoner spent the next several years playing on various radio shows, and in 1954, got his break when he began appearing on *Ozark Jubilee*, the first nationally televised country-music show. He had his first hit record with the 1955 single "A Satisfied Mind," which reached No. 1 on the country-music charts and cemented his career in Nashville. As with subsequent hits, Wagoner penned songs that "often told dark tales of desperate people in stark terms that placed him in the gothic tradition of country music," noted his *Los Angeles Times* obituary.

In 1960, Wagoner debuted with his own syndicated half-hour series for television, *The Porter Wagoner Show*. There were weekly featured guests as well as Wagoner's performances with his backing band, the Wagonmasters. He continued to record Top Ten hits, and also cut a few gospel records in the 1960s with the Blackwood Brothers Quartet, which gave him the only Grammy Award wins of his career. In 1967, he became one of the first country-music stars to make a concept album—borrowed from the rock music genre of the era—with *Soul of a Convict and Other Great Prison Songs*.

That same year, Wagoner replaced his regular female performer on his television show with a 21-year-old newcomer named Dolly Parton. Their duets on the show received an enthusiastic response, and led to several hit singles, including "Burning the Midnight Oil" and "Please Don't Stop Loving Me." They also won three Country Music Association (CMA) awards together for best vocal or duo between 1968 and 1971.

Parton left the show in 1974 to pursue a solo career, and "there were lawsuits and countersuits between the two in a six-year legal tangle over business interests that produced not a few tabloid headlines," reported *New York Times* obituary writer Douglas Martin. "One reported that Mr. Wagoner's wife had found him and Ms. Parton in bed and had shot both." In an interview years later, Wagoner dismissed that rumor, though he remarked coyly, "she didn't even hit Dolly."

There were long periods during Wagoner's career when he did not perform live or record any new songs. In later songs, he wrote lyrics about time spent in a Nashville psychiatric facility, and these appeared on *The Rubber Room: The Haunting Poetic Songs of Porter Wagoner, 1966-1977*. His show ended in 1981 after a 21-year run—at the time, it was the longest-running country-music series on television—but he still appeared regularly with the Grand Ole Opry. A flamboyant performer, Wagoner was known for his trademark blond pompadour hairstyle and custom-made rhinestone two-piece suits. He was inducted into the Country Music Hall of Fame in 2002, and four years later suffered an intestinal aneurysm that nearly killed him. After a surprising recovery, he released his final record, *The Wagonmaster*, in June of 2007, and a month later performed at Madison Square Garden in New York City as the opening act for the White Stripes, the rock duo.

Wagoner was heartened by a new generation of fans of his music, some of whom had not even been born when his television series went off the air in 1981. "The young people I met backstage, some of them were 20 years old," he told a reporter a day of the White Stripes show, according to CNN.com. "They wanted to get my autograph and tell me they really liked me. If only they knew how that made me feel—like a new breath of fresh air." Wagoner died later that year on October 28, 2007, two months after his 80th birthday, from lung cancer. Survivors include his three children from his second marriage to Ruth Williams in 1946, Richard, Denise, and Debra. His plain but plaintive singing style had enriched the lives of several generations of country-music fans, and Wagoner often said that he found success only when he realized what his strengths as a performer were. "I don't try to show off a so-called beautiful voice, because I don't feel my voice is beautiful," he said, according to his *Los Angeles Times* obituary. "I believe there is a different kind of beauty, the beauty of being honest, of being yourself, of singing like you feel it." **Sources:** CNN.com, http://www.cnn.com/2007/SHOWBIZ/Music/10/29/obit.wagoner.ap/index.html (October 29, 2007);

Entertainment Weekly, November 9, 2007, pp. 11-12; *EW.com,* http://popwatch.ew.com/popwatch/ 2007/10/porter-wagoner-.html (October 29, 2007); *Los Angeles Times,* October 29, 2007, p. B7; *New York Times,* October 30, 2007, p. C19; *Times* (London), October 30, 2007, p. 61.

—Carol Brennan

Jane Wyatt

Born Jane Waddington Wyatt, August 12, 1910, in Campgaw, NJ; died October 20, 2006, in Bel Air, CA. Actress. Though actress Jane Wyatt initially turned down the role of Margaret Anderson on the 1950s TV show, *Father Knows Best,* her husband convinced her to reconsider the part. Her acceptance of the role made her an instant celebrity and the character became one of the most beloved fictional mothers in pop culture history. Wyatt won three Emmy awards for her work on *Father Knows Best.*

Wyatt was born in 1910 in Campgaw, New Jersey. Her father was Christopher Wyatt, a wealthy investment banker. Her mother was Euphemia Van Rensselaur Wyatt, a playwright, drama critic, and editor. Wyatt's childhood was one of affluence and she grew up in New York City. When she came of age, her name was added to the New York Social Register.

Wyatt entered Barnard College, where she studied history. She took a few drama courses and decided to pursue an acting career. After two years at Barnard, she dropped out to enter the apprentice school at the Berkshire Playhouse, located in Stockbridge, Massachusetts. When Wyatt began working as an understudy on Broadway, the New York Social Register removed her name. She was reinstated when she married Edgar Bethune Ward in 1935.

Wyatt made her debut in the Broadway play, *Give Me Yesterday.* She later joined the cast of the comedic play *Dinner At Eight,* and went on tour as well. Her performance led to her Hollywood debut in the 1934 film *One More River.*

Wyatt is best known for playing the role of Sondra in 1937's *Lost Horizon,* co-starring with Ron Colman. She appeared in films alongside stars such as Ethel Barrymore, Gary Cooper, and Cary Grant. Most of the characters Wyatt played were girlfriends, wives,

and mothers of upstanding leading men. The *Washington Post* referred to her as one "who specialized in playing well-bred ingénues on stage and film."

While Wyatt's television debut was not on the show *Father Knows Best,* it was the program for which she is best known. *Father Knows Best* began on radio in 1949. When the producers decided to move the program to television, they approached Wyatt to play the mother, Margaret Anderson, but she declined. She told the *Toronto Star,* as quoted in the *Los Angeles Times,* "I'd been doing a lot of live TV drama in which I was the star. I didn't want to be just a mother." After a few months, her husband convinced her to reconsider the role and she changed her mind. She joined Robert Young, who played the father, Jim Anderson. Young was the only actor from the radio program to make the switch. The children, played by Elinor Donahue, Billy Gray, and Lauren Chapin, rounded out the cast.

Father Knows Best aired on CBS in the 1954-1955 season. CBS removed the program from the schedule the following season, but so many people protested it was picked up by NBC. The show, however, ended its run on CBS in 1960, but reruns continued to air in primetime for three more years.

While many viewers during the 1950s enjoyed the television show, critics claimed it was not a realistic portrayal of family life. The show even came under fire later in the 20th century by feminists who thought the Margaret Anderson character was always subordinate to her husband; Wyatt disagreed. According to the *Los Angeles Times,* she stated "She was the power behind the throne. She helped her husband out. Mother always knew best, too."

In addition to *Father Knows Best,* two reunion TV movies aired in the 1970s, *The Father Knows Best Reunion,* and *Father Knows Best: Home for Christmas.* The show has aired around the world. Wyatt found out how popular the show was in Peru, when she found herself surrounded by fans. The sitcom aired there as *Papa Lo Sabe Todo.*

Though she was a regular in film, Wyatt was happy to find work in television and on stage when she was blacklisted for protesting the House Un-American Activities Committee hearings. She also came under fire for being linked to the Lab Theater when she performed in the plays *Volpone* and *The Cherry Orchard.* Wyatt was also labeled prematurely anti-fascist because she spoke against Adolf Hitler before the United States had joined World War II.

Wyatt continued working and she guest-starred on the TV series, *Star Trek,* where she portrayed half-Vulcan Spock's human mother. She reprised the role for the film *Star Trek IV: The Voyage Home*. Wyatt continued doing regional theater and made guest appearances on television shows. One of her last roles was playing the wife of Dr. Daniel Auschlander on the hospital serial, *St. Elsewhere*. Wyatt's work on *Father Knows Best* garnered her three Emmy awards. She also received a citation from the California Assembly. The show itself won the Sylvania Award for Excellence.

In 1990 Wyatt said in an interview, according to *Entertainment Weekly*, that she had little in common with her most famous character. "I never vacuumed at home wearing my pearls. In fact, I never vacuumed at all; I was always working at the studio." She died in her home in Bel Air, California, on October 20, 2006. She was 96. Her husband preceded her in death, and she is survived by two sons, three grandchildren, and five great-grandchildren. **Sources:** *Chicago Tribune*, October 23, 2006, sec. 1, p. 11; *Entertainment Weekly*, November 3, 2006, p. 23; *Los Angeles Times*, October 23, 2006, p. B11; *New York Times*, October 23, 2006, p. A22; *Times* (London), October 26, 2006, p. 76; *Washington Post*, October 23, 2006, p. B4.

—*Ashyia N. Henderson*

Jane Wyman

Born Sarah Jane Mayfield, January 5, 1917, in St. Joseph, MO; died of natural causes, September 10, 2007, in Rancho Mirage, CA. Actress. Performing through six decades in Hollywood and on television, Jane Wyman was an Oscar-winning actress best known for her role as a deaf-mute girl who was abused and raped in *Johnny Belinda*. Often cast in the role of a long-suffering woman who stubbornly survives against the odds, Wyman was internationally known for her character, Angela Channing, which she played for nearly a decade on the soap opera *Falcon Crest*.

Wyman is also known as the first ex-wife of an American president. Married to Ronald Reagan when both were actors, Wyman was known for her silence on their relationship after they were divorced, and walked out of interviews that sought gossip about her ex-husband. "It's not because I'm bitter or because I don't agree with him politically," she explained in an interview, quoted on CNN.com. "But it's bad taste to talk about ex-husbands and ex-wives, that's all. Also, I don't know a damn thing about politics."

Despite her high profile, many of the details of Wyman's early life are hard to pin down. She claimed to have been born in 1914, but later sources have said that she was actually born in 1917, and that her false birth date was given so that she could get married at only 16 years of age. However, details on this first marriage (which ended in divorce) are also elusive. She may have also lied about her age in order to get work in Hollywood while still a minor: Her first film was produced in 1932.

Born Sarah Jane Mayfield, Wyman was the child of Manning Mayfield and Gladys Christian, who divorced when Wyman was four. When Wyman's father died of pneumonia, Wyman was entrusted with neighbors, the Fulks, who raised her. For years, she went by Sarah Jane Fulks, and when her adoptive father died when Wyman was eleven, she moved with the Fulks to Los Angeles.

Wyman returned to Missouri for school, but she moved back to Los Angeles where she wanted to make it in Hollywood, dying her hair blonde and working a variety of jobs while hoping to win a role in a film. She secured a position as a chorus girl and received a role as a dancer in *The Kid from Spain*. This was the beginning of her regular work in Hollywood, and though Wyman battled with shyness, she covered her insecurities with bravado. "Were all the other dancers prettier? Never mind," she once said, quoted in the *Times* of London. "I covered up by becoming the cockiest of all, by talking the loudest, laughing the longest, and wearing the curliest, most blatantly false eyelashes in Hollywood." Her attitude eventually won her a position as a contract actress at Warners, where, appearing as Jane Wyman, she performed as fast-talking lady reporters and sidekicks.

In 1938, Wyman appeared opposite Reagan in *Brother Rat,* and she and Reagan became a couple after she finalized her divorce to her second husband in 1939. They were Hollywood darlings, popularized by gossip columnist Louella Parsons. Reagan's career soared while Wyman remained a B-movie actress, and the two married in 1940. They had one daughter, adopted a son, and lost a second daughter to premature birth. In 1945, while Reagan was in the army during World War II, Wyman had her first breakthrough as a serious actress, playing the part of the girlfriend to an alcoholic in *The Lost Weekend*. In her next film, Wyman played her first Oscar nominated role in *The Yearling*.

As Wyman's career progressed, her relationship with Reagan began to fall apart, particularly after she was cast in *Johnny Belinda*. Reagan was becoming more interested in politics, and Wyman was completely ambivalent. Instead, she focused on her role as a deaf-mute girl, seldom speaking at home and learning sign language. "I learned the all-important thing: A deaf person hears with her eyes, just as a blind person sees with his ears," Wyman was quoted as having said in the *Los Angeles Times*. By the time the film came out, she and Reagan had finalized their divorce. *Johnny Belinda* received 12 Oscar nominations, and Wyman received the Oscar for best actress. Her speech was short; according to the *Times* of London she said, "I won this award for keeping my mouth shut, so I think I'll do it again now."

Several other Oscar nominations followed as Wyman took further roles of women under adversity. In 1952, Wyman married Fred Karger, Marilyn Monroe's sometimes boyfriend, and made the move to television. She and Karger divorced in 1954, remarried in 1963, and were divorced again, but Wyman's relationship with television was more stable. From 1955 through 1958, she was the host of *Fireside Theater*, which became *The Jane Wyman Theater*, a drama series that featured a short movie, often starring Wyman, every week. She left that position due to the enormous amount of work required, filming additional movies and television appearances throughout the 1960s and 1970s. Her last film, *How to Commit Marriage* with Bob Hope, appeared in 1969.

In 1981, Wyman took a role completely against her previous type: She became the controlling matriarch of *Falcon Crest*, a drama and soap opera that had similar themes to *Dallas*. On taking the role, she summed up her career in an interview, quoted at CNN.com: "I've been through four different cycles in pictures: the brassy blonde, then came the musicals, the high dramas, then the inauguration of television." When the show went off the air in 1990, Wyman largely retired from public life. She put her efforts into her paintings, many of which sold through a California gallery, and focused on volunteer work for the Arthritis Foundation.

Wyman "was not only a fine actress but a darling, dear lady," Paramount producer A. C. Lyles told the *Los Angeles Times*. "I think she was an inspiration to all young actresses because she started as a minor actress and worked her way through the ranks to become not only one of Hollywood's prominent leading ladies but an Academy Award winner." Over the course of her 54-year career, Wyman made 86 films and 350 television episodes. After years of failing health, she died in her home in Rancho Mirage, California. Wyman is survived by her son, Michael Reagan. **Sources:** CNN.com, http://www.cnn.com/2007/SHOWBIZ/Movies/09/10/obit.wyman.ap/index.html (September 10, 2007); *Entertainment Weekly*, September 21, 2007, p. 20; *Los Angeles Times*, September 11, 2007, p. B8; *New York Times*, September 11, 2007, p. C11; *Times* (London), September 11, 2007.

—Alana Joli Abbott

Cumulative Nationality Index

This index lists all newsmakers alphabetically under their respective nationalities. Indexes in softbound issues allow access to the current year's entries; indexes in annual hardbound volumes are cumulative, covering the entire *Newsmakers* series.

Listee names are followed by a year and issue number; thus **1996**:3 indicates that an entry on that individual appears in both 1996, Issue 3, and the 1996 cumulation. For access to newsmakers appearing earlier than the current softbound issue, see the previous year's cumulation.

AFGHAN
Karzai, Hamid **2002**:3

ALGERIAN
Zeroual, Liamine **1996**:2

AMERICAN
Aaliyah **2001**:3
Abbey, Edward
Obituary **1989**:3
Abbott, George
Obituary **1995**:3
Abbott, Jim **1988**:3
Abdul, Paula **1990**:3
Abercrombie, Josephine **1987**:2
Abernathy, Ralph
Obituary **1990**:3
Abraham, S. Daniel **2003**:3
Abraham, Spencer **1991**:4
Abrams, Elliott **1987**:1
Abrams, J. J. **2007**:3
Abramson, Lyn **1986**:3
Abzug, Bella **1998**:2
Achtenberg, Roberta **1993**:4
Ackerman, Will **1987**:4
Acuff, Roy
Obituary **1993**:2
Adair, Red **1987**:3
Adams, Amy **2008**:4
Adams, Don
Obituary **2007**:1
Adams, Patch **1999**:2
Adams, Scott **1996**:4
Adams, Yolanda **2008**:2
Adams-Geller, Paige **2006**:4
Addams, Charles
Obituary **1989**:1
Adler, Jonathan **2006**:3
Adu, Freddy **2005**:3
Affleck, Ben **1999**:1
AFI **2007**:3
Agassi, Andre **1990**:2
Agatston, Arthur **2005**:1
Agee, Tommie
Obituary **2001**:4

Agnew, Spiro Theodore
Obituary **1997**:1
Aguilera, Christina **2000**:4
Aiello, Danny **1990**:4
Aikman, Troy **1994**:2
Ailes, Roger **1989**:3
Ailey, Alvin **1989**:2
Obituary **1990**:2
Ainge, Danny **1987**:1
Akers, John F. **1988**:3
Akers, Michelle **1996**:1
Akin, Phil
Brief Entry **1987**:3
Alba, Jessica **2001**:2
Albee, Edward **1997**:1
Albert, Eddie
Obituary **2006**:3
Albert, Marv **1994**:3
Albert, Stephen **1986**:1
Albom, Mitch **1999**:3
Albrecht, Chris **2005**:4
Albright, Madeleine **1994**:3
Alda, Robert
Obituary **1986**:3
Alexander, Jane **1994**:2
Alexander, Jason **1993**:3
Alexander, Lamar **1991**:2
Alexie, Sherman **1998**:4
Ali, Laila **2001**:2
Ali, Muhammad **1997**:2
Alioto, Joseph L.
Obituary **1998**:3
Allaire, Jeremy **2006**:4
Allaire, Paul **1995**:1
Allard, Linda **2003**:2
Allen, Bob **1992**:4
Allen, Debbie **1998**:2
Allen, Joan **1998**:1
Allen, John **1992**:1
Allen, Mel
Obituary **1996**:4
Allen, Ray **2002**:1
Allen, Steve
Obituary **2001**:2
Allen, Tim **1993**:1
Allen, Woody **1994**:1

Allen Jr., Ivan
Obituary **2004**:3
Alley, Kirstie **1990**:3
Allred, Gloria **1985**:2
Allyson, June
Obituary **2007**:3
Alsop, Marin **2008**:3
Alter, Hobie
Brief Entry **1985**:1
Altman, Robert **1993**:2
Altman, Sidney **1997**:2
Alvarez, Aida **1999**:2
Ambrose, Stephen **2002**:3
Ameche, Don
Obituary **1994**:2
Amory, Cleveland
Obituary **1999**:2
Amos, Tori **1995**:1
Amos, Wally **2000**:1
Amsterdam, Morey
Obituary **1997**:1
Anastas, Robert
Brief Entry **1985**:2
Ancier, Garth **1989**:1
Anderson, Brad **2007**:3
Anderson, Gillian **1997**:1
Anderson, Harry **1988**:2
Anderson, Laurie **2000**:2
Anderson, Marion
Obituary **1993**:4
Anderson, Poul
Obituary **2002**:3
Anderson, Tom and Chris DeWolfe **2007**:2
Andreessen, Marc **1996**:2
Andrews, Lori B. **2005**:3
Andrews, Maxene
Obituary **1996**:2
Angelos, Peter **1995**:4
Angelou, Maya **1993**:4
Angier, Natalie **2000**:3
Aniston, Jennifer **2000**:3
Annenberg, Walter **1992**:3
Anthony, Earl
Obituary **2002**:3
Anthony, Marc **2000**:3
Antonini, Joseph **1991**:2

Bundy, McGeorge
  Obituary **1997**:1
Bundy, William P.
  Obituary **2001**:2
Bunshaft, Gordon **1989**:3
  Obituary **1991**:1
Burck, Wade
  Brief Entry **1986**:1
Burger, Warren E.
  Obituary **1995**:4
Burk, Martha **2004**:1
Burnett, Carol **2000**:3
Burnison, Chantal Simone **1988**:3
Burns, Charles R.
  Brief Entry **1988**:1
Burns, Edward **1997**:1
Burns, George
  Obituary **1996**:3
Burns, Ken **1995**:2
Burns, Robin **1991**:2
Burr, Donald Calvin **1985**:3
Burroughs, William S. **1994**:2
Burroughs, William S.
  Obituary **1997**:4
Burrows, James **2005**:3
Burstyn, Ellen **2001**:4
Burton, Jake **2007**:1
Burton, Tim **1993**:1
Burum, Stephen H.
  Brief Entry **1987**:2
Buscaglia, Leo
  Obituary **1998**:4
Buscemi, Steve **1997**:4
Busch, August A. III **1988**:2
Busch, August Anheuser, Jr.
  Obituary **1990**:2
Busch, Charles **1998**:3
Busch, Kurt **2006**:1
Bush, Barbara **1989**:3
Bush, George W., Jr. **1996**:4
Bush, Jeb **2003**:1
Bush, Millie **1992**:1
Bushnell, Candace **2004**:2
Bushnell, Nolan **1985**:1
Buss, Jerry **1989**:3
Butcher, Susan **1991**:1
Butler, Brett **1995**:1
Butler, Octavia E. **1999**:3
Butterfield, Paul
  Obituary **1987**:3
Buttons, Red
  Obituary **2007**:3
Bynes, Amanda **2005**:1
Caan, James **2004**:4
Cabot, Meg **2008**:4
Caen, Herb
  Obituary **1997**:4
Caesar, Adolph
  Obituary **1986**:3
Cage, John
  Obituary **1993**:1
Cage, Nicolas **1991**:1
Cagney, James
  Obituary **1986**:2
Cain, Herman **1998**:3
Calhoun, Rory
  Obituary **1999**:4
Caliguiri, Richard S.
  Obituary **1988**:3
Callaway, Ely
  Obituary **2002**:3

Calloway, Cab
  Obituary **1995**:2
Calloway, D. Wayne **1987**:3
Cameron, David
  Brief Entry **1988**:1
Cammermeyer, Margarethe **1995**:2
Campanella, Roy
  Obituary **1994**:1
Campbell, Bebe Moore **1996**:2
Campbell, Ben Nighthorse **1998**:1
Campbell, Bill **1997**:1
Canfield, Alan B.
  Brief Entry **1986**:3
Cannon, Nick **2006**:4
Cantrell, Ed
  Brief Entry **1985**:3
Caplan, Arthur L. **2000**:2
Capriati, Jennifer **1991**:1
Caras, Roger
  Obituary **2002**:1
Caray, Harry **1988**:3
  Obituary **1998**:3
Carcaterra, Lorenzo **1996**:1
Card, Andrew H., Jr. **2003**:2
Carell, Steve **2006**:4
Carey, Drew **1997**:4
Carey, Mariah **1991**:3
Carey, Ron **1993**:3
Carlin, George **1996**:3
Carlino, Cristina **2008**:4
Carlisle, Belinda **1989**:3
Carlson, Richard **2002**:1
Carmona, Richard **2003**:2
Carnahan, Jean **2001**:2
Carnahan, Mel
  Obituary **2001**:2
Carney, Art
  Obituary **2005**:1
Carpenter, Mary-Chapin **1994**:1
Carradine, John
  Obituary **1989**:2
Carson, Ben **1998**:2
Carson, Johnny
  Obituary **2006**:1
Carson, Lisa Nicole **1999**:3
Carter, Amy **1987**:4
Carter, Benny
  Obituary **2004**:3
Carter, Billy
  Obituary **1989**:1
Carter, Chris **2000**:1
Carter, Gary **1987**:1
Carter, Jimmy **1995**:1
Carter, Joe **1994**:2
Carter, Nell
  Obituary **2004**:2
Carter, Ron **1987**:3
Carter, Rubin **2000**:3
Carter, Stephen L. **2008**:2
Carter, Vince **2001**:4
Caruso, David **1994**:3
Carver, Raymond
  Obituary **1989**:1
Carvey, Dana **1994**:1
Case, Steve **1995**:4 **1996**:4
Casey, William
  Obituary **1987**:3
Cash, Johnny **1995**:3
Cash, June Carter
  Obituary **2004**:2
Cassavetes, John
  Obituary **1989**:2

Cassidy, Mike **2006**:1
Cassini, Oleg
  Obituary **2007**:2
Castelli, Leo
  Obituary **2000**:1
Castellucci, Cecil **2008**:3
Castillo, Ana **2000**:4
Catlett, Elizabeth **1999**:3
Cattrall, Kim **2003**:3
Caulfield, Joan
  Obituary **1992**:1
Cavazos, Lauro F. **1989**:2
Caviezel, Jim **2005**:3
Centrello, Gina **2008**:3
Cerf, Vinton G. **1999**:2
Chabon, Michael **2002**:1
Chaing Kai-Shek, Madame
  Obituary **2005**:1
Chamberlain, Joba **2008**:3
Chamberlain, Wilt
  Obituary **2000**:2
Chamberlin, Wendy **2002**:4
Chancellor, John
  Obituary **1997**:1
Chaney, John **1989**:1
Channing, Stockard **1991**:3
Chao, Elaine L. **2007**:3
Chapman, Tracy **1989**:2
Chappell, Tom **2002**:3
Chappelle, Dave **2005**:3
Charles, Ray
  Obituary **2005**:3
Charron, Paul **2004**:1
Chase, Chevy **1990**:1
Chast, Roz **1992**:4
Chastain, Brandi **2001**:3
Chatham, Russell **1990**:1
Chaudhari, Praveen **1989**:4
Chavez, Cesar
  Obituary **1993**:4
Chavez, Linda **1999**:3
Chavez-Thompson, Linda **1999**:1
Chavis, Benjamin **1993**:4
Cheadle, Don **2002**:1
Cheatham, Adolphus 'Doc'
  Obituary **1997**:4
Cheek, James Edward
  Brief Entry **1987**:1
Chen, Steve and Chad Hurley **2007**:2
Chenault, Kenneth I. **1999**:3
Cheney, Dick **1991**:3
Cheney, Lynne V. **1990**:4
Cher **1993**:1
Chesney, Kenny **2008**:2
Chia, Sandro **1987**:2
Chihuly, Dale **1995**:2
Chiklis, Michael **2003**:3
Child, Julia **1999**:4
Chisholm, Shirley
  Obituary **2006**:1
Chittister, Joan D. **2002**:2
Chizen, Bruce **2004**:2
Cho, Margaret **1995**:2
Chouinard, Yvon **2002**:2
Christopher, Warren **1996**:3
Chu, Paul C.W. **1988**:2
Chung, Connie **1988**:4
Chyna **2001**:4
Cisneros, Henry **1987**:2
Claiborne, Liz **1986**:3
Clancy, Tom **1998**:4

Dawson, Rosario **2007**:2
Day, Dennis
  Obituary **1988**:4
Day, Pat **1995**:2
Dean, Howard **2005**:4
Dean, Laura **1989**:4
Dearden, John Cardinal
  Obituary **1988**:4
DeBartolo, Edward J., Jr. **1989**:3
DeCarava, Roy **1996**:3
De Cordova, Frederick **1985**:2
Dee, Sandra
  Obituary **2006**:2
Deen, Paula **2008**:3
Dees, Morris **1992**:1
DeGeneres, Ellen **1995**:3
de Kooning, Willem **1994**:4
  Obituary **1997**:3
De La Hoya, Oscar **1998**:2
Delany, Dana **2008**:4
Delany, Sarah
  Obituary **1999**:3
de la Renta, Oscar **2005**:4
DeLay, Tom **2000**:1
Dell, Michael **1996**:2
DeLuca, Fred **2003**:3
De Matteo, Drea **2005**:2
DeMayo, Neda **2006**:2
de Mille, Agnes
  Obituary **1994**:2
Deming, W. Edwards **1992**:2
  Obituary **1994**:2
Demme, Jonathan **1992**:4
Dempsey, Patrick **2006**:1
De Niro, Robert **1999**:1
Dennehy, Brian **2002**:1
Dennis, Sandy
  Obituary **1992**:4
Denver, Bob
  Obituary **2006**:4
Denver, John
  Obituary **1998**:1
De Palma, Brian **2007**:3
de Passe, Suzanne **1990**:4
Depp, Johnny **1991**:3
Dern, Laura **1992**:3
Dershowitz, Alan **1992**:1
Desormeaux, Kent **1990**:2
Destiny's Child **2001**:3
Deutch, John **1996**:4
Devine, John M. **2003**:2
DeVita, Vincent T., Jr. **1987**:3
De Vito, Danny **1987**:1
Diamond, I.A.L.
  Obituary **1988**:3
Diamond, Selma
  Obituary **1985**:2
Diaz, Cameron **1999**:1
DiBello, Paul
  Brief Entry **1986**:4
DiCaprio, Leonardo Wilhelm **1997**:2
Dickerson, Nancy H.
  Obituary **1998**:2
Dickey, James
  Obituary **1998**:2
Dickinson, Brian **1998**:2
Dickinson, Janice **2005**:2
Diebenkorn, Richard
  Obituary **1993**:4
Diemer, Walter E.
  Obituary **1998**:2
Diesel, Vin **2004**:1

DiFranco, Ani **1997**:1
Diggs, Taye **2000**:1
Diller, Barry **1991**:1
Diller, Elizabeth and Ricardo
  Scofidio **2004**:3
Dillon, Matt **1992**:2
DiMaggio, Joe
  Obituary **1999**:3
Di Meola, Al **1986**:4
Dinkins, David N. **1990**:2
Disney, Lillian
  Obituary **1998**:3
Disney, Roy E. **1986**:3
Divine
  Obituary **1988**:3
Dixie Chicks **2001**:2
Dr. Demento **1986**:1
Dr. Dre **1994**:3
Doctorow, E. L. **2007**:1
Doherty, Shannen **1994**:2
Dolan, Terry **1985**:2
Dolan, Tom **2001**:2
Dolby, Ray Milton
  Brief Entry **1986**:1
Dole, Bob **1994**:2
Dole, Elizabeth Hanford **1990**:1
Dolenz, Micky **1986**:4
Domar, Alice **2007**:1
Donahue, Tim **2004**:3
Donahue, Troy
  Obituary **2002**:4
Donghia, Angelo R.
  Obituary **1985**:2
Donnellan, Nanci **1995**:2
Dorati, Antal
  Obituary **1989**:2
Dorris, Michael
  Obituary **1997**:3
Dorsey, Thomas A.
  Obituary **1993**:3
Doubleday, Nelson, Jr. **1987**:1
Douglas, Buster **1990**:4
Douglas, Marjory Stoneman **1993**:1
  Obituary **1998**:4
Douglas, Michael **1986**:2
Douglas, Mike
  Obituary **2007**:4
Dove, Rita **1994**:3
Dowd, Maureen Brigid **1997**:1
Downey, Bruce **2003**:1
Downey, Morton, Jr. **1988**:4
Downey, Robert, Jr. **2007**:1
Dravecky, Dave **1992**:1
Drescher, Fran **1995**:3
Drexler, Clyde **1992**:4
Drexler, Millard S. **1990**:3
Dreyfuss, Richard **1996**:3
Drysdale, Don
  Obituary **1994**:1
Duarte, Henry **2003**:3
Dubrof, Jessica
  Obituary **1996**:4
Duchovny, David **1998**:3
Dudley, Jane
  Obituary **2002**:4
Duff, Hilary **2004**:4
Duffy, Karen **1998**:1
Dukakis, Michael **1988**:3
Dukakis, Olympia **1996**:4
Duke, David **1990**:2
Duke, Doris
  Obituary **1994**:2

Duke, Red
  Brief Entry **1987**:1
Duncan, Tim **2000**:1
Duncan, Todd
  Obituary **1998**:3
Dunham, Carroll **2003**:4
Dunham, Katherine
  Obituary **2007**:2
Dunlap, Albert J. **1997**:2
Dunne, Dominick **1997**:1
Dunst, Kirsten **2001**:4
Dupri, Jermaine **1999**:1
Durocher, Leo
  Obituary **1992**:2
Durrell, Gerald
  Obituary **1995**:3
Duval, David **2000**:3
Duvall, Camille
  Brief Entry **1988**:1
Duvall, Robert **1999**:3
Dworkin, Andrea
  Obituary **2006**:2
Dykstra, Lenny **1993**:4
Dylan, Bob **1998**:1
Earle, Sylvia **2001**:1
Earnhardt, Dale
  Obituary **2001**:4
Earnhardt, Dale, Jr. **2004**:4
Eastwood, Clint **1993**:3
Eaton, Robert J. **1994**:2
Eazy-E
  Obituary **1995**:3
Eberhart, Richard
  Obituary **2006**:3
Ebersole, Christine **2007**:2
Ebert, Roger **1998**:3
Ebsen, Buddy
  Obituary **2004**:3
Eckert, Robert A. **2002**:3
Ecko, Marc **2006**:3
Eckstine, Billy
  Obituary **1993**:4
Edelman, Marian Wright **1990**:4
Ederle, Gertrude
  Obituary **2005**:1
Edmonds, Kenneth 'Babyface' **1995**
  :3
Edwards, Bob **1993**:2
Edwards, Harry **1989**:4
Efron, Zac **2008**:2
Eggers, Dave **2001**:3
Ehrlichman, John
  Obituary **1999**:3
Eilberg, Amy
  Brief Entry **1985**:3
Eisenman, Peter **1992**:4
Eisenstaedt, Alfred
  Obituary **1996**:1
Eisner, Michael **1989**:2
Eisner, Will
  Obituary **2006**:1
Elders, Joycelyn **1994**:1
Eldridge, Roy
  Obituary **1989**:3
Elfman, Jenna **1999**:4
Ellerbee, Linda **1993**:3
Elliott, Missy **2003**:4
Ellis, Perry
  Obituary **1986**:3
Ellison, Larry **2004**:2
Ellison, Ralph
  Obituary **1994**:4

Fulghum, Robert **1996**:1
Funt, Allen
  Obituary **2000**:1
Furman, Rosemary
  Brief Entry **1986**:4
Furyk, Jim **2004**:2
Futrell, Mary Hatwood **1986**:1
Futter, Ellen V. **1995**:1
Gabor, Eva
  Obituary **1996**:1
Gacy, John Wayne
  Obituary **1994**:4
Gaines, William M.
  Obituary **1993**:1
Gale, Robert Peter **1986**:4
Galindo, Rudy **2001**:2
Gallagher, Peter **2004**:3
Gallo, Robert **1991**:1
Galvin, John R. **1990**:1
Galvin, Martin
  Brief Entry **1985**:3
Gandolfini, James **2001**:3
Gandy, Kim **2002**:2
Ganzi, Victor **2003**:3
Garbo, Greta
  Obituary **1990**:3
Garcia, Andy **1999**:3
Garcia, Cristina **1997**:4
Garcia, Jerry **1988**:3
  Obituary **1996**:1
Garcia, Joe
  Brief Entry **1986**:4
Gardner, Ava Lavinia
  Obituary **1990**:2
Gardner, David and Tom **2001**:4
Gardner, Randy **1997**:2
Garner, Jennifer **2003**:1
Garnett, Kevin **2000**:3
Garofalo, Janeane **1996**:4
Garr, Teri **1988**:4
Garrison, Jim
  Obituary **1993**:2
Garson, Greer
  Obituary **1996**:4
Garzarelli, Elaine M. **1992**:3
Gates, Bill **1993**:3 **1987**:4
Gates, Robert M. **1992**:2
Gathers, Hank
  Obituary **1990**:3
Gault, Willie **1991**:2
Gayle, Helene **2008**:2
Gebbie, Kristine **1994**:2
Geffen, David **1985**:3 **1997**:3
Gehry, Frank O. **1987**:1
Geisel, Theodor
  Obituary **1992**:2
Gellar, Sarah Michelle **1999**:3
Geller, Margaret Joan **1998**:2
Gentine, Lou **2008**:2
George, Elizabeth **2003**:3
Gephardt, Richard **1987**:3
Gerba, Charles **1999**:4
Gerberding, Julie **2004**:1
Gere, Richard **1994**:3
Gergen, David **1994**:1
Gerstner, Lou **1993**:4
Gertz, Alison
  Obituary **1993**:2
Gerulaitis, Vitas
  Obituary **1995**:1
Getz, Stan
  Obituary **1991**:4

Giamatti, A. Bartlett **1988**:4
  Obituary **1990**:1
Giannulli, Mossimo **2002**:3
Gibson, Althea
  Obituary **2004**:4
Gibson, Kirk **1985**:2
Gibson, William Ford, III **1997**:2
Gifford, Kathie Lee **1992**:2
Gilbert, Walter **1988**:3
Gilford, Jack
  Obituary **1990**:4
Gill, Vince **1995**:2
Gillespie, Dizzy
  Obituary **1993**:2
Gillespie, Marcia **1999**:4
Gillett, George **1988**:1
Gilruth, Robert
  Obituary **2001**:1
Gingrich, Newt **1991**:1 **1997**:3
Ginsberg, Allen
  Obituary **1997**:3
Ginsberg, Ian **2006**:4
Ginsburg, Ruth Bader **1993**:4
Gioia, Dana **2008**:4
Gish, Lillian
  Obituary **1993**:4
Giuliani, Rudolph **1994**:2
Glaser, Elizabeth
  Obituary **1995**:2
Glass, David **1996**:1
Glass, Ira **2008**:2
Glass, Philip **1991**:4
Glasser, Ira **1989**:1
Glaus, Troy **2003**:3
Glazman, Lev and Alina Roytberg
  2007:4
Gleason, Jackie
  Obituary **1987**:4
Glenn, John **1998**:3
Gless, Sharon **1989**:3
Glover, Danny **1998**:4
Glover, Savion **1997**:1
Gobel, George
  Obituary **1991**:4
Gober, Robert **1996**:3
Goetz, Bernhard Hugo **1985**:3
Goizueta, Roberto **1996**:1
  Obituary **1998**:1
Gold, Thomas
  Obituary **2005**:3
Goldberg, Gary David **1989**:4
Goldberg, Leonard **1988**:4
Goldberg, Whoopi **1993**:3
Goldblum, Jeff **1988**:1 **1997**:3
Golden, Thelma **2003**:3
Goldhaber, Fred
  Brief Entry **1986**:3
Goldman, William **2001**:1
Goldman-Rakic, Patricia **2002**:4
Goldwater, Barry
  Obituary **1998**:4
Gomez, 'Lefty'
  Obituary **1989**:3
Gooden, Dwight **1985**:2
Gooding, Cuba, Jr. **1997**:3
Goodman, Benny
  Obituary **1986**:3
Goodman, Drew and Myra **2007**:4
Goodman, John **1990**:3
Goody, Joan **1990**:2
Goody, Sam
  Obituary **1992**:1

Gorder, Genevieve **2005**:4
Gordon, Dexter **1987**:1 **1990**:4
Gordon, Gale
  Obituary **1996**:1
Gordon, Jeff **1996**:1
Gordon, Michael **2005**:1
Gore, Albert, Jr. **1993**:2
Gore, Albert, Sr.
  Obituary **1999**:2
Gore, Tipper **1985**:4
Goren, Charles H.
  Obituary **1991**:4
Gorman, Leon
  Brief Entry **1987**:1
Gossett, Louis, Jr. **1989**:3
Gottlieb, William
  Obituary **2007**:2
Gould, Chester
  Obituary **1985**:2
Gould, Gordon **1987**:1
Gould, Stephen Jay
  Obituary **2003**:3
Goulet, Robert
  Obituary **2008**:4
Grace, J. Peter **1990**:2
Grace, Topher **2005**:4
Graden, Brian **2004**:2
Grafton, Sue **2000**:2
Graham, Bill **1986**:4
  Obituary **1992**:2
Graham, Billy **1992**:1
Graham, Donald **1985**:4
Graham, Heather **2000**:1
Graham, Katharine Meyer **1997**:3
  Obituary **2002**:3
Graham, Lauren **2003**:4
Graham, Martha
  Obituary **1991**:4
Gramm, Phil **1995**:2
Grammer, Kelsey **1995**:1
Granato, Cammi **1999**:3
Grandin, Temple **2006**:1
Grange, Red
  Obituary **1991**:3
Grant, Amy **1985**:4
Grant, Cary
  Obituary **1987**:1
Grant, Charity
  Brief Entry **1985**:2
Grant, Rodney A. **1992**:1
Graves, Michael **2000**:1
Graves, Nancy **1989**:3
Gray, Hanna **1992**:4
Gray, John **1995**:3
Gray, Macy **2002**:1
Gray, Spalding
  Obituary **2005**:2
Grazer, Brian **2006**:4
Graziano, Rocky
  Obituary **1990**:4
Green, Richard R. **1988**:3
Greenberg, Hank
  Obituary **1986**:4
Greenberg, Robert **2003**:2
Green Day **1995**:4
Greene, Brian **2003**:4
Greenspan, Alan **1992**:2
Greenwald, Julie **2008**:1
Gregorian, Vartan **1990**:3
Gregory, Cynthia **1990**:2
Gregory, Dick **1990**:3
Gregory, Rogan **2008**:2

McGowan, William **1985**:2
McGowan, William G.
  Obituary **1993**:1
McGrath, Judy **2006**:1
McGraw, Phil **2005**:2
McGraw, Tim **2000**:3
McGraw, Tug
  Obituary **2005**:1
McGreevey, James **2005**:2
McGruder, Aaron **2005**:4
McGuire, Dorothy
  Obituary **2002**:4
McGwire, Mark **1999**:1
McIntyre, Richard
  Brief Entry **1986**:2
McKee, Lonette **1996**:1
McKenna, Terence **1993**:3
McKinney, Cynthia A. **1997**:1
McKinney, Stewart B.
  Obituary **1987**:4
McLaughlin, Betsy **2004**:3
McMahon, Jim **1985**:4
McMahon, Vince, Jr. **1985**:4
McMillan, Terry **1993**:2
McMillen, Tom **1988**:4
McMurtry, James **1990**:2
McMurtry, Larry **2006**:4
McNamara, Robert S. **1995**:4
McNealy, Scott **1999**:4
McNerney, W. James **2006**:3
McRae, Carmen
  Obituary **1995**:2
McSally, Martha **2002**:4
McVeigh, Timothy
  Obituary **2002**:2
Meadows, Audrey
  Obituary **1996**:3
Meier, Richard **2001**:4
Meisel, Steven **2002**:4
Mellinger, Frederick
  Obituary **1990**:4
Mello, Dawn **1992**:2
Mellon, Paul
  Obituary **1999**:3
Melman, Richard
  Brief Entry **1986**:1
Melton, Douglas **2008**:3
Meltzer, Brad **2005**:4
Mengers, Sue **1985**:3
Menninger, Karl
  Obituary **1991**:1
Menuhin, Yehudi
  Obituary **1999**:3
Merchant, Ismail
  Obituary **2006**:3
Merchant, Natalie **1996**:3
Meredith, Burgess
  Obituary **1998**:1
Merkerson, S. Epatha **2006**:4
Merrick, David
  Obituary **2000**:4
Merrill, James
  Obituary **1995**:3
Merritt, Justine
  Brief Entry **1985**:3
Messick, Dale
  Obituary **2006**:2
Messing, Debra **2004**:4
Metallica **2004**:2
Meyers, Nancy **2006**:1
Mfume, Kweisi **1996**:3
Michelman, Kate **1998**:4

Michener, James A.
  Obituary **1998**:1
Mickelson, Phil **2004**:4
Midler, Bette **1989**:4
Mikan, George
  Obituary **2006**:3
Mikulski, Barbara **1992**:4
Milano, Alyssa **2002**:3
Milbrett, Tiffeny **2001**:1
Milburn, Rodney Jr.
  Obituary **1998**:2
Millan, Cesar **2007**:4
Milland, Ray
  Obituary **1986**:2
Millard, Barbara J.
  Brief Entry **1985**:3
Miller, Andre **2003**:3
Miller, Ann
  Obituary **2005**:2
Miller, Arthur **1999**:4
Miller, Bebe **2000**:2
Miller, Bode **2002**:4
Miller, Dennis **1992**:4
Miller, Frank **2008**:2
Miller, Merton H.
  Obituary **2001**:1
Miller, Nicole **1995**:4
Miller, Rand **1995**:4
Miller, Reggie **1994**:4
Miller, Roger
  Obituary **1993**:2
Miller, Sue **1999**:3
Mills, Malia **2003**:1
Mills, Wilbur
  Obituary **1992**:4
Milosz, Czeslaw
  Obituary **2005**:4
Minner, Ruth Ann **2002**:2
Minnesota Fats
  Obituary **1996**:3
Minsky, Marvin **1994**:3
Misrach, Richard **1991**:2
Mitchell, Arthur **1995**:1
Mitchell, George J. **1989**:3
Mitchell, John
  Obituary **1989**:2
Mitchell, Joni **1991**:4
Mitchelson, Marvin **1989**:2
Mitchum, Robert
  Obituary **1997**:4
Mizrahi, Isaac **1991**:1
Moakley, Joseph
  Obituary **2002**:2
Moby **2000**:1
Modano, Mike **2008**:2
Mohajer, Dineh **1997**:3
Molinari, Susan **1996**:4
Monaghan, Tom **1985**:1
Mondavi, Robert **1989**:2
Monica **2004**:2
Mo'Nique **2008**:1
Monk, Art **1993**:2
Monroe, Bill
  Obituary **1997**:1
Monroe, Rose Will
  Obituary **1997**:4
Montana, Joe **1989**:2
Montgomery, Elizabeth
  Obituary **1995**:4
Moody, John **1985**:3
Moody, Rick **2002**:2

Moog, Robert
  Obituary **2006**:4
Moon, Warren **1991**:3
Moonves, Les **2004**:2
Moore, Archie
  Obituary **1999**:2
Moore, Clayton
  Obituary **2000**:3
Moore, Demi **1991**:4
Moore, Julianne **1998**:1
Moore, Mandy **2004**:2
Moore, Mary Tyler **1996**:2
Moore, Michael **1990**:3
Moore, Rachel **2008**:2
Moose, Charles **2003**:4
Moreno, Arturo **2005**:2
Morgan, Dodge **1987**:1
Morgan, Robin **1991**:1
Morita, Noriyuki 'Pat' **1987**:3
Moritz, Charles **1989**:3
Morris, Dick **1997**:3
Morris, Doug **2005**:1
Morris, Henry M.
  Obituary **2007**:2
Morris, Kathryn **2006**:4
Morris, Mark **1991**:1
Morrison, Sterling
  Obituary **1996**:1
Morrison, Toni **1998**:1
Morrison, Trudi
  Brief Entry **1986**:2
Morrow, Rob **2006**:4
Mortensen, Viggo **2003**:3
Mosbacher, Georgette **1994**:2
Mos Def **2005**:4
Mosley, Walter **2003**:4
Moss, Cynthia **1995**:2
Moss, Randy **1999**:3
Motherwell, Robert
  Obituary **1992**:1
Mott, William Penn, Jr. **1986**:1
Mottola, Tommy **2002**:1
Mourning, Alonzo **1994**:2
Moyers, Bill **1991**:4
Moynihan, Daniel Patrick
  Obituary **2004**:2
Mulcahy, Anne M. **2003**:2
Muldowney, Shirley **1986**:1
Mulkey-Robertson, Kim **2006**:1
Mullis, Kary **1995**:3
Mumford, Lewis
  Obituary **1990**:2
Muniz, Frankie **2001**:4
Murdoch, Rupert **1988**:4
Murphy, Brittany **2005**:1
Murphy, Eddie **1989**:2
Murray, Arthur
  Obituary **1991**:3
Murray, Bill **2002**:4
Musburger, Brent **1985**:1
Muskie, Edmund S.
  Obituary **1996**:3
Mydans, Carl
  Obituary **2005**:4
Nader, Ralph **1989**:4
Nagin, Ray **2007**:1
Nair, Mira **2007**:4
Nance, Jack
  Obituary **1997**:3
Napolitano, Janet **1997**:1
Nardelli, Robert **2008**:4
Natsios, Andrew **2005**:1

Wynn, Stephen A. **1994**:3
Wynonna **1993**:3
Xzibit **2005**:4
Yamaguchi, Kristi **1992**:3
Yamasaki, Minoru
  Obituary **1986**:2
Yankovic, 'Weird Al' **1985**:4
Yankovic, Frank
  Obituary **1999**:2
Yard, Molly **1991**:4
Yeager, Chuck **1998**:1
Yearwood, Trisha **1999**:1
Yetnikoff, Walter **1988**:1
Yoakam, Dwight **1992**:4
Yokich, Stephen P. **1995**:4
York, Dick
  Obituary **1992**:4
Young, Coleman A.
  Obituary **1998**:1
Young, Loretta
  Obituary **2001**:1
Young, Robert
  Obituary **1999**:1
Young, Steve **1995**:2
Youngblood, Johnny Ray **1994**:1
Youngman, Henny
  Obituary **1998**:3
Zagat, Tim and Nina **2004**:3
Zahn, Paula **1992**:3
Zamboni, Frank J.
  Brief Entry **1986**:4
Zamora, Pedro
  Obituary **1995**:2
Zanker, Bill
  Brief Entry **1987**:3
Zanuck, Lili Fini **1994**:2
Zappa, Frank
  Obituary **1994**:2
Zech, Lando W.
  Brief Entry **1987**:4
Zellweger, Renee **2001**:1
Zemeckis, Robert **2002**:1
Zerhouni, Elias A. **2004**:3
Zetcher, Arnold B. **2002**:1
Zevon, Warren
  Obituary **2004**:4
Ziff, William B., Jr. **1986**:4
Zigler, Edward **1994**:1
Zinnemann, Fred
  Obituary **1997**:3
Zinni, Anthony **2003**:1
Ziskin, Laura **2008**:2
Zito, Barry **2003**:3
Zucker, Jeff **1993**:3
Zucker, Jerry **2002**:2
Zuckerberg, Mark **2008**:2
Zuckerman, Mortimer **1986**:3
Zwilich, Ellen **1990**:1

ANGOLAN
Savimbi, Jonas **1986**:2 **1994**:2

ARGENTINIAN
Barenboim, Daniel **2001**:1
Bocca, Julio **1995**:3
Duhalde, Eduardo **2003**:3
Herrera, Paloma **1996**:2
Maradona, Diego **1991**:3
Pelli, Cesar **1991**:4
Sabatini, Gabriela
  Brief Entry **1985**:4

Timmerman, Jacobo
  Obituary **2000**:3

AUSTRALIAN
Allen, Peter
  Obituary **1993**:1
Allenby, Robert **2007**:1
Anderson, Judith
  Obituary **1992**:3
Bee Gees, The **1997**:4
Blanchett, Cate **1999**:3
Bloom, Natalie **2007**:1
Bond, Alan **1989**:2
Bradman, Sir Donald
  Obituary **2002**:1
Byrne, Rhonda **2008**:2
Clavell, James
  Obituary **1995**:1
Freeman, Cathy **2001**:3
Gibb, Andy
  Obituary **1988**:3
Gibson, Mel **1990**:1
Helfgott, David **1997**:2
Hewitt, Lleyton **2002**:2
Hughes, Robert **1996**:4
Humphries, Barry **1993**:1
Hutchence, Michael
  Obituary **1998**:1
Irwin, Steve **2001**:2
Jackman, Hugh **2004**:4
Kidman, Nicole **1992**:4
Klensch, Elsa **2001**:4
Larbalestier, Justine **2008**:4
Ledger, Heath **2006**:3
Luhrmann, Baz **2002**:3
McMahon, Julian **2006**:1
Minogue, Kylie **2003**:4
Mueck, Ron **2008**:3
Murdoch, Rupert **1988**:4
Norman, Greg **1988**:3
Powter, Susan **1994**:3
Rafter, Patrick **2001**:1
Rush, Geoffrey **2002**:1
Summers, Anne **1990**:2
Travers, P.L.
  Obituary **1996**:4
Tyler, Richard **1995**:3
Urban, Keith **2006**:3
Webb, Karrie **2000**:4

AUSTRIAN
Brabeck-Letmathe, Peter **2001**:4
Brandauer, Klaus Maria **1987**:3
Djerassi, Carl **2000**:4
Drucker, Peter F. **1992**:3
Falco
  Brief Entry **1987**:2
Frankl, Viktor E.
  Obituary **1998**:1
Hrabal, Bohumil
  Obituary **1997**:3
Jelinek, Elfriede **2005**:3
Lamarr, Hedy
  Obituary **2000**:3
Lang, Helmut **1999**:2
Lorenz, Konrad
  Obituary **1989**:3
Mateschitz, Dietrich **2008**:1
Perutz, Max
  Obituary **2003**:2
Porsche, Ferdinand
  Obituary **1998**:4

Pouillon, Nora **2005**:1
Puck, Wolfgang **1990**:1
Strobl, Fritz **2003**:3
von Karajan, Herbert
  Obituary **1989**:4
von Trapp, Maria
  Obituary **1987**:3
Wiesenthal, Simon
  Obituary **2006**:4

BANGLADESHI
Nasrin, Taslima **1995**:1
Yunus, Muhammad **2007**:3

BARBADIAN
Rihanna **2008**:4

BELARUSSIAN
Lukashenko, Alexander **2006**:4

BELGIAN
Clijsters, Kim **2006**:3
Henin-Hardenne, Justine **2004**:4
Hepburn, Audrey
  Obituary **1993**:2
Verhofstadt, Guy **2006**:3
von Furstenberg, Diane **1994**:2

BOLIVIAN
Morales, Evo **2007**:2
Sanchez de Lozada, Gonzalo **2004**:3

BOSNIAN
Izetbegovic, Alija **1996**:4

BRAZILIAN
Cardoso, Fernando Henrique **1996**:4
Castaneda, Carlos
  Obituary **1998**:4
Collor de Mello, Fernando **1992**:4
Fittipaldi, Emerson **1994**:2
Ronaldinho **2007**:3
Ronaldo **1999**:2
Salgado, Sebastiao **1994**:2
Senna, Ayrton **1991**:4
  Obituary **1994**:4
Silva, Luiz Inacio Lula da **2003**:4
Xuxa **1994**:2

BRITISH
Adamson, George
  Obituary **1990**:2
Baddeley, Hermione
  Obituary **1986**:4
Beckett, Wendy (Sister) **1998**:3
Branson, Richard **1987**:1
Chatwin, Bruce
  Obituary **1989**:2
Cleese, John **1989**:2
Cummings, Sam **1986**:3
Dalton, Timothy **1988**:4
Davison, Ian Hay **1986**:1
Day-Lewis, Daniel **1989**:4 **1994**:4
Dench, Judi **1999**:4
Egan, John **1987**:2
Eno, Brian **1986**:2
Ferguson, Sarah **1990**:3
Fiennes, Ranulph **1990**:3
Foster, Norman **1999**:4
Gift, Roland **1990**:2

Goodall, Jane **1991**:1
Hamilton, Hamish
  Obituary **1988**:4
Harrison, Rex
  Obituary **1990**:4
Hawking, Stephen W. **1990**:1
Hockney, David **1988**:3
Hoskins, Bob **1989**:1
Hounsfield, Godfrey **1989**:2
Howard, Trevor
  Obituary **1988**:2
Ireland, Jill
  Obituary **1990**:4
Knopfler, Mark **1986**:2
Laing, R.D.
  Obituary **1990**:1
Lawrence, Ruth
  Brief Entry **1986**:3
Leach, Robin
  Brief Entry **1985**:4
Lennox, Annie **1985**:4 **1996**:4
Livingstone, Ken **1988**:3
Lloyd Webber, Andrew **1989**:1
Macmillan, Harold
  Obituary **1987**:2
MacMillan, Kenneth
  Obituary **1993**:2
Maxwell, Robert **1990**:1
Michael, George **1989**:2
Milne, Christopher Robin
  Obituary **1996**:4
Moore, Henry
  Obituary **1986**:4
Murdoch, Iris
  Obituary **1999**:4
Norrington, Roger **1989**:4
Oldman, Gary **1998**:1
Olivier, Laurence
  Obituary **1989**:4
Philby, Kim
  Obituary **1988**:3
Rattle, Simon **1989**:4
Redgrave, Vanessa **1989**:2
Rhodes, Zandra **1986**:2
Roddick, Anita **1989**:4
Runcie, Robert **1989**:4
  Obituary **2001**:1
Saatchi, Charles **1987**:3
Steptoe, Patrick
  Obituary **1988**:3
Stevens, James
  Brief Entry **1988**:1
Thatcher, Margaret **1989**:2
Tudor, Antony
  Obituary **1987**:4
Ullman, Tracey **1988**:3
Wilson, Peter C.
  Obituary **1985**:2
Wintour, Anna **1990**:4

BRUNEI
Bolkiah, Sultan Muda Hassanal **1985**
  :4

BULGARIAN
Christo **1992**:3
Dimitrova, Ghena **1987**:1

BURMESE
Suu Kyi, Aung San **1996**:2

CAMBODIAN
Lon Nol
  Obituary **1986**:1
Pol Pot
  Obituary **1998**:4

CAMEROONIAN
Biya, Paul **2006**:1

CANADIAN
Altman, Sidney **1997**:2
Arbour, Louise **2005**:1
Atwood, Margaret **2001**:2
Balsillie, Jim and Mike Lazaridis
  2006:4
Barenaked Ladies **1997**:2
Black, Conrad **1986**:2
Bouchard, Lucien **1999**:2
Bourassa, Robert
  Obituary **1997**:1
Bourque, Raymond Jean **1997**:3
Burr, Raymond
  Obituary **1994**:1
Campbell, Kim **1993**:4
Campbell, Neve **1998**:2
Campeau, Robert **1990**:1
Candy, John **1988**:2
  Obituary **1994**:3
Carrey, Jim **1995**:1
Cavanagh, Tom **2003**:1
Cerovsek, Corey
  Brief Entry **1987**:4
Charney, Dov **2008**:2
Cherry, Don **1993**:4
Chretien, Jean **1990**:4 **1997**:2
Christensen, Hayden **2003**:3
Coffey, Paul **1985**:4
Copps, Sheila **1986**:4
Cronenberg, David **1992**:3
Cronyn, Hume
  Obituary **2004**:3
Crosby, Sidney **2006**:3
Dewhurst, Colleen
  Obituary **1992**:2
Dion, Celine **1995**:3
Doherty, Denny
  Obituary **2008**:2
Eagleson, Alan **1987**:4
Ebbers, Bernie **1998**:1
Egoyan, Atom **2000**:2
Erickson, Arthur **1989**:3
Fonyo, Steve
  Brief Entry **1985**:4
Foster, David **1988**:2
Fox, Michael J. **1986**:1 **2001**:3
Frank, Robert **1995**:2
Frye, Northrop
  Obituary **1991**:3
Fuhr, Grant **1997**:3
Furtado, Nelly **2007**:2
Garneau, Marc **1985**:1
Gatien, Peter
  Brief Entry **1986**:1
Giguere, Jean-Sebastien **2004**:2
Gilmour, Doug **1994**:3
Gold, Christina A. **2008**:1
Graham, Nicholas **1991**:4
Granholm, Jennifer **2003**:3
Green, Tom **1999**:4
Greene, Graham **1997**:2
Greene, Lorne
  Obituary **1988**:1

Gretzky, Wayne **1989**:2
Haggis, Paul **2006**:4
Haney, Chris
  Brief Entry **1985**:1
Harper, Stephen J. **2007**:3
Harris, Michael Deane **1997**:2
Hayakawa, Samuel Ichiye
  Obituary **1992**:3
Hennessy, Jill **2003**:2
Hextall, Ron **1988**:2
Hull, Brett **1991**:4
Jennings, Peter Charles **1997**:2
Johnson, Pierre Marc **1985**:4
Jones, Jenny **1998**:2
Juneau, Pierre **1988**:3
Jung, Andrea **2000**:2
Karsh, Yousuf
  Obituary **2003**:4
Keeler, Ruby
  Obituary **1993**:4
Kent, Arthur **1991**:4 **1997**:2
Kielburger, Craig **1998**:1
Kilgore, Marcia **2006**:3
Korchinsky, Mike **2004**:2
Lalonde, Marc **1985**:1
Lang, K.D. **1988**:4
Lanois, Daniel **1991**:1
Lavigne, Avril **2005**:2
Lemieux, Claude **1996**:1
Lemieux, Mario **1986**:4
Leávesque, Reneá
  Obituary **1988**:1
Levy, Eugene **2004**:3
Lewis, Stephen **1987**:2
Mandel, Howie **1989**:1
Markle, C. Wilson **1988**:1
Martin, Paul **2004**:4
McKinnell, Henry **2002**:3
McLachlan, Sarah **1998**:4
McLaren, Norman
  Obituary **1987**:2
McLaughlin, Audrey **1990**:3
McTaggart, David **1989**:4
Messier, Mark **1993**:1
Morgentaler, Henry **1986**:3
Morissette, Alanis **1996**:2
Moss, Carrie-Anne **2004**:3
Mulroney, Brian **1989**:2
Munro, Alice **1997**:1
Myers, Mike **1992**:3 **1997**:4
Nickelback **2007**:2
O'Donnell, Bill
  Brief Entry **1987**:4
O'Hara, Catherine **2007**:4
Ondaatje, Philip Michael **1997**:3
Parizeau, Jacques **1995**:1
Peckford, Brian **1989**:1
Peterson, David **1987**:1
Pocklington, Peter H. **1985**:2
Pratt, Christopher **1985**:3
Raffi **1988**:1
Randi, James **1990**:2
Reisman, Simon **1987**:4
Reitman, Ivan **1986**:3
Reuben, Gloria **1999**:4
Rhea, Caroline **2004**:1
Richard, Maurice
  Obituary **2000**:4
Richards, Lloyd
  Obituary **2007**:3
Roy, Patrick **1994**:2
Rypien, Mark **1992**:3

Mubarak, Hosni **1991**:4
Rahman, Sheik Omar Abdel- **1993**:3

ENGLISH
Adams, Douglas
  Obituary **2002**:2
Ali, Monica **2007**:4
Altea, Rosemary **1996**:3
Amanpour, Christiane **1997**:2
Ambler, Eric
  Obituary **1999**:2
Ames, Roger **2005**:2
Amis, Kingsley
  Obituary **1996**:2
Amis, Martin **2008**:3
Andrews, Julie **1996**:1
Ashcroft, Peggy
  Obituary **1992**:1
Ashwell, Rachel **2004**:2
Atkinson, Rowan **2004**:3
Banksy **2007**:2
Barker, Clive **2003**:3
Baron Cohen, Sacha **2007**:3
Barrett, Syd
  Obituary **2007**:3
Bates, Alan
  Obituary **2005**:1
Beckham, David **2003**:1
Bee Gees, The **1997**:4
Bell, Gabrielle **2007**:4
Berners-Lee, Tim **1997**:4
Blair, Tony **1996**:3 **1997**:4
Bloom, Orlando **2004**:2
Bonham Carter, Helena **1998**:4
Bowie, David **1998**:2
Broadbent, Jim **2008**:4
Brown, Gordon **2008**:3
Brown, Tina **1992**:1
Burgess, Anthony
  Obituary **1994**:2
Burnett, Mark **2003**:1
Bush, Kate **1994**:3
Caine, Michael **2000**:4
Campbell, Naomi **2000**:2
Carey, George **1992**:3
Charles, Prince of Wales **1995**:3
Child, Lee **2007**:3
Choo, Jimmy **2006**:3
Christie, Julie **2008**:4
Clapton, Eric **1993**:3
Coldplay **2004**:4
Collins, Jackie **2004**:4
Comfort, Alex
  Obituary **2000**:4
Cook, Peter
  Obituary **1995**:2
Cooke, Alistair
  Obituary **2005**:3
Costello, Elvis **1994**:4
Cowell, Simon **2003**:4
Craig, Daniel **2008**:1
Crawford, Michael **1994**:2
Crick, Francis
  Obituary **2005**:4
Crisp, Quentin
  Obituary **2000**:3
Cushing, Peter
  Obituary **1995**:1
Davis, Crispin **2004**:1
Dee, Janie **2001**:4
Diana, Princess of Wales **1993**:1
  Obituary **1997**:4

Dido **2004**:4
Driver, Minnie **2000**:1
Duran Duran **2005**:3
Dyson, James **2005**:4
Elliott, Denholm
  Obituary **1993**:2
Entwistle, John
  Obituary **2003**:3
Everett, Rupert **2003**:1
Everything But The Girl **1996**:4
Faldo, Nick **1993**:3
Fforde, Jasper **2006**:3
Fielding, Helen **2000**:4
Fiennes, Ralph **1996**:2
Finney, Albert **2003**:3
Fonteyn, Margot
  Obituary **1991**:3
Freud, Lucian **2000**:4
Frieda, John **2004**:1
Fuller, Simon **2008**:2
Furse, Clara **2008**:2
Galliano, John **2005**:2
Gielgud, John
  Obituary **2000**:4
Goldsworthy, Andy **2007**:2
Gordon, Michael **2005**:1
Grant, Hugh **1995**:3
Gray, David **2001**:4
Green, Philip **2008**:2
Greene, Graham
  Obituary **1991**:4
Guinness, Alec
  Obituary **2001**:1
Haddon, Mark **2005**:2
Hadid, Zaha **2005**:3
Hamilton, Lewis **2008**:4
Harris, Richard
  Obituary **2004**:1
Harrison, George
  Obituary **2003**:1
Harvey, Polly Jean **1995**:4
Headroom, Max **1986**:4
Hebard, Caroline **1998**:2
Hempleman-Adams, David **2004**:3
Hicks, India **2008**:2
Hill, Benny
  Obituary **1992**:3
Hindmarch, Anya **2008**:2
Hollinghurst, Alan **2006**:1
Hornby, Nick **2002**:2
Houser, Sam **2004**:4
Hoyle, Sir Fred
  Obituary **2002**:4
Hughes, Ted
  Obituary **1999**:2
Hume, Basil Cardinal
  Obituary **2000**:1
Humphry, Derek **1992**:2
Hurley, Elizabeth **1999**:2
Irons, Jeremy **1991**:4
Izzard, Eddie **2008**:1
Jacques, Brian **2002**:2
Jagger, Jade **2005**:1
John, Elton **1995**:4
Kerr, Deborah
  Obituary **2008**:4
Kinsella, Sophie **2005**:2
Knightley, Keira **2005**:2
Lane, Ronnie
  Obituary **1997**:4
Lasdun, Denys
  Obituary **2001**:4

Laurie, Hugh **2007**:2
Law, Jude **2000**:3
Lawson, Nigella **2003**:2
Leach, Penelope **1992**:4
Leakey, Mary Douglas
  Obituary **1997**:2
le Carre, John **2000**:1
Lessing, Doris **2008**:4
LeVay, Simon **1992**:2
Lewis, Lennox **2000**:2
Lively, Penelope **2007**:4
Lupino, Ida
  Obituary **1996**:1
Lyne, Adrian **1997**:2
MacArthur, Ellen **2005**:3
Major, John **1991**:2
Malone, Jo **2004**:3
Marber, Patrick **2007**:4
Marsden, Brian **2004**:4
McCall Smith, Alexander **2005**:2
McCartney, Paul **2002**:4
McCartney, Stella **2001**:3
McDonagh, Martin **2007**:3
McDowall, Roddy
  Obituary **1999**:1
McEwan, Ian **2004**:2
McKellen, Ian **1994**:1
Mercury, Freddie
  Obituary **1992**:2
Milligan, Spike
  Obituary **2003**:2
Minghella, Anthony **2004**:3
Mirren, Helen **2005**:1
Molina, Alfred **2005**:3
Montagu, Ashley
  Obituary **2000**:2
Moore, Dudley
  Obituary **2003**:2
Morrissey **2005**:2
Moss, Kate **1995**:3
Newkirk, Ingrid **1992**:3
Newton-John, Olivia **1998**:4
Nolan, Christopher **2006**:3
Northam, Jeremy **2003**:2
Nunn, Trevor **2000**:2
Oasis **1996**:3
Ogilvy, David
  Obituary **2000**:1
Oliver, Jamie **2002**:3
Osborne, John
  Obituary **1995**:2
Osbournes, The **2003**:4
Owen, Clive **2006**:2
Owen-Jones, Lindsay **2004**:2
Palmer, Robert
  Obituary **2004**:4
Park, Nick **1997**:3
Patten, Christopher **1993**:3
Penrose, Roger **1991**:4
Pleasence, Donald
  Obituary **1995**:3
Pople, John
  Obituary **2005**:2
Porter, George
  Obituary **2003**:4
Princess Margaret, Countess of
  Snowdon
  Obituary **2003**:2
Pullman, Philip **2003**:2
Queen Elizabeth the Queen Mother
  Obituary **2003**:2
Radcliffe, Daniel **2007**:4

Cuaron, Alfonso **2008**:2
Esquivel, Juan **1996**:2
Felix, Maria
  Obituary **2003**:2
Fox, Vicente **2001**:1
Garcia, Amalia **2005**:3
Graham, Robert **1993**:4
Hayek, Salma **1999**:1
Kahlo, Frida **1991**:3
Ochoa, Lorena **2007**:4
Paz, Octavio **1991**:2
Salinas, Carlos **1992**:1
Santana, Carlos **2000**:2
Tamayo, Rufino
  Obituary **1992**:1
Zedillo, Ernesto **1995**:1

MONACO
Albert, Prince of Monaco **2006**:2
Rainier III, Prince of Monaco
  Obituary **2006**:2

MONGOLIAN
Enkhbayar, Nambaryn **2007**:1

MOROCCAN
Elbaz, Alber **2008**:1
King Hassan II
  Obituary **2000**:1
Lalami, Laila **2007**:1

MOZAMBICAN
Chissano, Joaquim **1987**:4
Dhlakama, Afonso **1993**:3
Guebuza, Armando **2008**:4
Machel, Samora
  Obituary **1987**:1

NAMIBIAN
Nujoma, Sam **1990**:4

NEPALI
Shah, Gyanendra **2006**:1

NEW ZEALANDER
Campion, Jane **1991**:4
Castle-Hughes, Keisha **2004**:4
Crowe, Russell **2000**:4
Frame, Janet
  Obituary **2005**:2
Jackson, Peter **2004**:4
Kleinpaste, Ruud **2006**:2
Shipley, Jenny **1998**:3

NICARAGUAN
Astorga, Nora **1988**:2
Cruz, Arturo **1985**:1
Obando, Miguel **1986**:4
Ortega, Daniel **2008**:2
Robelo, Alfonso **1988**:1

NIGERAN
Abacha, Sani **1996**:3
Babangida, Ibrahim Badamosi **1992**
  :4
Obasanjo, Olusegun **2000**:2

Okoye, Christian **1990**:2
Olajuwon, Akeem **1985**:1
Sade **1993**:2
Saro-Wiwa, Ken
  Obituary **1996**:2
Yar'Adua, Umaru **2008**:3

NIGERIAN
Olopade, Olufunmilayo **2006**:3

NORWEGIAN
Brundtland, Gro Harlem **2000**:1
Cammermeyer, Margarethe **1995**:2
Olav, King of Norway
  Obituary **1991**:3
Stoltenberg, Jens **2006**:4

PAKISTANI
Bhutto, Benazir **1989**:4
Zia ul-Haq, Mohammad
  Obituary **1988**:4

PALESTINIAN
Abbas, Mahmoud **2008**:4
Arafat, Yasser **1989**:3 **1997**:3
Freij, Elias **1986**:4
Habash, George **1986**:1
Husseini, Faisal **1998**:4
Nidal, Abu **1987**:1
Sharon, Ariel **2001**:4
Terzi, Zehdi Labib **1985**:3

PANAMANIAN
Blades, Ruben **1998**:2

PARAGUAYAN
Stroessner, Alfredo
  Obituary **2007**:4

PERUVIAN
Fujimori, Alberto **1992**:4
Garcia, Alan **2007**:4
Perez de Cuellar, Javier **1991**:3
Testino, Mario **2002**:1

POLISH
Begin, Menachem
  Obituary **1992**:3
Eisenstaedt, Alfred
  Obituary **1996**:1
John Paul II, Pope **1995**:3
Kaczynski, Lech **2007**:2
Kieslowski, Krzysztof
  Obituary **1996**:3
Kosinski, Jerzy
  Obituary **1991**:4
Masur, Kurt **1993**:4
Niezabitowska, Malgorzata **1991**:3
Rosten, Leo
  Obituary **1997**:3
Sabin, Albert
  Obituary **1993**:4
Singer, Isaac Bashevis
  Obituary **1992**:1
Walesa, Lech **1991**:2

PORTUGUESE
Saramago, Jose **1999**:1

PUERTO RICAN
Alvarez, Aida **1999**:2
Del Toro, Benicio **2001**:4
Ferrer, Jose
  Obituary **1992**:3
Julia, Raul
  Obituary **1995**:1
Martin, Ricky **1999**:4
Novello, Antonia **1991**:2
Trinidad, Felix **2000**:4

ROMANIAN
Basescu, Traian **2006**:2
Ceausescu, Nicolae
  Obituary **1990**:2
Codrescu, Andreá **1997**:3

RUSSIAN
Brodsky, Joseph
  Obituary **1996**:3
Gorbachev, Raisa
  Obituary **2000**:2
Gordeeva, Ekaterina **1996**:4
Grinkov, Sergei
  Obituary **1996**:2
Kasparov, Garry **1997**:4
Kasyanov, Mikhail **2001**:1
Konstantinov, Vladimir **1997**:4
Kournikova, Anna **2000**:3
Lapidus, Morris
  Obituary **2001**:4
Lebed, Alexander **1997**:1
Primakov, Yevgeny **1999**:3
Putin, Vladimir **2000**:3
Rostropovich, Mstislav
  Obituary **2008**:3
Safin, Marat **2001**:3
Sarraute, Nathalie
  Obituary **2000**:2
Schneerson, Menachem Mendel
  1992:4
  Obituary **1994**:4
Sharapova, Maria **2005**:2
Titov, Gherman
  Obituary **2001**:3

RWANDAN
Kagame, Paul **2001**:4

SALVADORAN
Duarte, Jose Napoleon
  Obituary **1990**:3

SAUDI
Fahd, King of Saudi Arabia
  Obituary **2006**:4

SCOTTISH
Coldplay **2004**:4
Connery, Sean **1990**:4
Ferguson, Craig **2005**:4
Ferguson, Niall **2006**:1
Franchitti, Dario **2008**:1

Cumulative Occupation Index

This index lists all newsmakers alphabetically by their occupations or fields of primary activity. Indexes in softbound issues allow access to the current year's entries; indexes in annual hardbound volumes are cumulative, covering the entire *Newsmakers* series.

Listee names are followed by a year and issue number; thus **1996**:3 indicates that an entry on that individual appears in both 1996, Issue 3, and the 1996 cumulation. For access to newsmakers appearing earlier than the current softbound issue, see the previous year's cumulation.

ART AND DESIGN

Adams, Scott **1996**:4
Adams-Geller, Paige **2006**:4
Addams, Charles
  Obituary **1989**:1
Adler, Jonathan **2006**:3
Agnes B **2002**:3
al-Ani, Jananne **2008**:4
Albou, Sophie **2007**:2
Allard, Linda **2003**:2
Alvarez Bravo, Manuel
  Obituary **2004**:1
Anderson, Laurie **2000**:2
Ando, Tadao **2005**:4
Appel, Karel
  Obituary **2007**:2
Arman **1993**:1
Armani, Giorgio **1991**:2
Ashwell, Rachel **2004**:2
Aucoin, Kevyn **2001**:3
Avedon, Richard **1993**:4
Azria, Max **2001**:4
Badgley, Mark and James Mischka
  2004:3
Baldessari, John **1991**:4
Ball, Michael **2007**:3
Banks, Jeffrey **1998**:2
Banksy **2007**:2
Barbera, Joseph **1988**:2
Barks, Carl
  Obituary **2001**:2
Barnes, Ernie **1997**:4
Barry, Lynda **1992**:1
Bean, Alan L. **1986**:2
Beene, Geoffrey
  Obituary **2005**:4
Bell, Gabrielle **2007**:4
Bellissimo, Wendy **2007**:1
Beuys, Joseph
  Obituary **1986**:3
Bird, Brad **2005**:4
Blahnik, Manolo **2000**:2
Blass, Bill
  Obituary **2003**:3
Bohbot, Michele **2004**:2
Bontecou, Lee **2004**:4
Boone, Mary **1985**:1

Borofsky, Jonathan **2006**:4
Botero, Fernando **1994**:3
Bourgeois, Louise **1994**:1
Bowie, David **1998**:2
Boynton, Sandra **2004**:1
Breathed, Berkeley **2005**:3
Brown, Bobbi **2001**:4
Brown, Howard and Karen Stewart
  2007:3
Brown, J. Carter
  Obituary **2003**:3
Bunshaft, Gordon **1989**:3
  Obituary **1991**:1
Calatrava, Santiago **2005**:1
Cameron, David
  Brief Entry **1988**:1
Campbell, Ben Nighthorse **1998**:1
Campbell, Naomi **2000**:2
Cardin, Pierre **2003**:3
Cartier-Bresson, Henri
  Obituary **2005**:4
Cassini, Oleg
  Obituary **2007**:2
Castelli, Leo
  Obituary **2000**:1
Catlett, Elizabeth **1999**:3
Cavalli, Roberto **2004**:4
Chagall, Marc
  Obituary **1985**:2
Chalayan, Hussein **2003**:2
Chast, Roz **1992**:4
Chatham, Russell **1990**:1
Chia, Sandro **1987**:2
Chihuly, Dale **1995**:2
Chillida, Eduardo
  Obituary **2003**:4
Choo, Jimmy **2006**:3
Christo **1992**:3
Claiborne, Liz **1986**:3
Clemente, Francesco **1992**:2
Cole, Anne **2007**:3
Cole, Kenneth **2003**:1
Cooper, Alexander **1988**:4
Crumb, R. **1995**:4
Dali, Salvador
  Obituary **1989**:2
Davis, Paige **2004**:2

DeCarava, Roy **1996**:3
de Kooning, Willem **1994**:4
  Obituary **1997**:3
de la Renta, Oscar **2005**:4
Diebenkorn, Richard
  Obituary **1993**:4
Diller, Elizabeth and Ricardo
  Scofidio **2004**:3
Dolce, Domenico and Stefano
  Gabbana **2005**:4
Donghia, Angelo R.
  Obituary **1985**:2
Duarte, Henry **2003**:3
Dubuffet, Jean
  Obituary **1985**:4
Dunham, Carroll **2003**:4
Ecko, Marc **2006**:3
Eisenman, Peter **1992**:4
Eisenstaedt, Alfred
  Obituary **1996**:1
Eisner, Will
  Obituary **2006**:1
Elbaz, Alber **2008**:1
Ellis, Perry
  Obituary **1986**:3
Engelbreit, Mary **1994**:3
Erickson, Arthur **1989**:3
Erte
  Obituary **1990**:4
Eve **2004**:3
Fekkai, Frederic **2003**:2
Ferre, Gianfranco
  Obituary **2008**:3
Ferretti, Alberta **2004**:1
Field, Patricia **2002**:2
Finley, Karen **1992**:4
Fisher, Mary **1994**:3
Ford, Tom **1999**:3
Foster, Norman **1999**:4
Frank, Robert **1995**:2
Frankenthaler, Helen **1990**:1
Freud, Lucian **2000**:4
Frieda, John **2004**:1
Gaines, William M.
  Obituary **1993**:1
Galliano, John **2005**:2
Gaultier, Jean-Paul **1998**:1

Rodriguez, Narciso **2005**:1
Ronson, Charlotte **2007**:3
Rosenberg, Evelyn **1988**:2
Rosenthal, Joseph
  Obituary **2007**:4
Rosenzweig, Ilene **2004**:1
Rosso, Renzo **2005**:2
Rothenberg, Susan **1995**:3
Rouse, James
  Obituary **1996**:4
Rowley, Cynthia **2002**:1
Rykiel, Sonia **2000**:3
Saatchi, Charles **1987**:3
Salgado, Sebastiao **1994**:2
Scavullo, Francesco
  Obituary **2005**:1
Schnabel, Julian **1997**:1
Schulz, Charles
  Obituary **2000**:3
Schulz, Charles M. **1998**:1
Schwartz, Allen **2008**:2
Segal, Shelli **2005**:3
Serrano, Andres **2000**:4
Shaw, Carol **2002**:1
Sherman, Cindy **1992**:3
Simpson, Lorna **2008**:1
Skaist-Levy, Pam and Gela Taylor
  2005:1
Slick, Grace **2001**:2
Smith, Paul **2002**:4
Smith, Willi
  Obituary **1987**:3
Spade, Kate **2003**:1
Spiegelman, Art **1998**:3
Sprouse, Stephen
  Obituary **2005**:2
Starck, Philippe **2004**:1
Stefani, Gwen **2005**:4
Stefanidis, John **2007**:3
Stella, Frank **1996**:2
Sui, Anna **1995**:1
Takada, Kenzo **2003**:2
Tamayo, Rufino
  Obituary **1992**:1
Tange, Kenzo
  Obituary **2006**:2
Taniguchi, Yoshio **2005**:4
Temperley, Alice **2008**:2
Testino, Mario **2002**:1
Thiebaud, Wayne **1991**:1
Tillmans, Wolfgang **2001**:4
Tompkins, Susie
  Brief Entry **1987**:2
Touitou, Jean **2008**:4
Trudeau, Garry **1991**:2
Truitt, Anne **1993**:1
Tunick, Spencer **2008**:1
Twombley, Cy **1995**:1
Tyler, Richard **1995**:3
Ungaro, Emanuel **2001**:3
Valli, Giambattista **2008**:3
Valvo, Carmen Marc **2003**:4
Varvatos, John **2006**:2
Venturi, Robert **1994**:4
Versace, Donatella **1999**:1
Versace, Gianni
  Brief Entry **1988**:1
  Obituary **1998**:2
Von D, Kat **2008**:3
von Furstenberg, Diane **1994**:2
Von Hellermann, Sophie **2006**:3

Vreeland, Diana
  Obituary **1990**:1
Wagner, Catherine F. **2002**:3
Walker, Kara **1999**:2
Wang, Vera **1998**:4
Warhol, Andy
  Obituary **1987**:2
Washington, Alonzo **2000**:1
Waterman, Cathy **2002**:2
Watterson, Bill **1990**:3
Wegman, William **1991**:1
Westwood, Vivienne **1998**:3
Whitney, Patrick **2006**:1
Wilson, Peter C.
  Obituary **1985**:2
Winick, Judd **2005**:3
Wintour, Anna **1990**:4
Witkin, Joel-Peter **1996**:1
Yamasaki, Minoru
  Obituary **1986**:2
Yeang, Ken **2008**:3

BUSINESS

Abraham, S. Daniel **2003**:3
Ackerman, Will **1987**:4
Adams-Geller, Paige **2006**:4
Adler, Jonathan **2006**:3
Agnelli, Giovanni **1989**:4
Ailes, Roger **1989**:3
Akers, John F. **1988**:3
Akin, Phil
  Brief Entry **1987**:3
Albou, Sophie **2007**:2
Albrecht, Chris **2005**:4
Allaire, Jeremy **2006**:4
Allaire, Paul **1995**:1
Allard, Linda **2003**:2
Allen, Bob **1992**:4
Allen, John **1992**:1
Alter, Hobie
  Brief Entry **1985**:1
Alvarez, Aida **1999**:2
Ames, Roger **2005**:2
Amos, Wally **2000**:1
Ancier, Garth **1989**:1
Anderson, Brad **2007**:3
Anderson, Tom and Chris DeWolfe
  2007:2
Andreessen, Marc **1996**:2
Annenberg, Walter **1992**:3
Antonini, Joseph **1991**:2
Aoki, Rocky **1990**:2
Arad, Avi **2003**:2
Aretsky, Ken **1988**:1
Arison, Ted **1990**:3
Arledge, Roone **1992**:2
Armstrong, C. Michael **2002**:1
Arnault, Bernard **2000**:4
Ash, Mary Kay **1996**:1
Ashwell, Rachel **2004**:2
Aurre, Laura
  Brief Entry **1986**:3
Ball, Michael **2007**:3
Ballmer, Steven **1997**:2
Balsillie, Jim and Mike Lazaridis
  2006:4
Banks, Jeffrey **1998**:2
Barad, Jill **1994**:2
Barksdale, James L. **1998**:2
Barnes, Brenda C. **2007**:4
Barrett, Craig R. **1999**:4

Bauer, Eddie
  Obituary **1986**:3
Beals, Vaughn **1988**:2
Becker, Brian **2004**:4
Beene, Geoffrey
  Obituary **2005**:4
Beers, Charlotte **1999**:3
Bellissimo, Wendy **2007**:1
Ben & Jerry **1991**:3
Benetton, Luciano **1988**:1
Berliner, Andy and Rachel **2008**:2
Berlusconi, Silvio **1994**:4
Berman, Gail **2006**:1
Bern, Dorrit J. **2006**:3
Bernhard, Wolfgang **2007**:1
Besse, Georges
  Obituary **1987**:1
Bezos, Jeff **1998**:4
Bieber, Owen **1986**:1
Bikoff, J. Darius **2007**:3
Bikoff, James L.
  Brief Entry **1986**:2
Black, Carole **2003**:1
Black, Cathleen **1998**:4
Black, Conrad **1986**:2
Bloch, Henry **1988**:4
Bloch, Ivan **1986**:3
Bloom, Natalie **2007**:1
Bloomberg, Michael **1997**:1
Bohbot, Michele **2004**:2
Boiardi, Hector
  Obituary **1985**:3
Bolkiah, Sultan Muda Hassanal **1985**:4
Bond, Alan **1989**:2
Bose, Amar
  Brief Entry **1986**:4
Boyer, Herbert Wayne **1985**:1
Boyle, Gertrude **1995**:3
Boynton, Sandra **2004**:1
Brabeck-Letmathe, Peter **2001**:4
Bradley, Todd **2003**:3
Branson, Richard **1987**:1
Bravo, Ellen **1998**:2
Bravo, Rose Marie **2005**:3
Breitschwerdt, Werner **1988**:4
Brennan, Edward A. **1989**:1
Brennan, Robert E. **1988**:1
Bronfman, Edgar, Jr. **1994**:4
Brooks, Diana D. **1990**:1
Brosius, Christopher **2007**:1
Brown, Howard and Karen Stewart
  2007:3
Brown, John Seely **2004**:1
Brown, Tina **1992**:1
Buffett, Jimmy **1999**:3
Buffett, Warren **1995**:2
Burnison, Chantal Simone **1988**:3
Burns, Robin **1991**:2
Burr, Donald Calvin **1985**:3
Burton, Jake **2007**:1
Busch, August A. III **1988**:2
Busch, August Anheuser, Jr.
  Obituary **1990**:2
Bushnell, Nolan **1985**:1
Buss, Jerry **1989**:3
Cain, Herman **1998**:3
Callaway, Ely
  Obituary **2002**:3
Calloway, D. Wayne **1987**:3
Campeau, Robert **1990**:1

Demme, Jonathan **1992**:4
Dempsey, Patrick **2006**:1
Dench, Judi **1999**:4
Deneuve, Catherine **2003**:2
De Niro, Robert **1999**:1
Dennehy, Brian **2002**:1
Dennis, Sandy
  Obituary **1992**:4
De Palma, Brian **2007**:3
Depardieu, Gerard **1991**:2
Depp, Johnny **1991**:3
Dern, Laura **1992**:3
De Vito, Danny **1987**:1
Diamond, I.A.L.
  Obituary **1988**:3
Diamond, Selma
  Obituary **1985**:2
Diaz, Cameron **1999**:1
DiCaprio, Leonardo Wilhelm **1997**:2
Diesel, Vin **2004**:1
Dietrich, Marlene
  Obituary **1992**:4
Diggs, Taye **2000**:1
Diller, Barry **1991**:1
Dillon, Matt **1992**:2
Disney, Roy E. **1986**:3
Divine
  Obituary **1988**:3
Doherty, Shannen **1994**:2
Donahue, Troy
  Obituary **2002**:4
Douglas, Michael **1986**:2
Downey, Robert, Jr. **2007**:1
Drescher, Fran **1995**:3
Dreyfuss, Richard **1996**:3
Driver, Minnie **2000**:1
Duchovny, David **1998**:3
Duff, Hilary **2004**:4
Duffy, Karen **1998**:1
Dukakis, Olympia **1996**:4
Dunst, Kirsten **2001**:4
Duvall, Robert **1999**:3
Eastwood, Clint **1993**:3
Ebersole, Christine **2007**:2
Ebsen, Buddy
  Obituary **2004**:3
Efron, Zac **2008**:2
Egoyan, Atom **2000**:2
Eisner, Michael **1989**:2
Elliott, Denholm
  Obituary **1993**:2
Ephron, Henry
  Obituary **1993**:2
Ephron, Nora **1992**:3
Epps, Omar **2000**:4
Estevez, Emilio **1985**:4
Evans, Robert **2004**:1
Eve **2004**:3
Everett, Rupert **2003**:1
Fairbanks, Douglas, Jr.
  Obituary **2000**:4
Fallon, Jimmy **2003**:1
Fanning, Dakota **2005**:2
Farley, Chris
  Obituary **1998**:2
Farrell, Colin **2004**:1
Farrow, Mia **1998**:3
Favreau, Jon **2002**:3
Fawcett, Farrah **1998**:4
Feldshuh, Tovah **2005**:3
Felix, Maria
  Obituary **2003**:2

Fell, Norman
  Obituary **1999**:2
Fellini, Federico
  Obituary **1994**:2
Ferguson, Craig **2005**:4
Ferrell, Will **2004**:4
Ferrer, Jose
  Obituary **1992**:3
Ferrera, America **2006**:2
Fetchit, Stepin
  Obituary **1986**:1
Fey, Tina **2005**:3
Fforde, Jasper **2006**:3
Field, Sally **1995**:3
Fiennes, Ralph **1996**:2
Fierstein, Harvey **2004**:2
Finney, Albert **2003**:3
Fishburne, Laurence **1995**:3
Fisher, Carrie **1991**:1
Flanders, Ed
  Obituary **1995**:3
Fleiss, Mike **2003**:4
Fleming, Art
  Obituary **1995**:4
Flockhart, Calista **1998**:4
Fonda, Bridget **1995**:1
Ford, Faith **2005**:3
Ford, Glenn
  Obituary **2007**:4
Ford, Harrison **1990**:2
Fosse, Bob
  Obituary **1988**:1
Foster, Jodie **1989**:2
Fox, Michael J. **1986**:1 **2001**:3
Fox, Vivica **1999**:1
Franciscus, James
  Obituary **1992**:1
Frank, Robert **1995**:2
Frankenheimer, John
  Obituary **2003**:4
Franz, Dennis **1995**:2
Fraser, Brendan **2000**:1
Freeman, Morgan **1990**:4
Freleng, Friz
  Obituary **1995**:4
Fugard, Athol **1992**:3
Gabor, Eva
  Obituary **1996**:1
Gallagher, Peter **2004**:3
Garbo, Greta
  Obituary **1990**:3
Garcia, Andy **1999**:3
Gardenia, Vincent
  Obituary **1993**:2
Gardner, Ava Lavinia
  Obituary **1990**:2
Garner, Jennifer **2003**:1
Garofalo, Janeane **1996**:4
Garr, Teri **1988**:4
Garson, Greer
  Obituary **1996**:4
Gassman, Vittorio
  Obituary **2001**:1
Geffen, David **1985**:3 **1997**:3
Gellar, Sarah Michelle **1999**:3
Gere, Richard **1994**:3
Gibson, Mel **1990**:1
Gielgud, John
  Obituary **2000**:4
Gift, Roland **1990**:2
Gilford, Jack
  Obituary **1990**:4

Gish, Lillian
  Obituary **1993**:4
Gleason, Jackie
  Obituary **1987**:4
Gless, Sharon **1989**:3
Glover, Danny **1998**:4
Gobel, George
  Obituary **1991**:4
Godard, Jean-Luc **1998**:1
Godunov, Alexander
  Obituary **1995**:4
Goldberg, Leonard **1988**:4
Goldberg, Whoopi **1993**:3
Goldblum, Jeff **1988**:1 **1997**:3
Gong Li **1998**:4
Gooding, Cuba, Jr. **1997**:3
Goodman, John **1990**:3
Gordon, Dexter **1987**:1 **1990**:4
Gordon, Gale
  Obituary **1996**:1
Gossett, Louis, Jr. **1989**:3
Goulet, Robert
  Obituary **2008**:4
Grace, Topher **2005**:4
Graham, Heather **2000**:1
Graham, Lauren **2003**:4
Grant, Cary
  Obituary **1987**:1
Grant, Hugh **1995**:3
Grant, Rodney A. **1992**:1
Gray, Spalding
  Obituary **2005**:2
Grazer, Brian **2006**:4
Greene, Graham **1997**:2
Greene, Lorne
  Obituary **1988**:1
Grier, Pam **1998**:3
Griffith, Melanie **1989**:2
Grodin, Charles **1997**:3
Grusin, Dave
  Brief Entry **1987**:2
Guest, Christopher **2004**:2
Guggenheim, Charles
  Obituary **2003**:4
Guinness, Alec
  Obituary **2001**:1
Gyllenhaal, Jake **2005**:3
Hackett, Buddy
  Obituary **2004**:3
Hackman, Gene **1989**:3
Hagen, Uta
  Obituary **2005**:2
Haggis, Paul **2006**:4
Hall, Anthony Michael **1986**:3
Hall, Arsenio **1990**:2
Hallstrom, Lasse **2002**:3
Hamilton, Margaret
  Obituary **1985**:3
Hammer, Jan **1987**:3
Hanks, Tom **1989**:2 **2000**:2
Hannah, Daryl **1987**:4
Hannigan, Alyson **2007**:3
Harden, Marcia Gay **2002**:4
Hargitay, Mariska **2006**:2
Harmon, Mark **1987**:1
Harris, Ed **2002**:2
Harris, Richard
  Obituary **2004**:1
Harrison, Rex
  Obituary **1990**:4
Harry, Deborah **1990**:1

Hart, Kitty Carlisle
    Obituary **2008**:2
Hartman, Phil **1996**:2
    Obituary **1998**:4
Harwell, Ernie **1997**:3
Hatcher, Teri **2005**:4
Hathaway, Anne **2007**:2
Hawke, Ethan **1995**:4
Hawn, Goldie Jeanne **1997**:2
Hayek, Salma **1999**:1
Hayes, Helen
    Obituary **1993**:4
Hayes, Isaac **1998**:4
Haysbert, Dennis **2007**:1
Hayworth, Rita
    Obituary **1987**:3
Heche, Anne **1999**:1
Heckerling, Amy **1987**:2
Heigl, Katharine **2008**:3
Hemingway, Margaux
    Obituary **1997**:1
Hennessy, Jill **2003**:2
Henson, Brian **1992**:1
Henson, Jim **1989**:1
    Obituary **1990**:4
Hepburn, Audrey
    Obituary **1993**:2
Hepburn, Katharine **1991**:2
Hershey, Barbara **1989**:1
Heston, Charlton **1999**:4
Hewitt, Jennifer Love **1999**:2
Hill, George Roy
    Obituary **2004**:1
Hill, Lauryn **1999**:3
Hines, Gregory **1992**:4
Hoffman, Dustin **2005**:4
Hoffman, Philip Seymour **2006**:3
Holmes, John C.
    Obituary **1988**:3
Hope, Bob
    Obituary **2004**:4
Hopkins, Anthony **1992**:4
Horne, Lena **1998**:4
Hoskins, Bob **1989**:1
Hou Hsiao-hsien **2000**:2
Houseman, John
    Obituary **1989**:1
Howard, Ron **1997**:2
Howard, Trevor
    Obituary **1988**:2
Hudson, Jennifer **2008**:1
Hudson, Kate **2001**:2
Hudson, Rock
    Obituary **1985**:4
Huffman, Felicity **2006**:2
Humphries, Barry **1993**:1
Hunt, Helen **1994**:4
Hunter, Holly **1989**:4
Hurley, Elizabeth **1999**:2
Hurt, William **1986**:1
Huston, Anjelica **1989**:3
Huston, John
    Obituary **1988**:1
Hutton, Timothy **1986**:3
Ice Cube **1999**:2
Ice-T **1992**:3
Ireland, Jill
    Obituary **1990**:4
Irons, Jeremy **1991**:4
Irving, John **2006**:2
Itami, Juzo
    Obituary **1998**:2

Ives, Burl
    Obituary **1995**:4
Izzard, Eddie **2008**:1
Jackman, Hugh **2004**:4
Jackson, Peter **2004**:4
Jackson, Samuel L. **1995**:4
Janney, Allison **2003**:3
Jarmusch, Jim **1998**:3
Jay, Ricky **1995**:1
Jillian, Ann **1986**:4
Johansson, Scarlett **2005**:4
Johnson, Beverly **2005**:2
Johnson, Don **1986**:1
Jolie, Angelina **2000**:2
Jones, Cherry **1999**:3
Jones, Tommy Lee **1994**:2
Jonze, Spike **2000**:3
Jordan, Neil **1993**:3
Jovovich, Milla **2002**:1
Joyce, William **2006**:1
Judd, Ashley **1998**:1
Julia, Raul
    Obituary **1995**:1
Kahn, Madeline
    Obituary **2000**:2
Kanakaredes, Melina **2007**:1
Kasem, Casey **1987**:1
Katzenberg, Jeffrey **1995**:3
Kaufman, Charlie **2005**:1
Kavner, Julie **1992**:3
Kaye, Danny
    Obituary **1987**:2
Kazan, Elia
    Obituary **2004**:4
Keaton, Diane **1997**:1
Keaton, Michael **1989**:4
Keeler, Ruby
    Obituary **1993**:4
Keitel, Harvey **1994**:3
Keith, Brian
    Obituary **1997**:4
Kelly, Gene
    Obituary **1996**:3
Kerr, Deborah
    Obituary **2008**:4
Kidman, Nicole **1992**:4
Kilmer, Val **1991**:4
King, Alan
    Obituary **2005**:3
King, Stephen **1998**:1
Kinski, Klaus **1987**:2
    Obituary **1992**:2
Kline, Kevin **2000**:1
Knight, Wayne **1997**:1
Knightley, Keira **2005**:2
Knotts, Don
    Obituary **2007**:1
Kramer, Larry **1991**:2
Kramer, Stanley
    Obituary **2002**:1
Kubrick, Stanley
    Obituary **1999**:3
Kulp, Nancy
    Obituary **1991**:3
Kurosawa, Akira **1991**:1
    Obituary **1999**:1
Kutcher, Ashton **2003**:4
LaBeouf, Shia **2008**:1
Lahti, Christine **1988**:2
Lake, Ricki **1994**:4
Lamarr, Hedy
    Obituary **2000**:3

Lamour, Dorothy
    Obituary **1997**:1
Lancaster, Burt
    Obituary **1995**:1
Lane, Diane **2006**:2
Lane, Nathan **1996**:4
Lange, Jessica **1995**:4
Langella, Frank **2008**:3
Lansbury, Angela **1993**:1
Lansing, Sherry **1995**:4
LaPaglia, Anthony **2004**:4
Lardner Jr., Ring
    Obituary **2001**:2
Larroquette, John **1986**:2
Lasseter, John **2007**:2
Laurie, Hugh **2007**:2
Law, Jude **2000**:3
Lawless, Lucy **1997**:4
Lawrence, Martin **1993**:4
Leary, Denis **1993**:3
LeBlanc, Matt **2005**:4
Ledger, Heath **2006**:3
Lee, Ang **1996**:3
Lee, Brandon
    Obituary **1993**:4
Lee, Jason **2006**:4
Lee, Pamela **1996**:4
Lee, Spike **1988**:4
Leguizamo, John **1999**:1
Leigh, Janet
    Obituary **2005**:4
Leigh, Jennifer Jason **1995**:2
Lemmon, Jack **1998**:4
    Obituary **2002**:3
Leno, Jay **1987**:1
Leone, Sergio
    Obituary **1989**:4
Levinson, Barry **1989**:3
Levy, Eugene **2004**:3
Lewis, Juliette **1999**:3
Lewis, Richard **1992**:1
Li, Jet **2005**:3
Liberace
    Obituary **1987**:2
Liman, Doug **2007**:1
Ling, Bai **2000**:3
Linklater, Richard **2007**:2
Lithgow, John **1985**:2
Little, Cleavon
    Obituary **1993**:2
Liu, Lucy **2000**:4
Livingston, Ron **2007**:2
LL Cool J **1998**:2
Lloyd Webber, Andrew **1989**:1
Locklear, Heather **1994**:3
Loewe, Frederick
    Obituary **1988**:2
Logan, Joshua
    Obituary **1988**:4
Lohan, Lindsay **2005**:3
Long, Nia **2001**:3
Long, Shelley **1985**:1
Lopez, Jennifer **1998**:4
Lord, Jack
    Obituary **1998**:2
Lords, Traci **1995**:4
Louis-Dreyfus, Julia **1994**:1
Lovett, Lyle **1994**:1
Lowe, Rob **1990**:4
Loy, Myrna
    Obituary **1994**:2
Lucas, George **1999**:4

Ludacris **2007**:4
Luhrmann, Baz **2002**:3
Lupino, Ida
   Obituary **1996**:1
Lynch, David **1990**:4
Lyne, Adrian **1997**:2
Mac, Bernie **2003**:1
MacDonald, Laurie and Walter
   Parkes **2004**:1
MacDowell, Andie **1993**:4
MacMurray, Fred
   Obituary **1992**:2
MacRae, Gordon
   Obituary **1986**:2
Macy, William H. **1999**:3
Madonna **1985**:2
Maguire, Tobey **2002**:2
Maher, Bill **1996**:2
Mako
   Obituary **2007**:3
Malkovich, John **1988**:2
Malle, Louis
   Obituary **1996**:2
Mamet, David **1998**:4
Mancini, Henry
   Obituary **1994**:4
Mandel, Howie **1989**:1
Mantegna, Joe **1992**:1
Marber, Patrick **2007**:4
Marin, Cheech **2000**:1
Markle, C. Wilson **1988**:1
Marsalis, Branford **1988**:3
Marshall, Penny **1991**:3
Martin, Dean
   Obituary **1996**:2
Martin, Dean Paul
   Obituary **1987**:3
Martin, Steve **1992**:2
Marvin, Lee
   Obituary **1988**:1
Masina, Giulietta
   Obituary **1994**:3
Mastroianni, Marcello
   Obituary **1997**:2
Matlin, Marlee **1992**:2
Matthau, Walter **2000**:3
Matuszak, John
   Obituary **1989**:4
McConaughey, Matthew
   David **1997**:1
McCrea, Joel
   Obituary **1991**:1
McDonagh, Martin **2007**:3
McDonnell, Mary **2008**:2
McDormand, Frances **1997**:3
McDowall, Roddy
   Obituary **1999**:1
McGillis, Kelly **1989**:3
McGinley, Ted **2004**:4
McGregor, Ewan **1998**:2
McGuire, Dorothy
   Obituary **2002**:4
McKee, Lonette **1996**:1
McKellen, Ian **1994**:1
McLaren, Norman
   Obituary **1987**:2
McMahon, Julian **2006**:1
Meadows, Audrey
   Obituary **1996**:3
Merchant, Ismail
   Obituary **2006**:3

Meredith, Burgess
   Obituary **1998**:1
Merkerson, S. Epatha **2006**:4
Messing, Debra **2004**:4
Meyers, Nancy **2006**:1
Midler, Bette **1989**:4
Milano, Alyssa **2002**:3
Milland, Ray
   Obituary **1986**:2
Miller, Ann
   Obituary **2005**:2
Miller, Frank **2008**:2
Milligan, Spike
   Obituary **2003**:2
Minghella, Anthony **2004**:3
Minogue, Kylie **2003**:4
Mirren, Helen **2005**:1
Mitchum, Robert
   Obituary **1997**:4
Miyazaki, Hayao **2006**:2
Molina, Alfred **2005**:3
Mo'Nique **2008**:1
Montand, Yves
   Obituary **1992**:2
Montgomery, Elizabeth
   Obituary **1995**:4
Moore, Clayton
   Obituary **2000**:3
Moore, Demi **1991**:4
Moore, Dudley
   Obituary **2003**:2
Moore, Julianne **1998**:1
Moore, Mandy **2004**:2
Moore, Mary Tyler **1996**:2
Moore, Michael **1990**:3
Morita, Noriyuki 'Pat' **1987**:3
Morris, Kathryn **2006**:4
Morrow, Rob **2006**:4
Mortensen, Viggo **2003**:3
Mos Def **2005**:4
Moss, Carrie-Anne **2004**:3
Murphy, Brittany **2005**:1
Murphy, Eddie **1989**:2
Murray, Bill **2002**:4
Myers, Mike **1992**:3 **1997**:4
Nair, Mira **2007**:4
Nance, Jack
   Obituary **1997**:3
Neeson, Liam **1993**:4
Nelson, Harriet
   Obituary **1995**:1
Nelson, Rick
   Obituary **1986**:1
Nelson, Willie **1993**:4
Newman, Paul **1995**:3
Newton-John, Olivia **1998**:4
Nichols, Mike **1994**:4
Nicholson, Jack **1989**:2
Nixon, Bob **2006**:4
Nolan, Christopher **2006**:3
Nolan, Lloyd
   Obituary **1985**:4
Nolte, Nick **1992**:4
North, Alex **1986**:3
Northam, Jeremy **2003**:2
Norton, Edward **2000**:2
O'Connor, Donald
   Obituary **2004**:4
O'Donnell, Rosie **1994**:3
O'Hara, Catherine **2007**:4
Oldman, Gary **1998**:1
Olin, Ken **1992**:3

Olin, Lena **1991**:2
Olivier, Laurence
   Obituary **1989**:4
Olmos, Edward James **1990**:1
O'Sullivan, Maureen
   Obituary **1998**:4
Ovitz, Michael **1990**:1
Owen, Clive **2006**:2
Paar, Jack
   Obituary **2005**:2
Pacino, Al **1993**:4
Page, Geraldine
   Obituary **1987**:4
Pakula, Alan
   Obituary **1999**:2
Palance, Jack
   Obituary **2008**:1
Paltrow, Gwyneth **1997**:1
Panettiere, Hayden **2008**:4
Pantoliano, Joe **2002**:3
Park, Nick **1997**:3
Parker, Mary-Louise **2002**:2
Parker, Sarah Jessica **1999**:2
Parker, Trey and Matt Stone **1998**:2
Parks, Bert
   Obituary **1992**:3
Parks, Gordon
   Obituary **2006**:2
Pascal, Amy **2003**:3
Patrick, Robert **2002**:1
Paxton, Bill **1999**:3
Payne, Alexander **2005**:4
Peck, Gregory
   Obituary **2004**:3
Peete, Holly Robinson **2005**:2
Penn, Sean **1987**:2
Perez, Rosie **1994**:2
Perkins, Anthony
   Obituary **1993**:2
Perry, Luke **1992**:3
Perry, Matthew **1997**:2
Perry, Tyler **2006**:1
Pesci, Joe **1992**:4
Peters, Bernadette **2000**:1
Peterson, Cassandra **1988**:1
Pfeiffer, Michelle **1990**:2
Phifer, Mekhi **2004**:1
Phillips, Julia **1992**:1
Phoenix, Joaquin **2000**:4
Phoenix, River **1990**:2
   Obituary **1994**:2
Picasso, Paloma **1991**:1
Pinchot, Bronson **1987**:4
Pinkett Smith, Jada **1998**:3
Pitt, Brad **1995**:2
Piven, Jeremy **2007**:3
Pleasence, Donald
   Obituary **1995**:3
Plimpton, George
   Obituary **2004**:4
Poitier, Sidney **1990**:3
Ponti, Carlo
   Obituary **2008**:2
Portman, Natalie **2000**:3
Potts, Annie **1994**:1
Preminger, Otto
   Obituary **1986**:3
Presley, Pricilla **2001**:1
Preston, Robert
   Obituary **1987**:3
Price, Vincent
   Obituary **1994**:2

Tilly, Jennifer **1997**:2
Timberlake, Justin **2008**:4
Tomei, Marisa **1995**:2
Travolta, John **1995**:2
Tucci, Stanley **2003**:2
Tucker, Chris **1999**:1
Tucker, Forrest
    Obituary **1987**:1
Turner, Janine **1993**:2
Turner, Kathleen **1985**:3
Turner, Lana
    Obituary **1996**:1
Turturro, John **2002**:2
Tyler, Liv **1997**:2
Ullman, Tracey **1988**:3
Umeki, Miyoshi
    Obituary **2008**:4
Union, Gabrielle **2004**:2
Urich, Robert **1988**:1
    Obituary **2003**:3
Usher **2005**:1
Ustinov, Peter
    Obituary **2005**:3
Valenti, Jack
    Obituary **2008**:3
Vanilla Ice **1991**:3
Van Sant, Gus **1992**:2
Vardalos, Nia **2003**:4
Varney, Jim
    Brief Entry **1985**:4
    Obituary **2000**:3
Vaughn, Vince **1999**:2
Ventura, Jesse **1999**:2
Vidal, Gore **1996**:2
Vidov, Oleg **1987**:4
Villechaize, Herve
    Obituary **1994**:1
Vincent, Fay **1990**:2
Voight, Jon **2002**:3
Walker, Nancy
    Obituary **1992**:3
Wallis, Hal
    Obituary **1987**:1
Warden, Jack
    Obituary **2007**:3
Warhol, Andy
    Obituary **1987**:2
Washington, Denzel **1993**:2
Wasserman, Lew
    Obituary **2003**:3
Waters, John **1988**:3
Waterston, Sam **2006**:1
Watson, Emily **2001**:1
Watts, Naomi **2006**:1
Wayans, Damon **1998**:4
Wayans, Keenen Ivory **1991**:1
Wayne, David
    Obituary **1995**:3
Weaver, Sigourney **1988**:3
Wegman, William **1991**:1
Weinstein, Bob and Harvey **2000**:4
Weintraub, Jerry **1986**:1
Weisz, Rachel **2006**:4
Whedon, Joss **2006**:3
Whitaker, Forest **1996**:2
White, Julie **2008**:2
Wiest, Dianne **1995**:2
Wilder, Billy
    Obituary **2003**:2
Wilkinson, Tom **2003**:2
Williams, Robin **1988**:4
Williams, Treat **2004**:3

Williams, Vanessa L. **1999**:2
Willis, Bruce **1986**:4
Wilson, Owen **2002**:3
Winfield, Paul
    Obituary **2005**:2
Winfrey, Oprah **1986**:4 **1997**:3
Winger, Debra **1994**:3
Winokur, Marissa Jaret **2005**:1
Winslet, Kate **2002**:4
Winters, Shelley
    Obituary **2007**:1
Wise, Robert
    Obituary **2006**:4
Wiseman, Len **2008**:2
Witherspoon, Reese **2002**:1
Wolfman Jack
    Obituary **1996**:1
Wong, B.D. **1998**:1
Woo, John **1994**:2
Wood, Elijah **2002**:4
Woods, James **1988**:3
Wyle, Noah **1997**:3
Wyman, Jane
    Obituary **2008**:4
Wynn, Keenan
    Obituary **1987**:1
Xzibit **2005**:4
Yeoh, Michelle **2003**:2
Young, Loretta
    Obituary **2001**:1
Young, Robert
    Obituary **1999**:1
Zanuck, Lili Fini **1994**:2
Zeffirelli, Franco **1991**:3
Zellweger, Renee **2001**:1
Zemeckis, Robert **2002**:1
Zeta-Jones, Catherine **1999**:4
Zhang, Ziyi **2006**:2
Ziskin, Laura **2008**:2
Zucker, Jerry **2002**:2

LAW

Abzug, Bella **1998**:2
Achtenberg, Roberta **1993**:4
Allred, Gloria **1985**:2
Andrews, Lori B. **2005**:3
Angelos, Peter **1995**:4
Archer, Dennis **1994**:4
Astorga, Nora **1988**:2
Babbitt, Bruce **1994**:1
Bailey, F. Lee **1995**:4
Baker, James A. III **1991**:2
Bikoff, James L.
    Brief Entry **1986**:2
Blackmun, Harry A.
    Obituary **1999**:3
Boies, David **2002**:1
Bradley, Tom
    Obituary **1999**:1
Brennan, William
    Obituary **1997**:4
Breyer, Stephen Gerald **1994**:4 **1997**:2
Brown, Willie **1996**:4
Brown, Willie L. **1985**:2
Burger, Warren E.
    Obituary **1995**:4
Burnison, Chantal Simone **1988**:3
Campbell, Kim **1993**:4
Cantrell, Ed
    Brief Entry **1985**:3
Carter, Stephen L. **2008**:2

Casey, William
    Obituary **1987**:3
Casper, Gerhard **1993**:1
Clark, Marcia **1995**:1
Clinton, Bill **1992**:1
Clinton, Hillary Rodham **1993**:2
Cochran, Johnnie **1996**:1
Colby, William E.
    Obituary **1996**:4
Cuomo, Mario **1992**:2
Darden, Christopher **1996**:4
Dees, Morris **1992**:1
del Ponte, Carla **2001**:1
Dershowitz, Alan **1992**:1
Deutch, John **1996**:4
Dole, Elizabeth Hanford **1990**:1
Dukakis, Michael **1988**:3
Eagleson, Alan **1987**:4
Ehrlichman, John
    Obituary **1999**:3
Ervin, Sam
    Obituary **1985**:2
Estrich, Susan **1989**:1
Fairstein, Linda **1991**:1
Fehr, Donald **1987**:2
Fieger, Geoffrey **2001**:3
Fitzgerald, Patrick **2006**:4
Florio, James J. **1991**:2
Foster, Vincent
    Obituary **1994**:1
France, Johnny
    Brief Entry **1987**:1
Freeh, Louis J. **1994**:2
Fulbright, J. William
    Obituary **1995**:3
Furman, Rosemary
    Brief Entry **1986**:4
Garrison, Jim
    Obituary **1993**:2
Ginsburg, Ruth Bader **1993**:4
Giuliani, Rudolph **1994**:2
Glasser, Ira **1989**:1
Gore, Albert, Sr.
    Obituary **1999**:2
Grisham, John **1994**:4
Harvard, Beverly **1995**:2
Hayes, Robert M. **1986**:3
Hill, Anita **1994**:1
Hills, Carla **1990**:3
Hirschhorn, Joel
    Brief Entry **1986**:1
Hoffa, Jim, Jr. **1999**:2
Hyatt, Joel **1985**:3
Ireland, Patricia **1992**:2
Ito, Lance **1995**:3
Janklow, Morton **1989**:3
Kennedy, John F., Jr. **1990**:1
    Obituary **1999**:4
Kennedy, Weldon **1997**:3
Kunstler, William **1992**:3
Kunstler, William
    Obituary **1996**:1
Kurzban, Ira **1987**:2
Lee, Henry C. **1997**:1
Lee, Martin **1998**:2
Lewis, Loida Nicolas **1998**:3
Lewis, Reginald F. **1988**:4
    Obituary **1993**:3
Lightner, Candy **1985**:1
Liman, Arthur **1989**:4
Lipsig, Harry H. **1985**:1
Lipton, Martin **1987**:3

MacKinnon, Catharine **1993**:2
Marshall, Thurgood
  Obituary **1993**:3
McCloskey, James **1993**:1
Mitchell, George J. **1989**:3
Mitchell, John
  Obituary **1989**:2
Mitchelson, Marvin **1989**:2
Morrison, Trudi
  Brief Entry **1986**:2
Nader, Ralph **1989**:4
Napolitano, Janet **1997**:1
Neal, James Foster **1986**:2
O'Connor, Sandra Day **1991**:1
O'Leary, Hazel **1993**:4
O'Steen, Van
  Brief Entry **1986**:3
Panetta, Leon **1995**:1
Pirro, Jeanine **1998**:2
Powell, Lewis F.
  Obituary **1999**:1
Puccio, Thomas P. **1986**:4
Quayle, Dan **1989**:2
Raines, Franklin **1997**:4
Ramaphosa, Cyril **1988**:2
Ramo, Roberta Cooper **1996**:1
Rehnquist, William H. **2001**:2
Reno, Janet **1993**:3
Rothwax, Harold **1996**:3
Scalia, Antonin **1988**:2
Scheck, Barry **2000**:4
Schily, Otto
  Brief Entry **1987**:4
Sheehan, Daniel P. **1989**:1
Sheindlin, Judith **1999**:1
Sirica, John
  Obituary **1993**:2
Skinner, Sam **1992**:3
Slater, Rodney E. **1997**:4
Slotnick, Barry
  Brief Entry **1987**:4
Souter, David **1991**:3
Spitzer, Eliot **2007**:2
Starr, Kenneth **1998**:3
Steinberg, Leigh **1987**:3
Stern, David **1991**:4
Stewart, Potter
  Obituary **1986**:1
Strauss, Robert **1991**:4
Tagliabue, Paul **1990**:2
Thomas, Clarence **1992**:2
Thompson, Fred **1998**:2
Tribe, Laurence H. **1988**:1
Vincent, Fay **1990**:2
Violet, Arlene **1985**:3
Wapner, Joseph A. **1987**:1
Watson, Elizabeth **1991**:2
White, Byron
  Obituary **2003**:3
Williams, Edward Bennett
  Obituary **1988**:4
Williams, Willie L. **1993**:1
Wilson, Bertha
  Brief Entry **1986**:1

MUSIC

Aaliyah **2001**:3
Abdul, Paula **1990**:3
Ackerman, Will **1987**:4
Acuff, Roy
  Obituary **1993**:2
Adams, Yolanda **2008**:2

AFI **2007**:3
Aguilera, Christina **2000**:4
Albert, Stephen **1986**:1
Allen, Peter
  Obituary **1993**:1
Alsop, Marin **2008**:3
Ames, Roger **2005**:2
Amos, Tori **1995**:1
Anderson, Marion
  Obituary **1993**:4
Andrews, Julie **1996**:1
Andrews, Maxene
  Obituary **1996**:2
Anthony, Marc **2000**:3
Apple, Fiona **2006**:3
Arlen, Harold
  Obituary **1986**:3
Arnaz, Desi
  Obituary **1987**:1
Arrau, Claudio
  Obituary **1992**:1
Arrested Development **1994**:2
Ashanti **2004**:1
Astaire, Fred
  Obituary **1987**:4
Autry, Gene
  Obituary **1999**:1
Backstreet Boys **2001**:3
Badu, Erykah **2000**:4
Baez, Joan **1998**:3
Bailey, Pearl
  Obituary **1991**:1
Baker, Anita **1987**:4
Barenboim, Daniel **2001**:1
Barrett, Syd
  Obituary **2007**:3
Bartoli, Cecilia **1994**:1
Basie, Count
  Obituary **1985**:1
Battle, Kathleen **1998**:1
Beastie Boys, The **1999**:1
Becaud, Gilbert
  Obituary **2003**:1
Beck **2000**:2
Bee Gees, The **1997**:4
Benatar, Pat **1986**:1
Bennett, Tony **1994**:4
Bentley, Dierks **2007**:3
Berio, Luciano
  Obituary **2004**:2
Berlin, Irving
  Obituary **1990**:1
Bernhard, Sandra **1989**:4
Bernstein, Elmer
  Obituary **2005**:4
Bernstein, Leonard
  Obituary **1991**:1
Berry, Chuck **2001**:2
Bjork **1996**:1
Black Eyed Peas **2006**:2
Blades, Ruben **1998**:2
Blakey, Art
  Obituary **1991**:1
Blige, Mary J. **1995**:3
Bolton, Michael **1993**:2
Bon Jovi, Jon **1987**:4
Bono **1988**:4
Bono, Sonny **1992**:2
  Obituary **1998**:2
Borge, Victor
  Obituary **2001**:3
Botstein, Leon **1985**:3

Bowie, David **1998**:2
Bowles, Paul
  Obituary **2000**:3
Boxcar Willie
  Obituary **1999**:4
Boyz II Men **1995**:1
Brandy **1996**:4
Branson, Richard **1987**:1
Braxton, Toni **1994**:3
Brooks, Garth **1992**:1
Brown, James **1991**:4
Brown, Les
  Obituary **2001**:3
Brown, Ruth
  Obituary **2008**:1
Buckley, Jeff
  Obituary **1997**:4
Buffett, Jimmy **1999**:3
Bush, Kate **1994**:3
Butterfield, Paul
  Obituary **1987**:3
Cage, John
  Obituary **1993**:1
Calloway, Cab
  Obituary **1995**:2
Cannon, Nick **2006**:4
Cardigans, The **1997**:4
Carey, Mariah **1991**:3
Carlisle, Belinda **1989**:3
Carpenter, Mary-Chapin **1994**:1
Carreras, Jose **1995**:2
Carter, Benny
  Obituary **2004**:3
Carter, Nell
  Obituary **2004**:2
Carter, Ron **1987**:3
Cash, Johnny **1995**:3
Cash, June Carter
  Obituary **2004**:2
Castellucci, Cecil **2008**:3
Cerovsek, Corey
  Brief Entry **1987**:4
Chapman, Tracy **1989**:2
Charles, Ray
  Obituary **2005**:3
Cheatham, Adolphus 'Doc'
  Obituary **1997**:4
Cher **1993**:1
Chesney, Kenny **2008**:2
Clapton, Eric **1993**:3
Clarke, Stanley **1985**:4
Clarkson, Kelly **2003**:3
Cleveland, James
  Obituary **1991**:3
Cliburn, Van **1995**:1
Clooney, Rosemary
  Obituary **2003**:4
Cobain, Kurt
  Obituary **1994**:3
Coldplay **2004**:4
Cole, Natalie **1992**:4
Collins, Albert
  Obituary **1994**:2
Combs, Sean 'Puffy' **1998**:4
Como, Perry
  Obituary **2002**:2
Connick, Harry, Jr. **1991**:1
Coolio **1996**:4
Copland, Aaron
  Obituary **1991**:2
Coppola, Carmine
  Obituary **1991**:4

Kelly, R. **1997**:3
Kendricks, Eddie
   Obituary **1993**:2
Kenny G **1994**:4
Keys, Alicia **2006**:1
Kid Rock **2001**:1
Kilmer, Val **1991**:4
King, Coretta Scott **1999**:3
Knopfler, Mark **1986**:2
Kravitz, Lenny **1991**:1
Kronos Quartet **1993**:1
Kurzweil, Raymond **1986**:3
Kyser, Kay
   Obituary **1985**:3
Lachey, Nick and Jessica Simpson
   2004:4
Lane, Burton
   Obituary **1997**:2
Lane, Ronnie
   Obituary **1997**:4
Lang, K.D. **1988**:4
Lanois, Daniel **1991**:1
Larson, Jonathan
   Obituary **1997**:2
Lauper, Cyndi **1985**:1
Lavigne, Avril **2005**:2
Lee, Peggy
   Obituary **2003**:1
Legend, John **2007**:1
Lennox, Annie **1985**:4 **1996**:4
Levine, James **1992**:3
Lewis, Henry
   Obituary **1996**:3
Lewis, Huey **1987**:3
Lewis, John
   Obituary **2002**:1
Liberace
   Obituary **1987**:2
Ligeti, Gyorgy
   Obituary **2007**:3
Living Colour **1993**:3
LL Cool J **1998**:2
Lloyd Webber, Andrew **1989**:1
Loewe, Frederick
   Obituary **1988**:2
Lohan, Lindsay **2005**:3
Lopes, Lisa
   Obituary **2003**:3
Lords, Traci **1995**:4
Love, Courtney **1995**:1
Loveless, Patty **1998**:2
Lovett, Lyle **1994**:1
Ludacris **2007**:4
Lynn, Loretta **2001**:1
MacRae, Gordon
   Obituary **1986**:2
Madonna **1985**:2
Makeba, Miriam **1989**:2
Mancini, Henry
   Obituary **1994**:4
Manson, Marilyn **1999**:4
Marky Mark **1993**:3
Marley, Ziggy **1990**:4
Maroon **2008**:1
Marsalis, Branford **1988**:3
Marsalis, Wynton **1997**:4
Martin, Dean
   Obituary **1996**:2
Martin, Dean Paul
   Obituary **1987**:3
Martin, Ricky **1999**:4
Master P **1999**:4

Masur, Kurt **1993**:4
Matthews, Dave **1999**:3
Mayer, John **2007**:4
McCartney, Linda
   Obituary **1998**:4
McCartney, Paul **2002**:4
McDuffie, Robert **1990**:2
McEntire, Reba **1987**:3 **1994**:2
McFerrin, Bobby **1989**:1
McGraw, Tim **2000**:3
McLachlan, Sarah **1998**:4
McMurtry, James **1990**:2
McRae, Carmen
   Obituary **1995**:2
Mehta, Zubin **1994**:3
Menuhin, Yehudi
   Obituary **1999**:3
Merchant, Natalie **1996**:3
Mercury, Freddie
   Obituary **1992**:2
Metallica **2004**:2
Michael, George **1989**:2
Michelangeli, Arturo Benedetti **1988**
   :2
Midler, Bette **1989**:4
Miller, Roger
   Obituary **1993**:2
Minogue, Kylie **2003**:4
Mintz, Shlomo **1986**:2
Mitchell, Joni **1991**:4
Moby **2000**:1
Monica **2004**:2
Monroe, Bill
   Obituary **1997**:1
Montand, Yves
   Obituary **1992**:2
Montoya, Carlos
   Obituary **1993**:4
Moog, Robert
   Obituary **2006**:4
Moore, Dudley
   Obituary **2003**:2
Moore, Mandy **2004**:2
Morissette, Alanis **1996**:2
Morris, Doug **2005**:1
Morrison, Sterling
   Obituary **1996**:1
Morrissey **2005**:2
Mos Def **2005**:4
Mottola, Tommy **2002**:1
Mutter, Anne-Sophie **1990**:3
Nelson, Rick
   Obituary **1986**:1
Nelson, Willie **1993**:4
New Kids on the Block **1991**:2
Newton-John, Olivia **1998**:4
Nickelback **2007**:2
Nilsson, Birgit
   Obituary **2007**:1
Nirvana **1992**:4
No Doubt **1997**:3
Norrington, Roger **1989**:4
North, Alex **1986**:3
Notorious B.I.G.
   Obituary **1997**:3 'N Sync **2001**:4
Nyro, Laura
   Obituary **1997**:3
Oasis **1996**:3
O'Connor, Sinead **1990**:4
O'Day, Anita
   Obituary **2008**:1
Ono, Yoko **1989**:2

Orbison, Roy
   Obituary **1989**:2
Ormandy, Eugene
   Obituary **1985**:2
Osborne, Joan **1996**:4
Osbournes, The **2003**:4
Ostin, Mo **1996**:2
OutKast **2004**:4
Owens, Buck
   Obituary **2007**:2
Paisley, Brad **2008**:3
Palmer, Robert
   Obituary **2004**:4
Parker, 'Colonel' Tom
   Obituary **1997**:2
Parton, Dolly **1999**:4
Pass, Joe
   Obituary **1994**:4
Pastorius, Jaco
   Obituary **1988**:1
Pavarotti, Luciano **1997**:4
Payton, Lawrence
   Obituary **1997**:4
Pearl, Minnie
   Obituary **1996**:3
Pearl Jam **1994**:2
Perkins, Carl
   Obituary **1998**:2
Petty, Tom **1988**:1
Phair, Liz **1995**:3
Phillips, John
   Obituary **2002**:1
Phillips, Sam
   Obituary **2004**:4
Pickett, Wilson
   Obituary **2007**:1
Pilatus, Robert
   Obituary **1998**:3
Pink **2004**:3
Pittman, Robert W. **1985**:1
Pogorelich, Ivo **1986**:4
Ponty, Jean-Luc **1985**:4
Presley, Lisa Marie **2004**:3
Preston, Billy
   Obituary **2007**:3
Preston, Robert
   Obituary **1987**:3
Pride, Charley **1998**:1
Prince **1995**:3
Public Enemy **1992**:1
Puente, Tito
   Obituary **2000**:4
Queen Latifah **1992**:2
Quinn, Martha **1986**:4
Rabbitt, Eddie
   Obituary **1998**:4
Raffi **1988**:1
Raitt, Bonnie **1990**:2
Ramone, Joey
   Obituary **2002**:2
Rampal, Jean-Pierre **1989**:2
Rascal Flatts **2007**:1
Rashad, Phylicia **1987**:3
Raskin, Jef **1997**:4
Rattle, Simon **1989**:4
Raven **2005**:1
Rawls, Lou
   Obituary **2007**:1
Red Hot Chili Peppers **1993**:1
Redman, Joshua **1999**:2
Reed, Dean
   Obituary **1986**:3

Reese, Della **1999**:2
Reznor, Trent **2000**:2
Rich, Buddy
  Obituary **1987**:3
Rich, Charlie
  Obituary **1996**:1
Richards, Keith **1993**:3
Riddle, Nelson
  Obituary **1985**:4
Rihanna **2008**:4
Rimes, LeeAnn **1997**:4
Robbins, Jerome
  Obituary **1999**:1
Robinson, Earl
  Obituary **1992**:1
Roedy, Bill **2003**:2
Rogers, Roy
  Obituary **1998**:4
Rollins, Henry **2007**:3
Rose, Axl **1992**:1
Rostropovich, Mstislav
  Obituary **2008**:3
Ruffin, David
  Obituary **1991**:4
RuPaul **1996**:1
Sade **1993**:2
Sagal, Katey **2005**:2
Sainte-Marie, Buffy **2000**:1
Salerno-Sonnenberg, Nadja **1988**:4
Salonga, Lea **2003**:3
Santana, Carlos **2000**:2
Satriani, Joe **1989**:3
Scholz, Tom **1987**:2
Schwarzkopf, Elisabeth
  Obituary **2007**:3
Seal **1994**:4
Seger, Bob **1987**:1
Segovia, Andreás
  Obituary **1987**:3
Selena
  Obituary **1995**:4
Serkin, Rudolf
  Obituary **1992**:1
Shaffer, Paul **1987**:1
Shakira **2002**:3
Shakur, Tupac
  Obituary **1997**:1
Shaw, Artie
  Obituary **2006**:1
Sherman, Russell **1987**:4
Shocked, Michelle **1989**:4
Shore, Dinah
  Obituary **1994**:3
Simmons, Russell and Kimora Lee **2003**:2
Simon, Paul **1992**:2
Simone, Nina
  Obituary **2004**:2
Sinatra, Frank
  Obituary **1998**:4
Sinopoli, Giuseppe **1988**:1
Smith, Jimmy
  Obituary **2006**:2
Smith, Kate
  Obituary **1986**:3
Smith, Will **1997**:2
Snider, Dee **1986**:1
Snoop Doggy Dogg **1995**:2
Snow, Hank
  Obituary **2000**:3
Solti, Georg
  Obituary **1998**:1

Sondheim, Stephen **1994**:4
Spears, Britney **2000**:3
Spector, Phil **1989**:1
Spice Girls **2008**:3
Springfield, Dusty
  Obituary **1999**:3
Staples, Roebuck 'Pops'
  Obituary **2001**:3
Stefani, Gwen **2005**:4
Stern, Isaac
  Obituary **2002**:4
Stewart, Rod **2007**:1
Sting **1991**:4
Stone, Joss **2006**:2
Strait, George **1998**:3
Streisand, Barbra **1992**:2
Strummer, Joe
  Obituary **2004**:1
Styne, Jule
  Obituary **1995**:1
Sun Ra
  Obituary **1994**:1
Suzuki, Sin'ichi
  Obituary **1998**:3
System of a Down **2006**:4
T. I. **2008**:1
Tan Dun **2002**:1
Tesh, John **1996**:3
Thomas, Michael Tilson **1990**:3
Tiffany **1989**:1
Timbaland **2007**:4
Timberlake, Justin **2008**:4
TLC **1996**:1
Tone-Loc **1990**:3
Torme, Mel
  Obituary **1999**:4
Tosh, Peter
  Obituary **1988**:2
Travis, Randy **1988**:4
Tritt, Travis **1995**:1
Tune, Tommy **1994**:2
Turner, Tina **2000**:3
Twain, Shania **1996**:3
Twitty, Conway
  Obituary **1994**:1
Tyner, Rob
  Obituary **1992**:2
U **2002**:4
Uchida, Mitsuko **1989**:3
Ullman, Tracey **1988**:3
Underwood, Carrie **2008**:1
Upshaw, Dawn **1991**:2
Urban, Keith **2006**:3
Usher **2005**:1
Valente, Benita **1985**:3
Vandross, Luther
  Obituary **2006**:3
Van Halen, Edward **1985**:2
Vanilla Ice **1991**:3
Vaughan, Sarah
  Obituary **1990**:3
Vaughan, Stevie Ray
  Obituary **1991**:1
Vega, Suzanne **1988**:1
Vollenweider, Andreas **1985**:2
von Karajan, Herbert
  Obituary **1989**:4
von Trapp, Maria
  Obituary **1987**:3
Wagoner, Porter
  Obituary **2008**:4

Walker, Junior
  Obituary **1996**:2
Washington, Grover, Jr. **1989**:1
Wasserman, Lew
  Obituary **2003**:3
Weintraub, Jerry **1986**:1
Wells, Mary
  Obituary **1993**:1
West, Dottie
  Obituary **1992**:2
West, Kanye **2006**:1
White, Barry
  Obituary **2004**:3
White Stripes, The **2006**:1
Williams, Joe
  Obituary **1999**:4
Williams, Pharrell **2005**:3
Williams, Vanessa L. **1999**:2
Willis, Bruce **1986**:4
Wilson, Brian **1996**:1
Wilson, Carl
  Obituary **1998**:2
Wilson, Cassandra **1996**:3
Wilson, Gretchen **2006**:3
Winans, CeCe **2000**:1
Winehouse, Amy **2008**:1
Winston, George **1987**:1
Winter, Paul **1990**:2
Womack, Lee Ann **2002**:1
Wynette, Tammy
  Obituary **1998**:3
Wynonna **1993**:3
Xenakis, Iannis
  Obituary **2001**:4
Xzibit **2005**:4
Yankovic, 'Weird Al' **1985**:4
Yankovic, Frank
  Obituary **1999**:2
Yearwood, Trisha **1999**:1
Yoakam, Dwight **1992**:4
Young, Neil **1991**:2
Zappa, Frank
  Obituary **1994**:2
Zevon, Warren
  Obituary **2004**:4
Zinnemann, Fred
  Obituary **1997**:3
Zwilich, Ellen **1990**:1

**POLITICS AND
GOVERNMENT--FOREIGN**
Abacha, Sani **1996**:3
Abbas, Mahmoud **2008**:4
Abdullah II, King **2002**:4
Adams, Gerald **1994**:1
Ahern, Bertie **1999**:3
Ahmadinejad, Mahmoud **2007**:1
Akihito, Emperor of Japan **1990**:1
al-Abdullah, Rania **2001**:1
al-Assad, Bashar **2004**:2
Albert, Prince of Monaco **2006**:2
Albright, Madeleine **1994**:3
Amin, Idi
  Obituary **2004**:4
Annan, Kofi **1999**:1
Aquino, Corazon **1986**:2
Arafat, Yasser **1989**:3 **1997**:3
Arens, Moshe **1985**:1
Arias Sanchez, Oscar **1989**:3
Aristide, Jean-Bertrand **1991**:3
Assad, Hafez
  Obituary **2000**:4

POLITICS AND GOVERNMENT--U.S.

Boyington, Gregory 'Pappy'
 Obituary **1988**:2
Bradley, Bill **2000**:2
Bradley, Tom
 Obituary **1999**:1
Brady, Sarah and James S. **1991**:4
Braun, Carol Moseley **1993**:1
Brazile, Donna **2001**:1
Bremer, L. Paul **2004**:2
Brennan, William
 Obituary **1997**:4
Brown, Edmund G., Sr.
 Obituary **1996**:3
Brown, Jerry **1992**:4
Brown, Ron **1990**:3
Brown, Ron
 Obituary **1996**:4
Brown, Willie **1996**:4
Brown, Willie L. **1985**:2
Browner, Carol M. **1994**:1
Buchanan, Pat **1996**:3
Bundy, McGeorge
 Obituary **1997**:1
Bundy, William P.
 Obituary **2001**:2
Bush, Barbara **1989**:3
Bush, George W., Jr. **1996**:4
Bush, Jeb **2003**:1
Caliguiri, Richard S.
 Obituary **1988**:3
Campbell, Ben Nighthorse **1998**:1
Campbell, Bill **1997**:1
Card, Andrew H., Jr. **2003**:2
Carey, Ron **1993**:3
Carmona, Richard **2003**:2
Carnahan, Jean **2001**:2
Carnahan, Mel
 Obituary **2001**:2
Carter, Billy
 Obituary **1989**:1
Carter, Jimmy **1995**:1
Casey, William
 Obituary **1987**:3
Cavazos, Lauro F. **1989**:2
Chamberlin, Wendy **2002**:4
Chao, Elaine L. **2007**:3
Chavez, Linda **1999**:3
Chavez-Thompson, Linda **1999**:1
Cheney, Dick **1991**:3
Cheney, Lynne V. **1990**:4
Chisholm, Shirley
 Obituary **2006**:1
Christopher, Warren **1996**:3
Cisneros, Henry **1987**:2
Clark, J. E.
 Brief Entry **1986**:1
Clinton, Bill **1992**:1
Clinton, Hillary Rodham **1993**:2
Clyburn, James **1999**:4
Cohen, William S. **1998**:1
Collins, Cardiss **1995**:3
Connally, John
 Obituary **1994**:1
Conyers, John, Jr. **1999**:1
Cornum, Rhonda **2006**:3
Cuomo, Mario **1992**:2
D'Amato, Al **1996**:1
Daschle, Tom **2002**:3
Dean, Howard **2005**:4
DeLay, Tom **2000**:1
Dinkins, David N. **1990**:2
Dolan, Terry **1985**:2

Dole, Bob **1994**:2
Dole, Elizabeth Hanford **1990**:1
Dukakis, Michael **1988**:3
Duke, David **1990**:2
Ehrlichman, John
 Obituary **1999**:3
Elders, Joycelyn **1994**:1
Engler, John **1996**:3
Ervin, Sam
 Obituary **1985**:2
Estrich, Susan **1989**:1
Falkenberg, Nanette **1985**:2
Farmer, James
 Obituary **2000**:1
Farrakhan, Louis **1990**:4
Faubus, Orval
 Obituary **1995**:2
Feinstein, Dianne **1993**:3
Fenwick, Millicent H.
 Obituary **1993**:2
Ferraro, Geraldine **1998**:3
Fish, Hamilton
 Obituary **1991**:3
Fitzgerald, A. Ernest **1986**:2
Fleischer, Ari **2003**:1
Florio, James J. **1991**:2
Flynn, Ray **1989**:1
Foley, Thomas S. **1990**:1
Forbes, Steve **1996**:2
Ford, Gerald R.
 Obituary **2008**:2
Foster, Vincent
 Obituary **1994**:1
Frank, Anthony M. **1992**:1
Frank, Barney **1989**:2
Franks, Tommy **2004**:1
Frist, Bill **2003**:4
Fulbright, J. William
 Obituary **1995**:3
Galvin, John R. **1990**:1
Garrison, Jim
 Obituary **1993**:2
Gates, Robert M. **1992**:2
Gebbie, Kristine **1994**:2
Gephardt, Richard **1987**:3
Gergen, David **1994**:1
Gingrich, Newt **1991**:1 **1997**:3
Giuliani, Rudolph **1994**:2
Glenn, John **1998**:3
Goldwater, Barry
 Obituary **1998**:4
Gore, Albert, Jr. **1993**:2
Gore, Albert, Sr.
 Obituary **1999**:2
Gramm, Phil **1995**:2
Granholm, Jennifer **2003**:3
Greenspan, Alan **1992**:2
Griffiths, Martha
 Obituary **2004**:2
Haldeman, H. R.
 Obituary **1994**:2
Hall, Gus
 Obituary **2001**:2
Harriman, Pamela **1994**:4
Harriman, W. Averell
 Obituary **1986**:4
Harris, Katherine **2001**:3
Harris, Patricia Roberts
 Obituary **1985**:2
Hastert, Dennis **1999**:3
Hatch, Orin G. **2000**:2

Hayakawa, Samuel Ichiye
 Obituary **1992**:3
Heinz, John
 Obituary **1991**:4
Heller, Walter
 Obituary **1987**:4
Helms, Jesse **1998**:1
Hills, Carla **1990**:3
Hiss, Alger
 Obituary **1997**:2
Holbrooke, Richard **1996**:2
Hughes, Karen **2001**:2
Hull, Jane Dee **1999**:2
Hundt, Reed Eric **1997**:2
Hyde, Henry **1999**:1
Inman, Bobby Ray **1985**:1
Jackson, Jesse **1996**:1
Jackson, Jesse, Jr. **1998**:3
Jackson, Thomas Penfield **2000**:2
Jeffords, James **2002**:2
Jeffrey, Mildred
 Obituary **2005**:2
Jindal, Bobby **2006**:1
Johnson, Lady Bird
 Obituary **2008**:4
Jordan, Barbara
 Obituary **1996**:3
Kassebaum, Nancy **1991**:1
Kemp, Jack **1990**:4
Kennan, George
 Obituary **2006**:2
Kennedy, Rose
 Obituary **1995**:3
Kerrey, Bob **1986**:1 **1991**:3
Kerry, John **2005**:2
Kessler, David **1992**:1
Keyes, Alan **1996**:2
Kirkpatrick, Jeane
 Obituary **2008**:1
Kissinger, Henry **1999**:4
Koop, C. Everett **1989**:3
Landon, Alf
 Obituary **1988**:1
Landrieu, Mary L. **2002**:2
Langevin, James R. **2001**:2
Lansdale, Edward G.
 Obituary **1987**:2
Levitt, Arthur **2004**:2
Lieberman, Joseph **2001**:1
Liman, Arthur **1989**:4
Lincoln, Blanche **2003**:1
Lindsay, John V.
 Obituary **2001**:3
Lodge, Henry Cabot
 Obituary **1985**:1
Lord, Winston
 Brief Entry **1987**:4
Lott, Trent **1998**:1
Luce, Clare Boothe
 Obituary **1988**:1
Lucke, Lewis **2004**:4
Manchin, Joe **2006**:4
Mankiller, Wilma P.
 Brief Entry **1986**:2
Mansfield, Mike
 Obituary **2002**:4
Martin, Lynn **1991**:4
Martinez, Bob **1992**:1
Matalin, Mary **1995**:2
Mathias, Bob
 Obituary **2007**:4
McCain, John S. **1998**:4

Costas, Bob **1986**:4
Crenna, Richard
Obituary **2004**:1
Day, Dennis
Obituary **1988**:4
Denver, Bob
Obituary **2006**:4
Dr. Demento **1986**:1
Donnellan, Nanci **1995**:2
Douglas, Mike
Obituary **2007**:4
Durrell, Gerald
Obituary **1995**:3
Edwards, Bob **1993**:2
Fleming, Art
Obituary **1995**:4
Ford, Tennessee Ernie
Obituary **1992**:2
Glass, Ira **2008**:2
Gobel, George
Obituary **1991**:4
Goodman, Benny
Obituary **1986**:3
Gordon, Gale
Obituary **1996**:1
Graham, Billy **1992**:1
Granato, Cammi **1999**:3
Grange, Red
Obituary **1991**:3
Greene, Lorne
Obituary **1988**:1
Griffin, Merv
Obituary **2008**:4
Gross, Terry **1998**:3
Harmon, Tom
Obituary **1990**:3
Harvey, Paul **1995**:3
Harwell, Ernie **1997**:3
Hill, George Roy
Obituary **2004**:1
Hollander, Joel **2006**:4
Hope, Bob
Obituary **2004**:4
Houseman, John
Obituary **1989**:1
Hughes, Cathy **1999**:1
Imus, Don **1997**:1
Ives, Burl
Obituary **1995**:4
Karmazin, Mel **2006**:1
Kasem, Casey **1987**:1
Keyes, Alan **1996**:2
King, Larry **1993**:1
Kyser, Kay
Obituary **1985**:3
Leávesque, Reneá
Obituary **1988**:1
Limbaugh, Rush **1991**:3
Magliozzi, Tom and Ray **1991**:4
Milligan, Spike
Obituary **2003**:2
Nelson, Harriet
Obituary **1995**:1
Olson, Johnny
Obituary **1985**:4
Osgood, Charles **1996**:2
Paar, Jack
Obituary **2005**:2
Paley, William S.
Obituary **1991**:2
Parks, Bert
Obituary **1992**:3

Parsons, Gary **2006**:2
Porter, Sylvia
Obituary **1991**:4
Quivers, Robin **1995**:4
Raphael, Sally Jessy **1992**:4
Raye, Martha
Obituary **1995**:1
Reagan, Ronald
Obituary **2005**:3
Riddle, Nelson
Obituary **1985**:4
Roberts, Cokie **1993**:4
Rollins, Henry **2007**:3
Saralegui, Cristina **1999**:2
Schlessinger, Laura **1996**:3
Seacrest, Ryan **2004**:4
Sedaris, David **2005**:3
Sevareid, Eric
Obituary **1993**:1
Shore, Dinah
Obituary **1994**:3
Smith, Buffalo Bob
Obituary **1999**:1
Smith, Kate
Obituary **1986**:3
Stern, Howard **1988**:2 **1993**:3
Swayze, John Cameron
Obituary **1996**:1
Toguri, Iva
Obituary **2007**:4
Tom and Ray Magliozzi **1991**:4
Totenberg, Nina **1992**:2
Wolfman Jack
Obituary **1996**:1
Young, Robert
Obituary **1999**:1

RELIGION
Abernathy, Ralph
Obituary **1990**:4
Altea, Rosemary **1996**:3
Applewhite, Marshall Herff
Obituary **1997**:3
Aristide, Jean-Bertrand **1991**:3
Beckett, Wendy (Sister) **1998**:3
Benson, Ezra Taft
Obituary **1994**:4
Bernardin, Cardinal Joseph **1997**:2
Berri, Nabih **1985**:2
Browning, Edmond
Brief Entry **1986**:2
Burns, Charles R.
Brief Entry **1988**:1
Carey, George **1992**:3
Chavis, Benjamin **1993**:4
Chittister, Joan D. **2002**:2
Chopra, Deepak **1996**:3
Clements, George **1985**:1
Cleveland, James
Obituary **1991**:3
Coffin, William Sloane, Jr. **1990**:3
Cunningham, Reverend William
Obituary **1997**:4
Curran, Charles E. **1989**:2
Daily, Bishop Thomas V. **1990**:4
Dalai Lama **1989**:1
Dearden, John Cardinal
Obituary **1988**:4
Dorsey, Thomas A.
Obituary **1993**:3
Eilberg, Amy
Brief Entry **1985**:3

Falwell, Jerry
Obituary **2008**:3
Farrakhan, Louis **1990**:4
Fox, Matthew **1992**:2
Fulghum, Robert **1996**:1
Graham, Billy **1992**:1
Grant, Amy **1985**:4
Hahn, Jessica **1989**:4
Harris, Barbara **1989**:3
Harris, Barbara **1996**:3
Healy, Timothy S. **1990**:2
Henry, Carl F.H.
Obituary **2005**:1
Huffington, Arianna **1996**:2
Hume, Basil Cardinal
Obituary **2000**:1
Hunter, Howard **1994**:4
Irwin, James
Obituary **1992**:1
Jackson, Jesse **1996**:1
Jefferts Schori, Katharine **2007**:2
John Paul II, Pope **1995**:3
Jumblatt, Walid **1987**:4
Kahane, Meir
Obituary **1991**:2
Khomeini, Ayatollah Ruhollah
Obituary **1989**:4
Kissling, Frances **1989**:2
Koresh, David
Obituary **1993**:4
Krol, John
Obituary **1996**:3
Lefebvre, Marcel **1988**:4
Levinger, Moshe **1992**:1
Macquarrie, John
Obituary **2008**:3
Mahesh Yogi, Maharishi **1991**:3
Mahony, Roger M. **1988**:2
Maida, Adam Cardinal **1998**:2
Malloy, Edward 'Monk' **1989**:4
McCloskey, James **1993**:1
Morris, Henry M.
Obituary **2007**:2
Mother Teresa **1993**:1
Obituary **1998**:1
Obando, Miguel **1986**:4
O'Connor, Cardinal John **1990**:3
O'Connor, John
Obituary **2000**:4
Osteen, Joel **2006**:2
Perry, Harold A.
Obituary **1992**:1
Peter, Valentine J. **1988**:2
Rafsanjani, Ali Akbar Hashemi **1987**
:3
Rahman, Sheik Omar Abdel- **1993**:3
Rajneesh, Bhagwan Shree
Obituary **1990**:2
Reed, Ralph **1995**:1
Reese, Della **1999**:2
Robertson, Pat **1988**:2
Robinson, V. Gene **2004**:4
Rogers, Adrian **1987**:4
Runcie, Robert **1989**:4
Obituary **2001**:1
Schneerson, Menachem Mendel
1992:4
Obituary **1994**:4
Scott, Gene
Brief Entry **1986**:1
Sentamu, John **2006**:2
Sharpton, Al **1991**:2

Radecki, Thomas
  Brief Entry **1986**:2
Ramaphosa, Cyril **1988**:2
Redmond, Tim **2008**:1
Reeve, Christopher **1997**:2
Ross, Percy
  Brief Entry **1986**:2
Rothstein, Ruth **1988**:2
Rowley, Coleen **2004**:2
Rubin, Jerry
  Obituary **1995**:2
Ruppe, Loret Miller **1986**:2
Sachs, Jeffrey D. **2004**:4
Sakharov, Andrei Dmitrievich
  Obituary **1990**:2
Salbi, Zainab **2008**:3
Sample, Bill
  Brief Entry **1986**:2
Sams, Craig **2007**:3
Saro-Wiwa, Ken
  Obituary **1996**:2
Sasakawa, Ryoichi
  Brief Entry **1988**:1
Schiavo, Mary **1998**:2
Seo, Danny **2008**:3
Shabazz, Betty
  Obituary **1997**:4
Sharma, Nisha **2004**:2
Sharpton, Al **1991**:2
Shcharansky, Anatoly **1986**:2
Shilts, Randy **1993**:4
  Obituary **1994**:3
Shocked, Michelle **1989**:4
Sidney, Ivan
  Brief Entry **1987**:2
Sinclair, Mary **1985**:2
Singer, Margaret Thaler
  Obituary **2005**:1
Slotnick, Barry
  Brief Entry **1987**:4
Slovo, Joe **1989**:2
Smith, Samantha
  Obituary **1985**:3
Snyder, Mitch
  Obituary **1991**:1
Sontag, Susan
  Obituary **2006**:1
Spong, John **1991**:3 **2001**:1
Steele, Shelby **1991**:2
Steinem, Gloria **1996**:2
Stephens, Arran and Ratana **2008**:4
Steptoe, Patrick
  Obituary **1988**:3
Stevens, Eileen **1987**:3
Stevens, James
  Brief Entry **1988**:1
Strong, Maurice **1993**:1
Strummer, Joe
  Obituary **2004**:1
Sullivan, Leon
  Obituary **2002**:2
Sullivan, Louis **1990**:4
Summers, Anne **1990**:2
Suu Kyi, Aung San **1996**:2
Sweeney, John J. **2000**:3
Szent-Gyoergyi, Albert
  Obituary **1987**:2
Tafel, Richard **2000**:4
Tambo, Oliver **1991**:3
Tannen, Deborah **1995**:1
Terry, Randall **1991**:4
Thomas, Clarence **1992**:2

Ture, Kwame
  Obituary **1999**:2
Unz, Ron **1999**:1
Verdi-Fletcher, Mary **1998**:2
Vitousek, Peter **2003**:1
Waddell, Thomas F.
  Obituary **1988**:2
Waters, Alice **2006**:3
Wattleton, Faye **1989**:1
Wei Jingsheng **1998**:2
Wells, Sharlene
  Brief Entry **1985**:1
West, Cornel **1994**:2
Whelan, Tensie **2007**:1
White, Ryan
  Obituary **1990**:3
Whitestone, Heather **1995**:1
Wiesenthal, Simon
  Obituary **2006**:4
Wigand, Jeffrey **2000**:4
Wildmon, Donald **1988**:4
Williams, Hosea
  Obituary **2001**:2
Williamson, Marianne **1991**:4
Willson, S. Brian **1989**:3
Wilmut, Ian **1997**:3
Wilson, William Julius **1997**:1
Wolf, Naomi **1994**:3
Woodruff, Robert Winship
  Obituary **1985**:1
Wu, Harry **1996**:1
Yard, Molly **1991**:4
Yeang, Ken **2008**:3
Yokich, Stephen P. **1995**:4
Youngblood, Johnny Ray **1994**:1
Yunus, Muhammad **2007**:3
Zamora, Pedro
  Obituary **1995**:2
Zech, Lando W.
  Brief Entry **1987**:4
Zigler, Edward **1994**:1

SPORTS
Abbott, Jim **1988**:3
Abercrombie, Josephine **1987**:2
Adu, Freddy **2005**:3
Agassi, Andre **1990**:2
Agee, Tommie
  Obituary **2001**:4
Aikman, Troy **1994**:2
Ainge, Danny **1987**:1
Akers, Michelle **1996**:1
Albert, Marv **1994**:3
Albom, Mitch **1999**:3
Ali, Laila **2001**:2
Ali, Muhammad **1997**:2
Allen, Mel
  Obituary **1996**:4
Allen, Ray **2002**:1
Allenby, Robert **2007**:1
Alter, Hobie
  Brief Entry **1985**:1
Angelos, Peter **1995**:4
Anthony, Earl
  Obituary **2002**:3
Aoki, Rocky **1990**:2
Arakawa, Shizuka **2006**:4
Armstrong, Henry
  Obituary **1989**:1
Armstrong, Lance **2000**:1
Ashe, Arthur
  Obituary **1993**:3

Auerbach, Red
  Obituary **2008**:1
Austin, 'Stone Cold' Steve **2001**:3
Axthelm, Pete
  Obituary **1991**:3
Azinger, Paul **1995**:2
Babilonia, Tai **1997**:2
Baiul, Oksana **1995**:3
Baker, Kathy
  Brief Entry **1986**:1
Barber, Tiki **2007**:1
Barkley, Charles **1988**:2
Barnes, Ernie **1997**:4
Baumgartner, Bruce
  Brief Entry **1987**:3
Becker, Boris
  Brief Entry **1985**:3
Beckham, David **2003**:1
Bell, Ricky
  Obituary **1985**:1
Belle, Albert **1996**:4
Benoit, Joan **1986**:3
Best, George
  Obituary **2007**:1
Bias, Len
  Obituary **1986**:3
Bird, Larry **1990**:3
Blair, Bonnie **1992**:3
Bledsoe, Drew **1995**:1
Boggs, Wade **1989**:3
Boitano, Brian **1988**:3
Bonds, Barry **1993**:3
Bonilla, Bobby **1992**:2
Bosworth, Brian **1989**:1
Boudreau, Louis
  Obituary **2002**:3
Bourque, Raymond Jean **1997**:3
Bowe, Riddick **1993**:2
Bowman, Scotty **1998**:4
Bradman, Sir Donald
  Obituary **2002**:1
Brady, Tom **2002**:4
Bremen, Barry **1987**:3
Brown, Jim **1993**:2
Brown, Paul
  Obituary **1992**:1
Bryant, Kobe **1998**:3
Burton, Jake **2007**:1
Busch, August Anheuser, Jr.
  Obituary **1990**:2
Busch, Kurt **2006**:1
Buss, Jerry **1989**:3
Butcher, Susan **1991**:1
Callaway, Ely
  Obituary **2002**:3
Campanella, Roy
  Obituary **1994**:1
Canseco, Jose **1990**:2
Capriati, Jennifer **1991**:1
Caray, Harry **1988**:3
  Obituary **1998**:3
Carter, Gary **1987**:1
Carter, Joe **1994**:2
Carter, Rubin **2000**:3
Carter, Vince **2001**:4
Chamberlain, Joba **2008**:3
Chamberlain, Wilt
  Obituary **2000**:2
Chaney, John **1989**:1
Chastain, Brandi **2001**:3
Chen, T.C.
  Brief Entry **1987**:3

Cherry, Don **1993**:4
Chyna **2001**:4
Clemens, Roger **1991**:4
Clijsters, Kim **2006**:3
Coffey, Paul **1985**:4
Collins, Kerry **2002**:3
Conigliaro, Tony
    Obituary **1990**:3
Conner, Dennis **1987**:2
Cooper, Cynthia **1999**:1
Copeland, Al **1988**:3
Cosell, Howard
    Obituary **1995**:4
Costas, Bob **1986**:4
Couples, Fred **1994**:4
Courier, Jim **1993**:2
Creamer, Paula **2006**:2
Crosby, Sidney **2006**:3
Cunningham, Randall **1990**:1
Curren, Tommy
    Brief Entry **1987**:4
Curtis, Ben **2004**:2
Damon, Johnny **2005**:4
Danza, Tony **1989**:1
Davenport, Lindsay **1999**:2
Davis, Eric **1987**:4
Davis, Terrell **1998**:2
Day, Pat **1995**:2
DeBartolo, Edward J., Jr. **1989**:3
De La Hoya, Oscar **1998**:2
Desormeaux, Kent **1990**:2
DiBello, Paul
    Brief Entry **1986**:4
DiMaggio, Joe
    Obituary **1999**:3
Djokovic, Novak **2008**:4
Dolan, Tom **2001**:2
Donnellan, Nanci **1995**:2
Doubleday, Nelson, Jr. **1987**:1
Douglas, Buster **1990**:4
Dravecky, Dave **1992**:1
Drexler, Clyde **1992**:4
Drysdale, Don
    Obituary **1994**:1
Duncan, Tim **2000**:1
Durocher, Leo
    Obituary **1992**:2
Duval, David **2000**:3
Duvall, Camille
    Brief Entry **1988**:1
Dykstra, Lenny **1993**:4
Eagleson, Alan **1987**:4
Earnhardt, Dale
    Obituary **2001**:4
Earnhardt, Dale, Jr. **2004**:4
Ederle, Gertrude
    Obituary **2005**:1
Edwards, Harry **1989**:4
Elway, John **1990**:3
Epstein, Theo **2003**:4
Esiason, Boomer **1991**:1
Evans, Janet **1989**:1
Ewing, Patrick **1985**:3
Fabris, Enrico **2006**:4
Faldo, Nick **1993**:3
Favre, Brett Lorenzo **1997**:2
Federer, Roger **2004**:2
Federov, Sergei **1995**:1
Fehr, Donald **1987**:2
Ferrari, Enzo **1988**:4
Fielder, Cecil **1993**:2
Fiennes, Ranulph **1990**:3

Firestone, Roy **1988**:2
Fittipaldi, Emerson **1994**:2
Flood, Curt
    Obituary **1997**:2
Flutie, Doug **1999**:2
Foreman, George **2004**:2
Foss, Joe **1990**:3
Fossett, Steve **2007**:2
Franchitti, Dario **2008**:1
Freeman, Cathy **2001**:3
Fuhr, Grant **1997**:3
Furyk, Jim **2004**:2
Galindo, Rudy **2001**:2
Garcia, Joe
    Brief Entry **1986**:4
Gardner, Randy **1997**:2
Garnett, Kevin **2000**:3
Gathers, Hank
    Obituary **1990**:3
Gault, Willie **1991**:2
Gerulaitis, Vitas
    Obituary **1995**:1
Giamatti, A. Bartlett **1988**:4
    Obituary **1990**:1
Gibson, Althea
    Obituary **2004**:4
Gibson, Kirk **1985**:2
Giguere, Jean-Sebastien **2004**:2
Gilmour, Doug **1994**:3
Glaus, Troy **2003**:3
Gomez, 'Lefty'
    Obituary **1989**:3
Gooden, Dwight **1985**:2
Gordeeva, Ekaterina **1996**:4
Gordon, Jeff **1996**:1
Graf, Steffi **1987**:4
Granato, Cammi **1999**:3
Grange, Red
    Obituary **1991**:3
Graziano, Rocky
    Obituary **1990**:4
Greenberg, Hank
    Obituary **1986**:4
Gretzky, Wayne **1989**:2
Griffey, Ken Jr. **1994**:1
Grinkov, Sergei
    Obituary **1996**:2
Gruden, Jon **2003**:4
Gumbel, Greg **1996**:4
Gwynn, Tony **1995**:1
Hagler, Marvelous Marvin **1985**:2
Hamilton, Lewis **2008**:4
Hamilton, Scott **1998**:2
Hamm, Mia **2000**:1
Hamm, Paul **2005**:1
Hanauer, Chip **1986**:2
Hardaway, Anfernee **1996**:2
Harkes, John **1996**:4
Harmon, Tom
    Obituary **1990**:3
Hart, Carey **2006**:4
Harwell, Ernie **1997**:3
Hasek, Dominik **1998**:3
Hawk, Tony **2001**:4
Hayes, Woody
    Obituary **1987**:2
Helton, Todd **2001**:1
Hempleman-Adams, David **2004**:3
Henderson, Rickey **2002**:3
Henin-Hardenne, Justine **2004**:4
Hernandez, Felix **2008**:2
Hernandez, Willie **1985**:1

Hershiser, Orel **1989**:2
Hewitt, Lleyton **2002**:2
Hextall, Ron **1988**:2
Hill, Grant **1995**:3
Hill, Lynn **1991**:2
Hingis, Martina **1999**:1
Hogan, Ben
    Obituary **1997**:4
Hogan, Hulk **1987**:3
Holtz, Lou **1986**:4
Holyfield, Evander **1991**:3
Howard, Desmond Kevin **1997**:2
Howser, Dick
    Obituary **1987**:4
Hughes, Sarah **2002**:4
Hull, Brett **1991**:4
Hunter, Catfish
    Obituary **2000**:1
Indurain, Miguel **1994**:1
Inkster, Juli **2000**:2
Irvin, Michael **1996**:3
Irwin, Hale **2005**:2
Ivanisevic, Goran **2002**:1
Iverson, Allen **2001**:4
Jackson, Bo **1986**:3
Jackson, Phil **1996**:3
Jagr, Jaromir **1995**:4
James, LeBron **2007**:3
Jenkins, Sally **1997**:2
Jeter, Derek **1999**:4
Johnson, Earvin 'Magic' **1988**:4
Johnson, Jimmie **2007**:2
Johnson, Jimmy **1993**:3
Johnson, Kevin **1991**:1
Johnson, Keyshawn **2000**:4
Johnson, Larry **1993**:3
Johnson, Michael **2000**:1
Johnson, Randy **1996**:2
Jones, Jerry **1994**:4
Jones, Marion **1998**:4
Jordan, Michael **1987**:2
Joyner, Florence Griffith **1989**:2
    Obituary **1999**:1
Joyner-Kersee, Jackie **1993**:1
Kallen, Jackie **1994**:1
Kanokogi, Rusty
    Brief Entry **1987**:1
Kasparov, Garry **1997**:4
Kelly, Jim **1991**:4
Kemp, Jack **1990**:4
Kemp, Jan **1987**:2
Kemp, Shawn **1995**:1
Kerr, Cristie **2008**:2
Kerrigan, Nancy **1994**:3
Kidd, Jason **2003**:2
King, Don **1989**:1
Kiraly, Karch
    Brief Entry **1987**:1
Kite, Tom **1990**:3
Klima, Petr **1987**:1
Knievel, Robbie **1990**:1
Knight, Bobby **1985**:3
Koch, Bill **1992**:3
Konstantinov, Vladimir **1997**:4
Kournikova, Anna **2000**:3
Kroc, Ray
    Obituary **1985**:1
Krone, Julie **1989**:2
Kruk, John **1994**:4
Krzyzewski, Mike **1993**:2
Kukoc, Toni **1995**:4
Laettner, Christian **1993**:1

Stewart, Payne
    Obituary 2000:2
Stewart, Tony 2003:4
Stockton, John Houston 1997:3
Stofflet, Ty
    Brief Entry 1987:1
Strange, Curtis 1988:4
Street, Picabo 1999:3
Strobl, Fritz 2003:3
Strug, Kerri 1997:3
Summitt, Pat 2004:1
Suzuki, Ichiro 2002:2
Swoopes, Sheryl 1998:2
Tagliabue, Paul 1990:2
Tarkenian, Jerry 1990:4
Taylor, Lawrence 1987:3
Testaverde, Vinny 1987:2
Teter, Hannah 2006:4
Thomas, Debi 1987:2
Thomas, Derrick
    Obituary 2000:3
Thomas, Frank 1994:3
Thomas, Isiah 1989:2
Thomas, Thurman 1993:1
Thompson, John 1988:3
Tomba, Alberto 1992:3
Torre, Joseph Paul 1997:1
Trask, Amy 2003:3
Trinidad, Felix 2000:4
Turner, Ted 1989:1
Tyson, Mike 1986:4
Unitas, Johnny
    Obituary 2003:4
Upshaw, Gene 1988:1
Van Dyken, Amy 1997:1
Van Slyke, Andy 1992:4
Vaughn, Mo 1999:2
Veeck, Bill
    Obituary 1986:1
Ventura, Jesse 1999:2
Villeneuve, Jacques 1997:1
Vincent, Fay 1990:2
Vitale, Dick 1988:4 1994:4
Waddell, Thomas F.
    Obituary 1988:2
Wade, Dwyane 2007:1
Wallace, Ben 2004:3
Walsh, Bill 1987:4
Wariner, Jeremy 2006:3
Warner, Kurt 2000:3
Webb, Karrie 2000:4
Webber, Chris 1994:1
Weber, Pete 1986:3
Weir, Mike 2004:1
Welch, Bob 1991:3
Wells, David 1999:3
Wescott, Seth 2006:4
Whaley, Suzy 2003:4
White, Bill 1989:3
White, Byron
    Obituary 2003:3
White, Reggie 1993:4
Wilkens, Lenny 1995:2
Williams, Doug 1988:2
Williams, Edward Bennett
    Obituary 1988:4
Williams, Ricky 2000:2
Williams, Serena 1999:4
Williams, Ted
    Obituary 2003:4
Williams, Venus 1998:2
Witt, Katarina 1991:3

Woodard, Lynette 1986:2
Woods, Tiger 1995:4
Woodson, Ron 1996:4
Worthy, James 1991:2
Yamaguchi, Kristi 1992:3
Yao Ming 2004:1
Young, Steve 1995:2
Yzerman, Steve 1991:2
Zamboni, Frank J.
    Brief Entry 1986:4
Zanardi, Alex 1998:2
Zatopek, Emil
    Obituary 2001:3
Zito, Barry 2003:3

TECHNOLOGY

Adair, Red 1987:3
Allaire, Jeremy 2006:4
Allaire, Paul 1995:1
Anderson, Tom and Chris DeWolfe
    2007:2
Andreessen, Marc 1996:2
Backus, John W.
    Obituary 2008:2
Balsillie, Jim and Mike Lazaridis
    2006:4
Barksdale, James L. 1998:2
Beal, Deron 2005:3
Belluzzo, Rick 2001:3
Berners-Lee, Tim 1997:4
Bezos, Jeff 1998:4
Bird, Brad 2005:4
Bloch, Erich 1987:4
Bose, Amar
    Brief Entry 1986:4
Boyer, Herbert Wayne 1985:1
Bradley, Todd 2003:3
Burum, Stephen H.
    Brief Entry 1987:2
Bushnell, Nolan 1985:1
Butterfield, Stewart and Caterina
    Fake 2007:3
Case, Steve 1995:4 1996:4
Cassidy, Mike 2006:1
Cerf, Vinton G. 1999:2
Chaudhari, Praveen 1989:4
Chen, Steve and Chad Hurley 2007
    :2
Chizen, Bruce 2004:2
Clarke, Richard A. 2002:2
Cray, Seymour R.
    Brief Entry 1986:3
    Obituary 1997:2
David, George 2005:1
Davis, Noel 1990:3
Dell, Michael 1996:2
De Luca, Guerrino 2007:1
Dolby, Ray Milton
    Brief Entry 1986:1
Donahue, Tim 2004:3
Dunlap, Albert J. 1997:2
Dzhanibekov, Vladimir 1988:1
Ellison, Larry 2004:2
Engibous, Thomas J. 2003:3
Engstrom, Elmer W.
    Obituary 1985:2
Evans, Nancy 2000:4
Fanning, Shawn 2001:1
Fender, Leo
    Obituary 1992:1
Filo, David and Jerry Yang 1998:3
Gardner, David and Tom 2001:4

Garneau, Marc 1985:1
Gates, Bill 1993:3 1987:4
Gould, Gordon 1987:1
Hagelstein, Peter
    Brief Entry 1986:3
Haladjian, Rafi 2008:3
Hewlett, William
    Obituary 2001:4
Hounsfield, Godfrey 1989:2
Inman, Bobby Ray 1985:1
Irwin, James
    Obituary 1992:1
Jacuzzi, Candido
    Obituary 1987:1
Jarvik, Robert K. 1985:1
Jemison, Mae C. 1993:1
Kamen, Dean 2003:1
Kilby, Jack 2002:2
Kimsey, James V. 2001:1
Kloss, Henry E.
    Brief Entry 1985:2
Koch, Bill 1992:3
Kurzweil, Raymond 1986:3
Kutaragi, Ken 2005:3
Kwoh, Yik San 1988:2
Lalami, Laila 2007:1
Lamborghini, Ferrucio
    Obituary 1993:3
Land, Edwin H.
    Obituary 1991:3
Langer, Robert 2003:4
Lanier, Jaron 1993:4
Ma, Jack 2007:1
Ma, Pony 2006:3
MacCready, Paul 1986:4
Malda, Rob 2007:3
McGowan, William 1985:2
McLaren, Norman
    Obituary 1987:2
Minsky, Marvin 1994:3
Moody, John 1985:3
Morita, Akio
    Obituary 2000:2
Morita, Akio 1989:4
Newman, Joseph 1987:1
Noyce, Robert N. 1985:4
Ollila, Jorma 2003:4
Pack, Ellen 2001:2
Palmisano, Samuel J. 2003:1
Parsons, Richard 2002:4
Peluso, Michelle 2007:4
Perlman, Steve 1998:2
Perry, William 1994:4
Pfeiffer, Eckhard 1998:4
Probst, Larry 2005:1
Ramsay, Mike 2002:1
Raskin, Jef 1997:4
Rifkin, Jeremy 1990:3
Ritchie, Dennis and Kenneth
    Thompson 2000:1
Roberts, Brian L. 2002:4
Roberts, Steven K. 1992:1
Rutan, Burt 1987:2
Schank, Roger 1989:2
Schmidt, Eric 2002:4
Scholz, Tom 1987:2
Schroeder, William J.
    Obituary 1986:4
Sculley, John 1989:4
Seidenberg, Ivan 2004:1
Semel, Terry 2002:2
Shirley, Donna 1999:1

Sinclair, Mary **1985**:2
Taylor, Jeff **2001**:3
Thomas, Edmond J. **2005**:1
Thompson, John W. **2005**:1
Tito, Dennis **2002**:1
Titov, Gherman
   Obituary **2001**:3
Tom and Ray Magliozzi **1991**:4
Toomer, Ron **1990**:1
Torvalds, Linus **1999**:3
Treybig, James G. **1988**:3
Walker, Jay **2004**:2
Wang, An **1986**:1
   Obituary **1990**:3
Wright, Will **2003**:4
Yamamoto, Kenichi **1989**:1
Zuckerberg, Mark **2008**:2

TELEVISION

Abrams, J. J. **2007**:3
Adams, Amy **2008**:4
Adams, Don
   Obituary **2007**:1
Affleck, Ben **1999**:1
Alba, Jessica **2001**:2
Albert, Eddie
   Obituary **2006**:3
Albert, Marv **1994**:3
Albom, Mitch **1999**:3
Albrecht, Chris **2005**:4
Alda, Robert
   Obituary **1986**:3
Alexander, Jane **1994**:2
Alexander, Jason **1993**:3
Allen, Debbie **1998**:2
Allen, Steve
   Obituary **2001**:2
Allen, Tim **1993**:1
Alley, Kirstie **1990**:3
Allyson, June
   Obituary **2007**:3
Altman, Robert **1993**:2
Amanpour, Christiane **1997**:2
Ameche, Don
   Obituary **1994**:2
Amsterdam, Morey
   Obituary **1997**:1
Ancier, Garth **1989**:1
Anderson, Gillian **1997**:1
Anderson, Harry **1988**:2
Anderson, Judith
   Obituary **1992**:3
Andrews, Julie **1996**:1
Angelou, Maya **1993**:4
Aniston, Jennifer **2000**:3
Apatow, Judd **2006**:3
Applegate, Christina **2000**:4
Arden, Eve
   Obituary **1991**:2
Arkin, Alan **2007**:4
Arledge, Roone **1992**:2
Arlen, Harold
   Obituary **1986**:3
Arnaz, Desi
   Obituary **1987**:1
Arnold, Tom **1993**:2
Arquette, Rosanna **1985**:2
Astin, Sean **2005**:1
Atkinson, Rowan **2004**:3
Autry, Gene
   Obituary **1999**:1

Axthelm, Pete
   Obituary **1991**:3
Aykroyd, Dan **1989**:3 **1997**:3
Azaria, Hank **2001**:3
Bacall, Lauren **1997**:3
Backus, Jim
   Obituary **1990**:1
Bacon, Kevin **1995**:3
Baddeley, Hermione
   Obituary **1986**:4
Bailey, Pearl
   Obituary **1991**:1
Bakula, Scott **2003**:1
Ball, Alan **2005**:1
Ball, Lucille
   Obituary **1989**:3
Baranski, Christine **2001**:2
Barbera, Joseph **1988**:2
Bardem, Javier **2008**:4
Barkin, Ellen **1987**:3
Barney **1993**:4
Baron Cohen, Sacha **2007**:3
Barr, Roseanne **1989**:1
Barrymore, Drew **1995**:3
Basinger, Kim **1987**:2
Bassett, Angela **1994**:4
Bateman, Jason **2005**:3
Bateman, Justine **1988**:4
Baxter, Anne
   Obituary **1986**:1
Beals, Jennifer **2005**:2
Beatty, Warren **2000**:1
Belushi, Jim **1986**:2
Belzer, Richard **1985**:3
Bergen, Candice **1990**:1
Berle, Milton
   Obituary **2003**:2
Berman, Gail **2006**:1
Bernardi, Herschel
   Obituary **1986**:4
Bernsen, Corbin **1990**:2
Bernstein, Leonard
   Obituary **1991**:1
Berry, Halle **1996**:2
Bialik, Mayim **1993**:3
Bird, Brad **2005**:4
Bishop, Joey
   Obituary **2008**:4
Bixby, Bill
   Obituary **1994**:2
Black, Carole **2003**:1
Blades, Ruben **1998**:2
Blaine, David **2003**:3
Blanc, Mel
   Obituary **1989**:4
Blanchett, Cate **1999**:3
Bloodworth-Thomason, Linda **1994**
   :1
Bloom, Orlando **2004**:2
Bochco, Steven **1989**:1
Bolger, Ray
   Obituary **1987**:2
Bonet, Lisa **1989**:2
Bono, Sonny **1992**:2
   Obituary **1998**:2
Booth, Shirley
   Obituary **1993**:2
Bourdain, Anthony **2008**:3
Bowen, Julie **2007**:1
Boyle, Lara Flynn **2003**:4
Boyle, Peter **2002**:3

Bradley, Ed
   Obituary **2008**:1
Bradshaw, John **1992**:1
Brady, Wayne **2008**:3
Braff, Zach **2005**:2
Brandy **1996**:4
Brenneman, Amy **2002**:1
Bridges, Lloyd
   Obituary **1998**:3
Brinkley, David
   Obituary **2004**:3
Broadbent, Jim **2008**:4
Brokaw, Tom **2000**:3
Bronson, Charles
   Obituary **2004**:4
Brooks, Mel **2003**:1
Brosnan, Pierce **2000**:3
Brown, Les **1994**:3
Brown, Ruth
   Obituary **2008**:1
Bruckheimer, Jerry **2007**:2
Buckley, Betty **1996**:2
Bullock, Sandra **1995**:4
Burnett, Carol **2000**:3
Burnett, Mark **2003**:1
Burns, George
   Obituary **1996**:3
Burns, Ken **1995**:2
Burr, Raymond
   Obituary **1994**:1
Burrows, James **2005**:3
Butler, Brett **1995**:1
Buttons, Red
   Obituary **2007**:3
Bynes, Amanda **2005**:1
Byrne, Rhonda **2008**:2
Caan, James **2004**:4
Caine, Michael **2000**:4
Calhoun, Rory
   Obituary **1999**:4
Campbell, Neve **1998**:2
Campion, Jane **1991**:4
Candy, John **1988**:2
   Obituary **1994**:3
Cannon, Nick **2006**:4
Carell, Steve **2006**:4
Carey, Drew **1997**:4
Carlin, George **1996**:3
Carney, Art
   Obituary **2005**:1
Carrey, Jim **1995**:1
Carson, Johnny
   Obituary **2006**:1
Carson, Lisa Nicole **1999**:3
Carter, Chris **2000**:1
Carter, Nell
   Obituary **2004**:2
Caruso, David **1994**:3
Carvey, Dana **1994**:1
Cassavetes, John
   Obituary **1989**:2
Cattrall, Kim **2003**:3
Caulfield, Joan
   Obituary **1992**:1
Cavanagh, Tom **2003**:1
Caviezel, Jim **2005**:3
Chancellor, John
   Obituary **1997**:1
Channing, Stockard **1991**:3
Chappelle, Dave **2005**:3
Chase, Chevy **1990**:1
Chavez, Linda **1999**:3

Cher **1993**:1
Cherry, Don **1993**:4
Chiklis, Michael **2003**:3
Child, Julia **1999**:4
Cho, Margaret **1995**:2
Chow Yun-fat **1999**:4
Christensen, Hayden **2003**:3
Chung, Connie **1988**:4
Clarkson, Kelly **2003**:3
Clarkson, Patricia **2005**:3
Clay, Andrew Dice **1991**:1
Cleese, John **1989**:2
Clooney, George **1996**:4
Close, Glenn **1988**:3
Coca, Imogene
    Obituary **2002**:2
Coco, James
    Obituary **1987**:2
Colasanto, Nicholas
    Obituary **1985**:2
Colbert, Stephen **2007**:4
Coleman, Dabney **1988**:3
Condon, Bill **2007**:3
Connery, Sean **1990**:4
Convy, Bert
    Obituary **1992**:1
Cook, Peter
    Obituary **1995**:2
Cooke, Alistair
    Obituary **2005**:3
Cooper, Anderson **2006**:1
Cooper, Chris **2004**:1
Copperfield, David **1986**:3
Coppola, Francis Ford **1989**:4
Corbett, John **2004**:1
Corwin, Jeff **2005**:1
Cosby, Bill **1999**:2
Cosell, Howard
    Obituary **1995**:4
Costas, Bob **1986**:4
Couric, Katherine **1991**:4
Cousteau, Jacques-Yves
    Obituary **1998**:2
Cowell, Simon **2003**:4
Cox, Courteney **1996**:2
Cox, Richard Joseph
    Brief Entry **1985**:1
Craig, Daniel **2008**:1
Crais, Robert **2007**:4
Crawford, Broderick
    Obituary **1986**:3
Crawford, Cindy **1993**:3
Crawford, Michael **1994**:2
Crenna, Richard
    Obituary **2004**:1
Crichton, Michael **1995**:3
Cronkite, Walter Leland **1997**:3
Crothers, Scatman
    Obituary **1987**:1
Crystal, Billy **1985**:3
Curry, Ann **2001**:1
Curtis, Jamie Lee **1995**:1
Cushing, Peter
    Obituary **1995**:1
Cyrus, Miley **2008**:3
Dalton, Timothy **1988**:4
Daly, Carson **2002**:4
Damon, Matt **1999**:1
Danes, Claire **1999**:4
Dangerfield, Rodney
    Obituary **2006**:1
Daniels, Faith **1993**:3

Daniels, Jeff **1989**:4
Danza, Tony **1989**:1
David, Larry **2003**:4
Davis, Bette
    Obituary **1990**:1
Davis, Geena **1992**:1
Davis, Paige **2004**:2
Davis, Sammy, Jr.
    Obituary **1990**:4
Day, Dennis
    Obituary **1988**:4
De Cordova, Frederick **1985**:2
Deen, Paula **2008**:3
DeGeneres, Ellen **1995**:3
Delany, Dana **2008**:4
De Matteo, Drea **2005**:2
Dempsey, Patrick **2006**:1
Denver, Bob
    Obituary **2006**:4
Depardieu, Gerard **1991**:2
Depp, Johnny **1991**:3
De Vito, Danny **1987**:1
Dewhurst, Colleen
    Obituary **1992**:2
Diamond, Selma
    Obituary **1985**:2
DiCaprio, Leonardo Wilhelm **1997**:2
Dickerson, Nancy H.
    Obituary **1998**:2
Dickinson, Janice **2005**:2
Diller, Barry **1991**:1
Disney, Roy E. **1986**:3
Doherty, Shannen **1994**:2
Dolenz, Micky **1986**:4
Douglas, Michael **1986**:2
Douglas, Mike
    Obituary **2007**:4
Downey, Morton, Jr. **1988**:4
Downey, Robert, Jr. **2007**:1
Drescher, Fran **1995**:3
Duchovny, David **1998**:3
Duff, Hilary **2004**:4
Duffy, Karen **1998**:1
Dukakis, Olympia **1996**:4
Duke, Red
    Brief Entry **1987**:1
Durrell, Gerald
    Obituary **1995**:3
Duvall, Robert **1999**:3
Eastwood, Clint **1993**:3
Ebersole, Christine **2007**:2
Ebert, Roger **1998**:3
Ebsen, Buddy
    Obituary **2004**:3
Efron, Zac **2008**:2
Eisner, Michael **1989**:2
Elfman, Jenna **1999**:4
Ellerbee, Linda **1993**:3
Elliott, Denholm
    Obituary **1993**:2
Engstrom, Elmer W.
    Obituary **1985**:2
Evans, Dale
    Obituary **2001**:3
Eve **2004**:3
Fallon, Jimmy **2003**:1
Fanning, Dakota **2005**:2
Farley, Chris
    Obituary **1998**:2
Fawcett, Farrah **1998**:4
Feldshuh, Tovah **2005**:3

Fell, Norman
    Obituary **1999**:2
Ferguson, Craig **2005**:4
Ferrell, Will **2004**:4
Ferrer, Jose
    Obituary **1992**:3
Ferrera, America **2006**:2
Fey, Tina **2005**:3
Field, Sally **1995**:3
Finney, Albert **2003**:3
Firestone, Roy **1988**:2
Fishburne, Laurence **1995**:3
Fisher, Carrie **1991**:1
Flanders, Ed
    Obituary **1995**:3
Flavor Flav **2007**:3
Fleiss, Mike **2003**:4
Fleming, Art
    Obituary **1995**:4
Flockhart, Calista **1998**:4
Fonda, Bridget **1995**:1
Ford, Faith **2005**:3
Ford, Glenn
    Obituary **2007**:4
Ford, Tennessee Ernie
    Obituary **1992**:2
Fosse, Bob
    Obituary **1988**:1
Foster, Jodie **1989**:2
Foster, Phil
    Obituary **1985**:3
Fox, Matthew **2006**:1
Fox, Michael J. **1986**:1 **2001**:3
Fox, Vivica **1999**:1
Foxworthy, Jeff **1996**:1
Foxx, Jamie **2001**:1
Foxx, Redd
    Obituary **1992**:2
Franciscus, James
    Obituary **1992**:1
Frankenheimer, John
    Obituary **2003**:4
Franz, Dennis **1995**:2
Freeman, Morgan **1990**:4
Freleng, Friz
    Obituary **1995**:4
Fuller, Simon **2008**:2
Funt, Allen
    Obituary **2000**:1
Gabor, Eva
    Obituary **1996**:1
Gallagher, Peter **2004**:3
Gandolfini, James **2001**:3
Garcia, Andy **1999**:3
Gardenia, Vincent
    Obituary **1993**:2
Garner, Jennifer **2003**:1
Garofalo, Janeane **1996**:4
Gellar, Sarah Michelle **1999**:3
Gere, Richard **1994**:3
Gifford, Kathie Lee **1992**:2
Gilford, Jack
    Obituary **1990**:4
Gillett, George **1988**:1
Gish, Lillian
    Obituary **1993**:4
Glass, Ira **2008**:2
Gleason, Jackie
    Obituary **1987**:4
Gless, Sharon **1989**:3
Glover, Danny **1998**:4

Langella, Frank **2008**:3
Lansbury, Angela **1993**:1
LaPaglia, Anthony **2004**:4
Larroquette, John **1986**:2
LaSalle, Eriq **1996**:4
Laurie, Hugh **2007**:2
Lawless, Lucy **1997**:4
Lawrence, Martin **1993**:4
Lawson, Nigella **2003**:2
Laybourne, Geraldine **1997**:1
Leach, Penelope **1992**:4
Leach, Robin
  Brief Entry **1985**:4
Leary, Denis **1993**:3
LeBlanc, Matt **2005**:4
Ledger, Heath **2006**:3
Lee, Jason **2006**:4
Lee, Pamela **1996**:4
Lee, Sandra **2008**:3
Leguizamo, John **1999**:1
Leigh, Jennifer Jason **1995**:2
Lemmon, Jack **1998**:4
  Obituary **2002**:3
Leno, Jay **1987**:1
Letterman, David **1989**:3
Levinson, Arthur D. **2008**:3
Levinson, Barry **1989**:3
Levy, Eugene **2004**:3
Lewis, Juliette **1999**:3
Lewis, Richard **1992**:1
Lewis, Shari **1993**:1
  Obituary **1999**:1
Liberace
  Obituary **1987**:2
Liguori, Peter **2005**:2
Liman, Doug **2007**:1
Ling, Lisa **2004**:2
Little, Cleavon
  Obituary **1993**:2
Liu, Lucy **2000**:4
Livingston, Ron **2007**:2
LL Cool J **1998**:2
Locklear, Heather **1994**:3
Lohan, Lindsay **2005**:3
Long, Shelley **1985**:1
Lopez, George **2003**:4
Lopez, Jennifer **1998**:4
Lord, Jack
  Obituary **1998**:2
Lords, Traci **1995**:4
Louis-Dreyfus, Julia **1994**:1
Loy, Myrna
  Obituary **1994**:2
Lucci, Susan **1999**:4
Ludacris **2007**:4
Lupino, Ida
  Obituary **1996**:1
Lynch, David **1990**:4
Mac, Bernie **2003**:1
MacFarlane, Seth **2006**:1
MacMurray, Fred
  Obituary **1992**:2
MacRae, Gordon
  Obituary **1986**:2
Macy, William H. **1999**:3
Madden, Chris **2006**:1
Madden, John **1995**:1
Maher, Bill **1996**:2
Mako
  Obituary **2007**:3
Malkovich, John **1988**:2
Malone, John C. **1988**:3 **1996**:3

Mandel, Howie **1989**:1
Mantegna, Joe **1992**:1
Marber, Patrick **2007**:4
Marchand, Nancy
  Obituary **2001**:1
Martin, Dean
  Obituary **1996**:2
Martin, Mary
  Obituary **1991**:2
Martin, Steve **1992**:2
Matlin, Marlee **1992**:2
Matthau, Walter **2000**:3
McCarthy, Jenny **1997**:4
McDonnell, Mary **2008**:2
McDormand, Frances **1997**:3
McDowall, Roddy
  Obituary **1999**:1
McGillis, Kelly **1989**:3
McGinley, Ted **2004**:4
McGraw, Phil **2005**:2
McGregor, Ewan **1998**:2
McKee, Lonette **1996**:1
McKellen, Ian **1994**:1
McMahon, Julian **2006**:1
Meadows, Audrey
  Obituary **1996**:3
Meltzer, Brad **2005**:4
Meredith, Burgess
  Obituary **1998**:1
Merkerson, S. Epatha **2006**:4
Messing, Debra **2004**:4
Midler, Bette **1989**:4
Milano, Alyssa **2002**:3
Millan, Cesar **2007**:4
Milland, Ray
  Obituary **1986**:2
Miller, Dennis **1992**:4
Milligan, Spike
  Obituary **2003**:2
Minogue, Kylie **2003**:4
Mirren, Helen **2005**:1
Mitchum, Robert
  Obituary **1997**:4
Molina, Alfred **2005**:3
Mo'Nique **2008**:1
Montgomery, Elizabeth
  Obituary **1995**:4
Moonves, Les **2004**:2
Moore, Clayton
  Obituary **2000**:3
Moore, Demi **1991**:4
Moore, Dudley
  Obituary **2003**:2
Moore, Julianne **1998**:1
Moore, Mary Tyler **1996**:2
Morita, Noriyuki 'Pat' **1987**:3
Morris, Kathryn **2006**:4
Morrow, Rob **2006**:4
Mortensen, Viggo **2003**:3
Mos Def **2005**:4
Moss, Carrie-Anne **2004**:3
Moyers, Bill **1991**:4
Muniz, Frankie **2001**:4
Murdoch, Rupert **1988**:4
Murphy, Brittany **2005**:1
Murphy, Eddie **1989**:2
Musburger, Brent **1985**:1
Myers, Mike **1992**:3 **1997**:4
Nance, Jack
  Obituary **1997**:3
Neeson, Liam **1993**:4

Nelson, Harriet
  Obituary **1995**:1
Nelson, Rick
  Obituary **1986**:1
Nelson, Willie **1993**:4
Newton-John, Olivia **1998**:4
Nichols, Mike **1994**:4
Nissel, Angela **2006**:4
Nixon, Bob **2006**:4
Nolan, Lloyd
  Obituary **1985**:4
Nolte, Nick **1992**:4
Northam, Jeremy **2003**:2
Norville, Deborah **1990**:3
Nye, Bill **1997**:2
O'Brien, Conan **1994**:1
O'Connor, Carroll
  Obituary **2002**:3
O'Donnell, Rosie **1994**:3
O'Hara, Catherine **2007**:4
Oldman, Gary **1998**:1
Olin, Ken **1992**:3
Oliver, Jamie **2002**:3
Olivier, Laurence
  Obituary **1989**:4
Olmos, Edward James **1990**:1
Olsen, Mary-Kate and Ashley **2002**:1
Olson, Johnny
  Obituary **1985**:4
Orbach, Jerry
  Obituary **2006**:1
O'Reilly, Bill **2001**:2
Osbournes, The **2003**:4
Osgood, Charles **1996**:2
Ostroff, Dawn **2006**:4
O'Sullivan, Maureen
  Obituary **1998**:4
Otte, Ruth **1992**:4
Ovitz, Michael **1990**:1
Owen, Clive **2006**:2
Owens, Buck
  Obituary **2007**:2
Paar, Jack
  Obituary **2005**:2
Palance, Jack
  Obituary **2008**:1
Paley, William S.
  Obituary **1991**:2
Palmer, Jim **1991**:2
Panettiere, Hayden **2008**:4
Pantoliano, Joe **2002**:3
Park, Nick **1997**:3
Parker, Sarah Jessica **1999**:2
Parker, Trey and Matt Stone **1998**:2
Parks, Bert
  Obituary **1992**:3
Pauley, Jane **1999**:1
Paulsen, Pat
  Obituary **1997**:4
Paxton, Bill **1999**:3
Peete, Holly Robinson **2005**:2
Peller, Clara
  Obituary **1988**:1
Penn, Sean **1987**:2
Pennington, Ty **2005**:4
Perez, Rosie **1994**:2
Perry, Luke **1992**:3
Perry, Matthew **1997**:2
Peterson, Cassandra **1988**:1
Pfeiffer, Michelle **1990**:2
Phifer, Mekhi **2004**:1
Philbin, Regis **2000**:2

Swayze, John Cameron
  Obituary **1996**:1
Swinton, Tilda **2008**:4
Sykes, Wanda **2007**:4
Tandy, Jessica **1990**:4
  Obituary **1995**:1
Tartakovsky, Genndy **2004**:4
Tartikoff, Brandon **1985**:2
  Obituary **1998**:1
Tautou, Audrey **2004**:2
Taylor, Elizabeth **1993**:3
Tellem, Nancy **2004**:4
Tesh, John **1996**:3
Thomas, Danny
  Obituary **1991**:3
Thompson, Emma **1993**:2
Thornton, Billy Bob **1997**:4
Tillstrom, Burr
  Obituary **1986**:1
Tilly, Jennifer **1997**:2
Timberlake, Justin **2008**:4
Tisch, Laurence A. **1988**:2
Tomei, Marisa **1995**:2
Totenberg, Nina **1992**:2
Travolta, John **1995**:2
Trotter, Charlie **2000**:4
Trudeau, Garry **1991**:2
Tucci, Stanley **2003**:2
Tucker, Chris **1999**:1
Tucker, Forrest
  Obituary **1987**:1
Turner, Janine **1993**:2
Turner, Lana
  Obituary **1996**:1
Turner, Ted **1989**:1
Ullman, Tracey **1988**:3
Umeki, Miyoshi
  Obituary **2008**:4
Underwood, Carrie **2008**:1
Urich, Robert **1988**:1
  Obituary **2003**:3
Usher **2005**:1
Ustinov, Peter
  Obituary **2005**:3
Vanilla Ice **1991**:3
Vardalos, Nia **2003**:4
Varney, Jim
  Brief Entry **1985**:4
  Obituary **2000**:3
Vaughn, Vince **1999**:2
Ventura, Jesse **1999**:2
Vidal, Gore **1996**:2
Vieira, Meredith **2001**:3
Villechaize, Herve
  Obituary **1994**:1
Vitale, Dick **1988**:4 **1994**:4
Von D, Kat **2008**:3
Wagoner, Porter
  Obituary **2008**:4
Walker, Nancy
  Obituary **1992**:3
Walters, Barbara **1998**:3
Wapner, Joseph A. **1987**:1
Ward, Sela **2001**:3
Warden, Jack
  Obituary **2007**:3
Washington, Denzel **1993**:2
Wasserman, Lew
  Obituary **2003**:3
Waterston, Sam **2006**:1
Wayans, Damon **1998**:4
Wayans, Keenen Ivory **1991**:1

Wayne, David
  Obituary **1995**:3
Weisz, Rachel **2006**:4
Weitz, Bruce **1985**:4
Whedon, Joss **2006**:3
Whitaker, Forest **1996**:2
White, Jaleel **1992**:3
White, Julie **2008**:2
Whiting, Susan **2007**:4
Whittle, Christopher **1989**:3
Wilkinson, Tom **2003**:2
Williams, Robin **1988**:4
Williams, Treat **2004**:3
Williams, Vanessa L. **1999**:2
Willis, Bruce **1986**:4
Wilson, Flip
  Obituary **1999**:2
Winfield, Paul
  Obituary **2005**:2
Winfrey, Oprah **1986**:4 **1997**:3
Winger, Debra **1994**:3
Winokur, Marissa Jaret **2005**:1
Wolfman Jack
  Obituary **1996**:1
Wong, B.D. **1998**:1
Woods, James **1988**:3
Wright, Steven **1986**:3
Wyatt, Jane
  Obituary **2008**:1
Wyle, Noah **1997**:3
Wyman, Jane
  Obituary **2008**:4
Wynn, Keenan
  Obituary **1987**:1
Xuxa **1994**:2
Xzibit **2005**:4
Yetnikoff, Walter **1988**:1
York, Dick
  Obituary **1992**:4
Young, Robert
  Obituary **1999**:1
Youngman, Henny
  Obituary **1998**:3
Zahn, Paula **1992**:3
Zamora, Pedro
  Obituary **1995**:2
Zeta-Jones, Catherine **1999**:4
Zucker, Jeff **1993**:3

THEATER

Abbott, George
  Obituary **1995**:3
Adjani, Isabelle **1991**:1
Albee, Edward **1997**:1
Albert, Eddie
  Obituary **2006**:3
Alda, Robert
  Obituary **1986**:3
Alexander, Jane **1994**:2
Alexander, Jason **1993**:3
Allen, Joan **1998**:1
Allen, Peter
  Obituary **1993**:1
Ameche, Don
  Obituary **1994**:2
Andrews, Julie **1996**:1
Angelou, Maya **1993**:4
Arden, Eve
  Obituary **1991**:2
Arkin, Alan **2007**:4
Ashcroft, Peggy
  Obituary **1992**:1

Atkinson, Rowan **2004**:3
Aykroyd, Dan **1989**:3 **1997**:3
Bacall, Lauren **1997**:3
Bacon, Kevin **1995**:3
Baddeley, Hermione
  Obituary **1986**:4
Bailey, Pearl
  Obituary **1991**:1
Ball, Alan **2005**:1
Bancroft, Anne
  Obituary **2006**:3
Barkin, Ellen **1987**:3
Barry, Lynda **1992**:1
Bassett, Angela **1994**:4
Bates, Alan
  Obituary **2005**:1
Bates, Kathy **1991**:4
Becker, Brian **2004**:4
Beckett, Samuel Barclay
  Obituary **1990**:2
Belushi, Jim **1986**:2
Bening, Annette **1992**:1
Bennett, Joan
  Obituary **1991**:2
Bennett, Michael
  Obituary **1988**:1
Bernardi, Herschel
  Obituary **1986**:4
Bernhard, Sandra **1989**:4
Bernstein, Leonard
  Obituary **1991**:1
Bishop, Andre **2000**:1
Bishop, Joey
  Obituary **2008**:4
Blackstone, Harry Jr.
  Obituary **1997**:4
Blanchett, Cate **1999**:3
Bloch, Ivan **1986**:3
Bloom, Orlando **2004**:2
Bogosian, Eric **1990**:4
Bolger, Ray
  Obituary **1987**:2
Bonham Carter, Helena **1998**:4
Booth, Shirley
  Obituary **1993**:2
Bowen, Julie **2007**:1
Bowie, David **1998**:2
Brady, Wayne **2008**:3
Branagh, Kenneth **1992**:2
Brandauer, Klaus Maria **1987**:3
Brando, Marlon
  Obituary **2005**:3
Broadbent, Jim **2008**:4
Brooks, Mel **2003**:1
Brown, Ruth
  Obituary **2008**:1
Brynner, Yul
  Obituary **1985**:4
Buckley, Betty **1996**:2
Bullock, Sandra **1995**:4
Burck, Wade
  Brief Entry **1986**:1
Burr, Raymond
  Obituary **1994**:1
Busch, Charles **1998**:3
Byrne, Gabriel **1997**:4
Caan, James **2004**:4
Caesar, Adolph
  Obituary **1986**:3
Cagney, James
  Obituary **1986**:2
Caine, Michael **2000**:4

Lange, Jessica **1995**:4
Langella, Frank **2008**:3
Lansbury, Angela **1993**:1
Larson, Jonathan
    Obituary **1997**:2
Lawless, Lucy **1997**:4
Leary, Denis **1993**:3
Leigh, Jennifer Jason **1995**:2
Lithgow, John **1985**:2
Little, Cleavon
    Obituary **1993**:2
Lloyd Webber, Andrew **1989**:1
Loewe, Frederick
    Obituary **1988**:2
Logan, Joshua
    Obituary **1988**:4
Lord, Jack
    Obituary **1998**:2
MacRae, Gordon
    Obituary **1986**:2
Macy, William H. **1999**:3
Maher, Bill **1996**:2
Malkovich, John **1988**:2
Maltby, Richard, Jr. **1996**:3
Mamet, David **1998**:4
Mantegna, Joe **1992**:1
Marber, Patrick **2007**:4
Marceau, Marcel
    Obituary **2008**:4
Marshall, Penny **1991**:3
Martin, Mary
    Obituary **1991**:2
McDonagh, Martin **2007**:3
McDonnell, Mary **2008**:2
McDormand, Frances **1997**:3
McDowall, Roddy
    Obituary **1999**:1
McGillis, Kelly **1989**:3
McGregor, Ewan **1998**:2
McKee, Lonette **1996**:1
McKellen, Ian **1994**:1
McMahon, Julian **2006**:1
Merkerson, S. Epatha **2006**:4
Merrick, David
    Obituary **2000**:4
Messing, Debra **2004**:4
Midler, Bette **1989**:4
Minghella, Anthony **2004**:3
Mirren, Helen **2005**:1
Molina, Alfred **2005**:3
Montand, Yves
    Obituary **1992**:2
Montgomery, Elizabeth
    Obituary **1995**:4
Moore, Dudley
    Obituary **2003**:2
Moore, Mary Tyler **1996**:2
Morrow, Rob **2006**:4
Mos Def **2005**:4
Moss, Carrie-Anne **2004**:3
Neeson, Liam **1993**:4
Newman, Paul **1995**:3
Nichols, Mike **1994**:4
Nolan, Lloyd
    Obituary **1985**:4
Nolte, Nick **1992**:4
North, Alex **1986**:3
Northam, Jeremy **2003**:2
Nunn, Trevor **2000**:2
O'Donnell, Rosie **1994**:3
Oldman, Gary **1998**:1
Olin, Ken **1992**:3

Olin, Lena **1991**:2
Olivier, Laurence
    Obituary **1989**:4
Orbach, Jerry
    Obituary **2006**:1
Osborne, John
    Obituary **1995**:2
O'Sullivan, Maureen
    Obituary **1998**:4
Owen, Clive **2006**:2
Pacino, Al **1993**:4
Page, Geraldine
    Obituary **1987**:4
Papp, Joseph
    Obituary **1992**:2
Parks, Suzan-Lori **2003**:2
Paulsen, Pat
    Obituary **1997**:4
Peck, Gregory
    Obituary **2004**:3
Penn, Sean **1987**:2
Penn & Teller **1992**:1
Perkins, Anthony
    Obituary **1993**:2
Perry, Tyler **2006**:1
Peters, Bernadette **2000**:1
Pfeiffer, Michelle **1990**:2
Picasso, Paloma **1991**:1
Pinchot, Bronson **1987**:4
Piven, Jeremy **2007**:3
Piven, Jeremy **2007**:3
Pleasence, Donald
    Obituary **1995**:3
Poitier, Sidney **1990**:3
Poston, Tom
    Obituary **2008**:3
Preminger, Otto
    Obituary **1986**:3
Preston, Robert
    Obituary **1987**:3
Price, Vincent
    Obituary **1994**:2
Prince, Faith **1993**:2
Quaid, Dennis **1989**:4
Radcliffe, Daniel **2007**:4
Radner, Gilda
    Obituary **1989**:4
Raitt, John
    Obituary **2006**:2
Randall, Tony
    Obituary **2005**:3
Rashad, Phylicia **1987**:3
Raye, Martha
    Obituary **1995**:1
Redford, Robert **1993**:2
Redgrave, Lynn **1999**:3
Redgrave, Vanessa **1989**:2
Reeves, Keanu **1992**:1
Reilly, Charles Nelson
    Obituary **2008**:3
Reilly, John C. **2003**:4
Reitman, Ivan **1986**:3
Reza, Yasmina **1999**:2
Richards, Lloyd
    Obituary **2007**:3
Richards, Michael **1993**:4
Ritter, John **2003**:4
Robbins, Jerome
    Obituary **1999**:1
Roberts, Doris **2003**:4
Roker, Roxie
    Obituary **1996**:2

Rolle, Esther
    Obituary **1999**:2
Rudner, Rita **1993**:2
Rudnick, Paul **1994**:3
Ruehl, Mercedes **1992**:4
Salonga, Lea **2003**:3
Sarandon, Susan **1995**:3
Schoenfeld, Gerald **1986**:2
Schreiber, Liev **2007**:2
Schwimmer, David **1996**:2
Scott, George C.
    Obituary **2000**:2
Seymour, Jane **1994**:4
Shaffer, Paul **1987**:1
Shanley, John Patrick **2006**:1
Shawn, Dick
    Obituary **1987**:3
Sheldon, Sidney
    Obituary **2008**:2
Shepard, Sam **1996**:4
Short, Martin **1986**:1
Silvers, Phil
    Obituary **1985**:4
Sinise, Gary **1996**:1
Slater, Christian **1994**:1
Smith, Anna Deavere **2002**:2
Snipes, Wesley **1993**:1
Sondheim, Stephen **1994**:4
Spacey, Kevin **1996**:4
Stamos, John **2008**:1
Stapleton, Maureen
    Obituary **2007**:2
Steiger, Rod
    Obituary **2003**:4
Stewart, Jimmy
    Obituary **1997**:4
Stewart, Patrick **1996**:1
Stiller, Ben **1999**:1
Sting **1991**:4
Stoppard, Tom **1995**:4
Streep, Meryl **1990**:2
Streisand, Barbra **1992**:2
Stritch, Elaine **2002**:4
Styne, Jule
    Obituary **1995**:1
Susskind, David
    Obituary **1987**:2
Swinton, Tilda **2008**:4
Tandy, Jessica **1990**:4
    Obituary **1995**:1
Taylor, Elizabeth **1993**:3
Taylor, Lili **2000**:2
Thompson, Emma **1993**:2
Tomei, Marisa **1995**:2
Tucci, Stanley **2003**:2
Tune, Tommy **1994**:2
Ullman, Tracey **1988**:3
Umeki, Miyoshi
    Obituary **2008**:4
Urich, Robert **1988**:1
    Obituary **2003**:3
Ustinov, Peter
    Obituary **2005**:3
Vardalos, Nia **2003**:4
Vogel, Paula **1999**:2
Walker, Nancy
    Obituary **1992**:3
Washington, Denzel **1993**:2
Wasserstein, Wendy **1991**:3
Waterston, Sam **2006**:1
Watts, Naomi **2006**:1

Lisick, Beth **2006**:2
Little, Benilde **2006**:2
Litzenburger, Liesel **2008**:1
Lively, Penelope **2007**:4
Logan, Joshua
  Obituary **1988**:4
Lord, Bette Bao **1994**:1
Louv, Richard **2006**:2
Ludlum, Robert
  Obituary **2002**:1
Lupino, Ida
  Obituary **1996**:1
Madden, Chris **2006**:1
Mahfouz, Naguib
  Obituary **2007**:4
Mailer, Norman **1998**:1
Mamet, David **1998**:4
Marchetto, Marisa Acocella **2007**:3
Martin, Judith **2000**:3
Mayes, Frances **2004**:3
Maynard, Joyce **1999**:4
McCall, Nathan **1994**:4
McCall Smith, Alexander **2005**:2
McCarthy, Cormac **2008**:1
McCourt, Frank **1997**:4
McDermott, Alice **1999**:2
McEwan, Ian **2004**:2
McGahern, John
  Obituary **2007**:2
McGraw, Phil **2005**:2
McKenna, Terence **1993**:3
McMillan, Terry **1993**:2
McMurtry, Larry **2006**:4
McNamara, Robert S. **1995**:4
Meltzer, Brad **2005**:4
Menchu, Rigoberta **1993**:2
Menninger, Karl
  Obituary **1991**:1
Merrill, James
  Obituary **1995**:3
Michener, James A.
  Obituary **1998**:1
Millan, Cesar **2007**:4
Miller, Arthur **1999**:4
Miller, Frank **2008**:2
Miller, Sue **1999**:3
Milne, Christopher Robin
  Obituary **1996**:4
Milosz, Czeslaw
  Obituary **2005**:4
Mina, Denise **2006**:1
Mo'Nique **2008**:1
Montagu, Ashley
  Obituary **2000**:2
Moody, Rick **2002**:2
Moore, Michael **1990**:3
Morgan, Robin **1991**:1
Morris, Henry M.
  Obituary **2007**:2
Morrison, Toni **1998**:1
Mortensen, Viggo **2003**:3
Mosley, Walter **2003**:4
Moyers, Bill **1991**:4
Munro, Alice **1997**:1
Murakami, Haruki **2008**:3
Murdoch, Iris
  Obituary **1999**:4
Narayan, R.K.
  Obituary **2002**:2
Nasrin, Taslima **1995**:1
Nemerov, Howard
  Obituary **1992**:1

Newkirk, Ingrid **1992**:3
Niezabitowska, Malgorzata **1991**:3
Nissel, Angela **2006**:4
Noonan, Peggy **1990**:3
Norton, Andre
  Obituary **2006**:2
Oates, Joyce Carol **2000**:1
Obama, Barack **2007**:4
O'Brien, Conan **1994**:1
Oe, Kenzaburo **1997**:1
Onassis, Jacqueline Kennedy
  Obituary **1994**:4
Ondaatje, Philip Michael **1997**:3
Ornish, Dean **2004**:2
Osborne, John
  Obituary **1995**:2
Osteen, Joel **2006**:2
Owens, Delia and Mark **1993**:3
Oz, Mehmet **2007**:2
Pagels, Elaine **1997**:1
Paglia, Camille **1992**:3
Palahniuk, Chuck **2004**:1
Pamuk, Orhan **2007**:3
Paretsky, Sara **2002**:4
Parker, Brant
  Obituary **2008**:2
Parks, Suzan-Lori **2003**:2
Patchett, Ann **2003**:2
Patterson, Richard North **2001**:4
Paz, Octavio **1991**:2
Percy, Walker
  Obituary **1990**:4
Peters, Tom **1998**:1
Phillips, Julia **1992**:1
Picoult, Jodi **2008**:1
Pilkey, Dav **2001**:1
Pipher, Mary **1996**:4
Plimpton, George
  Obituary **2004**:4
Politkovskaya, Anna
  Obituary **2007**:4
Porter, Sylvia
  Obituary **1991**:4
Post, Peggy **2001**:4
Potok, Chaim
  Obituary **2003**:4
Pouillon, Nora **2005**:1
Powter, Susan **1994**:3
Pratt, Jane **1999**:1
Proulx, E. Annie **1996**:1
Pullman, Philip **2003**:2
Pynchon, Thomas **1997**:4
Quindlen, Anna **1993**:1
Quinn, Jane Bryant **1993**:4
Ramsay, Gordon **2008**:2
Redfield, James **1995**:2
Reichs, Kathleen J. **2007**:3
Rendell, Ruth **2007**:2
Rey, Margret E.
  Obituary **1997**:2
Reza, Yasmina **1999**:2
Rice, Anne **1995**:1
Ringgold, Faith **2000**:3
Robbins, Harold
  Obituary **1998**:1
Roberts, Cokie **1993**:4
Roberts, Steven K. **1992**:1
Robinson, Peter **2007**:4
Roddenberry, Gene
  Obituary **1992**:2
Roizen, Michael **2007**:4
Rosenzweig, Ilene **2004**:1

Rossner, Judith
  Obituary **2006**:4
Rosten, Leo
  Obituary **1997**:3
Roth, Philip **1999**:1
Rowan, Carl
  Obituary **2001**:2
Rowland, Pleasant **1992**:3
Rowling, J.K. **2000**:1
Royko, Mike
  Obituary **1997**:4
Rudnick, Paul **1994**:3
Rushdie, Salman **1994**:1
Russo, Richard **2002**:3
Sacks, Oliver **1995**:4
Safire, William **2000**:3
Salk, Jonas **1994**:4
  Obituary **1995**:4
Salzman, Mark **2002**:1
Sapphire **1996**:4
Saramago, Jose **1999**:1
Saro-Wiwa, Ken
  Obituary **1996**:2
Sarraute, Nathalie
  Obituary **2000**:2
Satrapi, Marjane **2006**:3
Schaap, Dick
  Obituary **2003**:1
Schroeder, Barbet **1996**:1
Schulz, Charles M. **1998**:1
Sears, Barry **2004**:2
Sebold, Alice **2005**:4
Sedaris, David **2005**:3
Senghor, Leopold
  Obituary **2003**:1
Serros, Michele **2008**:2
Sethi, Simran **2008**:1
Sevareid, Eric
  Obituary **1993**:1
Shanley, John Patrick **2006**:1
Shawn, William
  Obituary **1993**:3
Sheldon, Sidney
  Obituary **2008**:2
Shepard, Sam **1996**:4
Shields, Carol
  Obituary **2004**:3
Shilts, Randy **1993**:4
  Obituary **1994**:3
Shreve, Anita **2003**:4
Shriver, Lionel **2008**:4
Silverstein, Shel
  Obituary **1999**:4
Singer, Isaac Bashevis
  Obituary **1992**:1
Siskel, Gene
  Obituary **1999**:3
Skinner, B.F.
  Obituary **1991**:1
Smiley, Jane **1995**:4
Smith, Kevin **2000**:4
Smith, Zadie **2003**:4
Sobol, Donald J. **2004**:4
Sontag, Susan
  Obituary **2006**:1
Southern, Terry
  Obituary **1996**:2
Sowell, Thomas **1998**:3
Spiegelman, Art **1998**:3

Cumulative Subject Index

This index lists all newsmakers by subjects, company names, products, organizations, issues, awards, and professional specialties. Indexes in softbound issues allow access to the current year's entries; indexes in annual hardbound volumes are cumulative, covering the entire *Newsmakers* series.

Listee names are followed by a year and issue number; thus **1996**:3 indicates that an entry on that individual appears in both 1996, Issue 3, and the 1996 cumulation. For access to newsmakers appearing earlier than the current softbound issue, see the previous year's cumulation.

ACLU
    See: American Civil Liberties Union

Acoustics
    Kloss, Henry E.
        Brief Entry **1985**:2

Acquired Immune Deficiency Syndrome [AIDS]

Saberhagen, Bret **1986**:1
Sanders, Deion **1992**:4
Santana, Johan **2008**:1
Schembechler, Bo **1990**:3
Schilling, Curt **2002**:3
Schmidt, Mike **1988**:3
Schott, Marge **1985**:4
Selig, Bud **1995**:2
Sheffield, Gary **1998**:1
Soriano, Alfonso **2008**:1
Sosa, Sammy **1999**:1
Spahn, Warren
   Obituary **2005**:1
Steinbrenner, George **1991**:1
Stewart, Dave **1991**:1
Thomas, Frank **1994**:3
Van Slyke, Andy **1992**:4
Vaughn, Mo **1999**:2
Veeck, Bill
   Obituary **1986**:1
Vincent, Fay **1990**:2
Welch, Bob **1991**:3
Wells, David **1999**:3
White, Bill **1989**:3
Williams, Ted
   Obituary **2003**:4
Zito, Barry **2003**:3

Basketball
Ainge, Danny **1987**:1
Allen, Ray **2002**:1
Auerbach, Red
   Obituary **2008**:1
Barkley, Charles **1988**:2
Bias, Len
   Obituary **1986**:3
Bird, Larry **1990**:3
Carter, Vince **2001**:4
Chaney, John **1989**:1
Cooper, Cynthia **1999**:1
Drexler, Clyde **1992**:4
Ewing, Patrick **1985**:3
Gathers, Hank
   Obituary **1990**:3
Hardaway, Anfernee **1996**:2
Jackson, Phil **1996**:3
James, LeBron **2007**:3
Johnson, Earvin 'Magic' **1988**:4
Johnson, Kevin **1991**:1
Johnson, Larry **1993**:3
Jordan, Michael **1987**:2
Kemp, Shawn **1995**:1
Kidd, Jason **2003**:2
Knight, Bobby **1985**:3
Krzyzewski, Mike **1993**:2
Kukoc, Toni **1995**:4
Laettner, Christian **1993**:1
Laimbeer, Bill **2004**:3
Leslie, Lisa **1997**:4
Lewis, Reggie
   Obituary **1994**:1
Majerle, Dan **1993**:4
Malone, Karl **1990**:1 **1997**:3
Maravich, Pete
   Obituary **1988**:2
McMillen, Tom **1988**:4
Mikan, George
   Obituary **2006**:3
Miller, Andre **2003**:3
Miller, Reggie **1994**:4
Mourning, Alonzo **1994**:2
Mulkey-Robertson, Kim **2006**:1
Nowitzki, Dirk **2007**:2

Olajuwon, Akeem **1985**:1
O'Malley, Susan **1995**:2
O'Neal, Shaquille **1992**:1
Palmer, Violet **2005**:2
Parker, Tony **2008**:1
Riley, Pat **1994**:3
Robinson, David **1990**:4
Rodman, Dennis **1991**:3 **1996**:4
Stern, David **1991**:4
Stockton, John Houston **1997**:3
Summitt, Pat **2004**:1
Swoopes, Sheryl **1998**:2
Tarkenian, Jerry **1990**:4
Thomas, Isiah **1989**:2
Thompson, John **1988**:3
Vitale, Dick **1988**:4 **1994**:4
Wade, Dwyane **2007**:1
Wallace, Ben **2004**:3
Webber, Chris **1994**:1
Wilkens, Lenny **1995**:2
Woodard, Lynette **1986**:2
Worthy, James **1991**:2
Yao Ming **2004**:1

Beatrice International
Lewis, Reginald F. **1988**:4
   Obituary **1993**:3

Benetton Group
Benetton, Luciano **1988**:1

Benihana of Tokyo, Inc.
Aoki, Rocky **1990**:2

Berkshire Hathaway, Inc.
Buffett, Warren **1995**:2

Bethlehem, Jordan, city government
Freij, Elias **1986**:4

Bicycling
Armstrong, Lance **2000**:1
Indurain, Miguel **1994**:1
LeMond, Greg **1986**:4
Roberts, Steven K. **1992**:1

Bill T. Jones/Arnie Zane & Company
Jones, Bill T. **1991**:4

Billiards
Minnesota Fats
   Obituary **1996**:3

Biodiversity
Wilson, Edward O. **1994**:4

Bioethics
Andrews, Lori B. **2005**:3
Bayley, Corrine
   Brief Entry **1986**:4
Caplan, Arthur L. **2000**:2

Biogen, Inc.
Gilbert, Walter **1988**:3

Biosphere 2
Allen, John **1992**:1

Biotechnology
Gilbert, Walter **1988**:3
Haseltine, William A. **1999**:2

Birds
Berle, Peter A.A.
   Brief Entry **1987**:3
Pough, Richard Hooper **1989**:1
Redig, Patrick **1985**:3
Toone, Bill
   Brief Entry **1987**:2

Birth control
Baird, Bill
   Brief Entry **1987**:2
Baulieu, Etienne-Emile **1990**:1
Djerassi, Carl **2000**:4
Falkenberg, Nanette **1985**:2
Morgentaler, Henry **1986**:3
Rock, John
   Obituary **1985**:1
Wattleton, Faye **1989**:1

Black Panther Party
Cleaver, Eldridge
   Obituary **1998**:4
Newton, Huey
   Obituary **1990**:1
Ture, Kwame
   Obituary **1999**:2

Black Sash
Duncan, Sheena
   Brief Entry **1987**:1

Blockbuster Video
Huizenga, Wayne **1992**:1

Bloomingdale's
Campeau, Robert **1990**:1
Traub, Marvin
   Brief Entry **1987**:3

Boat racing
Aoki, Rocky **1990**:2
Conner, Dennis **1987**:2
Copeland, Al **1988**:3
Hanauer, Chip **1986**:2
Turner, Ted **1989**:1

Bodybuilding
Powter, Susan **1994**:3
Reeves, Steve
   Obituary **2000**:4
Schwarzenegger, Arnold **1991**:1

Body Shops International
Roddick, Anita **1989**:4

Boston Bruins hockey team
Bourque, Raymond Jean **1997**:3

Bose Corp.
Bose, Amar
   Brief Entry **1986**:4

Boston Celtics basketball team
Ainge, Danny **1987**:1
Auerbach, Red
   Obituary **2008**:1
Bird, Larry **1990**:3
Lewis, Reggie
   Obituary **1994**:1

Maravich, Pete
Obituary **1988**:2

Boston, Mass., city government
Flynn, Ray **1989**:1
Frank, Barney **1989**:2

Boston Properties Co.
Zuckerman, Mortimer **1986**:3

Boston Red Sox baseball team
Boggs, Wade **1989**:3
Clemens, Roger **1991**:4
Conigliaro, Tony
Obituary **1990**:3
Damon, Johnny **2005**:4
Epstein, Theo **2003**:4
Henderson, Rickey **2002**:3
Ramirez, Manny **2005**:4
Vaughn, Mo **1999**:2
Williams, Ted
Obituary **2003**:4

Boston University
Silber, John **1990**:1

Bowling
Anthony, Earl
Obituary **2002**:3
Weber, Pete **1986**:3

Boxing
Abercrombie, Josephine **1987**:2
Ali, Laila **2001**:2
Armstrong, Henry
Obituary **1989**:1
Bowe, Riddick **1993**:2
Carter, Rubin **2000**:3
Danza, Tony **1989**:1
De La Hoya, Oscar **1998**:2
Douglas, Buster **1990**:4
Foreman, George **2004**:2
Graziano, Rocky
Obituary **1990**:4
Hagler, Marvelous Marvin **1985**:2
Holyfield, Evander **1991**:3
Kallen, Jackie **1994**:1
King, Don **1989**:1
Leonard, Sugar Ray **1989**:4
Lewis, Lennox **2000**:2
Moore, Archie
Obituary **1999**:2
Pep, Willie
Obituary **2008**:1
Robinson, Sugar Ray
Obituary **1989**:3
Trinidad, Felix **2000**:4
Tyson, Mike **1986**:4

Boys Town
Peter, Valentine J. **1988**:2

BrainReserve
Popcorn, Faith
Brief Entry **1988**:1

Branch Davidians religious sect
Koresh, David
Obituary **1993**:4

Brewing
Busch, August A. III **1988**:2
Coors, William K.
Brief Entry **1985**:1
Stroh, Peter W. **1985**:2

Bridge
Goren, Charles H.
Obituary **1991**:4

British Columbia provincial government
Vander Zalm, William **1987**:3

British royal family
Charles, Prince of Wales **1995**:3
Diana, Princess of Wales **1993**:1
Obituary **1997**:4
Ferguson, Sarah **1990**:3
Princess Margaret, Countess of Snowdon
Obituary **2003**:2
Queen Elizabeth the Queen Mother
Obituary **2003**:2
William, Prince of Wales **2001**:3

Broadcasting
Albert, Marv **1994**:3
Allen, Mel
Obituary **1996**:4
Ancier, Garth **1989**:1
Barber, Red
Obituary **1993**:2
Bell, Art **2000**:1
Brown, James **1991**:4
Caray, Harry **1988**:3
Obituary **1998**:3
Cherry, Don **1993**:4
Chung, Connie **1988**:4
Cosell, Howard
Obituary **1995**:4
Costas, Bob **1986**:4
Couric, Katherine **1991**:4
Daniels, Faith **1993**:3
Dickerson, Nancy H.
Obituary **1998**:2
Diller, Barry **1991**:1
Dr. Demento **1986**:1
Donnellan, Nanci **1995**:2
Drysdale, Don
Obituary **1994**:1
Edwards, Bob **1993**:2
Ellerbee, Linda **1993**:3
Firestone, Roy **1988**:2
Gillett, George **1988**:1
Goldberg, Leonard **1988**:4
Grange, Red
Obituary **1991**:3
Gumbel, Bryant **1990**:2
Gunn, Hartford N., Jr.
Obituary **1986**:2
Harvey, Paul **1995**:3
Hollander, Joel **2006**:4
Imus, Don **1997**:1
Jones, Jenny **1998**:2
Kasem, Casey **1987**:1
Kent, Arthur **1991**:4 **1997**:2
King, Larry **1993**:1
Kluge, John **1991**:1
Koppel, Ted **1989**:1
Kuralt, Charles
Obituary **1998**:3

Madden, John **1995**:1
Moyers, Bill **1991**:4
Murdoch, Rupert **1988**:4
Musburger, Brent **1985**:1
Norville, Deborah **1990**:3
Osgood, Charles **1996**:2
Paley, William S.
Obituary **1991**:2
Pauley, Jane **1999**:1
Pierce, Frederick S. **1985**:3
Povich, Maury **1994**:3
Quivers, Robin **1995**:4
Reasoner, Harry
Obituary **1992**:1
Riley, Pat **1994**:3
Rivera, Geraldo **1989**:1
Roberts, Cokie **1993**:4
Robertson, Pat **1988**:2
Sawyer, Diane **1994**:4
Sevareid, Eric
Obituary **1993**:1
Shriver, Maria
Brief Entry **1986**:2
Snyder, Jimmy
Obituary **1996**:4
Stahl, Lesley **1997**:1
Stern, Howard **1988**:2 **1993**:3
Swaggart, Jimmy **1987**:3
Tartikoff, Brandon **1985**:2
Obituary **1998**:1
Totenberg, Nina **1992**:2
Turner, Ted **1989**:1
Vitale, Dick **1988**:4 **1994**:4
Walters, Barbara **1998**:3
Zahn, Paula **1992**:3
Zucker, Jeff **1993**:3

Brokerage
Brennan, Robert E. **1988**:1
Fomon, Robert M. **1985**:3
Phelan, John Joseph, Jr. **1985**:4
Schwab, Charles **1989**:3
Siebert, Muriel **1987**:2

Brooklyn Dodgers baseball team
Campanella, Roy
Obituary **1994**:1
Drysdale, Don
Obituary **1994**:1

Brown University
Gregorian, Vartan **1990**:3

Buddhism
Dalai Lama **1989**:1

Buffalo Bills football team
Flutie, Doug **1999**:2
Kelly, Jim **1991**:4
Thomas, Thurman **1993**:1

Buffalo Sabres
Hasek, Dominik **1998**:3

Cabbage Patch Kids
Roberts, Xavier **1985**:3

Cable Ace Awards
Blades, Ruben **1998**:2
Carey, Drew **1997**:4
Cuaron, Alfonso **2008**:2

Central Intelligence Agency [CIA]
Carter, Amy **1987**:4
Casey, William
Obituary **1987**:3
Colby, William E.
Obituary **1996**:4
Deutch, John **1996**:4
Gates, Robert M. **1992**:2
Inman, Bobby Ray **1985**:1
Tenet, George **2000**:3

Centurion Ministries
McCloskey, James **1993**:1

Cesar Awards
Adjani, Isabelle **1991**:1
Deneuve, Catherine **2003**:2
Depardieu, Gerard **1991**:2
Tautou, Audrey **2004**:2

Chanel, Inc.
D'Alessio, Kitty
Brief Entry **1987**:3
Lagerfeld, Karl **1999**:4

Chantal Pharmacentical Corp.
Burnison, Chantal Simone **1988**:3

Charlotte Hornets basketball team
Bryant, Kobe **1998**:3
Johnson, Larry **1993**:3
Mourning, Alonzo **1994**:2

Chef Boy-ar-dee
Boiardi, Hector
Obituary **1985**:3

Chess
Kasparov, Garry **1997**:4
Polgar, Judit **1993**:3

Chicago Bears football team
McMahon, Jim **1985**:4
Payton, Walter
Obituary **2000**:2

Chicago Bulls basketball team
Jackson, Phil **1996**:3
Jordan, Michael **1987**:2
Kukoc, Toni **1995**:4
Pippen, Scottie **1992**:2

Chicago Blackhawks
Hasek, Dominik **1998**:3

Chicago Cubs baseball team
Caray, Harry **1988**:3
Obituary **1998**:3
Soriano, Alfonso **2008**:1
Sosa, Sammy **1999**:1

Chicago, Ill., city government
Washington, Harold
Obituary **1988**:1

Chicago White Sox baseball team
Caray, Harry **1988**:3
Obituary **1998**:3
Leyland, Jim **1998**:2

Thomas, Frank **1994**:3
Veeck, Bill
Obituary **1986**:1

Child care
Hale, Clara
Obituary **1993**:3
Leach, Penelope **1992**:4
Spock, Benjamin **1995**:2
Obituary **1998**:3

Children's Defense Fund [CDF]
Clinton, Hillary Rodham **1993**:2
Edelman, Marian Wright **1990**:4

Chimpanzees
Goodall, Jane **1991**:1

Choreography
Abdul, Paula **1990**:3
Ailey, Alvin **1989**:2
Obituary **1990**:2
Astaire, Fred
Obituary **1987**:4
Bennett, Michael
Obituary **1988**:1
Cunningham, Merce **1998**:1
Dean, Laura **1989**:4
de Mille, Agnes
Obituary **1994**:2
Feld, Eliot **1996**:1
Fenley, Molissa **1988**:3
Forsythe, William **1993**:2
Fosse, Bob
Obituary **1988**:1
Glover, Savion **1997**:1
Graham, Martha
Obituary **1991**:4
Jamison, Judith **1990**:3
Joffrey, Robert
Obituary **1988**:3
Jones, Bill T. **1991**:4
Lewitzky, Bella
Obituary **2005**:3
MacMillan, Kenneth
Obituary **1993**:2
Mitchell, Arthur **1995**:1
Morris, Mark **1991**:1
Nureyev, Rudolf
Obituary **1993**:2
Parsons, David **1993**:4
Ross, Herbert
Obituary **2002**:4
Takei, Kei **1990**:2
Taylor, Paul **1992**:3
Tharp, Twyla **1992**:4
Tudor, Antony
Obituary **1987**:4
Tune, Tommy **1994**:2
Varone, Doug **2001**:2

Christian Coalition
Reed, Ralph **1995**:1

Christic Institute
Sheehan, Daniel P. **1989**:1

Chrysler Motor Corp.
Eaton, Robert J. **1994**:2
Iacocca, Lee **1993**:1
Lutz, Robert A. **1990**:1
Nardelli, Robert **2008**:4

CHUCK
See: Committee to Halt Useless
College Killings

Church of England
Carey, George **1992**:3
Runcie, Robert **1989**:4
Obituary **2001**:1

**Church of Jesus Christ of Latter-Day
Saints**
See: Mormon Church

CIA
See: Central Intelligence Agency

Cincinatti Bengals football team
Esiason, Boomer **1991**:1

Cincinnati Reds baseball team
Davis, Eric **1987**:4
Rose, Pete **1991**:1
Schott, Marge **1985**:4

Cinematography
Burum, Stephen H.
Brief Entry **1987**:2
Markle, C. Wilson **1988**:1
McLaren, Norman
Obituary **1987**:2

Civil rights
Abernathy, Ralph
Obituary **1990**:3
Abzug, Bella **1998**:2
Allen Jr., Ivan
Obituary **2004**:3
Allred, Gloria **1985**:2
Aquino, Corazon **1986**:2
Baldwin, James
Obituary **1988**:2
Banks, Dennis J. **1986**:4
Blackburn, Molly
Obituary **1985**:4
Buthelezi, Mangosuthu Gatsha **1989**
:3
Chavez, Linda **1999**:3
Chavis, Benjamin **1993**:4
Clements, George **1985**:1
Connerly, Ward **2000**:2
Davis, Angela **1998**:3
Dees, Morris **1992**:1
Delany, Sarah
Obituary **1999**:3
Duncan, Sheena
Brief Entry **1987**:1
Farmer, James
Obituary **2000**:1
Faubus, Orval
Obituary **1995**:2
Glasser, Ira **1989**:1
Griffiths, Martha
Obituary **2004**:2
Harris, Barbara **1989**:3
Healey, Jack **1990**:1
Hoffman, Abbie
Obituary **1989**:3
Hume, John **1987**:1
Jordan, Vernon, Jr. **2002**:3
King, Bernice **2000**:2

King, Coretta Scott **1999**:3
Kunstler, William **1992**:3
Makeba, Miriam **1989**:2
Mandela, Winnie **1989**:3
Marshall, Thurgood
Obituary **1993**:3
McGuinness, Martin **1985**:4
Parks, Rosa
Obituary **2007**:1
Pendleton, Clarence M.
Obituary **1988**:4
Ram, Jagjivan
Obituary **1986**:4
Shabazz, Betty
Obituary **1997**:4
Sharpton, Al **1991**:2
Shcharansky, Anatoly **1986**:2
Simone, Nina
Obituary **2004**:2
Slovo, Joe **1989**:2
Stallings, George A., Jr. **1990**:1
Steele, Shelby **1991**:2
Sullivan, Leon
Obituary **2002**:2
Suzman, Helen **1989**:3
Ture, Kwame
Obituary **1999**:2
Washington, Harold
Obituary **1988**:1
West, Cornel **1994**:2
Williams, G. Mennen
Obituary **1988**:2
Williams, Hosea
Obituary **2001**:2
Wu, Harry **1996**:1

Civil War
Foote, Shelby **1991**:2

Claymation
Park, Nick **1997**:3
Vinton, Will
Brief Entry **1988**:1

Cleveland Ballet Dancing Wheels
Verdi-Fletcher, Mary **1998**:2

Cleveland Browns football team
Brown, Jim **1993**:2

Cleveland Cavaliers basketball team
James, LeBron **2007**:3
Wilkens, Lenny **1995**:2

Cleveland city government
Stokes, Carl
Obituary **1996**:4

Cleveland Indians baseball team
Belle, Albert **1996**:4
Boudreau, Louis
Obituary **2002**:3
Greenberg, Hank
Obituary **1986**:4
Lofton, Kenny **1998**:1
Veeck, Bill
Obituary **1986**:1

Cliff's Notes
Hillegass, Clifton Keith **1989**:4

Climatology
Thompson, Starley
Brief Entry **1987**:3

Clio Awards
Proctor, Barbara Gardner **1985**:3
Riney, Hal **1989**:1
Rivers, Joan **2005**:3
Sedelmaier, Joe **1985**:3

Cloning
Lanza, Robert **2004**:3
Wilmut, Ian **1997**:3

Coaching
Bowman, Scotty **1998**:4
Brown, Paul
Obituary **1992**:1
Chaney, John **1989**:1
Hayes, Woody
Obituary **1987**:2
Holtz, Lou **1986**:4
Howser, Dick
Obituary **1987**:4
Jackson, Phil **1996**:3
Johnson, Jimmy **1993**:3
Knight, Bobby **1985**:3
Leyland, Jim **1998**:2
Lukas, D. Wayne **1986**:2
Martin, Billy **1988**:4
Obituary **1990**:2
McCartney, Bill **1995**:3
Paterno, Joe **1995**:4
Schembechler, Bo **1990**:3
Shula, Don **1992**:2
Tarkenian, Jerry **1990**:4
Walsh, Bill **1987**:4

Coca-Cola Co.
Goizueta, Roberto **1996**:1
Obituary **1998**:1
Keough, Donald Raymond **1986**:1
Woodruff, Robert Winship
Obituary **1985**:1

Coleman Co.
Coleman, Sheldon, Jr. **1990**:2

Colorado Avalanche hockey team
Lemieux, Claude **1996**:1

Colorization
Markle, C. Wilson **1988**:1

Columbia Pictures
Pascal, Amy **2003**:3
Steel, Dawn **1990**:1
Obituary **1998**:2
Vincent, Fay **1990**:2

Columbia Sportswear
Boyle, Gertrude **1995**:3

Comedy
Adams, Don
Obituary **2007**:1
Alexander, Jason **1993**:3
Allen, Steve
Obituary **2001**:2

Allen, Tim **1993**:1
Allen, Woody **1994**:1
Anderson, Harry **1988**:2
Arnold, Tom **1993**:2
Atkinson, Rowan **2004**:3
Baron Cohen, Sacha **2007**:3
Barr, Roseanne **1989**:1
Bateman, Jason **2005**:3
Belushi, Jim **1986**:2
Belzer, Richard **1985**:3
Benigni, Roberto **1999**:2
Berle, Milton
Obituary **2003**:2
Bernhard, Sandra **1989**:4
Bishop, Joey
Obituary **2008**:4
Black, Jack **2002**:3
Bogosian, Eric **1990**:4
Borge, Victor
Obituary **2001**:3
Brooks, Albert **1991**:4
Brooks, Mel **2003**:1
Burns, George
Obituary **1996**:3
Burrows, James **2005**:3
Busch, Charles **1998**:3
Butler, Brett **1995**:1
Buttons, Red
Obituary **2007**:3
Candy, John **1988**:2
Obituary **1994**:3
Carey, Drew **1997**:4
Carney, Art
Obituary **2005**:1
Carrey, Jim **1995**:1
Carvey, Dana **1994**:1
Chappelle, Dave **2005**:3
Chase, Chevy **1990**:1
Cho, Margaret **1995**:2
Clay, Andrew Dice **1991**:1
Cleese, John **1989**:2
Colbert, Stephen **2007**:4
Cook, Peter
Obituary **1995**:2
Cosby, Bill **1999**:2
Crystal, Billy **1985**:3
Dangerfield, Rodney
Obituary **2006**:1
DeGeneres, Ellen **1995**:3
Diamond, Selma
Obituary **1985**:2
Dr. Demento **1986**:1
Fallon, Jimmy **2003**:1
Farley, Chris
Obituary **1998**:2
Fey, Tina **2005**:3
Ford, Faith **2005**:3
Foster, Phil
Obituary **1985**:3
Foxworthy, Jeff **1996**:1
Foxx, Jamie **2001**:1
Foxx, Redd
Obituary **1992**:2
Franken, Al **1996**:3
Gleason, Jackie
Obituary **1987**:4
Gobel, George
Obituary **1991**:4
Goldberg, Whoopi **1993**:3
Gordon, Gale
Obituary **1996**:1
Gregory, Dick **1990**:3

Department of Health and Human Services [HHR]
Kessler, David **1992**:1
Sullivan, Louis **1990**:4

Department of Housing and Urban Development [HUD]
Achtenberg, Roberta **1993**:4
Harris, Patricia Roberts
Obituary **1985**:2
Kemp, Jack **1990**:4
Morrison, Trudi
Brief Entry **1986**:2

Department of the Interior
Babbitt, Bruce **1994**:1

Department of Labor
Dole, Elizabeth Hanford **1990**:1
Martin, Lynn **1991**:4

Department of State
Christopher, Warren **1996**:3
Muskie, Edmund S.
Obituary **1996**:3

Department of Transportation
Dole, Elizabeth Hanford **1990**:1
Schiavo, Mary **1998**:2

Depression
Abramson, Lyn **1986**:3

Desilu Productions
Arnaz, Desi
Obituary **1987**:1
Ball, Lucille
Obituary **1989**:3

Detroit city government
Archer, Dennis **1994**:4
Maida, Adam Cardinal **1998**:2
Young, Coleman A.
Obituary **1998**:1

Detroit Lions football team
Ford, William Clay, Jr. **1999**:1
Sanders, Barry **1992**:1
White, Byron
Obituary **2003**:3

Detroit Pistons basketball team
Hill, Grant **1995**:3
Laimbeer, Bill **2004**:3
Rodman, Dennis **1991**:3 **1996**:4
Thomas, Isiah **1989**:2
Vitale, Dick **1988**:4 **1994**:4
Wallace, Ben **2004**:3

Detroit Red Wings hockey team
Bowman, Scotty **1998**:4
Federov, Sergei **1995**:1
Ilitch, Mike **1993**:4
Klima, Petr **1987**:1
Konstantinov, Vladimir **1997**:4
Yzerman, Steve **1991**:2

Detroit Tigers baseball team
Fielder, Cecil **1993**:2
Gibson, Kirk **1985**:2
Greenberg, Hank
Obituary **1986**:4

Harwell, Ernie **1997**:3
Hernandez, Willie **1985**:1
Ilitch, Mike **1993**:4
Monaghan, Tom **1985**:1
Schembechler, Bo **1990**:3

Digital Equipment Corp. [DEC]
Olsen, Kenneth H. **1986**:4

Diets
Agatston, Arthur **2005**:1
Atkins, Robert C.
Obituary **2004**:2
Gregory, Dick **1990**:3
Ornish, Dean **2004**:2
Powter, Susan **1994**:3
Sears, Barry **2004**:2

Dilbert cartoon
Adams, Scott **1996**:4

Dinosaurs
Bakker, Robert T. **1991**:3
Barney **1993**:4
Crichton, Michael **1995**:3
Henson, Brian **1992**:1

Diplomacy
Abrams, Elliott **1987**:1
Albright, Madeleine **1994**:3
Astorga, Nora **1988**:2
Baker, James A. III **1991**:2
Begin, Menachem
Obituary **1992**:3
Berri, Nabih **1985**:2
Carter, Jimmy **1995**:1
de Pinies, Jamie
Brief Entry **1986**:3
Dubinin, Yuri **1987**:4
Ghali, Boutros Boutros **1992**:3
Gromyko, Andrei
Obituary **1990**:2
Harriman, Pamela **1994**:4
Harriman, W. Averell
Obituary **1986**:4
Harris, Patricia Roberts
Obituary **1985**:2
Holbrooke, Richard **1996**:2
Jumblatt, Walid **1987**:4
Kekkonen, Urho
Obituary **1986**:4
Keyes, Alan **1996**:2
Kim Dae Jung **1998**:3
Lansdale, Edward G.
Obituary **1987**:2
Le Duc Tho
Obituary **1991**:1
Lewis, Stephen **1987**:2
Lodge, Henry Cabot
Obituary **1985**:1
Lord, Winston
Brief Entry **1987**:4
Luce, Clare Boothe
Obituary **1988**:1
Masako, Crown Princess **1993**:4
McCloy, John J.
Obituary **1989**:3
Molotov, Vyacheslav Mikhailovich
Obituary **1987**:1
Palme, Olof
Obituary **1986**:2

Paz, Octavio **1991**:2
Perez de Cuellar, Javier **1991**:3
Strauss, Robert **1991**:4
Taylor, Maxwell
Obituary **1987**:3
Terzi, Zehdi Labib **1985**:3
Williams, G. Mennen
Obituary **1988**:2
Zeroual, Liamine **1996**:2
Zhao Ziyang **1989**:1

Discovery Channel
Otte, Ruth **1992**:4

Disney/ABC Cable Networks
Cyrus, Miley **2008**:3
Efron, Zac **2008**:2
Jonas Brothers **2008**:4
Laybourne, Geraldine **1997**:1

DNA Testing
Scheck, Barry **2000**:4

DNC
See: Democratic National Committee

Documentaries
Burns, Ken **1995**:2
Moore, Michael **1990**:3

Dolby Laboratories, Inc.
Dolby, Ray Milton
Brief Entry **1986**:1

Domino's Pizza
Monaghan, Tom **1985**:1

Donghia Companies
Donghia, Angelo R.
Obituary **1985**:2

Drama Desk Awards
Allen, Debbie **1998**:2
Allen, Joan **1998**:1
Bishop, Andre **2000**:1
Brooks, Mel **2003**:1
Crisp, Quentin
Obituary **2000**:3
Ebersole, Christine **2007**:2
Fagan, Garth **2000**:1
Fierstein, Harvey **2004**:2
Foster, Sutton **2003**:2
Hoffman, Dustin **2005**:4
Janney, Allison **2003**:3
Kline, Kevin **2000**:1
Lane, Nathan **1996**:4
Langella, Frank **2008**:3
LaPaglia, Anthony **2004**:4
McDonagh, Martin **2007**:3
Nunn, Trevor **2000**:2
Peters, Bernadette **2000**:1
Salonga, Lea **2003**:3
Shanley, John Patrick **2006**:1
Smith, Anna Deavere **2002**:2
Spacey, Kevin **1996**:4
Waterston, Sam **2006**:1
Wong, B.D. **1998**:1

DreamWorks SKG
Katzenberg, Jeffrey **1995**:3
Ostin, Mo **1996**:2
Spielberg, Steven **1993**:4 **1997**:4

Hearst Magazines
Black, Cathleen **1998**:4
Ganzi, Victor **2003**:3

Heisman Trophy
Flutie, Doug **1999**:2
Howard, Desmond Kevin **1997**:2
Jackson, Bo **1986**:3
Testaverde, Vinny **1987**:2
Williams, Ricky **2000**:2

Helmsley Hotels, Inc.
Helmsley, Leona **1988**:1

Hemlock Society
Humphry, Derek **1992**:2

Herbalife International
Hughes, Mark **1985**:3

Hereditary Disease Foundation
Wexler, Nancy S. **1992**:3

Herut Party (Israel)
Levy, David **1987**:2

HEW
See: Department of Health,
Education, and Welfare

Hewlett-Packard
Fiorina, Carleton S. **2000**:1
Hewlett, William
Obituary **2001**:4
Packard, David
Obituary **1996**:3

HGS
See: Human Genome Sciences, Inc.

HHR
See: Department of Health and
Human Services

High Flight Foundation
Irwin, James
Obituary **1992**:1

Hitchhiking
Heid, Bill
Brief Entry **1987**:2

Hobie Cat
Alter, Hobie
Brief Entry **1985**:1
Hasek, Dominik **1998**:3

Hockey
Bourque, Raymond Jean **1997**:3
Cherry, Don **1993**:4
Coffey, Paul **1985**:4
Crosby, Sidney **2006**:3
Eagleson, Alan **1987**:4
Federov, Sergei **1995**:1
Fuhr, Grant **1997**:3
Giguere, Jean-Sebastien **2004**:2
Gilmour, Doug **1994**:3

Granato, Cammi **1999**:3
Gretzky, Wayne **1989**:2
Hextall, Ron **1988**:2
Hull, Brett **1991**:4
Jagr, Jaromir **1995**:4
Klima, Petr **1987**:1
Konstantinov, Vladimir **1997**:4
LaFontaine, Pat **1985**:1
Lemieux, Claude **1996**:1
Lemieux, Mario **1986**:4
Lindbergh, Pelle
Obituary **1985**:4
Lindros, Eric **1992**:1
Messier, Mark **1993**:1
Modano, Mike **2008**:2
Pocklington, Peter H. **1985**:2
Richard, Maurice
Obituary **2000**:4
Roy, Patrick **1994**:2
Sakic, Joe **2002**:1
Yzerman, Steve **1991**:2
Zamboni, Frank J.
Brief Entry **1986**:4

Honda Motor Co.
Honda, Soichiro
Obituary **1986**:1

Hong Kong government
Lee, Martin **1998**:2
Patten, Christopher **1993**:3

Horror fiction
Barker, Clive **2003**:3
Brite, Poppy Z. **2005**:1
Harris, Thomas **2001**:1
King, Stephen **1998**:1
Koontz, Dean **1999**:3
Stine, R. L. **2003**:1

Horse racing
Day, Pat **1995**:2
Desormeaux, Kent **1990**:2
Krone, Julie **1989**:2
Lukas, D. Wayne **1986**:2
McCarron, Chris **1995**:4
Mellon, Paul
Obituary **1999**:3
O'Donnell, Bill
Brief Entry **1987**:4
Pincay, Laffit, Jr. **1986**:3
Secretariat
Obituary **1990**:1
Shoemaker, Bill
Obituary **2004**:4

Houston Astros baseball team
Lofton, Kenny **1998**:1
Ryan, Nolan **1989**:4

Houston Oilers football team
Moon, Warren **1991**:3

Houston Rockets basketball team
Olajuwon, Akeem **1985**:1
Yao Ming **2004**:1

Houston, Tex., city government
Watson, Elizabeth **1991**:2
Whitmire, Kathy **1988**:2

HUD
See: Department of Housing and
Urban Development

Hustler Magazine
Flynt, Larry **1997**:3

Hugo Awards
Asimov, Isaac
Obituary **1992**:3

Human Genome Sciences, Inc. [HGS]
Haseltine, William A. **1999**:2

Huntington's disease
Wexler, Nancy S. **1992**:3

Hyatt Legal Services
Bloch, Henry **1988**:4
Hyatt, Joel **1985**:3

Hydroponics
Davis, Noel **1990**:3

IACC
See: International Anticounterfeiting
Coalition

IBM Corp.
See: International Business
Machines Corp.

Ice cream
Ben & Jerry **1991**:3

Ice skating
Arakawa, Shizuka **2006**:4
Baiul, Oksana **1995**:3
Gordeeva, Ekaterina **1996**:4
Grinkov, Sergei
Obituary **1996**:2
Hamilton, Scott **1998**:2
Hughes, Sarah **2002**:4
Kerrigan, Nancy **1994**:3
Lipinski, Tara **1998**:3
Thomas, Debi **1987**:2
Witt, Katarina **1991**:3
Yamaguchi, Kristi **1992**:3
Zamboni, Frank J.
Brief Entry **1986**:4

Imani Temple
Stallings, George A., Jr. **1990**:1

Immigration
Kurzban, Ira **1987**:2
Lewis, Loida Nicolas **1998**:3
Mahony, Roger M. **1988**:2

Imposters
Bremen, Barry **1987**:3

Inacomp Computer Centers, Inc.
Inatome, Rick **1985**:4

Indiana Pacers basketball team
Miller, Reggie **1994**:4

Indiana University basketball team
Knight, Bobby **1985**:3

Indonesia
Wahid, Abdurrahman **2000**:3

Insurance
Davison, Ian Hay **1986**:1
Hilbert, Stephen C. **1997**:4

Integrated circuit
Noyce, Robert N. **1985**:4

Intel Corp.
Barrett, Craig R. **1999**:4
Grove, Andrew S. **1995**:3
Noyce, Robert N. **1985**:4

Interarms Corp.
Cummings, Sam **1986**:3

International Anticounterfeiting Coalition [IACC]
Bikoff, James L.
Brief Entry **1986**:2

International Brotherhood of Teamsters
Carey, Ron **1993**:3
Hoffa, Jim, Jr. **1999**:2
Presser, Jackie
Obituary **1988**:4
Saporta, Vicki
Brief Entry **1987**:3

International Business Machines Corp. [IBM Corp.]
Akers, John F. **1988**:3
Chaudhari, Praveen **1989**:4
Gerstner, Lou **1993**:4
Kohnstamm, Abby **2001**:1
Palmisano, Samuel J. **2003**:1

International Creative Management Associates
Mengers, Sue **1985**:3

International Olympic Committee [IOC]
Eagleson, Alan **1987**:4
Samaranch, Juan Antonio **1986**:2

Internet
Allaire, Jeremy **2006**:4
Anderson, Tom and Chris DeWolfe **2007**:2
Beal, Deron **2005**:3
Berners-Lee, Tim **1997**:4
Butterfield, Stewart and Caterina Fake **2007**:3
Chen, Steve and Chad Hurley **2007**:2
Clark, Jim **1997**:1
Ebbers, Bernie **1998**:1
Evans, Nancy **2000**:4
Fanning, Shawn **2001**:1
Filo, David and Jerry Yang **1998**:3
Gardner, David and Tom **2001**:4
Haladjian, Rafi **2008**:3
Koogle, Tim **2000**:4

Ma, Jack **2007**:1
Malda, Rob **2007**:3
Nissel, Angela **2006**:4
Pack, Ellen **2001**:2
Peluso, Michelle **2007**:4
Pirro, Jeanine **1998**:2
Schmidt, Eric **2002**:4
Taylor, Jeff **2001**:3
Zuckerberg, Mark **2008**:2

Investment banking
Fomon, Robert M. **1985**:3

IOC
See: International Olympic Committee

IRA
See: Irish Republican Army

Irish Northern Aid Committee [NORAID]
Galvin, Martin
Brief Entry **1985**:3

Irish Republican Army [IRA]
Adams, Gerald **1994**:1
Galvin, Martin
Brief Entry **1985**:3
McGuinness, Martin **1985**:4

Jacuzzi Bros., Inc.
Jacuzzi, Candido
Obituary **1987**:1

Jaguar Cars PLC
Egan, John **1987**:2

Jane magazine
Pratt, Jane **1999**:1

Jewish Defense League
Kahane, Meir
Obituary **1991**:2

Joffrey Ballet
Joffrey, Robert
Obituary **1988**:3

Jolt Cola
Rapp, C.J.
Brief Entry **1987**:3

Joe Boxer Corp.
Graham, Nicholas **1991**:4

Judo
Kanokogi, Rusty
Brief Entry **1987**:1

Juno Awards
Furtado, Nelly **2007**:2
Lavigne, Avril **2005**:2
McLachlan, Sarah **1998**:4
Nickelback **2007**:2
Sainte-Marie, Buffy **2000**:1
Timbaland **2007**:4

Justin Industries
Justin, John Jr. **1992**:2

Kansas City Chiefs football team
Okoye, Christian **1990**:2
Thomas, Derrick
Obituary **2000**:3

Kansas City Royals baseball team
Howser, Dick
Obituary **1987**:4
Jackson, Bo **1986**:3
Saberhagen, Bret **1986**:1

Kelly Services
Kelly, William R.
Obituary **1998**:2

Khmer Rouge
Lon Nol
Obituary **1986**:1

Kitty Litter
Lowe, Edward **1990**:2

Kloss Video Corp.
Kloss, Henry E.
Brief Entry **1985**:2

K Mart Corp.
Antonini, Joseph **1991**:2
Stewart, Martha **1992**:1

Kraft General Foods
Fudge, Ann **2000**:3
Holden, Betsy **2003**:2
Rosenfeld, Irene **2008**:3

Ku Klux Klan
Duke, David **1990**:2

Labor
Bieber, Owen **1986**:1
Carey, Ron **1993**:3
Eagleson, Alan **1987**:4
Fehr, Donald **1987**:2
Feldman, Sandra **1987**:3
Hoffa, Jim, Jr. **1999**:2
Huerta, Dolores **1998**:1
Kielburger, Craig **1998**:1
Martin, Lynn **1991**:4
Nussbaum, Karen **1988**:3
Presser, Jackie
Obituary **1988**:4
Ramaphosa, Cyril **1988**:2
Rothstein, Ruth **1988**:2
Saporta, Vicki
Brief Entry **1987**:3
Steinberg, Leigh **1987**:3
Upshaw, Gene **1988**:1
Williams, Lynn **1986**:4

Labour Party (Great Britain)
Blair, Tony **1996**:3 **1997**:4
Jenkins, Roy Harris
Obituary **2004**:1
Livingstone, Ken **1988**:3
Maxwell, Robert **1990**:1

Martial arts
Chan, Jackie **1996**:1
Lee, Brandon
Obituary **1993**:4
Li, Jet **2005**:3

Maryland state government
Schaefer, William Donald **1988**:1

Massachusetts state government
Dukakis, Michael **1988**:3
Flynn, Ray **1989**:1
Frank, Barney **1989**:2
Moakley, Joseph
Obituary **2002**:2

Mathematics
Hawking, Stephen W. **1990**:1
Lawrence, Ruth
Brief Entry **1986**:3
Penrose, Roger **1991**:4
Pople, John
Obituary **2005**:2
Thom, Rene
Obituary **2004**:1
Wiles, Andrew **1994**:1

Mattel, Inc.
Barad, Jill **1994**:2
Eckert, Robert A. **2002**:3
Handler, Ruth
Obituary **2003**:3

Max Factor and Company
Factor, Max
Obituary **1996**:4

Maximilian Furs, Inc.
Potok, Anna Maximilian
Brief Entry **1985**:2

Mazda Motor Corp.
Yamamoto, Kenichi **1989**:1

McDonald's Restaurants
Kroc, Ray
Obituary **1985**:1

McDonnell Douglas Corp.
McDonnell, Sanford N. **1988**:4

MCI Communications Corp.
Cerf, Vinton G. **1999**:2
McGowan, William **1985**:2
McGowan, William G.
Obituary **1993**:1

MCP
See: Malawi Congress Party

Medicine
Adams, Patch **1999**:2
Baulieu, Etienne-Emile **1990**:1
Bayley, Corrine
Brief Entry **1986**:4
Blumenthal, Susan J. **2007**:3
Carson, Ben **1998**:2
Crichton, Michael **1995**:3

DeVita, Vincent T., Jr. **1987**:3
Duke, Red
Brief Entry **1987**:1
Elders, Joycelyn **1994**:1
Foster, Tabatha
Obituary **1988**:3
Gale, Robert Peter **1986**:4
Gallo, Robert **1991**:1
Hatem, George
Obituary **1989**:1
Healy, Bernadine **1993**:1
Hill, J. Edward **2006**:2
Hounsfield, Godfrey **1989**:2
Jacobs, Joe **1994**:1
Jarvik, Robert K. **1985**:1
Jemison, Mae C. **1993**:1
Jorgensen, Christine
Obituary **1989**:4
Keith, Louis **1988**:2
Kevorkian, Jack **1991**:3
Klass, Perri **1993**:2
Koop, C. Everett **1989**:3
Kopits, Steven E.
Brief Entry **1987**:1
Kwoh, Yik San **1988**:2
Langston, J. William
Brief Entry **1986**:2
Lorenz, Konrad
Obituary **1989**:3
Morgentaler, Henry **1986**:3
Novello, Antonia **1991**:2
Olopade, Olufunmilayo **2006**:3
Oz, Mehmet **2007**:2
Radocy, Robert
Brief Entry **1986**:3
Rock, John
Obituary **1985**:1
Rosenberg, Steven **1989**:1
Rothstein, Ruth **1988**:2
Sabin, Albert
Obituary **1993**:4
Sacks, Oliver **1995**:4
Schroeder, William J.
Obituary **1986**:4
Spock, Benjamin **1995**:2
Obituary **1998**:3
Steptoe, Patrick
Obituary **1988**:3
Sullivan, Louis **1990**:4
Szent-Gyoergyi, Albert
Obituary **1987**:2
Vagelos, P. Roy **1989**:4
Weil, Andrew **1997**:4
Wigler, Michael
Brief Entry **1985**:1

Men's issues
Bly, Robert **1992**:4
McCartney, Bill **1995**:3

Mercedes-Benz
See: Daimler-Benz AG

Merck & Co.
Vagelos, P. Roy **1989**:4

Metromedia, Inc.
Kluge, John **1991**:1

Miami Dolphins football team
Shula, Don **1992**:2

Miami, Fla., city government
Suarez, Xavier
Brief Entry **1986**:2

Michigan state government
Engler, John **1996**:3
Williams, G. Mennen
Obituary **1988**:2

Microelectronics and Computer Technologies Corp.
Inman, Bobby Ray **1985**:1

Microsoft Corp.
Ballmer, Steven **1997**:2
Belluzzo, Rick **2001**:3
Gates, Bill **1993**:3 **1987**:4
Stonesifer, Patty **1997**:1

Middle East
Arafat, Yasser **1989**:3 **1997**:3
Arens, Moshe **1985**:1
Assad, Hafez al- **1992**:1
Begin, Menachem
Obituary **1992**:3
Berri, Nabih **1985**:2
Freij, Elias **1986**:4
Ghali, Boutros Boutros **1992**:3
Hussein, Saddam **1991**:1
Hussein I, King **1997**:3
Obituary **1999**:3
Jumblatt, Walid **1987**:4
Khatami, Mohammed **1997**:4
Khomeini, Ayatollah Ruhollah
Obituary **1989**:4
Levy, David **1987**:2
Nidal, Abu **1987**:1
Rafsanjani, Ali Akbar Hashemi **1987**:3
Redgrave, Vanessa **1989**:2
Sarkis, Elias
Obituary **1985**:3
Schwarzkopf, Norman **1991**:3
Terzi, Zehdi Labib **1985**:3

Military
Abacha, Sani **1996**:3
Arens, Moshe **1985**:1
Aspin, Les
Obituary **1996**:1
Babangida, Ibrahim Badamosi **1992**:4
Boyington, Gregory 'Pappy'
Obituary **1988**:2
Cammermeyer, Margarethe **1995**:2
Cedras, Raoul **1994**:4
Cornum, Rhonda **2006**:3
Doe, Samuel
Obituary **1991**:1
Dzhanibekov, Vladimir **1988**:1
Fitzgerald, A. Ernest **1986**:2
Franks, Tommy **2004**:2
Galvin, John R. **1990**:1
Garneau, Marc **1985**:1
Hess, Rudolph
Obituary **1988**:1
Hope, Bob
Obituary **2004**:4
Hussein, Saddam **1991**:1
Inman, Bobby Ray **1985**:1
Jumblatt, Walid **1987**:4

NIH
See: National Institutes of Health

Nike, Inc.
Hamm, Mia **2000**:1
Knight, Philip H. **1994**:1 9 to 5
Bravo, Ellen **1998**:2
Nussbaum, Karen **1988**:3

Nissan Motor Co.
Ghosn, Carlos **2008**:3
Katayama, Yutaka **1987**:1

No Limit (record label)
Master P **1999**:4

Nobel Prize
Altman, Sidney **1997**:2
Arias Sanchez, Oscar **1989**:3
Axelrod, Julius
Obituary **2006**:1
Beckett, Samuel Barclay
Obituary **1990**:2
Begin, Menachem
Obituary **1992**:3
Bellow, Saul
Obituary **2006**:2
Blobel, Gunter **2000**:4
Carlsson, Arvid **2001**:2
Cela, Camilo Jose
Obituary **2003**:1
Coetzee, J. M. **2004**:4
Cram, Donald J.
Obituary **2002**:2
Crick, Francis
Obituary **2005**:4
Davis, Raymond, Jr.
Obituary **2007**:3
Ebadi, Shirin **2004**:3
ElBaradei, Mohamed **2006**:3
Fo, Dario **1998**:1
Friedman, Milton
Obituary **2008**:1
Gao Xingjian **2001**:2
Garcia Marquez, Gabriel **2005**:2
Grass, Gunter **2000**:2
Heaney, Seamus **1996**:2
Hounsfield, Godfrey **1989**:2
Jelinek, Elfriede **2005**:3
Kandel, Eric **2005**:2
Kilby, Jack **2002**:2
Kissinger, Henry **1999**:4
Kornberg, Arthur **1992**:1
Lederman, Leon Max **1989**:4
Lessing, Doris **2008**:4
Lewis, Edward B.
Obituary **2005**:4
Lorenz, Konrad
Obituary **1989**:3
Mahfouz, Naguib
Obituary **2007**:4
Menchu, Rigoberta **1993**:2
Milosz, Czeslaw
Obituary **2005**:4
Morrison, Toni **1998**:1
Mother Teresa **1993**:1
Obituary **1998**:1
Mullis, Kary **1995**:3
Nuesslein-Volhard, Christiane **1998**:1
Oe, Kenzaburo **1997**:1
Pamuk, Orhan **2007**:3

Pauling, Linus
Obituary **1995**:1
Paz, Octavio **1991**:2
Perutz, Max
Obituary **2003**:2
Pople, John
Obituary **2005**:2
Porter, George
Obituary **2003**:4
Prusiner, Stanley **1998**:2
Sakharov, Andrei Dmitrievich
Obituary **1990**:2
Saramago, Jose **1999**:1
Singer, Isaac Bashevis
Obituary **1992**:1
Suu Kyi, Aung San **1996**:2
Szent-Gyoergyi, Albert
Obituary **1987**:2
Trimble, David **1999**:1
Walesa, Lech **1991**:2
Wiesel, Elie **1998**:1
Yunus, Muhammad **2007**:3

NORAID
See: Irish Northern Aid Committee

**North Atlantic Treaty Organization
[NATO]**
de Hoop Scheffer, Jaap **2005**:1
Galvin, John R. **1990**:1

NOW
See: National Organization for
Women

NRA
See: National Rifle Association

NRC
See: Nuclear Regulatory
Commission

NPR
See: National Public Radio
Tom and Ray Magliozzi **1991**:4

NSF
See: National Science Foundation

Nuclear energy
Gale, Robert Peter **1986**:4
Hagelstein, Peter
Brief Entry **1986**:3
Lederman, Leon Max **1989**:4
Maglich, Bogdan C. **1990**:1
Merritt, Justine
Brief Entry **1985**:3
Nader, Ralph **1989**:4
Palme, Olof
Obituary **1986**:2
Rickover, Hyman
Obituary **1986**:4
Sinclair, Mary **1985**:2
Smith, Samantha
Obituary **1985**:3
Zech, Lando W.
Brief Entry **1987**:4

Nuclear Regulatory Commission [NRC]
Zech, Lando W.
Brief Entry **1987**:4

NUM
See: National Union of
Mineworkers

NWF
See: National Wildlife Federation

Oakland A's baseball team
Canseco, Jose **1990**:2
Caray, Harry **1988**:3
Obituary **1998**:3
Stewart, Dave **1991**:1
Welch, Bob **1991**:3
Zito, Barry **2003**:3

Oakland Raiders football team
Matuszak, John
Obituary **1989**:4
Trask, Amy **2003**:3
Upshaw, Gene **1988**:1

Obie Awards
Albee, Edward **1997**:1
Arkin, Alan **2007**:4
Baldwin, Alec **2002**:2
Bergman, Ingmar **1999**:4
Close, Glenn **1988**:3
Coco, James
Obituary **1987**:2
Daniels, Jeff **1989**:4
Dewhurst, Colleen
Obituary **1992**:2
Diller, Elizabeth and Ricardo
Scofidio **2004**:3
Dukakis, Olympia **1996**:4
Duvall, Robert **1999**:3
Ebersole, Christine **2007**:2
Ensler, Eve **2002**:4
Fierstein, Harvey **2004**:2
Fo, Dario **1998**:1
Fugard, Athol **1992**:3
Gray, Spalding
Obituary **2005**:2
Hoffman, Dustin **2005**:4
Hurt, William **1986**:1
Hwang, David Henry **1999**:1
Irwin, Bill **1988**:3
Kline, Kevin **2000**:1
Langella, Frank **2008**:3
Leguizamo, John **1999**:1
McDonagh, Martin **2007**:3
McDonnell, Mary **2008**:2
Merkerson, S. Epatha **2006**:4
Miller, Arthur **1999**:4
Pacino, Al **1993**:4
Parks, Suzan-Lori **2003**:2
Schreiber, Liev **2007**:2
Shanley, John Patrick **2006**:1
Shepard, Sam **1996**:4
Streep, Meryl **1990**:2
Tune, Tommy **1994**:2
Turturro, John **2002**:2
Vogel, Paula **1999**:2
Washington, Denzel **1993**:2
Waterston, Sam **2006**:1
White, Julie **2008**:2
Woods, James **1988**:3

Occidental Petroleum Corp.
Hammer, Armand
Obituary **1991**:3

Stroh Brewery Co.
Stroh, Peter W. **1985**:2

Students Against Drunken Driving [SADD]
Anastas, Robert
Brief Entry **1985**:2
Lightner, Candy **1985**:1

Submarines
Rickover, Hyman
Obituary **1986**:4
Zech, Lando W.
Brief Entry **1987**:4

Sun Microsystems, Inc.
McNealy, Scott **1999**:4

Sunbeam Corp.
Dunlap, Albert J. **1997**:2

Suicide
Applewhite, Marshall Herff
Obituary **1997**:3
Dorris, Michael
Obituary **1997**:3
Hutchence, Michael
Obituary **1998**:1
Quill, Timothy E. **1997**:3

Sundance Institute
Redford, Robert **1993**:2

Sunshine Foundation
Sample, Bill
Brief Entry **1986**:2

Superconductors
Chaudhari, Praveen **1989**:4
Chu, Paul C.W. **1988**:2

Supreme Court of Canada
Wilson, Bertha
Brief Entry **1986**:1

Surfing
Curren, Tommy
Brief Entry **1987**:4
Johnson, Jack **2006**:4

SWAPO
See: South West African People's Organization

Swimming
Ederle, Gertrude
Obituary **2005**:1
Evans, Janet **1989**:1
Van Dyken, Amy **1997**:1

Tampa Bay Buccaneers football team
Bell, Ricky
Obituary **1985**:1
Gruden, Jon **2003**:4
Johnson, Keyshawn **2000**:4
Testaverde, Vinny **1987**:2
Williams, Doug **1988**:2
Young, Steve **1995**:2

Tandem Computers, Inc.
Treybig, James G. **1988**:3

Teach for America
Kopp, Wendy **1993**:3

Tectonics
Rosendahl, Bruce R.
Brief Entry **1986**:4

Teddy Ruxpin
Kingsborough, Donald
Brief Entry **1986**:2

Tele-Communications, Inc.
Malone, John C. **1988**:3 **1996**:3

Televangelism
Graham, Billy **1992**:1
Hahn, Jessica **1989**:4
Robertson, Pat **1988**:2
Rogers, Adrian **1987**:4
Swaggart, Jimmy **1987**:3

Temple University basketball team
Chaney, John **1989**:1

Tennis
Agassi, Andre **1990**:2
Ashe, Arthur
Obituary **1993**:3
Becker, Boris
Brief Entry **1985**:3
Capriati, Jennifer **1991**:1
Clijsters, Kim **2006**:3
Courier, Jim **1993**:2
Davenport, Lindsay **1999**:2
Djokovic, Novak **2008**:4
Federer, Roger **2004**:2
Gerulaitis, Vitas
Obituary **1995**:1
Gibson, Althea
Obituary **2004**:4
Graf, Steffi **1987**:4
Henin-Hardenne, Justine **2004**:4
Hewitt, Lleyton **2002**:2
Hingis, Martina **1999**:1
Ivanisevic, Goran **2002**:1
Kournikova, Anna **2000**:3
Mauresmo, Amelie **2007**:2
Navratilova, Martina **1989**:1
Pierce, Mary **1994**:4
Riggs, Bobby
Obituary **1996**:2
Roddick, Andy **2004**:3
Sabatini, Gabriela
Brief Entry **1985**:4
Safin, Marat **2001**:3
Sampras, Pete **1994**:1
Seles, Monica **1991**:3
Sharapova, Maria **2005**:2
Williams, Serena **1999**:4
Williams, Venus **1998**:2

Test tube babies
Steptoe, Patrick
Obituary **1988**:3

Texas Rangers baseball team
Rodriguez, Alex **2001**:2
Ryan, Nolan **1989**:4

Texas State Government
Bush, George W., Jr. **1996**:4
Richards, Ann **1991**:2

Therapeutic Recreation Systems
Radocy, Robert
Brief Entry **1986**:3

Timberline Reclamations
McIntyre, Richard
Brief Entry **1986**:2

Time Warner Inc.
Ho, David **1997**:2
Levin, Gerald **1995**:2
Ross, Steven J.
Obituary **1993**:3

TLC Beatrice International
Lewis, Loida Nicolas **1998**:3

TLC Group L.P.
Lewis, Reginald F. **1988**:4
Obituary **1993**:3

Today Show
Couric, Katherine **1991**:4
Gumbel, Bryant **1990**:2
Norville, Deborah **1990**:3

Tony Awards
Abbott, George
Obituary **1995**:3
Alda, Robert
Obituary **1986**:3
Alexander, Jane **1994**:2
Alexander, Jason **1993**:3
Allen, Debbie **1998**:2
Allen, Joan **1998**:1
Arkin, Alan **2007**:4
Bacall, Lauren **1997**:3
Bailey, Pearl
Obituary **1991**:1
Bancroft, Anne
Obituary **2006**:3
Bates, Alan
Obituary **2005**:1
Bennett, Michael
Obituary **1988**:1
Bloch, Ivan **1986**:3
Booth, Shirley
Obituary **1993**:2
Brooks, Mel **2003**:1
Brown, Ruth
Obituary **2008**:1
Brynner, Yul
Obituary **1985**:4
Buckley, Betty **1996**:2
Burnett, Carol **2000**:3
Carter, Nell
Obituary **2004**:2
Channing, Stockard **1991**:3
Close, Glenn **1988**:3
Crawford, Cheryl
Obituary **1987**:1
Crawford, Michael **1994**:2
Cronyn, Hume
Obituary **2004**:3
Dench, Judi **1999**:4
Dennis, Sandy
Obituary **1992**:4

United Farm Workers [UFW]
Chavez, Cesar
Obituary **1993**:4
Huerta, Dolores **1998**:1

United Federation of Teachers
Feldman, Sandra **1987**:3

United Nations [UN]
Albright, Madeleine **1994**:3
Annan, Kofi **1999**:1
Arbour, Louise **2005**:1
Astorga, Nora **1988**:2
Bailey, Pearl
Obituary **1991**:1
de Pinies, Jamie
Brief Entry **1986**:3
Fulbright, J. William
Obituary **1995**:3
Ghali, Boutros Boutros **1992**:3
Gromyko, Andrei
Obituary **1990**:2
Kirkpatrick, Jeane
Obituary **2008**:1
Kouchner, Bernard **2005**:3
Lewis, Stephen **1987**:2
Lodge, Henry Cabot
Obituary **1985**:1
Perez de Cuellar, Javier **1991**:3
Terzi, Zehdi Labib **1985**:3

United Petroleum Corp.
Aurre, Laura
Brief Entry **1986**:3

United Press International [UPI]
Thomas, Helen **1988**:4

United Steelworkers of America [USW]
Williams, Lynn **1986**:4

University Network
Scott, Gene
Brief Entry **1986**:1

University of Chicago
Friedman, Milton
Obituary **2008**:1
Gray, Hanna **1992**:4

University of Colorado football team
McCartney, Bill **1995**:3

University of Las Vegas at Nevada basketball team
Tarkenian, Jerry **1990**:4

University of Michigan football team
Harmon, Tom
Obituary **1990**:3
McCartney, Bill **1995**:3
Schembechler, Bo **1990**:3

University of Notre Dame
Holtz, Lou **1986**:4
Malloy, Edward 'Monk' **1989**:4

University of Pennsylvania
Gutmann, Amy **2008**:4
Rodin, Judith **1994**:4

University of Tennessee
Alexander, Lamar **1991**:2

University of Wisconsin
Shalala, Donna **1992**:3

UNIX
Ritchie, Dennis and Kenneth
Thompson **2000**:1

Untouchables
Ram, Jagjivan
Obituary **1986**:4

UPI
See: United Press International

Urban design
Cooper, Alexander **1988**:4

USA Network
Herzog, Doug **2002**:4
Koplovitz, Kay **1986**:3

U.S. Civil Rights Commission
Pendleton, Clarence M.
Obituary **1988**:4

U.S. Department of Transportation
Peters, Mary E. **2008**:3
Slater, Rodney E. **1997**:4

U.S. House of Representatives
Abzug, Bella **1998**:2
Aspin, Les
Obituary **1996**:1
Bono, Sonny **1992**:2
Obituary **1998**:2
Clyburn, James **1999**:4
Collins, Cardiss **1995**:3
Conyers, John, Jr. **1999**:1
DeLay, Tom **2000**:1
Fenwick, Millicent H.
Obituary **1993**:2
Ferraro, Geraldine **1998**:3
Foley, Thomas S. **1990**:1
Frank, Barney **1989**:2
Fulbright, J. William
Obituary **1995**:3
Gephardt, Richard **1987**:3
Gingrich, Newt **1991**:1 **1997**:3
Gore, Albert, Sr.
Obituary **1999**:2
Hastert, Dennis **1999**:3
Hyde, Henry **1999**:1
Jackson, Jesse, Jr. **1998**:3
Jordan, Barbara
Obituary **1996**:3
Langevin, James R. **2001**:2
McCarthy, Carolyn **1998**:4
McKinney, Cynthia A. **1997**:1
McKinney, Stewart B.
Obituary **1987**:4
McMillen, Tom **1988**:4
Mfume, Kweisi **1996**:3
Mills, Wilbur
Obituary **1992**:4
O'Neill, Tip
Obituary **1994**:3

Pelosi, Nancy **2004**:2
Pepper, Claude
Obituary **1989**:4
Quayle, Dan **1989**:2
Ros-Lehtinen, Ileana **2000**:2
Roybal-Allard, Lucille **1999**:4
Sanchez, Loretta **2000**:3
Sanders, Bernie **1991**:4
Udall, Mo
Obituary **1999**:2
Waters, Maxine **1998**:4
Watts, J.C. **1999**:2

U.S. National Security Adviser
Berger, Sandy **2000**:1

U.S. Office of Management and Budget
Raines, Franklin **1997**:4

U.S. Postal Service
Frank, Anthony M. **1992**:1

U.S. Public Health Service
Koop, C. Everett **1989**:3
Novello, Antonia **1991**:2
Sullivan, Louis **1990**:4

U.S. Senate
Abrams, Elliott **1987**:1
Biden, Joe **1986**:3
Boxer, Barbara **1995**:1
Bradley, Bill **2000**:2
Braun, Carol Moseley **1993**:1
Campbell, Ben Nighthorse **1998**:1
Cohen, William S. **1998**:1
D'Amato, Al **1996**:1
Dole, Bob **1994**:2
Ervin, Sam
Obituary **1985**:2
Feinstein, Dianne **1993**:3
Fulbright, J. William
Obituary **1995**:3
Glenn, John **1998**:3
Goldwater, Barry
Obituary **1998**:4
Hatch, Orin G. **2000**:2
Heinz, John
Obituary **1991**:4
Helms, Jesse **1998**:1
Jackson, Jesse **1996**:1
Kassebaum, Nancy **1991**:1
Kemp, Jack **1990**:4
Lott, Trent **1998**:1
McCain, John S. **1998**:4
Mikulski, Barbara **1992**:4
Mitchell, George J. **1989**:3
Morrison, Trudi
Brief Entry **1986**:2
Muskie, Edmund S.
Obituary **1996**:3
Nunn, Sam **1990**:2
Pepper, Claude
Obituary **1989**:4
Quayle, Dan **1989**:2
Ribicoff, Abraham
Obituary **1998**:3
Snowe, Olympia **1995**:3
Thompson, Fred **1998**:2
Tower, John
Obituary **1991**:4

U.S. Supreme Court
Blackmun, Harry A.
Obituary **1999**:3

Brennan, William
    Obituary 1997:4
Breyer, Stephen Gerald 1994:4 1997
    :2
Burger, Warren E.
    Obituary 1995:4
Flynt, Larry 1997:3
Ginsburg, Ruth Bader 1993:4
Marshall, Thurgood
    Obituary 1993:3
O'Connor, Sandra Day 1991:1
Powell, Lewis F.
    Obituary 1999:1
Rehnquist, William H. 2001:2
Scalia, Antonin 1988:2
Souter, David 1991:3
Stewart, Potter
    Obituary 1986:1
Thomas, Clarence 1992:2

U.S. Trade Representative
    Barshefsky, Charlene 2000:4

U.S. Treasury
    Bentsen, Lloyd 1993:3

USW
    See: United Steelworkers of America

Utah Jazz basketball team
    Malone, Karl 1990:1 1997:3
    Maravich, Pete
        Obituary 1988:2
    Stockton, John Houston 1997:3

U2
    Bono 1988:4
    U 2002:4

Vampires
    Kostova, Elizabeth 2006:2
    Rice, Anne 1995:1

Venezuela
    Perez, Carlos Andre 1990:2

Veterinary medicine
    Redig, Patrick 1985:3

Viacom, Inc.
    Karmazin, Mel 2006:1
    Redstone, Sumner 1994:1

Vietnam War
    Dong, Pham Van
        Obituary 2000:4

Vigilantism
    Goetz, Bernhard Hugo 1985:3
    Slotnick, Barry
        Brief Entry 1987:4

Virgin Holdings Group Ltd.
    Branson, Richard 1987:1

Virginia state government
    Robb, Charles S. 1987:2
    Wilder, L. Douglas 1990:3

Vogue magazine
    Wintour, Anna 1990:4

Volkswagenwerk AG
    Bernhard, Wolfgang 2007:1
    Hahn, Carl H. 1986:4
    Lopez de Arriortua, Jose Ignacio
        1993:4

Volleyball
    Kiraly, Karch
        Brief Entry 1987:1

Voyager aircraft
    Rutan, Burt 1987:2

Vanity Fair magazine
    Brown, Tina 1992:1

Virtual reality
    Lanier, Jaron 1993:4

Wacky WallWalker
    Hakuta, Ken
        Brief Entry 1986:1

Wall Street Analytics, Inc.
    Unz, Ron 1999:1

Wallyball
    Garcia, Joe
        Brief Entry 1986:4

Wal-Mart Stores, Inc.
    Glass, David 1996:1
    Scott, H. Lee, Jr. 2008:3
    Walton, Sam 1986:2
        Obituary 1993:1

Walt Disney Productions
    Disney, Roy E. 1986:3
    Eisner, Michael 1989:2
    Iger, Bob 2006:1
    Katzenberg, Jeffrey 1995:3

Wang Laboratories, Inc.
    Wang, An 1986:1
        Obituary 1990:3

War crimes
    Barbie, Klaus
        Obituary 1992:2
    Hess, Rudolph
        Obituary 1988:1
    Karadzic, Radovan 1995:3
    Klarsfeld, Beate 1989:1
    Mengele, Josef
        Obituary 1985:2
    Milosevic, Slobodan 1993:2

Warnaco
    Wachner, Linda 1988:3 1997:2

Washington Bullets basketball team
    McMillen, Tom 1988:4
    O'Malley, Susan 1995:2

Washington, D.C., city government
    Barry, Marion 1991:1
    Williams, Anthony 2000:4

Washington Post
    Graham, Donald 1985:4
    Graham, Katharine Meyer 1997:3
        Obituary 2002:3

Washington Redskins football team
    Monk, Art 1993:2
    Rypien, Mark 1992:3
    Smith, Jerry
        Obituary 1987:1
    Williams, Doug 1988:2
    Williams, Edward Bennett
        Obituary 1988:4

Watergate
    Dickerson, Nancy H.
        Obituary 1998:2
    Ehrlichman, John
        Obituary 1999:3
    Ervin, Sam
        Obituary 1985:2
    Graham, Katharine Meyer 1997:3
        Obituary 2002:3
    Haldeman, H. R.
        Obituary 1994:2
    Mitchell, John
        Obituary 1989:2
    Neal, James Foster 1986:2
    Nixon, Richard
        Obituary 1994:4
    Thompson, Fred 1998:2

Water skiing
    Duvall, Camille
        Brief Entry 1988:1

Wayne's World
    Myers, Mike 1992:3 1997:4

WebTV Networks Inc.
    Perlman, Steve 1998:2

Wendy's International
    Thomas, Dave 1986:2 1993:2
        Obituary 2003:1

Who Wants to be a Millionaire
    Philbin, Regis 2000:2

Windham Hill Records
    Ackerman, Will 1987:4

Wine making
    Lemon, Ted
        Brief Entry 1986:4
    Mondavi, Robert 1989:2
    Rothschild, Philippe de
        Obituary 1988:2

WNBA
    See: Women's National Basketball
        Association

**Women's National Basketball
Association [WNBA]**
    Cooper, Cynthia 1999:1
    Laimbeer, Bill 2004:3
    Swoopes, Sheryl 1998:2

Cumulative Newsmakers Index

This index lists all newsmakers included in the entire *Newsmakers* series.

Listee names are followed by a year and issue number; thus **1996**:3 indicates that an entry on that individual appears in both 1996, Issue 3, and the 1996 cumulation.

Lee, Chang-Yuh
  See Lee, Henry C.
Lee, Henry C. 1938- **1997**:1
Lee, Jason 1970- **2006**:4
Lee, Martin 1938- **1998**:2
Lee, Pamela 1967(?)- **1996**:4
Lee, Peggy 1920-2002
  Obituary **2003**:1
Lee, Sandra 1966- **2008**:3
Lee, Shelton Jackson
  See Lee, Spike
Lee, Spike 1957- **1988**:4
Lee Jong-Wook 1945- **2005**:1
Lee Teng-hui 1923- **2000**:1
Lefebvre, Marcel 1905- **1988**:4
Legend, John 1978- **2007**:1
Leguizamo, John 1965- **1999**:1
Lehane, Dennis 1965- **2001**:4
Leibovitz, Annie 1949- **1988**:4
Leigh, Janet 1927-2004
  Obituary **2005**:4
Leigh, Jennifer Jason 1962- **1995**:2
Lelyveld, Joseph S. 1937- **1994**:4
Lemieux, Claude 1965- **1996**:1
Lemieux, Mario 1965- **1986**:4
Lemmon, Jack 1925- **1998**:4
  Obituary **2002**:3
Lemon, Ted
  Brief Entry **1986**:4
LeMond, Greg 1961- **1986**:4
LeMond, Gregory James
  See LeMond, Greg
L'Engle, Madeleine 1918-2007
  Obituary **2008**:4
Lennox, Annie 1954- **1985**:4 **1996**:4
Leno, James Douglas Muir
  See Leno, Jay
Leno, Jay 1950- **1987**:1
Leonard, Elmore 1925- **1998**:4
Leonard, Ray Charles
  See Leonard, Sugar Ray
Leonard, Sugar Ray 1956- **1989**:4
Leone, Sergio 1929-1989
  Obituary **1989**:4
Leopold, Luna 1915-2006
  Obituary **2007**:1
Lepore, Nanette 1964(?)- **2006**:4
Lerner, Michael 1943- **1994**:2
Lerner, Sandy 1955(?)- **2005**:1
Leslie, Lisa 1972- **1997**:4
Lessing, Doris 1919- **2008**:4
Letterman, David 1947- **1989**:3
LeVay, Simon 1943- **1992**:2
Leávesque, Reneá
  Obituary **1988**:1
Levin, Gerald 1939- **1995**:2
Levine, Arnold 1939- **2002**:3
Levine, James 1943- **1992**:3
Levinger, Moshe 1935- **1992**:1
Levinson, Arthur D. 1950- **2008**:3
Levinson, Barry 1932- **1989**:3
Levitt, Arthur 1931- **2004**:2
Levy, Burton
  See Lane, Burton
Levy, David 1938- **1987**:2
Levy, Eugene 1946- **2004**:3
Lewis, Edward B. 1918-2004
  Obituary **2005**:4
Lewis, Edward T. 1940- **1999**:4
Lewis, Henry 1932-1996
  Obituary **1996**:3
Lewis, Huey 1951- **1987**:3

Lewis, John 1920-2001
  Obituary **2002**:1
Lewis, Juliette 1973- **1999**:3
Lewis, Lennox 1965- **2000**:2
Lewis, Loida Nicolas 1942- **1998**:3
Lewis, Ray 1975- **2001**:3
Lewis, Reggie 1966(?)-1993
  Obituary **1994**:1
Lewis, Reginald F. 1942-1993 .... **1988**:4
  Obituary **1993**:3
Lewis, Richard 1948(?)- **1992**:1
Lewis, Shari 1934-1998 .... **1993**:1
  Obituary **1999**:1
Lewis, Stephen 1937- **1987**:2
LeWitt, Sol 1928- **2001**:2
Lewitzky, Bella 1916-2004
  Obituary **2005**:3
Leyland, Jim 1944- **1998**:2
Lhuillier, Monique 1971(?)- **2007**:4
Li, Jet 1963- **2005**:3
Liberace 1919-1987
  Obituary **1987**:2
Liberace, Wladziu Valentino
  See Liberace
Libeskind, Daniel 1946- **2004**:1
Lichtenstein, Roy 1923-1997 .... **1994**:1
  Obituary **1998**:1
Lieberman, Joseph 1942- **2001**:1
Ligeti, Gyorgy 1923-2006
  Obituary **2007**:3
Lightner, Candy 1946- **1985**:1
Liguori, Peter 1960- **2005**:2
Lilly, John C. 1915-2001
  Obituary **2002**:4
Lim, Phillip 1974(?)- **2008**:1
Liman, Arthur 1932- **1989**:4
Liman, Doug 1965- **2007**:1
Limbaugh, Rush **1991**:3
Lin, Maya 1960(?)- **1990**:3
Lincoln, Blanche 1960- **2003**:1
Lindbergh, Anne Morrow
  1906-2001
  Obituary **2001**:4
Lindberg, Pelle 1959-1985
  Obituary **1985**:4
Lindgren, Astrid 1907-2002
  Obituary **2003**:1
Lindros, Eric 1973- **1992**:1
Lindsay, John V. 1921-2000
  Obituary **2001**:3
Lindsay-Abaire, David 1970(?)- **2008**:2
Lines, Ray 1960(?)- **2004**:1
Ling, Bai 1970- **2000**:3
Ling, Lisa 1973- **2004**:2
Linklater, Richard 1960- **2007**:2
Lipinski, Tara 1982- **1998**:3
Lipkis, Andy
  Brief Entry **1985**:3
Lipsig, Harry H. 1901- **1985**:1
Lipton, Martin 1931- **1987**:3
Lisick, Beth 1969(?)- **2006**:2
Lithgow, John 1945- **1985**:2
Little, Benilde 1959(?)- **2006**:2
Little, Cleavon 1939-1992
  Obituary **1993**:2
Litzenburger, Liesel 1967(?)- **2008**:1
Liu, Lucy 1968- **2000**:4
Lively, Penelope 1933- **2007**:4
Livi, Yvo
  See Montand, Yves
Living Colour **1993**:3
Livingston, Ron 1968- **2007**:2

Livingstone, Ken 1945- **1988**:3
Lizhi, Fang
  See Fang Lizhi
LL Cool J 1968- **1998**:2
Lloyd Webber, Andrew 1948- **1989**:1
Lobell, Jeanine 1964(?)- **2002**:3
Locklear, Heather 1961- **1994**:3
Lodge, Henry Cabot 1902-1985
  Obituary **1985**:1
Loewe, Frederick 1901-1988
  Obituary **1988**:2
Lofton, Kenny 1967- **1998**:1
Lofton, Ramona
  See Sapphire
Logan, Joshua 1908-1988
  Obituary **1988**:4
Lohan, Lindsay 1986- **2005**:3
Long, Nia 1970- **2001**:3
Long, Shelley 1950(?)- **1985**:1
Longo, Robert 1953(?)- **1990**:4
Lon Nol
  Obituary **1986**:1
Lopes, Lisa 1971-2002
  Obituary **2003**:3
Lopes, Lisa 'Left Eye'
  See TLC
Lopez, George 1963- **2003**:4
Lopez, Ignacio
  See Lopez de Arriortua,
  Jose Ignacio
Lopez, Inaki
  See Lopez de Arriortua,
  Jose Ignacio
Lopez, Jennifer 1970- **1998**:4
Lopez, Nancy 1957- **1989**:3
Lopez de Arriortua, Jose Ignacio
  1941- **1993**:4
Lord, Bette Bao 1938- **1994**:1
Lord, Jack 1920-1998
  Obituary **1998**:2
Lord, Winston
  Brief Entry **1987**:4
Lords, Traci 1968- **1995**:4
Lorenz, Konrad 1903-1989
  Obituary **1989**:3
Lott, Trent 1941- **1998**:1
Louboutin, Christian 1963- **2006**:1
Louganis, Greg 1960- **1995**:3
Louis-Dreyfus, Julia 1961(?)- **1994**:1
Louv, Richard 1949- **2006**:2
Love, Courtney 1964(?)- **1995**:1
Love, Susan 1948- **1995**:2
Loveless, Patty 1957- **1998**:2
Lovett, Lyle 1958(?)- **1994**:1
Lovley, Derek 1954(?)- **2005**:3
Lowe, Edward 1921- **1990**:2
Lowe, Rob 1964(?)- **1990**:4
Lowell, Mike 1974- **2003**:2
Lowry, Adam and Eric Ryan **2008**:1
Loy, Myrna 1905-1993
  Obituary **1994**:2
Lucas, George 1944- **1999**:4
Lucci, Susan 1946(?)- **1999**:4
Luce, Clare Boothe 1903-1987
  Obituary **1988**:1
Lucid, Shannon 1943- **1997**:1
Lucke, Lewis 1951(?)- **2004**:4
Ludacris 1977- **2007**:4
Ludlum, Robert 1927-2001
  Obituary **2002**:1
Luhrmann, Baz 1962- **2002**:3
Lukas, D. Wayne 1936(?)- **1986**:2